CONCISE ENCYCLOPEDIA OF
BRAIN AND LANGUAGE

CONCISE ENCYCLOPEDIA OF BRAIN AND LANGUAGE

VOLUME EDITOR

PROFESSOR HARRY A. WHITAKER
Northern Michigan University
Marquette, MI
USA

ELSEVIER

AMSTERDAM • BOSTON • HEIDELBERG • LONDON • NEW YORK • OXFORD
PARIS • SAN DIEGO • SAN FRANCISCO • SINGAPORE • SYDNEY • TOKYO

Elsevier Ltd., The Boulevard, Langford Lane, Kidlington, Oxford, OX5 1GB, UK
Radarweg 29, PO Box 211, 1000 AE Amsterdam, Netherlands

Material in this work originally appeared in:
Encyclopedia of Gerontology, Ed. J. E. Birren, Elsevier Inc, 2007.
Encyclopedia of Language and Linguistics (2nd Edition), Ed. K. Brown, Elsevier Ltd, 2006.
Encyclopedia of Neuroscience, Ed. L. R. Squire, Elsevier Ltd, 2009.
Encyclopedia of the Neurological Sciences, Ed. M. J. Aminoff and R. B. Daroff, Elsevier Ltd, 2003.
Handbook of the Neuroscience of Language, Ed. B. Stemmer and H. A. Whitaker, Elsevier Ltd, 2008.

First edition 2010

Library of Congress Control Number: 2009937313

A catalogue record for this book is available from the British Library

ISBN 978-0-08-096498-0

10 11 12 13 14 10 9 8 7 6 5 4 3 2 1

This book is printed on acid-free paper
Printed and bound in the UK

THE EDITOR

Harry Whitaker lives in the Upper Peninsula of Michigan, where he is Professor of Psychology at Northern Michigan University. He earned a PhD from UCLA in 1969, subsequently held an NIH post-doctoral fellowship in Neurology and Speech Pathology at the Mayo Clinic, Rochester, Minnesota (1971–1972) and two NINCDS post-doctoral fellowships in Neurosurgery at the University of Washington School of Medicine, Seattle (1976–1977 and 1994–1995). In 2004 he was the Distinguished Visiting Professor in the Department of Psychological and Brain Sciences, University of Louisville. Whitaker founded the journal, *Brain and Language* in 1974 and was editor-in-chief until 2004; he founded the journal *Brain and Cognition* in 1982 and was editor-in-chief until 2002. He was elected fellow of the American Psychological Association, Division 6, Physiological and Comparative in 1986, and Division 26, History of Psychology, in 1997. Whitaker is a founding member and past-president of the International Society for the History of the Neurosciences and a member of the Memory Disorders Research Society. Since 1965 he has published over 115 research articles and book chapters in such journals as *Science, Neuropsychologia, Developmental Neuropsychology, Neuropsychiatry, Neuropsychology* & *Behavioral Neurology, Archives of Neurology, Nature, Brain, Cortex*, and *The Journal of Irreproducible Results*. He has edited or co-edited 16 books, most recently *Brain, Mind and Medicine: Essays in 18th Century Neuroscience*, Springer (2007), *Handbook of the Neuroscience of Language*, Elsevier (2008), and *Concise Encylopedia of Brain and Language*, Elsevier (2009).

COORDINATING EDITORS

James E. Birren Ed. *Encyclopedia of Gerontology*, Elsevier Inc, 2007.
Keith Brown Ed. *Encyclopedia of Language and Linguistics (2nd Edition)*, Elsevier Ltd, 2006.
Larry R. Squire Ed. *Encyclopedia of Neuroscience*, Elsevier Ltd, 2009.
Michael J. Aminoff Ed. *Encyclopedia of the Neurological Sciences*, Elsevier Ltd, 2003.
Robert B. Daroff Ed. *Encyclopedia of the Neurological Sciences*, Elsevier Ltd, 2003.
Brigitte Stemmer Ed. *Handbook of the Neuroscience of Language*, Elsevier Ltd, 2008.

CONTENTS

I

L

M

N

P

W

SUBJECT CLASSIFICATION

Note that entries highlighted in bold are used for classification purposes only and do not cross-reference content articles.

[1] Imaging Language in Brain

(a) Overview

Cognition, An Overview of Neuroimaging Techniques, S A Bunge, I Kahn

(b) Techniques and Results

Diffusion and Perfusion Imaging, A E Hillis
Direct Electrical Stimulation of Language Cortex, B Gordon, K Ledoux
Event-Related Potentials in the Study of Language, K Steinhauer, J F Connolly
Functional Magnetic Resonance Imaging (fMRI) Research on Language, U Hasson, S L Small
The Intracarotid Amobarbital Test (Wada Test) and Complementary Procedures to Evaluate Language Before Epilepsy Surgery, A I Tröster, K R Mohn
PET Research of Language, B Horwitz, R J S Wise
Transcranial Magnetic Stimulation (TMS) as a Tool for Studying Language, K E Watkins, J T Devlin

[2] Language Lateralization – Hemispheric Asymmetries

Apraxia, Handedness and Language Laterality, O Selnes
Anatomical Asymmetries Versus Variability of Language Areas of the Brain, O Selnes, H A Whitaker
Brain Asymmetry, Evolution, A W Toga, K L Narr, P M Thompson, E Luders
Dichotic Listening Studies of Brain Asymmetry, K Hugdahl
Handedness and Cerebral Laterality, D H Geschwind, E Crabtree
Hemispheric Specialization and Cognition, M T Banich
Imaging Brain Lateralization, B Stemmer
Imaging Brain Lateralization' Words, Sentences, and Influencing Factors in Healthy, Pathological, and Special Populations, B Stemmer
Interhemispheric Interaction in the Lateralized Brain, J B Hellige
Lateralization of Language across the Life Span, M Hiscock, M Kinsbourne

[3] Language Disorders

(a) General

Aphasia, Sudden and Progressive, M -M Mesulam
Category-Specific Knowledge, B Z Mahon, A Caramazza
Language and Discourse, S Bond Chapman, G Sparks
Language, Auditory Processes, D Gow, D Caplan
Language, Cortical Processes, D Caplan
Language Disorders, Aphasia, H A Whitaker
Language, Learning Impairments, J L Evans
Neuropragmatics, Disorders and Neural Systems, B Stemmer
Phonological, Lexical, Syntactic, and Semantic Disorders in Children, D L Molfese, M J Maguire, V J Molfese, N Pratt, E D Ratajczak, L E Fentress, P J Molfese
Primary Progressive Aphasia in Nondementing Adults, O Selnes, M Harciarek
Sign Language, disorders of, A Okrent

(b) Sentence – Semantic Levels

Agrammatism, G Miceli
Agrammatism I, Process Approaches, H Kolk
Agrammatism II, Linguistic Approaches, A Beretta
Sentence Comprehension, M C MacDonald, R S Sussman
Sentence Production, V S Ferreira

(c) Word Level

Anomia, A Kertesz
Lexical Impairments Following Brain Injury, R Casas, D Tranel
Morphology, Disorders of, G Jarema, G Libben
Proper and Common Names, Impairments, C Semenza
Word Production, R J Hartsuiker, G Vigliocco

(d) Phonology – Speech-levels

Fluency and Voice, Disorders of, D B Rosenfield
Phonological Impairments, Sublexical, H W Buckingham, S S Christman
Phonology, L Phengrasamy, B Miller
Speech Disorders, Overview, S Hari, B L Miller
Speech Impairments in Neurodegenerative Diseases/Psychiatric Illnesses, A Wisniecki, M Cannizzaro, H Cohen, P J Snyder
Speech Processes in Dysarthria, F R Boutsen

(e) Writing – Reading

Agraphia, S W Anderson, D Tranel, N L Denburg
Dyslexia and Dysgraphia, Developmental, V Molfese, D Molfese, A Molnar, J Beswick
Dyslexia, Neurodevelopmental Basis, G F Eden, D L Flowers
Reading and Acquired Dyslexia, H B Coslett
Written Language, Acquired Impairments of, C Luzzatti, H A Whitaker

[4] Neurological Disorders and Language

(a) Primarily Adult Focus

Agnosia, D Tranel, N L Denburg
Alzheimer's Disease, M D Greicius, H J Rosen, B L Miller
Amusia, C E Hou
Angular Gyrus Syndrome, A Boxer
Anosognosia, R P Friedland
Apraxia, Sensory System, L J Buxbaum, H B Coslett
Balint's Syndrome, R A Short, N R Graff-Radford
Behavior, Neuropathology of, G Tong, J Corey-Bloom
Cerebellum, Clinical Pathology, M Molinari, M G Leggio
Cognition in Aging and Age-Related Disease, E A Kensinger
Cognitive Impairment, D T Stuss
Cognitive Deficits in Schizophrenia, D S Manoach
Delirium and Language, Y Turgeon
Dementia and Language, J Macoir, Y Turgeon
Parkinson's Disease and Language, A I Tröster
Prosopagnosia, M J Farah, T E Feinberg
Synesthesia and Language, J Ward, R Cytowic

(b) Primarily Child Focus

Attention-Deficit/Hyperactivity Disorder (ADHD), S P Hinshaw
Autism and Asperger Syndrome, A Spectrum of Disability, H Cohen, S Rémillard
Landau Kleffner Syndrome, M A Mikati, R M Kurdi, A N Shamseddine
Language Following Congenital Disorders (not SLI), R Leech, F Dick
Mental Retardation, E H Sherr, D M Ferriero
Sturge–Weber–Dimitri Syndrome and Language, S Rémillard, H Cohen
Turner's Syndrome, J Ross

[5] Auditory system

Auditory Cortex Structure and Circuitry, D Barbour
Deafness, J E Hawkins
Sensory Aging, Hearing, M K Pichora-Fuller, E MacDonald

[6] Testing-Assessment of Aphasia

Classical Tests for Speech and Language Disorders, J Macoir, A Sylvestre, Y Turgeon
Mental Status Testing, K P Rankin
Neuropsychological Testing, D C Delis

[7] Treatment of Language and Cognitive Disorders

Remediation of Language Disorders in Adults, L R Cherney

[8] Recovery from Aphasia and Brain Damage

Brain Damage, Functional Reorganization, J Grafman, R Zahn, E Wassermann
Recovery of Language after Stroke or Trauma in Adults, S S Christman, F R Boutsen

[9] Psycholinguistic Principles

(a) General

Language Development, T H Mintz

(b) Speech

Speech Production, Adult, S M Barlow, S Stumm
Word Recognition, J Zevin

(c) Bilingualism

Bilingualism and Aphasia, P C M Wong

[10] Related Normal Processes

[11] Memory and Memory Disorders

(a) Normal Memory Processes

(b) Memory Disorders

INTRODUCTION

The Concise Encyclopedia of Brain and Language gathers into one volume a selection of articles from the recently published *Encyclopedia of Language and Linguistics* (2nd Edition), the *Encyclopedia of the Neurological Sciences*, the *Encyclopedia of Neuroscience*, the *Encyclopedia of Gerontology* and the *Handbook of the Neuroscience of Language*. The articles are broadly divided into 11 topics, listed here and outlined in greater detail immediately below: (1) functional and structural brain imaging of language, (2) hemispheric asymmetries and the lateralization of language, (3) disorders of language, (4) neurological symptoms and their language sequelae, (5) the auditory system, (6) testing, the assessment of language disorders, (7) the treatment and rehabilitation of persons with aphasia and cognitive disorders (8) recovery from aphasia and brain damage. The remaining three divisions broaden the scope of this collection of papers: (9) the principles of psycholinguistic analysis, essential for understanding language and language disorders, (10) normal brain processes that directly interact with the language system and (11) memory and memory disorders, understood since the 19th century to be inextricably bound up with language and language disorders.

In more detail, the first division of the *Concise Encyclopedia of Brain and Language* contains eight articles on imaging language in the brain; there is one overview article reviewing techniques in general and techniques specific to cognitive processing followed by seven articles covering all the major techniques used in language research: diffusion and perfusion imaging, direct electrical brain stimulation of both the cortical surface and deep structures, event-related (evoked) potentials, functional magnetic resonance imaging, the intracarotid sodium amobarbital procedure, positron emission tomography, and transcranial magnetic stimulation. The second division contains ten articles featuring brain hemispheric asymmetries and the lateralization of language representation, approached from a variety of behavioral and imaging techniques. Division three is the largest division, thirty two articles focusing on disorders of language. There are eleven general articles that review a variety of issues such as primary progressive aphasia, the clinical categorization of language disorders and the linguistic categorization of language disorders. There are sixteen articles which review aphasia at the sentence and semantic levels, the word level and at the levels of phonology and speech. An additional five articles deal specifically with disorders of reading, alexia, and writing, agraphia, in children and adults. The fourth division of the encyclopedia reviews a broad selection of neurological symptoms and their language concomitants; seventeen of these articles have an adult focus and seven of them a child focus. Among the neurological symptoms discussed are amusia, apraxia, Alzheimer's and other dementias, Balint's syndrome, cerebellar disorders, Parkinson's disease, agnosia including prosopagnosia, synesthesia, delirium, the autism spectrum including Asperger's syndrome attention deficit and hyperactivity disorders, Landau-Kleffner syndrome, Turner's syndrome and Sturge-Weber-Dimitri syndrome. The three articles of the fifth division discusses the structure and function of the normal and impaired auditory system. The three articles in division six cover the procedures for testing language and cognitive functions; both classic and modern tests are reviewed. Division seven reviews the remediation of language disorders in adults. Division eight comprises two articles that review the problem of recovery from brain damage and functional recovery of language after stroke or trauma. Division nine encompasses psycholinguistic principles for studying language and language processing, in four articles. The four articles of division ten review a variety of normal processes that interact with language: attention, emotion, consciousness and intelligence are highlighted in this section. The final division, eleven, contains thirteen articles on memory and memory disorders. All the major aspects of memory processes are covered: autobiographical, episodic, explicit and implicit, procedural, semantic, short term and working, spatial and visual-associative memory. Two articles review varieties of amnesia and their relation to language.

Considering the *Concise Encyclopedia of Brain and Language* overall, the first eight divisions successfully represent neurolinguistics as it is typically understood, providing the reader with a broad and up-to-date picture of the field. The last three divisions, however, extend the coverage of brain and language to critical ancillary areas: memory, psycholinguistics and normal brain processes all of which interrelate with language. An adequate contemporary understanding of brain and language is simply not possible without appropriate knowledge of the nature of memory, the nature of normal language processing and the brain correlates of normal cognitive functions.

Four aspects of research on brain and language that are particularly emphasized in this collection are: (1) all linguistic levels of language disorders are represented – phonological, syntactic, semantic, discourse and pragmatic, (2) thorough discussion of the variety of neurological impairments and syndromes that have correlated effects on language, (3) broad discussion of psycholinguistic processing at word and sentence levels, important for a proper, modern understanding of aphasia, and, (4) a carefully selected discussion of normal brain functions that are invariably concomitant with language processing, e.g. emotions, attention, memory, etc. The selection of articles on memory is particularly special to this collection, representing all aspects of normal and disordered memory processes. One of the more rapidly changing areas in modern cognitive neuroscience is brain imaging; both in techniques and analyses of imaging data, the selection of articles in this collection is intended to ground the reader in the most commonly used brain imaging techniques, fMRI, ERP, PET, TMS, etc. As well, these articles represent traditional, i.e. generally accepted, interpretations of imaging language processes.

Thus, despite the dynamic nature of this area of brain and language research, the present selection will ground the reader in this field, in preparation for understanding new discoveries and new analytic procedures as they evolve. Other highlights of this encyclopedia include extensive coverage of the lateralization of language, brain imaging and language disorders considered at all levels from the sound system to syntax, semantics, discourse and pragmatics. As well, neurological disorders that typically manifest language disturbances in addition to the primary disease, e.g., the various dementias, apraxia, agnosia and, of course, the schizophrenias, are given balanced coverage. The *Concise Encyclopedia of Brain and Language* thus furnishes the reader a uniquely broad coverage of key domains in modern cognitive neuroscience of language.

Harry A. Whitaker

CONTRIBUTORS

Contributor's affiliations are those applicable at the time of submitting their original chapters.

S W Anderson
University of Iowa Health Care, Iowa City, IA, USA

M T Banich
University of Colorado at Boulder, Boulder, CO, USA

D Barbour
Washington University in St. Louis, St. Louis, MO, USA

S M Barlow
University of Kansas, Lawrence, KS, USA

P J Bayley
University of California at San Diego, San Diego, CA, USA

M Benoit

A Beretta
Michigan State University, East Lansing, MI, USA

J Beswick
University of Louisville, Louisville, KY, USA

F R Boutsen
The University of Oklahoma Health Sciences Center, Oklahoma City, OK, USA

A Boxer

H W Buckingham
Louisiana State University, Baton Rouge, LA, USA

S A Bunge
University of California at Berkeley, Berkeley, CA, USA

L J Buxbaum
Moss Rehabilitation Research Institute and Thomas Jefferson University, Philadelphia, PA, USA

M Cannizzaro
Pfizer Global Research and Development, Groton, CT, USA and NeuroSolutions, Inc., Montreal, QC, Canada

D Caplan
Massachusetts General Hospital, Boston, MA, USA

A Caramazza
Harvard University, Cambridge, MA, USA

R Casas
University of Iowa, Iowa City, IA, USA

S B Chapman

L R Cherney
Northwestern University, Chicago, IL, USA

B J Cherry

S S Christman
The University of Oklahoma Health Sciences Center, Oklahoma City, OK, USA

H Cohen
NeuroSolutions, Inc., and Université de Québec à Montréal, Montréal, QC, Canada

J F Connolly
Université de Montréal, Montréal, QC, Canada

J Corey-Bloom

H B Coslett
University of Pennsylvania School of Medicine and Center for Cognitive Neuroscience, Philadelphia, PA, USA

E Crabtree

R Cytowic
Washington, DC, USA

D C Delis
University of California at San Diego, La Jolla, CA, USA; and San Diego veterans Affairs Healthcare System, San Diego, CA, USA

N L Denburg
University of Iowa Hospitals and Clinics, Iowa City, IA, USA

J T Devlin
University College London, London, UK

F Dick
University of London, London, UK; and University of California at San Diego, La Jolla, CA, USA

G F Eden
Georgetown University Medical Center, Washington, DC, USA

J L Evans
San Diego State University, San Diego, CA, USA

M J Farah

T E Feinberg

L E Fentress
University of Louisville, Louisville, KY, USA

V S Ferreira
University of California at San Diego, La Jolla, CA, USA

D M Ferriero

D L Flowers
Wake Forest University School of Medicine, Winston-Salem, NC, USA

K Foerde
University of California at Los Angeles, Los Angeles, CA, USA

A Fradera
King's College London, London, UK

R P Friedland

D H Geschwind

B Gordon
The Johns Hopkins University, Baltimore, MD, USA

D Gow
Massachusetts General Hospital, Boston, MA, USA

N R Graff-Radford

J Grafman
National Institute of Neurological Disorders and Stroke, Bethesda, MD, USA

M D Greicius

M Harciarek
University of Gdansk, Gdansk, Poland

S Hari

R J Hartsuiker
Ghent University, Ghent, Belgium

U Hasson
The University of Chicago, Chicago, IL, USA

J E Hawkins
Ann Arbor, MI, USA

J B Hellige
Loyola Marymount University, Los Angeles, CA, USA

A E Hillis
Johns Hopkins University, Baltimore, MD, USA

S P Hinshaw

M Hiscock
University of Houston, Houston, TX, USA

B Horwitz
National Institutes of Health, Bethesda, MD, USA

C E Hou

K Hugdahl
University of Bergen, Bergen, Norway

L F Jacobs

G Jarema
University of Montreal, Montreal, QC, Canada

I Kahn
Howard Hughes Medical Institute at Harvard University, Cambridge, MA, USA

E A Kensinger
Boston College, Chestnut Hill, MA, USA

A Kertesz

H M Kimura
University of Tokyo School of Medicine, Tokyo, Japan

M Kinsbourne
New School for Social Research, New York, NY, USA

H Kolk
University of Nijmegen, Nijmegen, The Netherlands

M D Kopelman
King's College London, London, UK

J H Kramer

M Kritchevsky
San Diego VA Healthcare System, San Diego, CA, USA

R M Kurdi
American University of Beirut, New York, NY, USA

K Ledoux
The Johns Hopkins University School of Medicine, Baltimore, MD, USA

K Lee

R Leech
University of London, London, UK

M G Leggio
University of Rome 'La Sapienza,' Rome, Italy

B Levine

G Libben
University of Montreal, Montreal, QC, Canada

B Libet[†]
Davis, CA, USA

[†]Deceased

E Luders
University of California at Los Angeles School of Medicine, Los Angeles, CA, USA

C Luzzatti
Universita' degli Studi di Milano-Bicocca, Milan, Italy

E MacDonald
University of Toronto, Toronto, ON, Canada

M C MacDonald
University of Wisconsin–Madison, Madison, WI, USA

J Macoir
Laval University, Quebec, QC, Canada

M J Maguire
University of Louisville, Louisville, KY, USA

B Z Mahon
Harvard University, Cambridge, MA, USA

D S Manoach
Massachusetts General Hospital, Charlestown, MA, USA

A Martin
National Institute of Mental Health, Bethesda, MD, USA

M -M Mesulam
Northwestern University Medical School, Chicago, IL, USA

G Miceli

M A Mikati
American University of Beirut, New York, NY, USA

B L Miller

H A Miller

T H Mintz
University of Southern California, Los Angeles, CA, USA

Y Miyashita
University of Tokyo School of Medicine, Tokyo, Japan

K R Mohn
University of North Carolina, Chapel Hill, NC, USA

D L Molfese
University of Louisville, Louisville, KY, USA

P J Molfese
University of Louisville, Louisville, KY, USA

V J Molfese
University of Louisville, Louisville, KY, USA

M Molinari
Santa Lucia Foundation, Rome, Italy

A Molnar
University of Louisville, Louisville, KY, USA

K Nakahara
University of Tokyo School of Medicine, Tokyo, Japan

K L Narr
University of California at Los Angeles School of Medicine, Los Angeles, CA, USA

A Okrent
The University of Chicago, Chicago, IL, USA

T Pasternak
University of Rochester, Rochester, NY, USA

L Phengrasamy

M K Pichora-Fuller
University of Toronto, Mississauga, ON, Canada

R A Poldrack
University of California at Los Angeles, Los Angeles, CA, USA

B R Postle
University of Wisconsin, Madison, Madison, WI, USA

A L Powell

N Pratt
University of Louisville, Louisville, KY, USA

K P Rankin

E D Ratajczak
University of Louisville, Louisville, KY, USA

S Rémillard
Université du Québec à Montréal, Montréal, Canada

P H Robert

H J Rosen

D B Rosenfield
The Methodist Hospital/Weill Cornell College of Medicine, Houston, TX, USA

J Ross

O Selnes
Johns Hopkins University School of Medicine, Baltimore, MD, USA

C Semenza
University of Trieste, Trieste, Italy

M C Shake
University of Illinois at Urbana–Champaign, Champaign, IL, USA

A N Shamseddine
American University of Beirut, New York, NY, USA

E H Sherr

R A Short

S L Small
The University of Chicago, Chicago, IL, USA

C N Smith
University of California at San Diego, San Diego, CA, USA

J Snedeker
Harvard University, Cambridge, MA, USA

P J Snyder
University of Connecticut, Storrs, CT, USA; Pfizer Global Research and Development, Groton, CT, USA; Université de Québec à Montréal, Montréal, QC, Canada

G Sparks

L R Squire
University of California at San Diego, San Diego, CA, USA

K Steinhauer
McGill University, Montréal, QC, Canada

B Stemmer
University of Montreal, Montreal, QC, Canada

E A L Stine-Morrow
University of Illinois at Urbana–Champaign, Champaign, IL, USA

S Stumm
University of Kansas, Lawrence, KS, USA

D T Stuss

R S Sussman
University of Wisconsin–Madison, Madison, WI, USA

E Svoboda

A Sylvestre
Laval University, Quebec, QC, Canada

P M Thompson
University of California at Los Angeles School of Medicine, Los Angeles, CA, USA

A W Toga
University of California at Los Angeles School of Medicine, Los Angeles, CA, USA

G Tong

D Tranel
University of Iowa Hospitals and Clinics, Iowa City, IA, USA

A I Tröster
University of North Carolina School of Medicine, Chapel Hill, NC, USA

Y Turgeon
Campbellton Regional Hospital, Campbellton, NB, Canada

G Vigliocco
University College London, London, UK

J Ward
University of London, London, UK

E Wassermann
National Institute of Neurological Disorders and Stroke, Bethesda, MD, USA

K E Watkins
University of Oxford, Oxford, UK

H A Whitaker
Northern Michigan University, Marquette, MI, USA

R J S Wise
Imperial College London, Hammersmith Hospital, London, UK

A Wisniecki
University of Connecticut, Storrs, and Pfizer Global Research and Development, Groton, CT, USA

P C M Wong
Northwestern University, Evanston, IL, USA

R Zahn
National Institute of Neurological Disorders and Stroke, Bethesda, MD, USA

J Zevin
Weill Medical College of Cornell University, New York, NY, USA

LIST OF ABBREVIATIONS

A	act (in speech act theory); actor (tagmemics); addressee; agent; agentive; argument; author
ABESS	abessive
ABL	ablative
ABS	absolutive
ACC	accusative
ACT	active; actor
Ad	adjunct
ADESS	adessive
ADJ	adjective, -ival
AdjP	adjective phrase
ADV	adverb(ial)
AdvP	adverbial phrase
AFF	affective; affix
AFFIRM	affirmative
AGR	agreement
AGT	agent
AI	Artificial Intelligence
ALL	allative
AM	amplitude-modulated (signal)
Amer	American
AN	adjective precedes noun (in word order typology)
ANIM	animate
ANN	artificial neural network
ANT	anterior
ANTI	antipassive
AOR	aorist
AP	atomic phonology
APG	arc pair grammar
APPL	applicative
ART	article
ASCII	American Standard Code for Information Interchange
ASL	American Sign Language
ASP	aspect(ual)
ASR	automatic speech recognition
ASSOC	associative
ATN	augmented transition network
ATR	advanced tongue root (distinctive feature)
ATTR	attribute
Auslan	Australian Sign Language
AUX	auxiliary
b.	born
BASIC	Basic All-purpose Symbolic Instruction Code
BEN	benefactive
BEV	Black English Vernacular
BNC	British National Corpus
BSE	base-form
BSL	British Sign Language
C	clause; coda (of syllable); codomain (set theory); complement(izer); consonant
c-command	constituent command
c-structure	constituent structure
CA	componential analysis; contrastive analysis; conversation analysis
CALL	computer assisted language learning
CAP	control agreement principle
CAT	category; computer-assisted translation
CAUS	causative
CCG	combinatory categorial grammar
CD	communicative dynamism; conceptual dependency
CF	characteristic frequency; constant frequency
CFG	context-free grammar
CFL	context-free language
CFPSG	context-free phrase structure grammar
CG	categorial grammar
CL	computational linguistics
CLASS	classifier
CN	common noun
COLL	collective
COM	comitative
COMP	comparative; complement(izer)
CONJ	conjunction/conjugation
CONS	consonantal
CONT	continuant; continuative
COP	copula
COR	coronal
CP	complement(izer) phrase

cps	cycles per second
CS	context-sensitive
CSG	context-sensitive grammar
CV	consonant vowel structure/sequence
CV phonology	skeletal phonology
D-structure	deep structure
d.	died
DA	discouse analysis
DAF	delayed auditory feedback
DAG	directed acyclic graph
DAT	dative
DCG	definite clause grammar
DD	discourse domain
DDG	daughter dependency grammar
DECL	declarative
DEF	definite
DEM	demonstrative
DESID	desiderative
DEST	destinative
DET	determiner
DG	dependency grammar
DIM	diminutive
DIR	direction(al)
DIST	distributive
DM	discourse marker
DO	direct object
dp	determiner phrase
DRS	discourse representation structure
DRT	discourse representation theory
DS	deep structure; direct speech
DTR	daughter (in HPSG)
DU	dual
DYN	dynamic
EA	error analysis
EAP	English for academic purposes
ECM	exceptional case marking
ECP	empty category principle
EEG	electroencephalography
EFL	English as a foreign language
EL	elative
ELT	English Language Teaching
EMG	electromyograph(y)
EMPH	emphatic
ENCL	enclitic
Eng	English
equi	equi NP deletion (= identity erasure transformation)
ERG	ergative
ESL	English as a second language
ESP	English for Specific/Special Purposes
ESS	essive
EST	Extended Standard Theory
etym	etymology
EXCL	exclusive
EXIST	existential
EXP	experiencer
F	false (in truth table); formant
f-structure	functional structure
F_0	fundamental frequency
F_1	first formant
F_2	second formant
F_3	third formant
FACT	factive
FDS	free direct speech
FEM	feminine
FFP	foot feature principle
FG	functional grammar
fig.	figure
FIN	finite
FIS	free indirect speech
fl.	*foruit, flourished,* lived
FLA	first language acquisition
FM	frequency modulation
FSP	functional sentence perspective
FSTN	finite state transition network
FUT	future
FUG	functional unification grammar
GB	government and binding (theory)
GB-phonology	government-based phonology
GEN	gender; genitive
GER	gerund
GN	genitive precedes noun (in word order typology)
GPSG	generalized phrase structure grammar
GR	grammatical relation
GS	generative semantics
H	head (of construction); hearer/reader; high/superposed (code/variety, in adiglossic situation); high (pitch/tone)
HABIT	habitual
HCI	human-computer interaction
HFC	head feature convention
HFP	head feature principle
HG	head grammar
HON	honorific
HPSG	head-driven phrase structure grammar
HUM	human
HYPOTH	hypothetical
Hz	hertz
IA	Item-and-Arrangement [model of grammatical description]
IC	immediate constituent
I-E	Indo-European
IELTS	[British Council] International English Language Testing System
iff	if and only if

IGNOR	ignorative
IL	interlanguage
ILL	illative
IMP	imperative
IMPERS	impersonal
IMPERF	Imperfect(ive)
INAN	Inanimate
INCL	Including; inclusive
INCORP	Incorporating
INDEF	Indefinite
INDIC	Indicative
INF	infinitival; infinitive
INFL	Inflection
INSTR	Instrumental
INTERJ	Integration
INTERROG	interrogative
INTRANS	Intransitive
IO	indirect object
IP	inflection phrase; Item-and-process [model of grammatical description]
IPA	International Phonetic Alphabet
IR	inflectional rule; internal reconstruction
IRR	irrealis
IRREG	irregular
IS	indirect speech
ISA	subsumption/subclass 'is a'
IT	Information Technology
ITER	iterative
K	set of situations (in speech act theory)
kHz	kilohertz
KWIC	keyword in context
L	language; low (pitch/tone); low/vernacular variety [in diglossia]
L1	first language
L2	second or foreign language
LAB	labial
LAD	language acquisition device
LARSP	language assessment, remediation, and screening procedure
LAT	lateral
LEX	lexicality (in HPSG)
LF	lexical function; logical form
LFG	Lexical Functional Grammar
lit.	literally
LMC	lower middle class
LOC	local; locative; locus
LP	language planning; linear precedence [statements]; linear prediction
LSP	language for special/specific purposes
LTAG	lexicalized tree adjoining grammar
LU	lexical unit
M	mid [tone]; Middle (in language names); modal
MASC	masculine
Mb	megabyte
MDS	multidimensional scaling
MG	Montague Grammar
MLAT	Modern Language Aptitude Test
MLU	mean length of utterance
MMC	middle-middle class
Mod	modern
MOD	modifier
MRI	magnetic resonance imaging
MT	mother tongue; machine translation
N	new (speaker); noun; nucleus (of syllable)
n.d.	no date
n.s.	new series
NA	noun precedes adjective (in word order typology)
NAS	nasal
NEG	negation; negative
NEUT	neuter
NG	noun precedes genitive (in word order typology)
NL	native language; natural language
NLG	natural language generation
NLP	natural language processing
NLU	natural language understanding
NMR	nuclear magnetic resonance
NN	neural net(work)
NNS	nonnative speaker
NOM	nominative; nominal(ization)
NP	noun phrase
NPrel	relative noun phrase
NRel	noun precedes relative clause (in word order typology)
NS	native speaker
nt	nonterminal
NT	New Testament
NUM	number
NVC	non-verbal communication
O	onset (of syllable)
OBJ	object
OBL	oblique
OBS	obstruent
obs.	obsolete
OCR	optical character recognition
OED	*Oxford English Dictionary*
OOP	object-oriented programming
OPT	optative
OSV	object-subject-verb (in word order typology)
OT	Old Testament; Optimality Theory
OV	object precedes verb (in word order typology)
OVS	object-verb-subject (in word order typology)
P	phrase; predicate

PA	pushdown automation
PART	participle; particle; partitive
PASS	passive
PAT	patient
PERF	perfect(ive)
PERS	person(al)
PET	positron-emission tomography
PF	phonetic form (in principles and parameters framework)
PHON	phonology
PIE	Primitive Indo-European; Proto-Indo-European
PL	plural
PM	phrase marker
Po	postposition
PO	primary object
POL	polite
POSS	possessive; possessor
POTEN	potential
PP	prepositional phrase
PP	past participle
PLUPERF	pluperfect
PRED	predicative
PREF	prefix
PREP	preposition
PRES	present
PRO	an unspecified NP
PRO	pronominal element; pronoun
PROG	progressive
ProgP	progressive phrase
PROHIB	prohibitive
PRESP	present participle
PS-rule	phrase structure rule
PSG	Phrase Structure Grammar
PTQ	[the] proper treatment of quantification [in English] (Montague grammar)
PURP	purpose; purposive
Q	question
QR	quantifier raising
QUANT	quantifier
QU	*wh*-marking
R-expression	referential/referring expression
R-graph	relational graph (in arc pair grammar)
RC	relative clause
RECIP	recipient/reciprocal
REFL	reflexive
reg	regular
ReIN	relative clause precedes noun (in sword order typology)
REP	repetitive
RES	resumptive/result
REST	Revised Extended Standard Theory
rev.	revised
RG	Relational Grammar
RNR	right node raising
RP	received pronunciation
RR	readjustment rule; redundancy rule
RST	Rhetorical Structure Theory
RT	reaction time; RTN recursive transition network
S	point of speech (temporal logic); sentence; sign (sign language); source; speaker; speaker/writer; standard (speaker); strong (syllable); subject (tagmemics); subject term (or conclusion in a syllogism)
S-structure	surface structure
SAE	Standard American English; standard average European OVhorO
SC	small clause; structural change
SD	structural description
SEM	semantics
SGML	standard generalized markup language
SIB	sibilant
sing	singular
SL	source language
SLA	second language acquisition
SLASH	unbounded dependency (in HPSG)
SON	sonorant
SOV	subject-object-verb (in word order typology)
SPEC	specifier
SS	surface structure
SSC	specified subject condition
Sta	statement
STAT	static
STRID	strident
SUBCAT	subcategorization
SUBJ	subject; subjunctive
SUBJUNC	subjunctive
SUBORD	subordinate, subordinative
SUF	suffix
SUP	supine
SUPERESS	superessive
SV	subject precedes verb (in word order typology)
SVO	subject-verb-object (in word order typology)
SYLL	syllabic; syllable
SYN	synonym; syntax
T	tense; text; time; transformation; tree; true (in truth table); tu (= familiar pronoun of address)
t	trace
T-rule	transformational rule
TAG	Tree-Adjoining Grammar
TAL	tree-adjoining language
TBU	tone-bearing unit

TC	total communication [approach] (in schools for the deaf)
TEFL	Teaching English as a foreign language
TEMP	temporal
TERM	terminative
TESOL	Teaching of English to Speakers of Other Languages
TG	Transformational Grammar
TGG	Transformational Generative Grammar
TL	target language
TNS	tense
TOEFL	Test of English as a Foreign Language
TOP	topic(alization)
TRANS	transitive
TRANSLV	translative
TYP	type
U	utterance
UCG	Unification Categorial Grammar
UG	Universal Grammar
UMC	upper middle class
V	verb(al); vowel; "you (= polite pronoun of address)
V-form	honorific form (of address)
VFORM	verb form
VIS	visual
VLSI	very large scale integration
VN	verbal noun
VO	verb precedes object (in word order typology)
VOC	vocalic
VOS	verb-object-subject (in word order typology)
VOT	voice onset time
VP	verb phrase
VS	verb precedes subject (in word order typology)
VSO	verb-subject-object (in word order typology)
W	weak (syllable)
WF	word formation
WFF	well-formed formula
WG	word grammar
WH-word	question word (*what, which,* etc.)
WP	Word-Paradigm (grammar)
0	zero (covert element)
1	first person
α	alpha, a variable
Σ	sentence; superfoot (in metrical phonology)
σ	syllable

A

Agnosia

D. Tranel and N. L. Denburg, University of Iowa Hospitals and Clinics, Iowa City, IA, USA

'Agnosia,' a neurological term of Greek origin (a + Greek *gnosis*), signifies a lack of knowledge and is virtually synonymous with an impairment of recognition. In the traditional literature, two types of agnosia were commonly described. 'Associative' agnosia referred to as failure of recognition that results from defective activation of information pertinent to a given stimulus. 'Apperceptive' agnosia referred to a disturbance of the 'integration' of otherwise normally perceived components of a stimulus.

Teuber in 1968 gave a narrower definition, in which agnosia was synonymous with having "normal percepts stripped of their meaning." In this sense, agnosia is conceptualized as a disorder of memory, and only associative agnosia qualifies for this stricter definition. In practical terms, however, it has been useful to retain the concept of apperceptive agnosia and to maintain a distinction between apperceptive and associative agnosia. In both conditions, recognition is disturbed. In the apperceptive variety, the problem can be traced, at least in part, to faulty perception, usually in reference to aspects of higher-order perceptual capacities (it is not appropriate to use the term agnosia for conditions in which perceptual problems are severe and obviously preclude the patient's apprehension of meaningful information). In associative agnosia, perception is largely intact, and the recognition defect is strictly or primarily a disorder of memory.

The difficulties of trying to separate apperceptive and associative forms of agnosia underscore the fact that the processes of perception and memory are not discrete. Rather, those processes operate on a physiological and psychological continuum, and demarcation of a clear separation point at which perceptual processes end and memory processes begin is simply not possible. Many patients with recognition defects will have elements of both conditions, that is, high-level perceptual problems and disturbances in memory. Some, however, can be classified unequivocally into one type or the other. For these reasons, the following operational definitions are appropriate. Associative agnosia is a modality-specific impairment of the ability to recognize previously known stimuli (or new stimuli for which learning would normally have occurred) that occurs in the absence of disturbances of perception, intellect, or language, and is the result of acquired cerebral damage. The designation appreciative agnosia applies when the patient meets the preceding definition in all respects except that perception is altered.

The term 'agnosia' should be restricted to situations in which recognition impairments are confined to one sensory modality, for example, vision, or audition, or touch. When recognition defects extend across two or more modalities, the appropriate designation is 'amnesia'. As noted, the term agnosia should not be used for patients in whom recognition defects develop in connection with major disturbances of basic perception. Nor should the term be applied to patients with major impairments of intellect. Finally, the term agnosia should be reserved for conditions that develop suddenly, following the onset of acquired cerebral dysfunction.

One other important distinction is between 'recognition' and 'naming.' The two capacities are often confused. It is true that recognition of an entity, under normal circumstances, is frequently indicated by naming (e.g., that is a 'groundhog' or that is 'Joe Montana'). Studies of brain-injured subjects, however, have shown clearly that recognition and naming are dissociable capacities, and the two terms should not be used interchangeably. Damage in the left inferotemporal region, for example, can render a patient incapable of naming a wide variety of stimuli, while leaving unaffected the patient's ability to recognize those stimuli. For the two preceding examples, for instance, the patient may produce the descriptions of 'that's a roly-poly animal that digs holes under barns and hibernates in the winter,' and 'that's the guy from Notre Dame who was a famous quarterback and won lots of football championships.' Both descriptions indicate unequivocal recognition of the specific entities, even if their names are never produced. In short, it is important to maintain a distinction between recognition, which can be indicated by any number of responses signifying that the patient understands the meaning of a particular stimulus, and naming, which may not, and need not, accompany accurate recognition. The patient with agnosia fails to experience familiarity with the stimulus, and is thus unable to evoke its meaning, use, or relevant relationships in both verbal and nonverbal terms.

In principle, agnosia can occur in any sensory modality, relative to any type of entity or event. In practice, however, some types of agnosia are far more frequent. 'Visual agnosia,' especially agnosia for faces ('prosopagnosia'), is the most commonly encountered form of recognition disturbance affecting a primary sensory modality. Visual agnosia is a disorder of recognition confined to the visual realm, in which a patient cannot arrive at the meaning of some or all categories of previously known nonverbal visual stimuli, despite normal or near-normal visual perception and intact alertness, attention, intelligence, and language. Most patients manifest a comparable defect in the anterograde compartment; that is, they cannot recognize new nonverbal, visual stimuli that would normally have been learned after adequate exposure.

The condition of 'auditory agnosia' is rarer, followed by the even less frequent 'tactile agnosia.' A frequently encountered condition which also conforms to the designation of agnosia is a disturbance in the 'recognition of illness,' or what has been termed 'anosognosia'.

It is important to distinguish anosognosia from several closely related conditions. One is 'anosodiaphoria', a term that refers to the condition in which a patient acknowledges, but fails to appreciate the significance of, acquired impairments in physical or psychological function. Although anosodiaphoria is not a true form of agnosia, in practice there is a certain degree of overlap between anosodiaphoria and anosognosia. In fact, it is common to observe that blatant forms of anosognosia, for example, denial of hemiplegia, tend to evolve over time, as the patient recovers, into various degrees of anosodiaphoria. Another condition refers to a disorder of body schema. Body schema disturbances are conditions in which patients become unable to localize various parts of their bodies. The most common manifestations are 'autotopagnosia,' 'finger agnosia,' and 'right–left disorientation' (the latter two being essentially partial forms of the first). Autotopagnosia refers to a condition in which the patient loses the ability to identify parts of the body, either to verbal command or by imitation. In its most severe form, the disorder affects virtually all body parts; however, this is quite rare, and it is far more common to observe partial forms of the condition, including deficits in finger localization (finger agnosia) and right–left discrimination.

Accurate detection and diagnosis of agnosia are important on several accounts. Both visual and auditory agnosia are strongly associated with the presence of bilateral cerebral disease, and the presence of one of these conditions can be a useful clue regarding the localization of brain dysfunction. This can be especially helpful in the early stages of acquired cerebral dysfunction, when even modern neuroimaging procedures may fail to detect a lesion. Such conditions furnish additional diagnostic clues because they are typically associated with cerebrovascular disease affecting the territories of the posterior or middle cerebral arteries. Furthermore, unilateral disease involving the dominant parietal lobe has recently been implicated in both tactile agnosia and apraxia. To avoid misdiagnosis, it is important to note that the complaints or behaviors of patients with agnosia can seem so bizarre as to raise questions about their veracity. There was, indeed, a time when it was doubted whether such conditions existed at all. That agnosic conditions do occur is no longer a contentious issue; nonetheless, clinicians may be skeptical of a patient who suddenly claims an inability to recognize familiar faces, despite normal vision, or of a patient who suddenly behaves as though all auditory information had lost its meaning. A particularly unusual case of agnosia was recently reported in which a child with sleep-induced electrophysiological abnormalities involving the occipitotemporal regions and episodic seizure disorder demonstrated stable defects in visual–spatial abilities, as well as visual agnosia.

Despite their relative rarity, agnosias have also proved to be important 'experiments of nature,' and they have assisted with the investigation of the neural bases of human perception, learning, and memory. Careful study of agnosic patients over the past couple of decades, facilitated by the advent of modern structural (computed tomography, magnetic resonance) and functional (positron emission tomography, functional magnetic resonance) neuroimaging techniques, and by the development of sophisticated experimental neuropsychological procedures, has yielded important new insights into the manner in which the human brain acquires, maintains, and retrieves various types of knowledge.

See also: Amnesia, Declarative and Nondeclarative Memory.

Further Reading

Bauer, RM and Demery, JA (2003). Agnosia. In: Heilman, KM and Valenstein, E (eds.) *Clinical Neuropsychology,* 4th edn., pp. 236–295. New York: Oxford University Press.

Caselli, RJ (1991). Rediscovering tactile agnosia. *Mayo Clinicical Proceedings* 66: 129–142.

Crutch, SJ, Warren, JD, Harding, L, and Warrington, EK (2005). Computation of tactile object properties requires the integrity of praxic skills. *Neuorpsychologia* 43: 1792–1800.

Damasio, AR and Damasio, H (1994). Cortical systems for retrieval of concrete knowledge: The convergence zone framework. In: Koch, C and Davis, JL (eds.) *Large-Scale Neuronal Theories of the Brain*, pp. 61–74. Cambridge, MA: MIT Press.

Damasio, AR, Damasio, H, Tranel, D, and Brandt, JP (1990). Neural regionalization of knowledge access: Preliminary evidence. *Symposia on Quantitative Biology* 55: 1039–1047.
Damasio, AR, Tranel, D, and Damasio, H (1990). Face agnosia and the neural substrates of memory. *Annual Review of Neuroscience* 13: 89–109.
Damasio, H, Grabowski, TJ, Tranel, D, Hichwa, RD, and Damasio, AR (1996). A neural basis for lexical retrieval. *Nature* 380: 499–505.
Denburg, NL and Tranel, D (2003). Acalculia and disturbances of the body schema. In: Heilman, KM and Valenstein, E (eds.) *Clinical Neuropsychology,* 4th edn., pp. 161–184. New York: Oxford University Press.
Eriksson, K, Kylliainen, A, Hirvonen, K, Nieminen, P, and Koivikko, M (2003). Visual agnosia in a child with non-lesional occipito-temporal CSWS. *Brain & Development* 25: 262–267.
Teuber, H-L (1968). Perception. In: Weiskrantz, L (ed.) *Analysis of Behavioral Change*, pp. 274–328. New York: Harper & Row.
Tranel, D and Damasio, AR (1985). Knowledge without awareness: An autonomic index of facial recognition by prosopagnosics. *Science* 228: 1453–1454.
Tranel, D and Damasio, AR (1996). The agnosias and apraxias. In: Bradley, WG, Daroff, RB, Fenichel, GM, and Marsden, CD (eds.) *Neurology in Clinical Practice,* 2nd edn., pp. 119–129. Stoneham, MA: Butterworth Publishers.
Vignolo, LA (1982). Auditory agnosia. *Philosophical Transactions of the Royal Society of London* 298: 49–57.
Warrington, EK and McCarthy, RA (1987). Categories of knowledge: Further fractionation and an attempted integration. *Brain* 110: 1273–1296.

Agrammatism I, Process Approaches

H. Kolk, University of Nijmegen, Nijmegen, The Netherlands

Agrammatism is a disorder that leads to difficulties with sentences. These difficulties can relate both to the correct comprehension and the correct production of sentences. That these difficulties concern sentences is evident from the fact that word comprehension and production can be relatively spared. Agrammatism occurs in many clinical populations. For Wernicke's aphasia, for instance, this has been established for both comprehension and production. Agrammatic comprehension has been demonstrated in Parkinson's patients, Alzheimer patients, and children with specific language disorders. However, agrammatism has been studied most systematically in patients with Broca's aphasia, and it is this group that is the focus of this article.

Agrammatism in Comprehension

The large majority of studies on agrammatism in Broca's aphasia have been on comprehension. An important impetus to these studies was the claim made by Zurif and Caramazza in the early 1970s that Broca's aphasics lack all knowledge of syntactical rules. It appeared that these patients were unable to comprehend reversible sentences such as 'the cat that the dog chased was black' (Caramazza and Zurif, 1976). The hypothesis that Broca's aphasics were 'asyntactic' led to three different reactions. The first was that this global characterization ignores the possibility that these patients may all be classifiable as Broca's aphasia but that their underlying deficits may be very different (Badecker and Caramazza, 1985). In support of the claim that agrammatism is not a unitary phenomenon, a number of studies have demonstrated that problems in comprehension can dissociate from problems in production (Miceli et al., 1983); that in production, problems with grammatical morphology can dissociate from problems with syntax *per se* (Miceli et al., 1983); and that there is large variation in the type of morphological errors within a group of patients (Miceli et al., 1989). (It should be noted that the latter findings were obtained from a large group of unselected aphasic patients, both fluent and nonfluent. However, grammatical deficits may manifest themselves very differently in fluent and nonfluent aphasia.) The critique by Badecker and Caramazza has widely been taken as a critique on neuropsychological group studies as such and has led to a substantial shift from group to case studies, particularly in the areas of reading, writing, and naming. Many researchers still insist on the usefulness of group studies in the case of agrammatism, maintaining that these patients share a number of important symptoms that need to be accounted for. A second reaction came from aphasiologists with a linguistic background. It held that instead of a loss of all syntax, only specific subsets of linguistic competence could be lost. In particular, when patients have to understand sentences with noncanonical word order, such as the ones employed by Caramazza and Zurif, they perform at chance, whereas they seem relatively unimpaired with canonical sentences (Grodzinsky, 1989). This approach has led to a large number of linguistically motivated studies of agrammatism, which are discussed in **Agrammatism II, Linguistic Approaches**.

The Mapping Hypothesis

A third type of reaction to the claim that 'grammar was gone' in agrammatism was that it is not so much the knowledge of grammatical rules that is impaired but the processing of this knowledge. The processing approach started with the seminal study by Linebarger et al. (1983), who observed that a number of agrammatic patients who performed at chance in comprehending reversible sentences with noncanonical word order were unimpaired in judging the grammaticality of the sentence. This dissociation led the authors to conclude that there could not be a loss of competence in agrammatism, as proposed by Caramazza and Zurif. Two possible accounts were suggested. The first was that the deficit did not relate to syntax as such but to the operations by which the syntactic level of representation (S-structure in transformational theory) was mapped onto the semantic level (D-structure) in order to assign thematic roles. Such mapping would be necessary for comprehension but not for grammaticality judgment; hence the dissociation. A second account had to do with mental resources. It is a well-known empirical phenomenon that carrying out two tasks simultaneously is more difficult than performing either task by itself – the so-called 'dual-task effect.' Comprehension can be regarded as a double task because it involves both syntactic and semantic processing, whereas grammaticality judgment presumably only depends on syntactic processing. A follow-up study provided evidence against the resource hypothesis (Schwarz et al., 1987). In this study, patients were asked to judge the plausibility of sentences. A comparison was made between simple actives, complex active sentences, and sentences with a noncanonical word order (e.g., passives and object gaps). Simple actives elicited relatively few errors, indicating that the problem was not with mapping as such. Sentences with a noncanonical word order elicited substantially and significantly more errors. This was attributed to the lack of syntactic transparency: Argument position in D- and S-structure is not the same, so mapping is complicated. Surprisingly, although complex sentences were somewhat more difficult than simple ones, the difference was not significant. This led to authors to reject the possibility that the dissociation between comprehension and grammaticality judgment was due to the cognitive resources of these patients being too limited to carry out two language tasks at once. The mapping hypothesis would therefore be the most appropriate account of agrammatic comprehension.

Kolk and Weijts (1996), however, argued that the way complexity was defined in the Schwartz et al. (1987) study may be less appropriate. To obtain a maximal complexity difference with a simple sentence, one should embed a relative clause between the agent noun phrase (NP) and the verb of this simple sentence, and this rarely occurred in the Schwartz et al. (1987) materials. When single-clause sentences were compared to sentences with center-embedded clauses, a significant complexity effect was obtained. It was concluded that (1) the resource hypothesis could not be rejected, and (2) in addition to word order, embedding is an important factor in agrammatic comprehension.

Of course, the mapping hypothesis was not ruled out by these results either. If one could think of the mapping process becoming more error prone, not only in the case of a noncanonical word order but also in the case of embedding, a mapping hypothesis could account for Kolk and Weijts's results. Such an hypothesis would be a resource limitation hypothesis, not a general one, as originally proposed, but a specific one related to the process of mapping syntactic structure onto thematic roles. Further research with the plausibility paradigm indeed led to such an hypothesis. Saffran et al. (1998) found that even single-clause sentences could pose serious difficulties to agrammatic patients. In particular, the patients found it very difficult to reject a sentence such as 'the painting disliked the artist,' performing just above chance. This is all the more remarkable since these sentences are nonreversible and active. Active nonreversible sentences generally produce very low error rates in a sentence picture matching task. It was argued that with these sentences, there is a strong bias to accept the interpretation indicated by the individual word meanings (an artist disliking a painting). Unimpaired individuals escape from this bias because syntactic analysis eliminates the interpretation that is inconsistent with the syntactic structure. In aphasics, this correcting influence is reduced "because of a pathological decrease in the spread of activation from the syntactic constituents to the units that represent syntactic roles" (Saffran et al., 1998, p. 290). [Kolk et al. (2003) present an event-related potential (ERP) study with normal persons, which represents a follow-up of the Saffran et al. (1998) study. The results of this study indicate that in normal persons semantic factors can overrule syntactic ones, even in unambiguous sentences.] Therefore, the authors maintained that the locus of the impairment is in the mapping stage. The nature of the impairment is conceived of differently: It has to do with resources. With this hypothesis, it is possible to account not only for the semantic bias effect observed in this experiment but also for the greater difficulty of sentences with a noncanonical word order in the traditional sentence picture matching tasks. Due to the fact that the first NP frequently carries the agent role, there is a bias both in normal and in aphasic people to interpret the first NP as an agent. As a consequence of their resource limitation, agrammatic patients have an even stronger bias to take the first NP as the agent of the verb, hence the canonicity effect.

The Resource Limitation Hypothesis

If indeed some sort of resource limitation is the underlying cause of agrammatism, as suggested by the outcome of the Saffran et al. (1998) study, it becomes interesting to again consider grammaticality judgment. Hartsuiker and Kolk (1998) used a word monitoring paradigm to study the detection of grammaticality and found that patients were able to detect ungrammaticalities in simple but not complex sentences. The normal participants did not show this complexity effect. In a recent ERP study, however, with subject and object-relative sentences, an effect of complexity on grammaticality detection was observed in normal participants (Kolk et al., 2003).

Further evidence for the presence of a resource limitation in agrammatism comes from studies on the interpretation of pronouns. For the proper interpretation of pronouns, it is essential that proper reference is made to persons, places, objects, or events in the contextual environment. This can only occur by means of integration of syntactic and discourse-related operations. From a resource-limitation standpoint, this means that pronoun interpretation should pose difficulties for agrammatic patients, particularly if the discourse operations are relatively complex (for a review, see Avrutin, 2000). In one study, it was found that sentences such as 'Who did the tiger chase?' were much less impaired than sentences such as 'Which lion did the tiger chase?' This contrast was explained by assuming that in the second sentence, reference is made to items, presupposed in the context, whereas in the first sentence there is no such presupposition. Difficulties with pronouns can also be demonstrated in sentences that, unlike the ones presented previously, do not involve argument movement. For instance, patients are much impaired when they have to establish reference for a pronoun in the presence of two possible antecedents: for example, 'First John hit Bill and than Mary hit him.' Similarly, more errors are made on nonreflexive (e.g., 'Is Mama Bear touching her?') than on reflexive pronouns (e.g., 'Is Mama Bear touching herself?'). The argument here is that with the reflexives, reference is to a unit present in the sentence itself – Mama Bear – and is therefore a purely syntactic operation. In the case of nonreflexive pronouns, on the other hand, reference has to be made to units present in the discourse and therefore requires syntax–discourse integration (Avrutin, 2000).

The Timing Hypothesis

Regarding the nature of the resource limitation, the most frequent approach has been to characterize it in terms of time (for a review, see Kolk, 1995). This means that the underlying deficit would relate either to a fast decay or to a slow retrieval of syntactic information. Either of these deficits would lead to a reduced period of time in which syntactic information is available for processes such as tree building the assignment of thematic roles, referential operations, and so on. This proposal has been implemented in a computational model that simulated the effects of varying degrees of fast decay or slow retrieval on tree building, assuming that a disruption of tree building would also negatively affect role assignment (mapping) and reference operations (syntax–discourse integration). The model was able to simulate the effects of variation in degree of severity and syntactic complexity on agrammatic error profiles, obtained in two earlier studies. Simulation was only successful when the timing disorder was assumed to affect syntactic phrasal categories and not when it affected function word categories alone. When phrasal categories were involved, it did not matter whether decay or retrieval rates were affected. The model bears close resemblance to the model of agrammatic comprehension by Haarmann et al. (1997). In this model, a limitation in the size of a pool of activation is responsible for agrammatic comprehension. This limitation leads to either a 'reduced efficiency,' which amounts to slower computation, or a reduced maintenance, comparable to fast decay. [Outside the sentence domain, Dell et al. (1997) simulated word production deficits in fluent aphasia using a similar contrast. The simulated deficits could consist of either 'a reduced connection strength,' leading to slower activation spreading, or fast decay. Interestingly, a later version of the model assumed only a single deficit – reduced connection strength – affecting either the phonological or the semantic level (Foygel and Dell, 2000).] The Haarmann et al. (1997) model constitutes an elaboration of the capacity model for normal sentence comprehension of Just and Carpenter (1992). [This model has been criticized by Caplan and Waters (1999), who argued for a subdivision of verbal working memory into one for automatic (e.g., structure building and role assignment) and one for controlled language processing (pragmatic and discourse related). Broca's aphasics should suffer from an impairment in the first type of working memory. From the evidence reviewed previously, it seems clear that Broca's aphasics are impaired on both syntactic and discourse-related operations. Furthermore, Kolk et al. (2003) present ERP evidence from normal people against this subdivision.] This model is about differences in the size of the activation pool within the normal population, between persons with a high versus a low working memory capacity. This implies that according to this theory, the agrammatic patients are not qualitatively but only quantitatively different from normal language users: They are at the lower end of a normal distribution of language capacity. Support for this hypothesis was provided by Miyake et al. (1994), who showed that when normal persons are presented with a large set of sentences of varying complexity at a very rapid rate, the error profile is highly similar to what has been found with aphasics.

A number of experimental studies have provided evidence for the timing hypothesis, particularly for the notion that syntactic processing is slowed down. This was done by means of various on-line techniques in which stimulus-onset asynchrony was manipulated, such as the syntactic priming paradigm (Kolk, 1995) and the crossmodal priming paradigm. Swinney et al. (1996) employed a crossmodal priming paradigm to study reactivation of moved arguments at their canonical site. They found that Broca's aphasics failed to show evidence for such reactivation. This failure is important because it could underlie the difficulties these patients have in comprehending sentences with moved arguments. Research, however, suggests that the failure is only a temporary one. When probed at later points in time, it appeared that patients did not show evidence for reactivation at the canonical site, nor at 300 ms after this site; at 500 ms, however, they did demonstrate reactivation of moved arguments.

Other support for the timing hypothesis comes from studies on ambiguity resolution. Research with normal persons has demonstrated that the interpretation of an ambiguous word is affected by the context in which it occurs. Therefore, in a sentence such as 'He made a phone call to the bank,' only the money-related meaning is activated. In an ERP study with Broca's aphasics, however, evidence was found for activation of both the appropriate and the inappropriate meaning (in the example given, the meaning related to river) at an interstimulus interval of 100 ms. After 1,250 ms, however, only the appropriate meaning was still active.

Two studies employed a word-monitoring paradigm and failed to find evidence for slow activation. This failure may have something to do with the nature of the word-monitoring paradigm. The priming results presented previously suggest that the delay may be as small as 500 ms. Given the fact that in these two studies, one or two other words intervened between the word containing the violation and the word to be monitored, the word-monitoring paradigm may not be sensitive enough to pick up a delay of this size.

Agrammatism in Production

Symptoms of agrammatic production have traditionally been assessed by means of analysis of spontaneous speech (Goodglass and Kaplan, 1983). Three main types of symptoms of spontaneous speech have been established in this way. The first is a reduced variety of grammatical form. The sentences that are produced have little subordination or phrasal elaboration. Because these symptoms relate to sentence form, we call them syntactic symptoms, where the term 'syntactic' is used in a purely descriptive way. Second is the omission of function words – articles, pronouns, auxiliaries, copulas, prepositions, and the like – and inflections. All these symptoms relate to grammatical morphology and are therefore referred to as morphological. The third is a slow rate of speech or nonfluency, referred to as the rate symptom. Whereas the previous symptoms have been established for English-speaking patients, similar symptoms occur in many other languages (Menn and Obler, 1990).

There has been some discussion in the literature on whether syntactic symptoms and morphological symptoms are caused by two independent deficits. This discussion was instigated by the case study of Miceli et al. (1983), who described an Italian-speaking patient as having "an almost pure morphological disorder" (p. 75), with syntax being almost entirely spared. Such a dissociation would indicate the existence of two independent deficits, a morphological and a syntactic one. However, the speech of this patient was characterized by a high number of nonfinite clauses, in which either the verb was lacking or the verb was used in the form of an infinitive or a past participle. For such clauses, it is difficult to argue that they are syntactically 'normal.' At least for languages such as English, Dutch, and German, a normal sentence must contain an inflected verb. In a further effort to find support for this double-deficit hypothesis, Rochon et al. (2000) conducted a large-scale factor analytic study that failed to support the hypothesis. Instead of a dissociation between syntactic and morphological symptoms, there was a dissociation between syntactic symptoms and symptoms related to inflection omission, on the one hand, and symptoms related to function word omission, on the other hand. It seems that the case for the existence of two independent grammatical deficits has not been made in a convincing way.

Variability of Symptoms

It is important to realize that these symptoms do not appear in an all-or-none fashion. Some patients show these symptoms slightly more often than a normal speaker, whereas other patients have them in almost all their utterances. A study of 22 Dutch-speaking Broca's aphasics examined the frequency of syntactic, morphological, and rate symptoms. With respect to syntactic symptoms, a mean percentage of embedded clauses of 6% was observed compared to 22% in a normal control group, but the frequency of this syntactic symptom varied from 0 to 21%. The same variability was apparent in the omission rate of grammatical morphology: It varied from 98 to 10%, almost as low as that for the control group, who omitted 8%. Finally, variability was also present in the rate symptom, which ranged from 23 to 90 words per minute, with the control group producing an average of 145 words per minute. Later work with a group of 37 English-speaking patients demonstrated similar variability (Rochon et al., 2000). As Rochon et al. (2000) indicated, there appears to be continuity on syntactic, morphological, and rate symptoms, both within the patient group and between the patient group and the normal controls. The implications of these observations are twofold. First, there is between-patient variation in the degree to which symptoms are present in individual patients. Second, because very few patients exhibit a particular symptom 100% of the time, there is within-patient variation: A symptom may be present on one occasion and fail to appear on other occasions. This probabilistic character of aphasic symptoms is not limited to sentence production. As noted by Goodglass (1993), inconsistency is the hallmark of aphasic behavior: A word that is appropriately produced or understood at one time will go wrong the next time and vice versa. At the same time, inconsistency is not a necessary outcome of brain dysfunction. It is not present in Alzheimer's disease, for instance, in which if a particular word is no longer understood, it will remain so on subsequent trials. This means that the variability of aphasic symptoms needs to be accounted for, as much as the symptoms.

The Timing Hypothesis

The most natural way to account for both within-patient and between-patient variability is to assume a resource limitation rather than a loss of some specific operation or set of operations. [Note that Friedmann and Grodzinsky (1997) made an attempt to account for between-patient variability (severity) by assuming loss of nodes at various heights in the syntactic tree. A loss at the level of tense or agreement node would lead to difficulties with inflection, whereas a loss at the level of the complementizer node would leave the ability to inflect intact but would make it possible for the patients to produce embedded clauses. This hypothesis predicts that when the agreement node is damaged, patients would only produce infinitives, in the case that their language has such infinitives. Data from Hofstede and Kolk (1994), however, indicate that the number of infinitives in the spontaneous speech of Dutch-speaking Broca's aphasics varies continuously: There is no bimodal distribution of patients who produce infinitives with a normal frequency and patients who produce infinitives in every utterance.]

As noted previously, to account for agrammatic comprehension, the resource limitation hypothesis has typically been worked our in terms of time, and this is also the case for agrammatic production. According to this hypothesis, fast decay or slow retrieval of grammatical information would disrupt the buildup of a syntactic tree. Such a disruption would harm not only comprehension but also production of sentences.

How does the temporal window hypothesis deal with variability? Between-subject variability was successfully implemented in the computer model referred to previously (Kolk, 1995) by making average decay or retrieval rates differ between simulated patients. Within-patient variability was simulated by making these rated vary stochastically around a mean.

To test applicability of the timing hypothesis to agrammatic production, Hartsuiker and Kolk (1998) employed a syntactic priming paradigm. In this paradigm, the participants repeated a sentence (e.g., 'The church was struck by the lightning'). After this, they were presented with a picture that they had to describe in one sentence (e.g., a picture of a cat chasing a dog). Normal participants tended to do this by employing the sentence form just presented to them. They did so despite the fact that they were unaware of the purpose of the experiment since they were told they were engaged in a study meant to test their memory for pictures. In a study of 12 Dutch-speaking agrammatics, the investigators found normal, and in one condition even better than normal, priming. Of particular interest are the results obtained with the production of passives. In the spontaneous speech of these patients, passives were extremely rare. In a picture description pretest, there was only a single occurrence of a passive construction in the whole group. After priming, however, passives appeared to be deblocked: 7 of 12 patients produced one or more passive constructions. These results fit the timing hypothesis quite well. If the computation of the constituent structure is delayed, priming speeds up this computation because the structural units have already reached a certain level of activation due to the previous repetition of this structure and it will generally take less time to bring these units to threshold.

According to the timing hypothesis, all operations that are necessary for planning a grammatical sentence have to be carried out within a limited amount of time. This means that not only syntactic but also conceptual or message-level operations could reduce the chance of computational simultaneity. Hartsuiker et al. (1999) carried out two experiments with Dutch agrammatic speakers in which they studied agreement inflection production. They drew upon a paradigm in which participants were presented with sentence fragments that had to be repeated and completed (e.g., 'The king of the colonies-was powerful'). One manipulation concerned the conceptual number of the head noun. This could be singular, as its grammatical number (e.g., 'the baby on the blankets'), or it could be plural (e.g., 'the label on the bottles'), unlike its grammatical number. In the latter example, although the head noun is grammatically singular, it is in fact referring to a multitude of labels, one on each bottle. Experiments with normal participants have demonstrated effects of conceptual plurality. In particular, they observed that in sentences with a head noun, which is grammatically singular but conceptually plural (e.g., 'the label on the bottles'), more agreement errors were made than in sentences without such a mismatch (e.g., 'the baby on the blankets'). This indicates that normal speakers take conceptual information into account when constructing subject–verb agreement. In two experiments with agrammatic speakers and normal controls, Hartsuiker et al. (1999) replicated this conceptual number effect in Dutch for the normal but not for the agrammatic speakers.

In fact, in the second experiment, which was better controlled, the agrammatics made fewer agreement errors in the mismatch condition than the normal controls. A subsequent comprehension test showed normal sensitivity in the agrammatics to the conceptual number variable. It was concluded that agrammatic speakers do not take into account conceptual information while constructing subject–verb agreement. They are unable to reach computational simultaneity of conceptual and syntactic information. This result parallels the difficulties agrammatic patients have with the interpretation of pronouns, which were discussed previously. Both appear to stem from the necessity to integrate two levels of representation: the syntactic and the discourse level in the case of comprehension and the syntactic and the message level in the case of production.

The Ellipsis Hypothesis

Ellipsis refers to well-formed incompleteness. So when a normal speaker utters 'everybody out,' he or she does not make a speech error. Linguistically, ellipsis can be defined by the absence of tense or finiteness. This means that in these utterances either a verb is lacking or an uninflected verb is used. Indefrey et al. (2001) studied the production of these constructions by German-speaking participants in a positron emission tomography study. Compared to complete sentences, the ones lacking finiteness elicited less brain activation. The area in which the blood flow response varied was the operculum in the left hemisphere, but in a replication the variation was observed in Broca's area. The ellipsis hypothesis holds that agrammatics overuse these little demanding elliptical constructions, presumably because they lack the capacity to generate sufficient brain activation to produce their complete counterparts. Various kinds of evidence support this hypothesis (Kolk, 1995). First, features of normal ellipsis – related to word order, subject omission, inflection omission, and so on – are also characteristic of the nonfinite constructions of agrammatic speakers. Second, categories of nonfinite constructions obtained from normal speakers, aphasics, and 2- and 3-year-old children have very similar distributions (Kolk, 2001). Third, substantial task effects are observed when spontaneous speech is compared to various kinds of picture description tasks, with the general trend being fewer omissions and more substitutions of grammatical morphology.

Task effects can be very large. For instance, a Dutch-speaking patient was observed who omitted finiteness in approximately 80% of his utterances in his spontaneous speech, and this omission rate decreased to almost zero not only in a picture description task but also in a condition in which the patient was requested to 'speak in complete sentences.' However, this shift to more complete sentences had a cost: It led to an increase in rate symptoms, as the patient paused longer between words and repeated more words. It may seem, therefore, that the rate symptoms are related to both the syntactic and the morphological symptoms. They would reflect a process of corrective adaptation to the timing deficit: A representation that is too complex disintegrates prematurely and the patient attempts to covertly repair the representation (for a further test of this hypothesis, see Oomen et al., 2001).

Conclusion

Studies on agrammatic comprehension indicate the existence of a processing bottleneck at the syntactic level. Effects of this bottleneck manifest themselves in tasks that primarily depend on the syntactic level but also in tasks that require the integration of this level with discourse and message levels of representation. The processing bottleneck appears to relate to temporal aspects of language processing.

See also: Agrammatism II, Linguistic Approaches.

Bibliography

Avrutin, S (2000). 'Comprehension of D-linked and non-D-linked wh-question by children and Broca's aphasics.' In: Grodzinsky, Y, Shapiro, L, and Swinney, D (eds.) *Language and the brain*, pp. 295–313. New York: Academic Press.

Badecker W and Caramazza, A (1985). 'On considerations of method and theory governing the use of clinical categories in neurolinguistics and cognitive neuropsychology: the case against agrammatism.' *Cognition* 20: 97–125.

Caplan, D and Waters, G (1999). 'Verbal working memory and sentence comprehension.' *Behavioral and Brain Sciences* 22: 77–94.

Caramazza, A and Zurif, EG (1976). 'Dissociation of algorithmic and heuristic processes in sentence comprehension: evidence from aphasia.' *Brain and Language* 3: 572–582.

Dell, GS, Schwartz, MF, Martin, N, Saffran, EM, and Gagnon, DA (1997). 'Lexical access in aphasic and non-aphasic speakers.' *Psychological Review* 104: 801–837.

Foygel, D and Dell, GS (2000). 'Models of impaired lexical access in speech production.' *Journal of Memory and Language* 43: 182–216.

Friedmann, N and Grodzinsky, Y (1997). 'Tense and agreement in agrammatic production: pruning the syntactic tree.' *Brain and Language* 56: 397–425.

Goodglass, H (1993). *Understanding aphasia.* New York: Academic Press.

Goodglass, H and Kaplan, E (1983). *The assessment of aphasia and related disorders,* 2nd edn. Philadelphia: Lea & Febiger.

Grodzinsky, Y (1989). 'Agrammatic comprehension of relative clauses.' *Brain and Language* 27: 135–159.

Haarmann, HJ, Just, MA, and Carpenter, PA (1997). 'Aphasic sentence comprehension as a resource deficit: a computational approach.' *Brain and Language* 59: 76–120.

Hartsuiker, RJ and Kolk, HJ (1998). 'Syntactic facilitation in agrammatic sentence production.' *Brain and Language* 62: 221–254.

Hartsuiker, RJ, Kolk, HHJ, and Huinck, P (1999). 'Agrammatic production of subject–verb agreement: the effect of conceptual number.' *Brain and Language* 69: 119–160.

Hofstede, BTM and Kolk, HHJ (1994). 'The effects of task variation on the production of grammatical morphology in Broca's aphasia: a multiple case study.' *Brain and Language* 46: 278–328.
Indefrey, P, Brown, CM, Hellwig, F, Amunts, K, Herzog, H, Seitz, RJ, and Hagoort, P (2001). 'A neural correlate of syntactic encoding during speech production.' *Proceedings of the National Academy of Sciences of the United States of America* 98: 5933–5936.
Just, M and Carpenter, P (1992). 'A capacity theory of comprehension: individual differences in working memory.' *Psychological Review* 99: 122–149
Kolk, HHJ (1995). 'A time-based approach to agrammatic production.' *Brain and Language* 50: 282–303.
Kolk, HHJ (2001). 'Does agrammatic speech constitute a regression to child language? A three-way comparison between agrammatic, child and normal ellipsis.' *Brain and Language* 77: 340–350.
Kolk, HHJ, Chwilla, DJ, van Herten, M, and Oor, PJW (2003). 'Structure and limited capacity in verbal working memory: a study with event-related potential.' *Brain and Language* 85: 1–36.
Kolk, HHJ and Weijts, M (1996). 'Judgements of semantic anomaly in agrammatic patients: argument movement, syntactic complexity and the use of heuristics.' *Brain and Language* 54: 86–135.
Linebarger, MC, Schwartz, M, and Saffran, E (1983). 'Sensitivity to grammatical structure in so-called agrammatic aphasia.' *Cognition* 13: 361–392.
Menn, L and Obler, L (1990). *Agrammatic aphasia: a cross language narrative source book.* Amsterdam: Benjamins.
Miceli, G, Mazzuchi, A, Menn, L, and Goodglass, H (1983). 'Contrasting cases of Italian agrammatic aphasia without comprehension disorder.' *Brain and Language* 35: 24–65.
Miceli, G, Silveri, MC, Romani, C, and Caramazza, A (1989). 'Variation in the pattern of omissions and substitutions of grammatical morphemes in the spontaneous speech of so-called agrammatic patients.' *Brain and Language* 26: 447–492.
Miyake, A, Carpenter, PA, and Just, MA (1994). 'Reduced resources and specific impairments in normal and aphasic sentence comprehension.' *Cognitive Neuropsychology* 12: 651–679.
Oomen, CCE, Postma, A, and Kolk, HHJ (2001). 'Prearticulatory and postarticulatory self-monitoring in Broca's aphasia.' *Cortex* 37: 627–641.
Rochon, E, Saffran, EM, Berndt, RS, and Schwartz, MF (2000). 'Quantitative analysis of aphasic sentence production: further development and new data.' *Brain and Language* 72: 193–218.
Saffran, E, Schwartz, MF, and Linebarger, MC (1998). 'Semantic influences on thematic role assignment: evidence from normals and aphasics.' *Brain and Language* 62: 255–297.
Schwartz, M, Linebarger, MC, Saffran, E, and Pate, D (1987). 'Syntactic transparency and sentence interpretation in aphasia.' *Language and Cognitive Processing* 2: 85–113.
Swinney, D, Zurif, E, Prather, P, and Love, T (1996). 'Neurological distribution of processing resources underlying language comprehension.' *Journal of Cognitive Neuroscience* 8: 174–184.

Agrammatism II, Linguistic Approaches

A. Beretta, Michigan State University, East Lansing, MI, USA

Introduction

The term agrammatism is used in a rather general way in the following discussion to refer to syntactic deficits of a sort that have been observed in Broca's aphasia. The term is used only to pick out certain phenomena as a focus of inquiry, without implying any exclusionary criteria or limitations on what counts as agrammatism or what does not. Agrammatic data form one piece of the neurolinguistic enterprise and are most useful only in conjunction with other data (from neuroimaging, from behavioral studies, and so forth).

The phenomena that constitute the focus of inquiry here are specific attempts to characterize the patterns of sparing and loss in Broca's aphasia in terms of linguistic theory. Although it may seem self-evident that any understanding of language sparing and language loss can only be as good as our theory of language, the fact is that the majority of researchers who have investigated agrammatism have ignored linguistic theory or have simply been unaware of its existence. Partly this is because many of those interested in agrammatism have primarily medical or clinical interests, partly because agrammatism predates linguistic theory by about a century, and partly because of sundry pragmatic considerations that need not detain us. Despite neglect in some quarters, linguistic theory nevertheless has been brought to bear on agrammatic phenomena, and a number of models have been proposed.

Before looking at some of these models, first it is necessary to consider what the nature of the enterprise is. Let us say that we have two bodies of knowledge that we may refer to, in broad terms, as brain theory and linguistic theory. In what ways can the study of agrammatism help to unify these two bodies of knowledge? Agrammatism involves abnormal brains and abnormal language, so we may rephrase the question as two related questions: (1) Do we expect to learn more about normal brains by looking at agrammatism?; and (2) Do we expect to learn more about the normal language faculty by looking at agrammatism? Answering either question in the affirmative would inevitably involve linking the two bodies of knowledge.

A sample of linguistic models of agrammatism is described in the next section, and thereafter this article returns to discussing these basic questions.

Linguistic Models of Agrammatism

Comprehension and production have been treated separately in research on agrammatism. This is because a number of Broca's aphasics who are impaired in their production but reportedly unimpaired in their comprehension have been identified. Therefore, this distinction is maintained here.

Comprehension

Quite a number of models of agrammatic comprehension have been proposed (Caplan and Futter, 1986; Druks and Marshall, 1995; Friederici and Gorrell, 1998; Grodzinsky, 1995; Hickok and Avrutin, 1995; Hickok et al., 1993; Linebarger et al., 1983; Mauner et al., 1993; Piñango, 2000; among others). More or less overtly, most of these models seek to partition the sentences that Broca's aphasics are good at from those sentences that they have difficulty with along a divide suggested by linguistic theory. The idea is that this will be informative about which aspects of language the impaired brain can no longer process, information that can potentially feed into both brain theory and linguistic theory. Just two of these models are discussed: the Trace-Deletion Hypothesis (Grodzinsky, 1995) and the Double-Dependency Hypothesis (Mauner et al., 1993).

This is not a random selection. The selection is intended to contrast a model that is constrained by linguistic theory and one that introduces nontheoretical components. This will serve to clarify what is important in the effort to find links between two bodies of knowledge, keeping our eyes on the prize.

Caramazza and Zurif (1976) showed that Broca's aphasics suffer from certain selective impairments in comprehension. At the time, this was a surprising finding because it had been believed for over a century that their comprehension was unimpaired. The fact that the disorder was selective is what made it potentially interesting from the perspective of linguistic theory. Caramazza and Zurif reported that on reversible sentence–picture matching tasks, Broca's aphasics did not know who was doing what to whom (who was the Agent and who was the Theme) in passive constructions and object-relative constructions – their performance was random. By contrast, they knew who was doing what to whom in active sentences and subject-relatives, where their performance was above chance. This pattern has since been observed very frequently in Broca's aphasics, such that it is now considered 'core' (though there is controversy regarding just how uniform this is).

One of the first attempts to characterize this core agrammatic pattern was the Trace-Deletion Hypothesis.

The Trace-Deletion Hypothesis (TDH)

The TDH is in two parts. The first specifies that in an agrammatic representation that is otherwise normal, traces in Θ-positions are deleted. This has the consequence that moved referential NPs lack information about thematic roles (like Agent or Theme) since that information is carried by the trace. The second part of the TDH indicates how NPs that lack a thematic role are assigned a role. The claim is that they are assigned a role by way of a default strategy: assign a referential NP a role by its linear position (e.g., first NP = Agent) if it does not already have a Θ-role (Grodzinsky, 1995). To see how this works, consider the following passive sentence:

1. [The boy]$_i$	was chased t_i	by the girl
Theme		Agent

In an unimpaired representation, the NP (*the boy*) moves from the object position to the front of the sentence. This movement leaves a trace (*t*) behind, in the object position. The role of Theme is assigned to the position occupied by the trace and conveyed to the moved NP via a chain shown by the coindexations (*i*) in (1). Now, let us turn to what happens in an agrammatic representation:

2. [The boy]	was chased *	by the girl
Default agent		Syntactic agent

Lacking trace (*), the chain is disrupted and the moved NP (*the boy*) is assigned the Agent role by the default strategy. The NP in the *by* phrase, which is not thought to have undergone movement, is assigned the Agent role in the normal way, syntactically. The upshot is that the representation contains two NPs, each competing for the role of Agent. On a standard sentence–picture matching task, the patient must guess which NP is Agent, and random performance follows, consistent with fact.

The TDH has been subject to severe criticism. A major flaw is that the deletion of trace does not, in fact, divide spared and impaired structures. Traces occur in virtually every sentence, but agrammatics do not have problems with virtually every sentence. To effect the division, in every instance, requires the effective agency of the totally atheoretical default strategy. There is no theory of strategies, and strategies do not form part of linguistic theory. The deletion of trace, on its own, has no consequences, yet trace is the only part of the TDH that is motivated by linguistic theory. Relevant consequences (i.e., partitioning the data into sentences agrammatics can understand and those they cannot) arise only by virtue of the atheoretical default strategy. Thus, if the aim of the study of agrammatism is to contribute to the linking of two bodies of knowledge, brain theory and linguistic theory, the problem is that, under the TDH, linguistic theory does not in fact do much work.

The Double-Dependency Hypothesis (DDH)

Partly motivated by the shortcomings of the TDH, the DDH (Mauner et al., 1993) sought to do away with any reliance on atheoretical strategies to partition agrammatic data and to account for those data entirely in terms of linguistic theory. At the heart of the proposal is the observation that there is a class of dependency relations, namely, those obtaining in syntactic chains that are assigned only one Θ-role, and that in relations of this kind, in agrammatism, the dependency between a referential NP and the foot of the chain is disrupted. This amounts to a loss of a constraint on coindexation. In sentences where there are **two** such dependencies, confusion arises over which NP is coindexed with what. Because the coindexation is semantically ambiguous, thematic role assignment is also ambiguous. This has the consequence that agrammatics must guess who is doing what to whom. By contrast, where there is only **one** such dependency, there is no possible ambiguity, so agrammatic interpretation should be normal. For an example with two dependencies, consider the following passive sentence:

3. $[\text{The dog}]_i$ was $\text{bitt}[\text{en}]_k$ t_i by $[\text{the cat}]_k$

In this sentence, the two dependencies correctly co-indexed in a normal representation are $\langle[\text{the dog}]_i, t_i\rangle$ and $\langle \text{en}_k, [\text{the cat}]_k\rangle$. The referential NP, *the dog*, and the foot of its chain, the trace *t*, form one dependency. The second dependency is between the referential NP, *the cat*, and the foot of its chain, the passive morphology *–en*. In an agrammatic representation, however, the ambiguous interpretation would permit not only the correct coindexations, as above, but would also allow the anomalous coindexations: $\langle[\text{the dog}]_i, \text{en}_k\rangle$ and $\langle t_i, [\text{the cat}]_k\rangle$.

The DDH succeeds in accounting for the core data (actives, passives, subject-relatives, and object-relatives) and a wide range of other data without resorting to strategies. Interestingly, this model survives stern cross-linguistic tests, with a variety of reversals of canonical word order, where all other models that incorporate linear-based strategies fail (Beretta, 2001).

Production

Traditional accounts of production deficits in agrammatism focus on the reduction in the range of syntactic forms that are available for deployment, the slow, effortful speech that is typically observed, and the loss or substitution of morphology (particularly function words and bound inflectional morphemes). Only the morphological deficit has received sustained attention in linguistic models, so here I describe two recent attempts to capture those phenomena: Hagiwara's (1995) model and Friedmann's (2001) tree-pruning hypothesis, both very similar models. The initial insight is due to Ouhalla (1993), who proposed that agrammatics lack all functional categories. Functional categories form the higher branches of the syntactic tree and Ouhalla's view was that nothing above VP survived in agrammatism. This turned out to be too all-or-nothing a characterization to accommodate the frequently observed sparing in many agrammatics of some functional categories. The models of Hagiwara and Friedmann are more flexible.

Hagiwara's Model

Like Ouhalla, Hagiwara's (1995) model locates agrammatic impairment in functional categories, but rather than lopping off all of the syntactic tree above VP, the model identifies a level for each agrammatic subject. Wherever in the tree that level is found to be for an individual, all elements dependent on nodes above it are lost and those dependent on nodes below it are spared. For example, Hagiwara reported Japanese subjects who had lost NegP but who retained the higher CP node. The model is framed in terms of increased processing costs for each application of a structure-building operation known in current linguistic theory as Merge (Chomsky, 1995).

Friedmann's Model

The tree-pruning hypothesis, like Hagiwara's, finds the level in the tree indicated by each individual agrammatic subject's performance on a range of tests. Friedmann (2001) reported a group of Hebrew-Arabic-speaking agrammatic subjects who made many errors of Tense but relatively few of subject–verb agreement. She argues that other studies in a range of languages offer a degree of support for this finding. She explains these findings by reference to a syntactic tree in which agreement (AgrP) is below Tense (TP). Agrammatics, it is suggested, cannot project to the higher Tense node.

What Does the Study of Agrammatism Tell Us about Brains or about Language?

What Does Evidence Organized by Linguistic Models of Agrammatism Reveal about Brains?

Brain theory deals with how brains get to accomplish the work they must do, from autonomic and somatic function to cognitive function. This work is accomplished by, among other things, patterns of firing of assemblies of feature-tuned neurons in particular regions. These patterns, it is thought, may constitute a neural code. The effort is to discover what the spatiotemporal neural codes are for any given function and how they instantiate behaviors. How can the study of agrammatism help with this? To the extent that we have a coherent theory of the normal language faculty, and to the extent that we have characterized abnormal agrammatic language correctly, then, whatever spatial and temporal neural information we find that produces observed behaviors should be relevant.

As a simple example, if someone acquires brain damage to a specific area, and if there are certain selective language deficits that we can observe in this person and which we can characterize properly, then this suggests that the lesioned area is implicated in the processing of those specific aspects of language that are compromised.

In this light, let us consider a contribution that comprehension models of the sort described above might reasonably make. Experiments testing these models involve Broca's aphasics who have lesions minimally encompassing Broca's area and its vicinity. Aspects of linguistic theory have been shown in some of these experiments to yield the requisite partitioning of data. The relevant aspects are a class of referential dependency relations (which involve more than trace–antecedent relations). Processing these dependency relations is problematic in agrammatism and is responsible for the observed pattern of sparing and loss. Therefore, it might be posited that Broca's area is implicated in the processing of these dependency relations. To the extent that this claim is justifiable, it constitutes an initial attempt to link something of what we know about brains (function is localized) and something of what we know about language (it involves the processing of a broad class of dependency relations).

The neuroimaging record lends some support to this view (e.g., Caplan et al., 1999; Stromswold et al., 1996; Just et al., 1996), though the picture is, unsurprisingly, far more complex (Caplan et al., 2001). The processing of dependencies apparently also implicates other areas of cortex. In addition, many other linguistic (and nonlinguistic) processes implicate the left inferior frontal cortex. Thus, whereas functional neuroimaging experiments suggest that a broad range of linguistic processing involves many brain regions, functional magnetic resonance imaging (fMRI) and positron-emission tomography (PET) studies coupled with the data from agrammatism confirm the importance of Broca's area and environs in the processing of relevant dependency relations.

The combination of data from well-motivated fMRI and PET experiments and data from principled studies of impaired subjects may be seen as preliminary, but it holds out promise for the future.

Apart from localization, agrammatic data, coupled with magnetoencephalography (MEG) and electroencephalography (EEG) experiments, ought to be revealing about some aspects of the temporal coding of language.

In principle, finding out more about brains by investigating agrammatism is at least possible. If we wish to know how a brain computes language, we must examine it computing language – and selectively failing to compute language in the normal ways.

What Does Evidence Organized by Linguistic Models of Agrammatism Reveal about Language?

It is quite common to read in the literature on agrammatism that agrammatic data provide a constraint on linguistic theory. Linguistic theory, it is asserted, must be compatible with the evidence from agrammatism. This is an interesting point of view, but one that needs to be thought through carefully. For instance, what happens if there is clear evidence from an agrammatic subject that conflicts with clear grammaticality judgment evidence? Is one form of evidence to be privileged over the other? Often, it is assumed that agrammatic data should be privileged because it is in some undefined sense more 'real' than grammaticality judgment data. But this view lacks merit. Any reasonable scientist will take evidence wherever it is to be found, and judgment data are the most obvious data presenting themselves to linguists. Grammaticality judgments are controlled experiments every bit as much as experiments with agrammatics. Any given experiment, whether it uses judgments of grammaticality, reaction times, or neuroimaging technologies, may yield findings that are either relatively clear or not, or may be based on predictions that follow from theory or not, or may suffer from methodological problems or not. Thus, experiments yielding different kinds of data may be well designed and executed or not, but there is nothing more real about one kind of data than another.

If agrammatic data ordered by linguistic theory are to be used to constrain linguistic theory, it is axiomatic that the agrammatic data actually **be** ordered by linguistic theory (and not by an atheoretical strategy, for example). Some models of agrammatism honor this simple logical requirement, but not all of them do. To the extent that this requirement is observed, agrammatic data can, in principle, be useful in testing linguistic theory, but it is worth stressing that the value of any experiment, involving agrammatic subjects or not, must be evaluated in the normal ways and weighed against other data.

An illustrative example is in order. The tree- pruning hypothesis makes a specific claim that agrammatic data act as a constraint on linguistic theory. It is argued that Pollock's (1989) ordering of functional nodes, with TP above AgrP, should be preferred to other accounts since because the agrammatic data favor this ordering. No mention is made of the arguments and evidence that have led linguists since Pollock to posit AgrP above TP, but even with the agrammatic evidence alone there are reasons to be cautious. First, it is not the case that subjects always make tense errors and never agreement errors. Rather, there is a statistically significant dissociation. In a verb completion test, Hebrew subjects made 41% errors on tense and 4% errors on agreement (Friedmann, 2001). However, as has been pointed out, this means that despite the supposed pruning of tense, "it is available more often than not" (Edwards and Lightfoot, 2000: 32). In a sentence completion task, Benedet et al. (1998) found very different percentages: 85% errors on tense and 58% errors on agreement among English-speaking agrammatics. In this case, even though agreement is supposedly intact, it is available **less** often than not. And Penke (2000) describes data from German, Italian, French, and Dutch that she interprets as being inconsistent with the tree-pruning hypothesis. In Korean, too, there are anomalous data. On the face of it, the agrammatic data do not seem consistent or clear enough to warrant an adoption of Pollock's hierarchy. In any case, however clear the agrammatic data may or may not be, they must be weighed against the linguistic evidence before it is possible to appraise their potential contribution.

However, it should not escape our attention that, in this case, the data are actually organized in syntactic terms and that this at least means that it is **possible** to assess the value of the data to linguistic theory.

Conclusion

In principle, the idea that the study of agrammatism might contribute to theories of brain and of language is an appealing one. In practice, perhaps unsurprisingly given current preliminary levels of understanding, it turns out to be very hard to make very precise contributions.

The study of agrammatism to map out cerebral localization of specific language function is best seen as complementary to imaging research. Lesions in agrammatic subjects tend to be too large to permit precise characterizations of the relation between location and aspects of language, but if careful attention is paid to the extent of the lesions and if this is informative about differences in performance patterns, as has been shown in studies by, for example, Baum et al. (1990) and Blumstein et al. (1994), then progress is possible. In combination with imaging studies, if these are more consistently motivated by linguistic theory than has typically been the case, an increased understanding of the spatial organization of language may emerge.

The study of agrammatism to find out more about temporal aspects of cortical language processing is also an area of inquiry that holds out considerable promise. On-line methods with agrammatics coupled with EEG/MEG studies of normal subjects are likely to be particularly useful.

Finally, although the two bodies of knowledge that are of interest in neurolinguistics (including agrammatism) are brain theory and linguistic theory, it is evident that the relationship between linguistic theory and language processing will need to be clarified if more rapid progress is to be made. After all, any task that agrammatic subjects or normal subjects in neuroimaging or electrophysiological studies can complete must be a performance task involving some sort of processing, and linguistic theory has traditionally been agnostic with regard to such processing. If it can be shown that the grammar and the parser are one and the same thing, as some have proposed, then it will make the whole neurolinguistic enterprise immeasurably more tractable. For an intriguing effort in this direction, see Phillips (2004), whose proposal is not just programmatic but is supported by a growing set of empirical data. Processing issues in agrammatism, clearly critical to the neurolinguistic enterprise, are addressed in **Agrammatism I, Process Approaches**.

See also: Agrammatism I, Process Approaches.

Bibliography

Baum, S, Blumstein, SE, Naeser, MA, et al. (1990). 'Temporal dimensions of consonant and vowel production: An acoustic and CT scan analysis of aphasic speech.' *Brain and Language* 39: 33–56.

Benedet, MJ, Christiansen, JA, and Goodglass, H (1998). 'A cross-linguistic study of grammatical morphology in Spanish- and English-speaking agrammatic patients.' *Cortex* 34: 309–336.

Beretta, A (2001). 'Linear and structural accounts of theta-role assignment in agrammatic aphasia.' *Aphasiology* 15: 515–531.

Beretta, A, Piñango, M, Patterson, J, et al. (1999). 'Recruiting comparative cross-linguistic evidence to address competing accounts of agrammatic aphasia.' *Brain and Language* 67: 149–168.

Beretta, A, Schmitt, C, Halliwell, J, et al. (2001). 'The effects of scrambling on Spanish and Korean agrammatic interpretation: Why linear models fail and structural models survive.' *Brain and Language* 79: 407–425.

Blumstein, SE, Burton, M, Baum, S, et al. (1994). 'The role of lexical status on the phonetic categorization of speech in aphasia.' *Brain and Language* 46: 181–197.

Caplan, D and Futter, C (1986). 'Assignment of thematic roles by an agrammatic aphasic patient.' *Brain and Language* 27: 117–135.

Caplan, D, Alpert, N, and Waters, G (1999). 'PET studies of syntactic processing with auditory sentence presentation.' *NeuroImage* 9: 343–351.

Caplan, D, Vijayan, S, Kuperberg, G, et al. (2001). 'Vascular responses to syntactic processing: Event-related fMRI study of relative clauses.' *Human Brain Mapping* 15: 26–38.

Caramazza, A and Zurif, E (1976). 'Dissociation of algorithmic and heuristic processes in sentence comprehension: Evidence from aphasia.' *Brain and Language* 3: 572–582.

Chomsky, N (1995). *The minimalist program.* Cambridge, MA: MIT Press.

Druks, J and Marshall, JC (1995). 'When passives are easier than actives: Two case studies of agrammatic comprehension.' *Cognition* 55: 311–331.

Edwards, S and Lightfoot, D (2000). 'Intact grammars but intermittent access.' *Behavioral and Brain Sciences* 23: 31–32.

Friederici, A and Gorrell, P (1998). 'Structural prominence and agrammatic theta-role assignment: A reconsideration of linear strategies.' *Brain and Language* 65: 252–275.

Friedmann, N (2001). 'Agrammatism and the psychological reality of the syntactic tree.' *Journal of Psycholinguistic Research* 30: 71–90.

Grodzinsky, Y (1995). 'A restrictive theory of agrammatic comprehension.' *Brain and Language* 50: 27–51.

Hagiwara, H (1995). 'The breakdown of functional categories and the economy of derivation.' *Brain and Language* 50: 92–116.

Hagiwara, H and Caplan, D (1990). 'Syntactic comprehension in Japanese aphasics: Effects of category and thematic role order.' *Brain and Language* 38: 159–170.

Hickok, G and Avrutin, S (1995). 'Representation, referentiality, and processing in agrammatic comprehension: Two case studies.' *Brain and Language* 50: 10–26.

Hickok, G, Zurif, E, and Canseco-Gonzales, E (1993). 'Structural description of agrammatic comprehension.' *Brain and Language* 45: 371–395.

Just, MA, Carpenter, PA, Keller, TA, et al. (1996). 'Brain activation modulated by sentence comprehension.' *Science* 274: 114–116.
Linebarger, M, Schwartz, M, and Saffran, E (1983). 'Sensitivity to grammatical structure in so-called agrammatic aphasics.' *Cognition* 13: 361–393.
Mauner, G, Fromkin, V, and Cornell, T (1993). 'Comprehension and acceptability judgments in agrammatism: Disruptions in the syntax of referential dependency.' *Brain and Language* 45: 340–370.
Ouhalla, J (1993). 'Functional categories, agrammatism and language acquisition.' *Linguistische Berichte* 143: 3–36.
Penke, M (2000). 'Unpruned trees in German Broca's aphasia.' *Behavioral and Brain Sciences* 23: 46–47.
Piñango, M (2000). 'Canonicity in Broca's sentence comprehension: The case of psychological verbs.' In: Grodzinsky, Y, Shapiro, L, and Swinney, D (eds.) *Language and the brain.* New York: Academic Press.
Phillips, C (2004). 'Linguistics and linking problems.' In: Rice, M and Warren, S (eds.) *Developmental language disorders: From phenotypes to etiologies.* Mahwah, NJ: Erlbaum.
Pollock, JY (1989). 'Verb movement, universal grammar and the structure of IP.' *Linguistic Inquiry* 20: 365–424.
Stromswold, K, Caplan, D, Alpert, N, et al. (1996). 'Localization of syntactic comprehension by positron emission tomography.' *Brain and Language* 52: 452–473.

Agrammatism

G. Miceli

Agrammatism is an aphasic disorder characterized by violations of grammatical rules in the subject's speech. Its most prominent feature is the difficulty using "function" words (freestanding grammatical morphemes, such as articles, prepositions, auxiliary verbs, and clitic pronouns; bound grammatical morphemes, such as verb and noun inflections, etc.), in the presence of relative sparing of "content" words (nouns, adjectives, and verbs). It frequently appears in the context of the nonfluent, dysarthric, and dysprosodic speech characteristic of Broca's aphasia. In its mildest form, it is characterized by fairly complex sentences with occasional omissions of function words (e.g., "Then admitted again. . .because pain always feel. Take pills but no sleep. . . . Then neurologist give sleeping pill, but I not sleep"). In more severe cases, speech consists of simple sentences lacking function words (e.g., "In the morning wear skirt. . .then bath. . .then wash. . .then exercise. . .always; then my daughter. . .go work). In the most severe cases, it is reduced to one-word utterances, often without recoverable grammatical structure (e.g., "Me. . .home. . .headache. . .dead!").

The features of agrammatic speech were first studied in German-speaking subjects in the early 1900s. However, the characterization of the disorder was critically influenced by later analyses conducted on English-speaking aphasics. Thus, for a long time the hallmark of agrammatism was deemed to be the omission of function words, both freestanding and bound to word roots. Studies conducted in the early 1980s on languages other than English (e.g., Italian, Hebrew, and German) forced the reconsideration of this view. They confirmed the widespread omission of freestanding grammatical words but documented substitutions (rather than omissions) of bound grammatical words. In these languages, which do not allow the production of uninflected roots (in Italian, *vol-* is the root of the verb *volare*, to fly, but is not a real word, whereas *talk-* is the root of the verb *to talk* but is also a real English word), inflected words usually occur in one of the infinitival or default forms. Additional deficits documented in agrammatic speech are omissions of main verbs and difficulties with word order or with case (in case-marked languages such as German).

The frequent association of agrammatic speech with Broca's aphasia influenced attempts to distinguish this disorder from paragrammatic speech, which would be characterized by substitutions (rather than omissions) of function words and by syntactically complex sentences, in the context of fluent spoken output. However, analyses of spontaneous speech consistently failed to demonstrate significantly different patterns of performance on function words in the two disorders. Thus, the apparent contrast between agrammatism and paragrammatism seems to result from associated symptoms (nonfluent speech in the former, and fluent speech in the latter) more than from theoretically meaningful distinctions.

Subjects who speak agrammatically usually also write ungrammatical sentences. Although detailed analyses of writing are far less numerous than similar analyses of speech, it has been suggested that in writing agrammatism is generally milder and grammatical words are more prone to substitutions (as opposed to omissions) than in speech. The co-occurrence of agrammatism in speech and in writing is not systematic, however, because there are reports of agrammatic speech associated with normal writing and of agrammatic writing associated with normal production of grammatical words in the context of neologistic jargonaphasia.

Subjects with agrammatic production frequently also present with agrammatic comprehension. It was claimed for a long time that agrammatic subjects have "good" comprehension of conversational speech, but this view was reconsidered when researchers started to evaluate comprehension by means of semantically reversible sentences. A sentence is semantically reversible when more than one of the noun arguments can be agent, theme, or beneficiary of the action denoted by the predicate verb. Thus, "The boy was kissed by the girl" is a semantically reversible sentence because in real life both boy and girl can perform the act of kissing, whereas "The apple was eaten by the boy" is semantically irreversible because the act of eating can only be performed by the boy. For the purpose of studies on agrammatism, reversible sentences have one crucial feature: Contrary to irreversible sentences, which can be interpreted correctly merely on the basis of encyclopedic knowledge (boy can eat apple, but the reverse is impossible), they can be comprehended only if grammatical rules are spared (word order and the morphology of the sentence). Thus, boy can kiss girl, and girl can kiss boy, but in the sentence "The boy was kissed by the girl" word order and passive morphology establish that it is the girl who is doing the kissing. Experimental investigations on groups of subjects proved that aphasics who produce ungrammatical sentences also fail to comprehend reversible sentences and other complex syntactic structures that require, among other things, a normal ability to process function words (e.g., those realizing the passive voice of a sentence). When presented with the sentence "The horse is chased by the cow," an agrammatic speaker might decide that horse, not cow, is doing the chasing, or he or she might assign an identical meaning to the sentences "The boy that the girl is chasing is fat" and "The boy that is chasing the girl is fat." As in the case of agrammatic speech and writing, the co-occurrence of agrammatic production and comprehension, however frequent, is by no means the rule. Several reports of subjects with flawless comprehension and agrammatic output unequivocally demonstrate that agrammatism can be restricted to production tasks.

Interpretations

Early accounts of agrammatism (and some recent proposals) focused on the production deficit. Deeply influenced by the co-occurrence of the disorder with the slow and effortful speech characteristic of Broca's aphasia, they invoked the notion of "economy of effort." In this view, the need to minimize articulatory effort leads the agrammatic speaker to plan very simple and agrammatic sentences or to produce simplified versions of sentences that at the planning stage are complex and grammatically correct. This results in utterances containing only the words that are essential in order to convey the message; after all, saying "Yesterday. . .wife. . .movie" is not much less informative than "Yesterday I went to see a movie with my wife." A distinct but somewhat related hypothesis assumes that in agrammatic subjects only words characterized by high values of stress and saliency (as defined by phonological, emotional, and motivational parameters) reach threshold for production.

Faced with the frequent association of agrammatic production and comprehension, later theories struggled to find a unitary account of the disorder. Agrammatism has been considered in turn the consequence of a phonological deficit, of a syntactic deficit, and of a lexical–semantic deficit. The phonological deficit hypothesis attributes agrammatism to a failure to process unstressed words (the so-called phonological nonwords) that do not alter the assignment of sentential stress and in most languages largely correspond to function words. In the presence of such deficit, producing or comprehending a sentence such as "The tiger is chased by the lion," in which "the," "is," "-ed," and "the" are phonological nonwords, is impossible. According to syntactic deficit theories, agrammatism results from the inability to process various aspects of grammar. Numerous proposals were made from this perspective. According to some authors, agrammatic subjects manage to construct partial representations of a sentence but cannot construct a global representation due to a syntactic disorder (or, in some cases, to a memory limitation). In a view inspired by Chomsky's *government and binding* theory, agrammatic subjects are unable to produce grammatical sentences and fail to comprehend complex grammatical structures because they cannot process phonological traces. According to others, agrammatism results from a difficulty in processing word order, which obviously results in failure to produce and comprehend reversible sentences such as "The man is kissed by the woman." In another view, the disorder underlying agrammatism affects a "central syntactic processor" responsible for processing function words in comprehension and production. A different theory proposes that agrammatism does not result from a deficit affecting function words but from the inability to map syntactic roles into semantic roles (in comprehension) and vice versa (in production). In a sentence such as "The man is kissed by the woman," "man" has the syntactic role of subject but the semantic role of theme. Erroneous mapping of syntactic into semantic roles (or vice versa) results in incorrectly assigning to "man" the role of agent instead of theme.

Each of these hypotheses focuses on a relevant aspect of agrammatism and provides a reasonable explanation for the performance observed in some subjects. However, and without exception, these theories fall short of a viable and comprehensive account. The reason is that agrammatism is a cognitively heterogeneous disorder: An agrammatic speaker may or may not be an agrammatic writer, and a subject with agrammatic production may or may not present with agrammatic comprehension. Furthermore, the functional deficits resulting in agrammatic production and in agrammatic comprehension differ across subjects. In-depth analyses of individual cases, based on extant theories of speech production and comprehension, have begun to document in further detail the range of distinct cognitive deficits that can result in agrammatic behavior. Agrammatic speech might result from one or more of the following (or perhaps other, not yet described, deficits): the inability to map semantic roles into syntactic roles, omission or substitution of function words as a consequence of selective damage to the mental vocabulary, the inability to insert grammatical words in the sentence frame even in the presence of spared function word vocabulary, or failure to retrieve the main verb. Similarly, agrammatic comprehension might result from reduced memory, from loss of syntactic abilities (both of which, albeit by different mechanisms, impair the construction of a complete structure for the stimulus sentence), from the inability to map syntactic roles into semantic roles, from the inability to understand the meaning of the main verb or of the inflectional endings of nouns or verbs, and so on. Also, in the presence of a subject with agrammatic comprehension and production, it is impossible to establish a priori whether the disorder results from damage to one and the same mechanism, is shared by both tasks, or results from separate impairments of production and of comprehension.

The implications of these observations are straightforward: Across-subject differences of the types previously mentioned cannot reflect random variation of performance across otherwise identical subjects, and they result from damage to distinct mechanisms. Thus, in order to understand grammatical disorders of language and their neural correlates, the most promising approach is to consider "agrammatism" as no more than a clinical label for a set of cognitively heterogeneous disorders and to concentrate on detailed studies of individual subjects. Analyses of aphasic performance based on computational theories of language production and comprehension will allow us to understand the functional mechanisms normally involved in speech processing, the types of damage to these mechanisms that result in the various forms of aphasic behavior, and their representation in the brain.

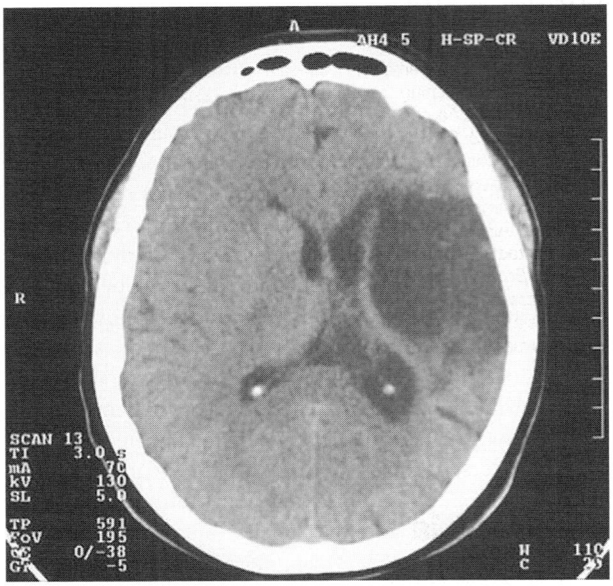

Figure 1 CT scan displaying the brain regions typically damaged in agrammatic aphasia.

Causes and Anatomical Correlates

The most frequent cause of agrammatism is a cerebrovascular accident in the superior division of the left middle cerebral artery supplying the frontal and rolandic structures (**Fig. 1**). Less frequent causes include brain tumors, traumatic head injuries, and focal degenerative diseases such as the nonfluent forms of primary progressive aphasia.

As expected on the basis of the co-occurrence of agrammatism and nonfluent aphasia, brain damage in these subjects often involves Broca's area and extends into adjacent cortical and subcortical structures of the frontal, superior temporal, and anterior parietal lobes and into the insula. Involvement of the left inferior frontal convolution in processing grammatical information is also suggested by recent neuroimaging studies showing activation of this area during tasks requiring syntactic processing. However, it is unclear which aspects of sentence processing are represented in these structures. For example, damage to the left frontal structures involved in agrammatism is also observed in subjects who are unable to name verbs in isolation, and damage to the perisylvian region without a prevalence of anterior lesions was documented in a large sample of subjects with agrammatic comprehension. In the two largest samples of agrammatic speakers reported so far, the largest lesion overlap was in the insula, and as many as 20% of the subjects had lesions outside Broca's area and located posteriorly. Also, neuroimaging data must be interpreted very cautiously because the structures in or adjacent to Broca's area (areas 44–46) activated by syntactic tasks also show activation during tasks that require processing of semantics, lexicon, phonology, and working memory. Currently, the most promising approach for the identification of the brain structures underlying language comprehension and production is to combine the neuroanatomical evidence collected in subjects suffering from damage to specific cognitive/linguistic mechanisms with the activation results obtained in normal subjects engaged in neuroimaging experiments.

See also: Agraphia; Anomia; Speech Disorders, Overview.

Further Reading

Badecker, W and Caramazza, A (1985). On considerations of method and theory governing the use of clinical categories in neurolinguistics and cognitive neuropsychology: The case against agrammatism. *Cognition* 20: 97–125.

Caplan, D, Hildebrandt, N, and Makris, N (1996). Location of lesions in stroke patients with deficits in syntactic processing in sentence comprehension. *Brain* 119: 933–949.

Caplan, D, Alpert, N, Waters, G, et al. (2000). Activation of Broca's area by syntactic processing under conditions of concurrent articulation. *Hum. Brain Mapp.* 9: 65–71.

Caramazza, A, Capitani, E, Rey, A, et al. (2001). Agrammatic Broca's aphasia is not associated with a single pattern of comprehension performance. *Brain Lang.* 76: 158–184.

Grodzinsky, Y, Pinango, MM, Zurif, EB, et al. (1999). The critical role of group studies in neuropsychology: Comprehension regularities in Broca's aphasia. *Brain Lang.* 67: 134–147.

Kean, ML (ed.) (1983). *Agrammatism.* New York: Academic Press.

Menn, L and Obler, LK (eds.) (1991). *Agrammatic Aphasia. A Narrative Sourcebook.* Philadelphia: Benjamins.

Miceli, G (1998). Grammatical disorders in aphasia. In: Denes, G and Pizzamiglio, L (eds.) *Handbook of Clinical and Experimental Neuropsychology.* London: Hove, Taylor & Francis.

Miceli, G, Silveri, MC, Romani, C, et al. (1989). Variation in the pattern of omissions and substitutions of grammatical morphemes in the spontaneous speech of so-called agrammatic patients. *Brain Lang.* 36: 447–492.

Agraphia

S. W. Anderson, D. Tranel, and N. L. Denburg, University of Iowa Health Care, Iowa City, IA, USA

Agraphia (a + Greek *graphein*) is a term used to denote an impairment of the ability to write caused by cerebral dysfunction. The term generally is reserved for instances of writing impairment due to a cerebral insult, acquired after the person has learned to write, that is, in someone who was previously literate. Writing impairments of developmental origin are usually considered part of dyslexia. Acquired impairments secondary to tremor, hemiparesis, or other basic motor defects are usually excluded from the definition of agraphia. Agraphia may involve impairment of one or multiple components of the psychomotor and linguistic aspects of writing, including grapheme formation, spelling, word selection, grammar, and spatial arrangement. Agraphia rarely occurs in isolation, and more often appears in the context of widespread language impairments, visuospatial defects, apraxia, dementia, or confusional states. The etiology may be virtually any cerebral disease, although stroke, traumatic brain injury, tumor, and Alzheimer's disease are the most frequent causes. Agraphia is often one of the early behavioral manifestations of cerebral dysfunction in acute confusional states of metabolic or toxic origin.

Much of the importance of agraphia in a clinical setting arises from the fact that collection of a writing sample is a simple, quick, and often highly informative procedure to include in a mental status examination, and generally can be obtained from even agitated or marginally cooperative patients. The task typically consists of having the patient copy a sentence, write a sentence to dictation, and spontaneously generate a sentence or two. Highly overlearned writing behaviors, such as writing one's name, may be preserved in agraphic patients and should not be used to infer normal writing ability.

The neural substrates of handwriting, a multifaceted and culturally transmitted skill which has risen to importance very late in the course of brain evolution, are far from 'hard wired.' Lesion studies have demonstrated variability across individuals in the nature and severity of agraphia stemming from damage to relevant brain areas, as well as considerable recovery of handwriting in the months following the onset of focal brain damage. The left dorsolateral frontal lobe, particularly the superior premotor region, is uniquely situated for the convergence of sequential motor activity of the dominant arm and hand together with activity of frontal and posterior language-related cortices, and damage to this region has been associated with severe and relatively circumscribed agraphia. However, agraphia also may arise from focal damage in left temporal and parietal regions, especially the perisylvian language-related cortices, as well as the left basal ganglia. **Figure 1** depicts a high left parietal lobe mass which resulted in agraphia.

Patients with severe agraphia may be unable to write even single letters. Milder versions of the condition may be manifest only as more subtle defects, such as an increased frequency of spelling errors. Written output, such as spelling, has been associated with damage to a network of brain regions in the left posterior frontal lobe involving Brodmann's area 44, 45, and 6. The ability to write numbers or other nonletter symbols is often defective in parallel with the impairment in writing letters and words, but in other cases these abilities may be dissociated. For example, number writing may be preserved

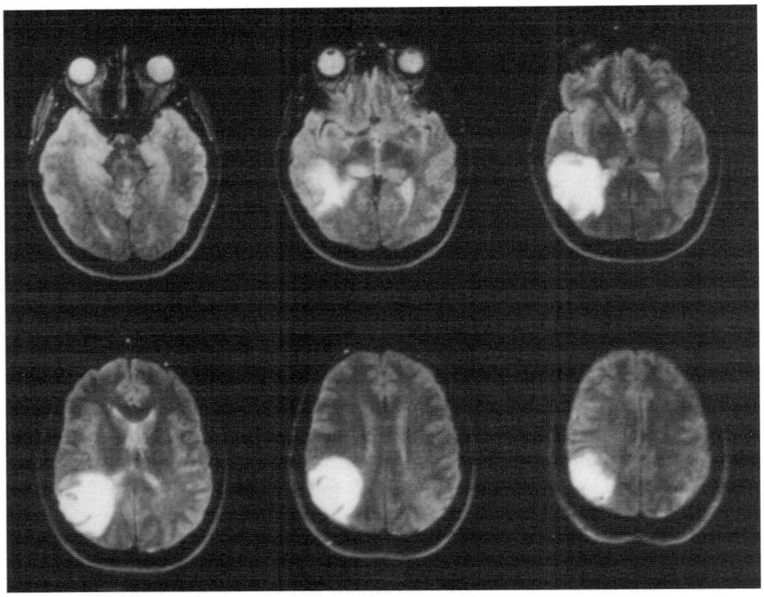

Figure 1 (See color plate 1.)

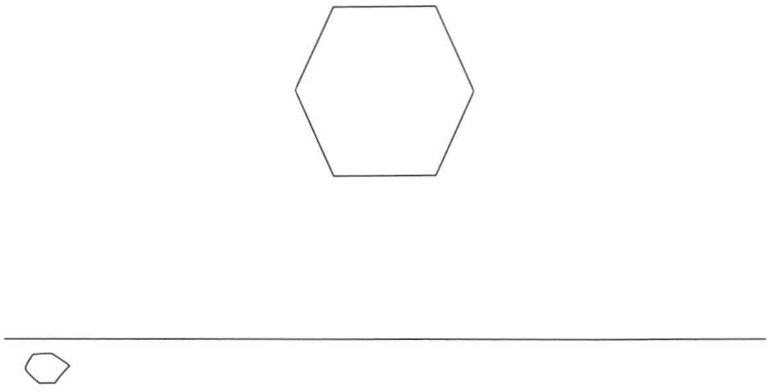

Figure 2

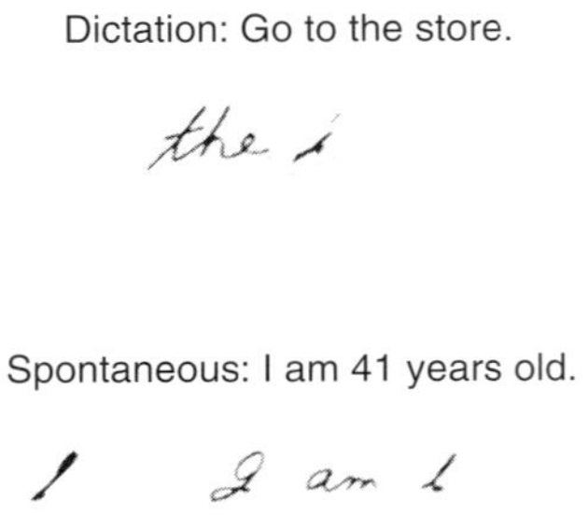

Figure 3

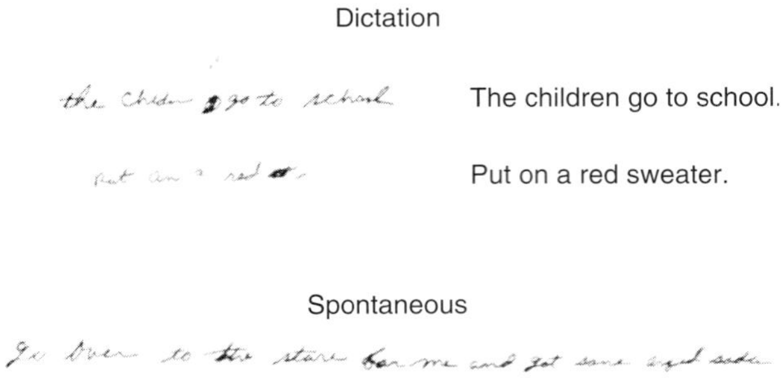

Figure 4

even if letter writing is impaired. Spatial agraphia involves an inability to maintain appropriate placement of written material on a page; this most often occurs as a progressive upward slant from the left to right side of the page and is associated with superior parietal lesions of the dominant hemisphere. Micrographia involves a progressive diminution of letter size of the course of a sentence, and is associated with parkinsonism or, less commonly, Alzheimer's disease. **Figure 2** is an illustration of micrographia: the original stimulus to be copied is in the upper panel, and the patient's rendering of the stimulus is in the bottom panel. A dysexecutive agraphia, or decrease in an individual's ability to express ideas in writing, may also occur following nonfocal brain damage, such as in the case of dementia or traumatic brain injury affecting prefrontal cortex.

We offer the following brief case to illustrate the nature of the writing impairments observed in agraphia. A middle-aged man with a high school degree suffered multiple strokes resulting in damage to each of the left frontal, temporal, and parietal brain regions. Examples of his writing during the acute epoch are presented in **Figure 3**. Writing during the chronic epoch (i.e., 3 months following the neurological event) indicated improvement, although he continued to perform at a level well below expectations (**Figure 4**).

Most patients with aphasia also have agraphia which parallels their defect in spoken language, although in individual cases written or spoken production may be relatively preserved. The syndrome of alexia with agraphia involves letter distortion and impaired spelling, in addition to reading impairment, and is associated with lesions in the left angular or supramarginal gyrus. In the so-called Gerstmann syndrome, loosely associated with dominant parietal lobe damage, agraphia appears in a constellation with acalculia, finger agnosia, and left–right disorientation. Callosal agraphia affecting the left hand only can follow lesions in the anterior half of the corpus callosum. Phonological agraphia involves a specific defect in phoneme-to-grapheme translation, expressed as an isolated inability to write pronounceable pseudowords, and appears with lesions in various left perisylvian regions.

With regard to treatment, a recent study indicated that rehabilitation is generally beneficial to patients with acquired agraphia, regardless of lesion location.

See also: Dyslexia, Neurodevelopmental Basis; Language, Cortical Processes.

Further Reading

Anderson, SW, Damasio, H, and Damasio, AR (1990). Troubled letters but not numbers: Domain specific cognitive impairments following focal damage in frontal cortex. *Brain* 113: 749–766.

Anderson, SW, Saver, J, Tranel, D, and Damasio, H (1993). Acquired agraphia caused by focal brain damage. *Acta Psychologica* 82: 193–210.

Ardila, A and Surloff, C (2006). Dysexecutive agraphia: A major executive dysfunction sign. *Internal Journal of Neuroscience* 116: 653–663.

Bub, D and Chertkow, H (1988). Agraphia. In: Boller, T and Grafman, J (eds.) *Handbook of Neuropsychology,* vol. 1. New York: Elsevier.

Chedru, F and Geschwind, N (1972). Writing disturbances in acute confusional states. *Neuropsychologia* 10: 343–353.

Hillis, AE, Chang, S, Breese, E, and Heidler, J (2004). The crucial role of posterior frontal regions in modality specific components of the spelling process. *Neurocase* 10: 175–187.

LaBarge, E, Smith, DS, Dick, L, and Storandt, M (1992). Agraphia in dementia of the Alzheimer type. *Archives of Neurology* 49: 1151–1156.

Leischner, A (1969). The agraphias. In: Vinken, PJ and Bruyn, GW (eds.) *Handbook of Clinical Neurology,* vol. 4. Amsterdam: North Holland.

Rapp, B (2005). The relationship between treatment outcomes and the underlying cognitive deficit: Evidence from the remediation of acquired dysgraphia. *Aphasiology* 19: 994–1008.

Roeltgen, DP (2003). Agraphia. In: Heilman, KM and Valenstein, E (eds.) *Clinical Neuropsychology,* 4th edn., pp. 126–143. New York: Oxford University Press.

Alzheimer's Disease

M. D. Greicius, H. J. Rosen, and B. L. Miller

Epidemiology and Genetics

Alzheimer's Disease (AD) is the most common cause of dementia, accounting for approximately two-thirds of all cases. Prevalence estimates of AD in the United States and Europe vary widely from 3.6 to 10.3% of people older than age 65. In the United States, estimates range from 1.5 to 4 million Americans affected with AD. A recent meta-analysis of 21 studies estimated a prevalence among white Americans of 1.7–1.9 million.

Ethnicity plays a role in prevalence, even when controlling for potential confounders, such as socioeconomic status and education. In particular, higher prevalence rates are reported among African Americans and Hispanics. Prevalence rates among Asian Americans are equivalent to or slightly lower than rates among whites. Gender also appears to play a role in prevalence, with most studies showing an increased frequency among women, unrelated to their increased longevity. Above and beyond the effects of ethnicity or gender, age has the strongest effect on prevalence. Prevalence approximately doubles every 5 years beyond age 65, and by age 85 at least one in four and perhaps closer to one in two people will have AD. Studies of incidence, the number of new cases of AD per year, are less numerous but have also shown an approximate doubling with age, increasing from approximately 1% in people aged 65–70 to 6–8% in people older than age 85.

The molecular genetics of AD contribute to some of the prevalence differences across ethnicity, gender, and age. It has been estimated that genetics account for 30–50% of the population risk for developing AD, with uncharacterized environmental risks making up the difference. Some studies examining concordance rates for AD among monozygotic twins suggest that the genetic component is even higher, approaching 70%. The bulk of this genetic burden is believed to be non-Mendelian, resulting from a combined effect of one or more incompletely penetrant genes.

However, in approximately 2% of cases AD is transmitted as an autosomal dominant disease with nearly complete penetrance. These autosomal dominant cases, usually early onset, are due to mutations in one of three genes. The β-amyloid precursor protein (APP) gene on chromosome 21 was the first to be identified and characterized, and new mutations in the gene continue to be identified. These mutations all result in excess production of Aβ42, the most neurotoxic of the three common forms of amyloid. APP gene mutations account for a small minority of the early onset autosomal dominant cases. Most of the documented early onset cases are due to mutations of Presenilin 1 (PS1), although a few cases have been caused by mutations in a homologous gene called Presenilin 2 (PS2). These genes, found on chromosomes 14 and 1, respectively, code for a pair of proteins with considerable homology that both seem to favor production of Aβ42.

A fourth gene, apolipoprotein E (apoE), has been implicated in the more common late-onset, sporadic form of AD and increases susceptibility to AD. The association between the apoE4 allele and AD was detected originally in a familial form of late-onset AD. Subsequently, this allele was found to be overrepresented in patients with sporadic, late-onset AD as well. At least one copy of the E4 allele is found in 45–60% of patients with AD but only in 20–30% of the general population. E4 homozygosity is found in 12–15% of patients with AD but only 2 or 3% of the general population. The largest study to examine the effect of the E4 allele was a meta-analysis that derived odds ratios (ORs) estimating the risk for AD associated with the various apoE genotypes. Among whites, the OR was 2.6 for the E2/E4 genotype, 3.2 for the E3/E4 genotype, and 14.9 for the E4/E4 genotype. Although the E4 effect was present in all ethnic groups included in this meta-analysis, it was attenuated among African Americans and Hispanics and amplified in Japanese. The E4 effect was found to be attenuated in patients older than age 70. Lastly, an increased effect of E4 was detected in women compared to men but not across all ethnic types, suggesting that apoE status accounts for some but certainly not all of the epidemiological differences seen with ethnicity, gender, and age.

Currently, the apoE4 allele is regarded as a susceptibility gene, neither necessary nor sufficient for the development of AD. Because of its poor sensitivity and specificity when used as an isolated diagnostic test, initial guidelines were adopted recommending that apoE screening not be used in clinical settings. A recent consortium report confirmed the poor sensitivity (65%) and specificity (68%) of apoE as an isolated diagnostic test, but it suggested that it may be used judiciously as an adjunct to the clinical diagnosis, noting that the test can add to the specificity of diagnosis when used in conjunction with clinical criteria.

Other potential susceptibility genes have been proposed, including α2-macroglobulin, interleukins-1 and -6, cathepsin D, and, most recently, cystatin C. Each gene has a plausible pathophysiological connection with AD, but the associations have not been widely reproduced. In some cases, as with α2-macroglobulin, the association has not held up in specific ethnic groups. In the future, it will be determined if these recently reported associations are as widely reproducible as that of apoE4.

Pathology

AD has a number of signature pathological findings. Grossly there can be generalized cortical atrophy, but this is typically most prominent in the medial temporal lobe and hippocampus. Microscopically, affected brain regions demonstrate granulovacuolar degeneration, Hirano bodies, neurofibrillary tangles (NFTs), and amyloid plaques. The true hallmarks of AD, however, are the NFTs and amyloid plaques. NFTs are collections of aggregated tau protein and neurofilaments found in neuronal cell bodies (**Figs. 1** and **2**). They are seen in the earliest stages of AD pathology, and the distribution and density of NFTs appear to be the best correlate of clinical presentation. Related neurofibrillary/tau protein changes that occur in AD include neuropil threads and neuritic plaques. The threads are due to collections of tau in neuronal dendrites. The neuritic plaques, although consisting primarily of amyloid protein, also have a component of dystrophic neurites that contain tau. Neuropil threads tend to occur early with NFTs, whereas neuritic plaques are typically found in later stages of AD. Amyloid plaques (**Fig. 1**) are extraneuronal aggregates of Aβ protein. There are two varieties of plaque—neuritic and diffuse. Diffuse plaques consist mainly of Aβ protein. They are considered less specific for AD and are commonly found in elderly patients without dementia. Neuritic plaques consist of Aβ protein aggregates that are mixed with other components, such as tau-containing dystrophic neurites. These are much less commonly found in cognitively intact elderly patients and hence considered more specific for AD.

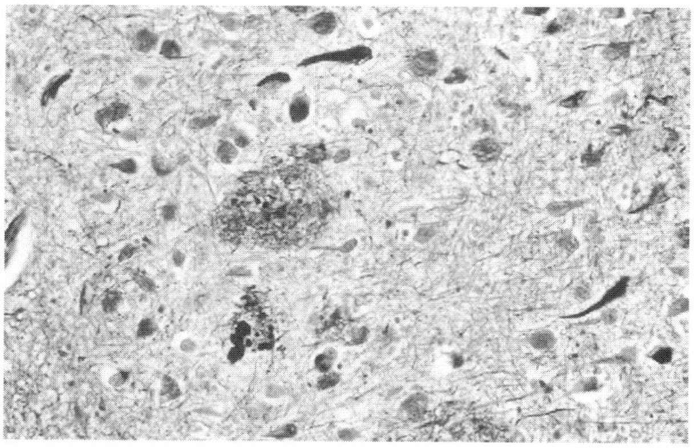

Figure 1 Bielschowsky silver staining reveals a typical Alzheimer's plaque (left of center). Several neurofibrillary tangles are also present. (See color plate 2.)

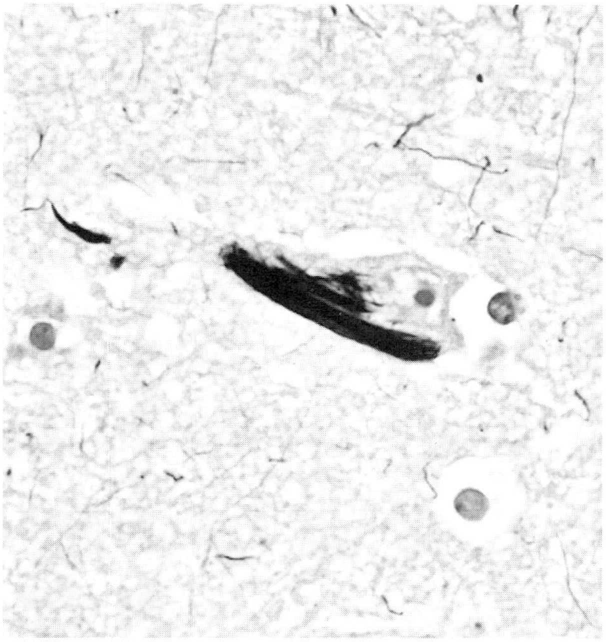

Figure 2 Magnified view of a neurofibrillary tangle (Bielschowsky stain). (See color plate 3.)

The Consortium to Establish a Registry for Alzheimer's Disease (CERAD) criteria use the frequency of NFTs and amyloid plaques to establish a probability scale for AD pathology ranging from normal brain to definite AD. The severity of AD pathology can also be determined by the location of NFTs in the brain. The Braak and Braak staging criteria reflect the degree to which AD pathology has spread from its typical starting point in the transentorhinal region (stages I and II) through the limbic system (stages III and IV) to more distant locations in the neocortex (stages V and VI). A recent consensus report on the postmortem diagnosis of AD used the CERAD criteria and Braak and Braak staging in combination to determine the likelihood that clinical dementia in life can be attributed to AD changes at autopsy.

Pathogenesis

The leading theory of AD pathogenesis favors amyloid over tau as the principal causative factor. Although there are arguments to be made against the amyloid hypothesis (amyloid deposition does not correlate closely with dementia severity, and neuropathological changes, including NFTs, can predate plaque deposition by several years), it remains the dominant theory. This is due mainly to the fact that all the known genetic factors that cause AD can be linked to amyloid. Conversely, AD pathology rarely occurs with the known tau mutations.

β-Amyloid protein, the main component of amyloid plaques, is a fragment of the APP protein. APP can be cleaved initially by either an α-secretase or a β-secretase. In either case, the resultant peptide is then cleaved again by γ-secretase. If APP is cleaved first by β-secretase and then by γ-secretase, an Aβ protein is formed. The Aβ protein can have either 40 or 42 amino acids (Aβ40 or Aβ42), depending on the site of cleavage. Although both forms have a tendency to aggregate, Aβ42, which has two additional hydrophobic amino acids, does so much more rapidly. Thus, a relative increase in levels of Aβ42 results in more rapid protein aggregation and formation of the early diffuse plaques. Formation of the Aβ42 nidus is believed to speed aggregation of Aβ40 such that more mature plaques will demonstrate an Aβ42 core surrounded by Aβ40. The aggregation of Aβ40 and Aβ42 precipitates further accumulation of a number of other proteins, including apoE, which are found in amyloid plaques. The deposition of plaques is believed to trigger a cascade of events, involving some combination of oxidative injury, cytoskeletal damage, and inflammatory responses, that ultimately ends in neuronal cell death.

The amyloid hypothesis is buttressed by its capacity to incorporate the various genetic defects associated with AD. Mutations in the APP gene can either decrease the rate of α-secretase activity or increase the rate of β-secretase activity. The presenilin proteins appear to act at the γ-secretase level, with recent evidence suggesting that they may even constitute the γ-secretase molecule. Some mutations inhibit the subsequent cleavage of C-100 (the β-secretase product) to Aβ40, thus favoring production of Aβ42. Others seem to promote directly the cleavage of C-100 to Aβ42. The apoE4 allele has been implicated in promoting amyloid deposition and possibly impairing clearance of amyloid plaques. Lastly, among the newer candidates for genetic risk factors in AD, α2-macroglobulin mutations appear to impair the clearance of Aβ plaques.

Diagnosis

A consensus on establishing the clinical diagnosis for AD was reached in 1984 with the development of the National Institute of Neurological and Communicative Disorders and Stroke and the Alzheimer's Disease and Related Disorders Association (NINCDS–ADRDA) criteria. To meet the diagnostic criteria for probable AD, a demented patient must have deficits in at least two areas of cognitive function, progressive worsening of memory and other cognitive functions, and onset between ages 40 and 90. In addition, there should be no disturbance of consciousness and no other neurological explanation for the cognitive decline. These criteria are weighted toward memory dysfunction, the most common presenting complaint in AD. The memory loss affects short-term memory disproportionately so that immediate memory and remote memory are often preserved early in the course. Following memory dysfunction, the typical patient will often develop additional deficits in a predictable order such that executive function, semantic processing, and visuospatial skills subsequently begin to decline.

Occasionally, as is seen with the focal variants of AD, memory loss is not a prominent early feature. Initially, isolated, focal impairments may occur in language, executive function, visuospatial skills, or praxis. In these cases, AD may mimic other focal degenerative disorders, such as frontotemporal dementia presenting with primary progressive aphasia or corticobasal degeneration presenting with apraxia. In addition to the classic neuropsychological symptoms, AD patients frequently develop psychiatric symptoms, particularly as the illness progresses. In addition to relatively mild behavioral problems, such as irritability and sleep disturbance, major depression occurs in up to 20% of patients, and in later stages up to 40% will have delusions. AD is slowly progressive but ultimately fatal. The average time to death following diagnosis is estimated to be 8 years.

The NINCDS–ADRDA criteria have been shown to have adequate sensitivity (90–95%) but poor specificity (60–70%). With the prospect of preventive interventions for AD, enhanced understanding of genetic risks, and growing awareness that many patients with minimal cognitive impairment progress to AD, techniques are being investigated that increase diagnostic specificity in demented and in at-risk individuals. Enormous effort has been made to increase specificity by using adjunctive testing, such as blood tests, cerebrospinal fluid analysis of Aβ42, and neuroimaging. As evidenced by the recent consensus report of the working group on molecular and biochemical markers of AD, most such efforts have not proven entirely successful. The consensus group did note that apoE genotyping improves specificity when used in conjunction with clinical criteria. Cerebrospinal fluid analysis of Aβ42 did not fulfill "criteria for a useful biomarker." In addition to biochemical markers, investigators have studied different neuroimaging techniques for diagnostic aids but with equally limited results. Positron emission tomography (PET) and single photon emission tomography have been used as adjunctive tests in patients with probable AD with the fairly consistent finding of decreased perfusion or metabolism in the temporoparietal regions. Measurements of hippocampal and entorhinal cortex atrophy using structural magnetic resonance imaging (MRI) have also been used to increase diagnostic accuracy. Studies of functional imaging using PET or MRI are still relatively few in number, but they suggest a pattern of increased activation in the earliest clinical and perhaps even preclinical state progressing to decreased activation once patients become more symptomatic. Currently, neuroimaging can only distinguish group differences and cannot be used with any certainty on an individual basis.

Treatment

Pharmacological treatments of AD can be classified as drugs that slow progression of disease, drugs that treat particular neuropsychiatric symptoms, and drugs that prevent disease. The most effective treatment in slowing progression of AD works through the cholinergic system. The cholinergic projections from the basal forebrain are known to be disproportionately affected early in AD and have been the target of pharmacological intervention for many years. Tacrine, a nonselective, reversible anticholinesterase, was approved for the treatment of AD in 1993, but is rarely used today, owing to its short half-life (requiring four daily doses), prominent peripheral cholinergic side effects (nausea, vomiting, and diarrhea), and its common elevation of liver function tests. Donepezil, a selective, reversible anticholinesterase approved for AD in 1996, has proven to be much better tolerated. Its longer half-life allows for once-daily dosing and it has milder peripheral cholinergic side effects allowing for approximately 80% of patients to complete the drug trial versus only 45% in the tacrine trial. In patients with mild to moderate AD treated for 24 weeks, donepezil improved cognitive scores on the ADAS by up to 4% and improved scores on the Clinician's Interview-Based Impression of Change Scale by 6%. A third anticholinesterase, rivastigmine, was recently approved for use in the United States. Trials using high doses have shown improvement on the ADAS cognitive subscale of approximately 5%, but there was a patient drop out rate of approximately 30–40% due to peripheral cholinergic side effects. The two other agents frequently used to slow progression of disease, α-tocopherol (vitamin E) and selegiline, are believed to work mainly as antioxidants. A large, placebo-controlled trial showed that either drug delayed the time to excessive dependence or death by approximately 200 days. Improvement was not detected on any cognitive scales. The major side effects were syncope and falls, again seen with either drug but more frequent with the combination of the two. The combination of the two drugs was not more effective than either drug alone, and this finding led to the routine recommendation of vitamin E (1000 IU twice daily) due to its lower cost and lower toxicity profiles.

Given our limited ability to slow the progression of AD, the symptomatic treatment of associated neuropsychiatric problems continues to be an important responsibility for clinicians. The treatment of depression in AD is best attempted with newer antidepressants with fewer side effects, such as the selective serotonin reuptake inhibitors and the newer mixed antidepressants with serotonin and noradrenergic boosting profiles. The other commonly used class of antidepressants, tricyclics, may have untoward cognitive effects owing to their anticholinergic properties. Delusions and severe agitation can be treated cautiously with antipsychotics, taking care to minimize sedation or extrapyramidal side effects. Although traditional agents such as haldol may work more quickly, atypical antipsychotics are probably better for long-term use. A recent randomized clinical trial of olanzapine, for example, showed it to be effective and well tolerated in nursing home-dwelling AD patients with psychosis or agitation. Management of sleep disturbances may involve mild sedatives such as trazodone but should not include anticholinergic compounds or prolonged use of benzodiazepines. Lastly, there is evidence that the anticholinesterases may also improve behavioral problems in AD, particularly apathy, visual hallucinations, and irritability.

Prevention of AD remains a distant goal. Evidence from both retrospective and prospective trials suggests that estrogen replacement may be effective in preventing or delaying the onset of AD in post-menopausal women. The methodological limitations of these observational studies preclude a definite recommendation at this time. Given the risks associated with estrogen replacement, randomized clinical trials will need to be carried out before a general consensus is reached. The role of inflammation in the pathogenesis of AD has prompted interest in anti-inflammatory agents and nonsteroidal anti-inflammatory drugs (NSAIDs) in particular. Retrospective and cross-sectional studies suggest that long-term NSAID use may delay or prevent AD. As with estrogen replacement, however, the risks associated with chronic NSAID use would require proof of their efficacy in a randomized clinical trial before they could be formally recommended. Recently, interest has turned to the prospect of immunizing patients against amyloid plaques. A mouse study showed that immunization with Aβ42 reduced AD-like pathology. Although the first trial testing of a vaccine in AD patients was halted due to adverse inflammatory reactions, it is hoped that refined formulations of the vaccine will prove both safe and efficacious. Another potential preventive therapy is the use of drugs that inhibit γ-secretase, the protease that leads to production of Aβ42. Several of these γ-secretase inhibitors are being developed by pharmaceutical companies, but none have yet reached the clinical trial stage.

See also: Anomia; Cognitive Impairment.

Further Reading

Braak, H and Braak, E (1991). Neuropathological staging of Alzheimer-related changes. *Acta Neuropathol* 82: 239–259.

Braak, H and Braak, E (1998). Diagnostic criteria for neuropathologic assessment of Alzheimer's disease. *Neurobiol. Aging* 18: S85–S88.

Farrer, LA, Cupples, LA, Haines, JL, et al. (1997). Effects of age, sex, and ethnicity on the association between apolipoprotein E genotype and Alzheimer disease: A meta-analysis. *J. Am. Med. Assoc.* 278: 1349–1356.

Hendrie, HC (1998). Epidemiology of dementia and Alzheimer's disease. *Am. J. Geriatric Psychiatry* 6: S3–S18.

Mayeux, R and Sano, M (1999) Drug therapy: Treatment of Alzheimer's disease. *N. Engl. J. Med.* 341: 1670–1679.

Mayeux, R, Saunders, AM, Shea, S, et al. (1998). Utility of the apolipoprotein E genotype in the diagnosis of Alzheimer's disease. *N. Engl. J. Med.* 338: 506–511.

Petersen, RC, Smith, G, Waring, SC, et al. (1999). Mild cognitive impairment. *Arch. Neurol.* 56: 303–308.

St. George-Hyslop, PH (2000). Molecular genetics of Alzheimer's disease. *Biol. Psychiatry* 47: 183–199.

Schenk, D, Barbour, R, Dunn, W, et al. (1999). Immunization with amyloid-beta attenuates Alzheimer-disease-like pathology in the PDAPP mouse. *Nature* 400: 173–177.

Selkoe, DJ (1997). Alzheimer's disease: Genotypes, phenotype, and treatments. *Science* 275: 630–631.

Selkoe, DJ (1998). The cell biology of amyloid precursor protein and presenilin in Alzheimer's disease. *Trends Cell Biol.* 8: 447–453.

Street, J, Clark, W, Gannon, KS, et al. (2000). Olanzapine treatment of psychotic and behavioral symptoms in patients with Alzheimer disease in nursing care facilities: A double-blind, randomized, placebo-controlled trial. The HGEU Study Group. *Arch. Gen. Psychiatry* 57: 968–976.

Amnesia, Functional

M. Kritchevsky, San Diego VA Healthcare System, San Diego, CA, USA

Published by Elsevier Ltd.

Introduction

Functional amnesia is an uncommon condition in which patients develop severe retrograde amnesia in the absence of significant anterograde amnesia and without any known brain injury or disorder. This nonneurological syndrome is variously referred to as psychogenic amnesia, hysterical amnesia, dissociative amnesia, and functional retrograde amnesia. Functional amnesia is easily distinguished from the neurological amnesic syndrome that is commonly seen with dysfunction of bilateral medial temporal lobe or bilateral medial diencephalic structures important for memory, in which patients have severe anterograde amnesia with variable retrograde amnesia. In contrast, functional amnesia may be indistinguishable from malingered amnesia. Functional amnesia is the disorder of memory that is most commonly popularized in literature and film, and it appears to be the condition that the majority of lay persons regard as amnesia.

Early descriptions of functional amnesia included large numbers of cases that were characterized primarily by a loss of personal identity. Memory for previously known facts and personal events sometimes was noted to be impaired as well. In 1982 the first case of functional amnesia that had been formally studied with neuropsychological testing was published. Subsequently many additional case studies have been described. In 2004 the first series of patients with functional amnesia who had been studied clinically and neuropsychologically in a systematic fashion was reported. The increasing understanding of functional amnesia has facilitated diagnosis of this condition, but treatment of many patients with functional amnesia has remained difficult.

Clinical Characteristics of the Patient with Functional Amnesia

The Clinical Picture of the Patient

The typical patient with functional amnesia presents with the sudden onset of retrograde amnesia without clinically significant anterograde amnesia. Most commonly, the retrograde amnesia affects all of the memories that occurred prior to the onset of amnesia, including memory for personal identity. Thus, the patient reports that he or she cannot remember their past. They do not know their name, where they were born, or where they were raised. They can not recall where they went to school, when or to whom they were married, where they live, or by whom they are employed. Once their identity is discovered, they do not recognize their name. When they meet their friends and family, they do not recognize them. In general, the loss of past memories affects public as well as personal material. For example, the patient will not recall or recognize previously known public figures such as sports figures, movie stars, and political leaders. They will not recall or recognize previously known public events such as wars or national disasters. Because the person with functional amnesia has no significant anterograde amnesia, they are able to relearn past memories. However, these newly learned memories typically have no sense of familiarity to them.

Uncommonly, the patient with functional amnesia has retrograde amnesia that affects only a period of time before the onset of memory loss. For example, if the period of amnesia is 2 years, then the patient will not recall or recognize memories that occurred during the 2-year period before the onset of amnesia. The patient will know their name and will have normal recollection of memories that occurred more than 2 years ago. However, he or she will give the year as 2 years earlier than the correct year, and will report their marital status, place of residence, and workplace as they were 2 years previously despite any significant changes that may have occurred since. The patient can relearn past memories, but the new memories will not have a sense of familiarity.

The patient with functional amnesia most often will report a complete loss of memories from the period of retrograde amnesia. However, on occasion a patient will be aware of one or more vague and incomplete memories from the period of amnesia.

At about the time of onset of functional amnesia, many patients have one or more abnormalities, in addition to the amnesia, that also appear to be psychogenic. These have included inability to name objects, inability to name numbers, difficulty with calculations, loss of ability to read and write, inability to move the eyes voluntarily during formal testing, bilateral leg weakness with inability to walk independently, weakness on one side of the body, and an inability to carry out previously familiar activities such as using a telephone or driving a car with a manual transmission. One patient has reported that he had to relearn the English language by reading a dictionary during the first 2 days of his amnesia. Another has reported that she could no longer remember the Spanish language, though she had been bilingual prior to the onset of her amnesia. With regard to anterograde amnesia, patients characteristically have good memory for events that occurred after the onset of amnesia. One patient has reported difficulty with new learning, and on neurological examination was poor at learning new verbal, but not nonverbal, material. However, like other patients with functional amnesia, he did not appear to be forgetful.

Occasionally, a patient with functional amnesia will present immediately after a period of sudden and unexpected travel during which they appear to have exhibited normal behavior. The period of travel is termed a fugue state, and whatever occurred during the fugue state will be included in the period of retrograde amnesia.

Risk and Precipitating Factors

Many patients with functional amnesia have significant premorbid psychiatric histories, including one or more of the following: alcohol abuse, other substance abuse, previous conversion symptoms, anxiety disorder, posttraumatic stress disorder, schizophrenia, depression, history of suicide attempt, and histrionic or borderline personality disorder. Many patients with functional amnesia have one or more of the following possible precipitating factors at the onset of amnesia: intoxication with alcohol, mild closed head injury, active depression, psychological stress, and involvement or alleged involvement in illegal activity.

Clinical Course

The clinical course of patients with functional amnesia is highly variable. Some patients appear to have a full recovery of their retrograde amnesia. In these cases the recovery most often occurs gradually over days to weeks. The recovery most often appears to consist of the gradual return of memories from throughout the period of amnesia. Rarely, the amnesia appears to resolve suddenly. Many patients have only a partial recovery of their lost memories. Sometimes this involves partial but incomplete recovery of memories from throughout the period of memory loss. In contrast, at times the initially extensive retrograde amnesia appears to shrink over a period of months to a shorter period of retrograde amnesia for a period of time (e.g., 6 months) immediately preceding the onset of amnesia. Some patients with functional amnesia report that they experience little or no recovery of their lost memories over an interval as long as 42 months. Patients who experience no significant recovery of memory occasionally appear to have established new personalities. It appears to be very uncommon for functional amnesia to suddenly and completely resolve in association with a mild head injury or a psychological catharsis.

The recovery of lost memories sometimes appears to have been facilitated by reacquainting the patient with their past, or by addressing and initiating treatment for ongoing psychological stressors. Also, sometimes hypnosis or an amobarbital interview appears to facilitate the recovery of lost memories. Memories initially remembered with these therapies sometimes are again inaccessible immediately following the session, but then rapidly return in the following days.

Recovery from retrograde amnesia should be distinguished from relearning lost memories. The patient with functional amnesia usually will report with confidence that a particular memory was relearned. They sometimes will recall the event of relearning and usually will report that the memory feels new and is unassociated with the familiar feel of an old memory.

Additional psychogenic cognitive deficits that are associated with the retrograde amnesia often resolve within hours to days of onset. General neurological deficits, particularly weakness, of psychogenic origin may persist throughout the course of the amnesia.

Laboratory Tests

In patients with functional amnesia, structural neuroimaging tests such as computed tomography (CT) and magnetic resonance imaging (MRI) brain scans are usually normal, though they occasionally show abnor-malities unrelated to the functional amnesia. Electroencephalography also is usually normal, but may show abnormalities that are unrelated to the amnesia. Functional neuroimaging tests such as single-photon computed tomography (SPECT), positron emission tomography (PET), or functional MRI brain scans have been reported to show abnormal findings related to the retrograde amnesia in some patients. The findings have not been consistent in the different patients studied. Although the demonstrated functional abnormalities may be related to the patients' retrograde amnesia, the presence of such abnormalities does not imply that functional amnesia is due to or associated with brain injury or disorder.

Differential Diagnosis

Malingered (intentionally feigned) amnesia also can present with the sudden onset of retrograde amnesia without clinically significant anterograde amnesia. In fact, it may be that a patient with malingered amnesia only can be distinguished from a patient with functional amnesia with certainty if the malingerer confesses. One clue that a patient has malingered amnesia may be the absence of a significant past psychiatric history. The precipitating factors for malingered amnesia may be similar to those for functional amnesia. One malingerer hit himself in the head with a bottle so there would be evidence of an appropriate precipitating factor for his amnesia.

Rare neurological patients have been reported to have significant retrograde amnesia with a lesser degree of anterograde amnesia. This may be associated with bilateral damage to the anterior or inferior temporal lobes. Personal identity probably is preserved, the retrograde amnesia covers a period of several years to several decades, and there is some degree of anterograde amnesia. Neuroimaging typically will reveal the responsible brain injury.

The neurological amnesic syndrome that is commonly seen with dysfunction of bilateral medial temporal lobe or bilateral medial diencephalic structures important for memory is easily distinguished from functional amnesia. Patients with the neurological amnesic syndrome have significant anterograde amnesia with variable retrograde amnesia.

Neuropsychological Findings in Patients with Functional Amnesia

In 2004, a series of ten patients who had initially been diagnosed with functional amnesia was published. The patients had been studied clinically and neuropsychologically in a systematic fashion. Nine of the patients presented with loss of past memories that extended into childhood and included loss of personal identity. One had retrograde amnesia that was limited to 2–3 years. Eight of the ten patients were thought to have definite functional amnesia. One of the patients (whose performance is noted by an asterisk in the figures) subsequently confessed that he had malingered his amnesia. The final patient was considered to be a possible malingerer. The patients ranged in age from 28 to 54 years (mean, 37 years). For the eight patients for whom the data were known, education ranged from 9 to 16 years (mean, 13 years). Eight patients were men and two women. Seven were tested neuropsychologically 1–14 days after the onset of amnesia. Three were tested 10 weeks to 9 months after the onset of amnesia. Five patients were tested between 1982 and 1985. The other five were tested between 1992 and 1995. Four men and one woman, matched to the patients with respect to age and education, served as controls. They were tested in 1996. The neuropsychological data presented in this section are from these patients and controls.

Retrograde Amnesia

Figure 1 shows the performance of nine of the ten patients on a test of past autobiographical memory. This test was not administered to the patient who had retrograde amnesia of only 2–3 years. Ten common words (e.g., bird, clock) were presented one at a time with the instruction to recall a specific personal event from any time in the past that involved the stimulus word. Subjects were asked to describe the memory in as much detail as possible and then to date the memory. When recall was not clearly specific to time and place, the examiner probed to elicit the most specific memory possible. Responses were scored on a 0–3 scale, with 3 representing a well-formed episodic memory. The patients performed more poorly than the controls, both without (t [12] = 3.2, $p < 0.01$) and with probing (t [12] = 2.7, $p < 0.05$) by the examiner. The two patients who obtained the best scores were tested 3 and 9 months after the onset of the amnesia. Their good performances resulted from their ability to recall memories from the period after the onset of their amnesia. On neurological examination, both of these patients exhibited significant loss of autobiographical memories for events that had occurred before the onset of amnesia.

Figure 2 shows the percentage of well-formed episodic memories that were recalled from different past time periods (0 days to > 20 years) on the test of past autobiographical memory. One patient, the malingerer, was unable to produce any well-formed recollections and was not included in this analysis. The remaining patients each recalled from three to ten memories. The patients differed markedly from the controls in that they recalled most of their memories from the most recent time period (patients, 78%; controls = 24%; t [11] = 3.1, $p < 0.01$) and very few of their memories from the most remote time period (patients, 3%; controls, 36%; t [11] = 3.2, $p < 0.01$). It was notable that all of the memories recalled by the patients from the most recent time period were drawn from the time after the onset of amnesia. Thus, compared with the controls, the patients had a striking tendency not to recall remote memories, but rather to draw their memories from the period after the onset of the amnesia.

Figures 3(a) and **3(b)** show the performance of four of the patients on a test of recall and recognition of

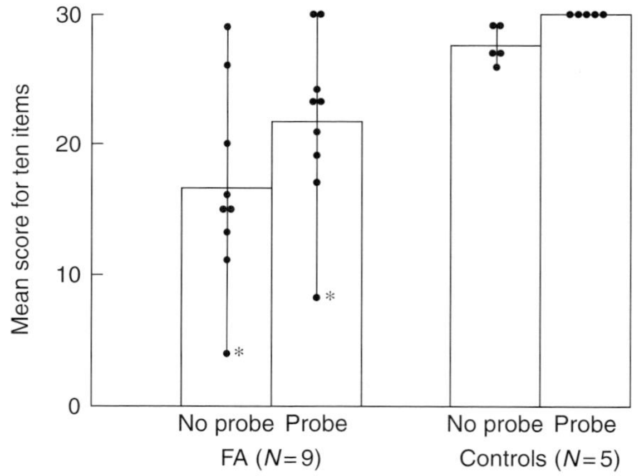

Figure 1 Patients with functional amnesia (FA) and controls were asked to recollect ten autobiographical episodes. Responses were scored (0–3) before (no probe) and after (probe) encouragement by the examiner to elicit as specific a recollection as possible. Each filled circle indicates the score for one subject. The asterisk indicates the score for the patient who later confessed that he had malingered his amnesia. Kritchevsky M, Chang J, and Squire LR (2004) Functional amnesia: Clinical description and neuropsychological profile of 10 cases. *Learning and Memory* 11: 213–226.

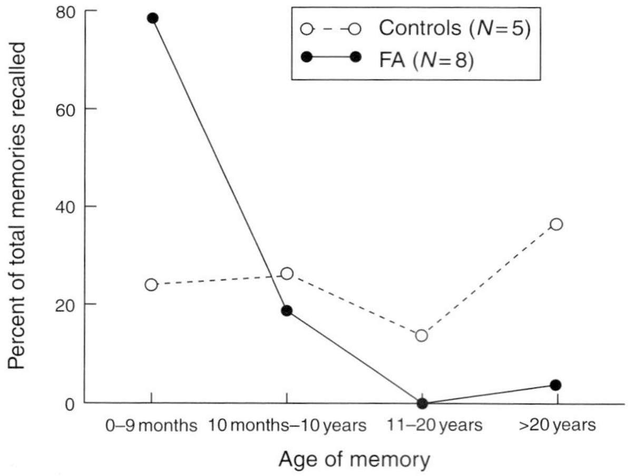

Figure 2 Percentage of memories that were recalled from the indicated time periods for patients with functional amnesia (FA) and controls. The data are based only on those recollections given a maximum score of 3 on the ten-item test of past autobiographical memory (**Figure 1**). The patient who later confessed that he had malingered his amnesia had no recollections that were given a three-point score. For the eight patients, all the memories from the 0–9 months time period were taken from the period after the onset of amnesia. Kritchevsky M, Chang J, and Squire LR (2004) Functional amnesia: Clinical description and neuropsychological profile of 10 cases. *Learning and Memory* 11: 213–226.

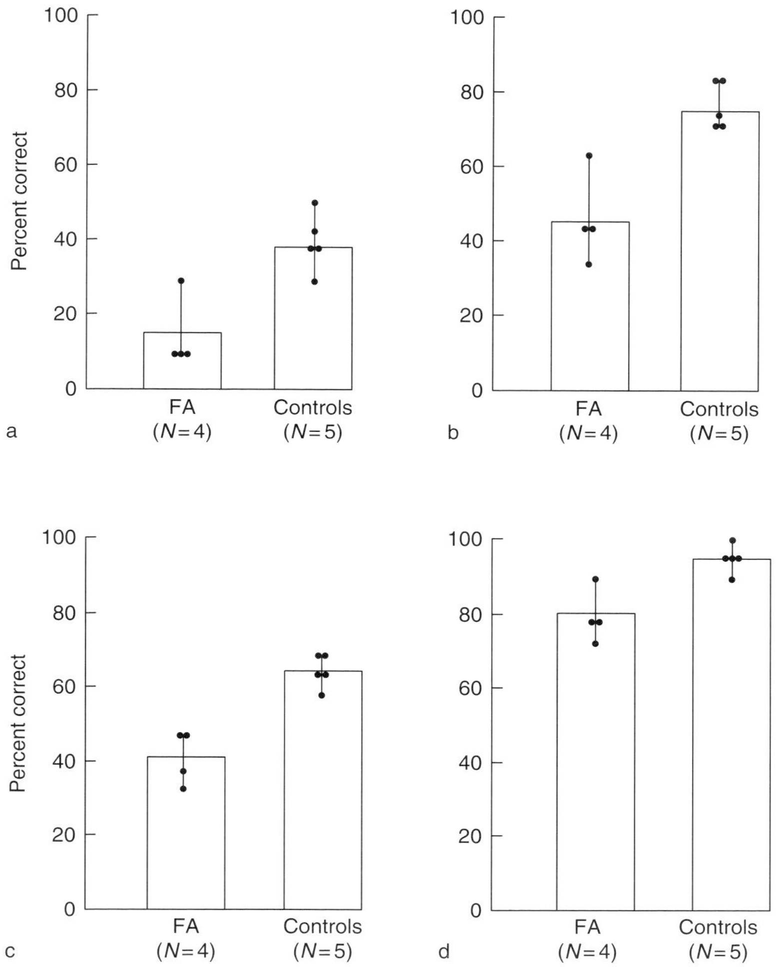

Figure 3 Performance on tests of remote memory for public events and famous faces. Patients with functional amnesia (FA) and controls were asked 24 questions about public events that had occurred during the two decades prior to testing (a) and then took a four-alternative, multiple-choice test about the same events (b). Subjects also were asked to identify 19 photographs of famous people who came into the news during the two decades before testing (c) and then to recognize the names that they could not recall (d). The recognition scores were based on the number of items recalled correctly plus the items that were recognized correctly. Chance = 25% for public events, 41.7% for famous faces. Each filled circle indicates the score for one subject. Kritchevsky M, Chang J, and Squire LR (2004) Functional amnesia: Clinical description and neuropsychological profile of 10 cases. *Learning and Memory* 11: 213–226.

public events. These patients were tested between 1992 and 1994. Twenty-four questions about public events that had occurred from 1970 to 1985 were asked. This test first was administered in a recall format (e.g., Who killed John Lennon?) and then, for each item that was not recalled or was incorrectly recalled, in a four-alternative, multiple-choice format (John Hinkley, Sara Jane Moore, David Roth, and Mark Chapman). The recognition score was based on the items that were recalled correctly plus the items that were recognized correctly. The four patients were impaired both at recall (16.7% correct for patients; 39.2% correct for controls; t [7] = 4.2, $p < 0.01$) and at recognition (44.8% correct for patients; 76.6% correct for controls; $t[7] = 4.2$, $p < 0.01$). One of these patients, who had retrograde amnesia of only 2–3 years, performed better than the other three. However, he still performed at the low end of the control range on recall (29.2%) and poorer than the controls on recognition (62.5%). The six other patients took a similar test consisting of 17–26 questions about the two most recent decades before the onset of their amnesia. They also scored poorly at recall (16.3% correct; one patient did not take the recall test) and at recognition (48.3% correct). One of these patients, the possible malingerer, had a score of 0% on the recall test and 11% on the recognition test (chance = 25%).

Figures 3(c) and **3(d)** show the performance of four of the patients on a test of recall and recognition of famous faces. These patients were tested between 1992 and 1994. Nineteen photographs of famous people who came into the news from 1970 to 1989 were shown. The test first was administered in a recall format and then, for each item that was not recalled or was incorrectly recalled, in a recognition format. For recognition, half the items were yes/no questions (e.g., Is this person's name Liza Minelli?) and half were three-alternative, multiple-choice questions (e.g., Liza Minelli, Ann Margaret, Helen Reddy). The recognition score was based on the items that were recalled correctly plus the items that were recognized correctly. As a group, the four patients were impaired both at recall (40.8% correct for patients; 64.2% correct for controls; $t\ [7] = 5.7$, $p < 0.01$) and at recognition (80.2% correct for patients; 94.7% for controls; $t\ [7] = 4.2$, $p < 0.01$). The six other patients took a similar test consisting of 20–27 faces from the two most recent decades before the onset of their amnesia. They also scored poorly as a group at recall (39.1% correct) and at recognition (77.8% correct; one patient did not take the recognition test). There was marked variability in the individual scores of the ten patients. Thus, both the recall and recognition scores of two patients (one of these was the malingerer) were as good as or better than the control scores. Also, the patient who had retrograde amnesia of only 2–3 years performed just below the controls at recall and obtained a perfect score at recognition. A fourth patient scored well enough on the recognition test to reach the low end of the control range. A fifth patient scored 0% correct at recall but nearly reached the control range at recognition. Finally, a sixth patient (the possible malingerer) scored 0% correct at recall and 18.5% correct at recognition (chance = 41.7%). His overall score on the public events and famous faces recognition tests was 2.75 standard deviations below the score that would have been expected from guessing.

Figure 4 shows the performance of nine of the ten patients on tests of identification of US and southern California cities. First, each subject was read the names of 16 real and 16 plausible US cities and associated states (e.g., Phoenix, Arizona, or Nelander, Michigan) and asked to identify whether each city name was real or fabricated. Then each subject was read a list of ten real and ten plausible southern California cities (e.g., Oceanside or Palmville) and again asked whether each city name was real or fabricated. The score on each test was the number of cities correctly identified. Overall, the patients performed similarly to the controls (US cities; $t[12] = 1.8$, $p = 0.09$; southern California cities, $p > 0.10$). However, two patients scored more than two standard deviations below the control mean on both tests. One of these, the possible malingerer, scored 47% correct on the US cities test and 30% correct on the southern California cities test (chance = 50% for each test).

In summary, all patients were impaired in their ability to recall autobiographical memories of specific events from their past. In contrast, there was marked variability in their performances on tests of their ability to recall and recognize public events and famous faces from the two decades before the onset of their amnesia. Thus, the possible malingerer scored significantly below chance on the recognition tests, and it is possible that he intentionally chose the wrong answers. Also, three patients (one was the malingerer) performed particularly well on the famous faces tests despite performing poorly on the public events tests. Another patient was unable to recall a single item on the famous faces test, but then did well on recognition of the faces. There was less variability in the patients' ability to distinguish names of real cities from the names of fictitious cities. Two patients, one the possible malingerer, performed abnormally on these tests.

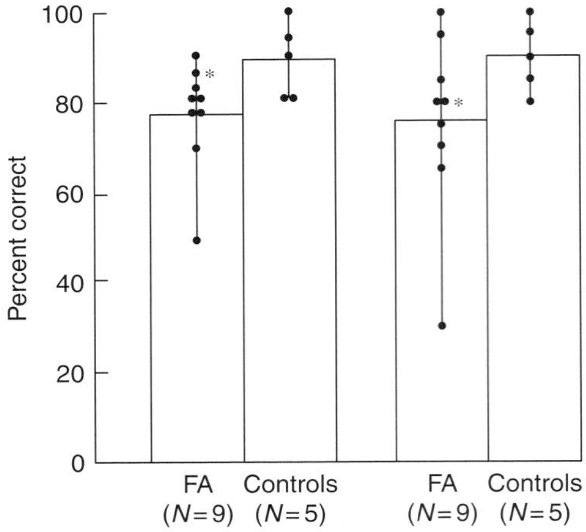

Figure 4 Patients with functional amnesia (FA) and controls were asked to identify the names of cities in the United States (left two bars) and the names of cities in southern California (right two bars) from lists of real and fictitious city names. Chance = 50%. Each filled circle indicates the score for one subject. The asterisk indicates the scores for the patient who later confessed that he had malingered his amnesia. Kritchevsky M, Chang J, and Squire LR (2004) Functional amnesia: Clinical description and neuropsychological profile of 10 cases. *Learning and Memory* 11: 213–226.

Anterograde Amnesia

Figure 5(a) shows the performance of the ten patients with functional amnesia on a test of story recall. A short prose passage was read to the patient. Recall was tested immediately and again after a 10–20 min delay. The score was the number of story segments correctly recalled. Overall, the patients were marginally impaired at immediate recall ($t\ [13] = 2.1$, $p < 0.06$) but similar to controls at delayed recall ($p > 0.10$). Nonetheless, there was considerable variability in the performance of individual patients. Six of the patients (including the malingerer and the possible malingerer) had immediate recall scores that were more than two standard deviations below the control mean. Only the malingerer had a delayed recall score that was more than two standard deviations below the control mean.

Figure 5(b) shows the performance of the ten patients on a test of paired associate learning. A series of ten noun–noun word pairs was presented verbally and

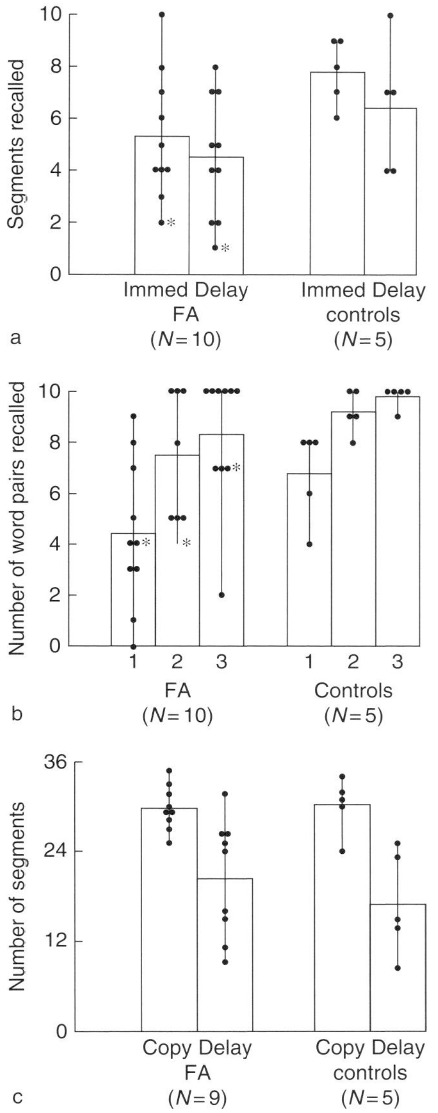

Figure 5 Performance of patients with functional amnesia (FA) and controls on tests of anterograde amnesia. (a) Story recall. Recall was tested immediately (Immed) and again after a delay of 10–20 min (Delay). (b) Paired-associate learning. Ten word pairs were presented on each of three study trials. (c) Copy of a complex diagram and reconstruction of the diagram from memory after 10–20 min (Delay). Maximum score = 36. Each filled circle indicates the score for one subject. The asterisk indicates the scores for the patient who later confessed that he had malingered his amnesia. He did not receive the diagram recall test. Kritchevsky M, Chang J, and Squire LR (2004) Functional amnesia: Clinical description and neuropsychological profile of 10 cases. *Learning and Memory* 11: 213–226.

visually on each of three study trials. After each study trial, the patient was shown the first word of each pair and asked to recall the second word. The score was the number of words correctly recalled on each trial. Patients and controls performed similarly overall ($F\ [1,13] = 2.7$, $p > 0.10$) and improved at a similar rate across the three trials ($F\ [2,26] = 0.5$, $p > 0.10$). There was some variability in the scores, with four of the patients (including the malingerer) having total number of words recalled across the three trials more than two standard deviations below the overall control mean.

Figure 5(c) shows the performance of nine of the patients on a test of recall of nonverbal material. This test was not administered to the malingerer. Each patient copied a complex diagram. After a 10–20 min delay and without forewarning, they were asked to reproduce the diagram from memory. The score was the number of parts of the diagram correctly recalled. The patients scored similarly to the controls, both when they copied the diagram and when they reconstructed it from memory ($p > 0.10$). No patient obtained a score on this test that was below the lowest score obtained by the controls.

In summary, the patients as a group performed well on tests of anterograde amnesia for verbal and nonverbal material. However, there was some variability among patients. Some appeared to have abnormal performances on immediate verbal memory for a prose passage or on paired associate learning. Despite these abnormal performances, no patient exhibited any difficulty learning and remembering day-to-day events after the onset of amnesia.

Etiology of Functional Amnesia

Functional amnesia is a nonneurological, conversion symptom-like disorder. The model for the amnesia is the amnesic syndrome that is popularized in literature and film, namely a loss of past memories that usually includes a loss of personal identity. Each patient has their own individual conception of what past memories should be lost, which leads to the striking variability in the clinical and neuropsychological findings of patients with functional amnesia. In functional amnesia, as in a conversion disorder, the patient is not intentionally producing the deficits. It has been proposed that posthypnotic amnesia might serve as a laboratory model of functional amnesia, and self-hypnosis is one possible mechanism of conversion disorder and of functional amnesia.

Evaluation and Treatment of the Patient with Functional Amnesia

The evaluation of the patient should begin with neurological and psychiatric histories. The patient may be able to provide some of this information, but early in the course of evaluation most of the history will come from family members, friends, and healthcare or legal professionals. Neurological and psychiatric examinations should be performed. Laboratory investigations usually are not required, but may be obtained in selected patients.

The patient should be treated in the same manner as a patient with a conversion disorder. They should be reassured that there is no evidence of serious or significant brain problem. Significant psychological stressors should be identified and treated. They should be informed that their memories may begin returning within days of the onset of the amnesia. Contact with friends and family members should be encouraged unless there is a contraindication. If there has been little or no return of past memories within about a week, then treatment with hypnosis or an amobarbital interview should be considered if the treating psychiatrist agrees. If psychologically painful memories are remembered during hypnosis or an amobarbital interview, then the patient will require careful observation to be sure that these memories do not lead to undue distress or even to a suicide attempt. Despite the best possible therapy, some patients have only partial recoveries and some patients do not appear to have any recovery from their functional amnesia.

See also: Cognition, An Overview of Neuroimaging Techniques; Memory Disorders.

Further Reading

Abeles, M and Schilder, P (1935). Psychogenic loss of personal identity. *Archives of Neurology and Psychiatry* 34: 587–604.

American Psychiatric Association (2000). Dissociative amnesia. *Diagnostic and Statistical Manual of Mental Disorders.* 4th edn., pp. 520–523. Arlington, VA: American Psychiatric Association.

Barnier, A (2002). Posthypnotic amnesia for autobiographical episodes: A laboratory model of functional amnesia? *Psychological Science* 13: 232–237.

Kanzer, M (1939). Amnesia: A statistical study. *American Journal of Psychiatry* 96: 711–716.

Kapur, N (1993). Focal retrograde amnesia in neurological disease: A critical review. *Cortex* 29: 217–234.

Kritchevsky, M, Chang, J, and Squire, LR (2004). Functional amnesia: Clinical description and neuropsychological profile of 10 cases. *Learning and Memory* 11: 213–226.

Kritchevsky, M, Zouzounis, J, and Squire, LR (1997). Transient global amnesia and functional retrograde amnesia: Contrasting examples of episodic memory loss. *Philosophical Transactions of the Royal Society of London B* 352: 1747–1754.

Schacter, DL, Wang, PL, Tulving, E, and Freedman, M (1982). Functional retrograde amnesia: A quantitative case study. *Neuropsychologia* 20: 523–532.

Yang, JC, Jeong, GW, Lee, MS, et al. (2005). Functional MR imaging of psychogenic amnesia: A case report. *Korean Journal of Radiology* 6: 196–199.

Amnesia, Declarative and Nondeclarative Memory

L. R. Squire, P. J. Bayley, and C. N. Smith, University of California at San Diego, San Diego, CA, USA

Introduction

Amnesia refers to difficulty in learning new information or in remembering the past. It is important to distinguish the amnesia that occurs following brain injury or disease (neurological amnesia) from the rarer functional (or psychogenic) amnesia that can occur as the result of an emotional trauma. Neurological amnesia has a variety of origins, including prolonged alcoholism, a temporary loss of blood supply or oxygen to the brain, and diseases such as herpes simplex encephalitis. All these conditions preferentially damage the medial temporal lobe or diencephalon. Neurological amnesia causes severe difficulty in learning new facts and events (anterograde amnesia). Amnesic patients also typically have some difficulty remembering facts and events that were acquired before the onset of amnesia (retrograde amnesia). Functional amnesia shows a different pattern of anterograde and retrograde memory impairment. Functional amnesia is characterized by a profound retrograde amnesia that is transient in some cases, and little or no anterograde amnesia is exhibited.

Functional Amnesia

Functional amnesia, also known as dissociative amnesia, is a dissociative psychiatric disorder that involves alterations in consciousness and identity. Although no particular brain structure or brain system is implicated in functional amnesia, the cause of the disorder must be due to abnormal brain function of some kind. Its presentation varies considerably from individual to individual, but in most cases, functional amnesia is preceded by physical or emotional trauma and occurs in association with some prior psychiatric history. Often, the patient is admitted to the hospital in a confused or frightened state. Memory for the past is lost, especially autobiographical memory and even personal identity. Semantic or factual information about the world is often preserved, though factual information about the patient's life may be unavailable. Despite profound impairment in the ability to recall information about the past, the ability to learn new information is usually intact. The disorder often clears, and the lost memories return. Occasionally, the disorder lasts longer, and sizable pieces of the past remain unavailable.

Etiology of Neurological Amnesia

Neurological amnesia results from a number of conditions, including Alzheimer's disease or other dementing illnesses, temporal lobe surgery, chronic alcohol abuse, encephalitis, head injury, anoxia, ischemia, infarction, and the rupture and repair of an anterior communicating artery aneurism. The common factor in all these conditions is that they disrupt normal function in one of two areas of the brain – the medial aspects of the temporal lobe and the diencephalic midline. Global amnesia results from bilateral damage, whereas material-specific amnesia results from unilateral damage. Typically, left-sided damage affects memory for verbal material, and right-sided damage affects memory for nonverbal material (e.g., the recall of faces and spatial layouts).

Anatomy

Well-studied cases of human amnesia and animal models of amnesia provide information about the neural connections and structures that are damaged in neurological amnesia. Damage limited to the hippocampus itself is sufficient to cause amnesia. For example, in one carefully studied case of amnesia (patient R.B.), the only significant damage was a bilateral lesion confined to the CA1 field of the hippocampus. The severity of memory impairment is exacerbated by additional damage outside the hippocampus. Thus, severe amnesia results when damage extends beyond the hippocampus to include adjacent structures in the medial temporal lobe, including the parahippocampal cortex, entorhinal cortex, and perirhinal cortex. Another well-studied case (H.M.) had surgery in 1953 to treat severe epilepsy. Most of the hippocampus and much of the surrounding medial temporal lobe cortices were removed bilaterally (the entorhinal cortex and most of the perirhinal cortex). Although the surgery was successful in reducing the frequency of H.M.'s seizures, it resulted in a severe and persistent amnesia.

Functional magnetic resonance imaging (fMRI) of healthy individuals who are engaged in learning and remembering reveals neural activity in the same structures that, when damaged, cause amnesia. It is also possible through structural imaging (MRI) to detect and quantify the neuropathology in amnesic patients. Many patients with restricted hippocampal damage have an average reduction in hippocampal volume of about 40%. Two such patients whose brains were available for detailed, postmortem neurohistological analysis (patients L.M. and W.H.) proved to have lost virtually all the neurons in the cornu ammonis (CA) fields of the hippocampus. These observations suggest that a reduction in hippocampal volume of approximately 40%, as estimated from MRI scans, likely indicates the near complete loss of hippocampal neurons. The amnesic condition is associated with neuronal death and tissue collapse, but the tissue does not disappear altogether because fibers and glial cells remain.

As questions about amnesia and the function of medial temporal lobe structures have become more sophisticated, it has become vital to obtain detailed, quantitative information about the damage in the patients being studied. In addition, single-case studies are not nearly so useful as group studies involving well-characterized patients. In the case of patients with restricted hippocampal damage, one can calculate the volume of the hippocampus itself as a proportion of total intracranial volume. One can also calculate the volumes of the adjacent medial temporal lobe structures (the perirhinal, entorhinal, and parahippocampal cortices), again in proportion to intracranial volume. Last, when there is extensive damage to the medial temporal lobe, it is important to calculate the volumes of lateral temporal cortex and other regions that might be affected. It is important to characterize patients in this way in order to address the kinds of questions now being pursued in memory research.

To understand the anatomy of human amnesia, and ultimately the anatomy of normal memory, animal models of human amnesia have been established in the monkey and in the rodent. In the monkey, following lesions of the bilateral medial temporal lobe or diencephalon, memory impairment is exhibited on the same kinds of tasks of new learning ability that human amnesic patients fail. Cumulative work with animal models suggests that the full medial temporal lobe memory system consists of the hippocampus and adjacent, anatomically related structures, including the entorhinal cortex, parahippocampal cortex, and perirhinal cortex (see **Figure 1**). When these adjacent structures are damaged, the severity of amnesia is greater than when only the hippocampus itself is damaged.

The important structures in the diencephalon are the mediodorsal thalamic nucleus, the anterior thalamic nucleus, the internal medullary lamina, the mammillary nuclei, and the mammillo-thalamic tract. Because diencephalic amnesia resembles medial temporal lobe amnesia in the pattern of sparing and loss, these two regions likely form an anatomically linked, functional system.

The Nature of Amnesia

It is important to appreciate that amnesic patients are not impaired at all kinds of memory. The major distinction is between declarative and nondeclarative memory. Only declarative memory is affected in amnesia. Declarative memory refers to the capacity to remember the facts and events of everyday life. It is the kind of memory that is meant when the term 'memory' is used in ordinary language. A declarative memory can be brought to mind as a conscious recollection. Declarative memory provides a

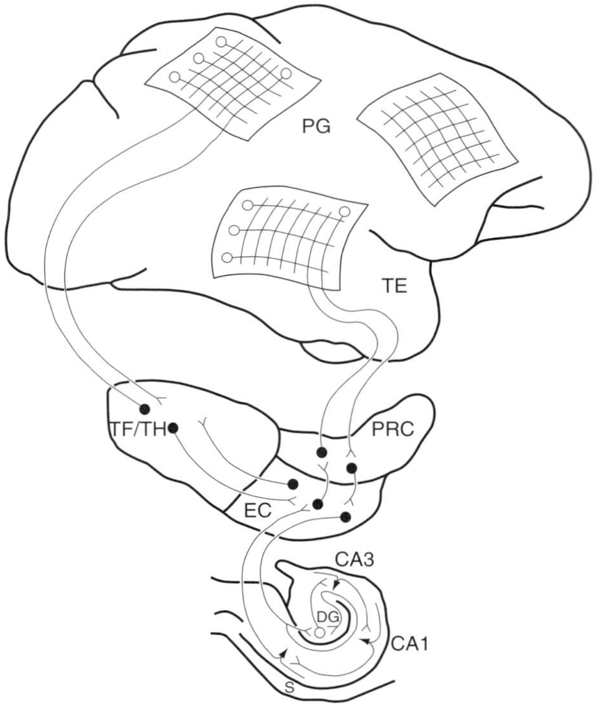

Figure 1 Schematic drawing of primate neocortex together with the structures and connections in the medial temporal region important for establishing long-term memory. The networks in the cortex show putative representations concerning visual object quality (in area TE) and object location (in area PG). If this disparate neural activity is to cohere into a stable long-term memory, convergent activity must occur along projections from these regions to the medial temporal lobe. Projections from neocortex arrive initially at the parahippocampal gyrus (TF/TH) and perirhinal cortex (PRC) and then at entorhinal cortex (EC), the gateway to the hippocampus. Further processing of information occurs in the several stages of the hippocampus, first in the dentate gyrus (DG) and then in the CA3 and CA1 regions. The fully processed input eventually exits this circuit via the subiculum (S) and the EC, where widespread efferent projections return to neocortex. The hippocampus and adjacent structures are thought to support the stabilization of representations in distributed regions of neocortex (e.g., TE and PG) and to support the strengthening of connections between these regions. Subsequently, memory for a whole event (for example, a memory that depends on representations in both TE and PG) can be revivified even when a partial cue is presented. Damage to the medial temporal lobe system causes anterograde and retrograde amnesia. The severity of the deficit increases as damage involves more components of the system. Once sufficient time has passed, the distributed representations in neocortex can operate independent of the medial temporal lobe. (This diagram is a simplification and does not show diencephalic structures involved in memory function.)

way to model the external world, and in this sense it is either true or false. The stored representations are flexible and can guide successful performance under a wide range of test conditions. Finally, declarative memory is especially suited for rapid learning and for forming and maintaining associations between arbitrarily different kinds of material (e.g., learning to associate two different words).

Anterograde Amnesia

Amnesia is characterized especially by profound difficulty in new learning. This impairment is referred to as anterograde amnesia. Amnesia can occur as part of a more global dementing disorder that includes other cognitive deficits, including impairments in language, attention, visuospatial abilities, and general intellectual capacity. However, amnesia can also occur in the absence of other cognitive deficits and without any change in personality or social skills. In this more circumscribed form of amnesia, patients have intact intellectual functions and intact perceptual functions, even on difficult tests that require the ability to discriminate between similar images containing overlapping features. Patients also have intact immediate memory (as measured, for example, by the ability to repeat a short string of digits). Their intact immediate memory explains why amnesic patients can carry on a conversation and appear quite normal to the casual observer. Indeed, if the amount of material to be remembered is not too large (e.g., a three-digit number), then patients can remember the material for minutes, or as long as they can hold it in mind by rehearsal. One would say in this case that the patients have carried the contents of immediate memory forward by engaging in explicit rehearsal. This rehearsal-based activity is referred to as working memory. The difficulty for amnesic patients arises when an amount of information must be recalled that exceeds immediate memory capacity (typically, when a list of eight or more items must be remembered) or when information must be recalled after a distraction-filled interval or after a long delay. In these situations, patients will remember fewer items than will their healthy counterparts.

Amnesic patients are impaired on tasks of new learning, regardless of whether memory is tested by free recall, recognition (e.g., presenting an item and asking whether it was previously encountered), or cued recall (e.g., asking for recall of an item when a hint is provided). In addition, the memory impairment involves not just difficulty in learning about specific episodes and events that occurred in a certain time and place (episodic memory), but also difficulty in learning factual information (semantic memory). Finally, the memory deficit is present regardless of the sensory modality in which information is presented (visual, auditory, olfactory, and so on).

Retrograde Amnesia

In addition to impaired new learning, amnesia also impairs memories that were acquired before the onset of amnesia. This type of memory loss is referred to as retrograde amnesia. Retrograde amnesia is usually temporally graded. That is, information acquired in the distant past (remote memory) is spared relative to more recent memory. The extent of retrograde amnesia can be relatively short and encompass only 1–2 years, or it can be more extensive and cover a much longer time. For example, an amnesic patient can have retrograde amnesia covering the previous one or two decades. In contrast, memories for the facts and events of childhood and adolescence can be intact. The severity and extent of retrograde amnesia is determined by the locus and extent of damage. Patients with restricted hippocampal damage have a limited retrograde amnesia covering a few years prior to the onset of amnesia. Patients with large medial temporal lobe damage have extensive retrograde amnesia covering decades.

The sparing of remote memory relative to more recent memory illustrates that the brain regions damaged in amnesia are not the permanent repositories of long-term memory. Instead, memories undergo a process of reorganization and consolidation after learning, during which time the neocortex becomes more important. During the process of consolidation, memories are vulnerable if there is damage to the medial temporal lobe or diencephalon. After sufficient time has passed, storage and retrieval of memory no longer require the participation of these brain structures. Memory is at that point supported by neocortex. The areas of neocortex important for long-term memory are thought to be the same regions that were initially involved in the processing and analysis of what was to be learned. Thus, the neocortex is always important, but the structures of the medial temporal lobe and diencephalon are also important during initial learning and during consolidation.

Spatial Memory

Discussions of amnesia have focused especially on the status of spatial memory because of the discovery of 'place cells' in the rodent hippocampus and the possible importance of the hippocampus in forming spatial maps. In human amnesia, spatial memory is impaired along with other forms of declarative memory. Patients have difficulty acquiring new spatial knowledge, and they are impaired in remembering recently acquired spatial knowledge. However, as is the case with other forms of declarative memory, remote spatial knowledge is intact. One well-studied patient with large medial temporal lobe lesions and severe amnesia (E.P.) was able to mentally navigate his childhood neighborhood, use alternate and novel routes to describe how to travel from one place to another, and point correctly to locations in the neighborhood while imagining himself oriented at some other location. These findings show that the medial temporal lobe is not needed for the long-term storage of spatial knowledge and does not maintain a spatial layout of learned environments that is necessary for successful navigation. Accordingly, the available data support the view that the hippocampus and related medial temporal lobe structures are involved in learning new facts and events, both spatial and nonspatial. Further, these structures are not repositories of long-term memory, either spatial or nonspatial.

Nondeclarative Memory

It is a striking feature of amnesia that many kinds of learning and memory are spared. Memory is not a unitary faculty of the mind but is composed of many parts that depend on different brain systems. Amnesia impairs only declarative memory and spares nondeclarative memory. Nondeclarative memory refers to a heterogeneous collection of abilities, all of which afford the capacity to acquire knowledge nonconsciously. Nondeclarative memory includes motor skills, perceptual and cognitive skills, priming, adaptation-level effects, simple classical conditioning, and habits, as well as phylogenetically early forms of experience-dependent behavior such as habituation and sensitization. In these cases, memory is expressed through performance rather than recollection, and performance does not require reflection on the past or even the knowledge that memory is being influenced by past events. For example, in the case of motor skills, one can learn how to ride a bicycle but be unable to describe what has been learned, at least not in the same sense that one might recall riding a bicycle on a particular day with a friend. Perceptual skills include such things as reading mirror-reversed print and searching a display quickly to find a hidden letter. In formal experiments, amnesic patients acquire perceptual skills at the same rate as individuals with intact memory, even though the patients may not remember performing the task.

Priming refers to an improved ability to identify a word or other item as a result of its prior presentation. For example, suppose that a line drawing of a dog, hammer, and airplane are presented in succession, with the instruction to name each item as quickly as possible. Typically, about 800 ms are needed to produce each name aloud. If in a later test these same pictures are presented intermixed with new drawings, the new drawings will still require about 800 ms to name, but now the dog, hammer, and airplane are named about 100 ms more quickly. The improved naming time occurs independent of whether one remembers having seen the items earlier. Furthermore, amnesic patients exhibit this effect at full strength, despite having a poor memory of seeing the items earlier. Priming effects of this kind can persist across intervals as long as several weeks. In formal experiments, severely amnesic patients had intact priming for recently presented words, even when the patients performed at guessing levels (50% correct) on tests that asked them to recognize which words were presented previously and which were not. This result shows that priming is fully independent of declarative memory.

Adaptation-level effects refer to changes in judgments about stimuli (e.g., their heaviness or size) that are caused by recent experience. For example, experience with light-weighted objects subsequently causes other objects to be judged heavier than they would be if the light-weighted objects had not been presented. Amnesic patients show this effect to the same degree as healthy individuals, though they have difficulty remembering what they have done.

Classical conditioning refers to the development of an association between a previously neutral stimulus and an unconditioned stimulus. One of the best-studied examples of classical conditioning in humans is eye-blink conditioning. In a typical conditioning procedure, a tone repeatedly precedes a mild air puff directed to the eye. After a number of pairings, the tone comes to elicit an eyeblink in anticipation of the air puff. Amnesic patients acquire the tone-air puff association at the same rate as healthy individuals do. In both groups, awareness of the temporal contingency between the tone and the air puff is unrelated to successful conditioning. Simple classical conditioning, where the tone overlaps with the air puff and terminates with it, is dependent on the cerebellum.

Habit learning refers to the gradual acquisition of associations between stimuli and responses, such as learning to make one choice rather than another. Habit learning depends on the neostriatum (basal ganglia). Many tasks can be acquired either declaratively, through memorization, or nondeclaratively, as a habit. For example, healthy individuals will solve many trial and error learning tasks quickly by simply engaging declarative memory and memorizing which responses are correct. In this circumstance, amnesic patients are disadvantaged. However, tasks can also be constructed that defeat memorization strategies, for example, by making the outcomes on each trial probabilistic. In such a case, amnesic patients and healthy individuals learn at the same gradual rate. It is also true that severely amnesic patients who have no capacity for declarative memory can gradually acquire trial-and-error tasks, even when the task can be learned declaratively by healthy individuals. In this case they succeed by engaging habit memory.

This situation is nicely illustrated by the eight-pair concurrent discrimination task, which requires individuals to learn the correct object for each of eight object pairs. Healthy individuals learn all eight pairs in a single test session. Severely amnesic patients acquire this same task over many weeks, even though at the start of each session they cannot describe the task, the instructions, or the objects. It is known that this task is acquired at a normal (slow) rate by monkeys with medial temporal lobe lesions and that monkeys with lesions of the neostriatum (basal ganglia) are impaired. Thus, humans appear to have a robust capacity for habit learning that operates outside awareness and independent of the medial temporal lobe structures that are damaged in amnesia.

These examples illustrate that nondeclarative memory is distinct from declarative memory. It is spared in amnesia, and it operates outside awareness. Nondeclarative forms of memory depend variously on the neostriatum, the amygdala, the cerebellum, and on processes intrinsic to neocortex (**Figure 2**).

Summary

The study of amnesia has illuminated the nature of memory disorders and has also led to a better understanding of the

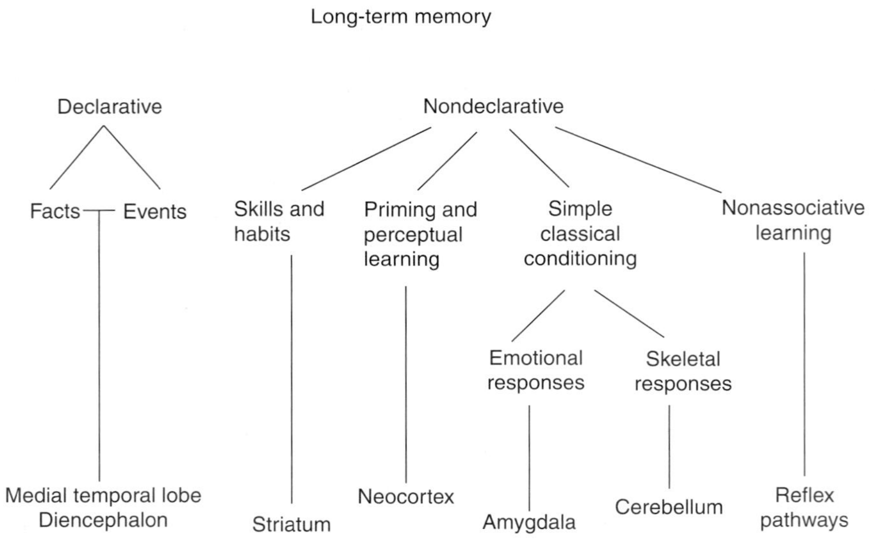

Figure 2 Classification of mammalian long-term memory systems. The taxonomy lists the brain structures thought to be especially important for each form of declarative and nondeclarative memory. In addition to the central role of the amygdala in emotional learning, it is able to modulate the strength of both declarative and nondeclarative learning.

neurological foundations of memory. Experimental studies in patients, neuroimaging studies of healthy volunteers, and related studies in experimental animals continue to reveal insights about what memory is and how it is organized in the brain. As more is learned about the neuroscience of memory, about how memory works, more opportunities will arise for achieving better diagnosis, treatment, and prevention of diseases and disorders that affect memory.

See also: Amnesia, Functional; Memory Disorders; Memory, Semantic.

Further Reading

Bayley, PJ, Frascino, JC, and Squire, LR (2005). Robust habit learning in the absence of awareness and independent of the medial temporal lobe. *Nature* 436: 550–553.

Bayley, PJ, Gold, JJ, Hopkins, RO, et al. (2005). The neuroanatomy of remote memory. *Neuron* 46: 799–810.

Eichenbaum, H and Cohen, NJ (2001). *From Conditioning to Conscious Recollection: Memory Systems of the Brain.* New York: Oxford University Press.

Gordon, B (1995). *Memory: Remembering and Forgetting in Everyday Life.* New York: Mastermedia.

Milner, B, Squire, LR, and Kandel, ER (1998). Cognitive neuroscience and the study of memory. *Neuron* 20(3): 445–468.

Schacter, DL (1996). *Searching for Memory: The Brain, the Mind, the Past.* New York: BasicBooks.

Squire, LR and Kandel, ER (2000). *Memory: From Mind to Molecules.* New York: W. H. Freeman.

Squire, LR and Schacter, DL (eds.) (2002). *The Neuropsychology of Memory,* 3rd edn. New York: Guilford Press.

Squire, LR, Stark, CE, and Clark, RE (2004). The medial temporal lobe. *Annual Review of Neuroscience* 27: 279–306.

Teng, E and Squire, LR (1999). Memory for places learned long ago is intact after hippocampal damage. *Nature* 400: 675–677.

Wais, PE, Wixted, JT, Hopkins, RO, and Squire, LR (2006). The hippocampus supports both the recollection and the familiarity components of recognition memory. *Neuron* 49: 459–468.

Relevant Websites

http://www.alzforum.org – Alzheimer's Research Forum.

http://whoville.ucsd.edu – Home page of Larry R. Squire.

http://www.nia.nih.gov – National Institute on Aging, Alzheimer's Disease Centers.

Amusia

C. E. Hou

Amusia can be defined as the loss of a preexisting musical talent. The deficit may manifest as an inability to perceive differences in the elements of music, to sing a song, or to play an instrument. Various classifications of the amusias have been developed based on motor versus sensory deficits, higher versus lower cognitive functions, or anatomical areas.

As one of the five primary senses, the perception of sound plays key roles in communication via speech or the appreciation of music. Any sound can be defined by its fundamental components: pitch, intensity, and timbre. Respectively, these are the sound's frequency, loudness, and overtone. Musical notes have additional properties that make them unique. A note is played or sung for a certain period of time, thus conferring the element of duration. Several musical notes combined simultaneously become a melody. Consecutive notes or melodies form a harmony. Finally, rhythm is the temporal sequence of musical notes or melodies.

Although sounds have bilateral representation in the cerebral cortex, some functions of the brain are unique to a particular hemisphere. For example, the dominant hemisphere controls comprehension and production of speech. However, the anatomical areas responsible for processing music are less defined. Various methods have been used to localize the process of musical perception and performance.

Intraoperative electrical stimulation of the brain by Penfield produced auditory hallucinations of voices or songs and caused some subjects to sing. The points of stimulation specific to music were found to be in the superior temporal gyrus of either hemisphere. Milner described impaired perception for timbre and poor tonal memory following right temporal lobectomies. Employing the dichotic listening technique in which different melodies were presented simultaneously in each ear, Kimura concluded that the left ear and right hemisphere were more effective in melodic perception.

Bever and Chiarello found a left hemispheric superiority for melody analysis in persons with musical experience when compared to musically naive listeners. They suggested that musical training increases the left hemisphere's contribution and develops a more detailed schema in melody analysis. This was later supported by functional imaging. Subjects using a nonanalytical strategy for tonal memory had greater right than left asymmetry. Those using an analytical strategy had increased metabolism in the left posterior superior temporal lobe.

Relatively few studies have dealt with the execution of music. Smith showed that singing was possible after resection of the left hemisphere. Bogen and Gordon injected amobarbital into the carotid artery to selectively depress either hemisphere and then assessed the quality of singing melodies without lyrics. Right hemispheric anesthesia produced monotone singing but did not affect the rhythm of singing or speech. Of the two patients that received left carotid injection, one produced melodic but slurred singing and the other could sing without difficulty. The nondominant hemisphere appears to be more important in the production of correct pitch and melody. They also suggested that singing may result from contributions of both hemispheres.

Oral-expressive or vocal amusia is perhaps the most frequently described motor amusia. Various permutations of the partial form may be seen: correct production of a tone but inability to carry a melody, correct production of a melody but inability to produce a tone, or production of a tune with inability to sing the words. Excluding those with aphasia, most cases of oral-expressive amusia result from anterior right hemispheric pathology. A singer was unable to sing or whistle after traumatic injury to the right frontal lobe. Following ligation of the right common carotid artery, a musician could not sing, whistle, or read a score. In both cases, the recognition of pitch and melody was intact.

Instrumental amusia is the loss of the ability to play a musical instrument. Key to this definition is the absence of dyspraxia for other motor skills. Botez and Wertheim reported on a 26-year-old man who had been playing the accordion since age 9. Following removal of an oligodendroglioma in the right frontal lobe, he could not accurately produce notes or songs on the accordion but did not show any motor apraxias. Also demonstrating oral-expressive amusia, he had difficulty singing or whistling in tune, but his perception of music was unaffected.

Musical agraphia is another form of motor amusia. In the primary form, a trained musician loses the skill to transcribe notes that are heard. Impaired copying of a score has also been reported as a form of musical agraphia. However, in most cases, musical agraphia may represent impaired visual–spatial skills rather than an amusia.

A commonly described sensory amusia is receptive amusia. In the most basic form, one cannot differentiate notes of various pitch and timbre. Tone-deaf persons often have difficulty with melodic appreciation. Reflecting the fact that receptive amusia may result from an auditory agnosia, there is a close association with understanding spoken language.

Musical alexia, another type of sensory amusia, afflicts musicians trained to read musical scores. An 1892 article described a singer who could not read a single note but was able to sing. Other patients with musical alexia also had receptive aphasias or other amusias.

The mixed motor and sensory amusias demonstrate impairments of both the execution and perception of music. Musical amnesia refers to the inability to name a tune or produce a melody. For example, musicians cannot write the score or singers cannot sing the tune when given the name of a familiar melody. Another mixed amusia is the disorder of rhythm, either impaired reproduction or discrimination of rhythmic patterns. Poor rhythm production is often the result of general motor apraxia.

As with many neurological functions, the loss of musical ability results primarily from destructive lesions, such as traumatic injury, tumors, and surgical resection. Ischemic stroke has also been reported to cause amusia. Infarction of the right temporal lobe has produced impaired tonal and timbre discrimination. In another case, an infarct in the right superior temporal and supramarginal gyri caused expressive and receptive amusia. The organist patient could sing and imitate nonmusical rhythms but had difficulty reproducing rhythms on the organ and identifying familiar melodies. A stroke in the left parietal area resulted in disturbed melody and rhythm production and recognition.

In contrast to structural and vascular damage, recent case reports suggest that musical functions are generally preserved in Alzheimer's-type dementia. Beatty described a musician who was able to play the trombone despite dementia that was diagnosed as Alzheimer's disease at autopsy.

Further Reading

Benton, AL (1977). The amusias. In: Critchley, M and Henson, RA (eds.) *Music and the Brain*, pp. 378–397. Springfield, IL: Thomas.

Bogen, JE and Gordon, HW (1971). Musical tests for functional lateralization with intracarotid amobarbital. *Nature* 230: 523–525.

Damasio, AR and Damasio, H (1977). Musical faculty and cerebral dominance. In: Critchley, M and Henson, RA (eds.) *Music and the Brain*, pp. 141–155. Springfield, IL: Thomas.

Kimura, D (1964). Left–right differences in the perception of melodies. *Q. J. Exp. Psychol.* 16: 355–358.

Mazziotta, JC, Phelps, ME, Carson, RE, et al. (1982). Tomographic mapping of human cerebral metabolism: Auditory stimulation. *Neurology* 32: 921–937.

Penfield, W and Perot, P (1963). The brain's record of auditory and visual experience. *Brain* 86: 595–696.

Anatomical Asymmetries Versus Variability of Language Areas of the Brain

O. Selnes, Johns Hopkins University, Baltimore, MD, USA
H. A. Whitaker, Northern Michigan University, Marquette, MI, USA

Introduction

Significant individual variability in the volume, weight, and morphology of the human brain has been recognized since the first detailed studies were performed as early as a century ago. Attempts to relate such variability in the size of the brain to functional properties have generally been predicated on the phrenological principle that a larger brain is a better brain. Despite improvements in the methods used for quantifying brain volume, evidence in support of this hypothesis remains weak. In addition to variability in overall brain volume, there is also variability in the degree of asymmetry between the two hemispheres of the brain. Mild asymmetry of paired structures is a common feature of all aspects of human anatomy, including the well-documented differences between the left and right hemispheres of the brain. Asymmetries favoring regions of the dominant (left) hemisphere known to be important for speech and language functions have been interpreted to reflect some as yet to be defined morphological marker of cerebral language dominance. The presence of similar asymmetries in nonhuman primates, however, has led some to question the relevance of such anatomical asymmetries for language functions. Anatomical differences between the left and right hemispheres of the brain have also been identified for regions not involved with speech and language functions. Such differences are present at multiple levels, including differences in overall volume and weight between the two hemispheres, and more regional asymmetries including specific subdivisions of the four major lobes of the brain, as well as in subcortical regions.

Individual Variability

Overall Brain Volume

Most earlier studies of the individual variability in the size, weight, and morphology of the human brain were based on autopsy materials. Such data were limited by several factors, including an autopsy bias towards older and less healthy individuals. With the advent of magnetic resonance imaging (MRI), recent studies of individual variability of the anatomy of the human brain have avoided these limitations. On the basis of volumetric MRI measures, the average total brain volume (excluding cerebrospinal fluid and the meningeal coverings) has been in the range 1250 to 1290 cm^3 for well-nourished males of predominantly European ancestry. For women, average brain volumes are approximately 130 cm^3 less. These MRI-based whole-brain volume estimates are generally smaller than previous measurements based on postmortem materials. Overall brain volume is closely related to body weight or body mass index. Although brain sizes at the extremes of the normal distribution (macro- and microcephaly) may be associated with cognitive abnormalities, the evidence that variations **within** the average range are correlated with intelligence or other cognitive functions remains difficult to interpret. Modest positive correlations between full-scale IQ and total gray matter volume have been reported in some studies (Bernard et al., 1993), suggesting that greater volume of brain tissue may be associated with higher level of intellectual functioning. It is not clear, however, how to reconcile such findings with reports that individuals with profound developmental disorders, such as autism, have larger brains than appropriate control subjects (Piven et al., 1996). Other investigations have focused more on regional microscopic anatomy in brains of gifted individuals in attempts to account for possible relationships between brain structure and mental skills (Bentivoglio, 1998; Witelson et al., 1999).

The volumes of individual lobes and other subdivisions of the brain are generally highly correlated with overall brain size. One notable exception to this rule is the occipital lobe. This may be because the occipital lobe is one of the regions of the brain that shows the greatest individual variability in both men and women. When adjusting for overall brain volume, there is a negative correlation between the frontal lobe and parietal lobe volume, which has been interpreted by some to suggest that the evolutionary expansion of the frontal lobes in humans may have come at the expense of a reduction in parietal lobe volume.

The volume of the lateral ventricles is highly variable, and in general is not associated with overall brain size. Attempts to correlate variability in the size of various brain regions with specific cognitive profiles, such as reading disability, have met with only variable degrees of success (Pennington et al., 1999).

Gyral Patterns and Regional Variability

The most striking individual differences in the gross morphology of the human brain are in the patterns of gyri and sulci. Although the subject of multiple investigations, the behavioral significance of this variability remains unknown (Whitaker and Selnes, 1976). There is some, although not complete, correspondence between the gyral pattern and the boundaries of cytoarchitectonic fields. While the greatest degree of individual differences is observed for the minor sulci and gyri, there is also considerable interindividual variability in the configuration of the Rolandic and Sylvian fissures. The gyral patterns of the cingulate region are likewise subject to a wide range of configurations (Paus et al., 1996; Ide et al., 1999).

The variability in configuration and size of specific brain regions involved in language was pointed out by early anatomists such as Constatin von Economo (1876–1931). For example, the planum temporale, which is located adjacent to the primary auditory cortex on the posterior portion of the supratemporal plane, shows particularly striking variability across individuals. The potential functional significance of such variability can best be evaluated in the context of the overall variability of the brain. There is considerable evidence that brain regions not related to language, such as the striate cortex, show a similar, if not greater, degree of variability.

White Matter Tracts

Considerable individual variability has been reported in the size of the corpus callosum, apparently related, at least in part, to variability in overall brain volume. There is no consensus regarding the relationship between callosal size and handedness. On the assumption that a larger volume of the corpus callosum may relate to improved interhemispheric integration, some studies have attempted to correlate overall callosum size with overall intellectual performance. A modest correlation between performance on some neuropsychological tests and callosal size has been found for women, but not for men (Davatzikos and Resnick, 1998). Interpretation of these findings is somewhat unclear because other investigators have reported a larger volume of the corpus callosum in dyslexic adults than in age-matched controls (Robichon and Habib, 1998). The results of studies attempting to correlate corpus callosum volume to measures of cerebral laterality, such as dichotic listening, have yielded somewhat conflicting results. There is some evidence, however, suggesting that a greater degree of asymmetry of perisylvian language regions is associated with a smaller volume of the corpus callosum. This may imply that as the degree of asymmetry between the two hemispheres has evolved, the degree of interhemispheric connectivity has gradually reduced. The development of the myelin of the corpus callosum is not complete until after age 10 years, which appears to coincide with the so-called critical period for language development. After this period, acquisition of phonological skills with a degree of competence comparable to that of a native speaker is no longer possible. Developmental studies have shown that the volume of the corpus callosum continues to increase until the middle of the second decade of life (Pujol et al., 1993). The high prevalence of bilateral language representation in individuals who are born without a corpus callosum has suggested to some that it may play a role in the development of unilateral language representation (Selnes, 1974).

Brain Asymmetries

The possibility of identifying regional brain structural correlates of language dominance was first introduced by the studies of Geschwind and Levitsky (Geschwind and Levitsky, 1968). They reported that in a sample of 100 autopsy brains, the planum temporale, located behind Heschl's gyrus on the supratemporal plane of the temporal lobe, was approximately one-third larger in the left hemisphere. This discovery stimulated considerable interest in defining the degree and pattern of language-related interhemispheric asymmetries, and subsequent autopsy and volumetric MRI studies have confirmed that the planum temporale is larger in the left hemisphere of the brain in 65% to 95% of cases.

Anatomical asymmetries involving the lateral aspect of the frontal cortex, including the anterior speech regions, have also been reported. Volumetric MRI of the third inferior frontal gyrus (Broca's area), have shown that this region is larger in the left hemisphere for most individuals. Broca's area is made up of two distinct subregions, the pars triangularis and the pars opercularis. Whereas the pars triangularis shows a consistent leftward asymmetry regardless of handedness, the directionality of the asymmetry of the pars opercularis appears to be predicted by handedness. It is larger on the left in right-handers, but larger on the right in left-handers (Foundas et al., 1998). Asymmetries at the microscopic level have also been demonstrated for both the posterior and anterior language areas (Amunts et al., 1999).

The functional significance of the structural asymmetry of the brain regions involved in language remains unclear. Most early studies hypothesized that the larger left planum temporale was a 'marker' of the left hemisphere specialization for language functions. The close proximity of the planum temporale to brain regions involved in comprehension of language (Wernicke's area) supported this argument. There is no direct evidence, however, that the planum temporale plays a specific role in language comprehension (Binder et al., 1996). Lesions restricted to this area do not appear to result in any linguistic deficits. There is also a mismatch between the approximate 65% prevalence of leftward anatomical asymmetry and the 95% prevalence of left hemisphere language dominance.

More recent studies have demonstrated that cortical asymmetries may be present even in the absence of any known asymmetry or lateralization at the functional level. Moreover, it has become increasingly clear that regional hemispheric asymmetries can best be interpreted in the context of overall hemisphere asymmetries. The overall volume of the right hemisphere is greater than that of the left, suggesting that, for most individuals, there is more brain tissue in the right than left hemisphere.

The right hemisphere on average extends further anteriorly, while the left hemisphere extends further posteriorly. Asymmetries involving the volume of white matter in the two hemispheres have also been described. For the frontal and temporal lobes, the volume of white matter is greater in the left hemisphere than the right (Pujol et al., 2002).

Subcortical Asymmetries

The roles of subcortical structures in speech and language functions have long been somewhat controversial. Current data suggest that subcortical lesions may influence the function of cortical regions through mechanisms of hypoperfusion (Hillis et al., 2004). Anatomical asymmetries at the subcortical level have been reported for the caudate nucleus, which shows a consistent right-greater-than-left volume. The volume of the insular cortex, which has been implicated in language functions, also shows an asymmetry in favor of the right being larger than the left (Watkins et al., 2001).

Although the hippocampus is not traditionally thought of as being part of the human language system, verbal memory is nonetheless an integral part of language. The vast majority of studies that have reported on asymmetries in the volume of the hippocampus have concluded that the right is larger than the left. This is perhaps somewhat surprising since we traditionally think of verbal memories as being more highly developed than visual memory systems.

White Matter Tract Asymmetries

Recent imaging techniques such as diffusion tensor imaging (DTI) allow more detailed quantification of specific white tracts of the brain. One recent study found an asymmetry of the arcuate fasciculus favoring the left hemisphere (Buchel et al., 2004). The arcuate fasciculus has long been thought to be involved in language functions, specifically in the ability to repeat auditory information. A lesion of the arcuate fasciculus was once believed to be the principal mechanism underlying the syndrome of conduction aphasia. However, more recent studies have questioned the role of the arcuate fasciculus in repetition (Selnes et al., 2002), and the significance of a more prominent left-hemisphere arcuate fasciculus is therefore unclear.

Asymmetry in Nonhumans

Although it was originally believed that the asymmetries of the temporal lobe regions involved in language were unique to man and not present in the great apes, more recent studies suggest that this may not be the case. Interpretation of these newer findings has been the subject of considerable debate, however. In the case of humans, the distribution of the asymmetry of the planum temporale involves approximately 65% with greater left than right, symmetry in 24%, and a larger volume on the right in 11%. In one series of great apes, 17 out of 18 were found to have a larger left than right planum temporale (Gannon et al., 1998). This has led some to suggest that the volume and degree of this particular region of the brain may not be directly related to the human capacity for language.

Conclusions

Considerable individual variability has been documented for both the macro- and microscopic anatomy of the brain. Asymmetries between the two hemispheres, with some favoring the left hemisphere, are also well documented. The functional significance of asymmetries involving language areas remains unknown. In many cases, regional variability is greater than that of interhemispheric asymmetries. While larger volumes of brain tissue have often been equated with greater functional propensities, the evidence for this remains controversial. Asymmetries at the gross morphological level can reflect differences in underlying neuronal or glial density, white matter tracts, or other components, and it is not known how each of these factors may contribute to the brain's overall cognitive capacity.

See also: Diffusion and Perfusion Imaging.

Bibliography

Amunts, K, Schleicher, A, Burgel, U, Mohlberg, H, Uylings, HB, and Zilles, K (1999). 'Broca's region revisited: cytoarchitecture and intersubject variability.' *Journal of Comparative Neurology* 412: 319–341.

Bentivoglio, M (1998). 'Cortical structure and mental skills: Oskar Vogt and the legacy of Lenin's brain.' *Brain Research Bulletin* 47: 291–296.

Bernard, LC, Houston, W, and Natoli, L (1993). 'Malingering on neuropsychological memory tests: potential objective indicators.' *Journal of Clinical Psychology* 49: 45–53.

Binder, JR, Frost, JA, Hammeke, TA, Rao, SM, and Cox, RW (1996). 'Function of the left planum temporale in auditory and linguistic processing.' *Brain* 119: 1239–1247.

Buchel, C, Raedler, T, Sommer, M, Sach, M, Weiller, C, and Koch, MA (2004). 'White matter asymmetry in the human brain: a diffusion tensor MRI study.' *Cerebral Cortex* 14: 945–951.

Davatzikos, C and Resnick, SM (1998). 'Sex differences in anatomic measures of interhemispheric connectivity: correlations with cognition in women but not men.' *Cerebral Cortex* 8: 635–640.

Foundas, AL, Eure, KF, Luevano, LF, and Weinberger, DR (1998). 'MRI asymmetries of Broca's area: the pars triangularis and pars opercularis.' *Brain and Language* 64: 282–296.

Gannon, PJ, Holloway, RL, Broadfield, DC, and Braun, AR (1998). 'Asymmetry of chimpanzee planum temporale: humanlike pattern of Wernicke's brain language area homolog.' *Science* 279: 220–222.

Geschwind, N and Levitsky, W (1968). 'Human brain: left–right asymmetries in temporal speech region.' *Science* 161: 186–187.

Hillis, AE, Barker, PB, Wityk, RJ, Aldrich, EM, Restrepo, L, Breese, EL, and Work, M (2004). 'Variability in subcortical aphasia is due to variable sites of cortical hypoperfusion.' *Brain and Language* 89: 524–530.

Ide, A, Dolezal, C, Fernandez, M, Labbe, E, Mandujano, R, Montes, S, Segura, P, Verschae, G, Yarmuch, P, and Aboitiz, F (1999). 'Hemispheric differences in variability of fissural patterns in parasylvian and cingulate regions of human brains.' *Journal of Comparative Neurology* 410: 235–242.

Paus, T, Tomaiuolo, F, Otaky, N, MacDonald, D, Petrides, M, Atlas, J, Morris, R, and Evans, AC (1996). 'Human cingulate and paracingulate sulci: pattern, variability, asymmetry, and probabilistic map.' *Cerebral Cortex* 6: 207–214.

Pennington, BF, Filipek, PA, Lefly, D, Churchwell, J, Kennedy, DN, Simon, JH, Filley, CM, Galaburda, A, Alarcon, M, and DeFries, JC (1999). 'Brain morphometry in reading-disabled twins.' *Neurology* 53: 723–729.

Piven, J, Arndt, S, Bailey, J, and Andreasen, N (1996). 'Regional brain enlargement in autism: a magnetic resonance imaging study.' *Journal of the American Academy of Child and Adolescent Psychiatry* 35: 530–536.

Pujol, J, Vendrell, P, Junque, C, Marti-Vilalta, JL, and Capdevila, A (1993). 'When does human brain development end? Evidence of corpus callosum growth up to adulthood.' *Annals of Neurology* 34: 71–75.

Pujol, J, Lopez-Sala, A, Deus, J, Cardoner, N, Sebastian-Galles, N, Conesa, G, and Capdevila, A (2002). 'The lateral asymmetry of the human brain studied by volumetric magnetic resonance imaging.' *Neuroimage* 17: 670–679.

Robichon, F and Habib, M (1998). 'Abnormal callosal morphology in male adult dyslexics: relationships to handedness and phonological abilities.' *Brain and Language* 62: 127–146.

Selnes, OA (1974). 'The corpus callosum: some anatomical and functional considerations with special reference to language.' *Brain and Language* 1: 111–139.

Selnes, OA, van Zijl, PC, Barker, PB, Hillis, AE, and Mori, S (2002). 'MR diffusion tensor imaging documented arcuate fasciculus lesion in a patient with normal repetition performance.' *Aphasiology* 16: 897–901.

Watkins, KE, Paus, T, Lerch, JP, Zijdenbos, A, Collins, DL, Neelin, P, Taylor, J, Worsley, KJ, and Evans, AC (2001). 'Structural asymmetries in the human brain: a voxel-based statistical analysis of 142 MRI scans.' *Cerebral Cortex* 11: 868–877.

Whitaker, HA and Selnes, OA (1976). 'Anatomic variations in the cortex: individual differences and the problem of the localization of language functions.' *Annals of the New York Academy of Sciences* 280: 844–854.

Witelson, SF, Kigar, DL, and Harvey, T (1999). 'The exceptional brain of Albert Einstein.' *Lancet* 353: 2149–2153.

Angular Gyrus Syndrome

A. Boxer

The angular gyrus syndrome is a constellation of neuropsychological deficits found in patients with damage to the dominant angular gyrus and surrounding brain regions. It has been defined as consisting of the following neuropsychological deficits: extrasylvian sensory aphasia (transcortical sensory aphasia), alexia with agraphia, plus components of Gerstmann's syndrome. Gerstmann's syndrome includes acalculia, agraphia, difficulty in distinguishing left from right, and finger agnosia. The angular gyrus syndrome is often associated with constructional disturbances such as constructional apraxia.

Damage to the inferior parietal lobe of the dominant hemisphere, which includes the angular gyrus, the supramarginal gyrus, and/or the white matter underlying these structures, produces the angular gyrus syndrome. In most patients the left hemisphere is dominant for language; thus, damage to the left angular gyrus region produces the syndrome (**Fig. 1**). Because the angular gyrus is functionally connected to both cerebral hemispheres, the deficits that comprise the angular gyrus syndrome are observed on both sides of the body. For example, finger agnosia is observed in both hands. Although each of the neuropsychological impairments that comprise this syndrome may exist independently, when they are found together they reliably indicate damage to the previously mentioned structures.

The most common cause of the angular gyrus syndrome is cerebrovascular disease, especially occlusion of the angular branch of the middle cerebral artery. Although the areas of pathology that produce the angular gyrus syndrome fall into a vascular watershed (between two cerebral artery distributions) area, such infarcts typically do not produce the syndrome because aphasia masks many of the deficits. Other lesions that have been reported to cause angular gyrus syndrome include neurodegenerative diseases such as Alzheimer's and frontotemporal dementia, developmental

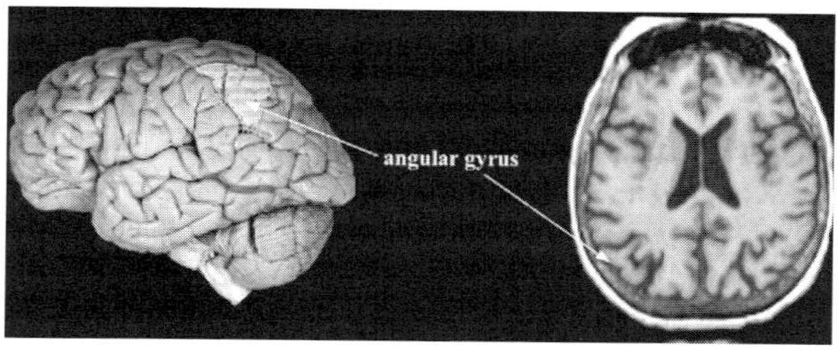

Figure 1 The approximate location of the left angular gyrus traced on the surface of the brain from a neurologically normal human cadaver (left) and an axial T1-weighted magnetic resonance imaging scan from a neurologically normal adult human male (right).

anomalies in children, arteriovenous malformations, brain tumors, trauma, abscesses, and gunshot wounds.

Components of the Angular Gyrus Syndrome

Extrasylvian (Transcortical) Sensory Aphasia

This language impairment is thought to be caused by a disconnection between sensory language processes and semantic knowledge of objects. Conversational speech is fluent; however, patients have severe problems with naming objects. The naming deficit may be category specific. There is often alienation of word meaning; that is, even after accurately repeating a word and demonstrating its use in a sentence, patients report that they do not understand it. Abundant use of one word, nonspecific filler words such as "one," "it," and "things," and paraphrasic errors result in an emptiness of spoken content. Speech may be verbose and uninhibited. By definition, repetition is always normal. Extrasylvian sensory aphasia is classically associated with echolalia; that is, patients will often incorporate words and phrases uttered by the examiner into their speech while apparently failing to understand the meaning of the words. Comprehension of spoken language is impaired, sometimes leading to misidentification of the language disorder as a psychogenic problem.

Alexia with Agraphia (Parietal–Temporal Alexia)

Alexia is the inability to read. In alexia with agraphia, the impairment in writing is equally severe to that in reading. Both the ability to read letters, words, numbers, and musical notation out loud, and the ability to comprehend them are impaired. Patients are often able to copy words; however, they are unable to spontaneously write them.

Acalculia

The inability to solve simple mathematical problems observed in patients with angular gyrus syndrome results from a combination of deficits. There is an anarithmetia, or basic disorder of computation, that results from damage to neural structures that store arithmetic facts and calculation procedures. These structures are thought to reside within the angular gyrus. Difficulties with reading and comprehension of numbers, which are components of extrasylvian sensory aphasia, also contribute to the acalculia.

Left–Right Confusion

Patients with angular gyrus syndrome have significant difficulty in distinguishing their own right from left as well as comprehending directional information in concrete and hypothetical tasks. Experimental evidence suggests that these deficits result from difficulties with the mental manipulation of spatial information.

Finger Agnosia

This is the inability to identify and localize fingers, both of one's own hands and those of the examiner. Finger agnosia appears to be related to autotopagnosia, the inability to localize body parts on one's own or another's body; however, the exact relationship is unclear.

Gerstmann's Syndrome

In 1930, Josef Gerstmann (1887–1969), a professor of neurology and psychiatry at the Maria–Thereisen–Schlossel in Vienna, described the constellation of symptoms that has since been referred to as Gerstmann's syndrome. He wrote that the syndrome of finger agnosia, agraphia, acalculia, and right–left disorientation "can be related to a focal disturbance in the area of transition between the angular and second occipital convolution" and is caused by "a unilateral lesion in the left hemisphere in right-handed individuals." Gerstmann believed that the phenomenological association of the four components of the syndrome reflected a common neuropsychological factor related to body image (*Grundstörung*), which was important for each of these functions. He postulated that the image of the hands and fingers was crucial for mathematical operations since children initially learn to do arithmetic by counting fingers.

For many years after its description, there was much controversy regarding the true nature of Gerstmann's syndrome. The debate focused on four major questions, which were recently summarized by Benton:

> (i) Whether the syndrome exists as a more or less autonomous combination of symptoms, unaccompanied by other behavioral indications of brain disease; (ii) whether the combination has specific neuroanatomic significance ... i.e., that it implies the presence of a focal lesion in the

territory of the angular gyrus; (iii) whether the syndrome has a special status compared with other combinations of deficits that are exhibited by patients with posterior perisylvian lesions of the left hemisphere; and (iv) whether the combination is the behavioral expression of a single underlying basic deficit (Grundstörung).

These objections were based on studies by Benton, Heimberger, and others that showed that the components of Gerstmann's syndrome were often associated with other neuropsychological deficits such as aphasia or apraxia, did not strongly correlate with each other, and were often not associated with angular gyrus lesions in a number of large series of brain-damaged patients.

A few cases of pure Gerstmann's syndrome have been described. All were associated with left parietal lobe damage involving the angular gyrus. Of note, one study used electrical stimulation of the cortex (during functional mapping prior to epilepsy surgery) to demonstrate an area in the transition zone between the left supramarginal and angular gyri that, when selectively inactivated, produced an isolated Gerstmann's syndrome. Nevertheless, the rarity of isolated Gerstmann's syndrome led Benson and colleagues to use the term angular gyrus syndrome to refer to the most common neuropsychological deficits associated with damage to the dominant angular gyrus and to reaffirm that their coincidence has strong localizing value.

See also: Agnosia; Agraphia.

Further Reading

Benson, DF and Ardila, A (1996). *Aphasia: A Clinical Perspective.* New York: Oxford Univ. Press.
Benson, DF, Cummings, JL, and Tsai, SY (1982). Angular gyrus syndrome simulating Alzheimer's disease. *Arch. Neurol.* 39: 616–620.
Benton, AL (1992). Gerstmann's syndrome. *Arch. Neurol.* 49: 445–447.
Farah, MJ and Feinberg, TE (2000). *Patient-Based Approaches to Cognitive Neuroscience.* Cambridge, MA: MIT Press.
Mayer, E, Martory, M-D, Pegna, AJ, et al. (1999). A pure case of Gerstmann syndrome with a subangular lesion. *Brain* 122: 1107–1120.
Morris, HH, Luders, H, Lesser, RP, et al. (1984). Transient neuropsychological abnormalities (including Gerstmann's syndrome) during cortical stimulation. *Neurology* 34: 877–883.
Pearce, JM (1996). Gerstmann's syndrome. *J. Neurol. Neurosurg. Psychiatry* 61: 56.

Anomia

A. Kertesz

Anomia is often defined two ways: (i) word finding difficulty in spontaneous or conversational speech and (ii) a failure to name objects presented on a naming task. Although these two phenomena are not exactly the same, they are considered to be manifestations of impaired word (lexical) access or lexical representation. Anomia is a universal disturbance of aphasia and dementia, and lexical processing is a major component of language in normals. Questions such as the following have interested philosophers, linguistics, and neurologists for centuries: How do we access words? Where are they stored in the brain? How do they come to the mind, selected from many others, and fit into a sentence? Theories of lexical access postulate that first the idea of the concept or an object is generated in various frontal, parietal, or temporal association areas depending on the stimulus. During conversation or responding to stimuli word concepts—"Wortbegriff" in Wernicke's terminology and "logogens" or "lexemes" in recent linguistic schemas—are generated at an incredibly rapid rate, and a word is selected for further processing. The selection process and its relationship to thought and to phonological output systems are extremely complex and much studied by the discipline of linguistics, particularly lexicosemantics.

Anomia in Aphasia

Anomia is a universal feature of aphasia, or central language deficit, and disturbances of word retrieval cut across all diagnostic classifications. Originally, aphasia was considered amnesia for words. Later, anomia became regarded as a symptom of various aphasic syndromes, and anomic aphasia was considered a diagnostic variety. Anomia is primarily considered the disturbance in retrieving words from a lexical store, but another consideration is a reduction of the lexical store. The first is often the feature of anomia, due to a focal lesion, and the second is more applicable in dementia or diffuse lesions. However, there is considerable overlap and uncertainty. Although anomia is a sine qua non of aphasia, anomic aphasia is not synonymous with aphasic anomia. Furthermore, anomia or word finding difficulty does not have to be associated with aphasia.

There is a general restriction of vocabulary, which is common to most aphasics, and in some there is a selective loss of the ability to name specific words. Many patients are anomic for specific items but can be fluent with relatively preserved conversational speech. More severely affected anomic patients have circumlocutory, uninformative empty speech, lacking the critical substantive words necessary to convey meaning. However, grammatical words, such as pronouns and auxiliary verbs, remain relatively intact, resulting in relatively preserved syntax and fluency. More severe cases of word finding difficulty are associated with logopenic or reduced speech output and decreased fluency.

What is retrieved and in what circumstances is dependent on the nature and the severity of the disease process and lesion size and location. For most patients, the frequent words of language are the best retained after brain damage or lost last in a progressive deficit, such as in dementia. There is a general frequency effect of common words retrieved better, but this is not as consistent as in reaction time experiments in normals. Often, features such as context, priming, stimulus characteristics, metatypicality, concreteness, manipulability, animateness, and grammatical class contribute to the accessibility of lexical items.

Clinicians have distinguished several varieties of anomia. Word production anomia ranges from the so-called "tip of the tongue" phenomenon, occurring in normal conversation, to the inability of a patient with frontal lesions or Broca's aphasia to produce a word spontaneously or confrontation with a stimulus. These patients are aware of the naming disturbance, they often insist they know the desired word, and prompting and cueing are often effective in retrieval. It has been postulated that word production is analogous to initiating nonverbal movements that may be impaired in frontal lobe lesions. This physiological activation phase of word retrieval has been separated experimentally from word selection, although the clinical boundaries are less clear. The tip of the tongue phenomenon often appears in combination with articulatory and phonemic paraphasias and word selection anomia in patients.

Word selection anomia is another variety characterized by the occasional semantic paraphasias and improved response to prompting. It is considered a disturbance at a more central stage of semantic specification, or a defect of retrieval from the internal lexicon. The spontaneous speech of these individuals is often loaded with circumlocutions and they use functional descriptions as replacement for a word. Many patients with pure anomia have comprehension problems in early stages and only with recovery pass on to the stage of residual anomia. Anomia and paraphasias may persist even when comprehension has recovered.

Category-specific anomia has been described for color-naming disturbance (color anomia and color agnosia) usually in occipital lesions, for finger naming (Gerstmann's syndrome), and for certain categories of nouns. Some of these were specifically related to certain anatomical structures. For instance, the difference in naming of animate and inanimate objects was based on superior or inferior location of the pathology in the dominant parietal lobe. The category specificity of naming was also demonstrated for nouns with preserved naming of letters and numbers. Recently, many dissociations have been found; for example, the loss of the meaning of vegetables and fruits with retention of naming of vehicles and tools is one of the most common dissociations originally described in association with temporal lesions. Some of these dissociations extend to the response modality with astonishing quadruple dissociations for categories in naming orally and in writing. Categories for persons were impaired in temporal polar lesions and for tools in inferior temporal regions. Intermediate temporal lesions resulted in combined loss of persons and fruits, and fruits and tools, but never the combination of persons and tools. Impaired retrieval of words denoting action was associated with damage to the left prefrontal and premotor regions. Recent functional activation studies also indicated that certain perceptual categories, such as unique persons, animals, and tools, have separable regions for storage in the left temporal lobe.

Other classifications of anomia include word-finding problems due to disconnection of cerebral structures, nonaphasic misnaming, and psychogenic misnaming. In the anomia of disconnection, observed after callosal lesions, blindfolded patients cannot name an object placed in the left hand, although they can select that object from an array of objects, indicating they perceived its characteristics without being able to label the object. When they are asked why they selected the object, they may give an explanation that is confabulatory. This indicates that the nondominant hemisphere continues to perform perceptual and matching tasks but cannot access verbal labels. Nonverbal recognition of an object can be dissociated from its access to the speaking hemisphere by the callosal sections. The perception, recognition, and selection of objects does not require verbal labels.

Nonaphasic misnaming has been described in acute confusional states. It has a confabulatory flavor, such as calling a physician a "repairman." The mechanism is considered to be related to decreased levels of consciousness or inattention interfering with memory and retrieval. Nonaphasic word-finding difficulty or lexical access inhibition by anxiety and stress, associated with distractibility or decreased level of alertness, is a common phenomenon that we all experience occasionally to a lesser or greater extent. Word finding with reaction times in normals is used in pharmacological experiments when medications such as hypnotics, neuroleptics, or narcotics are given to influence word retrieval. The results can be used to quantitate the effect of psychotropic drugs.

In modality-specific anomia, a dissociation between the effects of the modalities of presentation can be observed in the case of visual agnosia or optic aphasia when naming cannot be accomplished on visual stimulation but is prompt and clearly preserved in the tactile modality. The dissociation of visual and tactile naming is the sine qua non for the diagnosis of visual agnosia. Cognitive analysis of visual agnosia indicates that the deficit is at the level of recognition. Optic aphasia is sometimes also called visual anomia. In optic aphasia, the deficit is closer to language processing and the visual naming deficit is a modality-specific anomia. It is distinguished from visual agnosia by preserved description and demonstration of object use or correct answers to probe questions about it. Even though recognition has taken place, verbal labeling of the visually presented object is deficient.

Naming

Naming is a major item in aphasia testing, whether it is at the bedside using simple objects available to the clinician, such as a pen, comb, book, objects of clothing, and furniture, or items controlled for frequency, categories, stimulus complexity, phonological length, etc. presented under experimental conditions. The naming task, for instance, in the Western Aphasia Battery, uses 20 common objects controlled for frequency and selected for easy availability and manipulability. These objects are presented visually for 5–10 sec and a score of 3 is given for correct naming, 2 for recognizable phonemic paraphasia, and 1 if a phonemic or tactile cue is required. In the case of no response or an incorrect response, the patient is allowed to touch and manipulate the object. If this still does not result in lexical access, a phonemic prompt or a semantic cue is given. This allows not only a total object naming score but also analysis of naming deficit and the discovery of modality deficit anomia, tip of the tongue phenomena, and the effectiveness of cueing. Chronometric or timed, very brief tachistoscopic presentation of visual stimuli is often used for psycholinguistic studies of normal individuals. The reaction time measures to altered experimental conditions, such as priming or preceding the stimulus with a related word, are one of the most important tools of cognitive science. Priming can be phonological, semantic, auditory, or visual. Priming experiments in normals provide important information concerning the nature of word retrieval and semantic fields.

Word Fluency

Word fluency is a test of word finding in which patients are required to recall words in a certain category. This is also called word fluency in association. Some word fluency tests use initial letters or a phonological category, but this is more difficult for both aphasics and normals than a semantic category such as naming as many animals as the patient can name in 1 min. Tests of word fluency are very sensitive to a minimal amount of brain damage, be it due to head injury or early dementia. There is a significant difference in the word fluency performance of normals of various intellectual abilities or educational background. Anxiety and distractibility interfere with word fluency performance to a greater extent than with naming on stimulus.

Sentence completion is similar to word fluency in using semantic priming or word retrieval in syntactic association. Responsive speech also uses the context of the preceding sentence, and responding to it is easier than spontaneous word finding, or word fluency generation in categories ("Christmas is in the month of. . ."). Prompting, cueing, and priming are various methods of facilitating word retrieval. Various prompting or cueing of phonological or semantic associations are an important part of testing and treating aphasics.

Anomic Aphasia

The largest group of aphasics are variously categorized as anomic or amnesic aphasics, characterized by fluent speech with relatively little, if any, expressive or receptive difficulty. These patients have word-finding difficulty and a variable failure to name when confronted with a stimulus. Occasionally, there are verbal paraphasia or semantic substitutions, but usually there is no phonological or syntactic disturbance. Anomic aphasics have normal comprehension and repetition, and only their naming is impaired significantly. Anomic aphasia is often seen *de novo*, often as a result of recovery from Wernicke's, conduction, or transcortical aphasias. Occasionally, patients with Broca's aphasia recover toward the anomic type of aphasia. When anomic aphasia appears *de novo*, the etiology may not be a focal lesion but a metabolic or diffuse abnormality. Progressive anomic aphasia may be the presenting feature of degenerative illnesses, most notably primary progressive aphasia, a component of Pick's disease or frontotemporal dementia (FTD), or a slowly progressive brain tumor. It is also a common early feature of Alzheimer's disease (AD), but language impairment in AD usually follows significant episodic memory loss. Anomic aphasia due to strokes has a good prognosis, and word finding difficulty may recover with time, except for low-frequency items.

Goldstein described a variety of amnesic aphasia as an "impairment of abstract attitude," when a patient provided inappropriately specific names instead of the name of the general, base, or supraordinate category (polar bear instead of bear). Semantic specification depends a great deal on the nature of the stimulus and the circumstances of naming, such as the instructions given to the subjects. Typical exemplar from a supraordinate category is likely to be named as the category, whereas atypical exemplars or stimuli having specific visual identification may be named with a specific, subordinate, or proper name (A wren will be named a bird, but an ostrich will be named an ostrich). Henry Head described naming difficulty as nominal aphasia and considered it the most important component of semantic aphasia, which also included impaired understanding of names as part of the disturbance. Subsequently, this concept of central semantic disturbance was extended to semantic dementia, a progressive two-way loss of semantic fields in which both naming and comprehension are lost for even simple nouns.

Most clinicians and researchers of aphasia agree that naming disturbances are the least localizable function and, in fact, lesions from many areas of the brain, even for diffuse pathology such as in AD, can produce serious naming disturbances. However, very few would question that temporal, parietal, or perisylvian lesions interfere with lexical retrieval in a consistent fashion. Localization studies also suggest occasional separate but often overlapping regions for certain categories of items, especially in the temporal lobes.

Anomia in Dementia

Naming disorders in dementia have been examined in considerable detail. Alzheimer's disease patients initially have very little language disturbance, but they are forgetful of proper names, which is a borderline area between semantic and episodic memory. Although they are poor in generating names in controlled association, especially with phonological tasks such as a word starting with a certain letter, and they have word-finding difficulty in spontaneous speech, they still have relatively preserved naming of presented stimuli. However, later frequency-associated loss of naming occurs, and eventually both comprehension and naming of the same items indicate loss of semantic field. Much of the controversy regarding the study of naming or loss of semantic field in AD relates to the inclusion of patients in group studies at various stages of illness.

Word-finding difficulty is usually the beginning of the primary progressive aphasia (PPA), but episodic memory is preserved in contrast to AD. This condition is now recognized as the dominant temporal variety of Pick's disease or FTD. Most of these patients develop increasing difficulty with word access in spontaneous speech and also for naming stimuli. The result is a logopenic speech output that is relatively well articulated in most instances but soon becomes nonfluent. Some patients have a stuttering onset, but others develop agrammatism. In some cases, this proceeds to mutism without any development of articulatory disturbance or agrammatism. Meanwhile, comprehension is retained until the late stages. Similarly, progressive anomia is seen after the behavioral presentation, which is usually with apathy combined with disinhibition.

In contrast, the progressive fluent type of aphasia, or semantic dementia, retains syntactic organization and fluency. Although word retrieval may suffer initially, it is impaired proportionately with loss of comprehension for words. In fact, whole items disappear from the semantic field. Such patients would ask, "What is a steak?" when the word was mentioned, and they would be unable to name it on seeing the object. The auditory images or visual input fail to evoke lexical access, indicating a central loss of lexicon. Initially, this is restricted to nouns or things with preserved verbs, objectives, and connecting words; eventually, however, other elements of the language are affected and these patients also become logopenic and mute. Primary progressive or nonfluent aphasia tends to have more anterior atrophy in the frontotemporal region of the dominant hemisphere, whereas semantic dementia has dominant temporal atrophy. These anatomical distinctions tend to blur as the disease progresses.

Anatomy of the Mental Lexicon

Storage and memory for words and the representations of objects and concepts in the brain have been challenging for the neurological, psychological, and linguistic disciplines. Linguistic formulations (free from anatomical constraints) conceptualize a prelexical stage representing a thought. The lexeme is the selected meaning. The "lemma" in the next stage has certain grammatical attributes. Words are developed from the lemma by recursive inhibition from semantic, syntactic, and phonological mechanisms. These cascades of sequential and parallel processes, inspired by computer analogies, are a modern-day reincarnation of the steps in naming proposed by Pick a century ago. The role of internal auditory feedback in the selection of appropriate phonological and semantic attributes of words was first proposed by Wernicke. Physiological models postulate the simultaneous synthesis from multiple cortical activations with a major cross-modal link taking place, for instance, in the parietal lobe. The dominant hemispherical angular gyrus was singled out early as having a key function in complex, convergent, auditory–visual–spatial associations before reaching the motor system or generating words. Other favorite cortical areas for lexical storage are the inferior and middle temporal gyri, based on lesion evidence. It is believed that the representation of certain categories such as tools is located in the cortex, which is capable of receiving multiple sensory signals from the hand area, as well as the cortices of visual motor processing.

Naming of a word on sensory stimulation such as seeing an object can elicit a large number of visual, tactile, auditory, orthographic, olfactory, and emotional associations. Some of these act as inhibitory feedback to prevent a similar (semantically or phonologically) name from being produced. Naming evokes widespread functional activation in both hemispheres, as demonstrated by positron emission tomography scanning of glucose metabolism or cerebral blood flow and functional activation with magnetic resonance imaging. The results of these studies indicate the complexity of word selection and access.

A Single Lexicon or Multiple Mental Representation of Names?

Naming disturbances may represent impaired access (retrieval) or loss (impaired storage) of semantic information. When word-finding difficulty is variable and an item cannot be found or it is misnamed on one occasion and retrieved in another context, an access problem is postulated. On the other hand, if both naming and comprehension are impaired for the same item, loss of the semantic field is assumed. If anomia occurs consistently for an item in all stimulus modalities, then the argument is in favor of impairment of a unified, central or supramodality semantic field. In addition to a supramodality semantic field, lexicons are assumed in the visual orthographic and auditory modalities as well as for input and output modalities as evidenced from clinical and experimental observations.

The occurrence of category-specific and modality-specific anomia indicates that semantic memories are represented by categories and by various modalities of input separately. Interpretations include models of semantic representations, which are distributed according to functional, perceptual, and structural attributes when they are acquired and the modalities of acquisition, depending on the stimuli and the state of central processing. The phenomenon of mental imagery led to the dual-code hypothesis of semantic memory, which assumes that knowledge is represented internally by a verbal and pictorial code. The existence of a supramodality semantic field, however, is equally persuasive from evidence of supramodality impairment in aphasic anomia and semantic dementia. Thus, the psycholinguistic argument between dual, even multiple, semantic fields vs a central unified semantic lexicon continues.

See also: Agrammatism; Agraphia; Language and Discourse; Speech Disorders, Overview.

Further Reading

Caramazza, A and Hillis, AE (1991). Lexical organization of nouns and verbs in the brain. *Nature* 349: 788–790.
Dell, G (1986). A spreading activation theory of retrieval in sentence production. *Psychol. Rev.* 93: 283–321.
Glaser, WR (1992). Picture naming. *Cognition* 42: 61–105.
Goodglass, H, Kaplan, E, Weintraub, S, et al. (1976). The ''tip-of-the-tongue'' phenomenon in aphasia. *Cortex* 12: 145–153.
Goodglass, H and Wingfield, A (1997). Anomia—Neuroanatomical and Cognitive Correlates. San Diego: Academic Press.
Kertesz, A (1982). The Western Aphasia Battery. New York: Grune & Stratton (Psychological Incorporated).
Levelt, WJM (1989). Speaking. Cambridge, MA: MIT Press.
Pick, A (1913). Die Agrammatischen Sprachstörungen. Studien zur Psychologishen Grundlegung der Aphasielehre. Berlin: Springer.
Warrington, EK and Shallice, T (1984). Category specific semantic impairments. *Brain* 107: 829–854.
Wernicke, C (1874). Der Aphasische Symptomenkomplex. Breslau: Cohn & Weigart.

Anosognosia

R. P. Friedland

Anosognosia is a common behavioral phenomenon seen in people both with and without disease of the brain. It is a basic feature of human behavior for people to not readily accept bad things that happen to them. It has been said that when President George Bush did not recognize the challenge of Bill Clinton in the early stages of the campaign in the election of 1992, he suffered from "denial of presidential disability." People with serious medical illnesses often experience a period of varying length in which they fail to recognize the potential implications of their problems. This is an important issue in cancer, for example, when people fail to seek medical attention in the early stages of tumor growth when treatment is most effective. People with brain disease have patterns of response to illness that are often profound exaggerations of the denial seen in healthy people.

In 1924, Babinski and Joltrain coined the term anosognosia (literally, lack of knowledge of disease) to describe two patients with unawareness of left hemiplegia (paralysis of the left limbs), which had been previously reported by Pick in 1898. One would ignore commands to move her left hand and the other stated that she was not paralyzed. When asked what her trouble was she stated "pain in the back" and "phlebitis" as the difficulty, and when asked to move her paralyzed left arm she either did not respond or said "voilà, c'est fait." In 1918, Marie contributed to an extension of the concept of anosognosia, noting the lack of awareness of the hemianopia (deficit in one visual field) resulting from brain disease. Since that time, the manifestations of denial have been widely documented.

Patients may explicitly deny that there is anything wrong and may also minimize their difficulties. When asked "What is your main trouble? Why are you in the hospital?" a patient with left hemiplegia responds "My sister thought I should come in for some tests. I am hungry, when can I eat?" These patients characteristically do not learn from experience and often reject evidence of their disability as inconsequential. Other disabilities that patients with brain disease may deny include incontinence, involuntary movements, aphasia, and the fact of an operation. Denial syndromes also include lack of recognition of blindness [Anton's syndrome (1889), which was actually first noted by Von Monakow in 1885]. They may deny they are ill in any way and deny that they are in the hospital. These patients, despite their denial, remain in the hospital and usually cooperate in examinations, laboratory investigations, and even surgery. Patients with brain disease may deny or fail to recognize any form of disability.

Denial of illness is often accompanied by associated disorders, including unilateral neglect, confabulation, disorientation, hallucinations, acute confusional states, reduplication, and dementia. Confabulations in which the affected side is represented in metaphorical or allegorical language may be quite elaborate. Critchley describes patients who refer to their affected extremities with terms such as "silly Jimmy," "sloppy Joe," "fanny Anne," "the stinker," or "a piece of dead meat." One of Critchley's patients called his paralyzed arm "the Communist" because it refused to work. In 1974, Critchley coined the term misoplegia for morbid hatred of hemiplegia. These patients may also have disinhibited (ludic) behavior with inappropriate joking, referring to the examiner's health when asked how they feel or the examiner's vision when asked how well they see. Patients may also have reduplication for place, time, and person, nonaphasic misnaming, and marked mood changes including withdrawal. The disorientation for place seen in patients with denial usually indicates that the patient is somewhere else, implying that he or she is less ill. That is, the patient in the hospital often believes he or she is at home. As Hughlings Jackson stated in 1876, disorientation for place cannot be attributed to "confusion" unless one were to say that the patient is specifically confused only regarding the hospital name. In reduplication for place (closely related to disorientation), the patient usually states that there are two or more hospitals of the same or similar names. This phenomenon was described by Pick as "reduplicative paramnesia" in 1903. In nonphasic misnaming, the patient selectively misnames objects associated with the illness and personal identity.

In unilateral neglect, also know as hemi-inattention (a disturbance of the "body schema"), patients are neglectful of events in the external world on one side of space, usually on the same side as a lateralized motor or sensory deficit. Although unilateral neglect often accompanies denial of illness, denial often occurs without neglect. Neglect is often accompanied by constructional apraxia and other behavioral changes seen with denial of illness. Most patients with hemineglect also have a unilateral motor and sensory deficit on the same side and evidence of a disturbance of consciousness and sometimes an acute confusional state. These patients may also have dressing apraxia and topographical disorientation. Unilateral neglect was first reported by Hughlings Jackson in 1878 as "imperception." When asked to read, a patient with left neglect began in the right lower corner and tried to read backwards. She did not know places, persons, or objects and was withdrawn. She had difficulty in dressing and finding her way around the city. At autopsy, Sir William Gowers found a right temporal lobe glioma.

Patients with denial of illness and hemi-inattention may fail to recognize the limbs on one side of the body as their own. They may attend to events and people only on one side or respond only when addressed from one side. When drawing a figure, they may omit details on the neglected side. They may deviate their head and eyes constantly to the good side and fail to look at the effected side. Hemi-inattentive subjects may eat from only one side of the tray or shave completely only one side of the face. Critchley reported the case of an orchestra conductor who ignored the musicians on one side. A hemi-inattentive radiologist attended to only the right side of x-rays he was interpreting. This deficit is not caused solely by a motor or sensory loss because movement of the head and eyes can correct well for unilateral homonymous hemianopia when the patient has sufficient time. Patients with dense homonymous hemianopia often exhibit no evidence of visual hemineglect and are generally able to draw and read without asymmetry. The fact that neglect is not caused by motor or sensory loss alone is also illustrated by Critchley's glove test: When a patient with left neglect is asked to put on a pair of gloves, he or she characteristically uses the neglected left hand to put the glove on the "good" right hand. The defect that the patient denies may or may not be due to the same lesion in the nervous system that is necessary for the enduring maintenance of the denial. Thus, in a stroke patient with diabetes, the impaired vision of which the patient says he or she has no knowledge of and disregards may be due to retinal disease.

Patients may explicitly deny the presence of illness, such as when a hemiplegic patient states that he or she does not have any weakness in the affected extremity. There may also be implicit evidence of denial of illness as shown by a patient with hemiparesis who states that he or she has some stiffness in his or her arm from sleeping on it during the evening. Implicit denial may also be demonstrated as indifference or lack of concern. When one patient was asked if her left arm belonged to her, she said "my eyes and my feelings are not in agreement: and I must believe in what I feel. I sense in looking that they are as if they are mine, but I feel that they are not and I cannot believe my eyes." Patients persist in their misrepresentations and delusions despite evidence to the contrary because they have personal meaning. Denial, confabulation, reduplication, and symbolic disorientation may persist in part because they provide a sense of identity, combat feelings of unreality, and impart structure to what might otherwise be a mass of confusing information.

Lesions of the right hemisphere are more likely to cause denial and unilateral neglect than those of the left. Both Schilder and Goldstein discussed a motivational theory for anosognosia, suggesting a primary instinctive urge toward body integrity governing behavior. Schilder considered denial to be a form of "organic repression." Goldstein believed that denial represented a psychological defense mechanism often present in normal individuals, and that a "drive to self-actualization" was involved in the production of denial. Denial may be of value to the patient in assisting in the avoidance of a catastrophic reaction. Weinstein and associates found that patients with denial often have premorbid personalities (before development of altered brain function) that are compulsive and perfectionistic with a tendency to deny problems (regarding illness as a sign of failure and weakness). Weinstein and associates emphasized the positive, adaptive, conceptual, and symbolic aspects of denial of illness and unilateral neglect and that these manifestations may be in part "gestures in which the patient symbolizes the affected side, similar to the way he conceptualizes it verbally with delusions, confabulations, humor, and other forms of metaphorical expression." These are patients in whom "the idea of illness was incompatible with personal integrity" and who are conscientious, compulsive, efficiency-oriented people. Other patients with the same forms of altered brain function and neurological deficit, without such premorbid personalities, may show no explicit or implicit denial.

Denial of illness may occur with a lesion at any level of the central nervous system as long as there is an accompanying deficit in mental function. Lesions related to denial of illness syndromes are most commonly seen in the right hemisphere, including especially the parietal lobe, interparietal sulcus, supermarginal gyrus, and angular gyrus. Focal lesions causing denial more commonly involve the parietal–occipital cortex rather than the pre-Rollandic cortex or subcortical regions. However, denial may also be seen with damage to cortical white matter, frontal and temporal cortex, and occipital cortex. Mesulam proposed a model of neglect in which lesions of the cingulate, frontal, and reticular systems interrupt the "integrated network of modulation of directed attention within extrapersonal space." Heilman and associates proposed that denial and neglect represent a disorder in the orienting response caused by a lesion in a corticolimbic reticular loop.

Denial of illness may also occur in patients with Alzheimer's disease. Weinstein and colleagues found that denial was not related to severity of deficit in Alzheimer's disease. They concluded that denial or unawareness of dementia is not caused by the cognitive impairment alone because marked denial was encountered in patients with Mini-Mental Status Examination scores in the mid-20s (mild dementia), whereas awareness of disability was expressed by patients with scores as low as 7 (severe dementia). Most patients maintained their denial ratings over the course of the illness, indicating that disease progression alone does not necessarily produce denial. Persons with Alzheimer's disease who have poor awareness of their deficit may not understand the need for altered participation in activities, such as cooking, driving, and performing potentially hazardous tasks at work.

Denial of illness may have important practical consequences for the daily life of the patient. For example, a person with hemiplegia may not cooperate with physical therapy. However, anosognosia after acute brain lesions is usually a transient phenomenon and recedes along with the initial clouding of consciousness (as noted by Babinski). However, the selectivity of response to questions about disease in the patient with denial indicates that some discrimination is occurring. Patients often deny their disabilities in one context of language and acknowledge them in another. The recognition of disability may occur when the patient is speaking in anecdotes, clichés, humor, and other forms of idiomatic speech or "social language." Patients may deny illness in the presence of family members but acknowledge awareness of disability when interviewed alone.

Denial of illness is often shared by the patient and the family. This is illustrated by the case of a man with Alzheimer's disease who had difficulty driving because of dementia and needed his wife to shift for him: He made a left turn at the wrong time and caused an accident in which his wife died. It is important to include assessment of denial of illness in the patient evaluation and to conduct interviews with both the patient and the family members separately and together to acquire the needed information.

Acknowledgments

This work was supported in part by Grants PO 263-MO-818915 and UO1 AG1713-01A1 from the NIA, Grant P50

AG 08012 from the Alzheimer's Disease Research Center, the Mandel Foundation, the Nickman family, the Institute for the Study of Aging, and Philip Morris, USA.

Further Reading

Friedland, RP and Weinstein, EA (1977). Hemi-inattention and hemisphere specialization: Introduction and historical review. *Adv. Neurol.* 18: 1–31.

Heilman, KM (1991). Anosognosia: Possible neuropsychological mechanisms. In: Prigitano, GP and Schacter, DL (eds.) *Awareness of Deficit after Brain Injury*, pp. 53–62. New York: Oxford Univ. Press.

Shalev, RS (1985). Anosognosia: The neurological correlate of denial of illness. In: Edelstein, EL, Nathanson, DL, and Stone, AM (eds.) *Denial: A Clarification of Concepts and Research*, pp. 119–127. New York: Plenum.

Weinstein, EA (1969). Body schema in organic mental syndromes. *Handb. Clin. Neurol.* 4: 241–247.

Weinstein, EA and Kahn, RL (1955). *Denial of Illness: Symbolic and Physiological Aspects.* Springfield, IL: Thomas.

Weinstein, EA, Friedland, RP, and Wagner, EE (1994). Denial/unawareness of impairment in symbolic behavior in Alzheimer's disease. *Neuropsychiatry Neuropsychol. Behav. Neurol.* 7: 176–184.

Aphasia, Sudden and Progressive

M.-M. Mesulam, Northwestern University Medical School, Chicago, IL, USA

Introduction

Aphasia is an acquired disorder of language caused by brain damage. It is diagnosed when deficits are detected in naming, word choice, word comprehension, spelling, or syntax. Dysarthria and mutism do not, by themselves, lead to a diagnosis of aphasia. In approximately 90% of right handers and 60% of left handers, aphasia occurs only after lesions of the left hemisphere. For the majority of the population, the left hemisphere is therefore said to be dominant for language function. In some individuals no hemispheric dominance for language can be discerned, and in others (including a small minority of right handers) there is a right hemisphere dominance for language. A language disturbance occurring after a right hemisphere lesion in a right hander is called crossed aphasia.

Language is controlled by a large-scale distributed network, usually located within the left hemisphere, revolving around two perisylvian nodes. One extends into the temporoparietal junction and is known as Wernicke's area; the other extends into the inferior frontal gyrus and is known as Broca's area. These two areas are connected with each other as well as with multiple regions of the temporal, parietal, and frontal lobes. Wernicke's area can be considered the semantic-lexical pole of the language network, whereas Broca's area can be considered its syntactic-phonological pole. These specializations are relative rather than absolute. The network as a whole links sensory patterns corresponding to the words we hear and read into the distributed associations that encode their meaning. Damage to the language network can therefore have two major consequences. In some patients, the meanings of words cannot be decoded. In others, thoughts and experiences cannot be translated into statements that have the appropriate syntactic structure or semantic content. The location of the damage within the language network determines the type of aphasia experienced by the patient.

There are two major groups of acquired aphasias: those caused by cerebrovascular accidents and those caused by degenerative diseases. Aphasias caused by cerebrovascular accidents start suddenly and display maximal deficits at the onset. The underlying lesion is relatively circumscribed and associated with a total loss of neural function at the lesion site. These are the 'classic' aphasias in which relatively reproducible relationships between lesion site and aphasia pattern can be discerned. Aphasias caused by neurodegenerative diseases have an insidious onset and relentless progression so that the symptomatology changes over time. Since the neuronal loss within the areas encompassed by the neurodegeneration is partial and since it tends to include multiple components of the language network, distinctive clinical patterns and clinico-anatomical correlations are less obvious.

Clinical Examination

The clinical examination of language should include the assessment of naming, spontaneous speech, comprehension, repetition, reading, and writing. A deficit of naming (anomia) is the single most common finding in aphasic patients. When asked to name common objects (e.g., a pencil or wristwatch), the patient may fail to come up with the appropriate word, may provide a circumlocutious description of the object ('the thing for writing'), or may come up with the wrong word (paraphasia). If the patient offers an incorrect but legitimate word ('pen' for 'pencil'), the naming error is known as a semantic paraphasia; if the word approximates the correct answer but is phonetically inaccurate ('plentil' for 'pencil'), the error is known as a phonemic paraphasia. Asking the patient to name body parts, geometric shapes, and component parts of objects (e.g., lapel of coat, cap of pen) can elicit mild forms of anomia in patients who can otherwise name common objects. In most anomias, the patient cannot retrieve the appropriate name when shown an object but can point to the appropriate object when the name is provided by the examiner. This is known as a one-way (or retrieval-based) naming deficit. A two-way naming deficit exists if the patient can neither provide nor recognize the correct name, indicating the presence of a word comprehension impairment.

Spontaneous speech is described as fluent if it maintains appropriate output volume, phrase length, and melody or as nonfluent if it is sparse and halting and if average utterance length is less than four words. The examiner should also note whether the speech is paraphasic or circumlocutious; whether it shows a relative paucity of substantive nouns and action verbs compared to function words (prepositions, conjunctions); and whether word order, tenses, suffixes, prefixes, plurals, and possessives are used appropriately. Comprehension can be tested by assessing the patient's ability to follow the conversation, by asking yes/no questions ('Can a dog fly?,' 'Does it snow in summer?'), or by asking the patient to point to appropriate objects ('Where is the source of illumination in this room?'). Statements with embedded clauses or passive voice construction ('If a tiger is eaten by a lion, which animal stays alive?') help to assess the patient's ability to comprehend complex syntactic structure. Commands to close or open the eyes, stand up, sit down, or roll over should not be used to assess overall comprehension since appropriate responses aimed at such axial movements can be preserved in patients who otherwise have profound comprehension deficits.

Repetition is assessed by asking the patient to repeat single words, short sentences, or strings of words such as 'No ifs, ands, or buts.' The testing of repetition with tongue-twisters such as 'hippopotamus' or 'Irish constabulary' provides a better assessment of dysarthria than aphasia. Aphasic patients may have little difficulty with tongue-twisters but have a particularly hard time repeating a string of function words. It is important to make sure that the number of words does not exceed the patient's attention span. Otherwise, the failure of repetition becomes a reflection of the narrowed attention span (verbal working memory) rather than an indication of an aphasic deficit. Reading should be assessed for deficits in reading aloud as well as comprehension. Writing is assessed for spelling errors, word order, and grammar. Alexia describes an inability to read or comprehend written words; agraphia (or dysgraphia) is used to describe an acquired deficit in the spelling or grammar of written language.

Aphasias of Cerebrovascular Origin

Aphasias of cerebrovascular origin can be divided into central syndromes, which result from damage to the epicenters of the language network (Broca's and Wernicke's areas), and disconnection syndromes, which arise from lesions that interrupt the functional connectivity of these centers with each other and with the other components of the language network. The syndromes outlined in the following sections are idealizations; pure syndromes occur rarely.

Wernicke's Aphasia

In Wernicke's aphasia, comprehension is impaired for spoken and written language. Language output is fluent but is highly paraphasic and circumlocutious. The tendency for paraphasic errors may be so pronounced that it leads to strings of neologisms, which form the basis of what is known as jargon aphasia. Speech contains large numbers of function words (e.g., prepositions, conjunctions) but few substantive nouns or verbs that refer to specific actions. The output is therefore voluminous but uninformative. The patient does not seem to realize that his or her language is incomprehensible and may appear angry and impatient when the examiner fails to decipher the meaning of a severely paraphasic statement. Patients with Wernicke's aphasia cannot express their thoughts in meaning-appropriate words and cannot decode the meaning of words in any modality of input. This aphasia therefore has expressive as well as receptive components. Repetition, naming, reading, and writing are also impaired. The lesion site most commonly associated with Wernicke's aphasia is in the posterior portion of the language network and tends to involve at least parts of Wernicke's area.

Broca's Aphasia

In Broca's aphasia, speech is nonfluent, labored, interrupted by many word-finding pauses, and usually dysarthric. It is impoverished in function words. Abnormal word order and the inappropriate deployment of bound morphemes (word endings used to denote tenses, possessives, or plurals) lead to a characteristic agrammatism. Speech is telegraphic and pithy but quite informative. Output may be reduced to a grunt or single word ('yes' or 'no'), which is emitted with different intonations in an attempt to express approval or disapproval. In addition to fluency, naming and repetition are also impaired.

Comprehension of spoken language is intact, except for syntactically difficult sentences with passive voice structure or embedded clauses.

Global Aphasia

In global aphasia, speech output is nonfluent, and comprehension of spoken language is severely impaired. Naming, repetition, reading, and writing are also impaired. This syndrome represents the combined dysfunction of Broca's and Wernicke's areas and usually results from strokes that involve the entire middle cerebral artery distribution in the left hemisphere. Most patients are initially mute or say a few words, such as 'hi' or 'yes.'

Conduction Aphasia

In conduction aphasia, speech output is fluent but paraphasic, comprehension of spoken language is intact, and repetition is severely impaired. Naming and writing are also impaired. Reading aloud is impaired, but reading comprehension is preserved. The lesion sites spare Broca's and Wernicke's areas but may induce a functional disconnection between the two such that neural word representations formed in Wernicke's area and adjacent regions cannot be transmitted to Broca's area for assembly into corresponding articulatory patterns. Occasionally, a Wernicke's area lesion gives rise to a transient Wernicke's aphasia that rapidly resolves into a conduction aphasia. The paraphasic output in conduction aphasia interferes with the ability to express meaning, but this deficit is not nearly as severe as the one displayed by patients with Wernicke's aphasia.

Nonfluent Transcortical Aphasia (Transcortical Motor Aphasia)

The features of nonfluent transcortical aphasia are similar to those of Broca's aphasia, but repetition is intact and agrammatism may be less pronounced. The lesion site disconnects the intact language network from prefrontal areas of the brain and usually involves the anterior watershed zone between anterior and middle cerebral artery territories or the supplementary motor cortex in the territory of the anterior cerebral artery.

Fluent Transcortical Aphasia (Transcortical Sensory Aphasia)

The clinical features of fluent transcortical aphasia are similar to those of Wernicke's aphasia, but repetition is intact. The lesion site disconnects the intact core of the language network from other temporoparietal association areas. Infarctions in the posterior watershed zone are common causes.

Isolation Aphasia

Isolation aphasia, a rare syndrome, represents a combination of the two transcortical aphasias. Comprehension is severely impaired, and there is no purposeful speech output. The patient may parrot fragments of heard conversations (echolalia), indicating that the neural mechanisms for repetition are at least partially intact. This condition represents the pathologic function of the language network when it is isolated from other regions of the brain. Broca's and Wernicke's areas tend to be spared, but there is damage in surrounding frontal, parietal, and temporal cortex. Lesions are patchy and can be associated with anoxia, carbon monoxide poisoning, or complete watershed zone infarctions.

Anomic Aphasia

Anomic aphasia may be considered the 'minimal dysfunction' syndrome of the language network. Articulation, comprehension, and repetition are intact, but confrontation naming, word finding, and spelling are impaired. Speech is enriched in function words but impoverished in substantive nouns and verbs denoting specific actions. Language output is fluent but paraphasic, circumlocutious, and uninformative. The lesion sites can be anywhere within the left hemisphere language network, including the middle and inferior temporal gyri.

Pure Word Deafness

In pure word deafness, the most common lesions are either bilateral or left-sided in the superior temporal gyrus. The net effect of the underlying lesion is to interrupt the flow of information from the unimodal auditory association cortex to the language network. Patients have no difficulty understanding written language and can express themselves well in spoken or written language. They have no difficulty interpreting and reacting to environmental sounds since primary auditory cortex and subcortical auditory relays are intact. Since auditory information cannot be conveyed to the language network, however, the patient reacts to speech as if it were in an alien tongue that cannot be deciphered. Patients cannot repeat spoken language but have no difficulty naming objects.

Pure Alexia without Agraphia

Pure alexia without agraphia is the visual equivalent of pure word deafness. The lesions (usually a combination of damage to the left occipital cortex and to a posterior sector of the corpus callosum known as the splenium) interrupt the flow of visual input into the language network. There is usually a right hemianopia, but the core language network remains unaffected. The patient can understand and produce spoken language, name objects in the left visual hemifield, repeat, and write. However, the patient acts as if illiterate when asked to read even the simplest sentence because the visual information from the written words (presented to the intact left visual hemifield) cannot reach the language network. Objects in the left hemifield may be named accurately because they activate nonvisual associations in the right hemisphere, which, in turn, can access the language network through transcallosal pathways anterior to the splenium. Patients with this syndrome may also lose the ability to name colors, although they can match colors. This is known as a color anomia. The most common etiology of pure alexia is a vascular lesion in the territory of the posterior cerebral artery.

Neurodegenerative Aphasia

The language network can also become the target of dementia-causing neurodegenerative diseases. Dementia is a generic term used to designate a neurodegenerative disease that impairs intellect and behavior to the point at which customary activities of daily living become compromised. Alzheimer's disease is the single most common cause of dementia. The neuropathology of Alzheimer's disease causes the earliest and most profound neuronal loss in memory-related parts of the brain such as the entorhinal cortex and the hippocampus. This is why progressive forgetfulness for recent events and experiences is the cardinal feature of Alzheimer's disease. In time, the neuronal pathology in Alzheimer's disease spreads to the language network, and a progressive aphasia becomes added to the progressive amnesia. There are other patterns of dementia, however, in which neurodegeneration initially targets the language rather than the memory network of the brain, leading to the emergence of a progressive aphasia that becomes the most prominent aspect of the clinical picture during the initial phases of the disease. Primary progressive aphasia (PPA) is the most widely recognized syndrome with this pattern of selective language impairment.

Clinical Presentation and Diagnosis

The patient with PPA comes to medical attention because of word-finding difficulties, abnormal speech patterns, and spelling errors of recent onset. PPA is diagnosed when other mental faculties such as memory for daily events, visuospatial skills (assessed by tests of drawing and face recognition), and comportment (assessed by history obtained from a third party) remain relatively intact, when language is the only major area of dysfunction for the first few years of the disease, and when structural brain imaging does not reveal a specific lesion, other than atrophy, to account for the language deficit. Impairments in other cognitive functions may also emerge, but the language dysfunction remains the most salient feature and deteriorates most rapidly throughout the illness.

Language in PPA

The language impairment in PPA varies from patient to patient. Some patients cannot find the right words to express thoughts; others cannot understand the meaning of heard or seen words; still others cannot name objects in the environment. The language impairment can be fluent (i.e., with normal articulation, flow, and number of words per utterance) or nonfluent. The single most common sign of PPA is anomia, manifested by an inability to come up with the right word during conversation and/or an inability to name objects shown by the examiner. Asking the patient to name geometric shapes, body parts, or components of common objects reveals early stages of anomia. Many patients remain in an anomic phase throughout most of the disease and experience a gradual intensification of word-finding deficits to the point of near mutism. Others, however, proceed to develop distinct forms of agrammatism and/or word comprehension deficits. The agrammatism consists of inappropriate word order and misuse of small grammatical words. One patient, for example, sent the following e-mail to her daughter: 'I will come my house in your car and drive my car into chicago . . . You will back get your car and my car park in my driveway. Love, Mom.' Comprehension deficits, if present, start with an occasional inability to understand single low-frequency words and gradually progress to encompass the comprehension of conversational speech.

The impairments of syntax, comprehension, naming, or writing in PPA are no different than those seen in aphasias of cerebrovascular causes. However, they form slightly different patterns. According to a classification proposed by Gorno-Tempini and colleagues, three variants of PPA can be recognized: an agrammatic variant characterized by poor fluency and impaired syntax, a semantic variant characterized by preserved fluency and syntax but poor single-word comprehension, and a logopenic variant characterized by preserved syntax and comprehension but frequent word-finding pauses during spontaneous speech. The agrammatic variant is also known as progressive nonfluent aphasia, and the semantic variant as semantic dementia. The three

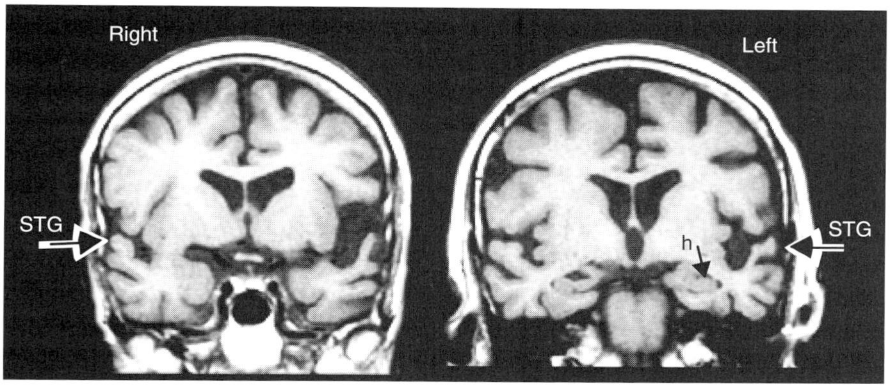

Figure 1 Coronal magnetic resonance image (MRI) of a primary progressive aphasia patient showing neuronal loss in the language network as indicated by atrophy of the left superior temporal gyrus (STG). The hippocampus (h) is intact.

variants display overlapping distributions of neuronal loss, but the agrammatic variant is most closely associated with atrophy in the anterior parts of the language network (where Broca's area is located), the semantic variant with atrophy in the temporal components of the language network, and the logopenic variant with atrophy in the temporoparietal component of the language network.

Pathophysiology

Patients with PPA display progressive atrophy (indicative of neuronal loss), electroencephalographic slowing, decreased blood flow (measured by single photon emission computed tomography) and decreased glucose utilization (measured by positron emission tomography) that are most pronounced within the language network of the brain (**Figure 1**). The abnormalities may remain confined to left hemisphere perisylvian and anterior temporal cortices for many years. The clinical focality of PPA is thus matched by the anatomical selectivity of the underlying pathological process.

Neuropathology

Approximately 30% of patients have shown the microscopic pathology of Alzheimer's disease, presumably with an atypical distribution of lesions. In the majority of cases, the neuropathology falls within the family of frontotemporal lobar degenerations and displays focal neuronal loss, gliosis, tau-positive inclusions, Pick bodies, and tau-negative ubiquitin inclusions. Apolipoprotein E and prion protein genotyping have shown significant differences between patients with typical clinical patterns of Alzheimer's disease and those with a diagnosis of PPA. The intriguing possibility has been raised that a personal or family history of dyslexia may be a risk factor for PPA, at least in some patients, suggesting that this disease may arise from a background of genetic or developmental vulnerability affecting language-related areas of the brain.

See also: Agraphia; Brain Damage, Functional Reorganization; Language, Auditory Processes; Lexical Impairments Following Brain Injury; Sentence Comprehension; Sentence Production; Word Learning; Word Production; Word Recognition.

Further Reading

Chawluk, JB, Mesulam, MM, Hurtig, H, et al. (1986). Slowly progressive aphasia without generalized dementia: Studies with positron emission tomography. *Annals of Neurology* 19: 68–74.

Gorno-Tempini, ML, Dronkers, NF, Rankin, KP, et al. (2004). Cognition and anatomy in three variants of primary progressive aphasia. *Annals of Neurology* 55: 335–346.

Kertesz, A, Hudson, L, Mackenzie, IRA, and Munoz, DG (1994). The pathology and nosology of primary progressive aphasia. *Neurology* 44: 2065–2072.

Knibb, JA, Xuereb, JH, Patterson, K, and Hodges, JR (2006). Clinical and pathological characterization of progressive aphasia. *Annals of Neurology* 59: 156–165.

Li, X, Rowland, LP, Mitsumoto, H, et al. (2005). Prion protein codon 129 genotype is altered in primary progressive aphasia. *Annals of Neurology* 58: 858–864.

Mesulam, M-M (2001). Primary progressive aphasia. *Annals of Neurology* 49: 425–432.

Mesulam, M-M, Johnson, N, Grujic, Z, and Weintraub, S (1997). Apolipoprotein E genotypes in primary progressive aphasia. *Neurology* 49: 51–55.

Mesulam, M-M, Johnson, N, Krefft, TA, et al. (2007). Progranulin mutations in primary progressive aphasia – The PPA1 and PPA3 families. *Archives of Neurology* 64: 43–47.

Rogalski, E and Mesulam, M-M (2007). An update on primary progressive aphasia. *Current Neurology and Neuroscience Reports* 7: 388–392.

Sonty, SP, Mesulam, M-M, Thompson, CK, et al. (2003). Primary progressive aphasia: PPA and the language network. *Annals of Neurology* 53: 35–49.

Weintraub, S, Rubin, NP, and Mesulam, MM (1990). Primary progressive aphasia. Longitudinal course, neuropsychological profile, and language features. *Archives of Neurology* 47: 1329–1335.

Apraxia, Handedness and Language Laterality

O. Selnes, Johns Hopkins University, Baltimore, MD, USA

Introduction

The term 'apraxia' refers to a distinct category of acquired central nervous system disorders that are characterized by an inability to carry out symbolic or purposeful motor actions, despite the absence of primary sensory or motor deficits.

The first use of the word 'apraxia' is attributed to the German philosopher and psychologist Heymann Steinthal (1823–1899), who used the term in an 1871 publication, but the behavioral phenomenon may have been described by the 'father' of British neurology, John Hughlings-Jackson (1835–1911), about five years earlier. He noted that some patients with aphasia were unable to perform certain types of voluntary movements to command, such as coughing or protruding their tongue, even though there was no evidence of weakness or paralysis. Moreover, patients could easily protrude their tongue spontaneously, as part of for example licking their lips after drinking.

The first systematic clinical studies of patients with apraxia were performed by Hugo Karl Liepman (1863–1925), a student of Carl Wernicke. He published his first case description of a 48-year-old man with unilateral apraxia in 1900. Liepman's theories were well received, but had relatively little impact on the scientific community until revived by the behavioral neurologist Norman Geschwind (1926–1984). In his article 'Disconnexion syndromes in animals and man' published in 1965, Geschwind described apraxia and other neurological syndromes that he hypothesized could be explained on the basis of an interruption of specific white matter pathways that interconnect different regions of the brain (Geschwind, 1965). The verbal instruction for a motor command is first processed in Wernicke's area in the posterior superior temporal lobe. The information is then relayed to the ipsilateral motor association cortex, most likely via the arcuate fasciculus. Performance of movements with the right hand is made possible when the information reaches the left primary motor cortex. In order to perform a movement command with the left hand, the additional step of transferring the information via the corpus callosum to the right motor association and primary motor cortex is required. Geschwind's theoretical account of apraxia thus had many similarities with that proposed by Carl Wernicke to explain various syndromes of aphasia.

Definition

Strictly speaking, apraxia means 'no action.' Geschwind defined apraxia as an acquired impairment in the execution of purposeful, learned movements in the absence of weakness, inattentiveness, or lack of cooperation. The term has also sometimes been used to describe unexplained clumsiness or lack of coordination, as in 'gait apraxia.' 'Apraxia of speech' is sometimes used to describe nonarticulatory abnormalities of phoneme sequencing (paraphasias) that are common in patients with conduction aphasia as well as other aphasia syndromes. Apraxic agraphia is a condition in which the patient has difficulty with the actual formation of letters, in the absence of difficulties with spelling or grammar. Patients with apraxic agraphia can therefore type or use a word processor without difficulty.

Testing for Apraxia

The bedside or clinic evaluation of apraxia relies on a set of semistandardized commands that are designed to explore the patient's ability to carry out specific movements involving the hands or face. A distinction between intransitive commands (not requiring an object), such as 'wave good-bye' or 'hitchhike,' and transitive commands ('use a hammer' or 'use a screwdriver') is typically made. Among the best-known standardized compilations of apraxia commands is the one included as part of the Boston Diagnostic Aphasia Exam (Goodglass and Kaplan, 1983). For research purposes, more detailed testing may include not only evaluating the patient's ability to carry out actions in response to verbal commands, but also the ability to imitate meaningful or meaningless movements or hand/finger postures performed by the examiner, and the ability to select the correct action from among multiple choices as demonstrated by the examiner (De Renzi, 1989). The most common errors in patients with apraxia include those of sequencing or timing, or using a body part as the tool (e.g., using the hand as a comb in response to 'show me how to comb your hair' instead of pretending to hold a comb.)

Subtypes of Apraxia

Several subtypes of apraxia are now recognized. First described by Arnold Pick (1851–1924), 'conceptual' or 'ideational apraxia' refers to the inability to perform commands that require multiple steps, such as folding a piece of paper, inserting it into an envelope and sealing the envelope. Although patients with ideational apraxia may be able to perform the individual components of the task, they have difficulties with the correct sequencing of the individual subcomponents. Ideational apraxia in its pure form is rare, and it may be more frequently observed in patients with diffuse cognitive impairment, such as dementia, than in patients with focal deficits secondary to stroke. 'Ideomotor apraxia' refers to an impairment of the timing, sequencing, and organization of gestures. Patients with this type of apraxia have difficulties demonstrating simple motor gestures, such as 'wave goodbye' and 'salute,' and the use of common tools, such as a hammer or screwdriver. This type of apraxia is usually associated with lesions involving the dominant parietal lobe.

A unique subtype of apraxia may occur with lesions that involve the anterior portions of the corpus callosum. It was first described by Liepman and Mass in 1907 and since that time, several case histories have been reported (Faglioni and Basso, 1985). Tumors, strokes, or traumatic lesions that interrupt the anterior portion of the corpus callosum can produce an apraxia that is limited to the left side of the body. No systematic case series have been published, and it is therefore not possible to determine how often such callosal lesions do not result in an apraxia (De Renzi, 1989). The presumed mechanism of callosal apraxia is that the lesion of the corpus callosum interrupts connections between language comprehension areas in the left hemisphere and motor areas controlling the left hand in the right hemisphere. In support of the verbal–motor disconnection hypothesis, a patient reported by Geschwind and Kaplan was unable to perform actions to verbal command, but was able to imitate gestures with his left hand (Geschwind and Kaplan, 1962). Other patients with callosal apraxia have not shown this dissociation between verbal and visual commands, however, but instead have shown left-hand apraxia regardless of stimulus modality. The hypothesis that a lesion of the corpus callosum by itself is sufficient to produce the syndrome of callosal apraxia has also been questioned in light of reports that patients with complete surgical lesions of this interhemispheric commissure (callosomectomy) typically do not show left-hand apraxia.

Patients with oral (sometimes also referred to as buccofacial) apraxia have difficulty performing movements involving the face, such as blowing out a match, sticking out their tongue, or whistling. Oral apraxia often coexists with Broca's aphasia, but it may also occur in the absence of aphasia. It is associated with lesions affecting the frontal operculum of the left hemisphere in right-handers.

Prevalence

Although apraxia is among the most common neuropsychiatric complications of stroke or other lesions involving the posterior left hemisphere in right-handers, the presence of the deficit is frequently overlooked for two reasons: first, the patient rarely complains of such symptoms, and second, because apraxia is most often associated with left hemisphere lesions, the symptoms may be masked or overshadowed by the co-occurring aphasia. The prevalence of apraxia among patients with a first left hemisphere stroke was reported to be 28% in one study (Donkervoort et al., 2000). Other studies that have included patients with both left and right hemisphere stroke have reported a prevalence rate of only 7% (Pedersen et al., 2001). This is consistent with the Liepman's original observation that apraxia occurs more frequently after left hemisphere stroke in right-handers.

Apraxia is also a common finding in some neurodegenerative disorders, including corticobasal degeneration and dementia with diffuse Lewy bodies. It occurs less frequently in conditions such as closed head injury or demyelinating disorders of the central nervous system.

Cerebral Dominance for Motor Learning

Apraxia was initially thought to be secondary to a disconnection of verbal and motor areas of the brain. According to this hypothesis, verbal input could be processed in the traditional speech comprehension areas of the superior temporal lobe, but apraxia would result if a lesion prevented this information from reaching appropriate motor areas for execution. Consistent with this interpretation was the observation that performance to visual demonstration was often intact, and performance with real objects was also typically better preserved. It soon became clear, however, that the majority of cases of apraxia could not be explained by disconnection alone. To account for such cases, Liepman developed the concept of cerebral dominance for motor learning and control. According to his theory, as one hemisphere becomes dominant for language functions, one of the two hemispheres similarly develops into the dominant one for motor functions. On the basis of studies of both right- and left-handed patients with apraxia, Liepman also noted a strong relationship between hemispheric dominance for motor programming and handedness. The vast majority of right-handers develop apraxia after lesions of the contralateral (left) hemisphere, while left-handers most often develop apraxia after right hemisphere lesions.

Dissociation of Language and Praxis

Because of the overlapping representations of language and praxis in the posterior regions of the left hemisphere, the vast majority of right-handers develop both apraxia and aphasia after left hemisphere lesions. In some patients, however, the representation of language functions and praxis are in separate hemispheres. Although rare, such cases have been very important for our understanding of the complex interrelationships of praxis, handedness, and hemispheric dominance for motor and language functions.

One such patient was described by Heilman and his colleagues. The patient was a left-handed man who had suffered a large cerebral infarction in the anterior right hemisphere. The infarction involved brain regions that would have resulted in severe Broca's aphasia if the lesion had been in the left hemisphere. The patient did develop a left hemiparesis, but no aphasia, suggesting that the intact left hemisphere was in fact the language-dominant hemisphere. He did, however, develop a significant apraxia involving his (nonparalyzed) right arm. This could be explained if one hypothesized that the repository of skilled movements was in the right hemisphere, contralateral to his dominant **left** hand (Heilman et al., 1973).

An opposite dissociation, apraxia but no aphasia after a large left hemisphere stroke in right-handers, is quite rare, but has been described in at least two cases. In one of these, the patient was a right-hander who suffered a massive left hemisphere stroke that involved most of the perisylvian language areas (Selnes et al., 1982). Surprisingly, this produced only a transient aphasia but a long-lasting apraxia. These findings were interpreted as a rare case of mixed or right hemisphere language dominance in a right-hander, but with motor skill dominance in the left hemisphere, contralateral to the dominant hand. A second patient with a similar dissociation between praxis and language was reported by Selnes and colleagues (Selnes et al., 1991). The patient was an 81-year-old right-handed male who suffered a massive left cerebral artery stroke. The radiological studies showed virtually complete destruction of the left hemisphere perisylvian language areas. Instead of the global aphasia that normally would have been associated with such a left hemisphere lesion in a right-hander, the patient developed a dense apraxia.

These cases of atypical language dominance in both right- and left-handers help demonstrate that aphasia and apraxia are dissociable, and provide support for the hypothesis that handedness is much more closely related to hemispheric laterality of motor control than to hemispheric laterality of language.

Anatomical Correlates

Although limb apraxia most often results from large lesions involving the dominant superior parietal lobe region, recent evidence suggests that apraxia may result from a spectrum of lesions affecting different nodes in a widely distributed network of higher-order motor functions. While frontoparietal regions may be the most crucial anchor points in this network, other nodes such as the supplementary motor area are now also recognized as being relevant for the neurological substrate of praxis.

See also: Anatomical Asymmetries Versus Variability of Language Areas of the Brain.

Bibliography

DeRenzi, E (1989). 'Apraxia.' In: Boller, F and Grafman, J (eds.) *Handbook of Neuropsychology*, pp. 245–263. Amsterdam: Elsevier.
Donkervoort, M, Dekker, J, Ende, E van den, Stehmann-Saris, JC, and Deelman, BG (2000). 'Prevalence of apraxia among patients with a first left hemisphere stroke in rehabilitation centres and nursing homes.' *Clinical Rehabilitation* 14: 130–136.
Faglioni, P and Basso, A (1985). 'Historical perspectives on neuroanatomical correlates of limb apraxia.' In: Roy, EA (ed.) *Neuropsychological studies of apraxia and related disorders*, pp. 3–44. Amsterdam: Elsevier.
Geschwind, N (1965). 'Disconnexion syndromes in animals and man.' *Brain* 88: 237–294.
Geschwind, N and Kaplan, E (1962). 'A human cerebral disconnection syndrome.' *Neurology* 12: 675–685.
Goodglass, H and Kaplan, E (1983). *The assessment of aphasia and related disorders,* 2nd edn. Philadelphia: Lea and Febiger.
Heilman, KM, Coyle, JM, Goneya, EF, and Geschwind, N (1973). 'Apraxia and agraphia in a left-hander.' *Brain* 96: 21–28.
Pedersen, PM, Jorgensen, HS, Kammersgaard, LP, Nakayama, H, Raaschou, HO, and Olsen, TS (2001). 'Manual and oral apraxia in acute stroke, frequency and influence on functional outcome: the Copenhagen Stroke Study.' *American Journal of Physical Medicine and Rehabilitation* 80: 685–692.
Selnes, OA, Pestronk, A, Hart, J, and Gordon, B (1991). 'Limb apraxia without aphasia from a left sided lesion in a right handed patient.' *Journal of Neurology, Neurosurgery & Psychiatry* 54: 734–737.
Selnes, OA, Rubens, AB, Risse, GL, and Levy, RS (1982). 'Transient aphasia with persistent apraxia.' *Archives of Neurology* 39: 122–126.

Apraxia, Sensory System

L. J. Buxbaum, Moss Rehabilitation Research Institute and Thomas Jefferson University, Philadelphia, PA, USA
H. B. Coslett, University of Pennsylvania School of Medicine and Center for Cognitive Neuroscience, Philadelphia, PA, USA

Historical Background

Limb praxis is subserved by a complex multicomponent system that provides a processing advantage to previously experienced, purposive movements. The term 'apraxia' was introduced by Steinthal in 1871. While this word, derived from Greek, means 'without action', the term is used to describe a decrease or disorder in the ability to perform skilled movements. Scientific and clinical interest in the disorder dates to the early twentieth century, when Liepmann reported patients with cerebral lesions who were unable to gesture to command or, in some instances, to imitation. Subsequently, Liepmann and Maas (1907) described a patient with a lesion of the corpus callosum who was unable to produce gestures with the left hand to verbal command. On the basis of these findings, Liepmann proposed that the left hemisphere was "dominant" for gesture in that it supported the learned "movement formulae" or "time-space-form picture of the movement" which specified the timing, trajectory, and content of learned movements.

Liepmann's ideas were extended by Geschwind (1965), who proposed a specific left hemisphere-based neural circuitry for movement representations. On his account, failure to produce a movement to command was attributable either to a disruption of Wernicke's area, with resultant failure to understand the command, or to a disconnection of the posterior language areas from motor cortex. A failure to imitate movements was attributed to a lesion involving the arcuate fasciculus, which was assumed to connect the visual association cortex to motor cortices.

Limb Apraxia Subtypes

Hugo Liepmann's description of three major forms of apraxia brought about a 'paradigmatic shift' in our understanding of motor control. These three types were 'limb kinetic apraxia' (LKA), 'ideational apraxia' (IA), and 'ideomotor apraxia' (IMA). To this triad, Gonzalez-Rothi, Heilman, and colleagues added another type, termed 'conceptual apraxia.' These types of apraxia are described briefly below.

LKA

Patients with LKA perform actions with slow, stiff, clumsy movements and exhibit impairment on tasks requiring rapid independent finger movements, such as rotating a coin between the thumb, index, and middle finger. Errors are more apparent in distal (finger) movements than in proximal movements. LKA is associated with lesions that include the primary motor cortex, premotor cortex, or descending corticospinal tract. It frequently occurs in patients with stroke and in degenerative disorders such as progressive supranuclear palsy and corticobasal degeneration.

IA

IA is defined as an impaired ability to carry out a sequence of acts that leads to a goal and that incorporates multiple objects, such as making a sandwich or lighting a candle. For example, a patient with IA might attempt to seal an envelope prior to inserting the letter. Another type of error exhibited in this disorder is illustrated in **Figure 1**.

IA is most frequently induced by bilateral damage and degenerative dementia. Injury to the frontal lobes is often also associated with temporal order processing deficits as well as impaired working memory, and thus one of the critical foci of dysfunction in IA may be in frontal-subcortical systems. The strongest predictor of errors in multistep, naturalistic action is overall severity of cognitive impairment and not lesion location.

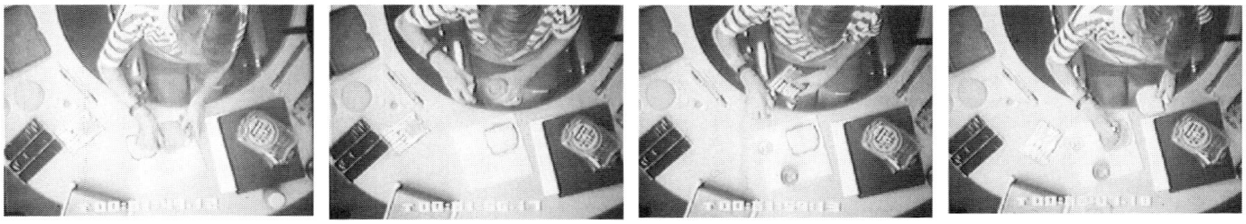

Figure 1 Photographs of a patient with conceptual apraxia making a sandwich with meat and mustard. She correctly places meat on a slice of bread, closes the sandwich, and opens a mustard jar. She replaces the mustard jar, reaches into a package of marking pens, retrieves a yellow marker, and proceeds to color the meat yellow. (See color plate 4.)

Conceptual Apraxia

Patients with conceptual apraxia make content errors in complex action – that is, they substitute incorrect objects or movements in their actions. For example, patients with conceptual apraxia may eat with a toothbrush. In some cases, underlying deficits in knowledge of specific tools or objects or the association of tools and objects has been demonstrated; these patients may misuse objects because they have lost knowledge regarding the function of the object. Conceptual apraxia also frequently co-occurs with IMA, and it has not been established whether these disorders can be reliably disambiguated.

Deficits in conceptual action knowledge have been associated with the dominant posterior parietal lobe and/or temporal parietal junction. On the other hand, errors apparently attributable to conceptual deficits frequently occur in patients whose lesions entirely spare brain regions typically associated with conceptual action knowledge (e.g., right parietal cortex).

IMA

IMA is a common disorder of complex skilled action not attributable to weakness, incoordination, or other elemental sensory or motor impairments. It is typically observed in individuals who have suffered left hemisphere strokes; IMA is observed in the actions of the 'unimpaired' left hand of approximately 50% of patients with left hemisphere stroke and commonly persists for at least 1 year after stroke. IMA is also common in Alzheimer's disease and in corticobasal degeneration. In stroke, it is usually a consequence of damage to the left inferior parietal lobe (and, on occasion, adjacent intraparietal sulcus and superior temporal gyrus) but has also been observed following left dorsolateral prefrontal, callosal, and subcortical damage (see **Figure 2**).

IMA is usually diagnosed on the basis of spatiotemporal errors in the production of gesture pantomime both to sight of objects and on imitation of others. That is, IMA is typically seen when a patient is asked to show how an object (e.g., scissors) would be used or when the patient is asked to copy a gesture produced by the examiner. Kinematic analyses have revealed that IMA patients pantomime skilled tool-use movements with abnormal joint angles and limb trajectories and uncoupling of the spatial and temporal aspects of movement (see **Figure 3**). Spatiotemporal errors persist to a lesser degree with actual tool use. The deficit is not restricted to meaningful movements and has also been observed in meaningless postures and sequences. IMA is also associated with cognitive deficits in declarative knowledge of the

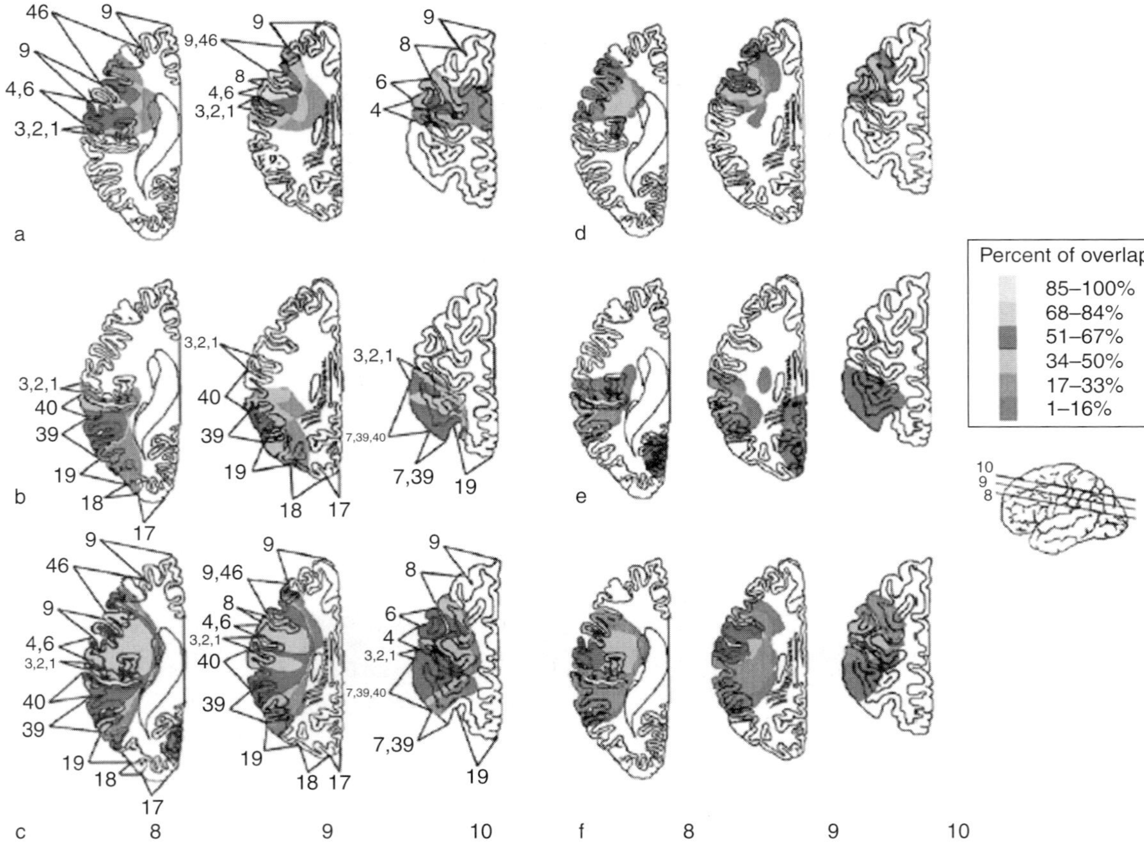

Figure 2 Maximal lesion overlap from 17 apraxic patients is shown in dorsolateral and inferior parietal regions. From Haaland KY, Harrington DL, and Knight RT (2000) Neural representations of skilled movement. *Brain* 123: 2306–2313. (See color plate 5.)

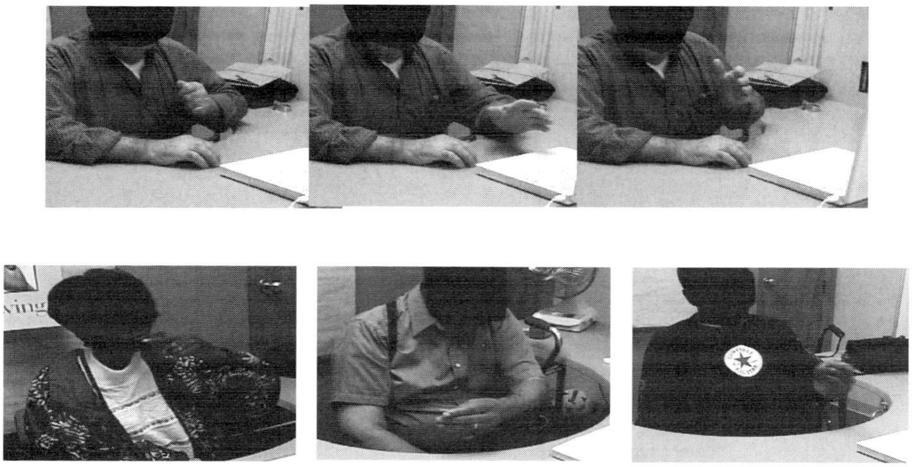

Figure 3 Typical errors in ideomotor apraxia. Top: Three still photographs from a videotape showing a sequence of postures produced by an apraxic patient in imitating a sawing movement. Note the typical hand posture error comprised of repeated hand opening with arm extension, despite the fact that the model maintained a closed grip throughout. Bottom left: Typical 'body-part-as-object' error in a toothbrushing pantomime. Bottom center: Typical arm posture error in imitating a scissoring movement. The model's movement was produced perpendicular to the body wall (from near to far) whereas the patient's movement proceeded left to right. Bottom right: Typical amplitude error in imitation of a hammering gesture. The model to be imitated demonstrated a large swing with peak amplitude at shoulder height, whereas the patient's maximal amplitude was at elbow height.

manipulation actions appropriate to objects, impairments in mechanical problem solving, deficits in motor planning, and difficulty learning new gestures.

The disorder may be attributed either to damage to stored spatiotemporal gesture representations in the left parietal lobe, sometimes called 'visuokinesthetic engrams,' or to disconnection of intact movement representations from motor output. The integrity of gesture representations is thought by many investigators to bear on the integrity of gesture recognition. In the case of damage to the representations, patients have impaired knowledge of the appropriate motor action to perform, as evidenced by deficits in gesture recognition (representational IMA). In the case of disconnection of intact engrams, patients have unimpaired knowledge of appropriate gestures, as evidenced by intact gesture recognition and ability to discriminate correct from incorrect gestures, but nevertheless perform with spatiotemporal errors (dynamic IMA).

In representational IMA, inability to discriminate correctly from incorrectly performed meaningful object-related hand movements correlates strongly with ability to produce the same movements, suggesting that the same representations may underlie both. In addition, representational IMA patients are significantly more impaired when producing object-related than symbolic, nonobject-related movements. This in turn suggests that the damaged system underlying representational IMA is specialized for movements related to skilled object use.

Disconnection and Dissociation Apraxias

Several apraxia patterns indicate that aspects of input to and output from the skilled action system are dissociable. Verbal–motor dissociation apraxia refers to a pattern of impairment in which patients are unable to gesture in response to command despite adequate comprehension and unimpaired ability to gesture to imitation. Heilman and colleagues posited that the lesion responsible for this apraxia subtype was in the angular gyrus, but they were unable to obtain neuroimaging data. Another reported pattern is seen in the tactile–motor and visuomotor dissociation apraxias, in which patients fail to gesture appropriately when holding tools or viewing tools, respectively, despite unimpaired object recognition and better gesture performance in the unaffected modality. In response to these and other patterns of dissociation, Gonzalez-Rothi, Heilman, and colleagues proposed a detailed diagrammatic model of IMA. Theoretical 'lesions' at various loci in the model appear to explain many of the observed dissociations.

Outstanding Issues in Diagnosis of Apraxia Subtype

Relevance of Recognition and Imitation Deficits for Diagnosis of IMA versus IA or Conceptual Apraxia

Historically, gesture recognition and imitation have both been used to distinguish between IMA and IA/conceptual apraxia. In Liepmann's account, patients with IA fail to reliably activate gesture engrams. Consequently, they perform normally when provided with the 'idea' of the movement; that is, when they are asked to imitate the movement of another person. Liepmann believed that, by contrast, patients with IMA suffered a disconnection of an intact idea (time–space–form picture of the movement) from motor innervatory patterns. Thus, on Liepmann's account, providing IMA patients with the 'idea' in the form of a gesture to imitate would not be of benefit.

On many contemporary accounts, it is representational IMA patients who fail to reliably activate gesture representations and who therefore may be able to imitate gestures. Recent evidence indicates that imitation may be accomplished either via gesture engrams (the so-called indirect or semantic route), or by way of a 'direct route' to action that enables imitation without access to meaning. (The direct route may bear a relationship to the putative 'mirror neuron' system discussed below.) Therefore, the ability to imitate may depend on the integrity of each of these routes. On the other hand, there is evidence that the direct route is not used for meaningful gestures even when it is intact, suggesting that there may be obligatory activation of the semantic route whenever familiar gestures are viewed.

Disagreement persists on whether gesture recognition problems signify IMA or IA. However, recent evidence from monkeys and humans indicates that the same representations are likely used for action recognition and production. In the macaque, cells in the inferior parietal lobule and in a sector of premotor cortex corresponding to Brodmann's areas 44 and 45 in humans respond both when the monkeys produce actions and when they observe the same specific actions performed by others ('mirror neurons'). In humans, there are strong correlations between action production and recognition for the same items. This suggests that gesture recognition problems may reflect degraded or inaccessible sensorimotor representations, a characteristic of IMA.

Relationship of Object Knowledge to Gesture Representations

Continued work is required to clarify the relationship of knowledge of appropriate object-oriented actions to the gesture engram system. In an influential paper on IA, De Renzi and Lucchelli proposed that the problem underlying deficient object use was a loss of knowledge of the manner in which objects are to be used, which they characterized as a semantic deficit. This emphasis on 'manner' of manipulation raises questions about the role gesture engrams might play in object-use knowledge. In contrast, other investigators view deficient recognition of the gestures associated with objects (that is, the manner of use) to be a symptom of the representational type of IM, and not IA.

Recent evidence suggests that different types of object knowledge may bear different relationships to apraxia. For example, knowledge of object function and knowledge of manner of object manipulation are dissociable. One might have knowledge of the function of an object (e.g., a knife is for cutting things) without knowledge that knives are often used with a back-and-forth, sawlike gesture. Patients with IMA tend to have the latter type, but not necessarily the former. Some reports indicate that patients with IMA may also be impaired in mechanical problem solving or the ability to infer function from structure.

Evidence for a relationship between function knowledge and performance on tasks involving multiple objects is equivocal. One potential source of confusion is that the relationship between functional knowledge and object use is sometimes assessed with single objects and sometimes with tasks involving multiple objects. In several studies using single object tests in patients with semantic dementia, a disorder with a predilection for the temporal lobes, a strong relationship has been reported. In other investigations, no relationship between single object use and functional knowledge has been found. There is stronger evidence that function knowledge is not well correlated with performance on tasks involving multiple objects. There are patients who make 'conceptual' errors on these tasks but who perform normally on semantic tests of functional and associative object knowledge, and others who perform nearly normally on tasks involving multiple objects or in real-life action, despite considerable semantic deficits.

Functional Implications of Limb Apraxia

Historically, most clinicians and researchers regarded IMA as a clinical oddity that had little significance in the real world. It appears that this view was derived from the notion that IMA was present when gestures to command and imitation were tested but improved when actions with actual objects were examined. A number of recent studies, however, have suggested that IMA is associated with deficits in activities of daily living. At least in some studies, participants with IMA are more likely to be impaired in object use, particularly in complex tasks, than nonapraxic participants who have suffered a stroke.

IMA in View of Recent Developments in the Motor Control Literature

Imitation

With the discovery of mirror neurons in the macaque premotor and parietal cortex that respond to both observed and performed actions, action imitation has emerged as an area of considerable interest in the neuroscience community. One important question concerns the degree to which imitation failure in IMA reflects damage to the mirror neuron system. Indeed, the neuroanatomic loci of lesions leading to IMA overlap considerably with the localization of mirror neurons (see **Figure 4**).

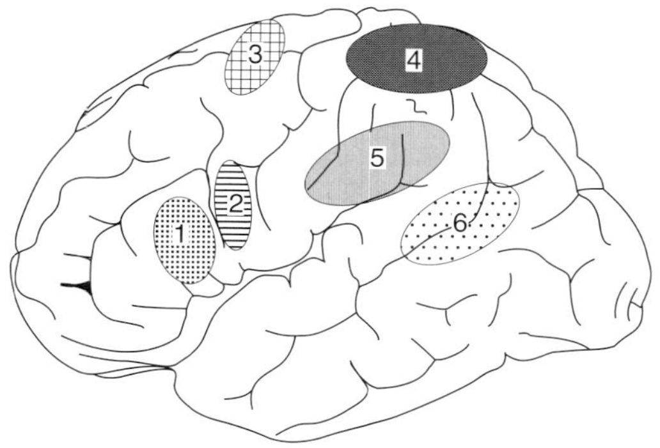

Figure 4 Mirror neuron cortical regions. From Brass M and Heyes C (2005) Imitation: Is cognitive neuroscience solving the correspondence problem? *Trends in Cognitive Sciences* 9(10): 489–495.

In addition, as noted, imitation and recognition impairments show a strong correspondence in IMA. On the other hand, IMA due to left parietal lesions frequently disrupts object-related (transitive) imitation far more than nonobject related, symbolic (intransitive) imitation. In addition, there is evidence of body part specificity in IMA imitation disruption that is not easily accommodated by putative damage to a mirror neuron system. Left hemisphere IMA patients tend to be significantly more impaired in imitation of hand postures than of finger positions, and in general, IMA appears to affect arm more than leg imitation. These dissociations could be accommodated by positing that effector-specific populations of mirror neurons might reside in different cortical regions in each hemisphere, but to this point there is little evidence for this possibility. Future investigations addressing these issues are required.

Object-Related Action

Recent evidence from single cell recordings in monkeys indicates that populations of neurons in the inferior premotor cortex (in an area with probable homolog of areas 44 and 45 in humans) as well as in the anterior intraparietal sulcus are active in response to objects that are graspable by the monkey observer. These have been termed 'canonical' neurons. Complementary studies using functional magnetic resonance imaging and transcranial magnetic stimulation in humans are consistent in suggesting that similar regions in the human brain are responsive to the structural properties (i.e., shape and size) of graspable objects. These populations appear to encode hand movement parameters (e.g., finger thumb aperture) for object grasping. In this context, there is considerable recent evidence that IMA patients, while intact in their ability to position the hand in response to object structure, are disproportionately impaired in hand shaping for functional object manipulation. The relationship of this pattern of performance to the 'canonical' neuron system is an additional area of interest for future investigation.

Spatiomotor Frames of Reference for Action

At least two different frames or reference or coordinate systems have been proposed for action. Many investigators have proposed that action may be planned in workspace-specified extrinsic coordinates. On this account, movements are planned with respect to a target that is coded in external space. Reaching to grasp a target would entail the creation of a spatial vector describing a desired movement's direction and amplitude. An alternative hypothesis proposes that movement control may occur in body-specified intrinsic coordinates; on this account, a movement plan would specify the positions of the shoulder, elbow, and wrist that would be needed to get the hand to the target. Extensive evidence for both types of control has led to a third group of accounts proposing that control is an interactive process that uses both extrinsic and intrinsic coordinate frames, depending in part on the demands of the task.

Recent evidence from IMA patients indicates that movements that may putatively rely strongly on extrinsic control (i.e., object-directed movements) are accurate, whereas movements not having external referents (i.e., body-directed movements) are characterized by spatial errors in hand configuration, wrist angle, hand orientation, and hand location. The possibility that IMA may in part reflect deficient coding of action in a body-centered framework is an area of active investigation in several laboratories.

Feedforward and Feedback-Driven Processes in IMA

The process of motor control is commonly subdivided into planning and online correction components. Planning is the preparation of a movement before movement initiation, whereas online correction refers to the adjustment of the movement plan during movement execution. There is evidence that IMA may be attributable in part to deficits in planning actions with relatively intact online correction. IMA patients are impaired in motor imagery, thought by several investigators to be a proxy for motor planning stages of action. They are also abnormally disrupted when visual feedback of movement is unavailable. This suggests that such patients may rely abnormally on visual feedback in the performance of skilled action.

Treatment of Limb Apraxia

The current literature on apraxia treatment is sparse. Approximately ten treatment efforts have been reported; in many cases, there is but a single study devoted to each treatment approach. The studies uniformly fall into the category of Phase I studies in which feasibility is assessed in small numbers of patients. Thus, it is difficult at this stage to draw conclusions about treatments that may hold particular promise.

In general, the few reported treatment approaches can be grouped into three categories: (1) studies that attempt to directly ameliorate deficient object-related gesture production with a variety of visual and tactile cues and feedback, (2) studies focusing on providing corrective feedback for errors in naturalistic multistep action, and (3) studies that attempt to prevent error from occurring (errorless learning approach). All the studies report at least some treatment benefit, but several difficulties obscure the interpretation of results. For example, apraxia type is frequently poorly characterized. Although gesture recognition is clearly an important index of the integrity of gesture representations (which in turn may have important implications for rehabilitation strategies), recognition testing is usually not performed. Only a few studies report generalization to untreated stimuli (or behaviors), maintenance of treatment effects, or impact on daily activities.

There is preliminary evidence based on these few studies that limb apraxia is amenable to treatment. The purpose of Phase I research, however, is to develop hypotheses, protocols, and methods; establish safety and activity; determine the best-outcome measures; identify responders versus nonresponders; determine optimal intensity and duration; and determine why the treatment is producing an effect. This suggests that further systematic inquiry is required to satisfy the objectives of Phase I research.

Testing for Limb Apraxia

Apraxia cannot be assessed in patients whose comprehension or cognitive deficits prevent them from understanding the task or whose visual deficits preclude identification of an object or gesture; before one tests for apraxia, these disorders must, therefore, be excluded. In order to identify apraxic patients and distinguish between the different types of apraxia described above, a testing battery should include at least the following components:

1. Assessment of manual dexterity (e.g., rotation of coin between fingertips).
2. Testing of gesture to command and to sight of object.
3. Imitation of meaningful and meaningless gestures.
4. Assessment of intrinsic egocentric spatial coding – that is, the ability to imitate meaningless static positions of the body such as holding the dorsum of the left hand against the right cheek.
5. Assessment of extrinsic egocentric spatial coding by reaching to touch or grasp objects.
6. Tests of functional semantic knowledge (e.g., which two of three pictured objects – paper clip, rubber band, and door lock – are used for the same purpose).
7. Tests of manipulation knowledge (e.g., which two of three pictured objects – saw, clothes iron, and watering can – is used with the same or similar gesture).
8. Perform a familiar multistep task such as preparing a cup of instant coffee.
9. Recognize gestures by naming a gesture or selecting which of two gestures is correctly performed.

Conclusions

Apraxia is a complex and heterogeneous disorder that has important clinical and scientific implications. Recent investigations of the disorder that are motivated by emerging accounts of motor control and planning are beginning to explicate the processing impairments underlying the apraxic disorders. The accumulating knowledge offers promise not only for the development of treatments for apraxia but also for greater understanding of the procedures by which actions are generated and the underlying neural basis.

Further Reading

Buxbaum, LJ, Johnson-Frey, SH, and Bartlett-Williams, M (2005). Deficient internal models for planning hand–object interactions in apraxia. *Neuropsychologia* 43: 917–929.
Buxbaum, LJ and Saffran, EM (2002). Knowledge of object manipulation and object function: Dissociations in apraxic and non-apraxic subjects. *Brain and Language* 82: 179–199.
Derenzi, E and Lucchelli, F (1988). Ideational apraxia. *Brain* 111: 1173–1185.
Goldenberg, G (2003). Apraxia and beyond: Life and work of Hugo Liepmann. *Cortex* 39: 509–524.
Goldenberg, G and Hagmann, S (1997). The meaning of meaningless gestures: A study of visuo-imitative apraxia. *Neuropsychologia* 35: 333–341.
Gonzalez Rothi, LJ, Ochipa, C, and Heilman, KM (1997). *A Cognitive Neuropsychological Model of Limb Praxis and Apraxia.* Hove: Psychology Press.
Haaland, KY, Harrington, DL, and Knight, RT (1999). Spatial deficits in ideomotor limb apraxia: A kinematic analysis of aiming movements. *Brain* 122: 1169–1182.
Haaland, KY, Harrington, DL, and Knight, RT (2000). Neural representations of skilled movement. *Brain* 123: 2306–2313.
Haaland, KY, Prestopnik, JL, Knight, RT, and Lee, RR (2004). Hemispheric asymmetries for kinematic and positional aspects of reaching. *Brain* 127: 1145–1158.
Heilman, KM, Rothi, LJ, and Valenstein, E (1982). Two forms of ideomotor apraxia. *Neurology* 32: 342–346.
Jeannerod, M (2003). Simulation of action as a unifying concept for motor cognition. In: Johnson-Frey, SH (ed.) *Taking Action: Cognitive Neuroscience Perspectives on Intentional Acts*, pp. 139–163. Cambridge, MA: MIT Press.
Johnson-Frey, S, Newman-Norland, R, and Grafton, S (2005). A distributed network in the left cerebral hemisphere for planning everyday tool use skills. *Cerebral Cortex* 15: 681–695.
Klatzky, R, Pellegrino, J, Mccloskey, B, and Lederman, S (1993). Cognitive representations of functional interactions with objects. *Memory & Cognition* 21: 294–303.
Leiguarda, RC and Marsden, DC (2000). Limb apraxias: Higher-order disorders of sensorimotor integration. *Brain* 123(5): 860–879.

Peigneux, P, Van Der Linden, M, Garraux, G, et al. (2004). Imagining a cognitive model of apraxia: The neural substrate of gesture-specific cognitive processes. *Human Brain Mapping* 21: 119–142.
Rizzolatti, G and Matelli, M (2003). Two different streams form the dorsal visual system: Anatomy and functions. *Experimental Brain Research* 153: 146–157.
Roy, EA and Square, PA (1985). Common considerations in the study of limb, verbal and oral apraxia. In: Roy, EA (ed.) *Neuropsychological Studies of Apraxia and Related Disorders*, pp. 111–164. Amsterdam: North-Holland.
Rumiati, RI and Humphreys, GW (1998). Recognition by action: Dissociating visual and semantic routes to action in normal observers. *Journal of Experimental Psychology: Human Perception and Performance* 24: 631–647.
Schwartz, MF and Buxbaum, LJ (1997). Naturalistic action. In: Rothi, LJG and Heilman, KM (eds.) *Apraxia: The Neuropsychology of Action*. East Sussex: Psychology Press.
Schwoebel, J, Buxbaum, L, and Coslett, HB (2004). Representations of the human body in the production and imitation of complex movements. *Cognitive Neuropsychology* 21: 285–299.
Sirigu, A, Duhamel, J-R, Cohen, L, Pillon, B, Dubois, B, and Agid, Y (1996). The mental representation of hand movements after parietal cortex damage. *Science* 273: 1564–1568.

Attention-Deficit/Hyperactivity Disorder (ADHD)

S. P. Hinshaw

Attention-Deficit/Hyperactivity Disorder (ADHD) is a syndrome of childhood constituting developmentally inappropriate, impairing, and cross-situational manifestations of inattention/disorganization, impulsivity, and motoric overactivity that cannot be better accounted for by known neurological disease or injury or by environmental trauma or deprivation. Since the advent of compulsory education in the 19th century, certain children's noteworthy problems of focusing attention and refraining from extraneous and disorganized motor behavior have become salient to society. During much of the 20th century, such appellations as minimal brain damage, minimal brain dysfunction, and hyperkinesis or hyperactivity were invoked as diagnostic terms to describe such deficits and problems. In 1980, the terminology shifted to attention deficit disorder, consistent with research pointing to problems in sustained attention and maintenance of arousal as the underlying deficits. The current nosological term, ADHD, as used in the American Psychiatric Association's *Diagnostic and Statistical Manual of Mental Disorders*, fourth edition, reflects the belief that difficulties in both attentional processing and hyperactive/impulsive behavior characterize most individuals who meet criteria for this diagnostic category. Research on the genetics, neurobiological underpinnings, and psychosocial correlates of ADHD has mushroomed in the past two decades.

ADHD received much attention in the latter part of the 20th century as scientific, clinical, and public awareness of this condition surged and as prescription rates for psychotropic medications (particularly stimulants) steadily increased. On one side are critics who contend that ADHD is a convenient psychiatric label used by society (i) to "medicalize" children's restlessness and inattention, which might be better explained by dysfunctional families, faulty schools, or societal pressures for academic success, and (ii) to legitimize pharmacological treatment for such problems. On the other side are scientists and clinicians who assert that ADHD is a real condition, with diagnostic validity and underlying neurobiological reality, for which successful treatments (both pharmacological and behavioral/psychological) are available. Indeed, a National Institutes of Health Consensus Development Conference, held during the late 1990s and focusing on the diagnosis and treatment of ADHD, concluded that the condition is a real, persistent syndrome that is substantially impairing but one for which thorough evaluation practices are needed to ensure accurate diagnosis.

Subtypes, Impairments, and Comorbidities

The constituent symptoms of ADHD are classified as inattentive/disorganized vs hyperactive/impulsive behavior patterns. Most referred cases show above-threshold levels of both symptom clusters, constituting the combined type. These individuals are usually salient to teachers and caregivers because of their high rates of disruptive behavior. In contrast, persons with high levels of inattention (but not hyperactivity/impulsivity), designated the inattentive type, display a lack of disruptive behavior and a sluggish cognitive tempo. Thus, ADHD is a heterogeneous condition. In the future, more precise subtypes (or even distinct disorders) are likely to emerge on the basis of neurobiologically sophisticated research.

Regardless of subtype, individuals with ADHD show clear impairment in academic achievement, interactions with family members, and peer relations. Severe inattention and impulse control problems do not bode well for classroom performance or formation of harmonious friendships. In addition, rates of accidental injury are well above norms, particularly for individuals with hyperactivity/impulsivity. Overall, ADHD impedes the attainment of competencies in key developmental domains.

Only rarely does ADHD exist in isolation from other psychiatric conditions. One-third of those with the diagnosis suffer from anxiety disorders, and one-half or more have oppositional defiant disorder or conduct disorder. This latter subgroup is at particularly high risk for substance abuse and delinquency. Indeed, the association of ADHD with common risk factors for antisocial behavior (low socioeconomic status, discordant family interactions, and poor verbal skills) tends to fuel an early onset and virulent course of such antisocial activities. Furthermore, ADHD may coexist with specific learning disorders (e.g., reading disability) or with neurological disorders such as Tourette's syndrome.

Assessment and Diagnosis

As for much of psychiatry, no conclusive biological test is available to confirm the diagnosis of ADHD. Furthermore, the core symptoms are ubiquitous, particularly in young children. Thus, evaluation of ADHD requires documentation of the presence of developmentally extreme levels of the constituent behavior patterns. Obtaining information from parents and teachers is necessary because cross-situational manifestations are required to meet diagnostic criteria and children with ADHD are notorious under-reporters of their own symptomatology. A thorough history, a family evaluation, and a medical examination are required to rule out neurological disease, sensory impairment, and such psychosocial influences as extreme family discord and child abuse. The practice of diagnosing ADHD within a brief office visit is not a valid diagnostic strategy.

Prevalence and Developmental Course

ADHD afflicts 3–7% of young persons. Among the combined type, the male:female ratio is approximately 3:1 or 4:1; in the inattentive type, the sex ratio may be closer to 2:1. Although it was formerly believed that ADHD remitted with the onset of puberty, well-controlled prospective studies confirm that the overwhelming majority of childhood cases persist until at least late adolescence, even though motoric overactivity per se tends to decrease with age. The absence of specific diagnostic criteria for adult manifestations of ADHD makes ascertainment of the prevalence into adulthood problematic, but ADHD clearly presents risks for lifelong adjustment problems. ADHD has been found to exist across diverse socioeconomic strata as well as throughout non-Western, nonindustrialized nations.

Risk and Etiological Factors

The heritability of the symptom dimensions underlying ADHD is quite strong, with a reported range from 0.6 to 0.9. Thus, ADHD appears to be more heritable than unipolar depression or schizophrenia and nearly as heritable as bipolar mood disorder. Recent molecular genetic work has featured susceptibility genes involved in dopamine neurotransmission, specifically the gene coding for the fourth subtype of dopamine receptors (*DR4R*) and the gene coding for the dopamine transporter (*DAT1*). Such risk factors as low birth weight and maternal tobacco use or use of alcohol or illicit substances may also predispose to ADHD. Although no direct evidence exists to implicate faulty parenting as a primary cause of ADHD, overly permissive, overly harsh, and/or inconsistent parenting may exacerbate temperamental traits (high activity level and intensity) related to ADHD, and such parenting is clearly implicated in the development of aggressive and antisocial behavior that frequently accompanies ADHD.

Neurobiological Underpinnings

At the level of neuroanatomy, small but reliable differences between ADHD and control samples have been found for total brain volume and, more specifically, for the caudate, corpus callosum, and right frontal regions. With regard to brain activity, positron emission tomography and functional magnetic resonance imaging investigations have implicated prefrontal, premotor, and frontal–striatal circuits in the pathophysiology of ADHD. Dopamine is the neurotransmitter system most heavily implicated in extant research, although interconnections with other neurotransmitter systems are clearly operative.

The core mechanism responsible for ADHD symtomatology is a point of contention. Competing theories implicate deficits in sustained attention, faulty inhibitory control, problems in frontally mediated executive functions (e.g., planning, working memory, and set shifting), erratic response to rewards, problems in regulating arousal, and motivational deficits. Among these, deficits in response inhibition and executive functions have generated the most research in recent years. A continuing challenge is the specification of underlying mechanisms and processes responsible for the varied and impairing symptomatology displayed in persons with ADHD.

Prevention and Intervention

Currently, prevention of ADHD is practically impossible because key risk and etiological factors are either not amenable to influence (e.g., susceptibility genes) or have proven difficult to address (e.g., low birth weight). Only two classes of treatment have shown consistent empirical support regarding intervention for ADHD: stimulant medications and behavioral treatment modalities that feature parent and teacher management training to promote more consistent environmental cues and rewards. Other approaches, such as dietary interventions or neurofeedback, must be considered preliminary because they lack consistent empirical support.

Once believed to exert a paradoxical response on individuals with ADHD, stimulants enhance dopaminergic transmission and positively influence attentional capacities and inhibitory control across persons with and without ADHD. Therefore, a positive response to these medications does not confirm a diagnosis of ADHD. The benefits of these agents for the core symptomatology and associated impairments have been repeatedly shown in carefully controlled investigations. Positive response rates are between 70 and 90%. Side effects are usually transitory and manageable with dose adjustment. Although stimulants clearly effect symptom control, their benefits disappear when medication treatment is terminated. Careful monitoring of stimulant treatment appears to markedly increase the likelihood of clinical benefit.

Behavioral treatments require effort on the part of parents and teachers to establish consistent, regular incentives for specified target behavioral, academic, and social goals for children and adolescents with ADHD. The benefits of these treatments are established, but the effects of behavioral intervention are typically smaller than those of medications, their use may be limited in families lacking socioeconomic resources, and the contingencies must remain in place for benefits to be maintained. The greatest likelihood of normalization of symptoms occurs when well-delivered medications and comprehensive behavioral programs are used in combination. At the level of service delivery, however, it appears that only a minority of children diagnosed with ADHD receive optimal medication or behavioral treatment. In addition, concern regarding possible overdiagnosis and inappropriately high rates of medication treatment in recent years must be balanced with the realization that ADHD is underdiagnosed and not treated at all in many sectors of the community. Public awareness of the reality of ADHD, as well as enforcement of appropriate standards for accurate evaluation and careful treatment monitoring related to ADHD, is crucial.

Conclusion

Although the subject of considerable controversy in recent years, ADHD is a valid psychiatric syndrome marked by developmentally extreme, cross-situational, and impairing symptoms in the areas of inattention/disorganization and hyperactivity/impulsivity. It is highly familial and yields marked dysfunction in key domains required for developmental competence. In addition, it is a lifelong condition in many if not most cases. Careful diagnostic assessment is required to distinguish ADHD from medical and psychosocial conditions that mimic its symptoms and to appraise comorbid diagnoses that may require separate treatment. Neural substrates include dopaminergic tracts in frontal–striatal regions that are responsible for executive functions and regulation of motor output. Inconsistent and erratic family socialization may exacerbate the child's temperamental proclivities. Effective treatment strategies include pharmacological intervention (mainly stimulant medication) and behavioral consultation with parents and teachers to aid the development of self-control. Combining these approaches yields the strongest likelihood of normalization of functioning, but both strategies appear to require long-lasting application if benefits are to be maintained. Further specification of precise neurobiological underpinnings, validated subtypes, and more efficacious treatment strategies are contingent on renewed research efforts into this prevalent and impairing disorder of childhood onset.

Further Reading

American Psychiatric Association (1994). *Diagnostic and Statistical Manual of Mental Disorders,* 4th ed. Washington, DC: American Psychiatric Press.

Barkley, RA (1997). *ADHD and the Nature of Self-Control.* New York: Guilford.

DeGrandpre, RJ and Hinshaw, SP (2000). ADHD: Serious psychiatric problem or all-American cop out? *Cerebrum* 2: 12–38.

Greenhill, LL and Osman, BO (eds.) (2000). *Ritalin: Theory and Practice,* 2nd ed. Larchmont, NY: Liebert.

Hinshaw, SP (1994). *Attention Deficits and Hyperactivity in Children.* Thousand Oaks, CA: Sage.

Hinshaw, SP, Klein, R, and Abikoff, HB (2002). ADHD: Nonpharmacologic treatments and their combination with medication. In: Nathan, PE and Gorman, J (eds.) *A Guide to Treatments That Work,* 2nd ed. New York: Oxford Univ. Press.

Jensen, PS, Martin, D, and Cantwell, DP (1997). Comorbidity in ADHD: Implications for research, practice, and DSM-V. *J. Am. Acad. Child Adolesc. Psychiatry* 36: 1065–1079.

Mannuzza, S and Klein, R (1999). Adolescent and adult outcomes in attention deficit hyperactivity disorder. In: Quay, HC and Hogan, AE (eds.) *Handbook of Disruptive Behavior Disorders*, pp. 279–294. New York: Guilford.

MTA Cooperative Group (1999). Fourteen-month randomized clinical trial of treatment strategies for attention deficit hyperactivity disorder. Moderators and mediators of treatment response for children with attention deficit hyperactivity disorder. *Arch. Gen. Psychiatry* 56: 1073–1096.

National Institutes of Health Consensus Development Statement (1999). Diagnosis and treatment of attention-deficit-hyperactivity disorder. *J. Am. Acad. Child Adolesc. Psychiatry* 39: 182–188.

Tannock, R (1998). Attention deficit hyperactivity disorder: Advances in cognitive, neurobiological, and genetic research. *J. Child Psychol. Psychiatry* 35: 65–99.

Auditory Cortex Structure and Circuitry

D. Barbour, Washington University in St. Louis, St. Louis, MO, USA

Introduction

The auditory system comprises neuronal circuits responsible for evaluating distant objects through mechanical (acoustic) vibrations transmitted to the observer via air or water. Acoustic vibrations are converted into neuronal signals by the ear, and these signals undergo multiple processing stages so that the organism can infer relevant information about the vibrations' source. Auditory cortex (ACx) of mammals represents the highest level of the conventionally described auditory system and one of the final stages of auditory processing before acoustic information has been sufficiently decoded to achieve cognitive awareness or to be acted upon in complex fashion. Many subcortical circuits extract various features from acoustic signals prior to ACx processing. These circuits have received the bulk of auditory research attention and consequently are better understood than are cortical circuits.

ACx represents the region of mammalian neocortex dedicated predominantly to the processing of auditory information and is located on the lateral surface of the brain, typically lateral or anterolateral to primary somatosensory cortex and anterior to primary visual cortex. Generally, ACx occupies a prominent position on the lateral surface of the telencephalon, and in primates (including humans) lies on the temporal lobe just inferior to and within the lateral sulcus (see **Figure 1**). In heavily convoluted primate brains, such as that of humans, much of ACx lies within the operculum of the lateral sulcus and is thus not visible from the external surface of the brain. Neuroanatomical studies indicate that ACx comprises several distinct areas that vary by species and that have individual functions that are still rather poorly understood. Organization of ACx demonstrates considerably more variation among species than does that of subcortical auditory nuclei.

Neuronal projections to the auditory cortex arise largely from the thalamus and other cortical areas, although inputs from other structures have been demonstrated. The various divisions of the medial geniculate body (MGB) of the thalamus represent ACx input arising directly from the ascending auditory pathway. These forward projections and (generally) reciprocal connections among distinct cortical areas define the region collectively referred to as ACx. Many of these distinct areas have unclear functions and await further physiological investigation to determine their contributions to auditory processing. Projections from ACx target other cortical areas, such as the frontal lobe, as well as each of the subcortical auditory nuclei.

Organization of Auditory Cortex

Thalamic Input

Distinct cortical areas are generally identified by architectonic differences and confirmed by neuroanatomical tracing studies and neurophysiological properties. Nonspecialized mammals have 10–15 distinct areas identifiable as ACx by their connections. These areas are typically subdivided into groups based upon their proximity and the types of subcortical projections they receive. One major source of thalamic input to ACx arises from the ventral division of the medial geniculate body (MGv), often referred to as the lemniscal pathway. This pathway appears to transmit strictly auditory information at short latencies using projection neurons having small receptive field sizes and arranged topographically in the thalamus. These neurons receive the bulk of their ascending input from topographically arranged neurons in the central nucleus of the inferior colliculus (ICc).

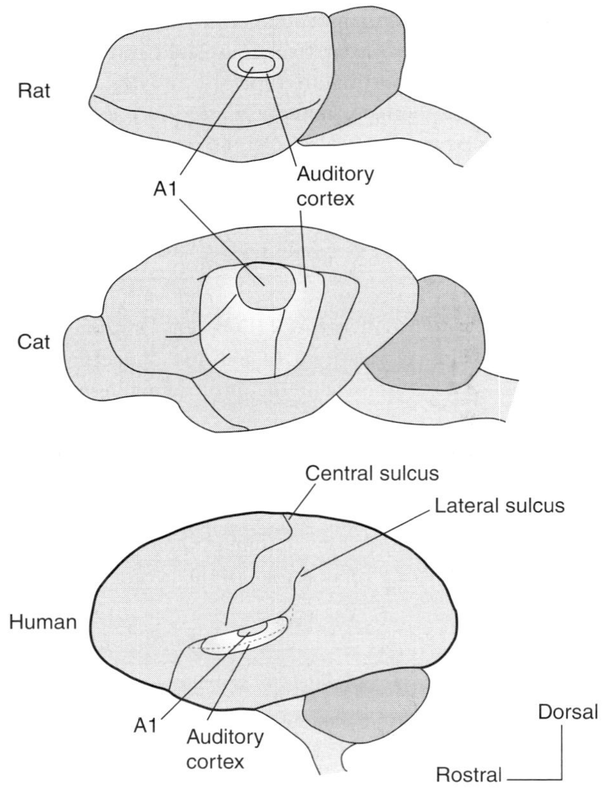

Figure 1 Approximate locations of auditory cortex on the surface of rat, cat, and human cortex. Some areas in the human brain are visible only by cutting away overlying brain tissue. A1 is the primary auditory cortex. Drawings not to scale.

Of the distinct thalamocortical pathways, the ventral pathway projects to fewer cortical areas and connects to these areas with relatively patchy distributions predominantly in cortical laminae 3b and 4.

Another major source of thalamic input to ACx arises from the dorsal division of the medial geniculate body (MGd), often referred to as one component of the paralemniscal or extralemniscal pathway. In some species, MGd has been shown to comprise multiple nuclei, each with potentially distinct cortical targets. The dorsal pathway contrasts with the ventral pathway in most if not all anatomical and physiological features. Compared with the ventral pathway, the dorsal pathway receives different, nontonotopic inputs from the inferior colliculus, projects largely to distinct areas of cortex, and sends less dense axonal collaterals more widely throughout most cortical laminae, although the largest projections are also to layers 3b and 4. The neurons composing this pathway exhibit less topographic organization, broader tuning, longer and more variable response latencies, and tendencies to habituate to ongoing stimuli. The projection patterns of the individual nuclei of the dorsal division appear to be more diverse than those of the ventral division.

The medial division of the medial geniculate body (MGm) comprises diverse cell types that represent another paralemniscal pathway. The MGm receives largely nontonotopic ascending auditory input and projects rather diffusely to multiple auditory cortical areas as well as nonauditory cortical areas and the amygdala. Its neurons typically respond at relatively short latencies (although with potential cell-to-cell variation) and some project with large axons, possibly indicating a fast connection from thalamus to cortex. Medial pathway projections to ACx are densest in cortical lamina 1a and possibly 6 and otherwise tend to be very sparse and fairly evenly distributed over the remaining laminae.

Other subcortical structures project to ACx in at least some species, although relatively little is known about the nature and effects of most of these projections. These projections likely underlie associative, learning, and sensory integration functions.

Area Parcellation

Distinct areas of auditory cortex are typically discerned by cytoarchitectural differences with adjacent areas and the pattern of thalamic input. Additional criteria for distinctiveness typically include variation in functional responses, although most of the anatomically determined areas of auditory cortex have yet to be explored physiologically in any detail. Primary auditory cortex (A1) receives its largest subcortical input from MGv, as typically do several other areas, the designations of which vary by species. Determination of A1 follows historically from its local architectonic distinctiveness, MGv input, and similarity in appearance to other koniocellular primary sensory areas. In addition, certain developmental stages in some species yield differential staining properties of A1, with stains differentiating a variety of molecules, such as cytochrome oxidase, acetylcholinesterase, parvalbumin, and neurofilament protein. Homology of areas labeled A1 among multiple species may be open to reinterpretation because of the plurality of cortical areas receiving substantial organized MGv input, particularly in primates.

Nomenclature of both area names and groupings varies by species. In primates, three groups of areas have been delineated based largely upon architecture, thalamocortical connections, interconnections with one another, and physiology. The core group stretches from anteriolateral to posteromedial along the lateral sulcus, contains tonotopically organized areas (including A1), and receives most of its thalamocortical input from MGv (see **Figure 2**). Two additional area groups situated just medial and lateral to the core are collectively referred to in modern parcellation

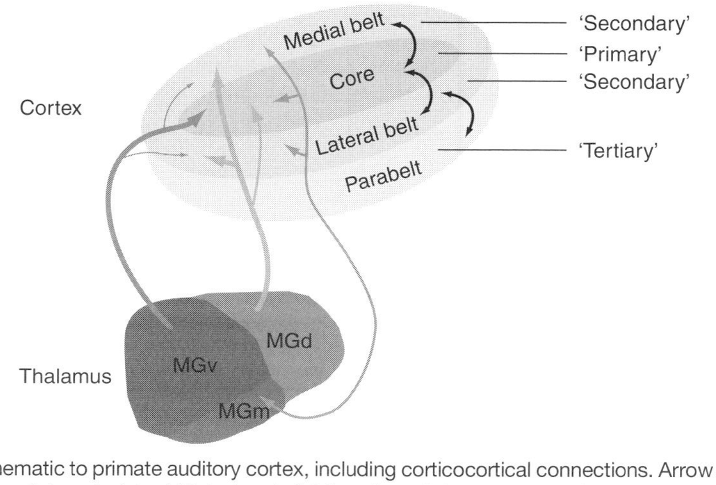

Figure 2 Thalamic input schematic to primate auditory cortex, including corticocortical connections. Arrow size approximates projection size; MGv, ventral division of medial geniculate; MGd, dorsal division of medial geniculate; MGm, medial division of medial geniculate.

schemes as 'the belt.' Belt areas receive little MGv input and substantially greater MGd and MGm input than do the core areas. These areas appear to be tonotopically organized but are difficult to study with classical, simple sound stimuli. Lateral to the lateral belt areas lie the parabelt areas, which receive no MGv projections and scattered MGd and MGm input. The internal organization of parabelt areas remains largely unknown.

Connections of Auditory Cortex

Local Structure of Primary Auditory Cortex

A1 represents both the most studied auditory cortical area and is the focus of the most research. For many years even such a basic organizational structure as tonotopy – the topographic representation of the cochlea – of A1 was debated because of the great variety of functional responses encountered during physiological experiments. Many modern lines of evidence, however, demonstrate tonotopy in A1, but other potential topographic structures remain unclear. In tonotopic areas, each sound frequency is represented in a narrow strip along the surface of the cortex (see **Figure 3**), and many attempts have been made to identify other sound properties that may be mapped along each of these strips. Many sound properties are known to be mapped nonrandomly onto the surface of A1, and computational studies imply that this relatively large number (>5) makes it unlikely that any one of these parameters is mapped orthogonally to the tonotopic axis.

Local horizontal connections in A1 tend to be patchy along the lengths of the isofrequency strips; when coupled with the patchiness of the MGv inputs, this finding implies that nonfrequency processing subunits may be spatially segregated in A1. Spatial segregation of processing appears to be true for frequency, as well, and evidence exists for substantial local frequency interactions in A1, currently of unknown function but potentially for the sensitive detection of frequency modulation sweeps and extraction of harmonicity underlying the perception of pitch – both important components of species-specific vocalizations. The patchiness of other stimulus parameters, such as neuronal receptive field bandwidth, is predicted by computational topographic models.

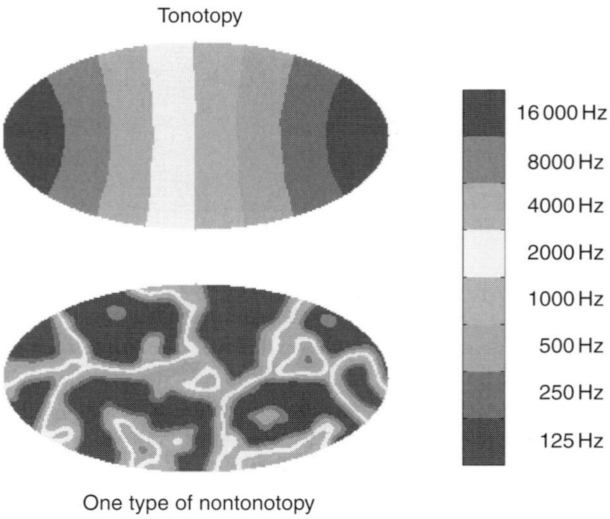

Figure 3 Model tonotopic and nontonotopic representations of sound frequency in a cortical area. (See color plate 6.)

Local connections within cortical columns of A1 remain to be further elucidated, but, as with other primary sensory areas, it is likely that specificity of interlaminar connections in A1 will become more apparent with further experimentation. Layer 4 cells tend to receive most of their excitatory input from other layer 4 cells. Layer 2/3 pyramidal cells appear to receive most of their excitatory input from either other layer 2/3 cells or layer 4 cells, reminiscent of the lemniscal/paralemniscal projection dichotomy apparent in rodent barrel cortex. How these local intracolumnar connections interface with thalamocortical and corticocortical connections remains unknown, but potentially they represent multiple modes of information transfer through A1 to other cortical areas.

Interconnections between Areas of Auditory Cortex

Auditory cortical interconnections follow the parcellation created by thalamocortical projections. The core areas in primates, which receive their major thalamocortical input from MGv, tend to interconnect densely. Core areas also interconnect with nearby belt areas, but not with parabelt areas. Belt areas appear to interconnect with most or all adjacent auditory areas (**Figure 4**). In terms of hierarchical auditory cortical processing, therefore, the belt areas appear to represent an obligatory intermediate step. This arrangement of cortical area interconnection may be unique to the auditory system.

Projections among auditory cortical areas tend to be topographic in nature, connecting subregions of each tonotopic area that correspond to similar frequencies, as assessed by physiological recordings. A similar topography appears to exist even for areas that show little or no clear frequency tuning, implying that the topographic nature of the projections reflects cortical circuits implementing more than simple frequency extraction. The persistence of topographical projections in absence of clear frequency tuning may ultimately provide some insight into the sensory transformations occurring between interconnected areas of auditory cortex.

Topography of projections across the midline to the contralateral auditory cortical areas follows the same general guidelines for ipsilateral connections, including

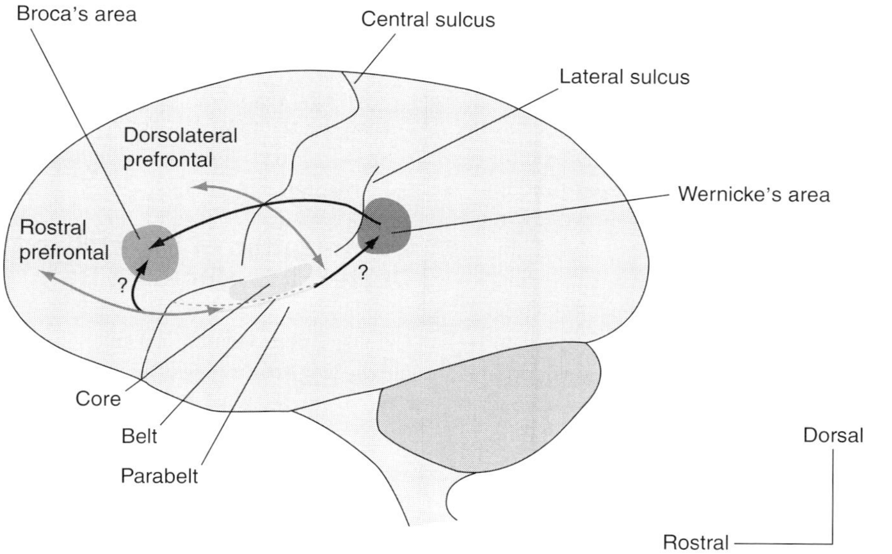

Figure 4 Projections from lateral belt to frontal and parietal lobes in primates. Frontal lobe projections are from experiments in monkeys. Wernicke's and Broca's areas have been demonstrated only in humans, but auditory cortex projections to Wernicke's and Broca's areas have not been conclusively demonstrated in humans.

area specificity and topography. Layer 2/3 pyramidal neurons project to other auditory cortical areas and to the contralateral hemisphere, as do some layer 5a pyramidal cells and possibly some cell types in layer 4. The proportion of auditory interhemispherical projections far outweighs the proportions of similar connections in other sensory modalities, indicating that ACx of both hemispheres represents fairly integrated processing circuits. It should be noted that unlike the visual system, many subcortical auditory nuclei receive input from both sensory organs (ears), as many of these circuits are used to compute the spatial layout of sound sources in the environment relative to the organism's head.

Cortical Projections Beyond Auditory Cortex

Auditory cortical areas in primates are known to project to various nonauditory frontal and parietal lobe areas shown to be involved in cognitive functions rather than audition. While core auditory cortex areas appear to interconnect substantially only with one another and nearby belt fields, the lateral belt and parabelt areas have been shown in monkeys to project to multiple targets in the frontal lobe, in addition to interconnections with one another. At least two projection pathways from lateral belt and parabelt areas to the frontal lobe have been elucidated in macaque monkeys. The anterior lateral belt and parabelt areas appear to send projections predominantly to the rostral prefrontal areas, while the posterior belt and parabelt areas appear to target mainly the dorsolateral prefrontal cortex and adjacent areas. The parabelt areas appear to send more projections to the frontal lobe than do the belt areas. All of the projections appear to be topographic in nature, with nearby auditory cortex neurons projecting to nearby frontal lobe neurons.

It has been proposed, based upon primate functional imaging studies, visual cortex projections, and limited electrophysiology, that the posterior belt/parabelt projections to the dorsolateral prefrontal cortex constitute a 'dorsal stream' representing predominantly spatial information. Conversely, the anterior belt/parabelt projections to the rostral prefrontal areas have been proposed to constitute a 'ventral stream' representing predominantly identifying information about the physical objections producing the sounds. Alternate interpretations for the information transmitted by these projections also exist, including representations of speaker identity. It is likely that future experimentation will reveal a greater complexity of information processing and transfer through auditory cortex to higher cognitive cortical areas than is implied by the 'two-stream' model.

Projections to Subcortical Nuclei

The ascending auditory pathway appears to have multiple projection streams that all converge initially in the inferior colliculus (IC) and again in the MGB. In other words, the IC and MGB are obligatory synapses for ascending auditory projections. In contrast, descending corticofugal projections, which represent a numerically large proportion of total auditory projections, project monosynaptically all the way to the earliest auditory brain stem nuclei. It appears, however, that few individual cortical neurons project to multiple subcortical auditory stations.

Most of the descending corticothalamic projections tend to mirror the ascending projections. In other words, thalamic nuclei that tend to send large projections to a particular auditory cortical area also tend to receive large projections from that cortical area. Like the ascending projections, these descending projections tend to be topographic, even for areas currently without clear functional organization. Not surprisingly, core areas such as A1 tend to project largely to MGv, although substantial divergence in corticothalamic projections exist such that A1 sends some projections to multiple nuclei of the MGB.

Descending corticocollicular projections appear to be organized topographically, much as are the corticothalamic pathways, but are smaller in total number and tend to target paralemniscal IC nuclei. Corticofugal projections to the brain stem represent a numerically small subset of the overall descending projections, terminating largely in the superior olivary complex (SOC) and the cochlear nuclei (CN). Most of these descending projections to all subcortical targets appear to be ipsilateral.

The cortical laminar locations of the corticofugal cells are infragranular (laminae 5 and 6) and tend to be located in specific sublaminar distributions. Corticothalamic cells tend to reside in layer 5b and throughout layer 6. Corticocollicular cells tend to reside in laminae 5 in regions that contain relatively few corticothalamic projections, although some IC-projecting cells are found in deep layer 6b. Few cortical cells appear to project to both the MGB and the IC. Cortical projections to SOC and CN are typically located in deep layer 5b.

The lack of extensive populations of cortical neurons sending projections to multiple subcortical stations argues that these corticofugal projections represent parallel descending pathways, each performing a distinct function. Details of the nature of these functions await further experimentation, but apparently dynamic and plastic modification of spectral tuning and neuronal dynamic range represents a major role of at least some of these pathways.

Other Circuitry

Other interconnections with ACx not described in detail here exist to various degrees throughout development and in the adult. Most of these connections are presumed to have modulatory roles on the encoding of acoustic stimuli, but most remain to be studied. Cholinergic projections from the basal forebrain play an active role in cortical plasticity, particularly in the developing animal but to some extent also in the adult. Dopaminergic, serotonergic, and norepinephrinergic projections to auditory cortex also exist and have yet to be studied extensively. The thalamic reticular nucleus (TRN) receives both ascending and descending auditory collateral input and appears to negatively modulate MGB responses. Interconnections with the limbic system, especially prevalent in nonprimary auditory cortex, presumably play a critical role in adding proper behavioral context to acoustic perception and memories, although little is known about how this phenomenon actually occurs. The auditory system at several levels, including cortex, interfaces with other sensory systems, most likely to integrate perception of space and object identity.

Organization of Specialized Auditory Cortex: Echolocating Bats

Extensive neuroanatomical and neurophysiological research on the acoustic processing and behavior of echolocating bats over the past half-century has revealed a tightly integrated neuronal system exquisitely adapted for one critical behavior. When seeking prey, the echolocating bat emits a series of vocalizations with stereotypical energy signatures. These energy signatures are modified by the size, shape, and velocity of the target and are reflected back to the bat's ears. Bats process this information extremely rapidly and use it to alter their own flight velocity to intercept desirable targets.

The subcortical auditory nuclei and auditory cortical areas of several species of echolocating bats have been studied successfully, thanks largely to the presence of their prey-seeking ethology and their stereotyped vocalizations. Use of species-specific vocalizations to probe physiological responses has resulted in marked advances in understanding the hierarchical processing of echolocating calls throughout the auditory system. In fact, more is known about the encoding of this specialized behavior in ACx than about any other auditory cortical phenomenon.

Knowledge of bat auditory processing of more general acoustic processing tasks, such as passive listening or species-specific vocalizations, generally does not surpass the equivalent knowledge in less specialized species. In fact, the auditory areas that seem to respond in such specific ways in echolocation tasks often respond in rather complex ways to more general tasks – much as is the case for other mammals. Nevertheless, it is hoped by many that adopting similar experimental techniques of studying behaving animals with relevant tasks and acoustic stimuli, such as species-specific vocalizations, will eventually lead to an improved knowledge of acoustic coding in these less specialized species.

Physiology of Unspecialized Auditory Cortex

Early studies of A1 using cortical surface electrodes revealed an apparent cochleotopic (tonotopic) topography. Later studies using penetrating microelectrodes recoding single neurons revealed much greater complexity than the surface electrodes hinted at and fueled claims that no such tonotopy existed. Tonotopy of A1 was eventually demonstrated unequivocally, and today many lines of evidence demonstrate this feature. The difficulty of determining such a basic organizational structure as tonotopy foreshadowed the difficulties in studying physiological responses from a cortical region where complexity, variability, and lack of clear organizing principles appear to dominate. Many attempts to assign unique processing features to A1 and other auditory cortical areas have been made, although a viable comprehensive theory regarding even the major role of A1 remains elusive.

The extraction of sound pitch or the perception of a single fundamental frequency for complex sounds represents a well-known psychophysical phenomenon. Imaging studies that show a functional signal in or near A1 in response to acoustic stimuli eliciting a sensation of pitch fail to reveal a similar source of subcortical activity. It is possible that one role of auditory cortex is to reassemble acoustic information decomposed in previous processing stages into relevant percepts, including the dimension of pitch. It has been speculated that pitch may represent only one dimension of an inherent musical processing ability implemented by circuits in ACx designed to process naturally occurring stimuli.

Experimentally, individuals exposed to many examples of repeated sounds with an occasional low-probability sound typically reveal a particular electroencephalogram (EEG) signal localized to auditory cortex in a phenomenon called mismatched negativity (MMN). Research into this phenomenon has led to theories that auditory cortex may carry recent acoustic history in its firing pattern in order to reassemble multiple streams of information over time, such as melodies, vocalization patterns, or sentences. Auditory stream analysis is a popular theory for the role of auditory cortex, although many of the properties of phenomena such as MMN can be found in subcortical structures or even simpler neural networks, such as the retina.

Different auditory cortex areas exhibit different responses to classes of species-specific vocalizations, leading to the theory that cortex is responsible for extracting information relevant to vocalizations. No models have been proposed for how this type of hierarchical processing may take place, and data upon which to build such models are currently sparse.

Nonauditory cortical areas that are known to be involved with the processing of human speech and language include Wernicke's area at the temporoparietal junction and Broca's area in the lateral frontal cortex (see **Figure 4**). These areas are located in the same cerebral hemisphere as one another and define the dominant hemisphere for humans, who have high degrees of brain lateralization. (Most individuals are left-hemisphere dominant.) Wernicke's area is involved with language comprehension, and impairment of function in this area induces a language deficit or aphasia that results in fluent speech lacking syntactical meaning. Broca's area is involved with speech production, and impairment of function in this area induces an aphasia that results in nonfluent, halting speech. These areas are connected by a projection pathway called the arcuate fasciculus, and impairment of function of this pathway preserves language comprehension and speech production but induces a so-called conduction aphasia whereby affected individuals have difficulty repeating complex utterances. (Conduction aphasias are likely to be caused by damage to other structures, as well.) Nonhuman primate analogs of Wernicke's and Broca's areas have yet to be convincingly demonstrated. It is assumed that auditory cortex connects to Wernicke's and Broca's areas in humans, but these projections have not been fully characterized.

Outstanding Questions

The auditory system differs from other sensory systems in the number and complexity of its subcortical nuclei and circuits. Bilateral information is represented at a very early stage in the auditory pathway, largely to calculate sound direction by circuits accurately measuring timing differences to microsecond resolution. Many other stimulus features appear to be extracted subcortically as well, including those that would be useful in acoustic recognition tasks. An obvious question arising from this observation is the appropriate analogy between auditory cortical areas and the processing regions of other sensory systems, notably the somatosensory and visual systems. All three of these systems project through the thalamus, but A1 is situated at least four or five spiking synapses from the periphery, unlike other primary sensory areas. The cytoarchitectural appearance of koniocellular primary auditory cortex, its cellular arrangement, and its subcortical interconnections appear to match well with those of the other two sensory systems, so the anatomical analogy seems appropriate.

On the other hand, statistical evaluations of the physiological filter elements most efficient in encoding natural stimuli indicate that the auditory nerve may actually generate an output analogous to that of primary visual cortex. If the assumption is correct – that the role of the early visual system is to neuronally construct efficient filters to encode visual scenes – then this comparison has some merit. Much of the subcortical auditory circuitry has no relevance for visual processing, especially given that binocular interactions are first seen in primary visual cortex.

Describing the responses of A1 neurons has been challenging and at times frustrating for decades – even more so for nonprimary auditory cortical areas. Is it appropriate to think of A1 in nonspecialized mammals as equivalent to a visual association area that requires appropriate stimuli and behavioral contexts to successfully study? Or perhaps a reductionist view is more appropriate: A1 may be responsible for creating particular 'filters' used to deconstruct stimuli and pass on to other areas for further processing, as V1 and bat A1 appear to do.

Questions and proposals such as these reflect at least part of the future research on high-level sensory coding in the auditory system, and begin to be resolved with continued efforts to discern what unique processing is performed by A1.

See also: Language, Auditory Processes; Sensory Aging, Hearing.

Further Reading

Doucet, JR, Molavi, DL, and Ryugo, DK (2003). The source of corticocollicular and corticobulbar projections in area Te1 of the rat. *Experimental Brain Research* 153(4): 461–466.

Doucet, JR, Rose, L, and Ryugo, DK (2002). The cellular origin of corticofugal projections to the superior olivary complex in the rat. *Brain Research* 925(1): 28–41.

Griffiths, TD (2003). Functional imaging of pitch analysis. *Annals of the New York Academy of Sciences* 999: 40–49.

Hu, B (2003). Functional organization of lemniscal and nonlemniscal auditory thalamus. *Experimental Brain Research* 153(4): 543–549.

Huang, CL and Winer, JA (2000). Auditory thalamocortical projections in the cat: Laminar and areal patterns of input. *Journal of Comparative Neurology* 427(2): 302–331.

Kaas, JH and Hackett, TA (2000). Subdivisions of auditory cortex and processing streams in primates. *Proceedings of the National Academy of Sciences of the United States of America* 97(22): 11793–11799.

Kaur, S, Lazar, R, and Metherate, R (2004). Intracortical pathways determine breadth of subthreshold frequency receptive fields in primary auditory cortex. *Journal of Neurophysiology* 91(6): 2551–2567.

Kaur, S, Rose, HJ, Lazar, R, et al. (2005). Spectral integration in primary auditory cortex: Laminar processing of afferent input. *in vivo and in vitro. Neuroscience* 134(3): 1033–1045.

Lee, CC and Winer, JA (2005). Principles governing auditory cortex connections. *Cerebral Cortex* 15(11): 1804–1814.

Lewicki, MS (2002). Efficient coding of natural sounds. *Nature Neuroscience* 5(4): 356–363.

Penagos, H, Melcher, JR, and Oxenham, AJ (2004). A neural representation of pitch salience in nonprimary human auditory cortex revealed with functional magnetic resonance imaging. *Journal of Neuroscience* 24(30): 6810–6815.

Peretz, I and Zatorre, RJ (2005). Brain organization for music processing. *Annual Review of Psychology* 56: 89–114.

Romanski, LM, Bates, JF, and Goldman-Rakic, PS (1999). Auditory belt and parabelt projections to the prefrontal cortex in the rhesus monkey. *Journal of Comparative Neurology* 403(2): 141–157.

Schreiner, CE, Read, HL, and Sutter, ML (2000). Modular organization of frequency integration in primary auditory cortex. *Annual Review of Neuroscience* 23: 501–529.

Schwartz, O and Simoncelli, EP (2001). Natural signal statistics and sensory gain control. *Nature Neuroscience* 4(8): 819–825.

Smith, PH and Populin, LC (2001). Fundamental differences between the thalamocortical recipient layers of the cat auditory and visual cortices. *Journal of Comparative Neurology* 436(4): 508–519.

Suga, N (1990). Biosonar and neural computation in bats. *Scientific American* 262(6): 60–68.

Suga, N (1994). Processing of auditory information carried by species-specific complex sounds. In: Gazzaniga, MS (ed.) *The Cognitive Neurosciences*, pp. 295–313. Cambridge, MA: MIT Press.

Suga, N, Xiao, Z, Ma, X, et al. (2002). Plasticity and corticofugal modulation for hearing in adult animals. *Neuron* 36(1): 9–18.

Winer, JA (2005). Decoding the auditory corticofugal systems. *Hearing Research* 207(1–2): 1–9.

Winer, JA, Miller, LM, Lee, CC, et al. (2005). Auditory thalamocortical transformation: Structure and function. *Trends in Neuroscience* 28(5): 255–263.

Autism and Asperger Syndrome, A Spectrum of Disability

H. Cohen and S. Rémillard, Université du Québec à Montréal, Montréal, Canada

Autism spectrum disorder (ASD) is a severe developmental disorder, first labeled and described by Kanner in 1943. The onset of ASD occurs before age 3 and persists throughout life. A male predisposition exists with a ratio of approximately 3 to 1. The prevalence of this disorder is approximately 1 of every 1000 births. According to the *Diagnostic and statistical manual,* 4th edition (DSM-IV; American Psychological Association), and the *International classification of diseases,* 10th edition (ICD-10; World Health Organization), this disorder is part of the Pervasive Developmental Disorders category and is characterized by three main disabilities: (1) failure to develop normal social interactions and relationships, (2) language delay and communication disability, and (3) restricted, repetitive, and stereotyped behaviors. Mental retardation is frequently associated with autism. Approximately 75% of individuals with autism have severe mental retardation (also known as low-functioning autism; LFA), and the rest have mild retardation or average intelligence (also called high-functioning autism; HFA). Approximately 10% of individuals with ASD may have very low levels of intellectual abilities, but show excellent rote memory and possess isolated savant skills, such as calendar calculations, exceptional musical or drawing abilities (Volkmar and Pauls, 2003).

Individual differences in ASD are also observed in language development. Some children with autism never develop speech, whereas others become verbally fluent but still have problems with comprehension and language use. As the manifestation of autism varies in degree of severity and from one individual to another, it is generally assumed that there is a spectrum of autistic disabilities ranging from LFA to HFA and Asperger's syndrome (AS). The distinction between LFA and HFA consists mainly of the fluency and flexibility of expressive language skills (Lord and Paul, 1997). LFA individuals may be mute or may acquire only minimum speech characterized by echolalia (the immediate repetition of what is said by another person) without any apparent communication purpose. HFA individuals develop speech, but tend to show idiosyncratic use of words and phrases and have difficulty participating in conversation (Bushwick, 2001). Asperger's syndrome constitutes a milder variant of the autism spectrum and, like the autistic disorder, is characterized by social disability and restricted stereotyped behaviors. However, AS individuals do not show mental retardation and language acquisition delay as in autism (Volkmar and Klin, 2000). Consequently, AS is often not diagnosed until late childhood or even adulthood. The prevalence of AS is higher than that of autism and is estimated at 3 of 1000 births. Although the cause of ASD is unknown, there is strong evidence for a genetic contribution to the development of the disorder. The concordance rate for monozygotic twins is very high (i.e., over 90%; Volkmar and Pauls, 2003).

Neuroanatomic and neuroimaging investigations have revealed functional and structural brain abnormalities in individuals with ASD, such as hyperserotonemia, reduced volume of cerebellar vermis, and abnormalities in cell structure in the hippocampus and amygdala (Beauman and Kemper, 2003). High rates of seizures have also been observed in individuals with ASD. The similarity of autistic impairments with frontal lobe and right hemisphere lesions (Martin and McDonald, 2003) and Landau–Kleffner syndrome (Levisohn, 2004) has been highlighted.

Abnormal auditory cortical processing of complex sounds in children with autism has also been revealed in a positron–emission tomography activation study and confirmed previous results obtained in adults. This irregular processing seen in both adults and children with autism could be involved in inadequate behavioral responses to sounds and in language impairments characteristic of autism (Boddaert et al., 2004). In addition, a language-association cortex asymmetry was revealed in autism and specific language impairment (SLI), suggesting a phenotypic link between autism with language impairment and SLI. Language-impaired boys with both autism and SLI had reversal of asymmetry on frontal language-related cortex, whereas linguistically unimpaired ASD boys had asymmetry similar to that found in the control group. It would appear that this asymmetry reversal is more a reflection of language impairment than specifically linked to autism diagnosis (De Fosse et al., 2004).

Language in ASD and Asperger's Syndrome

As most autistic children are usually diagnosed around 3 or 4 years of age, few investigations have been conducted with younger children. However, retrospective analyses of home videotapes of 1 year old children later diagnosed with ASD and parental reports of their child's language have provided useful information about the preverbal phase of the autistic disorder. Lord et al. (2004) reported that parents often observe word loss in the second year of life in children with autism. In addition, 1 year old autistic children are less responsive to their names or attend less to people than do typically developing children. The autistic child's failure to orient preferentially to speech, share attention, and use eye gaze to disambiguate an adult's intention may be the earliest signs of the disorder and constitute particularly strong handicaps for the acquisition of language (Dawson et al., 2004; Rollins and Snow, 1998).

Language impairment is an important part of the diagnostic in autistic spectrum disorders. As already mentioned, many children with autism may never learn to speak or show any attempt to communicate through compensating gestures or body expressions. Those children who acquire speech, approximately 50% of autistic individuals (Minshew et al., 1992), show striking peculiarities such as unusual intonation, severe difficulties in social use of language (pragmatics), echolalia, neologisms, and pronominal reversal (e.g., using 'you' instead of 'I').

Comprehension of language is often more delayed than expression in individuals with autism. As reported by Bartak et al. (1977), children with autism show more severe deficits in speech comprehension when compared to other mentally retarded children, matched for nonverbal cognitive level, as well as to normally developing children (Tager-Flusberg, 1981). More recently, a study of 134 children with autism, without severe mental retardation, showed that word comprehension and sentence comprehension were more delayed than word production, in contrast with the performance of the normative sample as measured by the MacArthur Communicative Development Inventory (Charman et al., 2003).

The phonological processing of 80 probands with ASD and 59 healthy controls was thoroughly assessed by Bishop et al. (2004). In that study, the parents of the participants completed a battery of tests including verbal and performance IQ, nonword repetition, nonsense passage reading, and a questionnaire about history of language and literacy problems. Interestingly, verbal IQ was the only measure to show any familiality within the index group. It appears that phonological processing impairments are not part of the ASD phenotype.

Pragmatic Language

Most individuals with a diagnosis of HFA and AS eventually develop good verbal skills (although delayed in HFA), with the ability to engage in relatively fluent and articulate speech, but still show marked deficits in pragmatic language abilities (i.e., the appropriate use of language in social context; Happé, 1993; Martin and McDonald, 2003). The language of individuals with AS is often described as pedantic, tangential, and overtalkative. These individuals also tend to have an overliteral understanding of what is said. In addition, individuals with AS have difficulty with the pragmatic interpretation of nonliteral utterances, such as metaphors, irony, and narrative humor (Happé, 1993; Martin and McDonald, 2003).

The ability to repair communicative breakdown is an important pragmatic skill. A number of studies have consistently shown that individuals with ASD generally recognize communicative breakdown and adequately respond to requests for clarifications (RQCL) with a variety of repair strategies. However, Volden (2004) has shown that children with ASD were more likely than language age-matched peers to respond to an RQCL with an inappropriate response.

Prosody

Segmental or articulatory aspects of speech have been reported to be generally appropriate for the developmental levels of people with HFA or AS (Bishop, 2003; Tager-Flusberg, 1981). However, abnormal suprasegmental aspects of speech, or prosody, constitute another characteristic frequently observed in autism (McCaleb and Prizant, 1985; McCann and Peppé, 2003; Rutherford et al., 2002; Tager-Flusberg, 1981). Therefore, abnormal tone, pitch, and modulation of speech are common. Specifically, studies on the use of contrastive stress (a component of prosody used to highlight an important word in an utterance, as the focus of attention) showed that individuals with autism tend to use stress in an atypical way (McCaleb and Prizant, 1985). Children with autism misassigned stress twice as often as typically developing children. However, as contrastive stress is dependent on the pragmatic intention of the speaker, a deficit in that aspect of prosody may be in fact a pragmatic deficit. In addition, Rutherford et al. (2002) investigated the affective aspects of prosody. They asked participants to listen to 40 stimuli and then decide which of two adjectives best described the affective content of the stimuli. Their results suggest an impairment in the comprehension of prosodic affect in individuals with HFA and AS.

Verbal Semantic Processing

According to Charman et al. (2003), children with autism have a broadly similar pattern of acquisition of different word categories and types than typically developing children. Lopez and Leekam (2003) reported no difficulty in a word-priming task as HFA and typically developing children showed similar facilitation effects. They all identified words related to a prime faster than words preceded by a neutral prime.

The fact remains that specific difficulties in semantic aspects of language have been reported in individuals with autism. The observed impairments refer to the understanding of particular types of words (i.e., terms with social or emotional content). As measured by the British Picture Vocabulary Scale, individuals with autism showed specific difficulties in understanding emotion-related terms, but not with emotion-unrelated ones (Hobson and Lee, 1989). Other studies have reported a specific impairment with terms having deictic function (terms that change their meaning according to the context in which they are used, e.g., 'you,' 'now,' 'there,' 'this'; Charman et al., 2003). Individuals with HFA also showed impairment in processing lexical ambiguous sentences (Jolliffe and Baron-Cohen, 1999) and interpretation of homographs (Happé, 1997); both tests involve the ability to adequately interpret the context in order to understand the meaning of the sentences.

Syntactic Aspect of Language

Syntactic development has not been well studied in autism. There is considerable individual variation in grammatical skill among children with autism. Many children never acquire productive syntax, but others show relatively high achievement (Rollins and Snow, 1998). Generally, in fluent HFA, sentences are grammatically intact. Dawson et al. (2004) and Rollins and Snow (1998) have shown that the establishment and manipulation of joint attention (the ability to coordinate attention between another person and an object or event of interest) may be a pragmatic skill prerequisite to the development of productive syntax. Their observations showed a strong association between pragmatic and morphosyntactic skills with autistic children who rarely established a joint focus of attention (Rollins and Snow, 1998).

Theoretical Understanding of Autism

Three hypotheses have been suggested to explain the cognitive and social features of autism. The first and most prominent position on the causation of social impairment in autistic disorder is the theory of mind hypothesis (ToM; i.e., a deficit in mental inference ability). This model suggests that an inability to attribute mental states to others (i.e., intentions, desires, feelings, and beliefs) leads to difficulties in effective communication and therefore in social interactions (Volkmar and Pauls, 2003). The ToM hypothesis has been widely studied using the standard False Belief Task (Martin and McDonald, 2003). Children with autism characteristically fail this test (Happé, 1993). In addition, Happé (1993) observed a strong association between ToM deficits and pragmatic comprehension in autism. The level of ToM complexity (first- or second-order intentions) is related to the ability to understand similes (a literal level of comprehension), metaphors (first-order intention), or irony (second-order intention). However, Ozonoff et al. (1991) found that adolescents diagnosed with AS do not fail ToM tasks as children with autism do, suggesting that they possess an understanding of mental states. However, AS children still have major difficulties with social interactions. Despite strong evidence of an association between ToM deficits and communication difficulties in autism, this model is somewhat limited in the explanation of their impaired social interactions.

A second hypothesis, the weak central coherence hypothesis (WCC), was proposed by Frith (1989) to explain the tendencies of people with autism to pay preferential attention to parts rather than global coherent patterns of information. This hypothesis takes into account their pragmatic deficit – an impairment in the ability to use language appropriately in context – and also their superior capacities of recalling and processing information. Because this theory suggests that autistic individuals pay preferential attention to segments rather than whole features of objects, it can explain the superior performance of autistic individuals over normal healthy controls, as on the Block Design subtest of the Wechsler Adult Intelligence Scale (WAIS), for example. However, some authors have found that global processing was intact in individuals with autism (e.g., Ropar and Mitchell, 2001). Thus, the WCC remains a controversial hypothesis.

The impaired executive functions hypothesis in autism is a third explanatory perspective of a primarily social impairment. Executive functions underlie planning, social judgment, insight, inhibition, flexibility, and working memory mediated by the frontal lobes. Consequently, the obsessive desire for sameness, restricted interests, and stereotyped and rigid behaviors that characterize individuals with autism have been associated with a deficit in executive function skills, which may explain their poor social skills. In order to assess executive dysfunction in autism, Ozonoff and McEvoy (1994) used the Wisconsin Card Sorting Test (WCST) and the Tower of Hanoi Test. In contrast to typically developing controls, children with autism showed a poor performance on both of these executive function tests. Nevertheless, executive function deficits are not specific to autism and a more recent study showed that there exists an association between performance on the WCST and social impairment in autism, but no relationship with communication impairment (Liss et al., 2001).

Treatment and Prognosis

Autism spectrum disorder is a lifelong disability. Although the symptoms may improve with age, most individuals with ASD or AS still show impairments in social and occupational functioning later in life. Onset of speech before the age of 5 (Venter et al., 1992) and joint attention abilities (Dawson et al., 2004) have been associated with a good prognosis. To date, there is no recognized medical treatment for the core deficits in autism. However, developmental, behavioral, and educational therapeutic programs have met with some success in helping reduce behavior problems and in fostering communication. Positive effects with significant improvement in language and social behavior have been reported with individual and intensive interventions dispensed early in childhood (Howling, 2003). However, clinical intervention should also focus on utterances that disrupt the conversational flow and that generate severe social penalties for the speaker with ASD (e.g., Volden, 2004).

Bibliography

Bartak, L, Rutter, M, and Cox, A (1977). 'A comparative study of infantile autism and specific developmental receptive language disorders.' *Journal of Autism and Childhood Schizophrenia* 7: 383–396.

Beauman, ML and Kemper, TL (2003). 'The neuropathology of the autism spectrum disorders: What have we learned?' *Autism: Neural Basis and Treatment Possibilities: Novartis Foundation Symposium* 251: 112–127.

Bishop, DVM (2003). 'Autism and specific language impairment: Categorical distinction or continuum?' *Autism: Neural Basis and Treatment Possibilities: Novartis Foundation Symposium* 251: 213–226.

Bishop, DV, Maybery, M, Wong, D, Maley, A, Hill, W, and Hallmayer, J (2004). 'Are phonological processing deficits part of the broad autism phenotype?' *American Journal of Medical Genetics* 128B: 54–60.

Boddaert, N, Chabane, N, Belin, P, Bourgeois, M, Royer, V, Barthelemy, C, Mouren-Simeoni, MC, Philippe, A, Brunelle, F, Samson, Y, and Zilbovicius, M (2004). 'Perception of complex sounds in autism: abnormal auditory cortical processing in children.' *American Journal of Psychiatry* 161: 2117–2120.

Bushwick, NL (2001). 'Social learning and the etiology of autism.' *New Ideas in Psychology* 19: 49–75.

Charman, T, Drew, A, Baird, C, and Baird, G (2003). 'Measuring early language development in preschool children with autism spectrum disorder using the MacArthur Communication Development Inventory (Infant Form).' *Journal of Child Language* 30: 213–236.

Dawson, G, Toth, K, Abbott, R, Osterling, J, Munson, J, Estes, A, and Liaw, J (2004). 'Early social attention impairments in autism: Social orienting, joint attention, and attention to distress.' *Developmental Psychology* 40: 271–283.

De Fosse, L, Hodge, SM, Makris, N, Kennedy, DN, Caviness, VS, Jr, McGrath, L, Steele, S, Ziegler, DA, Herbert, MR, Frazier, JA,

Tager-Flusberg, H, and Harris, GJ (2004). 'Language-association cortex asymmetry in autism and specific language impairment.' *Annals of Neurology* .

Frith, U (1989). *Autism and Asperger syndrome.* London: MRC Cognitive Development Unit.

Happé, FGE (1993). 'Communicative competence and theory of mind in autism: A test of relevance theory.' *Cognition* 48: 101–119.

Happé, FGE (1997). 'Central coherence and theory of mind in autism: Reading homographs in context.' *British Journal of Developmental Psychology* 15: 1–12.

Hobson, RP and Lee, A (1989). 'Emotion-related and abstract concepts in autistic people: Evidence from the British Picture Vocabulary Scale.' *Journal of Autism and Developmental Disorders* 19: 601–623.

Howling, P (2003). 'Can early interventions alter the course of autism?' *Autism: Neural Basis and Treatment Possibilities: Novartis Foundation Symposium* 251: 250–258.

Jolliffe, T and Baron-Cohen, S (1999). 'A test of central coherence theory: Linguistic processing in high-functioning adults with autism or Asperger syndrome: Is local coherence impaired?' *Cognition* 71: 149–185.

Levisohn, PM (2004). 'Electroencephalography findings in autism: Similarities and differences from Landau–Kleffner syndrome.' *Seminars in Pediatric Neurology* 11: 218–224.

Liss, M, Fein, D, Allen, D, Dunn, M, Feinstein, C, Morris, R, Waterhouse, L, and Rapin, I (2001). 'Executive functioning in high-functioning children with autism.' *Journal of Child Psychology and Psychiatry and Allied Disciplines* 42: 261–270.

Lopez, B and Leekam, SR (2003). 'Do children with autism fail to process information in context?' *Journal of Child Psychology and Psychiatry* 44: 285–300.

Lord, C and Paul, R (1997). 'Language and communication in autism.' In: Cohen, DJ and Volkmar, FR (eds.) *Handbook of autism and pervasive developmental disorders* (2nd edn.), pp. 195–225. New York: John Wiley & Sons.

Lord, C, Shulman, C, and DiLavore, P (2004). 'Regression and word loss in autistic spectrum disorders.' *Journal of Child Psychology and Psychiatry* 45: 936–955.

Martin, I and McDonald, S (2003). 'Weak coherence, no theory of mind, or executive dysfunction? Solving the puzzle of pragmatic language disorders.' *Brain and Language* 85: 451–466.

McCaleb, P and Prizant, B (1985). 'Encoding of new versus old information by autistic children.' *Journal of Speech and Hearing Disorders* 50: 230–240.

McCann, J and Peppé, S (2003). 'Prosody in autism spectrum disorders: A critical review.' *International Journal of Language and Communication Disorders* 38: 325–350.

Minshew, NJ, Goldstein, G, Muenz, LR, and Payton, JB (1992). 'Neuropsychological functioning in non-mentally-retarded autistic individuals.' *Journal of Clinical and Experimental Neuropsychology* 14: 749–761.

Ozonoff, S and McEvoy, RE (1994). 'A longitudinal study of executive function and theory of mind development in autism.' *Development and Psychopathology* 6: 415–431.

Ozonoff, S, Rogers, SJ, and Pennington, BF (1991). 'Asperger's syndrome: Evidence of an empirical distinction from high-functioning autism.' *Journal of Child Psychology and Psychiatry* 32: 1107–1122.

Rollins, PR and Snow, CE (1998). 'Shared attention and grammatical development in typical children and children with autism.' *Journal of Child Language* 25: 653–673.

Ropar, D and Mitchell, P (2001). 'Susceptibility to illusions and performance on visuospatial tasks in individuals with autism.' *Journal of Child Psychology, Psychiatry and Allied Disciplines* 42: 539–549.

Ruttherford, MD, Baron-Cohen, S, and Wheelwright, S (2002). 'Reading the mind in the voice: A study with normal adults and adults with Asperger syndrome and high functioning autism.' *Journal of Autism and Developmental Disorders* 32: 189–194.

Tager-Flusberg, H (1981). 'On the nature of linguistic functioning in early infantile autism.' *Journal of Autism and Developmental Disorders* 11: 45–56.

Venter, A, Lord, C, and Schopler, E (1992). 'A follow-up study of high functioning autistic children.' *Journal of Child Psychology and Psychiatry* 33: 489–507.

Volden, J (2004). 'Conversational repair in speakers with autism spectrum disorder.' *International Journal of Language and Communication Disorders* 39: 171–189.

Volkmar, FR and Klin, A (2000). 'Diagnostic issues in Asperger syndrome.' In: Klin, A, Volkmar, FR, and Sparrow, SS (eds.) *Asperger syndrome*, pp. 25–71. New York: Guilford Press.

Volkmar, FR and Pauls, D (2003). 'Autism.' *The Lancet* 362: 1133–1141.

B

Balint's Syndrome

R. A. Short and N. R. Graff-Radford

Balint's syndrome is an intriguing disorder of visuospatial attention. The ability to focus attention is necessary to make sense of the constant bombardment of sensory stimuli that occurs in everyday life. For example, in a crowded, noisy room we are usually still able to attend to the conversation at hand. Similar mechanisms allow us to focus on specific visual stimuli. However, this sometimes leads to the phenomenon of looking but not seeing. Many of us have had the experience of looking for an object such as a jar of mayonnaise in the refrigerator, being unable to locate it, and then having one's spouse grab the jar right in front of one's eyes. Patients with Balint's syndrome have an extreme form of looking but not seeing along with several other related deficits. Balint's syndrome is used in the neurological literature to designate a triad of visuospatial defects referred to as simultanagnosia, optic ataxia, and ocular apraxia. Patients with this triad of signs usually have brain lesions at the junction of the occipital and parietal lobes of both hemispheres. This entry describes the syndrome from a historical perspective, defines its individual components, and discusses the presentation and etiologies of the syndrome.

Historical Perspective

Reszo Balint (1874–1929), a Hungarian physician, is best known for a description of the components of a syndrome that bears his name. In 1909, he reported a man with three related but distinct visuospatial abnormalities that were individually designated as a spatial disorder of attention (simultanagnosia), optic ataxia, and psychic paralysis of gaze (ocular apraxia). At autopsy the man had multiple brain lesions, including bilateral nearly symmetrical softening of the posterior parietal, upper temporal, and occipital lobes. These lesions likely resulted from strokes because the patient also had severe atherosclerotic disease of the cerebral circulation. In 1918, Gordon Holmes reported six soldiers with missile wounds to occipital regions; each had "disturbances of visual orientation" similar to the patient of Balint's. An autopsy was performed on two of these patients and each had bilateral lesions involving the parieto-occipital area. However, the term Balint's syndrome did not appear in the literature until 1954, when it was used by Hecaen and de Ajuraguerra to describe four patients who had some similarities to Balint's patient. Subsequent studies and case reports have established Balint's syndrome as referring to the previously mentioned triad of impairments and implying lesions in specific brain areas. However, there are reasons to question whether this triad of signs meets the strict operational criteria for a syndrome.

Simultanagnosia

Balint claimed that his patient "could see one and only one object at a single time, no matter what size." What Balint referred to as a spatial disorder of attention has generally become known as simultanagnosia. Simultanagnosia is an inability to recognize multiple elements in a simultaneously displayed visual presentation. To demonstrate simultanagnosia, the patient is asked to describe a complex visual scene that has multiple items in all four quadrants of the visual field. A patient with simultanagnosia will be able to describe a single element of the scene but will have difficulty in directing attention to and describing other parts of the scene or the picture as a whole. Although visual field defects sometimes occur with the syndrome, they are not severe enough to account for the difficulty in describing the scene. Intact visual fields are demonstrated by displaying an object at different time points in each of the different fields on a plain background. The ability to recognize only one object at a time does not seem to be entirely dependent on the size or even complexity of the object. In 1959, Luria reported a patient with Balint's syndrome who could only see one circle when presented a piece of paper with two circles drawn on it. However, when the circles were connected with a line the patient reported seeing an object that looked like a dumbbell or spectacles. Typically, patients do not have impairment of object recognition or severe language problems that would interfere with their ability to describe what they are visualizing.

Ocular Apraxia

Balint's patient also had "psychic paralysis of gaze," which is now known as ocular apraxia. Ocular apraxia is the inability to voluntarily direct one's fixation of gaze from one object to another. This is demonstrated by having the patient fixate on one object and then introducing a second object in another part of the visual field and asking the patient to direct his or her gaze toward the second object. Patients will have difficulty in directing their gaze even if told where to look. Patients may have other eye movement abnormalities, such as difficulty in maintaining visual fixation and poor tracking eye movements. Each of these eye movement abnormalities can be attributed to the patient's impaired spatial representation of the visual scene. In fact, eye movements that are not visually dependent are intact so that the patient can direct his or her gaze to a part of his or her body or to sounds.

Optic Ataxia

Optic ataxia is an impairment of pointing toward or reaching for objects. This defect can be demonstrated by asking the patient to touch with his or her fingertip a small object that he or she has visually fixated on. The patient will make a smooth hand movement but will miss the target. As in ocular apraxia, movements that are not visually guided are intact. Patients can point toward their own body parts or toward the source of a sound.

Presentation and Etiology

Depending on the severity of the impairments, the patient's complaints will range from mild difficulty seeing with no functional impairment to being essentially blind. Patients have been reported to complain that objects seem to appear and disappear spontaneously. One patient reported watching a television show when, to her surprise, a character involved in a heated argument suddenly went flying across the room from a punch thrown by a character not seen. Here, two patients illustrating the clinical presentation of Balint's syndrome are briefly described.

The first patient was a 70-year-old woman who was admitted to the hospital because of severe headaches and transient left side weakness. She was diagnosed with an inflammatory vasculitis of the central nervous system. During her hospital stay, she began complaining of difficulty seeing, which she could not describe more in depth. Examination showed that she had normal visual acuity, visual fields, and a mild simultanagnosia, ocular apraxia, and optic ataxia. **Figure 1** shows the magnetic resonance image (MRI) of the patient showing bilateral lesions of the parieto-occipital junction.

The second patient was a 55-year-old woman evaluated for 5 years of progressively distorted vision. For example, she was unable to see two cars at an intersection and had almost stepped from a curb into an approaching car but her husband pulled her to safety. She also had difficulty performing manual tasks under visual guidance, such as reaching for utensils. On examination, when she was shown a picture of a man jogging next to an elephant, she said that she saw a man jogging outside but did not describe the elephant. When asked whether she saw an animal, she said that she saw only a blur of colors. She also had optic ataxia and mild language and memory difficulties. Her MRI showed prominent occipitoparietal atrophy (**Fig. 2**). The cause of her deficits is most likely a degenerative condition such as Alzheimer's disease because we have three similar cases who have come to autopsy and all had Alzheimer's disease.

The parieto-occipital areas most consistently involved in patients with Balint's syndrome are the angular gyrus, cuneus (Brodmann's area 19), and precuneus (Brodmann's area 7). Bilateral lesions restricted to these areas are quite rare, and patients often have confounding visual, sensory (such as hemineglect), and language impairments.

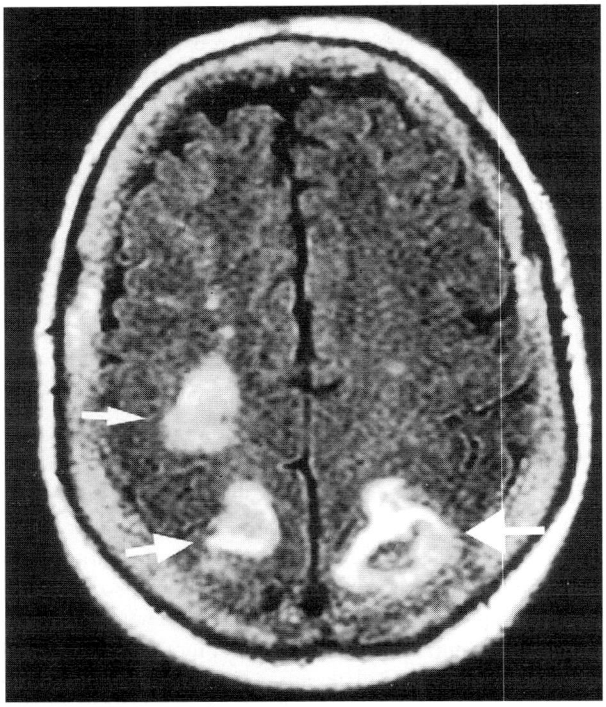

Figure 1 MRI of a 70-year-old patient. Large arrows indicate lesions in the parieto-occipital region. The small arrow indicates the lesion causing the left-sided weakness.

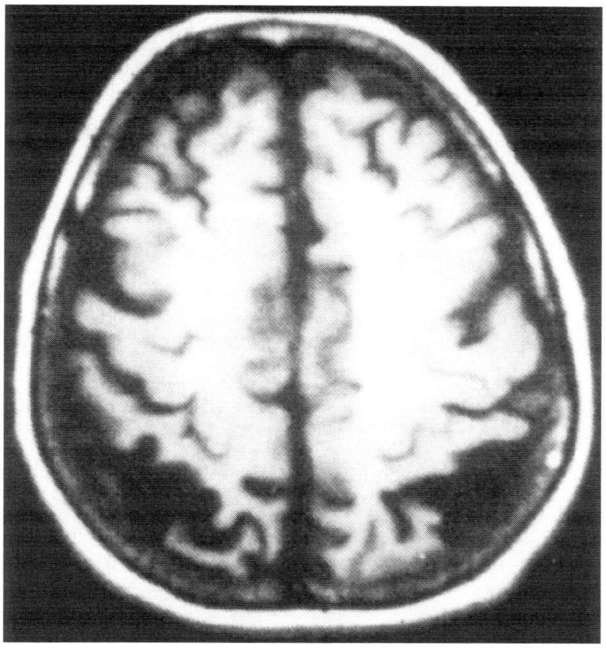

Figure 2 MRI of a 55-year-old patient. Note the marked atrophy in the parieto-occipital region.

Etiologies of these brain lesions include strokes (most commonly from a transient global cerebral hypoperfusion causing border zone infarcts), head trauma, primary and metastatic brain tumors, HIV encephalitis, progressive multifocal encephalopathy, and carbon monoxide poisoning. As illustrated in the second case, neurodegenerative illnesses such as Alzheimer's disease or Creutzfeldt–Jakob disease can also cause Balint's syndrome.

Conclusion

Balint's syndrome refers to a unique triad of visuospatial abnormalities. Most patients have had brain injuries to the parieto-occipital area of both cerebral hemispheres. Patients with these abnormalities can essentially attend to only one visual stimulus at a time, which may leave them profoundly impaired in a world that requires simultaneous synthesis of both entire visual scenes and individual components.

Acknowledgments

This work was supported in part by NIA Grant AG16574 and the State of Florida Alzheimer's Disease Initiative Program.

See also: Agnosia; Angular Gyrus Syndrome.

Further Reading

Ayuso-Peralta, L, Jimenez-Jimenez, FJ, Tejeiro, J, et al. (1994). Progressive multifocal leukoencephalopathy in HIV infection presenting as Balint's syndrome. *Neurology* 44: 1339–1340.
Damasio, AR (1985). Disorders of complex visual processing: Agnosia, achromatopsia, Balint's syndrome, and related difficulties of orientation and construction. In: Mesulam, MM (ed.) *Principles of Behavioral Neurology.* Philadelphia: Davis.
Graff-Radford, NR, Bolling, JP, Earnest, F, et al. (1993). Simultanagnosia as the initial sign of degenerative dementia. *Mayo Clin. Proc.* 68: 955–964.
Hijdra, A and Meerwaldt, JD (1984). Balint's syndrome in a man with border-zone infarcts caused by atrial fibrillation. *Clin. Neurol. Neurosurg.* 86: 51–54.
Luria, AR (1959). Disorders of "simultaneous perception" in a case of bilateral occipito-parietal brain injury. *Brain* 83: 437–449.
Montero, J, Pena, J, Genis, D, et al. (1982). Balint's syndrome. Report of four cases with watershed parieto-occipital lesions from vertebrobasilar ischemia or systemic hypotension. *Acta Neurol. Belgica* 82: 270–280.
Rafal, RD (1997). Balint syndrome. In: Feinberg, TE and Farah, MJ (eds.) *Behavioral Neurology and Neuropsychology.* New York: McGraw-Hill.
Rizzo, M (1993). "Balint's syndrome" and associated visuospatial disorders. *Baillieres Clin. Neurol.* 2: 415–437.

Behavior, Neural Basis of

M. Benoit and P. H. Robert

Behavior is generally defined as the sum of actions and psychomotor reactions that can be objectively observed and interpreted and that interfere with the subject's environment. In its broader interpretation, this term includes functions as diverse as motor activity, language, socially oriented actions, and affectivity expression. Some types of behavior are considered goal oriented because their sensory, psychomotor, emotional, and cognitive components contribute harmoniously to the individual's specific plans. They represent the more hierarchical form of action.

Some behaviors are exhibited only in specific situations in reaction to a type of stimulus (e.g., an impulsive or violent reaction to frustration). A behavioral pathology will reflect cognitive failure, abnormal personality traits, and/or a neurobiological dysfunction. One of the main purposes of cognitive neuroscience is to assess normal and disturbed behaviors and to highlight their probable relationship with normal and abnormal brain functioning (i.e., to link mind and brain).

The history of the presumed relationships between brain function and behavior has involved two opposing views. The first maintains that most motor, perceptive, and cognitive functions can be attributed to specific areas of the brain. This position was born with the phrenology doctrine, which tried to correlate the shapes of the skull with the underlying cortical areas and, to some extent, with the traits of character that these cortical areas were supposed to serve. Although now considered spurious, phrenology largely influenced emerging neurology, whose first solid conclusions were based on the established link between a localized lesion and a particular deficit. One of the first such links was established by Paul Broca, a French anthropologist and surgeon who, in the 19th century, discovered the existence of a brain region dedicated to language. A lesion in this particular cortical area consistently induced a form of aphasia. In keeping with this localization concept, it was assumed that the larger the lesion, the more severe the subsequent deficit. This is particularly relevant to certain instrumental functions, such as language, primary sensory perceptions, and motor components of action.

In the second point of view, the pioneers of neurology suspected that complex or subtle cognitive functions required collaboration between multiple brain regions. The concept of distributed processing still dominates the neural basis of cognition and behavior. This view, which is similar to the concept of plasticity, suggests that the brain can compensate for local dysfunction by activating alternative pathways or systems.

Phylogenesis provides information on the functional organization of the brain. The relationships between the anatomy and function of the brain derive from specific phylogenetic development. The brain can be divided anatomically into three main cores that appeared successively during evolution, giving rise to the concept of the "triune brain." The inner layer emerged in reptiles, and it contains neuronal groups serving consciousness, metabolism, and the main vegetative functions, namely the reticular core, the cranial nerves, and the hypothalamus. This corresponds in primates and humans to the brainstem and part of the basal diencephalic structures. These structures are crucial in arousal mechanisms and biological (e.g., metabolic) motivation processes.

The paramedian layer is essentially composed of the basal ganglia, limbic structures (hippocampus, amygdala, and emerging tracts), and olfactory cortex. It is involved in mnemonic and emotional aspects of motivation, motor coordination, and affective components of action and thought.

The most highly evolved outer layer developed in late mammals but has only achieved its particular predominance and organization in humans. It is mainly composed of the neocortex, which is differentiated into the primary sensorimotor cortex and associative regions, with the latter occupying the larger part of the cortex. Behavior results from synergistic interactions between these three main cores of the brain.

The hierarchical nature of brain organization confers a high degree of coherence on information processing. Some cortical association areas are considered as unimodal (i.e., process information arising from specific perceptual modalities; **Fig. 1**). Dysfunction of these regions will induce specific or behavioral deficits. For example, damage to Wernicke's area situated at the posterior part of the temporal lobe is responsible for relatively pure fluent aphasia.

Conversely, a second type of association cortex processes information in a heteromodal way and thus in a more integrated mode. For instance, the parietoparietal associative cortex integrates information from all primary and secondary sensory cortices, and its dysfunction may reduce or abolish the "sense of meaning" of the incoming sensory information. This may produce alexia (deficit of word meaning), anomia (e.g., deficit of naming objects or colors), agnosia (loss of recognition of objects or living things) when left-sided, whereas right-sided lesions will affect visuospatial construction and orientation.

Brain functioning can be understood in the form of structured neural networks, which run from the top to the bottom of the central nervous system and vice versa, but that also run within specific brain cores that will be systematically organized (e.g., the limbic system, basal ganglia group, and prefrontal lobe circuits). Because of the complexity of neuronal circuitry, it appears that behavioral abnormalities may arise from lesions or dysfunction in specific crucial areas (e.g., amnesia after bihippocampal damage) and from abnormalities in one or several sites of

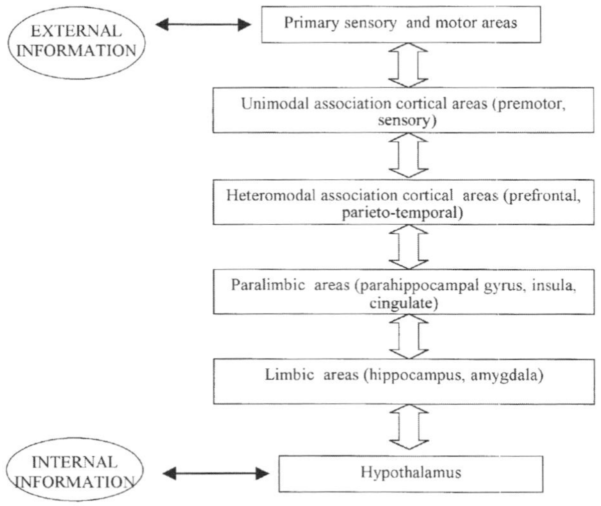

Figure 1 Hierarchical conception of the cortex (adapted from Mesulam, 1985).

a large network. Generally, behavior depends on neural parallel distributed processing, which means that most cognitive and behavioral functions are served by not only multiple serial but also parallel neural pathways.

The brain structures and circuits that play a key role in complex behaviors (i.e., frontal subcortical circuits and the limbic system) are discussed next. Then, examples of dysfunction in these circuits and their clinical consequences are presented. There is compelling anatomical evidence that most complex behaviors are based on the functioning of cortical–subcortical circuits, particularly involving the frontal lobes.

Frontal Subcortical Circuits

Alexander et al. introduced the concept of parallel and segregated frontal–subcortical circuits. These authors described five circuits that unite specific regions of the frontal cortex with the basal ganglia and the thalamus via circuits that mediate motor activity and behavior. Two circuits are involved in motor activity and eye movements, which respectively originate in the supplementary motor area and the frontal eye fields. The remaining three circuits originate in the dorsolateral prefrontal (Brodmann's areas A9 and A10), lateral orbitofrontal (A10 and A11), and anterior cingulate cortex (A24) (**Fig. 2**).

Each of these three circuits circumnavigates the same member structures, including the frontal lobe, striatum (caudate and putamen), globus pallidus, substantia nigra, and thalamus, but the relative anatomical positions of the circuits are preserved as they pass through different parts of the subcortical area. For instance, the dorsolateral frontal cortex projects to the dorsolateral region of the caudate nucleus, the orbital frontal regions to the ventral caudate, and the anterior cingulate to the medial striatum. In parallel to a principal direct loop, each of these circuits has an indirect pathway that includes the subthalamic nucleus (**Fig. 3**).

The effect of the direct loop is to activate the thalamus, which in turn activates the original cortical area as the indirect subthalamic pathway inhibits the thalamus. This organization contributes to modulating the activity of each circuit, which will depend on the relative activity of each loop.

The three nonmotor frontal circuits can be functionally dissociated. The dorsolateral prefrontal subcortical circuit mediates executive functions (i.e., functions permitting the adaptation of many behavioral responses to environmental constraints or changes), cognitive strategies and their behavioral responses when solving complex problems, and generation and monitoring of complex motor or behavioral programs. The role of this system in the control and planning of actions over time is preponderant and is crucial for the relative independence of the subject from environmental contingencies.

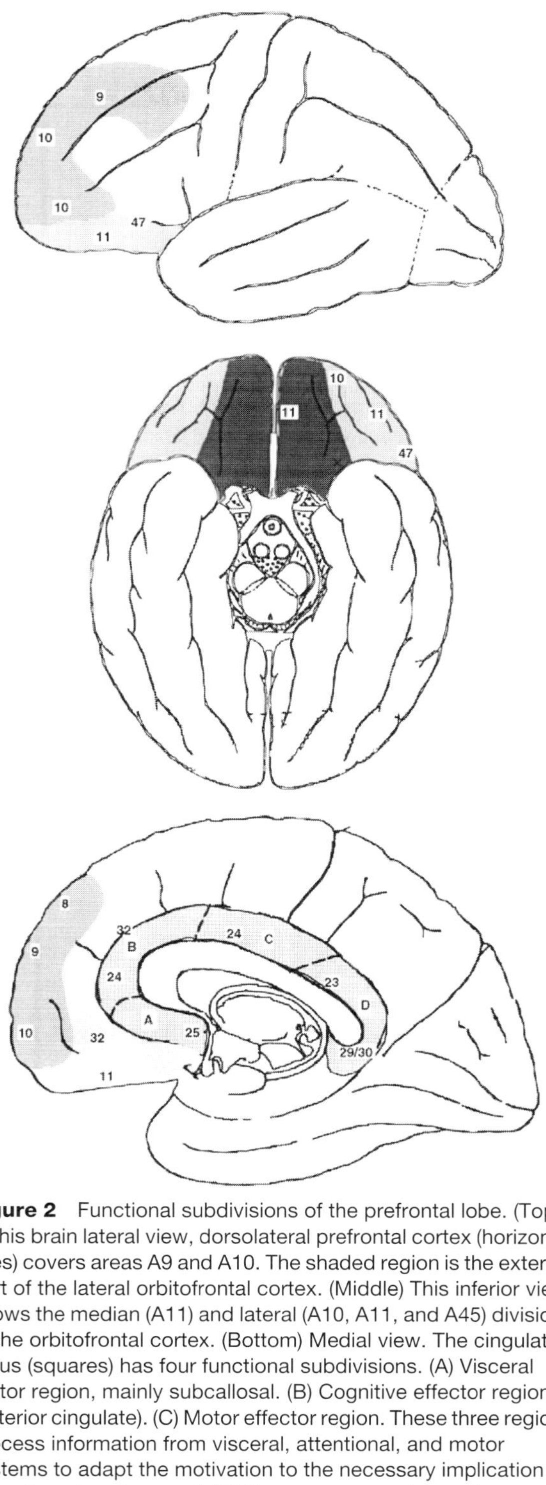

Figure 2 Functional subdivisions of the prefrontal lobe. (Top) In this brain lateral view, dorsolateral prefrontal cortex (horizontal lines) covers areas A9 and A10. The shaded region is the external part of the lateral orbitofrontal cortex. (Middle) This inferior view shows the median (A11) and lateral (A10, A11, and A45) divisions of the orbitofrontal cortex. (Bottom) Medial view. The cingulate gyrus (squares) has four functional subdivisions. (A) Visceral motor region, mainly subcallosal. (B) Cognitive effector region (anterior cingulate). (C) Motor effector region. These three regions process information from visceral, attentional, and motor systems to adapt the motivation to the necessary implication in the external environment. (D) Sensory-processing region or posterior cingulate involved in sensory and memory processes (adapted from Mega and Cummings, 1997).

The orbitofrontal cortex is functionally divided into lateral and medial parts, from which derive two overlapping circuits. The lateral orbitofrontal cortex mediates the emotional aspects of behavior. By linking appropriate

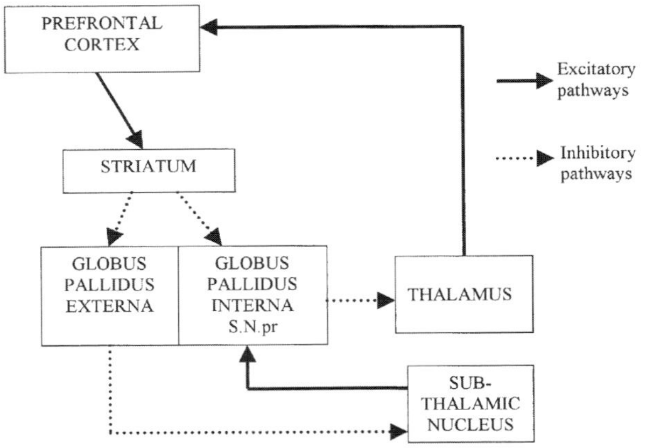

Figure 3 General anatomical and biochemical organization of frontal–subcortical circuits. S.N. pr, substantia nigra pars reticulata.

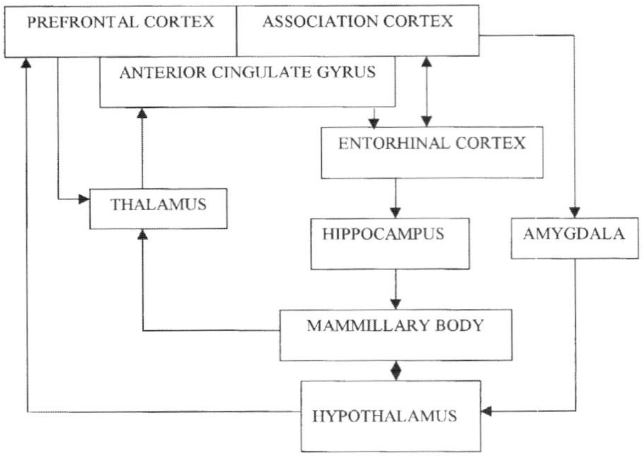

Figure 4 Limbic circuit. The inner loop corresponds to Papez's circuit, involved in memory processes. The outer loop is centered by amygdala and processes emotional patterns linked with experience coming from the association cortex.

behavioral and emotional responses to external and social cues, it plays an essential role in emotional adaptation to the environment and in sociability. It exerts some control over visual and auditory sensory processing (external flow of information) through its direct input from auditory (A22) and visual (A20 and A21) associative temporal areas.

Conversely, the medial orbitofrontal cortex, also called the paralimbic cortex because of its major connections with other limbic structures, integrates more information about the visceral and emotional state of the body, by which its controls motivational input. It receives input from the amygdala, entorhinal cortex, anterior cingulate, and temporal pole.

Because these orbitofrontal circuits receive emotional experiences from different origins (i.e., from the external and internal milieu), they are involved in emotionally and socially appropriate behavior.

The anterior cingulate subcortical circuit serves motivated behavior and is tightly connected to the limbic system, of which it is considered to be a part. Afferents come from the hippocampus, associative limbic cortex in the parahippocampal gyrus, and the amygdala, which provide the anterior cingulate with emotional aspects of the experience and internal motivation. It appears that the anterior cingulate cortex, located at the intersection of the prefrontal cortex with the limbic system and basal ganglia, is an important node linking attention, motivation, affect, and consciousness of the experience. The principal behavioral disorder associated with anterior cingulate dysfunction is apathy.

Limbic System

The limbic system includes a group of midbrain structures particularly involved in emotion, memory, and motivation processes. In neomammals and primates, the limbic structures (**Fig. 4**) form an intermediate level between the internal layers (reticulated area and hypothalamus) and the external layers (sensorimotor and associative cortices and corpus callosum). The limbic system components, especially those located in the medial temporal regions (hippocampus and immediately adjacent structures, parahippocampal cortices, and mammillary bodies), were long thought to be involved only in memory processes. The amygdala has been associated with affective and emotional components of memory.

It is now clear that the limbic system is a necessary pathway in the processing of behavior through two superimposed circuits:

- A hippocampus-centered circuit, originating in the primary sensory cortex and projecting to the prefrontal cortex (dorsolateral and cingulate) but also to the hypothalamus. It comprises the loop described by Papez that contributes to conscious encoding of experiences in suitable attentional conditions, which is the first step of memorization. It is involved in explicit cognitive processes and motivation, in relation with memorized experiences.
- An amygdala circuit that more specifically serves information processing with emotional patterns. The amygdala receives information about internal motivation and the visceral state of the organism but also receives information on the external milieu because of multiple afferents from all the unimodal associative areas. Its interaction with hippocampal formation will determine the motivational significance of the current internal and external state and play a role in the learning of new experiences with emotional coloration. Through its main connections with the prefrontal cortex (medial orbitofrontal), this subsystem computes current information and compares it with remote experience. The result of this comparison and its relevance to the presumed result will control the response by activation or inhibition.

The amygdala has been viewed as a "motivational rheostat." It appears that most behaviors are to some extent dependent on this type of comparison and on permanent access to emotionally charged memorized data.

These two circuits share certain pathways and structures but work in synergy. As the amygdala–prefrontal circuit assesses how relevant sensory stimuli are to the organism, the hippocampal–cingulate division participates in episodic encoding, intentional selection, and habituation. They form part of the frontal–subcortical circuits, and dysfunction of limbic systems will share some features with described prefrontal syndromes.

Damage to the hippocampal division (e.g., after extensive medial temporal lobe ablation) will cause severe anterograde amnesia. Deficient conscious encoding of the experience will interfere with behavior. Lesions of the amygdala are responsible for Kluver–Bucy syndrome, which in humans is associated with placidity, elimination of previous aggressiveness, and lack of association with implicit visceral or affective information.

With the basal ganglia, this limbic system forms a system involved in goal-directed behavior. The hippocampal and amygdala structures are tightly connected to the ventral striatopallidal complex (nucleus accumbens, olfactory tubercle, and ventral pallidum)—a system thought to play an important role in conditioned behaviors. It is assumed that these basal ganglia are crucial in controlling drive-related action. These stimuli can be generated internally through the hypothalamus or externally through the limbic system and neocortex.

The frontal and limbic circuits form closed loops but are also interconnected at the cortical limb or in the basal ganglia (especially the substantia nigra pars reticulata and globus pallidus interna). These links are functionally crucial. For instance, motor cortex projections to the substantia nigra relay information to the associative prefrontal cortex about current motor processes. Reciprocally, projections from the associative prefrontal cortex to the globus pallidus interna may activate the closed motor circuit (e.g., for the execution of learned motor programs). The associative prefrontal cortex is also informed by the limbic prefrontal cortex, through the substantia nigra, on the global motivational state and will therefore control the execution of motor programs by its direct or indirect projections to the motor cortex.

Neurochemistry

Frontal–subcortical structures are linked by excitatory pathways (glutamatergic) and inhibitory pathways (mainly GABAergic), organized in a closed loop to which a secondary subthalamic loop is connected. Other intrinsic and extrinsic pathways exert neuro-modulation of these circuits.

Dopamine projections enhance frontal cortical activity, mainly through three distinct pathways. One pathway arises from the substantia nigra pars compacta, innervating the striatum and contributing to thalamocortical activation. This nigrostriatal system is involved in movement control and is affected in Parkinson's disease, but it is also involved in motivation and cognition. Two circuits originate from the ventral tegmental area and project to the mesial limbic system (nucleus accumbens, amygdala, and hippocampus) and the entire prefrontal cortex. They play a determining role in emotional expression and motivation. For example, a reduction in the activity of the mesocortical pathway will result in a paucity of affect and loss of motivation and planning, whereas secondary overactivity of the mesolimbic system will produce disturbances of thought and perceptions (generally delusions and hallucinations). These radically opposing disorders may coexist in schizophrenia, a frequent and disabling psychosis in which dopaminergic dysfunction is thought to be a core biological disturbance.

Acetylcholine exerts its activation effect from two cholinergic systems: the basal forebrain system (Meynert's nucleus basalis and septum median nuclei) and the pedunculopontotegmental complex. The first system projects to the major part of neocortex and the hippocampus, and it plays a role in the modulation of brain excitability, learning, and memory. The deficit of this system present in Alzheimer's disease is at least partly responsible for many of the memory and behavioral disturbances.

Serotonin pathways, arising from the raphe nuclei in the brainstem, project to the entire cortex and are primarily involved in the regulation of the sleep–wake cycle. They are also important in mood regulation and, to some extent, in affective behaviors because they reduce aggressive and impulsive tendencies.

Clinical Syndromes

Focal lesions, in particular cortical or subcortical areas, may induce behavioral or thought disorders that depend on the degree of specialization of the affected zone, the extension and rapidity of the lesion, and compensation by other linked structures. Behavioral symptoms can also occur in dysfunctions not associated with detectable anatomical lesions, such as in psychiatric disorders. Different types of disorders are shown in **Table 1**.

Conclusion

In summary, the links between brain and behavior derive from a hierarchical organization in which some areas are important for specialized functions, and their lesions are responsible for circumscribed neurological disorders. In contrast, higher cognitive functions and complex

Table 1 Neuropsychiatric Clinical Syndromes

Affected circuit	*Distributed functions*	*Disorders*
Dorsolateral prefrontal	Executive dysfunction	Deficit of search and organizational strategies (memory, drawing, speech)
		Environmental dependency (utilization behavior)
		Perseverations, difficulties in cognitive shifting
	Affective disorders	Depression, anxiety
		Lack of insight and shelf-care
Lateral orbitoprefrontal	Personality disorders	Familiarity, lack of social adaptation
		Disinhibition, impulsivity
	Mood disorders	Euphoria or mood lability
Anterior cingulate	Behavioral and affective disorders	Apathy, slowness, akinetic mutism
		Lack of motivation
		Indifference to painful stimuli
Subcortical syndromes	Motor function	Akinesia, rigidity (Parkinson's disease)
		Involuntary movements (tremor, dystonia, dyskinesia)
	Behavioral and cognitive disorders	Lack of motivation, psychomotor poverty
		Progressive dementia
		Delusions, hallucinations (schizophrenia)
Limbic syndromes	Behavioral and cognitive disorders	Apathy (anterior cingulate)
		Memory deficits (hippocampal complex)
		Kluver–Bucy syndrome (amygdala)
		Delusions (mesolimbic pathway)
		Obsessive–compulsive disorder (mesial orbitofrontal)
	Mood disorders	Depression, mania, anxiety

actions depend more on parallel and superimposed circuits than on limited areas, accounting for the unlimited diversity of normal and abnormal thought and behavior.

See also: Behavior, Neuropathology of.

Further Reading

Alexander, GE, DeLong, MR, and Strick, PL (1986). Parallel organization of functionally segregation circuits linking basal ganglia and cortex. *Annu. Rev. Neurosci.* 9: 357–381.

Chow, TW and Cummings, JL (1998). Frontal–subcortical circuits. In: Miller, BL and Cummings, JL (eds.) *The Human Frontal Lobes*, pp. 3–26. New York: Guilford.

Cummings, JL (1993). Frontal–subcortical circuits and human behavior. *Arch. Neurol.* 50: 873–880.

Devinsky, O, Morrell, M, and Vogt, B (1995). Contributions of anterior cingulate cortex to behaviour. *Brain* 118: 279–306.

Duffy, JD (1997). The neural substrates of motivation. *Psychiatric Ann.* 27: 24–29.

Joel, D and Weiner, I (1994). The organization of the basal ganglia–thalamocortical circuits: Open interconnected rather than closed segregated. *Neuroscience* 63: 363–379.

MacLean, PD (1970). The triune brain, emotion and scientific bias. In: Schmitt, FO (ed.) *The Neurosciences: Second Study Program*, pp. 336–349. New York: Rockefeller Univ. Press.

Mega, MS, Cummings, JL, Salloway, S, and Malloy, P (1997). The limbic system: An anatomic, phylogenetic, and clinical perspective. *J. Neuropsychiatry Clin. Neurosci.* 9: 315–330.

Mesulam, MM (1985). Patterns in behavioral neuroanatomy: association areas, the limbic system, and hemispheric specialization. In: Mésulam, MM (ed.) *Behavioral Neurology*, pp. 1–70. Philadelphia: Davis.

Mesulam, MM (1995). The cholinergic contribution to neuromodulation in the cerebral cortex. *Semin. Neurosci.* 9: 23–28.

Nieuwenhuys, R (1995). Chemoarchitecture of brain. *Chemoarchitecture of Brain.* New York: Springer-Verlag.

Behavior, Neuropathology of

G. Tong and J. Corey-Bloom

The neuropathology of behavior concerns those brain lesions that underlie the human cognitive dysfunctions (e.g., language impairment, memory loss, and dementia) in addition to the neuropathological changes that accompany human aging.

The actions of the human brain subserve not only relatively simple behaviors, such as eating, smiling, and walking, but also complex behaviors, such as learning, memory, thinking, and feeling. The intellectual and emotional human behaviors are so elaborate and diverse that attempts to relate the impairment of specific cognitive abilities to lesions in discrete parts of the brain have only been partially successful. For example, language dysfunction is closely associated with diseases involving the dominant cerebral hemisphere, particularly the perisylvian regions of the frontal, temporal, and parietal lobes. Loss of capacity for reading and calculation is related to lesions in the left posterior hemisphere. Impairment in drawing or constructing simple and complex figures is observed with parietal lobe lesions, more often in the nondominant than dominant hemispheres. Disinhibition, impairment in planning and executing multistepped processes, and loss of social graces are associated with pathology of the frontal lobe.

Dementia involves acquired cognitive impairment and behavioral alterations of multiple domains. Adult-onset dementing disorders are one of the major medical problems of modern society. Until the past decade, neurodegenerative diseases, including Alzheimer's disease, were considered to be among the most obscure and intractable disorders in medicine. In many neurodegenerative diseases, it is still the neuropathologist who makes the definitive diagnosis at biopsy or autopsy. There have been considerable advances in neuropathology that, coupled with clinical–pathological correlation, molecular genetics, cellular and molecular biological techniques, and elucidation of neurotransmitters and their receptors, have contributed to the understanding of dementing disorders.

Neuropathological Changes in the Elderly Human Brain

A realistic definition of normal aging acknowledges that structural alterations, although present, are not necessarily associated with detectable clinical manifestations. At autopsy, the brains of elderly persons often show a number of changes—shrinkage of the overlying folds (gyri) and widening of the sulci, thickening of the arachnoid, an increase in size of the arachnoid granulations, and enlargement of the cerebral ventricles. Brain weights in apparently mentally normal individuals start to decline at 40–50 years of age at a rate of approximately 2 or 3% per decade and eventually reach a value of approximately 10% below maximum by the ninth decade of life. It is unclear what contributes to the brain atrophy—decreasing neuron numbers and/or size or alterations in nonneuronal elements. Changes in neuron numbers, dendrites, axons, cell bodies, and synapses have been described.

Neuron Numbers

Whether there is neuronal loss associated with normal aging remains controversial. Although the majority of early studies indicated a substantial age-related decline in neuron number in the cerebral cortex, recent studies reveal only neuron shrinkage accompanied by an overall preservation of, or perhaps only a slight decrease in, cell number.

Dendritic Changes

Dendrites comprise approximately 95% of the total receptive surface that neurons offer for contact with one another; therefore, maintenance of the size and integrity of the dendritic tree is paramount to ensure that the integrative capacity of individual nerve cells, brain regions, or the system as a whole remains effective. Studies of the extent of dendritic changes in human aging have yielded widely differing results by different investigators. Early work suggested that a reduction in the size of dendritic trees occurred with aging in both the cerebral cortex and the hippocampus. However, recent studies demonstrate a net dendritic growth in pyramidal cells that may reflect a compensatory response on the part of surviving cells to the loss of their neighbors.

Axonal and Synaptic Changes

Less is known concerning changes in axons and synapses with aging. Several studies have revealed an age-related decrease in synaptic density and a compensatory increase in the contact length of residual synapses.

Cell Body Changes

Several investigations have shown a reduction in the size of cell bodies with aging, although the structural and molecular counterparts of this neuronal atrophy are unknown. Other cell body changes include the formation and accumulation of inclusions, such as Lewy bodies and neurofibrillary tangles (NFTs), and increases in the amount of neuropigments. In addition, diffuse amyloid plaques are frequently seen, although usually to a mild extent, in the brains of normal elderly persons.

Alzheimer's Disease

By far the most common dementing disorder in the elderly is Alzheimer's disease (AD). This progressive dementing syndrome is characterized clinically by early and prominent memory loss, visuospatial impairment, disorientation, and language dysfunction. A definitive diagnosis of AD can only be made by biopsy or autopsy. In AD, macroscopic examination of the brain shows cortical atrophy that is much more severe than in age-matched controls and often most evident in the temporal and, to a lesser degree, frontal lobes. The brain is reduced in weight, and there is accompanying ventricular dilatation.

The basal ganglia may also appear atrophied. Microscopic examination of the brain shows extensive neuronal loss that is most evident in the hippocampus and frontal and temporal cortex and is accompanied by astrocytosis. These changes involve other cortical areas and subcortical gray matter structures, such as the amygdala and nucleus basalis. The major neuropathological features of AD are neocortical, hippocampal, and entorhinal NFTs and neuritic plaques. Other abnormalities found in AD include synaptic changes, granulovacuolar bodies, and Hirano bodies:

NFTs

NFTs are intracytoplasmic neuronal inclusions that are most numerous in the hippocampus and temporal cortex. Tangles are elongated, flame-shaped structures composed of paired helical filaments. Their precise chemical composition is unknown; however, a hyperphosphorylated form of tau (a microtubule-associated protein) and neurofilament protein are present. NFTs also contain ubiquitin, a polypeptide of 76 amino acids, whose function is to label effete or redundant proteins for proteolysis.

Amyloid Plaques

These are complex extracellular structures that occur most frequently in the hippocampus and cerebral cortex but are also present in deep gray matter structures (e.g., the nucleus basalis and amygdala). Two types of plaques can be identified morphologically: neuritic (or senile) and diffuse plaques. The neuritic plaque is a relatively large and complex structure. There is an amyloid core, formed from β-amyloid protein (Aβ protein, a cleaved product of β-amyloid precursor protein), surrounded by an accumulation of irregular neuritic processes derived from degenerating axons and dendrites. Activated microglia and, less frequently, reactive astrocytes are present at the periphery of the plaque. Diffuse plaques consist of a loose accumulation of Aβ protein, but these accumulations are not accompanied by dystrophic neurites. The amyloid deposition in the diffuse plaque does not have a dense central core. Diffuse plaques are now recognized to be an age-related phenomenon.

Synaptic Changes

One of the neuropathological features of AD is a major loss of synapses in the cerebral cortex. This synapse loss outweighs that of neuronal loss and leads to a decline in the ratio between neuronal and synaptic densities.

Granulovacuolar Bodies

Granulovacuolar bodies are enlarged lysosome-like structures within which a central dot-like inclusion is identifiable. Their precise nature and mechanism of formation are unknown.

Hirano Bodies

Hirano bodies are brightly stained eosinophilic inclusions with a rod-shaped structure that are found within the cytoplasm of hippocampal neurons. These inclusions are composed predominately of α-actinin, but their mechanism of formation is unknown.

Frontotemporal Lobar Degeneration

Frontotemporal lobar degeneration (FTLD) consists of a group of dementing disorders that cause frontal and anterior temporal lobe degeneration. At least three prototypic neurobehavioral syndromes have been described: frontotemporal dementia (FTD; also called frontal type of FTLD), progressive nonfluent aphasia (PA), and semantic dementia (SD). Clinical features of the most common form, FTD, include relatively early onset (mean age of onset is 54 years); striking behavioral and personality changes (including disinhibition, distractibility, emotional blunting, and lack of insight and judgment); language dysfunction; impairments in attention, abstraction, planning, and problem solving; memory decline; and often family histories of dementia. The clinical features of PA include nonfluent, hesitant, distorted spontaneous speech, impaired repetition, and relatively preserved comprehension. Fluent anomic aphasia with impaired comprehension and loss of knowledge are core features of SD. Although each of these syndromes has a characteristic clinical profile, pathologically each may be accompanied by a number of non-AD, and even AD, neuropathological changes. There is no good clinical–pathological correlation between the clinical syndrome and subtype of FTLD pathology.

At least five distinct neuropathological patterns are associated with the clinical features of FTLD. The most common pattern is microvacuolar degeneration and gliosis lacking distinctive inclusions. It is characterized by neuronal loss and spongiform changes, accompanied by varying degrees of astrocytosis affecting mainly laminae I–III of the anterior cingulated gyrus and the frontal and anterior temporal lobes. There is a paucity of neuritic plaques and NFTs. There are no Pick bodies, cortical Lewy bodies, or inflated neurons. A second type, a pattern of Pick's disease histology, is characterized by intense astrocytic gliosis in the presence of intraneuronal Pick inclusion bodies and inflated neurons in all layers of the hippocampal dentate gyrus and frontotemporal cortex. Pick bodies are rounded, well-circumscribed, basophilic, cytoplasmic intraneuronal inclusions. They are argyrophilic and, on immunocytochemistry, give a positive staining reaction for tau and ubiquitin. Pick cells are distended neurons with a characteristic ballooned shape. A third pattern consists of motor neuron degeneration at the cervical and thoracic levels in addition to ubiquitin-positive inclusions in cortical layer II and hippocampal dentate granule cells. A fourth pattern includes familial FTD with characteristic tau-positive inclusion in neurons and glial cells. The final pattern consists of corticobasal degeneration in the presence of tau-positive but ubiquitin-negative inclusions in cortical layer II and the substantia nigra, with ballooned achromatic neurons and astrocytosis.

Dementia with Parkinsonism

Some neurodegenerative disorders with dementia have prominent parkinsonian symptoms. Many patients with AD, for example, develop signs of parkinsonism as the disease progresses; conversely, many patients with idiopathic Parkinson's disease (PD) become demented at later stages. Numerous neuropathological studies have demonstrated an overlap between the histopathological findings of AD and PD (the hallmark of which is the subcortical Lewy body). In fact, there is a spectrum of neurodegenerative disorders with Lewy bodies, comprising idiopathic PD, diffuse Lewy body disease, and the Lewy body variant (LBV) of AD. In addition, some neurodegenerative diseases (e.g., progressive supranuclear palsy, corticobasal degeneration, and dementia pugilistica) have prominent parkinsonism but lack Lewy body pathology.

Lewy bodies are rounded intracytoplasmic inclusions, usually circular in outline, with a brightly eosinophilic, hyaline core surrounded by a pale halo. Their precise chemical composition is unknown, but they are composed of filamentous structures and give a positive reaction for neurofilament protein, ubiquitin, and α-synuclein.

Parkinson's Disease with Dementia

Dementia is commonly associated with PD as the illness progresses, often 10 years after disease onset. The dementia associated with PD is generally characterized by impairment of executive functions, visuospatial skills, free-recall memory, and verbal fluency, consistent with a pattern of frontal/subcortical dementia. The neuropathological hallmark of PD is the presence of Lewy bodies in the substantia nigra, locus ceruleus, and other brainstem and diencephalic nuclei. There is also evidence of neuronal loss accompanied by gliosis. Neocortical Lewy bodies are distinctly uncommon.

Diffuse Lewy Body Disease

The clinical presentation of dementia with Lewy bodies includes a fluctuating course, visual hallucinations and other psychotic symptoms, and parkinsonian signs. In diffuse Lewy body disease (DLBD), the memory loss is usually less severe. Neuropathologically, DLBD is characterized by the presence of Lewy bodies not only in the pigmented nuclei in the brainstem and diencephalon but also widely distributed throughout the cerebral cortex. Neuropathological findings of AD are usually absent.

Lewy Body Variant of AD

The clinical presentation of LBV is often indistinguishable from that of DLBD, although patients may have evidence of a greater memory deficit. The neuropathological features of LBV are abundant neocortical and brainstem Lewy bodies accompanied by sufficient pathological findings of AD, including senile plaques and NFTs.

Progressive Supranuclear Palsy

Progressive supranuclear palsy is a neurodegenerative disease involving the brainstem, basal ganglia, and cerebellum with gradually progressive vertical supranuclear gaze palsy; parkinsonism (characterized by bradykinesia, gait disorder, postural instability with falls, axial rigidity, and neck dystonia); cognitive decline (especially frontal lobe dysfunction); and pseudobulbar palsy, including dysarthria and dysphagia. The neuropathological features are numerous NFTs in selected structures of the basal ganglia and brainstem, granulovacuolar degeneration, and neuronal loss and fibrillary gliosis associated with the degeneration of various fiber tracts.

Corticobasal Degeneration

This uncommon disorder is characterized clinically by parkinsonism and signs of cortical dysfunction, including apraxia, alien hand syndrome, cortical sensory loss, and dementia. The neuropathological features are cortical atrophy, neuronal loss, and astrocytosis in the cerebral cortical layer II and substantia nigra, with variable numbers of ballooned achromatic neurons that are tau positive but ubiquitin negative.

Dementia Pugilistica

Dementia pugilistica is a clinical–pathological entity occurring in boxers who have experienced repeated head injury. The neuropathological features include a large and fenestrated septum cavum; degeneration of the substantia nigra and basal ganglia; numerous NFTs in the hippocampus, parahippocampal gyrus, amygdala, and temporal neocortex; β-amyloid deposits in the form of diffuse plaques widely distributed throughout the cerebral cortex; and marked loss of Purkinje cells, accompanied by astrocytosis, in the cerebellum.

Vascular Dementia

Cerebrovascular disease is a common cause of morbidity in the elderly. Vascular dementia, especially in association with AD (mixed dementia), accounts for approximately 10–15% of all cases of dementia. A broad spectrum of heterogeneous vascular lesions can be associated with a decline in cognitive functioning.

Multi-infarct Dementia

Multi-infarct dementia is characterized clinically by a progressive stepwise impairment in cognitive functions accompanied by focal neurological symptoms and signs. Unlike AD, memory loss is not usually predominant over other cognitive impairments. The neuropathological features include numerous infarcts in the brain, although the extent and distribution of the infarcts demonstrate considerable variability from case to case.

Binswanger's Disease

This uncommon form of vascular dementia occurs most frequently in the elderly and in patients with poorly controlled hypertension and diabetes mellitus. Dementia, apathy, lack of drive, mild depression, pseudobulbar state, and gait disorder are common clinical characteristics. The neuropathological features include extensive ischemic damage in the subcortical white matter. Such lesions produce widespread loss of axons and demyelinization accompanied by astrocytosis, with relative sparing of the overlying cerebral cortex. Hyalination and intimal fibrosis of the proximal middle cerebral artery and lenticulostriate perforating arteries are also observed.

Lacunar State

The clinical features of lacunar state are dementia, lack of volition, akinetic mutism, hemiparesis, dysarthria, pseudobulbar palsy, small-stepped gait, and urinary incontinence. The neuropathological features are multiple lacunar infarcts in the basal ganglia, thalamus, internal capsule, corona radiata, and frontal subcortical white matter. The ischemic lesions affect especially the prefrontal subcortical circuit, which explains the cognitive, behavioral, and clinical features.

Cadasil

CADASIL is an acronym for cereberal autosomal dominant arteriopathy with subcortical infarcts and leukoencephalopathy. An autosomal dominant disease resulting from mutations in the *notch 3* gene, CADASIL is characterized by recurrent small strokes, often beginning in early adulthood, and subcortical dementia. The neuropathological features include numerous partially cavitated infarctions in the white matter and basal ganglia, with loss of axons and myelin. The media of the small vessels in the regions of infarction contain basophilic granular deposits accompanied by degenerating smooth muscle fibers.

See also: Alzheimer's Disease; Behavior, Neural Basis of.

Further Reading

Feinberg, TE and Farah, MJ (eds.) (1997). Behavioral Neurology and Neuropsychology, pp. 497–638. New York: McGraw-Hill.
Graham, DI and Lantos, PL (eds.) (1997). Greenfield's Neuropathology, 6th ed. New York: Oxford Univ. Press.
Hodges, JR and Miller, R (2001). The classification, genetics and neuropathology of frontotemporal dementia. Introduction to the special topic papers: Part I. *Neurocase* 7: 31–35.
Jellinger, KA and Bancher, C (1998). Neuropathology of Alzheimer's disease: A critical update. *J. Neural Transm.* 54: S77–S95.
Markesbery, WR (ed.) (1998). Neuropathology of Dementing Disorders, pp. 121–143. London: Arnold.

Bilingualism and Aphasia

P. C. M. Wong, Northwestern University, Evanston, IL, USA

Bilingual individuals, sometimes referred to as multilinguals or polyglots, are broadly defined as individuals who know (and use) two or more languages. These individuals possibly acquire (or are still acquiring) the two or more languages at different times in their lives and use these languages at different levels of proficiency. Although the term 'perfect bilingual' has been used to refer to individuals who are equally proficient in the languages they know, often proficiency and use depend on the social/functional situations (e.g., work vs. family settings). Thus, it has been argued that bilinguals are not truly 'two monolinguals in one person' but are holistic, unique, and specific speaker–hearers (Grosjean, 1989). In the case of aphasia (language deficits as a result of brain damage), the various languages can be affected and recovered differently. Consequently, assessing and rehabilitating bilingual aphasics warrant considerations that are different from (or additional to) those associated with monolingual aphasics.

Bilingualism and the Brain

In order to better understand how neurological injuries may affect the linguistic abilities of individuals who speak more than one language, it is important to consider how multiple languages may be organized in the brain. Traditionally, the debate has been centered on 'language laterality' or 'hemispheric specialization'; that is, whether one side of the brain (the left side) is mostly responsible for both languages, whether the right hemisphere contributes in the case of bilinguals more so than in monolinguals, and whether one hemisphere contributes mostly to only one language (Paradis, 1990). Although the issue of laterality has some bearing on predicting the presence or absence of aphasia as a result of brain injury, it only considers the brain in very gross neuroanatomic terms (i.e., left and right hemispheres). Recently, the precise neuroanatomic circuits within and across cerebral hemispheres have been considered, as have other structures in the nervous system, along with factors such as language use, age of acquisition, proficiency, and level and medium of exposure, which potentially have more extensive clinical implications. Recent neuroimaging studies, although involving only isolated linguistic tasks, suggest that attained proficiency and the age of language acquisition may be determining factors in whether the two languages are subserved by the same neural circuits. Wong et al. (2005) found that even though both native Mandarin-speaking and English-speaking adults (who do not speak Mandarin) were able to discriminate Mandarin lexical tone patterns, a feature of the Mandarin language, the two groups used regions near the inferior frontal gyrus but in opposite hemispheres when doing so, presumably due to their corresponding attained proficiency or lack thereof in Mandarin.

Kim et al. (1997) found that early but not late bilinguals showed spatially overlapping brain activations in the left inferior frontal gyrus associated with sentence generation in first (L1) and second (L2) languages. Late bilinguals also showed activation in the left inferior frontal gyrus, but the centers of activation were further apart relative to the early bilinguals. However, since early bilinguals tend to have a higher level of proficiency in both languages, other studies have suggested that attained proficiency might be the most important factor in determining whether or not the two languages are subserved by the same neural circuit (Perani et al., 1998; for a review, see Abutalebi et al., 2001). Converging evidence on brain and bilingualism is being built and shows great promise for the effective assessment and rehabilitation of bilingual aphasics, especially when combined with existing knowledge in the neurobiology of monolingual aphasia. For example, studies suggest that perilesional areas may be recruited in aphasia recovery (Warburton et al., 1999). If, as Kim et al. (1997) suggested, L1 and L2 in late bilinguals (who likely speak L2 with relatively low proficiency) are in the same gross neuroanatomic region but nonoverlapping, then one language may be associated with the perilesional areas, areas that surround the injured area, in certain instances of brain injury (i.e., one language might be more preserved). Consequently, relying on these perilesional areas (and the less disrupted language) in rehabilitation of these individuals might be more productive than rehabilitation of their early bilingual or even monolingual counterparts whose injury might have caused disruption of all language(s) they speak. It is important to note that although some ideas have been proposed (Green and Price, 2001), little evidence exists to support one rehabilitation strategy over another in bilingual aphasia.

Types of Bilingual Aphasias and Patterns of Recovery

Different types of bilingual aphasia, as well as different patterns of recovery, have been reported, involving not only speaking and understanding speech but also reading and writing (Streifler and Hofman, 1976). In addition to cases in which the two or more languages are equally impaired, it has been reported that some individuals showed selective aphasia in which signs of aphasia were evident in one language but not the other (Paradis & Goldblum, 1989). Differential aphasia has also been reported where different types of aphasia were shown in different languages (Albert and Obler, 1978; Silverberg and Gordon, 1979) – for example, conduction aphasia in one language and global aphasia in another. In addition, some individuals showed involuntary blending of grammatical elements (e.g., syntactic and morphologic units) of two languages (Glonig & Glonig, 1965; Perecman, 1984) – for example, combining syllables of two languages, thus creating a new word (Paradis, 1998). This is different from 'code switching,' which involves the alternative use of two or more languages in the same conversation (Milroy and Myusken, 1995). Code switching can function to convey emotional content, to emphasize or clarify the references being made, and to quote (De Fina, 1989), and it is considered to be an important aspect of normal bilingual discourse in many communities (Heller, 1995). Patterns of code switching were also found to be different between bilingual aphasics and normal individuals (De Santi et al., 1995; Muñoz et al., 1999).

It has been suggested that the degree and type of linguistic impairments in bilingual aphasics may be specific to the structures of the language. For example, it has been found that although Mandarin–Cantonese bilinguals showed impairment in the production of lexical tones (pitch patterns used to contrast word meaning), a greater degree of deficit was found in Cantonese production, possibly because Cantonese contains six tonal contrasts, whereas Mandarin contains only four (Lim and Douglas, 2000). In Friulian–Italian bilingual aphasics, the most frequently made errors in Friulian but not Italian involved the omission of the second obligatory pronoun, which is a typical feature of Friulian but not Italian (Fabbro and Frau, 2001). In other words, a type of linguistic impairment may not be apparent in one language because it does not occur as often (or at all) in that language. This also reinforces the idea of assessing multiple languages in bilingual aphasic individuals because impairments in one language do not necessarily predict the same impairments in the other.

With regard to patterns of recovery, as well as improvements in both languages in terms of comparable rate and extent (parallel recovery), individuals show the following kinds of recovery: selective recovery, when only one language improves; successive recovery, when one language improves before the other language; or differential recovery, when one language improves more so than the other. Most interestingly, some individuals show antagonistic recovery, namely improvement in one language but deterioration in another (Paradis and Goldblum, 1989). Some even demonstrate alternating antagonism, in which the improvement–deterioration pattern of the two languages alternates (Paradis et al., 1982). It has also been reported that some individuals showed paradoxical recovery, namely when the patient recovered a 'dead' language – that is, a language the individual once had some knowledge of but had never used it premorbidly for ordinary communicative purposes. For example, Grasset (1884) reported a case of a monolingual French-speaking Catholic woman who started to speak single Latin words and prayers (the language of the church) a few days following a left-hemisphere stroke but was unable to speak French. It is worth noting that it is not known what single factor influences the pattern of recovery (Paradis, 1998). For example, it is not always the case that the language spoken most proficiently premorbidly will be the language affected the most or the least by brain injury or the language that will be recovered first.

Bilingual Aphasia Assessment

When evaluating a bilingual aphasic individual, various important issues warrant special considerations. First, a 'direct translation' is not the same as cross-language equivalency. Different languages have different (non-overlapping) grammatical structures and vocabulary that can potentially influence how thoughts are expressed; consequently, certain linguistic impairments may or may not manifest themselves depending on the language, as suggested previously in the Mandarin–Cantonese and Friulian–Italian bilingual cases. Furthermore, languages are used in different social and cultural contexts, resulting in context-dependent interpretations even for the same utterance. Second, because bilingual aphasics use the two or more languages in different social settings, and because the two or more languages can be affected and recovered differently, all languages the individuals speak premorbidly need to be assessed in order to gain a more complete picture of the aphasia. Third, in addition to any formal measures, a thorough case history detailing use and proficiency of each language needs to be taken because it can potentially affect the rehabilitation process.

Different formal/standardized test batteries are available for assessing aphasics who speak different languages. These include tests that are originally constructed in English but then translated into other languages with considerations of the appropriate linguistic and cultural contexts and/or normative data for the specific groups. For example, there is a Cantonese version of the Western Aphasia Battery (Yiu, 1992), a Spanish version of the Boston Naming Test (Taussig et al., 1992), and a Japanese version of the Communication Abilities in Daily Living (Sasanuma, 1991). In addition, there are also tests designed for assessing bilingual individuals, including the Bilingual Aphasia Test developed by Paradis and colleagues for more than 65 languages and 170 specific language-pair combinations [e.g., an Urdu version (Paradis and Janjua, 1987) and a Bulgarian–French version (Paradis and Parcehian, 1991)] and the Multilingual Aphasia Examination in Chinese, French, German, Italian, Portuguese, and Spanish (Rey and Benton, 1991).

Rehabilitation

Traditional approaches employed in aphasia rehabilitation still apply to rehabilitating bilingual aphasic individuals, such as language stimulation approaches that emphasize individual linguistic units and processes such as grammar and naming, as well as compensatory approaches that target the individual's participation in vocational and social settings despite linguistic impairments. However, additional challenges exist when more than two languages are present. For example, should rehabilitation focus on one or two languages? If one, which one? No one set of widely accepted guidelines exists for selecting one or all languages in aphasia rehabilitation, and evidence and arguments exist for either consideration (Bond, 1984; Chlenov, 1948; Linke, 1979; Wald, 1958). Similarly, it is still unclear whether skills acquired from the rehabilitation of one language can be transferred to another. Evidence suggests that skill transfer across affected languages may be optimal if the languages are closely related (e.g., Spanish and Italian) (Paradis, 1998). As stated previously, different individuals use their multiple languages in different social and vocational settings. In rehabilitation, the affected individual and her or his family should be counseled to consider the preponderating need of one language over another. For example, the social penalty of linguistic impairments in English may be greater for Spanish–English bilinguals whose immediate peers are English-speaking, even though Spanish might be the more proficient language.

Conclusion

Basic knowledge of how multiple languages are represented in the brain and what factors influence representation undoubtedly have bearing on the clinical process. Moreover, careful documentation of linguistic impairment characteristics and the course of recovery in the two languages can also inform us about how the brain is organized. With increasing interaction between individuals from diverse linguistic and cultural backgrounds, due to factors such as immigration, globalization, and state unionization, the number and proportion of individuals who know and use more than one language will most likely increase. The clinical population as well as clinical needs will likewise increase. Thus, a greater basic and clinical understanding of bilingualism and the brain is warranted.

Bibliography

Abutalebi, J, Cappa, F, and Perani, D (2001). 'The bilingual brain as revealed by functional neuroimaging.' *Bilingualism: Language and Cognition* 4(3): 179–190.

Albert, M and Obler, L (1978). The bilingual brain. New York: Academic Press.

Bond, S (1984). *Bilingualism and aphasia: word retrieval skills in a bilingual anomic aphasic.* Unpublished master's thesis, Denton: North Texas State University.

Chlenov, L (1948). 'Ob Afazii u Poliglotov.' *Izvestiia Akademii Pedagogucheskikh NAUK RSFSR* 15: 783–790. [Translated version: Hervouet-Zieber T (1983). 'On aphasia in polyglots.' In Paradis, M (ed.). 446–454.]

De Fina, A (1989). 'Code-switching: grammatical and functional explanations.' *Ressenga-Italiana-di-Linguistica* 32: 107–140.

DeSanti, S, Obler, L, and Sabo-Abramson, H (1995). 'Discourse abilities and deficits in multilingual dementia.' In: Paradis, M (ed.) *Aspects of bilingual aphasia*, pp. 224–235. San Diego: Singular.

Fabbro, F and Frau, F (2001). 'Manifestations of aphasia in Friulian.' *Journal of Neurolinguistics* 14: 255–279.

Gloning, I and Gloning, K (1965). 'Aphasien bei Polyglotten. Beitrag zur Dynamik des Sprachabbaus sowie zur Lokalisationsfrage dieser Störunge.' *Wiener Zeitschrift für Nervenheilkunde* 22: 362–397. [Translated version: Greenwood, A and Keller, E (1983). 'Aphasias in polyglots. Contribution to the dynamics of language disintegration as well as to the question of the localization of these impairments.' In Paradis, M (ed.). 681–716.]

Grasset, J (1884). 'Contribution clinique à l'étude des aphasies (cécité et surdité verbales).' *Montpellier Médical,* January (Observation II), 33–34. [Translated version: Mitchell, C (1983). 'Clinical contribution to the study of aphasias.' In Paradis, M (ed.). 15.]

Green, D and Price, C (2001). 'Functional imaging in the study of recovery patterns in the bilingual aphasia.' *Bilingualism: Language and Cognition* 4(2): 191–201.

Grosjean, F (1989). 'Neurolinguists, beware! The bilingual is not two monolinguals in one person.' *Brain and Language* 36: 3–15.

Heller, M (1995). 'Codeswitching and the politics of language.' In Milroy, L and Muysken, P (eds.) *One speaker, two languages.* Cambridge: Cambridge University Press. 115–135.

Kim, K, Relkin, N, and Lee, K (1997). 'Distinct cortical areas associated with native and second languages. *Nature (London)* 388: 171–174.

Lim, V and Douglas, J (2000). *Impairment of lexical tone production in stroke patients with bilingual aphasia.* Academy of Aphasia meeting at the School of Human Communication Sciences, Australia: La Trobe University.

Linke, D (1979). 'Zur Therapie polyglotter Aphasiker.' In: Peuser, G (ed.) *Studien zur Sprachtherapie.* Munich: Wilhelm Fink Verlag.

Milroy, L and Myusken, P (1995). 'Introduction: codeswitching and bilingualism research.' In: Milroy, L and Myusken, P (eds.) *One speaker, two languages*, pp. 1–14. Cambridge, UK: Cambridge University Press.

Muñoz, M, Marquardt, T, and Copeland, G (1999). 'A comparison of the codeswitching patterns in aphasic and neurologically normal bilingual speakers of English and Spanish.' *Brain and Language* 66: 249–274.

Paradis, M (ed.) (1983). *Readings on aphasia in bilinguals and polyglots.* Montreal: Didier.

Paradis, M (1990). 'Language lateralization in bilinguals: enough already!' *Brain and Language* 39: 576–586.

Paradis, M (1998). 'Acquired aphasia in bilingual speakers.' In: Sarno, M (ed.) *Acquired aphasia,* 3rd edn., pp. 531–549. New York: Academic Press.

Paradis, M and Goldblum, M (1989). 'Selective crossed aphasia followed by reciprocal antagonism in a trilingual patient.' *Brain and Language* 15: 55–69.

Paradis, M, Goldblum, M, and Abidi, R (1982). 'Alternate antagonism with paradoxical translation behavior in two bilingual aphasic patients.' *Brain and Language* 15: 55–69.

Paradis, M and Janjua, N (1998). *Bilingual Aphasia Test.* (Urdu version). Hillsdale, NJ: Lawrence Erlbaum.

Paradis, M and Parcehian, P (1991). *Bilingual Aphasia Test* (Bilingual-French version). Hillsdale, NJ: Lawrence Erlbaum.

Perani, D, Paulesu, E, Galles, NS et al. (1998). 'The bilingual brain. Proficiency and age of acquisition of the second language.' *Brain and Language* 121(10): 1841–1852.

Perecman, E (1984). 'Spontaneous translation and language mixing in a polygot aphasic.' *Brain and Language* 2: 43–63.

Rey, G and Benton, A (1991). *Examen de afasia multilingue: manual de intrucciones.* Iowa City, IA: AJA Associates.

Sasanuma, S (1991). 'Aphasia rehabilitation in Japan.' In: Sarno, M and Woods, D (eds.) *Aphasia rehabilitation: views from the Asian-Pacific region.* San Diego: Academic Press.

Silverberg, R and Gordon, H (1979). 'Different aphasia in two bilingual individuals.' *Neurology* 29: 51–55.

Streifler, M and Hofman, S (1976). 'Sinistrad mirror writing and reading after brain concussion in a by-systemic (oriento-occidental) polyglot.' *Cortex* 12: 356–364.

Taussig, I, Henderson, V, and Mack, W (1988). *Spanish translation and validation of a neuropsychological battery: performance of Spanish- and English-speaking Alzheimer's disease patients and normal comparison subjects. Paper presented at the meeting of the Gerontological Society of America*, San Francisco.

Wald, I (1968). Problema afazii poliglotov. *Voprosy Kliniki I Patofiziologii Afazii*. 140–176.
Warburton, E, Price, C, and Swinburn, K (1999). 'Mechanisms of recovery from aphasia: evidence from positron emission tomography studies. *Journal of Neurology, Neurosurgery, and Psychiatry* 66: 155–161.
Wong, PCM, Parsons, LM, Martinez, M, and Diehl, RL (2004). 'The role of the insula cortex in pitch pattern perception: the effect of linguistic contexts.' *Journal of Neuroscience* 24: *9153–9160*.
Yiu, EM-L (1992). 'Linguistic assessment of Chinese-speaking aphasics: development of a Cantonese aphasia battery.' *Journal of Neurolinguistics* 7: 379–424.

Brain Asymmetry, Evolution

A. W. Toga, K. L. Narr, P. M. Thompson, and E. Luders, University of California at Los Angeles School of Medicine, Los Angeles, CA, USA

The structural and functional specialization of the two cerebral hemispheres has warranted a tremendous amount of research during the past century. A number of everyday occurrences, whether we are consciously aware of them or not, provide evidence for asymmetrical behavioral traits: the foot preference of the snowboarder, the ear preference of the cell phone user, or the inclination for most people to use their right hands for fine motor activities. Neuroimaging and lesion studies of the brain confirm hemispheric specialization (or lateralization) for specific behavioral functions and show pronounced asymmetries in the structure of some brain regions in the two hemispheres.

Behavioral Traits: Language and Handedness

The most recognized manifestations of functional lateralization are the dominance of the left hemisphere for handedness and language. Approximately 90% of the population is right-handed, with the motor control of the right hand confined to brain regions in the left hemisphere that include the precentral gyrus or primary motor cortices. Observations that language is more severely impaired in response to tumors or strokes in the left hemisphere, as first reported by nineteenth-century anatomists Broca and Wernicke, also confirm that language functions are lateralized to the left hemisphere in most individuals. Specifically, the brain regions supporting language production and some aspects of syntactic processing are localized primarily in anterior left hemisphere regions that include the opercular and triangular sections of the inferior frontal gyrus (Broca's area). Language comprehension, such as understanding spoken words, is processed in the left posterior section of the superior temporal gyrus and around the temporoparietal junction (Wernicke's area). Interestingly, language dominance and handedness are not perfectly correlated. Approximately 97% of right-handers have their speech and language localized in the left hemisphere, whereas 3% demonstrate right hemisphere lateralization or bilateral language representation. These relationships degrade to 70% (right-lateralized) versus 30% (left-lateralized) in left-handed individuals.

Structural Asymmetries

Asymmetric behavioral traits and functional lateralization appear to be accompanied by hemispheric differences in brain structure. Although cursory examination of the human brain fails to expose profound left–right differences, more careful comparisons of the two hemispheres reveal a variety of asymmetric features. Macroscopic asymmetries (e.g., of fissurization) are complemented by microscopic asymmetries (e.g., of dendritic arborization) and by neurochemical asymmetries (e.g., in dopaminergic sensitivity). The first structural hemispheric differences were described in the late 1800s. They were macroscopic and concerned regions surrounding the Sylvian fissure, a deep sulcus on the lateral surface of the brain which separates the temporal lobe from the frontal and parietal lobe. Subsequently, increasingly more features of the brain have been shown as structurally asymmetric. Findings based on simple visual inspections have been confirmed and complemented by observations from manual region-of-interest analyses and from contemporary computational image analysis methods that allow whole-brain measurements. However, the results across laboratories are not always consistent, and the functional significance of structural asymmetries is not always obvious or agreed upon.

Petalias and Related Asymmetries

Among the most prominent observations of brain asymmetry are the right frontal and left occipital protrusions of the surface of one hemisphere relative to the other

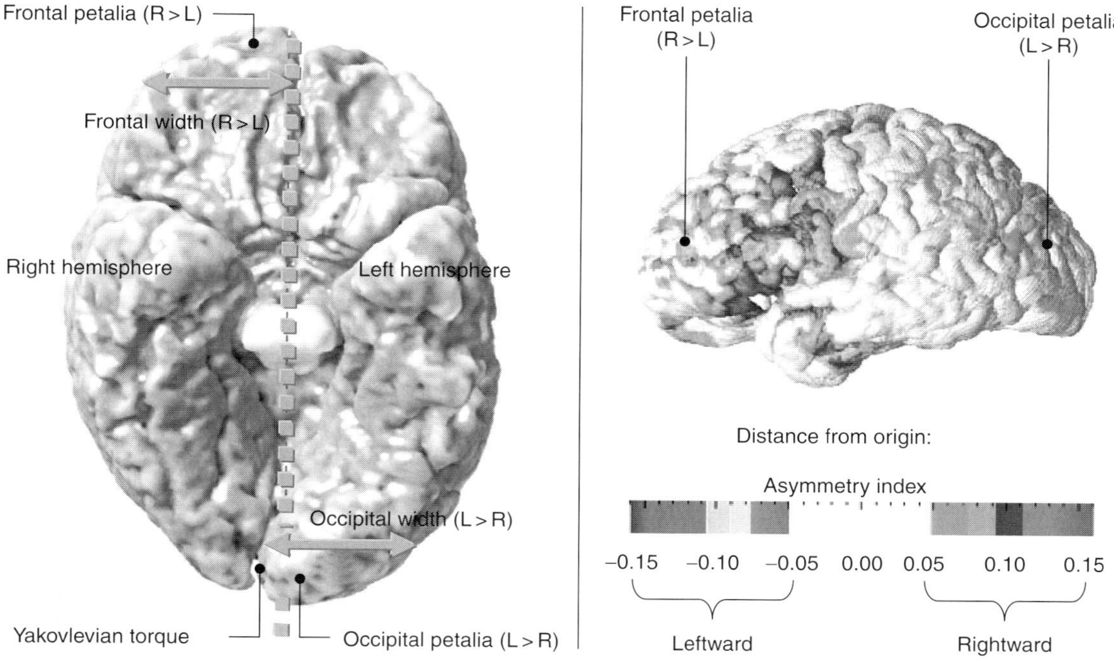

Figure 1 Petalia asymmetry. (Left) A three-dimensional rendering of the inferior surface of the human brain exaggerated to illustrate prominent asymmetries found in the gross anatomy of the two brain hemispheres. Noticeable protrusions of the hemispheres, anteriorly (R > L) and posteriorly (L > R), are observed, as well as differences in the widths of the frontal (R > L) and occipital lobes (L > R). A twisting effect is also observed, known as Yakovlevian torque, in which the left occipital lobe is splayed across midline and skews the interhemispheric fissure in a rightward direction. (Right) The magnitude and direction of hemispheric shape differences, which are estimated by measuring distances from a central point (origin) in the brain to thousands of spatially equivalent cortical surface locations in each hemisphere and by comparing these distances using an asymmetry index. The color scale illustrates anterior protrusions of hemispheric shape in the right hemisphere and posterior protrusions of hemispheric shape in the left hemisphere in one individual. (See color plate 7.)

(**Figure 1**). These protrusions also induce imprints on the inner skull surface, known as petalias. Several studies have shown that these petalias are more prominent in right-handers. A second feature, sometimes regarded as separate from the frontal and occipital protrusions, is that the right frontal region is often wider than the left, whereas the left occipital region is often wider than the right (**Figure 1**). Another related prominent geometric distortion of the hemispheres is known as Yakovlevian anticlockwise torque. This prenatally established pattern encompasses the features described previously and includes the frequent extension of the left occipital lobe across the midline (over the right occipital lobe), bending the interhemispheric fissure toward the right (**Figure 1**). As a consequence, structures surrounding the right Sylvian fissure are also torqued forward relative to their counterparts on the left.

Sylvian Fissure and Related Asymmetries

At the posterior limit, the right Sylvian fissure curves upward more anteriorly than the left Sylvian fissure in the majority of brains. The Sylvian fissure also typically follows a steeper trajectory in the right hemisphere, whereas it extends further posteriorly and is longer in horizontal length in the left hemisphere (**Figure 2**). In addition to shape asymmetries in the Sylvian fissure, neuroscientists have noted that on the superior surface of the temporal lobe, buried within the Sylvian fissure, there is typically only one transverse gyrus in the left hemisphere, whereas there are two on the right. These transverse gyri (Heschl's gyri) constitute primary auditory cortex. In addition, the extent or area of the cortical surface posterior to the first gyrus of Heschl, a brain region known as the planum temporale (PT), exhibits a hemisphere-specific gross morphology. The PT, a structure involved in the analysis of sound amplitude and frequency, is commonly observed as larger in the left hemisphere. This leftward asymmetry appears to be related to the degree of handedness, with right-handers exhibiting stronger leftward asymmetries than left-handers. Finally, Broca's area (the pars opercularis and pars triangularis of the inferior frontal gyrus, respectively) has been shown to be larger in volume in the left hemisphere than its homolog in the right hemisphere, although opposing results exist.

Notably, the structural asymmetries of Heschl's gyri, the PT, and Broca's area – all brain regions involved in auditory processing or speech perception and production – might constitute the anatomical substrate for language lateralization. In support of this hypothesis,

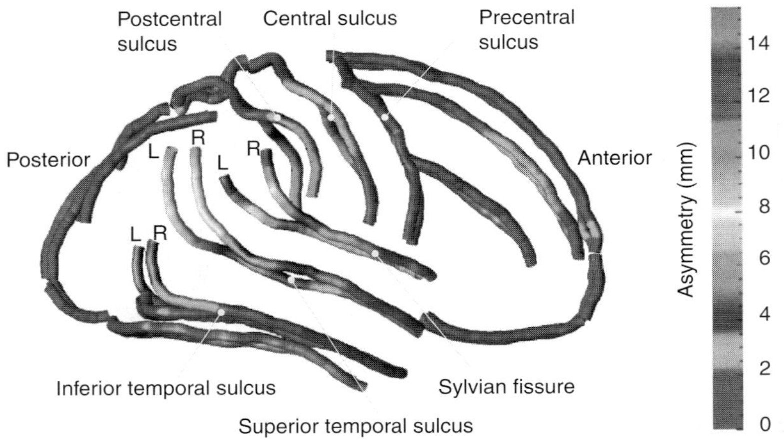

Figure 2 Sulcal asymmetry. From a lateral view, the average shape of the major sulci and fissures for 15 subjects are shown for both the left and the right hemisphere by looking through the brain. The color bar further indexes the magnitude of shape differences between matching sulci in each hemisphere. Note the typical hemispheric differences of the Sylvian fissure (longer in the left (L) and steeper and curving upward more anteriorly in the right (R)), where these asymmetries are largely mirrored in the superior and inferior temporal sulci. Finally, the trajectory of the postcentral sulcus appears to shift more anteriorly in the right hemisphere as opposed to the left hemisphere. (See color plate 8.)

investigators have observed that verbal fluency and the asymmetry of the pars triangularis are correlated in subjects with above average intelligence. In addition, language lateralization appears to follow the direction of the PT asymmetry. Moreover, others have demonstrated a strong leftward PT asymmetry among subjects with left hemisphere speech representation but no consistent PT asymmetry among subjects with right hemisphere speech representation in a sample of left-handers only.

Central Sulcus and Related Asymmetries

The postcentral gyrus is shown to exhibit structural hemispheric asymmetries in the majority of individuals, where the trajectory of the postcentral sulcus appears to shift more anteriorly in the right hemisphere as opposed to the left (**Figure 2**). This asymmetry may be associated with slope and horizontal length asymmetries of the Sylvian fissure and temporal sulci and may reflect asymmetries in the parietal operculum that complement PT asymmetries in right-handed subjects.

Whereas some neuroscientists have reported that the central sulcus is generally deeper and larger in the right hemisphere, other investigators have observed a rightward asymmetry of the central sulcus in left-handers only, or even a pronounced leftward asymmetry in right-handers. In fact, this latter macrostructural leftward asymmetry was complemented by a microstructural leftward asymmetry in neuropil volume (i.e., tissue compartment containing dendrites, axons, and synapses) in the primary motor cortex located in the precentral gyrus.

Other asymmetries have been detected in subcortical regions that are more proximal to the motor effectors. For example, the right cortical spinal tract is found to be larger than the left in 75% of subjects, and the left pyramid crosses more rostrally and is larger than the right in 82–87% of subjects. Possibly related to asymmetries in regions that supplement motor function, a rightward asymmetry in callosal regions that contain predominantly projections from the motor cortices (e.g., callosal anterior body) has been reported. Finally, anterior cerebellar volumes have been observed as larger in the right hemisphere, whereas posterior cerebellar volumes are reported as larger in the left.

Ventricular Asymmetries

Some hemispheric differences in brain structure may go unnoticed in individual subjects due to the high intersubject variability of anatomy. Population-based brain atlases overcome this problem by averaging three-dimensional models of anatomy across hundreds, or even thousands, of subjects while storing statistics on anatomic variation. Ventricular asymmetry is an example of a statistically significant effect that becomes clear in a group average brain map but is not universally apparent in individual subjects. As demonstrated in **Figure 3**, the left lateral ventricle is typically wider and larger than the right, and the left posterior horn is longer in normal adults. This finding is consistent with volumetric measures and may reflect rapid, asymmetric growth in the overlying language systems; it can occasionally be seen in the embryonic brain, using ultrasound, as early as 29–31 weeks postconception.

Tissue Component Asymmetries

Investigators have also examined the asymmetry of brain tissue compartments; they observed significant hemispheric differences of gray matter (GM) in frontal, temporal, parietal, and occipital regions, that include Heschl's gyrus, the PT, the amygdala, and the

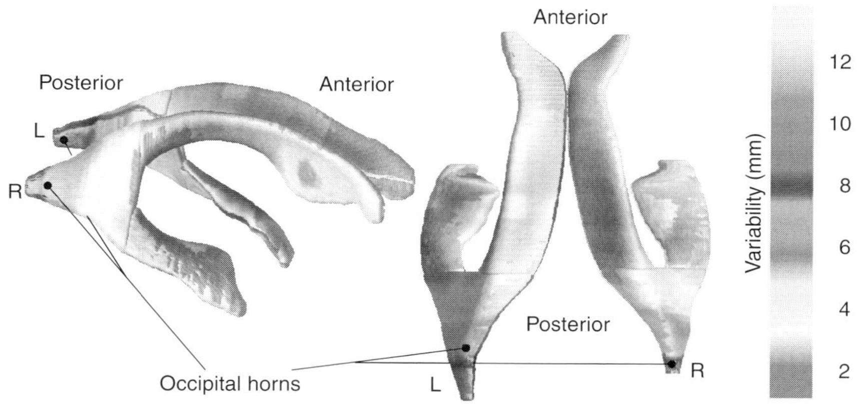

Figure 3 Ventricular asymmetry. The anatomy of the lateral ventricles is shown across subjects ($N = 40$) in three-dimensional view. These maps of average ventricular anatomy show that the left ventricle is larger than the right ventricle. The anatomic asymmetry is clearly localized to the occipital horn, which extends (on average) 5.1 mm more posteriorly on the left than the right. This is consistent with the petalia and torque effects described previously. This asymmetry may go unnoticed in individual subjects due to the high intersubject variability of anatomy. (See color plate 9.)

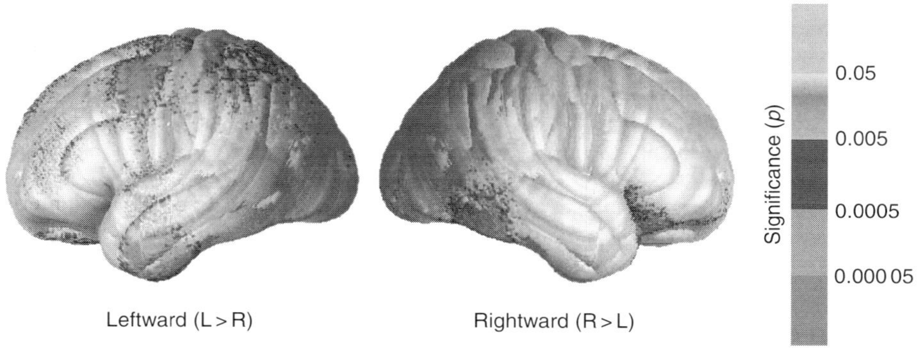

Figure 4 Cortical thickness asymmetry. Statistical maps demonstrating significant hemispheric differences of cortical thickness in a large sample of subjects ($N = 60$). The left brain demonstrates leftward (L > R) asymmetries in the anterior temporal lobe, including the inferior, middle, and superior temporal gyri and the precentral gyrus extending anteriorly to adjacent regions. Two additional larger clusters favoring the left are apparent in the middle frontal gyrus and superior parietal lobe (extending more diffusely inferiorly, covering the inferior parietal lobe and supramarginal gyrus). Smaller clusters of leftward asymmetry are evident in superior frontal regions very close to the midline extending along the longitudinal fissure and in the orbital gyrus. The right brain demonstrates significant rightward asymmetries (R > L) in the posterior inferior temporal lobe and inferior frontal gyrus (comprising the pars orbitalis, triangularis, and opercularis and extending into the extreme anterior tip of the temporal lobe) and near the frontal pole. In general, leftward asymmetries are spread over larger regions than rightward asymmetries. (See color plate 10.)

hippocampus (L > R), as well as in inferior and medial temporal gyrus regions, the lateral thalamus, and the anterior cingulum (R > L). Recent analyses have shown hemispheric differences with respect to the thickness of the cortex, where some regions exhibit pronounced thickness asymmetries that resemble GM asymmetries while other regions reveal distinct asymmetries (**Figure 4**).

Determining Factors of Brain Asymmetries

Heredity versus Environment

Perisylvian asymmetries are already present in children. Their magnitude, however, appears to increase throughout childhood and the teenage years, even after adjusting for developmental increases in brain volume. This suggests that there may be hemispheric differences in white matter maturation, perhaps during the many regional growth spurts in myelination that occur in childhood. It is not certain which factors determine the initiation or amplification of cerebral asymmetries. It appears unlikely that hemispheric differences are solely genetically predetermined. For example, an individual's genotype may not be the only determinant for laterality because many identical twins are discordant for handedness and differ considerably in their expression of PT asymmetry. However, genetic factors appear to influence hemispheric volumes twice as strongly in right-handed twin pairs than in twin pairs with at least one left-hander (non-right-handers). Investigators have hypothesized that the decrement in genetic control of cerebral volumes in non-right-handed twin pairs supports the existence of a 'right-shift' genotype in the majority of the population (expressed as a right hand/left hemisphere bias) that is lost in non-right-handers. Thus, genes appear to be significant contributors to brain and behavioral asymmetries, where the degree of genetic determination also depends on brain structure. For example, GM volumes in perisylvian areas are reported to be under predominantly genetic control, whereas gyral and sulcal patterns have been demonstrated as much less heritable. A number of potential nongenetic contributors to variations in brain asymmetry, including fetal orientation, hormones, and functional adaptations, are discussed later. In addition, gender-specific asymmetries and disturbances in asymmetries as may be associated with some specific diseases are explained.

Fetal Orientation

Asymmetric influences in the prenatal environment may lead to perceptual and motor asymmetries. Two-thirds of fetuses are confined to a leftward fetal position in the third trimester, with their right side facing outward. Lateralization of language perception may result from asymmetries in their auditory experience. For example, the right ear may be better positioned to discriminate high-frequency speech sounds. It has also been argued that asymmetrical vestibular stimulation *in utero* may produce behavioral motor asymmetries later in life. Finally, the exposure to ultrasound in fetal life has been suggested to increase the chances of being left-handed by approximately 30%.

Hormones

In male rats, the right neocortex is thicker than the left. Female rats, on the other hand, display a nonsignificant trend toward the opposite pattern. Notably, castration at birth, which prevents the flow of androgens from the testis to the brain, blocks the formation of the normal rightward brain asymmetry in male rats. Similarly, neonatal ovariectomy reverses the female pattern to the male pattern. Interestingly, maternal environmental or nutritional stress has been demonstrated to reverse the male-typical asymmetry in fetal male rats to the female pattern by both shifting and depressing a testosterone surge that normally occurs on gestational day 18. These findings suggest that levels of androgenic and ovarian sex steroids, before and after birth, play a role in modulating brain asymmetry, at least in rodents.

In humans, the hormonal determinants for sex-specific symmetries are less understood. In their widely cited theory of cerebral lateralization, Geschwind and Galaburda suggested that elevated testosterone levels might be responsible for deviations from the normal dominance pattern (i.e., right-handedness and leftward language dominance, as well as rightward visuospatial dominance). According to this theory, if testosterone levels are higher than normal *in utero*, consequences include a smaller left hemisphere and even anomalous dominance due to a delay of left-hemispheric growth. This model has been posited to explain the different maturational rates of the sexes (with females generally maturing faster) and also to explain the relative advantage males show for right hemisphere visuospatial tasks and that females show for left hemisphere linguistic tasks. It has also been used to explain the greater incidence of left-handedness in males. Finally, hormonal influences might largely determine gender-specific structural asymmetries, as outlined next.

Gender-Specific Asymmetries

Gender differences in structural asymmetries, with larger interhemispheric differences in males compared to females, have been widely replicated where sex-dependent patterns appear to be complemented by behavioral and neuroactivational scores. To explain greater functional lateralization in men compared to women, it has been suggested that either the functions of the hemispheres are less sharply differentiated in women than in men or, alternatively, that larger commissural systems in women may act to reduce the difference in lateralized response scores between hemispheres. Sex differences in brain organization, both within and between hemispheres, are thought to underlie sex differences in motor and visuospatial skills, linguistic performance, and vulnerability to deficits following stroke and other focal lesions.

With emphasis on structural asymmetries, a larger right hemisphere volume has been identified in male fetuses, but no equivalent pattern has been reported in adults. Other studies have shown a significantly deeper central sulcus in the left hemisphere than in the right, but only in male right-handers; interhemispheric asymmetry was reported absent in female right-handers. Similarly, a larger leftward GM asymmetry in males compared to females has been observed in a region posterior to the central sulcus. Possibly related to these findings, pronounced rightward parasagittal asymmetries have been detected in the anterior callosal body in males but appear to a much lesser degree in females (**Figure 5**). Other observations of sexually dimorphic cerebral asymmetries include pronounced rightward asymmetries of the planum parietale in right-handed men compared to right-handed women, whereas left-handed subjects demonstrate the opposite pattern. Gender-dependent asymmetries of the inferior parietal lobe and PT, with males having significantly larger leftward asymmetries and females showing reversed, diminished, or no asymmetries, have also been reported. Greater lateralization of right frontal petalias (in right-handers and left-handers) and occipital petalias

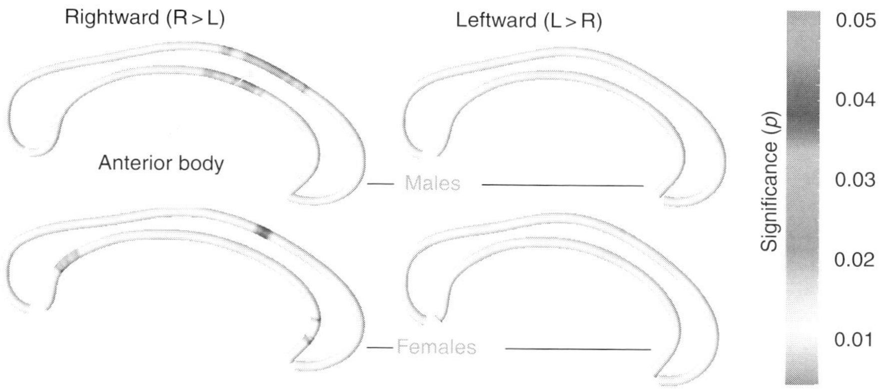

Figure 5 Callosal asymmetry. Statistical maps demonstrating significant gender-specific asymmetries in a large sample of subjects (30 men and 30 women). Differences between callosal thicknesses were measured in the left and right hemispheres several millimeters apart from the midsagittal plane. Rightward asymmetries are largely increased in men, supporting the assumption of a sexually dimorphic organization of male and female brains that involves hemispheric relations and is reflected in the organization and distribution of callosal fibers. (See color plate 11.)

(in left-handers only) in men compared to women further confirm previous findings of greater frontal and occipital asymmetries in men and reductions of the typical asymmetries in women.

Although the majority of studies suggest diminished asymmetries in female brains, a number of studies also exist that either failed to detect significant gender effects with respect to hemispheric differences or revealed even more pronounced asymmetries in females. A study that analyzed hemispheric differences with respect to the thickness of the cortex observed asymmetry profiles that were similar in both sexes. Notwithstanding, hemispheric differences appeared slightly pronounced in males compared to females, albeit a few regions also indicated greater asymmetry in females compared to males.

Functional Adaptation

Experience-dependent plasticity and asymmetric behaviors may also induce different neuronal changes in the two hemispheres. In rats, the asymmetric use of only one forelimb in the postweaning period induces an asymmetrically larger neuropil volume and lower cell packing density in the motor cortex. In mice with a hereditary asymmetry in their whisker pads, a dominant right whisker pad has been associated with left paw preference. Limb preference may therefore be associated with asymmetries in sensory input, although it is not known whether this relationship is causal.

In humans, professional right-handed keyboard players who had received intensive bimanual training from early childhood are more symmetrical in hand skill tests. Moreover, the absolute length of the central sulcus appears related to the age of commencement of musical training such that those musicians who had started early in life with musical training exhibited the longest sulcus on both sides. These findings suggest that some brain asymmetries are not necessarily genetically determined and may result from lateralized motoric activity and/or sensory stimulation.

Aberrant Asymmetries and Disease

Reduced or even inverted volume asymmetries of the PT have been reported in some subjects with reading disorders or developmental dyslexia, as well as in some people with unusual right-hemispheric dominance for speech. Analogously, functional magnetic resonance imaging studies have shown a pattern of brain activation in stutterers that is shifted toward the right in both motor and auditory language areas. This may suggest an inherent difference in the way in which normal subjects and stutterers process language.

Controversy surrounds reports of altered brain asymmetry in schizophrenia. For example, it has been proposed that altered anatomical and functional asymmetries in schizophrenia constitute a genetic and evolutionary basis for the disease that has developed in concert with hemispheric specialization for language. It has also been suggested that schizophrenia is due to an anomaly of cerebral dominance, in which an agnosic right shift gene is suggested to be a major contributor toward schizophrenia pathophysiology. Observations of altered structural asymmetries in patients with schizophrenia include the reversal of normal petalias; disproportionately reduced left hemisphere temporal lobe volumes; reduced asymmetries of the PT, the superior temporal gyrus, and the Sylvian fissure; and alterations in hemispheric gyrification indices. Findings indicating intact structural lateralization in schizophrenia, however, are not uncommon. For example, one study failed to detect schizophrenia-related changes in cortical thickness asymmetries in a large sample of schizophrenia patients compared to demographically similar healthy comparison subjects (**Figure 6**). Thickness asymmetries, however, were shown to vary by disease status in non-dextrals.

Some diseases appear to progress asymmetrically. Patients with semantic dementia generally show asymmetric anterolateral temporal atrophy (typically worse on the left side) with relative sparing of the hippocampal formation. In Alzheimer's disease, a spreading wave of GM loss emerges initially in entorhinal and temporal-parietal cortices, sweeping into frontal and ultimately sensorimotor territory as the disease progresses. This sequence occurs in both hemispheres, but left hemisphere regions are affected earlier and more severely. The right hemisphere follows a similar pattern approximately 2 years later (**Figure 7**). Furthermore, cerebrospinal fluid volumes in the Sylvian fissure appear to rise more sharply on the left than the right in patients with dementia compared to normal controls. Additional left-greater-than-right metabolic dysfunctions in a group of patients with early dementia have been observed using positron emission tomography. These disease-related asymmetries suggest either that the left hemisphere is more susceptible than the right to neurodegeneration in Alzheimer's disease or that left hemisphere pathology results in greater structural change and lobar metabolic deficits.

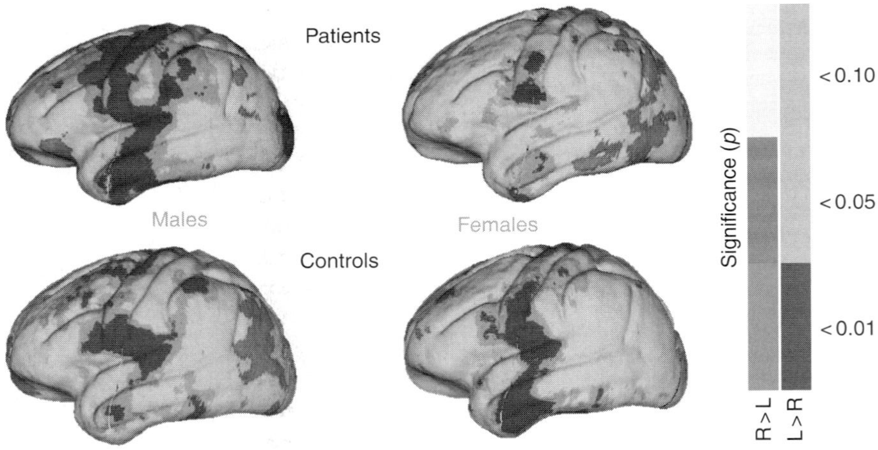

Figure 6 Cortical thickness asymmetry in schizophrenia. Statistical maps show significant hemispheric differences in cortical thickness within groups defined by sex and a diagnosis of schizophrenia ($N = 150$). The patterns of cortical thickness asymmetries appear similar in all groups (leftward asymmetries of thickness in sensorimotor and perisylvian cortices and rightward cortical thickness asymmetries in posterior temporoparietal cortices). Notably, these patterns were not shown to differ statistically in patients with schizophrenia compared to demographically similar healthy comparison subjects. (See color plate 12.)

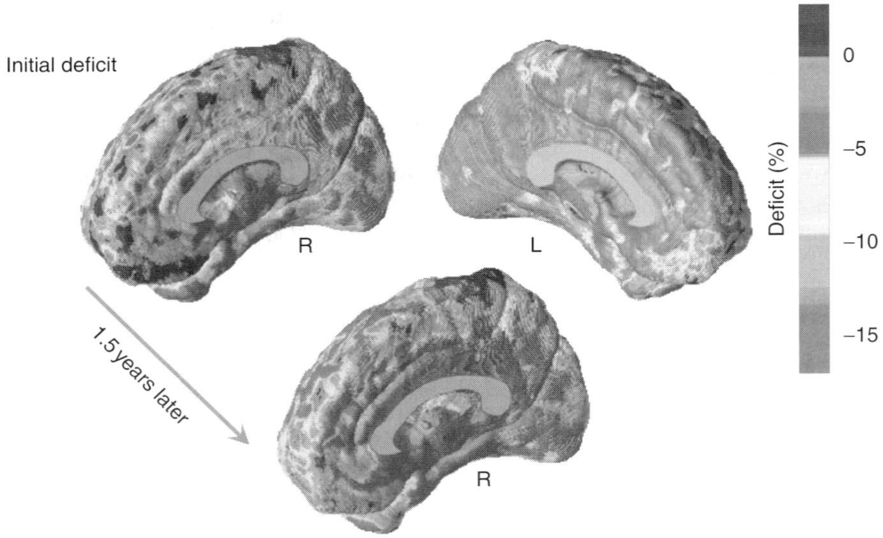

Figure 7 Asymmetrical progression of Alzheimer's disease. These maps show the average profile of GM loss in a group of patients with mild to moderate Alzheimer's disease ($N = 17$) compared to a group of healthy age- and gender-matched controls ($N = 14$). Initially, the right hemisphere (R) is much less severely affected than the left (L), but after 1.5 years the deficit progresses to encompass more of the right hemisphere. (See color plate 13.)

Evolutionary Origins of Anatomical Asymmetries

Brain Size Expansion

Increasing brain size in humans is possibly one of the driving forces in the phylogeny of hemispheric specialization. For example, it has been suggested that the massive evolutionary expansion of the brain may have resulted in a level of complexity where duplication of structures was no longer efficient. Functional incompatibility or the need for simultaneous parallel processing related to increasing cognitive capacities during the course of evolution might also constitute driving forces for the emergence of functionally separated systems. Due to competition for space within the brain, different functions might have been confined to different hemispheres (rather than to different networks within a hemisphere). As a possible consequence, the right hemisphere in humans outperforms the left in the analysis of spatial relations and also shows a tendency for global processes (e.g., with respect to attention and memory storage). The left hemisphere, on the other hand, is specialized in language and shows superiority in categorizing (as opposed to global processing).

Time limits associated with the transfer of information across the corpus callosum between the brain hemispheres may also favor development of unilateral networks in larger brains. It has been reported that more asymmetrical brains have a corpus callosum with a reduced midsagittal area relative to more symmetrical ones. In addition, there exists an inverse relationship between forebrain size and relative callosal size accounting for relatively smaller callosal areas in larger brains. Since smaller callosal areas may reflect fewer or thinner fibers connecting the two hemispheres, this suggests the degree of interhemispheric connectedness decreases with increased brain size.

Left-Hemispheric Dominance for Language

The evolutionary development of language in humans may have led to marked volume asymmetries in structures crucial for speech production and perception as well as for motor dominance. For example, in humans, the left PT – an extension of Wernicke's posterior receptive language area – is up to 10 times larger than its right hemisphere counterpart and is perhaps the most functionally significant human brain asymmetry. Language is commonly lateralized to the left hemisphere, and some argue that this is advantageous: (1) it avoids competition between hemispheres for control of the muscles involved in speech, and (2) it may be more efficient to transfer language information between collections of focal areas in a single hemisphere. The main pitfall in arguing that left hemisphere dominance provides an evolutionary advantage is that bilateral language representation, or rightward dominance, is also common. In addition, leftward dominance does not, in general, provide a cognitive advantage.

Left-Hemispheric Dominance for Handedness

A hypothesis first proposed by Condillac in 1746 suggests that the left hemisphere's dominance for language processing evolved from its control of the right hand. The left-hemispheric programming of skilled movement and gesture may have evolved to encompass control of the motor systems involved in speech. Broca's area, in particular, is a premotor module that sequences complex articulations that are not limited to speech. Great apes, including chimpanzees and gorillas, also have an enlarged area 44 (Broca's area). This area controls muscles of the face and vocal tract but is not as well connected with the homolog of Wernicke's area as it is in humans. It has been suggested that nonhuman primates developed a homolog of Broca's area due to a link between primate vocalization and gesture: captive apes usually gesture with the right hand as they vocalize. Research on indigenous gestural languages invented by children in Taiwan and in Nicaragua provides some evidence for the innate relation between gesture and language. Functional neuroimaging studies also suggest that deaf subjects using a gestural sign language activate many of the systems involved in verbal language production. These congruencies in functional anatomy may support the hypothesis that verbal language evolved from gestural language as an outgrowth of the already asymmetric motor control system. It was proposed that language is a relatively recent evolutionary adaptation (not more than 200 000 years old), where the Neanderthal vocal tract was incapable of articulating the range of modern human speech sounds.

Brain Asymmetries in Nonhuman Species

Functional asymmetries in the brain were initially thought to be uniquely human, reflecting unique processing demands required to produce and comprehend language. Nonetheless, functional and structural asymmetries have been identified in nonhuman primates and many other species. For example, Japanese macaques exhibit a right ear advantage for processing auditory stimuli, passerine birds produce song primarily under left hemisphere control, and frogs utilize their left hemisphere to control clasping vocalizations. Moreover, with respect to structural asymmetries, cerebral petalias are seen in phylogenetically older primates (and other species), as evidenced by endocasts from fossilized cranial bones. Similarly, the PT asymmetry also appears in higher nonhuman primates. In most great apes, the Sylvian fissure is longer and straighter on the left side than on the right. It has also been observed that the right hemisphere is generally larger than the left in rats, mice, rabbits, and cats. Although asymmetries in nonhuman species can be strikingly similar to those in humans, asymmetries defined in animal studies may not be easy to extrapolate to humans because the precursors of language-related asymmetries in humans may not be present in other species. The mechanisms that underlie some cerebral asymmetries in humans might differ substantially from those that underpin brain asymmetry in other mammals. Notwithstanding, the existence of hemispheric differences in nonhumans indicates that brain asymmetry is neither unique to humans nor completely dependent on the development of language.

Acknowledgments

This work was supported by NIBIB/NINDS/NIMG grant P01 EB001955 and NIH/NCRR resource grant P41 RR013642. Additional support was provided by the National Institutes of Health through the NIH Roadmap for Medical Research grant U54 RR021813. Additional support was also provided by the National Institute of Mental Health grant K01 MH073990.

See also: Brain Damage, Functional Reorganization; Dichotic Listening Studies of Brain Asymmetry; Hemispheric Specialization and Cognition.

Further Reading

Galaburda, AM and Geschwind, N (1981). Anatomical asymmetries in the adult and developing brain and their implications for function. *Advances in Pediatrics* 28: 271–292.
Geschwind, N and Galaburda, AM (1987). *Cerebral Lateralization: Biological Mechanisms, Associations, and Pathology.* Cambridge: MIT Press.
Hellige, JB (1990). Hemispheric asymmetry. *Annual Review of Psychology* 41: 55–80.
Hugdahl, K and Davidson, RJ (2003). *The Asymmetrical Brain*. Cambridge, MA: MIT Press.
Previc, FH (1991). A general theory concerning the prenatal origins of cerebral lateralization in humans. *Psychological Review* 98: 299–334.
Toga, AW and Thompson, PM (2003). Mapping brain asymmetry. *Nature Reviews Neuroscience* 4: 37–48.
Zilles, K, Dabringhaus, A, Geyer, S, et al. (1996). Structural asymmetries in the human forebrain and the forebrain of non-human primates and rats. *Neuroscience and Biobehavioral Reviews* 20: 593–605.

Relevant Websites

http://www.loni.ucla.edu – Laboratory of Neuro Imaging, UCLA.
http://nihroadmap.nih.gov – National Institutes of Health Roadmap for Medical Research.

Brain Damage, Functional Reorganization

J. Grafman, R. Zahn, and E. Wassermann, National Institute of Neurological Disorders and Stroke, Bethesda, MD, USA

Published by Elsevier Ltd.

Introduction

Recent research in cognitive neuroscience has made great strides in assigning behavioral functions to discrete areas of the brain and describing the knowledge, representational elements, and processes that are subserved by the tissue within their borders. Although much work remains to be done to provide a complete functional atlas of the thinking brain, one fact is generally accepted about how representational knowledge is stored. That is, the brain appears to be composed of modular networks within which a particular representational element is homogeneously represented. Such elements may range in complexity from the edge detectors, used in visual processing and stored in the occipital cortex, to high-level plan representations used to guide behavior and stored in the prefrontal cortex. To perform a cognitive or perceptual function, sets of modules are activated in concert. Thus, the human brain can be subdivided into functional modules, which must be combined to perform a task.

Neuroplasticity is a term used to describe structural and functional changes at the genetic, molecular, neuronal, system, and behavioral levels. Such changes may reflect new experience and learning or can occur as a reaction to brain damage. Although a great deal of scientific literature describes neuroplasticity at the molecular, structural, and system levels in animals, we focus on neuroplastic changes at the system level that can be observed in humans. Current thinking about systems neuroplasticity suggests that at least four kinds of neuroplastic changes operate at the representational module level after brain damage: (1) homologous area adaptation, (2) cross-modal reassignment, (3) potentiation of topographic representations, and (4) compensatory masquerade.

Homologous Area Adaptation

One form of neuroplasticity, homologous area adaptation, appears to prevail before children reach puberty and underlies the observation that damage to a particular brain region can be compensated for by shifting its functions to other brain areas, often to the homologous region of the opposite hemisphere. An implication of this mechanism is that the brain area accepting the new operation will be more 'crowded' with functional representations (both the new and the 'usual' representations are now stored in a region that before stored only the usual representation). This crowding leads to a sparser or 'lower resolution' representation of knowledge or sensory input within both modules and makes degraded performance or interference likely when the two functions are activated simultaneously. This form of neuroplastic change is reported less often in adults. This may be because regions of the developing brain are less 'committed' to specific cognitive processes, because they have not yet been encountered in school (e.g., mathematics) or demanded by the environment (e.g., complex social interactions).

We studied an adolescent who had incurred a severe right parietal lobe brain injury as a young child. Despite the severity and location of the injury, evaluation showed that the boy had developed essentially normal visuospatial function but had impaired arithmetic skills. We inferred that at the time of injury, the left parietal region assumed some of the functions normally stored in the right parietal lobe. Because most calculation skill is acquired in school, the injury and plastic change occurred before the age of arithmetic acquisition. Thus, we argued, spatial processes had claimed the left parietal region before arithmetic instruction, making it more difficult for the patient to learn and store mathematical facts. Functional magnetic resonance imaging (fMRI) of his brain activity during arithmetic processing indicated that he activated the left parietal lobe (among other regions). This finding implied that that the left parietal lobe was still programmed to store arithmetic facts even though it was now also committed to spatial processing, leading to the degradation of the subject's arithmetic ability.

Some investigators have claimed that the proportion of a functional region that is damaged determines the amount of homologous region adaptation that occurs. The underlying principle is as follows. Neighboring and homologous cortical regions have primary and secondary, or latent, functional assignments. Usually the secondary function is inhibited competitively by output from the nearby or contralateral brain region where that function is primary. Therefore, cortical regions are only able to express their secondary functions when competitive inhibition is removed. Given this logic, plasticity might be promoted by incurring complete rather than partial damage to a particular brain region, because when the damaged region is completely incapacitated, it cannot inhibit the expression of its usual function elsewhere in the brain.

We studied another patient who suffered a large infarction that destroyed most of the left cerebral hemisphere, although he had some spared and functionally active islands of tissue in the left parietal and frontal areas. This patient could read words but not nonwords, and he had great difficulty calculating. On fMRI, word reading activated a broadly distributed network of areas in the right hemisphere. Attempts to read nonwords were unsuccessful and did not produce significant activation in either hemisphere. This suggested that the right hemisphere had assumed some functions of the left hemisphere. However, although the left hemisphere substrate for reading known words was destroyed, allowing the right hemisphere to assume its function, the additional ability to read nonwords (a crucial skill reflecting the ability to learn to read new words) did not transfer and was lost with the injury. This indicates that functional neuroplasticity may be more limited in adults. Interestingly, during fMRI scanning, while the patient was performing arithmetic fact verification, both right and left parietal lobe activation was found. However, the left parietal activation was found in locations around the periphery of the area in the brain devoted to this ability. Even with this pattern, the patient performed poorly, although his accuracy increased slightly after a week of training with a concomitant increase in cortical activation. We suspect that the remaining left parietal tissue was inadequate for accurate calculation but still inhibited the right parietal cortex from assuming more of a role in calculation.

Cross-Modal Reassignment

A second form of neuroplasticity, cross-modal reassignment, involves the introduction of new sensory inputs to a brain region that has been deprived of its main sensory input. For example, positron emission tomography (PET) and fMRI studies of tactile discrimination have shown that adults who became blind early in childhood have somatosensory input to area V1 of the occipital cortex, whereas sighted controls do not. Presumably, in the blind, such input succeeds in activating the representations stored in area V1, because the cognitive operations in that area are somewhat independent of the modality of input, and their function is helpful in making the discriminations between geometric patterns required for reading Braille characters. In this study, only tactile discrimination of Braille letters, as opposed to simply palpating fields of nonsense dots or performing verbal language tasks, activated V1 in the early blind. In contrast, in sighted people exposed to the same stimuli and tasks, the V1 activation was absent and there was evidence of decreased activation in area V1 (suggesting that recruiting the brain regions that usually process the tactile input (e.g., parietal cortex) ordinarily inhibits or depotentiates the visual system). The fact that visual cortex activation is important in Braille reading and may account for the superior ability of blind subjects was demonstrated in a study in which transcranial magnetic stimulation (TMS) was delivered over the occipital cortex. This stimulation, designed to interfere with cortical processing, dramatically impaired the performance of the early blind but not sighted or late-life blinded individuals. The fact that such cross-modal sensory plasticity is possible and requires an early lesion suggests that afferent connections from multiple sensory sources may be latent in cortical areas such as V1, which is considered by most clinicians to be rigidly assigned to visual processing. Presumably these secondary inputs atrophy over time under the competitive influence of the primary input. Undoubtedly, limits exist to this form of neuroplasticity. For example, color processing cells in the occipital cortex are so specialized for visual input that they would be unlikely to accept other forms of sensory input.

Potentiation of Topographic Representations

This form of neuroplasticity involves changes within brain regions devoted to a particular kind of knowledge or operation. Studies in the motor cortex indicate that the intracortical connections devoted to a processing function may become temporarily enhanced or even enlarged with skill acquisition or frequent exposure to a stimulus. This enhancement may, in turn, result in topographic expansion of the area of cortex devoted to the function or representation. In two studies using two different techniques (TMS and electroencephalography (EEG)), we demonstrated that repetition of a cued sequence of key presses caused increasing excitability of neurons in the representation of the performing hand in the early stages of learning while the pattern was still implicit (i.e., the subjects did not become aware of the pattern, but their responses were becoming faster). When learning became explicit (i.e., the subjects could produce it without cueing), the excitability of the hand representation returned to baseline. This type of change, measured as a larger EEG potential before movement and a larger muscle response to TMS of the hand representation, could result from topographic expansion of this representation by unmasking of latent connections within the cortex or from the cortex to the spinal cord. Although EEG and TMS cannot measure motor map size, changes seen in fMRI studies during, and even weeks after, motor learning seem to bear this out. Evidence suggests that rapid enlargement of cortical maps can persist in individuals who develop or are trained in a particular skill that they use routinely. The meaning of map expansion is still unclear. One possible explanation for a change in map size is that continual input may overload the processing capacity of a local cortical network and signal it to expand by recruiting new neurons from adjacent tissue into the network to handle the increased load. Another possibility is that before enough synaptic change has occurred for the minimal necessary volume of cortex to perform the skill, an enlarged area of the network is recruited. With increasing practice, the system becomes more and more efficient, restricting activity to a few highly dedicated and stimulus specific neural elements.

Compensatory Masquerade

The fourth form of neuroplasticity, compensatory masquerade, means the novel use of an established and intact cognitive process to perform a task previously dependent on an impaired cognitive process. This can be a subtle change detectable only with fine-grained cognitive tasks. For example, there may be a single route from home to the office. One way to navigate that route may depend most upon spatial processes, is implicitly stored, and is performed rapidly. Another way to get to work would depend on verbal labeling of landmarks that are remembered explicitly and processed more deliberately. A large brain injury may affect both way-finding processes, but typically one is relatively spared. The patient may then be able to use the spared strategy to navigate the same route that was previously dependent on the impaired strategy. Unless a neuropsychologic study carefully evaluated both processes in some detail, an observer could be misled into thinking that a more fundamental form of neuroplasticity had occurred (e.g., homologous area adaptation).

Discussion

We have reviewed four major forms of neuroplasticity that can be studied and promoted in healthy human volunteers and patients after brain damage. The neurophysiologic processes that underlie plasticity continue to be studied at the level of synaptic physiology and ultrastructure after repeated stimulation.

Recently it has become clear that neurogenesis, synapse formation, and remodeling of axons and dendrites occur in adult human brains. Neurogenesis in adulthood appears to occur in both the hippocampus and subventricular zone. It is unclear what functional role new neurons play in previously existing networks. It would appear that neurogenesis and cortical rewiring would be ideal mechanisms to assist brain regions partially damaged by stroke and other lesions to recover their functions. However, because recovery of function after brain injury is rarely if ever complete, their contributions to recovery of function appear to be restricted. The neuroanatomical, physiological, and molecular bases of these restrictions to plasticity are the focus of intense investigation.

By focusing on the four forms of plasticity previously outlined, fundamental questions about how functional cooperation between brain regions is achieved can be asked. Why does the ability to shift functions between sites decline over development and aging? This may be the result of the necessity to stabilize connectivity between maturing brain areas dedicated to particular functions. The increasing degree and stability of this connectivity suggests that the networks themselves make a commitment to a particular functional representation. If functional substitution was permitted beyond the early stages of the formation of these networks, then continuous and substantial reorganization of distributed networks would be required for their efficient operation. Therefore, it is likely that the increasing connectivity required for learning is directly related to the increasing functional commitment of brain areas throughout life.

A second question about plasticity emerges from the observation of cross-modal activation of V1 in the early blind. Traditional notions about deafferentation lead one to expect atrophy and or 'denervation hypersensitivity' of a maladaptive kind in the visual areas of the blind. Instead, evidence suggests that the modality-independent processing capabilities of the visual cortex (e.g., discrimination of width, angles, feature conjunctions) can be used to process spatial information from more than one source. This is a remarkable departure from the idea that cortical functions are assigned to areas entirely based on input routing rather than processing architecture.

Clinical approaches to enhancing recovery of cognitive function in patients recovering from brain injury have historically been implemented in an atheoretical way. Early approaches relied simply on massed repetitive practice in various domains of function (e.g., memory, attention). More recent efforts at rehabilitation have begun to use treatments motivated by cognitive theory. Despite this increasing sophistication, there have been too few clinical trials that included large numbers of subjects or adequate controls, and most rehabilitation studies have compared programs of stimulation to supposedly neutral interactions or to no intervention at all rather than investigating the validity of specific interventions on specific outcomes. Furthermore, the therapeutic strategies used in these studies were not always developed with systems and cognitive neuroscience findings in mind. Although some recent counterexamples exist, the rehabilitation field has often lagged behind other specialties in clinical neuroscience in adapting laboratory findings to the clinic.

Fortunately, many conceptual frameworks for neuroplasticity exist that could lead to new rehabilitation methods. We suggest that proven methods for inducing changes in the cortical topography at the network level and rerouting or unmasking latent input and output to the affected network should guide the development of new rehabilitation techniques. Testing of paradigms designed to cause and manipulate neuroplasticity in healthy volunteers and patients will help investigators find the optimal conditions for neuroplastic change. Such paradigms may also lead to 'challenge' studies using pharmacologic and other agents to enhance or prevent neuroplastic changes. Indeed, the future looks promising as we probe the limits of functional neuroplasticity in adult humans while answering fundamental questions about the stable and dynamic topography of information processing.

See also: Brain Asymmetry, Evolution.

Further Reading

Aglioti, S, Bonazzi, A, and Cortese, F (1994). Phantom lower limb as a perceptual marker of neural plasticity in the mature human brain. *Proceedings of the Royal Society of London, Series B: Biological Sciences* 255(1344): 273–278.

Buonomano, DV, Hickmott, PW, and Merzenich, MM (1997). Context-sensitive synaptic plasticity and temporal-to-spatial transformations in hippocampal slices. *Proceedings of the National Academy of Sciences of the United States of America* 94(19): 10403–10408.

Chklovskii, DB, Mel, BW, and Svoboda, K (2004). Cortical rewiring and information storage. *Nature* 431: 782–788.

Chugani, HT, Muller, RA, and Chugani, DC (1996). Functional brain reorganization in children. *Brain Development* 18(5): 347–356.

Cohen, LG, Celnik, P, Pascual-Leone, A, et al. (1997). Functional relevance of cross-modal plasticity in blind humans. *Nature* 389(6647): 180–183.

Debanne, D (1996). Associative synaptic plasticity in hippocampus and visual cortex: Cellular mechanisms and functional implications. *Reviews in Neuroscience* 7(1): 29–46.

Donoghue, JP (1995). Plasticity of adult sensorimotor representations. *Current Opinion in Neurobiology* 5(6): 749–754.

Gilbert, CD (1996). Plasticity in visual perception and physiology. *Current Opinion in Neurobiology* 6(2): 269–274.

Goldman, S and Plum, F (1997). Compensatory regeneration of the damaged adult human brain: Neuroplasticity in a clinical perspective. *Advances in Neurology* 73: 99–107.

Gould, E, Reeves, AJ, Graziano, MSA, and Gross, CG (1999). Neurogenesis in the neocortex of adult primates. *Science* 286: 548–552.

Grafman, J and Litvan, I (1999). Evidence for four forms of neuroplasticity. In: Grafman, J and Christen, Y (eds.) *Neuronal Plasticity: Building a Bridge from the Laboratory to the Clinic*, pp. 131–140. Berlin: Springer.

Heiss, WD and Teasel, RW (2006). Brain recovery and rehabilitation. *Stroke* 37: 314–316.

Ide, CF, Scripter, JL, Coltman, BW, et al. (1996). Cellular and molecular correlates to plasticity during recovery from injury in the developing mammalian brain. *Progress in Brain Research* 108: 365–377.

Karni, A, Meyer, G, Rey-Hipolito, C, et al. (1998). The acquisition of skilled motor performance: Fast and slow experience-driven changes in primary motor cortex. *Proceedings of the National Academy of Sciences of the United States of America* 95: 861–868.

Keyvani, K and Schallert, T (1998). Plasticity-associated molecular and structural events in the injured brain. *Journal of Neuropathology and Experimental Neurology* 61(10): 831–840.

Klintsova, AY and Greenough, WT (1998). Synaptic plasticity in cortical systems. *Current Opinion in Neurobiology* 9: 203–208.

Kolb, B, Gibb, R, and Robinson, TE (1998). Brain plasticity and behavior. *Current Directions in Psychological Science* 12(1): 1–5.

Levin, HS, Scheller, J, Rickard, T, et al. (1998). Dyscalculia and dyslexia after right hemisphere injury in infancy. *Archives of Neurology* 53(1): 88–96.

Leviton, A, Bellinger, D, Pagano, M, and Rabinowitz, M (1998). Models of delayed recovery. *Journal of Child Neurology* 10(5): 385–391.

Lledo, PM, Alonso, M, and Grubb, MS (1998). Adult neurogenesis and functional plasticity in neuronal circuits. *Nature Reviews Neuroscience* 7: 179–193.

Melzack, R, Israel, R, Lacroix, R, and Schultz, G (1998). Phantom limbs in people with congenital limb deficiency or amputation in early childhood. *Brain* 120(Pt 9): 1603–1620.

Merzenich, M, Wright, B, Jenkins, W, et al. (1998). Cortical plasticity underlying perceptual, motor, and cognitive skill development: Implications for neurorehabilitation language comprehension in language-learning impaired children improved with acoustically modified speech. *Cold Spring Harbor Symposium on Quantitative Biology* 61(5245): 1–8.

Merzenich, MM, Jenkins, WM, Johnston, P, et al. (1998). Temporal processing deficits of language-learning impaired children ameliorated by training. *Science* 271(5245): 77–81.

Pascual-Leone, A, Grafman, J, and Hallett, M (1998). Modulation of cortical motor output maps during development of implicit and explicit knowledge. *Science* 263(5151): 1287–1289.

Plaut, DC (1998). Relearning after damage in connectionist networks: Toward a theory of rehabilitation. *Brain and Language* 52(1): 25–82.

Rauschecker, JP (1998). Mechanisms of compensatory plasticity in the cerebral cortex. *Advances in Neurology* 73: 137–146.

Romero, SG, Manly, CF, and Grafman, J (1998). Investigating cognitive neuroplasticity in single cases: Lessons learned from applying functional neuroimaging techniques to the traditional neuropsychological case study framework. *Neurocase* 8(5): 355–368.

Rosenzweig, MR and Bennett, EL (1998). Psychobiology of plasticity: Effects of training and experience on brain and behavior. *Behavioral Brain Research* 78(1): 57–65.

Sadato, N, Pascual-Leone, A, Grafman, J, et al. (1998). Activation of the primary visual cortex by Braille reading in blind subjects. *Nature* 380(6574): 526–528.

Seitz, RJ and Freund, HJ (1998). Plasticity of the human motor cortex. *Advances in Neurology* 73: 321–333.

Taub, E, Uswatte, G, and Elbert, T (1998). New treatments in neurorehabilitation founded on basic research. *Nature Reviews Neuroscience* 3(3): 228–236.

Ward, NS (1998). Neural plasticity and recovery of function. *Progress in Brain Research* 150: 527–535.

Wood, JN and Grafman, J (1998). Human prefrontal cortex: Processing and representational perspectives. *Nature Reviews Neuroscience* 4(2): 139–147.

Zhuang, P, Toro, C, Grafman, J, et al. (1998). Event-related desynchronization (ERD) in the alpha frequency during development of implicit and explicit learning. *Journal of Electroencephalography and Clinical Neurophysiology* 102(4): 374–381.

C

Category-Specific Knowledge

B. Z. Mahon and A. Caramazza, Harvard University, Cambridge, MA, USA

Principles of Organization

Theories of the organization of conceptual knowledge in the brain can be distinguished according to their underlying principles. One class of theories, based on the neural structure principle, assumes that the organization of conceptual knowledge is governed by representational constraints internal to the brain itself. Two types of neural constraints have been invoked: modality-specificity and domain-specificity. The second class of theories, based on the correlated structure principle, assumes that the organization of conceptual knowledge in the brain is a reflection of the statistical co-occurrence of object properties in the world. Neuropsychological evidence, and more recently findings from functional neuroimaging, have figured centrally in attempts to evaluate extant theories of the organization of conceptual knowledge. Here we outline the main theoretical perspectives as well as the empirical phenomena that have been used to inform these perspectives.

Modality-Specific Hypotheses

The first class of theories based on the neural structure principle assumes that the principal determinant of the organization of conceptual knowledge is the sensory-motor modality (e.g., visual, motor, verbal) through which the information was acquired or is typically processed. For instance, the knowledge that hammers are shaped like a T would be stored in a semantic subsystem dedicated to representing the visual structure of objects, while the information that hammers are used to pound nails would be represented in a semantic subsystem dedicated to functional knowledge of objects. There have been many proposals based on the modality-specific assumption (Beauvois, 1982; Warrington and McCarthy, 1983, 1987; Warrington and Shallice, 1984; Allport, 1985; Martin et al., 2000; Humphreys and Forde, 2001; Barsalou et al., 2003; Cree and McRae, 2003; Crutch and Warrington, 2003; Gallese and Lakoff, in press). One way to distinguish between these proposals concerns whether, and to what extent, conceptual knowledge is assumed to be represented independently of sensory-motor processes. At one extreme are theories that assume conceptual content reduces to (i.e., actually **is**) sensory-motor content (e.g., Allport, 1985; Pulvermuller, 2001; Barsalou et al., 2003; Gallese and Lakoff, in press). Central to such proposals is the notion of simulation, or the automatic reactivation of sensory-motor information in the course of conceptual processing. Toward the other end of the continuum are modality-based hypotheses of the organization of conceptual knowledge that assume that sensory-motor systems may be damaged without compromising the integrity of conceptual knowledge (Martin et al., 2000; Plaut, 2002; Crutch and Warrington, 2003; for discussion, see Mahon and Caramazza, in press).

Domain-Specific Hypotheses

A second class of proposals based on the neural structure principle assumes that the principal determinant of the organization of conceptual knowledge is semantic category (e.g., Gelman, 1990; Carey and Spelke, 1994; Caramazza and Shelton, 1998; Kanwisher, 2000). For instance, in this view, it may be argued that conceptual knowledge of conspecifics and conceptual knowledge of animals are represented and processed by functionally dissociable processes/systems. Crucially, in this view, the first order principle of organization of conceptual processing is semantic category and not the modality through which that information is typically processed. One proposal along these lines, the Domain-Specific Hypothesis (Caramazza and Shelton, 1998), argues that conceptual knowledge is organized by specialized (and functionally dissociable) neural circuits innately determined to the conceptual processing of different categories of objects. However, not all Domain-Specific theories assume that the organization of the adult semantic system is driven by innate parameters (e.g., Kanwisher, 2000).

Feature-Based Hypotheses

The class of hypotheses based on the correlated structure principle has focused on articulating the structure of semantic memory at the level of semantic features. There are many and sometimes diverging proposals along these lines; common to all of them is the assumption that the relative susceptibility to impairment (under conditions of neurological damage) of different concepts is a function of statistical properties of the semantic features that comprise those concepts. For instance, on some models, the degree to which features are shared by a number of concepts is contrasted with their relative distinctiveness (Devlin et al., 1998; Garrard et al., 2001; Tyler and Moss, 2001). Another dimension that is introduced by some theorists concerns dynamical properties of damage in the system; for instance, Tyler and Moss assume that features that are more correlated with other features will be more resistant to damage, due to greater reciprocal activation (or support) from those features with which they are correlated (but see Caramazza et al., 1990). Distinctive features, on the other hand, will not receive as much reciprocal support, and will thus be more susceptible to damage. More recently, theorists have expanded on the original proposal of Tyler and colleagues, adding dimensions such as familiarity, typicality, and relevance (e.g., Cree and McRae, 2003; Sartori and Lombardi, 2004). Feature-based models of semantic memory have in general emphasized an empirical, bottom up, approach to modeling the organization of semantic memory, usually drawing on feature generation tasks (e.g., Garrard et al., 2001; Tyler and Moss, 2001; Cree and McRae, 2003; Sartori and Lombardi, 2004). For this reason, feature-based models have been useful in generating hypotheses about the types of parameters that may contribute to the organization of conceptual knowledge.

Clues from Cognitive Neuropsychology

Neuropsychological studies of patients with semantic impairments have figured centrally in developing and evaluating the hypotheses outlined above. Of particular importance has been a clinical profile described as category-specific semantic deficit. Patients with category-specific semantic deficits present with disproportionate or even selective difficulty for conceptual knowledge of stimuli from one semantic category compared to other semantic categories. For instance, the reports of category-specific impairment by Warrington and her collaborators (e.g., Warrington and McCarthy, 1983, 1987; Warrington and Shallice, 1984) documented patients who were impaired for living things compared to nonliving things, or the reverse: greater difficulty with nonliving things than living things. Since those seminal reports, the phenomenon of category-specific semantic deficit has been documented by a number of investigators (for recent reviews of the clinical evidence, see Humphreys and Forde, 2001; Tyler and Moss, 2001; Capitani et al., 2003).

The clinical profile of category-specific semantic deficits is in itself quite remarkable, and can be striking. Consider some aspects of the following case of category-specific semantic deficit for living animate things. Patient EW (Caramazza and Shelton, 1998) was 41% correct (7/16) for naming pictures of animals but was in the normal range for naming pictures of non-animals (e.g., artifacts, fruit/vegetables) when the pictures from the different semantic categories were matched jointly for familiarity and visual complexity. EW was also severely impaired for animals (60%; 36/60 correct) in a task in which the patient was asked to decide, yes or no, whether the depicted stimulus was a real object or not. In contrast, EW performed within the normal range for making the same types of judgments about non-animals. On another task, EW was asked to decide whether a given attribute was true of a given item (e.g., Is it true that eagles lay eggs?). EW was severely impaired for attributes pertaining to animals (65% correct) but within the normal range for non-animals. EW was equivalently impaired for both visual/perceptual and functional/associative knowledge of living things (65% correct for both types of knowledge) but was within the normal range for both types of knowledge for non-animals.

The phenomenon of category-specific semantic deficits frames what has proven to be a rich question: How could the conceptual system be organized such that various conditions of damage can give rise to conceptual impairments that disproportionately affect specific semantic categories? There is emerging consensus that any viable answer to this question must be able to account for the following three facts (for discussion, see Caramazza and Shelton, 1998; Tyler and Moss, 2001; Capitani et al., 2003; Cree and McRae, 2003; Samson and Pillon, 2003).

Fact I: The grain of the phenomenon: Patients can be disproportionately impaired for either living animate things (i.e., animals) compared to living inanimate things (i.e., fruit/vegetables (e.g., Hart and Gordon, 1992; Caramazza and Shelton, 1998) or living inanimate things compared to living animate things (e.g., Hart et al., 1985; Crutch and Warrington, 2003; Samson and Pillon, 2003). Patients can also be impaired for nonliving things compared to living things (Hillis and Caramazza, 1991).

Fact II: The profile of the phenomenon: Category-specific semantic deficits are not associated with disproportionate impairments for modalities or types of information (e.g., Caramazza and Shelton, 1998; Laiacona and Capitani, 2001; Farah and Rabinowitz, 2003; Samson and Pillon, 2003). Conversely, disproportionate impairments for modalities or types of information are not necessarily associated with category-specific semantic deficits (e.g., Lambon-Ralph et al.,1998; Miceli et al., 2001).

Fact III: The severity of overall impairment: The direction of category-specific semantic deficits (i.e., living things worse than nonliving things, or vice versa) is not related to the overall severity of semantic impairment (Garrard et al., 1998; Zannino et al., 2002).

Explaining Category-Specific Semantic Deficits

Most of the empirical and theoretical work in category-specific semantic deficits has been driven by an attempt to evaluate a theoretical proposal first advanced by Warrington, Shallice, and McCarthy (Warrington and McCarthy, 1983, 1987; Warrington and Shallice, 1984): the Sensory/Functional Theory. The Sensory/Functional Theory is an extension of the modality-specific semantic hypothesis (Beauvois, 1982) discussed above. In addition to assuming that the semantic system is functionally organized by modality or type of information, the Sensory/Functional Theory assumes that the recognition/identification of items from different semantic categories (e.g., living things compared to nonliving things) differentially depends on different modality-specific semantic subsystems. In general, Sensory/Functional theories assume that the ability to identify/recognize living things differentially depends on visual/perceptual knowledge, while the ability to identify/recognize nonliving things differentially depends on functional/associative knowledge (for data and/or discussion of the assumption that different types or modalities of information are differentially important for different semantic categories, see Farah and McClelland, 1991; Caramazza and Shelton, 1998; Garrard et al., 2001; Tyler and Moss, 2001; Cree and McRae, 2003). There are several versions of the Sensory/Functional Theory, each of which has emphasized a different correspondence between the type or modality of information and the category of items that differentially depends on that type of information. For instance, it has been proposed that color information is more important for fruit/vegetables than animals (e.g., Humphreys and Forde, 2001; Cree and McRae, 2003; Crutch and Warrington, 2003) while biological motion information is more important for animals than for fruit/vegetables (e.g., Cree and McRae, 2003). Another version of the Sensory/Functional Theory (Humphreys and Forde, 2001) holds that there is greater perceptual crowding (due to greater perceptual overlap) at a modality-specific input level for living things than for nonliving things. Thus, damage to this visual modality-specific input system will disproportionately affect processing of living things compared to nonliving things (see also Tranel et al., 1997; Dixon, 2000; Laws et al., 2002).

Common to theories based on the Sensory/Functional Assumption is that at least some category-specific semantic deficits can be explained by assuming damage to the modality or type of information upon which recognition/identification of items from the impaired category differentially depends (for discussion see Humphreys and Forde, 2001). Other authors have argued that the fact that category-specific semantic deficits are not necessarily associated with deficits to a modality or type of knowledge (see Fact II above) indicates that the phenomenon does not provide support for Sensory/Functional theories (for discussion, see Caramazza and Shelton, 1998; Tyler and Moss, 2001; Capitani et al., 2003; Cree and McRae, 2003; Samson and Pillon, 2003).

Caramazza and Shelton (1998) argued for a Domain-Specific interpretation of category-specific semantic deficits that emphasized the hypothesis that the grain of category-specific semantic deficits will be restricted to a limited set of categories. Specifically, because the Domain-Specific Hypothesis (Caramazza and Shelton, 1998) assumes that the organization of conceptual and perceptual processing is determined by innate constraints, the plausible categories of category-specific semantic impairment are 'animals,' 'fruit/vegetables,' 'conspecifics,' and possibly tools. Recent discussion of this proposal (Caramazza and Mahon, in press; see also Shelton et al., 1998) has capitalized on using the category 'conspecifics' as a test case. Consistent with expectations that follow from the Domain-Specific Hypothesis, patients have been reported who are relatively impaired for knowledge of conspecifics but not for animals or objects (e.g., Kay and Hanley, 1999; Miceli et al., 2000) as well as the reverse: equivalent impairment for animals and objects but spared knowledge of conspecifics (Thompson et al., 2004). Thus, the domain of conspecifics can be spared or impaired independently of both objects and other living things, and importantly, an impairment for conspecifics is not necessarily associated with a general impairment for living things compared to nonliving things.

Another line of research has sought an account of category-specific semantic deficits in terms of feature-based models of semantic memory organization. For instance, the Organized Unitary Content Hypothesis (OUCH) (Caramazza et al., 1990) makes two principal assumptions. First, conceptual features corresponding to object properties that often co-occur will be stored close together in semantic space; and second, focal brain damage can give rise to category-specific semantic deficits either because the conceptual knowledge corresponding to objects with similar properties is stored in adjacent neural areas, or because damage to a given property will propagate damage to highly correlated properties. While the original OUCH model is not inconsistent with the currently available data from category- specific semantic deficits, it is too unconstrained to provide a principled answer to the question of *why* the various facts are as they are.

Other feature-based models have emphasized the differential susceptibility to impairment of different types of semantic features. These models often assume random (or diffuse) damage to a conceptual system that is not organized by modality or object domain. For instance, in order to account for category-specific semantic deficits, the semantic memory model advanced by Tyler and Moss (2001) makes three assumptions bearing on the relative susceptibility to impairment of different classes of semantic features: (a) Living things have more shared features than nonliving things, or put differently, nonliving things have more distinctive/informative features than living things; (b) For living things, biological function information is highly correlated with shared perceptual properties (e.g., can see/has eyes). For artifacts, function information is highly correlated with distinctive perceptual properties (e.g., used for spearing/has tines). (c) Features that are highly correlated with other features will be more resistant to damage than features that are not highly correlated (see also Devlin et al., 1998; Garrard et al., 2001; Cree and McRae, 2003). This proposal, termed the Conceptual Structure Account, predicts that a disproportionate deficit for living things will be observed when damage is relatively mild, while a disproportionate deficit for nonliving things will only arise when damage is so severe that all that is left in the system are the highly correlated shared perceptual and function features of living things. Recent work investigating the central prediction of the theory through cross sectional analyses of patients at varying stages of Alzheimer's disease has not found support for this prediction (Garrard et al., 1998; Zannino et al., 2002).

Clues from Functional Neuroimaging

Increasingly, the neuropsychological approach is being complemented by functional neuroimaging studies of category-specificity. There is a large body of evidence from functional neuroimaging that demonstrates differentiation by semantic domain within modality-specific systems specialized for processing object form and object-associated motion. Specifically, within the ventral object processing system, areas on the inferior surface of the temporal lobes process object-associated form and texture, while areas on the lateral surfaces of the temporal lobes process object-associated movement (Kourtzi and Kanwisher, 2000; Beauchamp et al., 2002, 2003). Within both form/texture- and motion-specific areas of the ventral object processing system, there is differentiation by semantic category. On the inferior surface of the temporal lobe (e.g., fusiform gyrus), more lateral areas are differentially involved in the processing of living things, while more medial regions are differentially involved in the processing of nonliving things. Furthermore, human face stimuli, in comparison to non-face stimuli (including animals without faces), differentially activate distinct regions of the inferior temporal cortex (Kanwisher et al., 1999). On the lateral surface of the temporal lobes, more superior regions (e.g., superior temporal sulcus) are differentially involved in the processing of motion associated with living things, while more inferior regions (e.g., middle temporal gyrus) are differentially involved in the processing of motion associated with nonliving things (for review, see Kanwisher, 2000; Martin and Chao, 2001; Beauchamp et al., 2002, 2003; Bookheimer, 2002; Caramazza and Mahon, 2003, in press).

All of the theoretical frameworks outlined above have been applied to the data from functional neuroimaging. One widely received view, the Sensory/Motor Theory, developed by Martin, Wiggs, Ungerleider, and Haxby (1996; see also Martin et al., 2000) assumes that conceptual knowledge of different categories of objects is stored close to the modality- specific input/output areas that are active when we learn about and interact with those objects. Other authors have interpreted these patterns of activation within a Domain-Specific Framework (e.g., Kanwisher, 2000; Caramazza and Mahon, 2003, in press), while still others have interpreted these findings within a distributed semantic memory model that emphasizes experience-dependent and/or feature-based properties of concepts (e.g., Tarr and Gauthier, 2000; Levy et al., 2001; Martin and Chao, 2001; Bookheimer, 2002; Devlin et al., 2002). Regardless of what the correct interpretation of these functional neuroimaging data turns out to be, they suggest a theoretical approach in which multiple dimensions of organization can be distinguished. In particular, whether the category- specific foci of activation are interpreted within the Domain-Specific Framework or within a feature-based framework, these data suggest the inference that the organization of conceptual knowledge in the cortex is driven both by the type or modality of the information as well as its content-defined semantic category.

Conclusion

The three proposals that we have reviewed (the Sensory/Functional Theory, the Domain-Specific Hypothesis, and the Conceptual Structure Account) are contrary hypotheses of the causes of category-specific semantic deficits. However, the individual assumptions that comprise each account are not necessarily mutually contrary as proposals about the organization of semantic memory. In this context, it is important to note that each of the hypotheses discussed above makes assumptions at a different level in a hierarchy of questions about the organization of conceptual knowledge. At the broadest level is the question of whether or not conceptual knowledge is organized by Domain-Specific constraints. The second question is whether conceptual knowledge is represented in modality-specific semantic stores specialized for processing/storing a specific type of information, or is represented in an amodal, unitary system. The third level in this hierarchy of questions concerns the organization of conceptual knowledge within any given object domain (and/or modality-specific semantic store): the principles invoked by feature-based models may prove useful for articulating answers to this question (for further discussion of the various levels at which specific hypotheses have been articulated, see Caramazza and Mahon, 2003).

Different hypotheses of the organization of conceptual knowledge are more or less successful at accounting for different types of facts. Thus, it is important to consider the specific assumptions made by each hypothesis in the context of a broad range of empirical phenomena. The combination of neuropsychology and functional neuroimaging is beginning to provide promising grounds for raising theoretically motivated questions concerning the organization of conceptual knowledge in the human brain.

Acknowledgments

Preparation of this manuscript was supported in part by NIH grant DC04542 to A. C., and by an NSF Graduate Research Fellowship to B. Z. M. Portions of this article were adapted from Caramazza and Mahon (2003) and Caramazza and Mahon (in press).

Bibliography

Allport, DA (1985). 'Distributed memory, modular subsystems and dysphasia.' In: Newman and Epstein (eds.) *Current perspectives in dysphasia*. New York: Churchill Livingstone.

Barsalou, LW, Simmons, WK, Barbey, AK, and Wilson, CD (2003). 'Grounding conceptual knowledge in the modality-specific systems.' *Trends in Cognitive Sciences* 7: 84–91.

Beauchamp, MS, Lee, KE, Haxby, JV, and Martin, A (2002). 'Parallel visual motion processing streams for manipulable objects and human movements.' *Neuron* 34: 149–159.

Beauchamp, MS, Lee, KE, Haxby, JV, and Martin, A (2003). 'FMRI responses to video and point-light displays of moving humans and manipulable objects.' *Journal of Cognitive Neuroscience* 15: 991–1001.

Beauvois, MF (1982). 'Optic aphasia: a process of interaction between vision and language.' *Proceedings of the Royal Society (London)* B298: 35–47.

Bookheimer, S (2002). 'Functional MRI of language: new approaches to understanding the cortical organization of semantic processing.' *Annual Review of Neuroscience* 25: 151–188.

Capitani, E, Laiacona, M, Mahon, B, and Caramazza, A (2003). 'What are the facts of category-specific deficits? A critical review of the clinical evidence.' *Cognitive Neuropsychology* 20: 213–262.

Caramazza, A, Hillis, AE, Rapp, BC, and Romani, C (1990). 'The multiple semantics hypothesis: Multiple confusions?' *Cognitive Neuropsychology* 7: 161–189.

Caramazza, A and Shelton, JR (1998). 'Domain specific knowledge systems in the brain: the animate-inanimate distinction.' *Journal of Cognitive Neuroscience* 10: 1–34.

Caramazza, A and Mahon, BZ (2003). 'The organization of conceptual knowledge: the evidence from category-specific semantic deficits.' *Trends in Cognitive Sciences* 7: 325–374.

Caramazza A & Mahon BZ (in press). 'The organization of conceptual knowledge in the brain: the future's past and some future directions.' *Cognitive Neuropsychology*.

Carey, S and Spelke, E (1994). 'Domain-specific knowledge and conceptual change.' In: Hirschfeld, LA and Gelman, SA (eds.) *Mapping the mind: domain-specificity in cognition and culture*. pp. 169–200. New York: Cambridge University Press.

Cree, GS and McRae, K (2003). 'Analyzing the factors underlying the structure and computation of the meaning of chipmunk, cherry, chisel, cheese, and cello (and many other such concrete nouns).' *Journal of Experimental Psychology: General* 132: 163–201.

Crutch, SJ and Warrington, EK (2003). 'The selective impairment of fruit and vegetable knowledge: a multiple processing channels account of fine-grain category specificity.' *Cognitive Neuropsychology* 20: 355–373.

Devlin, JT, Gonnerman, LM, Anderson, ES, and Seidenberg, MS (1998). 'Category-specific semantic deficits in focal and widespread brain damage: a computational account.' *Journal of Cognitive Neuroscience* 10: 77–94.

Devlin, JT, Russell, RP, Davis, MH, Price, CJ, Moss, HE, Fadili, MJ, and Tyler, LK (2002). 'Is there an anatomical basis for category-specificity? Semantic memory studies in PET and fMRI.' *Neuropsychologia* 40: 54–75.

Dixon, MJ (2000). 'A new paradigm for investigating category-specific agnosia in the new millennium.' *Brain and Cognition* 42: 142–145.

Farah, MJ and McClelland, JL (1991). 'A computational model of semantic memory impairment: modality specific and emergent category specificity.' *Journal of Experimental Psychology: General* 120: 339–357.

Farah, MJ and Rabinowitz, C (2003). 'Genetic and environmental influences on the organization of semantic memory in the brain: is "living things" an innate category?' *Cognitive Neuropsychology* 20: 401–408.

Gallese V & Lakoff G (in press). 'The brain's concepts: the role of the sensory-motor system in conceptual knowledge.' *Cognitive Neuropsychology*.

Garrard, P, Patterson, K, Watson, PC, and Hodges, JR (1998). 'Category specific semantic loss in dementia of Alzheimer's type. Functional-anatomical correlations from cross sectional analyses.' *Brain* 121: 633–646.

Garrard, P, Lambon-Ralph, MA, Hodges, JR, and Patterson, K (2001). 'Prototypicality, distinctiveness, and intercorrelation: analyses of semantic attributes of living and nonliving concepts.' *Cognitive Neuropsychology* 18: 125–174.

Gelman, R (1990). 'First principles organize attention to and learning about relevant data: number and the animate-inanimate distinction as examples.' *Cognitive Science* 14: 79–106.

Hart, J, Berndt, RS, and Caramazza, A (1985). 'Category-specific naming deficit following cerebral infarction.' *Nature* 316: 439–440.

Hart, J and Gordon, B (1992). 'Neural subsystems for object knowledge.' *Nature* 359: 60–64.

Hillis, AE and Caramazza, A (1991). 'Category-specific naming and comprehension impairment: a double dissociation.' *Brain* 114: 2081–2094.

Humphreys, GW and Forde, EM (2001). 'Hierarchies, similarity, and interactivity in object recognition: "Category-specific" neuropsychological deficits.' *Behavioral and Brain Sciences* 24: 453–509.

Kanwisher, N (2000). 'Domain specificity in face perception.' *Nature* 3: 759–763.

Kanwisher, N, Stanley, D, and Harris, A (1999). 'The fusiform face area is selective for faces, not animals.' *Neuroreport* 10: 183–187.

Kay, J and Hanley, JR (1999). 'Person-specific knowledge and knowledge of biological categories.' *Cognitive Neuropsychology* 16: 171–180.

Kourtzi, Z and Kanwisher, N (2000). 'Activation in human MT/MST by static images with implied motion.' *Journal of Cognitive Neuroscience* 12: 48–55.

Laiacona, M and Capitani, E (2001). 'A case of prevailing deficit for non-living categories or a case of prevailing sparing of living categories?' *Cognitive Neuropsychology* 18: 39–70.

Lambon-Ralph, MA, Howard, D, Nightingale, G, and Ellis, AW (1998). 'Are living and non-living category-specific deficits causally linked to

impaired perceptual or associative knowledge? Evidence from a category-specific double dissociation.' *Neurocase* 4: 311–338.
Laws, KR, Gale, TM, Frank, R, and Davey, N (2002). 'Visual similarity is greater for line drawings of nonliving than living thing: the importance of musical instruments and body parts.' *Brain and Cognition* 48: 421–423.
Levy, I, Hasson, U, Avidan, G, Hendler, T, and Malach, R (2001). 'Center-periphery organization of human object areas.' *Nature Neuroscience* 4: 533–539.
Mahon BZ & Caramazza A (in press). 'The orchestration of the sensory-motor systems: clues from neuropsychology.' *Cognitive Neuropsychology.*
Martin, A and Chao, LL (2001). 'Semantic memory and the brain: structure and processes.' *Current Opinion in Neurobiology* 11: 194–201.
Martin, A and Weisberg, J (2003). 'Neural foundations for understanding social and mechanical concepts.' *Cognitive Neuropsychology* 20: 575–587.
Martin, A, Ungerleider, LG, and Haxby, JV (2000). 'Category specificity and the brain: the sensory/motor model of semantic representations of objects.' In: Gazzaniga, MS (ed.) *The new cognitive neurosciences.* Cambridge, MA: MIT Press.
Martin, A, Wiggs, CL, Ungerleider, LG, and Haxby, JV (1996). 'Neural correlates of category-specific knowledge.' *Nature* 379: 649–652.
Miceli, G, Capasso, R, Daniele, A, Esposito, T, Magarelli, M, and Tomaiuolo, F (2000). 'Selective deficit for people's names following left temporal damage: an impairment of domain-specific conceptual knowledge.' *Cognitive Neuropsychology* 17: 489–516.
Miceli, G, Fouch, E, Capasso, R, Shelton, JR, Tamaiuolo, F, and Caramazza, A (2001). 'The dissociation of color from form and function knowledge.' *Nature Neuroscience* 4: 662–667.
Plaut, DC (2002). 'Graded modality-specific specialization in semantics: a computational account of optic aphasia.' *Cognitive Neuropsychology* 19: 603–639.
Pulvermuller, F (2001). 'Brain reflections of words and their meaning.' *Trends in Cognitive Science* 5: 517–524.
Samson, D and Pillon, A (2003). 'A case of impaired knowledge for fruit and vegetables.' *Cognitive Neuropsychology* 20: 373–401.
Sartori, G and Lombardi, L (2004). 'Semantic relevance and semantic disorders.' *Journal of Cognitive Neuroscience* 16: 439–452.
Shelton, JR, Fouch, E, and Caramazza, A (1998). 'The selective sparing of body part knowledge: a case study.' *Neurocase* 4: 339–351.
Tarr, MJ and Gauthier, I (2000). 'FFA: a flexible fusiform area for subordinate-level visual processing automatized by expertise.' *Nature Neuroscience* 3: 764–769.
Thompson, SA, Graham, KS, Williams, G, Patterson, K, Kapur, N, and Hodges, JR (2004). 'Dissociating person-specific from general semantic knowledge: roles of the left and right temporal lobes.' *Neuropsychologia* 42: 359–370.
Tranel, D, Logan, CG, Frank, RJ, and Damasio, AR (1997). 'Explaining category-related effects in the retrieval of conceptual and lexical knowledge for concrete entities.' *Neuropsychologia* 35: 1329–1339.
Tyler, LK and Moss, HE (2001). 'Towards a distributed account of conceptual knowledge.' *Trends in Cognitive Science* 5: 244–252.
Warrington, EK and McCarthy, R (1983). 'Category specific access dysphasia.' *Brain* 106: 859–878.
Warrington, EK and McCarthy, R (1987). 'Categories of knowledge: further fractionations and an attempted integration.' *Brain* 110: 1273–1296.
Warrington, EK and Shallice, T (1984). 'Category-specific semantic impairment.' *Brain* 107: 829–854.
Zannino, GD, Perri, R, Carlesimo, GA, Pasqualettin, P, and Caltagirone, C (2002). 'Category-specific impairment in patients with Alzheimer's disease as a function of disease severity: a cross-sectional investigation.' *Neuropsychologia* 40: 2268–2279.

Cerebellum, Clinical Pathology

M. Molinari, Santa Lucia Foundation, Rome, Italy
M. G. Leggio, University of Rome 'La Sapienza,' Rome, Italy

Published by Elsevier Ltd.

Introduction

When clinicians examine a patient for signs of cerebellar disease, they follow a procedure that developed from the observations of Luigi Luciani (1840–1919), Joseph Babinski (1857–1932), Andre Thomas (1867–1961), and Gordon Holmes (1876–1965). The notion of the pivotal function of the cerebellum in motor coordination and fine-tuning of movements originated from their pioneering work. The motor aspects of cerebellar functioning dominated cerebellar studies almost completely until the 1980s, when the importance of nonmotor cerebellar functions was recognized. As the spectrum of cerebellar functions enlarged, classical theories of cerebellar functioning were questioned so thoroughly that now there is little consensus over the basic rules controlling cerebellar physiology and the influence of this cerebral structure on other circuits in the central nervous system (CNS). To complicate matters even more, cerebellar symptoms, although similar independently of the etiology, may differ in their pattern of onset and recovery. Differences have been evidenced between focal acute and chronic degenerative pathologies as well as between developmental and adult lesions. Namely, acute vascular lesions have an abrupt, even dramatic, onset often followed over weeks or months by a progressive lessening of symptoms and even to quite complete clinical recovery. Degenerative pathologies behave in the opposite way, with rather slow onset and progressive development into a disabled state. Cerebellitis and cerebellar localization of more diffuse CNS pathologies, such as multiple sclerosis, tend to present acute onset and little if any recovery, even after stabilization of the primary pathology. During development, a very different clinical picture emerges from lack of development of the cerebellum or from acquired damage. Given this complex framework, our comprehension of the pathophysiology of cerebellar motor symptoms is still poor. However, cerebellar signs and symptoms are remarkably similar no matter what the disease process and, at least for the motor domain, are well defined and substantially the same as those listed by Holmes in 1939. In the present article, motor symptoms and related clinical signs, together with cognitive and behavioral impairments related to cerebellar diseases, are presented.

Common symptoms in the case of acute onset include headache, vertigo, nausea, and vomiting. However, these symptoms can depend on an increase in intracranial pressure resulting from expanding mass lesions or on secondary hydrocephalus due to a block of cerebrospinal fluid (CSF) flux in the aqueduct. Therefore, they cannot be considered specific to damage of the cerebellum *per se*. Since signs and symptoms related to cerebellar damage are remarkably the same no matter what the disease process, in this article they are not related to differences in pathological processes affecting the cerebellum. Different clinical scales have been developed to provide reliable and valid measures of the severity of cerebellar symptoms. Diseases specifically involving the cerebellum are listed in **Table 1**.

Motor Symptoms

In the motor domain, cerebellar symptoms are ipsilateral to the side of the cerebellar lesion and can be grouped as follows: (1) modified muscle tone, (2) impaired motor coordination, (3) tremor, (4) oculomotor disturbances, (5) stance and gait disturbances, and (6) speech disorders.

Muscle Tone

Some researchers believe that a reduction in muscle tone is linked to direct cerebellar influence on the spinal gamma loop; however, this interpretation has been questioned. More recently, the absence of facilitatory cerebellar influence over the contralateral motor cortex has been cited to explain cerebellar hypotonia. Although hypotonia is often intense in children, in adults it is usually associated with severe cerebellar damage or occurs in the acute stage of the disease. The following clinical tests are used diagnostically.

Gordon Holmes sign

Patients place their elbows on a table and keep their forearms and hands extended upward. If hypotonia is present the hands slowly close, drooping down toward the arms, because the patients are unable to hold the antigravity posture.

Pendulousness

When an extremity is displaced passively, so that it swings freely, there is a regular, precise pendulous motion that diminishes in a steady, even manner. Upper extremities are tested by moving the standing patient's shoulders back and forth. Lower extremities are tested with the patient sitting on the edge of a bed with their legs hanging freely. The examiner briskly flips one leg and lets it swing. In patients with cerebellar disease, pendulousness is increased.

Postural asymmetries

In unilateral lesions, side differences in muscle tone can induce postural asymmetries.

Table 1 The most common examples of cerebellar pathology

Pathology	*Description*
Developmental	Complete or partial absence of the cerebellum (agenesis), Dandy–Walker syndrome
Degenerative	Genetic disorders including spinocerebellar atrophies, Friedreich ataxia, ataxia telangiectasia, Refsum syndrome, amaurotic familial idiocy, multiple sclerosis, Wilson's disease, tuberous sclerosis, carcinomatous diffuse corticocerebellar degeneration
Infectious	Bacterial (abscesses, tuberculosis, syphilis, whooping cough), fungal infections, parasitic infestations (cysticercosis, malaria), viral infections (mumps, viral encephalitis, poliomyelitis, kuru, Creutzfeldt–Jakob disease, looping ill)
Toxic and metabolic	Ethanol, dilantin, carbon tetrachloride, anoxia, hypoglycemia, vitamin deficiencies (B_1, B_{12}), hypothyroidism, heat stroke
Vascular diseases	Thrombosis, embolism of superior cerebellar, anterior inferior cerebellar, or posterior inferior cerebellar branches of the basilar or vertebral arteries, transient ischemic episodes in these arterial territories, hemorrhage
Trauma	Restricted to the cerebellum; usually results from penetrating wounds and typically involves vessels and parenchyma
Tumors	Metastatic from primary sites elsewhere in the body; astrocytoma (slow growing, cystic, common in children); medulla blastoma (invasive, rapidly growing, most commonly occurs in children); ependymomas, vascular malformations, and hemangioblastoma; acoustic neuroma

Modified from Dow RS (1987) Cerebellum, pathology: Symptoms and signs. In: Adelman G (ed.) *Encyclopedia of Neuroscience*, pp. 203–206. Boston: Birkhäuser.

Pendular tendon reflexes

Especially for patellar and triceps reflexes, reflex responses are characterized by limb oscillation around the position at rest.

Impairment of Motor Coordination

Impaired synchrony of agonist and antagonist muscle interplay is considered to be the neurophysiological basis of the motor coordination deficits observed in cerebellar pathologies classically grouped under the term 'ataxia.' Ataxia, from the Greek *αταξια* (i.e., lack of order), refers to a lack of motor coordination and can be evidenced by several clinical tests that explore limb functions.

Heel–knee–shin/toe square-drawing tests

The patient, lying supine on a bed or sitting on a chair, flexes one leg at the hip, knee, and ankle so that the heel traces a path lightly along the top of the opposite shin and then extends to all joints to retrace the line. In normal persons the path is straight and the motion continuous, with smooth and accurate termination and reversal at the endpoint. In patients with ipsilateral damage of the cerebellum the moving limb commonly overshoots the endpoint (knee, ankle) and the path oscillates from side to side. The oscillation is rough, as if several rhythms were intermixed; the turnarounds look distinctly like 'bounces.' Although lateral deviations are the most conspicuous variations, to-and-fro variations also occur; up-and-down variations are damped by contact with the shin. In drawing a square, the patient is asked to follow the examiner's finger and/or to trace an imaginary square in the air with the big toe. Here again, in cerebellar disease one sees overshooting of the endpoint, with side-to-side oscillation that characteristically increases as the target is approached.

Finger–nose–finger test

The patient reaches out and uses his extended forefinger to touch the examiner's forefinger and then touches his own nose, repeating the process. The abnormalities to be looked for are (1) tremor at 3–6 Hz, which is primarily side to side and up and down, (2) overshooting the target position, which may then be corrected by a movement, and (3) in chronic cases, a tendency to 'decompose' the movement (moving first one joint then another seriatim).

Rebound

The examiner holds the cerebellar patient's wrists and asks her to pull against the resistance. Without warning the examiner suddenly releases his hold. The patient is unable to cease agonist and initiate antagonist muscle actions rapidly enough, and the patient's arms fly toward her and may even hit her in the face. In a similar test, the cerebellar patient is asked to hold outstretched a leg or an arm. The examiner then briskly taps a distal spot on the limb from a variety of different directions. The normal response is to deviate minimally from the initial position and return to it promptly, using a rapid increase first in agonist and then in antagonist muscle activity, to return to and hold the position without overshooting or oscillation. In cerebellar patients, a greater displacement occurs; the return overshoots the initial position, followed by one or more beats of oscillation.

Finger-to-finger and finger-to-thumb tests

The patient is asked to tap the pad of his thumb on the pads of each of the digits from 2 to 5 and then return from 5 to 2 in rapid succession. Cerebellar disease is characterized by slowing down, a lack of fixed rhythm and imprecise placing of the thumb on the fingertips. Actually, it is rare that these signs are greatly affected by cerebellar disease, possibly due to the surviving ability of the motor cortex to control single digits normally (the thumb may be held fixed while the fingers move at the metacarpophalangeal (MCP) joint only). A more sensitive test was devised by C M Fisher in which the nail of the index finger is tapped rapidly and repeatedly on the skin-crease at the top joint of the thumb. What is observed in cerebellar disease is slowing, irregularity in the amplitude of the excursion and the rhythm of subsequent excursions, and great variation in the position of the index 'hits' to either side of the thumb-crease target. The first test uses the stereotyped mechanisms of single-digit movement built into the motor cortex. The endpoint is primarily controlled by digit length. This test is more specific for lesions of the motor cortex than for lesions of the cerebellum. The second test requires coordinated action across proximal interphalangeal (PIP) and MCP joints (and lumbricals and long flexors) to an arbitrary endpoint and tests the integrity of the dentate nucleus in the lateral cerebellum.

Rapid, alternating movements

The capacity to develop alternating movements is tested by pronation–supination movements. The patient is asked to keep his forearms vertical and to perform pronation–supination movements with his hands. This function can also be tested by asking the patient to slap the palm and the back of one hand alternately on the palm of the other hand or on the thigh. Irregular rhythm and amplitude of excursion with slowing and frequent repeated 'wrong moves' are looked for, especially since the task performance is prolonged.

Tremor

Although the pathophysiology of cerebellar tremor has been addressed by numerous experimental and clinical studies, it is still a matter of debate. In general, it is thought to be generated within central motor loops.

Intention or kinetic tremor

This type of tremor is tested using the finger–nose and heel–knee test. It may be present throughout the entire movement or only at the beginning, but it is particularly evident at the end of the movement. Intention tremor tends to worsen in the days or weeks after acute cerebellar lesion.

Postural tremor

This type of tremor, defined also as 'action tremor,' appears during performance of postural tasks that require precision. It is tested by asking the patient either to keep her arm outstretched or, in a supine position, her legs held fixed against gravity.

Palatal tremor

This type of tremor is characterized by short, rhythmic, involuntary movements of the soft palate often associated with hypertrophy of the contralateral inferior olive.

Oculomotor Disturbances

In cerebellar pathologies, oculomotor deficits are usually related to involvement of the dorsal vermis or the fastigial nucleus, the folliculus and paraflocculus, and/or the uvula and the nodulus in the pathological process. Disorders of fixation, pursuit, and saccades, together with the development of nystagmus and skew deviation, are often observed. During fixation, brief oscillations (flutter), usually horizontally conjugated and present in both the light and the dark, can be observed. Nonsmooth pursuit, characterized by a stepwise decomposition of movement, is frequently observed in cerebellar diseases, but with low specificity. Also, in saccadic movements, the characteristic overshooting observed in limb movements (i.e., ocular hypermetria) can be present.

Equilibrium and Stance

The patient is in a standing position with his eyes first open and then shut. This test was originally devised by Moritz Romberg (1795–1873) to distinguish diseases of peripheral nerves or spinal afferent somatosensory pathways from diseases of the cerebellum. Patients with somatosensory disturbances can stand well with their eyes open but may fall when their eyes are closed. Patients with cerebellar disease may be unstable with their eyes open as well as closed; unlike normal persons, they cannot use somesthesis, vestibular information, or vision for equilibrium and stance. With acute unilateral cerebellar damage, the patient falls toward the side of the lesion. Equilibrium has been clinically tested in patients with cerebellar lesions by measuring postural sway on a force-sensing platform. Lesions of the flocculo-nodular lobe and posterior vermis (which projects heavily to the lateral vestibular nucleus) cause an irregular course sway (back and forth and side to side), as does damage to the membranous labyrinths, which is indistinguishable from 'vestibular ataxia.' Damage to the anterior lobe cortex (alcoholic cerebellar degeneration; late-life atrophy) causes back-and-forth oscillation of the trunk.

Gait

Gait is tested by observing the patient walking in a straight line, in tandem, and backwards. Gait is impaired if ataxia is present. The latter produces irregular steps, often with a broad base, staggering with clumsy corrections, altered rhythm, and irregular, often reduced, speed. Locomotion increases the tendency to fall to the side of the cerebellar lesion, especially in tandem walking. When mild unilateral damage is present, patients start to fall to the side of the lesion, sense the impending fall (vestibular sense is intact), and voluntarily correct themselves with a wider step to that side. The spinal cord contains many of the mechanisms necessary for stance and locomotion; spinal cats can make rudimentary walking movements. Results of animal studies show that stance and gait are specifically controlled by vestibular and fastigial nuclei: cells fire during walking; lesions cause falls to that side. Neurophysiological data in patients suggest that the cerebellum intervenes to adjust movements related to many joints, especially to accommodate external constraints.

Speech

Cerebellar damage affects both motor and cognitive aspects of speech. Dysarthria, cerebellar mutism, agrammatism, and reduced verbal fluency are symptoms of impaired speech reported after cerebellar damage.

Dysarthria

Patients with cerebellar disease can have what is called a scanning dysarthria. This impairment is characterized by difficulty in articulating sounds into words. The problem is not at the language level – that is, in choosing and saying words correctly or in making sentences and paragraphs out of them. The patient is asked to use lips (mi-mi-mi), tongue (la-la-la), pharynx (go-go-go), and larynx (kay-kay-kay) to make sounds involving relatively smaller groups of muscles, together with those moving the thorax and diaphragm. These utterances may sound normal or may be unevenly spaced across time. Saying a sample sentence is relatively more impaired. The utterance is monotonous, lacking normally modulated inflexion of volume, and is slow and slightly slurred. The impaired patient sounds illiterate, painfully and slowly reading from a text one word at a time (hence, scanning). The topography of cerebellar control over motor aspects of speech is not clear. Holmes found this symptom mostly with midline lesions. Working in the 1970s, Richard Lechtenberg and Sid Gilman also found local lesions to be very close to the midline, with a somewhat larger percentage in the left intermediate than in the right zone. This was somewhat surprising since language is located predominantly in the left cerebral hemisphere and thus one would expect its articulation to be located in the known crossed projection zone in the right cerebellar hemisphere. There are also recent reports of patients with lesions limited to the right cerebellar hemisphere.

Cerebellar mutism

The term 'mutism' refers to the inability of an alert patient to produce verbal output. The cerebellar form of mutism has been attributed to lesions of the cerebellar vermis or the cerebellar hemispheres and refers to a complete but transient loss of speech followed by dysarthria, usually after surgery for posterior fossa tumors, cerebellar hemorrhage, or trauma, or in infectious or postinfectious cerebellar syndromes. Cerebellar mutism has often been reported in children and adolescents, but rarely in adults; although it is believed to be due to lost coordination of orofacial movements, the issue is still being debated.

Agrammatism

Agrammatic deficits have been reported in patients with right cerebellar lesions, and the role of the cerebellum in grammar has been recently reviewed. In general, all authors report agrammatism in spontaneous speech with or without involvement of sentence comprehension. In agreement with current theories on agrammatism, it was previously found that cerebellar processing did not affect syntactic knowledge but rather affected sentence construction.

Verbal fluency

Verbal fluency is the ability to generate lists of words according to a given rule. The latter can be either a letter of the alphabet (e.g., retrieval of words that begin with the letter F) or a semantic category (e.g., retrieval of words from the semantic category of 'animals'). There are consistent reports that verbal fluency is reduced after cerebellar damage; also, functional neuroimaging data demonstrate cerebellar activation during verbal fluency tasks. In particular, verbal fluency is impaired in a modality-specific manner, with reduced phonemic rule performance and spared semantic rule performance.

Cognition and Emotion

As early as the nineteenth century there were speculations that the cerebellum might play a role in higher mental processes. However, the notion that the cerebellum might have a nonmotor function only became influential about 50 years ago. Subsequently, the advent of functional neuroimaging techniques, demonstrating cerebellar activation in a variety of cognitive, nonmotor tasks, and the discovery of reciprocal connections between the lateral cerebral hemispheres and the contralateral frontal and parietal cerebral association cortex provided strong support for clinical evidence of cognitive defects in cerebellar pathologies. Today, the number of studies addressing the cerebellar role in emotion and cognition has increased enormously and clinical data and neuroimaging evidence converge in supporting cerebellar influence on quite disparate functions, such as attention, cognitive flexibility, linguistic processing, mental imaging, sensory discrimination, visuospatial processing, timing, and verbal memory, as well as working memory.

Cerebellar Role in Motor Learning

Animal and human studies have shown that the cerebellum is involved in and needed for a variety of different motor tasks, including modification of vestibuloocular reflex gain, adaptation of saccade endpoint to target, associative conditioning of a blink reflex, and gaze–arm calibration in prism-adapted reaching and throwing. Neurophysiological and functional neuroimaging observations in humans indicate the importance of the cerebellum in implicit/procedural learning, and lesion studies indicate procedural learning impairment in cerebellar-lesioned subjects. Although these observation have not yet proved to be of any clinical relevance, knowledge of the characteristics of motor and procedural learning impairment is of clinical relevance, especially in rehabilitation settings.

Localization: Body Maps and Motor Modes

Holmes found little evidence for localization of functions in the cerebellum. Although clinical symptoms are not very useful for a lobular localization of cerebellar damage, there are general indications that medial lesions affect posture and gait while more lateral lesions affect voluntary limb movements. Animal studies have conclusively shown that the flocculus and the nodulus (vestibulocerebellum) control antigravity stance and eye and head movements in response to vestibular information; the vermis and fastigial nucleus control antigravity stance and saccadic eye movements; the intermediate zone cerebellar cortex and interposed nuclei control agonist–antagonist muscle coordination; and the lateral hemisphere cortex and dentate nuclei control combined activities of synergistic muscles in multijointed reaching toward and grasping of objects in space. Further, animal studies strongly support a scheme of localization of functions and of body parts. In macaques, a somatotopic map of muscle actions is seen within each of the fastigial, interposed, and dentate nuclei, with anterior lower extremity, posterior head, medial distal, and lateral proximal parts; the upper extremity is represented in the midportion. The advent of functional neuroimaging and the availability of a detailed atlas of human cerebellar folia have made it possible to collect localization data. Consequently, there is growing evidence of different maps in the cerebellum.

Sensorimotor Maps

Motor and kinesthetic tasks activate the rostral and caudal spinocerebellum with two distinct homuncular representations. One is located upside down in the superior cerebellum and the other, smaller one is in the inferior cerebellum.

The somatotopic map closely resembles that observed in macaques. Correlations between clinical findings and magnetic resonance imaging (MRI)-based cerebellar lesions provide support for a localization data diagnosis based on clinical evidence.

Localization of Cognitive Functions

Activation studies consistently demonstrate cerebellar activation in different cognitive functions and provide support for the development of topographic maps of the cognitive cerebellum, which evidence the following findings: explicit memory retrieval in vermal lobules IV–VIIA and in the left hemisphere, mainly in Crus I; sequence learning bilaterally in Crus I and in vermal lobule VI; language and working memory functions in vermal lobules IV–VIIA and Crus I of the right hemisphere; and verbal working memory in HVIIB of the right hemisphere. This functional topography has not yet been confirmed by clinically relevant data coupling cerebellar damage with cognitive symptoms.

Further Reading

Akshoomoff, NA, Courchesne, E, and Townsend, J (1997). Attention coordination and anticipatory control. *International Review of Neurobiology* 41: 575–598.
Bower, JM and Parsons, LM (2003). Rethinking the 'lesser brain'. *Scientific American* 289(2): 50–57.
Desmond, JE and Fiez, JA (1998). Neuroimaging studies of the cerebellum: Language, learning and memory. *Trends in Cognitive Sciences* 2(9): 355–362.
Dow RS (1987) Cerebellum, pathology: Symptoms and signs. In: Adelman G (ed.) *Encyclopedia of Neuroscience*, pp. 203–206. Boston: Birkhäuser.
Dow, RS and Moruzzi, G (1958). *The Physiology and Pathology of the Cerebellum.* Minneapolis, MN: University of Minnesota Press.
Grodd, W, Hulsmann, E, and Ackermann, H (2005). Functional MRI localizing in the cerebellum. *Neurosurgery Clinics of North America* 16(1): 77–99.
Holmes, G (1939). The cerebellum of man. *Brain* 62: 1–30.
Ito, M (2005). Bases and implications of learning in the cerebellum – adaptive control and internal model mechanism. *Progress in Brain Research* 148: 95–109.
Justus, T (2004). The cerebellum and English grammatical morphology: Evidence from production, comprehension, and grammaticality judgments. *Journal of Cognitive Neuroscience* 16(7): 1115–1130.
Leggio, MG, Silveri, MC, Petrosini, L, et al. (2000). Phonological grouping is specifically affected in cerebellar patients: A verbal fluency study. *Journal Neurology, Neurosurgery & Psychiatry* 69: 102–106.
Leiner, HC, Leiner, AL, and Dow, RS (1986). Does the cerebellum contribute to mental skills? *Behavioral Neuroscience* 100(4): 443–454.
Manto, MU and Pandolfo, M (2002). *The Cerebellum and Its Disorder.* Cambridge, UK: Cambridge University Press.
Middleton, FA and Strick, PL (1997). Dentate output channels: Motor and cognitive components. *Progress in Brain Research* 114: 553–566.
Molinari, M, Filippini, V, and Leggio, MG (2002). Neuronal plasticity of interrelated cerebellar and cortical networks. *Neuroscience* 111(4): 863–870.
Molinari, M, Leggio, MG, Solida, A, et al. (1997). Cerebellum and procedural learning: Evidence from focal cerebellar lesions. *Brain* 120(10): 1753–1762.
Ramnani, N (2006). The primate cortico-cerebellar system: Anatomy and function. *Nature Reviews Neuroscience* 7(7): 511–522.
Restuccia, D, Marca, GD, Valeriani, M, et al. (2007). Cerebellar damage impairs detection of somatosensory input changes. A somatosensory mismatch-negativity study. *Brain* 130: 276–287.
Schmahmann, JD (1997). The cerebellum and cognition. *International Review of Neurobiology* 41: 31–60.
Schmahmann, JD, Doyon, J, Toga, AW, et al. (2000). *MRI Atlas of the Human Cerebellum.* San Diego: Academic Press.
Silveri, MC, Leggio, MG, and Molinari, M (1994). The cerebellum contributes to linguistic production: A case of agrammatic speech following a right cerebellar lesion. *Neurology* 44(11): 2047–2050.
Thach, WT and Bastian, A (2004). Role of the cerebellum in the control and adaptation of gait in health and disease. *Progress in Brain Research* 143: 353–366.

Classical Tests for Speech and Language Disorders

J. Macoir, Laval University, Quebec, QC, Canada
A. Sylvestre, Laval University, Quebec, QC, Canada
Y. Turgeon, Campbellton Regional Hospital, Campbellton, NB, Canada

Introduction

The evaluation of speech and language is one of the most important tasks of speech-language pathologists and professionals from a variety of disciplines and backgrounds (neuropsychologists, physicians, nurses, etc.). The assessment session is often the first contact with clients and also constitutes the starting point of all clinical interventions. Because of the absence of biological markers or simple assessment methods, the early detection or diagnosis of speech and language problems remains dependent on various indirect assessments (i.e., speech or language functioning must be inferred from the client performance in various tasks devised to explore the different areas of this functioning) performed to identify specific impairments and eliminate other possible causes.

There are various purposes to conduct speech-language assessments. The main goal of screening is to determine whether a client has a problem or not. The output of this type of assessment is a 'pass' or 'fail' result, based on an established criterion that could lead to a more extensive or a follow-up assessment. Diagnosis and differential diagnosis assessments are usually performed to label the communication problem and/or to differentiate it from other disorders in which similar characteristics are usually reported.

Another important purpose to evaluation is to provide clinicians with a detailed description of the client's baseline level of functioning in all areas of communication in order to identify affected and preserved components, to plan for treatment, to establish treatment effectiveness, or to track progress over time through periodic re-evaluations. These types of assessment require the clinician to consider all aspects of communication, including the different areas of speech (e.g., articulation, voice, resonance) and language (e.g., lexical access, comprehension, written spelling), but also important related abilities and components such as pragmatics, cognitive functions (e.g., attention, memory, visual perception), emotions, awareness of deficits, etc. The selection of evaluation tools is also conditioned by the specific objectives of assessments. Screening for a speech or language disorder is usually performed with standardized screening measures whereas standardized norm-referenced tests are used for diagnosis and differential diagnosis assessments as well as for clinical treatment purposes (baseline, effectiveness, progress).

Reference Models for the Assessment of Speech and Language Impairment

The choice of a particular method of assessment, the selection of evaluation tools as well as the interpretation of results, is highly dependent not only on the clinician's own conception of speech and language functioning but also on the reference to a clinicopathological or cognitive model of assessment.

In the clinicopathological model, speech and language problems are considered as essential characteristics of clinical syndromes. These clinical syndromes are organized and classified according to neurological-neuropathological characteristics (e.g., deterioration of cortical tissue in a specific brain area) and according to semiology (e.g., sensitive and motor deficits, visuospatial deficits, language deficits, etc.). For the purpose of assessment, the emphasis is put on the precise identification of the diagnostic label that best corresponds to the observed deficits as well as to the identification of the possible etiology. For example, within this model, the general assessment process of an aphasic person essentially consists of (1) gathering case history data (e.g., cerebrovascular accident in the left frontal area), (2) administrating a specific test battery (e.g., the Boston Diagnostic Aphasia Examination [BDAE]; Goodglass et al., 2000), (3) confronting the results and description of behavior (e.g., impaired fluency, impaired articulatory agility, relatively good auditory comprehension, agrammatism) with the classification of neurogenic acquired deficits of language, and (4) specifying the precise aphasic label (Broca's aphasia) that best fits these characteristics. If screening or labeling is the main goal of the assessment, the clinicopathological model is probably the best option. It is, however, certainly not so if the purpose of the evaluation is to localize the functional origin of deficits or to guide clinical practice. Knowing that a person presents with a Broca's aphasia may not be much help in identifying the specific components of language that are totally or partially affected or preserved. It also does not tell the clinician what intervention goals are appropriate, what treatment approaches will succeed best.

Instead of resorting to a medical assessment model, clinicians may use cognitive neuropsychological models, directly derived from information-processing theories, to evaluate language. In these models, cognitive functions, including language, are sustained by specialized interconnected processing components, represented in functional architecture models. For example, as shown on **Figure 1**, the ability to orally produce a word in picture naming is conceived as a staged process in which the activation flow is initiated in a conceptual-semantic component and ends with the execution of articulation mechanisms.

An assessment process based on cognitive neuropsychological models consists in the localization of the impaired and preserved processing components for each language modality. This localization is performed through

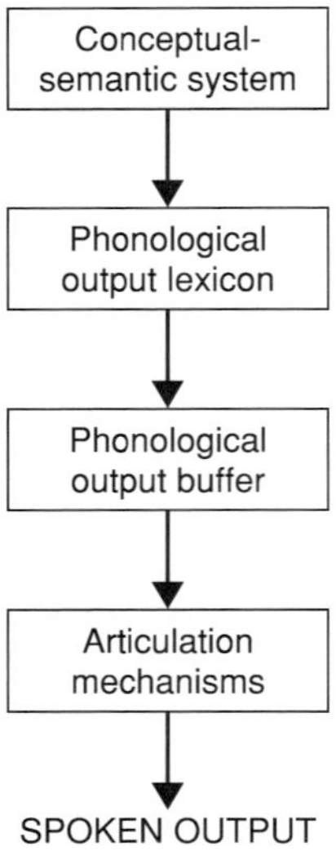

Figure 1 Schematic depiction of the cognitive neuropsychological model of spoken picture naming.

the administration of specific tasks or test batteries (e.g., Psycholinguistic Assessments of Language Processing in Aphasia [PALPA]; Kay et al., 1992) aiming at the evaluation of each component and route of the model. For example, the evaluation of naming abilities in an aphasic person could be performed by the administration of tasks exploring the conceptual-semantic (e.g., semantic questionnaire), phonological output lexicon (e.g., picture-naming task controlled for frequency, familiarity, etc), and phonological output buffer (e.g., repetition of words and nonwords controlled for length) components. Important information regarding the level of impairments also arises from error analysis. With the same example, an anomic behavior could arise from distinct underlying deficits (e.g., in the activation of conceptual-semantic representations or in retrieving phonological forms of words in the output lexicon), leading to distinct types of errors (e.g., semantic substitutions, phonemic errors). The complete cognitive assessment process should allow the clinician to understand the client's deficits (i.e., surface manifestations, underlying origins, affected components) as well as to identify the strengths and weaknesses in his communication abilities. When recommended, the treatment may focus on the impaired levels of processing (i.e., function restoration) or on alternative processing routes (i.e., function reorganization) that will allow the client to communicate successfully.

Classical Tests for the Assessment of Aphasia

Aphasia is the most common disorder of communication resulting from brain damage (i.e., stroke, brain tumor, head trauma, infections). This affection mainly involves language problems of production and comprehension as well as disturbances in reading and spelling.

Bedside and Screening Tests

The patient's symptoms change rapidly during the first days and weeks following the brain damage. Moreover, patients are often too ill to complete an exhaustive aphasia examination and bedside or screening instruments may be useful to advise relatives and health care professionals about the global communication profile and the best means to communicate in functional situations. These instruments are also useful to help clinicians to determine the necessity of performing a more thorough and extensive assessment of language or to establish the priority of patients on a waiting list. In addition to actual screening tests (e.g., Aphasia Screening Test; Reitan, 1991; for an extensive list see Murray and Chapey, 2001 and Spreen and Risser, 2003), clinicians also may administer shortened versions of comprehensive tests of aphasia (e.g., short form of the Token Test; Spellacy and Spreen, 1969; for an extensive list see Murray and Chapey, 2001). As pointed out by Spreen and Risser (2003), although bedside and screening tests may be used to identify language impairments in moderate and severe aphasics (language is obviously affected, even in simple and natural communication situations), they are inappropriate or of little use to distinguish the responses of individuals with mild deficits from those with normal language skills.

Comprehensive Examinations and Aphasia Batteries

As compared to bedside and screening tests, the main purpose of comprehensive examinations of aphasia is to provide an extensive description of language skills through the administration of tests designed to explore the different areas of language (i.e., spontaneous speech, naming, oral expression, auditory and written comprehension, repetition, reading, and writing). According to the reference model of assessment, the output of a comprehensive examination may consist in the identification of a particular diagnostic of aphasia with the description of severity of deficits in each language area (clinico-pathological approach), or in the localization of specific impairments affecting functional processing components of language skills (cognitive neuropsychological approach).

There are several classical comprehensive examinations and aphasia batteries. The most widely used in clinical and research settings in English are BDAE (Goodglass et al., 2000), the Western Aphasia Battery (Kertesz, 1982), and the Aphasia Diagnostic Profiles (Helm-Estabrooks, 1992). All these standardized test batteries comprise different subtests (e.g., BDAE has 27 subtests) that assess all the dimensions of language in order to diagnose and classify aphasic syndromes according to clinical localization-based classifications (i.e., Broca's, Wernicke's aphasia, etc.). For a complete description and a critical review of these instruments, and others not reported here, see Spreen and Strauss (1998), Murray and Chapey (2001), and Spreen and Risser (2003). PALPA (Kay et al., 1992) is a comprehensive test battery directly derived from the cognitive neuropsychology approach of assessment. This aphasia battery, commonly used in the United Kingdom, consists in a set of resource materials comprising 60 rigorously controlled tests that enable the user to select tasks "that can be tailored to the investigation of an individual patient's impaired and intact abilities." The scoring and analysis of errors give the clinician a detailed profile of language abilities, including reading and written spelling, which can be interpreted within current cognitive models of language. As compared to classical batteries of aphasia, the versatile and flexible nature of PALPA is, however, lessened by the lack of standardization and validity/reliability measures.

Tests for the Assessment of Specific Aspects of Language

Specific aspects of language behavior can also be assessed through the administration of several tests. These are often used to complete aphasia batteries but some of them also are used as screening tests. Clinicians may select these tests according to the different aspects of language they want to explore in depth, but also according to the underlying theoretical model of assessment. For example, comprehension may be tested through the administration of specific tests aiming at the discrimination of phonemic sounds (Phoneme Discrimination Test; Benton et al., 1994), semantics (Pyramids and Palm Trees Test; Howard and Patterson, 1992), sentence length and syntactic complexity (Auditory Comprehension Test for Sentences; Shewan, 1979), commands (Token Test; De Renzi and Vignolo, 1962), or narrative discourse (Discourse Comprehension Test; Brookshire and Nichols, 1993). Other tests are available for measuring verbal expression, spoken and written naming, verbal fluency, reading, writing, gestural abilities, etc. An extensive list of specific language function tests can be found in Spreen and Strauss (1998), Murray and Chapey (2001), and Spreen and Risser (2003).

The Assessment of Functional Communication

Traditional tests provide useful information on linguistic abilities and language impairments in aphasia. However, performance on these tests does not necessarily predict how a person will communicate in more naturalistic settings and everyday life. Instead of focusing on the importance and the nature of deficits, the functional communication approach of assessment aims at the impact of these deficits on the person's activities and participation in society. Functional communication skills may be assessed with specific structured tests or by rating scales and inventories of communication profiles. Structured tests such as Communication Activities of Daily Living 2 (Holland et al., 1999) and the Amsterdam–Nijmegen Everyday Language Test (Blomert et al., 1994) have been devised to explore functional communication skills using role-play in daily life activities (shopping, dealing with a receptionist, etc.) and have shown themselves to be useful to track progress over time. However, while they are certainly more ecological than comprehensive examinations and tests for specific aspects of language, structured tests of functional communication do not necessarily give reliable views of the communication skills of a person in real-life situations. In this respect, rating scales and inventories of communication profiles are closer to functional situations. For example, the Functional Assessment of Communication Skills for Adults (Frattali et al., 1995) is a rating protocol of 43 items, on a seven-point scale, based on the observations made by the speech-language pathologist or other significant person in the following four domains: social communication (e.g., 'refers to familiar people by name'); communication of basic needs (e.g., 'makes needs to eat'; reading, writing, and number concepts (e.g., 'writes messages'); and daily planning (e.g., 'tells time'). For a more extensive description of these functional communication tools, and others not described here, see Murray and Chapey (2001) and Spreen and Risser (2003).

Classical Tests for the Assessment of Speech and Language Impairment in Children

The assessment of language and communication in children can take place from infancy through adolescence, when cognitive abilities are developing. Therefore, the language assessment process must not only inform on current specific abilities, but has also to capture changes over time in the level, sequence, and rate of acquisition. The interrelationship between language and other cognitive and social skills is also of primary importance. As a part of a larger process, usually performed by different professionals, the evaluation of language in children should be completed by an assessment of nonverbal communication, play and social skills, perception, attention and memory, behavior, etc. Moreover, because of the major influence it has on child development, the evaluation also has to consider the familial and social environment, especially with respect to adult–child interaction. The different components (e.g., sensitivity, promptness) as well as the context (e.g., physical settings, types of play, activities) in which this interaction takes place should be analyzed through specific assessment tools or through direct observation.

The assessment of preschool children (children aged 2 to 5 years) and school-age children (5 to 10 or 12 years) is usually based upon a combination of parent interviews, standardized tests, criterion-referenced instruments, developmental scales, and observations. All these tools and methods aim to explore both receptive and expressive language abilities in semantics, morphology, syntax, phonology, and pragmatics. Collecting a communication sample is also a frequently used method to analyze communication in terms of sentence length, intelligibility of speech, vocabulary, and conversational strengths and weaknesses. Similarly to tests for aphasia, preschool and school-age tests can be divided into two major categories: screening and diagnostic tests. The purpose of screening tests is to determine if the child's communication should be explored more extensively for the presence of a possible impairment. On the other hand, the main purposes of diagnostic tests is to establish the presence or absence of a deficit in one or more areas of language, to identify a possible difference in language development, to determine the child's eligibility for clinical services, and to identify the targets for intervention. These instruments are devised to assess language development by reference to the parameters of the normal range.

Screening Tests

Screening tests are usually inexpensive and require minimal time for administration and interpretation of results. Many norm-referenced standardized instruments may be used to establish the child's general level of expressive and receptive language functioning as well as other areas of functioning. For example, the Denver Developmental Screening Test II (Frankenburg et al., 1990), a standardized screening battery for children from birth to age 6, is designed to test the child's abilities in the following four sectors: personal-social, fine motor, gross motor, and language (including expressive-receptive vocabulary). Screening tests may also consist in large batteries exploring language and cognitive functions through tasks of general verbal and nonverbal intellectual abilities. For example, the Wechsler Intelligence Scale for Children IV (Wechsler, 2004) is the most widely used measure of verbal and nonverbal intelligence in individuals from age 6 years 0 months to 16 years 11 months. As a screening tool, this battery consists in 16 subtests of verbal comprehension, perceptual reasoning, working memory, and processing speed skills.

For school-age children, some large screening batteries specifically concern academic achievement. That is, for example, the case with the Peabody Individual Achievement Test – Revised (PIAT-R; Markwardt, 1998), which provides a screening measure of achievement in the areas of mathematics, reading recognition and comprehension, spelling, and general information. However, most of the tasks of these large screening batteries are multifactorial and are therefore not appropriate to assess specific language or cognitive processes. For this purpose, clinicians may select among various specific screening tests for preschool and school-age children that focus only on language. Most of these instruments are designed to explore the different language components. That is the case, for example, with the Fluharty Preschool Speech and Language Screening Test II (Fluharty, 2001), which explores articulation, expressive and receptive vocabulary, and composite language in children from 2 to 6 years old. An exhaustive list of norm-referenced standardized screening tests of language can be found in Paul (2001).

Comprehensive Examinations and Batteries

As for screening, some diagnostic tools are designed to explore language skills as well as other aspects of development. That is the case, for example, with the Communication and Symbolic Behavior Scales Developmental Profile (Wetherby and Prizant, 1998), which includes tasks exploring expressive and receptive language, symbolic play, and nonverbal communication in children from 6 to 24 months old. Another example is the Rossetti Infant-Toddler Language Scale (Rossetti, 1990), which is used to assess attachment, play, gestures, and pragmatics, as well as language comprehension and expression in children from birth to 3 years old. There are also several standardized comprehensive batteries of language processing that comprise tests exploring exclusively some or all of the language areas. That is the case, for example, with the Preschool Language Scale 4 (Zimmerman et al., 2002), which is used to identify specific strengths and weaknesses in receptive and expressive language skills in children from birth to 6 years 11 months. The Clinical Evaluation of Language Fundamentals 4 (Semel et al., 2003) is a multidimensional battery that can be used in individuals between the ages of 5 and 21 years to explore semantics, expressive and receptive language, and syntax, as well as working memory. The Comprehensive Assessment of Spoken Language (Carrow-Woolfolk, 1999), designed for children from age 3 to 21, is another comprehensive battery of language skills, comprising 15 tests that provide an assessment of expressive and receptive skills in four language categories: lexical/semantic, syntactic, supralinguistic, and pragmatics. An extensive list of available comprehensive examinations and batteries of language for children can be found in McCauley (2001), Paul (2001), Mattis and Luck (2002), and Haynes and Pindzola (2003).

Tests for Specific Aspects of Language

Different components of language can be affected with more or less intensity in children according to the origin of developmental disorders. Therefore, the in-depth assessment of language and communication disorders in children is a critical component in the clinical process. Core tests can be used to evaluate each of the language areas in order to identify specific impairments, establish baselines, and identify precise therapeutic and intervention goals. For example, there are several core tests and instruments for the evaluation of word retrieval (e.g., naming and verbal fluency tests), phonology (e.g., word and nonword repetition tests), receptive and expressive vocabulary (e.g., word definition tests), receptive and expressive syntax and morphology (e.g., sentence-to-picture matching tests), and pragmatic skills (e.g., narrative production, story comprehension tests).

A combination of different tests, each focusing on specific language components, may also be used to establish such a language and communication profile. For example, to assess vocabulary, clinicians may select the following standardized norm-referenced specific tests: the Expressive One-Word Picture Vocabulary Test Revised (Gardner, 2000), to exclusively explore expressive vocabulary in individuals ages 2 years 0 months through 18 years 11 months;

or the Peabody Picture Vocabulary Test (Dunn and Dunn, 1997), to exclusively explore receptive vocabulary in individuals from age 2 years 6 months to adult. A more complete description of available diagnostic tests adapted to preschool and school-age children can be found in McCauley (2001), Paul (2001), Mattis and Luck (2002), and Haynes and Pindzola (2003).

The Assessment of Reading and Writing

The relationship between language acquisition and academic achievement is well established. Developmental disorders of language in preschool children are frequently associated with later difficulties in learning to read and write. The most common referral for a speech-language pathology assessment concerns school-age children who encounter problems in progressing beyond the developing language phase and present with difficulties in learning and acquiring communicative and academic skills. As for other populations, but especially at this stage of development, a significant difficulty in assessing school-age children arises because of important comorbidity between language and learning disorders and other cognitive and clinical pathological profiles, such as attention deficit/hyperactivity or executive function disorders. Therefore, the assessment process should include specific tests of language and communication but also instruments designed for exploring other cognitive functions, such as attention, working memory, and executive functions. In addition to formal tests, another important source of information also comes from structured interviews of the child himself, his parents and his teacher. With respect to language, phonological processing deficits are considered as an underlying cause of dyslexia and also play a role in developmental disorders of spelling. For example, dyslexic children often show problems with word and nonword repetition tasks, phonological awareness tasks (e.g., word and nonword segmentation tasks, phoneme manipulation, etc.), and working memory tasks for verbal material (i.e., word or digit span tasks). The semantic processing is another cognitive area highly related to reading and writing. School-age children usually learn new words through reading and writing. Those who encounter problems in reading and writing often present with poor vocabulary as well as with difficulty in word association and comprehension. Therefore, the assessment procedure for written language problems should be part of a more exhaustive evaluation of language and cognition. It should also include a close control of psycholinguistic parameters (e.g., orthographic regularity, lexical frequency) that are known to play an important role in written and spoken word recognition, reading comprehension, phoneme–grapheme conversion, decoding, etc. However, very few standardized assessment tools fulfill these conditions. As an exception, French-speaking clinicians may use the Batterie d'Évaluation du Langage Écrit et de Ses Troubles (Mousty et al., 1994), a written-language-testing battery based on current models of reading and writing, to assess children between the ages of 7 and 12 years. In addition to experimental tasks, one can resort to standardized achievement or specific tests of reading and writing skills. Among the most used of achievement tests are PIAT-R (Markwardt, 1998), which comprises subtests of reading comprehension, reading recognition, and spelling, and the Wide Range Achievement Test (Wilkinson, 1993), a brief test measuring reading recognition, spelling, and arithmetic computation. For a description of specific clinical tests of reading and writing, see Spreen and Strauss (1998) and Bailet (2001).

Classical Tests for the Assessment of Speech and Language Impairment in Special Populations

Referral for speech-language assessment not only concerns aphasia and developmental deficits of language but also involves individuals of different age groups presenting with various language and communication problems. In children and adolescents, these references include language deficits in pervasive developmental disorders (e.g., autism, Asperger's disorder), mental retardation, attention deficit/hyperactivity disorder, specific language impairment, sensory deficits (hearing loss, blindness), acquired disorders (e.g., traumatic brain injury), stuttering, etc. In adults, referral for a speech-language evaluation may be required for language and communication deficits following right hemisphere damage, traumatic brain injury, Alzheimer's disease and other forms of dementia (e.g., primary progressive aphasia, semantic dementia), stuttering and other fluency problems, etc.

In children, adolescents, and adults, clinical assessments may also concern such speech problems as dysarthria, following a stroke and neurodegenerative illnesses or accompanying cerebral palsy, acquired or developmental apraxia of speech, etc. In addition to the conventional evaluation of basic language (or speech) skills, the assessment procedure in all these special populations involves specific aspects and particularities of speech and language. For example, because of the absence of biological markers or simple diagnosis methods, the early detection of dementia often depends on various assessment tools, including language and cognitive tests performed to exclude other possible disease processes or identify specific forms of a given disease. In that particular domain, the assessment of speech and language usually includes tests allowing for differential diagnosis. For example, tests that specifically tap either semantic processing or written spelling can contribute to differentiating common disease processes in the elderly population. Semantic deficits are prominent characteristics of individuals diagnosed with Alzheimer's disease and these individuals usually differ from patients diagnosed with vascular dementia or frontotemporal dementia because of the presence of surface dysgraphia, a specific spelling disorder.

It is obviously not possible to exhaustively describe here the various tests adapted to special populations. The reader will find a more complete description of such tests in McCauley (2001), Paul (2001), Haynes and Pindzola (2003), and Spreen and Risser (2003).

Conclusion

Language production and comprehension are complex cognitive skills that should not be considered in isolation in assessment procedures. The interrelation between language and other cognitive functions has to be captured, particularly with respect to the possible influence of attention, working memory, and executive functions on linguistic abilities. If possible, clinicians should always select valid and reliable norm-referenced tests to assess language and communication. Resorting to theoretical models of language functioning also appears of primary importance and may sometimes condition the utilization of experimental, well-controlled, assessment tasks. A comprehensive assessment of language and communication is more than just an evaluation of specific skills in terms of preservation or impairment of processing components and surface structures. The scope of assessment should be widened in order to provide information about physical, social, and emotional contexts of communication, cultural differences, and economic factors. The combination of these data, obtained through assessment tools and direct observations, should then allow the clinician to establish a complete portrait of functional communication abilities.

See also: Dementia and Language; Phonological Impairments, Sublexical; Phonological, Lexical, Syntactic, and Semantic Disorders in Children; Primary Progressive Aphasia in Nondementing Adults; Proper and Common Names, Impairments; Speech Impairments in Neurodegenerative Diseases/Psychiatric Illnesses.

Bibliography

Bailet, LL (2001). 'Written language test reviews.' In: Bain, AM, Bailet, LL, and Moats, LC (eds.) *Written language disorders*. pp. 221–248. Austin: Pro-Ed.

Benton, AL, Hamsher, K, Varney, NR, and Spreen, O (1994). *Contributions to neuropsychological assessment,* 2nd edn. New York: Oxford University Press.

Blomert, L, Kean, ML, Koster, C, and Schokker, J (1994). 'Amsterdam–Nijmegen Everyday Language Test: construction, reliability, and validity.' *Aphasiology* 8: 381–407.

Brookshire, R and Nichols, LE (1993). *The Discourse Comprehension Test.* Minneapolis: BRK.

Carrow-Woolfolk, E (1999). *Comprehensive Assessment of Spoken Language.* Circle Pines, MN: American Guidance Service.

DeRenzi, E and Vignolo, L (1962). 'The token test: a sensitive test to detect receptive disturbances in aphasics.' *Brain* 85: 665–678.

Dunn, LM and Dunn, LM (1997). *Peabody Picture Vocabulary Test.* Circle Pines, MN: American Guidance Service.

Fluharty, NB (2001). *Fluharty Preschool Speech and Language Screening Test II.* Austin: Pro-Ed.

Frankenburg, W, Dodds, J, Archer, P, Bresnick, B, Maschka, P, Edelman, N, and Shapiro, H (1990). *Denver II: screening manual.* Denver: Denver Developmental Materials.

Frattali, CM, Thompson, CK, Holland, AL, Wohl, CB, and Ferketic, MM (1995). *Functional Assessment of Communication Skills for Adults.* Rockville, MD: American Speech-Language-Hearing Association.

Gardner, MF (2000). *Expressive One-Word Picture Vocabulary Test – Revised.* Novato, CA: Academic Therapy.

Goodglass, H, Kaplan, E, and Barresi, B (2000). *Boston Diagnostic Aphasia Examination,* 3rd edn. Philadelphia: Lippincott Williams & Wilkins.

Haynes, WO and Pindzola, HR (2003). *Diagnosis and evaluation in speech pathology,* 6th edn. Boston: Allyn & Bacon.

Helm-Estabrooks, N (1992). *Aphasia Diagnostic Profiles.* Chicago: Riverside Publishing.

Holland, AL, Frattali, CM, and Fromm, D (1999). *Communication Activities of Daily Living,* 2nd edn. Austin: Pro-Ed.

Howard, D and Patterson, KE (1992). *The Pyramids and Palm Trees Test.* Oxford: Harcourt Assessment.

Kay, J, Lesser, R, and Coltheart, M (1992). *Psycholinguistic Assessments of Language Processing in Aphasia (PALPA).* Hove, England: Lawrence Erlbaum Associates.

Kertesz, A (1982). *Western Aphasia Battery.* New York: Grune & Stratton.

Markwardt, FC (1998). *Peabody Individual Achievement Test Revised.* Circle Pines, MN: American Guidance Service.

Mattis, S and Luck, DZ (2002). 'Neuropsychological assessment of school-aged children.' In: Segalowitz, SJ and Rapin, I (eds.) *Handbook of neuropsychology: child neuropsychology 1.* New York: Elsevier Science.

McCauley, RJ (2001). *Assessment of language disorders in children.* Mahwah, NJ: Lawrence Erlbaum Associates.

Mousty, P, Leybaert, J, Alégria, J, Content, A, and Morais, J (1994). *Batterie d'Évaluation du Langage Écrit et de ses Troubles.* Brussels: Laboratoire de Psychologie Expérimentale, Université Libre de Bruxelles.

Murray, LL and Chapey, R (2001). 'Assessment of language disorders in adults.' In: Chapey, R (ed.) *Language intervention strategies in aphasia and related neurogenic communication disorders* (4th edn.), pp. 55–126. Philadelphia: Lippincott Williams & Wilkins.

Paul, R (2001). *Language disorders from infancy through adolescence: Assessment and intervention,* 2nd edn. Toronto: Mosby.

Reitan, RM (1991). *Aphasia Screening Test.* Tucson: Reitan Neuropsychology Laboratory.

Rossetti, L (1990). *Rossetti Infant-Toddler Language Scale.* East Moline, IL: LinguiSystems.

Semel, E, Wiig, EH, and Secord, WA (2003). *Clinical Evaluation of Language Fundamentals,* 4th edn. Toronto: Psychological Corporation.

Shewan, CM (1979). *Auditory Comprehension Test for Sentences (ACTS).* Chicago: Biolinguistics Clinical Institutes.

Spellacy, F and Spreen, O (1969). 'A short form of the Token Test.' *Cortex* 5: 390–397.

Spreen, O and Risser, AH (2003). *Assessment of aphasia.* New York: Oxford University Press.

Spreen, O and Strauss, E (1998). *A compendium of neuropsychological tests,* 2nd edn. New York: Oxford University Press.

Wechsler, D (2004). *The Wechsler Intelligence Scale for Children: Fourth edition integrated.* San Antonio, TX: Harcourt Assessment.

Wetherby, AM and Prizant, BM (1998). *Communication and Symbolic Behavior Scales-Developmental Profile.* Chicago: Applied Symbolix.

Wilkinson, GS (1993). *Wide Range Achievement Test 3.* San Antonio, TX: Harcourt Assessment.

Zimmerman, IL, Steiner, VG, and Pond, RE (2002). *Preschool Language Scale,* 4th edn. San Antonio, TX: Harcourt Assessment.

Cognition in Aging and Age-Related Disease

E. A. Kensinger, Boston College, Chestnut Hill, MA, USA

Introduction

As the average age of the population increases, there is growing interest in understanding the cognitive and neural changes that accompany aging. It is now clear that significant cognitive decline is not an inevitable consequence of advancing age. This realization has spurred researchers to examine what separates high-performing older adults from lower-performing older adults and to investigate how the changes with successful aging differ from those that result from age-related disease. Data acquired using behavioral testing, functional neuroimaging, and structural neuroimaging are beginning to inform these issues, although a number of questions remain.

Cognitive Declines with Healthy Aging

Not all cognitive domains are affected equally by age, and not all cognitive processes show age-related decline. If an older adult were asked to list the cognitive declines that have been most notable to him or her, it is likely that at least one of the following would make the list: problems paying attention to relevant information and ignoring irrelevant information in his or her environment, word-finding difficulties, or problems remembering the context in which information was learned.

Much of the research within the field of cognitive aging is focused on understanding whether the pattern of age-related cognitive decline can be explained by domain-general (or 'core') cognitive changes or whether changes in domain-specific processes are required to describe the data.

Domain-General Theories of Cognitive Aging

Domain-general theories of aging are based on the hypothesis that there is a shared ability that cross-cuts all of the tasks on which older adults are impaired: these theories suggest that although aging affects a range of cognitive functions, there is one central or core deficit underlying the myriad changes. This article focuses on three core deficits that have been proposed to explain the pattern of age-related declines: changes in sensory perception, changes in inhibitory ability, and changes in speed of processing.

Sensory deficits

The sensory deficit hypothesis of aging proposes that the cognitive changes with aging may be attributed to changes in sensation (i.e., deficits in vision and hearing). Indeed, aging is associated with dramatic sensory declines: by the eighth decade of life, the majority of older adults have significant hearing loss and a reduced ability to discriminate colors and luminance. Support for the hypothesis that these sensory deficits may underlie cognitive changes has come from two lines of research. First, across a wide range of cognitive tasks, older adults' performance correlates strongly with their sensory abilities. Second, in young adults, cognitive impairments can arise when the to-be-processed stimuli are degraded. For example, when asked to remember words pronounced against a noisy background, or when asked to match digits and symbols written in low-contrast font, young adults perform comparably to older adults. Thus, it is plausible that age-related deficits on many cognitive tasks stem, at least in part, from reductions in sensory processing. For example, changes in audition may result in older adults' slowed performance on tasks requiring auditory processing and could explain older adults' poorer memory for auditory information. It is also possible, however, that in at least some instances the correlation derives from a common influence underlying both the sensory and cognitive changes. For example, individuals who have greater brain atrophy or dysfunction may be more likely to have both sensory deficits and cognitive impairments. Regardless of the precise mechanism through which sensory deficits relate to cognitive ones, evidence of significant sensory changes with age underscores the importance of modifying testing procedures to minimize the influence of sensory deficits on older adults' cognitive test performance (e.g., using louder or higher-contrast stimuli).

Inhibition

Hasher, Zacks, and colleagues have proposed that older adults' cognitive deficits may relate to their inability to ignore irrelevant information in the environment while focusing attention on goal-relevant information. If an older adult is seated at a restaurant that has many tables in close proximity to one another, he or she may have difficulty paying attention to the conversation at his or her table while ignoring the conversations at nearby tables. In the laboratory, inhibitory deficits can result in responses to previous (but not current) targets. For example, after reading the sentence "Before going to bed, please turn off the STOVE," older adults will be more likely than young adults to believe that the target word was LIGHT rather than STOVE. The age-related increase in this type of error is thought to occur because older adults have a hard time inhibiting the strong association present in the 'garden path sentence' (e.g., between the idea of going to bed and the idea of turning off the light). Inhibitory deficits also frequently emerge when older adults are required to task-switch or to set-shift. On these tasks, older adults must first pay attention to one aspect of a stimulus (e.g., match items based on their shape) and then another (e.g., match items based on their color). Older adults often have a harder time than young adults when they must ignore the previously relevant dimension (e.g., the shape of the items) and instead focus their attention on another stimulus attribute (e.g., the color of the items).

These data clearly indicate that inhibitory deficits can occur on a range of tasks requiring the ability to selectively attend to information in the environment or to inhibit a strong association or response. However, inhibitory deficits may impair performance not only on tasks that directly assess inhibitory ability, but also on assessments of working memory capacity: if older adults have a hard time distinguishing relevant from irrelevant information, this likely means that they store task-irrelevant information, reducing the storage capacity available for task-relevant information.

Speed of processing

Older adults have a slower speed of processing than young adults. This slowed processing is noted at the motor level, but it also is apparent at a cognitive level. For example, older adults will tend to be slightly slower than young adults when they must slam on the brakes at a red light; this slowing may primarily be due to motor changes, because the association of red = stop remains very strong with aging. The reaction time differences between young and older adults will be exaggerated, however, if older adults must decide whether to slam on the brakes or to hit the gas as they approach a light that has just turned yellow. This additional slowing likely results because of the increased cognitive processing that must occur before the appropriate action can be selected.

Salthouse and colleagues have suggested that this decline in processing speed may underlie the age-related changes in cognitive function. It is apparent how slowed speed of processing could be detrimental to performance on any type of timed task. Importantly, however, a slower speed of processing could also manifest itself on nontimed tasks. For example, imagine that I read aloud the following arithmetic problem, and ask you to solve it in your head, with no time limit: "Jimmy walks up to a store counter with three packs of gum, each costing 50 cents. He gives the sales clerk $5. Because the clerk is out of dollar bills, she gives Jimmy his change in quarters. How many quarters does Jimmy receive from the sales clerk?" On the face of it, this is a task of working memory ability (the ability to store various pieces of information and to update the information as you work through the problem) that might be thought of as being independent from a measure of speed of processing, because there is no time limit for solving the task. However, if it takes someone a little longer to process the phrase "Jimmy walks up to a store counter with three packs of gum," it is possible that they will have a harder time attending to the phrase "costing 50 cents." Similarly, if it takes someone longer to multiply 3 by 50, it is possible that by the time that calculation is completed they will have forgotten the amount of money that Jimmy gave to the clerk. In other words, cognitive performance can suffer because the slowed mental operations cannot be carried out within the necessary time frame, and because the increased time between mental operations can make it more difficult to access previously processed information. Thus, a slower speed of processing may lead to a poorer encoding of information and a reduced ability to store information. In support of the hypothesis that processing speed changes may underlie much of the cognitive decline with aging, controlling for speed of processing often eliminates age differences on cognitive tasks, and longitudinal studies have shown a strong relation between changes in speed of processing and changes in performance on a large number of cognitive tasks.

Domain-Specific Theories of Cognitive Aging

In contrast to the domain-general theories of cognitive aging, domain-specific theories propose that some age-related declines may not be explained by core deficits that affect all aspects of cognition, but rather by changes that have a larger impact on one area of cognition than on another.

Word-finding difficulties and transmission deficits

Older adults often have difficulties retrieving the appropriate name for a person, place, or thing. These word-finding problems can be manifest in various ways: excessive use of pronouns (due to difficulty generating the proper nouns), decreased accuracy and increased reaction time when asked to name items, and increased tip-of-the-tongue experiences. The tip-of-the-tongue state occurs when a person has access to a word's meaning, but not the phonological features of the word. The word seems just out of reach. Older adults tend to have more tip-of-the-tongue experiences than young adults, particularly for proper names, and the accuracy of the phonological information available during a tip-of-the-tongue state (e.g., the first letter of the word, the number of syllables) tends to be more accurate for young adults than for older adults.

Burke, MacKay, and colleagues have suggested that these word-finding difficulties result from the fact that, with age, the links connecting one unit to another within the memory system become weaker. Thus, more links must be active in order for older adults to generate the correct name for an object or a person. This transmission deficit will mean that older adults will be relatively good at generating words when there are lots of links converging onto the word but will show larger impairments when trying to generate words that have fewer associated links. Most everyday objects have many semantic associations (e.g., individuals know that apples are red, of waxy texture, round, etc.). This convergence onto the word 'apple' (referred to by Burke and colleagues as summation of priming) makes it relatively easy to generate the name of the object. In contrast, proper names (with the exception of nicknames) are arbitrary and do not benefit from the same summation of priming (e.g., there is nothing that is required for someone to be a Jane vs. a Linda). Consistent with a transmission deficit, older adults remain relatively good at generating words of everyday objects for which they know a lot of semantic information but show larger impairments when asked to generate proper nouns.

Contextual memory and associative binding deficits

Episodic memory can be thought of as including memory for two different types of information: memory for the item previously encountered (which typically can be based on familiarity) and memory for the broader context in which that item was encountered (which requires recollection). For example, when I pass by someone on the street, I might recognize that I have seen the person before (item memory). I also may remember that I met the person at a recent conference (an item–context association) or that the person is my colleague's husband (an item–item association).

Older adults remain quite good at using familiarity to recognize previously encountered people or items. However, older adults are particularly impaired at using recollection to remember the contextual details of an event. They seem to have difficulties binding together multiple event details into one cohesive memory. These deficits arise when trying to remember both item–item associations and item–context associations ('source' memory). Naveh-Benjamin and colleagues have proposed that this associative memory deficit underlies older adults' episodic memory difficulties.

Two broad types of memorial deficits may underlie this decreased ability to remember item–item or item–context associations. First, older adults have difficulties initiating effective encoding 'strategies' that would promote memory for the associative details of an experience (as proposed by Craik, Jennings, and colleagues). When they are given a strategy to use as they learn information (e.g., if they are asked to tell a story that binds the item to its context), older adults often perform as well as young adults on tasks requiring associative or contextual memory. Thus, at least some of the age-related deficits in remembering contextual details seem to result from deficits at encoding. Second, older adults seem to have difficulties either in forming a long-lasting 'bond' between an item and its context, or in retrieving that bound representation. Thus, given retrieval support (e.g., an untimed recognition task), older adults will tend to perform better than when given little retrieval support (e.g., a recall task).

Preserved Cognitive Function with Healthy Aging

Although the previous sections have focused on age-related declines, aging is not associated with across-the-board deficits in cognitive. In fact, some aspects of cognition remain markedly stable, or even improve, as individuals age.

Crystallized Intelligence

Crystallized intelligence refers to the ability to retrieve and use information that has been acquired throughout a lifetime. It often is contrasted with fluid intelligence, the ability to store and manipulate new information. As discussed earlier, fluid intelligence processes tend to be disrupted by healthy aging. Crystallized intelligence, in contrast, remains stable across the life span. Thus, older adults are very good (often better than young adults) at defining words, answering questions that rely on general world knowledge (e.g., "Who wrote the 'Star Spangled Banner'?"), detecting spelling errors, or carrying out skills related to jobs that they have held for many years.

Emotion Regulation

Another important area of preservation (or enhancement) is within the realm of emotion regulation. After about the age of 60, the ability to regulate emotion seems to start to improve. Thus, older adults show lower rates of depression than young adults. Compared to young adults, their good moods last longer, and they are able to rebound more quickly from negative mood states. Older adults seem to focus more on positive information in their environment and to choose activities (e.g., spending time with close family or friends) based on their potential for emotional fulfillment.

At least some aspects of memory for emotional information also seem to be preserved with aging. While older adults tend to show overall poorer memory than young adults on a variety of tasks requiring retrieval of contextual information, studies of 'flashbulb memories'

(memories for a public event that was highly surprising and emotional) have suggested that older adults, like young adults, are more likely to remember contextual details if the event contains emotional relevance than if it does not. The emotional memory benefit for older adults may be particularly pronounced for positive information, although a number of studies have suggested that older adults receive a memory boost when asked to remember negative experiences as well.

Neural Changes with Healthy Aging

Although healthy aging is associated with brain changes, not all regions are affected equally. To date, the vast majority of studies investigating the neural changes with healthy aging have used structural magnetic resonance imaging (MRI) (allowing examination of the volume of various brain regions) and functional MRI (fMRI)or positron emission tomography (PET) (allowing indirect measurements of neural activity as individuals are performing a task). These studies have suggested that the largest changes in structure and function occur in the prefrontal cortex and in the medial temporal lobe, while other cortical and subcortical regions remain relatively preserved across the life span. Current research also is focused on examining how the connections between regions are affected by aging. Diffusion tensor imaging studies are being conducted to examine age-related changes in white matter tracks, and structural equation modeling of fMRI and PET data is being used to investigate age-related changes in the functional connections between brain regions. These methods may provide new insights into the neural changes that mediate older adults' cognitive decline.

Changes in Prefrontal Cortex

The prefrontal cortex shows notable changes with aging. At a structural level, there is evidence of atrophy, both in the gray matter and in the white matter. The gray matter declines may reflect reductions in the number of cells (due to cell death) or may be a sign of neuronal shrinkage. The white matter changes reflect axonal abnormalities and may result in slowed neurotransmission. It is plausible that these white matter changes may mediate the cognitive slowing that accompanies healthy aging.

Prefrontal function also is altered with aging. Across a range of working memory and episodic memory tasks, older adults seem to show a different pattern of prefrontal activity than young adults, with reduced activity in some prefrontal regions and increased activity in other regions. As noted by Cabeza and colleagues, particularly in the prefrontal cortex, older adults often show a hemispheric asymmetry reduction. In other words, on tasks leading to unilateral prefrontal activity in young adults, older adults will tend to show bilateral recruitment. It is not yet clear whether this bilateral recruitment reflects compensatory activation, or whether it is a result of pathological changes (e.g., hemispheric release from inhibition). Some of the strongest evidence in favor of the compensatory view has come from studies comparing the pattern of neural recruitment in older adults who perform a task as well as young adults (high performers) and in older adults who perform the task more poorly (low performers). These studies have found that the high performers tend to recruit the prefrontal cortex bilaterally, whereas the low performers show unilateral prefrontal activity. To the extent that the prefrontal activity underlies the initiation of goal-relevant task strategies, it would make sense that the older adults who recruit additional prefrontal regions would be those who would be best able to perform the tasks. Nevertheless, future studies are required to clarify whether this compensatory hypothesis can account for all of the findings of bilateral prefrontal recruitment with age.

Medial Temporal Lobe Changes

The hippocampus proper is the other region that shows large age-related change. While there are structural changes in the hippocampus, it is not clear whether there is significant cell loss in the hippocampus with aging, or whether the structural changes are related more to neuronal atrophy (shrinkage). There also is ambiguity regarding the regions of the hippocampus that are most affected by aging. High-resolution MRI, allowing the distinction of the various hippocampal subfields (CA1, CA3, dentate gyrus, subiculum) may allow better assessment of the structure (and function) of these regions.

Functionally, the hippocampus tends to be under-recruited by older adults during both the encoding and the retrieval phases of recollective or associative memory tasks, and these functional changes often correlate with the older adults' reduced performance on the tasks. Given the critical role of the hippocampus in forming vivid and detailed memories, it makes sense that the functional and structural changes in this region would correspond with older adults' difficulties in remembering the context in which information was learned.

Changes in Emotion Processing Regions

The fact that older adults show improved emotion regulation, and a memory enhancement for many types of emotional information, is consistent with the neural evidence indicating that emotion processing regions (particularly the amygdala and orbitofrontal cortex) are relatively spared in healthy aging. The amygdala shows minimal atrophy with healthy aging; its atrophy is on par with the decline in whole-brain volume (with a 1–3% reduction in volume every decade). Similarly, the orbitofrontal cortex seems to undergo little volumetric decline with age, particularly as compared to other regions of the prefrontal cortex.

Mild Cognitive Impairment

As discussed previously, some cognitive impairment is a natural part of the aging process. For some adults, however, advancing age is associated with fairly severe impairments in recent memory. Although the deficits do not impair their ability to function in daily life (and thus they do not meet the criteria for dementia), these individuals have cognitive impairments that exceed those that typically accompany healthy or successful aging. 'Benign senescent forgetfulness' was the first term used (by Kral and colleagues) to describe these individuals' impairments, although there were no strict diagnostic criteria associated with the concept. 'Age-associated memory impairment' (proposed by Crook and colleagues) was the first attempt at a standardized definition, requiring an individual to have subjective memory complaints and to perform at least 1 standard deviation below the mean for young adults on a standardized memory task. This concept was criticized by a number of researchers, who believed that the concept was too restrictive. Mild cognitive impairment (MCI) (defined by the Mayo Clinic Alzheimer's Disease Research Center) is the most recent in a series of attempts to characterize these individuals who straddle the boundary between healthy aging and dementia. A diagnosis of MCI requires subjective memory complaints and impairment in one area of cognition (scores must be more than 1.5 standard deviations below age-scaled norms), but with deficits not severe enough to interfere with activities of daily living or to result in a diagnosis of dementia.

There has been tremendous interest in defining this group of individuals, because as treatments that slow or reverse the development of Alzheimer's disease (AD) become available, it will be critical to have a method for diagnosing individuals at risk for, or in the prodromal stages of, the disease. Individuals with MCI seem to be an excellent population to be the targets of such treatments, because they are at increased risk for development of dementia, and of AD in particular. In fact, by some estimates, the vast majority of patients with MCI will eventually meet the diagnostic criteria for dementia.

The link between MCI and AD is supported not only by the high conversion rate, but also by the overlapping neuropathological and genetic features. Like AD patients, those with MCI have significant structural and functional changes in the medial temporal lobe. They also have alterations in the concentration of amyloid beta protein, the protein associated with neuritic plaque formation in AD. Moreover, the $\varepsilon 4$ allele of the apolipoprotein E, associated with an increased risk of developing AD, is overrepresented among individuals with MCI.

Alzheimer's Disease

AD was first described by Alois Alzheimer in 1907. In the landmark publication, Alzheimer reported a case study of a woman with severe psychiatric symptoms and memory deficits. An autopsy conducted upon her death revealed a large quantity of intracellular neuritic plaques and extracellular neurofibrillary tangles, now recognized as the pathologic hallmarks of AD.

Cognitive Changes in AD

Although dementia (a loss of intellectual function severe enough to interfere with daily activities) can result from a variety of etiologies, AD is by far the most common cause, accounting for an estimated two-thirds of all cases of dementia. Because AD can only be confirmed at autopsy, its clinical diagnosis must be an exclusionary one. Thus, the clinical profile of AD requires memory impairment plus decline in one other area of cognition (language, motor function, attention, executive function, personality, or object recognition). The deficits must have a gradual onset, and they must progress continually and irreversibly. When these criteria are met, a diagnosis of 'probable' AD is given. When made by a trained clinician, this diagnosis will be accurate in the vast majority (80–90%) of cases.

Episodic memory

In contrast to healthy older adults, who remain able to successfully remember previously encountered information (though perhaps not the context in which it was encountered), the most notable deficit for patients with mild AD is an inability to remember information encountered in the recent past. This deficit extends across different types of encoding tasks (e.g., incidental or intentional; deep or shallow processing) and exists regardless of the stimulus materials (e.g., pictures, words, faces, autobiographical events, emotional stimuli) or the task's retrieval demands (e.g., recall, forced-choice recognition, yes–no recognition). In fact, deficits in episodic memory tend to be the best way of distinguishing people with AD from healthy older adults.

Semantic memory

In contrast to episodic memory, semantic memory (general world knowledge) is relatively spared with mild AD. As the disease progresses, however, significant semantic deficits arise. The deficits are particularly pronounced on word-finding tasks, with the extent of such deficits being useful for tracking the severity of AD. Current research is examining the extent to which the breakdown in semantic memory is due to changes in the structure of the memory networks (i.e., to a problem with the storage of such knowledge) or to difficulties retrieving the stored information (i.e., a problem with access).

Working memory and executive function

In addition to deficits in long-term memory, Alzheimer's patients also show deficits in the online processing of information (working memory). Deficits are particularly pronounced on tasks requiring dual-task performance, suggesting that a primary deficit in AD may be in executive functions, the ability to flexibly shift attention and to attend to goal-relevant information.

Neural Changes in AD

Although plaques and tangles often are apparent throughout the brain in the later stages of AD, early in the course of the disease, the medial temporal lobe regions are those most affected. Even early in the disease, the hippocampal formation shows marked atrophy, and a volumetric reduction in the entorhinal cortex (which serves as the site of input to the hippocampus) is one of the best indicators that an individual has early AD. Given the essential role of the hippocampus for memory formation and retrieval (as demonstrated by the link between hippocampal damage and amnesia), it makes sense that patients with mild AD would be best identified by their difficulties remembering recently learned information (as discussed previously).

The amygdala is another region of the medial temporal lobe that is affected early in the disease process. This region, through its interactions with other medial temporal lobe structures, is thought to be essential for enhancing individuals' memories for highly emotional events. It is likely because of the amygdalar damage that patients with AD do not show a memory benefit for emotional information.

In addition to the medial temporal lobe changes, the nucleus basalis also shows significant cell loss in mild AD. This region of the ventral forebrain contains many of the brain's cholinergic neurons; thus, the damage to this region impedes cholinergic neurotransmission. Many of the first approved therapies for AD have been aimed at increasing the amount of acetylcholine in the brain, by blocking the function of acetylcholine esterase (the enzyme that breaks down the neurotransmitter acetylcholine). The minimal effectiveness of these acetylcholine esterase inhibitors in affecting cognitive function in AD patients suggests that the acetylcholine deficiency is not the only cause of the cognitive dysfunction in AD (and, indeed, at least by late-stage AD, there is marked depletion of other neurotransmitters, including norepinephrine, dopamine, and serotonin). The underwhelming effect of the cholinesterase inhibitors has led to continued research on alternate therapeutic options for AD, which may prove to be more effective in altering the progression of the disease.

Neural Changes in Later-Stage AD

In later stages of the disease, there is increased atrophy throughout the medial temporal lobe, and the cellular abnormalities also become apparent in the frontal lobe and throughout the temporal lobe. Because the frontal lobe is essential for higher-level executive functions, and the temporal neocortex is critical for the ability to retrieve semantic information, the advancing neuropathology in these regions clearly is linked to the cognitive deficits that arise in moderate AD. By the very late stages of AD, neuropathology is abundant throughout the cortical and subcortical structures, even within primary sensory regions (e.g., auditory, visual, and motor cortex).

Individual Differences in Aging

Unlike many diseases or illnesses that can be linked to a specific cause, MCI and AD appear to arise due to a combination of many factors, both environmental and biological. Research has begun to elucidate some of the traits that can increase the likelihood of disease development ('risk factors' such as prior head injury, mutations in the apolipoprotein, presenilin-1, and presenilin-2 genes, or having the ε4 allele of apolipoprotein E) or that seem to reduce the probability of disease ('protective factors' such as high education level, intake of antioxidants, or having the ε2 allele of apolipoprotein E). Research continues to investigate the reliability of these factors in predicting disease development and to examine whether any of the protective factors can alter disease progression once the pathological hallmarks of disease are present.

More broadly, researchers are beginning to recognize the necessity of taking an individual-differences approach to understanding the cognitive and neural changes that accompany aging. Research is now exploring the potential differences between high-performing and low-performing older adults. It is plausible that a better understanding of what differentiates the most successful agers from those who age less gracefully will lead to ideas for behavioral or neurobiological interventions that can boost the performance of individuals who experience significant age-related cognitive decline.

See also: Cognition, An Overview of Neuroimaging Techniques.

Further Reading

Burke, DM and Mackay, DG (1997). Memory, language, and ageing. *Philosophical Transactions of the Royal Society of London, B Series (Biological Sciences)* 352: 1845–1856.

Cabeza, R (2002). Hemispheric asymmetry reduction in older adults: The HAROLD model. *Psychology and Aging* 17: 85–100.

De Toledo-Morrell, L, Goncharova, I, Dickerson, B, Wilson, RS, and Bennett, DA (2000). From healthy aging to early Alzheimer's disease: *In vivo* detection of entorhinal cortex atrophy. *Annals of the New York Academy of Sciences* 911: 240–253.

Grady, CL and Craik, FIM (2000). Changes in memory processing with age. *Current Opinion in Neurobiology* 10: 224–231.

Kensinger, EA (2006). Remembering emotional information: Effects of aging and Alzheimer's disease. In: Welsh, EM (ed.) *Frontiers in*

Alzheimer's Disease Research. Hauppauge, NY: Nova Science Publishers.

Li, KZH and Lindenberger, U (2002). Relations between aging sensory/ sensorimotor and cognitive functions. *Neuroscience and Biobehavioral Reviews* 26: 777–783.

Light, L (1992). The organization of memory in old age. In: Craik, FIM and Salthouse, TA (eds.) *The Handbook of Aging and Cognition*, pp. 111–165. Hillsdale, NJ: Erlbaum.

Mather, M and Carstensen, LL (2005). Aging and motivated cognition: The positivity effect in attention and memory. *Trends in Cognitive Sciences* 9: 296–502.

Park, DC and Gutchess, AH (2002). Aging, cognition, and culture: A neuroscientific perspective. *Neuroscience and Biobehavioral Reviews* 26: 859–867.

Salthouse, TA (1996). The processing-speed theory of adult age differences in cognition. *Psychological Review* 103: 403–428.

Cognition, An Overview of Neuroimaging Techniques

S. A. Bunge, University of California at Berkeley, Berkeley, CA, USA
I. Kahn, Howard Hughes Medical Institute at Harvard University, Cambridge, MA, USA

Anatomical Techniques

Anatomical techniques are used in a variety of ways in the service of the study of cognition, for example, to localize neuropathies in patients with cognitive disabilities or to compare the size of specific brain structures between groups of subjects through volumetric analysis. Additionally, anatomical techniques are used in conjunction with functional techniques in order to localize brain activity.

The earliest technique for imaging brain structure was computed tomography (CT). Today, it has been largely replaced by the much more powerful technique of magnetic resonance imaging (MRI). MRI provides excellent detailed structural information and enables the naked eye to distinguish gray matter (neuronal cell bodies) from white matter (myelinated tracts). New anatomical techniques, such as diffusion tensor imaging, have been developed to specifically visualize myelinated tracts. These methods can be used to track the normal and abnormal development of neural pathways in childhood.

Functional Techniques

Functional techniques have been the dominant force in cognitive neuroscience because they enable us to determine when and where neural activity in the brain is associated with the ability to perform a particular cognitive task. These techniques allow us to examine the workings of the human brain throughout the life span, in sickness and in health.

It is common to design several task variants that differ slightly in terms of task requirements. On the basis of this approach, differences in brain activation between the task variants enable us to isolate brain structures that are implicated in hypothesized cognitive processes. For example, if one wanted to identify brain regions involved in actively maintaining information in mind (referred to as working memory), one might parametrically vary the number of items (or the load) that subjects needed to maintain and then identify brain regions in which the level of activation varied according to working memory load. Although parametric variation is arguably the most powerful functional brain imaging manipulation, a more standard approach is to compare two task variants that differ only in that task 1 but not task 2 is hypothesized to engage a specific cognitive process. This approach relies on the assumption of 'pure insertion'; that is, the assumption that the insertion of the new task requirement affects only the cognitive process of interest.

Classes of Functional Neuroimaging Techniques

A variety of noninvasive functional neuroimaging techniques are available for use in humans (**Figure 1**); these techniques are categorized into two main classes. The first consists of methods for directly measuring electrical activity associated with neuronal firing, such as electroencephalography (EEG) and magnetoencephalography (MEG). The second main class consists of methods for indirectly measuring neuronal activity, which operate under the principle that neural activity is supported by increased local blood flow and metabolic activity. These methods include positron emission tomography (PET), functional magnetic resonance imaging (fMRI), and near-infrared spectroscopy (NIRS). More information on each of these methods is provided in the following sections.

Direct measures of neural activity: EEG and MEG

EEG is the oldest functional brain imaging technique, dating back to Berger's discovery in 1929 that brain electrical activity could be recorded from electrodes placed

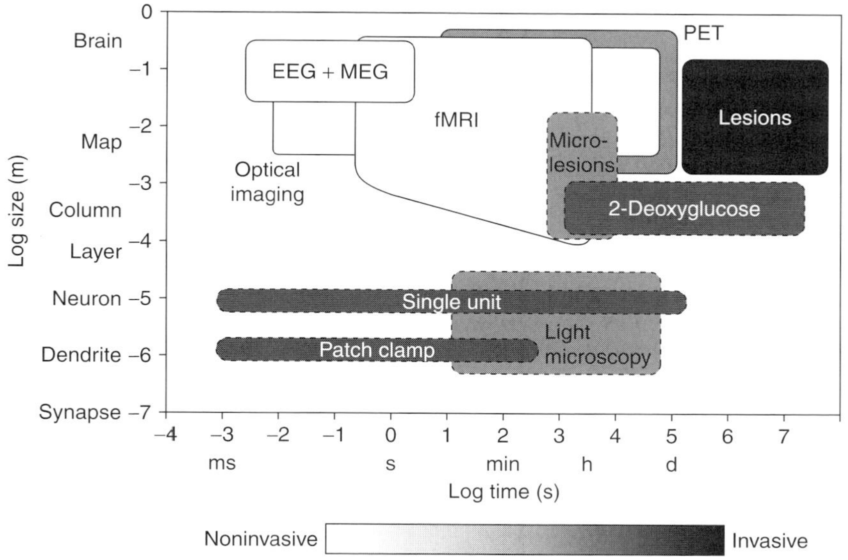

Figure 1 Relative spatial and temporal sensitivities of different functional brain imaging techniques. The level of invasiveness of each technique is indicated by a grayscale; more highly invasive techniques are shown in darker gray. Techniques used in animals only are outlined with a dashed line. Adapted from Cohen MS and Bookheimer SY (1994) Localization of brain function using magnetic resonance imaging. *Trends in Neuroscience* 17(7): 268–277.

on the scalp. This technique is still widely used today because of its ability to provide real-time measurements of brain activity. EEG records transient electrical dipoles generated by the net flow of electrical current across the cellular membrane during neuronal depolarization associated with postsynaptic potentials. Global EEG is used to measure neural activity during different brain states, such as sleeping and waking. A more powerful tool for cognitive neuroscience than global EEG measurements consists of event-related potentials, which refer to EEG activity averaged over a series of instances (or trials) triggered by the same event (e.g., the presentation of a visual stimulus).

Whereas EEG records the electrical activity associated with neuronal depolarization, the newer technique of MEG records the magnetic field produced by this electrical activity. The signal measured by both techniques results primarily from the activity of pyramidal neurons, which constitute roughly 70% of cells in the neocortex and are oriented perpendicular to the cortical sheath. EEG records electrical activity oriented perpendicular to the surface of the brain, whereas MEG records activity oriented parallel to the surface of the brain. Thus, EEG measures the activity of pyramidal cells in cortical gyri and the depths of the sulci, whereas MEG is sensitive primarily to the activity of pyramidal cells in the superficial parts of the sulci, and it is therefore more limited in its scope.

The major challenge with both EEG and MEG is referred to as the 'inverse problem,' which is the challenge of identifying the source of the underlying signal. This source can be a great distance from the point on the scalp at which it is measured, and it is affected by factors such as head shape and dipole location and orientation. Thus, it is necessary to build source localization algorithms to determine the likely source of a signal. One advantage of MEG over EEG is that the signal is less sensitive to factors such as head shape. Thus, the two techniques are complementary in that EEG samples from more neurons, but MEG is less sensitive to signal distortion. As such, some researchers take the approach of measuring EEG and MEG simultaneously to take advantage of what each technique has to offer.

Indirect measures of neural activity: PET

Roy and Sherrington first showed in 1890 that brain stimulation led to a local increase in blood flow to active populations of neurons. Landau and others subsequently used radioactive tracers to measure regional cerebral blood flow (rCBF) in animals (1955), and in 1963 this technique was first applied to humans. The most widely used radioactive tracer is $^{15}O_2$, an oxygen molecule in which one electron has been removed from the atom to give an unstable form that will emit one positron to revert to the stable form $^{16}O_2$. In a PET scan, a small amount of radioactive tracer is injected into a vein. The tracer enters the brain after approximately 30 s, and in the following 30 s radiation in the brain rises to its maximal value; a picture of the rCBF is taken during this time frame.

The greatest advantage of PET over the more recent method of fMRI is the choice of radioactive tracer. Researchers can synthesize radiopharmaceutical compounds that bind to dopamine or serotonin receptors (C-11 or F-18 *N*-methylspiperone), opiate receptors (C-11 carfentanil), etc. PET is likely to continue to be important for understanding the role of various neurotransmitters in cognition. However, there are several disadvantages of PET that have led to its being surpassed by fMRI as the most widely used indirect measure of brain activity. The first of these is cost; PET facilities require not only a PET camera but also a cyclotron, which is used to produce the radioactive tracers. The second disadvantage is the poor temporal resolution – on the order of 1 min compared to 6–8 s for fMRI. Finally, PET is more invasive than fMRI, requiring the injection of a radioactive tracer (albeit one with a half-life of a few minutes), and thus it is not suitable for use in children or other special populations.

Indirect measures of neural activity: fMRI

fMRI is currently the most widely used brain imaging technique for a number of reasons, including (1) widespread availability of MRI scanners and technology, (2) relatively low cost per scan, (3) the lack of recognized risks for properly screened subjects, (4) good spatial resolution, and (5) better temporal resolution than other indirect neuroimaging methods.

In addition to observing that brain activity was associated with local changes in blood flow, Roy and Sherrington noted that the increase in total oxygenated blood delivered far exceeded the demand. It is this surplus of oxygen that is detected with fMRI, with what is known as the blood oxygen-level dependent (BOLD) contrast. Oxygenated hemoglobin, or oxyhemoglobin, has magnetic properties different from those of deoxyhemoglobin. Thus, the deployment of a strong magnetic field (typically 1.5–4 tesla when used in humans) enables one to measure changes in the ratio of oxy- to deoxyhemoglobin in local draining venules and veins. An increase in blood flow in response to a specific stimulus (be it brain stimulation or the presentation of a visual or auditory stimulus) is referred to as a hemodynamic response. This response is sluggish with respect to the underlying neural activity; for example, the hemodynamic response in visual cortex to a brief (e.g., 30 ms) visual stimulus peaks roughly 4–6 s after the onset of the stimulus.

Related Techniques

Perfusion fMRI enables direct measurement of the hemodynamic response, unlike BOLD fMRI, which relies on the comparison of hemodynamic responses under different conditions. This technique is less widely used than BOLD fMRI because of its much lower sensitivity. Magnetic resonance spectroscopy is used to measure the relative concentration and distribution of specific ions or compounds, such as hydrogen, phosphorus, or carbon.

Optical Brain Imaging

NIRS operates according to the same principle as optical brain imaging techniques that have been used in animals. Both techniques capitalize on the fact that changes in hemoglobin concentration in cortical tissue affect the absorption of infrared light by the tissue. However, NIRS is noninvasive, whereas optical imaging in animals is accomplished by exposing the surface of the brain. Because the cortical surface is not exposed in NIRS, light scattering by the skull leads to reduced spatial resolution.

During the past few years, Gratton, Fabiani, and colleagues have developed a new analytic approach to the analysis of optical data, known as the event-related optical signal (EROS). The EROS signal is based on measures of the optical properties of cortical tissue, which change when the tissue is active. The changes in these optical properties are likely to be due to changes in light scattering as a function of neuronal activity. Because this type of optical signal is directly linked to neural activity, rather than blood flow, it provides a much higher temporal resolution than the signal typically analyzed in NIRS studies. Additionally, the EROS signal has a high degree of spatial resolution, in that it can be localized to an area of less than 1 cm^3.

A drawback of all three optical imaging techniques noted previously is that they can only be used to measure activity on or near the surface of the brain (within 3–5 cm of the surface). However, these techniques are advantageous in that they are relatively inexpensive and completely noninvasive. Furthermore, because these techniques are not as sensitive to head movement as fMRI, they hold much promise for the study of clinical populations and children.

Trade-Offs between Temporal and Spatial Resolution

Direct measures of neural activity, such as EEG and MEG, have exquisite temporal resolution. They are sensitive to changes in neural activity on a millisecond resolution. However, these methods have poor spatial resolution in that it is difficult to pinpoint the precise origin of the signal. In contrast, indirect measures of neural activity have better spatial resolution than EEG or MEG but poor temporal resolution. The spatial and temporal characteristics of these various methods are shown in **Figure 1**. Thus, there is currently a trade-off between high temporal precision and high spatial precision. One solution to this problem is to use fMRI data to limit the possible sources of neural activity in EEG and MEG data; another – and even more challenging – solution is multimodal imaging, for example, the concurrent acquisition of fMRI and EEG data.

Advantages and Limitations of Neuroimaging Techniques

To date, much of what we know about the functions of different brain regions comes from neuropsychological studies in humans and lesion studies in animals. A distinct drawback of neuroimaging techniques is that, unlike neuropsychological and lesion techniques, they cannot demonstrate the necessity of a brain region for a specific cognitive process. However, neuroimaging techniques can demonstrate that humans without neurologic damage routinely recruit this region to perform the task. Moreover, it is possible to compare levels of activation across individuals and to state that greater activation of this region is associated with better performance on a task. Better yet, it is possible to compare activation between trials within an individual and to state that on trials in which the subject made an error, activation was lower in this region than on trials in which the subject performed correctly. Thus, functional brain imaging techniques can be used to characterize a region's contribution to specific cognitive processes. Moreover, brain imaging techniques can be paired with techniques for temporarily disrupting neural activity in a temporally and spatially precise manner (transcranial magnetic stimulation).

There are several important advantages of neuroimaging techniques over neuropsychological ones. First, neuropsychological studies necessarily rely on the output of behavior as the critical dependent measure, whereas neuroimaging studies can focus on cognitive processes that take place prior to – or are not associated with – a behavioral response. For example, it is impossible to determine whether lesions that result in a long-term memory impairment are associated with a deficit at encoding and/or retrieval. With brain imaging, however, one can identify brain regions associated with the effective encoding of memories separately from brain regions associated with effective retrieval.

Second, neuroimaging techniques enable us to identify the entire neural circuit underlying a cognitive process. Lesion studies in animals can accomplish this only piecemeal by lesioning each area in turn. Neuropsychological studies in humans would be hard-pressed to accomplish this at all, given the limited availability of patients with specific brain lesions. This point is an important one because with lesion studies it is possible to completely overlook – or instead to overestimate – the contributions of a specific region to cognitive function. For example, the hippocampus has long been thought to be the primary structure contributing to the encoding and retrieval of memories. However, brain imaging has demonstrated that in the healthy brain, prefrontal cortex routinely contributes to memory encoding and retrieval.

The third point is also related to the limited availability of neuropsychological patients: neuroimaging techniques enable one to examine the role of a given human brain region in cognition even if one does not have access to specific patient groups. Moreover, it can be very difficult (or next to impossible, depending on the brain region) to find a patient with a lesion limited to the region in which one is interested because most brain lesions are rather coarse. Furthermore, cortical reorganization can lead to recovery of function over time, which could lead one to assume mistakenly that a lesioned brain region is not normally involved in a specific cognitive process.

Finally, neuroimaging techniques with high temporal resolution, such as EEG and MEG, provide us with important clues about brain mechanisms. It is helpful to say that brain regions X and Y are involved in memory retrieval, but if we can say that brain region X is active a short time after region Y, we can begin to gain insight into the cascade of events leading to memory retrieval.

A common criticism of neuroimaging studies is that they can be highly unconstrained and atheoretical. Like any scientific tool, however, brain imaging can be used wisely or foolishly. Certainly, many exploratory brain imaging studies have been conducted, particularly in the initial phase of brain imaging, when it was important to validate the new techniques. However, the second generation of imaging studies, starting in the late 1990s, has been much more focused. On the whole, cognitive neuroscientists carefully devise experimental manipulations designed to test psychological theories or specific predictions about brain function. Brain imaging techniques are likely to be an important force in cognitive neuroscience for the foreseeable future.

Contributions to the Study of Cognition

Neuroimaging research has been used to enrich our understanding of the neural basis of a wide variety of cognitive abilities, including attention, language, and memory. In addition, neuroimaging techniques have been used to gain insight into the etiology of neurobehavioral disorders, for surgical planning, and to assess functional recovery after brain damage.

One area in which neuroimaging studies are making important contributions is that of memory. For example, studies of long-term semantic memory have begun to uncover the ways in which stored information is organized in the brain. These studies show that different attributes of an object are stored in a distributed manner across several brain regions, with visual form information stored in a region that processes form, and functional information stored near a region that processes motion. Furthermore, studies of memory encoding have been able to pinpoint the precise regions for which level of activation during stimulus processing predicts subsequent memory for that stimulus. Additionally, studies of memory retrieval are being used to adjudicate between models of episodic memory positing that recollection (i.e., distinct remembrance of an item and the context in which it was previously encountered) and familiarity (a vague sense that the item has previously been encountered) are either distinct processes or merely on a continuum of memory retrieval. These examples show how brain imaging studies can be used to test or adjudicate between psychological models.

Perhaps the most important contribution of neuroimaging to the field of cognition will be in the study of higher cognitive functions, which are not highly developed in nonhuman species and are therefore best studied in humans. Carefully designed brain imaging experiments have begun to fractionate the cognitive processes that underlie language, reasoning, problem solving, and other high-level mental functions, but further investigation is necessary.

Further Reading

Andreassi, JL (1995). *Psychophysiology: Human Behavior & Physiological Response,* 3rd edn. Hillsdale, NJ: Lawrence Erlbaum.

Cohen MS and Bookheimer SY (1994) Localization of brain function using magnetic resonance imaging. *Trends in Neuroscience* 17(7): 268–277.

Frith, CD and Friston, KJ (1997). Studying brain function with neuroimaging. In: Rugg, M (ed.) *Cognitive Neuroscience*, pp. 169–195. Cambridge, MA: MIT Press.

Kutas, M and Dale, A (1997). Electrical and magnetic readings of mental functions. In: Rugg, M (ed.) *Cognitive Neuroscience*, pp. 197–242. Cambridge, MA: MIT Press.

Levy, I, Hasson, U, Avidan, G, Hendler, T, and Malach, R (2001). Center-periphery organization of human object areas. *Nature Neuroscience* 4(5): 533–539.

Raichle, ME (1998). Behind the scenes of functional brain imaging: A historical and physiological perspective. *Proceedings of the National Academy of Sciences of the United States of America* 95(3): 765–772.

Rorden, C and Karnath, HO (2004). Using human brain lesions to infer function: A relic from a past era in the fMRI age? *Nature Reviews Neuroscience* 5(10): 813–819.

Wilkinson, D and Halligan, P (2004). The relevance of behavioural measures for functional-imaging studies of cognition. *Nature Reviews Neuroscience* 5(1): 67–73.

Cognitive Deficits in Schizophrenia

D. S. Manoach, Massachusetts General Hospital, Charlestown, MA, USA

Why Study Cognitive Deficits in Schizophrenia?

For many years, schizophrenia was considered to be a profound mystery, beyond the reach of science. Over the past several decades, major advances in the neurosciences have drastically changed the way schizophrenia is viewed, have deepened our understanding of it, and have led to better treatments. Most of all, it has become abundantly clear that schizophrenia is a brain disease. It is characterized by 'positive' psychotic symptoms such as hallucinations and delusions and by 'negative' symptoms such as amotivation, social withdrawal, and apathy. Positive symptoms are the most dramatic manifestations of schizophrenia and have been the primary focus of drug development. They can be effectively managed by medications in the majority of individuals, but a full return to premorbid levels of function is rare. The focus on symptoms has contributed to a relative neglect of the subtler but severely disabling cognitive deficits until recently.

Since the initial conceptualization of the disease as 'dementia praecox,' cognitive dysfunction has been recognized as integral to schizophrenia. Rather than being an epiphenomenon of psychosis, cognitive deficits reflect the pathology that gives rise to schizophrenia. They are probably more closely related to predisposing genes and are better predictors of social function and outcome than are the symptoms that define schizophrenia. Increasingly, the goal of schizophrenia research is to understand the nature and neural basis of cognitive deficits and to effectively treat them. Aside from the obvious benefits of treatment, there are other important reasons to understand cognitive deficits. First, because cognitive abnormalities predate the onset of illness, they may identify individuals at high risk for developing schizophrenia and enable early intervention. Second, their presence in healthy relatives of individuals with schizophrenia suggests that cognitive deficits are markers of genetic vulnerability to illness that can help to identify genes that confer increased risk of schizophrenia. Third, schizophrenia is a heterogeneous illness, and identifying core cognitive deficits and their genetic bases may lead to more valid subtyping, which has important implications for treatment and prognosis. In summary, understanding cognitive deficits, along with relatively preserved abilities in schizophrenia, will implicate underlying neural circuitry, guide the search for neuropathology, lead us to susceptibility genes, and thereby provide clues to etiology (or etiologies) and contribute to a theoretical understanding of this enigmatic disorder.

Article Overview

The literature documents impairments in a wide range of neurocognitive functions in schizophrenia. In fact, most meta-analytic studies of cognition in schizophrenia demonstrate that no domain tested is spared. The aim of this article is not to provide an exhaustive list of cognitive deficits; rather it is to highlight a subset that seems most central to schizophrenia and that holds the most promise for shedding light on its pathophysiology. One criterion for identifying core deficits is whether they are present in increased rates in healthy relatives of patients with schizophrenia. This would suggest that they are markers of genetic vulnerability to illness, or 'cognitive endophenotypes.' The endophenotype concept in psychiatry is discussed in the section titled 'Cognitive endophenotypes.' Meta-analytic studies of relatives show the strongest effect sizes for impairments on tasks with high executive function demands, such as set-switching, inhibition, and working emory (see 'Executive function deficits'). Disturbances of memory, thought, and language are described in the sections titled 'Declarative memory' and 'Thought, language, and semantic memory disturbances.' The section titled 'Challenges and potential confounds in the study of cognition' outlines some of the difficulties in identifying specific cognitive deficits. And the section that asks 'Are there fundamental deficits that give rise to widespread cognitive disturbance?' considers whether there are more elementary deficits that can parsimoniously account for the range of cognitive dysfunction. Finally, the advent of sophisticated neuroimaging techniques and the revolution in genetics hold tremendous promise for illuminating the neural basis of cognitive deficits in schizophrenia (discussed in the section titled 'Promising advances in the study of cognition').

Cognitive Endophenotypes

Schizophrenia arises from a poorly understood and complex interaction of multiple genetic, environmental, and epigenetic risk factors. Identifying genes that predispose to schizophrenia will lead to early identification of individuals at risk, foster a better understanding of schizophrenia at a molecular level, improve pharmacotherapy, and guide the development of preventive interventions. Since only a small portion of individuals who have genes that predispose to schizophrenia will become ill, we cannot rely on the presence of symptoms alone to identify individuals who carry susceptibility genes. Because cognitive deficits are associated with illness within families and are present at a higher rate among family members than in the general population, they are can be used to identify individuals who lack any overt symptoms of illness but who carry susceptibility genes. These cognitive deficits can be considered endophenotypes, or markers of genetic vulnerability to illness. (The endophenotype concept was first presented in relation to psychiatric disorders by Gottesman and Shields in 1972.) Endophenotypes are manifestations of pathology that may not be obvious without specialized testing and that are thought to be more closely related to the genes that predispose to illness than are symptoms. Because endophenotypes fill gaps in the causal chain between genes and more distal, complex disease manifestations such as symptoms, they may provide clues to etiology. The characteristics of useful endophenotypes are listed in **Figure 1**. Candidate cognitive endophenotypes include deficits in executive functions such as working memory and inhibition. Abnormalities in several psychophysiological measures have also been proposed as candidate endophenotypes. These include smooth pursuit eye tracking, the P300 event-related potential, and indices of sensorimotor gating such as backward masking, prepulse inhibition of the startle blink, and gating of the auditory P50 event-related potential component. These abnormalities in early information processing are mentioned here because they might have ramifications for cognitive processing down the line, although such links are still more theoretical than established.

Executive Function Deficits

Executive functions are a diverse set of cognitive abilities that allow flexible rather than reflexive responses to events. They are necessary for coordinating thought and action in the pursuit of goals. These goals may be immediate, such as finding food, but they are often remote, higher order goals such as earning an academic degree. Executive functions include switching flexibly from one task to another; inhibiting strongly called for, but inappropriate, response tendencies; problem-solving; planning; and using context to select an appropriate response. The prefrontal cortex is thought to play a pivotal role in mediating executive function on the basis of studies of monkey neurophysiology, frontal lesion patients, and human neuroimaging. Neuroimaging studies consistently implicate prefrontal neural circuitry in the executive function deficits of schizophrenia.

In schizophrenia, executive function deficits are reflected in behavior that is stimulus-bound rather than guided by context, perseverative, and stereotyped. The seminal studies that first established a direct link between deficient executive function and abnormal prefrontal activity employed

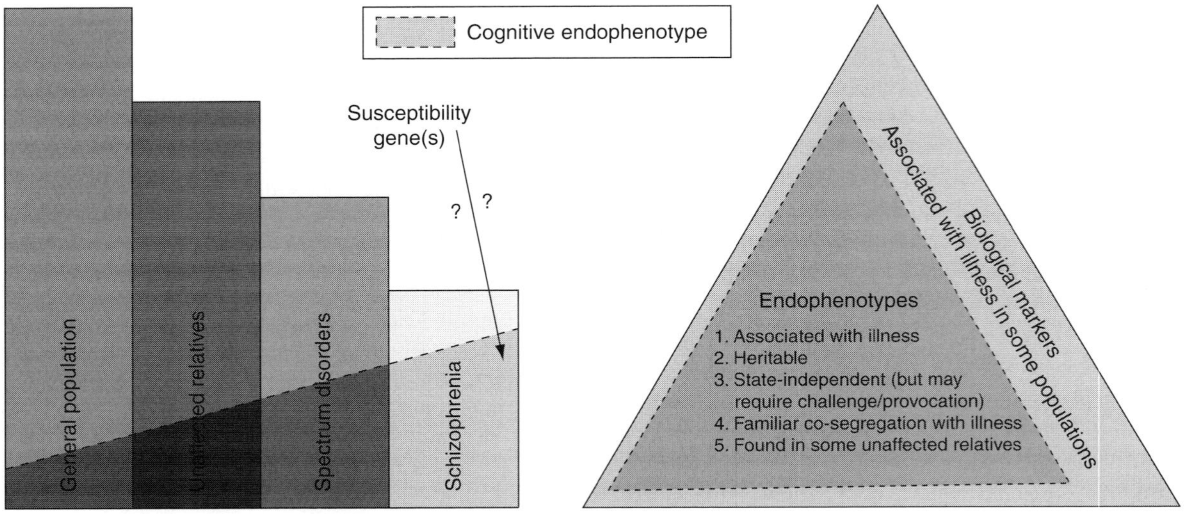

Figure 1 A schematic model of the frequency (left) and characteristics (right) of a cognitive endophenotype (e.g., inefficient working memory, formal thought disorder, antisaccade errors). It is most frequent in schizophrenia, then in schizophrenia spectrum disorders, then in unaffected family members, and then in the general population. It is presumed to reflect the influence of a susceptibility gene or genes. Enodophenotypes are a subset of biological markers that can be distinguished by the criteria listed, which suggests that they are genetic in origin (as opposed to primarily environmental, epigenetic, or multifactorial). The right side of the figure is adapted from Gould TD and Gottesman II (2006) Psychiatric endophenotypes and the development of valid animal models. *Genes, Brain, and Behavior* 5: 113–119 with permission from I. Gottesman, who owns the copyright.

the Wisconsin Card Sort Test (WCST) (**Figure 2**). Although clinically rich and sensitive to prefrontal network dysfunction, the WCST is a complex, multidimensional task that requires sustained attention, concept formation, performance monitoring, task switching, and working memory for successful performance. Therefore, poor performance and differential brain activation in schizophrenia compared to healthy individuals cannot be attributed to a specific deficit. More-recent studies employ tasks that constrain demands to identify specific executive processes that are intact or impaired.

Inhibition

Inhibition is the ability to suppress automatic or prepotent responses (e.g., looking toward a suddenly appearing object). Individuals with schizophrenia consistently show increased errors and frequently also show increased latencies for correct responses on tasks requiring inhibition, such as the Stroop interference paradigm, the go, no-go task, and the antisaccade task (**Figure 3**). In real life, deficits in inhibition might translate into behavior that is impulsive and stimulus-bound.

Task Switching

Task switching refers to moving flexibly from one set of rules to another in response to changing environmental contingencies. Task switching requires processes that are not necessary when simply repeating the same task and generally incurs costs in the form of increased response latency and errors. Clinical observations of perseveration – the contextually inappropriate and unintentional repetition of responses – and performance of neuropsychological tests such as the WCST have led to the presumption of task-switching deficits in schizophrenia. Using tasks that isolate cognitive processes, however, several groups have reported that task switching is normal. For example, while performing random sequences of prosaccades and antisaccades (**Figure 3**), patients showed normal task-switching costs. But unlike healthy

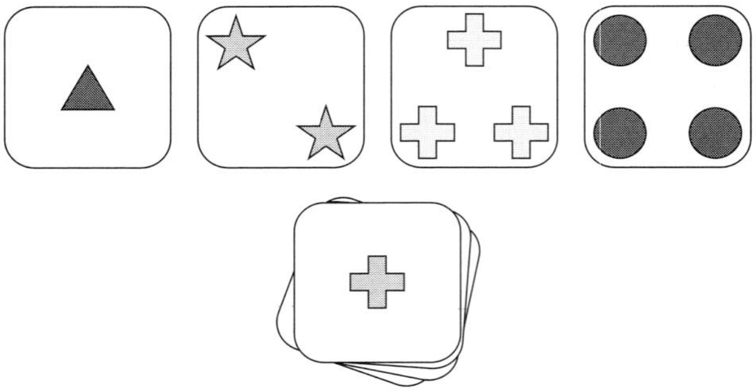

Figure 2 WCST: the participant is presented with four prototype cards and given a stack of cards to match to one of the prototypes by placing it beneath the prototype in a separate pile. The participant is not told the sorting rule (color, shape, or number) but has to figure it out on the basis of feedback from the examiner (i.e., a statement indicating that the match was correct or incorrect). If participants make a mistake, they must try again with the next card. Following ten correct sorts, unbeknownst to the participant, the rule changes, and the participant must again figure out the operative sorting rule based on feedback.
(See color plate 14.)

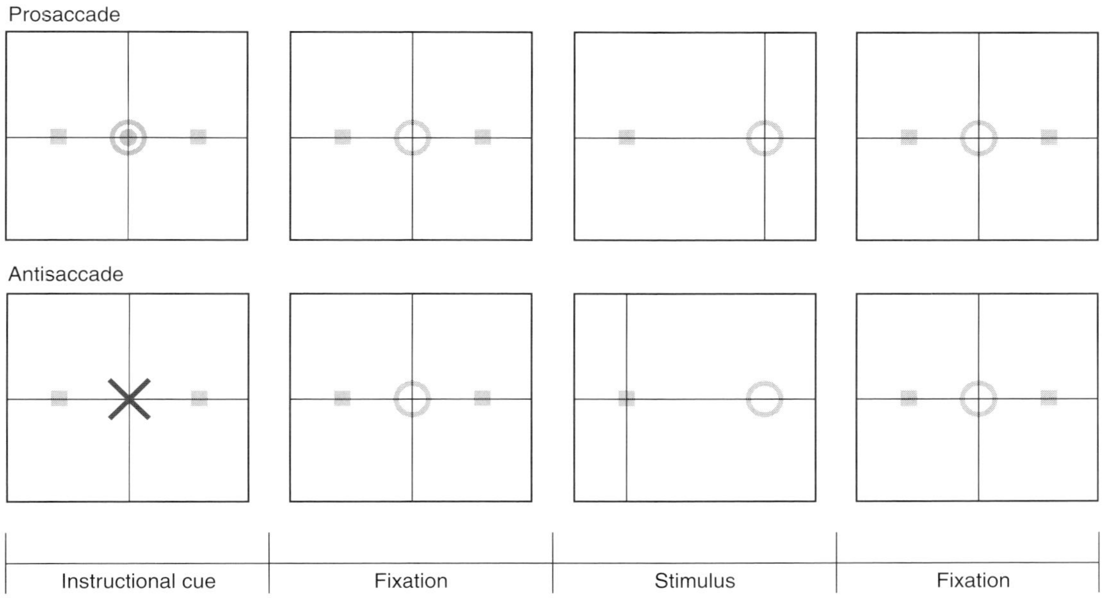

Figure 3 An example antisaccade paradigm. The cross hair represents the point of regard. A trial begins with a visual cue instructing either a prosaccade or an antisaccade (in this case an orange circle for prosaccades and a blue X for antisaccades). Following the disappearence of the cue, participants maintain fixation on the center until a stimulus appears over one of the two peripheral dots, the side randomly determined. Participants are instructed to look toward the suddenly appearing stimulus on prosaccade trials. For antisaccade trials, they are instructed to look in the opposite direction. After stimulus offset, fixation returns to the center as participants await the beginning of the next trial. While prosaccades are a relatively automatic response, antisaccades require executive control. To perform an antisaccade correctly one must suppress the prepotent response of looking toward a suddenly appearing stimulus (i.e., prosaccade) and generate the novel behavior of looking in the opposite direction. Out come measurements include directional accuracy of the saccadic eye movement and latency to initiate the saccade. Individuals with schizophrenia generally perform normally on prosaccade trials but show increased errors (failures of inhibition) and, depending on task parameters, may also show increased latency for correct responses on antisaccade trials. (See color plate 15.)

individuals, their errors tend to be in the same direction of the prior saccade. This suggests an abnormally strong influence of the prior response. Thus, instead of reflecting a problem with switching rules, perseveration may reflect an unwanted repetition of responses. Such dissociations between intact and impaired ability suggest that there are selective impairments of executive function in schizophrenia that can help pinpoint dysfunction in specific neural circuitry.

Working Memory

Working memory refers to actively holding information 'online' in the mind's eye and manipulating it in the service of guiding behavior. It is hypothesized to be a temporary store whose contents are continually updated and scanned in response to immediate information processing demands. Daily activities, from mentally rehearsing a phone number to considering alternative perspectives and outcomes, depend on it. In schizophrenia, there is abundant evidence of both behavioral impairment and anomalous patterns of brain activity during working memory performance. What is less clear is whether particular subcomponents of working memory are differentially affected. Working memory is comprised of distinct stages (encoding, maintaining and manipulating information, and then selecting the appropriate response) and operates on different domains of information (e.g., spatial, verbal, and object features). Neuroimaging and neurophysiological evidence suggests that different stages and domains of working memory require different strategies and cognitive processes for success and are therefore associated with distinct patterns of neural activity, although there is also a great deal of overlap in these patterns. Regardless of which subcomponents of working memory are disrupted in schizophrenia, impoverished internalized representations may lead to behavior that is unduly driven by external stimuli.

Response Monitoring

To perform well on any challenging task, it is necessary for one to evaluate one's performance so as to learn from errors and, if an error was made, slow down on the next try. These processes – performance evaluation, reinforcement learning, and remedial performance adjustment on the subsequent trial (i.e., post-error slowing) – are all thought to rely on the anterior cingulate cortex. Diminished performance evaluation and diminished reinforcement learning in schizophrenia are presumed on the basis of relative reductions in anterior cingulate cortex activity and error-related negativity (ERN) following error commission on a range of cognitive tasks. ERN is an event-related potential that is thought to reflect error-based reinforcement learning, or the modification of stimulus–response mappings in order to optimize behavioral outcomes. In spite of these abnormalities, post-error slowing and error positivity (PE), an event-related potential associated with both error awareness and posterror slowing, are often found to be intact. Such dissociations have been observed within single studies and suggest that performance evaluation and remediation are implemented by separate systems, only one of which may be impaired in schizophrenia. Because response monitoring is essential to optimal performance, a deficit could lead to generalized performance impairments and contribute to rigid, perseverative behavior.

Declarative Memory

Clinical observation suggests that individuals with schizophrenia have problems with memory. But memory is a broad term that encompasses the myriad ways that experience leaves durable traces in the brain. Declarative memory, particularly for verbal materials, has been a focus of research and is found to be deficient. Declarative memory includes both episodic memory (memory for events) and semantic memory (memory for facts) and can be divided into stages that engage distinct neural circuits: acquiring and organizing new information (encoding), filing and retaining it (storage), and retrieving it when necessary. Encoding and retrieval are both active processes that are vulnerable to disruptions of attention and depend on prefrontal networks. The storage of new information, in contrast, is not under voluntary control and is critically dependent on hippocampal mediation. There is ample evidence of deficient encoding and retrieval in schizophrenia, but in spite of reports of structural and functional hippocampal abnormalities, storage deficits, as distinct from encoding and retrieval deficits, are mild or nonexistent.

Thought, Language, and Semantic Memory Disturbances

In addition to abnormalities in the content of thought (i.e., delusions and hallucinations), individuals with schizophrenia also have abnormalities in the form of thought. Formal thought disorder refers to impairments in the organization and control of thoughts as expressed through language. It ranges in severity and type, from disturbances of logical concept formation to peculiar word usage. Although viewed as a symptom, formal thought disorder has cognitive origins, and milder manifestations have been documented in healthy relatives, suggesting that it may be an endophenotype. Whether formal thought disorder reflects a primary thought or language disturbance has been debated since it was first described by Bleuler as "loosening of associations." Although not specific to schizophrenia – it is seen in other psychotic disorders, and even healthy individuals show instances of thought slippage – qualitatively, the flavor of formal thought disorder in schizophrenia is unique. It is frequently characterized by confusion, instability, and unusual word and phrase usage, in contrast to, for example, the loosely combined ideas and jocularity often seen in mania. At its most extreme, language is incoherent. Milder manifestations include vagueness (language that lacks specific information) or its opposite, overly specific and excessively qualified speech (e.g., a four-legged pig).

Even patients without overtly thought disordered language may show abnormalities of language production and comprehension at the levels of individual words, sentences, and discourse. Studies examining the organization and retrieval of individual words from semantic memory suggest that there is no loss of lexico-semantic knowledge in schizophrenia, but that the storage and/or access to words is less organized than in healthy individuals. At the level of whole sentences, patients have difficulty in the 'online' use of semantic context to constrain their expectations of what will follow, and this impairs comprehension. This may arise because patients have difficulty in building up context, due to deficits in combining semantic with syntactic information within sentences and in generating bridging inferences across sentences. This can lead sentence and discourse processing to be inappropriately dominated by semantic associative relationships between individual words at the expense of constructing a more complete meaning.

Challenges and Potential Confounds in the Study of Cognition

Characterizing deficient versus preserved cognitive abilities has proved an elusive goal in schizophrenia, and the literature is replete with ambiguous or contradictory results. Several factors contribute to this difficulty.

Heterogeneity

Schizophrenia is a heterogeneous illness with no known etiology or pathognomomic signs. In most cognitive studies, only a subset of patients shows deficits on any given measure, and the particular subset showing a deficit varies from measure to measure. Thus, compared with demographically matched healthy individuals, patients with schizophrenia show a greater range of values on outcome measurements ranging from simple reaction time to indices derived from neuroimaging studies. The effects of course variables (e.g., first episode vs. chronic, acute exacerbation vs. partially remitted state), medication, severity of illness, and the interaction of illness with factors that normally contribute to individual differences (e.g., gender, age, intelligence) also contribute to measurement heterogeneity. Thus, depending on the composition of the sample, a particular cognitive deficit may or may not be detectable.

Paradoxically, in spite of this heterogeneity, schizophrenia has defied meaningful subdivision. Most subtyping schemes are based on phenomenology rather than biology, lack temporal stability, and fail to provide an adequate account of the variability in neuroanatomic abnormalities, cognitive dysfunction, outcome, response to medications, and other signs of schizophrenia. The failure of phenomenology to map onto specific biological substrates suggests that it may not be the most valid organizing principle for illness heterogeneity. Identifying core cognitive deficits that can be mapped onto specific neural substrates may lead to more meaningful subtyping.

Variability

In addition to showing a wide range of performance across individuals, there is more variable cognitive performance within individuals, both within a single session (i.e., from trial to trial) and over separate sessions (i.e., test–retest) compared with demographically matched healthy individuals. For example, while performing a working memory task, patients with schizophrenia show greater variability of response time within a single session and reduced test–retest reliability of brain activation across sessions. Even the demonstration of hand preference on simple tasks is less stable over two sessions. Increased variability and unreliability of performance are among the most consistent findings in schizophrenia research. Although frequently viewed as a measurement confound, it may be more productive to regard variability as intrinsic to schizophrenia and as having a neurological basis that requires explanation. This is supported by findings that frontal lobe damage in humans leads to increased variability of cognitive performance.

Amotivation

Amotivation is a core negative symptom of schizophrenia that makes it difficult to determine whether poor performance reflects a true deficit or that the patient was unwilling or unable to exert the effort necessary for optimal performance. Because tasks differ in the amount of effort required, amotivation may be more detrimental to the performance of some tasks than to others.

Medications

Antipsychotic medications have thus far targeted symptoms rather than cognition, and there is a vast and often contradictory literature on whether conventional antipsychotics impair cognition and whether atypical agents might improve it. Adjunctive anticholinergic drugs may also be detrimental to memory and other cognitive abilities.

Generalized Deficit

Meta-analytic studies demonstrate widespread cognitive dysfunction, suggesting that schizophrenia is characterized by a global blunting of performance. In addition to potential impairments attributable to amotivation and medication, patients may appear to have a generalized cognitive deficit because schizophrenia interferes with education and occupational attainment and many cognitive measurements are sensitive to these factors. In addition, acute psychosis and associated disruptions of attention may prevent optimal engagement in cognitive testing. For these reasons, simply demonstrating that patients perform worse on a particular task is not terribly revealing.

To some extent, the concept of a 'generalized deficit' is a straw man. Existing data do not support such a simplistic explanation. And a generalized deficit cannot account for the findings of highly selective cognitive deficits in unaffected relatives. Sorting out cognitive deficits that reflect the pathology of schizophrenia from those that are epiphenomena of having and being treated for a severe, chronic mental illness is an ongoing challenge. Strategies for identifying specific deficits in schizophrenia include demonstrating a pattern of both proficient and deficient performance across tasks that are matched for discriminating power and finding tasks on which a cognitive abnormality is actually advantageous to performance. Successful employment of this superiority strategy is illustrated by a series of numerosity studies in which the intact perceptual organizational ability of controls interfered with the rapid counting of elements (i.e., perceptual gestalts had to be broken for elements to be counted). Because patients failed to form gestalts, they were faster at counting.

Are There Fundamental Deficits That Give Rise to Widespread Cognitive Disturbance?

The seeming generality of neurocognitive deficits in schizophrenia leaves one searching for a parsimonious explanation – are there more-basic problems that can organize and account for the diverse deficits seen? Some investigators have hypothesized that many cognitive deficits stem from deficient working memory, which leads to a failure to guide behavior on the basis of internalized representations such as schemata and ideas. Deficits earlier in the information processing pipeline, such as in sensorimotor gating, have been proposed to account for higher order difficulties in inhibiting thoughts, speech, and action. While a theoretical case can be made for a number of integrative explanations, empirical evidence of links between elementary and higher order deficits is lacking.

Attention

A wide range of cognitive deficits in schizophrenia could be viewed as failures of the effective deployment and control of attention. The term attention refers to a broad array of cognitive functions that enable the individual to select relevant aspects of either the internal or external milieu (i.e., thoughts or environmental stimuli) for further processing while keeping others at bay. Particularly during acute phases of schizophrenia, patients describe difficulties filtering the continuous barrage of stimuli present at every moment and focusing on what is relevant. For example, they may have difficulty selectively attending to the voice of the person addressing them rather than to noise from the refrigerator. Inattention, however, cannot account for findings of deficits when attention is controlled or for information processing deficits on measurements that minimize its contribution, such as the auditory mismatch negativity, an event-related brain potential that is sensitive to stimulus deviation from a repetitive pattern and that is reduced in chronic schizophrenia.

Deficient Automation

In healthy individuals, practice can increase the speed of performance and reduce both the variability of responses and the error rate, reflecting a shift from controlled to more automatic processing and a corresponding shift in the brain networks that support performance. Tasks, or components of tasks, that have become automated proceed efficiently with reduced demands on attention. If schizophrenia were characterized by deficient automation, increased attention would be required for task components that should have been automated, and consequently fewer resources would be available for other, higher-order task demands. Although there are only a few studies of automation *per se* in schizophrenia, deficient automation provides a plausible account for increased variability and unreliability of performance across a range of tasks.

Context Processing

As illustrated in the section titled 'Executive function deficits,' the balance between past and present influences on behavior is upset in schizophrenia. Patients have trouble learning from error feedback, suggesting that the influence of previous experience is too weak. On the other hand, they also show perseveration of responses from trial to trial, indicating that the influence of the recent past is too strong and/or the influence of the current contingency is too weak. These difficulties in appropriately using information from both the past and the present to optimize behavior can be said to reflect deficient context processing. A number of executive functions are subsumed under the term 'context processing' (e.g., working memory since a representation of context has to be held online). Computational models have shown that a deficit in a single context processing module can mimic patient performance on a variety of cognitive tasks.

Promising Advances in the Study of Cognition

Imaging Genetics

An extremely promising avenue of research, made possible by advances in genetics, links variability in cognitive function and associated brain activation to genetic variation. This work is strengthening the case for suspected susceptibility genes and identifying potential mechanisms for the development of schizophrenia. For example, in groundbreaking work, Egan and colleagues in 2001 reported that a common functional polymorphism in the catechol-*O*-methyltransferase (COMT) gene, which reduces the amount of dopamine available in the synapses of the prefrontal cortex, and is slightly more common in individuals with schizophrenia than their unaffected family members, was associated with both poorer performance of the WCST and increased prefrontal cortical activation during performance of a working memory task in both patients with schizophrenia and healthy control participants. This suggest that prefrontal cortex function is influenced by genes that increase susceptibility to schizhophrenia. Increased prefrontal activation is thought to reflect inefficient function (i.e., increased resources are necessary to support a given level of performance). Several groups have shown that prefrontal inefficiency is also present in unaffected siblings of schizophrenia patients. The siblings showed greater activation than controls even though their task performance did not diffuse (**Figure 4**). These findings suggest that physiological indices derived from neuroimaging, because they more directly reflect the effects of genes (e.g., increased metabolism of dopamine), may prove more sensitive endophenotypes than behavioral ones.

Failures to find increased frequencies of the high risk COMT polymorphism in schizophrenia in some studies (e.g., of Asian populations) are not surprising given the number of factors that contribute to variability in association studies and point to the need for caution in

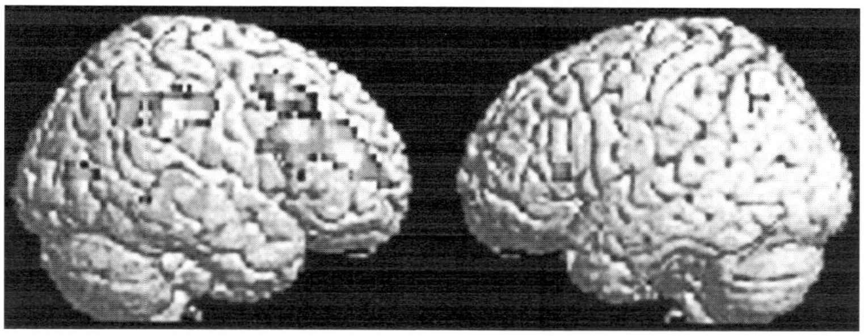

Figure 4 Regions of increased, inefficient fMRI activation in the unaffected siblings of schizophrenia patients relative to demographically matched control participants during performance of a working memory paradigm. Behavioral performance did not discriminate between the groups, but fMRI activation did, suggesting that imaging indices may be more sensitive to genetic risk for schizophrenia. Regions of increased activation include right dorsolateral and ventrolateral prefrontal cortices. Statistical group difference maps are rendered onto canonical single-participant lateral brain surfaces. Adapted from figure 2 in Callicott JH, Egan MF, Mattay VS, et al. (2003) Abnormal fMRI response of the dorsolateral prefrontal cortex in cognitively intact siblings of patients with schizophrenia. *American Journal of Psychiatry* 160: 709–719. (See color plate 16.)

generalizing these findings. In addition, particular polymorphisms account for only a small portion of the variance in cognitive performance and regional activation, as would be expected in a complex, multigenetic illness. A gene such as COMT likely interacts with other genetic and environmental factors to either diminish or exacerbate its effect on brain function, and investigations of the effects of gene–gene and gene–environment interactions on cognition are just getting under way.

Neuroimaging Advances

Neuroimaging findings continue to form the crux of many theoretical conceptualizations of schizophrenia, and continued technical advances hold tremendous promise for understanding its pathophsiology. The search for the neural basis of cognitive dysfunction in schizophrenia has evolved from key brain regions (e.g., prefrontal cortex or hippocampus) to also considering the integrity of neural circuits and the timing of neuronal processes across different regions. Advances in functional magnetic resonance imaging (fMRI) are providing ever higher spatial resolution. In combination with methods that provide high temporal resolution such as magnetoencephalography and electroencephalography, it is possible to examine the neural correlates of cognitive processes at each stage of performance and pinpoint exactly where and when they go awry. Complementary structural MRI can reveal morphological correlates of abnormal activation and cognitive performance. Since performance of even simple cognitive tasks is the product of coordinated activity in a distributed network, it is also of interest to assess the integrity of white matter, which can be done *in vivo* using a relatively new MRI technique, diffusion tensor imaging. Recent evidence suggests that white matter physiology contributes to individual differences in cognitive processing in health, and an emerging literature in schizophrenia links regionally reduced white matter integrity to cognitive dysfunction. By impairing communication in local circuitry and between connected brain regions, white matter pathology may contribute to cognitive dysfunction in schizophrenia. Together, these techniques can identify the functional and structural correlates of cognitive dysfunction, guide the search for neuropathology, and provide targets for intervention aimed at improving cognition in schizophrenia.

Further Reading

Callicott, JH, Egan, MF, Mattay, VS, et al. (2003). Abnormal fMRI response of the dorsolateral prefrontal cortex in cognitively intact siblings of patients with schizophrenia. *American Journal of Psychiatry* 160: 709–719.

Cirillo, MA and Seidman, LJ (2003). Verbal declarative memory dysfunction in schizophrenia: From clinical assessment to genetics and brain mechanisms. *Neuropsychology Review* 13: 43–77.

Egan, MF, Goldberg, TE, Kolachana, BS, et al. (2001). Effect of COMT Val108/158 Met genotype on frontal lobe function and risk for schizophrenia. *Proceedings of the National Academy of Sciences of the United States of America* 98: 6917–6922.

Gottesman, II and Gould, TD (2003). The endophenotype concept in psychiatry: Etymology and strategic intentions. *American Journal of Psychiatry* 160: 636–645.

Gould TD and Gottesman II (2006) Psychiatric endophenotypes and the development of valid animal models. *Genes, Brain, and Behaviour* 5: 113–119.

Green, MF (1998). *Schizophrenia from a Neurocognitive Perspective.* Boston: Allyn and Bacon.

Green, MF (2001). *Schizophrenia Revealed: From Neurons to Social Interactions.* New York: W. W. Norton.

Heinrichs, RW (2005). The primacy of cognition in schizophrenia. *American Psychologist* 60: 229–242.

Lee, J and Park, S (2005). Working memory impairments in schizophrenia: A meta-analysis. *Journal of Abnormal Psychology* 114: 599–611.

Knight, RA and Silverstein, SM (2001). A process-oriented approach for averting confounds resulting from general performance deficiencies in schizophrenia. *Journal of Abnormal Psychology* 110: 15–30.

Kuperberg, G and Caplan, D (2003). Language dysfunction in schizophrenia. In: Schiffer, RB, Rao, SM, and Fogel, BS (eds.) *Neuropsychiatry,* 2nd edn., pp. 444–466. Philadelphia: Lippincott Williams and Wilkins.

Manoach, DS (2003). Prefrontal cortex dysfunction during working memory performance in schizophrenia: Reconciling discrepant findings. *Schizophrenia Research* 60: 285–298.
Mathalon, DH, Fedor, M, Faustman, WO, et al. (2002). Response-monitoring dysfunction in schizophrenia: An event-related brain potential study. *Journal of Abnormal Psychology* 111: 22–41.
Montague, PR, Hyman, SE, and Cohen, JD (2004). Computational roles for dopamine in behavioural control. *Nature* 431: 760–767.
Nuechterlein, KH, Barch, DM, Gold, JM, et al. (2004). Identification of separable cognitive factors in schizophrenia. *Schizophrenia Research* 72: 29–39.
Snitz, BE, Macdonald, AW III, and Carter, CS (2006). Cognitive deficits in unaffected first-degree relatives of schizophrenia patients: A meta-analytic review of putative endophenotypes. *Schizophrenia Bulletin* 32: 179–194.
Stuss, DT, Murphy, KJ, Binns, MA, et al. (2003). Staying on the job: The frontal lobes control individual performance variability. *Brain: A Journal of Neurology* 126: 2363–2380.

Relevant Website

http://www.schizophreniaforum.org – Schizophrenia Research Forum.

Cognitive Impairment

D. T. Stuss

A theory of brain organization is a necessary framework for understanding cognitive impairment after brain damage. One model views cognitive functioning as hierarchically arranged with four levels. This entry briefly describes the impairments associated with the two lower levels in order to provide a context for understanding the higher and more elusive cognitive deficits associated with damage to the frontal lobes.

A Model of Cognition

General arousal is the lowest of the four levels in this model. An intact arousal system is necessary for consistent consciousness. This lower level, involving the brainstem reticular system, specific brainstem nuclei, and their projections to the thalamus and cortex, allows simple responses to incoming information. The second level involves the sensory and motor regions of the brain. At this level, information is processed for perception and complex motor activity. Herein lies the content of activated consciousness. The third level, related to the prefrontal cortex, mediates the executive or control functions of the brain. These control functions integrate the information provided by perception to produce goal-directed behavior. The final level also involves the frontal lobe, with the right frontal lobe playing a crucial role. This is the level of self-reflective awareness.

The hierarchy functions through bottom-up direction from simpler perceptual and cognitive processes to higher level processing and top-down control of lower levels to serve the goals of higher levels.

The Model in Action

Level 1: Arousal and Activation

Disorders of arousal necessarily have a devastating general impact on cognitive function. Coma, in which an individual is almost completely unresponsive, is the most extreme deficit. Between coma and normal arousal/wakefulness exists a continuum of states. Stupor is the state in which only intense stimuli evoke cortical activity, and then only briefly. Obtundation or torpor is characterized by responsiveness that is slow and poorly integrated. With damage in the brainstem reticular activating system, a patient may be able to pay attention for a brief period but soon succumbs to a more somnolent state due to a deficit in ongoing alertness (tonic attention). If the pathology is restricted to the diffuse thalamic projection system, the patient will have intact tonic alertness but be distractible due to impaired phasic attention. This type of wandering attention occurs in delirium or confusion. These patients represent a diagnostic challenge to the examiner assessing cognitive abilities since their impairments are pervasive, and an incomplete examination may suggest a focal disorder or a progressive dementing illness. The previously mentioned disorders of arousal should be differentiated from akinetic mutism, in which there is impaired ability to respond but normal arousal and intact cortical functioning.

Level 2: Content of Activated Consciousness

At this level, incoming information is perceived. Specific aspects of information are processed in different posterior brain regions. This is the level of knowledge or content. Experience constructs models of the outside world that help guide behavior. Information at this level is processed automatically and relatively rapidly.

Cognitive impairment secondary to brain damage at this second level is commonly classified according to the domain affected. The separation of impairments related to the different sensory modalities is clear: visuoperceptual, visuospatial, and visuoconstructive disorders; disorders of the somatosensory system; and impairments in the auditory system. There are also separate modules for language, memory, attention, and other functions that are superordinate to the sensory or perceptual domains. Impaired modular processes are described in relation to the cognitive domain in question:

1. *Amnesia*: Deficit in learning new information and, often, retrieving information from long-term memory
2. *Aphasia*: Loss or impairment of language
3. *Alexia*: Dysfunction in the comprehension of written language
4. *Agraphia*: Disturbances in writing
5. *Acalculia*: Impairment in numerical computations
6. *Apraxia*: Disorders of skilled movement that cannot be reduced to more elementary factors, such as motor weakness and impaired comprehension
7. *Agnosia*: Failure of recognition that cannot be explained by impaired perception, comprehension, and so on
8. *Neglect*: Difficulty in reporting, responding, or orienting to information in a side opposite to a lesion.

With each domain there may be multiple varieties of disorders. For example, many varieties of language disorders have been described, such as Wernicke's aphasia and anomic aphasia.

Level 3: Prefrontal Cortex and Supervisory Control

At the third level, the frontal lobes integrate information that has been evaluated in the posterior parts of the brain to prepare appropriate responses. The processes at this level include executive, supervisory, and control functions. These are necessary for selecting which information to attend to, activating or inhibiting behavior, and resolving discrepancies between various sources of information. These regulatory processes form a consistent model for dealing with the information provided by the second level. A useful approach to this level of cognition is to examine how damage to the frontal lobes impairs the effective functioning of the particular cognitive domains.

Anterior Attention Functions: Damage to the frontal lobes frequently results in impaired performance on attentional tasks. However, the impairment depends on the task, the complexity of the demands, and the location of the lesion within the frontal lobes. Most patients with frontal lobe damage are not impaired on simpler tasks such as forward digit span. Sustained attention (ability to identify target stimuli over a prolonged period of time) impairment can occur, most often after right frontal lobe damage. Tasks requiring attentional switching, such as in the shifting response categories in the Wisconsin Card Sorting Test, are sensitive to pathology in dorsolateral frontal and superior medial (but not inferior medial) frontal regions. Switching deficits can occur after inferior medial pathology, but the tasks that reveal this deficit are not cognitive in nature; they require affective feedback.

The frontal lobes are also involved in the selective attention and the inhibition of irrelevant stimuli. Deficits in these functions result in omitted responses to important stimuli or enhanced reactivity to irrelevant information. The dorsolateral frontal and supplementary motor areas, as well as the anterior cingulate gyrus, are necessary for these functions. Pathology may diminish the initial response to novel stimuli as well as reduce habituation to repeated stimuli. Difficulty in detecting targets contralateral to the lesion is observed, but supposedly unattended stimuli on the same side may evoke a larger than expected electrophysiological response. This inhibition or filtering impairment is more noticeable after right frontal lobe lesions. Exaggerated interference effects have also been reported after ventral medial frontal pathology.

This selective attention/inhibitory deficit after frontal lobe damage may be particularly noticeable in visual-directed attention tasks. The right frontal lobe normally provides the exploratory motor functions of a complex directed attention network. The frontal lobes are important for the stability of gaze fixation and in the use of preparatory directional cues to direct responses to a target location. Damage in the dorsolateral frontal eye field, supplementary motor area, and, apparently, the anterior cingulate gyrus results in impairment in the inhibition of inappropriate oculomotor responses to external stimuli and slowness in moving the eyes voluntarily away from a cue.

The context of the examination is often important. Sustained attention deficits are usually elicited when the task is simpler and the stimuli are presented slowly. If task complexity is manipulated, inhibitory deficits may be shown to be related to different regions of the frontal lobe. When the task is simple, deficits may be more focally limited to right frontal lobe damage. When the task is more complex, impairment may be observed after damage in most frontal brain regions (but not all posterior brain regions).

Frontal Lobe Language Functions: Excluding motor deficits (e.g., articulation problems) and Broca's aphasia, which is secondary to pathology involving a relatively large area of the left frontal lobe and surrounding regions, the language deficits related to the frontal lobes can be grouped very globally as activation and formulation (paralinguistic) deficits. Activation deficits can be tested by requiring the patient to generate a list of words beginning with a specific letter (phonological or literal fluency) or from a specific semantic category (semantic or category fluency). Impaired performance in phonological and semantic fluency occurs after right or left superior (but not inferior) medial frontal, left dorsolateral frontal, and left posterior lesions. Damage to the right dorsolateral area affects primarily semantic fluency. Clinically, difficulty in eliciting extended but normal language due to an activation problem usually involving lesions of medial frontal regions (anterior cingulate gyrus and supplementary motor area) is called dynamic aphasia. Transcortical motor aphasia, with notably truncated spontaneous language as well as other deficits, may occur after damage to the left dorsolateral frontal lobe (Brodmann areas 44, 46, 6, and 9).

The formulation problems, or disorders of discourse, are generative and narrative in nature. They reflect problems in planning and goal attainment. At the level of sentence generation and spontaneous utilization of complex syntax, deficits have only been described with left-sided lesions. At the level of story narrative, lesions in left dorsolateral and prefrontal regions may produce impairments. Left-sided lesions result in simplification and repetition (perseveration) of sentence forms and omissions of elements. Right-sided lesions cause amplification of details, wandering from the topic, and insertion of irrelevant elements, all leading to loss of narrative coherence.

Control of Memory: Memory dysfunction after frontal lobe damage also depends on test demands and on the lesion location. Generally, damage to the frontal lobes, other than the septal areas related to the hippocampal/medial temporal memory system, does not result in amnesia. On most traditional memory tests, particularly recognition memory, patients with frontal lobe lesions perform normally or near normally. Pathology in the left dorsolateral frontal area can affect memory encoding, which may be related to the level of language dysfunction.

The major memory deficit after frontal damage is impaired efficiency at encoding and retrieval, likely due to a deficiency in the strategic use of memory or the capacity to "work with memory" rather than an impairment in memory functions per se. There is general agreement that the left frontal lobe is involved in episodic (memories that are personal and related to particular times and places—episodes) encoding and semantic (content or knowledge-based information) retrieval, and the right frontal lobe is involved in episodic retrieval. Patients with frontal lobe lesions, particularly dorsolateral, are also impaired on conditional associative learning, which is the ability to learn associations between arbitrary stimuli.

Working with memory is different from working memory, defined as the capacity to hold information temporarily while performing some operation on that information. Goldman-Rakic suggested that working memory is the major function of the frontal lobes, particularly the dorsolateral regions. However, not all cognitive deficits observed in patients with frontal damage can be reduced to impairment in working memory.

Level 4: Self-Awareness and Metacognition

The fourth level of cognition, also requiring the frontal lobes, is where a "person" is defined and not where individual cognitive operations exist. In fact, performance on intelligence and standard neuropsychological tests, including traditional tests of frontal lobe function, is often normal in patients with disorders at this level of cognition. However, the changes may be so significant that others may consider the individual not to be the same person, as noted in Harlow's classic description of Phineas Gage ("He was no longer Gage").

The prefrontal cortices represent the end point for the interpretation of external percepts, merged with visceral input and integrated with emotional states for the preparation and execution of responses. The full integration of subjective experience requires integration in the frontal lobes, with perhaps a preeminent role of the ventral medial, particularly the right, frontal lobe at this highest level.

Some patients with ventral medial frontal lobe damage have been characterized as having an acquired sociopathy. These patients may appear totally self-interested. They may be humorless or, conversely, show inappropriate jocularity. At other times, impulsive outbursts of anger or inappropriate, irresponsible, and sometimes risky behavior are evident. The ability to understand the feelings of others (empathy) and to demonstrate appropriate emotional responses (sympathy) may be deficient. Although there is some superficial similarity to sociopathic behavior, frontal lobe patients usually exhibit no intentional antisocial behavior. Moreover, specific contexts or conditions such as unstructured environments may be required to elicit these behaviors.

The frontal lobes provide the self-reflective ability of the individual to use past personal knowledge to understand current behaviors and to select and guide future responses to integrate the personal self into a social context. This self-reflectiveness, or autonoetic consciousness, is the basis for memory related to personal, warm, and emotionally relevant past episodes. The right frontal lobe may play a particularly important role in episodic memory, autonoetic consciousness, and self-awareness.

Conclusion

Damage in various parts of the brain results in different forms of impairment. Understanding the distinction among these levels of cognitive function, as well as their interactions, provides the clinician with the knowledge to direct treatment. Disorders of arousal must be assessed first since they provide the necessary energy for the other processes to function. Much research has been done on impairments related to more posterior brain regions—those disorders described as related to level two. The most difficult functions to understand and assess are those related to the frontal lobes, associated with the third and fourth levels in the model. At the third level, impairment in different executive processes can be dissociated. There is no general frontal syndrome. Dysfunction at the fourth level impairs the highest of human functions—those related to abilities that define an individual personality: social cognition, autonoetic consciousness, and self-awareness.

See also: Agnosia; Agraphia.

Further Reading

Alexander, MP, Benson, DF, and Stuss, DT (1989). Frontal lobes and language. *Brain Lang.* 37: 656–691.
Boller, F and Grafman, J (eds.) (1994). *Handbook of Neuropsychology,* Vol 9. Amsterdam: Elsevier.
Damasio, AR (1996). The somatic marker hypothesis and the possible functions of the prefrontal cortex. *Philos. Trans. R. Soc. London Biol.* 351: 1413–1420.
Fuster, JM (1997). *The Prefrontal Cortex,* 3rd ed. Philadelphia: Lippincott-Raven.
Goldman-Rakic, PS (1996). Regional and cellular fractionation of working memory. *Proc. Natl. Acad. Sci. USA* 93: 13473–13480.
Grafman, J, Holyoak, KJ, and Boller, F (eds.) (1995). *Annals of the New York Academy of Sciences,* Vol. 769. New York: New York Academy of Sciences.
Levin, HS, Eisenberg, HM, and Benton, AL (eds.) (1991). *Frontal Lobe Function and Dysfunction.* New York: Oxford Univ. Press.
Passingham, R (1993). *The Frontal Lobes and Voluntary Action.* New York: Clarendon.
Perecman, E (ed.) (1987). *The Frontal Lobes Revisited.* New York: IRBN.
Stuss, DT and Alexander, MP (2000). Executive functions and the frontal lobes: A conceptual view. *Psychol. Res.* 63: 289–298.
Stuss, DT and Benson, DF (1986). *The Frontal Lobes.* New York: Raven Press.
Wheeler, M, Stuss, DT, and Tulving, E (1997). Toward a theory of episodic memory: The frontal lobes and autonoetic consciousness. *Psychol. Bull.* 121: 331–354.

Consciousness, Neural Basis of Conscious Experience

B. Libet[†], Davis, CA, USA

Basic Definitions and Concepts

Conscious or subjective experience or awareness is clearly accessible only introspectively to the individual having the experience. Consequently, the valid operational definition of it in scientific investigations is the introspective report by the individual, under conditions of reliability and credibility. That requires the availability of human study participants, awake and forthcoming, in whom simultaneous observations and manipulations of neural functions can be made. This combination of requirements imposes severe limitations on potential studies.

The observer must ask the individual the appropriate question about the latter's conscious experience and be confident that the individual understands the question. The report is often most conveniently verbal, but it may be nonverbal (e.g., a sign made by a finger) if the latter clearly represents the individual's introspective experience. Any report should be made only after sufficient time for introspection and not as part of any speedy reaction-time procedure. The issue of the accuracy and reliability of the individual's communication of introspective experience must be dealt with in each study individually. Suitable control tests can in fact be devised, and satisfactory reliability of reports is obtainable.

Physical Nature; System Property

Conscious subjective experience is a primary phenomenon whose nature cannot be defined by any other externally observable event, whether molecular or behavioral. Subjective experience arises as a system property of appropriate neural activities in the brain. It is a 'nonphysical' event, in that it cannot be detected or described by direct physical measurements, although a correlation with neural patterns may be discernible in relation to an individual's report of an experience. It is well known that the properties of a system are not predictable from those of the elements in the system. A 'nonphysical' property could, in principle, appear as a system property of the 'physical' neuronal activities. Even a complete knowledge of the observable neural processes in the brain of another individual would not in itself tell us what that individual is experiencing or feeling.

There are no *a priori* rules governing the relationship between conscious mental events and brain events; the

[†]Deceased.

rules must be discovered. The phenomenon of subjective referral of a sensory experience in the spatial dimension illustrates this principle. The spatial configuration of a subjectively experienced visual image, for example, is considerably different from the configuration of the brain neuronal activities that accompany and represent the sensory input and give rise to the visual images; the image that is seen, subjectively, is quite different from the neuronal pattern for that image. The cerebral neuronal representation is actually a spatial distortion of the original image coming into the eye, but subjectively the image is 'referred' to the original source of the input in a way that corrects the neuronal distortion. Direct electrical stimulation of primary sensory cortex provides an even more obvious demonstration of this; a stimulus applied to the lateral portion of the postcentral gyrus produces a sensation that is felt to be located not at the stimulated site of the brain, but is rather subjectively referred to, and felt in, the hand or arm and in a direction reversed from the postcentral representation. Clearly, a complete knowledge of the neuronal representation would not, without validation by the individual's report, tell us where or what sensation is being subjectively experienced. Similarly, the experience of color cannot be described by finding that certain neural units may respond to specific frequency bands of the light spectrum.

Although each individual has access to and can be certain about only his own conscious experiences and feelings, we do commonly concede and accept the premise that other human beings have their subjective experiences (except for those of us who want to adopt Bishop Berkeley's solipsism as a serious view of life). We are also confident that one person can communicate something about his subjective experiences to another. But the validity of what is communicated depends upon the degree to which both individuals have had similar or related experiences. A congenitally completely blind person can never share the conscious experience of a visual image, regardless of how detailed a verbal description he is given by a sighted individual. The same limitation applies to all experiences in less dramatic, more subtle ways. For example, electrical stimulation of somatosensory cortex can produce sensations related to but sufficiently different from those generated by normal sensory input, so that the individuals could only relate some roughly understandable approximation of these experiences to the experimental observer, in whom similar modes of sensory generation had never been employed.

Reports of Conscious Experience versus Behavioral Detection

There is an imperative corollary of the foregoing operational definition of conscious experience: any measured indicator that can be dissociated from or independent of subjective awareness would be invalid, not acceptable as a primary indicator of subjective experience. This would even include behavioral responses that depend on cognitive and decision-making processes, unless these were validated by the primary evidence of the individual's introspective reports. For example, we have all had the experience of driving an automobile and becoming subjectively engrossed in thoughts not related to the mechanics of driving; nevertheless, the driving proceeds while all sorts of sensory signals are being properly recognized, evaluated, and acted upon (usually successfully), without any consciously introspective awareness or later recallability. Among experimental paradigms, signal detection studies provide sophisticated examples of a generally unacceptable approach to conscious experiences. The forced-choice responses in such studies could be made independent of introspective awareness of the signal, although they may be excellent indicators of whether some type of detection has occurred. Even when individuals are giving confidence ratings of their responses in a signal detection study, they are rating their forced choices and are not necessarily directly reporting their subjective experiences. There is, in fact, evidence that signal detection can occur with signals that are distinctly below the threshold required for any conscious awareness of the signal. Indeed, most sensory signals probably do not reach conscious awareness; however, many of them lead to modified responses and behaviors, as in simple everyday postural and walking activities, and have therefore clearly been detected and utilized in complex brain functions.

Do Animals Have Conscious Experience?

There is no way to answer this in any absolute sense. But it should be clear that it is difficult, if not impossible, to carry out valid studies of conscious experience in nonhuman animals. Obviously, we cannot meaningfully ask an animal to report about a shared introspective experience, the validity of which we have confidence. Second, as just noted, complicated cognitive and purposeful behaviors can proceed even in human beings without introspective awareness of them, and so we cannot safely assume that such behaviors in animals are expressing subjective experience. Some investigators and writers have proposed that adaptive, problem-solving behaviors in animals indicate conscious thought and experience. However, even in humans, the most complex and even mathematical problem solving can and often does proceed at unconscious levels, as has been repeatedly described by many creative thinkers, artists, and others. Again, one must be careful to hold to the primary criterion of conscious experience *per se*, as a phenomenon that cannot automatically be described by any nonvalidated behavioral expression.

Are Computers Conscious?

Some enthusiasts of machines with artificial intelligence have tended to equate complexity of abstract processing with the existence of conscious experience. As we have noted, there is no such necessary connection even in the human brain. Again, there is the fundamental error in assuming that conscious experience can be identified based on purely behavioral criteria, whether for humans or machines. It has been argued that a machine might eventually be constructed with such sophistication that an external observer could not distinguish its behavior and responses from those of a human being. Even if we grant such a possibility, for the sake of argument, such an apparent identity of behavioral responses does not require that the two systems, machine and human brain, are alike in every respect. In fact, they are constituted differently and operate with different mechanisms. The unique makeup of the brain, and indeed certain special neuronal actions in it (see later), may be essential correlates of what we recognize as conscious subjective experience.

Studies of Neural Basis

Effects of Cerebral Lesions

It was, of course, long known that lesions of the cerebral cortex that destroyed a primary sensory area resulted in severe sensory impairment. For example, with loss of striate cortex area 17 patients are blind; that is, they report being unaware of signals in the affected visual field. But further analyses are showing that these patients can detect signals without any reportable awareness, by pointing correctly to them in forced-choice tests; this is the 'blindsight' phenomenon. In a related manner, patients with lesions that abolish their reportable awareness of differences in color can correctly discriminate among different colors in forced-choice tests, and with lesions that obliterate conscious identifiability of the shapes and locations of objects, patients can retain correct visuomotor guidance (of their hands) to these objects. A similar discrepancy, between conscious and unconscious (or nonconscious) processes, can be produced by lesions in the frontal medial cortex: patients exhibit the 'alien-hand sign,' in which the affected arm and hand perform spontaneous purposeful-looking movements that are not consciously willed or amenable to direct conscious control. A variety of other cerebral lesions can produce other interesting distortions of, or losses in, various kinds of awareness.

The foregoing kinds of findings in neuropsychology indicate cortical areas that are necessary for developing conscious experiences of sensory and volitional events. But they do not demonstrate that these areas are sufficient for this function; that is, they do not show where the conscious experience actually forms or arises. This distinction between necessity and sufficiency has at times been neglected, leading to potentially erroneous conclusions about the 'seat of consciousness'; it presents a problem that is difficult to address experimentally. Also, the neuropsychological findings do not themselves provide evidence on the physiological activities and interactions of the neuronal groups involved in the conscious process.

Regional Cerebral Blood Flow and Metabolism

The ability to measure regional cerebral blood flow (rCBF) and relating this to psychological functions in awake humans was introduced over 25 years ago by N Lassen and D Ingvar. The analysis has since been technically improved, as to localizability and quantitativeness, by the introduction of positron emission topography (PET) scan and by the coupling of this with the structural mapping by magnetic resonance imaging (MRI). These techniques are essentially noninvasive, except for the administration of presumably harmless tagged agents, and have thus opened a highly productive avenue for studying brain activity in the awake and responsive human. However, while these methods tell us which areas or nuclei in the brain are changing in their rate of metabolism, they do not give information on the physiological dynamics involved; that is, the information is essentially topographical. The timing of the change is also still only possible to within some seconds, for PET scans, but MRIs are faster. The rCBF studies in which individuals are asked to perform conscious mental operations are of special interest to the issue of brain and conscious experience. In one such study, individuals were asked to imagine moving their fingers without actually moving them; a selective increase in blood flow appeared in the supplementary motor area (SMA). Such findings might bear on the question of whether and where a conscious mental function can initiate or influence neural processes. The time resolution of the rCBF method, however, as well as the absence of indicators of the precise relative timing of the onset of the mental imagining, vitiate any answers to the question. It has been shown experimentally that conscious intention to move, for example, actually follows onset of electrophysiological activity associated specifically with the volitional process.

It should be noted that, although the machine for the functional MRI (fMRI) responses can show changes within a few milliseconds, the relevant fMRI responses cannot appear for perhaps 1000 ms or more after the relevant neuronal event. This is because fMRI measures a local change in blood flow or in some neural metabolite. Such changes require a substantial time to become evident after the relevant neural event has initiated the processes that produce them. That is, the time of a relevant fMRI change is delayed by the slower circulatory and metabolic changes that follow the neural activity, even though the machine itself can be very fast. Timing of the relevant neuronal activities can only be obtained by direct recordings of the electrical or magnetic changes that immediately are manifested by the relevant neural activities.

Electrophysiological Stimulation and Recording

The numerous studies with extracranial (scalp) recordings of event-related potentials (ERPs) over recent decades have not generally been sufficiently relevant to the issue of conscious experience. This is partly because the associated psychological tasks for the study participants were mostly those of detection of, recognition of, and responsiveness to signals, functions that could all potentially be performed unconsciously unless direct introspective reports of awareness are demanded. Scalp recordings also suffer from uncertainties of localization of the neuronal sources of the ERPs, although this is improving with recent technological advances. Whether the recording of magnetic rather than electrical fields will improve localizability significantly remains to be seen. Also, even when conscious reports are appropriately included, it is extraordinarily difficult to design experiments that may indicate causal interrelationships, as there is little possibility to manipulate one of the independent variables, the cerebral neural activity.

Intracranial electrodes can greatly improve both the localizability of electrical manifestations and the ability to manipulate neuronal functions in some quantitative fashions by electrical stimulation. On the other hand, the availability of such electrodes in loci suitable for study in awake, responsive patients is not common, and the kinds of experimental procedures permitted by the therapeutic and risk factors are greatly restricted. Fruitful experimental avenues have, however, been found. Stimulation can elicit conscious experiences, especially when applied in the cerebral sensory systems. It can also reversibly interfere with or 'disrupt' normal cerebral functions. This latter ability can be used to investigate functions of cerebral areas where stimulation does not itself elicit any conscious responses; it has been employed fruitfully in recent years by GA Ojemann and colleagues to analyze the language functions of temporal (and other) cortical areas.

Many neural responses to stimulation can develop without leading to any conscious experience. For example, stimulating the cortical surface can produce large electrophysiological direct cortical responses (DCRs) with no awareness by the individual. Similarly, the primary evoked potential elicited by a peripheral sensory stimulus leads to no conscious sensation if the appropriate later event-related potentials do not accompany the primary one. Unique kinds and durations of neuronal activities appear to be required to elicit a conscious sensory experience, but not unconscious forms of stimulus detection.

In recent years the ability to deliver brief magnetic pulses repetitively has been achieved, thus permitting effective stimulation of a cortical area with a magnetic device placed on the overlying scalp. This makes it possible to stimulate the cortex without the invasive surgery required to place an electrical stimulating wire in a local region, expanding the pool of potential individuals greatly, to include normal individuals. However, magnetic stimulation may be deficient in some important ways, relative to an intracranial electrical stimulator. Stimulation with an electrode inserted intracranially can be more localizable and affect more identifiable groups of stimulated neural elements. Also, one can be more certain of a threshold level for eliciting a neural or a subjective response; with a magnetic stimulus, it is possible that each single stimulus pulse at an apparently threshold level is actually producing an undetected series of repetitive neural responses.

Time Factors in Conscious and Unconscious Mental Functions

Neural Delay for Sensory Experience

Substantial duration of specific cerebral activations, of up to about 500 ms, have turned up experimentally as one of the most interesting neuronal requirements. This implies there is a substantial delay before neuronal adequacy for a sensory experience is achieved. However, further evidence indicates there is a subjective referral of the experience back to the time of the initial sensory signal that normally arrives at the cerebral cortex within 15–25 ms after a sensory stimulus; the primary evoked potential represents the response to this early signal, which comes up by way of the fast, specific projection system. Subjectively, then, the skin sensation would appear to have no significant delay, even though the experience is not neuronally elicitable until some hundreds of milliseconds later. Such a subjective referral in the temporal dimension is analogous to that in the spatial dimension. Both referrals serve to project the subjective image closer to the spatial and temporal features of the real stimuli, even though the adequate neuronal representation distorts both the spatial pattern and the timing of the process.

Neural Delay for Intention to Act

When individuals perform a self-initiated voluntary motor act, a slow surface-negative potential is recordable at the vertex (the 'readiness potential,' or RP); this begins 550 ms before the muscle is activated, in a fully spontaneous act. However, conscious intention to act appears only 350 ms after onset of the RP, although 200 ms before the act. This indicates that initiation of a voluntary act is made unconsciously by the brain before there is any awareness of the wish to act. But, also, there is time after conscious intention appears during which the volitional process could be consciously stopped or vetoed.

'Time-On' Theory for Conscious versus Unconscious Functions

Based on their earlier lines of evidence indicating a requirement for a substantial duration of neural activities in order to elicit a conscious experience, whether a sensation or intention (to move now), in 1991 Libet and colleagues devised and tested a theory to explain how the brain may distinguish between conscious and unconscious mental functions. The theory proposes the duration, or 'time-on,' of appropriate neural activities as one controlling factor in achieving this distinction: durations must exceed minimum values of up to about 500 ms to achieve conscious awareness of a mental process, but durations distinctly below those minimum values can mediate unconscious mental functions (without awareness). A specific experimental test of the proposal was carried out in relation to detection of a sensory signal with and without awareness.

Unity of Conscious Experience

One of the most mysterious and seemingly intractable problems in the mind–brain relationship is that of the unitary and integrated nature of conscious experience. This phenomenon is somehow a product of a brain with an estimated 100 billion neurons, each of which may have thousands of interconnections with other neurons. There is increasing evidence that many functions of cerebral cortex are localized, apparently organized into specialized columns of neurons. In spite of the enormously complex array of structures and functions, whatever does reach awareness is experienced as unified and integrated.

A recent neurophysiological observation may offer one possible route to investigating the issue of experiential integration, or, as it is often referred to, the 'binding problem.' This is the discovery by Charles M Gray and Wolf Singer of widespread synchronization of oscillatory neuronal electrical potentials in response to a visual image. It has led to some speculation that a 'correlation' model (based on the widely occurring synchronization of some activities) might represent the neural coding for a unified mental image in an otherwise chaotic background. This speculation is still to be tested.

A testable field theory

We may view subjective experience as if it were a field, produced by appropriate though multifarious neuronal activities of the brain. This conscious mental field (CMF) would have the attribute of a unitary, integrated experience or awareness, and it would also have a causal ability to affect or alter neuronal function. The theory of a CMF makes some crucial experimental predictions. If local areas of cerebral cortex could independently contribute to or alter the larger, unitary CMF, it should be possible to demonstrate such contributions when (1) that cortical area is completely isolated or cut off from neuronal communication with the rest of the brain, but (2) the area remains *in situ*, alive, and kept functioning in some suitable manner that sufficiently resembles its normal behavior. A fuller discussion of this theory and the experimental design to test it have been previously elaborated. The point here is to show that it is possible to formulate a theory and design an experimental test of it, even when the theory deals with the profound issues of conscious unity and with the question of whether the conscious function can actually influence brain function.

Further Reading

Amassian, VE, Somasundaram, M, Rothswell, JC, et al. (1991). Parasthesias elicited by single pulse magnetic coil stimulation of motor cortex in susceptible humans. *Brain* 114: 2505–2520.

Ciba Foundation Symposium 174 (1993). *Experimental and Theoretical Studies of Consciousness* (Nagel T, chair). Chichester: Wiley.

Eccles, JC (1994). *How the Self Controls Its Brain.* Berlin: Springer.

Goldberg, G, Mayer, NH, and Toglia, JU (1981). Medial frontal cortex infarction and the alien hand sign. *Archives of Neurology* 38: 683–686.

Ingvar, D and Phillipson, L (1977). Distribution of cerebral blood flow in the dominant hemisphere during motor ideation and motor performance. *Annals of Neurology* 2: 230–237.

Libet, B (1973). Electrical stimulation of cortex in human subjects, and conscious sensory aspects. In: Iggo, A (ed.) *Handbook of Sensory Physiology, Volume 2, Somatosensory System*, pp. 743–790. Berlin: Springer.

Libet, B (1985). Unconscious cerebral initiative and the role of conscious will in voluntary action. *Behavioral and Brain Sciences* 8: 529–566.

Libet, B (1993). *Neurophysiology of Consciousness.* Boston, MA: Birkhauser.

Libet, B (1994). A testable field theory of mind–brain interaction. *Journal of Consciousness Studies* 1: 119–126.

Libet, B (2006). Reflections on the interaction of the mind and brain. *Progress in Neurobiology* 78(3–5): 322–326.

Libet, B, Alberts, WW, Wright, EW, et al. (1975). Cortical representation of evoked potentials relative to conscious sensory responses and of somatosensory qualities in man. In: Kornhuber, HH (ed.) *The Somatosensory System*, pp. 291–308. Stuttgart: G. Thiene.

Libet, B, Wright, EW, Jr., Feinstein, B, et al. (1979). Subjective referral of the timing for a conscious sensory experience, a functional role for the somatosensory specific projection system in man. *Brain* 102: 191–222.

Libet, B, Pearl, DK, Morledge, DE, et al. (1991). Control of the transition from sensory detection to sensory awareness in man by the duration of a thalamic stimulus. The cerebral time-on factor. *Brain* 114: 1731–1759.

Nagel, T (1979). *Mortal Questions.* Cambridge: Cambridge University Press.

Ojemann, GA, Fedio, P, and van Buren, JM (1968). Anomia from pulvinar and subcortical parietal stimulation. *Brain* 91: 99–116.

Penfield, W (1958). *The Excitable Cortex in Conscious Man.* Liverpool: Liverpool University Press.

Weiskrantz, L (1986). *Blindsight: A Case Study and Implications.* Oxford: Clarendon.

D

Deafness

J. E. Hawkins, Ann Arbor, MI, USA

Deafness (anacusis) is the complete inability to hear speech and other sounds, however much they may be amplified. Persons with partial deafness (hypoacusis, dysacusis) are described colloquially as being hard of hearing, or clinically as having a hearing loss. Such deficiencies are all too common, especially in developed countries, with their overcrowded cities, excessive environmental noise and other forms of pollution, and their 'diseases of civilization.' In the United States alone, more than 20 million persons over 3 years of age have trouble hearing. Thus, some 8% of us are, like Chaucer's Wyf of Bathe, 'som-deel deef.' As our population ages and noise levels continue to rise, these figures can only increase. Moreover, some 4.8 million persons are deaf in the proper, absolute sense of that word. Comparable estimates are available for the UK, where the total number of deaf persons has been calculated to be 1 774 000. This figure includes 15 000 deaf mutes; 30 000 totally deaf; 70 000 'deaf to all natural speech' (who could hear speech amplified by hearing aids); and 1 659 000 persons who are hard of hearing.

Assessment of Hearing

The degree of auditory impairment, or hearing loss, is usually estimated by subjective audiometry, using pure tones and speech at precisely measured intensities. Thresholds, that is, sound pressure levels at which tones are just audible, or speech barely intelligible, are compared with established average normal values. The difference in decibels (dB) is the patient's hearing level. The audiogram (**Figure 1**) shows hearing levels for tones over a range of about six octaves, including the frequencies between 125 and 4000 Hz, which are most important for speech and music. Hearing levels between 0 and 20 dB ISO (i.e., based on the audiometric calibration of the International Standards Organization) are generally considered normal; those between 20 and 40 dB represent a mild hearing loss. Between 40 and 55 dB the loss is regarded as moderate, between 55 and 70 dB as moderately severe. Hearing levels between 70 and 90 dB indicate that the loss is severe and, above 90 dB, that the loss is profound. In these terms, deafness can be defined as a hearing level of 92 dB or more.

Other types of screening tests are used for identifying neonates who are at risk for hearing problems. One important test is based on otoacoustic emissons (OAEs) measured from the external ear canal with a microphone. Normal OAEs indicate normal middle-ear function and normal function of the inner ear at least for the outer hair cells, which are the likely generators of OAEs. Brain stem response measures are also used for hearing screening. The neuronal potentials of the brain stem, as elicited by brief sounds, are recorded with one electrode on the skin over the mastoid process and another on the scalp at the vertex. Normal brain stem responses indicate normal function of the middle ear, inner ear, auditory nerve, and certain important pathways within the brain stem. In electrocochleography (EcoG), the responses of the inner ear (cochlear microphonics and nerve action potentials) are recorded from the cochlea with a fine needle electrode piercing the tympanic membrane to make contact with its bony wall at the promontory. Pain is minimal for the adult, but for children sedation or anesthesia is advisable. On occasion, measurement of the threshold for the acoustic reflex, the brief contraction of the stapedius muscle of the middle ear in response to sudden sounds of high intensity, can be informative.

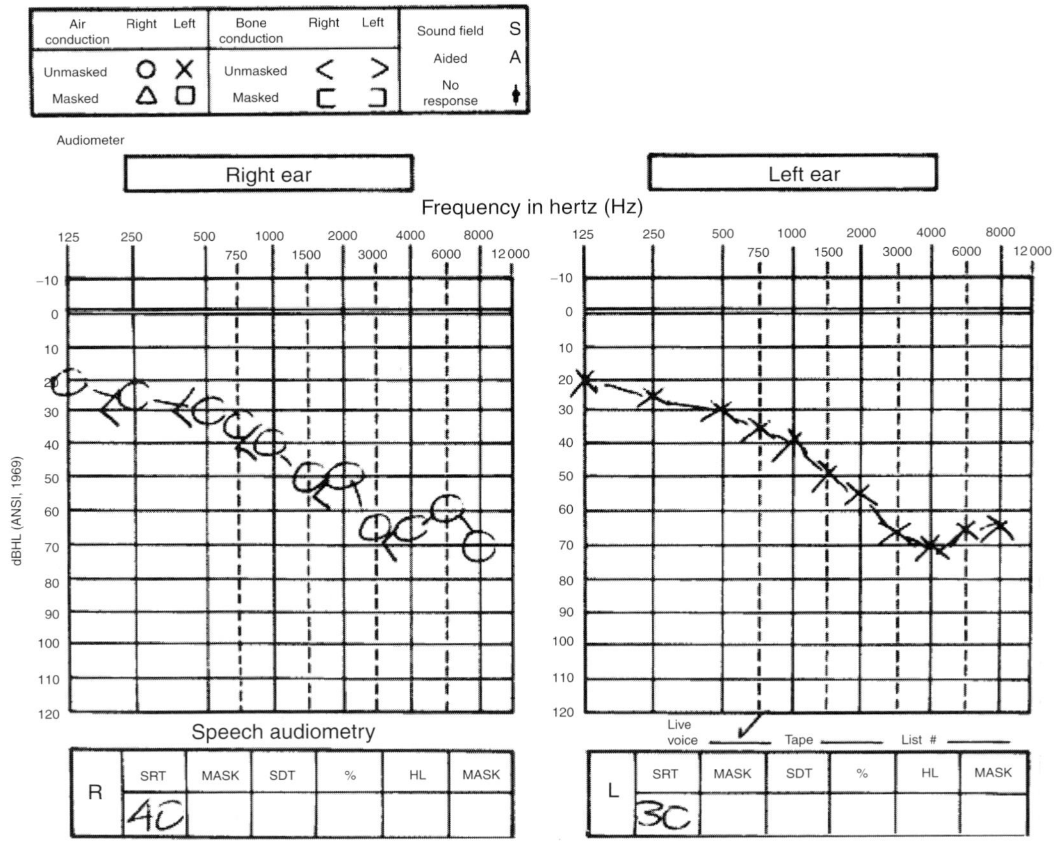

Figure 1 Audiogram showing moderate, symmetrical, sensorineural hearing loss in an octogenarian subject of the NIDCD-sponsored 'Old Time Ears Project' (a functional and histopathological study of presbycusis by CI Berlin and JB Nadol). Speech reception thresholds (SRT) for spondees are 40 and 30 dB. In addition to presbycusis, the hearing loss suggests the lasting effects of numerous experimental exposures some 50 years ago to intense tones and noise and possibly those of still earlier quinine treatment for malaria. Nowadays the subject finds binaural hearing aids of help in the theatre and lecture room, but not essential for ordinary conversation. Published with permission.

Causes of Impaired Hearing

When deafness is congenital, as it is in 1 or 2 in 1000 births, it is generally of genetic origin. The majority of such cases of hereditary hearing loss are nonsyndromic, that is, not accompanied by other structural or functional anomalies. Others may be the result of one or another of a large number of genetically determined syndromes involving malformation of the external or middle ear, or degenerative changes in the cochlea. The loss may be associated with visual defects, as in retinitis pigmentosa (Usher syndrome); musculoskeletal malformations, as in mandibulofacial dysostosis (Treacher–Collins syndrome) and osteogenesis imperfecta; pigmentary abnormalities, as in the Waardenburg syndrome; renal disease, as in the Alport syndrome; metabolic disorders such as goiter, as in Pendred's syndrome; various neurological conditions; or trisomy 13, 18, and 21. Also, maternal disease during pregnancy (e.g., rubella and syphilis) or perinatal conditions (e.g., jaundice, anoxia, and trauma) may be responsible. When hearing impairment is acquired, it may be attributable to one or more well-recognized causes, including viral or bacterial disease (e.g., mumps, measles, herpes zoster oticus, meningitis, and syphilis), or head injury with temporal bone fracture. Other causes include ototoxic medications, in particular the aminoglycosidic antibiotics such as neomycin or gentamicin (especially when used with a loop diuretic), the antitumor agent cisplatin, the antimalarial quinine, or even aspirin in large doses. Occupational or recreational exposure to high levels of noise sooner or later produces hearing loss, not least among today's youth. In adults, otosclerosis and Meniere's disease can be causes of impaired hearing, with the aging process itself the most common cause of all. In presbyacusis, which may have a genetic, an environmental, or a temporal basis, both ears tend to be equally affected (**Figure 1**). In Meniere's disease and sudden deafness, the loss is often confined to one ear. In Meniere's there may also be evidence of an autoimmune condition. In sudden deafness a viral infection may be responsible, or possibly occlusion of a small artery supplying the membranous labyrinth. Infection with cytomegalovirus can also be a cause of adult deafness, especially in AIDS.

Sites and Types of Abnormality

The site of hearing impairment is usually peripheral rather than central, that is, in the outer, middle, or inner ear rather than in the brain stem or higher centers. If the cochlea is normal but sounds are prevented from reaching it by malformation or blockage of the external canal or injury to the drum membrane or the chain of ossicles, the hearing loss is said to be of the conductive type. Thresholds for airborne sounds tend to be reduced more or less equally at all frequencies, but the loss is not complete. Hearing by bone conduction, that is, with a vibrator held against the mastoid process, the forehead, or the teeth, may be normal. For such a patient, a hearing aid to amplify sounds is often of great help. Surgical repairs, as in Wullstein's and Zöllner's types of tympanoplasty, can restore sound conduction by the ossicular chain and thus give significant hearing improvement. In otosclerosis (more appropriately called otospongiosis, as in French usage), the impairment is most often of the conductive type. Sounds are prevented from reaching the cochlea because the stapes footplate is unable to vibrate, being sealed in the oval window by deposits of newly formed, abnormal bone. Fortunately, an effective surgical treatment is available. In this stapedectomy, the fixed and immobile stapes are removed from the oval window and the opening into the vestibule is covered with a membrane consisting of vein, fascia, or other suitable material. As a substitute for the stapes, a short length of wire or plastic is attached to the long process of the incus to make contact with the new membrane. Like tympanoplasty, stapedectomy has proved to be a dramatic advance in surgery for the betterment of hearing in patients with conductive hearing loss.

Sensorineural Impairment

In sensorineural hearing impairment, there are usually pathological changes in both the cochlea and its nerve, but the middle ear may be intact. Most often, extensive loss of the sensory hair cells and supporting cells of the organ of Corti has occurred, with secondary degeneration of at least some of the cochlear nerve fibers and spiral ganglion cells. This most prevalent type of hearing loss occurs with aging and after injury by intense noise or ototoxic medications. The changes tend to occur first in the basal turn of the cochlea, which responds to the higher frequencies of sound, but they may spread to involve the upper turns and thus affect hearing for lower frequencies as well. A slow progression of this type of change is commonly observed in presbyacusis, the hearing loss associated with aging and earlier in life with certain genetic disorders. During treatment with an ototoxic antibiotic, especially in combination with a loop diuretic, a similar but rapidly progressive loss of hearing can occur. The sensory epithelium of the cochlea may also degenerate in the wake of viral diseases such as mumps; in the late stage of Meniere's disease; in sudden deafness; and in the destructive capsular form of otosclerosis, which is not limited to the oval window and stapes but may extend so far as to violate the periosteal lining of the bony labyrinth and injure Corti's organ as well (**Figures 2** and **3**). Because the resulting impairment is both conductive and sensorineural in character, it is called mixed. In man and other mammals, sensorineural loss is permanent because the hair cells do not regenerate. Ongoing studies in several laboratories have shown that in birds the sensory cells can reappear after noise or ototoxic injury. There is a hope that gene transfer or stem cell treatment may eventually be devised to encourage human hair cells to regenerate and replace their losses after injury. Because sensorineural change tends to diminish hearing for the higher frequencies, presbyacusic

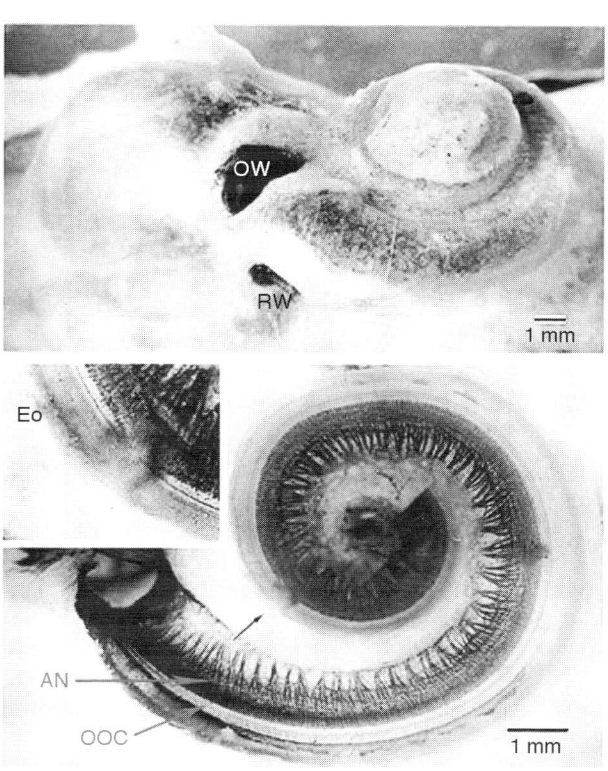

Figure 2 A case of deafness in a 73-year-old woman with capsular otosclerosis who had also received ototoxic aminoglycosides for sepsis following surgery. Top, Otic capsule, right ear, thinned by drilling and with stapes removed, showing otosclerotic focus surrounding both oval window (OW) and round window (RW). Bottom, Basal turn of cochlea. The organ of Corti (OOC) is clearly absent from most of the basal half-turn. The auditory-nerve fibers (AN) coursing across the osseous spiral lamina.were stained with osmium; their density is less than normal in most of the basal half-turn. At dark arrow, Endosteum (Eo) is thickened and connective tissue has grown onto the basilar membrane as a result of the otosclerosis. From Johnsson LG, Hawkins JE Jr. et al. (1982) Cochlear and otoconial abnormalities in capsular otosclerosis with hydrops. *Annals of Otology, Rhinology and Laryngology* 91(supplement 97): 3–15.

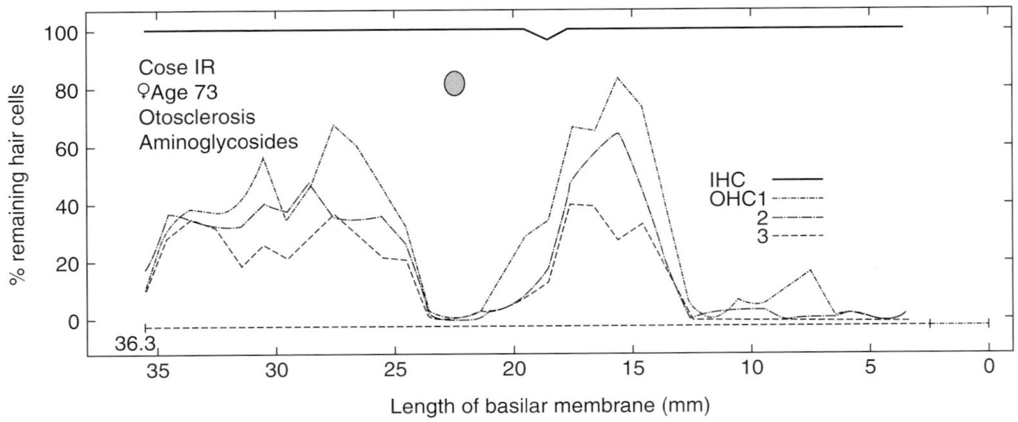

Figure 3 Corresponding cytocochleogram of the same ear as **Figure 2**. The *x*-axis plots the length of the basilar membrane from the cochlea's basal end (0 mm) to the apex (36.3 mm). There is a loss of outer hair cells from the basal turn (below 13 mm), attributable to ototoxic agents, and from the second turn (18–25 mm) in the region of the thickened endosteum, attributable to the capsular otosclerosis. Inner hair cells are present except for the most basal 3 mm of Corti's organ, where nerve fibers have also degenerated. Reprinted from Johnsson LG, Hawkins JE Jr., et al. (1982) Cochlear and otoconial abnormalities in capsular otosclerosis with hydrops. *Annals of Otology, Rhinology and Laryngology* 91(supplement 97): 3–15, with permission.

and other patients with this form of impairment have difficulty in understanding sibilant and fricative speech sounds and in distinguishing among unvoiced stop consonants. They are at a particular disadvantage when trying to converse in noisy surroundings and in groups. A hearing aid may be helpful in a church, theater, or lecture hall, but the results are often disappointing because of the user's inability to resolve the spectral details of speech sounds, especially in the presence of noise, despite amplification.

Sensorineural impairment of hearing may be accompanied by the sometimes distressing symptom called tinnitus, a subjective ringing in the ears that may also take the form of a buzzing or roaring noise. Tinnitus often accompanies attacks of Meniere's disease, in which the acuity of hearing tends to vary (fluctuant hearing loss). It also occurs during quinine treatment for malaria and salicylate treatment for arthritis. Furthermore, tinnitus may also be present after injury by noise, and unless the impairment is symmetrical, sounds may produce an unpleasant sensation of dissimilar pitch in the two ears (diplacusis). Unilateral tinnitus when hearing thresholds are near normal may indicate a problem with the auditory nerve. Such a retrocochlear lesion may be produced by a tumor such as an acoustic neuroma, which can interrupt conduction in the auditory nerve. A final characteristic symptom of sensorineural hearing loss is an unusually rapid increase in the perceived loudness of sound as its intensity level is increased: a phenomenon known as the recruitment of loudness.

Animal Models for Deafness

Animal models are very important tools for the study of normal hearing and disease processes. Genetic forms of deafness and their underlying otopathology have historically been studied in certain types of domestic and laboratory animals that are either born deaf or become deaf at an early age. Among these are blue-eyed white cats; waltzer, shaker, and other strains of mice; Dalmatian dogs; and Hedlund mink. The changes seen in the inner ear can resemble closely those occurring in certain types of congenitally deaf patients. Molecular biological techniques can be used to knock out (or over-express) a protein in mouse models. The resulting loss of function can lead to important knowledge of the role of that protein in the normal ear. Noise-induced and ototoxic hearing losses have been studied experimentally in a variety of species to understand why humans who are exposed to such conditions lose their hearing. Presbyacusic changes in the cochlea vary with the species examined. In the dog they more nearly resemble those found in aging human ears, whereas those seen in the largely vegetarian rhesus monkey tend to be milder and less extensive.

The Cochlear Prosthesis

In deafened patients, even with extensive degeneration or absence of cochlear hair cells, it is often possible to restore a significant degree of useful hearing by surgically implanting a cochlear prosthesis. This device consists of a microphone, a speech processor, and an array of up to 24 tiny metal electrodes inserted through the round window of the cochlea into scala tympani. These electrodes stimulate the remaining nerve fibers, bypassing the missing hair cells. Most patients who have received an implant have emerged from a world of silence. Many are able to carry on a normal conversation. Lip-reading ability is usually enhanced. Over 60 000 implants have been placed over the past 20 years. In the past, the prosthesis scored its greatest successes in patients who had become deaf after learning to speak. Now, striking results are being obtained even in congenitally deaf infants and children, provided they receive the implant during the optimal period for language learning. Many such operations are now performed around the age of 12 months. In some patients, a cochlear implant will not work because there is no functioning auditory nerve. In these patients, an auditory brain stem implant (ABI) is placed in the cochlear nucleus in the brain stem. ABI users have not generally had speech perception as good as that possible with a cochlear implant One challenge of the future will be to improve such devices to allow speech perception for all forms of deafness.

Further Reading

Ballantyne, J Martin, MC, and Martin, A (eds.) (1993). *Deafness*, 5th edn. London: Whurr.

Chen, CY, Halpin, C, and Rauch, SD (2003). Oral steroid treatment of sudden sensorineural hearing loss: A ten year retrospective analysis. *Otology and Neurotology* 24: 728–733.

Cheng, AG, Cunningham, LL, and Rubel, EW (2005). Mechanisms of hair cell death and protection. *Current Opinion in Otolaryngology and Head and Neck Surgery* 13: 343–348.

Colletti, V and Shannon, RV (2005). Open set speech perception with auditory brainstem implant? *Laryngoscope* 115: 1974–1978.

Dennis, JM and Neely, JG (1991). Basic hearing tests. *Otolaryngology Clinics of North America* 24: 253–276.

Forge, A and Schacht, J (2000). Aminoglycoside antibiotics. *Audiology and Neurotology* 5: 3–22.

Goldfarb, A and Avraham, KB (2002). Genetics of deafness: Recent advances and clinical implications. *Journal of Basic and Clinical Physiology and Pharmacology* 13: 75–88.

Hawkins, JE and Johnsson, LG (1985). Otopathological changes associated with presbyacusis. *Semin Hearing* 6: 115–133.

Johnsson, LG, Hawkins, JE, Jr., Rouse, RC, and Linthicum, FH, Jr. (1982). Cochlear and otoconial abnormalities in capsular otosclerosis with hydrops. *Annals of Otology, Rhinology and Laryngology* 91(supplement 97): 3–15.

Kawamoto, K, Ishimoto, S, Minoda, R, Brough, DE, and Raphael, Y (2003). Math1 gene transfer generates new cochlear hair cells in mature guinea pigs *in vivo*. *Journal of Neuroscience* 23: 4395–4400.

Linthicum, FH (1993). Histopathology of otosclerosis. *Otolaryngology Clinics of North America* 26: 335–352.

Morton, CC and Nance, WE (2006). Newborn hearing screening – A silent revolution. *New England Journal of Medicine* 354: 2151–2164.

National Institutes of Health (2000) *Healthy People 2010, Vol. II, 28: Vision and Hearing*. http://www.healthypeople.gov/document/html/volume2/28vision.htm (accessed Jul. 2008).

Niparko, JK, Kirk, KI, Mellon, NK, Robbins, AM, Tucci, DL, and Wilson, DL (eds.) (2000). *Cochlear Implants. Principles and Practices*. Philadelphia: Lippincott Williams & Wilkins.

Ohlemiller, KK (2006). Contributions of mouse models to understanding of age- and noise-related hearing loss. *Brain Research* 1091: 89–102.

Pickles, JO (2004). Mutation in mitochondrial DNA as a cause of presbyacusis. *Audiology and Neurotology* 9: 23–33.

Schuknecht, HF (1993). *Pathology of the Ear*, 2nd edn. Philadelphia: Lea and Febiger.

Talaska, AE and Schacht, J (2007). Mechanisms of noise damage to the cochlea. *Journal of Audiological Medicine* 5: 3–9.

Whitehead, ML, Lonsbury-Martin, BL, Martin, GK, and McCoy, MJ (1996). Otoacoustic emissions: Animal models and clinical observations. In: Van De Water, T, Popper, AN, and Fay, RR (eds.) *Clinical Aspects of Hearing*, pp. 199–257. New York: Springer.

Willott, JF (2007). Factors affecting hearing in mice, rats, and other laboratory animals. *Journal of American Association for Laboratory Animal Science* 46: 23–27.

World Health Organization (2006). Deafness and hearing impairment. Fact sheet N°300. http://www.who.int/mediacentre/factsheets/fs300/ (accessed Jul. 2008).

Delirium and Language

Y. Turgeon, Campbellton Regional Hospital, Campbellton, Canada

Delirium is an acute state of confusion characterized by disturbances in consciousness and cognitive functioning. Acute confusional state is used interchangeably with delirium and both conditions have been referred to as transient cognitive disorder (for reviews, see Levkoff et al., 1986; Lipowski, 1990; Tune and Ross, 1994).

Several studies have examined the prevalence and incidence of delirium. In a study with 325 participants, Levkoff et al. (1992) showed that, of the study participants, 10.5% met the criteria for delirium according to the third version of the *Diagnostic and statistical manual of mental disorders* (DSM-III) at initial evaluation, whereas 31.3% developed delirium subsequently. An additional 110 participants presented with symptoms of delirium without fully meeting the DSM-III criteria. Generally, among older adults who are hospitalized in medical units, approximately 10% are reported to present delirium on admission and another 10 to 15% may develop delirium while hospitalized (APA, 1994).

Delirium is most often reported among the elderly population and special populations, such as terminally ill or postoperative patients. Nevertheless, children can present cardinal features of delirium (Trzepacz, 1996; Prugh et al., 1980). In a 4 year retrospective study of the clinical presentation and symptoms of delirium in children and adolescents, Turkel et al. (2003) showed that symptoms of psychosis and disorientation were less distinctive in that population. However, they concluded that for the most part the presentation and course of pediatric delirium were similar to those of delirium in adults. They also established support for the usefulness of the current *Diagnostic and standard manual of mental disorders* (DSM) in the pediatric population.

Delirium typically has a sudden onset, a sharp rise, a fluctuating course, and a brief duration. Symptoms may arise abruptly (e.g., following a stroke or a head injury) or can be gradual (e.g., in older adults receiving multiple medications, experiencing pain, or experiencing a sensory loss). Reports on the onset and course of delirium are numerous and some have reported that delirium is worse at night, a phenomenon known as sundowning (Evans, 1987). In general, delirium develops over periods of time that vary from a few hours to a few days. If left untreated, symptoms may last several days or weeks, even months, especially in individuals with coexisting cognitive disorders due to a persisting or evolving medical condition. Prolonged memory impairment and incomplete recovery are common in similar cases (APA, 1994).

A number of conditions can cause delirium. The DSM-IV lists four subtypes of delirium according to presumed etiologies: delirium due to a general medical condition, substance-induced delirium, delirium due to multiple etiologies, and delirium not otherwise specified (if the cause is indeterminate). The most common etiologies for delirium include chemical intoxication (e.g., alcohol intoxication and withdrawal), metabolic disorders (e.g., hypoglycemia), structural brain diseases (e.g., vascular infarction, hemorrhage, brain tumors, brain abscesses), infections (e.g., acute meningitis, encephalitis), medications (e.g., anticholinergics), and environmental factors. Environmental factors include prior recent acute-care hospital admission and increased number of medications. Other major precipitating factors are advanced age, institutionalization, pre-existing cognitive impairment, dehydration, pain, and sensory loss. Rahkonen et al. (2000) examined delirium in elderly people without severe predisposing disorders. Among 51 healthy seniors, the most important primary causes of delirium were infections and strokes.

Diagnostic Criteria and Differential Diagnosis

The current diagnostic criteria for delirium are based on the *Diagnostic and statistical manual of mental disorders* (DSM-IV) and the *International classification of diseases* (ICD–10). The DSM-IV criteria focus on three essential features of delirium: a disturbance of consciousness (i.e., reduced awareness to the environment) with reduced attention (Criterion A); a change in cognition or the development of a perceptual disturbance that is not accounted for by a pre-existing, established, or evolving dementia (Criterion B); and a disturbance that develops over a short period of time and fluctuates over the course of the day (Criterion C).

A study by Laurila et al. (2004) asserted that a clouding of consciousness, perceptual disturbances, and disorganized thinking are the most significant contributors to delirium diagnosis according to the DSM-IV among individuals with dementia. In a cross-sectional study, the authors compared the usefulness of criteria from earlier versions of the DSM and the ICD–10. They established that the DSM-IV criteria of delirium identified new, often nondemented, subjects as being confused, whereas the criteria from ICD–10 were overly restrictive.

Delirium is ordinarily associated with changes in sleep–wake patterns, disorientation to time and space, disordered or incoherent speech, visual hallucinations, and marked alterations in psychomotor activity. Individuals suffering from delirium commonly display neuropsychological deficits on tasks of attention and concentration, memory, language and visual spatial functions. The clinical presentation of delirium is heterogeneous by nature and may vary and change rapidly. The severity and progression of symptoms may vary noticeably from patient to patient and in the same patient at different times during the day, even within short periods of time.

It may be difficult to differentiate persisting delirium from dementia that occurs in clear consciousness. Dementia is most often characterized by a slow onset and a gradual rise and predominantly affects memory. Several screening instruments for delirium have been developed. The Delirium Rating Scale (Trzepacz et al., 1987) and the Confusion Assessment Method (Inouye et al., 1990) have become widely used assessment tools in medical units. Simple bedside tests of attention have also been reported to aid in identification of delirium in older adults (O'Keeffe and Gosney, 1997).

Changes in consciousness and cognitive functioning in delirium can arise in the absence of prior cognitive disorders or can be superimposed on conditions that present with cognitive impairment. The symptoms of delirium have been examined among elderly inpatients with or without dementia. Cole et al. (2002) studied the prevalence, frequencies, and coexistence of delirium symptoms in individuals with and without dementia. These researchers determined that symptoms appeared to be similar among both groups, although individuals with dementia had increased psychomotor agitation at the time of diagnosis and elevated levels of disorganized thinking and disorientation at subsequent assessment.

The clinical presentation of delirium often manifests signs and symptoms such as changes in personality associated with irritability, inappropriate behavior, and psychotic characteristics, including hallucinations and paranoia. Differential diagnoses also include other psychiatric disorders such as depression, substance intoxication, substance withdrawal, malingering, and factice disorders (APA, 1994).

Communication and Language in Delirium

The assessment of language impairment and communication disorders contributes to the diagnosis of delirium. Language disturbance is a cardinal feature of Criterion B in DSM-IV. However, formal assessment of language impairment in individuals with symptoms of delirium can be complicated if the individual is unable to interact for the purpose of communication. If the individual presents with a reduced awareness, diminished responsiveness, and reduced ability to be attentive (Criterion A), the assessment of language disturbance, other than a change in cognition, will be limited. In similar circumstances, a bedside interview that includes informal interaction, as well as a few simple, but strategic tasks, is enough to establish the presence or absence of language disturbance and thus facilitate the diagnosis and later management of delirium. Beeson and Rapcsak (1998) suggested that the assessment of language impairment in individuals suffering from delirium be delayed because it does not provide a valid basis for assessment. Also, the examiner may consider an exhaustive review of an individual's medical files to obtain information from other sources, such as family members or caregivers.

The abrupt onset and fluctuating nature of delirium make formal assessment difficult. Nevertheless, the assessment of language impairment in individuals suffering from delirium, although limited, can be achieved with the use of a few tasks that target major domains of linguistic behavior, namely, conversational speech, auditory comprehension, confrontational naming, repetition, and reading and writing.

In comparison with the study of speech and language disturbance in the dementias, there is limited research that aims specifically at characterizing communication and language in delirium. This does not indicate an absolute lack of empirical data, as language disturbances in individuals suffering from delirium have been discussed as part of related research on dementia and other psychiatric disorders, including psychosis. Alternatively, language impairments in delirium, as in some psychiatric disorders, have been described as concurring with a global failure in cognitive processing, more specifically attention and perceptual deficits. However, a few patterns of language disturbances in delirium emerge from the literature.

Chedru and Geschwind (1972) provided one of the first descriptive studies of cognitive disorders in delirium, including speech and language. These authors reported that impaired reading, writing, and verbal fluency were the most common linguistic abnormalities in delirium. They also determined that individuals suffering from delirium exhibited naming and repetition abnormalities, but that spontaneous speech was relatively preserved. Naming deficits were often present. Wallesch and Hundsalz (1994) reported impairment on a naming and a language comprehension task in a small group of individuals suffering from delirium. They compared a group of individuals diagnosed with delirium with a group diagnosed with probable Alzheimer's disease (AD). They found that the number of naming errors was comparable for both groups. They found an effect of word frequency on naming success only for the AD group. In contrast, unrelated naming errors were significantly more frequent in the delirium group. Wallesch and Hundsalz (1994) showed that some of the overall unrelated naming errors in participants presenting with delirium were caused by visual misperceptions, thus supporting nonlinguistic influences on language. Additionally, behavioral strategies aiming at the target were more frequently exhibited by AD participants, among whom the lack of such strategies is consistent with a reduced clarity of awareness of the environment and diminished attention.

A number of studies have found writing deficits in participants presenting with delirium participants. Macleod and Whitehead (1997) have shown that writing is the most impaired of the language modalities in delirium. In a 6 month study, they compared the performance of a small group of individuals diagnosed with acute delirium with that of a control group. Their results provided further support for the predominance of writing impairments in delirium. They also showed that reading was the least impaired of linguistic functions. Additionally, Macleod and Whitehead (1997) used a short and simple test to substantiate writing errors in delirium, especially among frail and dying individuals. They requested each participant in their study to simply write their name and address. Interestingly, they found that the writing errors were invariably motor and that the most consistent error was the reduplication of letters. The fact that none of the individuals suffering from delirium could write their name and address without obvious motor errors is further support of a nonlinguistic influence on language in delirium. Aakerlund and Rosenberg (1994) have found similar results in postoperative delirium. They found that all individuals who developed postoperative delirium had severely impaired writing, with features such as reluctance to write, motor disability, and spatial disturbances. None of the individuals without delirium developed these disturbances. Their results suggested that testing of writing ability may be useful in the diagnosis of delirium.

Conclusion

Delirium is a highly variable clinical phenomenon that is difficult to study. More well-controlled and systematic studies are needed to fully describe and explain speech and language impairment in delirium.

See also: Dementia and Language.

Bibliography

Aakerlund, PL and Rosenberg, J (1994). 'Writing disturbances: An indicator for postoperative delirium.' *International Journal of Psychiatry in Medicine* 24(3): 245–257.

American Psychiatric Association (APA) (1994). *Diagnostic and statistical manual of mental disorders,* 4th edn. Washington, DC: American Psychiatric Association.

Beeson, PM and Rapcsak, SZ (1998). 'The aphasias.' In: Snyder, PJ and Nussbaum, PD (eds.) *Clinical neuropsychology: A pocket handbook for assessment*, pp. 211–239. Washington, DC: American Psychological Association.

Chedru, F and Geschwind, N (1972). 'Disorders of higher cortical functions in acute confusional states.' *Cortex* 10: 395–411.

Cole, MG, McCusker, J, Dendukuri, N, and Han, L (2002). 'Symptoms of delirium among elderly medical inpatients with or without dementia.' *Journal of Neuropsychiatry & Clinical Neurosciences* 14(2): 167–175.

Evans, LK (1987). 'Sundown syndrome in institutionalized elderly.' *Journal of the American Geriatrics Society* 35: 101–108.

Inouye, SK, van Dyck, CH, Alesi, CA, Balkin, S, Siegal, AP, and Horwitz, RI (1990). 'Clarifying confusion: The confusion assessment method: A new method for detecting delirium.' *Annals of Internal Medicine* 113: 941–948.

Laurila, JV, Pitkala, KH, Strandberg, TE, and Tilvis, RS (2004). 'Delirium among patients with and without dementia: Does the diagnosis according to the DSM-IV differ from the previous classifications?' *International Journal of Geriatric Psychiatry* 19(3): 271–277.

Levkoff, SE, Besdine, RW, and Wetle, TT (1986). 'Acute confusional states (delirium) in the hospitalized elderly.' *Annual Review of Gerontology and Geriatrics* 6: 1–26.

Levkoff, SE, Evans, DA, Liptzin, B, Cleary, PD, Lipsitz, LA, Wetle, TT, Reilly, CH, Pilgrim, DM, Schor, J, and Rowe, J (1992). 'Delirium. The occurrence and persistence of symptoms among elderly hospitalized patients.' *Archives of Internal Medicine* 152: 334–340.

Lipowski, ZJ (1990). *Delirium: Acute confusional states.* New York: Oxford University Press.

Macleod, AD and Whitehead, LE (1997). 'Dysgraphia and terminal delirium.' *Palliative Medicine* 11(2): 127–132.

O'Keeffe, ST and Gosney, M (1997). 'Assessing attentiveness in older hospital patients: Global assessment versus test of attention.' *Journal of the American Geriatrics Society* 45(4): 470–473.

Prugh, DG, Wagonfeld, S, Metcalf, D, and Jordan, K (1980). 'A clinical study of delirium in children and adolescents.' *Psychosomatic Medicine* 42(I/II): 177–195.

Rahkonen, T, Makela, H, Paanila, S, Halonen, P, Sivenius, J, and Sulkava, R (2000). 'Delirium in elderly people without severe predisposing disorders: Etiology and 1-year prognosis after discharge.' *International Psychogeriatrics* 12(4): 473–481.

Trzepacz, PT (1996). 'Delirium: Advances in diagnosis, pathophysiology, and treatment.' *Psychiatric Clinics of North America* 19(3): 429–448.

Trzepacz, PT, Baker, RW, and Greenhouse, J (1987). 'A symptom rating scale for delirium.' *Psychiatry Research* 23: 89–97.

Tune, L and Ross, C (1994). 'Delirium.' In: Coffey, CE and Cummings, JL (eds.) *Textbook of geriatric psychiatry*, pp. 351–365. Washington, DC: American Psychiatric Press.

Turkel, SB, Braslow, K, Tavare, CJ, and Trzepacz, PT (2003). 'The Delirium Rating Scale in children and adolescents.' *Psychosomatics: Journal of Consultation Liaison Psychiatry* 44(2): 126–129.

Wallesch, CW and Hundsalz, A (1994). 'Language Function in Delirium: A comparison of single word processing in acute confusional states and probable Alzheimer's Disease.' *Brain and Language 46,* 592–606.

Dementia and Language

J. Macoir, Laval University, Quebec, Quebec, Canada
Y. Turgeon, Campbellton Regional Hospital, Campbellton, New Brunswick, Canada

Introduction

Dementia is a generalized loss of functions that results from cerebral disease. Dementia occurs in absence of acute confusion (i.e., the deficits do not occur exclusively during the course of a delirium). According to the American Psychiatric Association's *Diagnostic and statistical manual of mental disorders* (DSM-IV), a dementia syndrome is characterized by multiple deficits in cognition, including memory impairment, which are the direct consequence of physiological changes. The DSM-IV criteria require that these deficits must be of a sufficient magnitude to impair social or occupational function. Historically, diagnostic classifications for dementia have included subtypes based on characteristics such as typical symptoms presentation, the progression and course of the disease, and psychiatric and behavioral features, as well as presumed causes (e.g., a general medical condition, persisting effects of a substance, multiple etiologies). The concept of dementia has evolved over the past hundred years. It has long been associated with a progressive decline of cognitive functions and with an irreversible course. Nowadays, definitions of dementia are descriptive and rely on typical symptoms presentation, and thus do not necessarily imply a progressive degeneration. However, the primary progressive dementias are most common and often present with language and communication disorders.

As the population in Western countries ages, the prevalence of progressive dementias resulting from brain diseases increases. Recent epidemiologic studies have suggested that the prevalence of dementia in industrialized countries is approximately 1.5% at age 65 years, rising to approximately 25% by age 80 years (Lobo et al., 2000). For example, according to the Canadian Study of Health and Aging (1994), more than 364 000 Canadians over 65 suffer from dementia. Among these individuals,

65% presented with dementia of the Alzheimer's type (DAT) whereas the remaining suffer from vascular dementia (VaD) and other forms of dementia. Moreover, it is predicted that over three-quarters of a million Canadians will have Alzheimer's disease and related dementias by the year 2031. Thus, progressive dementia is becoming an increasingly important public health concern across the world.

Diagnostic Criteria and Differential Diagnosis

In recent years, with the growing concern for early diagnosis of progressive dementia (i.e., dementia resulting from a gradual degeneration of the brain), several researches have been conducted on prodromal forms of dementia. Mild cognitive impairment (MCI) refers to the clinical condition between normal aging and DAT in which persons experience memory loss to a greater extent than one would expect for age, yet they do not meet currently accepted criteria for clinically probable Alzheimer's disease. Work from Petersen and colleagues on MCI provided for the diagnostic criteria that are commonly accepted (Petersen et al., 2001; Petersen, 2004). Recent studies suggest that a percentage of individuals presenting with mild cognitive impairment later developed typical symptoms of progressive dementia, especially DAT. According to Petersen et al. (2001), a clinical diagnosis of MCI requires a memory complaint, preferably corroborated by an informant, and an impaired memory function. Although a subtype of MCI may present with cognitive deficits other than memory, the amnesic type presents with salient memory failures in conjunction with a preserved general cognitive functioning and intact performance in activities of daily living. Individuals diagnosed with MCI are, however, not demented.

Because of the absence of biological markers or simple diagnostic methods, the early detection of dementia relies on various assessments, performed to rule out other possible causes and to identify specific forms of the disease (i.e., differential diagnosis). Neuropsychological testing plays an important role in the assessment of individuals with cognitive impairment. A large number of studies have sought to identify the neuropsychological features that distinguish the different forms of dementia. What emerges from these studies are descriptions of cognitive functioning among which some distinctions are useful for the differential diagnosis of dementia. For example, there are remarkable differences between patients with DAT and VaD with respect to verbal long-term memory and executive functions. However, these patients also presented with similar language, constructional ability, attention, and memory deficits (Looi and Sachdev, 1999).

This inconsistency and overlapping of cognitive deficits is certainly due to the important heterogeneity of neuropsychological manifestations in the early stages of the disease (for a review, see Rosenstein, 1998) as well as to methodological problems, including the application of diagnostic criteria, selection of neuropsychological tests (aiming at large cognitive domains instead of more precise components of cognition) and lack of adequate matching of patients groups. As we mentioned above, the definition of dementia continues to evolve. Current studies have refined clinical criteria of dementia and, for example, have made possible the distinction between the different presentations of frontal lobe disease.

Language Disorders in the Major Forms of Dementia

With respect to language impairments, neuro-epidemiological and neuropsychological studies propose clinical linguistic profiles usually associated with common forms of dementias. Recent neuropsycholinguistic studies also largely contribute to a better characterization of language deficits in dementia by specifically identifying functional localization of impaired and preserved processing components and subcomponents of the linguistic processing system. In the following sections we will review current data on language and communication disorders in the most frequent primary progressive syndromes of dementia, namely DAT, VaD and dementia with Lewy Bodies, as well as in specific forms of frontotemporal lobe disease, namely frontotemporal dementia (FTD), progressive nonfluent aphasia (PNA) and semantic dementia (SD).

Language Disorders in Dementia of the Alzheimer Type

DAT presents with an association of cardinal features that allow for differential diagnosis. It also refers to probable Alzheimer's disease because pathological verification is necessary for a definitive diagnosis, that is, a primary degenerative dementia with a distinctive pathology (i.e., neurofibrillary tangles and senile plaques). According to McKhann and colleagues, a diagnosis of probable Alzheimer's disease requires that an individual presents with a dementia syndrome established by clinical examination and documented by screening tests and procedures such as the Mini-Mental State Examination and confirmed by neuropsychological tests (McKhann et al., 1984). Furthermore, cognitive deficits in two or more areas of cognition are required. A progressive worsening of memory and other cognitive functions characterizes the progression of the disease. These symptoms occur in clear consciousness and usually onset between age 40 and 90 years. There must be an absence of systemic disorders or other brain diseases that in and of themselves could account for the progressive deficits in memory and cognition (For a review of concepts and diagnostic criteria of DAT, see Kennedy et al., 2001).

As for other types of dementia, DAT does not begin with global impairment in cognitive functions, but usually progresses through different stages. The most pervasive characteristic of DAT is undoubtedly a progressive episodic memory loss associated with decline in other cognitive areas. During the prodromal stage, which generally lasts about 2 years, cognitive problems are usually too mild to clearly distinguish from age-related changes and are not always identified through extensive testing. With respect to language, DAT patients often complain about word retrieval difficulties at this stage of the disease. They also sometimes report having difficulties in initiating conversation or understanding inferences or humor. Language deficits are usually more prominent after approximately 2 or 3 years from onset. Symptoms of anomia are more marked, especially for less used vocabulary. In conversations, patients mainly produce circumlocutions as well as generic and imprecise terms while semantic errors are still scarce. At this stage of illness, phonetic, phonemic, and syntactic aspects of language are preserved. The patients perform relatively normally in tests exploring reading aloud, repetition, and auditory comprehension. However, they may show signs of impairment in writing, confrontation naming and fluency tasks. Language is much more affected in the middle or intermediate stage of DAT, a stage that generally occurs between the third and the fifth year from onset. Phonetic and phonological abilities are still preserved but spontaneous speech is characterized by severe reduction, stereotyped utterances, and important anomia manifested in the production of verbal and semantic paraphasias as well as by occasional neologisms. Repetition and reading aloud are still often preserved while there is an important worsening of comprehension and spelling. In the final stage of the disease (after the fifth to six year post onset), all linguistic abilities are impaired. There is a severe deficit of comprehension and oral expression is impossible or limited to automatisms, verbal perseverations or stereotyped expressions.

Even if a large proportion of DAT patients presented with this standard description of language impairments, recent group studies have shown that there is an important lack of homogeneity across patients, with respect to (1) the evolution of the disease, (2) the relative preservation or damage of the different cognitive functions, and (3) the relative preservation or damage of specific components in each cognitive function, including language (e.g., Schwartz, 1990; Price et al., 1993). By resorting to cognitive models of language processing, neuropsycholinguistic studies have largely contributed to the identification of functional origins of language deficits in DAT. What emerges from these studies is that the main impact of the disease falls on semantic memory, a component of explicit long-term memory which contains the permanent information related to objects, concepts, words, and their meanings. Because of its central role to the processing of language, the deficit affecting semantic memory leads to important difficulties in word comprehension and production. Therefore, when tested with comprehensive batteries of language, DAT patients usually show poor performance in picture naming, word–picture matching, picture or word sorting, and semantic questionnaires, even at the first stage of the disease. Moreover, the consistency for individual items across tests (i.e., the same items are preserved or damaged across tests), as well as the relative preservation of superordinate knowledge as compared to specific and detailed knowledge (e.g., knowing that a zebra is an animal but not that it has stripes or lives in Africa), is suggestive of a deterioration of semantic representations instead of access damage to preserved semantic representations. This question is, however, controversial, other researchers having reported experimental data that rather support a normal organization of semantic memory and an access deficit in DAT (For an extensive discussion, see Luzzatti, 1999). Furthermore, with respect to semantic memory, recent studies have also investigated whether the semantic loss in DAT affects some categories more than others. Most of these studies conclude that DAT patients perform worse on biological concepts (i.e., animals, fruits, vegetables, etc.) than on artifacts (i.e., vehicles, furniture, tools, etc.) (e.g., Chertkow and Bub, 1990). However, the opposite pattern was also found in other studies, while yet others failed to demonstrate any category effects. (For a review, see Whatmough and Chertkow, 2002.)

Articulatory, phonological, and syntactic abilities are usually considered unscathed until the final stage of DAT. Recent studies, however, showed that, with the progression of the disease, these abilities may be damaged. For example, Croot and her colleagues (Croot et al., 2000) have shown that, in less typical cases of DAT, phonological and articulatory abilities may be impaired, sometimes as a selective deficit. Syntactic processes required for sentence production (e.g. Bates et al., 1995) and sentence comprehension (e.g., Waters, et al., 1995) may also be compromised in some cases of DAT, even at the early stage of the disease. Whether this deficit is really syntactic in nature or is more explicable in terms of working memory disorder or in terms of semantic interpretative processing remains unresolved.

Studies on reading and writing impairments in DAT also reflect a relative lack of consistency. As mentioned earlier, according to the standard clinical portrait of DAT, reading and spelling abilities are considered to be largely preserved in patients even at rather advanced stages of the disease. In contrast to this classical conception, several recent single-case and group studies, resorting to cognitive neuropsychological or to paralleled-distributed-processing models have shown that the ability to read aloud and to spell words is frequently affected in DAT. These patients often demonstrate characteristics of surface alexia and surface agraphia: they are better at reading/spelling orthographically regular than irregular words (i.e., words with exceptional or unpredictable sound-to-spelling and spelling-to-sound correspondences), they show a preserved ability to read/write nonwords, and they tend to produce regularization errors in reading (e.g., bread → /brid/) and phonologically plausible errors in spelling (e.g., crane → CRAIN). Recent group studies, however, have shown that different patterns of written language impairment may be observed in DAT, a result that contradicts the hypothesis that the disease selectively impairs lexical-semantic routes of reading and writing (for a discussion and a review, see Luzzatti, 1999; Graham, 2000; Noble et al., 2000).

Language Disorders in Vascular Dementia

The concept of VaD significantly changed in the 1990s with the publication of international diagnostic criteria (e.g., Roman et al., 1993). VaD may result from an array of causes. It includes all dementias following ischemic or hemorrhagic cerebrovascular accidents, i.e., single vascular insult (most typically to a critical area of the brain), repeated cerebral infarction (also referred to as multi-infarct dementia), and chronic ischemia without discrete infarction. According to Roman et al. (1993), a diagnosis of probable VaD requires a loss of cognitive ability (i.e., a decline in memory and intellectual abilities that impairs functioning in daily living). The decline should be demonstrated by a loss of memory and deficits in at least two other cognitive domains. Additionally, cerebrovascular disease (CVD) must be defined by the presence of focal neurological signs consistent with stroke (with or without a history of stroke) and relevant evidence of CVD on computerized tomography or other cerebral imagery techniques. A temporal relation between dementia and CVD as shown by onset of dementia within 3 months following a documented stroke, abrupt deterioration in cognitive functions, or fluctuating, stepwise progression of cognitive deficits is also required (for a review, see Bowler and Hachinski, 2003).

In contrast with the extensive literature on language deficits in DAT, the patterns of cognitive deterioration in other forms of dementia are much less known. Consequently, the identification of clear neuropsychological differences between the major progressive dementias remains difficult to establish. In VaD, for example, most of the reported descriptions related to cognitive deficits concern behavioral manifestations and large cognitive domains. The most commonly reported cognitive impairments in VaD are bradyphrenia (i.e., slowed cognition), dysexecutive symptoms (e.g., difficulty in problem solving and planning), and decreased initiation and spontaneity. There are very few studies that have systematically described language disorders in VaD. Most of them were conducted in an attempt to differentiate VaD from DAT. The majority of these studies suggested that there was no significant difference in language function between the two dementia syndromes. However, in a few recent studies, VaD patients performed better than DAT patients in initial-letter-based verbal fluency tests (e.g., Lafosse et al., 1997), an assessment task that is usually thought to reflect executive dysfunction. As compared to DAT too, anomia is less severe in VaD patients. On a qualitative point of view, they also show a very similar pattern of general naming errors (i.e., visuoperceptual, semantic, and phonemic) when compared to DAT (e.g., Lukatela et al., 1998).

As of now, the nature and the prevalence of reading and writing deficits in VaD remain almost completely unknown. A few recent studies that have included reading and writing tasks in the neuropsychological assessment found that both abilities appeared to be more impaired in VaD. It is, however, impossible to clearly determine the functional origins of written language deficits. For written spelling, different investigations are suggestive of peripheral impairments (e.g., difficulty in writing letters and copying of sentences). Others found that, as compared to DAT, VaD patients produced more spelling errors and produced grammatically less complex sentences, therefore suggesting a central origin of the deficit (see Graham, 2000).

Finally, as compared to DAT, the speech of individuals with VaD is less empty and conveys more information but they tend to produce shorter and less grammatically complex phrases (Powell et al., 1988). The same authors also have shown that VaD patients often present with abnormal prosody and articulation.

Language Disorders in Dementia with Lewy Bodies

Together with DAT and VaD, DLB is another common form of progressive dementia. However, this entity is a relatively recent one, and as such, there is debate on its classification. DLB is commonly regarded as a Parkinson-plus syndrome that bears the clinical features of both Alzheimer's disease and Parkinson's disease. Pathologically, the cortical neurons of individuals presenting with DLB contain, as the name implies, Lewy bodies or intracytoplasmic inclusion bodies. Clinically, the disease presents with a grouping of distinctive symptoms. According to McKeith et al. (1996), the clinical presentation must include a dementia plus two of the following: a fluctuating cognition with pronounced variations in attention and alertness, recurrent visual hallucinations, and spontaneous motor features of parkinsonism (i.e., parkinsonian extrapyramidal symptoms) (for a review see Salmon et al., 2001).

In comparison with DAT, relatively little is known about the cognitive deficits in DLB. A few retrospective studies have compared the performance of DAT and neuropathologically confirmed DLB on a range of neuropsychological assessment, including language. As with DAT, DLB patients show significant impairments in all areas of cognition. Both groups display similar deficits in episodic memory and language (confrontation naming, semantically based verbal fluency) while attention, initial-letter-based verbal fluency, visuoperceptual/spatial abilities, and psychomotor speed are usually more affected in DLB. There is almost no study that specifically addresses the question of the deterioration of language abilities in DLB. As an exception, Lambon Ralph and his colleagues (Lambon Ralph et al., 2001) have recently tested the hypothesis that semantic processing is affected in DLB. Through a group study of 10 DLB and 10 DAT patients, they have shown that semantic impairment is not limited to DAT. Both demented groups exhibited impaired performance in a semantic assessment battery. However, while DAT patients showed equivalent deficit in every modality, DLB patients demonstrated more severe deficits when they were presented with pictures than with words, a performance interpreted by the authors as the result of a combination of semantic and visuoperceptual impairment.

Language Disorders in Frontotemporal Lobe Disease

FLTD lobe disease refers to a heterogeneous group of neurodegenerative disorders and has been known under several different names, including frontal lobe dementia, Pick complex, and, more recently, frontotemporal lobar degeneration. FTLD is often used as an umbrella term to cover the different, but related, clinical presentations that involve a degeneration of the frontal and temporal lobes of the brain (McKhann et al., 2001). According to recent updating of diagnostic criteria (Neary et al., 1998; McKann et al., 2001), three main types of FTLD may be described: (1) frontotemporal dementia or frontal lobe dementia (FTD), (2) progressive fluent aphasia or semantic dementia (SD), and (3) progressive nonfluent aphasia (PNA). However, there is still a lack of consensus on the clinical classification of the FTLDs (for a discussion and a review, see Hodges and Miller, 2001). In the following subsections, we will briefly review current data on language and communication disorders in the three main types of frontotemporal lobe disease.

Language Disorders in Frontotemporal Dementia

According to Neary et al. (1998), FTD is marked by character changes and a disordered social conduct. These are the dominant features initially and throughout the disease's course. A diagnosis of FTD requires an insidious onset and gradual progression, an early decline in social interpersonal conduct, an early impairment in regulation of personal conduct, and an early emotional blunting and loss of insight (see Hodges and Miller, 2001). The detection of cognitive deficits at the early stage of the disease often remains problematic. Some patients show evident cognitive deficits at presentation while others may perform almost perfectly on a general neuropsychological battery. With respect to specific cognitive areas, memory is considered to be relatively spared in FTD but recent studies have shown that patients may present with impaired episodic and working memory, with a pattern different to what was encountered in DAT. In comparison to DAT too, instrumental functions of perception, spatial skills, and praxis are usually intact or relatively well preserved. Language also appears to be largely spared in FTD patients, who often show a reduction in spontaneous speech but perform normally on tests exploring lexical-semantic abilities (e.g., naming, word–picture matching).

Language Disorders in Semantic Dementia

SD is a clinical syndrome that results from a degenerative disease of the temporal lobes. The core features of SD include: (1) the selective impairment of semantic memory, causing important difficulties in word production and comprehension, (2) the relative sparing of the grammatical and phonological structure of language, (3) normal perceptual skills and nonverbal problem-solving ability, and (4) relatively spared autobiographical and episodic memory (for a review, see Hodges et al., 1998). In other words, semantic dementia is marked by a selective impairment of semantic memory with a relative sparing of nonsemantic aspects of language.

As already mentioned, semantic memory occupies a central place in cognition and language processing. Therefore, SD patients experience important deficits in every cognitive task requiring the activation of semantic representations. Spontaneous speech is usually fluent, well articulated and grammatically correct but present many signs of word-finding difficulties: miscarried sentences, latencies, and occasional semantic paraphasias. Repetition is typically well preserved for both words and nonwords while the ability to repeat short sentences or strings of unrelated words depends on the deterioration/preservation of their meaning. SD patients usually complain about loss of memory for words. This deficit is obvious in tests of naming to definition and confrontation naming in which patients mainly produce semantic errors consisting in the production of a superordinate (lion → animal) or a category coordinate (lion → tiger) concept. This pattern of errors reflects a loss of attribute knowledge along with preservation of general superordinate information. SD patients are also impaired on tests of verbal and nonverbal semantic memory. Spoken and written single-word comprehension is affected in tasks of word–picture matching, synonymy judging, word sorting, etc. The centrality of the semantic deficit is also confirmed by tests exploring nonverbal semantic knowledge, such as tests of semantic relatedness judgment on pictures, picture sorting, etc. Whether the semantic deficit in SD is more severe for one category of items than another (i.e., category specific) is also discussed in the literature (for a review see Garrard et al., 2002).

Reading and spelling impairments have also been reported in many cases of SD. These patients often demonstrate surface alexia and surface agraphia characteristics. A relationship between semantic impairment on the one hand and impaired word reading (e.g., Funnel, 1996) and impaired word spelling (e.g., Macoir and Bernier, 2002) on the other has been proposed. This hypothesis is questioned, however, since there have been cases reported in which irregular words are read or spelled correctly without any evidence of comprehension.

Language Disorders in Progressive Nonfluent Aphasia

In 1982, Mesulam reported six patients who showed a syndrome of slowly progressive language impairment without associated cognitive or behavioral disorders. This progressive nonfluent aphasia (PNA) shares the features of FTD but a disorder of expressive language is the dominant feature initially and throughout the course of the disease (Neary et al., 1998). Other aspects of cognition are intact or relatively well preserved. A diagnosis of PNA also requires an insidious onset and gradual progression with primarily nonfluent spontaneous speech and at least one of the following: agrammatism, phonemic paraphasias, and anomia. Other clinical features as the presence of stuttering or oral apraxia and the preservation of social skills also support the diagnostic.

Patients with PNA present with complaints of difficulties in expressing themselves and finding words. Their spontaneous speech is markedly slow, hesitant, and sometimes agrammatic. Articulation as well as prosody is affected. Semantic errors and circumlocutions are rare but patients often produce phonological errors. Other patients sometimes present with stuttering or slow dysprosodic speech with verbal apraxia. Because of the spoken output deficit, PNA patients perform poorly on words, nonwords, sentence reading aloud, and repetition tests. Naming tasks are also affected, with word-finding difficulties and production of phonological errors. Their performance is, however, unaffected in every test of semantic memory. Except for complex syntactic structures, comprehension is normal in the early stages of the disease. With disease progression, the breakdown of phonological abilities gradually compromises speech comprehension and production. At later stages, patients also present with difficulties in other cognitive areas.

Conclusions

In this article, we have briefly described verbal communication disorders accompanying the major forms of primary progressive dementia as well as vascular dementia. These disorders are often prominent symptoms of the disease and may occur as early symptoms. We have shown that substantial information is available for language disturbances in DAT, SD, and PNA. In contrast with the extensive literature on these dementing illnesses, relatively little is known about the patterns of language deterioration in other forms of dementia. For example, the few available descriptions of cognitive deficits in LBD, VaD and FTD mainly concern behavioral manifestations and large cognitive domains. More specific abilities are almost completely ignored and it is still difficult to identify functional deficits to language components.

The concept of dementia continues to evolve. Current studies have refined clinical criteria of dementia and, for example, have made possible the distinction between the different forms of FTD. An improvement in clinical diagnosis should result from the study of more specific subcomponents of the different cognitive domains. In this respect, cognitive neuropsychology is surely useful in that it allows the fractionation of many cognitive domains into specialized subcomponents that can be selectively impaired by a neurological affection. For example, such an approach has led to extensive descriptions of language deficits in DAT and semantic dementia. Moreover, further research is also needed to better characterize the effect of the progression of the disease on the various language abilities and components.

See also: Classical Tests for Speech and Language Disorders; Delirium and Language; Primary Progressive Aphasia in Nondementing Adults; Speech Impairments in Neurodegenerative Diseases/Psychiatric Illnesses.

Bibliography

American Psychiatric Association (1994). *Diagnostic and statistical manual of mental disorders,* 4th edn. Washington, DC: American Psychiatric Association.

Bates, E, Harris, C, Marchman, V, Wulfeck, B, and Kritchevsky, M (1995). 'Production of complex syntax in normal aging and Alzheimer's disease.' *Language and Cognitive Processes* 10: 487–539.

Bowler, JV and Hachinski, V (2003). 'Current criteria for vascular dementia: a critical appraisal.' In: Bowler, JV and Hachinski, V (eds.) *Vascular cognitive impairment: preventable dementia*, pp. 1–11. New York: Oxford University Press.

Canadian Study of Health and Aging (1994). 'The Canadian Study of Health and Aging: Risk factors for Alzheimer's disease in Canada.' *Neurology* 44: 2073–2080.

Chertkow, H and Bub, D (1990). 'Semantic memory loss in dementia of Alzheimer's type: what do various measures measure?' *Brain* 113(2): 397–417.

Croot, K, Hodges, JR, Xuereb, J, and Patterson, K (2000). 'Phonological and articulatory impairment in Alzheimer's disease: a case series.' *Brain and Language* 75: 277–309.
Forde, EME and Humphreys, GW (eds.) (2002). *Category-specificity in brain and mind.* New York: Psychology Press.
Funnel, E (1996). 'Response biases in oral reading: an account of the co-occurrence of surface dyslexia and semantic dementia.' *Quarterly Journal of Experimental Psychology* 49A: 417–446.
Garrard, P, Lambon Ralph, MA, and Hodges, JR (2002). 'Semantic dementia: a category-specific paradox.' In: Forde and Humphreys (eds.) 149–180.
Graham, NL (2000). 'Dysgraphia in dementia.' *Neurocase* 6: 365–376.
Hodges, JR (ed.) (2001). *Early-onset dementia: A multidisciplinary approach.* New York: Oxford University Press.
Hodges, JR and Miller, B (2001). 'Frontotemporal dementia (Pick's disease).' In: Hodges, JR (ed.) 284–303.
Hodges, JR, Garrard, P, and Patterson, K (1998). 'Semantic dementia.' In: Kertesz, A and Munoz, DG (eds.) *Pick's disease and Pick complex*, pp. 83–104. New York: Wiley-Liss.
Kennedy, AM, Rossor, MN, and Hodges, JR (2001). 'Familial and sporadic Alzheimer's disease.' In: Hodges, JR (ed.) 263–283.
Lafosse, JM, Reed, BR, Mungas, D, Sterling, SB, Wahbeh, H, and Jagust, WJ (1997). 'Fluency and memory differences between ischemic vascular dementia and Alzheimer's disease.' *Neuropsychology* 11: 514–522.
Lambon Ralph, MA, Powell, J, Howard, D, Whitword, AB, Garrard, P, and Hodges, JR (2001). 'Semantic memory is impaired in both dementia with Lewy bodies and dementia of Alzheimer's type: a comparative neuropsychological study and literature review.' *Journal of Neurology, Neurosurgery, and Psychiatry* 70: 149–156.
Lobo, A, Launer, LJ, Fratiglioni, L, Andersen, K, Di Carlo, A, Breteler, MMB, Copeland, JRM, Dartigues, J-F, Jagger, C, Martinez-Lage, J, Soininen, H, and Hofman, A (2000). 'Prevalence of dementia and major subtypes in Europe: a collaborative study of population-based cohorts.' *Neurology* 54(suppl. 5): S4–S9.
Looi, JCL and Sachdev, PS (1999). 'Differentiation of vascular dementia from AD on neuropsychological tests.' *Neurology* 53: 670–678.
Lukatela, K, Malloy, P, Jenkins, M, and Cohen, R (1998). 'The naming deficit in early Alzheimer's and vascular dementia.' *Neuropsychology* 12: 565–572.
Luzzatti, C (1999). 'Language disorders in dementia.' In: Denes, G and Pizzamiglio, L (eds.) *Handbook of clinical and experimental neuropsychology*, pp. 809–846. Hove, England: Psychology Press.
Macoir, J and Bernier, J (2002). 'Is surface dysgraphia linked to semantic impairment? Evidence from a patient with semantic dementia.' *Brain and Cognition* 48: 452–457.
McKeith, IG, Galasko, D, Kosaka, K, Perry, EK, Dickson, D W, Hansen, LA, Salmon, DP, Lowe, J, Mirra, SS, Byrne, EJ, Lennox, G, Quinn, NP, Edwardson, JA, Ince, PG, Bergeron, C, Burns, A, Miller, BL, Lovestone, S, Collerton, D, Jansen, EN, Ballard, C, de Vos, RA, Wilcock, GK, Jellinger, KA, and Perry, RH (1996). 'Consensus guidelines for the clinical and pathologic diagnosis of dementia with Lewy bodies DLB: report of the consortium on DLB international workshop.' *Neurology* 47: 1113–1124.
McKhann, G, Drachman, D, Folstein, M, Katzman, R, Price, D, and Stadlan, EM (1984). 'Clinical diagnosis of Alzheimer's disease: report of the NINCDS-ADRADA Work Group under the auspices of Department of Health and Human Services Task Force on Alzheimer's Disease.' *Neurology* 34: 939–944.
McKhann, GM, Albert, MS, Grossman, M, Miller, B, Dickson, D, and Trojanowski, JQ (2001). 'Clinical and pathological diagnosis of frontotemporal dementia: report of the Work Group on Frontotemporal Dementia and Pick's Disease.' *Archives of Neurology* 58(11): 1803–1809.
Mesulam, MM (1982). 'Slowly progressive aphasia without generalized dementia.' *Annals of Neurology* 11: 592–598.
Neary, D, Snowden, JS, Gustafson, L, Passant, U, Stuss, D, Black, S, Freedman, M, Kertesz, A, Robert, PH, Albert, M, Boone, K, Miller, BL, Cummings, J, and Benson, DF (1998). 'Frontotemporal lobar degeneration: a consensus on clinical diagnostic criteria.' *Neurology* 51(6): 1546–1554.
Noble, K, Glosser, G, and Grossman, M (2000). 'Oral reading in dementia.' *Brain and Language* 74: 48–69.
Petersen, RC (2004). 'Mild cognitive impairment as a diagnostic entity.' *Journal of Internal Medicine* 256: 183–194.
Petersen, RC, Doody, R, Kurz, A, Mohs, RC, Morris, JC, Rabins, PV, Ritchie, K, Rossor, M, Thal, L, and Winblad, B (2001). 'Current concepts in mild cognitive impairment.' *Archives of Neurology* 58: 1985–1992.
Powell, AL, Cummings, JL, Hill, MA, and Benson, DF (1988). 'Speech and language alterations in multi-infarct dementia.' *Neurology* 38: 717–719.
Price, BH, Gurvit, H, Weintraub, S, Geula, C, Leimkuhler, E, and Mesulam, M (1993). 'Neuropsychological patterns and language deficits in 20 consecutive cases of autopsy confirmed Alzheimer's disease.' *Archives of Neurology* 50: 931–937.
Roman, GC, Tatemichi, TK, Erkinjuntti, T, Cummings, JL, Masdeu, JC, Garcia, JH, Amaducci, L, Orgogozo, JM, Brun, A, and Hofman, A (1993). 'Vascular dementia: diagnostic criteria for research studies. Report of the NINDS-AIREN International Workshop.' *Neurology* 43: 250–260.
Rosenstein, LD (1998). 'Differential diagnosis of the major progressive dementias and depression in middle and late adulthood: a summary of the literature of the early 1990s.' *Neuropsychology Review* 8: 109–167.
Salmon, DP, Galasko, D, and Hansen, LA (2001). 'Dementia with Lewy bodies.' In: Hodges (ed.) 304–318.
Schwartz, MF (1990). *Modular deficits in Alzheimer-type dementia.* Cambridge, MA: MIT-Bradford.
Waters, GS, Caplan, D, and Rochon, E (1995). 'Processing capacity and sentence comprehension in patients with Alzheimer's disease.' *Cognitive Neuropsychology* 12: 1–30.
Whatmough, C and Chertkow, H (2002). 'Category-specific recognition impairments in Alzheimer's disease.' In: Forde, EME and Humphreys, GW (eds.) 181–210.

Dichotic Listening Studies of Brain Asymmetry

K. Hugdahl, University of Bergen, Bergen, Norway

Dichotic Stimuli

The stimuli typically used in dichotic listening (DL) studies consist of presentations of pairwise combinations of consonant–vowel (CV) syllables that are made up of the six stop-consonants /b/, /d/, /g/, /p/, /t/, and /k/, and the vowel /a/. Thus, examples of DL stimulus pairs are /ba/–/pa/, /ga/–/pa/, and so on. Another often-used variant of the DL test is the so-called fused rhymed words test. These stimuli are computer synthesized and consist of consonant–vowel-consonant (CVC) pairs. The stimuli are synthesized so that the nondistinctive components of each pair are identical (e.g., /aba/–/aka/). The temporal and auditory spectral overlap between numbers of each pair in this test is so great that they fuse into a single auditory percept.

The Dichotic Test Situation

Preparation of dichotic stimulus materials requires computer editing on each trial of the two CV syllables. The most important aspect of the editing procedure is the synchronization of the onset of the energy release in the two syllables in a pair. The syllables are synchronized on both the consonant and vowel segments, which usually requires access to speech synthesis analysis capability. **Figure 1** shows a computer display of the syllables /ba/ (top) and /pa/ (bottom) that are synchronized on both the consonant and vowel onset.

DL Paradigms

The most commonly used paradigms in DL laterality studies are the free-report paradigm, the forced-attention paradigm, the fused-rhymed paradigm, and the target-monitoring paradigm. In the free-report paradigm, individuals are required to report the items that they heard on each trial as accurately as possible. Only those trials in which a person can identify one item, but not the other, correctly reveal information about brain laterality. Thus, as a general rule, only single-correct trials should be analyzed. An alternative is to instruct the person to answer only for one item on each trial. The experimenter then calculates number of correct reports from the right and left ears, separately. The free-report paradigm requires that the person has intact speech and can give an oral answer. Thus, the free-report paradigm is less well suited for the study of laterality in clinical populations with speech dysfunctions.

In the target-monitoring paradigm, some of the items in the list to be presented are selected as 'targets,' and the person is instructed to indicate (manually or orally) whenever he/she detects a target. Usually CVC syllables or words are used in the target-monitoring paradigm. The target-monitoring paradigm has the advantage that it can be used also with persons who lack expressive speech.

The fused-rhymed paradigm is similar to the free-report paradigm except for the important distinction that the two sounds presented at the ears fuse into a coherent perceptual unit. A characteristic of the fused-rhymed paradigm is that although individuals subjectively report that they hear only one sound, they report this to be the right-ear item.

The forced-attention paradigm allows for the study of attentional influences on brain laterality. The paradigm involves instructing the individual to pay attention only to the right ear, and report only from that ear in half of the trials, and to pay attention to and report only from the left ear in the other half of the trials. Often there is a third condition included whereby the person is not given any specific instructions. In that case, each instructional condition then applies to a third of the trials.

The Right-Ear Advantage

Irrespective of whether nonfused CV syllables or fused CVC syllables are used, the typical outcome in a standard

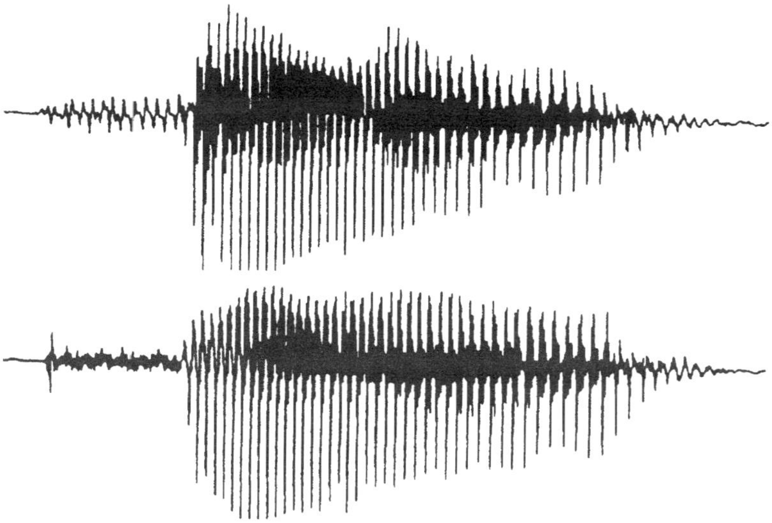

Figure 1 Computer display of the CV syllables /ba/ (top) and /pa/ (bottom) synchronized at the energy release at both consonant and vowel onset segments.

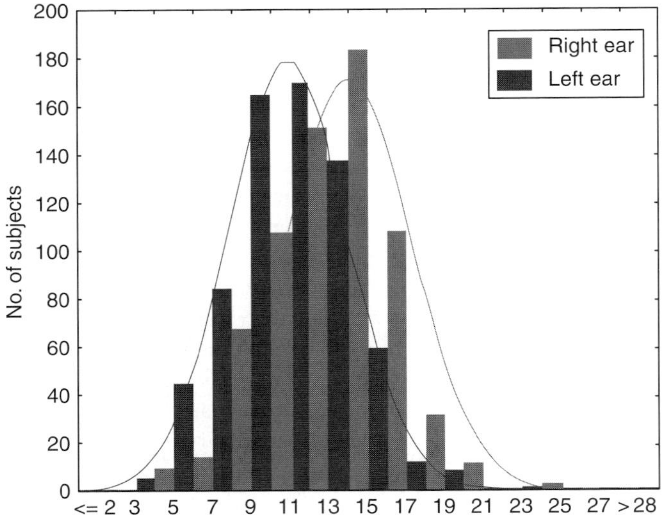

Figure 2 Number of adult study participants ('subjects'; *y*-axis) plotted against correctly reported CV syllables presented in the right ear (light distribution) and left ear (dark distribution), respectively. Data from 694 right-handed adults.

DL test is a greater percentage of correct reports from the right ear, as compared to the left ear. This is called a right-ear advantage (REA) and is a robust empirical finding in both right- and left-handed persons. The REA is most easily seen in response to the consonant, and is difficult to observe in response to the vowel in a CV syllable. It has thus been argued that the REA might reflect hemisphere specialization for rapidly changing auditory stimuli, such as the rapid formant transition seen in the stop consonants. **Figure 2** shows the distributions for correctly reported items from the right-ear (light) and left-ear (dark) stimuli from 694 right-handed adults. Note the apparent shift to the right for the right-ear stimulus distribution.

Attentional Factors

DL also indicates dynamic laterality factors, such as attention, which may modulate a structurally based laterality when the individual shifts attention to the right or left side in auditory space. In the typical DL test, one-third of the trials involve a 'nonforced' attentional condition, where individuals are not given any particular instructions regarding deployment of attention. In one-third of the trials the person is instructed to attend to and report from the right ear (forced-right attention), and in one-third of the trials the person is instructed to attend to and report from the left ear (forced-left attention). The REA is increased during the forced-right attention condition, and a left-ear advantage (LEA) is observed during the forced-left attention condition. Thus, attentional factors can sometimes override the basic REA asymmetry, providing evidence for a 'top-down' instruction-driven modulation of a 'bottom-up' stimulus-driven laterality effect. Studies in our laboratory have, however, shown that top-down modulation is reduced in children, particularly before literacy, and in psychiatric patients. The switching of an REA to an LEA during forced-left attention is also dramatically reduced in patients with right-sided brain damage.

Neuroanatomical Basis

The REA is believed to be caused by the fact that although auditory input is transmitted to both auditory cortices in the temporal lobes, the contralateral projections are stronger and more preponderant, interfering with the ipsilateral projections. The advantage for the contralateral auditory projections means that the language-dominant left hemisphere receives a stronger signal from the right ear. The contralateral signal from the left ear to the right hemisphere must first pass the corpus callosum in other to be processed in the left hemisphere. Following the same logic, an LEA indicates the right hemisphere to be language dominant, and a no-ear advantage (NEA) indicates a bilateral language dominance.

In an O^{15}-positron emission tomography (PET) study in our laboratory using a DL target monitoring paradigm, we compared brain activation to CV syllables and musical stimuli that were presented dichotically. The CV syllables and musical stimuli showed opposite activation asymmetries in the temporal lobe. Greater activation was observed in the left superior temporal gyrus to the CV syllable stimuli, while greater activation was observed in corresponding right temporal lobe areas to the musical stimuli. Interestingly, overall activation and the intensity of activation were greater in response to the CV syllable stimuli compared with the musical stimuli. This may indicate specialized cortical networks in the left hemisphere for the processing of linguistic stimuli, also including the planum temporale area. The PET data are shown in **Figure 3**.

Validity and Reliability

The REA to dichotic presentations of CV syllables is usually about 20% in order of magnitude for oral reports, with about 50–70% correct reports from the right ear and 30–50% correct reports from the left ear. The REA is observed in about 85–90% of right-handed persons, and in about 65% of left-handed persons. The magnitude of the REA may, however, vary considerably among individuals within a given ear advantage direction. Scatterplots of DL correct reports from the right and left ears for more than 1000 persons, both children and adults, are seen in **Figure 4**.

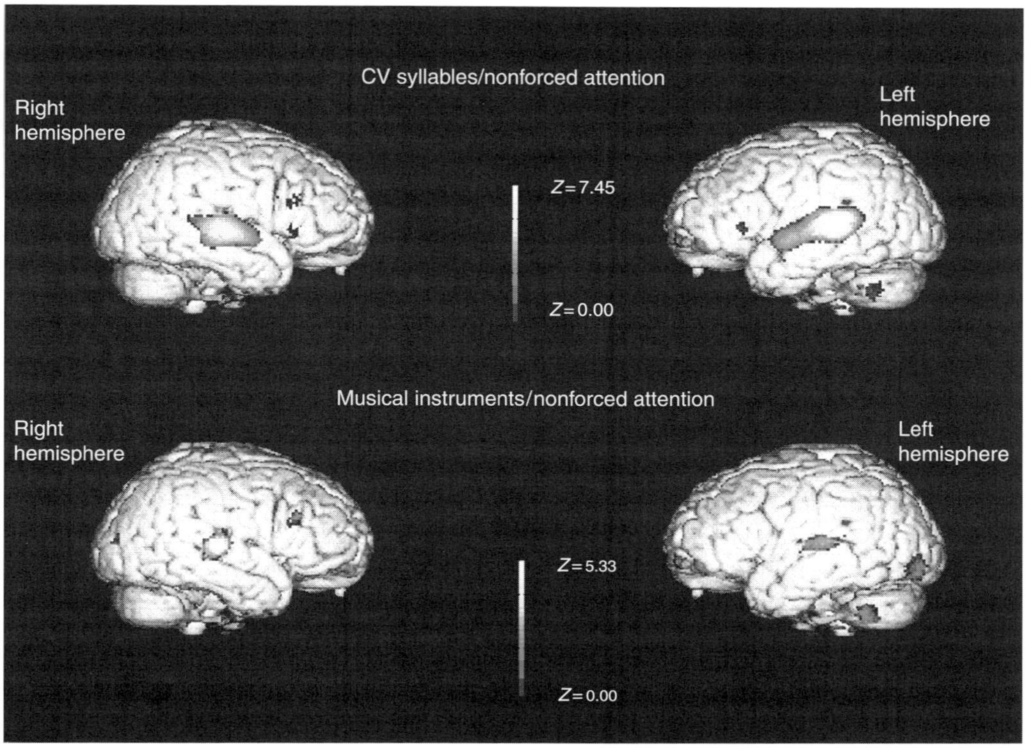

Figure 3 ^{15}O-PET brain activation data in response to CV syllables and musical stimuli. Note the leftward asymmetry for the CV syllable stimuli, and rightward asymmetry for the musical stimuli. Reproduced from Hugdahl K, Brønnick K, Law I, et al. (1999) Brain activation during dichotic presentations of consonant–vowel and musical instruments stimuli: A ^{15}O-PET study. *Neuropsychologia* 37: 431–440, with permission from Elsevier. (See color plate 17.)

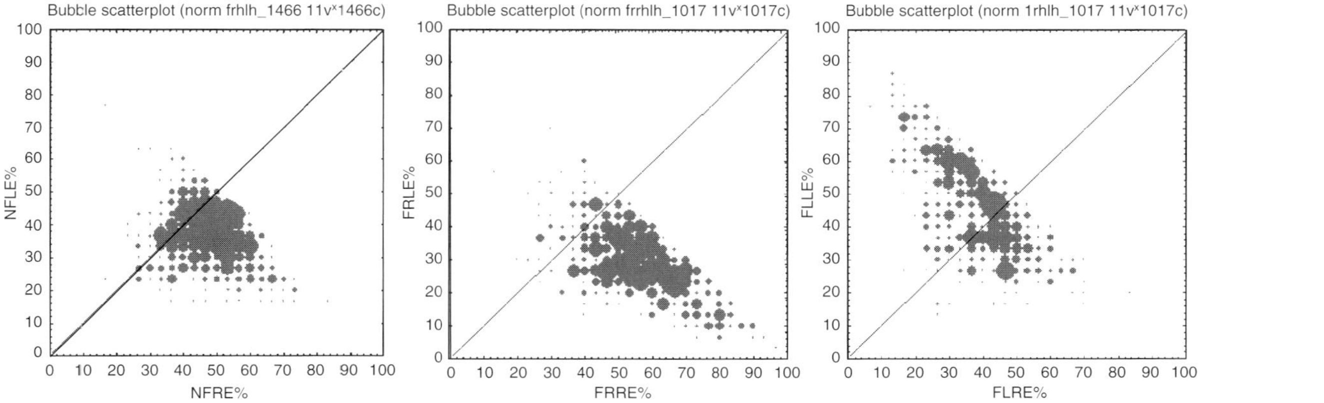

Figure 4 Scatterplots of left- and right-ear correct reports in normal right- and left-handed persons. RE%, % correct right ear reports; LE%, % correct left ear reports, NF, nonforced attention; FR, attention forced to right-ear stimulus; FL, attention forced to left-ear stimulus.

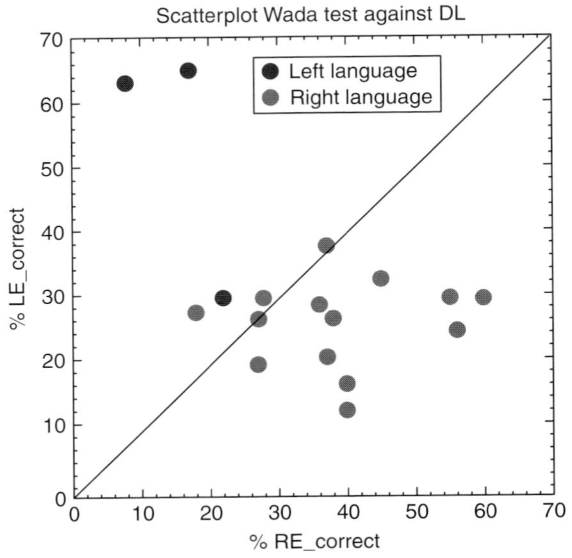

Figure 5 Wada test validation of DL scores from 17 adolescent epileptic patients. Overall, 94% of the group was correctly classified. Data courtesy of Göran Carlsson and Paul Uvebrant, Kiel, Germany, and Göteborg, Sweden. (See color plate 18.)

The 85% of right-handed subjects to be identified as left-hemisphere-language dominant by the DL technique is about 10% lower than what is obtained when invasive techniques, like the Wada test, are used. The Wada test involves selective injection of a barbiturate into the right or left hemisphere, 'silencing' the injected hemisphere for about 10 min. The 10% discrepancy between DL and the Wada test probably reflects that DL, in addition to indicating cortical function, also reflects subcortical thalamic influences on language lateralization. DL also picks up perceptual language laterality in addition to expressive speech laterality, whereas the Wada test is an exclusive test of speech laterality. Measures of test–retest reliability vary between 0.70 and 0.90 across different studies. The variation across studies may stem from differences in the reliability index used. However, a study from our laboratory showed that of 17 epileptic patients undergoing both the Wada test for language dominance and DL, 94% of the cases were correctly classified with the DL technique from a stepwise discriminant analysis. The DL results are shown in **Figure 5**, together with an indication of left- (blue dots) or right- (red dots) hemisphere speech according to the Wada test.

Calculation of DL Scores

The ear advantage in DL may be calculated in different ways. The most straightforward and simple method is to calculate the number of correct reports from each ear. Since this measure does not compensate for differences in overall performance (i.e., total correct reports) among individuals, some authors favor an index score, where right-ear minus left-ear scores are divided by the sum total of left-ear plus right-ear scores. Still another way of handling DL scores is to display the number of individuals that show a particular ear advantage in scatterplots, as shown in **Figure 4**.

Arousal and Activation

DL scores may be affected by factors other than brain laterality, and it has been shown that individual differences in arousal or activation may attenuate the REA. Specifically, experimental manipulations whereby the persons are made to believe that they will receive an electric shock to their hand whenever they make an error have been shown to drastically attenuate the REA. This is probably caused by an increase in both brain stem reticular and right-hemisphere activation (right hemisphere being particularly sensitive for emotional events), which interferes with left-hemisphere processing of the contralateral right-ear signal.

Studies with the forced-attention paradigm have generally revealed that the REA is not an attentional artifact, with right-handed persons attending to the right side in space, which causes the right-ear signal to be better perceived and reported. Experimental manipulations whereby the person is explicitly instructed to turn his/her head and eyes toward the right or left side in space do not seriously affect the REA.

Developmental Effects

The REA to CV syllables can be observed in children as young as 3 years of age, and is frequently reported in 5-year-old children. The magnitude of the REA does not change with age, but stays rather constant. However, the overall level of performance increases with increasing age. Furthermore, preliterate children also report more items from the right ear during testing following instructions to focus attention to the left ear, as in the forced-attention paradigm. The constancy of the REA across different age levels is taken as an indication that brain laterality is not subject to ontogenetic development, and that it is present already at the infant stage.

Sex Differences and Handedness Effects

Males and females differ regarding several cognitive processes (language, visuospatial skills) that are differentially mediated by the left and right hemispheres. The sexes also differ in disorders related to hemisphere differences in brain function. Various disorders such as dyslexia, hyperactivity, and stuttering occur more frequently among boys than girls. Aphasia is also more commonly seen in males than in females after unilateral left-sided lesions. All this evidence points to the hypothesis that females are either less lateralized than males for certain cognitive functions, or that they have a more diffuse cortical organization for cognitive function.

Similar patterns of responding have been obtained in DL tests, with a greater proportion of males than females showing a REA to CV syllables. Males as a group also show a greater mean REA in the standard free-report DL paradigm. It is known that there are differences in cortical organization between right- and left-handers. Only about 65–70% of left-handers are left-hemisphere dominant for language, compared to 95–99% of right-handers. It then follows that right- and left-handers should also differ in their DL performance to CV syllables. Although not all studies have found significant group-mean differences in ear advantage magnitudes between handedness groups, almost every study has reported a tendency for attenuation of the REA in left-handers compared to right-handers. Usually the difference in the magnitude of the REA between right- and left-handers is in the order of 10–15%. The higher proportion of right-handers showing an REA also seem to be independent of the testing procedure or the kind of paradigm used.

Clinical Populations

Commissurotomized patients with sectioning of the corpus callosum show almost complete suppression of the left-ear signal. This is termed 'paradoxical left-ear extinction' and is explained with reference to Kimura's model of suppression of the ipsilateral auditory pathways under dichotic competition. Thus, in a patient with a split brain, the right-ear signal reaches the left temporal cortex unopposed by the ipsilateral right-ear signal. However, the left-ear signal reaches the right hemisphere, and because of the sectioning of the corpus callosum, it cannot be relayed to the left hemisphere for processing.

DL has been used to assess anomalous brain laterality patterns in, for example, stuttering and dyslexia. Although several studies have reported reduced REA magnitudes in these groups, the evidence is not convincing and more research is needed. The DL technique has also been used in studies of schizophrenia and in affective disorders, under the assumption that these disorders are related to left- and right- hemisphere dysfunctions, respectively. The DL data support a notion that schizophrenia may be associated both with left-hemisphere overactivation and with an interhemispheric transfer deficit, although the findings to some extent are controversial.

Nonverbal Stimuli and Lateralization of Affect

Studies of lateralization of affect have involved both the expression of an emotion, as in facial emotional expressions, and the perception of affect, as in the presentation of an emotional stimulus. To summarize, most studies have revealed a right-hemisphere superiority for both expression and perception of affective, or emotional, events. One question that still arouses controversy in the literature is whether the right-hemisphere superiority for emotional processing is valid for both positive and negative emotions.

DL studies of affect have employed either verbal stimuli differing in prosody (vocal intonation), or nonspeech sounds, such as crying or laughing. DL studies with nonspeech sounds have in general revealed a left-ear advantage in most persons, supporting right-hemisphere processing superiority for these kinds of stimuli. DL studies of differences in prosody to speech sounds have also revealed a larger proportion of persons with an LEA than an REA. However, it is at present unclear whether this is specifically tied to the prosodic component in speech, or whether it is related to an overall right-hemisphere specialization for emotional processing.

See also: Brain Asymmetry, Evolution; Hemispheric Specialization and Cognition; Neuropsychological Testing.

Further Reading

Bruder, GE (1988). Dichotic listening in psychiatric patients. In: Hugdahl, K (ed.) *Handbook of Dichotic Listening: Theory, Methods, and Research*, pp. 527–564. Chichester, UK: Wiley.

Bryden, MP (1988). An overview of the dichotic listening procedure and its relation to cerebral organization. In: Hugdahl, K (ed.) *Handbook of Dichotic Listening: Theory, Methods, and Research*, pp. 1–44. Chichester, UK: Wiley.

Clark, CR, Geffen, LB, and Geffen, G (1988). Invariant properties of auditory perceptual asymmetry assessed by dichotic listening. In: Hugdahl, K (ed.) *Handbook of Dichotic Listening: Theory, Methods, and Research*, pp. 71–83. Chichester, UK: Wiley.

Green, MF, Hugdahl, K, and Mitchell, S (1994). Dichotic listening during auditory hallucinations in schizophrenia. *American Journal of Psychiatry* 151: 357–362.

Hugdahl, K (1995). Dichotic listening: Probing temporal lobe functional integrity. In: Davidson, RJ and Hugdahl, K (eds.) *Brain Asymmetry*, pp. 123–156. Cambridge, MA: MIT Press.

Hugdahl, K (ed.) (1988). *Handbook of Dichotic Listening: Theory, Methods, and Research.* Chichester, UK: Wiley.

Hugdahl, K and Andersson, L (1986). The 'forced-attention paradigm' in dichotic listening to CV-syllables: A comparison between adults and children. *Cortex* 22: 417–432.

Hugdahl, K, Brønnick, K, Law, I, et al. (1999). Brain activation during dichotic presentations of consonant–vowel and musical instruments stimuli: A ^{15}O-PET study. *Neuropsychologia* 37: 431–440.

Hugdahl, K, Carlsson, G, Uvebrant, P, et al. (1997). Dichotic listening performance, intracarotid amobarbital injections in children/adolescent: Comparisons pre- and post-operatively. *Archives of Neurology* 54: 1494–1500.

Hugdahl, K, Helland, T, Færevåg, MK, et al. (1995). Absence of ear advantage on the consonant–vowel dichotic listening test in adolescent and adult dyslexics: Specific auditory–phonetic dysfunction. *Journal of Clinical and Experimental Neuropsychology* 17: 833–840.
Hugdahl, K, Nordstrand, L, and Engstrand, O (1986). A graphic-interactive CAD system for dichotic stimulus alignment (CADDIC). *Psychological Reports, 7, no. 3.* Bergen: University of Bergen.
Hugdahl, K and Wester, K (1992). Dichotic listening studies of brain asymmetry in brain damaged patients. *International Journal of Neuroscience* 63: 17–29.
Wexler, BE and Halwes, T (1983). Increasing the power of dichotic methods: The fused rhymed words test. *Neuropsychologia* 21: 59–66.

Diffusion and Perfusion Imaging

A. E. Hillis, Johns Hopkins University, Baltimore, MD, USA

The classic method of identifying brain/language relationships is to identify brain-damaged patients with impairment in a particular language task (e.g., word comprehension), and then to determine the site of damage common to those patients by autopsy or structural imaging. It is reasoned that the area of the brain most commonly damaged among patients with the impaired language task must be the area responsible for the task that was disrupted. This reasoning seems straightforward. However, a limitation of this lesion/deficit methodology is that structural imaging and autopsy do not always reveal the entire region of the brain that is dysfunctional and that may contribute to the impairment. That is, strokes are often surrounded by hypoperfused tissue getting enough blood to survive, but not enough to function, which may cause language deficits. However, it is now possible to identify dysfunctional regions of brain that may be responsible for particular language impairments, using imaging that reveals both infarct and regions of low blood flow. While position emission tomography (PET) imaging is the current ‘gold standard’ for identifying dysfunctional brain tissue, it has drawbacks, including high expense, exposure to radiation, and a relatively long duration of the scan. Recent advances in magnetic resonance imaging (MRI), including dynamic contrast perfusion-weighted imaging (PWI) and arterial spin labeling (ASL) perfusion imaging, permit rapid identification of regions of low blood flow without exposure to radiation. In the same scanning session, diffusion-weighted imaging (DWI) can identify regions of dense ischemia or infarct that are unlikely to survive. DWI reveals areas of reduced diffusion associated with cytotoxic edema in acute stroke. Together with conventional MRI scans that reveal areas of old stroke or other brain damage, DWI and PWI may reveal the entire area of dysfunctional brain in the first hours after onset of stroke, allowing one to identify regions critical for specific functions before reorganization or therapy after stroke. This article will illustrate how such imaging can be used to evaluate the neural basis for language.

Dynamic Contrast Perfusion-Weighted Imaging

Dynamic contrast PWI requires intravenous injection of a bolus of contrast material (gadolinium). Images taken in rapid succession track the flow of contrast material in the brain. A variety of brain maps can be reconstructed that reveal different hemodynamic measures. These reconstructions include: (1) time-to-peak (TTP) maps, which show the peak arrival time of gadolinium in each voxel of the image; (2) mean-time-to-transit (MTT) maps, which show the mean time between arrival and clearance of the contrast material in each voxel; (3) cerebral blood volume (CBV) maps, which show the amount of gadolinium in each voxel between arrival and clearance; and (4) cerebral blood flow (CBF) maps, which estimate the rate of blood flow in each voxel. Most of the studies described in this article that utilize PWI have identified areas of relative hypoperfusion using TTP maps (defining hypoperfusion as more than 2.5 s delay in TTP, relative to the homologous region in the intact hemisphere). This approach has been demonstrated to reveal neural areas that are dysfunctional. However, other approaches (e.g., using MTT) may be equally useful for defining regions of dysfunctional tissue, while still others (e.g., use of CBV or CBF maps) may be better at revealing regions of the brain that will ultimately succumb to infarction in acute stroke.

Use of PWI and DWI to Identify Neural Bases of Lexical Processing

Neural regions of infarct and/or hypoperfusion associated with impairments of specific components of lexical processing have been identified through: (1) relatively detailed analysis of performance across lexical tasks to identify the impaired and spared components of lexical processing in patients within 24 hours of onset of stroke;

and (2) DWI and PWI to identify the regions of hypoperfusion and/or infarct at the same time as the language impairment. Associations between imaging abnormalities in regions of interest (or individual voxels) and deficits are tested with Fisher's exact tests. When possible, intervention is provided to restore blood flow to hypoperfused areas that are not yet infarcted. Cases of successful reperfusion provide additional evidence that a particular brain region is essential for a specific cognitive function if that function is impaired when the region is hypoperfused and recovers as soon as the region is reperfused (Hillis et al., 2002c, 2003).

To illustrate, in two large studies of patients within 24 hours of onset of stroke, the area of hypoperfusion and/or infarct most strongly associated with impaired access to lexical phonological representations for output (anomia) was Brodmann's area (BA 37) (posterior inferior temporal gyrus; Hillis et al., 2002b), whereas the area most strongly associated with lexical-semantic impairment, characterized by poor spoken and written word comprehension, was left BA 22 (posterior superior temporal gyrus) (Hillis et al., 2002a, 2002b). Furthermore, reperfusion of BA 22 resulted in recovery of word comprehension, and reperfusion of BA 37 resulted in recovery from anomia (Hillis et al., 2002c, also illustrated in **Figure 1**). Other regions have been demonstrated to be critical for access to phonological representations of verbs, orthographic representations for reading and spelling, and articulatory mechanisms for speech production using this methodology (Hillis et al., 2002a, 2002b, 2004a, 2004b).

Based on the finding that the presence of hypoperfusion in BA 22 was associated with the presence of word comprehension deficits, the relationship between severity of hypoperfusion in this region with severity of word comprehension impairment was then evaluated to determine if PWI could be used as a semiquantitative measure of dysfunction in a cortical region. From a consecutive series of 80 patients with acute ischemic stroke, 29 patients who showed no infarct in BA 22 were selected (because in the presence of infarct, the degree of hypoperfusion would be irrelevant to tissue function). The severity of hypoperfusion in BA 22 was determined by a technician blinded to language testing, who measured the mean time to peak arrival of gadolinium across the voxels in BA 22. There was a very strong correlation ($r = 0.84$; $p < 0.000001$) between the error rate in word comprehension (measured with spoken word/picture verification) and the severity of hypoperfusion in BA 22, indicating that PWI TTP maps can be used as a semiquantitative measure of regional dysfunction (Hillis et al., 2001).

Use of PWI and DWI to Reevaluate Hypotheses about Brain–Behavior Relationships

While some of the lesion/deficit associations identified by carrying out language testing, DWI, and PWI in acute

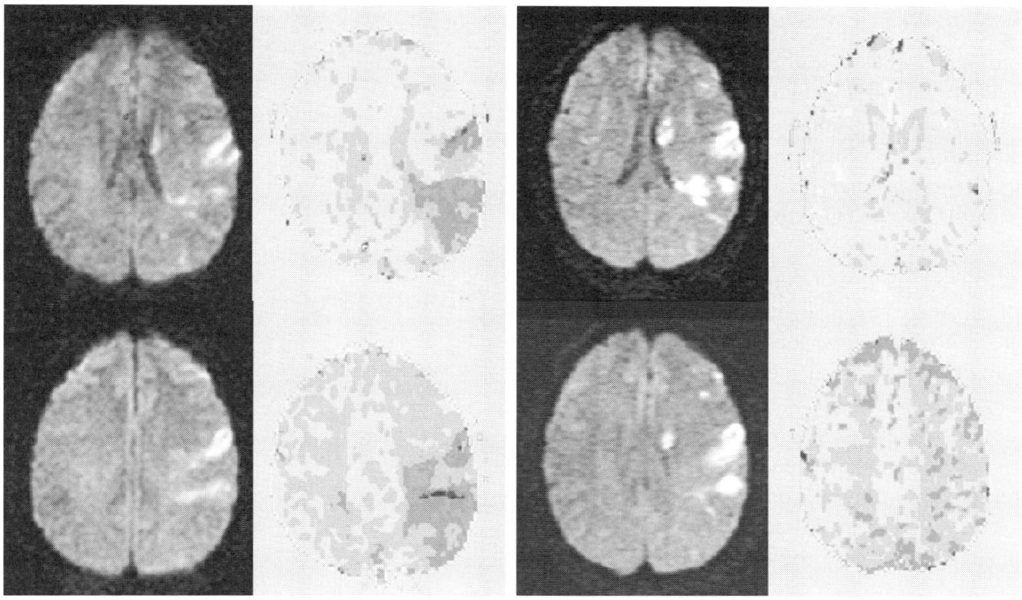

Figure 1 PWI and DWI scans of a patient with severe impairments in oral and written naming and reading on day 1 of her stroke, which improved on day 2. Panel A: DWI scans done within 1 hour of testing show an acute infarct in left motor strip and patchy areas of left BA 37 and 40; PWI scans show low blood flow (darker regions) in left BA 37, 39 (angular gyrus), and 40. Panel B: After intervention to improve perfusion, her deficit in oral naming partially resolved, and her deficit in written word comprehension completely resolved. Repeat PWI within 12 hours of initiation of treatment showed reperfusion of left angular gyrus in association with recovered written word comprehension, confirming the essential role of left angular gyrus in reading. Impaired access to phonological representations for naming only partially recovered with reperfusion of BA 37, since this region was partially infarcted before and after treatment.

stroke have confirmed previous notions of the role of cortical regions in various language functions (e.g., the critical role of BA 22 in word comprehension), other results have conflicted with results from chronic lesion/deficit studies. To illustrate, numerous previous studies have reported aphasia after stroke restricted to subcortical structures. However, a study of consecutive patients with infarcts restricted to left subcortical tissue – the basal ganglia, thalamus, or surrounding white matter – demonstrated that aphasia occurred only when there was concomitant cortical hypoperfusion, and aphasia resolved when blood flow was restored to the cortex, as demonstrated by repeat PWI (Hillis et al., 2002d). The aphasia in these cases of subcortical stroke was attributed to cortical hypoperfusion caused by arterial stenosis that independently caused the subcortical infarct. The aphasia was not attributed to diaschisis (hypometabolism of the cortex caused by reduced input from the subcortical region that was infarcted), since the language impairment resolved when blood flow was restored to the cortex, despite the continued presence of the subcortical infarct that would have continued to cause diaschisis. Furthermore, the variable forms of aphasia due to similar subcortical stroke can be explained by different regions of hypoperfusion on PWI (Hillis et al., 2004c).

Arterial Spin Labeling Perfusion Imaging

Another method of perfusion MRI is known as arterial spin labeling (ASL) (Alsop et al., 2000). ASL does not require injection of contrast and provides a quantitative measure of cerebral blood flow by measuring the flow rate of molecules that are 'spin labeled' at the carotid artery. ASL perfusion imaging is more time consuming than PWI (and requires greater cooperation of the patient/subject to remain still during the time for imaging), but can be useful for identifying the neural substrates of language. For example, in ASL studies of dementia, Grossman et al. (2001) reported that reduced blood flow in the left temporal lobe around the superior temporal sulcus correlated with impairment of word meaning in patients with Alzheimer's disease, and reduced blood flow in left inferior frontal and dorsolateral prefrontal cortex correlated with poor scores on sentence comprehension in patients with frontotemporal dementia. These studies provide evidence that ASL can be useful for identifying regions of poor perfusion responsible for language deficits associated with brain damage.

ASL can also be used to reveal areas of increased blood flow with 'activation' of particular areas in response to a functional task. While the blood oxygen level dependent (BOLD) effect typically used in fMRI reveals areas where blood flow increases out of proportion to oxygen extraction, ASL more directly measures the blood flow response. Although ASL has not yet been used extensively to study areas of activation during language tasks in normal subjects, activation studies of motor and visual tasks demonstrate that ASL may be more sensitive and reliable than traditional fMRI using the BOLD effect (Aguirre et al., 2002).

Summary and Future Directions

Neuroimaging techniques are changing rapidly. Recent developments allow imaging of brain regions with reduced blood flow or very recent ischemia that may contribute to the patient's language impairments in acute stroke. This PWI and DWI imaging, when carried out at the same general time as language testing, can be used to identify associations between regions of neural dysfunction and impairments of very specific language functions, before reorganization or therapy. Importantly, this methodology can also confirm the necessity of the region for a particular language function by determining if the language function recovers when the region is reperfused. Quantitative perfusion imaging, ASL, can also be used to identify areas of reduced blood flow associated with deficits in chronic stroke or dementia, or to identify areas of increased blood flow associated with 'activation' during specific language tasks in normal or brain-damaged subjects. Another recently developed imaging technique, DTI, can reveal lesions of particular white matter tracks, to identify the role of these tracks in language processing (e.g., Selnes et al., 2002). Further refinements of these imaging modalities and additional applications in linguistic research are likely to emerge in the coming years, along with new MRI techniques for measuring blood flow and oxygen extraction ratios that vary as a function of brain activity.

Bibliography

Aguirre, GK, Detre, JA, and Zarahn, E (2002). 'Experimental design and the relative sensitivity of BOLD and perfusion fMRI.' *Neuroimage* 15(3): 488–500.

Alsop, DC, Detre, JA, and Grossman, M (2000). 'Assessment of cerebral blood flow in Alzheimer's disease by spin-labeled magnetic resonance imaging.' *Annals of Neurology* 47(1): 93–100.

Grossman, M, Alsop, DC, and Detre, JA (2001). 'Perfusion fMRI using arterial spin labeling in Alzheimer's disease and frontotemporal dementia: correlations with language.' *Brain and Language* 79: 94–95.

Hillis, AE, Wityk, RJ, and Tuffiash, E (2001). 'Hypoperfusion of Wernicke's area predicts severity of semantic deficit in acute stroke.' *Annals of Neurology* 50: 561–566.

Hillis, AE, Kane, A, and Tuffiash, E (2002a). 'Neural substrates of the cognitive processes underlying spelling: evidence from MR diffusion and perfusion imaging.' *Aphasiology* 16: 425–438.

Hillis, AE, Tuffiash, E, and Wityk, RJ (2002b). 'Regions of neural dysfunction associated with impaired naming of actions and objects in acute stroke.' *Cognitive Neuropsychology* 19: 523–534.
Hillis, AE, Kane, A, and Tuffiash, E (2002c). 'Reperfusion of specific brain regions by raising blood pressure restores selective language functions in subacute stroke.' *Brain and Language* 79: 495–510.
Hillis, AE, Wityk, RJ, and Barker, PB (2002d). 'Subcortical aphasia and neglect in acute stroke: the role of cortical hypoperfusion.' *Brain* 125: 1094–1104.
Hillis, AE, Wityk, R, and Barker, PB (2003). Neural regions essential for writing verbs.' *Nature Neuroscience* 6: 19–20.
Hillis, AE, Work, M, and Breese, EL (2004a). 'Re-examining the brain regions crucial for orchestrating speech articulation.' *Brain* 127: 1479–1487.
Hillis, AE, Chang, S, and Breese, E (2004b). 'The crucial role of posterior frontal regions in modality specific components of the spelling process.' *Neurocase* 10: 175–187.
Hillis, AE, Barker, PB, and Wityk, RJ (2004c). 'Variability in subcortical aphasia is due to variable sites of cortical hypoperfusion.' *Brain and Language* 89: 524–530.
Selnes, OA, van Zijl, P, and Barker, PB (2002). 'MR diffusion tensor imaging documented arcuate fasciculus lesion in a patient with normal repetition performance.' *Aphasiology* 16: 897–902.

Direct Electrical Stimulation of Language Cortex

B. Gordon and K. Ledoux, The Johns Hopkins University, Baltimore, MD, USA

Introduction

Direct cortical electrical stimulation (DCES) was originally developed to map the location of sensory, motor, memory, and particularly language functions in the brains of patients being considered for resectional surgery. During the procedure, areas of the brain are stimulated by electrical current, while the patient (who is awake for the mapping procedure) is asked to engage in different behaviors (such as moving a finger or speaking out loud). Under these conditions the stimulation generally produces what is in effect a temporary, localized functional lesion. The effects of the stimulation on the target behaviors are observed to determine which types of behavior are dependent upon the brain region being stimulated. DCES is thus used to try to predict what deficits might result from permanent resection of brain regions, to inform the risk/benefit analysis of any contemplated resections. Individualized mapping, on a subject-by-subject basis, has proven necessary because individuals often prove to have significant deviations from standardized functional-neuroanatomic maps. In addition to this clinical use, DCES as a research tool has led to an increased understanding of the processing components involved in language and of their neuroanatomic associations.

Description of the Technique

DCES is applied through electrodes resting directly on the surface of the cortex. The technique thus requires some access to the cortical surface, and is limited to patients undergoing surgical exposure of the cortex for clinical reasons. Electrode placement is determined clinically to best characterize the areas to be resected and their participation in critical functions in that individual. Language mapping is generally indicated when considering resection of the language-dominant hemisphere. Most frequently, electrodes in studies of language localization using DCES have been placed in perisylvian regions: the superior and middle temporal gyri, portions of the inferior temporal gyrus, the angular gyrus, inferior parietal regions, and the posterior inferior frontal lobe. However, more diverse areas (for instance, the basal temporal regions) have also been explored in a number of studies.

During both intraoperative and extraoperative testing procedures (see **Box 1**), electrical current is usually delivered across bipolar electrode contacts, using short-duration square-wave pulses of alternating polarity. The effect of stimulation generally appears to be extremely focal, limited to the cortical tissue immediately subjacent to the electrode pair, and also largely to the cortical gray matter. Additionally, under routine testing conditions, the effects of stimulation appear to have nearly immediate onset as well as nearly immediate offset. Cortical electrical stimulation as generally used is not believed to permanently alter or damage the underlying tissue, based on both animal studies and histopathologic studies of stimulated human brain tissue.

In the most common scenario during language testing, onset of the presentation of the electrical current is timed to coincide with or precede the onset of stimulus presentation for a given trial of a language task. For example, during an object naming task, stimulation might be timed

Box 1 Intraoperative versus extraoperative testing

Two general methods of DCES have been used, intraoperative and extraoperative. In the intraoperative method, stimulation is applied at the time of the craniotomy. The patient is sedated during the first part of the operation when the skull and dura are opened. Then, the patient is tapered off general anesthesia until awake and able to respond. A second approach, the extraoperative one, has relied on implanted electrode arrays that allow stimulation testing after the patient has recovered from the initial surgery. Such arrays are most commonly implanted to record EEG activity at the surface of the brain to best localize epileptiform activity, but can also be used for stimulation mapping. During an initial surgery, electrode arrays are inserted and are left in place. The patient remains in the hospital for the period during which the electrodes remain in place, generally several days to 2 weeks (depending upon clinical needs). The electrodes (and any cerebral tissue identified for resection) are removed during a second, final, surgery.

Intraoperative testing can provide smaller interelectrode distances than those generally allowed by subdural arrays. Additionally, the surgeon has flexibility in independently selecting electrode sites based on the functional anatomy that has been determined from prior testing, a feature not possible with a chronically implanted array. The mapping offered by the intraoperative procedure may thus be more detailed, in some respects. However, the extraoperative technique, with its grids or strips, can potentially provide coverage of much wider cortical areas (such as occipital areas or inferior temporal areas). The time available for electrical stimulation testing is generally much greater with the extraoperative procedure, and the conditions of testing may be more amenable to experimental control outside of the operating room. The patient's ability and willingness to cooperate may also be improved by extraoperative testing. Finally, extraoperative testing allows repeated stimulation, over time, at the same site(s).

to the presentation of the picture to be named. Alternatively, some researchers have varied the onset of stimulation relative to presentation of the behavioral stimulus in order to assess its effect at different processing stages during the language task (see, e.g., Hart et al., 1998). Stimulation is terminated upon response, or, in cases of a lack of response, after a pre-determined period of time. For maximal safety, the duration of any single train of electrical stimulation is kept relatively brief, generally below 10–15 s, and often less than 5 s. This factor has led to the selection or design of language tasks with trials that can be meaningfully accomplished within this time frame. The most common language task used in conjunction with DCES is visual confrontation naming, in which a picture of an object is presented, and the patient is asked to name it; others include single word reading, sentence reading, naming to definition, writing, auditory comprehension, spontaneous speech, auditory repetition, syllable discrimination, and verbal working memory tasks. Extensive pretesting is usually done to familiarize the patient with the tasks and to establish baseline levels of performance. Generally, stimulation is applied during some trials, and not during others; behavioral performance is compared across the two conditions.

The effects of stimulation may be positive or negative. *Positive effects* are the elicitation of motor movements, sensations, or, at times, behaviors. An example would be the occurrence of visual phenomena (such as geometric patterns) with stimulation of occipital areas, or clonic and tonic motor activity with stimulation of motor cortex. *Negative effects* involve the temporary disruption of an ongoing behavior upon stimulation. An example is the inhibition of rapid alternating finger movements during stimulation. In many cases, the patient can immediately resume the disrupted behavior upon cessation of stimulation. Negative effects therefore are in essence functional "lesions," extremely proscribed in their location and duration. The detection of negative effects requires the active initiation of different behaviors by the awake patient in order to determine if those behaviors are disrupted by stimulation.

The effect of DCES on language functions is generally a negative one. For example, upon stimulation, the patient may experience a complete inability to continue the language task in which he or she is engaged. At times, this effect may be one of interference more than a complete block, such that response times are slowed, hesitations are observed, paraphasias are produced, or pronunciation is noticeably difficult. These effects will often resolve immediately upon (or very shortly after) cessation of the electrical current.

An example may help to illustrate the procedure and its effects. Suppose a patient undergoing DCES was asked to engage in a confrontation naming task. She would be shown pictures of objects and asked to name each one out loud. She would have been extensively pre-tested on the pictures to be sure that she knew all the objects, and she might have been trained to use a particular phrase in naming them: "This is a ———." During DCES, stimulation would be applied randomly during some (but not all) trials, probably timed to the presentation of the picture. On trials without stimulation, we would expect the patient to be able to respond correctly, and without hesitation or speech error. (These trials serve as important controls, to ensure the patient is capable of performing the task correctly under what are often stressful conditions.) On trials with stimulation, a number of things might occur. The patient might not be able to speak at all, in which case the site of stimulation might be labeled as involved in basic mechanisms of speech production. The patient might be able to say the trained phrase "This is a...", but may then have trouble naming the object; she might even say things like, "I know what it is, I just can't get to it..." This might be scored as a specific deficit in naming (as opposed to general speech arrest). The patient might make phonological errors ("gat" instead of "cat") or semantic errors ("dog" instead of "cat"), indicating the involvement of the stimulation site in specific component processes of naming. She might be delayed significantly in naming the object, but be able finally to produce its name. Or she might show naming behavior that is not in any appreciable way different from her performance on non-stimulation trials, suggesting no role for this particular stimulation site in the naming process.

Our increased understanding of the nature of language representation in the brain from studies of DCES, then, has been based on inferences similar to those made when studying organic brain lesions: that the disruption of language behavior by a lesion in a given brain region strongly suggests the essential involvement of that region in that behavior.

Comparison to other Techniques

DCES offers distinct advantages and disadvantages when compared to other functional-neuroanatomic methods usable with human subjects. Probably its most striking advantage over other methods in general is that it is not only a lesional method, which allows direct interpretation of the results, but one in which the "lesion" is relatively small ($\sim 1\ cm^2$), temporary, movable, and repeatable in the same subject. Most discrete lesions in human subjects are otherwise the result of accidental conditions such as ischemic or hemorrhagic stroke, trauma, or encephalitis. Such lesions occur without planned localization, follow their own neuroanatomic distribution, tend to be much larger than the functional lesions induced by DCES, and are irreversible. Also, the effects of natural lesions are typically studied at least days after onset; only the rarest circumstances allow study of their effects within hours. As a result of the time delay, there is an opportunity for functional reorganization with accidental lesions that is less of a concern with DCES.

However, DCES also has a number of disadvantages. Its effects may not be purely "lesional" at the neural level, even though they may appear to be so behaviorally. It may also have distant effects, both positive and negative, which are not easily appreciated during its application. And perhaps most importantly, the opportunity to use DCES is relatively rare, and arises only in special populations: those in whom direct cortical recording of possible seizure activity is felt to be necessary, and those in whom functional mapping is necessary as part of pre-surgical planning. Most such cases have had uncontrollable epilepsy; some have had tumors; some both. It is still unclear how representative the functional neuroanatomic organization of such patients will be of individuals without these conditions. Most research has failed to show a relationship between the extent of an epileptic focus and language localization, as might be expected if epilepsy forced reorganization. But this fundamental limitation of cortical stimulation studies cannot be eliminated.

Two methods that bypass this limitation, and allow studies of normal subjects, are functional neuroimaging (using methods such as fMRI) and transcranial magnetic stimulation (TMS). Functional neuroimaging and DCES result in fundamentally different types of data. Functional neuroimaging shows the areas that can be active during a given task (those that *participate* in the task), while DCES marks the areas without which a given task cannot be accomplished (those that are *necessary* for the task). A more direct analog of DCES is therefore TMS, which has now been widely used in a variety of studies. TMS is similar to DCES in that the effects of TMS can be stimulatory or inhibitory. TMS offers the inestimable advantage over DCES of being usable in healthy participants. It has disadvantages relative to DCES in having presumably larger volumes of current induction and difficulties controlling the exact location of the current pulse in the brain.

Selected Findings with Cortical Stimulation Technique

In addition to the clinical use, findings from DCES have also contributed to insights about the processing components involved in language and of their neuroanatomic associations.

Correspondence with the Classic Functional-Neuroanatomic Model

What might be called the classic model of neuroanatomic localization of language functions was generally derived from single-case and group studies of patients with language deficits acquired following relatively large, permanent focal lesions due to ischemic infarctions. In this model, language functions are localized primarily to a region of the inferior frontal gyrus (Broca's area) and a posterior region of the superior temporal lobe (Wernicke's area) in the left (dominant) hemisphere. This model is broadly supported by the findings from DCES studies. Stimulation-induced interference effects have been demonstrated for most language tasks in most individuals at inferior frontal and posterior temporal sites (e.g., Ojemann et al., 1989; Ojemann, 1991). When assessed on multiple language tasks, a high number of sites that show stimulation deficits across tasks fall within the traditional Broca's and Wernicke's areas (Ojemann, 1991). (See **Box 2** for language mapping in the non-dominant hemisphere.)

Lesion Effects and Aphasia

The behavioral deficits arising from temporary functional lesions created during cortical stimulation often resemble those observed following accidental lesions, and their

Box 2 Language mapping in the non-dominant hemisphere

Most of the electrical cortical stimulation studies discussed in the main text have been limited to the language-dominant (generally left) hemisphere. A handful of studies have explored language localization in the non-dominant hemisphere. Andy and Bhatnagar (1984) found sites throughout the non-dominant cortex at which naming performance was impaired with stimulation. Boatman et al. (1998) studied a right-handed patient with seizures. Although cortical stimulation testing was conducted only over the left-hemisphere, bilateral intracarotid sodium amobarbital testing allowed some conclusions to be drawn about speech processing in both hemispheres. Syllable discrimination remained intact following injection to each hemisphere, suggesting that each hemisphere could independently support acoustic–phonetic processing as needed for that task. Subsequently, however, electrical stimulation of the left hemisphere impaired syllable discrimination, leading the researchers to posit preferential processing by left hemisphere mechanisms despite bilateral speech perception capabilities in this patient. Jabbour et al. (2005) looked at language localization in the right hemisphere of patients in whom a language-dominant hemisphere had not been demonstrated, that is, they performed DCES in six patients who had been classified as having bilateral language representation by the intracarotid amobarbital procedure. Four of the six patients showed right-hemisphere language areas analogous to those classically described in the left hemisphere (in frontal and temporal regions). One patient showed involvement of widespread right-hemisphere sites in language (at which, however, stimulation did not always evoke errors), and in the final patient, no right-hemisphere language sites were identified (possibly due to the placement of the electrodes). The significance of such right-hemisphere language sites in these patients (with bilateral language representation) is unknown; these sites might duplicate left-hemisphere areas, or language abilities in such individuals might require an interaction of areas across the hemispheres.

Andy, O.J., & Bhatnagar, S. (1984). Right-hemispheric language evidence from cortical stimulation. *Brain and Language, 23*, 159–166.

Boatman, D., Hart, J., Lesser, R.P., Honeycutt, N., Anderson, N.B., Miglioretti, D., & Gordon, B. (1998). Right hemisphere speech perception revealed by amobarbital injection and electrical interference. *Neurology, 51*, 458–464.

Jabbour, R.A., Hempel, A., Gates, J.R., Zhang, W., & Risse, G.L. (2005). Right hemisphere language mapping in patients with bilateral language. *Epilepsy and Behavior, 6*, 587–592.

localization supports interpretations of these disorders within the classical model. For example, deficits in language production and comprehension of the sort demonstrated in many Broca's aphasics have been reported with electrical stimulation of Broca's area (Schaffler et al., 1993). Stimulation of either Broca's area or Wernicke's area has been shown to result in deficits in language comprehension; however, production deficits in those same patients arose only with stimulation of Broca's area (Schaffler et al., 1996), a pattern that is again commensurate with the findings of neuropsychological studies of Broca's and Wernicke's aphasias.

Another example comes from studies of the angular gyrus, both in patients with epilepsy (Morris et al., 1984), and in patients with tumors located near this region (Roux et al., 1999). This area is thought to be the site of damage producing the varied symptoms of Gerstmann syndrome (finger agnosia, right/left disorientation, acalculia, and agraphia). This association was supported by the demonstration of similar deficits with stimulation of the angular gyrus. Additionally, such deficits were elicited with stimulation outside the angular gyrus, and deficits in other behaviors (reading, color naming) were elicited with stimulation of the angular gyrus. These results might help explain why Gerstmann syndrome can result from damage outside the angular gyrus, and why damage to the angular gyrus can result in other behavioral deficits.

In another example, stimulation of sites in and around classical Wernicke's area during multiple language tasks (including auditory comprehension, repetition, and spontaneous speech tasks) was shown to produce patterns of performance similar to those reported in transcortical sensory aphasia (TSA). TSA is characterized by impaired auditory comprehension with intact repetition and overall fluent speech. Interestingly, the precision of electrical stimulation allowed a test of one hypothesis of the neurological basis of TSA. Previous researchers had suggested that the impaired comprehension with intact repetition of TSA arose due to the isolation (by lesion) of an intact Wernicke's area, which would result in the disconnection of phonology and lexical semantics. That TSA was induced with stimulation of Wernicke's area alone suggests that its sparing is not a necessary condition for this type of aphasia (Boatman et al., 2000).

Finally, the category-specific naming deficits that have been reported in some patients with accidental lesions have also been elicited during DCES; for example, one patient showed category-specific disruption of living objects but not non-living objects upon stimulation of a site in the inferior temporal lobe. (Upon subsequent resection of this region, the patient exhibited similar category-specific deficits in naming; Pouratian et al., 2003.)

In summary, then, electrical stimulation studies have shown broad support for the classic model of localization of language functions. The temporary lesions produced by DCES have frequently been shown to result in behavioral deficits that are similar to those observed in patients with chronic organic lesions, and frequently support the interpretation of aphasic syndrome deficits within the classic neurologic model.

Divergence from the Classic Neurologic Model

Discreteness of Representation

The results of cortical stimulation studies of language, however, also demand some refinements to the classic neurological model. The sites at which stimulation interference effects are observed are remarkably localized and discrete. Sites of 1–2 cm^2 have been identified as showing task-specific susceptibility to stimulation; immediately adjacent sites may not show effects of stimulation at all. Virtually no patients have demonstrated stimulation-related errors on language tasks at all sites throughout Broca's and Wernicke's areas as classically defined. Instead, small language-related regions exist in and around these zones, adjacent to other tissue within these areas that does not show interference upon stimulation. This discreteness of localization has led some to suggest a mosaic organization of the sites involved in a given language process (Ojemann et al., 1989; Ojemann, 1991).

An example of the discreteness of localization of function was reported by Boatman and colleagues (Boatman et al., 1997; Boatman, 2004). They performed a series of cortical stimulation studies of speech perception processes in which they specifically targeted acoustic–phonetic processing using an auditory syllable discrimination task. Acoustic–phonetic processing involves the discrimination of speech sounds based on phonetic features such as voicing or manner of articulation. This type of processing is thus one of the earliest, low-level stages of speech perception. Patients were asked to indicate whether syllables that they heard were the same or different; when different, the syllables differed by basic acoustic–phonetic features of consonants. Across studies, performance on this syllable discrimination task was disrupted by stimulation of a relatively localized region of the middle-posterior superior temporal gyrus in all patients tested. An important component of the perception of speech, then, was localized discretely to a specific cortical area (Boatman et al., 1997; Boatman, 2004).

Individual Variability within Anterior and Posterior Language Areas

Another divergence from the classic neurological model comes from the finding of a high degree of individual variability in the localization of essential language sites in cortex. Although most (not all) patients show an area of language localization anteriorly in frontal regions and posteriorly in temporal regions, the exact location of these areas varies widely. For some patients, language areas are identified within traditional Broca's and Wernicke's areas (although, as mentioned, rarely across these entire regions); for others, language regions may be slightly adjacent to these centers, and some patients will not show representation near these centers at all. Ojemann et al. (1989), in a review of cortical stimulation results of 117 patients tested at their center, showed that the area of greatest overlap of interference effects during naming across patients was the inferior posterior frontal cortex (Broca's area). But even at this site, 21% of the 82 patients tested with stimulation during naming did not show interference effects. Of the other 34 zones in which stimulation effects were tested, none was shown to lead to disruption of naming in more than 50% of the patients tested. The prediction of the precise location of language-essential cortex in any individual patient based on anatomical landmarks alone is therefore impossible with current methods.

Language Representation Outside of Classical Language Regions

Sites of language interference upon stimulation are also not confined to Broca's and Wernicke's areas. Stimulation of regions surrounding the Sylvian fissure in all directions has been shown to interfere with language processing on a number of different tasks. Outside of Broca's area, stimulation-induced language deficits have been evoked at sites throughout the frontal lobe (including along the superior and middle frontal gyri). Within the temporal lobe, stimulation effects have been demonstrated outside of Wernicke's area, at sites along anterior regions of the superior temporal gyrus and all along the middle temporal gyrus. Inferiorly, stimulation effects have been reported in the basal temporal language area, including inferior temporal gyrus, fusiform gyrus, and parahippocampal gyrus. Cortical stimulation interference effects have been demonstrated all along the supramarginal gyrus and in more superior parietal regions, as well as at regions at the end of the Sylvian fissure, at the posterior temporal–occipital junction.

Different Stimulation Sites for Different Language Tasks

A comparison of the sites that, when stimulated, lead to disruption of a given language task with the sites disrupted during another language task will sometimes demonstrate sites of overlap, but also, frequently, sites that are not common to the two (Ojemann et al., 1989; Ojemann, 1991; Ojemann et al., 2002). Presumably, to some extent, this finding reflects the fact that different tasks are the product of a variable mixture of different language processes (phonologic, orthographic, semantic, and so forth), which in turn may be differentially localized in the brain. Naming and reading, for example, are believed to share at least some component processes, including semantic identification (when reading for meaning) and phonological output. Other component processes (such as orthographic identification in the case of reading) may be unique to one or the other task. When naming and reading are tested in the same patients, some sites may show stimulation-induced interference during both tasks, and may thus be sites of localization of some common component processes. Frequently, sites are also tested at which naming deficits are observed in the face of intact reading performance, and vice versa. These sites might be separated by as little as 1 cm, but show precisely differential effects for the two tasks. These sites, then, might best be described as localizing processes that are unique to each task. Other tasks that have been compared within the same patients, and that have demonstrated both overlap and separation in localization, include naming and verb generation; naming and single word comprehension; naming, reading, and writing; and speech perception and production.

If DCES causes interference with basic components of language processes that might or might not be common to different language tasks, we might also expect that more complex tasks (that require the integration of several basic component processes for their execution) would recruit larger areas of cortex than simple tasks that more purely tap one component process. If so, larger areas of cortex should be susceptible to interference effects during more complex tasks than during simpler tasks. An example of such a finding was demonstrated using speech perception tasks of increasing complexity during DCES (Boatman, 2004). As mentioned previously, low-level acoustic–phonetic processing was localized to a circumscribed region of midposterior superior temporal gyrus. The more complex phonological processing demanded by phoneme identification tasks (which includes low-level acoustic–phonetic processing plus higher-level speech identification processes) was disrupted by stimulation of a broader region, which included the middle-posterior superior temporal gyrus site critical to acoustic–phonetic processing, but which also included regions within other temporal areas, and within the frontal and parietal lobes. Finally, the still higher-level process of accessing lexical-semantic systems, as assessed by sentence comprehension tasks, showed the broadest cortical distribution, with stimulation-induced deficits arising at multiple sites throughout the temporal, parietal, and frontal lobes, but again encompassing those disrupted by the lower-level tasks (Boatman, 2004). Thus, component processes that are essential to higher-level processes may have the most precise cortical representation, and complex tasks that require the integration of several component processes may be represented over larger cortical regions.

Differential localization has also been reported when language tasks are presented in two different languages, or in different sensory modalities. Stimulation studies with bilingual patients, tested in both of the languages in which they are proficient, have sometimes shown sites in which naming or reading is disrupted in both languages, but have also shown sites in which language behavior is disrupted in one language but not the other (see, e.g., Lucas et al., 2004; Walker et al., 2004). Overlapping and specific sites have been demonstrated in proficient patients tested with both spoken language and signed language (see, e.g., Corina et al., 1999). Similar findings have been reported when language functions were tested across two different modalities; for example, Roux et al. (2006) found sites at which color naming was impaired when stimuli were presented visually, but not when presented auditorily (e.g., a question such as, "What color is grass?"). Hamberger et al. (2001) reported finding sites susceptible to stimulation during auditory confrontation naming only in anterior temporal sites, with both auditory and visual naming disrupted at posterior temporal sites.

Cognitive Efficiency and Precision of Localization

Several findings suggest that greater efficiency in a cognitive operation may be correlated with greater precision in cortical localization. Women were more likely than men to have language areas only in the frontal lobes; that is, women were more likely to show greater precision of cortical representation of language than were men (Ojemann, 1991). Taken together with the common finding of higher verbal skills in women than in men, this finding may suggest a correlation between cognitive efficiency and precise localization. Ojemann (1991) also found that patients with high verbal IQs (measured pre-operatively) devoted less total surface area to naming than did patients with lower verbal IQs. Additionally, some bilingual patients studied showed greater cortical representation (i.e., a larger number of disrupted sites) for the language in which they were least proficient. Ojemann et al. (2002) showed a decrease in the number of sites of interference of a verb generation task as participants become more practiced with the task. These results suggest a positive correlation between proficiency and precision of localization. They are countered, however, by the results of a cortical stimulation study in pediatric patients, in which fewer sites of stimulation-induced errors in naming were identified in children than in adults (and indeed, the youngest children in the study showed fewer sites than the older children; S. Ojemann et al., 2003). The question of whether total cortical area of representation reflects one's behavioral proficiency in a given cognitive realm remains open to future study.

Electrical Stimulation and Subcortical Structures

Increasingly, our understanding of the role of subcortical structures and connecting pathways in language is being informed by studies using electrical stimulation techniques. Already, our understanding of the role of subcortical structures has benefited from research with depth electrodes, placed intraoperatively (for days or weeks) or chronically implanted, usually for the treatment of dyskinesia or chronic pain. A number of studies, for example, have implicated a role for the thalamus in language and verbal memory functions (see, e.g., Bhatnagar & Mandybur, 2005). Another line of work has extented the intraoperative stimulation technique to the white matter tracts lying beneath resected tissue. Stimulation is applied to white matter areas as they are exposed during the resection, with the clinical goal of further mapping essential functions within these tracts while maximizing the resection (especially of tumors). Mapping of the subcallosal fasciculus, the periventricular white matter, and the arcuate fasciculus has provided insight into the role of these subcortical pathways in different types of aphasia (Duffau et al., 2002). Similarly, the mapping of a pathway connecting Broca's area (proposed as an area of articulatory rehearsal) and the supramarginal gyrus (proposed as a potential phonological store) suggests an anatomical basis for the phonological loop (Duffau et al., 2003). Another promising method of studying subcortical pathways was described by Henry et al. (2004), who combined intraoperative cortical stimulation and diffusion tensor MRI fiber tracking methodologies to establish connections among essential cortical sites. Matsumoto et al. (2004) developed a refined cortico-cortical evoked potential (CCEP) method for studying neuronal connectivity. DCES was used to identify language areas in each patient. Single pulse electrical stimuli were then delivered to these areas, and the resulting electrical activity, time-locked to the stimulus, at other regions throughout the cortex (as detected by the electrocorticogram) was averaged to derive the CCEP. Such measures will increase our understanding of the critical connections among cortical language areas.

Challenges and Future Directions

Further refinement of the language tasks used during cortical stimulation testing might improve our understanding of the localization of language functions, especially in light of the suggestion of a correlation between task complexity and the number of cortical regions disrupted by stimulation. Psycholinguistic theories of language processing can point researchers in directions of the types of associations and dissociations for which one might seek evidence of neural representation. Using a conjunction of tasks, or stimuli that vary along psychologically meaningful dimensions, might allow a hierarchical investigation to isolate some of the cognitive psychological subprocesses thought to underlie tasks like reading or naming. Some of the stimulation studies reviewed above have adopted this approach to draw refined conclusions about language processing (see, e.g., Hart et al., 1998), but there is much more work that could be done.

Future developments with structural and functional imaging techniques may eventually obviate or at least minimize the need for cortical mapping with DCES. Recently, several groups have explored the possibility of using functional neuroimaging techniques as an alternative to or in conjunction with electrical stimulation mapping for the identification of eloquent areas in surgical patients (see, e.g., Bookheimer et al., 1997; FitzGerald et al., 1997, McDermott et al., 2005; Medina et al., 2005). The use of such technologies in studies of language processing in normal adults has become quite sophisticated, and has greatly expanded our understanding of language lateralization and localization. The application of these techniques to the preoperative determination of essential language areas in surgical patients shows a great deal of promise, and offers a number of advantages over the stimulation method (not least of which is their non- or minimally invasive nature, but also including patient comfort, speed of acquisition, and the ability to map the entire brain, not just those areas exposed by craniotomy). At present, though, functional neuroimaging seems best placed to complement stimulation mapping, by identifying areas that are most likely to be important to language in a given individual and that therefore should be tested by stimulation. Such an approach might reduce the number of electrodes needing to be placed and the amount of stimulation testing to be done.

Finally, increased understanding of cortical plasticity might come from studies of DCES. Gordon et al. (1999) described patients who acquired reading deficits following surgical resection, and followed the recovery of these functions during an extended post-operative period. These patients had undergone cortical stimulation testing with several language tasks (including reading) prior to resection. The relationship between the cortical stimulation results and the recovery of reading function in these patients is being analyzed retrospectively in an attempt to better understand the mechanisms by which such recovery might occur. Duffau et al. (2002) had the opportunity to perform cortical mapping on a set of three patients twice. Based on the results of the initial mapping, the patients' tumors were not completely resected in order to spare eloquent areas. Because of tumor recurrence, the cortical mapping was performed a second time, 12–24 months after the first. Duffau et al. (2002) reported evidence of functional reorganization of the language, sensory, and motor maps in these patients over the 12–24 month intervals, such that areas that had shown essential function on the first mapping were negative on the second. To a certain extent, these mappings were validated when tumor resections were done, guided by the results of the stimulation mappings, and proved to be without neurological sequelae. Although the opportunities for multiple mappings are rare, the information provided from such studies could prove very informative.

Direct electrical stimulation of the human cortex therefore continues to be refined as a useful tool for exploring the functional components of language, and their relationship to brain regions, and for refining our understanding of this uniquely human ability and its brain substrates.

References

Bhatnagar, SC and Mandybur, GT (2005). Effects of intralaminar thalamic stimulation on language functions. *Brain and Language* 92: 1–11.

Boatman, D (2004). Cortical bases of speech perception: Evidence from functional lesion studies. *Cognition* 92: 47–65.

Boatman, D, Gordon, B, Hart, J, Selnes, O, Miglioretti, D, and Lenz, F (2000). Transcortical sensory aphasia: Revisited and revised. *Brain* 123: 1634–1642.

Boatman, D, Hall, C, Goldstein, MH, Lesser, R, and Gordon, B (1997). Neuroperceptual differences in consonant and vowel discrimination as revealed by direct cortical electrical interference. *Cortex* 33: 83–98.

Bookheimer, SY, Zeffiro, TA, Blaxton, T, Malow, BA, Gaillard, WD, Sato, S, Jufta, C, Fedio, P, and Theodore, WH (1997). A direct comparison of PET activation and electrocortical stimulation mapping for language localization. *Neurology* 48: 1056–1065.

Corina, DP, McBurney, SL, Dodrill, C, Hinshaw, K, Brinkley, J, and Ojemann, G (1999). Functional roles of Broca's area and SMG: Evidence from cortical stimulation mapping in a deaf signer. *Neuroimage* 10: 570–581.

Duffau, H, Capelle, L, Sichez, N, Denvil, D, Lopes, M, Sichez, JP, Bitar, A, and Fohanno, D (2002). Intraoperative mapping of the subcortical language pathways using direct stimulations: An anatomofunctional study. *Brain* 125: 199–214.

Duffau, H, Denvil, D, and Capelle, L (2002). Long term reshaping of language, sensory, and motor maps after glioma resections: A new parameter to integrate in the surgical strategy. *Journal Neurology Neurosurgery Psychiatry* 72: 511–516.

Duffau, H, Gatignol, P, Denvil, D, Lopes, M, and Capelle, L (2003). The articulatory loop: Study of the subcortical connectivity by electrostimulation. *Neuroreport* 14: 2005–2008.

FitzGerald, DB, Cosgrove, GR, Ronner, S, Jiang, H, Buchbinder, BR, Belliveau, JW, Rosen, BR, and Benson, RR (1997). Location of language in the cortex: A comparison between functional MR imaging and electrocortical stimulation. *American Journal of Neuroradiology* 18: 1529–1539.

Gordon, B, Boatman, D, Lesser, RP, and Hart, J, Jr. (1999). Recovery from acquired reading and naming deficits following focal cerebral lesions. In: Broman, S and Fletcher, JEE (eds.) *The changing nervous system: Neurobehavioral consequences of early brain disorders*, pp. 199–213. New York: Oxford University.

Hamberger, MJ, Goodman, RR, Perrine, K, and Tamny, T (2001). Anatomic dissociation of auditory and visual naming in the lateral temporal cortex. *Neurology* 56: 56–61.

Hart, J, Jr., Crone, NE, Lesser, RP, Sieracki, J, Miglioretti, DL, Hall, C, Sherman, D, and Gordon, B (1998). Temporal dynamics of verbal object comprehension. *Proceedings of the National Academy of Sciences of the United States of America* 95: 6498–6503.

Henry, RG, Berman, JI, Nagarajan, SS, Mukherjee, P, and Berger, MS (2004). Subcortical pathways serving cortical language sites: Initial experience with diffusion tensor imaging fiber tracking combined with intraoperative language mapping. *Neuroimage* 21: 616–622.

Lucas, TH, II, McKhann, GM, II, and Ojemann, GA (2004). Functional separation of languages in the bilingual brain: A comparison of electrical stimulation language mapping in 25 bilingual patients and 117 monolingual control patients. *Journal of Neurosurgery* 101: 449–457.

Matsumoto, R, Nair, DR, LaPresto, E, Najm, I, Bingaman, W, Shibasaki, H, and Luders, HO (2004). Functional connectivity in the human language system: A cortico-cortical evoked potential study. *Brain* 127: 2316–2330.

McDermott, KB, Watson, JM, and Ojemann, JG (2005). Presurgical language mapping. *Current Directions in Psychological Science* 14(6): 291–295.

Medina, LS, Bernal, B, Dunoyer, C, Cervantes, L, Rodriguez, M, Pacheco, E, Jayakar, P, Morrison, G, Ragheb, J, and Altman, N (2005). Seizure disorders: Functional MR imaging for diagnostic evaluation and surgical treatment—Prospective study. *Radiology* 236: 247–253.

Morris, HH, Luders, H, Lesser, RP, Dinner, DS, and Hahn, J (1984). Transient neuropsychological abnormalities (including Gerstmann's syndrome) during cortical stimulation. *Neurology* 34(7): 877–883.

Ojemann, GA (1991). Cortical organization of language. *Journal of Neuroscience* 11: 2281–2287.

Ojemann, GA, Ojemann, J, Lettich, E, and Berger, M (1989). Cortical language localization in left, dominant hemisphere: An electrical stimulation mapping investigation in 117 patients. *Journal of Neurosurgery* 71: 316–326.

Ojemann, JG, Ojemann, GA, and Lettich, E (2002). Cortical stimulation mapping of language cortex using a verb generation task: Effects of learning and comparison to mapping based on object naming. *Journal of Neurosurgery* 97: 33–38.

Ojemann, SG, Berger, MS, Lettich, E, and Ojemann, GA (2003). Localization of language function in children: Results of electrical stimulation mapping. *Journal of Neurosurgery* 98: 465–470.

Pouratian, N, Bookheimer, SY, Rubino, G, Martin, NA, and Toga, AW (2003). Category-specific naming deficit identified by intraoperative stimulation mapping and postoperative neuropsychological testing: Case report. *Journal of Neurosurgery* 99(1): 170–176.

Roux, FE, Boetto, S, Sacko, O, Chollet, F, and Tremoulet, M (1999). Writing, calculating, and finger recognition in the region of the angular gyrus: A cortical stimulation study of Gerstmann syndrome. *Journal of Neurosurgery* 99: 716–727.

Roux, FE, Lubrano, V, Lauwers-Cances, V, Mascott, CR, and Demonet, JF (2006). Category-specific cortical mapping: Color-naming areas. *Journal of Neurosurgery* 104: 27–37.

Schaffler, L, Luders, HO, and Beck, GJ (1996). Quantitative comparison of language deficits produced by extraoperative electrical stimulation of Broca's, Wernicke's, and basal temporal language areas. *Epilepsia* 37: 463–475.

Schaffler, L, Luders, HO, Dinner, DS, Lesser, RP, and Chelune, GJ (1993). Comprehension deficits elicited by electrical stimulation of Broca's area. *Brain* 116: 695–715.

Walker, JA, Quinones-Hinojosa, A, and Berger, MS (2004). Intraoperative speech mapping in 17 bilingual patients undergoing resection of a mass lesion. *Neurosurgery* 54: 113–118.

Further Reading

Duffau, H, Capelle, L, Sichez, JP, Faillot, T, Abdennour, L, Law Koune, JD, Dadoun, S, Bitar, A, Arthuis, F, Van Effenterre, R, and Fohanno, D (1999). Intra-operative direct electrical stimulations of the central nervous system: The Salpêtrière Experience with 60 patients. *Acta Neurochirurgica* 141: 1157–1167.
A review of the intraoperative stimulation research done at the Hôpital de la Salpêtrière, primarily with patients with tumors and vascular malformations. A nice overview of the clinical implications of the technique.

Gordon, B, Boatman, D, Hart, J, Jr., Miglioretti, D, and Lesser, RP (2001). Direct cortical electrical interference (stimulation). In: Berndt, RS (ed.) *Handbook of neuropsychology,* 2nd edn. Vol. 3, pp. 375–391. Amsterdam: Elsevier.
An overview of the methodology of, and one institution's experience with, extraoperative direct cortical electrical stimulation done through subdural electrode arrays, using relatively extensive language testing protocols.

Ojemann, GA (1983). Brain organization for language from the perspective of electrical stimulation mapping. *Behavioral and Brain Sciences* 6: 189–206.
A detailed account, with commentaries by many other investigators, of the seminal findings of Ojemann and his colleagues with intraoperative direct cortical electric stimulation mapping of language and related functions.

Ojemann, GA (2003). The neurobiology of language and verbal memory: Observations from awake neurosurgery. *International Journal of Psychophysiology* 48: 141–146.
A recent, accessible summary of the pioneering work of one of the most important researchers in the field. A good launching point for those interested in delving further into the study of language processing by electrical stimulation.

Dyslexia and Dysgraphia, Developmental

V. Molfese, D. Molfese, A. Molnar, and J. Beswick, University of Louisville, Louisville, KY, USA

Developmental dyslexia and developmental dysgraphia have been the focus of much interest from researchers, clinicians, and educators. Findings from research investigations have yielded information with important implications for our understanding of learning abilities as well as disabilities, of brain structure and function, and of assessment and intervention approaches. The word 'developmental' preceding the terms 'dyslexia' and 'dysgraphia' distinguishes this subtype of the disabilities as occurring as a result of abnormal learning during the normal course of development despite adequate learning and instructional opportunities and normal intelligence. This subtype is differentiated from acquired dyslexia and dysgraphia, which are disabilities arising as a result of brain injury, neurological conditions, or diseases, and entail a loss of previously intact skills. Dyslexia is frequently used to refer to disorders in reading skills and dysgraphia is used to refer to disorders in writing skills. These two disabilities may exist in isolation but more commonly they are 'comorbid,' that is, occurring with other disabilities, such as dyscalculia (mathematics), dyspraxia (motor), and attention deficit disorder with and without hyperactivity. It is these relations between underlying cognitive mechanisms and brain processing areas subserving reading and writing skills that have intrigued researchers and that have particular relevance to clinicians and educators.

Developmental dyslexia has been found to be the underlying basis for most cases of poor reading skills identified in the early childhood period and beyond. There has been extensive research on the causes of dyslexia and numerous theories have been proposed, such as the phonological processing theory, the temporal auditory processing theory, and the visual processing deficits theory. The phonological processing theory focuses on the abilities to link speech and print that are important for decoding words, the fundamental skill for reading. Phonological processing problems can occur at many levels, including phonological awareness (understanding that words are composed of individual sounds), phonological retrieval (the ability to quickly and automatically name letters, objects, numbers, or colors), and phonological memory (the ability to code phonological information [e.g., a string of words or nonwords] into working or short-term memory). Phonological processing deficits as a basis for dyslexia have received a great deal of research support (for reviews see Fletcher et al., 1999) and it is generally accepted that dyslexia has a basis in deficits in phonological processing and other specific language skills (Catts, 1996).

Theories of temporal auditory processing deficits have also been hypothesized as underlying dyslexia. Tallal (1980) has proposed that dyslexic children have difficulty in processing complex auditory tones when they are presented in quick succession but not when presented at slower rates. While research provides some support for a link between deficits in auditory temporal processing and dyslexia (Hari and Renvall, 2001), other researchers argue that processing difficulties for dyslexics may be due to speech-related processing problems rather than to general auditory processing problems (Mody et al., 1997).

Deficits in visual processes also have been hypothesized as causes of dyslexia. Indeed, some of the earliest writings link visual problems with dyslexia (Bronner, 1917) and some evidence of the continuing view of a visual deficit as a basis for dyslexia persists in commercial products involving colored or other corrective lenses for people with dyslexia. Problems related to visual processing and dyslexia have been researched in studies of visual discrimination, visual memory, letter reversals, eye movement dysfunctions, or visual processing problems related to magnocellular pathway disruption. Research using functional brain-imaging techniques has explored relations between visual motion processing and dyslexia (Eden et al., 1996). However, findings across studies have been inconsistent on the impacts of visual problems in reading skills, especially in comparison with the more consistent findings of the impacts of phonological deficits on reading skills (Fletcher et al., 1999).

Genetics

Researchers have looked for the causes for dyslexia in genetics and family studies. These studies have supported a genetic basis for dyslexia (Pennington, 1999). In studies of identical and fraternal twins, Gayan and Olson (2001) found that genetic influences on phonological awareness and decoding skills range from 60% to 70% and deficits in word reading range from 50% to 60%. However, the role of the environment in these studies may be understated in accounting for only 30% to 50% of the variance because the environments within samples are similar and individual differences in the consequences of environmental impacts (e.g., due to perinatal risks or insults) also tend to be similar. There is evidence from this and other research studies that genes play an important but not exclusive role in developmental dyslexia (Gallagher et al., 2000).

Linkage analyses have been used in studies of families with a history of dyslexia to locate genes and regions along genes that are responsible for dyslexia. Gayan and Olson (1999) identified genes on chromosome 6 that relate to deficiencies in phonological skills. Others have found genes on chromosome 6 related to phonological awareness and genes on chromosome 15 that link to word reading (Grigorenko et al., 1997). Schulte-Korne et al. (1998) reported a link between poor spelling skills and chromosome 15. Although work is continuing to link specific gene regions to dyslexia, there is growing converging evidence supporting linkages between chromosomal regions and various phenotypes of dyslexia (Demonet et al., 2004; Pennington, 1999). Ongoing behavior genetics work is seeking to understand how the genetic base for susceptibility to dyslexia interacts with environmental conditions to influence the expression of different levels of reading skills.

Brain Structure and Function

Numerous investigations of brain differences in dyslexic compared to nondyslexic populations have been published and have included studies of brain structure (i.e., different parts of the brain, such as the cerebellum) and brain function (i.e., the behaviors that are controlled by different brain structures, such as voluntary control of movements). Differences in the size of brain regions and structures have been reported, but replicability of such findings across studies is inconsistent (Filipek, 1995). Pennington (1999) reported a behavior genetics study of size variations in brain structure of reading-disabled and control subjects. Evidence of genetic influences on the subcortex and genetic plus environment influences on the cortex was found, supporting the hypothesis that some brain structure differences related to reading skills are genetically influenced.

Brain function differences have also been studied. In studies of developmental dyslexia, children at risk for dyslexia due to family history, as well as longitudinal studies of children later identified as dyslexic readers, have been reported. For example, Molfese (2000) reported that event-related potentials (ERPs) recorded to speech and nonspeech sounds in the newborn period are highly predictive of reading skills up to eight years later. In these studies, auditory ERPs were recorded from left and right frontal, temporal, and parietal scalp regions during the newborn period and these children were subsequently tested within 2 weeks of their eighth birthday using a variety of reading and language measures. By eight years of age, a group of 48 children, comprising 17 dyslexics, seven poor readers, and 24 typical readers, was identified. The results indicated faster latencies in brain responses for the typical readers compared to dyslexic and poor readers. These data extended findings previously reported (Molfese and Molfese, 1985) on the strong relationship between neonatal speech discrimination and preschool language skills.

Similar findings are reported in studies of children at risk for dyslexia because of family history but whose eventual reading status was not yet known because of the young age of the children. Brain responses to speech sounds in these at-risk infants were identified that reliably characterized differences between them and the brain responses of control infants (e.g., Guttorm et al., 2003). Distinctive hemisphere differences were found such that atypical responses to speech sounds were predictive of receptive vocabulary and verbal memory skills in the preschool period. It is anticipated that these measures will link with future difficulties that these children are likely to have in learning to read. Similar findings are reported in studies using auditory mismatch negativity as a method to investigate sensitivity to differences in specific speech sounds. These studies are consistent in finding that both children who are at risk because of their family history of dyslexia and children with dyslexia process speech sounds differently than do not-at-risk and typical reading children. The findings from these studies also support the growing evidence of a phonological processing basis for reading skills.

Dysgraphia

Developmental dysgraphia is a disorder of handwriting or written language that is present from childhood and is manifested in both spelling and motor coordination disabilities, resulting in slow, irregular, or illegible handwriting. The American Psychiatric Association establishes developmental dysgraphia as a "disorder of written expression" if the disability interferes with academic achievement or daily living activities. Lyon (1996) estimated that 8% to 15% of schoolchildren have writing disorders. A number of different types of dysgraphia are referenced in the literature, such as phonological dysgraphia (difficulty sounding out and writing words, especially in writing nonwords) and lexical dysgraphia (difficulty writing words letter by letter or in picturing words). Gubbay and deKlerk (1995) report that certain types of language-based dysgraphia (phonological, lexical, and dyslexic) and nonlanguage-based dysgraphia (motor apraxia and constructional apraxia) were more frequently found in a sample of schoolchildren compared to Gerstmann (characterized by dyscalculia, difficulties distinguishing right from left, and finger agnosia), semantic (characterized by semantic errors in writing), ideational (characterized by difficulties in spontaneous writing or drawing by not transcribing or copying), and other types of dysgraphia.

Differences in a variety of writing skills of children with dysgraphia have been studied and compared to control children in an effort to better understand the differences that exist. Vlachos and Karapetsas (2003) studied Greek schoolchildren (6 years 6 months to 12 years 5 months) who were diagnosed with dysgraphia alongside controls matched for sex, age, handedness, and grade. The children were tested in copying complex figures and during mnemonic reproduction (copying from memory). While no differences were found in their ability to copy the figures, the children with dysgraphia had poorer performance on the mnemonic task. The findings point to the involvement of visual memory skills in addition to other visual or perceptual processing problems. Furthermore, children with dysgraphia are characterized by writing errors in which they may reverse letters and numbers, write letters and words backwards, write letters out of order, leave words or letters unfinished, and mix print with cursive, upper with lower case, sizes of letters, and slants of letters. Simner and Eidlitz (2000) reported that four types of writing errors produced by a group of 320 first-grade children were particularly characteristic of children with dysgraphia. The children showed distortions in letter shape, distortions in relative size of letter parts, irregular spacing between letters, and crowding of words within sentences. Deuel et al. (1999) found that school-aged children with dysgraphia were distinguishable from their schoolmates by their motor acts when forming letters (e.g., where they started writing letters, redrawing already written letters, and the addition of extra elements unrelated to proper letter construction).

Researchers (e.g., Bowers et al., 2003; Gubbay and de Klerk, 1995) recommend that several different tasks be used to diagnose dysgraphia, such as writing text from dictation, text generation and copying, fine motor and visual-perceptual skills, writing speed, spelling, and memory tests. All of these tasks can be used to explore the visual, motor, lexical, and memory aspects of writing. Posture, pencil grip, tremor, and specific motor behaviors in writing are also aspects that should be considered in diagnosing dysgraphia. Finally, because writing, reading, and oral language skills are related, the capabilities and disabilities in these three skill areas should also be evaluated.

From the research literature, a variety of different theories of writing disorders have been identified. Bowers et al. (2003) identified four theories: memory or working memory deficits, fine motor impairments, information-processing deficiencies, and neurological impairments. Swanson and Berninger (1996) have found that problems or deficits in working memory (information storage and processing) and short-term memory (information storage and reproduction) are linked to text writing and transcribing. Other researchers have also reported a link between memory span or capacity and writing behaviors (Torrance and Galbraith, 2005). The fine motor impairments theory focuses on the sequencing of fine motor skills that affect poor handwriting as well as the speed and spatial accuracy of writing skills. Researchers report that difficulties inhibiting and controlling motor movements impact handwriting skills and that the motor movement demands of writing impacts composition skills (Jones and Christiensen, 1999). For example, working memory has limited capacity for information processing. If working memory must be used for performing basic skills, such as forming each letter in a word, then there is less capacity for higher order thinking needed to understand what was written as well as for performing more complex, multistep tasks such as are needed for composition.

Information-processing theories focus on sequencing difficulties encountered in writing. Problems in sequencing and organizing thoughts and writing behaviors implicate executive function skills, such as initiative, set shifting, and sustaining attention, which have been found to differentiate poor from good writers (Hooper et al., 2002). The neurological impairment theory looks at the different brain areas and systems involved in writing and hypothesizes that there are dysfunctions in how the areas and systems interact. Bowers et al. (2003) reported from their study of a referred sample of individuals with learning or academic problems that all the models they tested, with the exception of the neurological model, were related to writing behaviors.

Research on Dyslexia and Dysgraphia

Spelling disabilities are a good illustration of how reading and writing skills intersect. Spelling difficulties have been found to characterize most children who are diagnosed with dyslexia, or dysgraphia, or both. Because spelling relies on knowledge about the structure of language, deficits in the knowledge or use of this information are reflected in spelling errors. At a basic level, spelling involves incorporating phonological information from spoken language into written language. That is, beginning spellers must learn to translate the phonemes of spoken language into the letters and words of a written language. As young children become aware of the orthographic and morphologic structures of their spoken language, these too become incorporated into writing. Studies of spelling that have compared the skills of children with disabilities to those of younger children whose spelling skills are at a comparable level have found evidence that different linguistic components play a role in spelling skills.

Bourassa and Treiman (2001) reviewed the research evidence on linguistic factors affecting spelling and could not find evidence of clear-cut differences between children with spelling disabilities and spelling level controls based on phonological, orthographic, and morphologic bases *per se*. However, there was evidence of deficits appearing in some aspects of phonological, orthographic, and/or morphological skills in poor spelling. These deficits appeared to be related to the problems poor spellers have in accurately analyzing and consistently incorporating sounds, syllables, and morphemes into written language. Other researchers have investigated whether differences in auditory temporal processing skills underlie spelling disabilities as they are believed to underlie reading disabilities. Schulte-Korne et al. (1998b) studied children and adults with spelling and reading disabilities. However, no evidence was found that differences in auditory temporal processing skills distinguished children with spelling disabilities from control participants.

Researchers have been interested in understanding how information-processing demands of reading and writing tasks affect children's spelling abilities. For example, the processing demands of tasks differ and when the number of tasks needing to be engaged in concurrently increases, there are limitations on how individuals are able to perform the tasks. In the case of individuals with reading or writing disabilities, the multiple demands of reading or writing tasks create situations where some aspects of tasks may be attended to at the cost of less attention to other tasks. Mather (2003) studied competing task demands, also called dual task interference, in three groups of children. One group had poor reading and poor spelling skills (dyslexic), the second group had good reading and poor spelling skills (dysgraphic), and the third group had good reading and good spelling skills (controls). It was hypothesized that when these children (11 to 14 years) were engaged in performing two tasks concurrently, one task (tapping) would interfere with the performance of the other task (line orientation judgments). Information about hemisphere processing of verbal and nonverbal stimuli was inferred from the interference data. Concurrent task performance was hypothesized to vary according to how the two hemispheres of the brain are involved in processing the tasks. The results showed that children with dyslexia and dysgraphia differed from the controls in showing marked reductions in the rate of left-hand tapping while making line orientation judgments compared to the rate of right-hand tapping during the same judgment task. These findings were interpreted as reflecting differences in how children with dyslexia and dysgraphia process information in their left hemispheres and may reflect a limitation in left hemisphere processing.

In a more direct study of brain hemisphere processing, Richards et al. (1999) included children with dyslexia alongside controls matched for age, IQ, and head size. Brain activation was recorded during lexical, rhyming, and tone judgment tasks. Pairs of words and nonwords that were either rhyming or nonrhyming as well as pairs of tones were judged as the same or different. MRI was used to determine task-related differences in the brain processing of the children. Greater activation was noted in areas of the left hemisphere of the children with dyslexia and seems to indicate that these children were exerting greater mental effort during the phonological (rhyming) task, despite making more errors in judgment, compared to the control group. No group differences in brain activation were noted for the other conditions. Studies such as these point to possible brain-processing limitations linked to language and seem to reinforce phonological processing as an important skill that characterizes children who are dyslexic and/or dysgraphic.

Interventions – Dyslexia and Dysgraphia

Intervention approaches for dyslexia and dysgraphia must begin with diagnosing the capabilities and deficits of children in reading and writing skills. Knowing that there are skills needed for both reading and writing proficiency and additional skills that are specific to reading and writing proficiencies helps to focus diagnosis and intervention on targeted abilities. There is a large literature on intervention approaches for dyslexia and/or dysgraphia (for a review see Berninger et al., 2003). Early diagnosis with explanation to the child, parents, and teachers is important for intervention success.

Among the different approaches to intervention are several that focus on the facilitating effects of reading and spelling interventions. Treiman (1998) reviewed an extensive literature to reveal how learning to spell benefits reading skills, such as phonemic awareness and segmentation, real word and pseudoword reading, and the alphabetic principle. Indeed, it is clear from the review that the skills gained by young children from spelling transfer to reading skills more than the reverse (i.e., reading skills transferring to spelling). Graham et al. (2003) reported an intervention approach with a focus on reading, writing, and spelling skills. Second-grade children with reading and writing problems, some of whom had diagnosed learning and behavior disabilities, participated in a spelling program. Compared to children in the control condition, who received mathematics instruction, the children in the spelling program showed improved skills in spelling, sentence writing, and word reading, with improved word-reading skills still seen 6 months after treatment. Castle et al. (1994) also reported benefits of an intervention focusing on phonemic awareness and letter–sound associations with kindergarten children who had poor phonemic awareness skills. Compared to the children in the control group, who spent time writing stories and inventing spellings, the children in the experimental group showed more pre-/posttest gains in phonemic awareness skills and on real word and pseudoword spelling tests. Clearly, there are advantages to interventions for young children that integrate skills needed for reading, writing, and spelling.

Other researchers have examined how the changes in reading and writing skills that are found from interventions are reflected in brain processing. Berninger et al. (2003) investigated changes in brain functioning of children with dyslexia before and after participation in a comprehensive reading instruction program. Children with dyslexia were compared to their age-matched controls on a number of measures. In addition to poor reading skills, the children with dyslexia also had low scores on phonological coding, rapid automatic naming, and spelling compared to both population means and the matched controls. Children with dyslexia participated in a 28-hour program across 14 days involving linguistic awareness, alphabetic principle, fluency, and reading comprehension. The children in the matched control group did not receive any treatment. Pre-/posttreatment improvements were noted for the children with dyslexia in skills on three tasks: pseudoword reading, letter–phoneme matching (judging whether the letters in two words represented the same sound), and letter matching (judging whether two letter strings matched exactly). In addition, fMRI data obtained from the children with dyslexia and the matched controls showed that the quantity and pattern of brain activation in multiple brain areas of the children with dyslexia after participation in the treatment program resembled that of the control children.

Consistent with these findings are those of Temple et al. (2003), who investigated how a remediation program influenced the oral language and reading skills of children with dyslexia and whether fMRI measures of brain processing reflected the influences of the remediation. Children with dyslexia were matched according to age, sex, handedness, and nonverbal IQ to controls. Remediation focused on auditory processing and oral language skills using computer-based training in specific skill areas. After training, significant changes in behavioral scores for the children with dyslexia were noted for real word and pseudoword reading, and reading comprehension, with scores of the dyslexic group moving into the normal range. Data obtained by fMRI showed increased brain activation in multiple brain areas of the children with dyslexia, and the magnitude of activation increase was correlated with improved oral language skills. While these findings do not indicate that the brain processing of children with dyslexia was normalized by the treatment programs they participated in, there is clear indication that brain processing is influenced by treatment, such that there are changes in areas and levels of activation.

Together, studies of children with developmental dyslexia and developmental dysgraphia provide evidence of how these disabilities are manifested in behavior and also how they impact children's lives inside and outside of the classroom. These studies have also been helpful in understanding the similarities and differences in skills and skill development in children with disabilities and those of typical developing children. The focus of researchers not only on identification and diagnosis of disabilities but also on the identification and/or development of effective treatment programs for children is encouraging for children, parents, clinicians, and researchers.

Acknowledgments

This work was supported in part by a grant (R215R000023) from the U.S. Department of Education to Dr. Victoria Molfese and by the University of Louisville.

See also: Classical Tests for Speech and Language Disorders; Phonological, Lexical, Syntactic, and Semantic Disorders in Children.

Bibliography

Aylward, EH, Richards, TL, Berninger, VW, Nagy, WE, Field, KM, Grimme, AC, Richards, AL, Thomson, JB, and Cramer, SC (2003). 'Instructional treatment associated with changes in brain activation in children with dyslexia.' *Neurology* 61: 212–219.

Berninger, V, Nagy, W, Carlisle, J, Thomson, J, Hoffer, D, Abbott, S, et al. (2003). 'Effective treatment for dyslexics in grades 4 to 6.' In: Foorman, B (ed.) *Preventing and remediating reading difficulties: bringing science to scale*, pp. 382–417. Timonium, MD: York Press.

Bourassa, D and Treiman, R (1991). 'Spelling development and disability: The importance of linguistic factors.' *Language, Speech and Hearing Services in Schools* 32: 172–181.

Bowers, TG, DeMulder, J, Struck, DM, and Bedard, B (2003). 'Expressive writing disorders: an analysis of the theoretical views.' *Perceptual and Motor Skills* 96: 528–538.

Bronner, A (1917). *The psychology of special abilities and disabilities*. Boston: Little, Brown.

Castle, JM, Riach, J, and Nicholson, T (1994). 'Getting off to a better start in reading and spelling: the effects of phonemic awareness instruction within a whole language program.' *Journal of Educational Psychology* 86: 350–359.

Catts, H (1996). 'Defining dyslexia as a developmental language disorder: an expanded view.' *Topics in Language Disorders* 16: 14–29.

Deuel, RK, VanMier, H, Gopalan, B, and Stallings, G (1999). *Children writing: motor performance in dysgraphics and controls*. Presentation at the American Academy of Neurology Meeting, San Diego.

Demonet, J, Taylor, M, and Chaix, Y (2004). 'Developmental dyslexia.' *Lancet* 363: 1451–1460.

Eden, GF, VanMeter, JW, Rumsey, JM, Maisog, JM, Woods, RP, and Zeffiro, TA (1996). 'Abnormal processing of visual motion in dyslexia revealed by functional brain imaging.' *Nature* 382: 66–69.

Filipek, PA (1995). 'Neurobiological correlates of developmental dyslexia: what do we know about how dyslexics' brains differ from those of normal readers?'. *Journal of Child Neurology* 10: 562–569.

Fletcher, J, Foorman, B, Shaywitz, S, and Shaywitz, B (1999). 'Conceptual and methodological issues in dyslexia research: A lesson for developmental disorders.' In: Tager-Flusberg, H (ed.) *Neurodevelopmental disorders*, pp. 271–305. Cambridge, MA: MIT Press.

Gallagher, A, Frith, U, and Snowling, MJ (2000). 'Precursors of literacy-delay among children at genetic risk of dyslexia.' *Journal of Child Psychology and Psychiatry* 41: 203–213.

Gayan, J and Olson, RK (1999). 'Reading disability: evidence for a genetic etiology.' *European Child and Adolescent Psychiatry* 8: 52–55.

Gayan, J and Olson, RK (2001). 'Genetic and environmental influences on orthographic and phonological skills in children with reading disabilities.' *Developmental Neuropsychology* 20(2): 487–511.
Graham, S, Harris, K, and Fink-Chorzempo, B (2003). 'Extra spelling instruction: promoting better spelling, writing and reading performance right from the start.' *Teaching Exceptional Children* 35: 66–68.
Grigorenko, EL, Wood, FB, Meyer, MS, Hart, LA, Speed, WC, Shuster, A, and Pauls, DL (1997). 'Susceptibility loci for distinct components of developmental dyslexia on chromosomes 6 and 15.' *American Journal of Human Genetics* 60: 27–39.
Gubbay, SS and deKlerk, NH (1995). 'A study and review of developmental dysgraphia in relation to acquired dysgraphia.' *Brain and Development* 17: 1–8.
Guttorm, TK, Leppänen, PHT, Eklund, KM, Poikkeus, AM, Lyytinen, P, and Lyytinen, H (2003). *'Brain responses to changes in vowel duration measured at birth predict later language skills in children with familial risk for dyslexia.'* Manuscript submitted for publication.
Hari, R and Renvall, H (2001). 'Impaired processing of rapid stimulus sequences in dyslexia.' *Trends in Cognitive Science* 5: 525–532.
Hooper, SR, Swartz, CW, Wakely, MB, deKruif, RE, and Montgomery, JW (2002). 'Executive functions in elementary school children with and without problems in written expression.' *Journal of Learning Disabilities* 25: 57–68.
Jones, D and Christensen, CA (1999). 'Relationship between automaticity in handwriting and students' ability to generate written text.' *Journal of Educational Psychology* 91: 44–49.
Lyon, G (1996). 'Learning disabilities.' *Special Education for Students with Disabilities* 6: 54.
Mather, D (2003). 'Dyslexia and dysgraphia: More than written language difficulties in common.' *Journal of Learning Disabilities* 4: 307–317.
Mody, M, Studdert-Kennedy, M, and Brady, S (1997). 'Speech perception deficits in poor readers: auditory processing or phonological coding.' *Journal of Experimental Child Psychology* 64: 199–231.
Molfese, DL (2000). 'Predicting dyslexia at 8 years of age using neonatal brain responses.' *Brain and Language* 72: 238–245.
Molfese, D and Molfese, V (1985). 'Electrophysiological indices of auditory discrimination in newborn infants: the bases for predicting later language development?' *Infant Behavior and Development* 8: 197–211.
Pennington, BF (1999). 'Dyslexia as a neurodevelopmental disorder.' In: Tager-Flusberg (ed.) 307–330.
Richards, TL, Dager, SR, Corina, D, Serafini, S, Heide, A, Steury, K, Strauss, W, Hayes, CE, Abbott, RD, Craft, S, Shaw, D, Posse, S, and Berninger, VW (1999). 'Dyslexic children have abnormal brain lactate response to reading-related language tasks.' *American Journal of Neuroradiology* 20: 1393–1398.
Schulte-Korne, G, Grimm, T, Nothen, M, Muller-Mysok, B, Cichon, S, Vogt, I, Propping, P, and Remschmidt, H (1998a). 'Evidence for linkage of spelling disability to chromosome 15.' *American Journal of Human Genetics* 63: 279–282.
Schulte-Korne, G, Deimel, W, Bartling, J, and Remschmidt, H (1998b). 'Role of auditory temporal processing for reading and spelling disability.' *Perceptual and Motor Skills* 86: 1043–1047.
Simner, ML and Eidlitz, MR (2000). 'Towards an empirical definition of developmental dysgraphia: preliminary findings.' *Canadian Journal of School Psychology* 16: 103–110.
Swanson, HL and Berninger, VW (1996). 'Individual differences in children's working memory and writing skills.' *Journal of Experimental Child Psychology* 63: 358–385.
Tager-Flusberg, H (ed.) (1999). *Neurodevelopmental disorders.* Cambridge, MA: MIT Press.
Tallal, P (1980). 'Auditory temporal perception, phonics, and reading disabilities in children.' *Brain and Language* 56: 334–353.
Temple, E, Deutsch, GK, Poldrack, RA, Miller, SL, Tallal, P, Merzenich, MM, and Gabrieli, JDE (2003). 'Neural deficits in children with dyslexia ameliorated by behavioral remediation: evidence from functional MRI.' *Proceedings of the National Academy of Sciences* 100: 2860–2865.
Torrance, M and Galbraith, D (2005). 'The processing demands of writing.' In: MacArthur, C, Graham, S, and Fitzgerald, J (eds.) *Handbook of writing research.* New York: Guilford.
Treiman, R (1998). 'Why spelling? The benefits of incorporating spelling into beginning reading instruction.' In: Metsala, J and Ehri, L (eds.) *Word recognition in beginning literacy*, pp. 289–313. Mahwah, NJ: Lawrence Erlbaum Associates.
Vlachos, F and Karapetsas, A (2003). 'Visual memory deficit in children with dysgraphia.' *Perceptual and Motor Skills* 97: 1281–1288.

Dyslexia, Neurodevelopmental Basis

G. F. Eden, Georgetown University Medical Center, Washington, DC, USA
D. L. Flowers, Wake Forest University School of Medicine, Winston-Salem, NC, USA

Introduction

Developmental dyslexia, also referred to as reading disability, is an unexpected reading problem that cannot be attributed to poor intellectual ability or educational shortcomings. Unlike acquired reading disorders such as alexia (acquired dyslexia), this reading disability is developmental in nature and accounts for about 80% of all learning disabilities. The 5–12% of the population affected with developmental dyslexia struggles to attain proficient levels of reading accuracy and fluency, without which they are prevented from deriving meaning from text. The identification of individuals with dyslexia and research into its etiology have been complicated by variations among researchers and educators in placing boundaries between dyslexic and typical readers. Further, although individuals with dyslexia have traditionally been distinguished from those poor readers with lower cognitive capacities or those lacking appropriate reading instruction, avenues for improving reading in these populations may follow similar paths. The most popular approach to counter dyslexia entails explicit instruction in phonological representation (i.e., phonological code). This approach has been reinforced by the positive relationship observed between phonological skills and reading proficiency in the majority of children during the early school grades. Further, functional brain imaging studies have revealed lower brain activity in dyslexic people during the performance of skills invoking phonological representations, and more recently, brain imaging techniques have been employed to study the functional anatomy of reading interventions. Linkage studies continue to reveal candidate genes, pointing to the multigenetic nature of dyslexia and its heterogeneous phenotype. The behavioral manifestations of dyslexia also include deficits in sensorimotor performance which, much like the language-based deficits, have been tied to perturbations in brain function. Together, this information about the behavioral manifestations and biological markers of dyslexia is being used to ensure better identification of dyslexia and more effective treatment strategies.

Behavioral Profile of Developmental Dyslexia

Definition of Developmental Dyslexia

There are numerous definitions of dyslexia. One formulated in 2002 by a working group commissioned by the National Institutes of Health and the International Dyslexia Association specifies the following:

> Dyslexia is a specific learning disability that is neurological in origin. It is characterized by difficulties with accurate and/or fluent word recognition and by poor spelling and decoding abilities. These difficulties typically result from a deficit in the phonological component of language that is often unexpected in relation to other cognitive abilities and the provision of effective classroom instruction. Secondary consequences may include problems in reading comprehension and reduced reading experience that can impede growth of vocabulary and background knowledge.

This definition serves researchers and practitioners. It reflects four decades of behavioral research indicating that the word-decoding and reading-fluency deficiencies observed in dyslexia are the symptoms of an underlying deficit in phonological processes. The definition is therefore now more specific than earlier definitions were in identifying one of the cognitive deficits and less specific about the role of IQ. Previous versions of the definition operated using a discrepancy definition. Under that model, IQ measures provided a benchmark of expected achievement against which to measure actual reading achievement. Typically in the United States, a discrepancy of least one standard deviation (15 standard score points) defines dyslexia for inclusion of a student in research studies or allocation of resources by school systems. However, the existence of a strong correlation between IQ and reading achievement biases against identifying individuals with dyslexia, in part because responses to verbal portions of the IQ test are influenced by reading experience. In addition, some of the core deficits exhibited by individuals with dyslexia are shared by poor readers with lower IQ (known as garden-variety poor readers), and these deficits are typically the focus of applied interventions (e.g., phonological coding). Hence IQ is no longer included in the above definition. From an educational perspective, these interventions are now administered in the school systems under a 'response to intervention' model, which in itself selects for those children who fail to benefit from standard instruction, with the next stage being implemented for those students who fail to show sufficient gains at the previous level. Finally, the more recently derived data from neuroscience research indicating anatomical differences in the brains of individuals with dyslexia has motivated the inclusion of the now widely accepted notion that developmental dyslexia has a neurobiological origin. However, measures of brain function are not currently used to diagnose dyslexia. Hence the current definition of developmental dyslexia has been shaped by a convergence of research findings and the practical aspects of educational reality.

Cognitive Characteristics of Developmental Dyslexia

For the majority of children, early phonological coding skills predict the course of their later reading development. These skills encompass sound manipulation at the phoneme level (phonemic awareness), rapid naming of letters and numbers (phonological retrieval), and short-term verbal memory (phonological recoding). Children who fail to show awareness of the phonemic structure of spoken words at the kindergarten level are more likely to struggle in acquiring grapheme–phoneme correspondence rules, and this affects their long-term ability to decode words. These observations have led to ways by which to identify children with dyslexia early, as those children with poor phonological representation are considered to be at higher risk for reading disability, even prior to the advent of formal schooling. This longitudinal research, together with the fact that treatments aimed at promoting the phonological code are fairly successful in helping children with reading disabilities, has given rise to the notion that a phonological core-deficit hypothesis represents the best explanation for dyslexia.

However, while phonological processes are impaired in many poor readers, these children may also exhibit deficits in other language-related processes, including vocabulary, morphology and syntax, and text comprehension. Likewise, measures of vocabulary and grammar attained at kindergarten are strongly associated with reading outcome in second grade. Finally, skills in the domain of orthography, such as the ability to name words based on visual information or appreciating letter patterns that are legitimate, affect reading fluency and reading comprehension in the later grades.

In sum, the most prominent cognitive deficit associated with dyslexia is that pertaining to phonological coding. However, it should not go unnoticed that other language skills make strong predictions for later reading development and that the process of reading itself promotes phonological representation. Hence it would be fair to say that dyslexia is associated with a number of language-based deficits, with poor decoding serving as the identifying feature. However, because the definition of dyslexia is largely exclusionary, it is not surprising that the result is the identification of heterogeneous populations of dyslexics. This in turn results in variability in the description of the dyslexic phenotype. Although the phonological and other language deficits are prominent and most are directly related to the process of reading acquisition, other behavioral manifestations have been observed and will be described next.

Sensorimotor Characteristics of Developmental Dyslexia

While the behavioral measures of phonological coding described above have provided a strong theoretical framework at the cognitive level, this approach has not been able to address other diverse symptoms observed in dyslexia outside the domain of language. Psychophysical studies in the domain of vision and audition have suggested aberrations within lower-level, perceptual systems, and impaired motor performance in individuals with dyslexia also suggest the possibility of motor system involvement. The hypotheses put forward in this area of research are sometimes based on systems, such as the magnocellular-based visual perceptual hypothesis, or on concepts (such as temporal integration) or are directly linked to locations in the brain (e.g., parietal and cerebellar deficits).

It was first demonstrated by Lovegrove and colleagues using psychophysical experimental techniques that magnocellular visual system function is altered in individuals with dyslexia. These studies were largely confirmed by data acquired using neuroanatomical (altered magnocellular layers in the lateral geniculate nucleus at postmortem), electrophysiological, and functional neuroimaging techniques comparing dyslexics with nondyslexics. For example, the perception of visual motion, which relies on magnocellular function, usually induces a robust activation response in the dorsal visual stream, including parietal cortex and area MT/V5. However, in individuals with dyslexia, this activity is reduced or absent (see **Figure 1**). These results raise the question of the nature of the relationship between dorsal stream function, which is highly developed for visuospatial perception in human and nonhuman primates, and reading, a skill that is uniquely human and has come into use very recently. The dual symptomatology of impaired visual motion perception and phonological processing could be due to the close proximity of brain regions functionally specialized for these divergent tasks, resulting in equal susceptibility under circumstances of brain perturbation. Another possibility is that visual perception that requires tracking of rapidly changing information is impaired because of systematic differences in sensory systems that handle rapidly changing information. While neither of these hypotheses has been confirmed, this latter idea has some parallels with a hypothesis that has emerged from the study of auditory perception in children with reading problems.

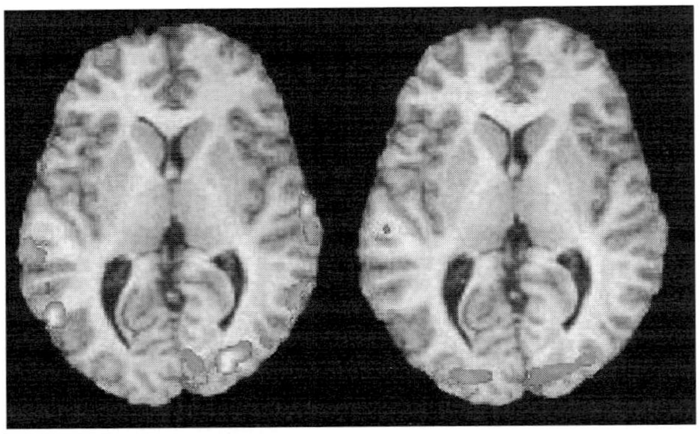

Figure 1 Horizontal sections of the brain reveal that typical adult readers (left) display activity in visual cortex, including area MT/V5, during the perception of visual motion. Adults with dyslexia (right) lack this activity. From Eden GF, VanMeter JW, Rumsey JW, Maisog J, and Zeffiro TA (1996) Abnormal processing of visual motion in dyslexia revealed by functional brain imaging. *Nature* 348: 66–69. (See color plate 19.)

In this case, the poor readers were children with a primary diagnosis of specific language impairment (SLI; see the section titled 'Comorbid disorders') and were found to require longer intervals in order to accurately perceive the sequence of rapid successive auditory inputs. This work by Tallal and colleagues also suggested a link between early sensory processing of nonverbal sounds and phonological processing. This led to an intervention strategy in which children completed exercises devised to improve processing of rapidly presented successive acoustic stimuli and to improve speech perception. However, while initial laboratory work showed promise for improving language function in children with SLI, independent, randomized controlled studies have not yet demonstrated any long-term benefits to reading. Nevertheless, the temporal-deficit hypothesis continues to be actively investigated and provides an interesting model by which to examine whether the remediation of behavioral deficits observed in dyslexia generalize to improvements in other domains, specifically reading.

On the other hand, a locus-specific theoretical framework for understanding the behavioral manifestations of dyslexia has been built around the cerebellum. Nicolson and Fawcett, for example, have argued that reading and phonological deficits arise in parallel with poor skill automaticity, the latter being dependant on cerebellar integrity. While this work is supported by behavioral and functional brain imaging results, the claims that reading gains can be brought about via regimens that target functions carried out by the cerebellum have been controversial.

The appeal of most brain-based research is that it ties into well-characterized neural functions and frequently offers an explanation for the numerous deficits noted in dyslexia. However, a common weakness of this research is that the causal relationship between sensorimotor deficits and reading has not been demonstrated. To do so would require the examination of behavioral deficits over a wide age range or longitudinally, in large participant groups. Only in this way can it be established whether a perceptual deficit plays a causal role in disrupting phonological coding abilities. Research of this type is ongoing and will undoubtedly provide a clearer picture of the direction of causality among these factors.

Biological Basis of Developmental Dyslexia

Brain-Based Evidence

A landmark study by Galaburda and colleagues in 1985 revealed microscopic anomalies in the brains of individuals with dyslexia examined at postmortem (see **Figure 2**). As the appropriate brain imaging tools became available, this finding provided the impetus for a large number of investigations into the anatomical and physiological integrity of reading-impaired participants *in vivo*. Since then, an abundance of investigations using functional neuroimaging (positron emission tomography and functional magnetic resonance imagery) have reported anomalous patterns of activation associated with reading and phonological representation in adults with persistent and compensated developmental dyslexia. Although these studies have varied in their use of tasks (e.g., the detection or judgment of rhymes, nonword reading, and implicit reading) and in terms of the languages spoken by the participants, their respective observations have largely been consistent. The most common finding for differential brain activity between dyslexic and nondyslexic participants falls into left-hemisphere perisylvian regions. Differences in task-related signal change in the left parietal cortex are commonly reported in children and adults with dyslexia. It is important that these differences are not the result of lower task performance by the dyslexic participants or simply the consequence of impoverished reading experience. In addition, there are reports of altered involvement of the left inferior frontal gyrus in dyslexia (some report hypo- and others hyperactivation) and underactivity in the left occipitotemporal junction (BA 37), the latter being a common finding. For example, during the performance of reading tasks, dyslexic adults from different countries showed common underactivity in this region despite their differences in language experience (see **Figure 3**).

Considering the number of brain regions identified in these studies, it is conceivable that dyslexia may arise in a number of different ways. Further, the loci at which functional differences are observed do not necessarily represent the original site of perturbation. However, recent MRI studies measuring fractional anisotropy (estimating white matter integrity) do concur with the physiological differences observed in left temporal parietal in dyslexia. Therefore, not only do functional and anatomical findings converge, but also data emerging from genetic research are beginning to offer a gene-based explanation for the neuronal migrations that may lie behind these neuroanatomical and neurophysiological differences observed in dyslexia.

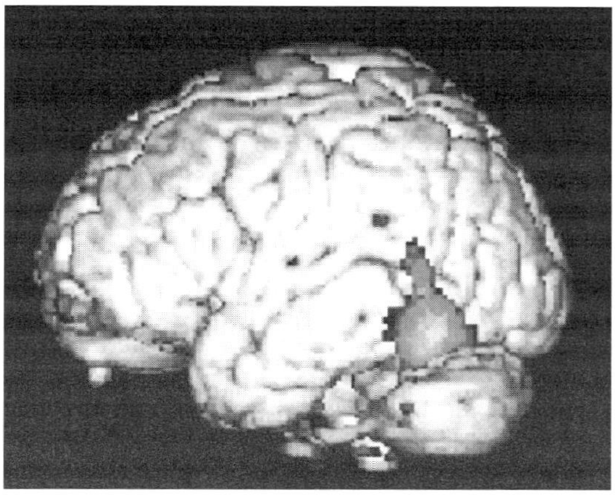

Figure 2 An example of a brain examined at postmortem. The individual was diagnosed as having had dyslexia. Developmental anomalies consist of neuronal ectopias and architectonic dysplasias. Adapted from Galaburda AM, Sherman GF, Rosen GD, Aboitiz F, and Geschwind N (1985) Developmental dyslexia: Four consecutive patients with cortical anomalies. *Annals of Neurology* 18: 222–233. (See color plate 20.)

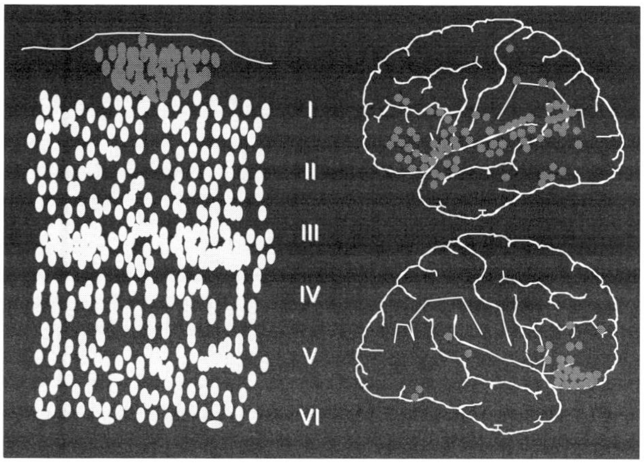

Figure 3 During word processing, dyslexics in French-, Italian-, and English-speaking countries, despite their inherent differences in language systems, all exhibit less activity than controls at the occipitotemporal junction of the left hemisphere. From Paulesu E, Demonet J-F, Fazio F, et al. (2001) Dyslexia: Cultural diversity and biological unity. *Science* 291(5511): 2165–2167.

Genetic Evidence

There is abundant evidence that component reading skills which influence reading acquisition are strongly influenced by genes; however, it is already clear that the elusive 'dyslexia gene' is a myth. That is, at least seven regions of susceptibility have been identified by linkage studies (on chromosomes 1, 2, 3, 6, 15, 18, and X), and four candidate genes (on chromosomes 3, 6, and 15) have been associated with dyslexia phenotypes. This complexity may help explain the co-occurrence of dyslexia with other learning and developmental disorders. In any case, there is hope that genetic screening, together with other information, will help to identify individuals at risk for dyslexia well before reading problems emerge in the classroom.

Consistent with human postmortem reports of migration anomalies as well as with animal models, the candidate genes implicate abnormalities in the coding of axonal guidance and neuronal migration. In the present case, they are believed to be involved in the abnormal organization of cortical networks that contribute to the component skills of reading acquisition. As a caveat, however, it must be noted that the known functions of the candidate genes might be expected to lead to a general rather than to a specific disorder. Furthermore, it seems likely at this stage of research that the culprits are mutations in regions that regulate the candidate genes.

Dyslexia in Different Languages and Orthographies

How many of the reading problems encountered by individuals with dyslexia are unique to the English language? Although most of the language-based deficits described above have been reported for dyslexia in a variety of different countries and the neurobiological basis for these problems is shared in large part among users of the alphabet (see **Figure 3**), there are differences in the rate of reading acquisition that can be attributed to variations in language characteristics. For example, it has been argued by Ziegler and Goswami that the differences in syllable structure and the consistency by which phonology is mapped to orthography will affect the rate at which children reach reading proficiency (e.g., faster in German than in English). It is interesting that skills such as phonological coding also play a role in logographic writing systems, such as Chinese, although in this case the role of orthography clearly is more dominant. Not surprisingly, Chinese reading, compared with English reading, evokes greater responses in the visual system and less activity in the superior temporal lobe regions that are associated with phonological processing in the alphabetic languages. Struggling Chinese readers show less activity in frontal systems thought to be responsible for the mapping of orthography to phonology and orthography to semantics (see **Figure 4**). In other words, dyslexia is omnipresent, and while there are common elements that support reading across languages and writing systems, there are also unique differences in the brain signatures for reading, each of which is most likely susceptible to changes that could result in reading disability.

Comorbid Disorders

Developmental Dyslexia and Attention-Deficit/Hyperactivity Disorder

It has been suggested that as many as 40% of children with dyslexia also have attention-deficit/hyperactivity disorder

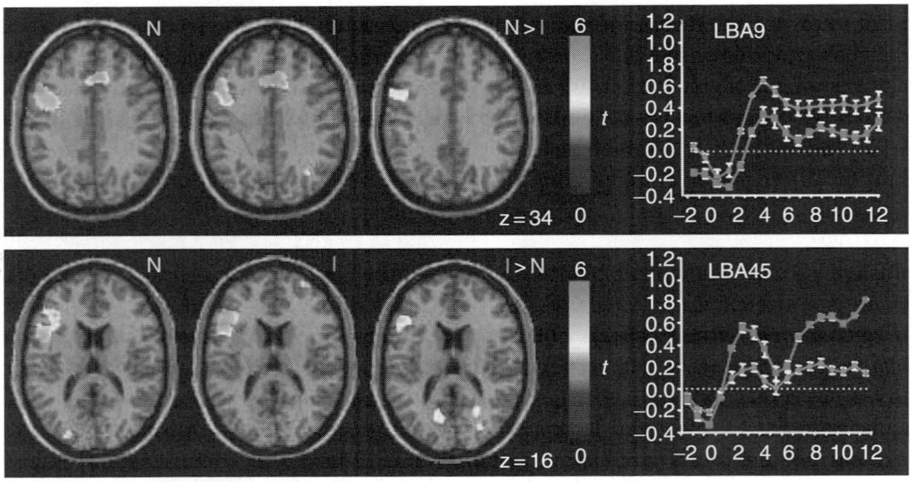

Figure 4 During a homophone judgment task, Chinese normal (blue) and impaired readers (red) differ in brain activity in left-middle frontal gyrus (top panel) and inferior frontal gyrus. From Siok WT, Perfetti CA, Jin Z, and Tan LH (2004) Biological abnormality of impaired reading is constrained by culture. *Nature* 431(7004): 71–76. (See color plate 21.)

(ADHD). Because these disorders have been seen both alone and together, there has been some debate as to whether they were entirely independent. More recently, a common etiology to their co-occurrence has been supported by genetic evidence of susceptibility regions on chromosomes 2, 8, 14, and 15. Separately, either disorder can affect learning or either can affect focus of attention, thus making their independent and collective contributions particularly difficult to identify. Obviously, the importance of correct diagnosing has obvious treatment implications, whether academic, behavioral, or pharmacological. Few neuroimaging studies have focused on the question of a common etiology, as opposed to independent etiologies, of ADHD and dyslexia, with the former focusing on frontal and subcortical function and the latter on language substrates.

Developmental Dyslexia and SLI

Approximately 50% of children diagnosed with SLI in early childhood will develop learning difficulties, particularly in reading, especially if the language impairment is severe and is still present on school entry. Dyslexia is not the inevitable outcome of SLI, however, and dyslexic individuals do not necessarily have a history of SLI – evidence that the two disorders are independent. Brain imaging studies support the proposition that phonological deficits and language comprehension are served by different neural networks, further support for independent etiologies. Like ADHD, SLI has been studied alone and in combination with dyslexia. Although phonological-awareness problems might be expected to be associated with SLI, studies have found only mild deficits in that group on measures of phonological-coding skills. In contrast, dyslexic participants with or without comorbid SLI have poorer phonological skills. The separate and combined aspects of these often coexisting disorders make it prudent to adopt specific intervention strategies to address their respective deficits, highlighting phonological processes on one hand and listening comprehension on the other.

Therapeutic Approaches to Developmental Dyslexia

Given the plurality of weaknesses in addition to reading problems that are observed in individuals with dyslexia, the necessity for multiple treatment strategies may seem pressing. As discussed above, programs that emphasize phonological coding are known to facilitate reading acquisition. However, targeting just this one domain is not sufficient. Although gains in phonological representation can bring about growth in multiple aspects of reading, they do not generalize to all aspects of reading. For example, promoting reading fluency and reading comprehension in addition to phonology requires other types of intervention approaches. Studies targeting domains of reading other than phonological coding, such as orthography, are less numerous. Increasingly, successful treatment methods represent a combination of training approaches (combining phonics, phonemic awareness, fluency, vocabulary, and reading comprehension), which, although logical from an educational perspective, complicates any experimental approach to identify independent contributors of reading recovery. It is interesting that the methods by which these instructions are delivered in clinics or classrooms often involve 'multisensory' enhancing techniques, whereby the same principles are taught by reliance on several sensory systems, through speaking (audition), visual imagery or visual representation touch, and motor system involvement (writing, air writing, or body movements that correspond to the number of syllables or phonemes in a given word). These observations from the classroom are ripe for neuroscientific inquiry, based on our understanding of neural responses under conditions of single versus multiple sensory stimulation in the auditory and visual systems.

Evaluating the benefits of various remediation strategies for dyslexia is beyond the scope of this article; a thorough review of representative therapies has been published by Alexander and colleagues. From the neuroscientific perspective, it is of value to establish the neural correlates of successful reading interventions as these provide important insight not only into brain mechanisms of dyslexia but also into behavioral plasticity. Based on a rich animal and human literature of training-induced brain plasticity and functional reorganization following rehabilitation from cerebral injury, one can consider several paths that would lead to changes following successful reading intervention in developmental dyslexia. One is a mechanism by which brain regions with known anomalies in dyslexia are shown to establish a more typical response. An alternative brain response could involve the manifestation of brain activity in brain regions not typically associated with the reading process. Such compensatory strategies have been described for stroke patients in brain regions contralateral to the injury (and which encompassed the site typically activated by the now relearned skill). Functional brain imaging technology has allowed these models to be subjected to the test. For example, in a study comparing dyslexic adults with persistent reading problems following 120 h of intensive reading intervention to a matched group of dyslexics receiving no intervention at all, the intervention group was found to have increased activity in bilateral parietal and right perisylvian cortex following the intervention (see **Figure 5**). These results suggest that the significant gains in reading enjoyed by the intervention group could be attributed to right hemisphere compensation combined with increases in a more typically reading-related left hemisphere brain

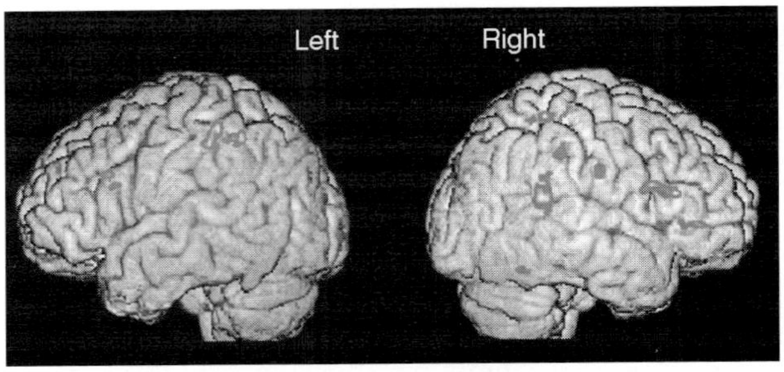

Figure 5 Functional anatomy of phonological manipulation following reading remediation (Group X Session interaction) revealed increases during phonological manipulation in left parietal cortex and fusiform gyrus. Right hemisphere increases included posterior superior temporal sulcus/gyrus and parietal cortex. Reprinted from Eden GF, Jones KM, Cappell K, et al. (2004) Neural changes following remediation in adult developmental dyslexia. *Neuron* 44(3): 411–422. (See color plate 22.)

region. Several functional brain imaging studies have also been conducted in children receiving reading interventions, and a review of this small literature suggests a role for age (or brain maturation) in directing the pattern of treatment-induced brain plasticity. This, however, does not mean that changes in brain activity necessarily guarantee behavioral gains, and results from these studies are meaningful only if the studies follow rigorous research practices, such as the use of controlled, randomized experimental designs.

Summary

Developmental dyslexia has been studied in the context of learning, development, experiential factors, genetic influences, and brain function. For all children, a mastery of reading requires the integration and coordination of sensorimotor and cognitive processes. How these fail to operate at an optimal level to bring about accurate and fluent reading in the context of normal cognitive function and appropriate teaching methods continues to be questioned from the viewpoint of behavior and brain function. Avenues of remediation within both cognitive and sensorimotor domains are under active investigation to establish the efficacy of these approaches as well as to discover their neuronal targets. Investigations into the hereditary mechanisms of reading deficits hold the promise of strengthening the understanding of the neural mechanisms of dyslexia. Together, behavioral and physiological studies continue to aid in the early identification of dyslexia and best avenues for its treatment.

See also: Language Development; Language, Cortical Processes; Language, Learning Impairments.

Further Reading

Alexander, AW and Slinger-Constant, AM (2004). Current status of treatments for dyslexia: Critical review. *Journal of Child Neurology* 19(10): 744–758.

Bradley, L and Bryant, P (1983). Categorizing sounds and learning to read: A causal connection. *Nature* 301: 419–421.

Eckert, M (2004). Neuroanatomical markers for dyslexia: A review of dyslexia structural imaging studies. *Neuroscientist* 10(4): 362–371.

Eden, GF, Jones, KM, Cappell, K, et al. (2004). Neural changes following remediation in adult developmental dyslexia. *Neuron* 44(3): 411–422.

Eden, GF and Moats, L (2002). The role of neuroscience in the remediation of students with dyslexia. *Nature Neuroscience* 5(supplement): 1080–1084.

Fisher, SE and DeFries, JC (2002). Developmental dyslexia: Genetic dissection of a complex cognitive trait. *Nature Review Neuroscience* 3(10): 767–780.

Galaburda, AM, LoTurco, J, Ramus, F, Fitch, RH, and Rosen, DG (2006). From genes to behavior in developmental dyslexia. *Nature Neuroscience* 9(10): 1213–1217.

Lovegrove, WJ, Bowling, A, Badcock, D, and Blackwood, M (1980). Specific reading disability: Differences in contrast sensitivity as a function of spatial frequency. *Science* 210(4468): 439–440.

Nicolson, R, Fawcett, AJ, and Dean, P (2001). Dyslexia, development and the cerebellum. *Trends in Neuroscience* 24(9): 515–516.

Paulesu, E, Demonet, J-F, Fazio, F, et al. (2001). Dyslexia: Cultural diversity and biological unity. *Science* 291(5511): 2165–2167.

Rutter, M, Caspi, A, Fergusson, D, et al. (2004). Sex differences in developmental reading disability: New findings from 4 epidemiological studies. *Journal of the American Medical Association* 291(16): 2007–2012.

Schatschneider, C, Fletcher, JM, Francis, DJ, Carlson, CD, and Foorman, BR (2004). Kindergarten predictions of reading skills: A longitudinal comparative analysis. *Journal of Educational Psychology* 96(2): 265–282.

Siok, WT, Perfetti, CA, Jin, Z, and Tan, LH (2004). Biological abnormality of impaired reading is constrained by culture. *Nature* 431(7004): 71–76.

Vellutino, FR, Fletcher, JM, Snowling, MJ, and Scanlon, DM (2004). Specific reading disability (dyslexia): What have we learned in the past four decades? *Journal of Child Psychology and Psychiatry* 45(1): 2–40.

Ziegler, JC and Goswami, U (2005). Reading acquisition, developmental dyslexia, and skilled reading across languages: A psycholinguistic grain size theory. *Psychological Bulletin* 131(1): 3–29.

Relevant Website

http://www.interdys.org – International Dyslexia Association.

E

Event-Related Potentials in the Study of Language

K. Steinhauer, McGill University, Montréal, Québec, Canada
J. F. Connolly, Université de Montréal, Montréal, Québec, Canada

Introduction

Investigating how the brain accomplishes language comprehension is a particular challenge compared to other areas of cognitive neuroscience. Animal models are of limited value given that no other species has a comparably complex communication system. On the other hand, areas as distinct as sensory physiology and formal linguistics contribute important details to our understanding of language processes in the brain. Most ERP research discussed here is strongly rooted in psycholinguistic models of word recognition, syntactic parsing, and the online integration of information. This work provides a solid foundation upon which to examine cognitive factors and the brain mechanisms involved in the transformation of a low-level signal into the highly complex symbolic system we know as human language.

Three major goals of using neuroimaging are to understand *where* language is processed in the brain and *when* and *how* the different levels of linguistic processing unfold in time. Thanks to their ability to provide continuous online measures with an excellent temporal resolution, even in the absence of behavioral tasks, ERPs contribute primarily to the second and third goals and can add the valuable perspective of real-time brain dynamics underlying linguistic operations. We will concentrate on these by making reference to a number of established "ERP components," that is, characteristic brain potentials at the scalp assumed to reflect specific neurocognitive processes, and, on occasion, corresponding event-related magnetic field (ERMF) research. We will outline the factors that influence these brain responses, and by inference, the linguistic processes they reflect. As ERP and ERMF measures are not completely without power in addressing *where* in the brain certain language functions may occur, those aspects will briefly be mentioned as well.

ERP research in linguistics has historically had a strong element of component discovery since the first "language" component, the "semantic" N400, was observed (Kutas & Hillyard, 1980). In the intervening years additional ERP components associated with acoustic–phonetic, phonological, orthographic, prosodic, and syntactic processes have been discovered. Those of them concerned with basic operations such as phoneme discrimination or word segmentation tend to be early (100–200 ms), fast, and automatic. Other components reflect integration or revision processes and tend to have larger latencies (up to 1 s). Parallel processes can be distinguished primarily in terms of ERP scalp distributions.

A recent theme that has gained increasing prominence is the degree to which these "linguistic" components are actually domain specific. Most of them have been described initially as being related to language processes only. However, subsequent research has usually weakened the case for domain specificity. For example, the P600 (Osterhout & Holcomb, 1992) had been linked to syntactic processing. More recently, however, it has been proposed that language and music share processing resources and that a functional overlap exists between neural populations that are responsible for structural analyses in both domains (Patel et al., 1998). It will become apparent that most "linguistic" ERP components may also be associated with non-linguistic functions. It might even be proposed that some of them might be more accurately thought of as domain-non-specific responses that reflect basic operations critical for, but not limited to, linguistics processes.

Language-Related Components and their Functional Significance

The following subsections will discuss which ERP components have contributed to our understanding of psycholinguistic processes in phonology, lexical/conceptual semantics, syntax, as well as their respective interactions.

The N100: An Exogenous Component with Linguistic Functions?

The complexity of examining language functions with ERP is captured very well by the first component that we will discuss, the N100: a *N*egativity peaking around *100* ms. Long considered an exogenous response sensitive to the physical features (e.g., loudness or brightness) of an auditory, visual, or tactile stimulus, it has more recently been linked to word segmentation processes (Sanders & Neville, 2003). Noting the disagreement in the literature as to whether continuous speech stimuli elicit the early sensory components (including the N100), these studies sought to clarify whether word onsets within a context of continuous speech would elicit the early sensory or "obligatory" components. This work also examined whether the hypothesized word onset responses were related to segmentation and word stress. ERPs to word initial and word medial syllables were obtained within different types of sentence context. It was found that word onset syllables elicited larger anterior N100 responses than word medial syllables across all sentence conditions.

Word onsets in continuous speech can vary in their physical characteristics (e.g., loudness, duration) by virtue of whether the syllable is stressed or unstressed. Thus, word onset effects on the N100 were examined as a function of word stress with the finding that stressed syllables evoked larger N100 responses than unstressed syllables at electrode sites near the midline. Such an effect was expected given the physical differences that exist between stressed and unstressed syllables. However, it was concluded that the N100 was monitoring more than the physical characteristics of the stressed and unstressed syllables because the N100 to these stimuli showed a different scalp distribution compared to that seen for the N100 to word onset and word medial syllables which had been equated for physical characteristics. Further evidence for a language-related role for the N100 was found in an examination of Japanese–English bilinguals who failed to show N100 segmentation effects to English stimuli similar to native English speakers. This observation contrasts with the finding that the Japanese–English bilinguals showed clear N100 responses to sentence onsets thus exhibiting normal acoustic ERPs. The conclusion was made that non-native speakers do not use the acoustic differences as part of a speech comprehension system in the same manner as native speakers. Although these effects require replication as a final confirmation, they nevertheless demonstrate very well the neural flexibility involved in language function as well as the "multipurpose" nature of some ERP components that can reflect simple acoustic processing or complex linguistic segmentation. This work also demonstrates quite well the importance of evaluating all aspects of an ERP component insofar as the primary difference between the N100 as an acoustic or language component was its scalp distribution and thus, by implication, its neural generators.

Prelexical Expectations: The Phonological Mapping Negativity

Terminal words of spoken sentences that violate contextually developed phonological expectations (as in *1b*) elicit this fronto-centrally distributed ERP component that peaks in the late 200 ms range (270–310 ms) and is earlier than and distinct from the N400 reflecting pure semantic anomalies (*1c*) (see also Section 2.3). In combined violations of phonological and semantic expectations (*1d*), the Phonological mapping negativity (PMN) precedes the N400 (**Figures 1** and **2(b)**).

(1a) Father carved the turkey with a knife (expected word: knife)
(1b) The pigs wallowed in the pen (mud)
(1c) The gambler had a streak of bad luggage (luck)
(1d) The winter was harsh this allowance (year)

This component was labeled the phonological mismatch negativity (PMN) (Connolly & Phillips, 1994, from which the above examples are taken) although this was a misleading description of its behavior inasmuch as it is found to occur in response to all sentence-ending words but is larger to those that violate phonological expectations and is *not* related to the mismatch negativity (MMN; **Box 1**). Thus, the PMN now refers to the phonological *mapping* negativity as this phrase better describes its behavior. The PMN appears to be modality specific (auditory) and prelexical as it is equally responsive to words and nonwords. It also appears to be related to phonological awareness, responds to single phoneme violations of localized expectations, and is insensitive to phonologically correct pattern masking (e.g., Connolly et al., 1992). Preliminary data indicate it is absent in many poor and dyslexic readers. Using both magnetoencephalography (MEG) and high-resolution (hr)ERP, the PMN has been localized predominantly to left perisylvian regions (Kujala et al., 2004; **Figure 1**) and the left inferior frontal area (Broca's area) as well as left inferior parietal region (D'Arcy et al., 2004; **Figure 2(c)**). The MEG findings also indicate that the PMN is anterior to both the N1 and N400 in MEG responses (Kujala et al., 2004). Other work (Newman et al., 2003) has used a phoneme deletion paradigm to isolate the PMN from frequently occurring larger negativities (e.g., the semantic N400 discussed in the next section).

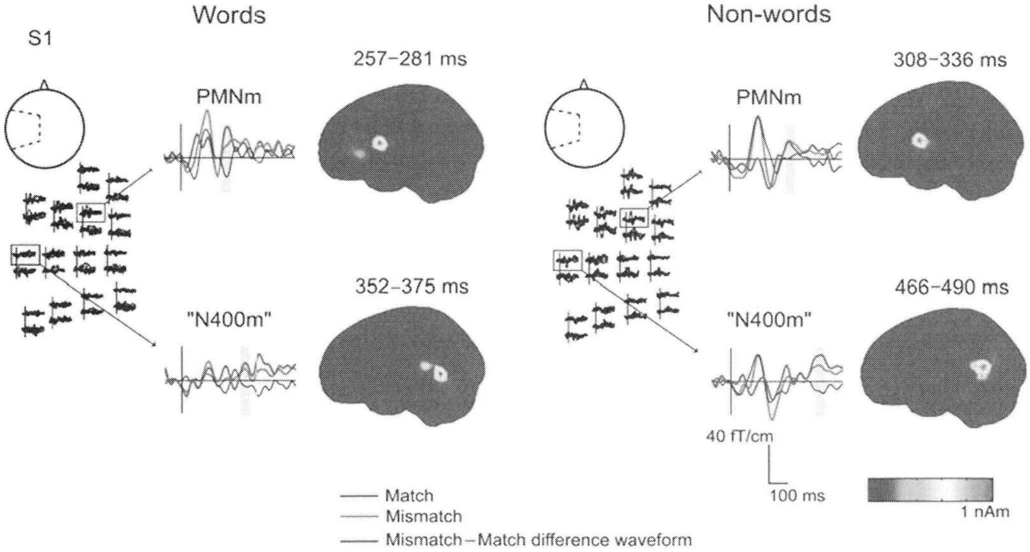

Figure 1 Phonological mapping negativity (PMN) and semantic N400. MEG responses to words (left) and non-words (right) for one participant for those left-hemisphere channels showing maximum amplitude for the magnetic PMN (PMNm) and the N400-like response. The corresponding estimates of the PMN- and N400m-like response sources (over a 25 ms time window centered at the peak of the response) are depicted in the brain images. The gray vertical bars indicate the 50 ms time periods within which significant PMNm- and N400m-like responses occurred. *Source*: Modified after Kujala et al., 2004. (See color plate 23.)

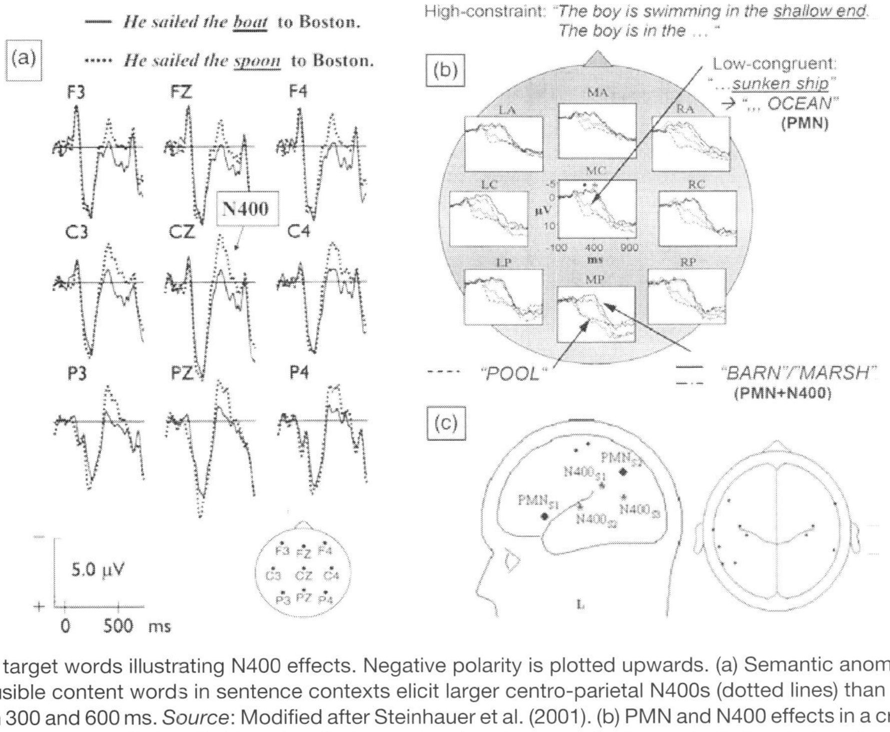

Figure 2 ERPs to target words illustrating N400 effects. Negative polarity is plotted upwards. (a) Semantic anomaly in sentences. Semantically implausible content words in sentence contexts elicit larger centro-parietal N400s (dotted lines) than plausible words (solid lines) between 300 and 600 ms. *Source*: Modified after Steinhauer et al. (2001). (b) PMN and N400 effects in a cross-modal priming study in which written sentences that ended in subordinate words primed superordinate words that ended spoken sentences. Exemplar-subordinate probabilities for congruent endings determined high-constraint primes (shallow end) or a low-constraint primes (sunken ship) which primed auditory target words in the paired sentences (in capitals) that were either congruent (Pool/Ocean) or not (Barn/Marsh). While incongruent targets (e.g., Barn/Marsh) always elicited PMNs and N400s, congruent targets following low-constraint contexts (Ocean) yielded PMNs only (L = left, R = right, M = middle, A = anterior, C = central, P = parietal). *Source*: Modified after D'Arcy, 2004. (c) Source localization revealed distinct neural generators for PMN and N400 components, primarily in the left hemisphere.

Box 1 The mismatch negativity

The mismatch negativity (MMN) is a pre-attentive response to discriminable auditory differences between a frequently occurring "standard" stimulus and a rare "deviant" stimulus – the so-called oddball paradigm (Näätänen et al., 2001). Panel a in the figure shows ERPs at midline electrodes for standard stimuli (85%, solid line) and deviant stimuli (15%, dotted line) in an auditory oddball. In panel b the difference wave (deviant minus standard) at frontal electrode FZ displays a large MMN and in panel c the voltage map between 140 and 190 ms post stimulus onset illustrates the frontal distribution of the MMN (Steinhauer, unpublished data). Within language research the MMN has been used to study categorical phoneme perception, most recently also probing the audio–visual McGurk–MacDonald effect (Massaro, 1998). This effect is achieved by having a subject watch a speaker articulate a syllable that differs from what is recorded on the audio channel the subject hears. The effect occurs when the subject sees the speaker articulate/ka/ but hears /pa/ – this combination results in the perception of /ta/. Examination of the McGurk–MacDonald effect has led one group to suggest the existence of an "audio–visual" MMN that has generators different to or overlapping with those that produce the purely acoustic MMN (Colin et al., 2002). They argue that, since their audio–visual stimuli had no acoustic deviants and the visual stimuli *per se* were incapable of eliciting MMNs, the visual stimuli required an appropriate auditory context within which a MMN was generated to an illusory deviant auditory percept. Also, they suggest that the MMN must result from an automatic, precognitive comparison between phonetic traces held in short-term memory.

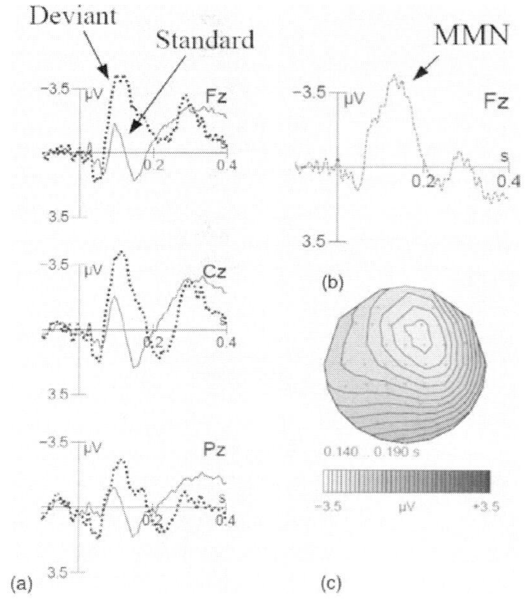

Colin, C., Radeaua, M., Soquetc, A., Demolinc, D., Colind, F., & Deltenre, P. (2002). Mismatch negativity evoked by the McGurk–MacDonald effect: a phonetic representation within short-term memory. *Clinical Neurophysiology, 113*, 495–506.

Massaro, D.W. (1998). *Perceiving talking faces: From speech perception to a behavioural principle*. Cambridge, MA: MIT Press.

Näätänen, R., Tervaniemi, M., Sussman, E., Paavilainen, P., & Winkler, I. (2001). "Primitive intelligence" in the auditory cortex. *Trends in Neurosciences, 24*, 283–288.

These findings have confirmed the PMN as a prelexical response reflecting a compulsory stage of word processing that is sensitive to top-down phonological expectations established by the experimental circumstances. Current thinking is that the PMN reflects phoneme awareness and the consequent phonological processing activity. Although influenced by top-down phonological expectations, once a violation of expectations is perceived the PMN does not appear to be sensitive to gradations of phonological relatedness but rather shows an "all-or-none" response that is equally large for all violations. The PMN may reflect a phonological stage of word processing that operates at the level of transforming acoustic input into phonological code assisting in the establishment of a lexical cohort. It is also compatible with the data to suggest that the PMN may reflect the earliest point at which top-down contextual information influences bottom-up processes at or just prior to the Isolation Point within, for example, a version of the Cohort Model (Connolly & Phillips, 1994).

Lexico-Semantic Integration: The N400 Component

This typically centro-parietal and slightly right-lateralized component peaks around 400 ms and was first observed to sentence-ending words that were incongruous to the semantic context of the sentences in which they occurred (e.g., in examples *1c* and *1d* above) (Kutas & Hillyard, 1980; Steinhauer & Friederici, 2001; D'Arcy et al., 2004; **Figure 2(a)** and **(b)**). More generally, the N400 amplitude seems to reflect costs of lexical activation and/or semantic integration, such as in words terminating low versus high contextually constrained sentences (Connolly et al., 1992). Other work has proposed that the N400 is larger to open- than closed-class words and in a developing sentence context becomes progressively smaller to such words as sentence context develops and provides contextual constraints (Van Petten & Luka, 2006). A particularly important report has demonstrated similarities between open- and closed-class words on the N280/Lexical Processing Negativity (LPN) and the N400 (Münte et al., 2001). It was found that the N280/LPN responded to both word classes. The N400 was also seen with both classes (albeit smaller to closed-class words, as mentioned above, due to their reduced semantic complexity), reinforcing the view that neither component offers support for different neural systems being involved in the processing of word class. In word-pair semantic priming paradigms (e.g., *bread–butter* versus *bread–house*) the N400 amplitude to the second word was reduced when it was related to the prime (Van Petten & Luka, 2006). N400s have also been shown to be larger to concrete than abstract words and to words with higher density orthographic neighborhoods (Holcomb et al., 2002). Word frequency appears to affect N400 amplitude, being larger for low than high frequency words. However, this effect disappears when the words are placed in a sentence context; a finding that has been interpreted as suggesting the N400 word frequency effect is probably semantically based (Van Petten & Luka, 2006).

The issue of domain specificity refers to a recurring theme about whether N400 activation reflects activity in an amodal conceptual-semantic system. Two studies exemplify work in the area. Also, both studies directly address the issue of "other" negativities (such as the PMN in the work already described) associated with the N400 and of conceptualizing the N400 as a response composed of distinct sub-processes rather than a monolithic process.

Based on earlier work that used line drawings of objects within an associate priming paradigm that required participants to indicate whether they recognized the second item in each pair, McPherson and Holcomb (1999) used color photos of identifiable and unidentifiable objects in three conditions in which an identifiable object preceded a related identifiable object, an unrelated identifiable object, and an unidentifiable object. Replicating earlier work, they found both a negativity at 300 ms as well as an N400 to the unrelated and unidentifiable objects. The N400 exhibited an atypical frontal distribution that was attributed to the frontal distribution of the adjoining negativity at 300 ms. An argument was made that as no equivalent of the N300 had been seen to linguistic stimuli it might be a response specific to objects/pictures. We now know that a similar response is seen to linguistic stimuli but that fact does not invalidate the proposal that the "N300" may be object/picture specific. Again, the possibility is raised that both the PMN and N300 may reflect the action of similar neural populations that reflect pre-semantic processes (phonological and object based, respectively) that facilitate subsequent semantic evaluation of a stimulus.

In a similar vein, simple multiplication problems in which the answer is incorrect exhibit an N400 that is smaller if the incorrect solution is conceptually related to one of the operands in a manner similar to contextual modulation of the language-related N400 (Niedeggen et al., 1999). The explanation of this N400 effect is a combination of activation spread and controlled processing mechanisms. A particularly interesting aspect of this study is that the authors take the position that treating the N400 as a unitary monolithic phenomenon is likely to be incorrect. They divided the N400 component into three sections: the ascending limb, the peak, and the descending tail of the waveform. Having done this, they demonstrate that the ascending limb appears related to automatic aspects of activation spread while the descending limb is associated with the more controlled processing functions. This study represents another instantiation of a recurring theme: the N400 is not a unitary phenomenon and/or there are other independent but related components (PMN, N300, N280/LPN) that play an important role in how the process(es) reflected by the N400 fulfills its functional duties within a broadly defined conceptual-semantic system. A final note regarding these earlier components is that they are often difficult to observe in grand averages due, as Münte and colleagues suggest, to their overlap with the larger N400. Connolly and colleagues have made a similar argument regarding the PMN and added that these responses may show individual differences in processing speeds, for example, leading to their "loss" in grand averages despite being clear in individual's waveforms.

Finally, the importance of the conceptual system(s) reflected by the N400 is emphasized by the fact that it has become one of the principal components utilized in recent research using ERPs as clinical assessment tools in brain-injured populations (**Box 2**).

Left Anterior Negativities (LANs) and P600s in Morpho-Syntactic Processing

In order to understand the difference between *John is hitting the ball* and *John was hit by the ball* our brain is not only required to identify the conceptual meaning of content words (*John, hit, ball*) but it also needs to analyze the grammatical relations between them. This syntactic parsing of the hierarchical structure of utterances will reveal whether *John* is the agent of the action, and whether this action is continuing or has been completed. Parsing takes place incrementally in real time at rates of approximately three words per second and involves (1) the analysis of word order and word category information including function words (*is, the, was, by*) and (2) the checking of certain features that need to be congruent between linked sentence constituents (e.g., subject–verb agreement in English).

The most common way of studying ERP correlates of morpho-syntactic processing has utilized violation paradigms. The rationale is that violations should disrupt or increase the workload of the brain systems underlying the type of processing that is of interest. These changes are intended to elicit a specific differential ERP. Two such ERP components have indeed been identified as markers of two stages of syntactic processing: an early, often left-lateralized anterior negativity (LAN) typically occurring between 100 and 500 ms that has been linked to automatic first pass parsing, and a late centro-parietal positive component between 500 and 1000 ms (P600), that may reflect rather controlled attempts to reanalyze and fix the anomaly at a later stage (**Figure 3**). The qualitative differences between these two components and the semantic N400 have been taken as evidence that syntactic and semantic information are processed differently in the brain (Osterhout & Holcomb, 1992).

Box 2 Clinical assessment of language using cognitive ERP

Unlike the history of evoked potentials in assessing sensory function (EP; Chiappa, 1997) cognitive ERP have only recently been employed to examine patients' language abilities and the functional integrity of systems upon which language depends. The failure to employ ERP in clinical settings was partially due to the outdated belief that these components were insufficiently reliable in their occurrence, physical characteristics (such as latency), and functional specificity. Today, however, a high level of specificity and replicability have been established, in some cases by adapting psychometrically valid neuropsychological tests for computer presentation and simultaneous ERP recording. These tests provide a method for neuropsychological assessment of patients who are otherwise impossible to assess due to the severity of their brain injuries, for example, after stroke (D'Arcy et al., 2003). The link between basic research and clinical application is exemplified by an auditory ERP study that tested semantic and phonological sentence processing in a traumatic brain injury patient in a persistent vegetative state (Connolly et al., 1999). The top part of the figure shows axial computerized tomography (CT) scans of patient's head. Left brain is on the right side of scan, the entry wound is left frontal. Three-dimensional figures in the bottom part depict N400 responses in the left (T3–F3) and right (T4–F4) hemisphere to sentences such as *The gambler had a streak of bad luggage* (see Sections 2.2 and 2.3). Amplitude is on left vertical axis, scalp location on bottom axis, and time (ms) on right axis. Despite his apparent vegetative state, the patient exhibited classic N400 responses to the semantically incongruous sentence endings. Having demonstrated the patient's comprehension abilities were intact, the inference was drawn that he was mentally intact and possessing sufficient mental resources to merit rehabilitation (ultimately highly successful) instead of the scheduled discharge to a long-stay facility and the associated poor prognosis for patients in such conditions.

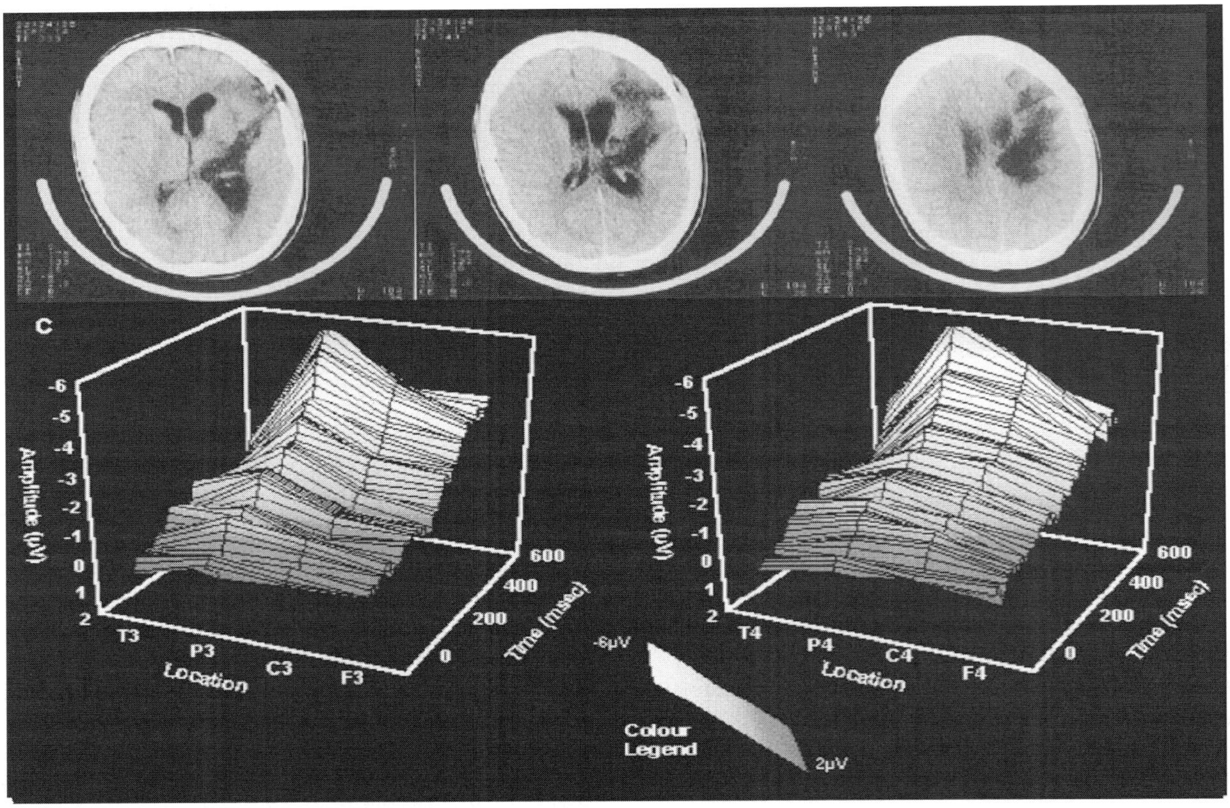

Chiappa, K.H. (1997). *Evoked potentials in clinical medicine* (3rd edn). New York: Lippincott-Raven.

Connolly, J.F., Mate-Kole, C.C., & Joyce, B.M. (1999). Global aphasia: An innovative assessment approach. *Archives of Physical Medicine and Rehabilitation, 80*, 1309–1315.

D'Arcy, R.C.N., Marchand, Y., Eskes, G.A., Harrison, E.R., Phillips, S.J., Major, A., & Connolly, J.F. (2003). Electrophysiological assessment of language function following stroke. *Clinical Neurophysiology, 114*, 662–672.

Early and Other Left Anterior Negativities

LANs have primarily been reported for outright syntactic violations and not, for example, for structure ambiguities. Typical conditions eliciting LANs are word category violations (in *2a,b*; Neville et al., 1991; Friederici, 2002) and violations of number agreement between the subject and verb (*2c*). (*Note*: an asterisk "*" marks the ungrammatical word.)

(*2a*) *He criticized Max's * of proof the theorem*

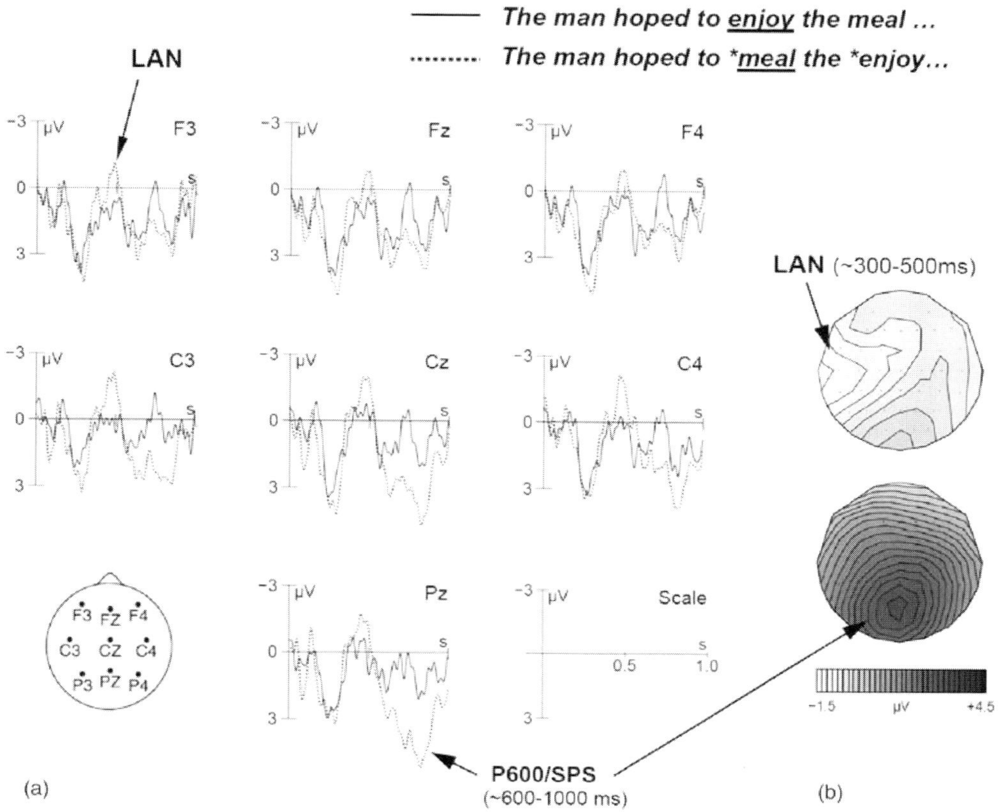

Figure 3 Biphasic LAN and P600 pattern elicited by syntactic word category violations in an English reading study. Negative polarity is plotted upwards. (a) ERP plots of the ungrammatical target words (dotted lines) show a LAN effect between 300 and 500 ms, that is in a similar time interval as the N400 (see Figure 2(a)), which was followed by a late posterior P600/SPS between 600 and 1000 ms. (b) Voltage maps of the difference waves (violation minus correct control) illustrate the scalp distribution of both ERP components (Steinhauer, unpublished data).

*(2b) Die Bluse wurde am *ge-bügelt* (The blouse was at the *ironed)
*(2c) The children *plays in the garden*

Among these, only word category violations (*2a,b*) have been found to yield a particularly early LAN (ELAN) between 100 and 300 ms, which appeared more reliable in auditory than visual studies, and has been linked to neural generators in Broca's area and the anterior temporal lobe. Some models suggest that this ELAN is distinct from other later LAN effects and reflects interruptions of highly automatic processes during the very first phase of building up a phrase structural representation that is required in subsequent processing stages. Within this framework, other morpho-syntactic operations (and respective violations) affecting agreement features or verb arguments which already depend on a phrase marker, are processed in parallel to semantic information, and elicit the later LANs between 300 and 500 ms (concurrently with the semantic N400; Rossi et al., 2005). Unlike P600s (see Section 2.6), ELANs were not influenced by the relative proportion of violations in an experiment, suggesting their "autonomous" status independent of processing strategies (Hahne & Friederici, 1999).

In psycholinguistics, the short latency of the "syntactic" ELAN component has been of theoretical importance as it lent strong empirical support to so-called syntax first models that claim an initial autonomy phase for the syntactic parsing device, as opposed to more interactive models. However, the short ELAN latency has convincingly been shown to depend on the rapid availability of word category information in the respective experimental paradigms (e.g., the prefix *ge* in the prevailing German paradigm in (*2b*)), rather than the proposed early stage of processing *per se*. In absence of such early phonological markers, word category violations elicit LANs in the typical 300–500 ms time window of other morpho-syntactic violations (Hagoort et al., 2003), even though primacy of syntactic over semantic processes may still hold. The critical impact of phonological markers on the ELAN latency raises yet another issue; since the German prefix *ge* is not restricted to verb forms (and, therefore, is not a reliable word category marker), the ELAN likely reflects violations of phonological expectations related to word category violations rather than an automatic response to syntactic violations as such. This in itself, however, is remarkable as it suggests an extremely early phonological mismatch/detection mechanism based on experimental processing regularities and resulting expectations, modulating the ERP in less than 200 ms. Such an account may also explain the modality differences, that is, the greater robustness of ELANs in auditory experiments. Compatible with this notion are studies that reported a similar early anterior negativity over the right hemisphere (ERAN (early right-anterior negativity)) for certain musical violations (Patel et al., 1998). Hagoort et al. (2003) set out to replicate ELAN effects in a Dutch reading study that avoided word initial markings of the word category. As expected, they observed an anterior negativity only between 300 and 500 ms which, moreover, was bilaterally distributed rather than left lateralized. Lau et al. (2006) found that clear LAN-like effects occurred only if local phrase structure imposed high constraints on the target word, whereas less predictable structures resulted in attenuated LAN effects. Predictability and expectations may be crucial to our understanding of LAN-like effects in morpho-syntactic processing more generally. Previous reviews have argued that failure to replicate [E]LANs was due to the failure to create outright syntax violations. However, even the standard paradigm used to successfully elicit ELAN effects in German in (*2b*) does actually not meet this particular criterion (see (*3*)). That is, at the position of the supposed "outright violation" sentences can still be completed such that a syntactically correct (although semantically somewhat odd) sentence results:

(*3*) *Die Bluse wurde am gebügelt noch festlicher wirkenden Jackett mit Nadeln befestigt*
The blouse was to the ironed even more festive seeming jacket with pins fixed (Literal translation)
The blouse was pinned to the jacket which, after being ironed, appeared even more festive (Paraphrase)

The adverbial and adjectival use of participles in German illustrated in (*3*) poses a major problem to the traditional interpretation of ELAN components. Based on word category information alone, the brain has simply no reason to assume an outright syntax violation, unless (a) it either knows in advance that such sentences are not included in the experiment (i.e., a pragmatic constraint) or (b) it uses prosodic cues (or punctuation) to determine that the sentence will not be continued beyond the past participle. In this latter case, however, the word category is entirely irrelevant as *any* single-word completion following *am* would cause a syntax violation.

To summarize, whereas the ELAN appears to be related to violations of expected speech sounds or orthographic patterns in particularly constrained structural environments, the somewhat later anterior negativities between 300 and 500 ms may be more directly linked to structural/syntactic processes proper. Several current models have associated these later LAN components with (the interruption of) proceduralized cognitive operations such as rule-based sequencing or structural unifications, either within the linguistic domain or across cognitive domains (see Chapter 18, this volume; Hoen & Dominey, 2000). In fact, there exist a few reports of LAN-like effects for non-linguistic sequencing (Hoen & Dominey, 2000). A rule-based interpretation of LANs beyond syntax would also be compatible with LAN effects found for over-regularizations in morphophonology (e.g., *childs* instead of *children*).

Working Memory

In the previous section we discussed rule-based accounts of LAN-like components. Another account explains these components in terms of working memory (WM) load increases. This appears appropriate for syntactic structures involving long-distance dependencies (such as *wh* questions) and may, in fact, refer to a distinct set of left anterior negativities. LAN effects reflecting WM load usually tend to display broader distributions and longer durations than the focal, transient morpho-syntactic LAN components (Martin-Loeches et al., 2005). Whether a unified WM-based LAN interpretation could appropriately account for LANs elicited by word category or agreement violations remains a controversial issue.

Scalp Distribution of LAN Components

Despite their name, the scalp distribution of LAN-like components is not always left lateralized, nor is it always frontal. Factors underlying this variability are not well understood, nor are the reasons explaining why the same paradigm employed for eliciting LANs in some studies fail to do so in others (Lau et al., 2006). The consistency of phonological or orthographic markings along with predictable sentence structures may be important for the elicitation of ELAN components. Recent data indicate that left lateralization of LANs may be modulated by linguistic proficiency levels even in native speakers (Pakulak & Neville, 2004).

P600/Syntactic Positive Shift

The second syntax-related ERP component is a late positivity between 500 and 1000 ms, dubbed the P600 (Osterhout & Holcomb, 1992) or *syntactic positive shift* (SPS), which may be preceded by [E]LAN components (**Figure 3**). The P600/SPS has been linked to more controlled processes during second pass parsing and, unlike LANs, is often found to be modulated by non-syntactic factors including semantic information, processing strategies, and experimental tasks. P600 components have been found across languages for a large variety of linguistic anomalies, such as (a) nonpr-preferred "garden path" sentences that require structural reanalyses due to local ambiguities (Osterhout & Holcomb, 1992; Mecklinger et al., 1995; Steinhauer et al., 1999) and (b) most types of morpho-syntactic violations (such as those in *1a, b, c*). Kaan et al. (2000) demonstrated that structurally more complex sentences may evoke a P600 even in the absence of any violation or ambiguity. Taken together, these findings would suggest that the P600/SPS is a rather general marker for structural processing.

The considerable range of (linguistic) phenomena eliciting P600 effects raised the question of whether this response was language-specific at all. A direct comparison of linguistic and musical violations found P600-like waveforms in *both* domains; moreover, their amplitudes displayed parametric modulation as a function of violation strength (Patel et al., 1998) – a finding that clearly questions the P600 as a language-specific response. It was suggested the P600/SPS may rather be viewed as a member of the *P300 family* of WM-related components, providing a parsimonious domain-general P600 account (Coulson et al., 1998; but see Friederici et al., 2001). Studies examined if the P600 behaved like a P300 and shared its topographical profile, but the overall results were inconclusive. For example, increasing the probability of violations did reduce the P600 amplitude in some studies (pro P300 interpretation) but not in others (contra P300) (Friederici et al., 2001). Patient data showed that basal ganglia lesions affect only the P600 but not the parietal P300 (Kotz et al., 2003), suggesting a dissociation of the components. Current thinking is that the P600 should not be viewed as a monolithic component, but may occasionally comprise P3b-like subcomponents. This hypothesis was strongly supported by a study using temporal–spatial principle component analysis (PCA) to tease apart P600 subcomponents (Friederici et al., 2001). In fact, the authors suggested that P600 subcomponents may reflect the diagnosis of syntactic problems, attempts to fix them, secondary checking processes, and phonological revisions.

Verb Argument Structure Violations and Thematic Roles

Verb argument structure violations seem to elicit more complex patterns than other violations, arguably because they affect thematic role assignments (i.e., "who did what to whom?") in addition to syntactic aspects. These effects also vary across languages. A German study found that, whereas violating the case of an object noun phrase (NP) by swapping dative and accusative case markings elicited a LAN/P600, violating the *number* of arguments by adding a direct object NP to an intransitive verb, as in *(4)*, evoked an N400/P600 instead (Friederici & Frisch, 2000).

*(4) Sie weiß, dass der Kommissar (NOM) den Banker (ACC) *abreiste (V)*
She knows that the inspector (NOM) the banker (ACC) departed (V, intransitive)

Revisions of case assignment elicited N400 effects (sometimes without P600s), while thematic role revisions yielded P600-like positivities (sometimes without preceding negativities) (Bornkessel & Schlesewsky, 2006; Kuperberg et al., 2006). The most striking findings in this respect have been unexpected P600s instead of N400s for sentences in which the thematic roles violated animacy constraints as in *(5)*.

(5) For breakfast the eggs would only #eat toast and jam.

Several research groups have suggested that these findings may require a reinterpretation of P600 (sub)components, for example in terms of a re-checking mechanism in cases of conflicts between the syntactic parser and a parallel thematic evaluation heuristics (e.g., van Herten et al., 2005).

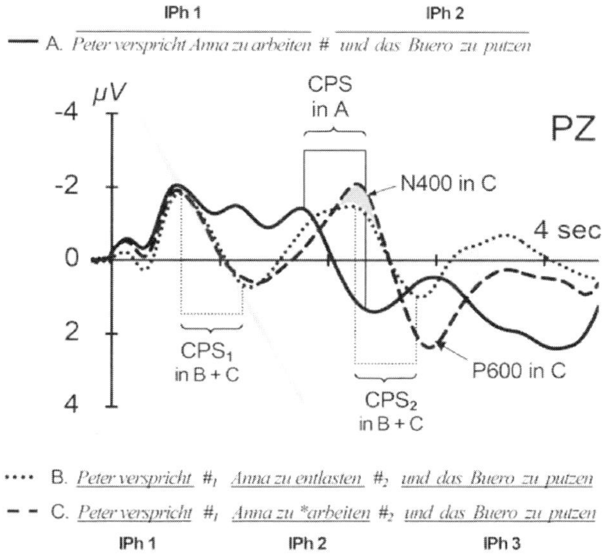

Figure 4 Illustration of the closure positive shift (CPS) at prosodic boundaries of spoken German sentences, and a prosody-induced syntax violation negative polarity is plotted upwards. Boundary positions and intonational phrases (IPh) are aligned to the time axis. Sentence A (solid line) has only one prosodic boundary (#) after the verb "arbeiten," while B (dotted line) and violation condition C (dashed line) have two such boundaries. At each boundary position a large CPS component was elicited in each condition. Magnitude and slope of the CPS (illustrated by the thick gray line at CPS1) are very similar at all boundary positions. In C, the syntax-prosody mismatch on the verb "arbeiten" additionally elicited an N400/P600 pattern which superimposes the second CPS. Waveforms represent a grand average ERP at PZ across 40 subjects and approximately 5000 trials per condition. Prosodic boundary information is not only important during language learning but also guides the listener's syntactic analysis and sentence comprehension. *Source*: Modified after Steinhauer (2003) and Steinhauer et al. (1999). Translation of sentences: A. Peter promises Anna to work # and to clean the office. B. Peter promises # to support Anna # and to clean the office. C. Peter promises # * [to work Anna] # and to clean the office. (Conditions A and C are lexically identical and differ only prosodically.)

Interactions Between Syntax, Semantics, Discourse, and Prosody

Some of the most interesting questions in psycholinguistics concern the integration and interplay of different kinds of information, such as syntax and semantics. Can the syntactic parser be viewed as an autonomous, encapsulated module, as suggested by some "syntax first" models? Or rather is there a continuous multidirectional exchange of all varieties of information as proposed by interactive models? How do N400, LANs, and P600s interact in the case of double violations?

As far as the incoming target word itself is concerned, most available data suggest an early stage of largely parallel semantic/thematic and morpho-syntactic processing followed by a later integration stage (P600 interval) that allows for interaction between different types of information. Thus double violations typically tend to elicit additive effects of a syntactic LAN/P600 pattern and a semantic N400 with possible non-additive modulations of the P600 (Osterhout & Nicol, 1999; Gunter et al., 1997).

One exception, however, is that unlike other syntax violations, word category violations seem to require

Box 3 Order of emerging ERP components in language development

Language-related ERP components emerge during childhood in a temporal order that nicely corresponds to the development of respective linguistic and cognitive subdomains. As a general pattern, ERP components in childhood are initially larger and more broadly distributed both spatially and temporally and develop the more focused and specialized ERP profiles of adults usually until puberty (Holcomb et al., 1992; Mills et al., 1997; Hahne et al., 2004). The diagram illustrates the timeline of cognitive development and the emergence of corresponding ERP components during the first 3 years of life (adapted from Friederici, 2006). The MMN reflecting one's ability to discriminate sounds is the earliest ERP response and is already present in newborns. During the first months, babies are able to discriminate phonemes of all natural languages. However, at about 10 months a particular specialization for sound distinctions important in their mother tongue is reflected by larger and more robust MMN effects whereas speech sounds that do not belong to the phonemic inventory of their first language lose the ability to elicit MMNs (categorical perception). The next ERP response found in infants is the CPS reflecting prosodic phrasing. The CPS is present no later than at 8 months, that is, when infants are able to distinguish between adequate and inadequate pausing in speech. As large prosodic boundaries typically coincide with syntactic boundaries and the presence of function words, the presence of the CPS component may indicate the onset of "phonological bootstrapping" in language acquisition. The lexico-semantic N400 component emerges at 12–14 months, just after infants have started to babble. The N400 was observed when infants saw a picture of an animal or simple object (e.g., a dog) and heard a word that did not match (e.g., pencil). Last, LAN and P600 responses to simple syntactic violations develop only 1 year later, at an age of 24 months (P600) and 32 months (LAN).

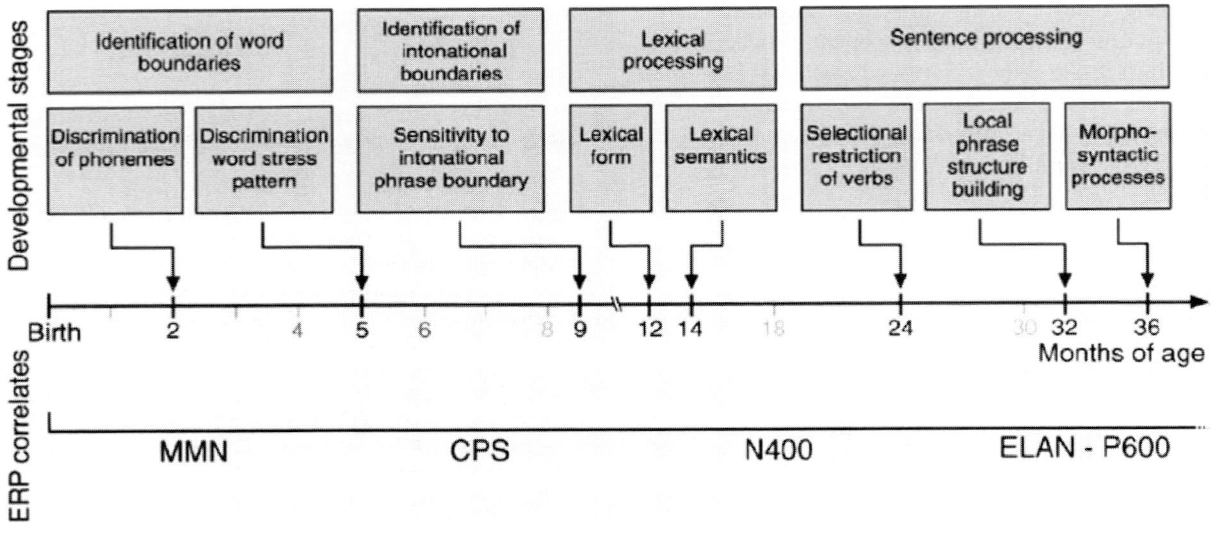

Friederici, A.D. (2006). Neurophysiological markers of early language acquisition: From syllables to sentences. *Trends in Cognitive Science*, *9*(10), 481–488.

Hahne, A., Eckstein, K., & Friederici, A.D. (2004). Brain signatures of syntactic and semantic processes during children's language development. *Journal of Cognitive Neuroscience*, *16*(7), 1302–1318.

Holcomb, P.J., Coffey, S.A., & Neville, H.J. (1992). Visual and auditory sentence processing: A developmental analysis using event-related brain potentials. *Developmental Neuropsychology*, *8*(2/3), 203–241.

Mills, D.L., et al. (1997). Language comprehension and cerebral specialization from 13 to 20 months. *Developmental Neuropsychology*, *13*, 397–445.

immediate phrase structural revision and thus temporarily block further semantic processing during this period (thereby preventing or delaying N400 effects of the semantic incongruency). Thus, in a standard grammaticality judgment task, these double violations did not elicit a late N400-like response until a P600 reflecting a structure revision had already occurred (Friederici et al., 1999). This suggests that semantic integration in sentences is at least partly guided by syntactic structure. Typical N400s were observed only if semantic task instructions explicitly required instant semantic integration. Conversely, in order for semantic information to be able to influence syntactic parsing decisions, it must be available much earlier in the sentence, or may not show an effect at all. A study on German "garden path" sentences by Mecklinger et al. (1995) demonstrated that even reliable semantic plausibility information failed to facilitate syntactic reanalysis suggesting that initial syntactic analyses are relatively independent from local semantic information.

However, there are at least two types of contextual information that have been shown to radically change initial parsing preferences: referential support and prosodic cues. First, van Berkum et al. (1999) demonstrated that a discourse providing either one or two potential referents for a NP determined whether readers were biased toward a complement clause or relative clause reading. If a context

Box 4 ERP components in second language: evidence for "critical periods?"

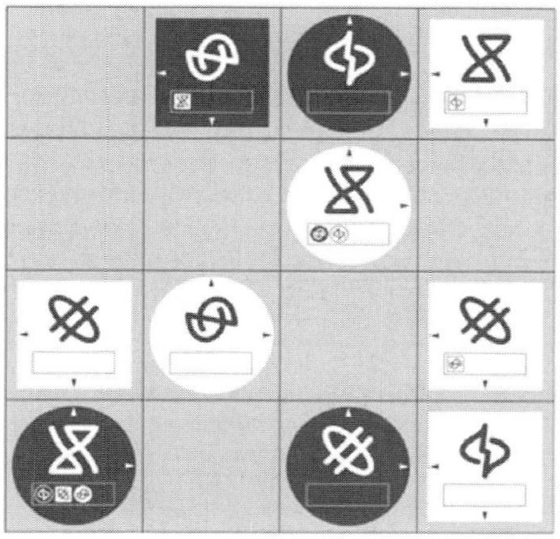

(a)

The content words and their semantics

Nouns (N)	
tok	(object identifier)
plox	(object identifier)
gum	(object identifier)
trul	(object identifier)
Verbs (v)	
prez	capture
pel	release
glif	swap
rix	buy
Adjectives (M)	
füne	round
böke	square
Adverbs (m)	
rüfi	vertically
nöri	horizontally

(b)

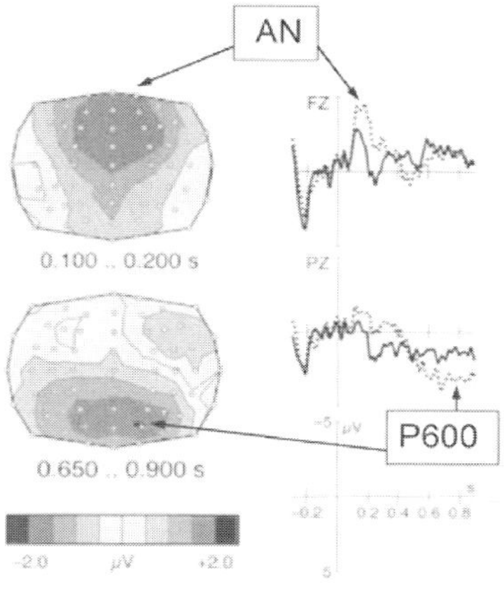

(c)

Native-like mastery of a language seems almost impossible if this language was not acquired early in childhood. This observation is often explained with an early "critical period" (CP) during which the brain is particularly well prepared to learn the sounds, words, and grammatical rules. An ERP study by Weber-Fox and Neville (1996) tested Chinese subjects who had learned English at different ages, and found support for a CP in syntactic but not semantic processing. Semantic anomalies elicited native-like N400s in all groups, but even short delays in age of exposure to English prevented LANs in syntax conditions. More posterior and right-lateralized negativities, delayed P600/SPS components, or no ERP effects were found instead. Data seemed to indicate that late L2 learners are unable to do early automatic parsing and rely on compensatory brain mechanisms that are distinct from those of native speakers. Alternatively, ERPs might primarily reflect the level of proficiency which was at least partially confounded with age of exposure. To tease these factors apart, Friederici et al. (2002) trained adult subjects in the artificial miniature language "Brocanto" to native-like proficiency. A computer-implemented chess-like board game (panel a) was employed to engage subjects in speaking Brocanto: sentences referred to the moves of the game (panel b). After training, high proficient subjects displayed the typical "native-like" ERP patterns of syntactic processing (panel c): an early anterior negativity (AN) followed by a P600, here shown for a syntactic subcondition that was controlled for transfer effects between first language (German) and second language (Brocanto). Subsequent studies investigating adult L2 learners of *natural* languages found similar but mixed evidence (Clahsen & Felser, 2006; Steinhauer et al., 2006). Overall, while ERP support for a CP in L2 grammar learning appeared unambiguous by 2001, more detailed research and new paradigms have raised new controversies.

Clahsen, H., & Felser, C. (2006). Grammatical processing in language learners. *Applied Psycholinguistics*, *27*(1), 3–42.

Friederici, A.D., Steinhauer, K., & Pfeifer, E. (2002). Brain signatures of artificial language processing: Evidence challenging the critical period hypothesis. *Proceedings of the National Academy of Sciences*, *99*(1), 529–534.

Steinhauer, K., White, E., King, E., Cornell, S., Genesee, F., & White, L. (2006). The neural dynamics of second language acquisition: Evidence from event-related potentials. *Journal of Cognitive Neuroscience*, Supplement 1, 99.

Weber-Fox, C.M., & Neville, H.J. (1996). Maturational constraints on functional specializations for language processing: ERP and behavioral evidence in bilingual speakers. *Journal of Cognitive Neuroscience*, *8*(3), 231–256.

Source: Modified after Friederici et al. (2002); Figures 2 and 4.

sentence had introduced "*two* girls" in the discourse, a singular NP "*the* girl" required further specification, thus favoring the (usually non-preferred) relative clause reading (as indicated by an enhanced P600/SPS component). Second, Steinhauer et al. (1999) demonstrated that prosodic information in speech can dramatically alter parsing preferences typical for reading. This study showed that the presence or absence of an intonational phrase boundary determined whether the following NP was parsed as the object of either a preceding verb or a subsequent verb. Introducing prosodic boundaries between verbs and their object NPs caused a prosody-induced verb argument structure violation which elicited an N400/P600 pattern to the incompatible verb (*cf.* condition C in **Figure 4**). These two studies demonstrate that at least some kinds of context information can immediately influence the syntactic parsing mechanism.

Prosodic Phrasing: The Closure Positive Shift

The Steinhauer et al. (1999) study discussed above also identified a novel ERP correlate of prosodic processing, which was labeled the *closure positive shift* (CPS; **Figure 4**). This component is reliably elicited at prosodic boundaries and is assumed to reflect prosodic phrasing (closure of intonational phrases) in listeners cross-linguistically. Unlike most other language-related components, it is independent of linguistic violations. In both first and second language acquisition the CPS is among the first brain responses observed (see **Boxes 3** and **4**) and may help learners identify syntactic phrase boundaries and even word boundaries. The CPS is also elicited (1) by boundaries in delexicalized and hummed sentence melodies and (2) during silent reading, both at comma positions and when subjects were instructed to reproduce prosodic boundaries at specific positions (Steinhauer & Friederici, 2001). The former finding suggests that the CPS is independent of lexical/syntactic information and may be domain general; the latter one establishes a link between covert prosody and punctuation (in reading and writing). By revealing that, and how, prosody guides language processing, ERPs have addressed longstanding issues in psycholinguistics.

Challenges and Future Directions

During the last 25 years, electrophysiological investigations have contributed to our understanding of the various processes involved in speech and text comprehension, their roles in language development and clinical applications. In all of these areas there remain many new and interesting challenges to be met.

What different kinds of cognitive subprocesses contribute to the classical ERP components discussed above? Do language-specific ERP (sub)components exist?

What more can ERPs tell us about shared domain space amongst language, music, and other cognitive domains?

How can we move beyond "violation paradigms" in isolated words and sentences towards more ecologically valid paradigms of language processing?

What are the differential effects of explicit (e.g., classroom) versus implicit (e.g., immersion-like) training environments on L2 acquisition? How do they affect which brain systems are involved in language?

References

Bornkessel, I and Schlesewsky, M (2006). The extended argument dependency model: A neurocognitive approach to sentence comprehension across languages. *Psychological Review* 113(4): 787–821.

Connolly, J, Phillips, N, Stewart, S, and Brake, W (1992). Event-related potential sensitivity to acoustic and semantic properties of terminal words in sentences. *Brain and Language* 43(1): 1–18.

Connolly, JF and Phillips, NA (1994). Event-related potential components reflect phonological and semantic processing of the terminal word of spoken sentences. *Journal of Cognitive Neuroscience* 6(3): 256–266.

Coulson, S, King, JW, and Kutas, M (1998). ERPs and domain specificity: Beating a straw horse. *Language and Cognitive Processes* 13(6): 653–672.

D'Arcy, RCN, Connolly, JF, Service, E, Hawco, CS, and Houlihan, ME (2004). Separating phonological and semantic processing in auditory sentence processing: A high-resolution event-related brain potential study. *Human Brain Mapping* 22(1): 40–51.

Friederici, AD (2002). Towards a neural basis of auditory sentence processing. *Trends in Cognitive Sciences* 6(2): 78–84.

Friederici, AD and Frisch, S (2000). Verb-argument structure processing: The role of verb-specific and argument-specific information. *Journal of Memory and Language* 43: 476–507.

Friederici, AD, Steinhauer, K, and Frisch, S (1999). Lexical integration: Sequential effects of syntactic and semantic information. *Memory and Cognition* 27(3): 438–453.

Friederici, AD, Mecklinger, A, Spencer, KM, Steinhauer, K, and Donchin, E (2001). Syntactic parsing preferences and their on-line revisions: A spatio-temporal analysis of event-related brain potentials. *Cognitive Brain Research* 11(2): 305–323.

Gunter, TC, Stowe, LA, and Mulder, G (1997). When syntax meets semantics. *Psychophysiology* 34(6): 660–676.

Hagoort, P, Wassenaar, M, and Brown, C (2003). Syntax-related ERP-effects in Dutch. *Cognitive Brain Research* 16(1): 38–50.

Hahne, A and Friederici, AD (1999). Electrophysiological evidence for two steps in syntactic analysis: Early automatic and late controlled processes. *Journal of Cognitive Neuroscience* 11(2): 194–205.

Hoen, M and Dominey, PF (2000). ERP analysis of cognitive sequencing: A left anterior negativity related to structural transformation processing. *Neuroreport* 11(14): 3187–3191.

Holcomb, P, Grainger, J, and O'Rourke, T (2002). An electrophysiological study of the effects of orthographic neighborhood size on printed word perception. *Journal of Cognitive Neuroscience* 14(6): 938–950.

Kaan, E, Harris, A, Gibson, E, and Holcomb, P (2000). The P600 as an index of syntactic integration difficulty. *Language and Cognitive Processes* 15(2): 159–201.

Kotz, SA, Frisch, S, von Cramon, DY, and Friederici, AD (2003). Syntactic language processing: ERP lesion data on the role of the basal ganglia. *Journal of the International Neuropsychological Society* 9(7): 1053–1060.

Kujala, A, Alho, K, Service, E, Ilmoniemi, RJ, and Connolly, JF (2004). Activation in the anterior left auditory cortex associated with phonological analysis of speech input: Localization of the phonological mismatch negativity response with MEG. *Cognitive Brain Research* 21(1): 106–113.

Kuperberg, GR, Caplan, D, Sitnikova, T, Eddy, M, and Holcomb, PJ (2006). Neural correlates of processing syntactic, semantic, and thematic relationships in sentences. *Language and Cognitive Processes* 21(5): 489–530.
Kutas, M and Hillyard, SA (1980). Reading senseless sentences: Brain potentials reflect semantic incongruity. *Science* 207(1): 203–205.
Lau, E, Stroud, C, Plesch, S, and Phillips, C (2006). The role of structural prediction in rapid syntactic analysis. *Brain and Language* 98(1): 74–88.
Martin-Loeches, M, Muñoz, F, Casado, P, Melcon, A, and Fernandez-Frias, C (2005). Are the anterior negativities to grammatical violations indexing working memory? *Psychophysiology* 42(5): 508–519.
McPherson, WB and Holcomb, PJ (1999). An electrophysiological investigation of semantic priming with pictures of real objects. *Psychophysiology* 36(1): 53–65.
Mecklinger, A, Schriefers, H, Steinhauer, K, and Friederici, AD (1995). Processing relative clauses varying on syntactic and semantic dimensions: An analysis with event-related potentials. *Memory and Cognition* 23(4): 477–494.
Münte, TF, Wieringa, BM, Weyerts, H, Szentkuti, A, Matzke, M, and Johannes, S (2001). Differences in brain potentials to open and closed class words: Class and frequency effects. *Neuropsychologia* 39(1): 91–102.
Neville, H, Nicol, JL, Barss, A, Forster, KI, and Garrett, MF (1991). Syntactically based sentence processing classes: Evidence from eventrelated brain potentials. *Journal of Cognitive Neuroscience* 3(2): 151–165.
Newman, RL, Connolly, JF, Service, E, and McIvor, K (2003). Influence of phonological expectations during a phoneme deletion task: Evidence from event-related brain potentials. *Psychophysiology* 40(4): 640–647.
Niedeggen, M, Rosler, F, and Jost, K (1999). Processing of incongruous mental calculation problems: Evidence for an arithmetic N400 effect. *Psychophysiology* 36(3): 307–324.
Osterhout, L and Holcomb, PJ (1992). Event-related brain potentials elicited by syntactic anomaly. *Journal of Memory and Language* 31: 785–806.
Osterhout, L and Nicol, J (1999). On the distinctiveness, independence, and time course of the brain responses to syntactic and pragmatic anomalies. *Language and Cognitive Processes* 14(3): 283–317.
Pakulak, E and Neville, H (2004). *Individual differences in online syntactic processing in monolingual adults as reflected by ERPs*, pp. 149. 17th Annual CUNY Conference on Human Sentence ProcessingMaryland, USA: College Park.
Patel, AD, Gibson, E, Ratner, J, Besson, M, and Holcomb, PJ (1998). Processing syntactic relations in language and music: An event-related potential study. *Journal of Cognitive Neuroscience* 10(6): 717–733.
Rossi, S, Gugler, MF, Hahne, A, and Friederici, AD (2005). When word category information encounters morphosyntax: An ERP study. *Neuroscience Letters* 384(3): 228–233
Sanders, LD and Neville, HJ (2003). An ERP study of continuous speech processing. II. Segmentation, semantics, and syntax in non-native speakers. *Cognitive Brain Research* 15(3): 214–227.
Steinhauer, K (2003). Electrophysiological correlates of prosody and punctuation. *Brain and Language* 86: 142–164.
Steinhauer, K and Friederici, A (2001). Prosodic boundaries, comma rules, and brain responses: The closure positive shift in ERPs as a universal marker for prosodic phrasing in listeners and readers. *Journal of Psycholinguistic Research* 30(3): 267–295.
Steinhauer, K, Alter, K, and Friederici, AD (1999). Brain potentials indicate immediate use of prosodic cues in natural speech processing. *Nature Neuroscience* 2(2): 191–196.
Steinhauer, K, Pancheva, R, Newman, AJ, Gennari, S, and Ullman, MT (2001). How the mass counts: An electrophysiological approach to the processing of lexical features. *Neuroreport* 12(5): 999–1005.
van Berkum, JJ, Hagoort, P, and Brown, C (1999). Semantic integration in sentences and discourse: Evidence from the N400. *Journal of Cognitive Neuroscience* 11(6): 657–671.
van Herten, M, Kolk, HHJ, and Chwilla, DJ (2005). An ERP study of P600 effects elicited by semantic anomalies. *Cognitive Brain Research* 22(2): 241–255.
Van Petten, C and Luka, BJ (2006). Neural localization of semantic context effects in electromagnetic and hemodynamic studies. *Brain and Language* 97(3): 279–293.

Further Reading

Brown, CM and Hagoort, P (eds.) (2000). *The neurocognition of language.* Oxford, UK: Oxford University Press.
This work provides a critical overview of how neurocognitive methods have been used to address psycholinguistic research questions in listeners, readers, and speakers, focusing in particular on electrophysiological techniques (EEG, ERPs, MEG). The book first introduces the reader to linguistic theory, psycholinguistics, and cognitive neuroscience, and then explains how current theories and models have been tested using brain imaging and ERPs.
Handy, TC (ed.) (2005). *Event-related potentials: A methods handbook.* Cambridge, MA: The MIT Press.
Provides a good introduction to the world of ERP recording, analysis, and evaluation.
Nunez, PL and Srinivasan, R (2006). Electric fields of the brain: The neurophysics of EEG. Oxford, UK: Oxford University Press.
The definitive and comprehensive text on the EEG signal from the relevant principles of physics to the analysis of the response with extensive discussion of issues related to recording the EEG (e.g., choosing the best reference)
Rugg, MD and Coles, MGH (1996). Electrophysiology of mind. Oxford, UK: Oxford University Press.
Despite its age, this classic book is one of the best introductions to ERPs in cognitive neuroscience.
Zani, A and Proverbio, A (eds.) (2003). *The cognitive electrophysiology of mind and brain.* Amsterdam: Academic Press.
An introduction to EEG/ERP and MEG measures in perception, language, and memory.

F

Fluency and Voice, Disorders of

D. B. Rosenfield, The Methodist Hospital/Weill Cornell College of Medicine, Houston, TX, USA

Definition

There are multiple definitions of stuttering (Bloodstein, 1995; Conture, 2001). At issue is the question of what a 'stutter' is. If a child bounces on a sound, or someone repeats a whole word, is that a stuttered dysfluency? Should investigators consider dysfluency in adult stutterers isomorphic to the effortless dysfluency ('normal fluency of childhood') seen frequently among children? How we answer these questions affects our inquiries into the etiology of dysfluency.

Children who stutter (those with developmental stuttering [DS]) have difficulty producing the intended sounds and words. Their language is normal, but their speech is not. Location of stuttered dysfluencies in DS is not random. These are located at the beginning of sentences and phrases and are associated with part-word repetitions, as opposed to repetition of whole words or phrases. Sometimes the child will back up in sentence production and repeat whole phrases in an effort to overcome the dysfluency. However, the core problem of the dysfluency (i.e., definition) remains the repetition of a single sound or a fragment of a word (Bloodstein, 1995).

In an effort to overcome these dysfluencies, the stuttering child often engages in circumlocutions, substituting one word for the other. Thus, a child who stutters might say "g-g-g ... see you later," instead of continuing to stutter on the /g/ of 'goodbye.' Acoustic analysis indicates that when the child attempts to say "g-g-goodbye," the initial /g/ sound in the stuttered dysfluency differs from that in his final, fluently produced target word. This is in addition to the 'secondary characteristics' of stuttering, which refers to facial distortions in an effort to force out the appropriate sound. Whatever stuttering behavior one produces, that behavior reflects the underlying difficulty producing the sound, with a superimposed maneuver to achieve fluent speech (Bloodstein, 1995; Rosenfield, 2001).

Identification of the locus of the dysfluency is difficult. If a stutterer says "s-s-sound," where is the actual dysfluency? Many investigators formerly contended that the dysfluency was on the /s/, but most now maintain the deficit is on the transition from one sound to the next. The stutterer is able to say the /s/ but not the /*ound*/. The stutterer's strategy to attain fluent output can result in repeating the /s/ until the transition into the following /*ound*/ is secured (Rosenfield, 1997, 2001).

Clinical Features of Stuttering

The locations of stutterers' dysfluencies are nonrandom and occur where fluent speakers' occasional dysfluencies also occur – at the beginning of sentences and phrases (**Figure 1**). Thus, one seldom hears a stutterer say, "Go to the hospital-l-l-l." Rather, a stutterer says, "G-g-go to the hospital" (Bloodstein, 1995).

Stuttering is usually worse under stress, consistent with stuttering being a disturbance of the neuromotor system. Motor systems are affect-sensitive systems and worsen with stress. Stutterers seldom repeat whole words. The dysfluent output is usually word fragments. The sounds (fragments, part-words) differ from the target sounds the stutterers are trying fluently to produce (Bloodstein, 1995; Conture, 2001; Rosenfield, 2001).

Several maneuvers increase fluency in stutterers, the most potent of which is singing. Stutterers' speech also considerably improves with choral reading, speaking in cadence with a metronome, or when loud, broadband noise prohibits them from hearing their own speech. Delayed auditory feedback improves stuttering, as does speaking during inhalation or repeating the same passage (adaptation effect) (Bloodstein, 1995).

Genetics

There is a strong male prevalence among stutterers. Eighty percent of children 'outgrow' their stutter, but

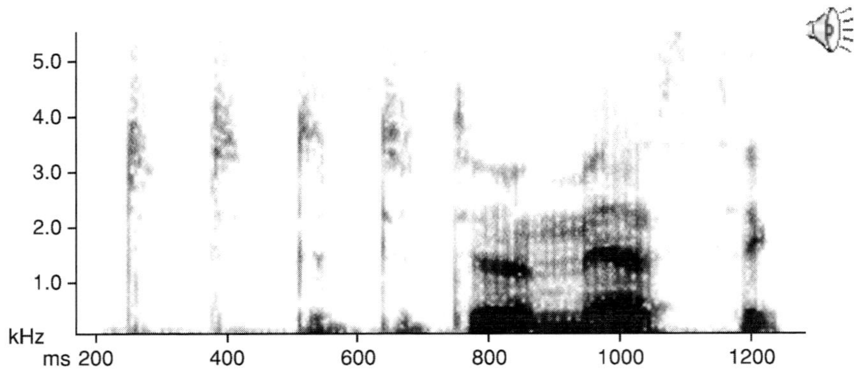

Figure 1 This is a spectrogram of a stutterer saying, 'domestic.' He repeats the /d/ sound several times before he fluently achieves his target word, 'domestic.'

20% do not. This confounding variable necessitates the importance of identifying current stutterers as well as past stutterers in any genetic investigation. Genetic investigations in stuttering have often focused on concordance rates among monozygotic versus dizygotic twin pairs, as well as analyses of pedigrees in different families. Many investigations of stuttering among twins are hampered by small sample size, as well as difficulty ascertaining twin status and assessing speech disruption. Howie (1981), directly examining twin pairs of stutterers, observed that 63% of 16 monozygotic twin pairs and 19% of 13 dizygotic twin pairs were concordant for stuttering. Andrews et al. (1991), investigating 3800 twins through self-employed reporting, determined 20% concordance among 50 monozygotic twin pairs and 3% concordance among 85 dizygotic twin pairs. These investigations indicate that heredity is an important factor in the genesis of stuttering but may not be a sufficient condition, as the concordance among homozygous (identical, same genetic code) twins was not 100%. Thus, environmental factors may also be a factor in the genesis of stuttering.

Another focus of genetic investigation of stuttering involves analysis of stuttering aggregates within families. Relatives of persons who stutter have an increased risk of stuttering, ranging from a three- to a 10-fold increase. The segregation patterns of stuttering in these families do not indicate a single-gene, fully penetrable transmission model of inheritance, such as autosomal dominant, autosomal recessive, or x-linked. Current studies indicate a diallelic model, with penetrance affected by whether a parent stutters and by the sex of that parent stutterer (penetrance is higher among male stuttering parents; Cox et al., 1984; MacFarlane et al., 1991; Ambrose et al., 1993; Viswanath et al., 2001).

Brain Imaging

Employing volumetric magnetic resonance imaging, Foundas et al. (2001) observed abnormalities in stutterers' brains. Stutterers had qualitative differences in frontal lobe gyral patterns, involving Broca's area, and quantitative differences in the posterior temporal lobe regions, involving Wernicke's area. Given that most right-handed fluent speakers have a larger left superior posterior temporal area (Brodmann's Area 22, Planum Temporale), primarily consisting of Wernicke's area, the most robust finding of the researchers was that Wernicke's area on the left and its corresponding area on the right were bilaterally larger but less asymmetric in stutterers than in normal speakers.

Foundas et al. (2001) suggest that these brain abnormalities permit normal development of language but can produce abnormalities in the motor output of language – primarily speech. They query whether the perisylvian (includes Broca's and Wernicke's areas) speech-language cortex compromise contributes to an instability in interaction between an outer 'linguistic' loop and an inner 'phonatory' loop, resulting in stuttering (discussed below in greater detail; Nudelman et al., 1992; Anderson et al., 1999). They note that abnormalities in the anatomic substrates of language might be different among stutterers, with some having difficulty in processing speech-motor control as a result of aberrancies in frontal opercular areas, and others having a compromise near the Wernicke's area.

Sommer et al. (2002) also detected abnormalities in the structure of stutters' brains. Employing diffusion tensor imaging of the brain, a technique that highlights white-matter neural fibers, these researchers noted that stutterers had fewer white-matter fibers in the left brain immediately below the representation of the tongue and laryngeal areas, leading the authors to posit a disconnection between the representation of the oropharynx (Brodmann's area 43) and the sensorimotor cortex.

In addition to the above investigations of abnormal brain structure in stuttering, which could cause or result from stuttered speech, there have been investigations of possible altered brain function in stuttering, primarily employing positron emission tomography (PET) or functional magnetic resonance imaging (fMRI). PET experiments, including reading aloud, reading silently, and choral reading, indicate different activation patterns in stutterers versus nonstutterers (Fox et al., 1996; Braun et al., 1997; DeNil et al., 2000). Despite differences in experimental design, these investigations highlight the fact that right-handed stutterers lateralize activations to the right hemisphere, in contrast to nonstutterers, who lateralize activations to the left hemisphere. Fox et al. (1996) noted that stuttering during solo reading induced widespread activation of motor systems in both the cerebrum and cerebellum, with a right dominance. Consistent with this finding, Braun et al. (1997) noted in stutterers that regional responses were absent, bilateral, or lateralized to the right hemisphere when the subject engaged in speech production during stuttering episodes. DeNil et al. (2000) supports this conclusion by observing a proportionately greater right-hemisphere activation in stutterers while they read individual words overtly or covertly, in contrast to proportionately greater activation in the left hemisphere in nonstutterer controls. Fox et al. (1996) and Braun et al. (1997) reach similar conclusions with regard to fluency evoked by chorus reading and prolonged speech. These studies indicate that brain activation patterns of stutterers differ from those of nonstutterers not only during stuttered speech but also during fluency.

Some investigators attempt to combine the excellent spatial resolution capability of fMRI with the excellent temporal resolution of magneto-encephalography (MEG), a technique permitting investigation of the timing of cortical activation sequences in various tasks. MEG provides excellent temporal resolution, with good accuracy of localization of active cortical areas, and is useful for characterizing an activation sequence from visual perception to oral output and for identifying cortical correlates of the disorders of these processes. Salmelin et al. (2000) had stutterers and controls read isolated nouns aloud in a delayed reading paradigm. The stutterers were fairly fluent in this task. Despite similar overt performance between the two groups, however, the cortical-evoked patterns revealed clear differences both in the evoked responses, which were time locked to word presentation and mouth movement onset, and in the task-related suppression of 20-Hz oscillations. Within the first 400 milliseconds after seeing the word, processing in fluent speakers advanced from the left inferior frontal cortex (articulatory programming) to the left lateral central sulcus and dorsal premotor cortex (motor preparation). This sequence was reversed in stutterers: they had early left motor cortex activation followed by delayed left inferior frontal signals. Stutterers seem to initiate motor programming before preparation of the articulatory code. Suppression of motor cortical 20-Hz rhythms, caused by neuronal-related processing of tasks, occurred bilaterally in stutterers and fluent speakers, but the suppression was dominant in the right hemisphere in the stutterers, whereas it was dominant in the left hemisphere in fluent speakers. Accordingly, the right frontal cortex was very active during speech DS but did not generate synchronous time-locked responses. The authors postulate a dysfunctional network of the left inferior frontal cortex and right motor/premotor cortex network in stutterers.

Theories of Stuttering

Stutterers have difficulty controlling their laryngeal sound source. Investigators have shown that the adductor as well as the abductor muscles of the larynx cocontract during dysfluencies, rendering normal speech output impossible. When stutterers try to 'fake' these dysfluencies, or if fluent speakers try to produce these cocontractions, they do not produce them. The electromyographic relationship between laryngeal abductor and adductor muscles is abnormal during moments of the stutterer's dysfluency (reviewed in Bloodstein, 1995). Further, other investigators have observed that stutterers with laryngeal cancer who subsequently underwent laryngectomy and spoke with an electronic voicer were all totally fluent with this electronic voicing apparatus (Rosenfield and Freeman, 1983).

There have been theories that aberrant cerebral laterality of language causes stuttering. There are multiple extensions of theories of handedness, resulting in the exploration of cerebral laterality as a cause for stuttering. Because right handedness reflects left laterality for language, and left-handedness reflects mixed or right laterality for language, some query whether stutterers lack normal language laterality for language. Investigations exploring handedness and laterality testing, ranging from dichotic listening to presentation of visual stimuli to competing hemispheres, have made this theory enticing, but it has not been confirmed. Being left- or right-handed has never been demonstrated to be a necessary or sufficient condition for stuttering (reviewed in Bloodstein [1995] and in Rosenfield [1997]).

Some maintain that stuttering relates to abnormalities in auditory self-monitoring of speech. When loud, broadband noise prohibits a stutterer from hearing his speech, fluency markedly improves. This has also been observed with delayed auditory feedback – a setting in which a stutterer hears what he says 250 milliseconds after he or she speaks. Frequency-altered feedback, in which the person who stutters hears what he or she just said with an altered frequency, also promotes fluency (Kalinowski et al., 2000). Disruption of auditory processing and input is further highlighted by investigations of dichotic presentation of meaningful linguistic stimuli; many stutterers lack the normal left-brain (i.e., right-ear) advantage (Curry and Gregory, 1969; Rosenfield and Goodglass, 1977; Hall and Jerger, 1978).

Other investigators contend that stuttering reflects periodic irregularities in the timing of muscle movements within the speech motor control system (SMCS) (Zimmermann, 1980). When background muscle tension is elevated, as may be the case in DS (Freeman and Ushijima, 1978), high-precision adjustments needed during speech are difficult to perform, and movements are not smooth. Stutterers have poor coordination of antagonist laryngeal muscles (Freeman and Ushijima, 1978) and are systematically slower in initiating phonation than are fluent speakers (Bloodstein, 1995). Caruso (1991) suggests that the supplementary motor area is dysfunctional in stuttering, resulting in poor motor planning of the speech output.

The above theories primarily note a difference between a group of stutterers and nonstutterers and posit mechanisms that are not common to all the stutterers, as some of the stutterers do not have the abnormalities noted. One theory, which lacks anatomic or actual physiologic verification, does explain the necessary and sufficient conditions for a dysfluency to occur. It is complex, involves mathematical modeling, and involves control theory. We present here a basic discussion of control theory and its subsequent modeling of the necessary and sufficient conditions for stuttered dysfluencies to occur.

Employing control theory, researchers (Nudelman et al., 1989; Rosenfield et al., 1991) model the speech motor control system as consisting of two nested loops – an inner phonatory loop that produces sound, and an outer linguistic loop that selects the sounds to be produced. Stuttering occurs when the timing between these 'functional loops' is disrupted; evidence indicates that stutterers have a slowing within the outer loop. Some data (Anderson et al., 1999; Foundas et al., 2001) suggests that perisylvian speech-language cortex mediates the outer loop, whereas cortico-striatal-thalamo-cortical circuits mediate the inner loop. Anderson et al. (1999) have further corroborated this hypothesis by noting that dopamine blockade and Parkinson disease slow the inner cortical-basal ganglia loop, reducing dysfluency in stuttering.

We have developed an animal model of stuttering (**Figures 2–7**), hoping to investigate the neurophysiology and neuropharmacology underlying fluent and dysfluent production of birdsong. Whereas human beings have a unique system of language, animals have a system of communication. An animal can signal danger or food to another animal, but it is not able to produce a rich language akin to ours. Within this context, however, some animals do share with us mechanisms of sound production. For instance, Zebra finches (*Taenopygia guttata*) share with human beings many features pertaining to communication and sound production. Both have critical periods during development, during which they must hear the sounds of their respective communication/language they are to produce, and there are specific periods during which they must hear these sounds and practice them. For instance, a Zebra finch must hear songs from its adult tutors by day 65 and practice them by day 90. If disruption in hearing or social isolation prohibits this time course, the animal will not learn normal adult bird song. Similarly, young children must hear and practice the sounds they are to make if they are to acquire the language of their parents.

Zebra finches and humans have a spectrally and temporally diverse sound output (i.e., multiple frequencies and changes in frequencies over time). Both the finches and humans have brains that control these sound outputs, and both have an established hierarchy (reviewed in Helekar et al., 2000, 2003).

Our laboratory has demonstrated that ~5% of Zebra finches born to normal parents and raised among normals

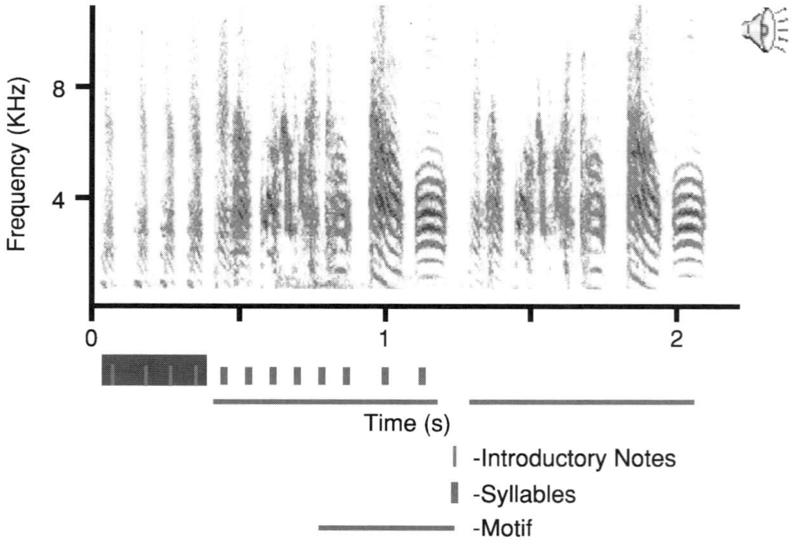

Figure 2 Normal Zebra finch birdsong. These are spectrograms of birdsong, the horizontal axis again reflects time, and the vertical axis reflects frequencies. Note that the Zebra finch bird song is spectrally complex and changes over time, sharing these properties with humans.

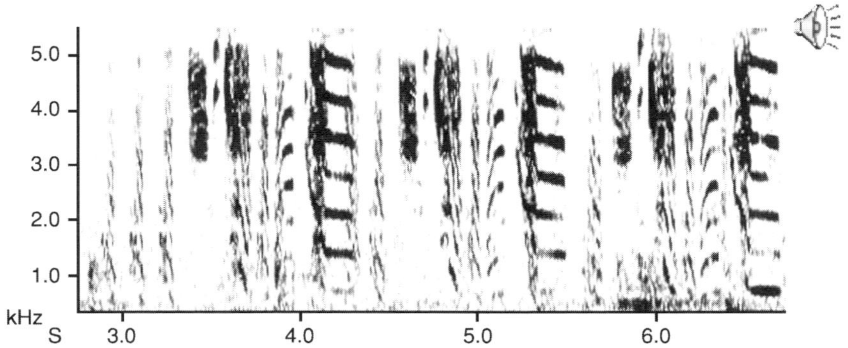

Figure 3 Another spectrogram of normal Zebra finch birdsong demonstrating spectral complexity and temporal changes.

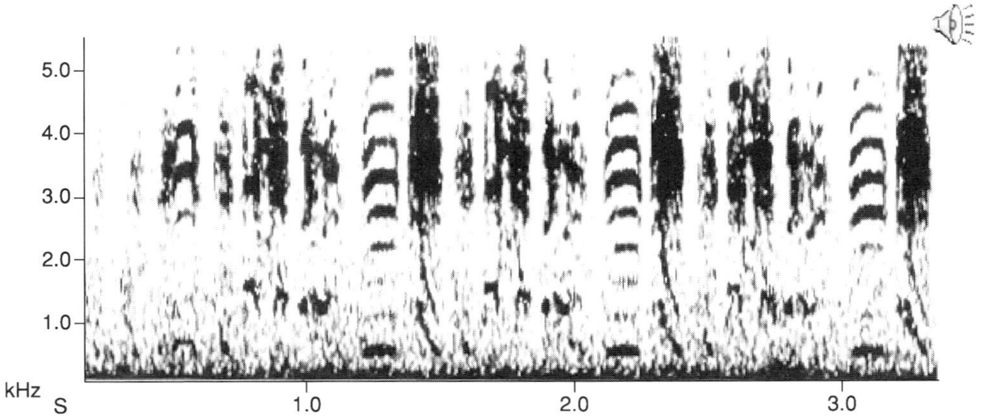

Figure 4 Spectrogram of normal Zebra finch birdsong.

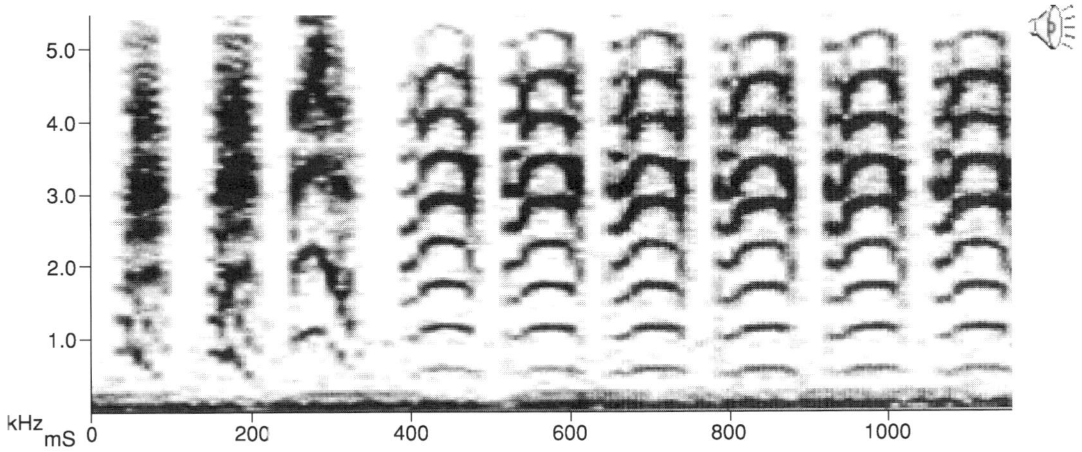

Figure 5 These spectrograms describe phonatory iterations in a bird. Note the repetition of the 'syllable' at the end of each motif.

will have phonatory iterations similar to stuttering. When these birds raise other birds, born to normals, ~60% of these birds stutter. However, although the latter have multiple phonatory iterations, they do not repeat the spectral content of the birds from which they learned to stutter. In other words, they learn to make an error in timing, but not in the frequency domain. They have considerable improvement in these abnormal repetitions when they are placed in isolation or among normal singers. Thus, there appears to be a 'rule to repeat' in birdsong. Some birds (~5%) are born repeaters, perhaps reflecting a genetic mandate. Other birds learn to repeat

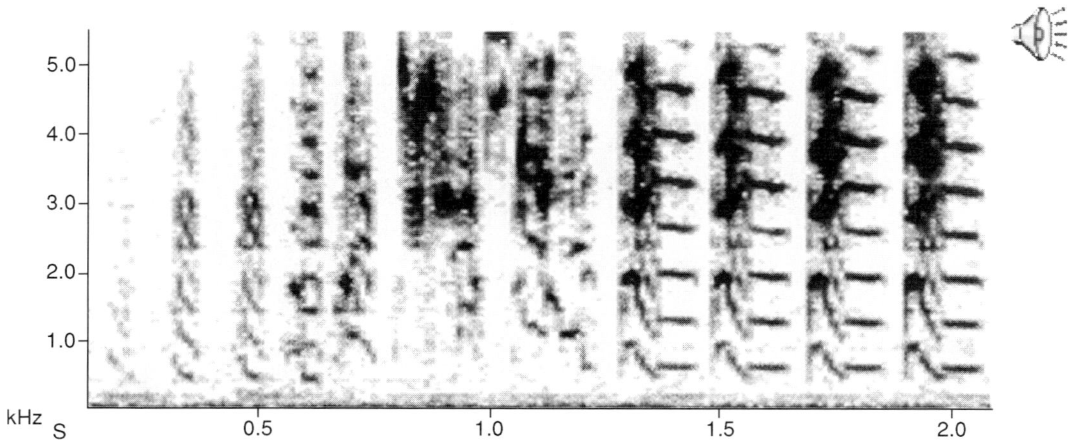

Figure 6 These spectrograms describe phonatory iterations in a bird. Note the repetition of the 'syllable' at the end of each motif.

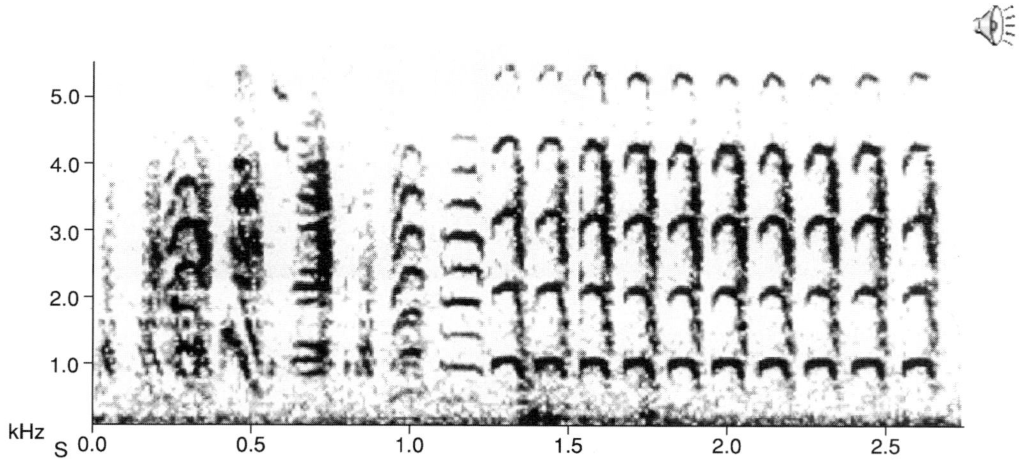

Figure 7 These spectrograms describe phonatory iterations in a bird. Note the repetition of the 'syllable' at the end of each motif.

abnormally and can improve toward normalcy with time but still exhibit stuttering (Helekar et al., 2003).

Zebra finches provide a good animal model of stuttering. Similar to human stutterers, the birds' stuttering is position specific, although it is at the end of the motif, whereas humans stutter at the beginning of sentences and phrases at the end of a motif (see **Figures 5, 6** and 7). The birds' and humans' errors are repetitive and nonvoluntary, as indicated by the regularity of the iterations (Helekar et al., 2000). One presumes that the birds, similar to humans, prefer not to stutter, given that the tutored repeaters improve significantly when they are placed among normal singing adults (Helekar et al., 2003). It is not known whether the birds that stutter are distraught by their abnormal iterations or whether their colleagues perceive them as different. We are currently investigating this.

If one disregards the abstract linguistic and cognitive elements of speech and focuses on vocal motor components, songbird vocalization can provide substantial insight into human speech motor control disorders. Similarities between birdsong and speech can help understand the pathophysiology of human dysfluencies and possibly in testing neuromotor theories of stuttering.

Acquired Stuttering

Acquired stuttering (AS) was initially reported by Rosenfield in 1972 and has been substantiated by many other investigators. As noted in that report, AS differs from DS in that a person with the former is dysfluent throughout the sentence, stutters when he or she sings, and is oftentimes not emotionally disturbed by his or her dysfluencies. AS can result from injury to the brain in either hemisphere or in multiple locations. The injury is usually mild. The prognosis is good if the damage is unilateral but less so if brain damage is bilateral. In some AS patients, there may be psychogenic factors (Helm et al., 1978; Rosenfield and Barroso, 2000).

Table 1 Differential diagnosis of dysfluency

	Developmental stuttering	*Acquired stuttering*	*Cluttering*
Locus of lesion	Unknown	Usually cortical, but subcortical cases have been reported	Unknown
Cause	Unknown	Vascular, metabolic tumor	Unknown
Duration	80% of children outgrow; adults have a worse prognosis	Unilateral: good prognosis; bilateral: poor prognosis	Varies
Locus of dysfluency	Beginning of sentence or phrase	Frequently scattered throughout sentence	Varies
Singing	Fluent	May improve somewhat, but still not totally fluent	Varies
Onset	Subacute	Subacute or acute	Gradual
Reaction to dysfluencies	Anxious	Not anxious	Not usually concerned

Whereas people with DS have difficulty achieving the target sound (i.e., "ba-ba-ba-book"), those with AS achieve the target sound, but repeat it (i.e., "boo-boo-book"). This difference is often clinically perceptible at the bedside.

Cluttering is sometimes confused with stuttering. Clutterers produce abnormal speech, characterized by excessive speed, repetition, interjections, drawling, disturbed prosody, and monotonous sound. Sometimes, they also have inconsistent articulatory disturbances. Some investigators contend that clutterers also have grammatical difficulties, are hyperactive, and have poor concentration and poorly integrated thought processes. Many clutterers omit sounds, syllables, and whole words and invert the orders of sound, repeat the initial sound, and prolong several syllables of the word. Their rate of speech is usually very rapid, and the listener often complains about the rapidity of the speech. As opposed to people with DS, clutterers frequently lack concern about their speech deficits (see **Table 1**; Bloodstein, 1995).

Conclusion

Stuttering is a complex disturbance reflecting abnormal cerebral processing of speech-related signals. There is probably a strong genetic component to stuttering, based at a minimum on studies of twin pairs, but a genetic predisposition may not be sufficient to cause stuttering. The current investigation, employing clinical studies as well as genetic and brain imaging studies, coupled with studies in animals, may provide more insight into this pan-cultural, global disturbance.

Acknowledgments

This work was sponsored by the National Institutes of Health Grant 1-R03-DC04778-01A1, the M. R. Bauer Foundation, and the Lowin Family Research Foundation.

See also: Apraxia, Handedness and Language Laterality; Imaging Brain Lateralization.

Bibliography

Ambrose, Yairi, and Cox (1993).

Anderson, JM, Hughes, JD, Rothi, LJ, Crucian, GP, and Heilman, K (1991). 'Developmental stuttering and Parkinson's disease: the effects of levodopa treatment.' *Journal of Neurology, Neurosurgery, and Psychiatry* 66: 776–778.

Anderson, JM, Hughes, JD, Rothi, LJ, Crucian, GP, and Heilman, KM (1999). 'Developmental stuttering and Parkinson's disease: the effects of levodopa.' *Journal of Neurology, Neurosurgery, and Psychiatry* 66: 776–778.

Andrews (1991).

Bloodstein, O (1995). *A handbook on stuttering.* San Diego, CA: Singular.

Botas, A, Espino, G, Rosenfield, DB, and Helekar, SA (2001). 'Reduction of female-directed song motifs induced by repeated singing in laboratory-bred zebra finches.' *Neuroscience Letters* 297: 203–206.

Braun, AR, Varge, M, Stager, S, et al. (1997) 'Alerted patterns of cerebral activity during speech and language production in developmental stuttering: a PET study.' *Brain 120*, 762–784.

Caruso, AJ (1991). 'Neuromotor processes underlying stuttering.' In: Peters, HFM, Halstijn, W, and Starkweather, CW (eds.) *Speech Motor Control in Stuttering*, pp. 101–116. Amsterdam: Elsevier.

Conture, EG (2001). *Stuttering, its nature, diagnosis, and treatment.* Needham Heights, MA: Allyn and Bacon.

Cox, Kramer, and Kidd (1984).

DeNil, LF, Kroll, RM, Kapur, S, and Houle, S (2000). 'A positron emission tomography study of silent and oral reading of single words in stuttering and nonstuttering adults.' *Journal of Speech, Language & Hearing Research* 43: 1038–1053.

Foundas, AL, Bollich, AM, Corey, DM, Hurley, M, and Heilman, KM (2001). 'Anomalous anatomy of speech-language areas in adults with persistent developmental stuttering.' *Neurology* 57: 207–215.

Fox, PT, Ingham, RJ, Ingham, JC, et al. (1996). 'A PET study of the neural systems of stuttering.' *Nature* 382: 158–161.

Freeman, FJ and Ushijima, T (1978). 'Laryngeal muscle activity during stuttering.' *Journal of Speech, Language & Hearing Research* 21: 538–562.

Helekar, SA, Espino, GG, Botas, A, and Rosenfield, DB (2003). 'Development and adult phase plasticity of syllable repetitions in the birdsong of captive zebra finches (*Taeniopygia guttata*).' *Behavioral Neuroscience* 117: 939–951.

Helekar, SA, Marsh, S, Viswanath, NS, and Rosenfield, DB (2000). 'Acoustic pattern variations in the female-directed birdsongs of a colony of laboratory-bred zebra finches.' *Behavioral Processes* 49: 99–110.

Helm, NA, Butler, RB & Benson, DF (1978). 'Neurogenic acquired stuttering.' *Neurology 5*, 269–279.
Howie, PM (1981). 'Concordance for stuttering in monozygotic and dizygotic twin pairs.' *Journal of Speech, Language & Hearing Research* 24: 317–321.
Kalinowski, J, Armson, J, Mieszkowski, M, Stuart, A, and Gracco, V (1993). 'Effects of alterations in auditory feedback and speech rate on stuttering frequency.' *Language and Speech* 36: 1–16.
Kalinowski, J, Dayalu, VN, Stuart, A, Rastatter, MP, and Rami, MK (2000). 'Stutter-free and stutter-filled speech signals and their role in stuttering amelioration for English speaking adults.' *Neuroscience Letters* 293: 115–118.
MacFarlane, et al. (1991).
Nudelman, HB, Herbrich, KE, Hoyt, BD, and Rosenfield, DB (1992). 'Phonatory response times of stutterers and fluent speakers to frequency-modulated tones.' *Journal of the Acoustical Society of America* 92: 1882–1888.
Nudelman, HB, Hoyt, B, Herbrich, KE, and Rosenfield, DB (1989). 'A neuroscience model of stuttering.' *Journal of Fluency Disorders* 14: 399–427.
Porfert, AR and Rosenfield, DB (1978). 'Prevalence of stuttering.' *Journal of Neurology, Neurosurgery, and Psychiatry* 41: 954–956.
Rosenfield, DB (1972). 'Stuttering and cerebral ischemia.' *New England Journal of Medicine* 287: 991.
Rosenfield, DB (1997). In: 'Stuttering.' In Schachter, S and Devinsky, O (eds.) *Behavioral neurology and the legacy of Norman Geschwind*, pp. 101–111. Philadelphia: Lippincott-Raven.
Rosenfield, DB (2001). 'Do stutterers have different brains?' *Neurology* 57: 171–172.
Rosenfield, DB and Barroso, AO (2000). 'Difficulties with speech and swallowing.' In: Bradley, WG, Darroff, RB, Fenichel, GM, and Marsden, CD (eds.) *Neurology in clinical practice: principles of diagnosis and management,* 3rd edn., chapter 13, pp. 171–186. Boston: Butterworth-Heinemann.
Rosenfield, DB and Freeman, FS (1983). 'Stuttering onset after laryngectomy.' *Journal of Fluency Disorders* 8: 265–268.
Rosenfield, DB and Viswanath, NS (2002). 'Neuroscience of stuttering.' *Science* 295: 973–974.
Rosenfield, DB, Fann, WE, and Viswanath, NS (2001). 'Resolution of stuttering following neurologic disease.' In: Bosshardt, HG, Yaruss, JS, and Peters, HFM (eds.) *Fluency disorders: theory, research, treatment and self-help; proceedings of the Third World Congress on Fluency Disorders in Nyborg, Denmark*, pp. 99–101. Amsterdam: Nijmegen University Press.
Rosenfield, DB, Viswanath, NS, Callis-Landrum, L, DiDanato, R, and Nudelman, HB (1991). 'Patients with acquired dysfluencies: what they tell us about developmental stuttering.' In: Peters, HFM, Halstijn, W, and Starkweather, CW (eds.) *Speech motor control in stuttering*, pp. 277–284. Amsterdam: Elsevier.
Rosenfield, DB, Viswanath, NS, and Helekar, SA (2001). 'An animal model of stuttering.' In: Bosshardt, HG, Yaruss, JS, and Peters, HFM (eds.) *Fluency disorders: theory, research, treatment and self-help; Proceedings of the Third World Congress on Fluency Disorders in Nyborg, Denmark*, pp. 119–122. Amsterdam: Nijmegen University Press.
Salmelin, R, Schnitzler, A, Schmitz, F, and Freund, H-J (2000). 'Single work reading in developmental stutterers and fluent speakers.' *Brain* 123: 1184–1202.
Sommer, M, Kooh, MA, Paulus, W, Weller, C, and Buchal, C (2002). 'Disconnection of speech relevant brain areas in persistent developmental stuttering.' *Lancet* 360: 380–383.
Sommer, M, Koch, MA, Paulus, W, Weiller, C, and Buchel, C (2002). 'Disconnection of speech-relevant brain areas in persistent developmental stuttering.' *Lancet* 360: 380–383.
Viswanath, NS and Rosenfield, DB (1999). 'Stuttering.' In: Adelman, G and Smith, BH (eds.) *Encyclopedia of neuroscience*, pp. 1961–1963. Amsterdam: Elsevier Science.
Viswanath, NS, Rosenfield, DB, Alexander, JP, Lee, HS, and Chakraborty, R (2001). 'Genetic basis of developmental stuttering – preliminary observations.' In: Bosshardt, HG, Yaruss, JS, and Peters, HFM (eds.) *Fluency disorders: theory, research, treatment and self-help; proceedings of the Third World Congress on Fluency Disorders in Nyborg, Denmark*, pp. 102–108. Amsterdam: Nijmegen University Press.
Viswanath, NS, Karmonik, C, King, D, Rosenfield, DB, and Mawad, M (2003). 'Functional magnetic resonance imaging (fMRI) of a stutterer's brain during overt speech.' *Journal of Neuroimaging* 13: 280–281.
Zimmermann, G (1980). 'Stuttering: A disorder of movement.' *Journal of Speech, Language & Hearing Research* 23: 122–126.

Functional Magnetic Resonance Imaging (fMRI) Research on Language

U. Hasson and S. L. Small, The University of Chicago, Chicago, IL, USA

Introduction

The advancement of non-invasive imaging methods such as positron emission tomography (PET) and functional magnetic resonance imaging (fMRI) has made it possible to study the neurophysiological basis of language. These studies, in areas such as speech recognition, parsing (lexical) semantic memory, sentence and discourse comprehension and production, are informative for both the psychologist and the neuroscientist. On one hand, they constrain cognitive theory, and on the other, they represent the essential constituent of theory development in the neurophysiology of language.

That said, newcomers to fMRI quickly discover that fMRI studies differ in the extent to which their results have implications for cognitive (functional) theories of language. Likewise, studies differ in how informative they are for understanding the anatomy and physiology of the brain. For instance, many neuroscientists focus their research on the role of particular brain structures (e.g., the inferior frontal cortex), and in their work they will define that region as a "region of interest" (ROI) and exclusively report neural activity in that region across different language tasks, ignoring other regions. This type of investigation is useful for the development of neurobiological theories, but may be less important for development of functional theories, as it does not adequately characterize the full network of regions that work together collaboratively to perform tasks. Analogously, some psychologists focus on the degree to which brain activation patterns differ under varying experimental conditions in order to support or refute psycholinguistic theories, but put less emphasis on thorough neurophysiological description of these differences. Although theory development in psychology and linguistics, as well as basic findings in neurophysiology are all valuable uses of functional imaging, much of the field strives for results that are at the intersection of the two and thus can help integrate theories of brain and function. In this review, we focus on four central research themes underlying language processing in the brain. These include (a) sub-lexical speech perception, (b) single-word comprehension, (c) sentence processing (syntactic and semantic) and (d) discourse.

Recognizing Auditory Input as Speech

When individuals are presented with spoken, non-meaningful sub-lexical speech stimuli such as consonant-vowel syllables, numerous brain regions demonstrate reliable activity. An important subset of these areas is more activated by such stimuli than by non-speech stimuli. One of the main goals of research in speech perception is to clarify how the acoustic input is represented phonetically and comes to be understood as speech.

Certain brain regions are thought of as specialized for auditory processing. These regions, located bilaterally on the supratemporal plane include (a) transverse temporal gyrus of Heschl; thought to be the site of the primary (or core) auditory cortex in the human, and (b) auditory association cortexes; the planum polare (anterior to Heschl's) and planum temporale (posterior to Heschl's). The core and association regions differ in their functional properties: the primary area is sensitive to pure frequencies, but not complex sounds, whereas the association areas show the opposite pattern.

Drawing on comparative studies with primates, it has been suggested that specialization for speech (as contrasted with generic auditory processing) begins at the level of the auditory association cortex. In primates, the auditory cortex anterior to the core region has been shown to differentiate among diverse monkey calls (Rauschecker & Tian, 2000). A number of studies suggest that humans also have a comparable neural pathway in which acoustic information is understood at a more abstract level, as an "auditory object." These studies have shown that regions on the anterior part of the left superior temporal gyrus (STG) and superior temporal sulcus (STS) of the lateral temporal cortex are more sensitive to auditory speech than to stimuli with similar acoustic complexity (Scott & Johnsrude, 2003). To this extent, auditory processing in the human seems to match that of primates.

However, there are a number of problems with this account. First, while primates show rudimentary higher-level auditory processing in auditory regions anterior to auditory cortex, in humans such processing is also found in the planum temporale posterior to auditory cortex (Griffiths & Warren, 2002). This region may be particularly sensitive to speech input (Vouloumanos et al., 2001), and it seems to process auditory input in a specialized way when it could potentially contain speech (Meyer et al., 2005). The posterior left STG could also be implicated in some of these higher-level functions (Narain et al., 2003). Another problem with this account is interpretive: the argument is based on the finding that speech stimuli evoke more activity than non-speech stimuli in anterior regions of temporal cortex. However, this finding could originate not from specialized mechanisms for perceiving sound categories, but from the fact that speech processing necessitates discriminating among highly similar sound categories. That is, speech comprehension might be a quantitatively more difficult categorization task, but not one that is qualitatively different than other complex auditory discrimination tasks (Belin et al., 2004).

While auditory processing largely activates temporal regions, audiovisual speech evokes different patterns of neural activity. In a pivotal study, Calvert et al. (1997) demonstrated that many brain regions involved in auditory speech perception are also activated during silent lip reading, and further research suggested that the left STS is particularly important for integrating auditory and visual input (Calvert et al., 2000). In that region, neural activity during presentation of auditory input was strongly affected by whether it was accompanied by a matching or mismatching visual stimulus. Finding an interaction between auditory and visual information in STS suggested that integration of auditory and visual input occurs relatively late in the processing stream, after both auditory and visual input have been independently elaborated in areas involved in lower-level processing (Calvert et al., 2000), but there is some debate on this issue (see **Box 1**). Audiovisual speech perception may also rely on premotor and motor cortexes, as these show greater activity for audiovisual speech than for either auditory or visual speech tracks presented separately (Skipper et al., 2005).

Word Representation: Form and Meaning

In addition to phonological knowledge, word comprehension entails accessing semantic knowledge. There has

Box 1 Dynamics of auditory and visual integration during audiovisual speech comprehension

How are auditory and visual inputs integrated during audiovisual speech comprehension? Initial findings pointed to the STS as such an integration hub (Calvert et al., 2000). Because this region processes sensory input once it has been analyzed in lower-level, unimodal regions, it was thought that integration takes place relatively late in the processing stream. However, there is some controversy on this issue. First, visual information can affect neural activity in brain areas involved in the earliest stages of acoustic processing (the brainstem; Musacchia et al., 2006) and also in the primary auditory cortex (Pekkola et al., 2003). Second, methods sensitive to the timeline of processing (e.g., magnetoencephalography) indicate that visual information affects auditory processing in the vicinity of the primary auditory cortex before it affects processing in STS (Mottonen et al., 2004). Thus, the stage of processing at which visual information integrates with auditory input during speech processing is still a matter of ongoing research.

Calvert, G. A., Campbell, R., & Brammer, M. J. (2000). Evidence from functional magnetic resonance imaging of crossmodal binding in the human heteromodal cortex. *Current Biology, 10*(11), 649–657.

Mottonen, R., Schurmann, M., & Sams, M. (2004). Time course of multisensory interactions during audiovisual speech perception in humans: A magnetoencephalographic study. *Neuroscience Letters, 363*(2), 112–115.

Musacchia, G., Sams, M., Nicol, T., & Kraus, N. (2006). Seeing speech affects acoustic information processing in the human brainstem. *Experimental Brain Research, 168*(1), 1–10.

Pekkola, J., Ojanen, V., Autti, T., Jaaskelainen, I. P., Mottonen, R., Tarkiainen, A., & Sams, M. (2003). Primary auditory cortex activation by visual speech: An fMRI study at 3 T. *Neuroreport, 16*(2), 125–128.

been considerable work on the organization of lexical semantic knowledge (semantic memory) in the brain, on the basis of both lesion studies and imaging methods. Brain regions have been identified that are relatively selective to living versus non-living categories, or concrete versus abstract nouns (see, Martin & Chao, 2001 for review). Understanding the organization of semantic knowledge in the brain is fundamental for understanding neural activity during word comprehension, as this is the type of information that single words denote.

One of the major goals of imaging research is to understand how semantic knowledge is accessed and manipulated during language comprehension. The main difficulty in answering this question is that word comprehension (whether presented in auditory or visual modality) entails phonological processing of the sort discussed in the previous section and semantic processing having to do with the access and manipulation of information. Consequently, it is not possible to tell which brain regions are specifically involved in semantic processing by observing brain activity during the processing of a single-word. Much of the research of semantic access has been engrossed in developing methods to address this issue.

One solution has been to manipulate the task under which words are processed. In an early study (Demb et al., 1995), words were visually presented to participants, who performed one of two tasks: in the more complex task they judged whether the word was abstract or concrete, and in the simpler task they judged whether the word was presented in upper- or lower-case. Both tasks entail processing of the printed word and making a judgment, but clearly diverge in their semantic processing demands. In that study, a region in left inferior frontal gyrus (IFG) showed more neural activity in the complex task than in the simple task. Furthermore, repeated performance of the more complex task resulted in decreased neural activity in the same IFG region (a phenomenon called *repetition suppression*), but repeated performance of the simpler task did not result in repetition suppression. Because the words were printed in both task conditions, the suppression found only for the more difficult task suggests that this suppression reflects easier semantic processing related to repetition rather than easier phonological processing. A later study (Poldrack et al., 1999) largely replicated these findings, demonstrating greater IFG activity in a semantic task (abstract/concrete judgment for printed words) than in a phonologically oriented task (counting a word's syllables). However, this study further revealed an interesting partitioning between the more anterior and more posterior parts of IFG: whereas the more posterior part (~BA 44) showed above-baseline activity for both phonological and semantic tasks, the more anterior part (~BA 47/45) showed above-baseline activity only for the semantic task. A study by Wagner et al., (2000) made a similar point. In that study, participants made a semantic judgment for visually presented words. Some of these words had been seen before (repeated items) whereas others had not (novel items). The crucial manipulation depended on the context in which the words that were now repeated were previously presented: in one condition, these words were presented in the context of the identical semantic judgment task; in the other condition, they were presented in the context of a different, non-semantic task (upper-case/lower-case judgment). In the anterior portion of left IFG, repeated presentation of words resulted in reduced neural activity, but only when these words were repeated in the context of the same task as they were presented before. In contrast, a different pattern of repetition was evident for posterior IFG: that region demonstrated less neural activity for the repeated words independently of whether they were previously presented in the same or different task. Thus, the posterior part of IFG seemed to benefit from repeated exposure to a word independent of the task in which it was presented – consistent with its role in phonological processing.

There is much debate on the nature of semantic processes subserved by the anterior and posterior parts of IFG. One topic of debate addresses the nature of the semantic processes indexed by activity in anterior left IFG. The details of this debate are outside the scope of the current chapter, and it has yet to be seen whether all the suggested functions play a fundamental role in natural language comprehension. Another point of contention is whether the purported anterior–posterior distinction indeed reflects a dichotomy that is based solely on a semantics versus phonology continuum. With respect to this matter, Gold et al. (2005) have shown that the anterior part of left IFG (~BA 45/47) was also reliably active during a phonological task in which participants were asked to "regularize" words that have irregular orthography-to-phonology mappings (e.g., participants were asked to pronounce *pint* in a way that rhymes with *hint*). Gold et al.'s findings are consistent with the hypothesis that activity in anterior IFG indexes general types of controlled processing, rather than solely access to semantic knowledge.

Few fMRI studies have examined how access and selection of semantic meanings take place during natural sentence processing. In one such study (Rodd et al., 2005), participants either heard sentences that contained a few ambiguous words (e.g., The *shell* was *fired* towards the *tank*) or sentences with less lexical ambiguity (Her secrets were written in her diary). They conducted two experiments, each with a different task: in one, participants actively listened to the sentences knowing they had to answer a question about them. In the other, they passively listened to the sentences. In the active task experiment, high-ambiguity sentences were associated with more IFG activity (bilaterally) than the low-ambiguity sentences. In contrast, in the passive task experiment, differences were found in left inferior frontal sulcus (IFS) and in left middle temporal gyrus (MTG) but not in IFG. (Furthermore, these results were found using a somewhat less conservative analysis method.)

While the role of left IFG in semantic processing has been extensively studied, it is far from the only region that is involved in semantic processing of single words. Indeed, quite a few other regions have been identified in the literature: Wagner et al. (2000) report decreased activity in the left STG and MTG and the left superior and middle frontal gyri (SFG, MFG) when words are repeated in the context of the same task. Poldrack et al. (1999) report a greater increase in activity during semantic compared to phonetic tasks bilaterally in SFG, MFG and in the medial frontal gyrus (among other regions; that study imaged only the frontal parts of the brain).

Another paradigm used in studying word comprehension is the semantic priming method. As established by decades of behavioral research, processing a word is easier if a semantically related word has just been previously presented (the target word is then said to be "primed" by the previous one). It is reasonable to assume that on the neural level, accessing a word is more efficient when the word's meaning has been recently primed. This logic has lead to a number of investigations into the neural mechanisms underlying semantic priming: specifically, brain regions showing less activity for primed than unprimed words have been linked to semantic retrieval of words' meanings. In one study, Copland et al. (2003) presented participants with words such as *money* or *river* after these words were primed by a word such as *bank*. When neural activity for these words was compared to that of a word semantically unrelated to *bank* (e.g., *sky*), both semantically related words demonstrated neural facilitation in the left MTG and left anterior IFG (BA 47/11). However, not all studies of semantic priming have found facilitation in left IFG, and some have also revealed facilitation in temporal cortex (*cf.* Hasson et al., 2006, for a recent review).

From Words to Sentences: Syntactic Processing

Beyond the single-word level, a large body of research has focused on the neural mechanisms underlying semantic and syntactic aspects of sentence comprehension. This is possibly due to the relatively entrenched dichotomy between semantic and syntactic processes in certain linguistic and philosophical theories.

Many studies have attempted to identify neural correlates of syntactic complexity. In an early study, Just et al. (1996) presented participants with three sorts of sentences that differed in their structural complexity because they either contained conjoined clauses, subject-relative clauses or object-relative clauses. In brain regions roughly corresponding to Broca's and Wernicke's area (bilaterally), the volume of neural activity increased with sentence complexity. Given that three experimental conditions contained the same content words, the authors argued that the complexity of the sentence was responsible for the increased neural activity, but did not speculate on specific component functions these regions perform.

Expanding on the issue of structural complexity, some researchers have put forward the stronger claim that certain theoretical constructs of syntactic theories are related to neuronal regions (a regular relationship between subcomponents of syntactic theory and brain loci; Grodzinsky & Friederici, 2006, p. 240). Notably, Grodzinsky has argued that there are different types of dependency relations in sentences, and that parsing these relations is associated with a distinct pattern of neural activity. To examine this claim, Ben-Shachar et al. (2003) studied neural activity during comprehension of sentences that, from a linguistic perspective, either contained or did not contain a particular syntactic transformation. In that study, sentences that contained transformations were associated with increased neural activity in left IFG and bilaterally in posterior STS, which was taken to indicate their involvement in this very specific type of syntactic processing. Yet, a detailed examination of the results reveals an interesting pattern: in both regions, sentences with transformations showed above-baseline activity, but sentences without transformations showed below-baseline activity. This pattern is intriguing; if these regions were indeed involved in general syntactic processing, we would expect that in both conditions neural activity would be reliably above baseline. Instead, only the more difficult syntactic conditions were associated with above-baseline activity. Similar findings are seen in a study where participants were presented with either subject-relative or more complex object-relative sentences (Cooke et al., 2002). Both types of sentences could contain either few or many words between the antecedent and the gap. In this study, only the most difficult condition, consisting of object-relative sentences with long antecedent-gap linkages, showed above-baseline activity in left IFG. Taken together, these findings may indicate that the increased activity associated with complex transformation indicates a categorically different mode of operation in left IFG, rather than a qualitative increase in activity that is related to syntactic complexity.

Indeed, identifying brain regions that differentiate between sentences of different syntactic complexity can be interpreted in at least two ways: on the more syntax-specific interpretation, this effect could indicate that certain brain regions are specialized in carrying out formal syntactic operations. On a more general interpretation, syntactic difficulty increases the demands on working memory, which in turn results in increased neural activity. A number of studies have tried to differentiate these two components, and some findings suggest that the syntactic effects in left IFG may reflect *maintenance* of dislocated arguments in working memory (Cooke et al., 2002; Fiebach et al., 2005). Thus, there is considerable debate on the explanation of syntactic transformation effects, and future research is needed to address this issue.

A different approach to studying syntactic processing was used by Dapretto and Bookheimer (1999): participants were presented with pairs of statements and determined whether the two statements had the same meaning. In one of the conditions these statements had different syntactic forms (e.g., *the policeman arrested the thief*; *the thief was arrested by the policeman*), and in another condition they were based on word substitutions (*the lawyer questioned the witness*; *the attorney questioned the witness*). When sentence-pairs differed in syntax, there was relatively increased activity in posterior IFG, whereas when they differed in the noun used, there was more activity in anterior IFG. This finding supports the purported dissociation between posterior and anterior aspects of IFG we have discussed.

Temporal regions may also be involved in syntactic processing. Left STG demonstrates less activity during blocks of sentences that share the same syntactic structure compared to blocks where different structures are mixed (Noppeney & Price, 2004). Both left STG and left IFG show increased activity for sentences that are more difficult to parse, independent of whether they are presented in spoken or written form (Constable et al., 2004). When compared to simple correct sentences, sentences that include semantic or syntactic violations are associated with increased activity in posterior STG (for both types of violations) and in anterior STG (for syntactic violations; Friederici et al., 2003). Other findings on the involvement of STG in syntactic processing are reviewed in Grodzinsky and Friederici (2006).

From Words to Sentences: Semantic Processing of Sentences

As we have discussed, there is some debate on whether there are brain regions that are specialized for syntactic functions. That is, it is unclear whether the theoretical element referred to as "syntax" has a unique/privileged status in the brain. There is much less debate on whether there are brain regions particularly important for semantic processing of sentences, which in this chapter will subsume processes that underlie the ability to comprehend the meaning of sentences.

In psychology, the study of sentential semantic processing often refers to the online processes by which the cognitive system constructs the meaning of sentences, and to the nature of the end product that results (e.g., is it "image-like," or a-modal/propositional in nature). Neuroscientists tackle questions that overlap to some extent. These include, but are not limited to (a) identifying regions involved in establishing sentence meaning, (b) establishing whether these regions play a language-specific role in a more general role in meaning construction, (c) understanding the processing of literal and non-literal meanings or (d) studying if sentence comprehension activates modality-specific networks related to the content of those sentences (e.g., do sentences speaking of action activate action-related motor regions, see **Box 2**).

One method that may identify brain regions involved in semantic processing is to present sentences in visual and auditory form and characterize the brain regions active for both. Using this method, Constable et al. (2004) revealed reliable activity to spoken and printed sentences predominantly in left hemisphere regions, including STG, MTG and IFG. However, this activity is likely to index both semantic and syntactic processing. The anterior left IFG may play a particularly important role in the integration of semantic and syntactic processes. Vandenberghe et al. (2002) have shown that activity in this region is sensitive to whether a sentence has a canonical grammatical structure, but *only* when the words in the sentences can be put

Box 2 Meaning and embodied representations

Does the comprehension of action sentences rely on a-modal semantic representations, or on more action-like simulations of the situations described in those sentences? This longstanding question in cognitive science has been recently addressed by neuroimaging studies. Interestingly, these suggest that action sentences systematically activate brain regions associated with observation and execution of physical actions. Sentences referring to actions performed by the mouth, hand and leg evoke greater activity in posterior left IFG than abstract sentences (Tettamanti et al., 2005). In monkeys, this region has been found to contain neurons that fire during both observation and execution of certain goal-directed actions (Rizzolatti & Craighero, 2004). Thus, in humans this region may code actions at a level that is abstract enough to be accessible to language. Furthermore, the sentences referring to leg, mouth and hand differentially activated premotor regions associated with actions of these afferents. Other research shows that brain regions differentially sensitive to observation of mouth, foot and hand actions are also differentially sensitive to sentences mentioning actions performed by these effectors (Aziz-Zadeh et al., 2006). Such studies suggest that language comprehension, at least in the action domain, is supported by motor systems used to perform the actions referred to in those sentences, which is consistent with theoretical approaches in the "embodied cognition" framework.

Aziz-Zadeh, L., Wilson, S. M., Rizzolatti, G., & Iacoboni, M. (2006). Congruent embodied representations for visually presented actions and linguistic phrases describing actions. *Current Biology, 16*(18), 1818–1823.

Rizzolatti, G., & Craighero, L. (2004). The mirror-neuron system. *Annual Review of Neuroscience, 27*(1), 169–192.

Tettamanti, M., Buccino, G., Saccuman, M. C., Gallese, V., Danna, M., Scifo, P., Fazio, F., Rizzolatti, G., Cappa, S. F., & Perani, D. (2005). Listening to action-related sentences activates fronto-parietal motor circuits. *Journal of Cognitive Neuroscience, 17*(2), 273–281.

together to form a meaningful sentence; when they cannot, then this region is not sensitive to grammaticality.

Finding that a brain region is active during the presentation of linguistic information does not necessarily mean that this region performs a function that is uniquely linguistic. Emphasizing this point, Humphries et al. (2001) presented participants with narrative information either via sentences (e.g., the sentence *there was a gunshot and then somebody ran away*) or via sound effects (presenting the sound of a gunshot followed by the sound of fading footsteps). Perhaps the most striking result of the study was not the difference between the two conditions, but the fact that both resulted in above-baseline activity in middle (auditory) and posterior regions of the temporal lobe and left IFG. The direct contrast between the conditions did reveal increased neural activity for the sentence condition in the anterior temporal lobes (bilaterally), posterior STS and a few other regions, suggesting these are particularly important for accessing or integrating information presented in linguistic form.

Semantic integration processes have also been studied by examining neural processing of sentences that contain different types of violations. Kuperberg et al. (2000) contrasted brain activity during comprehension of normal sentences, with that seen during comprehension of sentences with different sorts of meaning or syntax violations (e.g., *the man buried/slept/drank the guitar*). In their study, the left IFG was particularly sensitive to the differences between normal- and meaning-violated sentences, but the fusiform gyrus was also sensitive to this difference. In another study (Friederici et al., 2003), semantic violations were associated with increased activity in the middle portion of MTG as well as the Insula (bilaterally).

Several studies have examined sentential processing by identifying brain regions that show decreased activity to sentences when they are presented for a second time. Currently, the results of such studies support a role for temporal regions in sentential semantics. Stowe et al. (1999) used a visual presentation method, and compared the initial reading of sentences or mixed-word lists to their repeated presentation. They found decreased activity in cortical areas including the left fusiform gyrus (extending to the inferior parietal lobule and MTG; i.e., relatively posterior regions), left lingual gyrus and right STG/MTG. However, similar repetition effects were found for sentences and for mixed-word lists suggesting that the regions in which the repetition effects were found were not necessarily involved in sentence-level semantic processes (in that study, the lag between the initial and repeated presentations was 44 min, which could have contributed to diminished accessibility of the sentence meaning). Hasson et al. (2006) presented auditory sentences twice; these sentences either contained or did not contain subordinate clauses. Repetition of both types of sentences was associated with reduced activity bilaterally in temporal regions. However, in the right lingual gyrus they found decreased activity for repetition of non-subordinate-clause sentences, but repetition enhancement for repetition of subordinate-clause sentences. The authors also found that repetition was associated with decreased activity in left IFG, but only when the sentences were repeated in the context of an active task demanding an explicit sensibility judgment. No repetition effects in IFG were found during passive listening.

From Sentences to Discourse

Comprehension of connected sentences in the context of discourse entails discourse-level processes that are absent during comprehension of single sentences. Experimental cognitive research of discourse comprehension has examined many such processes, for example, those involved in integration of content across sentences. The understanding of the neural underpinnings of these processes is only in its initial stages.

Integration of sentential information with prior knowledge is fundamental to discourse comprehension. How does this occur? St. George et al. (1999) presented participants with texts that were difficult to comprehend unless presented with a title that summarized what the text was about. Temporal regions in the right hemisphere showed greater activity for untitled than for titled stories, but temporal regions on the left showed the opposite pattern. However, another study that used a conceptually similar manipulation in which texts were clarified with a picture revealed different results (Maguire et al., 1999). In this study, unusual texts were either clarified by preceding them with a descriptive photo or not. It was found that clarifying a text's meaning resulted in increased activation in medial brain regions. Similarly, in examining comprehension of narratives versus unlinked sentences, Xu et al. (2005) found increased activity in the anterior temporal pole, and medial prefrontal cortex (bilaterally) among other regions. One way to summarize these disparate findings is that the comprehension of meaningful narratives is associated with increased neural activity as compared to less meaningful ones, although at present, the nature of the specific manipulation seems to affect the anatomical pattern of results more than does the presence of textual clarification *per se.*

World knowledge is critical for deciphering causal relationships between sentences. Neural regions involved in establishing a causal link between two sentences were first examined by Mason and Just (2004), who presented pairs of sentences varying in causal strength. They found that neural activity in temporal regions in the right hemisphere as well as regions in right IFG was mediated by the strength of the causal link between two sentences. When the sentences were moderately related (as opposed to highly related or distantly related) these regions demonstrated the greatest number of active voxels. In that study, it was the moderate-link condition that most strongly demanded construction of a causal scenario from world knowledge. Yet, a different study using a highly similar methodology (Kuperberg et al., 2006) revealed quite different findings: while the moderate-link condition was associated with the highest activity in certain regions, these did not overlap with those reported by Mason and Just.

A number of studies have attempted to identify brain regions involved in integrating consecutive discourse ideas. Ferstl et al. (2005) found that hearing a statement that is inconsistent with prior discourse context was associated with increased neural activity in the vicinity of the right anterior temporal pole and bilaterally in anterior IFG. Individual differences in perceiving inconsistencies were linked to activity in dorso-medial prefrontal cortex. Another study demonstrated that transitions between narrative events during reading are associated with increased activity in midline and right temporal regions (Speer et al., 2007).

The emerging picture from studies of discourse comprehension is that discourse-level relations in text affect activity in brain regions that are not typically involved in the comprehension of single, context-independent sentences. Furthermore, in contrast to the relatively entrenched position that language is mainly left lateralized, discourse relations seem to affect activity bilaterally (Jung-Beeman, 2005).

Challenges and Future Directions

One of the main challenges facing future research is establishing how and whether language processing capitalizes on more general functions. As reviewed, extracting speech categories from the auditory input may rely on general mechanisms. Similarly, accessing semantic knowledge via words likely depends to some extent on general mechanisms mediating access to semantic knowledge whether triggered verbally or by other means (e.g., pictures or gestures). Compositional processes at the sentence level may share common functions and neural basis with processes mediating music comprehension, comprehension of meaningful sound sequences or even pantomime sequences. On the discourse level, establishing consistency or inconsistency with prior information could rely on neural substrates with a general role in noticing unexpected stimuli in an input stream. Thus, understanding the relation between language comprehension and related domains would be an essential step towards establishing what types of neural processing are more or less specialized for language comprehension.

Another research direction that is developing to be of major interest will address how non-verbal input such as hand gestures or face movements affect the neural processing of language. The presence of gestures can serve to emphasize or add to information conveyed verbally. Thus, the presence of gesture will result in increased activity in certain regions (as more information is processed), but less activity in others, as interpretation *per se* may be easier. Understanding how such integration takes place will enhance understanding of both verbal and non-verbal processing.

Finally, we expect that much research effort will be dedicated to understanding the extent to which language comprehension relies on more basic perceptual or motor systems, and the specific circumstances in which these systems play a greater or lesser role. In particular, it would be important to explicate how activity in such areas serves language comprehension, and whether their activity is sensitive to higher level, a-modal functions expressed by language, such as negation.

To summarize, the neurophysiology of language has benefited greatly from fMRI research to date. The challenges facing this research in the future are interesting, and successfully dealing with those challenges is likely to lead to a much better understating of the human language system.

References

Belin, P, Fecteau, S, and Bedard, C (2004) Thinking the voice: Neural correlates of voice perception. *Trends in Cognitive Science* 8(3): 129–135.

Ben-Shachar, M, Hendler, T, Kahn, I, Ben-Bashat, D, and Grodzinsky, Y (2003). The neural reality of syntactic transformations. *Psychological Science* 14: 433–440.

Calvert, GA, Bullmore, ET, Brammer, MJ, Campbell, R, Williams, SCR, McGuire, PK, et al. (1997). Activation of auditory cortex during silent lipreading. *Science* 276(5312): 593–596.

Calvert, GA, Campbell, R, and Brammer, MJ (2000). Evidence from functional magnetic resonance imaging of crossmodal binding in the human heteromodal cortex. *Current Biology* 10(11): 649–657.

Constable, RT, Pugh, KR, Berroya, E, Mencl, WE, Westerveld, M, Ni, W, and Shankweiler, D (2004). Sentence complexity and input modality effects in sentence comprehension: An fMRI study. *Neuroimage* 22(1): 11–21.

Cooke, A, Zurif, EB, DeVita, C, Alsop, D, Koenig, P, Detre, J, Gee, J, Pinãngo, M, Balogh, J, and Grossman, M (2002). Neural basis for sentence comprehension: Grammatical and short-term memory components. *Human Brain Mapping* 15(2): 80–94.

Copland, DA, de Zubicaray, GI, McMahon, K, Wilson, SJ, Eastburn, M, and Chenery, HJ (2003). Brain activity during automatic semantic priming revealed by event-related functional magnetic resonance imaging. *Neuroimage* 20(1): 302–310.

Dapretto, M and Bookheimer, SY (1999). Form and content: Dissociating syntax and semantics in sentence comprehension. *Neuron* 24(2): 427–432.

Demb, JB, Desmond, JE, Wagner, AD, Vaidya, CJ, Glover, GH, and Gabrieli, JD (1995). Semantic encoding and retrieval in the left inferior prefrontal cortex: A functional MRI study of task difficulty and process specificity. *Journal of Neuroscience* 15(9): 5870–5878.

Ferstl, EC, Rinck, M, and von Cramon, DY (2005). Emotional and temporal aspects of situation model processing during text comprehension: An event-related fMRI study. *Journal of Cognitive Neuroscience* 17(5): 724–739.

Fiebach, CJ, Schlesewsky, M, Lohmann, G, von Cramon, DY, and Friederici, AD (2005). Revisiting the role of Broca's area in sentence processing: Syntactic integration versus syntactic working memory. *Human Brain Mapping* 24(2): 79–91.

Friederici, AD, Rüschemeyer, S-A, Hahne, A, and Fiebach, CJ (2003). The role of left inferior frontal and superior temporal cortex in sentence comprehension: Localizing syntactic and semantic processes. *Cerebral Cortex* 13(2): 170–177.

Gold, BT, Balota, DA, Kirchhoff, BA, and Buckner, RL (2005). Common and dissociable activation patterns associated with controlled semantic and phonological processing: Evidence from fMRI adaptation. *Cerebral Cortex* 15(9): 1438–1450.

Griffiths, TD and Warren, JD (2002). The planum temporale as a computational hub. *Trends in Neurosciences* 25(7): 348–353.

Grodzinsky, Y and Friederici, AD (2006). Neuroimaging of syntax and syntactic processing. *Current Opinion in Neurobiology* 16(2): 240–246.

Hasson, U, Nusbaum, HC, and Small, SL (2006). Repetition suppression for spoken sentences and the effect of task demands. *Journal of Cognitive Neuroscience* 18(12): 2013–2029.

Humphries, C, Willard, K, Buchsbaum, B, and Hickok, G (2001). Role of anterior temporal cortex in auditory sentence comprehension: an fMRI study. *Neuroreport* 12(8): 1749–1752.

Jung-Beeman, M (2005). Bilateral brain processes for comprehending natural language. *Trends in Cognitive Sciences* 9: 512–518.

Just, MA, Carpenter, PA, Keller, TA, Eddy, WF, and Thulborn, KR (1996). Brain activation modulated by sentence comprehension. *Science* 274(5284): 114–116.

Kuperberg, GR, McGuire, PK, Bullmore, ET, Brammer, MJ, Rabe-Hesketh, S, Wright, IC, Lythgoe, DJ, Williams, SRC, and David, AS (2000). Common and distinct neural substrates for pragmatic, semantic, and syntactic processing of spoken sentences: An fMRI study. *Journal of Cognitive Neuroscience* 12(2): 321–341.

Kuperberg, GR, Lakshmanan, BM, Caplan, DN, and Holcomb, PJ (2006). Making sense of discourse: An fMRI study of causal inferencing across sentences. *Neuroimage* 33: 343–361.

Maguire, EA, Frith, CD, and Morris, RGM (1999). The functional neuroanatomy of comprehension and memory: The importance of prior knowledge. *Brain* 122: 1839–1850.

Martin, A and Chao, LL (2001). Semantic memory and the brain: Structure and processes. *Current Opinion in Neurobiology* 11(2): 194–201.

Mason, RA and Just, MA (2004). How the brain processes causal inferences in text. *Psychological Science* 15(1): 1.

Meyer, M, Zaehle, T, Gountouna, VE, Barron, A, Jancke, L, and Turk, A (2005). Spectro-temporal processing during speech perception involves left posterior auditory cortex. *Neuroreport* 16(18): 1985–1989.

Narain, C, Scott, SK, Wise, RJS, Rosen, S, Leff, A, Iversen, SD, and Matthews, PM (2003). Defining a left-lateralized response specific to intelligible speech using fMRI. *Cerebral Cortex* 13: 1362–1368.

Noppeney, U and Price, CJ (2004). An fMRI study of syntactic adaptation. *Journal of Cognitive Neuroscience* 16: 702–713.

Poldrack, RA, Wagner, AD, Prull, MW, Desmond, JE, Glover, GH, and Gabrieli, JDE (1999). Functional specialization for semantic and phonological processing in the left inferior prefrontal cortex. *Neuroimage* 10: 15–35.

Rauschecker, JP and Tian, B (2000). Mechanisms and streams for processing of "what" and "where" in auditory cortex. *Proceedings of the National Academy of Sciences* 97(22): 11800–11806.

Rodd, JM, Davis, MH, and Johnsrude, IS (2005). The neural mechanisms of speech comprehension: fMRI studies of semantic ambiguity. *Cerebral Cortex* 15(8): 1261–1269.

Scott, SK and Johnsrude, IS (2003). The neuroanatomical and functional organization of speech perception. *Trends in Neurosciences* 26(2): 100–107.

Skipper, JI, Nusbaum, HC, and Small, SL (2005). Listening to talking faces: Motor cortical activation during speech perception. *Neuroimage* 25: 76–89.

Speer, NK, Zacks, JM, and Reynolds, JR (2007). Human brain activity time-locked to narrative event boundaries. *Psychological Science* 18: 449–455.

St. George, M, Kutas, M, Martinez, A, and Sereno, MI (1999). Semantic integration in reading: Engagement of the right hemisphere during discourse processing. *Brain* 122: 1317–1325.

Stowe, LA, Paans, AMJ, Wijers, AA, Zwarts, F, Mulder, G, and Vaalburg, W (1999). Sentence comprehension and word repetition: A positron emission tomography investigation. *Psychophysiology* 36: 786–801.

Vandenberghe, R, Nobre, AC, and Price, CJ (2002). The response of left temporal cortex to sentences. *Journal of Cognitive Neuroscience* 14(4): 550–560.

Vouloumanos, A, Kiehl, KA, Werker, JF, and Liddle, PF (2001). Detection of sounds in the auditory stream: Event-related fMRI evidence for differential activation to speech and nonspeech. *Journal of Cognitive Neuroscience* 13(7): 994–1005.

Wagner, AD, Koutstaal, W, Maril, A, Schacter, DL, and Buckner, RL (2000). Task-specific repetition priming in left inferior prefrontal cortex. *Cerebral Cortex* 10: 1176–1184.

Xu, J, Kemeny, S, Park, G, Frattali, C, and Braun, A (2005). Language in context: emergent features of word, sentence, and narrative comprehension. *Neuroimage* 25(3): 1002–1015.

Further Reading

Hasson, U, Nusbaum, HC, and Small, SL (2007). Brain networks subserving the extraction of sentence information and its encoding to memory. *Cerebral Cortex* Advance Access published on March 19, 2007. DOI 10.1093/cercor/bhm016.

An examination of brain regions involved in the integration of discourse contents, and their encoding to memory. Highlights the role of temporal, frontal and midline brain regions in encoding discourse content.

Jung-Beeman, M (2005). Bilateral brain processes for comprehending natural language. *Trends in Cognitive Sciences* 9: 512–518.
A review of higher level language comprehension with emphasis on the role of the right hemisphere in semantic processing at the single word and discourse level.

Vigneau, M, Beaucousin, V, Herve, PY, Duffau, H, Crivello, F, Houde, O, Mazoyer, B, and Tzourio-Mazoyer, N (2006). Meta-analyzing left hemisphere language areas: Phonology, semantics, and sentence processing. *Neuroimage* 30(4): 1414–1432.
An analysis of data from 129 scientific reports of neural activity during language processing, broadly defined.

Xu, J, Kemeny, S, Park, G, Frattali, C, and Braun, A (2005). Language in context: Emergent features of word, sentence, and narrative comprehension. *Neuroimage* 25(3): 1002–1015.
A comprehensive fMRI study of the differences between single-word, single-sentence and discourse processing.

H

Handedness and Cerebral Laterality

D. H. Geschwind and E. Crabtree

The concept of laterality in cerebral functioning arose from the notion that brain functions were localized. Without the recognition of the relationship between specific brain regions and discrete functions, there would not have been the necessary context in which the issue of brain laterality could be discussed. In this regard, it is ironic that the early threads of modern functional localization may have been reborn in the science of phrenology introduced by Franz Joseph Gall in the early 19th century. Phrenology played an important role by challenging prevailing notions of more diffuse or esoteric underpinnings of human cognitive and behavioral capacities, although its true localizing value was absent.

In 1861, approximately 40 years later, Paul Broca presented his first and most famous patient, dubbed "Tan" for the major sound produced when this unfortunate patient attempted speech. Based on Tan and one other case, Broca posited a specific relationship between the left frontal lobe and spoken language. Brain specialization along the dorsal–ventral and rostral–caudal axes was well appreciated; but Broca's assertion was revolutionary in the context of the prevailing belief that the brain was a symmetrical organ. Broca's stunning observations provided the foundation for modern research in brain laterality and language.

In the ensuing decades, other cases supported Broca's seminal conclusions while expanding our understanding of the cerebral territory responsible for language. Similarly, other functions, such as visuospatial, and constructional abilities were localized to the right hemisphere, and different aspects of emotional function appear similarly lateralized. Whereas the asymmetry in structures such as the pars triangularis of the frontal lobe and planum temporale of the posterior temporal lobe supports an anatomical basis for language laterality, the structural–anatomical basis of emotional, constructional, and spatial functional laterality has not been as well established. Although the well-recognized asymmetries in perisylvian language regions are present prior to birth, precisely how anatomical asymmetry is involved in the organization of functional asymmetry for language observed in individuals is unknown.

However, functional brain laterality for language and other higher cognitive functions is so well established that a reference to another strongly lateralized human behavior, handedness, begins the discussion of every neurological patient. This practice sets the context for understanding the patient's condition, emphasizing the striking and undeniable link between brain function laterality and handedness. This association was introduced by Hughlings Jackson, who, following Broca, reported the case of a left-handed man with aphasia and a right-sided lesion, demonstrating a connection between hand dominance and language laterality.

Although these observations may have suggested that left-handers' brains are the mirror image of right-handers' brains, a large number of lesion studies have demonstrated a more complex relationship. Language is localized in the left hemisphere perisylvian regions of the majority (97%) of right-handers, whereas left-handers are far more likely than right-handers to have either right hemisphere or bilateral language. The organization of the left-hander's brain about the left–right axis is best explained by a loss of the strong bias toward leftward brain asymmetry that is present in right-handers, leading to a more symmetrical, less lateralized brain in left-handers. This likely underlies the more rapid recovery of many left-handers than right-handers from strokes or other injuries affecting language function. Moreover, the study of brain organization in some groups of patients with developmental language disorders, such as dyslexia, Klinefelter's syndrome, and autism, has suggested an increase in left-handedness and a tendency toward increased brain symmetry in language regions in some studies, again supporting the relationship between handedness, language, and brain asymmetry. The concept that certain functions are strongly lateralized to one hemisphere, perhaps not exclusively, is often referred to as cerebral dominance. Populations that differ from the standard pattern of lateralization or dominance (e.g., left-handers) are said to have anomalous dominance.

Most clinicians define handedness simply by the preferred hand for writing. For the most part, this simplification is meaningful. However, it does not take into account societal biases and training effects that may alter the writing hand, thus masking the true handedness of the individual, which may still be evident in less regimented activities such as household chores and sports. For this reason, hand preference inventories or skill tests are used in research.

One important issue is how handedness measures are used to classify subjects. For example, in how many activities must one prefer to use the left hand to be considered left-handed? The neurobehavioral and psychological literature supports the division of the population into strong right-handers (approximately 90–92% of people), those who use the right hand for almost all activities, and non-right-handers (approximately 8–10% of people, called left-handers), who may prefer the left hand for some or the majority of fine motor activities. This definition of left-handedness is supported by most research and correlates well with preferred writing hand, fine motor skill, structural brain asymmetry, and language functional laterality. Furthermore, left-handers overall show less strong hand bias in preference questionnaires and skill tests than do right-handers, consistent with the definition of non-right-handers and in parallel with the more symmetrical organization of their brains.

One evolutionary prediction based on the fundamental link between brain organization for language and human handedness is that left hemisphere language and the predominance of right-handers are an early and relatively stable feature in human populations. It is therefore not surprising that the historical record as far back as 15,000 BC demonstrates a fixed and relatively stable prevalence of right-handedness of approximately 90%, with no significant cross-cultural differences. This is in contrast to other species; although individual animals may show paw preference, the striking asymmetrical distribution of handedness seen in humans is not observed. Similarly, whereas human handedness runs in families, in animals paw preference does not appear to be influenced by previous generations.

These observations suggest that human handedness has a fundamental genetic basis. However, the nature of this genetic influence and its relationship with language and brain laterality has been a source of controversy. Furthermore, whether handedness is a continuum or simply two categories, left and right, remains controversial. To classify subjects into categories, one needs to define a cutoff—a process that can be considered arbitrary when applied to any complex behavior such as handedness. We routinely make arbitrary cutoffs as part of neurobehavioral diagnoses, such as when using the yardstick of level of functioning within society to define disease states such as dementia or dyslexia. However, we should recognize that there is often no clear biological evidence supporting the specific cutoffs that are used. Tests of relative hand skill, which simply measure dexterity and speed, often show two overlapping populations, each with a normal distribution. Further understanding of the environmental and genetic factors that underlie handedness and brain language dominance, providing a robust biological framework, will be necessary to answer satisfactorily the question of whether handedness is fundamentally continuous or dichotomous.

In this regard, two major biological models of brain asymmetry and handedness have been most influential. The first, known as the Geschwind–Galaburda hypothesis, attempts to incorporate alterations in typical cerebral dominance (the preeminence of one cerebral hemisphere over the other for a specific function such as language) with diverse associated conditions, such as specific learning disabilities and autoimmune disorders and left-handedness, into a neurodevelopmental model driven by *in utero* testosterone levels. This theory remains unproven but has sparked a large amount of research to test its predictions. Its strength lies in tying together seemingly unconnected clinical observations by postulating common fundamental developmental influences. The treatment of handedness and its relationship to cerebral dominance in the Geschwind-Galaburda model is largely influenced by a second major biological model of human handedness, the R-shift model proposed by Marian Annett.

The Right-shift theory postulates that human language dominance and handedness are biased to the left hemisphere due to the influence of a major gene, the R-shift gene. The absence of this influence tends toward random asymmetry or relative symmetry, which is the situation in most left-handers. To many geneticists, it is antiparadigmatic that a complex behavior such as handedness or a fundamental aspect of language would be attributed to a single major gene rather than to multiple genes interacting with the environment. This is certainly the case for other behavioral features or cognitive capacities in which multiple genetic loci have been implicated.

However, the R-shift model and other major gene models are supported by our knowledge of the development of visceral body asymmetry, where some of the molecular signaling pathways that contribute to symmetry breaking and organ asymmetry (visceral situs) have been identified. Loss-of-function mutations in single genes involved in these pathways can lead to mirror-image reversal of the viscera, organ duplication, or random organ placement. This is in agreement with the major gene models of handedness, in which the non-right-handed genotype that defines most left-handers results in a loss or reduction in directional bias or, in some cases, a total loss of positional information. In this manner, a relatively complex genetic phenotype is generated from a single mutation that operates stochastically.

It is also notable that three genes involved in visceral left–right axis development are asymmetrically expressed in a lower vertebrate diencephalon (zebrafish) during development. In addition to asymmetrically expressed genes, studies of lower vertebrates have demonstrated a critical role for the midline of the developing embryo in the development of asymmetry. Some of the genes involved in these complex signaling cascades underlying visceral asymmetry are involved in central nervous system patterning along the anterior–posterior and dorsal–ventral axes in vertebrates. However, the connection between genes involved in visceral asymmetry and cerebral laterality in humans has not been demonstrated.

Genetic influences on a particular trait, such as handedness or brain asymmetry, can be tested by studying how the phenotype (what is being measured or observed) varies as a function of genetic relatedness. In humans, this is accomplished by performing family or twin studies. Twin studies are powerful because twins share a similar environment *in utero*; however, dizygotic (DZ) twins share only half of their genes, whereas monozygotic (MZ) twins are genetically identical. Therefore, by comparing the extent to which a particular phenotype is shared among MZ and DZ twin pairs, one can estimate the heritability of that trait.

Meta-analyses of twin studies of handedness performed by Sicotte and Woods demonstrated a slight increase in left-handedness among twins, consistent with the possible contribution of pre- or perinatal injury (so-called pathological left-handedness) in a small percentage of twins. However, an increase in MZ twin similarity for handedness (concordance) relative to DZ twins was also demonstrated, supporting a genetic etiology for handedness. This is consistent with the conclusions of a large number of population-based or family studies that show significant familiality for handedness.

To further explore the genetic links between genes, handedness, and cerebral asymmetry, we studied cerebral lobar volumes as determined by magnetic resonance imaging in a large cohort of aging twins. This work confirmed the results of other studies showing a large genetic component to cerebral structure and cerebral volume overall. In addition, it demonstrated that twin pairs with the non-right-handed genetic makeup had more symmetrical, somewhat random hemisphere volumes, entirely consistent with models postulating a R-shift genetic influence that is lost in non-right-handers. Also, we found that shared environment, which likely represents *in utero* events in twins, had approximately twice the influence on left hemisphere frontal and temporal volumes than on those on the right. This could mean that hormonal or other factors have more influence on left hemisphere structures, such as those underlying language, supporting a potential role for prenatal testosterone or other alterations in the local biochemical milieu in language development. However, this effect of the environment on left hemisphere structure was not related to genetic handedness; therefore, it is likely independent of genetic factors contributing to cerebral laterality per se. Due to the availability of increasingly powerful biological and genetic methodologies, many of these relationships should soon be clarified.

See also: Behavior, Neural Basis of.

Further Reading

Alexander, MP and Annett, M (1996). Crossed aphasia and related anomalies of cerebral organization: Case reports and a genetic hypothesis. *Brain Language* 55: 213–239.

Annett, M (1985). *Left, Right, Hand and Brain: The Right Shift Theory.* London: Erlbaum.

Davidson, R and Hugdahl, K (1995). *Brain Asymmetry.* Cambridge, MA: MIT Press.

Galaburda, AM, LeMay, M, Kemper, TL, et al. (1978). Right-left asymmetries in the brain. *Science* 199: 852–856.

Geschwind, D and Iacoboni, M (1999). Structural and functional asymmetries of the frontal lobes. In: Miller, B and Cummings, J (eds.) *The Frontal Lobes*, pp. 45–70. New York: Guilford.

Geschwind, DH and Miller, BL (2001). Molecular approaches to cerebral laterality: Development and neurodegeneration. *Am. J. Med. Genet.* 101: 370–381.

Geschwind, DH, Miller, BL, DeCarli, C, et al. (2002). Heritability of lobar brain volumes in twins supports genetic models of cerebral laterality and handedness. *Proc. Natl. Acad. Sci. USA* 99: 3176–3181.

Geschwind, N and Galaburda, A (1985). Cerebral lateralization: Biological mechanisms, associations, and pathology. *Arch. Neurol.* 42: 428–458, 521–552.

McManus, IC (1991). The inheritance of left-handedness. *CIBA Foundation Symp.* 162: 251–267; discussion 267–281.

Schachter, SC, Galaburda, AM, and Ransil, BJ (1993). Associations of dyslexia with epilepsy, handedness, and gender. *Ann. N. Y. Acad. Sci.* 682: 402–403.

Sicotte, N, Woods, R, and Mazziotta, J (1999). Handedness in twins: A meta-analysis. *Laterality* 4: 265–286.

Yost, HJ (2001). Establishment of left-right asymmetry. *Int. Rev. Cytol.* 203: 357–381.

Hemispheric Specialization and Cognition

M. T. Banich, University of Colorado at Boulder, Boulder, CO, USA

Hemispheric Differences in Cognition

Discovery of Hemispheric Differences in Cognition

Paul Broca, a French neurologist and anthropologist, is generally considered the first person to have clearly illustrated hemispheric differences in cognitive function. As such, he is often said to have discovered the phenomenon. His critical insight derived from his visit with a patient who demonstrated an interesting dissociation in language abilities. Although able to understand what was said to him, the man had an inability to produce speech, being able only to utter the syllable 'tan.' Broca's postmortem analysis of his brain showed that damage was localized to the third convolution of the inferior frontal gyrus in the left hemisphere. Broca then went on to examine other patients who exhibited a similar cognitive profile – an inability to produce speech in the face of a retained ability to comprehend speech. In all cases, the damage was localized to the same region but, most important, always in the left hemisphere – a region now known as Broca's area. As a result of these findings, Broca proposed in 1863 that the left hemisphere is specialized, or dominant, for speech output. Thus, Broca's paper was the first systematic and compelling demonstration of hemispheric specialization of function. In fact, unlike most other aspects of hemispheric specialization, this one is absolute: the right hemisphere has no ability to control speech output in practically all right-handed individuals.

Evidence from Patients with Unilateral Brain Damage

As a result of Broca's discovery, the idea of cerebral dominance was overgeneralized. Probably because language was considered synonymous with thought, his work was interpreted to mean that the left hemisphere was dominant for all aspects of cognitive function. This idea only began to erode gradually over the next century as studies of patients with unilateral brain damage demonstrated different consequences depending on which hemisphere was damaged. As apparent to any neurologist or clinical neuropsychologist, left hemisphere damage usually results in deficits in the domains of verbal, sequential, and analytic processing. For example, aphasia is a common consequence of left hemisphere damage. In contrast, right hemisphere damage typically yields deficits in nonverbal, holistic, and Gestalt processing. For example, deficits in visuospatial processing are more often observed after right hemisphere damage.

Evidence from Split-Brain Patients

In the 1960s, research by Nobel laureate Roger Sperry and colleagues with split-brain patients dramatically demonstrated the relative specialization of the cerebral hemispheres. In these split-brain patients, the main nerve fiber tract connecting the cerebral hemispheres, the corpus callosum, is severed for the treatment of intractable epilepsy. As a result, higher order information, such as that about an item's identity (e.g., a car, the letter 'A,' and the face of Bill Clinton), cannot be transferred from one hemisphere to the other. Thus, information directed to a single hemisphere is functionally isolated to that hemisphere. This situation provides a unique opportunity to examine the relative specialization of the cerebral hemispheres because each hemisphere's capabilities can be examined in isolation from those of its partner. As a result, research with split-brain patients has yielded much important information about hemispheric specialization. Absolute differences have been demonstrated only for a couple of functions, namely speech output and phonological processing, which are under sole control of the left hemisphere. Both hemispheres can perform all other tasks, albeit with differing levels of ability and in different manners. Whereas the left hemisphere has a rich ability to perform most all language tasks, the vocabulary of the right hemisphere is much more limited, as is its ability to process complicated grammatical functions. On the other hand, the right hemisphere is superior at processing most types of spatial relationships, especially those involving three-dimensional relations or complicated geometries.

Perceptual Asymmetries in Neurologically Intact Individuals

The relative specializations of the cerebral hemispheres can also be demonstrated in neurologically intact individuals through the use of methods that essentially pit the hemispheres against one another. These methods, which include tachitoscopic presentation, dichotic listening, and dichaptic presentation, all take advantage of the neuroanatomical wiring of the human brain that transfers information from sensory receptors to the contralateral sensory cortex. In these methods, information is presented laterally so it is received either solely or predominantly by one hemisphere. Then behavioral performance, with regard to either reaction time or accuracy, can be examined depending on which hemisphere initially received the sensory information. These behavioral measures are often referred to as perceptual asymmetries because they reflect the asymmetry in the perception of information depending on the hemisphere to which information was initially directed. Even though the corpus callosum in neurologically intact individuals contains more than 250 million fibers by which the hemispheres can communicate, differences in performance are nonetheless observed. Typically, these effects are in the range of a 10% difference in accuracy in performance or a 20–50 ms difference in reaction time. These studies provide converging evidence with data obtained from patients with unilateral brain damage and from split-brain patients. Myriads of studies have confirmed a left hemisphere superiority for processing verbal information and a right hemisphere superiority for processing nonverbal material, regardless of sensory modality – visual, auditory, or tactile.

Neuroimaging Studies of Hemispheric Specialization

The surge in neuroimaging during the past decade has also served to emphasize that the specializations of the hemispheres are more relative than absolute. These studies have shown that for most all tasks, activation is bilateral, although not necessarily of equal extent nor intensity. Even classic language tasks, such as verbal word reading, activate both hemispheres, although the activation is more left-sided than right-sided. In addition, the complimentarity of the hemispheres is revealed by these studies. For example, single-word processing leads to greater left than right hemisphere activation, but understanding the nonliteral meaning of language, such as analogy or the moral of a story, leads to greater right than left hemisphere activation.

Asymmetries Related to Emotion and Emotional Processing

Hemispheric specialization is not limited to cognitive function; it is found for emotional processes as well. The majority of evidence suggests that the right hemisphere is specialized for the interpretation of emotional information, including information contained in tone of voice and facial expression. Moreover, it is also specialized for the production of emotional cues that serve a communicative function (e.g., a smile that sends a communicative signal to someone else letting him or her know you are happy or pleased).

In contrast, lateralization of mood – that is, the subjective experience of one's internal emotional state – appears to rely on a pattern of brain activation across prefrontal and parietal regions. A large body of research has indicated that asymmetry of activation of frontal regions of the brain is linked to mood states. Greater activation of left than right frontal regions is associated with positive mood and approach behaviors. In contrast, greater activation of the right than left frontal regions is associated with negative mood and avoidance behavior. Moreover, individual differences in these asymmetries have been linked to differences in temperament in infants and to susceptibility to depression in later life. Overlaid on these effects of valence (positive and negative) are differences in activation of right parietal regions, which are linked to arousal. Depressed mood is associated with decreased activity of right parietal regions, whereas the panic associated with heightened anxiety is associated with increased activity of right parietal regions.

Models of Hemispheric Specialization

The broad body of work – from patients with unilateral brain damage, split-brain patients, and studies of perceptual asymmetries with neurologically intact individuals – was originally framed with regard to differences in the type of material that each hemisphere is specialized to process. Initially, the left hemisphere was considered specialized for processing verbal materials, whereas the right hemisphere was considered specialized for processing nonverbal materials. However, in a series of studies in the late 1960s and early 1970s, studies with split-brain patients clearly demonstrated that in many cases both hemispheres were capable of processing a given type of material. What differed, however, was the manner in which they processed that material. This led to a new rubric for understanding hemispheric specialization. The left hemisphere was conceptualized to analyze information in an analytic, piecemeal, and local manner, whereas the right hemisphere was conceptualized to analyze information in a holistic and Gestalt manner. For example, although the right hemisphere of a split-brain patient is superior to the left at identifying a previously viewed face, both can do so. The right hemisphere appears to analyze the overall configuration of the face, such as whether the face is long and narrow or wide and round, and whether the eyes are wide set compared to the width of the face. In contrast, the left hemisphere processes the features or local details, such as the shape of the chin or the eyes. This shift in conceptualizing hemispheric specialization was important because it explained a potential advantage of a specialized brain, namely the ability of simultaneous dual processing. Practically all information can be processed independently and in a distinct manner by each hemisphere at the same time, providing two distinct ways of simultaneously understanding and interpreting the world.

With this conceptual shift, researchers began to explore hemispheric differences from a computational perspective, with the goal of determining the fundamental differences in computations performed by each hemisphere. One early theory suggested that the hemispheres differed in their ability to process low-level sensory information. In particular, the right hemisphere was conceived as being specialized for processing information of low visual spatial frequency – that is, information that does not shift from dark to light within a small degree of visual space. This information generally provides the general contours and outline of visual forms but not the details. In contrast, the left hemisphere was conceived as being specialized for processing information of high spatial frequency – that is, information that shifts quickly, within a given amount of visual space, from dark to light. Such information provides the detail in visual forms. Moreover, asymmetries in higher order cognitive function were posited to emerge from these sensory asymmetries. For example, the overall configuration of a face would be provided by visual information of low spatial frequency, whereas the detailed information would be provided by visual information of high spatial frequency.

This theory was highly influential and has been subsequently modified. Further research demonstrated that the hemispheres appear to be specialized not for the absolute frequency of sensory information but, rather, for the relative frequency, an effect that holds across different sensory modalities. For example, when individuals are presented with information of high auditory frequency, the left hemisphere exhibits a performance advantage for processing the higher half of those high auditory frequencies and the right hemisphere for processing the lower half of those high auditory frequencies. Findings such as these have been expanded to be accounted for by the double-filtering hypothesis, which argues that hemispheric differences arise from an attentional bias in the information that each processes. It is argued that the right hemisphere employs a low pass filter on incoming information, whereas the left hemisphere employs a high pass filter.

Other researchers have focused on why there might be a need to have distinct ways of processing information in each of the cerebral hemispheres. These theories have focused on how the hemispheres might insulate conflicting or independent processes from one another. For example, in the spatial domain it has been argued that the right hemisphere is specialized to coordinate spatial relationships, considered those that provide information about the distance between objects. In contrast, the left hemisphere is specialized for categorical spatial relations that describe the relationship between items (e.g., above, below, to the right of, and to the left of). These two ways of describing information are considered orthogonal to each other because knowing the coordinate information, such as that one item is 3 ft from another, provides no information about categorical information, such as if one item is behind the other. Computational models suggest that these two types of spatial processing are best supported by independent insulated processing systems because the representations required are mutually incompatible and/or create interference. Performance on spatial tasks is superior in a split rather than unitary computational model, suggesting that the hemispheres are specialized to allow for noninterference of processing.

Similar arguments have been made with regard to language processing. Even though the left hemisphere alone has control over speech output and phonological processing, its specialization for language is also relative. Whereas the left hemisphere has been found to be superior to the right hemisphere in aspects of grammar and syntax, the right hemisphere is superior at processing the nonliteral aspects of language, such as discourse, metaphor, and analogy. These differences may arise from incompatible means of semantic access and/or organization. The left hemisphere appears to access words in a very specific, precise, and local manner, whereas the right hemisphere accesses words in a more diffuse manner that allows activation for more far-flung associates. For example, if a paragraph was about gardening, the left hemisphere would quickly hone in on the particular meaning of 'bug' related to insects, whereas the right hemisphere would hold onto a more diffuse set of meanings, including not only the meaning related to insects but also that related to spying devices. As such, the right hemisphere would be better equipped to make connections across sentences and phrases that would allow for discourse and for nonliteral aspects of language comprehension.

Origins of Hemispheric Asymmetry

Although there was once speculation that cerebral asymmetry is a unique feature of the human brain, hemispheric asymmetry is observed in other species, including not only mammals but also fishes, reptiles, and amphibians. The asymmetries observed in behaviors range from those involved in courtship and copulation to escape behavior and limb use (i.e., 'handedness'). These asymmetries are found not only for an individual organism (i.e., a right-sided limb preference in a given animal) but also at the population level. For example, apes tend to use the left hand for stabilizing objects and the right hand for fine motor manipulation. Likewise, 59% of certain species of toad prefer to use their right paw to remove an object affixed to their head.

Because hemispheric asymmetries are observed in many other species, much theorizing has focused on how language processing becomes lateralized. Some theories posit that the association of fine motor coordination of the right hand associated with tool use served as the platform for the fine motor control that is associated with the vocalizations that underlie human language. Other theories posit that a lateralized gestural system, when linked to vocalizations, led to language lateralization. Cross-species support for such an idea is provided by research showing that cells in area F5 of the macaque monkey brain, a region homologous to Broca's area in humans, fire when a monkey sees someone else perform a grasping action similar to one which it has just performed. It has been argued that these 'mirror' neurons underlie the ability to form, through gesture, a common communicative system between individuals. Such a common communicative system would then have evolved to include vocalization. Supporting this idea, gestures linked to speech are produced with much more frequency by the right hand in humans and chimpanzees, whereas gestures that do not have a communicative value (e.g., straightening one's clothes) are not produced asymmetrically.

Developmental Issues and Hemispheric Specialization

Given the evidence for an evolutionary history of lateralization of functioning, it is not surprising that hemispheric asymmetries exist at birth. That is not to say, however, that this pattern cannot be modified by environmental factors. Evidence for an inborn pattern of asymmetry comes from numerous sources. First, gyral and sulcul patterns, which differ between right- and left-handers (who, as discussed later, differ in behavioral asymmetry) are present before birth and not modified thereafter. Second, the effects of hemispherectomy at birth differ depending on whether the left or right hemisphere is removed. Although individuals with only one hemisphere acquire both verbal and nonverbal skills, the degree to which these skills are acquired varies by the hemisphere removed. Individuals with only a right hemisphere perform, on average, better on spatial tasks than those with only a left hemisphere, whereas individuals with only a left hemisphere perform better on verbal tasks than those with only a right hemisphere. Third, asymmetries can be observed in the newborn. These include motoric asymmetries, behavioral asymmetries, and asymmetries in brain responses. For example, a larger evoked response is recorded over the left hemisphere to verbal materials and over the right hemisphere to nonverbal materials.

Thus, it appears that the basic blueprint of hemispheric specialization exists at birth. However, the nature of that blueprint can be altered by environmental factors. For example, it has been well documented that after damage to the left hemisphere during approximately the first 2 years of life, the right hemisphere can acquire the ability to control speech. Somewhat more ambiguous are findings that experience can influence the degree of perceptual asymmetry that is observed. For example, a greater left visual field advantage is observed for holistic processing of faces from a racial group with which one is familiar than for faces of a group with which one is not familiar. Whether this result indicates that the nature of hemispheric specialization is changed by experience, or whether more experience tends to engage more specialized processors in the brain, remains unclear.

The Effect of Handedness

One individual difference, that of handedness, has been clearly linked to patterns of hemispheric specialization for cognitive and emotional function. The relative specializations of the cerebral hemispheres described previously appear to hold only for individuals who are right-handed. In contrast, left-handed individuals, who comprise approximately 10% of individuals worldwide, can have a diverse pattern of lateral organization. This difference is well-known by neurologists and neuropsychologists who have long observed that handedness is an important factor in predicting the types of deficits and the amount of recovery that is likely to be observed after unilateral brain damage. However, there is much variability among left-handers regarding the type of lateralized brain organization they display. In some cases, it is similar to that of right-handers, with the left hemisphere specialized for verbal functions and the right for nonverbal functions. In other cases, it is the opposite, with the right hemisphere specialized for verbal function and the left for nonverbal function. It is estimated that such a brain organization is found in only 1% or 2% of right-handers. Finally, other left-handers exhibit a pattern in which both hemispheres appear to be able to process both verbal and nonverbal information, including speech output. Although much research has attempted to isolate a factor that can predict the type of brain organization a given left-hander will exhibit, for the most part, these efforts have failed. Currently, the leading model of the genetic basis of handedness and its relationship to lateralized brain organization suggests that handedness (and hence brain organization) is randomly distributed, unless one inherits a right-shift allele, which shifts handedness to the right hand and language to the left hemisphere. Such a model assumes that it was evolutionarily advantageous to have motor control of the right hand and control of language co-lateralized to the same hemisphere.

Interhemispheric Integration

After the explosion of research examining hemispheric specialization in the 1970s and 1980s, recent work has examined how the processing of the hemispheres is coordinated and the effects of integration of information between the cerebral hemispheres.

Interhemispheric integration occurs mainly via the massive bundle of nerve fibers connecting the cerebral hemispheres, the corpus callosum. Because information from the peripheral nerves is directed contralaterally, at least for vision, motor, and somatosensory information, integration of information across the hemispheres allows information from each sensory half-field to be bound together. For example, in the visual domain, information is represented contralaterally in V1, V2, and V3a/VP. In fact, there are few, if any callosal connections in BA 17. Representation of information from the ipsilateral visual field first appears at the level of V3a and V4v, which are brain regions whose cells have receptive fields that span the midline. This critical role of the callosum in fusing the sensory worlds is made apparent by split-brain patients who cannot bind information from different sensory fields. For example, if fixated on a central point and shown two items, one on each side visual midline so that they are projected to opposite hemispheres, a split-brain patient cannot determine if they are the same or different.

Although the callosum acts as a mechanism to transfer information between the hemispheres, this transfer involves time costs as well as degradation of information. Transfer of information via the corpus callosum takes approximately 5 ms via the large myelinated fibers that connect sensory and motor areas and 20–50 ms for small unmylineated fibers. The fidelity costs are apparent in old/new memory paradigms. If an item is presented in one visual field, correctly recognizing of that item as previously viewed is poorer if presented to the hemisphere that did not initially view the item as compared to the hemisphere. Such findings are consistent with theorizing that the representations supported by each of the hemispheres are different and are not completely interchangeable.

Integration of information across the cerebral hemispheres plays an additional role above and beyond that of binding together the visual world – that of attentional control. Evidence suggests that the cerebral hemispheres dynamically couple and decouple to meet task demands. When tasks involve relatively low attentional demands, performance is better when all the critical information needed for a decision (e.g., are these two items physically identical?) is directed to a single hemisphere compared to divided between them. It has been proposed that under such conditions, the processing capacity of a single hemisphere is adequate to meet the demands and the cost of interhemispheric communication takes a toll on performance. In contrast, when attentional demands are high, dividing processing between the hemispheres enables more resources to be brought to bear and the advantage provided by these additional resources more than outweighs the cost of callosal transfer. Such an outcome can occur because, as described previously, the specialization of the hemispheres is not absolute but relative, allowing both hemispheres to process almost all types of information. Thus, the additional resources provided by the partner hemisphere, even if not specialized for the task, can nonetheless have a major impact on performance. These findings are consonant with data from individuals in whom the corpus callosum is severed or damaged, such as occurs in multiple sclerosis. A common consequence of callosal damage or insufficiency is problems in attentional control. Although the neural mechanisms that allow the callosum to play such a role remain somewhat obscure, connectionist modeling suggests that the advantage afforded by dividing processing between the hemispheres is an emergent phenomenon of having two somewhat insulated and distinct processors.

Summary

Each of the human cerebral hemispheres has a distinct manner of processing information, with the left hemisphere more adept at attending to and processing more fine-grained information and the right hemisphere more adept at attending to and processing more coarse-grained information. This distinction holds for all types of information, whether verbal or spatial. The complimentarity of these modes of processing means that the human brain contains two processors, each of which provides a unique manner of understanding and interpreting the world. Moreover, this dichotomy and isolation of processing also provides for a system that can dynamically reconfigure to act in isolation or in tandem depending on attentional demands.

See also: Brain Asymmetry, Evolution; Cognition, An Overview of Neuroimaging Techniques; Dichotic Listening Studies of Brain Asymmetry.

Further Reading

Annett, M (2002). *Handedness and Brain Asymmetry: The Right Shift Theory.* New York: Psychology Press.

Banich, MT (1998). The missing link: The role of interhemispheric interaction in attentional processing. *Brain and Cognition* 36: 128–157.

Beeman, MJ and Chiarello, C (1998). Complementary right- and left-hemisphere language comprehension. *Current Directions in Psychological Science* 7: 2–8.

Corballis, MC (2003). From mouth to hand: Gesture, speech, and the evolution of right-handedness. *Behavioral and Brain Sciences* 26: 199–260.

Davidson, RJ (1992). Anterior cerebral asymmetry and the nature of emotion. *Brain & Cognition* 20: 125–151.

Hellige, JB (2001). *Hemispheric Asymmetry: What's Right and What's Left.* Cambridge, MA: Harvard University Press.

Hugdahl, K and Davidson, RJ (eds.) (2003). *The Asymmetrical Brain.* Cambridge: MIT Press.

Ivry, RB and Robertson, LC (1998). *The Two Sides of Perception.* Cambridge: MIT Press.

Keller, J, Nitschke, JB, Bhargava, T, et al. (2000). Neuropsychological differentiation of depression and anxiety. *Journal of Abnormal Psychology* 109: 3–10.

Kosslyn, SM (1987). Seeing and imagining in the cerebral hemispheres: A computational approach. *Psychological Review* 94: 148–175.
Levy, J, Trevarthen, C, and Sperry, RW (1972). Perception of bilateral chimeric figures following hemispheric deconnexion. *Brain* 95: 61–78.
Monaghan, P and Pollmann, S (2003). Division of labor between the hemispheres for complex but not simple tasks: An implemented connectionist model. *Journal of Experimental Psychology: General* 132: 379–399.
Sergent, J (1985). Influence of task and input factors on hemispheric involvement in face processing. *Journal of Experimental Psychology: Human Perception and Performance* 11: 846–861.
Trevarthen, C (1996). Lateral asymmetries in infancy: Implications for the development of the hemispheres. *Neuroscience & Biobehavioral Reviews* 20: 571–586.
Zaidel, E and Iacoboni, M (eds.) (2003). *The Parallel Brain: The Cognitive Neuroscience of the Corpus Callosum.* Cambridge: MIT Press.

I

Imaging Brain Lateralization

B. Stemmer, University of Montreal, Montreal, Canada

Although there are still debates on the specific networks in the left hemisphere that contribute to language processing, most researchers adhere to the view that 'low-level' processing, including phonological, morphological, syntactic, and semantic processing, predominantly engages the left hemisphere. (*see* **Imaging Brain Lateralization, Words, Sentences, and Influencing Factors in Healthy, Pathological, and Special Populations**.) Right hemisphere involvement or dominance is usually attributed to 'high-level' processing, involving, for example, the comprehension or production of discourse and pragmatic (including social) aspects of language.

Integrating Semantics

Meaning developing from incoming words through spoken or written sentences is integrated rapidly with global discourse-level semantic information, usually within less than 600 milliseconds (for a summary see van Berkum et al., 2003). For example, when hearing a sentence such as *Dutch trains are red*, the semantic content of the sentence (i.e., that Dutch trains are of red color) is rapidly understood. However, at the same time, every person familiar with Dutch trains will also know that this is not true because Dutch trains are, in fact, yellow. In this example, semantic information does not coincide with pragmatic world knowledge. The question, thus, is whether there is a distinction between the integration of linguistic meaning (semantic information) and world knowledge (pragmatic information). Some researchers don't think so. Using functional magnetic resonance imaging (fMRI) scanning and recording of event-related potentials (ERPs), Hagoort et al. (2004) compared semantic and world knowledge violations and their correct counterparts using sentences such as *The Dutch trains are yellow/white/sour and very crowded.* Applying fMRI and ERPs to the same stimuli provided the researchers with information on the time course of the ongoing processes as well as on the spatial distribution of the underlying neural substrates. They observed an ERP component (the N400) that is very sensitive to semantic integration processes occurring in a time window between 250 to 550 milliseconds after the critical stimulus for both world knowledge violation and semantic violation. This indicated that lexical-semantic knowledge and general world knowledge were both integrated in the same time frame during sentence interpretation. The neural substrates that were activated when the critical words occurred were identified with fMRI and were all shown to be in the left hemisphere (left inferior prefrontal cortex, BA45 and 47) for both the semantic and the world knowledge violation condition. These findings were viewed as evidence that the left hemisphere, and specifically the left inferior prefrontal cortex, plays a role in the integration of both world knowledge and lexical semantic knowledge.

It seems, though, that at least for the integration of lexical semantic knowledge (pragmatic knowledge has not been investigated), other brain areas – such as the left posterior fusiform gyrus and the anterior temporal lobe bilaterally (Kiehl et al., 2002) – are also implicated. A specific involvement of the right hemisphere in lexical semantic meaning integration has been suggested by Federmeier and Kutas (1999). They used the ERP technique while presenting the critical stimuli to single hemispheres. Participants had to read pairs of sentences with different endings, such as: '*Checkmate,' Rosaline announced with glee. She was getting to be really good at chess/ monopoly/ football.* The target word at the end of the sentence was either an expected word (*chess*) or an unexpected word, thus creating contextual violation. The unexpected word could be from an expected category (*monopoly*) or an unexpected category (*football*). The target words were presented to either the left or the right hemisphere. The authors found a negativity (the N400) for contextual violations. However, this component differed according to the side of presentation. With presentations to the left hemisphere, the negativity was reduced when violations occurred within a category (*monopoly*). With presentation to the right hemisphere, the negativity was of similar amplitude for both within-category and between-category violations. The authors concluded that both hemispheres process message-level meaning but that they use qualitatively different processing strategies in the way new information is integrated into the sentence context. The right hemisphere compares new information directly with the context information and follows an 'integrative' strategy whereas the left hemisphere compares whether the new information matches the expectation that has been built-up and is thus more 'predictive.'

Hemispheric sentence contribution during sentence comprehension is also influenced by the information that the sentence conveys, such as abstract information or information that can be visualized. For example, when reading or listening to high- or low-imagery sentences and making true/false judgments, both hemispheres are implicated, but it seems to be the left hemisphere (intraparietal sulcus, frontal operculum, temporal area) that generates the internal representations that are used in maintaining and communicating the sentence information – possibly reflecting working memory functions (Just et al., 2004).

In summary, lexical semantic and pragmatic information seems to be integrated very quickly and simultaneously during sentence processing. Specific neural substrates in the left hemisphere have been implicated in the integration of both types of information. For lexical semantic integration, involvement of the right hemisphere has also been shown. Little is known, however, about the neural substrates involved in the integration of pragmatic information. It seems that both hemispheres contribute to lexical semantic integration, with each hemisphere possibly using qualitatively different processing strategies to integrate new information into the sentence context.

Discourse-Related Studies

The idea that the right hemisphere is dominant for discourse and pragmatic processing is based on observations with patients who have suffered damage to the right hemisphere. Such patient studies, however, have not provided conclusive evidence for this idea inasmuch as discourse and pragmatic problems have also been observed in patients with bilateral frontal, left frontal, or diffuse damage to the brain. Several explanations for the observed impairments have been proposed and include an inability to appropriately draw inferences, to integrate information, or to construct mental models. We will explore whether neuroimaging techniques have clarified the contribution of each hemisphere to discourse and pragmatic processing.

It is obvious that a text is easier to comprehend when the topic under discussion is a familiar one. This is, in part, because information on familiar topics can be integrated and inferences drawn on these more easily. For example, it can be difficult to comprehend a text about how to use a video recorder when the headline is missing, that is, without a clarification of the general context of the following information. Several neuroimaging studies indicate right hemisphere dominance in tasks in which the theme or topic guides comprehension or requires topic maintenance (Caplan and Dapretto, 2001; St. George et al., 1999). The specific neural substrates activated within the right hemisphere show **rough** overlapping in right inferior frontal and temporal regions. Drawing inferences from a discourse to judge the theme or moral of a story is also associated with right hemisphere activation (orbital part of the inferior frontal gyrus, BA47; anterior portion of the middle temporal gyrus, BA21) (Nichelli et al., 1995). Note that besides right hemisphere activation, the left hemisphere language network is usually also activated, indicating the presence of low-level language processing, such as word retrieval and syntactic parsing. Both hemispheres (especially the dorsolateral prefrontal cortex) seem to be involved when the generation of an inference is necessary to maintain coherence in a text. Once an inference is successfully generated, the right hemisphere takes over to integrate the inference into the internal knowledge base of the reader/writer (Mason and Just, 2004). However, not all tasks that involve making inferences activate the right hemisphere. Deductive and syllogistic verbal reasoning tasks and the judgment of local coherence when reading sentences have been shown to activate specific regions in the left hemisphere (left frontal, left temporal, and left cingulate regions for deductive and syllogistic verbal reasoning and left frontomedian wall, posterior cingulate, and precuneal regions for judging coherence; Ferstl and von Cramon, 2001; Goel et al., 1998). One explanation of this left hemispheric involvement is that the generation processes involved in these tasks operate on easily available information and are relatively automatic. No high-level integration processes are necessary.

The comprehension of discourse and pragmatic aspects are also influenced by the way stress and intonation are used, and some models have proposed that prosody is lateralized to the right hemisphere, although the evidence is not clear cut (for a review see Baum and Pell, 1999). Right hemisphere activation is reported by one functional imaging study investigating recognition of emotional prosody by applying stress and intonation to words or sentences that conveyed the speaker's emotional state (anger, surprise, sadness, or happiness) (Buchanan et al., 2000). Increased activation was reported in the right inferior frontal gyrus and right inferior parietal regions. Considering that the right prefrontal cortex has generally been implicated in the processing of emotions, it remains open whether the observed right hemisphere activation is specific to prosody or to the emotional component involved. In a review of the literature, Baum and Pell (1999) concluded that a clear-cut division that assigns prosody to the right hemisphere is unwarranted.

Investigating the Pragmatics of Communication

When we talk about the pragmatics of communication, we talk about language in use and in context. That not everything that is said is meant in a direct, straightforward way is best exemplified when we use figurative language such as metaphors or irony. To comprehend the information the other person wants to convey entails inferring the other person's intention, or attributing mental states.

Attributing Mental States

We constantly draw on our experience and knowledge and on information from the environment to make sense of the world. Taking a different perspective and inferring the mental state of other people (that is, their intentions, knowledge, beliefs, or desires) is fundamental to successful interaction. Several neuroimaging studies have investigated the neural substrates underlying the attribution of mental states (such as discussed in the theory of mind; for a summary see Abu-Akel, 2003; Gallagher and Frith, 2003). Although neuroimaging studies do not always report corresponding regions of activation, there are three areas that have been reported to be consistently active in theory-of-mind tasks (for a summary see Gallagher and Frith, 2003, and **Figure 1**): the medial prefrontal cortex (in some studies slightly left lateralized), the right or bilateral superior temporal sulci, and the temporal poles bilaterally. The medial prefrontal cortex is associated with the ability to represent mental states that are 'decoupled' from reality. The superior temporal sulcus seems involved in processing explicit behavioral information such as the perception of intentional behavior, and the temporal poles have been implicated in the retrieval from memory of personal experiences.

Another interesting observation is that the brain reacts in characteristic manners when we predict other people's actions as opposed to when we predict our own. Predicting one's own actions preferentially activates the left dorsal premotor area, whereas predicting other people's actions activates the left paracingulate cortex, right superior temporal sulcus, and cerebellar vermis (Ramnani and Miall, 2004). Interestingly, when observing one's own action brain activation (left parietal, left operculum, and bilateral premotor cortex) starts earlier compared with watching other people's actions (Grèzes et al., 2004). The reason could be that when one observes one's own action, there is a closer match between simulated and perceived action than there is when one observes the actions of others.

It is important to realize that different types of theory-of-mind tasks may activate different neural substrates and that activation can occur at different points in time. Investigations using the EEG/ERP technique have identified two negative ERP components: one between 270 and 400 milliseconds when decoding others' emotional mental states and another around 800 milliseconds when making belief judgments (Liu et al., 2004; Sabbagh et al., 2004). Whereas the generator for the early negativity was identified in the right hemisphere (right orbitofrontal cortex

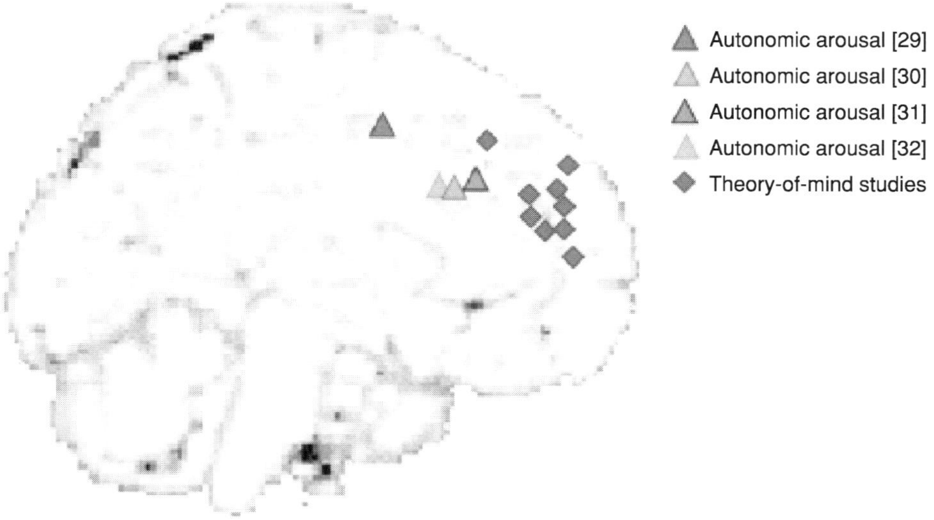

Figure 1 A summary and display of areas of activation found in the medial prefrontal cortex (anterior paracingulate) during theory-of-mind tasks. Also displayed are areas of activation in other areas of the medial prefrontal cortex (the anterior cingulate cortex) found to be associated with autonomic arousal, cognitive demand, and response conflict. [29] Critchley H D et al. (2000). 'Cerebral correlates of autonomic cardiovascular arousal: a functional neuroimaging investigation in humans.' *Journal of Physiology London 523*, 259–270. [30] Critchley H D et al. (2001). 'Neural activity in the human brain relating to uncertainty and arousal during anticipation.' *Neuron 29*, 537–545. [31] Duncan J and Owen A M (2000). 'Common regions of the human frontal lobe recruited by diverse cognitive demands.' *Trends in Neuroscience 23*, 475–483. [32] Barch D M et al. (2001). 'Anterior cingulate cortex and response conflict: effects of response modality and processing domain.' *Cerebellum Cortex 11*, 837–848. Taken from Gallagher HL & Frith C D (2003). 'Functional imaging of 'theory of mind'.' *Trends in Cognitive Science 7(2),* 77–83. © Elsevier, with permission. (See color plate 24.)

and right anterior medial temporal cortex), the late negativity was generated in the left hemisphere (left orbitofrontal cortex). Orbitofrontal activation has been associated with emotional processing (Damasio et al., 2000) whereas the right medial temporal activation would fit with other studies that implicate this region in theory-of-mind tasks.

Finally, the ability to infer other people's mental states has also been investigated in schizophrenic and autistic patients during imaging. Based on a nonverbal comic strip depicting a simple story, schizophrenic patients had to attribute intentions to others (Brunet et al., 2003). Compared with healthy participants, schizophrenic patients did not activate the right prefrontal cortex, a region that has been shown in several studies to be implicated in theory-of-mind tasks. Autistic patients, on the other hand, demonstrated activation patterns similar to those of healthy people in right hemispheric and bilateral regions, except that there was generally less activation (Castelli et al., 2002).

Investigating Figurative Language

Right hemisphere involvement in figurative language (such as in the comprehension or production of metaphors, humor, and idioms, or the making of requests) has been claimed ever since it was observed that some people with damage to the right hemisphere show problems interpreting figurative language appropriately. The idea of right hemisphere involvement in the comprehension of figurative language also has its roots in psycholinguistic models of figurative language comprehension.

A lively debate in psycho- and neurolinguistics has surrounded questions such as whether metaphors can be understood as quickly and automatically as regular sentences, whether specific processing stages are necessary for their comprehension, whether the same processes underlie the comprehension of different types of metaphors, and whether such differences are represented in different parts and sides of the brain (for a summary see Glucksberg, 2003). Despite the numerous psycho- and neurolinguistic studies, only a few neuroimaging studies have directly investigated this question. In a positron emission tomography (PET) study, participants had to make plausibility judgments while listening to sentences (plausible metaphors, implausible metaphors) and to random word strings. Greater activation in the right hemisphere (right inferior frontal gyrus, the right premotor cortex, and the right posterior temporal cortex) was found when comparing plausibility judgments of metaphoric sentences with those of literal sentences (Bottini et al., 1994).

Understanding jokes is, in a way, similar to metaphoric or other figurative language in that what is meant is not said. Comprehending jokes, however, involves more than just understanding what is meant. Neuroimaging studies using fMRI have identified dissociated neural substrates for a cognitive and an affective element of humor (Goel and Dolan, 2001; Moran et al., 2004; see **Figure 2**). Unfortunately, the neural substrates identified by the two groups do not correspond. For the affective component, one study described the medial ventral prefrontal cortex and bilateral cerebellum (Goel and Dolan, 2001) whereas the other study found the bilateral amygdala and bilateral insula to be activated (Moran et al., 2004). The left insular region (BA44/4) was also activated in the Goel and Dolan study (2001), but it was related to phonological, not affective, joke processing. For the cognitive component, both studies identified the posterior middle temporal gyrus to be implicated, but in the right hemisphere in one study (Moran et al., 2004) and in the left hemisphere in the other (Goel and Dolan, 2001). The left posterior inferior temporal gyrus (Goel and Dolan, 2001) and the left inferior frontal gryus (Moran et al., 2004) were also involved.

Taken together, the right hemisphere contributes to keeping track of the topic or theme of a discourse and to drawing high-level inferences, including attributing mental states to others and interpreting figurative language, and to integrating meaning into a larger discourse or

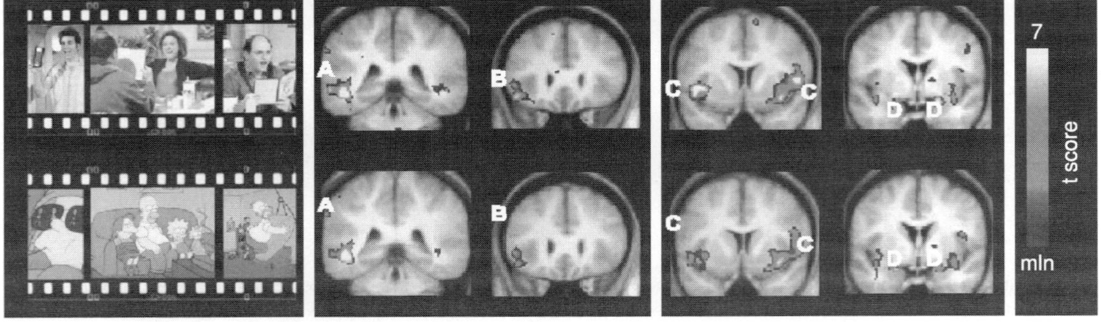

Figure 2 Displayed are averaged activation maps based on subjects viewing *Seinfeld* (upper panel) and *The Simpsons* (lower panel) sitcoms. A functional dissociation between humor detection and humor appreciation was described. In the coronal brain images, the left side of the image corresponds to the left hemisphere. In both studies, humor detection led to greater activation in the left posterior middle temporal gyrus and the left inferior frontal gyrus. By contrast, humor appreciation yielded greater activation bilaterally in the insular cortex and the amygdala. Taken from Moran et al. (2004). 'Neural correlates of human detection and appreciation.' *Neuroimage 21*, 1055–1060. © Elsevier, with permission. (See color plate 25.)

social context. The right hemisphere thus seems to be indispensable for successful pragmatic and social communication. Inconsistencies remain, however, concerning the specific neural substrates or networks involved. It is also possible that not all neural substrates and networks involved have yet been identified.

In addition to its role in low-level language processing, the left hemisphere is also involved in deductive and syllogistic reasoning processes and in establishing local coherence, that is, in low-level inferencing processes (for a summary see Bookheimer, 2002).

See also: Imaging Brain Lateralization, Words, Sentences, and Influencing Factors in Healthy, Pathological, and Special Populations.

Bibliography

Abu-Akel, A (2003). 'A neurobiological mapping of theory of mind.' *Brain Research Reviews* 43: 29–40.
Baum, S and Pell, MD (1999). 'The neural bases of prosody: insights from lesion studies and neuroimaging.' *Aphasiology* 13(8): 581–608.
Bookheimer, S (2002). 'Functional MRI of language: new approaches to understanding the cortical organization of semantic processing.' *Annual Reviews of Neuroscience* 25: 151–188.
Bottini, G, Corcoran, R, Sterzi, R, et al. (1994). 'The role of the right hemisphere in the interpretation of figurative aspects of language: a positron emission tomography activation study.' *Brain* 117: 1241–1253.
Brunet, E, Sarfati, Y, Hardy-Baylé, MC, et al. (2003). 'Abnormalities of brain function during a nonverbal theory of mind task in schizophrenia.' *Neuropsychologia* 41: 1574–1582.
Buchanan, T, Lutz, K, Mirzazade, S, et al. (2000). 'Recognition of emotional prosody and verbal components of spoken language: an fMRI study.' *Cognitive Brain Research* 9: 227–238.
Caplan, R and Dapretto, M (2001). 'Making sense during conversation: an fMRI study.' *Neuroreport* 12: 3625–3632.
Castelli, F, Frith, C, Happe, F, et al. (2002). 'Autism, Asperger syndrome and brain mechanisms for the attribution of mental states to animated shapes.' *Brain* 125(8): 1839–1849.
Damasio, AR, Grabowski, TJ, Bechara, A, et al. (2000). 'Subcortical and cortical brain activity during the feeling of self-generated emotions.' *Nature Neuroscience* 3(10): 1049–1056.
Federmeier, KD and Kutas, M (1999). 'Right words and left words: electrophysiological evidence for hemispheric differences in meaning processing.' *Cognitive Brain Research* 8(3): 373–392.
Ferstl, EC and von Cramon, Y (2001). 'The role of coherence and cohesion in text comprehension: an event-related fMRI study.' *Cognitive Brain Research* 11: 325–340.
Gallagher, HL and Frith, CD (2003). 'Functional imaging of 'theory of mind'.' *Trends in Cognitive Sciences* 7(2): 77–83.
Glucksberg, S (2003). 'The psycholinguistics of metaphor.' *Trends in Cognitive Sciences* 7(2): 92–96.
Goel, V and Dolan, RJ (2001). 'The functional anatomy of humor: segregating cognitive and affective components.' *Nature Neuroscience* 4(3): 237–238.
Goel, V, Gold, B, Kapur, S, et al. (1998). 'Neuroanatomical correlates of human reasoning.' *Journal of Cognitive Neuroscience* 10(3): 293–302.
Grèzes, J, Frith, CD, and Passingham, RE (2004). 'Inferring false beliefs from the actions of oneself and others: an fMRI study.' *Neuroimage* 21(2): 744–750.
Hagoort, P, Hald, L, Bastiaansen, M, et al. (2004). 'Integration of word meaning and world knowledge in language comprehension.' *Sciencexpress 18 March 2004*. www.sciencexpress.org.
Just, MA, Newman, SD, Keller, TA, et al. (2004). 'Imagery in sentence comprehension: an fMRI study.' *Neuroimage* 21: 112–124.
Kiehl, KA, Laurens, KR, and Liddle, PF (2002). 'Reading anomalous sentences: an event-related fMRI study of semantic processing.' *Neuroimage* 17: 842–850.
Liu, D, Sabbagh, MA, Gehring, WJ, et al. (2004). 'Decoupling beliefs from reality in the brain: an ERP study of theory of mind.' *Neuroreport* 15(6): 991–995.
Mason, RA and Just, MA (2004). 'How the brain processes causal inferences in text.' *Psychological Science* 15(1): 1–7.
Moran, JM, Gagan, SW, Adamas, RB , Jr, et al. (2004). 'Neural correlates of humor detection and appreciation.' *Neuroimage* 21: 1055–1060.
Nichelli, P, Grafman, J, Pietrini, P, et al. (1995). 'When the brain appreciates the moral of a story.' *NeuroReport* 6: 2309–2313.
Ramnani, N and Miall, RC (2004). 'A system in the human brain for predicting the actions of others.' *Nature Neuroscience* 7(1): 85–90.
Sabbagh, MA, Moulson, MC, and Harkness, KL (2004). 'Neural correlates of mental state decoding in human adults: an event-related potential study.' *Journal of Cognitive Neuroscience* 16(3): 415–426.
St. George, M, Kutas, M, Martinez, A, et al. (1999). 'Semantic integration in reading: engagement of the right hemisphere during discourse processing.' *Brain* 122: 1317–1325.
van Berkum, JJA, Brown, CB, Hagoort, P, et al. (2003). 'Event-related brain potentials reflect discourse-referential ambiguity in spoken language comprehension.' *Psychophysiology* 40: 235–248.

Imaging Brain Lateralization, Words, Sentences, and Influencing Factors in Healthy, Pathological, and Special Populations

B. Stemmer, University of Montreal, Montreal, Quebec, Canada

Classically, the brain has been divided into two sides – the right and the left. To the inexperienced eye, both sides look the same, although a closer look reveals subtle anatomical differences. For example, an anatomical area situated at the end of the superior temporal gyrus, the planum temporale, is much larger on the left than its right-sided homologue. In addition, Broca's speech area and the primary auditory cortex (Heschl's gyrus) are larger in the left hemisphere than in the right (for a summary, see Toga and Thompson, 2003). These anatomical structures surround or overlap brain regions important for language. It seems natural to ask whether these anatomical or structural differences are in any way reflected at a behavioral, functional, or even biochemical level (for a detailed discussion, see Hugdahl, 2000). Early models of brain asymmetry tried to establish such relationships primarily by observing the language performance of patients with damage to specific regions of the brain or behavioral tasks performed with healthy individuals. Based on such data, language production and some aspects of syntactic processing were suggested to be localized in the left side of the brain, and indeed, in particular, to areas of the inferior frontal gyrus (Broca's area). Language comprehension was localized in the posterior temporal–parietal region (Wernicke's area) (**Figure 1**).

Since the advent of neuroimaging techniques, new possibilities have opened up to investigate anatomical/structural and functional/behavioral relationships. Although these techniques allow, to some degree, to watch 'the brain in action,' each has its own strengths and weaknesses. As is the case with all complex techniques, data from each of these imaging methods need to be interpreted with those particular strengths and weaknesses in mind. The most common of these neuroimaging techniques are positron emission tomography (PET) and functional magnetic resonance imaging (fMRI); these are both particularly appropriate for discovering *where* in the brain specific events happen. Techniques based on electrical or magnetic signals (electroencephalogram (EEG) or magnetoencephalogram (MEG)), on the other hand, are more suitable in determining *when* they happen.

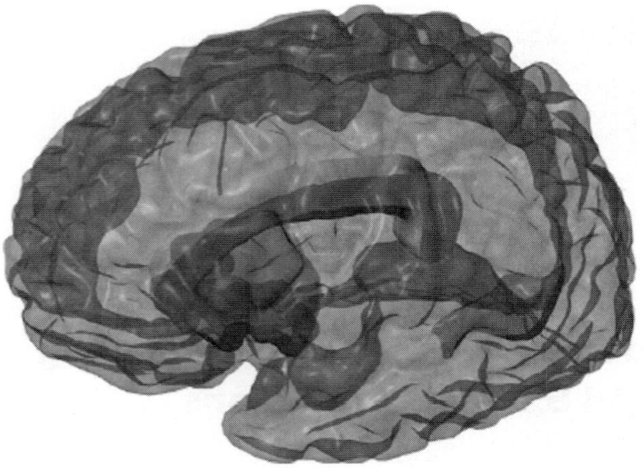

Figure 1 Anatomical sites of the classical language areas identified in a transparent surface model of the human cerebral cortex. Broca's speech area (green) and Wernicke's language-comprehension area (blue) are identified on a transparent surface model of the human cerebral cortex. All cortical regions are interconnected through the corpus callosum (yellow) with corresponding systems in the opposite brain hemisphere. From Toga A W and Thompson P M (2003). Mapping brain asymmetry. Reproduced with permission from Nature Reviews Neuroscience. Copyright (2003) Macmillan Magazines Ltd., www.nature. com/reviews. (See color plate 26.)

Research on the mind/brain–language relationship has not only produced a wealth of insights but also raised new questions or rephrased old ones. This article focuses on research that has used neuroimaging techniques (PET, fMRI, and EEG) to investigate language and, more specifically, explores what neuroimaging research has contributed to our understanding of what happens in the 'left' and 'right' side of the brain at the word and sentence level.

Imaging Single Word Lateralization

Imagine that you see a string of symbols such as *oppmtrgt* or *flower*. Approximately 200–250 ms after seeing these symbols or hearing the corresponding sounds, your brain has determined that one is a word and the other is a nonword; slightly more time is needed if the word is less frequently used (such as flower vs. tungsten). Approximately 400 ms after seeing or hearing a word, the brain has assigned some meaning to it. Where in the brain do these fast processes take place? Is one hemisphere more implicated than the other in these abilities? Generally, when people listen to speech stimuli, such as syllables, single words, pseudowords, foreign words, or sentences, most studies report involvement of both hemispheres; only a few report slightly more activity in the left hemisphere (Binder and Price, 2001) (**Figure 2**). During these listening tasks, the brain regions consistently activated according to fMRI or PET studies are in the superior temporal gyrus (including the planum temporale) of both hemispheres. Based on these observations, it has been suggested that the superior temporal region in both hemispheres plays a critical role in auditory perception but is less implicated in processing lexical–semantic or syntactic information. Lateralization to the left is associated with other aspects of auditory processing. For example, when healthy volunteers listen to tones, sounds of animals, instruments, and words, the highest activation for the perception of words is exhibited within the left superior temporal sulcus and in the left inferior frontal gyrus.

Phoneme processing is also lateralized to the left side of the brain. Areas of brain activation during phoneme processing involve the left frontal operculum (around the anterior insula and BA45) and a more posterior dorsal region near the inferior frontal gyrus/premotor boundary (BA44/6). Although the left supramarginal gyrus also seems to contribute to phoneme processing, this region is also activated in a variety of other tasks, such as pitch discrimination of auditory tones, reading visually presented words relative to picture naming, and reading pseudowords relative to words (for a summary, see Binder and Price, 2001).

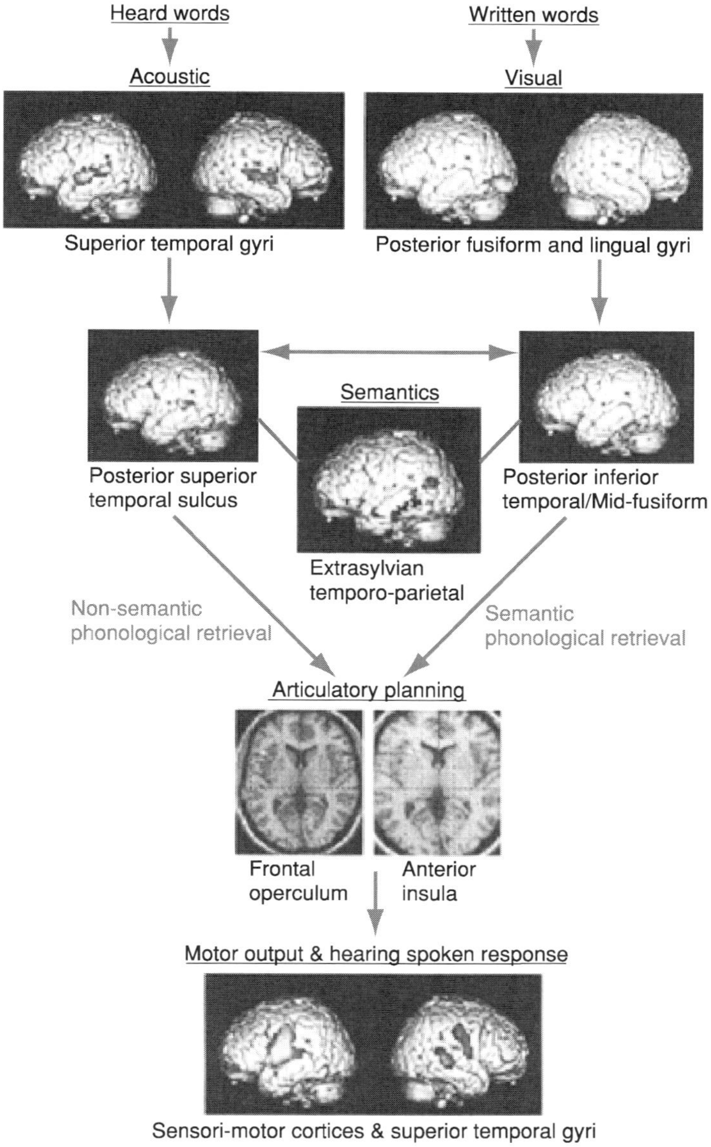

Figure 2 Summary of the results of functional imaging studies on word repetition, word retrieval, and word reading. The top row shows brain areas activated during the acoustic processing of heard words and visual processing of written words. Activation is predominantly bilateral. The second row, left side, shows brain activation related to the phonological processing of speech sounds relative to environmental sounds. In the center, semantic decisions relative to phonological decisions on the same words are shown, and the right side shows activation associated with retrieving the name (via lexical semantics) relative to seeing visual controls and saying 'Okay' or 'Yes.' Note that the activation is predominantly left lateralized. The third row presents transverse slices and shows activation in the left anterior insula and left frontal operculum during phonological output. Bilateral activation is shown in the fourth row and exhibits motor areas for articulation and auditory processing of spoken response for reading aloud relative to reading silently. The red arrows connect these areas to indicate the proposed model of auditory and visual word processing. From Price C J (2000). 'The anatomy of language: contributions from functional neuroimaging.' *Journal of Anatomy 197(5)*, 335–359. Reproduced with permission from Blackwell Publishing. (See color plate 27.)

Word generation (exemplified by tasks such as 'Name all words that start with F' or 'Name all animals you can think of') is a frequently used paradigm in functional imaging studies. This task involves phonological but also word retrieval processes and consistently produces activation in the left hemisphere (the frontal operculum and inferior frontal gyrus (BA44–47)). These areas overlap with regions that are also activated in phoneme processing. Additional areas of activation have been described in the posterior part of the middle frontal gyrus and inferior frontal sulcus, the mid-dorsal part of the precentral sulcus (BA6, 8, and 44) and the left posterior temporal lobe

(BA37). Some of these specific regions in the left hemisphere (left frontal operculum and the left posterior ventral temporal area) are activated independently of the type of stimulus cue or the modality in which the stimulus is presented. Evidence for this comes from studies on blind subjects when reading Braille (Büchel et al., 1998) or when comparing active generation of words with listening to words or semantic judgments on heard words (Warburton et al., 1996).

Tasks involving word meaning also invoke activation that is strongly lateralized to the left hemisphere. The single most consistently activated area within the left hemisphere is the angular gyrus (BA39). This region has been interpreted as a multimodal 'convergence' zone involved in storing or processing very abstract representations of sensory experience and word meaning. Other regions that are frequently activated with the meaning of words are those associated with memory functions, such as the dorsal prefrontal cortex (including medial aspects of BA8 and 9) (for a summary, Binder and Price, 2001).

It was previously mentioned that the extraction of word meaning is preferentially processed in the left hemisphere. The question arises, however, whether or not this is true for the whole spectrum of words ranging from abstract words (such as 'creativity') to concrete words (such as 'television'). Several nonimaging studies – often within the context of specific theories of word processing such as the dual coding model – have investigated the neural bases of abstract and concrete word processing. The dual coding model assumes that abstract words are represented only in verbal symbolic codes, whereas concrete words additionally activate nonverbal, imagery-based representations (Paivio, 1991). Within this framework, it has often been assumed that abstract words are represented in the left and concrete words in the right hemisphere. Neuroimaging studies investigating concrete and abstract nouns, however, have not shown such a clear-cut division. Most studies comparing concrete versus abstract nouns report increased activation for concrete nouns predominantly in the left hemisphere, and several studies have found greater activity for abstract than concrete words in the right hemisphere (for a summary, see Fiebach and Friederici, 2003) (**Figure 3**). Other researchers report no difference in activation between abstract and concrete nouns in the two hemispheres but differences within the left hemisphere. For example, a fMRI study using a lexical decision task (Fiebach and Friederici, 2003) reported a double dissociation within the left hemisphere: abstract words elicited increased activation in the pars triangularis (BA45) of the left inferior frontal gyrus and concrete words led to an activation increase in basal regions of the left temporal lobe.

Taken together, neuroimaging studies have shown that auditory perception involves both hemispheres, whereas phoneme processing and word processing engage predominantly the left hemisphere, regardless of the modality in which the stimulus is presented. The findings are inconsistent with regard to the processing of words with specific characteristics, such as concrete versus abstract words.

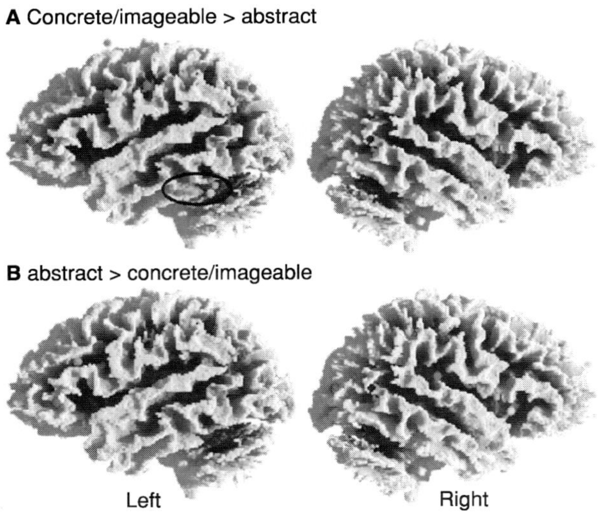

Figure 3 Fiebach and Friederici (2003) visualized brain areas exhibiting greater activity for concrete words than for abstract words (A) or greater activity for abstract than for concrete words (B). Each colored dot represents the results of a particular study reviewed by Fiebach and Friederici. Note that medial and subcortical activations are not displayed. Reproduced with permission from Fiebach C J and Friederici A D (2003). 'Processing concrete works: fMRI evidence against a specific right-hemisphere involvement.' *Neuropsychologia 42*, 62–70. © Elsevier. (See color plate 28.)

Imaging Sentence Lateralization

When listening to or reading sentences, we constantly determine 'Who did what to whom?' That is, we establish the meaning of the sentence. Is there a hemisphere that is dominant for these processes, and are there areas in the brain that are specialized for syntax alone? Traditionally, damage to the anterior regions of the left hemisphere has been associated with language problems as observed in patients with Broca's aphasia. Broca's aphasia was typically linked with damage involving the left inferior frontal cortex (BA44/45), leading to the idea that this was an area specialized for syntactic processing. Do imaging data support this idea? To test this idea with neuroimaging, one would need to design tasks that tease out syntactic processing alone. This, however, would be very difficult to accomplish, and it is thus not surprising that the different approaches and stimuli that have been used have not produced consistent activation patterns.

Some researchers compared simple versus complex sentences and reported activations predominantly in the left hemisphere (Broca's area (BA44/45), occasionally extending to BA47, 6, 9; left angular/supramarginal gyri (BA39, 40); and cingulate gyrus (BA23, 24, 31, 32)) (for a summary, see Kaan and Swaab, 2002). However, not all such studies have reported significant activation in Broca's area – an inconsistency that suggests that this region is not necessarily implicated in all aspects of syntactic processing. For example, Friederici et al. (2003), using fMRI, compared correct sentences to sentences with syntactic or semantic violations. Bilateral activation (midportion of superior temporal gyrus, insular cortices, and posterior superior temporal gyrus) was observed in sentences containing semantic violations, whereas sentences with syntactic violations activated only the left hemisphere (anterior and posterior portion of the superior temporal gyrus, left posterior frontal operculum adjacent to BA44, and basal ganglia). Activation in classical Broca's area was not observed.

Another question frequently asked concerns the relationship between syntax and semantics. Do they activate common or separate brain areas? Alas, neuroimaging research has produced mixed and partially inconsistent results. An interaction between syntax and semantics was reported in several regions of the left hemisphere, including Broca's region, the left cingulate, left posterior middle frontal gyrus, and left inferior parietal cortex (for a summary, see Ben-Shachar et al., 2004). It remains unclear, however, whether Broca's and Wernicke's areas are activated conjointly or whether each region is activated individually, and how specific this is for either syntax or semantics. Another series of studies also reported activation in the right hemisphere and indeed in the right homologue of Broca's and Wernicke's regions. A consistent set of brain regions was activated when comparing 'movement' sentences ('John gave the red book to the professor from Oxford'/ 'John gave to the professor from Oxford the red book') to 'nonmovement' sentences while manipulating topicalization and wh-questions (Ben-Shachar et al., 2004). In both conditions, activations included regions only in the left hemisphere (inferior fontal gyrus and ventral precentral sulcus) and bilaterally (posterior superior temporal sulcus). It was hypothesize that the bilateral posterior temporal activation was related to maintenance of the 'moving element' in memory.

Various researchers have suggested that the amount of material that is processed (i.e., the 'processing load') needs to be considered. In this context, the question has been raised to what degree Broca's area is involved in memory processes. For example, a sentence such as 'The student who imitated the professor dropped his books' (subject relative clause) seems to require less working memory resources than 'The student who the professor imitated dropped his books' (object relative clause). Several studies report activation in Broca's and Wernicke's areas. Investigating center-embedded subject- and object-relative clauses, McDonald and Christiansen (2002) found increased activation in both Broca's *and* Wernicke's areas for object-relative clauses compared to subject-relative clauses and for subject-relative clauses compared to active conjoined clauses. Similarly, comparing subject-relative clauses in Japanese (a verb-final language) and manipulating center-embedded vs. left-branching structures showed an increase in activation in the left inferior frontal gyrus (BA44 and BA45), the posterior portion of the left superior temporal gyrus (BA22; i.e., Wernicke's area), and the left dorsolateral prefrontal cortex (posterior part of BA9) (Inui et al., 1998). In Japanese, center-embedding with canonical word order seems to entail a greater working memory load than fronting an object in noncanonical word order. However, a series of PET studies comparing center-embedded object relatives ('The juice [that the child spilled] stained the rug') vs. right-branching subject relatives ('The child spilled the juice [that stained the rug]') performed by Caplan and colleagues consistently showed increased activation in Broca's area only, although the exact locus of activation withinBroca's area varied: the pars opercularis (BA44) (Caplan et al., 1998; Stromswold et al., 1996) and the pars triangularis (BA45) (Caplan et al., 1999, 2000).

Taken together, and consistent with some behavioral studies, these neuroimaging studies indicate that Broca's area is not involved in all aspects of syntactic processing. In addition, although functional neuroimaging studies investigating syntactic processing report predominantly left hemisphere activation, bilateral and right hemisphere activation is also reported. The observed activation patterns may indicate that different aspects of syntactic processing activate different parts of a network in both hemispheres (Kaan and Swaab, 2002). For example, incoming words of a sentence activate phonological, syntactic, and semantic information that may be reflected in the activation of the middle and superior temporal lobes in the left hemisphere. Other left hemisphere activation, such as that of the anterior temporal lobe, may reflect accessing stored information or encoding of information for later use. Increased processing load requires storing nonintegrated material in which the inferior frontal gyrus (Broca's area) might be implicated. Bilateral or right hemisphere activation may reflect aspects of prosody, discourse, and pragmatic integration processes but also control and memory processes.

Imaging Hemispheric Lateralization in Patients

Other questions of interest concern whether changes in language lateralization occur after damage to specific brain regions, such as in patients suffering from intractable epilepsy, children with extensive brain damage in early childhood, schizophrenic patients, or patients recovering from a stroke.

Defining Hemispheric Lateralization for Presurgical Patients

The gold standard to determine language lateralization in patients who need to undergo surgical intervention, such as tumor removal or epilepsy surgery, has been the Wada test, a procedure during which one hemisphere is selectively anesthetized. Since fMRI has become more available, the question as to whether noninvasive fMRI provides similar or possibly even better information than the Wada test has been raised. This seems, indeed, to be the case. Studies are consistent in their evaluation that there is good agreement between the Wada and the fMRI procedure (Adcock et al., 2003; Bazin et al., 2000; Binder et al., 1996; Gaillard et al., 2002; Sabbah et al., 2003; Yetkin et al., 1998). Some researchers even reported more sensitivity of the fMRI technique concerning the involvement of the nondominant right hemisphere (Adcock et al., 2003). It should also be noted that due to time constraints of the anesthetic agent used in Wada testing, rather simple language tasks had to be used. This limitation does not pertain to fMRI, which allows for more flexibility in language testing. Finally, several neuroimaging studies noted the higher variability of language dominance in epilepsy patients (Adcock et al., 2003; Sabbah et al., 2003; Springer et al., 1999).

Language Lateralization in Other Patients

It has been an accepted common wisdom that children recover faster or better after their brains have been damaged than do adults. For obvious reasons, there are only few neuroimaging studies with young children. One such study monitored the recovery of language abilities in a boy with intractable epilepsy before and after the left hemisphere was removed (Hertz-Pannier et al., 2002). After surgery, the boy showed rapid recovery of receptive language functions but slower and incomplete recovery of expressive language and reading as measured by fMRI. A year later, a shift of language-related networks to the right hemisphere (right inferior frontal, temporal, and parietal activation) during expressive and receptive tasks was observed in agreement with the notion of the superior plasticity of the child's brain and the ability of the right hemisphere to take over some expressive language functions. Another study (Holland et al., 2001) investigated developmental patterns of brain activation associated with a verb-generation task in 13 healthy children/adolescents aged 7–18 years using fMRI. The regions of activation found were similar to those of adults with predominantly left hemisphere activation (inferior frontal gyrus). Similar results were reported by Balsamo et al. (2002). Generally, it appears that the degree of lateralization increased with age and proficiency in language skills, leading to a shift in activation toward greater lateralization in the left hemisphere (Holland et al., 2001).

In schizophrenic patients, increased activation in the right hemisphere in response to low-level language tasks has been consistently reported (Artiges et al., 2000; Greene et al., 2001; Sommer et al., 2003). Some researchers have hypothesized that the increased activation reflects a failure to inhibit nondominant language areas in patients suffering from schizophrenia (Greene et al., 2001; Sommer et al., 2003).

Clinical recovery from aphasic syndromes can be observed over weeks, months, and even many years after a stroke. Imaging studies have tried to elucidate the neural mechanisms underlying this recovery (for a review of recovery and PET studies, see Heiss et al., 2003) (**Figure 4**). It has been suggested that recovery in right-handed, left hemisphere language-dominant patients includes undamaged portions of the language network in the left hemisphere and, to a lesser extent, homologous right hemisphere areas (Rosen et al., 2000). Although there might be some contribution by the right hemisphere, it is the reactivation of areas in the left hemisphere that seems essential for recovery of language functions. Predominant activation of structures in the affected hemisphere have been related to good recovery (Heiss et al., 2003).

Interestingly, pharmaceutical intervention in aphasic stroke patients with piracetam (a nootropic agent that has been shown to generally enhance cognitive functions in some patients) has been shown to improve language performance. This, in turn, was reflected in an increase in activation in the left hemisphere (left transverse temporal gyrus, left triangular part of the inferior frontal gyrus, and left posterior temporal gyrus), whereas a trend toward a decrease in activation was observed in the right hemisphere (right inferior frontal gyrus) (Heiss et al., 2003).

Imaging Special Populations

In addition to investigating the contribution of each hemisphere in patient groups, neuroimaging studies have also investigated whether the brain is lateralized differently in people with particular characteristics, such as in people using sign language or people who know more than one language.

Left hemisphere specialization for language has usually been demonstrated with regard to the vocal tract as the primary articulator. However, what if the articulator consists of hands, such as used by deaf users of American Sign Language? Whereas some functional neuroimaging studies have reported largely left-lateralized brain activity for signing, others have shown more right hemisphere involvement than is seen in spoken language (for a

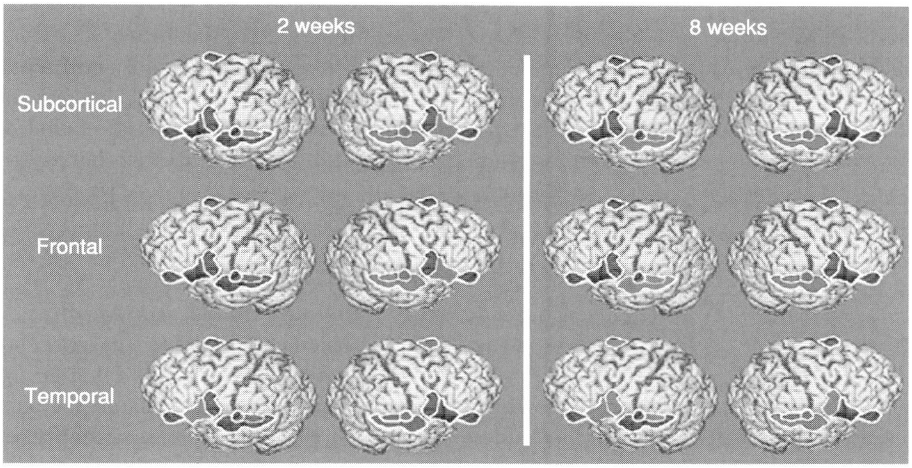

Figure 4 Results of a PET study in left hemisphere stroke patients with various aphasic syndromes. The patient group with subcortical and frontal lesions improved substantially and activated the right hemisphere (inferior frontal and right superior temporal gyri) at baseline. Left superior temporal gyrus activation occurred at follow-up. Patients with temporal lesions improved only in word comprehension and activated the left Broca area and supplementary motor areas at baseline. Precentral gyrus bilaterally and right superior temporal gyrus were activated at follow-up but not the left superior temporal gyrus. Reproduced with permission from Heiss et al. (2003). 'Disturbance and recovery of language function: correlates in PET activation.' *Neuroimage 20(1)*, 542–549. © Elsevier. (See color plate 29.)

summary, see Corina et al., 2003). This discrepancy has been attributed to interpretation problems due to different demands of the motor system involved in signing. Corina et al. (2003) performed a PET study using a lexical–semantic word generation task in deaf signers. They observed activation in the left hemisphere (dorsolateral prefrontal cortex (BA46)), dorsal operculum (pars triangularis and opercularis (BA44/45)), and ventral operculum (par orbitalis (BA47)) and concluded that linguistic–semantic processing relies on left hemisphere regions regardless of the modality in which a language is realized.

Numerous neuroimaging studies have investigated brain activation in people who know more than one language. Inconsistent results are found, however, when comparing these studies. Some researchers report no interhemispheric difference for different languages (Klein et al., 1999), whereas others report language-sensitive regions in second languages exclusively in the left hemisphere (Kim et al., 1997) or in both hemispheres (Dehaene et al., 1997), or report different findings for different participants (Chee et al., 2001). Reasons for these inconsistent results are probably due to variables that were not accounted for or are inconsistent in these studies; these include different scanning techniques; different tasks, stimuli, and paradigms used; different languages investigated; differences in proficiency level; differences in the age of acquisition of the nonnative language; differences in length of exposure to the second language; lack of distinction between male and female participants; and differences in methods of analyzing the neuroimaging data (e.g., ROI, individual vs. group data). Considerable variability among subjects in the precise spatial location, spatial extent, and magnitude of these activations has also been reported (for a summary, see Binder and Price, 2001). The importance of distinguishing the level of processing evoked by the task has been noted by Pillai et al. (2003). For example, right hemisphere activation occurred only in a phonological (rhyming) task and not in a semantic (verb–noun association) task in the nonnative (but not native) language. Involvement of the right hemisphere appears to be related to the cognitive demands of the tasks and possibly to the level of proficiency (Perani et al., 1998). In fact, level of proficiency has been shown to be more important than age of acquisition in eliciting specific patterns of brain activation. Left hemispheric dominance for the native as well as the nonnative language for high-proficiency adults who had acquired their second language late in life has been described by Perani et al. (1998). In addition, in these adults, some right hemisphere activation for one but not the other language was seen. These findings contrasted with adults exhibiting low language proficiency who showed different areas of activation for both languages only within the left hemisphere, regardless of age of acquisition of the nonnative language. Another factor that needs to be considered is which languages are compared. For example, in bilinguals, some right hemispheric involvement was found when reading Chinese, whereas reading in English recruited only regions in the left hemisphere (Liu and Perfetti, 2003). Generally, there seems to be little support for the hypothesis that languages learned later in life entail more right hemispheric involvement as both the native and the nonnative language recruit large brain areas in the left hemisphere (Vingerhoets et al., 2003).

Taken together, there is no evidence from imaging studies to support a specific role for the right hemisphere in bi- or multilingual people. Note, however, that we cannot draw any conclusions from these studies concerning the involvement of the right hemisphere or the interaction between the two hemispheres during the *process of learning* a foreign language at different stages in life.

Imaging Gender

A long-debated issue concerns an old hypothesis that language functions are more lateralized to the left side of the brain in men and represented more bilaterally in women. It has been shown that the left planum temporale is much larger than its right homologue in males, whereas in females this difference is not significant. This observation seems to provide some anatomical support for reduced asymmetry of lateralization for females for language tasks (Kulynych et al., 1994). However, neither nonimaging studies nor imaging studies have yielded consistent results (for a summary, see Binder and Price, 2001; Kansaku and Kitazawa, 2001; Kimura, 2000). Some neuroimaging studies that investigated low-level processing using a verb generation task, word completion task, or semantic word judgment task reported no lateralization differences in men or women (Buckner et al., 1995; Jaeger et al., 1998). Others, however, using rhyming judgments or passive listening to spoken narratives, found more bilateral activation in women than in men (Kansaku et al., 2000; Phillips et al., 2000).

Aside from methodological differences, another reason for these discrepant findings could be the different types of stimuli used and different task demands. In addition, many of these neuroimaging studies relied on group data. There is, however, evidence for high individual variation, as shown in a study by Vikingstad et al. (2000). Individual data demonstrated that the lateralization index varied continuously from left hemisphere dominant to bilateral representation. In males, language was primarily lateralized in the left hemisphere. In females, approximately half showed left lateralization and the other half bilateral representations. There is thus a possibility that more women than men show bilateral activation in language tasks. Lacking more evidence, however, there is no clear picture about language lateralization in men and women.

Imaging Handedness

There is a widely held belief that language is lateralized in the left side of the brain in right-handed people and in the right side in left-handers. Research, however, tells a somewhat different story: language is lateralized in the left in the majority of right- and left-handers. Functional imaging studies using low-level language tasks consistently report that in approximately 96% of right-handers, speech and language are lateralized to the left, and in the remaining 3% they are lateralized to the right or bilaterally. In left-handers, 70% show left lateralization and 30% right or bilateral lateralization (Pujol et al., 1999; Szaflarski et al., 2002; Toga and Thompson, 2003). IIn addition, family history of sinistrality strongly influences personal handedness and scores on the language laterality index (Szaflarski et al., 2002). Although these studies argue for a strong relationship between handedness and side of language lateralization, due to a lack of studies it would be premature to conclude that this relationship also holds at higher levels of language processing. Furthermore, brain damage may destabilize this otherwise strong relationship between handedness and language laterality. For example, in right-handed patients with epilepsy, language lateralization proved more variable than in healthy right-handed individuals (Springer et al., 1999). This variability in the epilepsy group was related to weaker right-handedness and also to age of brain injury.

See also: Imaging Brain Lateralization.

Bibliography

Adcock, JE, Wise, RG, Oxbury, JM, Oxbury, SM, and Matthews, PM (2003). 'Quantitative fMRI assessment of the differences in lateralization of language-related brain activation in patients with temporal lobe epilepsy.' *Neuroimage* 18(2): 423–438.

Artiges, E, Martinot, JL, Verdys, M, Attar-Levy, D, Mazoyer, B, Tzourio, N, Giraud, MJ, and Paillere-Martinot, ML (2000). 'Altered hemispheric functional dominance during word generation in negative schizophrenia.' *Schizophrenia Bulletin* 26(3): 709–721.

Balsamo, LM, Xu, B, Grandin, CB, Petrella, JR, Braniecki, S H, and Elliott, TK (2002). 'A functional magnetic resonance imaging study of left hemisphere language dominance in children.' *Archives of Neurology* 59(7): 1168–1174.

Bazin, B, Cohen, L, Lehericy, S, Pierrot-Deseilligny, C, Marsault, C, Baulac, M, and Le Bihan, D (2000). 'Study of hemispheric lateralization of language regions by functional MRI. Validation with the Wada test' (in French). *Revue Neurologique* 156(2): 145–148.

Ben-Shachar, M, Palti, D, and Grodzinsky, Y (2004). 'Neural correlates of syntactic movement: converging evidence from two fMRI experiments.' *Neuroimage* 21(4): 1320–1336.

Binder, J and Price, CJ (2001). 'Functional neuroimaging of language.' In: Cabeza, R and Kingstone, A (eds.) *Handbook of functional neuroimaging of cognition*, pp. 187–251. Cambridge: MIT Press.

Binder, JR, Swanson, SJ, Hammeke, TA, Morris, GL, Mueller, WM, Fischer, M, Benbadis, S, Frost, JA, Rao, S M, and Haughton, VM (1996). 'Determination of language dominance using functional MRI: a comparison with the Wada test.' *Neurology* 46(4): 978–984.

Büchel, C, Price, CJ, and Friston, KJ (1998). 'A multimodal language area in the ventral visual pathway.' *Nature* 394: 274–277.

Buckner, RL, Raichle, ME, and Ptersen, SE (1995). 'Dissociation of human prefrontal cortical areas across different speech production

tasks and gender groups.' *Journal of Neurophysiology* 74: 2163–2173.
Caplan, D, Alpert, N, and Waters, G (1998). 'Effects of syntactic structure and propositional number on patterns of regional cerebral blood flow.' *Journal of Cognitive Neuroscience* 10(4): 541–552.
Caplan, D, Alpert, N, and Waters, G (1999). 'PET studies of syntactic processing with auditory sentence presentation.' *Neuroimage* 9(3): 343–351.
Caplan, D, Alpert, N, Waters, G, and Olivieri, A (2000). 'Activation of Broca's area by syntactic processing under conditions of concurrent articulation.' *Human Brain Mapping* 9(2): 65–71.
Chee, MW, Hon, N, Lee, HI, and Soon, CS (2001). 'Relative language proficiency modulates BOLD signal change when bilinguals perform semantic judgments.' *Neuroimage* 13(6): 155–163.
Corina, DP, San jose-Robertson, L, Guillemin, A, High, J, and Braun, AK (2003). 'Language lateralization in a bimanual language.' *Journal of Cognitive Neuroscience* 15(5): 718–730.
Dehaene, S, Dupoux, E, Mehler, J, Cohen, L, Paulesu, E, Perani, D, van de Moortele, PF, Lehericy, S, and LeBihan, D (1997). 'Anatomical variability in the cortical representation of first and second language.' *Neuroreport* 8(17): 3809–3815.
Fiebach, CJ and Friederici, AD (2003). 'Processing concrete words: fMRI evidence against a specific right-hemisphere involvement.' *Neuropsychologia* 42: 62–70.
Friederici, AD, Rüschemeyer, S-A, Hahne, A, and Fiebach, CJ (2003). 'The role of left inferior frontal and superior temporal cortex in sentence comprehension: localizing syntactic and semantic processes.' *Cerebral Cortex* 13: 170–177.
Gaillard, WD, Balsamo, L, Xu, B, Grandin, CB, Braniecki, S H, Papero, PH, Weinstein, S, Conry, J, Pearl, PL, Sachs, B, Sato, S, Jabbari, B, Vezina, LG, Frattali, C, and Theodore, W H (2002). 'Language dominance in partial epilepsy patients identified with an fMRI.' *Neurology* 59(2): 256–265.
Greene, JD, Sommerville, RB, Nystrom, LE, Darley, JM, and Cohen, JD (2001). 'An fMRI investigation of emotional engagement in moral judgment.' *Science* 293(5537): 2105–2108.
Heiss, W, Thiel, A, Kessler, J, and Herholz, K (2003). 'Disturbance and recovery of language function: correlates in PET activation.' *Neuroimage* 20(1): S42–S49.
Hertz-Pannier, L, Chiron, C, Jambaque, I, Renaux-Kieffer, V, van de Moortele, P-F, Delalande, O, Fohlen, M, Brunelle, F, and Le Bihan, D (2002). 'Late plasticity for language in a child's non-dominant hemisphere: a pre- and post-surgery fMRI study.' *Brain* 125(2): 361–372.
Holland, SK, Plante, E, Weber Byars, A, Strawsburg, RH, Schmithorst, VJ, and Ball, WS, Jr (2001). 'Normal fMRI brain activation patterns in children performing a verb generation task.' *Neuroimage* 14(4): 837–843.
Hugdahl, K (2000). 'Lateralization of cognitive processes in the brain.' *Acta Psychologica* 105(2): 211–235.
Inui, T, Otsu, Y, Tanaka, S, Okada, T, Nishizawa, S, and Konishi, J (1998). 'A functional MRI analysis of comprehension processes of Japanese sentences.' *Neuroreport* 9(14): 3325–3328.
Jaeger, JJ, Lockwood, AH, van Valin, RD, Kemmerer, DL, Murphy, BW, and Wack, DS (1998). 'Sex differences in brain regions activated by grammatical and reading tasks.' *Neuroreport* 9: 2803–2807.
Kaan, E and Swaab, TY (2002). 'The brain circuitry of syntactic comprehension.' *Trends in Cognitive Sciences* 6(8): 350–356.
Kansaku, K and Kitazawa, S (2001). 'Imaging studies on sex differences in the lateralization of language.' *Neuroscience Research* 41: 333–337.
Kansaku, K, Yamaura, A, and Kitazawa, S (2000). 'Sex differences in lateralization revealed in the posterior language areas.' *Cerebral Cortex* 10: 866–872.
Kim, KHS, Relkin, NR, Kyoung-Min, L, and Hirsch, J (1997). 'Distinct cortical areas associated with native and second languages.' *Nature* 388(10): 171–174.
Kimura, D (2000). *Sex and cognition.* Cambridge: MIT Press.
Klein, D, Milner, B, Zatorre, RJ, Zhao, V, and Nikelski, J (1999). 'Cerebral organization in bilinguals: a PET study of Chinese–English verb generation.' *Neuroreport* 10: 2841–2846.
Kulynych, JJ, Vladar, K, Jones, DW, and Weinberger, DR (1994). 'Gender differences in the normal lateralization of the supratemporal cortex: MRI surface-rendering morphometry of Heschl's gyrus and the planum temporale.' *Cerebral Cortex* 4: 107–108.
Liu, Y and Perfetti, CA (2003). 'The time course of brain activity in reading English and Chinese: an ERP study of Chinese bilinguals.' *Human Brain Mapping* 18: 167–175.
McDonald, MC and Christiansen, MH (2002). 'Reassessing working memory: comment on Just and Carpenter (1992) and Waters and Caplan (1996).' *Psychological Review* 109(1): 35–54.
Paivio, A (1991). 'Dual-coding theory: retrospect and current status.' *Canadian Journal of Psychology* 45: 255–287.
Perani, D, Paulesu, E, Galles, NS, Dupoux, E, Dehaene, S, Bettinardi, V, Cappa, SF, Fazio, F, and Mehler, J (1998). 'The bilingual brain. Proficiency and age of acquisition of the second language.' *Brain* 121: 1841–1852.
Phillips, MD, Lurito, JT, Dzemidzic, M, Lowe, MJ, Wang, Y, and Mathews, VP (2000). 'Gender based differences in temporal lobe activation demonstrated using a novel passive listening paradigm.' *Neuroimage* 11: S352.
Pillai, JJ, Araque, JM, Allison, JD, Sethuraman, S, Loring, DW, Thiruvaiyaru, D, Ison, CB, Balan, A, and Lavin, T (2003). 'Functional MRI study of semantic and phonological language processing in bilingual subjects: preliminary findings.' *Neuroimage* 19: 565–576.
Pujol, J, Deus, J, Losilla, JM, and Capdevila, A (1999). 'Cerebral lateralization of language in normal left-handed people studied by functional MRI.' *Neurology* 52(2): 1038–1043.
Price, CJ (2000). 'The anatomy of language: contributions from functional neuroimaging.' *Journal of Anatomy* 197(5): 335–359.
Rosen, HJ, Petersen, SE, Linenweber, MR, Snyder, AZ, White, DA, Chaoman, L, Dromerick, AW, Fiez, JA, and Corbetta, MD (2000). 'Neural correlates of recovery from aphasia after damage to left inferior frontal cortex.' *Neurology* 55: 1883–1894.
Sabbah, P, Chassoux, F, Leveque, C, Landre, E, Baudoin-Chial, S, Devaux, B, Mann, M, Godon-Hardy, S, Nioche, C, Ait-Ameur, A, Sarrazin, JL, Chodkiewicz, JP, and Cordoliani, Y S (2003). 'Functional MR imaging in assessment of language dominance in epileptic patients.' *Neuroimage* 18(2): 460–467.
Sommer, IE, Ramsey, NF, and Kahn, RS (2003). 'Language lateralization in schizophrenia: an fMRI study.' *Schizophrenia Research* 52(1–2): 57–67.
Springer, JA, Binder, JR, Hammeke, TA, Swanson, SJ, Frost, JA, and Bellgowan, PS (1999). 'Language dominance in neurologically normal and epilepsy subjects: a functional MRI study.' *Brain* 122(11): 2033–2046.
Stromswold, K, Caplan, D, Alpert, N, and Rauch, S (1996). 'Localization of syntactic comprehension by positron emission tomography.' *Brain and Language* 52(3): 452–473.
Szaflarski, JP, Binder, JR, Possing, ET, McKiernan, KA, Ward, BD, and Hammeke, TA (2002). 'Language lateralization in left-handed and ambidextrous people: fMRI data.' *Neurology* 59(2): 238–244.
Toga, AW and Thompson, PM (2003). 'Mapping brain asymmetry.' *Nature Reviews Neuroscience* 4: 37–48.
Vikingstad, EM, George, KP, Johnson, AF, and Cao, Y (2000). 'Cortical language lateralization in right handed normal subjects using functional magnetic resonance imaging.' *Journal of the Neurological Sciences* 175(1): 17–27.
Vingerhoets, G, VanBorsel, J, Tesink, C, van den Noort, M, Deblaere, K, Seurinck, R, Vandemaele, P, and Achten, E (2003). 'Multilingualism: an fMRI study.' *Neuroimage* 20(4): 2181–2196.
Warburton, E, Wise, RJ, Price, CJ, Weiller, C, Hadar, U, Ramsay, S, and Frackowiak, RS (1996). 'Noun and verb retrieval by normal subjects: studies with PET.' *Brain* 119: 159–179.
Yetkin, FZ, Swanson, S, Fischer, M, Akansel, G, Morris, G, Mueller, W, and Haughton, V (1998). 'Functional MR of frontal lobe activation: comparison with Wada language results.' *American Journal of Neuroradiology* 19(6): 1095–1098.

Intelligence

A. L. Powell

Intelligence is defined as the ability to learn, understand, or deal with new or trying situations. It is also the ability to apply knowledge to manipulate one's environment. In agreement with this definition, intelligence is often viewed as an ability to perform specific tasks. It has come to mean different things to different people. Despite such ambiguity, tests of intelligence are commonly used to assess an individual's aptitude for an occupation or for education. Test scores are also used to select pupils for law, medicine, and graduate education. In addition to aptitude tests, tests like the Stanford–Binet intelligence test are used to quantify intelligence by deriving an individual's intelligence quotient (IQ). This approach is useful when monitoring a patient for cognitive changes over time that may be caused by brain injury or degeneration. Intelligence tests are used to determine whether a specific pattern of abnormal function is attributable to some specific cause. Consequently, intelligence tests may be potent guides to medical diagnosis or intervention. One key assumption underlying testing is the belief that a person's success (or failure) during testing is a true measure of their intellect. This reasoning suggests that higher scores equate with greater intelligence.

As noted previously, there are two categories of intelligence tests: those that evaluate patterns of ability (i.e., aptitude) and those that quantify the amount of intelligence (i.e., IQ). Aptitude tests estimate occupation and academic success and an individual's suitability for particular careers. Where the numbers of applicants exceed available positions, testing may help allocate resources. Competition for college entrance is an example for which testing has found broad acceptance with the wide use of devices such as the Scholastic Aptitude Test. Test results aid decisions about whom to admit (or reject) into undergraduate, law, medical, or graduate school. Such tests also help determine placement into honors, remediation programs, and promotion. Although aptitude tests correlate with academic success, the converse is not true: Poor test performance does not predict failure. In other words, aptitude tests are sensitive but not specific. Although they are often pivotal in admission and occupational decisions, there are lingering issues about what intellectual attribute is tested beyond the capacity to correctly answer questions.

A more controversial use of intelligence tests involves quantifying intelligence. A premise underlying this strategy is the belief in a monotonic and symmetrical relationship between test scores and intelligence: Those with higher scores have more intelligence and those with more intelligence have higher test scores. The converse view is also widely considered true: Those with low scores have less intelligence and those with less intelligence have low scores. Test scores and intelligence are thereby equated, but there are no data supporting this conviction. Also, the capacity to train and prepare oneself for the test and the widespread proliferation of businesses striving to prepare and educate individuals on how to obtain higher scores serve to cast doubt on this belief. In reality, there is no proof that a particular person who scores higher than another individual is more intelligent. Higher test scores do not necessarily indicate greater intelligence, or the converse, except when scores determine average tendencies in groups of individuals. There are several other problems with this notion. First, there is no standard test battery or attempt to normalize battery use. This lack of uniformity serves to increase variability and decrease reliability. Test battery composition, application, and interpretation vary widely. Also, test validity is highly dependent on the tester's training, experience, skill, and notions. By necessity, tests are not comprehensive. Furthermore, the tests evaluate arbitrary, but limited, cognitive ability. Complicating matters further is the varied approaches taken by the same tester administering the same battery. There is also a lack of correspondence between test scores and brain function; IQ measures socially relevant ability, which is adjusted for age, gender, and education, but does not evaluate brain function. Accordingly, they are psychological models of behavior. As such, intelligence tests are indirect correlates of intelligence reflecting an individual's insight and experience. In the presence of deficient understanding or experience, the product of testing becomes more unreliable. Since IQ scores depend on test-taking ability, test scores of untutored individuals increase with practice.

Another tenet underlying the use of such devices is that cognitive processes in different people are the same. However, there has been no discussion about whether this notion is correct. One is left to question whether it is appropriate to use written measures for all individuals, thereby neglecting possible innate relevant cognitive differences. The factual basis of this view is yet to be established, but when a small cohort of high-functioning individuals were asked to describe their thought processes, several different modes of thought were described. Some reported an auditive mode of thought, with thoughts composed of internally heard conversational speech. Others reported primarily pictorial modes, some with written elements, some scenic, and others with nameless symbols. Some respondents described a muscular component to thought, while others noted that their thinking composition included tastes or odors. On this basis alone, the practice of using written tests and applying the same criteria to interpret all test results must be questioned. One must further note the lack of a gold standard for tests. There is no available independent method to corroborate a numerical score. By way of analogy, a blood test indicating heart disease may be supported by independent tests of heart function, such as cardiac tissue and other measures, but there is no method to corroborate or refute claims made by intelligence tests. Lastly, effects of culture, native language, and ethnicity are generally neglected during test development and use. Cross-cultural validity is simply not factored into the process, which serves to further diminish the significance and meaning of test scores.

Fundamental Concepts

Several important concepts underlie the brain's capacity for intelligence. From this perspective, it is possible to derive a neurologically relevant definition. Such fundamental concepts help define the nature and limits of intelligence. The brain has three elemental demands placed on it. It must represent the world while evaluating its models for important patterns. The brain also manipulates, modifying the information it receives while concomitantly determining its significance. Lastly, the brain must allow safe and constructive interaction with the environment. The capacity to modify information is essential to intelligence. Although the demands placed on the brain are clear, there are prerequisites for success. For intellectual activity, there must be effective operation of appropriate brain circuits. The brain must also be capable of initiating and sustaining action and mental focus. Association cortices must be capable of effectively linking ideas, sensations (visual, auditory, olfactory, gustatory, somesthetic, or vestibular), emotions, and memories. Since spatial and temporal data processing occurs within association cortices, these areas must function well. Also, intelligence requires the capacity to combine and manipulate information; this capacity requires input from both halves of the brain through a rich cellular network of connecting neurons that are widely separated in the same and opposing hemispheres. Damage to this network will disrupt intelligence. Lastly, the capacity to learn is fundamentally important to intelligence. The capacity to communicate with symbols (i.e., language) allows efficient interaction with other individuals, and it also serves as an external information reservoir.

Heredity and Environment

That heredity plays an important role in determining one's potential intelligence is beyond dispute. However, genetic investigations have failed to identify smart genes, which are genes that confer brilliance on the possessor. Instead, given the complexity of the brain organization and the need for effective interaction among its many components, it is not surprising that genetic mutations of several genes are known to lessen the efficiency of brain operation and, in turn, to diminish potential intelligence. Mutational disorders range from subtle to dramatic and include trisomy 21, fragile-X syndrome, tuberous sclerosis, and autism. There are also important epigenetic factors—evident during the early years of life—that are necessary for normal development and organization. A rich array of neuronal networks develop, with many destined to be removed; the final product of such factors is that gyral and sulcal patterns of monozygotic twins, individuals with identical genetic constitution, will look different. Maturational factors such as myelin development, which is important for efficient signal transmission across the extensive neuron network, are known to continue for many years, peaking around the middle of the third decade of life.

A plethora of environmental factors also serve to lessen or optimize intellectual promise. Brain development and function can be disrupted in many ways *in utero*, during postnatal life, or much later. Consequently, an individual's intellect is the product of synergistic biochemical, maturational, epigenetic, physiological, and environmental factors that depend on nutrition, hormone levels, cell maturation, and development. In addition to these factors, operational activity and practice within brain circuitry serve to optimize neural efficiency. One must recognize that the presence and action of neurons are crucial. Neurons are limited to three functions: discharge, remain silent, and change likelihood of discharge. Repeated neuronal action facilitates future action. Cells are more efficiently recruited into action after discharging (i.e., neurons learn). For such reasons, there are many firing patterns, with the discharge pattern of cell populations defining meaning. Thus, although investigations continue to seek smart genes, it is more probable that the interplay between nature and nurture lessens intelligence from a potential ideal. Efficient and effective operation of a complex array of neuron networks underlies attainment of this ideal.

Products of Collaboration

There is no evidence that the brain creates information from nothing. Neurons respond to stimuli; it is this reaction that informs. When sensory input declines below critical levels, mental function is impaired and mental confusion is likely to ensue. Accordingly, intellectual activity is driven by sensory information. Within the cerebral cortex, sensory input is deconstructed into its components, such as shape, color, movement, texture, contrast, and borders. This deconstruction proceeds automatically and beyond conscious awareness. The same process of deconstruction appears to apply to all sensory information. Patterns of neuronal activity are then assessed for familiarity (i.e., signal versus noise). The left, or dominant, hemisphere favors discrete bits of information, such as elements of language and mathematics. The right hemisphere favors seamless patterns of information, such as faces, music, landmarks, odors, and emotions. In most individuals, creativity appears to depend more on right hemisphere structures, whereas logical thought is more dependent on the left hemisphere.

Once sensory input is analyzed, it is linked to other sensations in a matrix, forming a multimodal neural representation. To this matrix are added thoughts and various memories. The final product of this cascade is a synthetic, richly textured and unique personal product. Information becomes transformed. Sounds combine with letters and images, touch sensations, odors, experiences, and beliefs. Letters such as "C-A-T" are linked to images, sounds (verbal and nonverbal), odors, touch sensations, and memories. The mental product tied to other animals and attributes, such as animals with claws. This process flows without conscious awareness or volitional effort. The ability to link information is fundamentally creative, permitting one to conceive of a dog with the head of a cat and a raccoon's tail. It is also vital to the intellect.

Judgment

The subject of judgment is handled superficially during medical and psychiatric education. Common instructions taught to medical students regarding how to evaluate judgment involve an individual's response to questions about what to do when they find an addressed and stamped letter or how to respond to fire in a crowded theater. In psychology, however, there has been increasing attention paid to the capacity of individuals to make judgments under uncertain conditions. The capacity to judge is important with regard to intellectual behavior given the need to discriminate between potentially rewarding and detrimental circumstances. Judgment consists of the capacity to decide between alternatives in the presence of relevant background bias. One's course of action is largely predetermined by the decision; the decision, however, is made difficult by any ambiguity separating the alternatives.

Emotions

The role of emotion in intelligence is often ignored but is nonetheless important. Emotions establish the value of objects in the world. They determine what is desired and what is to be avoided. Drive (i.e., motivation) is largely emotional, serving to engage the impulse to act. Motivation provides the will to act, with the emotional state fueling motives and thereby stimulating or retarding intellectual activity. Emotions that shape cognition are diverse, including anger, agitation, and pleasure. In addition to their role in shaping value and motives, emotions help shape meaning, particularly during social interaction and communication. The significance of words and phrases is shaped and made to vary by melody, rate, loudness, and prosody. These attributes heavily depend on affective contributions. Patients who are unable to properly interpret or express emotions have a constricted intellectual universe and limited cognition. Similarly, the inability to express emotions decreases the range of intellectual options for the individual with consequent impact on social and intellectual well-being, often with devastating effect.

History of Neural Correlation

The Greeks speculated that the mind is composed of a series of innate powers or faculties that are localized in the hollow ventricles of the brain: sensation and imagination in the anterior chamber, reason in the middle, and memory in the posterior. Franz Josef Gall (1758–1828), the founder of phrenology (cranioscopic method), convinced the scientific community that "the brain is the organ of the mind." He argued for structure and function interdependence and the need to study the relationship. He was first to note how much man and animals have in common. As noted by George Lewes in 1871, in [Gall's] vision of psychology as a branch of biology, subject therefore to all biological laws, and to be pursued by biological methods, he may be said to have given the science its basis." Gall's reasoning was based on the following suppositions: Moral and intellectual faculties are innate; their manifestation depends on organization; the brain is the organ of all propensities, sentiments, and faculties; and the brain is composed of as many particular organs as there are propensities, sentiments, and faculties, which differ essentially from each other. He further assumed that

> As the organs and their localities can be determined by observation only, it is also necessary that the form of the brain or cranium should represent, in most cases, the form of the brain, and should suggest various means to ascertain the fundamental qualities and faculties, and the seat of their organs.

Consequently, the shape of a person's head, with its various bumps and ridges, was associated with 35 different mental faculties.

Gall first offered his views in private lectures held in Vienna, Austria, as early as 1803. What he taught was considered heretical by the imperial government and was banned. His views suggested that the mind was a consequence of an organic brain, an opinion that contradicted prevailing beliefs in an eternal, omniscient spirit that inhabits the brain and body. Gall's teachings were construed to be a threat to religious orthodoxy. He continued to lecture, managing to leave Austria as troops were sent to arrest him. He settled in Paris, where phrenology further developed and disseminated.

The next major advance in the neurology of intelligence was made by Paul Broca, who in the mid-19th century demonstrated the asymmetrical distribution of intellectual function within the human cortex; a lesion in the left third frontal gyrus was shown to be responsible for a patient's aphasia. By 1870, there was general acceptance of the correctness of Gall's idea of different brain areas having different functions. His view was accepted given the accumulated clinical and anatomical evidence provided by a number of investigators.

At the beginning of the 20th century, Paul Flechsig studied the order of myelin maturation after birth and concluded that the brain was organized into motor and sensory functions and into association tissue capable of merging products of different brain regions. He believed association areas formed the basis of intelligence and were divided into two regions—inferior parietal and prefrontal tissues. Later distinctions by other investigators included cell types and architecture and the staining characteristic of different regions of the brain. Investigations also evaluated the impact of surgical ablation of circumscribed cortex on intelligence. Concomitantly, the clinical study of epilepsy and stroke developed and allowed clinicians to correlate specific anatomical lesions and changed cognition. Additional insights were gained by electrically stimulating exposed cortex as early as 1874, with the number of studies increasing during the 20th century. During World Wars I and II, large numbers of nonlethal head wounds culminated in development of competing theories of intellectual ability, theories based on the structure and function of brain tissue.

Advances in technology fostered further insights, such as the invention of electroencephalography to record cortical activity and the development of x-ray techniques to view intact anatomy. Insight into the structure/function relationship dramatically increased with the introduction of single photon tomography in the 1950s, x-ray computed tomography in the 1970s, and magnetic resonance imaging and positron emission tomography in the 1980s. These techniques allow investigators to correlate the effects of regional damage on mental processes and capability.

History of IQ Tests

During the early 19th century, many investigators sought to develop pragmatic measures of intelligence, including Francis Galton, first cousin to Charles Darwin. At the end of the century, a request was made on behalf of the French government to Dr. Alfred Binet to develop a method of determining the intellectual development of children. This request was made in response to a newly enacted law mandating the education of all French citizens. Although initially reticent about the request, he decided to comply after being assured that the test would not be used to segregate or deny an education to low-functioning individuals. He determined age-appropriate behaviors, incorporating his findings into what later became the Binet–Simon Intelligence Test. After its publication in the early 20th century, it was rapidly translated into English and used in the United States. Lewis Terman was among the first to recognize its value. He tested large numbers of individuals to establish ranges of values for individuals with impaired, normal, and superior levels of intellectual function. His work was the basis for the Stanford–Binet Intelligence Test. These works were designed to yield an individual's IQ. IQ tests rapidly proliferated and were used extensively. Their use increased during enrollment of military recruits during World Wars I and II. The utility of testing was further aided by improvement in statistical techniques.

Neuroanatomy

Paul Flechsig described the important contribution of the association cortex to intelligence at the beginning of the 20th century. By the end of the century, the cytoarchitectonic flow of neural information, from its entry into the cerebral cortex to subsequent processing, was well established. According to current notions, entry of perceptual inputs into the cerebral cortex occurs within idiotypic cortex. These primary areas are contiguous with adjacent unimodal areas. Unimodal neurons in temporal, parietal, and occipital lobes communicate with the heteromodal cortex (of Flechsig) located in the superior temporal (gyrus supramarginalis) and inferior parietal (gyrus angularis) lobes. There is a structure and flow of information within such circuits. Incoming signals are evaluated for familiarity; in essence, the information is characterized as signal or noise. As information moves through the brain circuitry, it is progressively transformed. Inputs are initially modality specific within unimodal association homotypical isocortex but are progressively combined with other sense modalities. Within higher order heteromodal association areas, cross-sensory integration occurs. Data are delivered to paralimbic areas within anterior temporal lobes (amygdala, parahippocampus, and hippocampus) and inferior, medial, and lateral frontal lobe structures. The paralimbic regions serve are gates into the emotional, limbic brain; this region is also important for episodic memory. The flow of neural activity continues within the limbic areas (corticoid and allocortical tissue) and posterior basal frontal cortex (e.g., the septal nuclei and substantia innominata). Anatomical structures deep to the cortex, basal ganglia, thalamus, and cerebellum appear to play an essential role in cognition by regulating and coordinating the action with the cortex.

A clinical integration of structure and function by D. Frank Benson during the mid-1980s merits mention. He envisioned three brain areas by levels of function. The first level consisted of sensory areas of input, including primary visual (Brodmann area 17), auditory (Heschl's gyrus in Brodmann areas 40 and 42), and somesthetic (Brodmann areas 1–3) areas. He posited that the primary motor area (Brodmann area 4) functioned analogously to primary sensory areas, with progressively complex processing of sensory stimuli from unimodal to multimodal associations. Second, heteromodal association cortex was noted for its rich anatomical connection traversing different sensory modalities. Heteromodal association cortex was thought to include Brodmann areas 39 (angular gyrus), 40 (upper temporal gyrus supramarginalis), 36 (within the middle temporal gyrus), 7 (anterior segment of the upper parietal lobe), and a segment of Brodmann area 22 in the superior temporal lobe. Another region that appears to serve heteromodal functions is located within the dorsal prefrontal cortex. This site is essential for maintaining appropriate sequential order over several steps of mental processes. Lastly, supramodal association cortex (Brodmann areas 8, 9, 45, 46, and possibly 47 within the prefrontal cortex) may constitute an evolutionarily highest area of the brain. He believes that supramodal tissue provides executive control over other intellectual functions.

Conclusions

For more that 150 years there has been intense study of how brain action translates into intelligence; there was also parallel interest in practical measures of intelligence. Intelligence is now known to be the product of coordinated activity of connected neuron populations. It reflects the ability to combine and link sensations, memory, and thoughts, to discern patterns, and to anticipate outcome, as manifested by problem solving, creativity, insight, and the capacity to analyze.

See also: Behavior, Neural Basis of; Cognitive Impairment; Language and Discourse; Mental Retardation; Mental Status Testing.

Interhemispheric Interaction in the Lateralized Brain

J. B. Hellige, Psychology Department, Loyola Marymount University, Los Angeles, CA, USA

Introduction

A prominent characteristic of human brains is division of the cerebral cortex into left and right hemispheres, each constituting a somewhat separate information processing system with its own abilities, propensities and biases. Among the most dramatic hemispheric differences are those related to language. For example, language disorders are far more frequent and more serious after damage to certain areas of the left hemisphere than after damage to corresponding areas of the right hemisphere. In particular, left-hemisphere dominance for such things as speaking, reading words, using grammar and understanding word meaning has been established for some time. Despite this general picture of left-hemisphere superiority for language, there is also evidence of contributions from the right hemisphere. For example, functional neuroimaging studies typically show activation in many areas of both hemispheres as individuals perform a variety of language tasks. Indeed, when "language" is viewed more broadly for the purpose of communication, aspects of left-hemisphere dominance may even be complemented by right-hemisphere dominance for such things as intonation, emotional tone and building coherent meaning across sentences. Remarkably, the left and right hemispheres typically coordinate their various activities without effort, leading to a sense of unity in language processing and other domains. The present chapter outlines how this coordination takes place and considers more generally the variety of interhemispheric interactions in our lateralized brain.

The chapter begins with a brief overview of the nature of functional hemispheric asymmetry, with special emphasis on processes related to language. This is followed by a discussion of the advantages of having a lateralized brain and of the special challenges that laterality creates for interhemispheric interaction. Against this backdrop, I then review mechanisms of interhemispheric interaction, including discussion of the costs and benefits of distributing processing across both hemispheres as tasks become more or less demanding. Though there is a good deal of consistency from person to person, there is also sufficient individual variation in the efficiency of interhemispheric interaction to have important consequences for language and other activities. Thus, the chapter ends by considering several dimensions of individual variation and looking toward future issues related to interhemispheric interaction.

Functional Hemispheric Asymmetry

Hemispheric asymmetry or laterality is ubiquitous across information processing domains and across contemporary species. For example, within humans, functional hemispheric asymmetries are found in such varied domains as motor control, perception, memory, emotion and language. During the last 30 years, laterality studies have demonstrated that functional asymmetries are also ubiquitous across other species, with some of those asymmetries being similar to those found in humans. In fact, it has been hypothesized that all contemporary vertebrate groups have inherited a basic pattern of laterality from a common chordate ancestor.

In order to understand issues related to interhemispheric interaction, it is useful to consider certain general properties of contemporary hemispheric asymmetry. In addition to being ubiquitous across information processing domains, most hemispheric asymmetries in humans and other species are subtle rather than being all or none. That is, both sides of the brain typically have at least some competence to perform a task or to utilize a specific process, though one side or the other may be superior, preferred or dominant in some other measurable way. For example, for many people the right hand is better at a variety of fine-grained motor activities, but the left hand is not completely without competence for those same activities. In the visual domain, the left hemisphere is superior for processing small local details and the right hemisphere is superior for processing global configuration, but each hemisphere can handle both local and global information to a reasonable extent (see **Figure 1**). One exception to this property of subtlety may be overt speech, which is produced exclusively by the left hemisphere in most people. Even in this case, however, the right hemisphere is capable of producing speech in individuals who are born without a left hemisphere or if the left hemisphere is removed at a sufficiently young age.

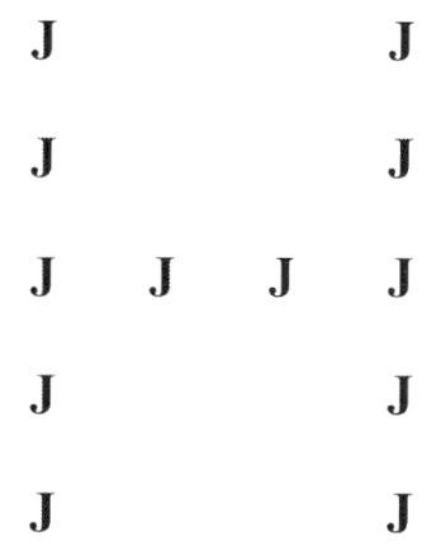

Figure 1 A large letter H (the global level) made up of small letter J's (the local level). When patients with left-hemisphere damage try to reproduce such figures, the intact right hemisphere correctly produces the global pattern (the large H), but ignores the small local details (the small J's). In contrast, in patients with right-hemisphere damage, the intact left hemisphere correctly produces the local detail (several small J's) but does not arrange them into the correct global pattern. In neurologically intact individuals, global and local levels are processed better when flashed briefly to the left visual field (right hemisphere) and right visual field (left hemisphere), respectively, and functional neuroimaging studies show that attending to global versus local levels produce greater activation in right and left hemispheres, respectively.

Evidence from individuals with unilateral brain injury, from split-brain patients and from neurologically intact individuals has identified additional aspects of left-hemisphere dominance for language, though in most of these other cases the right hemisphere is not completely without ability. The left hemisphere is typically better than the right for speech perception and other phonetic tasks such as rhyming and naming printed words and nonwords. The left hemisphere is also dominant for such things as determining whether a string of letters spells a word and for dealing with syntactic (grammatical) information in both the production and understanding of language.

In something of a complementary manner, the right hemisphere is thought to be superior to the left for a variety of additional communication-related factors. For example, studies with both brain-injured and neurologically intact individuals demonstrate right-hemisphere superiority for the production and perception of prosody or intonation in speech. Thus, the speech of patients with right-hemisphere injury is often described as monotonic, lacking vocal inflection and emotion. Such patients also have a difficult time identifying such things as emotion from the vocal inflections of others. Right-hemisphere damage also interferes with the ability to understand certain kinds of jokes that depend on the ability to build a context across sentences and to process the metaphoric meanings of words such as warm and cold (which can refer to feelings as well as to temperature). (For further discussion of language-related laterality, see Hellige, 2001; Banich, 2004.)

Advantages and Challenges of Hemispheric Asymmetry

The ubiquity of laterality suggests that it confers sufficient advantages to have evolved early and to have been sustained and exploited for millennia in many widely differing species. A long-standing idea is that hemispheric asymmetry is advantageous as a way of packing more abilities into a particular amount of neural tissue than would be the case if the two hemispheres were functionally identical. Thus, as one hemisphere becomes specialized for language, the other is freed to become specialized for other activities like localizing stimuli in space. Something akin to this idea of increased processing capacity can be extended to asymmetries that are subtle in the way discussed earlier.

Indications of hemispheric asymmetry in a number of domains suggest that left- and right-hemisphere superiorities complement each other, like two pieces of a puzzle (Hellige, 2001). In terms of speech perception, for example, left-hemisphere dominance for identifying such things as stop consonants (b, d, g, p, t, k) may arise because the left hemisphere is well adapted for processing the rapid acoustic changes that differentiate one such consonant from others. By way of contrast, right-hemisphere dominance for identifying emotional tone may arise because the right hemisphere is well adapted for processing acoustic changes over longer temporal intervals (Ivry & Robertson, 1998). Another language-related example is provided by hemispheric differences in semantic processing. When a word is presented, the left hemisphere very quickly restricts access to one possible meaning (either the dominant meaning or the meaning most consistent with the preceding words), whereas the right hemisphere maintains activation of many possible meanings for a longer period of time (Chiarello, 2003; see also **Box 1**).

Box 1 When is a bank not a bank? Or, what's right and what's left

"He did as he was told, put all of the money into a plain brown paper bag, and took the bag to the right bank, only to find the abductors waiting across the Seine river on the south side. 'Never again,' he mused 'will I forget that right and left refer to the north and south sides of the river rather than the other way round.' You just gotta love Paris." If you are like most people, when you read the word "bank" you immediately thought of an institution that houses money. That is, in fact, the most common meaning of the word "bank." Moreover, prior references to a bag of money created a context that was also biased toward that meaning. However, by the time you reached the end of the passage, you probably realized that the reference was actually to the bank alongside a river – the Right Bank of the Seine in Paris to be specific. There is good reason to believe that both brain hemispheres contributed to your performance and likely interacted with each other at various points along the way. When encountering an ambiguous word, the left hemisphere quickly restricts activation to the dominant meaning or the meaning most consistent with the context that has come before. This is typically very useful in quickly deciphering the intended meaning. In contrast, when encountering the same word, the right hemisphere maintains activation of multiple meanings, distant semantic relations and such things as metaphoric interpretation. This is also very useful in quickly resolving the confusion that occurs when information that comes in later is in conflict with the first meaning considered. By the way, chances are you also switched at some point from interpreting "right" as the opposite of "wrong" to "right" as the opposite of "left!" (see Chiarello, 2003).

Chiarello, C (2003). Parallel systems for processing language: Hemispheric complementarity in the normal brain. In: Banch, MT and Mack, M (eds.) *Mind, brain, and language: Multidisciplinary perspectives*, pp. 229–250. Lawrence Erlbaum Associates: Mahwah, NJ.

The computational network that is best adapted to one of two complementary processes may be different in subtle ways from the computational network that is best adapted to the other. An instructive example comes from studies of localizing visual stimuli in space. Specifically, the right hemisphere is dominant for processing information about metric distance or what is often referred to as coordinate spatial relations (e.g., determining the distance between a line and a dot), whereas the left hemisphere is dominant for processing information about categorical spatial relations (e.g., whether a dot is above or below a line) (Hellige, 2001, 2006; Kosslyn, 2006). In computer modeling studies, neural network simulations that were constructed to have relatively large overlapping "receptive fields" computed coordinate spatial information better than did neural network simulations that were constructed to have relatively small, non-overlapping "receptive fields," whereas exactly the reverse was found for the computation of categorical spatial relationships. Furthermore, these same simulation studies found that both categorical and coordinate performance was better when the networks were split so that some units contributed only to categorical processing and others contributed only to coordinate processing than when all units contributed to both types of spatial processing. Results like these illustrate how it can be advantageous for complementary processes to be segregated from each other so as to reduce maladaptive crosstalk. There is considerable evidence that two tasks performed simultaneously interfere with each other more when they require specialized abilities of the same hemisphere than when the processing load can be spread more evenly across both hemispheres. Thus, it is likely to be advantageous to have mutually inconsistent or complementary processes at least partially segregated into different hemispheres. Consistent with this possibility, greater cerebral lateralization for two complementary tasks in the domestic chick is associated with enhanced ability to perform those tasks simultaneously: finding food (for which the left hemisphere is typically dominant) and being vigilant for predators (for which the right hemisphere is typically dominant) (Rogers et al., 2004).

The foregoing considerations suggest that laterality may have emerged and been sustained as a way of packing more abilities into a finite amount of neural tissue and as a way of reducing maladaptive interaction between partially inconsistent, complementary neural computations. Along with these advantages, laterality poses challenges associated with the need for communication and collaboration between the two hemispheres. To some extent, the challenges are similar to those involved in connecting cortical areas within a single hemisphere. However, there are important differences. For one thing, each hemisphere is a relatively complete "brain" unto itself, with a broad range of abilities. Without appropriate interhemispheric interaction, this could lead to conflicts, with each hemisphere trying to seize control of processing to direct action toward different goals. Interhemispheric interaction is also demanded by many naturally occurring circumstances in which each hemisphere receives only a portion of the information that is required to identify a stimulus or perform a task. For example, in vision, the left half of centrally fixated objects and words projects directly to the right hemisphere and the right half projects directly to the left hemisphere so that integrating information across the visual midline must involve interaction of the two hemispheres. Interaction is also required when different processing components of a task are accomplished primarily or exclusively by different hemispheres, as when listening to your favorite comedienne tell her version of the "aristocrats" joke, during which the left hemisphere is likely to take the lead for phonetic, syntactic and certain semantic aspects of processing and the right hemisphere is likely to take the lead for processing intonation, prosodic cues to emotion and contextual clues to meaning. In addition, the fact that many functional asymmetries are subtle in the manner discussed earlier also raises the possibility that, when needed, tasks or processes that are typically performed by only one hemisphere can recruit help from the other hemisphere and thereby improve performance.

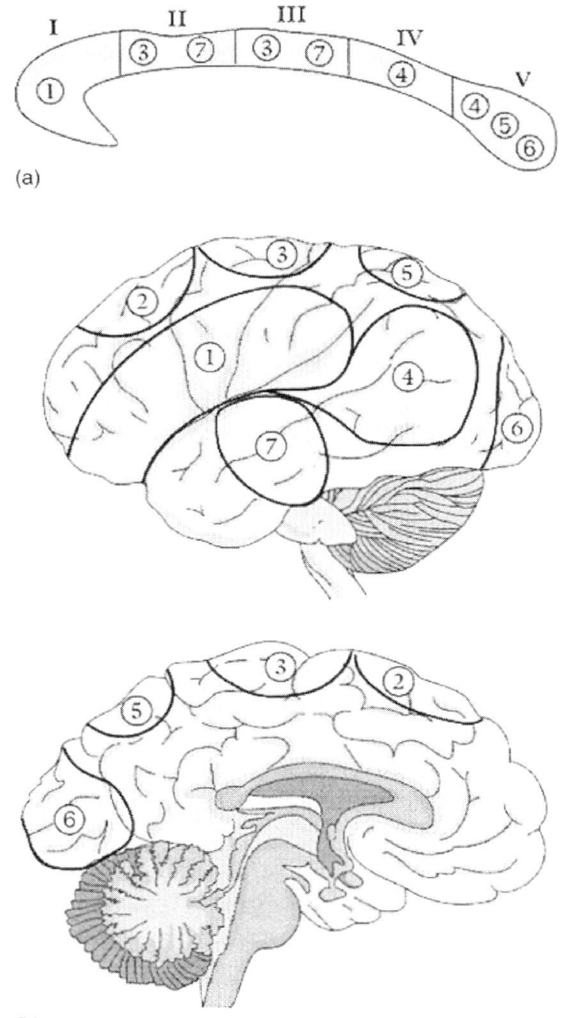

Figure 2 (a) Diagram of the corpus callosum. The number shown in each section indicates the brain region depicted in (b) (top, left hemisphere, lateral view; bottom, left hemisphere, midsagittal view), which are connected through that section of the corpus callosum. The connections occur in topographic manner: anterior sections (I) of the corpus callosum connect anterior sections of the brain (Region 1, which is frontal), middle sections of the callosum (II and III) connect brain regions that are more central (Regions 3 and 7) and posterior sections of the callosum (IV and V) connect posterior sections of the brain (Regions 4, 5 and 6). Some brain regions, such as the frontal region labeled 2, have few, if any, callosal connections. (Banich, M.T. (2004). *Cognitive neuroscience and neuropsychology* (2nd edn). Boston: Houghton Mifflin, © 2004 by Houghton Mifflin Company. Used with permission.)

Mechanisms of Interhemispheric Interaction

The largest fiber tract connecting the left and right hemispheres is the corpus callosum, consisting of between 200 and 800 million axon fibers. In general, anterior portions of the corpus callosum connect frontal and premotor regions of the two hemispheres, middle portions of the corpus callosum connect motor and somatosensory regions of the two hemispheres and posterior regions of the corpus callosum connect temporal, postparietal and peristriate regions of the two hemispheres (see **Figure 2**). Integrity of the corpus callosum is particularly important for the transfer of explicit, conscious information about the identity of stimuli. The corpus callosum has also been hypothesized to help regulate the state of asymmetric arousal between the two hemispheres and to serve as a kind of barrier between the hemispheres, minimizing potentially maladaptive crosstalk between the processes for which each hemisphere is dominant, though the specific mechanisms by which the corpus callosum accomplishes these different things are not yet fully understood (for more on the corpus callosum, see Hellige, 2001; Banich, 2004; Bloom & Hynd, 2005, and suggestions for further readings).

In addition to the corpus callosum, the two hemispheres are connected via the anterior commissure and via a number of subcortical pathways. Studies with split-brain patients, whose hemispheres can no longer communicate via the surgically severed corpus callosum, indicate that implicit (unconscious) information about stimulus identity, information about the location of objects in space, information about categories to which a stimulus belongs and contextual information about an object can be transmitted subcortically. Subcortical structures may also play a role in permitting each hemisphere to receive information about decisions made by the other hemisphere (for more, see Banich, 2004, and further readings).

This extensive system of callosal and subcortical connections allows the two hemispheres to bind the various aspects of language into a coherent experience, even though different aspects depend primarily on processing in one hemisphere. However, although the two hemispheres are capable of sharing many types of information, ranging from sensory input to complex decisions, cooperation at all levels does not necessarily take place all of the time. Thus, it is important to consider when the benefits of distributing processing across both hemispheres might be outweighed by the costs of interhemispheric transfer.

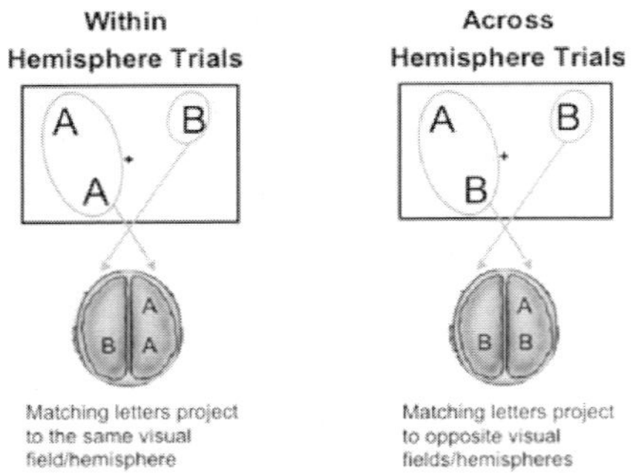

Figure 3 Example of an experimental paradigm used to investigate the costs and benefits of interhemispheric interaction. The task is to indicate whether the letter on the bottom matches either of the top two letters, which are always different from each other. The three letters are flashed on the viewing screen for a fraction of a second while the observer's eyes are fixated on the center cross. Thus, letters from each side of the screen project directly to only one brain hemisphere. Two types of matching trials are illustrated above. On within-hemisphere trials, the two letters that match are presented to the same side of the fixation cross and, thus, to the same brain hemisphere. Consequently, the match may be made without interhemispheric interaction. On across-hemisphere trials, the two letters that match are presented to opposite sides of the fixation cross and, thus, to different brain hemispheres. Consequently, interhemispheric interaction is required to make a match. If the costs of interhemispheric interaction outweigh the benefits of distributing processing across both hemispheres, performance should be better on within-hemisphere trials than on across-hemisphere trials. Exactly the opposite result should be obtained if the benefits of distributing processing across both hemispheres outweigh the costs of interhemispheric interaction.

Costs and Benefits of Interhemispheric Interaction

In order to examine the costs and benefits of interhemispheric interaction, it is instructive to compare performance of the same task under conditions that demand interhemispheric collaboration and conditions that do not. Many experiments of this sort take advantage of the fact that the visual projection pathways of humans are such that information from the right visual half-field projects directly to the left hemisphere and information from the left visual half-field projects directly to the right hemisphere. Thus, simultaneous lateralization of two stimuli to the same or opposite visual half-fields can determine whether interhemispheric collaboration is needed to determine whether the two stimuli match according to some criterion (see **Figure 3**). An important conclusion to emerge is that distributing information becomes more beneficial as tasks become more complex or demanding. That is, for very simple tasks (e.g., determining whether two uppercase letters are physically identical), performance is typically better when both matching items are presented to the same visual field and hemisphere than when one is presented to each visual field and hemisphere (a within-hemisphere advantage), suggesting that the costs of interhemispheric transfer outweigh the potential benefits of interhemispheric interaction. However, when processing demands become a bit greater (e.g., indicating whether two letters of different case have the same name), performance is typically better when one matching item is presented to each visual field and hemisphere than when they are both presented to the same visual field and hemisphere (an across-hemisphere advantage), suggesting that the benefits of spreading the processing load across both hemispheres now outweigh the costs of interhemispheric transfer. Dividing relevant input between the two hemispheres is also advantageous if it permits the hemispheres to engage in mutually inconsistent perceptual processes (e.g., one hemisphere restricts processing to upright letters while the other hemisphere restricts processing to inverted letters). Results such as these suggest why it may be advantageous to lateralize complementary or mutually exclusive aspects of language and communication to opposite hemispheres. (For more discussion and review, see Hellige, 2001; Banich, 2004; Patel & Hellige, 2007.)

A key idea to emerge from studies of interhemispheric interaction is that it becomes advantageous to spread processing across both cerebral hemispheres to the extent that a specific task or set of tasks overloads the processing resources of a single hemisphere. This possibility receives additional support from a set of computerized models that simulate two interconnected processing systems or "hemispheres" performing physical identity and name identity letter-matching tasks. In these models, an across-hemisphere advantage emerged spontaneously for the simulated name-identity task but not for the simpler physical-identity task, for which there tended to be a within-hemisphere advantage. Moreover, the complex task tended to involve both "hemispheres" even when the two matching stimuli were projected to the same side, a result similar to that found in an functional magnetic resonance imaging (fMRI) investigation of letter-matching tasks (Monaghan & Pollmann, 2003).

Box 2 Mixing stimulus formats: when are two hemispheres better than one?

Do the two stimuli shown below in column A refer to the same emotion? How about the two stimuli shown in column B? Column C? In each case, the answer is "yes." My colleagues and I have used stimuli like these to examine how mixing different stimulus formats influences the costs versus benefits of distributing processing across both brain hemispheres. When both items were of the same type (columns A and B), performance was better if one of the two matching stimuli was presented to each hemisphere than if both matching stimuli were presented to the same hemisphere. Despite being even more complex, when one item was a word and the other was a cartoon face (column C), the results were quite different. In fact, performance was better if both matching stimuli were presented to the same hemisphere than if one was presented to each hemisphere. Why? Uppercase and lowercase words are processed in common cortical areas, as are different cartoon faces. Thus, simultaneous processing of two words or two faces presented to the same hemisphere may overload that hemisphere, so that the benefits of spreading processing across both hemispheres outweigh the costs of interhemispheric interaction. In contrast, even though they may refer to the same emotion, words and faces are processed along different cortical routes, even when they are presented to the same hemisphere. Thus, within-hemisphere competition is minimized, so that any benefits of spreading processing across both hemispheres are overshadowed by the costs of interhemispheric interaction. Just as the division of labor between the two hemispheres can increase the overall processing capacity of the brain, the division of labor among more areas within a single hemisphere can increase the processing capacity of that hemisphere.

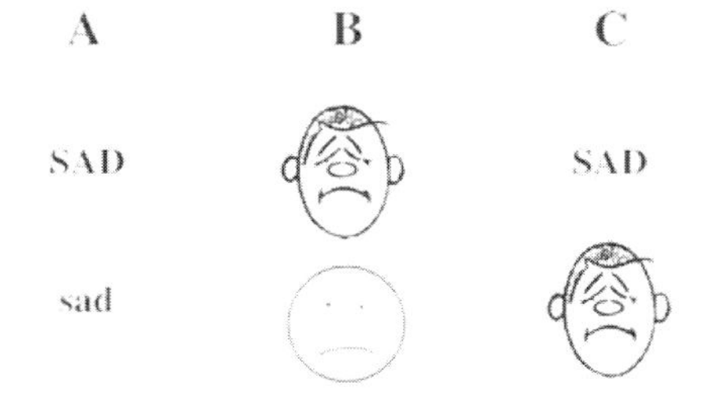

Mixing Stimuli that are Processed in Different Cortical Areas

Though within-hemisphere overload becomes more likely with increases in task complexity and task difficulty, neither difficulty nor complexity *per se* provides a sufficient explanation of the extent to which a task sufficiently overloads the resources of a single hemisphere so as to produce an across-hemisphere advantage. Consider experiments which mix stimulus formats that are processed via different cortical routes, even though they may eventually lead to a common abstract code. In one such experiment, observers were required to indicate whether two stimuli represented the same numeric quantity. Matching stimuli consisted of two digits, two dice-like dot patterns or a digit and a dice-like pattern (mixed-format condition). Despite added difficulty and complexity, the mixed-format condition produced a significant within-hemisphere advantage rather than the across-hemisphere advantage that would be expected for a task that, like matching different-case letters on the basis of name, cannot be performed on the basis of physical identity (Patel & Hellige, 2007). This counterintuitive within-hemisphere advantage persisted for the mixed-format condition even when the task required a more difficult and complex decision based on whether the two matching stimuli fell into the same magnitude category (small (1,2), medium (3,4), large (5,6)). Similar within-hemisphere advantages have been obtained in experiments that required observers to indicate whether items represented by a word and a picture came from the same semantic category (e.g., the word "coat" and a picture of a shoe) (Koivisto & Revensuo, 2003) and in experiments that required observers to indicate whether a word and a cartoon face depicted the same emotion (e.g., the word "sad" and a cartoon face with a sad expression; see **Box 2**). What all of these experiments have in common is the mixing of stimulus formats that are processed via different cortical routes, even within one hemisphere. Thus, a critical factor in determining the relative costs and benefits of interhemispheric interaction appears to be the extent to which multiple stimuli presented to the same hemisphere must compete for the same cortical route. In a sense, just as the division of labor between the two hemispheres can increase the overall processing capacity of the brain, the division of labor among more areas within a hemisphere can increase the processing capacity of that hemisphere. This may explain why such things as phonetic analysis, processing of syntax and extraction of word meaning, which depend on distinctive cortical areas, can all take place without interference within the normal left hemisphere.

Bihemispheric Redundancy Gain

Another experimental paradigm that has proven useful in the study of interhemispheric interaction compares performance on unilateral visual half-field trials with performance on redundant bilateral trials, on which exactly the same information is presented to both hemispheres. In a number of experiments, performance is found to be better on redundant bilateral trials (on which both hemispheres can contribute) than on either left or right visual field unilateral trials (a phenomenon referred to as bilateral or bihemispheric redundancy gain). With respect to language, such bihemispheric redundancy gain has been found for lexical decision tasks and for the identification of printed words and pronounceable nonwords, for handwritten cursive, and for a variety of languages including English, German, Hebrew, Arabic and Urdu (Adamson & Hellige, 2006; Hellige & Adamson, 2006; Hellige & Adamson, 2007). Factors that influence the balance of costs and benefits associated with interhemispheric interaction also seem to influence the magnitude of bihemispheric redundancy gain. For example, mixing stimulus formats on redundant bilateral trials (e.g., digits to one visual field and corresponding dice-like dot patterns to the other) reduces the amount of bilateral gain, even though the stimuli on both sides represent exactly the same abstract numeric information. In view of the fact that many if not most callosal fibers connect homologous regions of the two hemispheres, such results suggest that some of the interhemispheric interaction responsible for bilateral redundancy gain is greatest for homologous areas of the two hemispheres (see Marks & Hellige, 2003).

Individual Variation

Individuals differ in such things as the size and microstructure of the corpus callosum, the speed with which information about even simple stimuli can be transmitted through the corpus callosum and the efficiency of interhemispheric coordination for more complex tasks. These aspects of interhemispheric interaction appear to be related in important ways. For example, an increase in the size of the corpus callosum is thought to reflect greater potential for interhemispheric interaction. Faster transmission speed through the corpus callosum may also facilitate interhemispheric collaboration (e.g., Cherbuin & Brinkman, 2006). Further, individual differences in interhemispheric connectivity (as reflected by the microstructure of the corpus callosum) are related to language lateralization (as reflected by word generation) such that interconnectivity is stronger or faster in strongly left-dominant individuals compared to moderately left-dominant, bilateral or moderately right-dominant individuals (see Westerhausen et al., 2006).

Variation Across the Life Span

In considering individual variation in interhemispheric interaction, it is useful to begin with changes across the life span. The corpus callosum begins to become myelinated between the ages of 3 and 7 years, with myelination not being completed until about the age of puberty. (Myelin is a fatty sheath around neurons that greatly increases conduction speed.) Thus, at very young ages, the corpus callosum is not fully functional, making it difficult for young children to perform tasks that require information to be shared across the hemispheres. Above the age of 6 or 7 years, however, children, like adults, show an across-hemisphere advantage for name-identity letter matching but not for simpler physical-identity letter matching (see Banich et al., 2000). At the same time, there is variation among children in such things as the rate of myelination and in other aspects of callosal connectivity. Efficient callosal function may be particularly important during early stages of learning to read, as certain visual processes for which the right hemisphere is dominant must be coordinated with language processes for which the left hemisphere is dominant (see Banich, 2004).

At the other end of the life span, there is anatomical evidence of age-related changes in the corpus callosum, including some evidence of a reduction in size. Of course, there are also age-related changes within the hemispheres, which complicates behavioral predictions. For example, if the decline in callosal connectivity is great relative to within-hemisphere decline, then older individuals should show a larger within-hemisphere advantage than young adults for a simple physical-identity-matching task and a smaller across-hemisphere advantage than young adults for a more complex name-identity-matching task. On the other hand, if age-related declines within the hemispheres are large relative to the decline in callosal connectivity, then exactly the opposite might be expected. Empirical results have been mixed, and suggest that task complexity may be an important moderating factor. For example, older individuals do seem to show a larger within-hemisphere advantage than young adults for very simple physical-identity-matching tasks (e.g., Reuter-Lorenz et al., 1999; Cherry et al., 2005; Reuter-Lorenz & Mikels, 2005), consistent with an age-related decline in callosal connectivity. For a more difficult name-identity matching task, however, the results are less consistent. Reuter-Lorenz et al. found a larger across-hemisphere advantage for older individuals than for young adults. Cherry et al. found a similar difference for response accuracy, but exactly the opposite difference for reaction time. It may be that, as tasks become sufficiently complex, age-related declines within the hemispheres make it more effective to spread the processing load across both hemispheres, despite some age-related decline in callosal connectivity.

Cognition and Memory

There are a number of indications that interhemispheric interaction may be associated with individual differences in cognition and memory. For example, enhanced interhemispheric interaction characterizes the brains of mathematically gifted adolescents compared with adolescents and college students of average mathematical ability (Singh & O'Boyle, 2004). Whether similar findings characterize youth who are precocious in other domains (including language) remains to be determined.

Increased interhemispheric interaction also appears to be associated with better retrieval of episodic memories. Episodic memory refers to memory for personally experienced events occurring at specific times and places. Studies of brain activity indicate that encoding (i.e., storing) of episodic memories is associated with increased prefrontal activity in the left hemisphere whereas retrieving of episodic memories is associated with prefrontal activity in the right hemisphere. The fact that opposite hemispheres are associated with encoding and retrieval makes it likely that right-hemisphere retrieval mechanisms interact with memory traces encoded by the left hemisphere. Studies of individual variation have provided an important way of studying the association between interhemispheric interaction and episodic memory. The logic of such studies is based on findings that mixed-handedness (compared to strong right-handedness) is associated with increased size of the corpus callosum and with evidence suggesting that a larger corpus callosum is associated with greater interhemispheric interaction in neurologically normal individuals. With this in mind, it has been shown that mixed-handers, relative to strong right-handers, have better memory for both real-world and laboratory events, are less prone to false memories and show an earlier offset of childhood amnesia (i.e., they are able to recall events from younger ages; see **Box 3**). (For more review and discussion, see Christman et al., 2004; Propper et al., 2005; Christman et al., 2006.).

Box 3 Interhemispheric interaction and childhood amnesia

What is your earliest childhood memory? Not an event in your childhood that others have told you about, but one you actually remember. No matter how hard we try, we cannot remember events from the earliest years of our lives, a phenomenon referred to as childhood amnesia. Memory for personally experienced events (referred to as episodic memory) is hypothesized to rely on interhemispheric interaction, as right-hemisphere retrieval mechanisms operate on memory traces encoded primarily by the left hemisphere. Thus, individuals with more efficient interhemispheric interaction might be expected to show an earlier offset of childhood amnesia; that is, to recall events from a younger age than individuals with less efficient interhemispheric interaction. To test this possibility, Christman et al. (2006) elicited early childhood memories from college students who were either strongly right-handed or mixed-handed. They chose this classification because non-right-handedness is thought to be associated with increases in the size of the corpus callosum and with increased interhemispheric interaction. In fact, Christman et al. found that non-right-handers reported earlier episodic memories than did strong right-handers (the accuracy of those memories and the age at which the events occurred was verified by the participants' parents). In a second experiment, making bilateral saccadic eye movements (moving the eyes back and forth) for 30 s, which has been shown to momentarily enhance interhemispheric interaction, also led to reports of earlier episodic memories. Because eye movements made in young adulthood could not have affected the original encoding of childhood memories, interhemispheric interaction seems to have its effect by increasing the ability to retrieve those memories.

Christman, SD, Propper, RE, and Brown, TJ (2006). Increased interhemispheric interaction is associated with earlier offset of childhood amnesia. *Neurospychology,* 20: 336–354.

Cognitive Deficits and Emotional Disorders

Less efficient interhemispheric interaction is also hypothesized to be associated with a variety of cognitive deficits and emotional disorders. For example, a number of studies have reported areas of the corpus callosum to be smaller in individuals with developmental dyslexia, but there are also results to the contrary (for discussion, see Bloom & Hynd, 2005). Though it is not yet possible to reconcile the discrepant results, it may be that callosal connectivity is more important during the early stages of learning to read than it is for experienced readers or that only a subset of dyslexics has problems that relate to interhemispheric interaction. Reduced interhemispheric interaction, as reflected in corpus callosum morphology and in behavioral studies, is also thought to be associated with such disorders as schizophrenia (see Mohr et al., 2000; Caligiuri et al., 2005) and Tourette's syndrome (see Plessen et al., 2004), both of which are also associated with problems related to verbalization and language. Though there is evidence of corpus callosum involvement in patients with Alzheimer's disease, behavioral studies show comparable decline on within- and across-hemisphere conditions, perhaps because Alzheimer's disease produces a similar breakdown of cortical connections within and across hemispheres (Reuter-Lorenz & Mikels, 2005).

Gender

Though there are some indications of corpus callosum differences in men and women, many of the results are difficult to interpret in view of sex differences in overall brain size and in view of what may be complex and inconsistent interactions between sex and handedness. Behavioral studies of functional interhemispheric interaction have not produced consistent differences between men and women, though there is some indication that the efficiency of callosal transfer in women varies as the level of estradiol and progesterone vary over the menstrual cycle (Hausmann et al., 2006).

The foregoing examples illustrate the range of individual variation in efficiency of interhemispheric interaction.

To be sure, such studies shed light on the biological and behavioral mechanisms that make one person different from another or one group different from another. At the same time, the study of individual variation is an important converging technique that provides a way of testing theories about the nature and extent of interhemispheric interaction more generally. As such, investigations of individual variation will continue to be an important tool for learning more about brain-behavior relations.

Challenges and Future Directions

A great deal of progress has been made in understanding the neural mechanisms that underlie language and communication. Indeed, cognitive neuroscience has done a very good job of taking the brain apart by identifying specific processing modules. The rate of progress has accelerated with interdisciplinary approaches that attempt to combine different levels of analysis, including more sophisticated *in vivo* measures of brain structure, more clever behavioral manipulations, more sophisticated computational models and an increasing ability to put all of this information together. Modern functional imaging techniques make it clear that most tasks involve neural networks dispersed across both brain hemispheres. A significant challenge concerns the manner in which the different elements of these neural networks fit together and coordinate their activity – at both biological and behavioral levels. As outlined in this chapter, the need to understand integration across areas is particularly acute with respect to the two very general information processing systems characterized by the left and right hemispheres. Though understanding interhemispheric interaction poses continued challenges, the expanding array of tools holds promise for resolving significant issues. The next several years are likely to see the development of imaging techniques that provide even more detail about the microstructure of the corpus callosum and about the flow of activation across different regions of the corpus callosum as individuals perform tasks in real time. This, along with clever behavioral manipulations and modeling techniques will permit an even more detailed analysis of individual variation, addressing such important questions as the relationship between laterality and interhemispheric interaction and about the advantages of having an appropriately lateralized brain. The existence of laterality in so many animal species, some of which have good interhemispheric communication and some of which have virtually none, will also provide important converging tests among theoretical alternatives. All things considered, advances in these various areas provide reason for optimism as we put the brain back together again.

References

Adamson, MM and Hellige, JB (2006). Hemispheric differences for identification of words and nonwords in Urdu-English bilinguals. *Neuropsychology* 20: 232–248.

Banich, MT (2004). Cognitive neuroscience and neuropsychology. 2nd edn. Boston, MA: Houghton Mifflin.

Banich, MT, Passarotti, AM, and Janes, D (2000). Interhemispheric interaction during childhood: I. Neurologically intact children. *Developmental Neuropsychology* 18: 33–51.

Bloom, JS and Hynd, GW (2005). The role of the corpus callosum in interhemispheric transfer of information: Excitation or inhibition? *Neuropsychology Review* 15: 59–71.

Caligiuri, MP, Hellige, JB, Cherry, BJ, Kwok, W, Lulow, LL, and Lohr, JB (2005). Lateralized cognitive dysfunction and psychotic symptoms in schizophrenia. *Schizophrenia Research* 80: 151–161.

Cherry, BJ, Adamson, M, Duclos, A, and Hellige, JB (2005). Aging and individual variation in interhemispheric interaction and hemispheric asymmetry. *Aging, Neuropsychology, and Cognition* 12: 316–339.

Cherbuin, N and Brinkman, C (2006). Efficiency of callosal transfer and hemispheric interaction. *Neuropsychology* 20: 178–184.

Chiarello, C (2003). Parallel systems for processing language: Hemispheric complementarity in the normal brain. In: Banch, MT and Mack, M (eds.) *Mind, brain, and language: Multidisciplinary perspectives*, pp. 229–250. Mahwah, NJ: Lawrence Erlbaum Associates.

Christman, SD, Propper, RE, and Dion, A (2004). Increased interhemispheric interaction is associated with decreased false memories in a verbal converging semantic associates paradigm. *Brain and Cognition* 56: 313–319.

Christman, SD, Propper, RE, and Brown, TJ (2006). Increased interhemispheric interaction is associated with earlier offset of childhood amnesia. *Neurospychology* 20: 336–354.

Hausmann, M, Tegenthoff, M, Sanger, J, Janssen, F, Gunturkun, O, and Schwenkreis, P (2006). Transcallosal inhibition across the menstrual cycle: A TMS study. *Clinical Neurophysiology* 117: 26–32.

Hellige, JB (2001). Hemispheric asymmetry: What's right and what's left (Paperback edition). Cambridge, MA: Harvard University Press.

Hellige, JB (2006). Evolution of brain lateralization in humans. *Cognition, Brain, Behavior* 10: 211–234.

Hellige, JB and Adamson, MM (2006). Laterality across the world's languages. In: Brown, K (ed.) *Encyclopedia of language and linguistics,* 2nd edn., pp. 709–718. Oxford: Elsevier.

Hellige, JB and Adamson, MM (2007). Hemispheric differences in processing handwritten cursive. *Brain and Language* 102: 215–227.

Ivry, RB and Robertson, LC (1998). *The two sides of perception.* Cambridge, MA: MIT Press.

Koivisto, M and Revensuo, A (2003). Interhemispheric categorization of pictures and words. *Brain and Cognition* 52: 181–191.

Kosslyn, SM (2006). You can play 20 questions with nature and win: Categorical versus coordinate spatial relations as a case study. *Neuropsychologia* 44: 1519–1523.

Marks, NL and Hellige, JB (2003). Interhemispheric interaction in bilateral redundancy gain: Effects of stimulus format. *Neuropsychology* 17: 578–593.

Mohr, B, Pulvermüller, F, Cohen, R, and Rockstroh, B (2000). Interhemispheric cooperation during word processing: Evidence for callosal transfer of dysfunction in schizophrenic patients. *Schizophrenia Research* 46: 231–239.

Monaghan, P and Pollmann, S (2003). Division of labor between the hemispheres for complex but not simple tasks: An implemented connectionist model. *Journal of Experimental Psychology: General* 132: 379–399.

Patel, U and Hellige, JB (2007). Benefits of interhemispheric collaboration can be eliminated by mixing stimulus formats that involve different cortical access routes. *Brain and Cognition* 63: 114–127.

Plessen, KJ, Wentzel-Larsen, T, Hugdahl, K, Feineigle, P, Klein, J, Staib, LH, Leckman, JF, Bansal, R, and Peterson, BS (2004). Altered interhemispheric connectivity in individuals with Tourette's disorder. *American Journal of Psychiatry* 161: 2028–2037.

Propper, RE, Christman, SD, and Phaneuf, KA (2005). A mixed-handed advantage in episodic memory: A possible role of interhemispheric interaction. *Memory and Cognition* 33: 751–757.
Reuter-Lorenz, PA and Mikels, JA (2005). A split-brain model of Alzheimer's disease? Behavioral evidence for comparable intra and interhemispheric decline. *Neuropsychologia* 43: 1307–1317.
Reuter-Lorenz, PA, Stanczak, L, and Miller, AC (1999). Neural recruitment and cognitive aging: Two hemispheres are better than one, especially as you age. *Psychological Science* 10: 494–500.
Rogers, LJ, Zucca, P, and Vallortigara, G (2004). Advantages of having a lateralized brain. *Proceedings of the Royal Society B, Biology Letters* 271: 420–422.
Singh, H and O'Boyle, MW (2004). Interhemispheric interaction during global–local processing in mathematically gifted adolescents, averageability youth, and college students. *Neuropsychology* 18: 371–377.
Westerhausen R, Kreuder, F, Sequeria, SDS, Walter, C, Woener, W, Wittling, RA, Schweiger, E, and Wittling, W (2006). The association of macro- and microstructure of the corpus callosum and language lateralisation. *Brain and Language* 97: 80–90.

Further Reading

Rogers, LJ and Andrew, RJ (eds.) (2002). *Comparative vertebrate lateralization.* Cambridge, UK: Cambridge University Press.
Vallortigara, G and Regolin, L (2006). Animal brain lateralization: Cognitive, ontogenetic and phylogenetic aspects. *Cognition, Brain, Behavior* 10: 187–210.
Vallortigara, G and Rogers, LJ (2005). Survival with an asymmetrical brain: Advantages and disadvantages of cerebral lateralization. *Behavioral and Brain Sciences* 28: 575–589.
These books and articles provide thoughtful review and integration of research on laterality and interhemispheric interaction in non-human species.
Cutica, I, Bucciarelli, M, and Bara, BG (2006). Neuropragmatics: Extralinguistic pragmatic ability is better preserved in left-hemisphere-damaged patients than in right-hemisphere-damaged patients. *Brain and Language* 98: 12–25.
Ross, ED, Thompson, RD, and Yenkosky, J (1997). Lateralization of affective prosody in brain and the callosal integration of hemispheric language functions. *Brain and Language* 56: 27–54.
Soroker, N, Kasher, A, Giora, R, Batori, G, Corn, C, Gil, M, and Zaidel, E (2005). Processing of basic speech acts following localized brain damage: A new light on the neuroanatomy of language. *Brain and Cognition* 57: 214–217.
These articles provide more on possible hemispheric differences and interhemispheric interaction for prosodic and pragmatic aspects of language.
Aboitiz, F and Montiel, J (2003). One hundred million years of interhemispheric communication: The history of the corpus callosum. *Brazilian Journal of Medical and Biological Research* 36: 409–420.
Zaidel, E and Iacoboni, M (eds.) (2003). *The parallel brain: The cognitive neuroscience of the corpus callosum.* Cambridge, MA: MIT Press.
These articles and books provide more information on the corpus callosum and other biological mechanisms of interhemispheric interaction.
Bergert, S, Windmann, S, and Güntürkün, O (2006). Is interhemispheric communication disturbed when the two hemispheres perform on separate tasks? *Neuropsychologia* 44: 1457–1467.
Cherbuin, N and Brinkman, C (2006). Hemispheric interactions are different in left-handed individuals. *Neuropsychology* 20: 700–707.
Compton, RJ, Wilson, K, and Wolf, K (2004). Mind the gap: Interhemispheric communication about emotional faces. *Emotion* 4: 219–232.
Ratinckx, E and Brysbaert, M (2002). Interhemispheric Stroop-like interference in number comparison: Evidence for strong interhemispheric integration of semantic number information. *Neuropsychology* 16: 217–229.
Weems, SA and Zaidel, E (2005). Repetition priming within and between the two cerebral hemispheres. *Brain and Language* 93: 298–307.
These articles provide additional examples of behavioral investigations of interhemispheric interaction in language and other communication-relevant domains.

L

Landau Kleffner Syndrome

M. A. Mikati, R. M. Kurdi, and A. N. Shamseddine, American University of Beirut, New York, NY, USA

Definition and Epidemiology

Landau–Kleffner Syndrome (LKS), which was first described in 1957, is a childhood disorder manifesting two main symptoms: an acquired aphasia and a paroxysmal electroencephalogram (EEG) with spikes and spike slow waves that are often multifocal, most commonly seen in the temporal or temporo-parieto-occipital regions, and that are enhanced during sleep. This syndrome is also often associated with two other symptoms: behavioral problems and epileptic seizures. The International League Against Epilepsy (ILAE) defines this syndrome as "a childhood disorder in which an acquired aphasia, multifocal spikes, and spike and wave discharges are associated." Onset of LKS ranges from 3 to 8 years following a normal cognitive and language development. To date, the prevalence of LKS has not been determined. Eighty-one cases were reported between 1957 and 1980, and 117 cases between 1981 and 1991. It is worth noting that there are definitely many more cases than reported. During the past two decades, there has been increasing interest in LKS course, its pathogenesis, and treatment. Patry et al. in 1971 were the first to coin the term 'subclinical status epilepticus induced by sleep,' which was later referred to as 'electrical status epilepticus during slow-wave sleep' (ESES). Now it is known as epilepsy with 'continuous spikes and waves during slow-wave sleep' (CSWS). CSWS often occurs in LKS. The sex (male to female) ratio in LKS is 2:1. Family and medical history are usually, otherwise, negative, and there are usually no additional coexisting neurological symptoms other than those mentioned above (see **Table 1**).

Clinical Manifestations

Patients present with loss of expressive speech and auditory verbal agnosia. Behavioral and psychiatric disturbances are common. These include motor hyperactivity, impulsivity, and aggressive behavior. Anxiety can occur as a reaction to the sudden loss of understanding of spoken language that these patients experience. Language problems typically start as word deafness or auditory agnosia. Children do not respond to their parents' commands even with loud voices. The auditory agnosia may exacerbate to a stage that those children are unable to recognize even familiar sounds like bells or ringing phones. These patients are usually suspected to have hearing impairment. No abnormalities are found in audiograms or brain stem auditory evoked responses (BAERs). There are delays in long-latency cortical evoked responses which implicate posterior temporal regions' involvement. Permanent extinction of one ear contralateral to the involved temporal cortex is shown with dichotic listening tasks. Word deafness can extend to complete lack of response. Problems in expression such as frequent or even continuous misarticulations, use of telegraphic speech and flowing jargon, or even complete mutism often occur. The language problems of LKS resemble in many aspects those of the autism spectrum disorder. However, there are clear and well-defined differences. Autism patients suffer from problems in the development of spoken language and in the capability of starting a conversation. The language that the autistic child uses is stereotyped, repetitive, and characteristic. Confusion sometimes also arises from the fact that autistic patients can have seizures with frequent EEG discharges. In addition, at minimum, one-third of the autistic cases suffer from neurodevelopmental deterioration involving language, sociability, playing, and thinking skills. However, the language regression in autism occurs before 3 years of age, whereas the age of onset of LKS is typically 5–7 years. Autistic children suffer from early regression that involves losing single words, whereas children with LKS, who are older, suffer from more dramatic changes as they have acquired more vocabulary and language. Problems in reciprocal social relatedness and limited stereotypical forms of interests and behaviors that are associated with autism are not manifested

Table 1 Characteristic features of Landau–Kleffner syndrome, epilepsy with CSWS, and CSWS as an EEG finding

Characteristics	*LKS*	*ESES or epilepsy with CSWS*	*CSWS as an EEG finding*[a]
Age of onset	3–8 years	The first seizure occurs between the ages of 1 and 10 years, with a peak at 4–5 years	Usually in children
Symptoms	Auditory verbal agnosia and loss of expressive speech with behavioral psychiatric disturbances	Atypical absence seizures, seizures with falls, and sometimes absence status. Other seizure types commonly occur. Neuropsychological dysfunction as a rule is present	Depending on the epilepsy syndrome: LKS (in 80% of cases), ESES (in all cases), or BECTS (in occasional cases)
EEG features	Focal or multifocal epileptic discharges that occur most commonly in the temporal areas and that are consistently enhanced during sleep. EEG may also show CSWS (i.e., >85% of sleep dominated by continuous electrographic seizure activity) in 80% of cases.	In the waking state, focal and/or multifocal, and/or generalized diffuse spike wave activity. During sleep, the EEG shows continuous bilateral and diffuse slow spike wave activity persisting through all or most (>85%) the slow sleep stages (i.e., CSWS)	Spike wave activity constitutes more than 85% of slow-wave sleep time
Etiology	It is unknown in most cases (cryptogenic). Multiple etiologies: encephalitis, autoimmune mechanisms, and others	Posthemorhagic, postinfectious, hydrocephalus, focal cortical dysplasia, periventricular leukomalacia, perinatal occlusion of middle cerebral artery, arachoid cyst, congenital biopercular syndrome, and other etiologies	Depending on the epilepsy syndrome
Therapy	Anticonvulsants, corticosteroids, adrenocorticotropic hormone (ACTH), intravenous immunoglobulin, and surgical	Anticonvulsants, corticosteroids	Depending on the epilepsy syndrome
Prognosis	50% of the patients recover partially or suffer from permanent aphasia	In adulthood, 50% of patients suffer from speech abnormalities and behavioral problems	Depending on the epilepsy syndrome

[a]Can be seen in multiple epilepsy syndromes including BECTS, epilepsy with CSWS and LKS.

in LKS patients. Patients who fulfill the criteria of LKS, but who also have the behavioral problems of autism, are known as patients with the Landau–Kleffner variant.

Epileptic Manifestations

Seventy percent of patients with LKS have seizures. One-third of them have one seizure or a single status epilepticus event, usually at the onset of the syndrome. The other patients usually have occasional seizures between 5 and 10 years of age. Sporadic seizures persist in one-fifth of the patients after the age of 10 years. Seizures rarely occur by the time patients reach the age of 15 years. Seizures in LKS are mostly nocturnal simple partial motor seizures. Complex-partial seizures occur infrequently. Atonic seizures are common. The occurrence of generalized tonic-clonic seizures, atypical absences, and myoclonic-astatic seizures is noted less frequently. The prognosis is not dependent on the frequency and type of seizures. Seizures, but not aphasia, are usually controlled by the use of anticonvulsants.

EEG Findings

Focal or multifocal epileptic discharges commonly occur in the temporal areas. Paroxysmal activity is rarely precipitated by hyperventilation or photic stimulation, but is consistently enhanced during sleep, often leading to CSWS. Though common, the presence of CSWS is not essential to diagnose LKS as studies have shown that CSWS occurs in 80%, but not in all patients fulfilling the criteria of LKS. CSWS as an EEG finding is determined to be present when the spike wave activity constitutes more than 85% of slow-wave sleep time. The ILAE defines the epilepsy syndrome of "epilepsy with CSWS" as a condition that "results from the association of various seizure types, partial or generalized, occurring during sleep, and atypical absences when awake" and "despite the usually benign evolutions of seizures, prognosis is guarded because of the appearance of neuropsychologic disorders." The spike slow-wave activity is characterized by being bilateral and mainly generalized. In that respect, one should distinguish between epilepsy with CSWS as an epilepsy syndrome (as defined above) and CSWS as an

EEG finding (also as defined above). The epilepsy syndrome of CSWS resembles LKS clinically, but the difference between them arises from the EEG (which may not show CSWS in LKS), from the general mental deficiency in epilepsy with CSWS, and the serious comprehension problems (auditory agnosia) in LKS. Also, the two syndromes can be differentiated by their clinical profile when patients reach adulthood, whereby patients with epilepsy with CSWS suffer from global cognitive abnormalities, and those with LKS have these deficits restricted to speech abnormalities and behavioral problems.

Etiology and Pathogenesis

It is probable that LKS is a syndrome of multiple etiologies which are yet to be fully elucidated. This syndrome was initially assumed to be secondary to encephalitis because an initial report indicated the presence of encephalitic changes in a biopsy taken from the cortex of a case of LKS. Subsequent studies could not confirm the presence of encephalitic changes in pathological specimens taken from other patients. Autoimmune mechanisms have been reported to be potentially important, at least in some patients. Autoantibodies against each of the following – brain-derived neurotrophic factor, neuronal antigens, myelin, and brain endothelial cells – were found in the sera of some patients with LKS. Other possible etiologies have been implicated in different case reports. These include genetic predisposition, cerebral arteritis, toxoplasmosis, neurocysticercosis, temporal astrocytoma, temporal ganglioglioma, hemophilus influenzae meningitis, subacute sclerosing panencephalitis, inflammatory demyelinating disease, and abnormal zinc metabolism. The neurologic deficit in LKS is thought to be secondary to the frequent and at times continuous electroencephalographic discharges that inhibit the function of the speech centers. The pathophysiology of this electroencephalographic seizure activity is believed to be that thalamic-related neural generators of synchronous sleep-related EEG oscillations combine to promote electrographic seizure propagation during nonrapid eye movement sleep and drowsiness.

Laboratory and Radiological Studies

Cerebrospinal fluid (CSF), computed tomography (CT), and magnetic resonance imaging (MRI) usually show no abnormalities. In rare cases, there may be an elevation in CSF protein, changes in white matter, or structural lesions on CT or MRI scans. Occasionally, some enlargement or asymmetry of temporal horns may be present, and this is suspected to be due to the effects of long-term epileptic activity. Various studies using single photon emission computed tomography (SPECT) and positron emission tomography (PET) on LKS patients have demonstrated the presence of abnormalities in the temporal lobe in brain perfusion and in glucose metabolism. These include hypometabolism in middle temporal gyri on fluoro-deoxy glucose (FDG)-PET. Also, decreased temporoparietal perfusion was detected by SPECT. The exact relationship between LKS aphasia and hypometabolism or hypoperfusion of the temporal lobe is not known because these features are also seen in epileptic patients who do not manifest aphasia.

Diagnosis and Differential Diagnosis

Essentials for the diagnosis of LKS include (1) auditory agnosia with language regression and (2) epileptiform EEG abnormalities that exacerbate during sleep. The workup to define the underlying etiology, if one can be found, usually includes an MRI scan. On rare occasions, functional imaging, CSF studies, or arteriograms may be needed. These tests are, however, not essential for making the diagnosis of this syndrome. It is crucial to differentiate LKS and Landau–Kleffner variant from CSWS (see the earlier section 'EEG findings'), autism (see the earlier section 'Clinical manifestations'), and from benign rolandic epilepsy with centrotemporal spikes (BECTS) with exacerbation in sleep. In rare cases of BECTS, the strong activation during sleep of the centrotemporal EEG spike and wave activity results in cognitive decline and attention disorders. In the usual BECTS cases, the EEG shows normal background rhythms; spike foci can be unilateral or bilateral. It also shows typical morphology of high amplitude and diphasic waveforms. BECTS seizures are typically simple partial seizures that include speech arrest, excessive drooling, twitching of the face, stiffening of the tongue, or other sensomotor phenomena of the orofacial region and the regression is not verbal auditory agnosia. Their seizures can also, less frequently, be complex-partial, generalized, or partial with secondary generalization. Most patients keep a normal global intellectual efficiency and good long-term outcome. However, some, as mentioned above, may suffer from oromotor dysfunction, neuropsychological deficits, or attention deficits with learning disorders. This may be more common in BECTS with atypical features. Atypical BECTS features include leg jerking, unilateral body sensations, ictal blindness, epigastric pain, lateral body torsion, diurnal seizures only, status epilepticus, developmental delay, and attention-deficit disorder (ADD). Some patients can have additional neuropsychological problems such as cognitive dysfunction, auditory–verbal and visuospatial memory problems, and behavioral disturbances. BECTS can be aggravated by the administration of some antiepileptic drugs (AEDS) leading to the development of CSWS. Some patients presenting with typical BECTS may present later with atypical features. Moreover, a small number of patients with BECTS develop LKS years later. Landau–Kleffner variant patients manifest LKS features, but also have the behavioral problems of autism (see the earlier section 'Clinical manifestations'). These patients are managed predominantly as LKS patients and less as autism patients.

Therapy

General Principles

Therapy of LKS still has many controversial issues due to the complete lack of controlled clinical trials in this syndrome. The therapeutic approaches that are used are based on open label data usually collected from case reports involving small numbers of patients. There are essentially two main lines of therapy. Pharmacological treatment which includes anticonvulsants, corticosteroids, adrenocorticotropic hormone (ACTH), or intravenous immunoglobulin (IVIG), and surgical treatment. Surgical therapy is still largely controversial. In addition, while treating LKS, one should treat all its aspects including seizures, speech, and behavior. Controlling seizures is usually easy. Sometimes, improvement in EEG is associated with language restoration. Due to the fluctuating profile of LKS and its unpredicted remissions, it is difficult to assess the effectiveness of any treatment.

Antiepileptic Drugs

The conventional AEDs are effective in controlling seizures of LKS patients; however, their effect on aphasia is not consistent. Valproate (10–50 mg $kg^{-1}day^{-1}$), clobazam (1–1.6 mg $kg^{-1}day^{-1}$), and ethosuximide (20 mg $kg^{-1}day^{-1}$) were reported to be efficient in stopping seizures and in reducing language problems in about half of the patients that received them. Valproate at a dose of 20 mg $kg^{-1}day^{-1}$ was reported to be effective in ameliorating the speech problems, especially in patients whose aphasia started earlier. High dosage of oral diazepam (0.75 mg $kg^{-1}day^{-1}$ with a blood level of 100–400 ng ml^{-1}) given for six short cycles (3–4 weeks) was successful in treating ESES patients including one with LKS. Riviello from Children's Hospital, Boston, reported administering 1 mg kg^{-1}per dose of rectal or oral diazepam (up to a maximum of 40 mg) for patients with LKS or ESES on two consecutive nights with continuous video EEG monitoring for 2 days and pulse oximeter monitors for 4 h after the diazepam dose. The patients were administered 0.5 mg $kg^{-1}day^{-1}$ (up to a maximum of 20 mg) for 3–4 weeks, then the dose was tapered (2.5 mg per month). Eleven out of 13 patients responded to treatment and they had their language and EEG improved within a month. The use of ethosuximide (20 mg $kg^{-1}day^{-1}$) combined with either valproic acid, phenobarbital, carbamazepine, or a benzodiazepine, and that of vigabatrin combined with ethosuximide, carbamazepine, or clonazepam were also reported to be effective in some LKS patients. Also, lamotrigine monotherapy improved cognitive functions and language in some patients. Nicardipine (0.5–2 mg $kg^{-1}day^{-1}$) combined with conventional AEDs was reported to be effective in LKS patients. Felbamate given as polytherapy or monotherapy (60 mg $kg^{-1}day^{-1}$) was able to dramatically improve language skills and EEG in some patients. Sulthiame and levetiracetam (35–60 mg $kg^{-1}day^{-1}$) were reported to be effective in helping some LKS patients. The 4:1 ketogenic diet (4 parts saturated fats, 1 part proteins and carbohydrates) was reported to be an effective treatment of acquired epileptic aphasia patients. It is not recommended to use carbamazepine for LKS patients since it was found to often worsen this condition.

Corticosteroids and Adrenocorticotrophin Hormone

Corticosteroids and ACTH (50–80 μg day^{-1} given for 4 weeks to 3 months) have been reported to be useful in improving language, cognitive, and behavioral problems. It is not known which regimen is the most effective. Prednisone is given orally (2–3 mg kg^{-1} for 1–2 months, then tapered according to response) or given at a dose that ranges from 30 to 60 mg day^{-1}. Dexamethasone is often given in a dose of 4 mg day^{-1} for 2 weeks before being tapered off. Intravenous methyl prednisolone given as 20 mg kg^{-1} daily for 3 days, then every 4 days, followed by oral prednisolone 2 mg kg^{-1} daily for 1 month or given as 500 mg over 3 h daily for 5 days, followed by 250 mg infusion over 2 h once per month was reported to be effective in a few patients resistant to other therapies. Treatment with steroids usually needs to be prolonged for several months or for more than a year to avoid relapses. This prolonged steroid therapy may cause several side effects such as avascular necrosis of hip, hypertension, behavioral abnormalities, gastric ulcers, hyperglycemia, and immunosuppression. These side effects can be minimized by using every other day dosing or weekend pulse dosing.

Intravenous Immunoglobulin

Occasional cases of LKS respond to IVIG; usually given as 2 g kg^{-1} for 4–5 days). The response to IVIG, in those that do respond (and those are a small minority), is usually quick and dramatic starting by day 3 of the infusion and resulting in remission of speech within a few days to a few weeks. However, this at times usually lasts for 3–4 months, after which a second or a third course is needed to result in similar responses and eventually in a permanent remission.

Surgery

The surgical procedure that has been reported to improve the profile of LKS patients that have failed medical therapy is multiple subpial transection (MST). This procedure involves sectioning the horizontal interneurons, which is hoped to lead to a decrease in epileptic discharges originating from the speech cortex while maintaining the area's physiologic functions. MST was reported to result in eradication of continuous spike waves during sleep and in ameliorating the language functions in many of the above patients. However, MST is still viewed as an experimental procedure by many experts. In fact, it is usually required, before proceeding with MST, that the patient should fulfill several restrictive criteria. These include having normal developmental history of language and cognition before starting to lose language skills, normal nonverbal cognitive functions, unilateral intra- and perisylvian epileptogenic zone, and CSWS duration of less than 3 years. Vagal nerve stimulation (VNS) has recently been introduced as another type of surgery that could help LKS patients with refractory seizure. It was reported to decrease seizure frequency by half in three out of six children. Its effects on the aphasia still need to be determined.

Speech Therapy and Behavioral Intervention

Several interventions such as sign language, a daily diary of consecutive pictures of the classroom routine, auditory training starting with environmental sounds, and 'graphic conversation' technique have been found to be useful intervention tools. Even after LKS patients receive the appropriate treatment, they can still have problems related to processing oral language. Thus, even if they respond, there is still a need to use different methods to bypass the auditory channel of processing. Moreover, patients may need some behavioral modification techniques to deal with their behavioral problems. Medications to control hyperactivity and behavioral problems are also occasionally needed.

Evolution and Prognosis

Children with LKS may show complete recovery from aphasia months or years after the onset of LKS. Others, constituting around 50% of the patients, recover partially or suffer from permanent aphasia. Some cases are characterized by periods of fluctuating remissions and relapses. Prognosis is affected by many factors such as age of onset, type of language deficit, frequency and topography of EEG abnormalities, epilepsy duration, and effectiveness and side effects of AEDs. Outcomes can be as good as complete recovery and as bad as permanent aphasia. Most patients improve with some remaining moderate language problems. Moreover, one can expect better prognosis when the onset of language deficits takes place after the age of 6, and when speech therapy is started at an early stage. The relationship between the age of onset of language deficits and the end result is contrary to the situation of childhood aphasia after structural injury. The older the LKS patients, the greater their chance of language improvement. In aphasia that is associated with a lesion, the older the age at which the lesion appears, the lower the probability of language improvement. Improvement in EEG often precedes improvement in LKS-associated language disorders, but it does not guarantee the most favorable end point. In fact, some have found a strong relationship between the manifestation of language problems and EEG changes whereby improvement in both speech and EEG occurred at the same time, whereas others did not find such a relationship.

See also: Agnosia; Aphasia, Sudden and Progressive.

Further Reading

Hirsch, E, Marescaux, C, Maquet, P, et al. (1990). Landau–Kleffner syndrome: A clinical and EEG study of five cases. *Epilepsia* 31: 756–767.
Landau, WM and Kleffner, RF (1957). Syndrome of acquired aphasia with convulsive disorder in children. *Neurology* 7(8): 523–530.
Mikati, MA and Shamsuddine, AN (2005). Management of Landau–Kleffner syndrome. *Paediatric Drugs* 7(6): 377–389.
Pearl, PL, Carrazana, EJ, and Holmes, GL (2001). The Landau–Kleffner syndrome. *Epilepsy Currents* 1(2): 39–45.
Shouse, MN, Scordato, JC, and Farber, PR (2004). Sleep and arousal mechanisms in experimental epilepsy: Epileptic components of NREM and antiepileptic components of REM sleep. *Mental Retardation and Developmental Disabilities Research Reviews* 10(2): 117–121.
Steriade, M (2005). Sleep, epilepsy and thalamic reticular inhibitory neurons. *Trends in Neuroscience* 28(6): 317–324.

Language and Discourse

S. B. Chapman and G. Sparks

The gold standard for understanding the neurology of language has been derived almost exclusively from studies of lower levels of language (i.e., impaired syntax and semantics) in stroke-induced aphasia during the past century. In recent years, however, focus has shifted to explicate the neurology of higher levels of language function, specifically connected language or discourse. The shift in emphasis to discourse abilities evolved because of the rich diagnostic clues and functional treatment goals available from measuring this more naturally occurring unit of language. Discourse measures are sensitive to distinguishing normal cognitive aging in late life (> 80 years) from disease; early changes in progressive brain diseases, even in preclinical stages of diseases such as Alzheimer's disease and frontotemporal dementia; and mild impairment in stroke and traumatic brain injury in adults and children. Differential disruption in discourse has been associated with different sites of cortical involvement and distinct disease syndromes.

Discourse is the linguistic expression of ideas, wishes, and opinions in everyday life, typically conveyed as a sequence of sentences that has coherent organization and meaning. Discourse provides a window into the flow, misflow, or lack of flow of information that may occur as a consequence of brain damage. Discourse abilities entail a complex interplay of basic linguistic skills, cognitive processes, and information-handling abilities. Discourse is a generic term that refers to a variety of discourse types, such as descriptive, conversational, narrative, procedural, or expository. Each genre has unique cognitive and linguistic requirements. Discourse methodologies characterize breakdowns in productivity of ideas (fluency), organization of content, and coherence of thought. Whereas productivity of ideas refers to the fluency, quantity, and completeness of ideas, the organization of discourse expression refers to the sequential unfolding of information according to the degree to which each new unit of information is related to preceding content. Coherence corresponds to the global semantic representation (or the central meaning/gist) of a text. The ability to infer the gist-based meaning is the most critical discourse skill related to everyday communicative competence.

Discourse in Normal Cognitive Aging

Discourse has been used as a tool to identify spared and impaired cognitive–linguistic changes in cognitively normal aging. Increasing evidence indicates that cognitively normal adults are capable of deriving the gist from discourse text when the topic is within their general level of understanding or expertise. Preservation of discourse gist has been identified in cognitively normal seniors in their eighties and nineties. The ability to provide the gist for a discourse text is achieved through drawing inferences between the content in the text and real-world knowledge. In contrast, one of the most robust age-related declines is in detail-level processing because older adults recall fewer ideas from the text. It has been proposed that older adults may adopt a gist-based strategy, integrating old knowledge with new information, to compensate for declines in detail-level processing. Clearly, cognitively healthy older adults demonstrate a remarkable adaptive ability to derive a central or deeper meaning in the form of an interpretive response or summary statement and to maintain it across time delays.

Discourse of the Dementias

Alzheimer's Disease

Discourse abnormalities may be one of the earliest signs of Alzheimer's disease (AD), often measurable years before memory impairment is apparent. In contrast to the pattern of preserved gist-level processing in normal advanced aging, discourse gist is particularly vulnerable in the earliest stages of AD, and deficits are found in patients with mild cognitive impairment who may be in the preclinical stages of AD. Discourse changes in early AD include reduced embedding of ideas, impaired gist-level processing, and interruptions in the flow of information during verbal expression. As one would expect, detail-level processing of discourse is reduced in early AD. The degree of loss of detail-level discourse information is greater for AD patients, with increased time between task and testing, than for cognitively normal adults. The loss of gist is much greater in AD than in cognitively normal aging. For example, a person with AD may produce a gist-level response to discourse that includes incorrect information, is too concretely tied to details, or fails to infer between the text and world knowledge.

Frontotemporal Dementia (FTD)

Similar to AD, discourse in FTD is characterized by a significant impairment in the ability to derive the gist.

Counter to adults with AD, however, adults with FTD show relatively preserved comprehension and recall of details from meaningful discourse. Deficits in procedural discourse appear to be particularly revealing in patients in the early stages of FTD. Procedural discourse requires that an individual identify all the props needed to perform a task (e.g., scramble eggs) and then to carefully describe all the steps required to complete the task. Adults with FTD show reduced productivity in identifying the necessary props for the task. Additionally, they show a significant reduction in specificity of verbs used in the procedure compared to normal controls and to patients with AD. In patients with semantic dementia, which is a type of frontotemporal dementia, there is a loss of both nouns and verbs in discourse. In this disorder, patients are able to perform the task but have significant difficulties detailing the steps.

Discourse in Focal Neurological Injuries: Left Versus Right Hemisphere-Lesioned Patients

Discourse in individuals with aphasia due to left hemisphere lesions reveals a clear dissociation between lower levels of language and higher levels of discourse function. Patients with mild to moderate forms of nonfluent aphasia are typically able to derive and convey the central meaning of discourse despite a significant disruption in producing grammatically correct sentences and word-finding problems. Moreover, patients with primarily left hemisphere lesions understand the emotional content of discourse. This ability to decode the emotional content is prerequisite to discerning the central meaning of discourse because words do not always explicitly convey the intended meaning.

In contrast, individuals with right hemisphere damage show relatively intact use of grammar and vocabulary. Nonetheless, this population manifests deficits in processing larger language units, as demonstrated by deficits in expressing a coherent, central meaning from text. Patients with right hemisphere damage also show greater deficits in inferring the emotional content of discourse compared to patients with left brain injury.

Traumatic Brain Injury in Childhood

Children with severe traumatic brain injury exhibit significant difficulties conveying their ideas, despite normal or near normal performance on traditional language measures as early as 3 months postinjury. Discourse impairment is characterized by impaired sequential flow of ideas and marked disturbances in expressing the most central information. Children with traumatic brain injury rarely receive interventions to remediate these discourse deficits, which become increasingly more severe over time.

Conclusion

Advances in neurolinguistics in the area of discourse have proven beneficial to diagnosing and treating neurological diseases in several ways. First, discourse measures distinguish normal aging and early progressive brain disease even in the preclinical stages. Second, measures of discourse function can impact not only differential diagnosis but also functional abilities in everyday life. Discourse performance provides direct clues for treatment goals in different types of neurological disorders at all stages post-injury (at long-term follow-up) and at all severity levels. Finally, discourse measures may provide a useful measure of the effectiveness of emerging pharmaceuticals or brain treatments designed to enhance brain–behavior recovery (i.e., transplantation, excision, and stimulation of brain) on everyday life functions.

See also: Alzheimer's Disease; Cognitive Impairment; Intelligence; Speech Disorders, Overview.

Further Reading

Brownell, HH, Potter, HH, Bihrle, AM, et al. (1986). Inference deficits in right brain-damaged patients. *Brain Language* 27: 310–321.

Chapman, SB, Peterson-Highley, A, and Thompson, JL (1998). Discourse in fluent aphasia and Alzheimer's disease: Linguistic and pragmatic considerations. *J. Neurolinguistics* 11: 55–78.

Chapman, SB, Levin, HS, and Lawyer, SL (1999). Communication problems resulting from brain injury in children: Special issues of assessment and management. In: McDonald, S, Togher, L, and Code, C (eds.) *Communication Disorders following Traumatic Brain Injury*, pp. 235–269. Gloucester, UK: Psychology Press.

Joanette, Y and Brownell, HH (1990). *Discourse Ability and Brain Damage: Theoretical and Empirical Perspectives.* New York: Springer-Verlag.

Snowdon, DA, Kemper, SJ, Mortimer, JA, et al. (1996). Linguistic ability in early life and cognitive function and Alzheimer's disease in late life. *J. Am. Med. Assoc* 275: 528–532.

Ulatowska, HK and Chapman, SB (1994). Discourse macrostructure in aphasia. In: Bloom, RL, Obler, LK, DeSanti, S, and Ehrlich, J (eds.) *Discourse in Adult Clinical populations*, pp. 19–46. New York: Erlbaum.

Wingfield, A and Stine-Morrow, EAL (2000). Language and speech. In: Craik, FIM and Salthouse, TA (eds.) *The Handbook of Aging and Cognition,* 2nd ed., pp. 359–416. Mahwah, NJ: Erlbaum.

Language Development

T. H. Mintz, University of Southern California, Los Angeles, CA, USA

Introduction

The ability of human children to acquire a language is one of the hallmarks of the species. Within 24 h of being born, infants already show evidence of having learned aspects of the broad rhythmic structure of their mother tongue, most likely from hearing speech *in utero* during gestation. Infants continue to attend to the patterns in their language and start to learn a considerable amount about its structure well before they start combining words in their own speech. After just a few years, children will have mastered many of the complex grammatical structures in their language, and persistent systematic errors become rare as children approach their tenth birthday. Children exposed early on to additional languages will learn them without any significant added difficulty compared with monolingual acquisition, provided they have sufficient exposure to each language.

Language development in children is remarkable for its regularity across individuals and different languages, even when the languages are quite diverse. Children universally progress through many of the same stages, mastering certain components of the grammar before others and making characteristic errors in production and comprehension at each stage. Despite individual differences in intelligence and other abilities, and despite normal differences in language exposure, all children end up able to speak and understand their native language(s) fluently. This is in marked contrast to adult learners, who show much greater variability in learning processes and ultimate outcomes. Indeed, differences between children and adult learners in ultimate outcome, in the kinds of errors made, and in the stages of acquisition have led many researchers to conclude that there is a critical or sensitive period for language development. As in other developmental domains with critical periods, learning that takes place outside this period is more variable and less robust, leading to a greater range of outcomes and more idiosyncratic patterns of acquisition.

In addition to the uniform patterns of acquisition across languages, there are some aspects of language development that are tied more closely to structural properties of the particular language being learned. Comparing components that are more or less language dependent can lead to insights about the learning mechanisms involved in language development and the properties of the linguistic input to which learners attend.

This article gives an overview of early language development, discussing some key phenomena in acquisition and some major theoretical issues. Other articles offer more-detailed discussions of specific areas within language development.

Overview of Early Language Development

First Words

Linguistic structure

When acquiring a vocabulary, learners associate word forms with concepts related to their meanings. In addition, they store information about how words combine with other words to makes sentences. The combinatorial patterns in language are governed primarily by the categories of words rather than by words themselves; thus learners must represent category information. While all languages have categories for nouns and verbs, languages vary as to what other categories are differentiated grammatically, such as adjectives, adverbs, determiners, and so forth. For example, many languages have classifiers – words or morphemes (see the section titled 'Morphology') that occur obligatorily and specify general properties of objects (e.g., animate, long thin object) – but English does not have a classifier system. The presence or absence of a grammatical class in a language should not be confused with the language's ability to express related concepts. For example, in English one can talk about attributes generally designated by classifiers in other languages, but English uses phrases involving adjectives and nouns instead of a unique class of markers.

Production

Children produce their first words at approximately 1 year of age, although there is considerable variability in the onset of lexical production. These words are distinct from babbles in that they have referential content, although phonetically they may only approximate the target word form. Semantically as well, a word may only approximate the adult target. Thus, [dɔ] ('daw'), might be a 1-year-old's word for dog, but also for horses and other four-legged animals.

Children's productive vocabulary increases relatively slowly as the first 50–100 words are acquired. The initial cohort of words is primarily nouns. The early dominance of nouns appears to be a universal phenomenon and is attributed to the relative ease of determining a noun's referent (often a concrete object) versus a verb's referent (complex relationships between objects, internal mental states, etc.).

Perception

Although children generally do not produce their first words until they are approximately 1 year old, they segment the stream of continuous speech sounds into wordlike units much earlier. By 4.5 months, infants can recognize their own names embedded in fluent speech, and by approximately 7.5 months, their ability to segment words is much more fully developed. Thus, many months before producing their first words, infants become aware of the sound sequences that correspond to words in their language.

Morphology

Many words are made from smaller parts – sublexical meaning-bearing units called bound morphemes. Bound morphemes cannot exist alone as words but combine in systematic ways with stems to create words. For example, in English the morpheme *-ed* signifies past tense and affixes to the ends of verbal stems to produce past tense forms: *talk* + *-ed* → *talked*; the morpheme *–er* affixes to the end of verbal stems to produce related nouns: *talk* + *-er* → *talker*.

Although there is a relatively restricted range of functions or meanings associated with bound morphemes, individual languages differ as to what grammatical functions are marked morphologically. For example, many languages mark grammatical case – subject, object, possessor, and so forth – on nouns morphologically, but in English, case marking appears only on pronouns (e.g., *he* is in nominative case for subjects, *him* is in accusative case for objects), and case roles are determined structurally, using word order. Thus, in learning a language, children must learn what the bound morphemes are in their language, as well as the way in which these morphemes combine.

Production

The timing of children's first productive uses of grammatical morphemes depends on the language being learned. For example, while a typical 18-month-old learning English is unlikely to systematically vary tense or agreement marking on verbs – such as always saying *walk* instead of *walked*, *walks*, or *will walk*, and so forth – a Turkish-learning child will use past tense morphology by as young as 15 months. Cross-linguistic differences in children's mastery of grammatical components is unlikely to arise from differences in children's conceptual development or general manner of conceiving of events and relations across language. Rather, many such differences can be explained by formal differences in the morphological systems. Turkish has a richer inflectional system that morphologically marks case and number on nouns and tense, mood, aspect, and agreement on verbs. Moreover, in Turkish each marker is a unique morpheme, unlike in English. For example, the English morpheme *-s* marks both third person and singular, whereas in Turkish, one morpheme marks third person and another marks singular. Overall, then, there is a greater prevalence of bound morphemes in Turkish than in English. In addition, inflections in Turkish are phonetically more salient than in English: they are syllabic, containing unreduced vowels, and usually receiving stress. Finally, the near-perfect one-to-one mapping of morpheme to grammatical function in Turkish makes the morphological system less ambiguous than in languages like English (where, for example, *-s* marks both third-person singular on verbs and plural on nouns), which could make learning faster. Thus, language-specific factors such as the regularity of form, the uniqueness of form-to-meaning mappings, and the acoustic/phonetic salience of morphemes all influence the time course of morphological development.

Perception

Before children use morphology productively, they must identify the phonological forms that correspond to bound morphemes in their language. As discussed above, in languages in which grammatical morphemes are acoustically salient, regular, and unambiguous, detection of the forms and mastery of the form–meaning mappings proceed more rapidly than in languages that do not have these properties. Nevertheless, perception of morphological forms and dependencies of forms occurs well before the forms are used productively. In English, 18-month-old infants have been shown to be aware of the dependency between the auxiliary verb *is* and the main-verb ending,-*ing*, in present progressive sentences: they differentiate grammatical sentences such as *The baker is baking bread* from ungrammatical sentences such as *The baker can baking bread*, in which *can* and *-ing* are incompatible.

First Word Combinations

During the period of early vocabulary growth, children's utterances consist almost entirely of isolated words. Children between 18 and 24 months of age start to combine words, producing both one- and two-word utterances. During that time, children's vocabulary growth rate increases as well, with an increase in the ratio of verbs to nouns compared with prior periods. Early word combinations often combine nouns with verbs, as well as nouns with other nouns and sometimes adjectives. These multiword combinations show consistent ordering patterns that generally reflect the basic word order patterns of the exposure language. For example, the basic word order pattern in English transitive sentences is subject–verb–object (SVO). At the stage when English-learning children combine at maximum two words per utterance, they sequence verbs before nouns to express action–patient, action–theme, action–goal, and action–location relations, and they sequence nouns before verbs to express agent–action relations. For example, a child in this stage might produce 'kick ball' to indicate an action performed on a ball (action–patient), and 'baby kick' to refer to an agent performing an action. Noun–noun combinations also respect the basic word-order relations, so that in the example above, expressing both agent and patient would be accomplished by the utterance 'baby ball', in which the correct ordering relation between the two arguments is maintained but the verb is missing. The last example points to potential ambiguity in interpreting early child productions as there are also situations in which the same sequence of words ('baby ball') might express a possession relationship, that is, 'baby's ball,' without the possessive morpheme. Many analyses of children's speech thus consider the context of an utterance in determining its meaning and underlying structure. The researcher Lois Bloom pioneered this method of analysis, coined 'rich interpretation,' in the early 1970s. After carefully analyzing the situational contexts under which children's early utterances are produced, Bloom argued that children's two-word utterances express the same kinds of basic semantic and syntactic relations as adult sentences express – possessor, thing possessed, subject, direct object, indirect object, and so forth. While there was (and still is) disagreement about the particular categories and grammatical structure underlying children's early utterances, many researchers followed Bloom's lead in using context to infer structuring principles that would not be evident from analyzing the sequence of words alone.

Even languages that place few syntactic constraints on word order (marking subject, object, and direct object by case marking on nouns) have canonical word-order patterns that are governed by pragmatic and discourse constraints. For example, Turkish allows all possible orders of subject, verb, and object in transitive sentences; however, there is a statistical predominance of subject–object–verb (SOV) sequences, with SVO sequences being the second most frequent (and, indeed, Turkish is usually considered an SOV language, the most common type cross-linguistically). Children learning Turkish reflect these patterns in their own multiword utterances. Thus, word-order patterns are one of the first structural properties that young children attend to and master. Their representation of these patterns includes knowledge of how structural positions correspond to semantic roles, such as agent, patient, theme, goal, and location.

Gradual Development of Grammatical Constructions Involving Phrases

Most grammatical formalisms include categories for word sequences, or phrases, as well as for individual words, and many grammatical operations involve phrase-level constituents. For example, *the red dog* is a noun phrase (NP) in English, and it takes its category type from the phrase head (the noun, *dog*). Grammatical operations, such as question formation, operate on elements at this level: for example, the declarative *John sees the red dog* becomes *Who does John see?* in the interrogative, with the entire NP replaced by *who* (which is subsequently moved).

While phrases are an important structuring component in language, they are abstract entities, in that phrases – the boundaries between phrases, the category of phrases, and the hierarchical organization of phrases – are not explicitly marked in speech. Thus, part of what children must learn in acquiring a language is the internal organization of phrases and the sequencing of phrases within sentences. Children must also learn how grammatical operations manipulate phrases. In some cases, mastery develops in stages and suggests processes of reorganization in language development. Several examples are given in the next sections.

Question Formation

English-learning children go through several distinct stages in forming interrogative sentences, producing ungrammatical questions early on. For example, they produce sentence-initial *wh*-words without required auxiliaries: "what doing?" or "what you doing?" Next, they produce the auxiliary verbs but without the required inversion with the subject: "what you are doing?" Finally, they perform the required inversion of subject and auxiliary verb: "what are you doing?" Although there is individual variation across children in this general pattern, it is striking how predictable the development of question formation in English is. The stable pattern of errors has been used to argue for highly constrained mechanisms guiding learning, but the facts are also consistent with theories of language development that posit more general mechanisms that are sensitive to the statistical properties of the input. The acquisition of questions is also an example of the incremental development of linguistic capabilities.

In Chinese and Japanese (among other languages), forming questions does not involve moving words or inserting auxiliary verbs like *do*. Children learning such languages consistently produce well-formed questions before English-learners do. Comparing the course of development for similar syntactic functions across typologically different languages can give insights into the nature of the mechanisms and representations involved in acquisition because it provides evidence about the ease or difficulty with which different surface features are mastered to achieve similar linguistic functions.

Verb Complement Clauses

A phrase can have another phrase embedded within it. Examples are sentences with sentential complements, for example, *Mary saw (that) [Sam was sad]*, in which the embedded verb is tensed, and *Mary wanted [Sam to be happy]*, in which the embedded verb is infinitival. The function words *that* and *to* serve to mark embedded clauses, and their consistent use by children would be suggestive evidence that they have the adult complement structures in place. However, early productions of tensed complements occur without *that*, for example, *I know he sits here.* Although this appears to be a grammatical complement construction, some accounts of these early constructions propose that they involve two hierarchically adjacent phrases rather than one phrase embedded within a larger sentence. The structure of the last example would be similar to *He sits here, and I know this.* On that account, early utterances like those do not involve embedded clauses.

Similarly, children initially produce utterances such as "I want open it" or "I gonna get it" without the obligatory infinitival marker, *to*. The marker emerges gradually, first restricted only to a small set of matrix verbs (e.g., . . . *want to* . . .). But even in those constructions, it is rare for subjects to intervene between the main verb and *to*, with the result that the subject of the embedded clause is identical to the subject of the main clause (e.g., *I want (to) open it* vs. *I want Sam (to) open it*). These restricted aspects have led some researchers to claim that these utterances do not contain embedded complement clauses at all; they analyze the main verb as a modal verb that modifies the second verb (which would be analyzed as the main verb). In this view, *I want open it* is parallel structurally to *I can open it.* These accounts of early complement-like constructions claim that early utterances do not, in fact, involve embedded clauses.

In summary, mastery of complement phrases appears to be gradual and depends, in part, on the identity of the main verb. Even when children correctly produce and comprehend most complement constructions, some still cause difficulty. In particular, some main verbs are special, in that the embedded subject is not the subject of the embedded clause. Compare *Sam wanted Mary to set the table* with *Sam promised Mary to set the table.* In the first sentence, the embedded subject is the subject of the embedded complement, and this is the normal situation. However, in the second sentence, the matrix subject *Sam* is also the subject of the embedded clause. Children routinely interpret such sentences as though *Mary* is setting the table, and these errors can persist until about age 9.

Relative Clauses

Relative clauses are another kind of embedded clause that adds complexity to basic sentences, here within NPs. For example, the material after *that* in *the man that I know*, is a sentence embedded within an NP; the relativizers (*that*, *who*, etc.) are often optional. As with complement clauses, development of these structures in production is gradual. At first, children omit relativizers and generally modify only the last noun in a sentence, resulting in the modifying material occurring at the end of the utterance, which modifies the sentential object: "I see the car has the stripes." Later, they also produce relative clauses in subject position and are more likely to include *that* or other relative pronouns (e.g., *who*): "Man that I saw is leaving." Thus, as with complement clauses, the development of relative clauses in production is incremental.

Overregularization

There are regularities in the way a given language carries out grammatical functions. For example, in English, the past tense is formed by suffixing *-ed* onto a verb stem: *walk* → *walked.* In addition, there are exceptions to the regular patterns: the past tense of *go* is not *goed* but the irregular *went.* A universal phenomenon in language development is the overregularization of irregulars by children. When children initially produce an irregular, they may do so correctly, but as they start to learn more and more regular forms, and learn the generalized pattern, they sometimes apply the pattern to irregular forms – either to the stem (e.g., *goed*) or the irregular form itself (e.g., *wented*). These overgeneralization errors can persist in individuals for several years.

The phenomenon of overregularization has played an important role in the theorizing about language acquisition. Patterns of overregularization have been used as evidence in support of a variety of different architectures for lexical memory and related storage and access mechanisms, from general pattern associators that treat all stems and derivations equally, to specialized mechanisms that explicitly distinguish regular and irregular forms.

Nativism and Domain Specificity

One of the core questions in language acquisition research is the nature of the mechanisms and representations that make learning a first language possible. Central issues are nativism – the degree to which acquisition relies on innate mechanisms and representations – and domain specificity – the degree to which learning mechanisms are specific to language development. Although these issues are often conflated, they are two distinct theoretical claims.

It is clear that human language involves, to some degree, innate or biologically determined components that are present in humans but absent in other species. Inherent differences in cognitive architecture across species, in part, make human language qualitatively different from the natural communication systems of other species. (Clearly there are nonneurological biological differences between species that are relevant for language learning and use. Spoken language as we know it is not possible without a vocal tract capable of producing the necessary range of phonetic material, and a species without hands or the appropriate visual system would be unable to communicate using a signed language. But the crucial formal characteristics of human language are modality independent and in principle could be implemented in a variety of physical systems. It is these properties that arguably have an innate component in the cognitive architecture of humans.)

These innate components contribute to the highly systematic and uniform pattern of development cross-linguistically and to the inability of nonhuman species to achieve the same degree of mastery. What is generally debated is the content of the innate components: is there specialized functional machinery that is dedicated to the acquisition and/or use of language, or does language have the structure it does, and do children learn language the way they do, because of more-general properties of human cognition and/or human social interaction?

One of the most influential theories about the innate component was proposed in the 1960s by Noam Chomsky. Chomsky proposed that humans possess an innate, universal grammar (UG). In its standard conception, UG specifies the structural properties that all human languages share (and thus that putatively do not have to be learned), for example, that words are organized into phrases and phrases are organized into sentences, the kind of syntactic operations that words in certain phrasal positions can undergo, and so forth. UG also contains specialized mechanisms for learning the nonuniversal idiosyncrasies of the language to which the child is exposed (e.g., whether question formation involves inversion of the subject and auxiliary verb). The motivation for the theory is often referred to as the 'poverty of the stimulus' (POS) argument. The core of the argument states that the data from which children learn language – the utterances that they hear – are too variable and too underspecified to guarantee that all learners would converge on the correct grammar without specialized constraints and linguistic knowledge guiding learning. UG provided a description of these constraints.

Within this general theoretical framework, different theories were proposed for learning mechanisms that could determine the language-specific properties that were specified in (but also highly constrained by) UG. The content of UG and the associated learning mechanisms were described in the vocabulary of formal linguistic theory and were traditionally viewed as specific to language. But in a broader sense, UG could be construed as a set of constraints on possible inferences that can be made from linguistic input. Viewed in this way, it becomes reasonable to investigate alternative sources or descriptions of these constraints. For example, some constraints on learning and generalization could emerge from constraints in substrate learning components such as working memory, sequential processing, and so forth, and constraints governing their interaction. Some universal constraints on linguistic structure could arise from social and cultural phenomena, as opposed to specific cognitive structures for language. The computational problem of linking linguistic forms to meanings, sequencing these forms when producing utterances, and comprehending these sequences when listening to speech could lead to specific kinds of structures, in order to be carried out in real time by a human brain.

Nevertheless, many constraints on linguistic structure seem difficult to motivate from these other sources. For example, from sentence (2a), question (2b) is possible, but (2c) is ungrammatical. What could account for this difference?

(2a) Sam knows a man who likes wine.
(2b) Who does Sam know who likes wine?
(2c) What does Sam know a man who likes?

Grammatical theories account for this difference by positing constraints on grammatical operations and defined on the basis of syntactic structures; in other words, domain-specific constraints. It is not immediately obvious how the alternative sources of constraints just discussed could account for such phenomena, but a number of research programs are currently addressing just these questions.

Recovery from Errors and Negative Evidence

Part of the POS argument is the observation that a learner who was not adhering to the right structural constraints could posit grammars that overgenerate sentences. That is, the grammars would account for the utterances the child heard, but also ungrammatical utterances. This is not, in principle, an insurmountable problem. Having such a grammar, a child would be expected to make errors and produce ungrammatical sentences. But if the child received a corrective signal that the utterance was ill-formed – negative evidence – then the learner could update the grammar to rule out the ungrammatical utterance. This alternative has two essential components: (1) there must be reliable sources of feedback available to children when they make errors, and (2) the feedback should change the pattern of errors a child makes. If either of these points is not satisfied, then an alternative to a highly constrained learning mechanism becomes more difficult to maintain.

In fact, there is considerable evidence that none of these conditions are satisfied by the empirical data. A number of possible sources of negative evidence have been proposed, primarily involving the types of replies adults give in response to children's ungrammatical utterances (e.g., repeating the utterance with errors repaired, expanding the utterance, etc.), but caretakers vary widely in the kinds of responses they give to children's ungrammatical utterances, and so far no type of feedback has been shown to be reliable enough to be universally informative. Moreover, even in cases when children's errors are explicitly corrected, children very rarely alter their behavior, and the errors persist. When errors do cease, they do so without corrective feedback from adults.

Taken together, the reliability across children in the kinds of errors they make and their recovery from errors in the absence of negative evidence points to learning mechanisms that follow an internally constrained program. However, these facts are neutral as to the nature of the constraints and whether they are special to language or derive from more-general principles and properties of learning.

Cues to Structure

An important aspect of the POS argument is that utterances do not come marked with their structural description. For example, words are not inherently marked as noun, verb, adjective, and so forth, and phrasal constituency in utterances is not explicitly marked. If structure were transparent in the input, then the nature of the learning problem would be very different, as learners could simply 'read off' the structure from the utterance.

Researchers are examining the degree to which cues that correlate with important structural distinctions are available to infants and children acquiring a language. In many languages, there are bound morphemes that correlate strongly with lexical category (noun, verb, adjective, etc.). For example, case markers occur on nouns but not on verbs, and tense markers appear on verbs but not on nouns. Even though the correspondence between overt marker and lexical category may be many-to-one (e.g., because there are multiple nominal cases), as opposed to one-to-one (the simplest kind of cue), morphological markers could nevertheless be extremely useful cues to category membership.

However, not all languages have robust marking; as discussed earlier, languages like English have case marking only on pronouns, and verbal morphology is relatively impoverished. In addition, in some languages, morphemes that occur with different lexical categories are homophonous, and therefore ambiguous cues; in English, for example, *-s* is a plural marker on nouns (e.g., *cats*) and a third-person-singular agreement marker on verbs (e.g., *grows*). Therefore, while bound morphemes might provide useful category cues in some languages (e.g., Turkish), their usefulness might be limited in others. However, other cues, such as the co-occurrence patterns of words and phonological cues, have been shown to be informative for determining lexical categories.

Studies have also investigated whether prosodic information – information involving pitch, syllable duration, pause duration between words, and amplitude – could cue major phrase boundaries, such as boundaries separating subject NPs from the verb phrase. There is cross-linguistic evidence that combinations of cues involved in prosody are probabilistic indicators of phrase boundaries and could thus be used by children to aid in assigning structure to an utterance.

Another cue to phrase-level constituency that is available in some languages is inflectional marking, in particular, case marking within NPs. In German, for example, case is marked on articles and adjectives (both within an NP), and the case morpheme often (although not always) takes the same form on the article and adjective. For example, in the masculine declension, the definite article is *der* in the nominative case, and the corresponding ending on a following adjective would be *-er*; however, in the accusative case, the definite article is *den*, and the corresponding case marker on the adjective is *-en*. The phonological similarity of endings within a phrase (the article and adjective) could be used by learners as a cue to identify phrasal constituency. Even when within-constituent endings are not as similar phonologically, the endings covary within a phrasal constituent to a significant degree, and the patterns of dependency within phrases could be a more general cue to phrasal constituents.

Investigations into possible cues to structure are uncovering a variety of probabilistic cues inherent in the structure of utterances and in statistical patterns across utterances that learners could use to recover some aspects of the structural description of an utterance. To learn successfully using these cues, learners must attend to the relevant perceptual dimensions and process their input in specific ways. Experiments with infants and young children demonstrate that learners are indeed sensitive to many of the requisite properties and perform the necessary types of analysis on the basis of those properties. These lines of research are helping to specify the nature of the innate mechanisms involved in language learning. In some cases, the sensitivities and constraints are not clearly specific to language but rather could be viewed as more-general constraints on sequential processing, auditory perception, and categorization.

See also: Language in Aged Persons; Language, Auditory Processes; Language, Cortical Processes; Sentence Comprehension; Sentence Production; Word Learning.

Further Reading

Bates, E and Mac Whinney, B (1982). Functionalist approaches to grammar. In: Wanner, E and Gleitman, LR (eds.) *Language Acquisition: The State of the Art*. Cambridge: Cambridge University Press.

Bloom, L (1970). *Language Development: Form and Function in Emerging Grammar*. Cambridge, MA: MIT Press.

Crain, S (1991). Language acquisition in the absence of experience. *Behavioral and Brain Sciences* 14: 597–650.

Elman, JL, Bates, EA, Johnson, MH, Karmiloff-Smith, A, Parisi, D, and Plunkett, K (1996). *Rethinking Innateness: A Connectionist Perspective on Development*. Cambridge, MA: MIT Press.

Jackendoff, R (2002). *Foundations of Language*. New York: Oxford University Press.

Marcus, GF (1993). Negative evidence in language-acquisition. *Cognition* 46(1): 53–85.
McClelland, JL and Patterson, K (2002). Rules or connections in past-tense inflections: What does the evidence rule out? *Trends in Cognitive Sciences* 6(11): 465–472.
Newport, EL, Bavelier, D, and Neville, HJ (2001). Critical thinking about critical periods: Perspectives on a critical period for language acquisition. In: Dupoux, E and Mehler, J (eds.) *Language, Brain, and Cognitive Development: Essays in Honor of Jacques Mehler.* Cambridge, MA: MIT Press.
Pinker, S and Ullman, MT (2002). The past and future of the past tense. *Trends in Cognitive Sciences* 6(11): 456–463.
Slobin, DI (ed.) (1985). *The Cross-Linguistic Study of Language Acquisition, Vol. 1: The Data.* Hillsdale, NJ: LEA.

Language Disorders, Aphasia

H. A. Whitaker, Northern Michigan University, Marquette, WI, USA

This article is a revision of 'Aphasia Syndromes' in Encyclopedia of Language and Linguistics, 2nd edition, volume 1, pp 321–327, Copyright 2006, Elsevier Ltd.

Introduction

Kertesz (1979: p. 2) defined aphasia as "a neurologically central disturbance of language characterized by paraphasias, word finding difficulty, and variably impaired comprehension, associated with disturbance of reading and writing, at times with dysarthria, non-verbal constructional, and problem-solving difficulty and impairment of gesture." Goodglass and Kaplan (1983: p. 5) defined aphasia as "the disturbance of any or all of the skills, associations and habits of spoken or written language produced by injury to certain brain areas that are specialized for these functions." Basso and Cubelli (1999: p. 181) defined aphasia as "a disorder of verbal communication due to an acquired lesion of the central nervous system, involving one or more aspects of the processes of comprehending and producing verbal messages." Implicit in these definitions, of course, is a definition of language, itself a relatively complex concept.

The clinical syndromes of aphasia have been associated with particular anatomical loci in the central nervous system in the literature since the nineteenth century. Contemporary research, particularly aided with the used of modern brain-imaging techniques, suggests that in addition to the so-called classical language areas of the dominant (usually, left) hemisphere's cortex (Broca's area, Wernicke's area, etc.), many other areas of the central nervous system participate in language processing, including subcortical structures (including the basal ganglia, cerebellum and thalamus), other cortical areas of the dominant hemisphere (including inferior and mesial temporal lobe and insula) as well as various regions of the non-dominant hemisphere. This article focuses on aphasia as a behavior and not its anatomical substrate.

Approaches

In broad outline, there are two approaches to understanding the nature of aphasia. The first is concerned with functional components, what people do when engaged in language behaviors; the four modalities of language – speaking, listening, reading, and writing – are examples of functional components. Other functional components of language include being able to repeat what is said, initiating speech, speaking fluently, being able to name things and people, and being able to clearly articulate words. This approach to aphasia has typically been clinical; identifying impaired functional components of language in conjunction with impairments in one or more of the four modalities has led to a clinical classification of the aphasias that is used in assessment, rehabilitation, and research. An active area of research in this approach has been correlating the loci of brain lesions with functionally identified syndromes of aphasia.

The second approach might be termed neurolinguistic; it is concerned with the structure of language and which linguistic structures are impaired in aphasia. This approach begins with analyses of aphasic language in terms of linguistic levels – phonological, morphological, syntactic, semantic, and discourse – and then may take either an experimental or applied tack, correlating linguistic deficits, brain lesions, and clinical syndromes. The neurolinguistic approach typically furnishes linguistic details to the functional-clinical approach, particularly in research applications.

Studying the localization of lesions that cause aphasia was at one time of major clinical importance; modern imaging techniques, applied to both brain-damaged aphasic patients and non-brain-damaged experimental subjects, have shifted emphasis to questions of which parts of the brain subserve which language functions and/or which language structures. A reasonable goal would be to identify a unique brain structure and its connections, damage to which caused a well-defined clinical aphasia syndrome and a well-defined linguistic impairment.

Functional-Clinical Aphasia Syndromes

Broca's Aphasia

Broca's aphasia has also been called verbal aphasia, expressive aphasia, efferent motor aphasia, and motor aphasia. The primary modality of language that is affected is speech production, but writing is often affected, too. Comprehension of spoken language and reading are usually much better preserved. According to the older scheme of dividing the aphasias into fluent and non-fluent, Broca's aphasia is the common variant of non-fluent aphasia. Speech output tends to exhibit poorly articulated words with missing, added, or transposed sounds, and there is usually difficulty in initiating speech. The range of vocabulary is often reduced from premorbid levels, and speech output tends to rely a great deal on basic, highly familiar, and thus overlearned speech patterns. Speech is likely to be in short phrases with fewer words than expected, punctuated with frequent pauses. Commonly seen in Broca's aphasia is agrammatism, speech and writing in which the small elements of grammatical structure, typically the so-called function words such as articles, auxiliary verbs, and some prepositions, are omitted or unrecognized. Anomia is also fairly common, causing patients to struggle with finding the appropriate word, both in conversational speech and in confrontational naming. Although comprehension is noticeably better than production, some patients with Broca's aphasia have difficulty comprehending less frequent syntactic structures, although most demonstrate the ability to comprehend single nouns, verbs, or adjectives. Errors may occur in word order, which is called paragrammatism, but this is more common to Wernicke's aphasia (discussed next). Nouns tend to be preserved better than verbs and adjectives in Broca's aphasia, but grammatical function words are the most impaired. A concomitant of the shorter phrases and frequent pauses seen in Broca's aphasia is an impairment in prosody, alterations such as impaired inflection, pitch, and rhythm; this is commonly referred to as dysprosody. Repetition often shows the same impairments as in conversational speech. Writing in Broca's aphasia tends to be impaired analogously to speech output, but reading ability may be only mildly impaired; writing will exhibit misspellings, letter omissions, poor formation of letters, and agrammatism. Patients with Broca's aphasia are generally more aware that their speech and language is impaired than those with Wernicke's aphasia and thus may struggle to produce more correct responses.

The lesions typically leading to Broca's aphasia most often affect both the inferior frontal lobe and the anterior inferior portion of the parietal lobe; this is generally more extensive than the part of the third (inferior) frontal gyrus and surrounds that have been identified as Broca's area.

Wernicke's Aphasia

Wernicke's aphasia has also been called syntactic aphasia, acoustic aphasia, sensory aphasia, and receptive aphasia. The primary modality of language that is affected is speech perception, and reading may be affected, too. The ability to produce speech and the ability to write are usually much better preserved, although the content of speech and writing will likely be impaired. According to the older scheme of dividing the aphasias into fluent and non-fluent, Wernicke's aphasia is the common variant of fluent aphasia. The salient feature of Wernicke's aphasia is an impairment in understanding spoken language, particularly when the content of the spoken language is not predictable from the context or not otherwise highly familiar. In milder forms, comprehension may be contextually appropriate, e.g., a discussion of the weather, but lacking in details, e.g., unable to distinguish partially cloudy from overcast. On the other hand, the speech of the Wernicke's aphasic patient may appear articulatorily fluent but paraphasic, that is, an intrusion of non-words, words out of order, and word choices that are marginally related or unrelated to the topic of the conversation. Paraphasias may appear in any variety of aphasia, but they are typically more prevalent in Wernicke's aphasia. As in Broca's aphasia, grammar may be affected, rather than function words being omitted, they are more likely to be used improperly or added extraneously. Grammatical word order constraints may be violated, a syntactic impairment called paragrammatism. Wernicke's aphasic patients are not likely to use complex sentence structure but rather will resort to simple, common declarative word order. Occasionally, patients with Wernicke's aphasia may talk excessively, even to the point of adding unrecognizable syllables, words, or phrases to their speech, a phenomenon known as jargon aphasia. Most researchers consider jargon aphasia to be a subtype of Wernicke's aphasia. In jargon aphasia, the jargon aphasic errors may be literal (single sounds), verbal (added words that are recognizable), or neologistic (added words that are unrecognizable). The patient with Wernicke's aphasia may be able to write letters and words correctly as a motor action, but the output reflects the patient's fluent paraphasic speech, including a disorganized and rambling style, occasional to frequent repetitions of words or phrases, jargon aphasic errors, and a lack of recognizable content. Reading tends to follow auditory comprehension ability, typically impaired.

The lesions responsible for Wernicke's aphasia are typically in the middle to posterior temporal lobe, particularly the superior gyrus, but frequently the middle temporal gyrus as well. These lesions often continue back to the junctions of the temporal lobe with the occipital and inferior parietal lobes, in the areas named the supramarginal and angular gyri.

Conduction Aphasia

Conduction aphasia has also been called central aphasia, disorganized execution of the encoding program related to disturbed auditory feedback, repetition aphasia, and afferent motor aphasia. The primary function of language that is affected is the repetition of speech, whereas comprehension and production tend to be much less impaired. Conduction aphasic patients frequently attempt to correct their repetition errors, implying a better preserved comprehension. The repetition errors may be at the level of individual sounds or words; repetition may exhibit an agrammatic character. The speech of the patient with conduction aphasia is more often like that seen in Wernicke's aphasia but sometimes is like that seen in Broca's aphasia. In addition to the repetition deficit, patients with conduction aphasia are often afflicted with anomia; literal paraphasias (substitution of sounds) may intrude in both spontaneous speaking and in attempts to repeat what is heard. Within single words or very short phrases, articulatory fluency may be good, but patients with conduction aphasia typically display phonemic (or literal) paraphasias, a substitution of sounds. Although within-phrase syntactic patterns tend to be normal, many conduction aphasic patients have difficulty with sentences containing pronouns and grammatical function words, as well as polysyllabic words. Other characteristics that may be found include difficulties in writing, showing some forms of agraphia and ideomotor apraxia. Writing ability usually parallels speech output, showing deficits in spelling and letter omissions or substitutions. As is the case for Broca's aphasia, conduction aphasic patients are typically aware of their speech and language deficits.

The lesions leading to conduction aphasia tend to be located in and around the supramarginal gyrus and the arcuate fasciculus; the latter pathway connects the temporal lobe to the frontal lobe. Other lesions are along the border of the Sylvian fissure, extending to the subjacent white matter.

Anomic Aphasia

Anomic aphasia is also known as amnestic or amnesic aphasia, nominal aphasia, and semantic aphasia. The primary modality of language that is affected is speech production, restricted to the production of names, but it is most easily observed by asking an aphasic patient to name an object, so an input problem cannot be excluded. Anomia is described by the failure to name or to retrieve names, common and proper nouns; auditory comprehension is either unimpaired or only mildly impaired. One manifestation of anomic speech is a fluent output that lacks the nouns and verbs related to concepts. As a result, speech may be described as empty. Speech rate, articulation, and, surprisingly, grammar are typically normal, and the on-line deficits in word retrieval may be signaled by noticeable pauses. Accompanying impaired naming is the inability to comprehend nouns or verbs in isolation; however, object recognition is usually quite good. Although reading and writing are usually preserved, in severe cases of anomia there may be an anomic alexia or anomic agraphia. Some degree of anomia is found in virtually all varieties of aphasia; in part for that reason, no specific localization for the causative lesions has been or is likely to be documented.

Global Aphasia

Global aphasia has also been called total aphasia. All language modalities are affected in global aphasia to an equal degree, unlike the other aphasias, in which a processing disparity among the modalities is evident. The causative lesions leading to global aphasia are typically very large, subtending all or most of language cortex.

Single-Modality Functional-Clinical Aphasia Syndromes

There are a number of aphasia syndromes that predominantly affect a single language modality.

Apraxia of Speech

Apraxia of speech has also been called aphemia, verbal apraxia, articulatory apraxia, and anarthria. Not all researchers agree that this is an aphasia syndrome; it is included here because, by definition, motor control of the speech musculature is not affected in apraxia of speech, in other words, it is independent of dysarthria. Apraxia of speech often accompanies Broca's aphasia but may be an independent, modality-specific impairment. The modality affected is speaking, and the problems are best described as errors in the selection or ordering of sounds such that the resultant erroneous words either sound something like the target word but have the wrong meaning or are so distorted that they are no longer words of the language.

Alexia with Agraphia

Alexia and agraphia are, respectively, input and output impairments of written language. Alexia and agraphia may occur independently or together; alexia with agraphia has also been called parietal-temporal alexia, central alexia, semantic alexia, angular alexia, and letter blindness. The primary modalities of language that are affected are reading and writing. Patients suffering from alexia with agraphia display impairments in both reading and writing skills. In general, their ability to copy words tends to be better preserved than their spontaneous writing ability. The inability to read and write extends into domains other than visual language: numbers, musical notation, and chemical formulas can also be impaired. Speech output and auditory comprehension may be somewhat impaired but typically only in a mild form of anomia. Both the location and the size of the lesion will strongly influence the manifestation of any aphasia, but these are particularly relevant in the impairment described as alexia with agraphia; the causative lesions are predominantly found in the region of the angular gyrus.

Pure Word Deafness

Pure word deafness has also been called auditory agnosia, isolated speech deafness, and subcortical sensory aphasia; the modality affected is hearing. It causes patients to be unable to recognize speech sounds, while being able to hear non-language environmental noises, animal sounds, and music. Other language modalities – speech production, reading, and writing – generally remain intact. Lesions typically leave Wernicke's area undamaged, but destroy both Heschl's gyrus (primary auditory cortex) in the language hemisphere and the afferent auditory pathways coming from the non-language hemisphere. The functional result is that Wernicke's area behaves as though it is isolated from auditory language input; the patient can hear but cannot understand or repeat speech sounds. Except for the severely impaired input processing of speech, the patient with pure word deafness does not otherwise function like someone with Wernicke's aphasia. Auditory agnosia, which also reflects impaired processing of speech sounds, additionally reflects an impairment in processing non-language environmental sounds.

Agraphia

Agraphia, an inability to produce written language, has several neurolinguistic variants, which are discussed later in the neurolinguistic structures section. Functionally, it may appear as a written form of Broca's aphasia and, since written language so often mirrors spoken language, is typically associated with an aphasia. But, because writing also includes visuospatial skills as well as motor skills that differ from speech, impairments in spatial orientation or visual discrimination can cause agraphia without aphasia. Cases of pure agraphia frequently report damage within the frontal lobe, but a few cases have also shown damage within the left superior parietal lobe.

Alexia

Alexia is an acquired reading problem exhibited as an impaired ability to recognize words and/or letters, thus affecting the ability to extract meaning from written text. There are several varieties of alexia, including literal alexia (also referred to as letter blindness because the problem is primarily with individual letters), verbal alexia (also referred to as word blindness because whole words are primarily affected), general alexia (which refers to reading impairments that affect grammatical and/or semantic processing more than letters or words), and hemialexia, more commonly called neglect alexia (which refers to the impairment of attending to only half of a word or a line of text). In so-called pure alexia, written language stimuli are seen but not recognized as letters, as words, or both. In these cases, lesions tend to compromise the visual association cortex in the language hemisphere together with the callosal fibers projecting from the other hemisphere, effectively isolating central language brain areas from visual input. There is a variant of pure alexia called letter-by-letter reading; such patients seem to process words by reading one letter at a time aloud before the word is identified. In some cases of alexia patients may successfully comprehend words if they are spelled out loud or traced on the palm, thus bypassing visual input to access the language core brain regions.

Transcortical Aphasias

The transcortical aphasias are sometimes known as the echolalic aphasias; there are three types, transcortical sensory, transcortical motor, and mixed transcortical, the latter sometimes known as the isolation syndrome. The modalities of language that are affected are speech comprehension (transcortical sensory) and speech production (transcortical motor) in the context of a sometimes dramatic spared ability to repeat, thus contrasting with conduction aphasia. In discussing the transcortical aphasias, it is useful to consider the notion of the language core, the temporo-parieto-frontal cortex of the language-dominant hemisphere in which resides the ability to repeat what is heard as well as the ability to process the basic sounds and word and sentence structures of one's language. Originally, the term transcortical meant that an ability to reproduce the sound structure or representation of a word was preserved, in the context of being unable to construct its meaning; this could be considered analogous to an ability to repeat a word in a foreign language that one does not understand. The predominant anatomically distinguishing feature of these aphasias is that the causative lesions are largely extra-Sylvian in location, that is, outside the classic language core. The following provides a brief overview of the generally accepted classical forms of the transcortical aphasias.

Transcortical Sensory Aphasia

Transcortical sensory aphasia is an uncommon form of aphasia that may occur when a lesion functionally isolates Wernicke's areas from the rest of the brain, leaving the reception-to-output sufficiently unimpaired that repetition is preserved; neither speech comprehension nor spontaneous speech remain intact. The simplest way to describe transcortical sensory aphasia is to think of it as a form of Wernicke's aphasia in which the patient exhibits a severe comprehension deficit, but in which repetition, and thus articulation, is well preserved. In spite of intact articulation, the repeated speech of the transcortical sensory aphasic patient may be paraphasic, neologistic, anomic, and even echolalic. Typical output may appear to be uninhibited. Patients with transcortical sensory aphasia typically tend to be unaware of their impairment; as might be expected, their speech is occasionally misinterpreted as a psychogenic problem, such as schizophrenia. Writing ability is usually disturbed in a manner similar to that of patients with Wernicke aphasia.

Transcortical Motor Aphasia Transcortical motor aphasia, another form of the transcortical aphasias, is sometimes known as dynamic aphasia or anterior isolation syndrome. Functionally, the causal lesion separates the processing of speech from the mechanisms for initiating the action to speak. Patients with transcortical motor aphasia tend to appear mute, or nearly so, and may even have an associated general akinesia, an inability to initiate action. Although transcortical motor aphasia impairs the ability to initiate speech, once such patients begin talking, speech output is typically relatively intact. Comprehension will be relatively normal, as will repetition. Prosody, articulation, and grammatical structure remain quite preserved even if verbal output is interrupted by incomplete sentences, verbal paraphasias, or false starts. When asked to say something, or otherwise initiate a response without cues, these patients have a great deal of difficulty responding; however, when asked to repeat words, phrases, or sentences, performance is characteristically flawless. There is a range in ability in word retrieval, with some patients being able to perform well on tasks such as object naming. Verbal output may improve if related to common, repetitious material. The lesions that lead to transcortical motor aphasia are typically found on the mesial surface of the anterior left frontal lobe, near supplementary motor cortex, or along the lateral aspect of the left frontal lobe; in either case these lesions fall outside of what is traditionally thought of as Broca's area. Presumably the lesions impinge on an anterior cortical or subcortical site that forms part of a circuit linking the motor speech area with the supplementary motor area and certain limbic structures considered essential for the initiation of speech and other actions.

Mixed Transcortical Aphasia

Mixed transcortical aphasia, known also as the isolation syndrome, may be associated with Pick's disease or carbon monoxide poisoning affecting the so-called watershed region of the cerebral vasculature; the language core, the peri-Sylvan speech areas, are functionally isolated from other brain functions, particularly higher-order cognitive functions. The one remaining language function is a striking ability to repeat words, phrases, and on occasion whole sentences. The isolation syndrome is most clearly the functional opposite of conduction aphasia; the former patient can only repeat speech, while the latter cannot repeat speech. Although articulatory fluency generally remains well preserved, the quasi-automatic repetition, often a frank echolalia, is prominent in a context of few if any other intact language functions. There is typically a complete alexia and agraphia, with an occasional ability to scribble meaninglessly. As pointed out by Benson and Ardila, other than the ability to repeat, patients with mixed transcortical aphasia exhibit the characteristics common to global aphasia.

Neurolinguistic Structures

The second approach, a neurolinguistic analysis of the aphasias, focuses on which linguistic components of language are affected by brain damage, within the framework of five, sometimes six, components of language: (1) phonology, or the sound system, (2) morphology, or the structure of words, (3) syntax, or the grammatical system, (4) semantics, or the system of meaning, (5) narrative or discourse, or the component that strings sentences together in coherent syntactic and semantic structure, and (6) the pragmatic or language use system. Linguistic-based descriptions of aphasic errors are neutral as to whether the errors are seen in speech production or comprehension or in written language. It is typical that the degree of impairment (percentage of errors seen on testing) of linguistic components is different in different language modalities; for example, a Broca's aphasic patient is likely to exhibit more severe agrammatism in speaking than in comprehending. It is occasionally documented that the linguistic impairments are overwhelmingly in one modality (e.g., being able to recognize grammatical errors but being unable to avoid producing them); this can lead to interesting theoretical issues regarding the nature of the language core brain areas, which are beyond the scope of this article.

Phonological Disorders

Phonological disorders are typically described in terms of phonemes, the minimal significant unit of sound in a language, or graphemes, the equivalent for the writing system. Errors may be described as substitutions (e.g., *bit* for *pit*), omissions (e.g., *cook* for *crook*), or sequencing errors (e.g., *cattle* for *tackle*, as sounds). Other phonological errors include problems with the control of prosody: syllables may be shortened or lengthened incorrectly, pitch contours may signal a question when a statement was intended, or speech may be louder or quieter at inappropriate times.

Morphological Disorders

Morphological disorders affect a word's affixes, either (a) the inflectional affixes such as mark plural vs. singular, third person singular vs. first person singular, or past vs. present tense (e.g., *three cat* for *three cats, he will jumped* for *he will jump*) or (b) the derivational affixes such as mark words as nouns, verbs, or adjectives (e.g., *nationalness* for *nationality*).

Syntactic Disorders

Syntactic disorders, agrammatism, affect the grammatical structure of phrases and sentences. Obviously, if disorders of derivational or inflectional affixes discussed previously were to impact the grammatical correctness of a phrase or sentence (e.g., *he's a regularity guy* for *he's a regular guy*) one would speak of a syntactic deficit that manifested as a morphological error. The more common form of agrammatism is seen as the omission of grammatical function words (e.g., *boy hit ball* for *the boy was hit by the ball*), which clearly impacts the meaning of the sentence as well as its grammaticality; thus, as was the case with morphological disorders, syntactic disorders can overlap semantic disorders, too. A rarer form of syntactic disorder known as paragrammatism results in the inappropriate use and ordering of grammatical function words, rather than their omission (e.g., *in on a the by a flower pot* for *in the flower pot*). Additional syntactic disorders involve the simplification, ordering, substitution, or omission of phrase- and sentence-level structures that may interact with impairments in meaning. For example, if *what the pot put on the table was the boy* were substituted for *it was the pot that the boy put on the table*, or, *what the boy put on the table was the pot*, one would note that the grammatical errors of substitution and ordering resulted in a change in meaning. As will be readily surmised, agrammatism is frequently, though not exclusively, seen in Broca's aphasia; paragrammatism is less frequently seen in Wernicke's aphasia because word order violations are infrequently observed syntactic disorders.

Semantic Disorders

Semantic disorders can take any number of forms, depending upon what aspect of the semantic system is impaired. Substitution of similar-meaning words is common (e.g., *concert* for *orchestra*) as is the interchange of superordinates and subordinates (e.g., *animal* for *dog*). A common strategy for anomic patients is to substitute an indefinite noun for an inaccessible one (e.g., *something* or *stuff* in place of *shirt* or *clothes*). Semantic disorders may also impair knowledge of features of objects (e.g., being unable to indicate that a fire truck is red or that grass is green) or attribute incorrect features to objects (e.g., something inanimate is given attributes of being alive).

Narrative Disorders

Narrative or discourse disorders will affect the coherent stringing of sentences or phrases together in conversation, for example, changing a pronoun so that it no longer refers back to the person who is being discussed or inappropriately changing the time frame of a narrative. Pragmatic disorders refer to impairments in language use, for example, no longer understanding that the statement "I could use some salt on my roast beef" is an indirect request to another person to pass the salt shaker to the speaker. It will be immediately apparent that, just as with morphological and syntactic disorders, higher level problems with discourse and pragmatics may be described in terms of semantic or syntactic errors. The different linguistic components of language, levels, are simultaneously present when language is being used.

Alexias

The analysis of neurolinguistic structures has led to a syndrome classification of reading and writing disorders as follows. Three alexias have been defined in terms of the putative locus in a psycholinguistic model of reading: deep alexia, phonological alexia, and surface alexia.

Deep Alexia

Patients with deep alexia usually have sustained a lesion sufficiently large to produce an aphasia, frequently a Broca's aphasia; their reading is characterized by semantic errors in reading aloud (the error is semantically related to the target word) and may also show visual errors (the error is visually similar but otherwise unrelated to the target word), morphological errors (the error is a morphological variant of the target word), a concreteness effect (concrete words are easier to read than abstract ones), and difficulty in reading grammatical function words. Word frequency and word length may also impact the prevalence of reading errors. Patients with deep alexia are impaired in grapheme-to-phoneme conversion; as a result, they have a pronounced inability to read non-word letter strings that could be possible words in the native language (e.g., for English, the string *vib* or *phite*).

Phonological Alexia

Phonological alexic patients can read real words but because they also have a major problem with grapheme-to-phoneme conversion, they have difficulty reading pronounceable nonwords, as is the case with deep alexic patients. Patients with phonological alexia typically do not make the semantic errors seen in deep alexia; otherwise, the boundary between deep and phonological alexia is not always sharp and some patients seem to have many characteristics of both types. It has been reported that deep alexia may evolve to phonological alexia in the course of recovery.

Surface Alexia

Patients with surface alexia have a reading impairment characterized by their ability to read orthographically regular words (note that about 75% of the English lexicon is orthographically regular, e.g., words such as *top, jelly, sing*) but a pronounced difficulty reading orthographically irregular words (in English, words such as *pint, come, bury* are orthographically irregular). Errors made by surface alexic patients on irregular words tend to be regularizing errors, that is, pronouncing them as though they were orthographically regular. Surface alexic patients are able to read pronounceable nonwords, e.g., *heaf* would be read to rhyme with the word *leaf*, which is regular, but not *deaf*, which is irregular.

Agraphic Disorders

As with reading impairments, there are three main linguistic forms of agraphic disorders. The first is phonological agraphia, which is an impairment in writing pronounceable pseudowords to dictation, with a much better preserved ability to write real words and occasional difficulties with grammatical function words and abstract words. A second form is semantic agraphia, which can occur with focal lesions but is more commonly found in the early stages of senile dementia of the Alzheimer type; such patients may write real words and pseudowords normally to dictation, but they make frequent semantic errors in written confrontation naming or written descriptions. A third form is lexical agraphia; these patients preserve the phonological form of the word when writing, but produce spelling errors that normalize spelling to approximate to how the word sounds.

Conclusion

In conclusion, the main recommendations today for continued use of the functional/clinical aphasia syndromes, the so-called classical syndromes, reviewed here are convenience and consistency. A great deal of modern research in neurolinguistics, clinical neuropsychology, and the cognitive neurosciences employs the classical aphasia syndromes for identifying patient groups, notwithstanding the research in the late twentieth century that casts doubt upon the validity of the consistent location of causative lesions, other research that questions the logical coherence of the symptomatology of syndromes, and still other research that questions the possibility of studying groups of patients classified in terms of these syndromes. The most widely used test battery in the United States, the Boston Diagnostic Aphasia Examination (BDAE), from which the major aphasia syndrome typology originates, claims to be able to classify only about three-fourths of all patients with language impairments. One may still argue, and many contemporary publications will attest, that the patients who can be so classified into syndromes can, sensibly and statistically, be grouped under these headings for research purposes. In contrast, a linguistic typology of aphasia, a classification of neurolinguistic impairments, would only be challenged by a better linguistic theory. Such a classification does characterize aphasic impairments even if it does not neatly align with functional and clinical categories, nor does it neatly align with particular brain regions as revealed by lesion localization or imaging techniques. Caveat emptor.

Further Reading

Basso, A and Cubelli, R (1999). Clinical aspects of aphasia. In: Denes, G and Pizzamigliio, L (eds.) *Handbook of Clinical and Experimental Neuropsychology*, pp. 181–193. East Sussex, UK: Psychology Press.

Benson, FD and Ardila, A (1996). *Aphasia: A Clinical Perspective.* New York: Oxford University Press.

Caplan, D (2000). Aphasia. In: Kazdin, AE (ed.) *Encyclopedia of Psychology.* Washington, DC: American Psychological Association.

Coltheart, M (ed.) (1996). *Phonological dyslexia. Special issue of the Journal of Cognitive Neuropsychology.* (September).

Coltheart, M, Patterson, K, and Marshall, JC (eds.) (1980). *Deep Dyslexia.* London: Routledge and Kegan Paul.

Gonzalez-Rothi, LJ (1997). Transcortical motor, sensory, and mixed aphasia. In: LaPointe, LL (ed.) *Aphasia and Related Neurogenic Language Disorders,* 2nd edn. New York: Thieme.

Goodglass, H (1993). *Understanding Aphasia.* San Diego, CA: Academic Press Inc.

Goodglass, H and Kaplan, E (eds.) (1983). *The Assessment of Aphasia and Related Disorders,* 2nd edn. Philadelphia, PA: Lea & Febiger.

Kaplan, E, Gallagher, RE, and Glosser, G (1998). Aphasiarelated disorders. In: Sarno, MT (ed.) *Acquired Aphasia,* 3rd edn. San Diego, CA: Academic Press.

Kertesz, A (1979). *Aphasia and Associated Disorders.* New York: Grune and Stratton.

Patterson, K, Marshall, JC, and Coltheart, M (eds.) (1985). *Surface Dyslexia: Cognitive and Neuropsychological Studies of Phonological Reading.* London: Lawrence Erlbaum Associates.

Pratt, N and Whitaker, HA (2006). Aphasia syndromes. *Encyclopedia of Language and Linguistics,* 2nd edn. Amsterdam: Elsevier.

Whitaker, H and Whitaker, HA (eds.) (1976). *Studies in Neurolinguistics,* vol. 1. New York: Academic Press.

Language Following Congenital Disorders (not SLI)

R. Leech, University of London, London, UK
F. Dick, University of London, London, UK; and University of California at San Diego, La Jolla, CA, USA

Congenital developmental disorders can result in a wide range of language outcomes. At one extreme, children with some disorders never master complex language use. At the other extreme, after an initial period of delay, some children may achieve a language outcome indistinguishable from that of typically developing peers. Congenital disorders affecting language also vary considerably in terms of the underlying etiology; indeed, etiology of a congenital disorder is one of the most important determinants of the course of language development and eventual outcome. However, the relationship between the degree and location of frank neurological abnormality and the degree of corresponding language deficit is anything but straightforward.

In this article, we contrast the effects of two general classes of congenital disorder on language development: 'neurodevelopmental' disorders, such as Williams and Down syndromes and autistic spectrum disorder, and 'acquired' disorders, such as focal brain lesions (FLs) acquired in the pre- or perinatal period. The neurological sequelae of neurodevelopmental disorders often tend to be subtle, relatively widespread, and heterogeneous, at least on a gross anatomical level. For instance, people with autistic spectrum disorders (ASD) tend to have reduced volume in the cerebellar vermis but increased volume of the cerebral and possibly cerebellar white and gray matter. People with Williams syndrome (WS) appear to have particular cortical abnormalities in occipital and parietal regions but relatively preserved cortical structure in the superior temporal lobe, whereas people with Down syndrome (DS) appear to have dysmorphology in the medial temporal lobe. In addition, a number of postmortem studies suggest that ASD, WS, and DS may be associated with aberrant neuronal morphology, packing density, and columnar architecture, albeit in somewhat different forms. In contrast, children with perinatal FLs are assumed to have a typical neurodevelopmental trajectory and cerebral architecture except for the lesion immediately affected by the infarct (with potential longer-term quantitative changes in connecting white matter tracts and homologous gray matter regions).

A comparison of these two types of developmental disorders allows for an examination of the relationship between neural development, cerebral functional differentiation, and language acquisition across the first two decades of life. Importantly, the relative strengths and weaknesses that characterize the language profiles tend to change from infancy through toddlerhood and into late childhood, and they differ according to the etiology of the language disorder. In this article, we first trace the development (and possible neural and social underpinnings) of the linguistic strengths and weaknesses associated with three neurodevelopmental disorders (ASD, WS, and DS). We then discuss language acquisition in children with FLs, focusing not only on eventual outcome but also on the transient relationships between lesion side and site, and linguistic and nonlinguistic abilities over development.

Neurodevelopmental Disorders

As noted previously, the changes to brain structure and function that result from neurodevelopmental disorders tend to begin very early in development and to become more pervasive and more enigmatic. For instance, unlike FLs, it is not possible to diagnose developmental disorders from brain imaging because of high interindividual variability in the neural manifestation of the disorders. Children with neurodevelopmental disorders all tend to show atypical performance in many different social and cognitive skills including language. However, what makes the study of developmental disorders particularly informative is that different disorders have divergent profiles of strengths and weaknesses, not only in language processing but also in aspects of social and cognitive development that appear to be necessary for the early stages of language development. We highlight some of these early appearing social and cognitive deficits, and link them to possible linguistic deficits further 'downstream' in childhood. The following sections are roughly chronological, highlighting the diverging developmental paths in WS, DS, and ASD first in infancy and toddlerhood and later in school-age years and adolescence.

Language Learning in Infancy and Toddlerhood

Language is heavily dependent on social cognition in order to start developing. Early social skills, such as the ability of the infant to share attention with caregivers, are thought to play a substantial role in developing language and nonlinguistic communicative skills. Even in the first months of life, important social precursors to language already distinguish between infants with neurodevelopmental disorders and typically developing (TD) infants. For example, TD infants show a preference for their mother's speech, whereas infants with ASD show no such preference and seem to have very little interest in people and social interaction. These infants show poor levels of eye contact and gaze following, and they may even attempt to avoid the gaze of a caregiver. This early lack of social motivation and attention sharing, and later lack of social conventions such as turn-taking, provides a plausible explanation for the inability of approximately half of children with ASD to develop any kind of complex language. There is some speculation that low-level attentional switching deficits in ASD may contribute to the higher-level social deficits noted here, and that these may be linked to the cerebellar abnormalities characteristic of this syndrome.

In contrast, infants with WS are typified by their strong desire for social interaction and keen interest in faces. However, this preference also leads to poor gaze-following behavior because infants with WS prefer to look at the face of the caregiver as opposed to following the direction of gaze. Such atypical use of referential information by children with WS may in part explain their delays, relative to TD children, in early language comprehension and production. Infants with DS also enjoy interacting socially, although there is a delay in mutual eye contact, which may have an impact on subsequent dyadic interactions between infant and caregiver. Moreover, once these initial problems resolve, infants with DS seem to prefer to focus on the eyes as opposed to visually exploring the facial features of the caregiver, as TD infants do. Deviations in early interactive behavior can also be seen in more complicated triadic interactions between infant, caregiver, and object. For example, infants with WS struggle to switch their attention from the caregiver to an object. This problem with triadic interactions is thought to hinder the acquisition of conceptual knowledge of objects, contributing to a subsequent delay in vocabulary development. In general, ASD, WS, and DS are all characterized to varying degrees by some form of deficit in social skills, which are very important for structuring the early word and grammar learning of infants and young children.

Precursors of Expressive Language in Developmental Disorders

As for social cognition, infants with neurodevelopmental disorders diverge from TD infants in terms of their prelinguistic 'productive' abilities, such as babbling and gesturing. As before, the exact patterns and the mechanisms underlying these delays tend to vary with the type of disorder. For instance, for infants with DS, there is an average delay in the onset of babbling of 2 months, with subsequent delays in phonological development. These may be due to the articulatory difficulties, which frequently occur in conjunction with the disorder (because of differences in palate shape and tongue position), as well as to DS children's frequent problems with hearing loss due to chronic and severe otitis media (probably due to deformations of the eustachian tube).

Unlike their profile with babbling, young children with DS produce far more communicative gestures than those seen in TD, a behavior that may serve as a compensatory mechanism for delayed and error-prone phonological production. In contrast, young children with ASD and WS gesture very little. Use of referential pointing in WS does not appear until after the naming explosion, demonstrating that children with WS do not follow the typical language development trajectory and may be using atypical mechanisms for early referential language use.

Despite the differences between DS and WS, children with DS and WS show a similar delay in the onset of babbling. Furthermore, children with WS show early problems with speech segmentation, which is surprising given the relatively strong phonological abilities of older children with WS. This highlights the fact that the pattern of deficits and relative strengths in the adult does not imply that these same deficits and strengths are present earlier in development.

Word Comprehension and Production and Early Grammatical Development

Just as prelinguistic expressive skills in developmental disorders are delayed, so is the onset of first word comprehension and production. Both WS and DS children are severely delayed in word production, obtaining a vocabulary size of approximately 50 words approximately 2 years later than a TD child, who would produce this many words at approximately 16 months. After reaching this critical vocabulary size, the language profiles of DS and WS diverge. TD children demonstrate an almost lawful relationship between the size of their vocabularies and their productive grammatical complexity, implying that a certain level of vocabulary is necessary for complex language to get started. Similarly, children with WS follow the same relationship between vocabulary size and grammatical complexity as TD children (**Figure 1**), albeit one that is considerably delayed (i.e., young children with WS demonstrate similar complex language abilities as younger TD children with the same vocabulary level). In contrast, children with DS show an atypical relationship, with their grammatical complexity worse than would be predicted by their vocabulary size (**Figure 1**). For children with DS, syntactic development is slow and does not generally

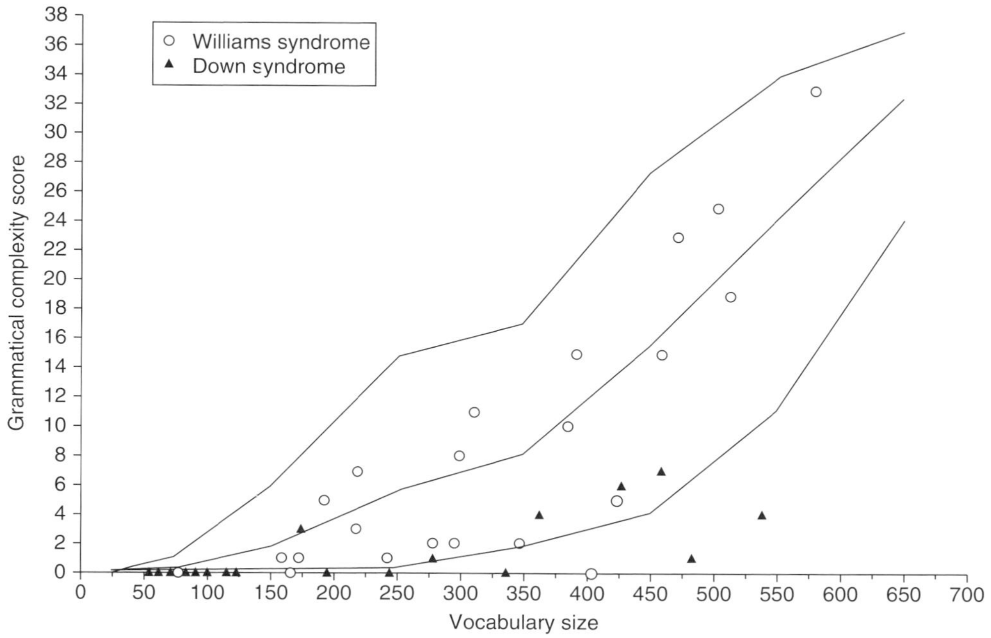

Figure 1 Vocabulary size vs. grammatical complexity. Children with WS show the same developmental trajectory as TD children (albeit one that is markedly delayed), whereas children with DS diverge from the typical trajectory, with less grammatical complexity thanwould be expected given their vocabulary size. The lines mark the 50th, 10th, and 90th percentiles for TD children. Redrawn from Bates and Goodman (1997).

result in these children consistently producing and understanding more complex forms. However, despite the differences in the rate of grammatical development between disorders, it has been suggested that, in general, children with developmental disorders acquire grammatical knowledge in approximately the same sequence as TD children.

Perhaps not surprisingly, there are profound differences in the ways that children with these neurodevelopmental disorders use language to communicate. For example, both children with DS and children with WS generally enjoy the opportunity to interact within a social environment, and their use of language is motivated through social exchanges in conversation. By contrast, language in many children with ASD, even when fluent and social, appears to lack a sense of reciprocity in conversational norms. Such a language profile is often linked to a significant discrepancy between verbal and nonverbal IQ. Overall, early communicative styles differ as substantially between disorders as do their social and grammatical abilities.

Later Language Learning

The profiles of strengths and weaknesses seen in different developmental disorders are not constant throughout the child's life. Instead, the relative strengths and weaknesses of early and late language abilities can be quite different as the multiple interacting linguistic and social factors underlying language acquisition unfold.

Williams Syndrome

The main feature of later language development in WS is delay. Despite this, relative to mental age-matched (MA) controls, school-age and adolescent children with WS may develop good semantic knowledge, an extensive vocabulary, and complex syntax, although their vocabulary skills generally exceed their syntactic ability relative to MA controls. In this regard, when narrating a picture book story, children with WS show a very similar profile of slowed morphosyntactic development as children with a seemingly very different developmental disorder, language impairment (LI). However, by age 10–12 years, children with WS (unlike those with LI) produce the same proportion of complex syntactic structures as typically developing controls, although there are subtle differences from TD children in their discourse structure. For instance, children with WS fail to establish ties between the protagonist's goals and his or her actions. Finally, as might be expected given their hypersocial nature, children with WS far surpass even typically developing children in their use of socially engaging cues when telling a story. Thus, part of the language profile of children with WS might be accounted for by nonlinguistic characteristics of the disorder, such as a strong desire for social interaction.

Down Syndrome

In general, older children with DS show the same sequence of developmental 'events' as do TD children but are generally very delayed. For example, children with DS usually produce the same pattern of phonological errors produced by younger TD children. However, when WS and DS children are compared across early and later childhood, there is a divergence of DS and WS developmental trajectories in different language domains. For instance, in early language development, children with WS and DS have a similar level of vocabulary, but by adolescence the vocabulary of children with WS exceeds that of those with DS. Thus, the performance of children with DS appears to asymptote at a lower level.

Autistic Spectrum Disorders

In contrast to DS, children with ASD exhibit severe pragmatic difficulties in comparison to MA controls, although there is major individual variability in language outcome. Whereas children with ASD will use language to manipulate their environment, their use of language to engage in conversation or express thoughts and emotional states is often limited. It has been suggested that autistic children may actually use their language knowledge to bootstrap their understanding of others' mental states. In terms of pragmatic ability, children with ASD struggle to understand figurative speech, such as 'It's raining cats and dogs', taking literal meanings from such sentences. Other characteristics of autistic speech include a flat pattern of intonation and echolalia (in which children repeat the verbal utterances of others). These may occur when the child is required to respond to a question or in the form of preconstructed speech during conversation.

Neurodevelopmental Disorders versus Acquired Disorders

Whereas the different neurodevelopmental disorders vary considerably in the profiles of relative strengths and weaknesses of language skills, almost all affected children fail to achieve the functional language outcome of TD children. This contrasts strikingly with children with pre- and perinatal FLs who generally fall within the normal range of language use despite the severity of their neurological damage. However, as with all such developmental disorders, a 'normal' language outcome may mask previous language delays and atypical trajectories in different aspects of language development. Thus, in the following sections we consider first the general language outcome of older children with FLs before discussing the more subtle lesion site-specific language problems observed during infancy and early childhood.

Acquired Language Disorders: Learning Language after Early Brain Injury

Pre- and perinatal focal lesions are typically the result of vascular insult (e.g., congenital arteriovenous malformation or pre- or perinatal stroke) and are exceedingly rare events, observed in approximately 1 or 2 of every 10 000 births. Of particular neuroscientific and clinical interest are cases of children with unilateral focal lesions because they generally occur without concomitant global neurological malformation (e.g., cortical dysplasias) and thus allow direct comparisons with results from adult neuropsychological patients with similar lesions.

Comparisons of children and adults with FLs have provided a unique perspective on the fundamental questions of neural development, plasticity, and domain specificity, particularly how these play out in the establishment of language function in the brain. Although the inherent variability in lesion site and size makes children with FLs far from a homogeneous group, results from 30 years of research paint a fairly consistent picture. In particular, the impressive but delayed language outcomes of children with congenital focal lesions suggest that many of the neural biases needed for language to start developing are very coarse indeed.

Lesion Location and Language Outcome

Based on the adult model, the language outcome of children with FLs should depend to a large degree on whether the injury is located in the left or the right hemisphere because left hemisphere injury in adults frequently leads to severe and lasting language problems. However, the overall picture from the literature on children with early focal lesions tends not to show consistent differences between early left and right hemisphere in terms of language processing. When sample sizes are large, and direct statistical comparisons between lesion groups are made, (i.e., right hemisphere damage (RHD) vs. left hemisphere damage (LHD), controlling for seizure history and lesion onset time), lesion side and site generally do not predict language proficiency. If differences are observed, they are noted only for a few language subscales and are considerably smaller than those observed in adults with commensurate injuries.

For instance, language studies on adult patients with focal lesions reveal a classic double dissociation, with RHD patients showing impaired comprehension of familiar phrases and idioms (e.g., 'It's like talking to a brick wall') with relatively preserved comprehension of novel literal phrases (e.g., 'She's looking down at her black cat'),

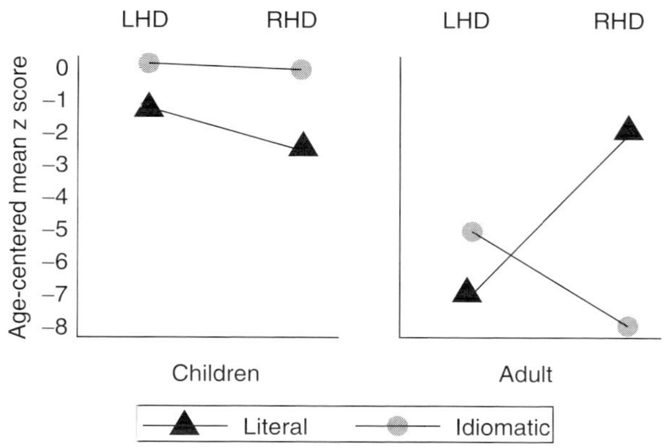

Figure 2 Accuracy in interpreting novel literal and idiomatic sentences, contrasting children and adults with left hemisphere damage (LHD) vs. right hemisphere damage (RHD). Redrawn from Kempler et al. (1999).

whereas LHD patients show the opposite pattern of deficits. In stark contrast, not only is there no difference between children with LHD and children with RHD on either measure but also both groups perform within the low-normal range for their age-matched controls, whereas their adult aphasic counterparts are massively impaired relative to healthy age-matched controls (**Figure 2**). This striking difference has been observed across a range of language tasks, such as narrating brief biographical sketches and online complex syntactic comprehension. As would be expected, adults with LHD are significantly more impaired than their RHD counterparts. However, comparisons between children with RHD and those with LHD reveal no differences. Indeed, in narration tasks, children with FLs differ very little from typically developing children, performing in the normal to low-normal range on a variety of measures. The only significant (but small) delays observed in children with FLs involved the production of somewhat fewer words and more omission errors than age-matched controls. Similarly, the syntactic comprehension of children with FLs to either hemisphere appears to be somewhat delayed but not deviant from the language trajectory of typically developing children.

Lesion Location and Language Acquisition in Infants

Although there are few, if any, apparent differences between language outcomes for children with LHD and those with RHD by the time they begin primary school, it is possible that younger children and toddlers with FLs may demonstrate more subtle and transient language difficulties associated with hemisphere- and site-specific damage. Beginning at the start of language development, prospective cross-sectional and cross-linguistic studies of children with FLs allow a direct contrast between various 'stages' of brain organization for language. Several studies have investigated the early language abilities of infants from 10 to 40 months old, from first word comprehension to production, multiword utterances, and grammatical development. The results of these studies serve as *prima facie* evidence against the theoretical notion that the developing brain is a conglomeration of inexorably maturing modules devoted to different processing needs.

Early in the development of language skills (10–18 months), some children with perinatal focal lesions show a delay in language comprehension as well as gestural communication. However, this delay is only observed in children with right hemisphere injury; those with LHD (even with left temporal damage) are within the normal range on word comprehension. Not only is this the opposite of what one would expect from an adult model of language comprehension, in which left temporal damage tends to correlate with comprehension disorders, but also this finding goes against the usual lesion correlate of deficits in gesture production and comprehension, which in adults are strongly associated with LHD.

For early single-word production in the same cohort of children (10–18 months), lesions to either hemisphere provoke delays in development but are particularly severe in children with left temporal damage. This again contrasts with the adult model, in which language production deficits tend to correlate with left frontal damage. Similarly, results from multiple studies show that left temporal damage continues to be a predictor of delayed language production somewhat later in development (e.g., 19–31 months). Toddlers with left temporal damage show impaired lexical production, with commensurate delays in grammatical development. In contrast to the left temporal findings, frontal damage to either hemisphere was also implicated in production delays – again unlike the adult model of left-lateralized frontal damage leading to production difficulties.

Neural Plasticity in Response to Focal Lesions

The low-normal language outcome of children with early onset FLs as well as the changing and distinctly non-adult-like profile of lesion site-to-language mappings over early development provide compelling evidence for the plasticity of the developing brain. These results also suggest that the usual pattern of brain organization for language (i.e., left hemisphere dominance) is neither inevitable nor even necessary for successful language processing. These findings suggest that there is considerable change in how the brain processes language, even well into the school-age years.

Clearly, these children's brains are organizing themselves differently than they would in typical development. Does this indicate that the brain is equipotential for language (i.e., any brain region can be equally co-opted into language processing), or are there early forming connections and architectures that make some developing brain regions more hospitable to language than others? More concretely, if left frontal and temporal regions are damaged early in development, will the brain regions enabling language function emerge throughout the brain (as one might predict given strict equipotentiality), or will contralateral regions homologous to those characteristically associated with language be recruited for language tasks?

This question has been investigated using positron emission tomography (PET) and functional magnetic resonance imaging (fMRI) on patients with early onset lesions. In a PET study, activation profiles for children with perinatal left and right focal lesions were compared on sentence listening and repetition tasks. Children and adolescents with early left hemisphere lesions showed extensive right lateralization of activation in both traditional perisylvian 'language' areas as well as much of the right temporal lobe (particularly the anterior temporal lobe), the angular gyrus, the precuneus, and the anterior cingulate. Roughly the opposite pattern was seen for the group with right hemisphere lesions. An fMRI study of five children with left periventricular lesions (causing hemiplegia but no epilepsy) showed a similar mirroring of typical left lateralized activation in a covert verb generation task.

Similarly, studies have directly compared typical adult language-related activation in children and adults with early and late-onset left hemisphere focal lesions, respectively. The expectation was that earlier injuries would allow greater potential for reorganization of function. Neurologically intact adults showed the usual left-lateralized perisylvian activation profile for sentence comprehension, whereas patients with early onset focal lesions showed a mirrored and right-lateralized profile, and late-onset patients show highly symmetrical perisylvian activation. The dramatic lateralization difference between the early and late-lesion groups suggests that at least some of the remarkable capacity of the early lesion group to acquire normal language may be due to development of these (or closely related) functions in the right hemisphere. These findings argue against the notion that language functions are inexorably hard-wired within specific left hemisphere regions; rather, they indicate that the brain has some flexibility to reorganize such cognitive functions, if necessary.

Interestingly, this early lesion-induced shift in interhemispheric activation is not seen in all domains, even in the face of early cerebral insult. One study comparing sentence listening with a basic motor task (finger tapping) in patients with relatively early onset left hemisphere lesions found strong rightward activation asymmetries for the language task (a pattern opposite that of healthy controls). However, the same participants showed strong leftward activation asymmetries in the motor task – a pattern very similar to controls. These results suggest that the development and commitment of neural resources for language is a protracted process – one that might be more flexible than the development of more developmentally and evolutionarily entrenched capacities such as the motor system. However, it is worth emphasizing that lesion-induced reorganization of language function appears to recruit roughly homologous regions in the right hemisphere rather than, for instance, co-opting left hemisphere visual and somatosensory regions to accomplish language tasks. This suggests that regions with certain patterns of cortical and subcortical connections may be more amenable than others to co-option or 'shared use' by language.

Conclusions

There are clear differences between 'acquired' and 'neurodevelopmental' congenital disorders, as well as considerable differences between the different neurodevelopmental disorders. The impressive language outcome in FLs is testament to remarkable abilities of an otherwise typically developing brain to adapt in the face of substantial neurological insult. This stands in stark contrast to the more complex and more pervasive language problems associated with children with ASD, WS, and DS, whose brains are following multiple and distinct atypical developmental pathways.

See also: Language Development; Language, Cortical Processes; Language, Learning Impairments; Sentence Comprehension; Sentence Production; Word Learning; Word Production; Word Recognition.

Further Reading

Bates, E and Roe, K (2001). Language development in children with unilateral brain injury. In: Nelson, CA and Luciana, M (eds.) *Handbook of Developmental Cognitive Neuroscience*, pp. 281–307. Cambridge, MA: MIT Press.

Karmiloff-Smith, A, Grant, J, Berthoud, I, Davies, M, Howlin, P, and Udwin, O (1997). Language and Williams syndrome: How intact is 'intact'? *Child Development* 68: 246–262.

Rice, ML, Warren, SF, and Betz, SK (2005). Language symptoms of developmental language disorders: An overview of autism, Down syndrome, fragile X, specific language impairment, and Williams syndrome. *Applied Psycholinguistics* 26: 7–27.

Singer Harris, N, Bellugi, U, Bates, E, Jones, W, and Rossen, M (1997). Contrasting profiles of language development in children with Williams and Down syndromes delay using parental report. *Developmental Neuropsychology* 13: 345–370.

Language in Aged Persons

E. A. L. Stine-Morrow and M. C. Shake, University of Illinois at Urbana–Champaign, Champaign, IL, USA

Introduction

Communicative competence is essential for effective functioning through adulthood. The ability to understand and remember language depends on a coordinated array of processing components that translate an orthographic or acoustic signal (i.e., printed symbols and speech sounds, respectively) into a representation of the meaning of written text or speech that changes dynamically as the signal unfolds in real time. Language production can be thought of as a reverse process, requiring message formulation from which a surface form is generated. Aging brings both growth (e.g., knowledge) and decline (e.g., speed of processing). As a result, there are a variety of changes in how language is processed, both normatively and in what is required for successful performance. In this article, we consider the nature of these changes. We first review prominent theories of cognitive aging and then present a conceptual model of language processing. We then consider how language comprehension, memory, and production change with age, taking into account data from behavioral paradigms, event-related potentials, and imaging.

Theories of Cognitive Aging

Although there are a number of competing theories for cognitive and brain mechanisms that underlie age-related changes in cognition, there is broad agreement that at a coarse level, age effects on cognition can be characterized as a result of two competing forces. On the one hand, senescence drives a decline in mental mechanics, the speed and accuracy with which elementary information processing components can be completed. On the other hand, there is accumulating evidence that the brain has immense potential for plasticity into late life so that experience-based growth in knowledge systems, skill, and expertise offers potential for growth. Language processing can potentially depend on both of these systems.

There are a variety of cognitive theories characterizing the specific nature of declines in mechanics with age, all of which have influenced both behavioral and neuroscience approaches to the study of language. The slowing hypothesis suggests that aging brings a systematic decrease in the speed with which mental operations can be performed. The working memory (WM) hypothesis posits that aging is associated with a decline in the capacity to perform basic processing operations and store their products (as might be required, for example, as one listens to a lecture and tries to construct an understanding of what is currently being discussed and integrate it with what has come before). The inhibition deficit (ID) hypothesis focuses on the important role that inhibitory function plays in effective language processing by suppressing irrelevant environmental input, inappropriate (or no longer appropriate) features of meaning, and incorrect interpretations. According to the ID account, inhibitory function is reduced with age, thus compromising comprehension by allowing irrelevant (or incorrect) information to be incorporated into the language representation – and consuming working memory capacity that might otherwise be used for effective processing. Finally, drawing on the WM hypothesis, the effortfulness hypothesis identifies sensory loss as critical to understanding the aging language system, not simply as a direct influence on the quality of signal, but as an influence on central resources that are strained by the attempt to interpret the muddy signal.

At the same time, aging may bring growth in vocabulary and some aspects of verbal ability, with evidence suggesting that such growth depends on habitual engagement with literacy-based activities. Particularized knowledge systems and expertise develop differentially as a consequence of occupational and leisure pursuits. Well-developed procedural skills, such as reading, can be well maintained into late life. Evidence suggests that language processing may impact the trajectory of mental mechanics as well, with several demonstrations of enhanced executive function among fluent bilinguals, who habitually manage two language systems.

Patterns of growth and decline are also evident in the aging brain, with selective changes in both brain structure and function. Consistent with the notion of age-related declines in controlled attention, as suggested by WM and ID accounts, the prefrontal cortex is the brain region most vulnerable to deterioration. Both evoked potential and imaging data very often show more diffuse activation in the aging brain, a pattern that has been explained alternately in terms of dedifferentiation (effectively, inhibition failure) and as compensatory recruitment.

The Nature of Language Processing

In both reading and speech understanding, the signal unfolds linearly in time. However, the structure of thought arising from this process is not linear and certainly represents information beyond the verbatim input. The task faced by theories of language comprehension, then, is to explain how this mental representation is constructed and updated over time during comprehension, as well as later when certain tasks require retrieval or use of the text representation. Contemporary models of language comprehension distinguish among distinct processes that operate in concert to construct different facets of the language representation. At the surface level, individual lexical items (words) are encoded from the orthographic or acoustic signal, and their meanings are activated. The stream is parsed into syntactically coherent segments (e.g., clauses and sentences) that establish the thematic roles (functions such as agent and object) for the constituents of the sentence. The semantic representation can be described in terms of integrated ideas (or propositions) that establish relationships among concepts given by the text, a representation called the textbase. Knowledge plays a role in facilitating integration, enabling elaborative inference, and evoking a simulation of the situation suggested by the text. Production can be described as the reverse of this process. To express a thought, a syntactic structure has to be formulated, particular lexical items must be selected to fill thematic roles (a process called lemma selection), and the phonology must be assembled (phonological encoding).

Age-Related Change in Language Processing

Language Comprehension and Memory

Consistent with the divergent age trajectories of mechanics and knowledge-based processes, aging appears to have the strongest impact on resource-consuming aspects of language processing.

Word processing

Vocabulary often shows an increase with age, particularly among those who read regularly. Word recognition appears to be highly resilient through late life. For example, word frequency effects (i.e., faster processing for more familiar words) in reading and word naming are typically at least as large for older adults as they are for young. Sublexical features (e.g., neighborhood density), however, may have a smaller effect on processing time on older readers, suggesting that accumulated experience with literacy may increase the efficiency of orthographic decoding.

By contrast, declines in auditory processing can make spoken word recognition more demanding so that more acoustic information is needed to isolate the lexical item. Such effects may not merely disrupt encoding of the surface form but also tax working memory resources that would otherwise be used to construct a representation of the text's meaning. For example, when elders with normal or impaired hearing listen to a word list and are interrupted periodically to report the last word heard, they may show negligible differences. However, if asked to report the last three words, hearing-impaired elders will likely show deficits. The explanation for such a provocative finding is that the hearing-impaired elders overcome a sensory loss at some attentional cost so as to exert a toll on semantic and elaborative processes that enhance memory. Presumably, the same mechanisms would operate in ordinary language processing.

At the same time, there is evidence that older adults can take differential advantage of context in the recognition of both spoken and written words, especially in noisy environments. Semantic processes at the lexical level also appear to be largely preserved. Semantic priming effects (i.e., facilitation in word processing by prior exposure to a related word) are typically at least as large among older adults as among the young. Also, in the arena of neurocognitive function, evoked potentials show similar lexical effects for young and old – a reduced N400 component for related words relative to unrelated controls. One area of difficulty that older adults may have in word processing is in deriving the meaning of novel lexical items from context, with research showing that older adults are likely to infer more generalized and imprecise meanings relative to the young – a difference that can be largely accounted for in terms of working memory deficits.

Syntactic processing

Syntax, or the set of rules directing appropriate formation of grammatical sentences, guides the near instantaneous and incremental processing of words into coherent chunks as we encounter them, a phenomenon often termed 'parsing.' Paradigms in neuroscience have shed some light on the influence of aging on brain activity during syntactic parsing. Most of this research indicates that initial parsing processes are fundamentally preserved with aging. Studies using functional magnetic resonance imaging (fMRI), for example, show that for simple sentences, the left perisylvian areas responsible for sentence processing produce similar patterns of activation for young and old. Also, attempts to understand ungrammatical sentences produce similar effects among young and old in evoked potentials – for example, exaggerated left anterior negativity to number violations or an exaggerated P600 to phrase structure violations. Other research with evoked potentials suggests a qualitative shift in brain region recruitment, with brain potentials to syntactic violations becoming less asymmetric and more frontal with age. Despite substantial preservation of certain aspects of syntactic processing, complex syntax can especially compromise the older adult's ability to interpret a sentence's meaning and remember it, a finding often attributed to processes downstream from the initial parse. Such effects may be due to cognitive constraints imposed by age-related declines in the working memory resources needed to retain the products of parsing in memory. For example, behavioral and imaging studies comparing the effects of syntactically simpler subject-relative sentences (e.g., 'The dog that chased the boy is friendly') to more complex object-relative sentences (e.g., 'The dog that the boy chased is friendly') suggest that age differences emerge primarily for more complex constructions. As syntactic structure becomes more complex, older adults are more likely to show comprehension errors (e.g., was it the boy who chased the dog or vice versa?) than younger adults and may show relatively less activation in the left peri-sylvian sentence processing region. However, variability among older adults is high, so there is typically a subset of elders who perform at least as well as the young. These high-comprehension older adults appear to achieve good performance in part by upregulating additional brain regions associated with verbal working memory (e.g., left dorsal portions of the inferior frontal cortex and right temporal–parietal regions).

Textbase processing

Older adults typically show poorer memory for the content expressed directly by the text. Online measures of reading (e.g., reading time and probed recognition) suggest that the fundamental mechanisms of the system used to construct an integrated representation of ideas are preserved. However, processes used to construct the textbase (e.g., to instantiate and integrate concepts in the text) are among the most resource-consuming of those required in language understanding and are hence the most vulnerable to aging. When reading is self-paced, older adults require more time for effective propositional encoding (e.g., as indexed by effective reading time, the time allocated per idea unit recalled). In listening, when the pace is controlled by the speaker, older adults may have particular difficulty in understanding and retaining the information, especially as propositional density (ideas expressed per word) is increased or in noisy environments. Older adults appear to have no difficulty drawing anaphoric inference (i.e., correctly identifying the referent when the pronoun is used to refer to a noun that was introduced earlier) over short distances, but they may have difficulty when the pronoun and referent are separated by intervening text so that the referent must be retained in working memory. Similarly, older adults may have difficulty in reactivating nouns during sentence comprehension in the way that younger adults do, which may compromise the ability to represent a coherent meaning. For example, younger adults trying to understand an object-relative construction, as described previously (e.g., 'The dog$_i$ that the boy chased t_i is friendly') will reactivate the object (e.g., dog) of the matrix clause following the verb (i.e., at t_i, the gap in the phrase structure that leaves a trace of the constituent moved in the relativized construction) and actually show facilitated processing of the object at the gap site. Older adults are less likely to reactivate the object as the noun-gap distance is increased (e.g., 'The dog$_i$ wearing the blue bandana that the boy chased t_i is friendly').

The general impression from the behavioral data that the semantic (textbase) representation is more fragmented and less distinctive among older adults is reinforced by evidence from evoked potentials. Semantic anomaly (e.g., 'The dog wearing the blue bandana is a tree') exaggerates the N400 component of the evoked potential for the anomalous word (in this case, 'tree') for both younger and older adults; however, the brain response to this anomaly is less pronounced among older adults. Such findings suggest that the encoding of the sentence context up to the anomalous word was not as distinctive among the older adults so that the perception of anomaly was not as strong when the implausible word was encountered. Interestingly, there is no evidence of a delayed response to the anomaly with age; rather, the data are more consistent with a reduced level of response. Contrary to early claims in the literature that aging brings no semantic deficits, it appears that difficulty in integrating concepts can lead to an impoverished semantic representation.

Ironically, older adults may ordinarily allocate less attention to textbase processing. This is demonstrated in reading time for naturalistic text, in which regression analysis is used to isolate the effects of textbase processes. For example, with lexical properties such as length and frequency controlled, reading time increases when new concepts are introduced or at the ends of syntactic constituents, which are sites at which readers pause briefly to integrate concepts into a coherent meaning. These data show that older readers may allocate less time to these processes. However, analogous to fMRI findings with sentence processing, older adults who show high levels of language memory performance often overallocate attention to these processing components or, as described later, may shift allocation to process more holistic features of the discourse. Some older adults do show very good language comprehension and memory, with data from behavioral studies and neuroimaging suggesting that compensatory recruitment of additional resources underlies their successful performance.

Less is known about the factors that engender this recruitment. However, age effects on language performance are often moderated by verbal ability: more verbal older adults are more likely to show event-related potential patterns similar to young, allocate resources to construct the textbase, and show relatively good textbase memory. To the extent that literacy activities are practiced across the life span, growth in knowledge-based systems may support language processing at different levels.

Situation model

Aside from deriving ideas directly from the text, language understanding also involves elaboration on these ideas based on existing knowledge. Some theories focus on the perceptual quality of this level of representation, which gives rise to a perceptual simulation of the events described by the text. For example, in narrative understanding, readers track the goals and emotional reactions of characters, as well as their movement through space and time. Behavioral methods to study this level of representation include probe recognition for objects in the narrative as well as reading time, both of which show subtle effects of situation model processing. Readers are slower to verify the existence (in the narrative world) of objects that are spatially distant from the protagonist relative to those that are nearby. Readers also slow down when new characters are introduced or when there is a spatial discontinuity (e.g., the locus of narrative events shifts from the village to the castle) or a temporal discontinuity (e.g., 'The next day . . .'). When the text describes a goal to be achieved (e.g., Susan intends to buy her mother a purse for her birthday), the goal is activated in memory until it is achieved so that concepts related to the goal are more quickly verified as long as the goal is open (e.g., the purse will be more quickly verified if Susan cannot find the purse when she goes to the store relative to a condition in which she succeeds in securing the gift). To the extent that these paradigms have been used to explore adult age differences in situation model processing, there has been very little evidence of developmental differences in situation construction and updating.

Outside of narrative comprehension, it appears that older adults also show the perceptual symbols effect, suggesting that fundamental processes of perceptual simulation are preserved. For example, adults are faster to verify that a pictured object was described in a sentence if the picture of the object represents its shape implied from the sentence (e.g., in encountering, 'She watched the egg frying in the pan,' readers are faster at verifying that the sentence described an egg if the drawing depicts a cracked egg with yolk and white relative to a picture of an egg in its shell, with the reverse effect for 'She watched the egg boiling in the pot'). According to perceptual symbol theory, response time is faster when the picture matches the shape implied by the sentence because sentence processing evokes a perceptual simulation of the events described so that the implied shape is more available when the picture is presented. This perceptual symbols effect is at least as large in the elderly as it is among the young.

Older adults may particularly rely on the situation model to support textbase processing. For example, in ambiguous text (e.g., 'The strength and flexibility of this equipment is remarkable. Not everyone is capable of using it even though most try at one point or another . . .'), older readers take differential advantage of titles (e.g., Driving a Car) that disambiguate the meaning to facilitate processing. Because the title renders the situation instantly transparent, both younger and older adults are more efficient in reading when it is available; however, older adults show this effect to a larger degree.

To the extent that the hallmark of situation model processing is an integration of textbase content with knowledge, one might expect that older adults would be particularly adept at inferential processing; however, this is not always the case. Although older adults are more likely to draw elaborative inference (e.g., in recall, to annotate their recollections with personal experiences or related information learned in another context), if inference is constrained so that it requires retrieval of textbase content, age deficits are the norm.

Discourse structures and context

Beyond sentence processing, different genres of text have characteristic forms. For example, narratives typically begin by introducing a setting and characters and proceed to describe a series of episodes in which goals or problems are introduced to be resolved, and so on. Expository texts have certain characteristic forms of argumentation (e.g., problem–solution and thesis–evidence). Older readers generally appear to track these larger discourse structures in the same way as the young. For example, scrambling a narrative so that the canonical form is disrupted will impair recall similarly for young and old. However, other research suggests that older readers may have more difficulty in remembering narratives relative to matched expository text, presumably because of the demands of establishing and tracking complex plot structures. For example, older adults are more likely to have difficulty when two plots are interwoven.

Recap

Collectively, these findings are generally consistent with what would be expected given declines in mechanics accompanied by experience-based growth in knowledge. The most resource-intensive aspects of language processing requiring the associationist connection of concepts in propositional encoding and storage in working memory show the largest age deficits. At the same time, sensory deficits may indirectly tax working memory by diverting resources to interpret muddy input. However, knowledge-based processes are largely preserved and may support these other processes.

Language Production

In contrast to comprehension, production shows more pronounced differences as a function of age at almost every level of analysis. In this domain, methodological approaches are almost exclusively behavioral, and even among behavioral measures, the focus has been on word production and on comparing global measures of spontaneous production (e.g., diaries) because of the problems associated with constraining production in a way that can be measured (although there are interesting recent innovations).

Word production stands in sharp contrast to receptive word processes in showing age differences. Picture naming is slower and likely to produce more errors among older adults. As do the young, older adults show effects of name agreement and word frequency on naming latency, suggesting that processes of lemma selection and phonological encoding are intact. Older adults may show relatively faster response time when name agreement is high, suggesting perhaps enhanced effects of knowledge on lemma selection. Aging is also likely to bring an increase in tip-of-the-tongue experiences, that feeling of knowing the word one wants to say (e.g., this experience is evoked among some people by asking them the name of a person who collects stamps) but not quite being able to come up with it (e.g., philatelist). Interestingly, spelling errors also increase with age. This asymmetry between comprehension and production has been explained in terms of transmission deficits between the phonological and semantic networks. It is assumed that connections among lexical and phonological units generally decrease with increased age and disuse. Although the semantic representation is rich in connections, phonological units are constrained (e.g., there are rich and variable ways to encode the concept of chocolate, but if one cannot activate /ch/, production is necessarily disrupted).

Cross-sectional studies of spontaneous production show that older adults generally produce shorter sentences with fewer complex syntactic constructions (e.g., embeddings and left-branching constructions). Diary studies have shown longitudinal change toward simpler syntactic forms and reduced information content as a function of normal aging, with declines exaggerated among those later diagnosed with Alzheimer's disease.

In constrained production (e.g., construct a novel sentence from a given set of target words), age differences may be negligible when the number of target words to be accommodated in the production is small; however, as the number of targets is increased, older adults are more likely to become dysfluent, presumably because of the greater demands on syntactic construction and proposition assembly. Another form of constrained production that has been explored with aging is to create a sentence to describe a picture. In this paradigm, too, older speakers are likely to produce dysfluencies. The monitoring of eye movements has been used to examine the extent to which older adults might plan their utterances ahead to enhance fluency, but evidence on this issue is not yet clear.

Finally, there have been several demonstrations in the contexts of laboratory tasks (e.g., text recall) that older speakers may be more likely to produce off-target speech. Whereas some have shown this to be related to independent estimates of inhibition and have labeled this phenomenon verbosity, other research has demonstrated that such age differences in such elaboration can be exaggerated for personal topics, suggesting that such patterns may be related to social demands rather than to individual differences in cognitive function. This issue remains to be resolved.

Conclusion

There appears to be a two-way street between the multidirectional change in adult cognition and language processing. Age-related declines in sensory processes and cognitive capacity impact the ability to derive meaning from text and spoken language, especially as syntactic structure becomes more complex or speech rate is increased. Age-related declines also impact name retrieval and the syntactic complexity of production. Knowledge-driven processes can offset these declines to a large degree so that in many arenas, aging individuals will show better performance than their younger counterparts. At the same time, language processing (e.g., habitual reading, or learning a second language) appears to exercise the cognitive system so as to contribute to cognitive vitality.

See also: Cognition in Aging and Age-Related Disease; Language Development; Language, Auditory Processes; Language, Cortical Processes; Sentence Comprehension; Sentence Production; Word Production; Word Recognition.

Further Reading

Bialystok, E, Craik, FIM, and Freedman, M (2007). Bilingualism as a protection against the onset of symptoms of dementia. *Neuropsycholgia* 45: 459–464.

Federmeier, KD, McLennan, DB, De Ochoa, E, and Kutas, M (2002). The impact of semantic memory organization and sentence context information on spoken language processing by younger and older adults: An ERP study. *Psychophysiology* 39: 133–146.

Federmeier, KD, Van Petten, C, Schwarz, TJ, and Kutas, M (2003). Sounds, words, sentences: Age-related changes across levels of language processing. *Psychology and Aging* 18: 858–872.

Griffin, ZM and Spieler, DH (2006). Observing the what and when of language production for different age groups by monitoring speakers' eye movements. *Brain and Language* 99: 272–288.

Johnson, RE (2003). Aging and the remembering of text. *Developmental Review* 23: 261–346.

Kemper, S and Mitzner, TL (2001). Language production and comprehension. In: Birren, JE and Schaie, KW (eds.) *Handbook of the Psychology of Aging,* 5th edn., pp. 378–398. New York: Academic Press.

Kemper, S, Thompson, M, and Marquis, J (2001). Longitudinal change in language production: Effects of aging and dementia on grammatical complexity and propositional content. *Psychology and Aging* 16: 600–614.

Meyer, BJF and Pollard, CK (2006). Applied learning and aging: A closer look at reading. In: Birren, JE and Schaie, KW (eds.) *Handbook of the Psychology of Aging,* 6th edn. New York: Elsevier.

Radvansky, GA, Zwaan, RA, Curiel, JM, and Copeland, DE (2001). Situation models and aging. *Psychology and Aging* 16: 145–160.

Stine-Morrow EAL (2007) The Dumbledore hypothesis of cognitive aging. *Current Directions in Psychological Science* 16: 289–293.

Stine-Morrow EAL, Miller LMS, Gagne DD, and Hertzog C (in press) Self-regulated reading in adulthood. *Psychology and Aging*.
Stine-Morrow, EAL, Miller, LMS, and Hertzog, C (2006). Aging and self-regulated language processing. *Psychological Bulletin* 132: 582–606.
Thornton, R and Light, LL (2005). Language comprehension and production in normal aging. In: Birren, JE and Schaie, KW (eds.) *Handbook of the Psychology of Aging,* 6th edn. New York: Academic Press.
Wingfield, A and Grossman, M (2006). Language and the aging brain: Patterns of neural compensation revealed by functional brain imaging. *Journal of Neurophysiology* 96: 2830–2839.
Wingfield, A and Stine-Morrow, EAL (2000). Language and speech. In: Craik, FIM and Salthouse, TA (eds.) *The Handbook of Aging and Cognition,* 2nd edn., pp. 359–416. Mahwah, NJ: Erlbaum.
Wingfield, A, Tun, PA, and McCoy, SL (2005). Hearing loss in older adults: What it is and how it interacts with cognitive performance. *Current Directions in Psychological Science* 14: 144–148.

Language, Auditory Processes

D. Gow and D. Caplan, Massachusetts General Hospital, Boston, MA, USA

Introduction

The auditory stimulus in speech perception is shaped and constrained by the acoustical properties of the human vocal tract. Speech is produced through the coordinated movement of the glottis, tongue, velum, lips, and jaw. The form of this signal is often understood in terms of a simple source-filter model in which acoustic energy produced by subglottal pressure and the vibration of the vocal folds, or turbulence produced when airflow is directed against a barrier, is given spectral shape by the natural resonances of coupled natural cavities created by different vocal tract configurations. The component sounds produced by articulation consist of simultaneous frequency-limited resonances with time-varying frequencies called formants, as well as silences, pops, clicks, and brief bursts of frequency-limited noise. Movement of articulators changes the shape of resonators, which in turn changes the frequencies of formants over time. Additionally, release of air when constrictions are released, or noise produced when constrictions are narrow but incomplete, produces noise. These sounds overlay an overall periodic structure caused by the opening and closing of the vocal folds during much of speech and a quasi-periodic structure caused by changes in subvocal pressure and vocal fold vibration.

While the specific acoustic form of spoken language reflects the microstructure of articulation defined in both time and space, this relation is complex. For example, the same [r] sound can be produced by radically different tongue movements. Conversely, the vocal tract configurations that produce [i] and [u] sounds in some contexts produce [j] and [w] sounds in others. This relationship is simplified somewhat by the fact that there is often a nonlinear or quantal relation between individual articulations and their acoustic consequences that maximizes the acoustic contrast between speech sounds, while providing relatively stable acoustic properties within them. For example, when producing a segment with the feature 'nasal,' such as [n], [m], or [ng], speakers move the velum to produce an opening between the oral and nasal cavities. While the act of opening involves a continuous articulation, there is a critical point at which the opening is large enough to allow acoustic coupling, which is marked by the appearance of a new spectral prominence, the nasal pole, which marks the segment as a nasal.

The primary computational problem posed by the perception of spoken language is created by the variability of the speech signal relative to the linguistic categories that are perceived by the listener. Spoken language is perceived as a sequence of more or less discrete events such as words, syllables, or component speech sounds. However, coarticulation, the overlapping articulation of adjacent speech sounds, often makes it impossible to draw a one-to-one mapping between a single speech sound and any interval of sound. Moreover, the acoustic realization of any unit of spoken language is highly variable, and may be influenced by a variety of factors including speaking rate, individual differences in vocal tract anatomy, language or dialect, articulatory style, the emotional state of the speaker, or social context.

Each level of linguistic representation is related to somewhat different properties of the speech signal, although these properties overlap. Word recognition relies on the perception of 'segmental' properties. These tend to be collections of relatively brief acoustic events. At typical natural speaking rates, speakers produce roughly 15 segments per second, with wide variability in the duration of different segments and temporal overlap in the distribution of properties associated with any one segment. At the level of sentence or discourse structure, 'suprasegmental' or intonational properties may provide information about syntactic constituent structure or the relative importance of individual words or phrases. These properties are typically defined over larger temporal regimens than segmental properties, and are encoded primarily in relative changes in pitch, intensity, and timing between different parts of an utterance.

These linguistic entities are perceived despite the enormous variance in how they are realized in the acoustic signal. Different research groups are currently pursuing four contrasting approaches to the issue of variance. One approach is to identify relatively invariant acoustic properties of speech sounds. While early research found an invariant correlate of one characteristic of a subset of syllable initial consonants, subsequent work has yielded few successes. A second approach focuses on possible normalization processes that may play a role in categorization or recognition. Work in this vein has demonstrated a variety of normalization processes, most notably processes of rate normalization in the classification of duration-dependent feature cues. A third approach is built on the premise that speech gestures are less variable than the acoustic forms produced by their combination. Within this approach, researchers are concerned with trying to determine whether speech perception is mediated by articulatory representations. Finally, a fourth approach suggests that words or other linguistic units are stored for the purpose of recognition in the form of multiple exemplars that present relatively veridical representations of individual tokens encountered in the past (similar to machine speech recognition). There is evidence that listeners have access to memory of specific speech tokens. However, it is not clear whether this type of memory plays a role in the online perception of spoken language. The ultimate solution to the variability problem may involve some combination of these approaches.

Unique Neural Mechanisms for Processing Language Acoustically?

At the earliest stages of processing, both speech and nonspeech stimuli are processed using the same pathways, and are subject to the same processes. Transduction of acoustic energy by cochlear hair cells with frequency-selective tuning curves breaks acoustic input down into a representation of the intensity of acoustic energy at different frequency bands. An unresolved question is whether complex stimuli like speech are represented entirely by the spatial pattern of activation across tonotopically organized cortex, the temporal pattern of neural activity, or both. At some point, the processing of acoustic signals as linguistic entities diverges from processing acoustic signals as other types of stimuli. But whether that point occurs at the stage of processing the acoustic signal itself, or only after linguistic categories have been activated, remains a debated issue.

For some time, a considerable number of researchers argued that listeners applied different analytic processes to sounds that were and were not speech. The existence of what were thought to be unique aspects of speech perception – such as the inability to discriminate synthesized acoustic signals that did not fall into different phonemic categories while being able to discriminate signals with equivalent acoustic differences when they were perceived as being linguistically different (so-called categorical perception) – was considered strong evidence for this position. Confidence in the implications of such findings eroded when it was discovered that nonhumans show comparable phonetic discrimination effects. Similarly, psychophysical evidence suggests that humans are able to resolve temporal order of linguistic events with substantially more precision than that of nonlinguistic events. This again suggests a relatively low-level divergence between linguistic and general auditory processing streams. However, it has been suggested that this difference may be related to differences in the ability of linguistic versus nonlinguistic components to be represented at more global levels.

More recently, the question has been addressed on the basis of the location of neural responses to processing acoustic properties of linguistic and nonlinguistic stimuli. A challenge facing this approach is to equate the complexity of the speech and nonspeech stimuli while at the same time eliminating speechlike properties from the nonspeech stimuli that could cause activity in areas that are in fact uniquely devoted to processing acoustic stimuli as speech. Different research groups have taken different positions on the appropriate control stimuli. Some results suggest that perception of segmental acoustic properties as meaningful speech uniquely involves a region in the left superior temporal lobe anterior to the primary auditory cortex, but the issue remains open. Even fewer studies have examined the question of whether processing of acoustic signals to yield intonation contours utilizes the same brain regions as processing of acoustic signals to yield nonlinguistic representations, such as musical structures. One study reported that one patient whose abilities to discriminate melodies was impaired had comparable difficulties with intonation contours, but whether the same parts of the complex lesion in this patient were responsible for both functional impairments is unclear; to our knowledge, no functional neuroimaging studies have addressed this question.

Segmental Processing

The targets of segmental perceptual processes are abstract representations of the sounds of words. Phonological theories are essentially unanimous in maintaining that the sounds of words consist of a number of structures. In many models, the critical structures are 'phonemes' – abstract segments representing idealized units of sound whose presence is required for a word to be individuated. For instance, the word 'cat' consists of three phonemes, [k], [æ], and [t], in that order. A change in one of these segments to another phoneme (e.g., of [k] to [s]) turns 'cat' into a different word or into a nonword. Phonemes, too, are conceived of as complexes of 'features' – characterizations of positions and trajectories of articulatory organs and qualities of the sounds thereby produced. Examples of such features are 'stopped' (indicating full closure of the vocal tract), 'high' (referring to the position of the body of the tongue), and 'voiced' (indicating vibration of the vocal cords). Like phonemes, phonological features are abstract entities, identified on the basis of many aspects of the sound patterns of words and other phenomena in a language. For instance, most models of features utilize a binary system, despite the continuous nature of articulatory postures, because generalizations that arise with respect to high-level phonological properties of words (e.g., effects of word formation on phonemes) can be best captured in such a system. Words also have phonological structure above the phoneme level, such as the level of syllables. In all languages, syllables in multisyllabic words have different degrees of prominence, represented as either lexical stress or tone patterns. English is a stress language (e.g., the difference between torment' [noun] and tor'ment [verb]); Chinese is a tone language (e.g., the word 'ma' can be produced with four different tones to mean 'mother,' 'hemp,' 'horse,' or 'scold').

The dominant view in psychology is that words are recognized by a process whose front end maps properties of the acoustic waveform onto phonological features and phonemes. Two literatures converge to support the significance of features in the representation of speech. A large body of work in acoustic-phonetics has identified acoustic characteristics that correspond to proposed features, and has demonstrated that systematic manipulation of these characteristics or cues leads to predictable changes in the perception of speech sounds or words. Similarly, linguists have shown that systematic variations in the sound patterns of the world's natural languages are best predicted and understood at a level of featural representation.

Based on the importance of features and feature cues in theory, the existence of phonetic feature detectors has been a subject of great interest. The strongest evidence for feature detectors comes from studies of selective adaptation effects. In selective adaptation experiments, listeners hear a series of words or syllables that share a common feature, and are then asked to make phonetic judgments about a continuum of speech sounds that differ in terms of that feature. For example, they may hear a series of syllables that begin with voiced consonants (e.g., [bu], [do], [ge]), and are then asked to categorize a series of syllables in which voicing cues are manipulated to create a continuum from [ba] to [pa]. Results show that categorization is shifted after adaptation, with listeners showing a

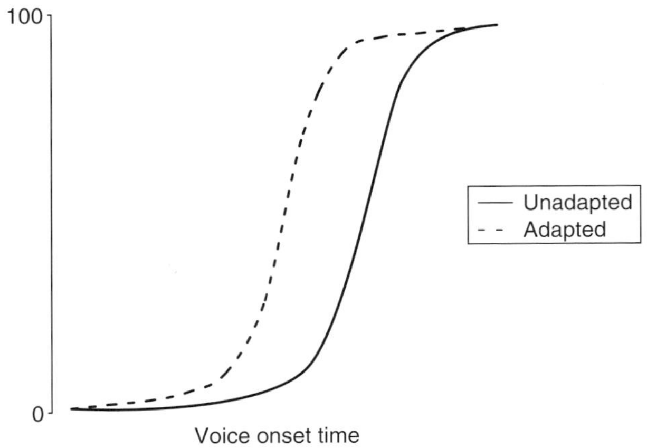

Figure 1 Schematic results showing categorical perception and selective adaptation effects in phoneme identification. Listeners are asked to identify tokens taken from a synthetic /ba/–/pa/ continuum created by increasing voice onset time. In the adaptation condition, listeners may first hear a series of consonant–vowel syllables with voiced onsets (e.g., *bu*, *do*, *ge*). Listeners in both conditions show identification curves consistent with categorical perception, but the function is shifted after adaptation as listeners show an increased bias toward perceiving segments as voiceless.

greater likelihood of classifying ambiguous segments as being unvoiced ([pa]) (**Figure 1**). This result is interpreted as the result of fatigue on the part of voicing detectors. Some observers have challenged this interpretation, noting that fatigue could be occurring at many levels, including the level of raw auditory representation, feature cue, feature, syllable, or, in some cases, lexical representation.

While there is little work directly examining neural responses to specific segmental features in humans, there are several studies that have looked at neural responses to phonetic feature cues in animals. In studies of the macaque, it has been shown that short voice onset time (a characteristic of segments like [b], [d], and [g]) produces a single onset transient in A1, while longer voice onset times (characteristic of voiceless segments such as [p], [t], and [k]) produce two transients. More recently, it has been found that voice onset time and aspiration (another acoustic characteristic associated with voicing) are represented in discrete tonotopic regions in A1 by synchronous activation patterns involving large populations of neurons.

Evidence from humans with normal and impaired language processing suggests that these temporospectral cues to feature identity appear to be integrated in unimodal auditory association cortex lying along the superior temporal sulcus immediately adjacent to the primary auditory koniocortex. Many language processes are lateralized, with the left hemisphere being the sole site in which they occur, but whether this is true of these early acoustic–phonetic mappings is an unsettled issue. Some researchers have suggested that the unconscious, automatic activation of features and phonemes, such as occurs as a stage in word recognition under normal conditions, occurs bilaterally, and that the dominant hemisphere is the sole site of phonemic processing that is associated with controlled processes (such as subvocal rehearsal) and conscious processes (such as explicit phoneme discrimination and identification, making judgments about rhyme, and other similar functions). Other researchers believe that even the unconscious processes that map acoustic properties onto phonological features and phonemes in the process of normal word recognition are lateralized. The evidence for the involvement of both hemispheres in these processes is stronger for vowels than for consonants. It has been suggested that this is because the left hemisphere is specialized for perceptual categorization of acoustic signals that is based upon rapidly changing acoustic properties, though a recent authoritative review downplays this possibility on the grounds that a left hemisphere advantage is only seen for linguistic stimuli and not nonlinguistic stimuli with such temporal characteristics.

The stage of processing that follows acoustic-phonemic processing is lexical access. Most models maintain that a language user has a store of the phonological properties of words in a long-term memory structure (the 'phonological input lexicon') and that acoustic-phonemic mapping identifies features and phonemes that in turn activate these representations. Other models conceive of the long-term representations of the forms of words as distributed sets of features without discernible listings of individual words. In these models, activation of the units over which features are distributed settles into stable patterns that suffice to activate semantic and syntactic features associated with individual words. Activation of items in a phonological input lexicon is not an entirely bottom-up process, however. Prevailing models maintain that bottom-up processes are supplemented top-down in important ways by information about words and context. Indeed, listeners fill in masked gaps in the middle of words so well that they are unable to discriminate masked gaps from masked segments (the 'phoneme restoration effect').

Based on functional neuroimaging results, activation of the long-term representations of the sound patterns of words is thought to occur in the left superior temporal gyrus. Scott and her colleagues have argued that there is a pathway along this gyrus and the corresponding left superior temporal sulcus such that word recognition occurs in a region anterior and inferior to primary auditory cortex, roughly corresponding to the parabelt region of auditory cortex in the monkey, and word meanings are activated yet further along this pathway in anterior inferior temporal lobe bilaterally (**Figure 2**). This pathway constitutes the auditory counterpart to the visual 'what' pathway in the inferior occipital-temporal lobe, in which cells respond to

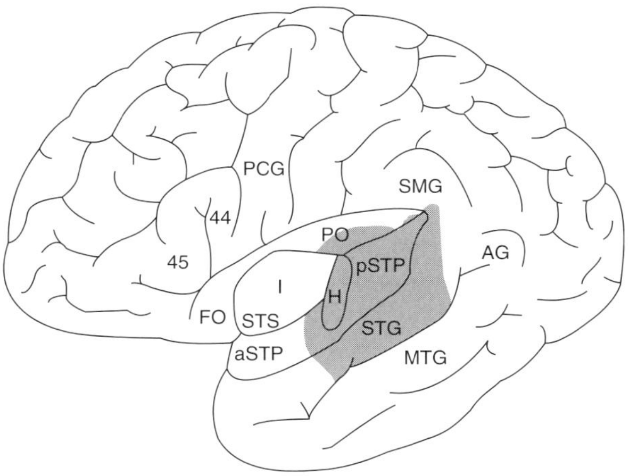

Figure 2 Depiction of the areas in the left superior temporal lobe that are involved in processing sounds and spoken words. PCG, precentral gyrus; SMG, supramarginal gyrus; AG, angular gyrus; MTG, middle temporal gyrus; aSTP and pSTP, anterior and posterior supratemporal planes; STS, superior temporal sulcus; FO, frontal operculum; PO, parietal operculum; H, transverse temporal gyrus of Heschi; STG, superior temporal gyrus. Reproduced from Hickok G and Poeppel D (2004) Dorsal and ventral streams: A framework for understanding aspects of the functional anatomy of language. *Cognition* 92: 67–99, with permission from Elsevier.

features of objects and objects themselves. In both the auditory and visual modalities, these temporal lobe pathways extract categories that are associated with meaning, with the difference being that the forms that are extracted from auditory stimuli are words, which are associatively linked to meaning, while those extracted from visual stimuli are structural descriptions of objects, which are partially constitutive of meaning.

The combination of bottom-up and top-down processing streams in language perception is one of the factors that makes it difficult to delineate the auditory component of language processing. Speech sounds map onto words, which in turn map onto representations of meaning, syntax, discourse, and world knowledge. To the extent that activation flows both ways between these representations, higher level representations may influence activation in auditory areas. Any understanding of auditory processing in language must involve an appreciation of these connections.

Speech perception is connected to speech production, especially during language acquisition, when imitation is crucial for the development of the child's sound inventory and lexicon. On the basis of lesions in patients with repetition disorders known as 'conduction aphasia,' the neural substrate for this connection has been thought to consist of the arcuate fibers of the inferior longitudinal fasciculus, which connect auditory association cortex (Wernicke's area in the posterior part of the superior temporal gyrus) to motor association cortex (Broca's area in the posterior part of the inferior frontal gyrus).

Recent functional neuroimaging studies and neural models have partially confirmed these ideas, providing evidence that integrated perceptual-motor processing of speech sounds and words makes use of a 'dorsal' pathway separate from that involved in word recognition. Again, the parallel with perception of visually presented objects has been emphasized, with the dorsal speech pathway corresponding to the parietal-based pathway that links object recognition with object use.

Once items are identified in the phonological input lexicon, it is possible, in principle, for a great deal of subsequent language processing to be carried out on syntactic and semantic properties of words and to be far removed from what would ordinarily be considered 'auditory' processing. However, the processes that construct the forms and meanings of sentences and discourse are not as independent of auditory processing as one might imagine. The products of segmental auditory processing, believed to be based in the dorsal pathway, play an important role with respect to these levels of language through subvocal rehearsal. The exact role of subvocal rehearsal in language comprehension is debated, but there is wide agreement that it is used as at least an ancillary mechanism to keep words in an active available form, to be reconsidered by comprehension mechanisms when structures are hard to build or have to be revised.

Suprasegmental (Intonational) Processing

Intonation (or prosody) refers to the pitch contours of words and phrases. Like lexical structures, intonational structures have been characterized in abstract representational terms, of which the Tones and Boundary Indices (ToBI) system is the most widely used. The ToBI assigns various levels of height to 'tones' that indicate intonational contours, and numerical levels to types of intonational breaks between words. For instance, the sentence "I like football, hockey, and soccer" might be spoken as one intonational phrase (IP), with several smaller intermediate phrases (ips), as in [$_{\text{IP}}$ [$_{\text{ip}}$I like football], [$_{\text{ip}}$hockey], [$_{\text{ip}}$and soccer]].

Like phonemes and their features, these tones and breaks are abstract characterizations of sound, and an active field of study investigates the mapping between them and acoustic properties. Many acoustic features of ToBI notational elements have begun to be identified. Some of these features are local. For instance, longer word nucleus duration and lower fundamental frequencies tend to occur at intonation phrase boundaries compared to intermediate phrase boundaries. The higher the pitch, or the bigger the pitch rise on a word, the more intonationally prominent the word is. Sentence-final rising intonation is associated with questions rather than statements. However, many ToBI notational elements are determined by relational properties of discontinuous portions of the acoustic waveform and features. For instance, whether a boundary is an intonational or an intermediate phrase boundary is determined in part by pitch, duration, and pause features adjacent to that boundary relative to these features at other boundaries.

Listeners use intonation to obtain information about syntactic and discourse structure. At the level of syntax, intonational boundaries are relevant to how phrases are attached to one another. For instance, the sentence "When the woman washed the clothes fell off the shelf," is usually initially misanalyzed, with listeners (and readers) taking 'the clothes' to be the object of 'washed,' and then are left with an apparently ungrammatical end to the sentence. A pause (or, in writing, a comma) after 'washed' indicates the clause boundary and makes the sentence understandable. At the level of discourse, intonation provides a great deal of information, including the focus of the discourse, the illocutionary force of a sentence (statement, question), and other semantic features. For instance, the sentence "Senator Eastland doesn't grow cotton to make money" is ambiguous, conveying either the sense that Senator Eastland grows cotton for some reason other than to make money or that Senator Eastland makes money by not growing cotton. An intonational contour that places a rising and then falling tone on 'cotton' followed by an intonational phrase break after 'cotton' leads to 'cotton' being the focus of the sentence. This leads to the usually unpreferred sense that the senator makes money by not growing cotton.

The mapping between intonation and other levels of linguistic structure is complex; intonational structures tend to correlate with, but not be isomorphic to, other structures. The sentence "The man who walked the dog that chased the squirrel tripped" consists of a series of relative clauses attached to noun phrases, and its syntactic structure can be roughly sketched as [$_{\text{S}}$ [$_{\text{NP}}$ The man who walked [$_{\text{NP}}$the dog that chased the squirrel]] tripped]. Its intonational contour, however, is different, grouping the objects of each clause with their verbs ([The man who walked the dog] [that chased the squirrel] tripped]). Intonation thus gives some strong and relatively direct cues regarding higher level linguistic representations (as in the case of focus) and some less direct cues as to these structures.

The neural basis of perceiving intonation has been less intensively studied than that of word-level phonology. These studies follow the same lines as those of segmental aspects of spoken language, dividing into those that that focus on the perception of the elements that determine intonational percepts and those that focus on the mapping of intonation onto higher linguistic categories.

One topic in the first set is pitch perception. Pitch is a derived percept that stands in a complicated relationship with its acoustic counterpart, fundamental frequency, or F0. The perceived pitch that creates intonation patterns is the product of vibration of the vocal cords, which pulse energy through the vocal tract as they open and close. Pitch information may be present throughout a wide frequency range due to the presence of harmonics – bands of energy found at integer multiples of the fundamental frequency. Behavioral evidence suggests that the perception of pitch in complex tone stimuli (including language) is a constructive process involving the full harmonic structure of a signal. Evidence for this view comes from the missing fundamental phenomenon in which listeners perceive pitch even when the fundamental is removed through filtering. Interestingly, pitch perception involves anatomically dissociable mechanisms in pitch-present versus missing fundamental stimuli, suggesting the existence of multiple cortical pitch extraction mechanisms. Evidence from imaging and lesion studies in humans and animals typically points to bilateral involvement of primary auditory cortex, with a dominant role in pitch perception played by the right hemisphere. So, for example, neurons in both left and right primary auditory cortex have been found that are sensitive to pitch change and pitch direction, but behavioral tasks involving the pitch direction discrimination appear to depend on intact right hemisphere primary auditory cortex. One of the great challenges in the study of the neural correlates of pitch perception has to do with the problem of encoding. While both temporal and place encoding models of cortical pitch representation has been proposed, it is clear that neither class of models adequately relates physiological data to psychophysical data across the relevant frequency span.

Turning to the mapping of intonational percepts onto other linguistic representations, studies are scarce and results are inconsistent. One study from our lab examined the processing of intonation in the context of linguistic processing. We found that syntactic statements pronounced with question intonational contours led to increased blood oxygen level-dependent (BOLD) activity in bilateral inferior frontal and temporal regions, compared to the corresponding statements with statement intonation. Other studies, however, have found only right hemisphere activation related to intonation signaling questions, albeit in different contrasts (contrasting sentences with intonation signaling a statement or question, against sentences with the same or different tone on the final word, in Chinese). One preliminary finding of interest is that different intonational features may activate different brain regions. For instance, in one study, the areas activated by Chinese listeners making judgments about the location of contrastive stress (relevant to discourse focus) were more left lateralized than the areas activated by the same listeners making judgments about whether an intonational contour expressed a question or a statement. Many aspects of design and analysis will need to be addressed before a clear picture is likely to emerge regarding this question.

Future Directions

This brief overview indicates that many basic questions about the processing of acoustic information to yield linguistic representations remain unanswered. The application to these questions of modern investigational methods in psychology, functional neuroimaging, and neurophysiology, though in its infancy, has already added enormously to the information we have about these processes and their neural bases. Beyond these areas lie questions about closely related matters, such as the processing of indexical information, emotional state, and other percepts as separate or related processing streams. Models of the neural mechanisms that are responsible for processing the acoustic stimulus in linguistic terms are guaranteed to deepen and change as these topics are further explored.

See also: Speech Production, Adult.

Further Reading

Beckman, ME, Hirschberg, J, and Shattuck-Hufnagel, S (2005). The original ToBI system and the evolution of the ToBI framework. In: Jun, S-A (ed.) *Prosodic Typology: The Phonology of Intonation and Phrasing*, pp. 9–54. Oxford: Oxford University Press.

Binder, JR, Frost, JA, Hammeke, TA, et al. (2000). Human temporal lobe activation by speech and nonspeech sounds. *Cerebral Cortex* 10: 512–528.

Doherty, CP, West, WC, Dilley, LC, et al. (2004). Question/statement judgments: An fMRI study of intonation processing. *Human Brain Mapping* 23: 85–98.

Gandour, J, Xu, Y, and Wong, D (2003). Neural correlates of segmental and tonal information in speech perception. *Human Brain Mapping* 20: 185–200.

Guenther, FH and Perkell, JS (2004). A neural model of speech production and its application to studies of the role of auditory feedback in speech. In: Maassen, B, Kent, R, Peters, H, et al. (eds.) *Speech Motor Control in Normal and Disordered Speech*, pp. 29–49. Oxford: Oxford University Press.

Hickok, G and Poeppel, D (2004). Dorsal and ventral streams: A framework for understanding aspects of the functional anatomy of language. *Cognition* 92: 67–99.

Johnson, K (2003). *Acoustics and Auditory Phonetics,* 2nd edn. Oxford, UK: Blackwell.

Okada, K, Smith, KR, Humphries, C, et al. (2003). Word length modulates neural activity in auditory cortex during covert object naming. *NeuroReport* 14: 2323–2326.

Patel, AD (2005). The relationship of music to the melody of speech and to syntactic processing disorders in aphasia. *Annals of the New York Academy of Sciences* 1060: 59–70.

Perkell, JS and Klatt, D (eds.) (1986). *Invariance and Variability of Speech Processes.* Hillsdale, NJ: Lawrence Erlbaum Assoc.

Perkell, JS, Matthies, ML, Svirsky, MA, et al. (1993). Trading relations between tongue-body raising and lip rounding in production of the vowel /u/: A pilot motor equivalence study. *Journal of the Acoustical Society of America* 93: 2948–2961.

Poeppel, D and Hickok, G (2004). Towards a new functional anatomy of language. *Cognition* 92: 1–12.

Scott, SK (2003). How might we best conceptualise speech perception? The view from neurobiology. *Journal of Phonetics* 31(3–4): 417–422.

Scott, SK, Blank, SC, Rosen, S, et al. (2000). Identification of a pathway for intelligible speech in the left temporal lobe. *Brain* 123: 2400–2406.

Scott, SK and Johnsrude, IS (2003). The neuroanatomical and functional organization of speech perception. *Trends in Neuroscience* 26(2): 100–107.
Scott, SK and Wise, RJS (2004). The functional neuroanatomy of prelexical processing of speech. *Cognition* 92: 13–45.
Stevens, KN (2000). *Acoustic Phonetics.* Cambridge, MA: MIT Press.
Tramo, MJ, Cariani, PA, Koh, CE, et al. (2005). Neurophysiology and neuroanatomy of pitch perception: Auditory cortex. *Annals of the New York Academy of Sciences* 1060: 148–174.
Zatorre, RJ, Evans, AC, Meyer, E, et al. (1992). Lateralization of phonetic and pitch processing in speech perception. *Science* 256: 846–849.
Zatorre, RJ, Evans, AC, and Meyer, E (1994). Neural mechanisms underlying melodic perception and memory for pitch. *Journal of Neuroscience* 14: 1908–1919.

Language, Cortical Processes

D. Caplan, Massachusetts General Hospital, Boston, MA, USA

The study of language–brain relationships is almost exclusively focused on the neural basis of the largely unconscious normal processes of speaking, understanding spoken language, reading, and writing. Data bearing these relations come from a variety of sources.

Correlating lesions with deficits provides evidence regarding brain areas that are necessary for a function. The original approach of postmortem analysis has largely been supplanted by magnetic resonance imaging (MRI), positron emission tomography (PET), and other imaging techniques. Data are also obtained by intraoperative stimulation, subdural electrode placement, and transcranial magnetic stimulation focally in normal individuals, which interfere with functions in most cases. The second approach to the study of language–brain relations is to record physiological and vascular responses to language processing in normal individuals using event-related potentials (ERPs) and magnetoencephalography (MEG), intraoperative and subdural recordings, optical imaging, and, most commonly, PET and functional MRI. Regions in which differences in neurovascular activity are associated with differences in performance on two tasks support the operations that differ in the two tasks. Functional neuroimaging in patients can reveal brain areas that are involved in an operation only postinjury.

Neural Structures Involved in Language

Beginning in the late nineteenth century, the application of deficit–lesion correlations based on autopsy to the problem of the regional specialization of the brain for language yielded important findings that remain undisputed. Chief among these is the fact that human language requires parts of the association cortex in the lateral portion of one cerebral hemisphere, usually the left in right-handed individuals. This cortex surrounds the Sylvian fissure and runs from the pars triangularis and opercularis of the inferior frontal gyrus (Brodman's area (BA) 45 and 44; Broca's area) through the angular and supramarginal gyri (BA 39 and 40) and into the superior temporal gyrus (BA 22; Wernicke's area) in the dominant hemisphere (**Figure 1**).

Data from other sources – deficit–lesion correlations based on antemortem neuroimaging and functional neuroimaging – have provided evidence that regions outside the peri-Sylvian association cortex also support language processing. Written language appears to involve cortex closer to the visual areas of the brain and sign language brain regions closer to those involved in movements of the hands than movements of the oral cavity. Some ERP components related to processing improbable or ill-formed language are maximal over high parietal and central scalp electrodes, suggesting that these regions may be involved in language processing. Both lesion studies in stroke patients and functional neuroimaging studies suggest that the inferior and anterior temporal lobe is involved in aspects of language processing. Injury to the supplementary motor cortex along the medial surface of

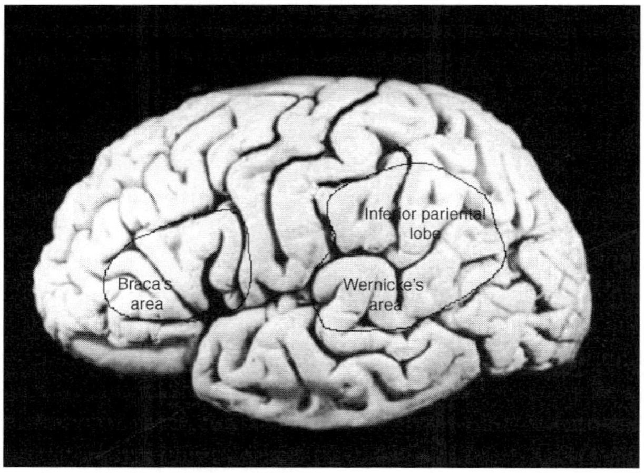

Figure 1 Depiction of the left hemisphere of the brain showing the main language areas.

the frontal lobe can lead to speech initiation disturbances; this region may be important in activating the language processing system, at least in production tasks. Activation studies have shown increased regional cerebral blood flow (rCBF) and blood oxygen level-dependent signal in the cingulate gyrus in association with many language tasks, although this activation appears to be nonspecific because it occurs in many nonlinguistic tasks as well. It has been suggested that it is due to increased arousal and deployment of attention associated with more complex tasks.

The same sources of data provide evidence that subcortical structures are also involved in language processing. Several studies report aphasic disturbances following strokes in the deep gray matter nuclei (the caudate, putamen, and parts of the thalamus). It has been suggested that subcortical structures involved in laying down procedural memories for motor functions, particularly the basal ganglia, are involved in 'rule-based' processing in language, such as regular aspects of word formation, as opposed to the long-term maintenance of information in memory, as occurs with simple words and irregularly formed words. The thalamus may play a role in processing the meanings of words. In general, subcortical lesions cause language impairments when the overlying cortex is abnormal (often, the abnormality can be seen only with metabolic scanning techniques) and the degree of language impairment is better correlated with measures of cortical than subcortical hypometabolism. It may be that subcortical structures serve to activate a cortically based language processing system but do not process language. In some activation studies involving language, the cerebellum also has increased rCBF. This may be a result of the role of this part of the brain in processes involved in timing and temporal ordering of events or because it is directly involved in language and other cognitive functions.

Ongoing studies have also clarified data regarding hemispheric dominance for language. In approximately 98% of right-handed individuals, the left hemisphere is dominant. Approximately 60–65% of non-right-handed individuals are left-hemisphere dominant, approximately 15–20% are right-hemisphere dominant, and the remainder appear to use both hemispheres for language processing. The relationship of dominance for language to handedness suggests a common determination of both, probably in large part genetic. The neural basis for lateralization was first suggested by Geschwind and Levitsky in 1968, who discovered that part of the language zone (the planum temporale, a portion of the superior temporal) was larger in the left than in the right hemisphere. Subsequent studies have confirmed this finding and identified specific cytoarchitectonically defined regions in this posterior language area that show this asymmetry. Several other asymmetries that may be related to lateralization have been identified. The exact relationship between size and function is not known. In general, however, relative size is a good predictor of lateralization and an example of the 'bigger is better' principle that applies elsewhere to communication systems (e.g., to song nuclei in birds).

An important finding is that the 'nondominant' hemisphere is involved in many language operations. Evidence from the effects of lesions and split brain studies, experiments using presentation of stimuli to one or the other hemisphere in normal subjects, and functional neuroimaging studies indicate that the nondominant hemisphere understands many words, perhaps representing them more generally than does the left hemisphere, and suggest that it is involved in other aspects of language processing as well. Some language operations may be carried out primarily in the right hemisphere. The best candidates for these operations are ones that pertain to processing the discourse level of language, especially revising inferences, interpreting nonliteral language, and appreciating humor.

Models of Organization of the Brain for Language Processing

Two general models of the relationship of areas of the brain to components of the language processing system have been developed. Localizationist theories maintain that language processing components are localized in specific parts of the brain. 'Holist' theories maintain that linguistic representations and processes require broad areas of the brain. Five basic models, which capture the set of logically possible relations of brain areas to language processes, can be extracted from these two conceptualizations: invariant localization, variable localization, even distribution, invariant uneven distribution, and variable uneven distribution.

Invariant localization hypothesizes that only a small area of the brain supports a function. Variable localization hypothesizes that different small areas of the brain support a function in different individuals. Distribution hypothesizes that a large region of the brain supports a function. Traditional distributed models assumed an even distribution of distributed functions: All parts of the region contributed equally to the function. If a function is evenly distributed throughout a region, there can be no individual variability in its neural basis. If a function is unevenly distributed throughout a region, it may be distributed the same way in everyone (invariant uneven distribution) or differently in different individuals (variable uneven distribution). Other models are extensions of these basic five. Degeneracy is a variant of localization in which more than one structure independently supports a function; degeneracy can either be invariant (the same areas independently support the function in everyone) or variable (different areas independently support the function in different people). Variable localization could be constrained so that a function is localized more often in one area than another.

It is not possible to review all the areas of language whose neurological basis has been studied. Here, syntactic processing is discussed.

Syntactic structures determine the relationships between words that allow sentences to convey propositional information – information about thematic roles (who is initiating an action, who is receiving it, etc.), attribution of modification (which adjectives are assigned to which nouns), scope of quantification, co-reference, and other relations between words. The propositional content of a sentence conveys a great deal of information beyond what is conveyed by words alone and is crucial to many human intellectual functions. Propositions are the source of much of the information stored in semantic memory. Because propositions can be true or false, they can be used in thinking logically. They serve the purpose of planning actions. They are the basic building blocks of much of what is conveyed in a discourse.

Unlike models of the neural basis for lexical access and lexical semantic processes, a variety of models have been proposed regarding the neural basis for syntactic processing. Of the five theories of functional neuroanatomy reviewed previously, four have been proposed regarding syntactic processing on the basis of deficit–lesion correlations: localizationist models that claim that Broca's area plays a critical role in connecting moved constituents and their antecedents; variable localization models; traditional, evenly distributed models; and invariant unevenly distributed models.

Evidence supporting these models is based on correlating deficits in syntactic comprehension with lesions. There is considerable disagreement about how to characterize these deficits. Syntactic comprehension deficits are typically established by showing that patients can understand sentences with simple syntactic structures (e.g., 'The boy chased the girl') and sentences with complex syntactic structures in which the relationships between the nouns and verbs can be inferred from knowledge of real-world events (e.g., 'The apple the boy ate was red') but not sentences with complex structures in which the relationships between the nouns and verbs depend on a syntactic structure that needs to be constructed (e.g., 'The boy the girl pushed was tall'). However, there are two issues that must be dealt with. First, it is not clear whether a patient with a performance of this type has a deficit in a particular parsing operation or has what might be called a reduction in the resources available to accomplish syntactically based comprehension. Second, there is virtually no consistency of individual patients' performances across tasks, raising questions about whether it is correct to say that a patient who fails on a particular structure has a parsing deficit.

Assuming, however, that performances such as those outlined previously on a single task are properly analyzed as deficits in particular parsing operations, the empirical basis that relates these deficits to lesions is so limited that none of the models that have been championed have been tested rigorously. The vast majority of claims about the neural basis for syntactic processing are based on patient data and do not examine lesions quantitatively. Many are based on the assumption that Broca's or nonfluent patients have 'anterior' lesions and Wernicke's, fluent, conduction and anomic patients have 'posterior' lesions, whereas the reality is far more complicated. We recently reported the most detailed study of patients with lesions whose syntactic comprehension has been assessed. Forty-two patients with aphasia secondary to left hemisphere strokes and 25 control subjects were studied for the ability to assign and interpret three syntactic structures (passives, object-extracted relative clauses, and reflexive pronouns) in enactment, sentence–picture matching, and grammaticality judgment tasks. Neither the most direct prediction made by distributed models (that lesion size correlates with performance level) nor the most commonly made claim about localization of syntactic operations (that the insertion of traces into syntactic structures occurs in Broca's area) have been tested quantitatively on the basis of radiological data. We recently began to address this question. We measured accuracy, reaction time, and self-paced listening times in picture matching and grammaticality judgment. We obtained MRI and 5-deoxyglucose PET data on 31 patients and 12 controls. The percentage of selected regions of interest that was lesioned on MRI and the mean normalized PET counts per voxel in regions of interest were calculated. In regression analyses, lesion measures in both peri-Sylvian and non-peri-Sylvian regions of interest predicted performance. Patients who performed at similar levels behaviorally had lesions of very different sizes, and patients with equivalent lesion sizes varied greatly in their level of performance. The data are consistent with a model in which the neural tissue that is responsible for the operations underlying sentence comprehension and syntactic processing is localized in different neural regions in different individuals.

Functional neuroimaging has supplanted deficit–lesion correlations as the principle source of information regarding the localization of syntactic processing in sentence comprehension. These studies have led to localizationist models. Many researchers advance models in which some aspect of parsing or sentence interpretation is localized in Broca's area or in portions of this region. Some authors have argued that the innate capacity that underlies the ability to acquire the syntax of natural language is localized in this region. However, despite the numerous advocates for localization of syntactic operations, most neuroimaging studies show that multiple cortical areas are activated in tasks that involve syntactic processing, and different areas have been activated in different tasks. Overall, these data suggest variation in the localization of the areas that are sufficient to support syntactic processing within the language area across the adult population, with perhaps some constraint on the areas in which processing is localized as a function of the proficiency of individuals to assign syntactic structure and determine the meaning of sentences.

Conclusion

Human language is a unique representational system that relates aspects of meaning to many types of forms (e.g., phonemes, lexical items, and syntax), each with its own complex structure. Deficit–lesion correlations and neuroimaging studies are beginning to provide data about the neural structures involved in human language. It appears that many areas of the brain are either necessary or sufficient in representing and processing language, with the left peri-Sylvian association cortex being the most important such region. How these areas act to support particular language operations is not understood. There is evidence for both localization of some functions in specific regions and either multifocal or distributed involvement of brain areas in other language functions. It may be that some higher level principles are operative in this domain. For instance, content-addressable activation and associative operations such as those that underlie phoneme recognition, lexical access, and lexical semantic activation may be invariantly localized, whereas combinatorial computational operations such as those that constitute the syntax of natural language may not. However, many aspects of these topics remain to be studied with tools of modern cognitive neuroscience.

See also: Language Development; Language in Aged Persons; Language, Auditory Processes; Sentence Comprehension.

Further Reading

Annett, M (1985). *Left, Right, Hand and Brain: The Right Shift Theory.* London: Erlbaum.

Beeman, M, Friedman, RB, Grafman, J, Perez, E, Diamond, S, and Lindsay, MB (1994). Summation priming and coarse semantic coding in the right hemisphere. *Journal of Cognitive Neuroscience* 6: 26–45.

Caplan, D, Hildebrandt, N, and Makris, N (1996). Location of lesions in stroke patients with deficits in syntactic processing in sentence comprehension. *Brain* 119: 933–949.

Caplan, D, Waters, G, Kennedy, D, et al. (2007). A study of syntactic processing in aphasia II: Neurological aspects. *Brain and Language* 101(2): 151–177.

Caramazza, A and Zurif, EB (1976). Dissociation of algorithmic and heuristic processes in language comprehension: Evidence from aphasia. *Brain and Language* 3: 572–582.

Damasio, AR and Damasio, H (1992). Brain and language. *Scientific American* 1992: 89–95.

Friederici, A (2002). Towards a neural basis of auditory sentence processing. *Trends in Cognitive Science* 6: 78–84.

Geschwind, N (1965). Disconnection syndromes in animals and man. *Brain* 88: 237–294, 585,644.

Geschwind, N and Galaburda, AM (1987). *Cerebral Lateralization: Biological Mechanisms, Associations and Pathology.* Cambridge, MA: MIT Press.

Grodzinsky, Y (2000). The neurology of syntax: Language use without Broca'a area. *Behavioral and Brain Sciences* 23: 47–117.

Kaan, E and Swaab, T (2002). The brain circuitry of syntactic comprehension. *Trends in Cognitive Sciences* 6(8): 350–356.

Kutas, M and Hillyard, SA (1980). Reading senseless sentences: Brain potentials reflect semantic incongruity. *Science* 207: 203–204.

Lashley, KS (1950). In search of the engram. *Society of Experimental Biology Symposium* 4: 454–482.

Mesulam, M-M (1990). Large-scale neurocognitive networks and distributed processing for attention, language, and memory. *Annals of Neurology* 28(5): 597–613.

Mohr, JP, Pessin, MS, Finkelstein, S, Funkenstein, HH, Duncan, GW, and Davis, KR (1978). Broca aphasia: Pathologic and clinical. *Neurology* 28: 311–324.

Ojemann, G (1983). Brain organization for language from the perspective of electrical stimulation mapping. *Behavioural and Brain Sciences* 6: 189–230.

Ojemann, G and Schoenfield-McNeill, J (1998). Neurons in human temporal cortex active with verbal associative learning. *Brain and Language* 64: 317–327.

Poizner, H, Klima, ES, and Bellugi, U (1989). *What the Hands Reveal about the Brain.* Cambridge, MA: MIT Press..

Rugg, MD and Coles, M (eds.) (1995). *Electrophysiology of Mind: Event-Related Brain Potentials and Cognition.* Oxford Psychology Series. Oxford: Oxford University Press.

Stromswold, K, Caplan, D, Alpert, N, and Rauch, S (1996). Localization of syntactic comprehension by positron emission tomography. *Brain and Language* 52: 452–473.

Tettamanti, M, Alkadhi, H, Moro, A, Perani, D, Kollias, S, and Weiniger, D (2002). Neural correlates for the acquisition of natural language syntax. *NeuroImage* 17: 700–709.

Language, Learning Impairments

J. L. Evans, San Diego State University, San Diego, CA, USA

In this article, the characteristics of a group of children with language learning impairments are described. These children do not have problems that are usually associated with language-learning impairments, such as hearing impairment, intellectual impairments, and/or neurological damage. In the research literature, 'specific language impairment' (SLI) is the most widely used term for this group of children, and it is the one that is used here.

The criteria for SLI are quite precise. They include Performance IQ in the normal range; normal hearing; no recent episodes of otitis media with effusion; no evidence of seizure disorders, cerebral palsy, or brain lesions; no medication for control of seizures; no oral–motor structural abnormalities; and no symptoms of impaired reciprocal social interactions (e.g., autism). Typically, nonverbal IQs of these children are on average 85–100, whereas standardized language assessment scores are 1.25 standard deviations or more below one's expectations. These children pass pure-tone hearing screenings at 20 dB in both ears at frequencies of 500, 1000, 2000, and 4000 Hz. They have no focal brain lesions, traumatic brain injury, cerebral palsy, or seizures. Important is the exclusion of children who have problems with volitional control of oral–motor structures, which does not rule out mild neuromaturational delays. Interestingly, some children with SLI may be more clumsy, have slower motor responses, and have poorer fine motor skills than peers.

A final exclusion criteria is the absence of all of the symptoms listed for pervasive developmental disorder 'not otherwise specified' in the *Diagnostic and Statistical Manual of Mental Disorders*. Hence, no problems using gaze and gestures to regulate social interactions, or stereotypic, repetitive motor movements characteristic of children with autism, are seen in these children. This is not to say that they do not experience substantial difficulties in social interactions as a result of their language disorders.

The prevalence of SLI is approximately 7% of school-aged children. Although it was commonly believed that the incidence of SLI is higher in males than females, large-scale epidemiological studies now report a ratio of SLI in males to females of 1.1:1. Thus, the 'often reported' higher rate of males to females with SLI may instead be a reflection of referral bias in the public schools, the over-identification of males with SLI, and the underidentification of female children with SLI. Approximately 70% of very young children (2-year-olds) who experience delays in language production may catch up to their peers by the time they are 3 or 4 years of age; however, if a child is still classified as having language difficulties by the time he or she is in kindergarten, it is likely that he or she will continue to have language impairments throughout adolescent and adulthood. This suggests that a 'wait-and-see' approach for children beyond the age of 4 years puts them at extreme risk for pervasive and continued language impairments and may result in significant costs to health care and educational systems.

Language Abilities of Children with SLI

The work reviewed here includes only studies investigating American- and British-English-speaking children with SLI (although cross-linguistic work suggests similar findings). Children with SLI have difficulty comprehending and producing new words. Vocabulary growth is slow, and expressive vocabulary, as measured by standardized assessments, is smaller than that of age-matched peers. First words appear at older ages in children with SLI, with the average age of first word being 23 months in contrast to 12 months for typically developing children. The types of words used by children with SLI, however, mirror those of typically developing children, with names of objects/animals/substances comprising approximately 55% of their first words, words referring to actions comprising 12% of first words, and words referring to properties of objects also comprising 12%. Moreover, verb stem errors are extremely rare in children with SLI, reportedly occurring in only 7:2998 verb tokens in the speech of preschool children with SLI.

Experimental word-learning studies show that children with SLI need, on average, at least twice the number of exposures to a novel word compared to their peers before they can successfully comprehend and/or produce it. The trajectory of word learning is also qualitatively different. Children with SLI exhibit a concave word learning trajectory, with initial performance being poor but improving rapidly with increased exposure, compared to typical children, whose word learning trajectory is convex, with rapid improvement in comprehension and production accuracy after initial exposure to novel words, followed by a leveling off and stabilizing of performance. Additional semantic cues presented with a novel word increase comprehension accuracy for children with SLI, whereas phonological cues increase production accuracy in these children but not in typical peers. Errors made by children with SLI in extending a newly learned word to a novel object mirror those of younger language-matched typical children, with the referent receiving the incorrect label when it is both perceptually and functionally similar to the target object. Studies of lexical abilities in school-aged children with SLI parallel the findings when these children were younger.

Difficulty acquiring and using grammatical morphology, including inflectional affixes such as past tense *-ed* and plural *s*, characterizes the difficulties seen in children with SLI and has been proposed as a possible phenotype marker for this disability. Typically developing children have acquired these morphological forms by the time they are approximately 4 years of age, whereas learning these forms is difficult for children with SLI, who are well into school-aged years before they learn them. On tasks designed to probe comprehension of various syntactic forms, young children with SLI are unable to identify syntax errors in sentences, such as tense marking and subject–verb agreements; have difficulty comprehending passive constructions; and rely heavily on comprehension strategies in the absence of full comprehension. Not surprising, children with SLI have more difficulty identifying syntactic violations despite easily identifying semantic violations.

In a given language, the use of grammatical morphology is highly predictable. Because of this regularity, its use is often viewed as being 'rule governed,' and children's use of these forms is an indication that they have inferred the 'rules' governing the generation of a given linguistic form. Moreover, in typically developing children, this rule can be extended to new and novel linguistic contexts, with such extensions providing critical evidence that the child has completely extracted the rule and is able to use the rule generatively (e.g., affixing plural *s* to 'wug'). In discrimination-learning studies, in which a child is asked to extract 'regularities' from recurring stimulus presentations and then extend them to new stimulus items consistently, children with SLI are unable to extend linguistic regularities from trained to untrained forms.

The use of argument structure by children with SLI in spontaneous and elicited utterances suggests that underlying knowledge of these forms in these children may be learned through exposure to specific verbs in individual sentence constructions. Although most argument structures are evident in the speech of children with SLI, they do not consistently produce these forms. For example, children with SLI produce elements that add substantially to the information content of an utterance but which are not obligatory. Although 7- to 9-year-old children with SLI resemble typical 5-year-olds in the rate at which they use adverbial forms to express temporal relationships, they are unable to provide additional contextual information when necessary (e.g., 'the dog left' is not sufficient).

Theoretical Accounts

A critical question with regard to this population is whether SLI is a primary deficit in an independent grammar module or whether more general-purpose processing mechanisms underlie the language impairments seen in these children. Several processing mechanisms have been proposed and include but are not limited to auditory processing deficits, limited verbal working memory, slower speed of processing, and generalized limited processing capacity.

Processing capacity and speed of processing accounts view processing as trade-offs between task demands and cognitive resources. Limited capacity accounts of SLI share the tenet that children have a fixed pool of operational resources available to perform computations, and when the demands of a task exceed available resources, both processing and storage of information will be degraded. A consistent finding across both verbal and nonverbal tasks that are designed to simultaneously tax the processing and storage of information in children with SLI is that when they are required to allocate more of their working memory resources to processing information, they are left with substantially fewer resources for the storage of information compared to their unimpaired peers. Processing capacity tasks have high specificity and sensitivity in the identification of children with SLI and account for a significantly greater proportion of the variance in language abilities in SLI than standardized measures of grammatical knowledge.

Speed of processing is often viewed as a processing resource in the sense that it is finite and the faster/slower processing is performed, the better/worse the resulting level of cognitive performance will be. Children with SLI are consistently slower than their peers across a myriad of verbal and nonverbal tasks. Both large-scale meta-analysis studies and direct comparisons of reaction time (RT) data for children with SLI show that their speed of processing information is between 20 and 30% slower than that of age-matched controls. One problem in invoking a general processing mechanism account of SLI is that it is not clear whether limited capacity and/or speed of processing reflect a fundamental limitation of the underlying cognitive system or if they are themselves emergent properties of the system, arising naturally as a consequence of interactions within the cognitive system. Limited capacity and speed of processing have been treated as separate constructs in the study of SLI.

Historically, slower reaction times in children with SLI have been interpreted as the processing of each successive step in a given task being slower by a constant proportion. By this account, the more complex the task (e.g., the greater the number of processing steps), the progressively slower reaction times will be for children with SLI. Importantly, RT data alone cannot rule out alternative slowing accounts, such as cognitive processes being slowed but speed of sensorimotor processes not being slowed, or slowing increasing proportionately with each successive processing step. Event-related potentials (ERPs) provide a means of examining speed of processing with and without higher cognitive processing. Comparisons of behavioral RTs and P300 latencies of children with SLI indicate that P300 ERP latencies are no slower than those of age-matched peers despite RTs being significantly slower. In contrast, N400 latencies, a measure of higher cognitive processing, are significantly longer in children with SLI compared to peers. Taken together, ERP data suggest that slowing in SLI may not be the primary deficit but an artifact of poorly specified and/or degraded extant knowledge in these children, requiring greater processing resources to maintain in active memory than for typically developing children.

Another hypothesized cause of SLI is impaired auditory processing. The nature of auditory processing difficulties in SLI remains open to debate, however. Some researchers have championed the idea that temporal processing deficits are the cause of SLI. Others have proposed reduced storage for phonological material in working memory or poorly specified long-term phonological representations. Studies of auditory processing accounts in children with SLI use several experimental methods, including temporal order judgment tasks, just noticeable difference tasks, phoneme identification tasks, categorical perception tasks, and mismatch negativity (MMN).

Some of the earliest studies of temporal order judgments in SLI showed that children with SLI did not differ from their peers in the interstimulus interval (ISI) needed to detect two separate tones; however, they needed much longer interstimuli durations to correctly report the order in which the tones appeared. Follow-up work has shown that children with SLI are able to successfully report the order of the steady-state vowels but not the order of the CV syllables. These data have been interpreted as a temporal processing deficit, specifically that children with SLI are unable to process rapidly changing acoustic features of speech stimuli.

In just noticeable differences tasks, children with SLI listen to pairs of stimuli and decide if they are the same or different. Typically, one of the pair is a clear exemplar of a given target stimuli, whereas the second is designed to contrast an acoustic dimension of interest. In these tasks, children with SLI require greater acoustic difference between stimulus pairs to discriminate stimuli (e.g., /ba/-/pa/ or /ba-da-ga/) compared to peers. Findings of phoneme-identification studies show the same pattern, in which children with SLI are able to easily distinguish phonemes that are spectrally dissimilar vowels [i] and [a] at both long and short durations, but they have difficulty distinguishing phonemes with greater spectral similarity (e.g., [i]-[I]). (An important finding from auditory processing work is that children with SLI who have both speech and language impairments (articulation impairments as well as language impairments) have greater difficulty with both identification and temporal order judgments.)

The extent to which children with SLI perceive speech sounds categorically has been studies extensively. What is interesting about studies of categorical perception in children with SLI is that, given the ubiquitous nature of categorical perception across species, a deficit in categorical perception in children with SLI would indicate a profound neurocognitive impairment in these children – a finding not in keeping with the perceptual and cognitive abilities seen in these children. Children with SLI consistently exhibit similar crossover points (CPs) as their peers in identification but show less-consistent labeling of unambiguous endpoint tokens and reduced discrimination. Historically, however, these studies of CP in children with SLI used synthetic speech stimuli. A series of CP studies comparing natural and synthesized speech stimuli revealed that poor speech discrimination is evident only for synthetic speech stimuli. The consistent finding of poor auditory processing under synthetic speech conditions suggests that the auditory 'perceptual' deficits in children with SLI are not the result of deficits in auditory processing *per se* but, rather, from increased processing demands inherent in synthesized speech.

MMN, a component of the auditory ERP that reflects the outcome of an automatic comparison processing between different acoustic stimuli, is a measure of sensory memory. Typically, it is elicited when a deviate stimuli occurs in a series of identical stimuli. Both pure tones and speech stimuli have been used in investigations of central auditory processing in children with SLI. Interestingly, children with SLI have attenuated amplitudes for MMNs to speech stimuli (e.g., /ba/ /da/ /ga/) compared to age-matched peers but not for simple tone stimuli differing in either frequency (1000 vs. 12 000) or duration (175 vs. 100 ms).

Classification and Labels

The study of SLI dates back to the first half of the nineteenth century with the introduction of the term congenital aphasia (the term 'hearing mutism' was used in Germany during this same time period). Other terms used in the late 1800s and early 1900s included delayed speech development, congenital auditory imperception, and congenital verbal auditory agnosia. Interestingly, because clear neurological damage was not evident in these children, as early as the 1880s it was suggested that attention and memory were possible underlying causes of the language disorder. At the turn of the century, English and French researchers began to use the term 'congenital aphasia.' In the 1960s, terms such as developmental aphasia and congenital aphasia began to disappear, and developmental dysphasia began to be used. This shift to *dys-* reflected the differentiation of children with neurological insults and 'acquired aphasia' from children who had language impairments in the absence of brain injury. The shift also reflected the emphasis in the 1960s on detailed description of the linguistic deficit profiles of these children as well. Currently, the terms 'language/learning disabled' or 'language/learning impaired' are often used in studying the academic skills of these children, reflecting the fact that having a label of 'language impaired' does not exclude these children from being labeled as learning disabled in schools. The term 'developmental language disorder with expressive and expressive–receptive subtypes' is also used in the *Diagnostic and Statistical Manual of Mental Disorders.*

Three different approaches characterize the grouping of children with SLI: clinical, psychometric, and linguistic classifications. Clinical taxonomies of language disorders, such as that proposed by Rapin and Allen, closely parallel acquired language disorders in adults with aphasia and include phonological, syntactic, semantic, and pragmatic skills. Alternatively, Aram and Nation classify children with SLI using standardized psychometric tests assessing phonological, syntactic, and semantic aspects of language. In contrast, Crystal, Fletcher, and Garman classify children with SLI based on linguistic measures that include assessment of semantic referencing, phonology, grammar, and structure building. These different approaches have yielded not only different labels for SLI but also different theoretical accounts of the disorders, as well as different subgroupings within SLI.

Neurobiological Correlates

A common but largely unsubstantiated hypothesis in the 1950s was that left hemisphere damage was the cause of SLI. The development of computed tomography scan technology allowed for direct investigation of the hypothesis that SLI was due to left hemisphere damage. However, these studies revealed a remarkable absence of neuroradiological abnormalities in children with SLI. Because research failed to demonstrate that the language disorders seen in children with SLI stemmed from focal brain damage, researchers compared the language abilities in children with known lateralized brain lesions to those of children with SLI. Interestingly, children with unilateral brain lesions manifest profiles of language disorders that are very similar to characteristics of children with SLI. One outcome of this research was a shift in focus from models of SLI that involved left hemisphere damage to models of SLI that involved bilateral or more diffuse areas of the brain.

In unimpaired individuals with normal language abilities, the planum temporale and pars triangularis are larger in the left hemisphere than the right. Children with SLI have abnormal asymmetry of the prefrontal region (right greater than left) and abnormal symmetry in the parietal region. Moreover, the area containing the left planum is significantly smaller in children with SLI, or reverse asymmetry is seen in the region containing the planum temporale in children with SLI. Quantitative anatomical differences in the brains of children with SLI and age-matched controls shows three majors differences: Children with SLI have significantly narrower right hemispheres, have significantly smaller pars triangularis in the left hemisphere, and do not have leftward asymmetry of the pars triangularis, planum temporale, and the planum compared to their age-matched peers. Whereas the left pars triangularis is significantly smaller in children with SLI, the right pars triangularis does not differ in children with SLI and their peers.

Cerebral blood flow measures (single-photon emission computed tomography) in phoneme discrimination indicate that children with SLI do not show predominant activation of the left hemisphere. Moreover, functional magnetic resonance imaging and event-related potential (ERP) studies of toddlers at risk for SLI (e.g., late talkers), children with SLI, and even parents of children with SLI exhibit different patterns of coordinating activation among brain regions relative to controls, suggesting the possibility of qualitatively different brain organization for language in this population.

Genetics and Heritability

There is a familial component to SLI. The concordance rate for monozygotic twins with SLI is almost 100%, and it is 50–70% for dizygotic twins. Molecular genetic studies implicate: (1) the linkage of a severe autosomal dominant speech and language disorder to the region of 7q31 (*SPCH1*) and (2) translocation in the *SPCH1* region and evidence of linkage on both chromosome 16q and 19q. Furthermore, work indicates that 16q and 19q may represent universally important loci in SLI and, more broadly, a risk factor for developmental language impairments. Importantly, in the SLI consortium study, there is no evidence for linkage to 7q near FOXP2, a gene that has been implicated in severe speech impairment and which is located in a region that may also include a major locus for autism. A study completing a genome scan for SLI used both dominant and recessive models for the three phenotype classifications: (1) clinical diagnosis, language impairment; (2) reading discrepancy; and (3) evidence for linkage between 13q21 using the recessive reading discrepancy model. Results from this study also suggest that additional loci, on 2p22 and 17q23, may comprise part of the phenotype of SLI.

SLI or Dyslexia?

One question is the extent to which SLI and dyslexia are distinct or overlapping disorders. On the one hand, SLI and dyslexia, by diagnostic criteria, are two distinct developmental language disorders, with SLI being characterized by semantics, syntax, and discourse processing difficulties, and dyslexia characterized by phonological processing deficits and problems in word reading. However, children with dyslexia exhibit deficits in semantics and syntax in addition to deficits in phoneme processing. Alternatively, children with SLI, in addition to language impairments, also exhibit substantial deficits in phonological processing. Reviews of behavioral, neurological, and genetic evidence, as well as large-scale epidemiological studies of children with SLI and dyslexia selected from a population-based sample, suggest that these two clinical populations represent two different but overlapping developmental disorders. In a large-scale population-based study, where the participant sample from which the children in the study were drawn included 527 school-aged children, the prevalence of dyslexia was examined in second, fourth, and eighth grade among children who were classified with SLI in kindergarten. A statistically significant, but limited, overlap between SLI and dyslexia existed, but the majority of the children with SLI did not have dyslexia during the school years.

An Implicit Learning Impairment?

Learning is a gradual, often unconscious process that initially is slow and inefficient, but with sufficient exposure it becomes automatic and efficient. Recent studies suggest that language impairments seen in SLI may be secondary to deficits in implicit learning. Procedural learning is the system involved in the learning of new cognitive and/or motor sequences. Grammar is also a regular pattern of sequences. Based on the idea that the lexical declarative memory system is relatively spared in children with SLI, it has been argued that the grammatical systems in these children are impaired, specifically due to neurological damage in the corticostriatum and association areas.

Research has begun to examine this directly using both statistical word learning (SWL) paradigms and a classic task of procedural learning of sequential pattern – the serial reaction time task (SRT). In SRT tasks, a child presses a button corresponding to a spatial location of a visual stimulus, trial by trial. Embedded within a random order of stimuli are patterns of locations. The learning of these embedded patterns within the sequence is evidenced by shorter reaction times of button pressing of the patterned sequence in contrast to the random sequences. Adolescent children with SLI are significantly impaired in their ability to learn the embedded sequence. Moreover, performance on the SRT task accounts for a significant amount of the variance in grammatical knowledge in these children.

Statistical word-learning paradigms also show that children with SLI are significantly impaired in the ability to implicitly discover word boundaries within continuous speech. Whereas school-aged children are able to implicitly learn novel words after only 3 min of exposure, performance of children with SLI after 20 min of exposure is at chance. Importantly, after double the exposure (40 min) to the same speech stream, the performance of children with SLI is greater than chance and no different from the performance of their peers. It is argued that implicit learning is such a primitive cognitive construct that there should be no differences across an individual's performance. However, ERP studies using the same SWL paradigm show that high word learners evidence rapid and early sensitivity to word boundaries seen in the N100 waveform prior to demonstrating this knowledge behaviorally in posttesting, whereas poor word learners do not. Clearly, a key aspect of learning language is the tracking of the regularities in the language input. One can see how impairment in the mechanisms involved in implicitly tracking the regularities in the language input could have profound implications for language learning and suggest a single mechanism account of the pattern of deficits seen both across language domains and developmentally over time in children with SLI.

See also: Dyslexia, Neurodevelopmental Basis; Language Development; Language Following Congenital Disorders (not SLI); Language, Cortical Processes; Sentence Comprehension; Sentence Production; Word Learning; Word Production; Word Recognition.

Further Reading

Barlett, CW, Flax, JF, Logue, MW, et al. (2002). A major susceptibility locus for specific language impairment is located on 13q21. *American Journal of Human Genetics* 71: 45–55.

Bishop, DVM, Bright, P, James, C, Bishop, SJ, and van der Lely, HKJ (2000). Grammatical SLI: A distinct subtype of developmental language impairment? *Applied Psycholinguistics* 21: 159–181.

Bishop, DVM and Leonard, LB (eds.) (2000). *Speech and Language Impairments in Children: Causes, Characteristics, Intervention and Outcome.* Hove: Psychology Press.

Catts, HW, Adlof, SM, Hogan, TP, and Ellis Weismer, S (2005). Are specific language impairment and dyslexia distinct disorders? *Journal of Speech, Language, and Hearing Research* 48: 1378–1396.

Coady JA and Evans JL (2007) The uses and interpretations of nonword repetition tasks in children with and without specific language impairment. *International Journal of Communication Disorders* 43: 1–40.

Coady, JA, Evans, JL, Mainela-Arnold, E, and Kluender, KR (2007). Children with specific language impairment perceive speech most categorically when tokens are natural and meaningful. *Journal of Speech, Language, and Hearing Research* 50: 41–57.

Ellis Weismer, S, Evans, J, and Hesketh, L (1999). An examination of verbal working memory capacity in children with specific language impairment. *Journal of Speech, Language, and Hearing Research* 42: 1249–1260.

Evans, JL, Viele, K, Kass, RE, and Tang, F (2002). Grammatical morphology and perception of synthetic and natural speech stimuli in children with specific language impairments. *Journal of Speech, Language, and Hearing Research* 45: 494–504.

Gauger, LM, Lambardino, LJ, and Leonard, CM (1997). Brain morphology in children with specific language impairment. *Journal of Speech, Language, and Hearing Research* 40: 1272–1284.

Hugdahl, K, Gundersen, H, Brekke, C, Thomsen, T, Rimol, LM, and Ersland, L (2004). fMRI brain activation in a Finnish family with specific language impairment compared with a normal control group. *Journal of Speech, Language, and Hearing Research* 47: 162–172.

Leonard, L (1998). *Children with Specific Language Impairment*. Cambridge, MA: MIT Press.

Leonard L, Ellis Weisner S, Miller C, Francis D, Tomblin B, and Kail R (2007) Speed of processing, working memory, and language impairment in children. *Journal of Speech, Language, and Hearing Research* 50: 408–428.

O'Brien, EK, Zhang, S, Nishimura, J, Tomblin, B, and Murray, C (2003). Association of specific language impairment (SLI) to the region of 7q31. *American Journal of Human Genetics* 74: 1536–1543.

Plante, E, Swisher, L, Vance, R, and Rapcsak, S (1991). MRI findings in boys with specific language impairment. *Erain and Language* 41: 52–66.
Rice, ML and Warren, SF (eds.) (2004). *Developmental Language Disorders: From Phenotypes to Etiologies.* Mahwah, NJ: Erlbaum.
SLI Consortium (2002). A genomewide scan identified two novel loci involved in specific language impairment. *American Journal of Human Genetics* 70: 384–398.
Tomblin, JB, Smith, E, and Zhang, X (1997). Epidemiology of specific language impairments: Prenatal and perinatal risk factors. *Journal of Communication Disorders* 30: 325–343.
Tomblin, JB, Zhang, X, Buckwalter, P, and O'Brien, M (2003). The stability of primary language disorder: Four years after kindergarten diagnosis. *Journal of Speech, Language, and Hearing Research* 46: 1283–1296.

Lateralization of Language across the Life Span

M. Hiscock, University of Houston, Houston, TX, USA
M. Kinsbourne, New School for Social Research, New York, NY, USA

Introduction

This chapter concerns the time course of language lateralization. It addresses primarily "when" questions. When are harbingers of language lateralization first observed in human development? When does lateralized language emerge? When is the lateralization of language complete? At what later stage of life, if any, does lateralization begin to change?

Different answers to these "when" questions may be represented on a graph in which degree of language lateralization is plotted against the years of a person's life. The most parsimonious explanation, and the explanation that we have favored in the past is known as "invariant lateralization." Invariant lateralization can be depicted as a horizontal line, for example, as line "a" in **Figure 1**. According to this viewpoint, signs of lateralization are already present at the time of birth, and the magnitude of differences between left and right sides of the brain remains constant throughout the life span.

The alternative point of view, of course, is that lateralization changes across the life span. There are two variants of this "age-dependent lateralization" position. The first, known as progressive lateralization, could be represented graphically as a monotonic increase in lateralization from a symmetric base state at birth to the mature state of left-sided language. Traditionally, progressive lateralization has been claimed to continue from the beginning of language development until pubescence (Lenneberg, 1967). However, some clinical evidence indicates that language lateralization is completed by the age of 4 or 5 years. It has also been suggested that the process continues throughout the life span. Although the increase in lateralization over time need not be linear, we represent the three hypothetical patterns of progressive lateralization as straight lines (lines "b," "c," and "d") in **Figure 1**.

The other variant of age-dependent lateralization is what we might call lateralized degeneration. This variant concerns only senescence. The central idea is that the functions of one cerebral hemisphere deteriorate before the functions of the other hemisphere. Typically, because certain nonverbal abilities appear to decline at an earlier age than most verbal abilities, it is claimed that the right hemisphere is the first to deteriorate. By virtue of its later or more subtle deterioration, the left hemisphere progressively becomes more "dominant" during the period of cognitive decline. This possibility is depicted as line "e"

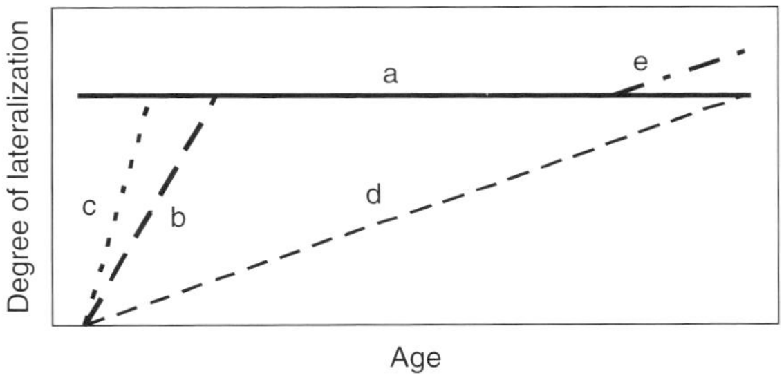

Figure 1 Curve "a" depicts the developmental invariance model, which posits that the left hemisphere is specialized for language at the time of birth or even prior to birth. The model predicts early emergence of lateralized precursors of language, and no increase or decrease in the degree of lateralization during development. The lateralization-by-puberty model is represented by curve "b", and the lateralization-by-five-years model is represented by curve "c". Both models exemplify progressive lateralization, in which the bilateral symmetry of infant's brain gradually develops into the lateralized adult state. Curve "d" represents a form of progressive lateralization in which the brain continues to become more strongly lateralized during maturity and even into senescence. The progressive degeneration model is represented by curve "e". According to this model, the functions of one hemisphere (usually the right) deteriorate more rapidly than the functions of the other, thus accentuating any differences between hemispheres.

in **Figure 1**. Asymmetry of deterioration is logically independent of asymmetric development and may be combined with any previous pattern of lateralization.

We begin with a brief summary of the empirical evidence regarding the genesis of hemispheric specialization. We consider (1) brain anatomy, (2) electrophysiological findings, (3) behavioral asymmetries, and (4) clinical evidence. We emphasize language lateralization but the coverage will by necessity be broader. We conclude the first part of the chapter by summarizing evidence that concerns differential decline.

In the second part of the chapter, we discuss complexities that make it difficult to interpret the available evidence. The emphasis then will shift from "when" questions to "what" questions. What do the early asymmetries mean? Exactly what is lateralized? What is the relationship between language lateralization and the skill with which language is used?

Box 1 Will brain imaging resolve questions about lateralization?

Do methods drive science? The history of lateralization studies suggests that this may be so. From the early nineteenth to mid-twentieth century, functional differences between the human hemispheres were inferred primarily from lesion studies. Though enormously informative, this method addressed mainly the binary question: is a function affected by left- or by right-sided damage? Twentieth century technologies such as electroencephalography, commissurotomy, and Wada test enabled more refined questions.

Functional imaging techniques herald a new era for lateralization studies. Most functional imaging studies thus far only confirm what is already known through other methods, but even this corroboration serves to solidify and elaborate earlier findings and also to validate the imaging methods themselves. Nonetheless, the new imaging technologies will permit researchers to examine more complex and refined propositions about lateralization. Two studies illustrate this prospect.

Liégeois et al. (2004) used functional magnetic resonance imaging (fMRI) to monitor the re-organization of language in children following early left-hemisphere damage. They found that children with lesions in or near the anterior language region continued to use the left hemisphere for expressive language. Unexpectedly, language was more likely to shift to the right hemisphere if the lesion in the left hemisphere was remote from classical language areas.

Reuter-Lorenz et al. (2000) used positron emission tomography (PET) to illuminate age-related changes in the lateralization of verbal and nonverbal working memory. Instead of the expected differential left (verbal) versus right (spatial) frontal lateralization as seen in young adults, the PET evidence for older participants indicated bilateral frontal activation for both spatial and verbal rehearsal.

The rapidly growing corpus of functional imaging studies points to progressive refinement in the answers that can be obtained, and in the models of cortical functioning that will result. It becomes possible to study differences between hemispheres simultaneously with differences within each hemisphere.

Liégeois, F., Connelly, A., Cross, J. H., Boyd, S.G., Gadian, D.G., Vargha-Khadem, F., & Baldeweg, T. (2004). Language reorganization in children with early-onset lesions of the left hemisphere: An fMRI study. Brain, 127, 1229–1236.

Reuter-Lorenz, P.A., Jonides, J., Smith, E.E., Hartley, A., Miller, A., Marshuetz, C., & Koeppe, R.A. (2000). Age differences in the frontal lateralization of verbal and spatial working memory revealed by PET. Journal of Cognitive Neuroscience, 12, 174–187.

Brain Development

Assertions about invariant or progressive lateralization are based on evidence of brain asymmetries during different stages of development. The evidence comprises anatomical, electrophysiological, behavioral, and clinical data.

Brain Anatomy

Asymmetries in the immature brain. Several anatomical asymmetries have been found in the neonatal brain (Spreen et al., 1995). These findings contradict the previously held belief that the two cerebral hemispheres in infancy are morphologically identical or nearly so. Asymmetries in some cerebral regions can be attributed to more widely spaced cortical columns on the larger side (Buxhoeveden & Casanova, 2000), but whether cortical volume is an index of any functional characteristic that differs between hemispheres remains to be established. One can only conclude that some of the anatomical asymmetries that characterize the adult human brain are neither absent nor less marked in the infant brain. A similar conclusion applies to the anticlockwise torque that is manifested as a wider frontal lobe on the right side and a greater anterior extension of the right frontal lobe, coupled with a wider posterior left hemisphere and a greater posterior extension of the left hemisphere. Irrespective of its functional significance, if any, in the adult human brain, a similar torque is observed in the immature human brain as well as in the ape brain.

Maturational gradients. Perhaps anatomical disparities between the hemispheres reflect differences in the rate of growth. However, findings are not unanimous as to which hemisphere grows more rapidly. The putative left-to-right gradient of an earlier era was superseded by subsequent evidence that the right cerebral cortex in fact develops more rapidly than the left, which is now commonly believed.

A difference between the maturation rates of the two hemispheres is but one aspect of brain development, and it may not be more important than other maturational gradients. In an attempt to consolidate all available data on the rate at which different brain regions mature, Best (1988) proposed a growth vector representing the resultant of four developmental dimensions: right-to-left, anterior-to-posterior, primary-to-secondary-to-tertiary, and basal-to-cortical. In addition, within each cerebral hemisphere, there are regional patterns in the development of myelination, in neuronal, dendritic, and axonal density, and in the width of different cortical layers.

Electrophysiological Evidence

A substantial body of evidence indicates that electrophysiological asymmetries are present in infancy. Much of this evidence has been reviewed by Molfese and Betz (1988) and by Segalowitz and Berge (1994). Numerous studies have shown consistent differences between the infant's hemispheres in electrophysiological responses to specific speech cues. Event-related potentials (ERPs) indicate that differences in voice onset time (e.g., the difference between "ba" and "pa") elicit an initial response from both hemispheres, followed by a response from the right hemisphere alone. Differences in place of articulation (e.g., the difference between "ba" and "ga") elicit a left-hemisphere response that is followed by a bilateral response. The ERP findings for infants are similar-but not identical- to those for adults.

Behavioral Evidence

Head turning and postural asymmetry. Whether turning spontaneously or in response to stimulation, most infants turn their heads to the right more often than to the left. This rightward bias is one of the earliest behavioral asymmetries to be manifested by the neonate, and it has been linked both to parental handedness and to the infant's subsequent hand preference.

When the infant is placed on his or her back with the head turned to one side, the arm and foot on that side often are extended, and the contralateral arm and foot are flexed. This so-called asymmetric tonic neck reflex (ATNR) occurs in the newborn infant and persists for at least the first 3 months of life, but certain aspects change during that time (Liederman, 1987). For instance, the ATNR is more evident in the legs of newborns than in their arms, whereas the opposite pattern is observed in infants older than 3 weeks. In infants between the ages of 3 and 10 weeks, head-turns to the nonpreferred side are more likely to elicit the ATNR than are head-turns to the preferred side, but this may not apply to neonates. Whether the predominant direction of the ATNR predicts subsequent handedness is a matter of dispute although, as noted previously, head turning by itself seems to bear a relationship to subsequent manual asymmetries.

Motor activity. Early indications of hand preference are of special interest because of theoretical and empirical links between handedness and language lateralization in the adult (e.g., Knecht et al., 2000; Annett, 2002). Unfortunately, the literature is replete with unresolved conceptual and methodological issues and seemingly inconsistent findings. Much of the evidence supports (Liederman's 1983) contention that most infant behavior is dominated by the left hemisphere and right hand. For instance, most infants hold objects for a longer time with the right hand than with the left hand, and most infants prefer the right hand for a variety of target-related actions that are performed during the first few months of life. A hand preference for unimanual manipulation of objects develops between the ages of 5 and 7 months, and a hand preference in tasks requiring bimanual manipulation develops by the age of 1 year.

Perception. Studies of auditory perception provide some of the most convincing evidence of early functional asymmetries. This evidence has been summarized by Best (1988). Using dishabituation paradigms to determine infants' ability to discriminate between two speech sounds, investigators have demonstrated an early right-ear advantage (REA) for detection of transitions between consonants (e.g., /ma/ to /da/) and a left-ear advantage (LEA) for transitions in musical timbre (for example, cello to bassoon). For instance, Best et al. observed an REA for speech syllables and an LEA for musical stimuli in infants 3 months of age and older. Although an LEA for musical stimuli was found in 2-month-old infants, a corresponding REA for speech perception has not been reported below the age of 3 months.

A study based on a novel behavioral method suggests that a speech-related brain asymmetry is present even in short-gestation infants. Using limb movements as a measure of immaturity, Segalowitz and Chapman (1980) found that repeated exposure to speech, but not to music, caused a disproportionate reduction of right-arm tremor in infants with an average gestational age of 36 weeks. This was taken as evidence that speech affected the left side of the brain more than the right side.

Other investigators have observed that neonates turn more often to the right than to the left when exposed to speech sounds. MacKain et al. (1983) reported that 6-month-old infants detect the synchronization of visual (articulatory) and aural components of adults' speech, but only when the adult is positioned to the infant's right. These findings suggest that speech sounds bias orientation to the right side of space, presumably because the left side of the infant's brain is more responsive than the right side to speech-specific activation. This language-specific asymmetry appears to complement a more pervasive left-hemisphere prepotency that biases orientation to the right.

Childhood laterality. In a review of auditory, visual, tactual, and dual-task laterality studies involving children between the ages of 2 and 12 years, Hiscock (1988) found no consistent evidence of age-related increases in laterality. Irrespective of the modality tested or the method employed, cross-sectional studies typically reveal the expected asymmetries in the youngest children tested,

Box 2 Measuring asymmetries and age differences in asymmetries: How hard can it be?

Kolb and Whishaw (2003) summarize attempts by different researchers to measure differences between the size of people's left and right feet. The upshot is that something as seemingly straightforward as measuring foot length may lead to disparate results. If so, how difficult might it be to measure differences between the structure or the functions of left and right regions of the brain?

The situation often becomes even more challenging when one compares groups. Consider the challenge of comparing the performance of younger and older children on a verbal dichotic listening test. Maybe the average 5-year-old reports 30% of left-ear words and 40% of right-ear words, whereas the average 10-year-old reports 60% of left-ear words and 80% of right-ear words. The REA is 10 percentage points for the 5-year-olds and 20 percentage points for the 10-year-olds. Yet, the ear differences are identical in magnitude if calculated as proportions of the overall score. The 10-year-olds are more asymmetric by one calculation but not by the other.

This scaling problem is sometimes compounded by floor and ceiling effects. Many laterality researchers have responded by using mathematical transformations (laterality indices) that adjust difference scores for the overall level of performance. Regrettably, no transformation is entirely neutral or applicable to all data (Kinsbourne & Byrd, 1985). Some investigators eschew parametric data analyses in favor of less informative alternatives such as tabulating the proportion of individuals in each age group who show an REA. We advocate a third approach that entails selecting two transformations that would be expected to bias the results in opposite directions (Kinsbourne & Hiscock, 1983). If both transformations lead to congruent results, the data can be interpreted accordingly. If not, the findings are considered inconclusive with regard to age-group differences.

Kinsbourne, M., & Byrd, M. (1985). Word load and visual hemifield shape recognition: Priming and interference effects. In M.I. Posner & O.S.M. Marin (Eds.), Mechanisms of attention: Attention and performance XI (pp. 529-543). Hillsdale, NJ: Erlbaum.

Kinsbourne, M., & Hiscock, M. (1983). The normal and deviant development of functional lateralization of the brain. In M.M. Haith & J.J. Campos (Eds.), Handbook of Child Psychology, Infancy and Developmental Psychobiology (Vol. 2, 4th edn, pp. 157-280). New York: Wiley.

Kolb, B., & Whishaw, I.Q. (2003). Fundamentals of human neuropsychology (5th edn). New York: Worth.

and those asymmetries are comparable in magnitude to the asymmetries found in older children.

Though few longitudinal studies of the REA for linguistic stimuli have been published, the results are similar to results from cross-sectional studies. When an age-related increase (or decrease) in laterality is observed, the change seems to reflect either the noisiness of the data or extraneous factors that covary with age. For example, a large-scale longitudinal study by Morris et al. (1984) yielded different developmental patterns of ear asymmetry for different subsamples. The authors attributed this variability to the lack of experimental control that is inherent in the free-report dichotic listening method.

Even if laterality remains invariant across the childhood years, a quantitative difference conceivably could exist between the asymmetry of children and of adults. However, direct comparisons of children and adults on dichotic listening tasks have not revealed any consistent difference in the magnitude of the REA.

Clinical Evidence

The literature on childhood aphasia, hemispherectomy, and recovery of function has been reviewed by a number of authors (e.g., Spreen et al., 1995; Bates et al., 1999; Vargha-Khadem, 2001). Even though the hypothesis of progressive lateralization drew much of its support from cases of aphasia in children following right-hemispheric lesions, the preponderance of evidence now suggests that persistent aphasia consequent to unilateral right-hemisphere damage is as infrequent in children as in adults.

Studies of cognitive functioning following unilateral lesions that use quantitative measures are limited by a reliance on IQ and academic achievement tests, which constitute neither sensitive nor comprehensive measures of linguistic and visuo-perceptual functioning. Such measures are not optimal for differentiating between left- and right-sided lesions. Despite this handicap, several studies do show associations between left-sided damage and verbal impairments, and between right-sided damage and nonverbal impairments. Some studies suggest that the effects of unilateral lesions are less selective when the damage is prenatal or perinatal than when it occurs later in development (Vargha-Khadem, 2001). Nonetheless, even unilateral brain lesions of prenatal or perinatal origin can lead to differential impairment of verbal and nonverbal functions. The development of expressive language, in particular, appears to be vulnerable to early left-sided brain damage (Bates et al., 1999).

The implications of hemispherectomy performed at different ages are difficult to specify, mainly because of extraneous factors that confound comparisons between hemispherectomy in children and in adults, but also because of the inferential limitations of small-sample and single-case studies. If any conclusion is justified by the available hemispherectomy evidence, it is that the right hemisphere of children exhibits an impressive ability to support "aspects of everyday verbal communication" when the left hemisphere is compromised (Devlin et al., 2003).

Changes Associated with Aging

Does the seemingly stable lateralization of the brain in early and middle adulthood change in senescence? The answer to this question is informed by studies of normal aging as well as by clinical studies.

Normal Aging

Physiological changes. Autopsy studies reveal no obvious predominance of neuropathology in either the left or the right hemisphere of the elderly (Esiri, 1994). Studies based on PET scanning report nearly identical levels of glucose metabolism in the left and right cerebral cortices and in the left and right basal ganglia of healthy elderly subjects. A study of 100 postmortem brains revealed comparable age-related decreases in cerebral volume within the left and right hemispheres (Witelson et al., 2006).

Behavioral changes. Various psychometric data, typically cross-sectional, establish that certain kinds of tasks are more prone than others to show age-related declines in average performance. The selectivity of decline is often interpreted as evidence that the right hemisphere deteriorates sooner or more precipitously than the left. For instance, scores on the performance (nonverbal) subtests of the Wechsler Adult Intelligence Scale decline more rapidly with increasing age than do scores on the verbal subtests. Much of this differential decline can be attributed to a cohort effect that affects nonverbal tests more strongly than verbal tests (Flynn, 2006). Nevertheless, a differential decrement of verbal and nonverbal skills has been confirmed by longitudinal data, which are not susceptible to cohort effects. Similarly, tests of "fluid" intelligence-the ability to solve problems requiring novel information and strategies-are more likely to show agerelated changes than are tests of "crystallized" intelligence-the ability to utilize previously acquired knowledge and strategies. Again, this pattern is frequently attributed to a greater deterioration of right-hemisphere functioning. Age-related decline in average performance on some tests of fluid intelligence is quite marked. On Raven's standard progressive matrices, an untimed test that contains seemingly novel problems, a raw score at the 50th percentile for 18-year-olds falls at the 95th percentile for 65-year-olds. Much of that difference, however, can be attributed to a cohort effect rather than to cognitive deterioration over time, and even the portion attributable to deterioration does not necessarily reflect asymmetrical deterioration.

Two of the most salient cognitive deficits observed among the elderly are reduced speed of processing (van Gorp et al., 1990) and reduced ability to perform complex or difficult tasks (Crossley & Hiscock, 1992). It is uncertain whether these deficits represent separate limitations or different manifestations of the same limitation. Furthermore, it remains to be established that either deficit implicates the deterioration of one hemisphere more than the other.

Clinical Evidence

Dementia. Alzheimer's disease (AD), especially early-onset AD, often affects object naming, spontaneous speech, and praxis. Although attributable to left-hemisphere disease, these deficits simply may be more noticeable than deficits associated with right-hemisphere disease. Right-hemispheric symptoms such as spatial confusion are also seen frequently. AD patients do not constitute a homogeneous group for laterality studies. Even though some individuals initially may exhibit cognitive profiles suggestive of asymmetric dysfunction, either hemisphere may be the more severely affected. Ultimately the pathology becomes diffuse and bilateral.

Aphasia. The relative incidence of different aphasia types appears to shift as a function of age. Expressive disorders and mixed aphasias (i.e., nonfluent speech with moderately impaired comprehension) predominate throughout the life span, but particularly during the first three decades of life. The incidence of global aphasia begins to rise in the fourth decade, and sensory (fluent) aphasias become relatively common during the seventh decade. These age-related shifts might be attributable to a gradually increasing degree of lateralization and focal brain organization: An initially bilateral and diffuse language substrate becomes unilateral and focal over time, with expressive functions lateralizing before receptive functions. Alternatively, the changing incidence rates might reflect regional changes in vulnerability to cerebral disease, changes in compensatory ability (i.e., in plasticity), or other variables.

Interpretive Complexities

The presence or absence of age-related changes in language lateralization is an old question that has attracted a large amount of research and clinical observation. Accordingly, a large corpus of relevant evidence has been accumulated. The evidence, as we have already seen, is often ambiguous. Some of the sources of ambiguity are discussed below.

General Problems in Studying Life-Span Development

Developmental patterns must be constructed. The ideal study of change across the life span would begin at conception and then continue longitudinally through successive stages of life. As a rule, the scientific examination of ontogenetic change in humans does not conform to this ideal but instead begins with the mature organism. As interesting characteristics are observed and investigated in the adult, certain development questions invariably arise. At what stage of development does this attribute become manifest? What are the mechanisms responsible for the emergence the characteristic? To what extent is the attribute influenced by exogenous or endogenous environmental factors? What evolutionary advantage, if any, is bestowed by the characteristic? How does the attribute change as the organism approaches the end of its life trajectory? Studies of young or middle-aged adults are then extended downward to infants and children, and upward to the elderly.

Life-span studies are constrained by methodological limitations. Unfortunately, the methods used with young or middle-aged adults often are not feasible for use with children or elderly people. Visual (tachistoscopic) experiments in which letters or words are presented to one visual half-field cannot be used with infants or young children who cannot read. Most elderly people can read, of course, but their ability to perform a visual task may be compromised by impairments of visual acuity. Dichotic listening is also problematic. Infant researchers have used habituation-dishabituation paradigms to study asymmetries of auditory perception in infants, and some of the infant studies have shown an REA for language sounds. Infant studies of this kind are difficult to do, however, and results will vary with the physiological and psychological state of the infant at the time of testing. It is especially difficult to test 1- and 2-year-olds, for whom infant methods are inappropriate and methods designed for older children may be unsatisfactory. Dichotic studies have been done successfully with 3-, 4-, and 5-year-olds, but even children in this age range do not respond well to the standard dichotic listening tests that are used with school-age children and adults. The elderly are difficult to assess because hearing impairment is common in older adults. fMRI is difficult to use with young children, but other functional imaging techniques (e.g., magnetic source imaging and functional transcranial Doppler sonography) seem to be more feasible.

Problems Related to the Study of Language Lateralization

Brain lateralization is an abstraction. The majority of adults have speech-related regions of cerebral cortex that are larger on the left hemisphere than on the right hemisphere (Dorsaint-Pierre et al., 2006). The majority of humans also are more skilled with the right hand than with the left and more likely to report linguistic signals from the right ear than from the left ear when the signals are presented in dichotic competition. Although there is reason to believe that different asymmetries may be correlated, associations among them are not strong nor are they universal (e.g., Knecht et al., 2000; Dorsaint-Pierre et al., 2006; Fernandes et al., 2006). What asymmetry best represents lateralization? Does any specific asymmetry adequately represent lateralization?

The loose association among different asymmetries illustrates two fundamental points. First, one must distinguish lateralization of the brain from specific manifestations of lateralization. Neuroanatomical asymmetry, handedness, and ear asymmetry are manifestations of a lateralized nervous system, but none is synonymous with lateralization. Lateralization is a construct, which is to say, an artifact. Nature may reveal concrete and specific markers of lateralization, such as handedness, but it is researchers who infer the existence of lateralization. The second truth is that none of the markers is definitive. Some may be better proxies than others, perhaps because they lend themselves to more precise measurement, but none is ideal. The implication of this distinction between construct and manifestations is that lateralized language may mean different things to different people.

It is not easy to specify what is lateralized. As Kinsbourne (1984) has pointed out, neuropsychologists have been more successful in specifying where functions are localized than in specifying the functions that are localized. The dichotomy between "what" and "where" underlies many of the most difficult questions concerning life-span development of hemispheric specialization. A misplaced emphasis on the question of "where" has led to disagreement about the lateralization of functions that are only vaguely defined. For instance, some dichotic listening tasks tap processes that are primarily auditory or phonetic, whereas others involve semantic and mnemonic processing. As a rule, however, investigators have assumed that a particular category of stimuli, such as digit names, represents the full spectrum of linguistic material.

Luria (1973) addressed this problem when he emphasized that the development of a new perceptual or motor skill entails first consolidating isolated elements of the function into an integrated and automatized series of elements and then linking the integrated elements into a network of superordinate functions. Luria made it clear that lesion studies cannot reveal the localization of a mental process unless the structure of the process is understood. Much of the research on age-related change in functional lateralization violates this basic Lurian caveat: Investigators have attempted to lateralize a function or set of functions without any independent knowledge as to how the functions are organized.

Processing asymmetries must be distinguished from activation asymmetries. Only in the ideal case would the pattern of regional brain activation match precisely an individual's cortical localization scheme. Once laterality of activation is distinguished from lateralized representation of various cortical functions (Segalowitz & Berge, 1994), it follows that age-related changes in one aspect of lateralization may be dissociated from changes in the other aspect. For example, markedly asymmetric activation in a patient with AD need not imply a corresponding shift of cortical functions to the more activated side. The asymmetry of activation may instead indicate that the locus of activation and locus of processing are not the same.

Change in lateralization is different from change in the microstructure of an activity. New components of a task may materialize as a consequence of maturation or practice, or existing components may become automatized. In addition, increasing proficiency might entail restructuring a task, as when material-appropriate strategies enhance reading. Other changes in task structure-compensatory as well as deleterious-presumably occur in senescence. Whenever there is an age-related change in the lateralization of an activity, it will be important to establish whether that change reflects a shifting brain basis for a fixed set of task components or a shifting set of task components.

Specialization versus plasticity. It is essential to distinguish between decreasing bilaterality of function (evidence of which might be found in normal children) and decreasing equipotentiality (which would be manifested only as differential outcomes following focal brain injury sustained at different ages). Failures to make that distinction have added confusion to the literature on childhood lateralization. The same problem is encountered when behavioral changes at the other end of the life span are being interpreted. A developmental shift toward bilateralization of a previously unilateral function is different in principle from deterioration of the unilateral function.

Individual- and population-level asymmetries. If evidence continues to support the existence of hemisphere-selective deficits in some patients with AD, it will be important to know whether the disease process itself is asymmetrical in those patients (at least, in the early stages of the disease), or whether the behavioral consequences of an invariably bilateral degenerative process depend on certain premorbid characteristics of the patient. Either answer would contribute significantly to our understanding of AD, but neither answer would support a claim that the left and right hemispheres-at the level of the population-are differentially vulnerable.

The implications of asymmetry are unclear. Failure to develop normal language skills often has been attributed either to an inadequate degree of lateralization or a deficiency in left-hemispheric function. Apparently neither explanation is correct. In a longitudinal study of children from birth until the age of 5 years, Molfese and Molfese (1997) found that individual differences in ERP recorded in the neonate could predict performance on language tests 5 years later. However, prediction did not depend entirely on lefthemisphere ERP. Electrical responses from both hemispheres contributed to the prediction of later language functioning. In another longitudinal study, Guttorm et al. (2005) similarly found a significant correlation between ERP to linguistic stimuli in neonates and measures of receptive language skill at the age of 2.5 years. In this study, it was right-hemisphere ERP that predicted receptive language ability. Lefthemisphere ERP predicted verbal memory at the age of 5 years.

Other evidence calls into question the notion of a specific association between brain lateralization and language. Indications of lateralization sometimes are found in the absence of language, and language sometimes is accompanied by bilateral brain activity. Vallortigara (2006) points out that, in various nonhuman species, the left side of the brain is specialized for processing complex auditory signals. Lateralized ERPs to speech cues have been recorded in dogs and rhesus monkeys, prompting Molfese and Betz (1988) to suggest that the critical difference between humans and nonhumans with respect to speech discrimination is reflected not by lateralized ERP components but instead by bilateral components that have been not been found in monkeys and dogs. The right hemisphere is implicated further in language processing by fMRI evidence indicating that bilingual adults have more bilateral and diffuse activation patterns when listening to their second language than when listening to their primary language (e.g., Dehaene et al., 1997).

Differential loss of skills does not necessarily mean differential deterioration of the cerebral hemispheres. The available evidence concerning cognitive changes during aging establishes only that certain measures-especially reaction time and dual-task performance-are more prone than others to show age-related declines in average performance. Even the widely accepted principle that fluid intelligence deteriorates more rapidly than crystallized intelligence remains open to question (van Gorp et al., 1990). Longitudinal data reveal that the rate of cognitive decline varies markedly among individuals.

Witelson et al. (2006) studied the postmortem brains of 100 individuals of known IQ. The correlation between postmortem cerebral volume and verbal IQ was +.51 for right-handed women and +.62 for right-handed men. The correlations were comparable irrespective of hemisphere. Moreover, there was a striking sex difference in the relationship between age and brain volume. Irrespective of hemisphere, brain volume decreased significantly with age in men but not in women. When considered together, the data present a peculiar pattern. Regardless of whether brain volume decreases with age (as in men) or does not change with age (as in women), verbal IQ-which is related to brain volume in both men and women-remains constant. Findings such as these are difficult to reconcile with any simple principle for relating the decline of cognitive ability to differential left- and right-hemisphere deterioration or even to concurrent deterioration of both hemispheres.

Challenges and Future Directions

Brain functions change over the life span as a consequence of maturation, experience, and disease, and those functional changes sometimes are associated with detectable re-organization of the neural substrate. Language is not exempt from this general principle. Only a dynamic substrate would support the acquisition of various culturally specified languages (sometimes in the same brain) and the idiosyncratic modification of those languages during the course of a person's life. Language representation is not hard-wired to the degree that destruction of the relevant left-hemispheric circuitry would always preclude the development or recovery of language. On the contrary, clinical evidence from various sources attests to the resilience of language in the aftermath of left-hemisphere damage, especially when the damage occurs pre- or perinatally.

Yet, the preponderance of evidence from studies of normal brains suggests that the lateralization of language ordinarily does not change during one's life. In the absence of pathology, language representation remains primarily lefthemispheric in the great majority of humans. Lateralized language is the default state, but insults to the brain under some circumstances may cause some or all components of language to be shifted to the opposite side. Neural plasticity allows the default state to be altered.

An obvious challenge, therefore, is to understand plasticity with respect to different facets of language, how plasticity itself changes across the life span, and the circumstances under which it results in interhemispheric (rather than merely intrahemispheric) re-organization of the neural substrate. Three contrasting models of life-span changes in plasticity are depicted in **Figure 2**. Curve "a" represents the capacity for new learning, or fluid intelligence, which may begin its gentle decline before the end of the third decade. Curve "b" depicts a gradual decline in plasticity with respect to various aspects of language that could account for the clinical observations on which the Lenneberg (1967) hypothesis rested. The decline in plasticity between language onset and pubescence commonly was misinterpreted as progressive lateralization. Curve "c" depicts a rapid decrease in plasticity between the perinatal period and the first birthday. This pattern is consistent with evidence indicating that the right hemisphere can support relatively normal development of expressive language only if the left hemisphere is damaged during the prenatal or perinatal period.

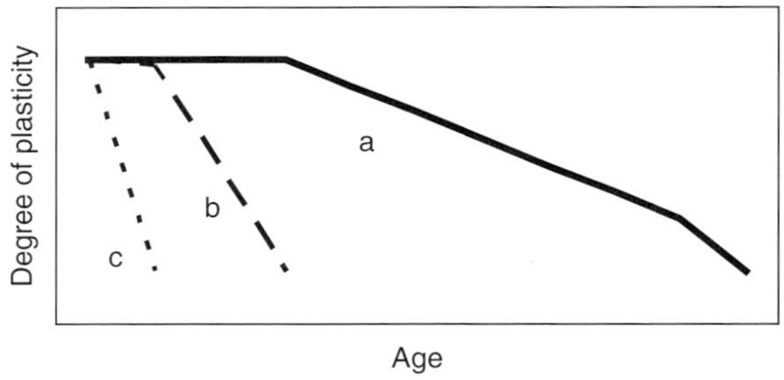

Figure 2 Curve "a" depicts a conventional model of plasticity, in which overall capacity for learning remains at a maximum for a number of years (perhaps until the end of the third decade), after which it begins to decline gradually. Curve "b", which may pertain to certain automatized phonological aspects of language, indicates a shorter period of maximal learning capacity (ending by pubescence), which is followed by a rapid decline in plasticity with respect to those aspects of language. Curve "c" depicts a decline in plasticity that begins prior to birth, and perhaps as soon as the neurons of the cerebral cortex begin to establish connections. This model corresponds to evidence of impaired expressive speech development in individuals who sustained left-hemisphere damage during the prenatal or perinatal stages.

Developmental invariance of lateralization, coupled with developmentally decreasing plasticity, has served as a broad heuristic device over the past few decades. Findings from a variety of experimental and clinical studies support this combination of concepts. To an increasing extent, structural and functional imaging techniques will enable researchers to ask more detailed and sophisticated questions about plasticity with respect to different components of language and the factors that determine whether some or all of those components will move to the opposite hemisphere following damage to the language-dominant hemisphere. Imaging studies will also be useful in addressing two other important questions that we have raised in this chapter: (1) the potential incongruence between the cortical substrate of language and the subcortical mechanism that differentially activates the left and right hemispheres; and (2) the causes and consequences of individual differences in language lateralization and plasticity.

References

Annett, M (2002). *Handedness and brain asymmetry: The right shift theory.* Hove, East Sussex, UK: Psychology Press.

Bates, E, Vicari, S, and Trauner, D (1999). Neural mediation of language development: Perspectives from lesion studies of infants and children. In: Tager-Flusberg, H (ed.) *Neurodevelopmental disorders*, pp. 533–581. Cambridge, MA: MIT Press.

Best, CT (1988). The emergence of cerebral asymmetries in early human development: A literature review and a neuroembryological model. In: Molfese, DL and Segalowitz, SJ (eds.) *Brain lateralization in children: Developmental implications*, pp. 5–34. New York: Guilford.

Buxhoeveden, D and Casanova, M (2000). Comparative lateralisation patterns in the language area of human, chimpanzee, and rhesus monkey brains. *Laterality* 5: 315–330.

Crossley, M and Hiscock, M (1992). Age-related differences in concurrenttask performance of normal adults: Evidence for a decline in processing resources. *Psychology and Aging* 7: 499–506.

Dehaene, S, Dupoux, E, Mehler, J, Cohen, L, Paulesu, E, Perani, D, et al. (1997). Anatomical variability in the cortical representation of first and second language. *Neuroreport* 8: 3809–3815.

Devlin, AM, Cross, JH, Harkness, W, Chong, WK, Harding, B, Vargha-Khadem, F, and Neville, BGR (2003). Clinical outcomes of hemispherectomy for epilepsy in childhood and adolescence. *Brain* 126: 556–566.

Dorsaint-Pierre, R, Penhune, VB, Watkins, KE, Neelin, P, Lerch, JP, Bouffard, M, and Zatorre, RJ (2006). Asymmetries of the planum temporale and Heschl's gyrus: Relationship to language lateralization. *Brain* 129: 1164–1176.

Esiri, MM (1994). Dementia and normal aging: Neuropathology. In: Huppert, FA, Brayne, C, and O'Connor, DW (eds.) *Dementia and normal aging*, pp. 385–436. Cambridge, UK: Cambridge University Press.

Fernandes, MA, Smith, ML, Logan, W, Crawley, A, and McAndrews, MP (2006). Comparing language lateralization determined by dichotic listening and fMRI activation in frontal and temporal lobes in children with epilepsy. *Brain and Language* 96: 106–114.

Flynn, JR (2006). Tethering the elephant: Capital cases, IQ, and the Flynn effect. *Psychology, Public Policy, and Law* 12: 170–189.
Guttorm, TK, Leppänen, PHT, Poikkeus, A-M Eklund, KM, Lyytinen, P, and Lyytinen, H (2005). Brain event-related potentials (ERPs) measured at birth predict later language development in children with and without familial risk for dyslexia. *Cortex* 41: 291–303.
Hiscock, M (1988). Behavioral asymmetries in normal children. In: Molfese, DL and Segalowitz, SJ (eds.) *Brain lateralization in children: Developmental implications*, pp. 85–169. New York: Guilford.
Kinsbourne, M (1984). *Why is neuropsychology progressing so slowly? Contemporary Psychology* 29: 793–794.
Knecht, S, Drager, B, Deppe, M, Bobe, L, Lohmann, H, Floel, A, Ringelstein, EB, and Henningsen, H (2000). Handedness and hemispheric language dominance in healthy humans. *Brain* 123: 2512–2518.
Lenneberg, E (1967). *Biological foundations of language*. New York: Wiley.
Liederman, J (1983). Mechanisms underlying instability in the development of hand preference. In: Young, G, Segalowitz, S, Corter, C, and Trehub, S (eds.) *Manual specialization and the developing brain*, pp. 71–92. New York: Academic Press.
Liederman, J (1987). Neonates show an asymmetric degree of head rotation but lack an asymmetric tonic neck reflex asymmetry: Neuropsychological implications. *Developmental Neuropsychology* 3: 101–112.
Luria, AR (1973). *The working brain: An introduction to neuropsychology*. New York: Basic Books. (B. Haigh, Trans.).
MacKain, K, Studdert-Kennedy, M, Spieker, S, and Stern, D (1983). Infant intermodal speech perception is a left hemisphere function. *Science* 214: 1347–1349.
Molfese, DL and Betz, JC (1988). Electrophysiological indices of the early development of lateralization for language and cognition, and their implications for predicting later development. In: Molfese, DL and Segalowitz, SJ (eds.) *Brain lateralization in children*, pp. 171–190. New York: Guilford.
Molfese, DL and Molfese, VJ (1997). Discrimination of language skills at five years of age using event-related potentials recorded at birth. *Developmental Neuropsychology* 13: 135–156.
Morris, R, Bakker, D, Satz, P, and Van der Vlugt, H (1984). Dichotic listening ear asymmetry: Patterns of longitudinal development. *Brain and Language* 22: 49–66.
Segalowitz, SJ and Berge, BEM (1994). Functional asymmetries in infancy and early childhood: A review of electrophysiologic studies and their implications. In: Davidson, RJ and Hugdahl, K (eds.) *Brain asymmetry*, pp. 579–615. Cambridge, MA: MIT Press.
Segalowitz, SJ and Chapman, JS (1980). Cerebral asymmetry for speech in neonates: A behavioral measure. *Brain and Language* 9: 281–288.
Spreen, O, Risser, AH, and Edgell, D (1995). *Developmental neuropsychology*. New York: Oxford University Press.
Vallortigara, G (2006). Cerebral lateralization: A common theme in the organization of the vertebrate brain. *Cortex* 42: 5–7.
Van Gorp, WG, Satz, P, and Mitrushina, M (1990). Neuropsychological processes associated with normal aging. *Developmental Neuropsychology* 6: 279–290.
Vargha-Khadem, F (2001). Generalized versus selective cognitive impairments resulting from brain damage sustained in childhood. *Epilepsia* 42(Suppl. 1): 37–40.
Witelson, SF, Beresh, H, and Kigar, DL (2006). Intelligence and brain size in 100 postmortem brains: Sex, lateralization and age factors. *Brain* 129: 386–398.

Further Reading

Bates, E, Vicari, S, and Trauner, D (1999). Neural mediation of language development: Perspectives from lesion studies of infants and children. In: Tager-Flusberg, H (ed.) *Neurodevelopmental disorders*, pp. 533–581. Cambridge, MA: MIT Press.
A scholarly review and interpretation of the extensive literature concerning effects of early brain lesions on different facets of language development.
Hiscock, M and Kinsbourne, M (1995). Phylogeny and ontogeny of cerebral lateralization. In: Davidson, RJ and Hugdahl, K (eds.) *Brain asymmetry*, pp. 535–578. Cambridge, MA: MIT Press.
A detailed critique of the claim that the lateralized brain of the adult human represents the culmination of phylogenetic and ontogenetic progressions from simple and symmetric to complex and asymmetric nervous systems.
Martins, IP (1997). Childhood aphasias. *Clinical Neuroscience* 4: 773–777.
A succinct review of the literature on childhood aphasia.
Van Gorp, WG, Satz, P, and Mitrushina, M (1990). Neuropsychological processes associated with normal aging. *Developmental Neuropsychology* 6: 279–290.
This cross-sectional study of 57- to 85-year-olds indicates that age-related decline in neuropsychological test performance is related to demand for processing speed rather than to specific task content.

Lexical Impairments Following Brain Injury

R. Casas and D. Tranel, University of Iowa, Iowa City, IA, USA

Lexical retrieval, which refers to the ability to retrieve words, is an essential component of language communication. Production of an appropriate word for a given stimulus involves activation of multiple processes in the brain. Damage to brain areas associated with the processes involved in lexical retrieval can lead to naming deficits that disrupt fluent speech, which can greatly encumber an individual's ability to communicate. Such impairments are common sequelae of brain injury and thus are an important topic of clinical and scientific inquiry. The types of brain injuries that commonly lead to impairments in lexical retrieval include stroke, head injury, surgical resection to treat pharmacoresistant epilepsy (left temporal lobectomy), and degenerative diseases that have a proclivity for left hemisphere regions important for lexical retrieval (including Pick's disease and Alzheimer's disease). This article summarizes the nature and types of lexical impairments that can occur as a result of damage to specific brain areas.

Deficits in lexical retrieval refer to the inability to provide names for things such as concrete entities (typically named by nouns), actions (typically named by verbs), or spatial relationships (typically named by prepositions). Defined as 'anomia' in the medical and scientific literature, lexical retrieval impairments are a frequent part of the symptom complex that characterizes patients with aphasia. In general, aphasia can be defined as an acquired disturbance of the comprehension and formulation of verbal messages following damage to language-related brain structures (typically in the left hemisphere). Lexical retrieval, which requires the capacity to retrieve a particular word to designate an entity or event at the appropriate level of specificity, is different from the ability to recognize the entity or event. Whereas 'naming' refers specifically to knowing what something is called, 'recognition' involves semantic understanding of the entity or event and, hence, the ability to retrieve conceptual knowledge for it. Patients with anomia have lost the ability to retrieve names of things, but they have not lost the ability to recognize what things are. Hence, even when they cannot name things, anomic patients can usually produce accurate descriptions of those things or indicate by gestures and other nonverbal forms of communication that they have normal knowledge of things. For example, when shown a picture of a camel, the patient may say, "That is an animal that has humps on its back, lives in the desert, and can go for a long time without water." When shown a picture of Bill Clinton, the patient may say, "That guy was a president; had an affair, had a southern accent." Similar 'subclinical' forms of lexical retrieval problems occur fairly frequently in the realm of normal experience, particularly under conditions of fatigue, distraction, or in connection with normal aging. A related phenomenon is 'tip-of-the-tongue' state, which occurs when normal individuals experience the inability to retrieve a particular name (especially proper names) even though they know perfectly well what it is that they are attempting to name.

Neuropsychological studies of naming and recognition suggest that these two processes may be subserved by partially distinct brain networks. Some evidence for the neural separation of the processes involved in lexical retrieval and recognition comes from category-related deficits that are limited to the verbal modality, such as the famous case of patient 'CP.' CP was selectively impaired in the naming of artifacts (man-made objects such as tools and utensils). Although CP was able to recognize objects, he could not name them, indicating a lexical rather than conceptual deficit. Interestingly, CP could recognize and name objects from other stimulus categories (e.g., familiar faces and animals). Additional evidence compatible with the neural separation between conceptual and lexical retrieval processes comes from research with patients suffering from semantic dementia, who often have bilateral temporal atrophy. Studies have shown that these patients are impaired in both naming and recognition, whereas patients with damage limited to the temporal region tend to be impaired in naming but not in recognition. Additional evidence for the neural separation between the systems subserving lexical retrieval and recognition comes from studies which examined lesion overlap in patients who showed only naming problems and patients who showed both naming and recognition problems.

Relative to the main types of aphasia syndromes, pure anomia in the absence of additional speech or linguistic deficits is fairly uncommon. It occurs far less frequently than most of the 'classic' aphasia syndromes, such as Broca's aphasia and Wernicke's aphasia. For those cases for which lexical impairments occur as an isolated manifestation of acquired brain dysfunction, the designation of 'anomic aphasia' applies. Studies of patients with anomic aphasia have identified distinct brain structures that are specialized for different categories of concrete entities (faces, landmarks, animals, tools, and fruits and vegetables) as well as for different types of words (i.e., words referring to concrete objects, actions, and spatial relationships). The classic aphasia syndromes are associated with brain damage in the vicinity of the Sylvian fissure in the left hemisphere (the left hemisphere is dominant for language in the vast majority (approximately 98%) of right-handed individuals and in the majority (approximately 70%) of left-handed individuals). Isolated defects in naming, however, which define anomic aphasia, are associated primarily with damage to structures in the left hemisphere outside the classic language regions. Specifically, anomic aphasia is most often caused by damage to the left anterior temporal lobe, the inferior and lateral aspect of the left temporal lobe, or the left occipitotemporal junction. Scientific investigations of patients with anomic aphasia, using modern neuroanatomical and neuropsychological techniques, have revealed a number of intriguing associations between specific brain structures and specific types of naming abilities. Studies in normal subjects, using functional neuroimaging procedures (positron emission tomography and functional magnetic resonance imaging), have corroborated several of these findings.

Category-specific lexical impairments following acquired brain injury have been observed and investigated by several researchers. With regard to the retrieval of words for various categories of concrete objects, work conducted in our laboratory has led to several general conclusions. First, there is strong left hemisphere specialization, as would be expected for word retrieval processes (although category-related word retrieval deficits have been reported in connection with right hemisphere lesions as well). Second, there is consistent evidence for category relatedness in the arrangement of systems that support word retrieval for different categories of concrete entities. Lesion studies have shown that defective naming of unique persons and unique landmarks is associated with lesions in the left temporal pole. Defective naming of animals is associated with lesions in left anterior inferior temporal (IT) areas, anterior insula, and the dorsal temporo-occipito-parietal junction. Defective naming of tools is associated primarily with lesions in the left posterior lateral temporo-occipito-parietal junction and with lesions in the inferior pre- and post-central gyri and the insula. Defective naming of fruits and vegetables is associated with lesions in left inferior pre- and post-central gyri and anterior insula. Defective naming of musical instruments is associated with lesions in the left temporal polar region and anterior IT, the posterolateral temporal region (close to the motion-related area known as MT), the insula, and the inferior pre- and post-central gyri. The degree of segregation for different categories varies, and is more or less defined, depending on the categories being contrasted. For example, the association between retrieval of proper names (persons and landmarks) and the left temporal polar region has been particularly strong, as has the association between retrieval of tool names and the left posterior lateral temporo-occipito-parietal junction. However, categories such as musical instruments and fruits and vegetables have not revealed highly localized and reliable neural correlates. Convergent findings have been reported by a number of other laboratories.

In addition to the category-specific distinctions for concrete entities, there are also intriguing distinctions between different types of words. For example, the brain regions that are important for retrieving words for concrete objects (nouns) are partially separate from those that are important for retrieving words for actions (verbs). As noted previously, the retrieval of words for actions is associated with neural structures in the frontal operculum (in front of the Rolandic sulcus) of the left frontal lobe. Researchers in our laboratory have conducted several studies focused on the neural correlates of retrieving words for actions. Specifically, these studies attempted to determine if the neural systems subserving lexical retrieval for objects and actions were segregated. They also investigated whether lexical retrieval for actions involved not only structures of the left inferior frontal gyrus, particularly the frontal operculum, but also intermediary structures located in left premotor/prefrontal areas. One such study used the lesion method and involved 75 subjects with focal, stable lesions in the left or right hemisphere. The experimental tasks were standardized procedures for measuring action and object naming. Results from the study indicated that lesions of the left anterior temporal and inferotemporal regions, which produce impairments in naming of concrete entities, did not cause action-naming deficits. Additionally, lesions associated with impaired action naming overlapped maximally in the left frontal operculum and in the underlying white matter and anterior insula. A follow-up analysis indicated that action-naming impairments, especially when they were disproportionate relative to concrete entity naming impairments, were associated with not only premotor/prefrontal lesions but also lesions of the left mesial occipital cortex and those of the paraventricular white matter underneath the supramarginal and posterior temporal regions.

Interestingly, some studies have suggested that noun–verb homophones (e.g., words such as 'hammer' or 'duck', which are used frequently as either nouns or verbs) are retrieved by the brain system that fits the context in which the word is being used. For example, if 'hammer' is being used as a noun, the temporal lobe system will be used, but if 'hammer' is being used as a verb, the frontal lobe system will be used. Such dissociations may appear rather curious on the surface, but there are compelling explanations and theories of why the brain has organized knowledge in different regions to subserve words from different grammatical categories. For example, factors such as whether an entity is unique (e.g., 'Tom Hanks') or nonunique (e.g., a screwdriver), whether it is living (e.g., pig) or nonliving (e.g., a hammer), whether it is manipulable (e.g., a wrench) or nonmanipulable (e.g., a giraffe), or whether it makes a distinctive sound (e.g., a rooster) or not (e.g., a thimble) are important in determining which neural structures will be used in the mapping and retrieval of knowledge for entities, including their names. The dissociation between deficits in naming objects and deficits in naming actions is also confirmed in studies of patients with degenerative conditions, such as variants of primary progressive aphasia. Also, patients with semantic dementia (SD) have been shown to be impaired in their semantic knowledge concerning objects. The speech of patients with SD is fluent but dramatically marked by anomia. Interestingly, SD is characterized by prominent atrophy in anterolateral temporal cortex (one of the brain structures that, when damaged, has been associated with category-specific lexical impairments for concrete entities) of either the left or both the left and the right hemispheres. Patients with progressive nonfluent aphasia (PNFA), on the other hand, tend to be more impaired in action rather than object naming. Their speech is nonfluent and effortful, with grammatical and phonological errors. PNFA is also characterized by neuronal loss most prominent in inferior frontal and superior temporal regions. These findings are in general agreement with the findings from focal lesion patients, as noted previously.

Very little research has explored which neural systems may be important for retrieving words for spatial relationships (locative propositions such as 'in,' 'on,' and 'around'). Our laboratory has carried out exploratory work on this domain. In one lesion study, the hypothesis that processing the meanings of locative prepositions depends on neural structures in the left inferior prefrontal cortex and left inferior parietal cortex was tested. Seventy-eight subjects with focal, stable lesions to various parts of the telencephalon and a comparison group of 60 normal participants performed tasks that required production, comprehension, and semantic analysis of locative prepositions. In support of the hypothesis, it was found that in subjects with impaired knowledge of locative prepositions, the highest region of lesion overlap was in the left frontal operculum and the left supramarginal gyrus, and in the white matter subjacent to these two areas.

A second study on six patients who had pervasive defects for locative prepositions confirmed that such defects were associated specifically with damage to the posterior left frontal operculum, white matter subjacent to this region, and white matter underneath the inferior parietal operculum. These patients did not have basic impairments in spatial processing or working memory, and they had relatively well-preserved conceptual knowledge for actions and various categories of concrete entities (e.g., persons, animals, and tools). All six patients, however, had defects in naming actions, and some also had defective naming of some categories of concrete entities. Overall, the findings converge well with results from functional imaging, and with results from classic cases in the aphasia-based literature, and suggest that the left inferior prefrontal and left inferior parietal regions have crucial, albeit not exclusive, roles in processing knowledge associated with locative prepositions.

The anomic deficits described throughout this article can occur in connection with any sensory modality – for example, when a person is attempting to name a picture of something, a sound, a smell, or something that is felt by the hand. Anomia can occur in the course of verbal discourse, such as when one is speaking and suddenly cannot retrieve the name for a particular concept that is part of the intended utterance. The majority of scientific inquiries into the phenomenon of anomia, however, have focused on the visual modality and have used paradigms in which subjects are presented pictures (or actual objects) and asked to name them. This format, known as 'visual confrontation naming,' is also the standard paradigm for assessing naming in patients with brain injuries. As a consequence, most of our current knowledge regarding the brain underpinnings of word retrieval and most theoretical accounts of this process are heavily tied to the visual modality. However, evidence suggests that the modality in which a stimulus is perceived may not make much difference. For example, retrieval of the name 'rooster' when confronted with a picture of a rooster, or when confronted with the characteristic sound of a rooster, appears to depend on the same left temporal lobe region.

For the majority of individuals, those who have not acquired a brain injury or do not suffer from a neurodegenerative disorder, lexical retrieval comes naturally and effortlessly. However, the relative ease with which most of us are able to provide names for various objects, actions, and entities is somewhat deceptive. There are a number of neural systems involved in the recognition and retrieval of appropriate word forms that, when disrupted by brain injury, can produce a variety of deficits. Lesion studies of patients with anomic aphasia have provided a unique opportunity to learn how the brain operates the processes associated with word retrieval. Results from these studies have identified different brain structures that are specialized for different types of words and different categories of entities. Future research on patients with anomic aphasia will continue to shed light on how the human brain operates language processes and, it is hoped, will help to inform rehabilitation efforts aimed at patients with acquired disturbances of naming.

See also: Aphasia, Sudden and Progressive; Language Development; Language Following Congenital Disorders (not SLI); Language, Cortical Processes; Language, Learning Impairments; Word Learning; Word Recognition.

Further Reading

Burke, DM, MacKay, DG, Worthley, JS, and Wade, E (1991). On the tip of the tongue: What causes word finding failures in young and older adults? *Journal of Memory and Language* 30: 542–579.
Carammaza, A and Hillis, A (1991). Lexical organization of nouns and verbs in the brain. *Nature* 349: 788–790.
Damasio, H, Grabowski, TJ, Tranel, D, Hichwa, R, and Damasio, A (1996). A neural basis for lexical retrieval. *Nature* 380: 499–505.
Dell, GS, Schwartz, MF, Martin, N, Saffran, EM, and Gagnon, DA (1997). Lexical access in aphasic and nonaphasic speakers. *Psychological Review* 104: 801–838.
Hillis, AE and Caramazza, A (1995). Representations of grammatical categories of words in the brain. *Journal of Cognitive Neuroscience* 7: 396–407.
Kemmerer, D (2005). The spatial and temporal meanings of English prepositions can be independently impaired. *Neuropsychologia* 43: 797–806.
Kemmerer, D and Tranel, D (2003). A double dissociation between the meanings of action verbs and locative prepositions. *Neurocase* 9: 421–435.
Knibb, JA, Xuereb, JH, Patterson, K, et al. (2006). Clinical and pathological characterization of progressive aphasia. *Annals of Neurology* 59: 156–165.
Levelt, WJM, Roelofs, A, and Meyer, AS (1999). A theory of lexical access in speech production. *Behavioral and Brain Sciences* 22: 1–75.
Martin, A, Wiggs, CL, Ungerleider, LG, and Haxby, JV (1996). Neural correlates of category-specific knowledge. *Nature* 379: 649–652.
Pulvermüller, F (1999). Words in the brain's language. *Behavioral and Brain Sciences* 22: 253–336.
Tranel, D (2006). Impaired naming of unique landmarks is associated with left temporal polar damage. *Neuropsychology* 20: 1–10.
Tranel, D, Adolphs, R, Damasio, H, and Damasio, AR (2001). A neural basis for the retrieval of words for actions. *Cognitive Neuropsychology* 18: 655–670.
Tranel, D, Damasio, H, and Damasio, AR (1997). A neural basis for the retrieval of conceptual knowledge. *Neuropsychologia* 35: 1319–1327.
Tranel, D, Grabowski, TJ, Lyon, J, and Damasio, H (2005). Naming the same entities from visual or from auditory stimulation engages similar regions of left inferotemporal cortices. *Journal of Cognitive Neuroscience* 17: 1293–1305.
Tranel, D and Kemmerer, D (2004). Neuroanatomical correlates of locative prepositions. *Cognitive Neuropsychology* 21: 719–749.

M

Memory Disorders

A. Fradera and M. D. Kopelman, King's College London, London, UK

Varieties of Amnesic Syndrome

The amnesic syndrome can be defined as an abnormal mental state in which memory and learning are affected out of all proportion to other cognitive functions in an otherwise alert and responsive patient. Various disorders can give rise to an amnesic syndrome, including the alcoholic Korsakoff syndrome, herpes encephalitis, severe hypoxia, certain vascular lesions, head injury, deep midline tumors, basal forebrain lesions, and occasionally the amnesic variant of mild cognitive impairment Alzheimer's dementia. These syndromes can produce both anterograde amnesia (AA), whereby memory is affected for events following the onset of the disorder, and retrograde amnesia (RA), affecting events from before the onset.

Korsakoff Syndrome

Korsakoff syndrome is the result of nutritional depletion (i.e., thiamine deficiency, due most commonly to alcohol abuse). Diagnosis typically follows an acute Wernicke encephalopathy involving confusion, ataxia, nystagmus, and ophthalmoplegia; however, onset can also be insidious, with little history of these features. Korsakoff patients will show intact short-term memory over spans of seconds but severe impairment for learning over longer periods, together with a retrograde memory loss that typically covers years or decades. Reasoning is broadly intact but patients will often exhibit some abnormal facets of cognition, including repetitive questioning and a dysexecutive profile that may alter behavior – for example, apathy or irritability – together with disorientation in time and its attribution; patients may also confabulate. Consistent with this, some degree of general cortical atrophy is usually observed, particularly in the frontal lobes.

The Korsakoff syndrome is notable in that there is a distinct neurochemical pathology, with important implications for treatment. Research on animals and on malnourished prisoners-of-war established thiamine depletion as the pathological basis for the acute Wernicke episode, and the subsequent (Korsakoff) memory impairment. The mechanisms by which thiamine depletion acts to produce the Wernicke–Korsakoff neuropathology is not fully understood, nor is the genetic contribution to acquiring the condition. Along with the mamillary bodies, the thalamus is considered the critical site of damage in producing the amnesia; early research suggested that damage to the medial dorsal nucleus was key, but more recent evidence points to the anterior principal nucleus.

Herpes Encephalitis

Herpes encephalitis (HSE) can give rise to a severe form of amnesic syndrome. The onset is typically abrupt, arising either from primary infection or reactivation of the virus from an earlier infection, and accompanied by acute fever, headache, nausea, and, in some cases, seizures and behavioral changes. Diagnosis is by the polymerase chain reaction (PCR) test or a raised titer of antibodies to the virus in the cerebrospinal fluid (CSF), but sometimes a presumptive diagnosis is made on the basis of the clinical picture as well as severe signal alteration in the temporal lobes on brain magnetic resonance imaging (MRI), associated with loss of tissue volume, hemorrhage, and edema.

The disorder will usually produce extensive temporal lobe damage that is usually bilateral, together with some general cortical atrophy and changes in orbitofrontal regions and surrounding frontal lobe. The medial temporal lobe structures are usually particularly severely affected (see **Figure 1**) including the hippocampi, amygdalae, and the entorhinal, perirhinal, and parahippocampal cortices – areas critical to memory formation. The disease may also implicate basal forebrain structures which give cholinergic outputs to the hippocampi.

Herpes encephalitis and the Korsakoff syndrome lead to a very similar memory disorder that reflects the fact

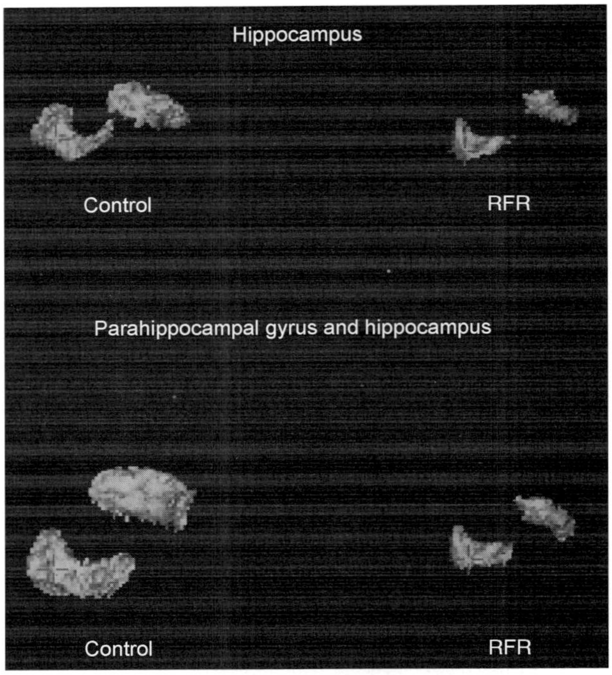

Figure 1 Three-dimensional surface renderings of the hippocampi (top) and the combined parahippocampal and hippocampal structures (bottom) in a healthy control volunteer (left) and in a herpes encephalitis patient (right). These images are taken from planimetric segmentations of the structures from three-dimensional magnetic resonance images. Reproduced from Kopelman MD, Lasserson D, Kingsley DR, et al. (2003) Retrograde amnesia and the volume of critical brain structures. *Hippocampus* 13: 879–891, with permission. (See color plate 30.)

that the hippocampi are linked to the thalami and mamillary bodies by several neural connections. These patients show similar forgetting rates. However, herpes patients typically show more severe involvement of early retrograde memories, a particular impairment for spatial memory (especially when the right hippocampus is implicated, which can result also in an impairment in face recognition) and a greater degree of semantic memory loss from concomitant damage to inferolateral temporal structures. These patients may, however, have a better insight into their memory disorder.

Severe Hypoxia

Severe hypoxia can give rise to an amnesic syndrome following carbon monoxide poisoning, cardiac and respiratory arrests, or suicide attempts by hanging or by poisoning with the exhaust pipe from a car. Drug overdoses may precipitate prolonged unconsciousness and cerebral hypoxia, and this quite commonly occurs in heroin abusers. The consequences of this can be quite variable, but typically severe hypoxia involves changes in the hippocampi, with evidence of loss of pyramidal cells in the CA1 region reported. Fluorodeoxyglucose–positron emission tomography (FDG–PET) studies have also shown reduced glucose metabolism in the thalamus.

Vascular Disorder

Vascular disorders can particularly affect memory, as opposed to general cognitive functioning, in cases of (1) thalamic, medial temporal, or retrosplenial infarction or (2) subarachnoid hemorrhage. Thalamic damage produces amnesia when there is anterior thalamic involvement, as this is where the mamillothalamic tract projects into the thalamus. The features of this disorder are an anterograde amnesia with a limited retrograde component (although when frontocortical projections are affected, a more extensive retrograde amnesia may be observed). Hippocampal damage is due to disruption of the supply from the anterior and posterior choroidal arteries, the latter being a branch of the posterior cerebral circulation; bilateral damage will produce a global amnesia whereas unilateral damage produces a more material-specific memory loss. The retrosplenium is also supplied from the posterior cerebral artery, and infarction or hemorrhage can produce amnesia by disrupting connections to the anterior thalamus, entorhinal, and parahippocampal cortices.

Subarachnoid hemorrhage following rupture of an aneurysm can result in memory impairment, whether the anterior cerebral or posterior cerebral circulation in the Circle of Willis is involved. Ruptured aneurysms in the anterior communicating artery can implicate the basal forebrain and ventromedial frontal structures. To produce a persistent amnesic syndrome it is thought critical that damage occurs to the septal nucleus of the basal forebrain, which provides cholinergic projections to the hippocampi.

Head Injury

Following head injury both transient and persisting amnesias can arise. Posttraumatic amnesia (PTA) is assumed to reflect the degree of underlying diffuse brain pathology (axonal shearing and tearing) resulting from rotational forces, but other pathological mechanisms include contrecoup damage, hypoxia, and intracranial hemorrhage. During PTA patients show accelerated forgetting of material, and following recovery from head injury memory impairments (in new learning) are the slowest cognitive function to improve. Head injury can also produce an RA which is usually fairly brief, but may be extensive in severe cases. Although most patients with head injury show a recovery over the course of 1–3 months, a proportion will show deficits that extend well beyond this. It appears that amnesia following head injury does not insulate against posttraumatic stress disorder (PTSD) for the event, as windows of experience tend to be preserved that allow the reexperiencing of emotionally harrowing elements of the event.

Transient Global Amnesia

Transient global amnesia (TGA) occurs over a period of several hours (average 4–6 h, up to 12 h), in which the sufferers (typically older males) retain their sense of personal identity but show a profound anterograde amnesia together with some degree of RA, typically more pronounced for episodes than for facts. This episode is sometimes preceded by headache or nausea, a stressful life event, a medical procedure, intense emotion, or vigorous exercise, and an episode of migraine may be a precipitating factor. TGA is currently understood to be due to transient dysfunction in limbic–hippocampal circuits, crucial to memory formation.

Transient Epileptic Amnesia

Transient epileptic amnesia refers to a small minority of TGA patients in whom epilepsy appears to be the underlying cause. Standard electroencephalogram (EEG) and computed tomography (CT) scan findings are often normal, but abnormalities may be found on sleep EEGs. Episodes may be ictal or postictal in nature. Memory deficits between attacks are sometimes reported, both for new learning and particularly gaps in past memory. One possible explanation for these gaps is that brief runs of seizure activity at a clinically undetectable level have disrupted normal encoding. Another is that the current epilepsy somehow prevents the retrieval of old, autobiographical memories. Automatisms and postictal confusional states that can arise from epilepsy are also associated with memory disruption: automatisms involve limbic structures that are otherwise responsible for memory formation, and hence amnesia for these periods is always present and is usually complete.

Summary of Amnesic Syndrome

The preceding examples of amnesic syndrome do not, of course, comprise a comprehensive list of the disorders which give rise to transient or persistent amnesia. What they have in common is the neuroanatomical basis for the memory disruption: temporary or permanent dysfunction or damage in medial temporal/diencephalic circuitry, or damage to the basal forebrain cholinergic inputs to that circuitry. Our discussion now turns to the different components of memory that can be affected by damage to this circuitry, and interactions with frontal lobe and temporal neocortical structures. These are anterograde and retrograde episodic memory deficits (see **Figure 2**), semantic memory deficits, and confabulatory episodes.

Various aspects of anterograde memory can be affected in amnesic disorders. Anterograde memory encompasses working memory – which holds information for brief periods of time (a matter of seconds) and allocates resources – and the more permanent episodic memory – which is explicit and refers to specific learned events. It also covers forms of memory whereby information is decoupled from its learning context, such as semantic memory for facts and knowledge, and implicit memory in the form of classical conditioning, procedural learning of perceptuo-motor skills, and priming effects.

Episodic Memory Deficits

There has been much debate about the nature of the episodic memory impairment in amnesia. An overview of the basic processes of memory is illustrative: memories must initially be registered in some way (encoded); they must be stored in an effective fashion, and they must be able to be recovered from the memory system (retrieval). Amnesia could in principle be due to problems at any or all of these stages.

It now seems unlikely that initial encoding is failing in amnesia, as memory performance is largely unaffected

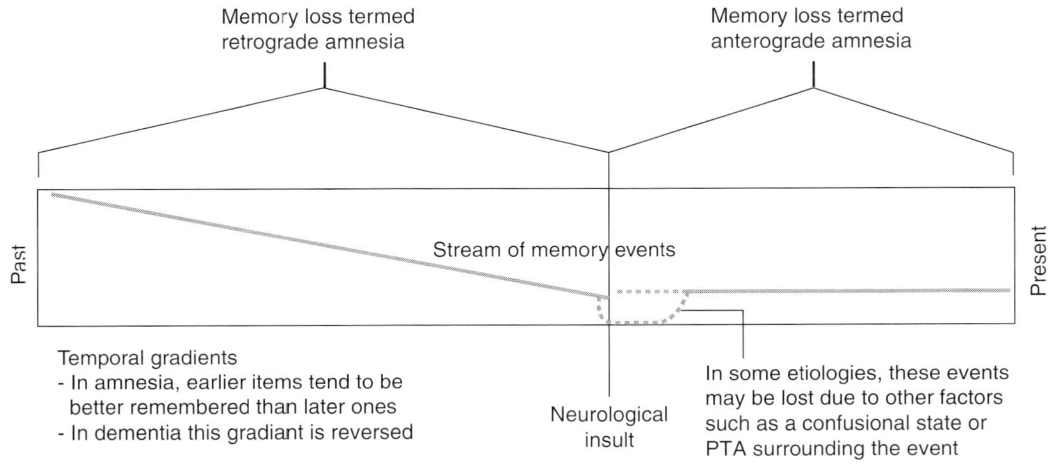

Figure 2 The taxonomy of episodic memory loss due to amnesia (PTA, posttraumatic amnesia). Lines with higher gradients denote better memory for that period.

by conditions that maximize encoding support for studied items; also, working memory can be preserved in the presence of profound amnesia. A more credible account is that disruption occurs later, during the transition of memories into long-term storage, termed consolidation, which may involve processes operating over hours as well as months or even years. The hippocampus has been identified as a critical site in terms of this consolidation, but the process and nature of the process are still under debate, particularly with regard to the implications of a longer term consolidation process for retrograde amnesia (discussed more fully later). Memories that are successfully consolidated into the store may be threatened by the failure of storage itself: this would be reflected by accelerated rates of forgetting. Following work with the medial temporal lobe patient HM and others, this account was put forward to distinguish hippocampal from diencephalic amnesia, but subsequent, more stringent studies found that differences in the forgetting rate of patients from controls were restricted to recall rather than recognition memory, and that this was true across both types of pathology.

A further account is that amnesia reflects a specific deficit in the acquisition of contextual information, in terms of the spatial and temporal information tying an item to the environment in which it was encountered. Such specific deficits are indeed found in amnesics, but not in all cases, and the patterns differ substantially across groups. In terms of the hippocampal lesion sites associated with amnesia, the account has been reformulated as a deficit in binding complex associations or relations (not merely between item and position, but between very different types of items, such as pairing words and pictures); amnesia is thought to disrupt the flexible association of items, and the composition of these items with respect to one another.

Finally, the impairment may lie at the final stage of memory processing, the retrieval of items from storage. The case for the pure retrieval hypothesis is made on the basis of findings showing that amnesics clearly have memory information but produce it inappropriately – for example, producing true memory items on a task that requires another type of item, as well as evidence that retrieval cues can improve performance. However, this pattern can also be seen in the performance of healthy participants, suggesting that it may be a consequence of poor memory rather than its cause. Cueing effects may also simply reflect priming effects – that is, an advantage to memory that is purely implicit in nature.

In summary, the balance of evidence seems to favor a primary role for an acquisition/consolidation problem, some slighter impairments in retention (forgetting), detectable only on recall testing, and a possibly secondary deficit in retrieval processes. Basic research has demonstrated a biological mechanism for consolidation and its disruption, and primate work indicates that medial temporal lobe damage disrupts pair-coding neuronal responses, a mechanism likely to be critical in the support of long-term memory representations. The disruption of acquisition in amnesia may be particularly characterized by a deficit in binding different types of material, including contextual information, and this relates to various distinctions drawn within episodic memory, which is now considered.

Explicit and Implicit Memory

Relative to explicit memory, implicit memory is generally much better preserved in amnesia. Patients show preserved perceptuo-motor skills, and respond appropriately to simple forms of classical conditioning (such as the eye-blink response). They also show priming effects (a more rapid response to an item on the basis of its prior presentation, or that of a similar item), suggesting that this process does not rely on diencephalic/medial temporal brain structures, but rather upon cortical regions. Cases have been described whereby perceptual priming is impaired, even in the face of preserved explicit memory; a role for occipital lobe circuits has been implicated in these cases. However, amnesic patients do show impaired priming in certain experimental conditions (e.g., in difficult tasks when baseline responding has been controlled) or in associative learning. This implicates a contribution of medial temporal/diencephalic structures to priming in these circumstances.

Recall and Recognition Memory

The distinction in memory between recall (items are directly retrieved from memory with little support from cues) and recognition (information is provided to an individual who must simply make a judgment as to whether it has been previously experienced) is of great current interest in contemporary research. At issue is whether amnesic patients may show a disproportionate impairment for one form over the other, suggesting that there may be distinct neural loci underlying these processes. One position is that recall is subserved by a set of neural structures comprising the hippocampi, fornices, mamillary bodies, mamillothalamic tract, and anterior thalami – structures which are crucial in attributing contextual information, including time and spatial location, to memory items, thereby allowing the items to be distinguished and retrieved in the manner required for recollection. Recognition is supported by brain regions (including the perirhinal cortex) which are critical for familiarity judgments. There is some evidence that hippocampal damage disproportionately affects recall memory, as in some cases of developmental amnesia.

An opposing position is that both recall and recognition are served by medial temporal lobe structures and that dissociations across recall and recognition tasks reflect the severity of amnesia. Particular support for this position is given by studies showing that damage limited to the hippocampal formation has produced impairments in recognition memory. This is a touchstone issue which is continuing to preoccupy researchers.

Remembering and Knowing; Recollection and Familiarity

Gardiner and Richardson-Klavehn have distinguished between the subjective states of remembering and knowing. Remembering (R) involves the reexperience of 'intensely personal experiences of the past,' whereas knowing (K) is when 'we are aware of knowledge that we possess but in a more impersonal way,' without the experience of reliving the acquisition of this knowledge. Do these types of memories arise from a single unitary process, from two independent but overlapping processes, or from entirely exclusive processes? Evidence that the same memory items can be variously experienced as R or K, depending on the passage of time, has been used to argue that the processes are not exclusive. Extensive work has examined how these concepts map onto the recall and recognition divisions of memory. It seems likely that both familiarity and recollection can contribute to recognition, with characteristics of performance varying according to the experience supporting it (e.g., judgments that rely upon recollection show greater levels of subjective confidence). Familiarity is not accompanied by the contextual detail required to spontaneously evoke a piece of memory information, whereas recall necessarily relies upon recollection. An analysis of data from several studies of amnesia (due to hippocampal or diencephalic damage) suggests that recollection is disrupted to a greater extent than is familiarity. This evidence leads to the possibility that a defining feature of amnesia is the loss of contextual/associational information, leading to a memory experience that is both impoverished and lacking the subjective experience of 'mental time travel' – the rich and fluid memorial reexperiencing of an event.

Semantic Memory Deficits

Semantic memory comprises knowledge of facts, concepts, and language, stored without corresponding information about the initial learning experience. The cognitive neuroscience of semantic memory – in particular, its relation to episodic memory – is an issue of current theoretical interest. There are several ways in which this issue has been investigated.

Semantic Dementia

Semantic dementia is a degenerative disorder that causes a progressive loss of semantic knowledge which can occur across both verbal and nonverbal domains. In the verbal domain, this leads to loss of word comprehension and naming, and increasingly degraded and empty speech, though the latter remains fluent and grammatical in output. Perceptual and reasoning abilities are also intact, and episodic memory is relatively preserved, as are some classes of knowledge, such as numerical information. The underlying pathology is generally confined to inferior and lateral temporal gyri, more commonly left-lateralized, although right-lateralized atrophy can occur, producing impairments in visual semantics.

Patients often show impaired knowledge of subordinate meaning categories relative to superordinate categories, such as loss of 'dog' but preservation of 'animal'; over time, however, superordinate knowledge may also succumb to the disease. This has been taken as evidence for a hierarchical organization of semantic memory, but it may reflect a more secure neural underpinning for the superordinates, due to their higher usage frequency or their greater degree of connectedness to other concepts. Crucial to the debate on memory systems is the fact that, when compared with amnesic disorders, there can be a classic double dissociation, in that semantic dementia results in semantic impairments with preserved episodes, whereas amnesia leads to episodic impairments with relatively preserved semantic information.

New Learning of Semantic Material in Amnesia

Individuals who suffer severe amnesia provide the opportunity to assess whether the acquisition of semantic material depends upon the episodic memory system. In principle, if new semantic knowledge can be acquired despite a very severe episodic memory deficit, it implies a separation of the neurobiological systems underlying semantic memory and episodic memory. A number of studies in the past 10 years suggested that patients who show severe episodic memory impairments may show significantly better performance on tasks of new vocabulary or recognizing public figures and events. For example, a densely amnesic individual with almost complete bilateral destruction of the hippocampi and severe atrophy of the perihippocampal tissue was tested on knowledge of vocabulary and famous individuals that had arisen since the onset of amnesia; he demonstrated access to explicit semantic knowledge in these domains, albeit at lower levels than within matched controls. However, this finding has been contested, due to some cases of medial temporal lobe amnesia apparently showing little ability to acquire new knowledge.

Cases of developmental amnesia have been studied recently, again offering the opportunity to assess current semantic memory when the acquisition of new episodic memories has been severely impaired. For example, the patient Jon, amnesic due to neonatal injury, is impaired on recall tasks and does not describe any subjective sense of episodic recollection. However, he has been able to perform relatively well in mainstream education – developing competencies in speech, reading, and writing, and scores within the normal range on measures of comprehension, world knowledge, and vocabulary that tap semantic information.

Retrograde Amnesia

In this section, we address amnesia for past events: its nature in different kinds of memory disorder, its implications for theories of memory storage, and whether it can occur in the absence of broader memory impairment.

Temporal Gradients

Investigations of remote memory loss have often striven to assess Ribot's law, expressed in 1882:

> The progressive destruction of memory follows a logical order . . . it begins at the most recent recollections which, being . . . rarely repeated and . . . having no permanent associations, represent organization in its feeblest form. (Théodule Ribot, 1839–1916)

This is reflected in a temporal gradient whereby the most recent memories are lost but more remote ones are intact. Such temporal gradients have been reported in a number of patients with amnesia of both temporal lobe and diencephalic origin, and a more gentle gradient is also observed in Alzheimer's dementia (see **Figure 3**).

What is the basis of these gradients? In Korsakoff patients, one possible explanation is that prolonged heavy drinking leading up to the Wernicke episode might result in a progressive anterograde memory loss over this period. However, this view is not supported by cases in which memories lost due to the syndrome are known to have been in the awareness of the individual prior to onset (e.g., memories were described in diary entries), nor by the fact that severity of drinking does not correlate with severity of retrograde deficit. Drinking may, at best, explain the relative steepness of the gradient compared with other syndromes, but not the gradient itself.

Consolidation theory suggests that the medial temporal/diencephalic system is responsible for both memory formation and consolidation of memories into permanence over a period of years, whereas older memories are permanently distributed through the neocortex. This consolidation/structural reallocation account is supported by findings of minimal RA when lesions are confined to the diencephalon or medial temporal lobe, whereas more substantial RA is underpinned by more extensive pathology, which at its extreme (when there is widespread damage of the kind observed in HSE or Alzheimer dementia) produces a flat temporal gradient. However, this consolidation process would operate over a much longer duration than that involved in transfer from short-term to long-term memory, and an extensive temporal gradient, going back 20–30 years, would imply that physiological consolidation occurs over very long durations, which is problematic for this account.

Another account is the multiple trace theory (MTT), in which the hippocampi are assumed to be continuously involved in the storage and retrieval (reactivation) of memory traces. This model proposes that activations within neocortical and other structures represent information, and that these are bound into a memory trace by hippocampal neurons, acting as an index or marker of the distributed memory information. Each reactivation of a memory trace results in the formation of multiple traces indexed by the hippocampus, and the extraction of more generalized factual information into semantic memory stores. In turn, the existence of multiple traces results

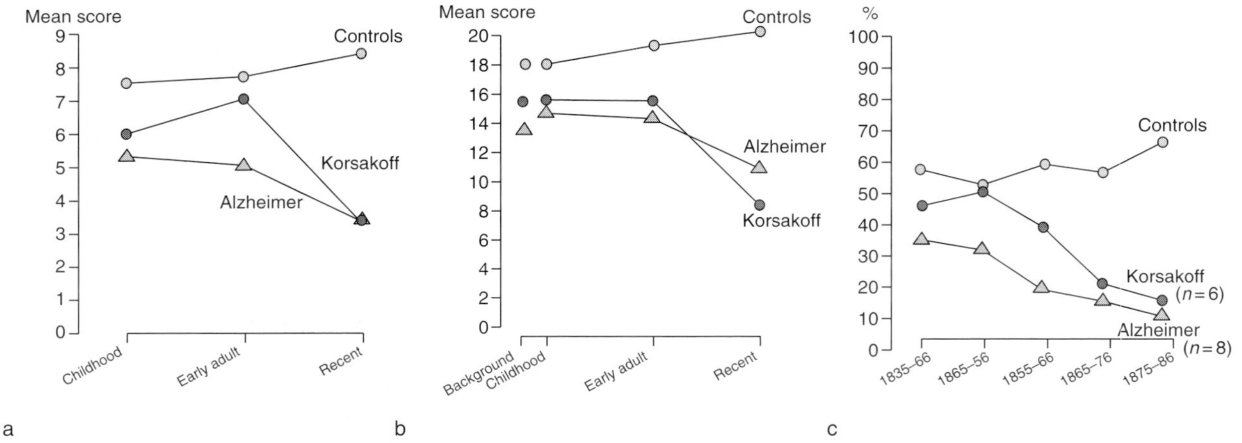

Figure 3 Temporal gradients across different tasks. Remote memory curves on different types of tasks obtained in healthy control participants, Korsakoff patients, and Alzheimer patients. (a) Autobiographical incident recall. (b) Personal semantic fact recall. (c) News event recall. Adapted from Kopelman MD (1989) Remote and autobiographical memory, temporal context memory, and frontal atrophy in Korsakoff and Alzheimer patients. *Neuropsychologia* 27: 437–460, with permission from Elsevier.

in temporal gradients with relative preservation of older (more rehearsed) memories, and the extent of RA would depend upon the size of the hippocampal lesion (with severe atrophy/damage leading to a flat gradient). However, past factual information is not coupled to the hippocampus and hence semantic memories can show a temporal gradient, even when severe hippocampal pathology results in a flat gradient for episodic memories.

A third theory is that, over time, episodic memories are recomposed in a semantic form, losing their vividness and contextual (episodic) aspects: a transformation of memories, rather than their replication. Semantic memories are better insulated from loss in brain damage, as they are presumably stored in more widespread and interconnected networks.

At the time of writing, these various positions remain as credible alternative theories of retrograde amnesia. In support of MTT are reports of patients with steep gradients for personal semantic facts together with flat autobiographical memory gradients, following medial temporal lobe damage. However, many such patients also have extensive damage elsewhere, and other patients with damage confined to the medial temporal lobe or diencephalon show a brief, graded RA – the latter is more consistent with the structural reallocation account of RA. Meanwhile, the episodic-to-semantic memory account – wherein early semanticized memories are easier to retrieve under suboptimal conditions – is consistent with evidence of a retrieval deficit in RA, and the weakness of the relationship between anterograde and retrograde deficits. However, temporal gradients can also be found within the semantic domain, such as for new word learning.

Focal Retrograde Amnesia

A number of cases in the literature have been reported to show a profound RA, with anterograde amnesia slight or absent. However, closer examination of these cases show they provide only limited evidence for the existence of a neurological focal retrograde amnesic syndrome. In a review of the literature, Kopelman found that in many cases the anterograde component was substantial, in others modest but certainly present, and that effort has not always been made to equate the difficulty of retrograde and anterograde tests, which may differentially rely on specific cognitive processes such as visual imagery. Accounts of focal RA have relied on impairments in semantic, autobiographical, or public event knowledge, and may have overemphasized isolated dips in performance in the absence of a more generalized impairment. Moreover, a thorough assessment of psychiatric state is rarely reported; this is relevant, as the retrograde impairment may reflect a psychological or simulated component (see **Figure 4**). The more convincing cases have included those who showed an initial anterograde amnesia

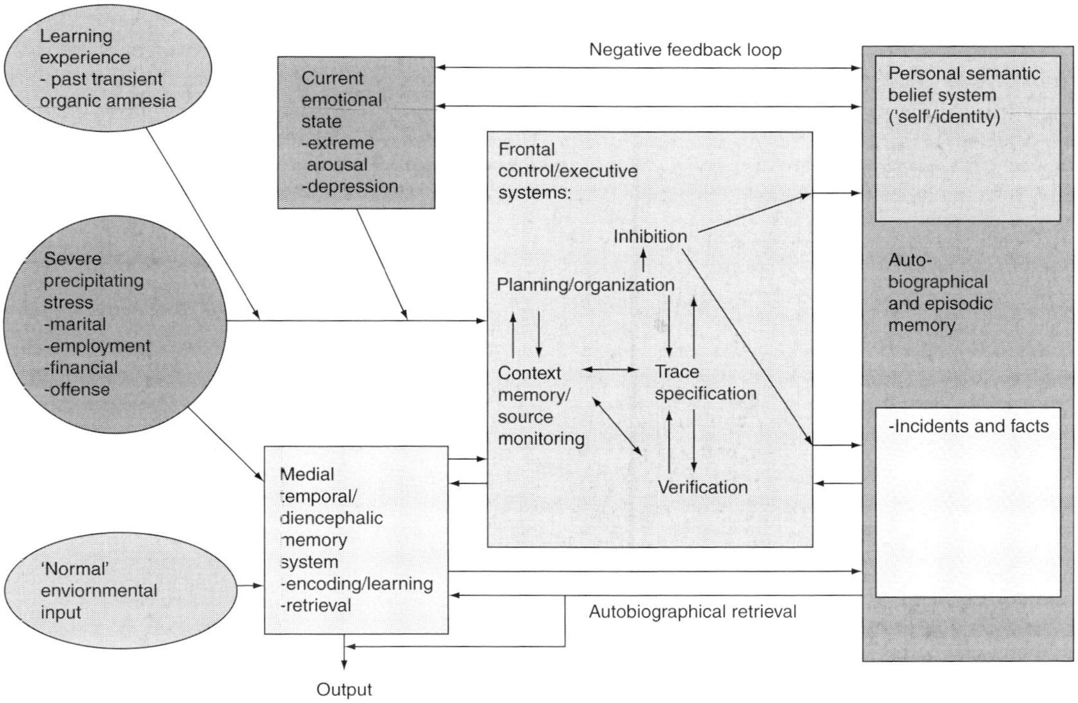

Figure 4 Social factors and brain systems influencing autobiographical memory retrieval and personal identity. The diagram shows frontal lobe processes (large light gray box) involved in confabulation (trace specification/verification; context memory/source monitoring), and social factors (ovals, circle) and brain systems (rectangles) involved in psychogenic amnesia: Inhibition leads to impaired retrieval of incidents and facts, and severe inhibition affects orientation in person. Adapted from Kopelman MD (2000) Focal retrograde amnesia and the attribution of causality: An exceptionally critical review. *Cognitive Neuropsychology* 17: 585–621.

which then abated, and cases of transient epileptic amnesia; however, the former may be better characterized as instances of failure to recover retrograde amnesia, and the latter could be explained as the consequence of periods of faulty encoding across the life span due to brief runs of seizure activity. Cases in which a psychological component made a substantial contribution are interesting in their own right and pose issues both for the clinician and for the researcher of memory. There is continuing debate as to whether psychogenic cases are underpinned by a neurophysiological component – such as in frontal control mechanisms – or whether their understanding is best attempted at a more cognitive or psychosocial level, such as memory suppression mechanisms deployed in response to certain stressors.

Confabulation and Memory Distortion

Confabulation was defined by Berlyne as "falsification of memory occurring in clear consciousness in association with an organically derived amnesia." He argued that it can arise either in a momentary fashion or as spontaneous outbursts from the patient. The former is far more common, and is characterized by the confabulated content being produced as a response to a demand for memory information unavailable to the subject. These provoked confabulations can be viewed as an extension of the kind of intrusion errors seen in recall memory performance by healthy individuals, as well as occasional fill-ins and guesses intended to smooth over awkwardness. Spontaneous confabulation is rarer, but when it occurs it tends to persist either over a short period of time, such as within a confusional state, or over more extended periods, in which case it is usually associated with ventromedial frontal lobe pathology.

A number of theories of spontaneous confabulation have been proffered. One is that the memory errors are the consequence of misattribution of context to memories, such that memories associated with a certain location or time are attributed to another (such as recalling a bank transaction and relocating this event to the current environment of a hospital). This idea originates from Korsakoff's descriptions of confabulations that were essentially confusions in time. Another possibility is that the fault lies not in context memory but within a broader evaluation of the origin of memories. According to this view, much of the patients' memorial information is impoverished or uncoupled from details of where or when it originated, from whom it was given, and whether the experience occurred at all, or was simply imagined. According to both of these views, the fault lies with the amount of memory information that is retrieved, whereby degraded information, or that uncoupled from associated information, results in confabulatory errors.

A further theory is that the stages of memory search and retrieval are disrupted such that memories are poorly selected, and then verified without adequate monitoring of their appropriateness. Initial memory search suffers either because of introduced noise or overbroad search criteria. Subsequent retrieval stages are also prone to failure, including checking that the memory accords with the initial goal of searching for it, as well as whether it is implausible or otherwise problematic. The patient thus produces erroneous memories that a healthy memory system would have halted within its verification system. Plausibility is given to this account by the fact that memory retrieval, information assessment, and judgments are all cognitive processes associated with frontal lobe function. There is also experimental evidence that confabulators make errors in memory judgments that are not dependent on context, but which depend upon accurate strategic retrieval, such as recalling details of fairy tales and bible stories.

Schnider has argued that the problem in confabulation is not in memory *per se*, but in a component of the brain's reward system that acts to suppress memory traces that do not pertain to current ongoing reality. According to this view, evoked memories are accompanied by mental associations to other more tangential memories; these are normally easily distinguished and inhibited when the individual wants to act or make a decision, but for confabulators these persist with a strong experiential sense of relevance (see **Figure 5** for a depiction of this). Schnider notes that a neuroanatomical site common to spontaneously confabulating patients is the orbitofrontal cortex, part of the anterior limbic system which orchestrates communication between the neocortex and the subcortical reward system, directly via the ventral striatum. He also provides data which demonstrate that spontaneous confabulators fail an experimental test distinguishing currently relevant from irrelevant memories. Later, they pass this test once their confabulating has resolved. However, some recent evidence contests the specificity of this linkage.

There has been recent evidence that confabulations may be biased toward emotionally motivated content. Patients will produce information that is self-enhancing – that they are younger than they truly are, that dead or distant relations are alive or near, or that the severity or awkwardness of their current situation is minimized. This may be because the damage to the executive system has eroded the distinctions between the idealized representation of self and the actual sense of self, such that idealizing distortions are more likely to be accepted than in healthy individuals.

Summary

The state of our understanding of memory disorders continues to develop. The natures of the various etiologies are well established and currently the focus of interest is upon the conceptual issues that underpin memory formation,

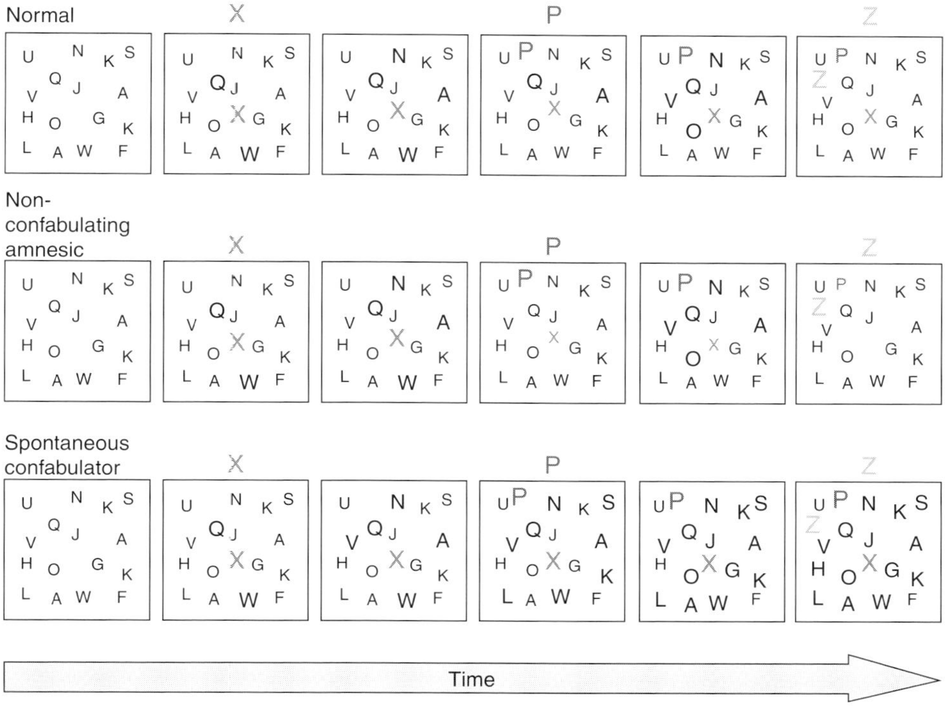

Figure 5 Model of 'now representation' in thinking. Any letter is meant to indicate an event or memory trace. The sizes of the letters indicate their saliency in thinking. Letters outside the boxes are external cues. In normal memory, traces are activated by external cues and associations with other activated cues. When the system is required to adapt to ongoing reality (a fresh cue), these items are then suppressed, with weaker (more tangential) traces fading quicker than recently seen ones; thus, the healthy brain remains in the 'now' but has access to the past. In amnesics, this process occurs, but the trace relating to the recently viewed item is lost at a rate similar to that for more tangential items, trapping amnesics in the 'now.' Spontaneous confabulators are unable to suppress the memories that are no longer currently relevant, allowing a tumult of traces to ensue.

loss, and confusion. The roles of the hippocampi in recollection and in recall memory and the putative hippocampal role in the reactivation or consolidation of memories are of crucial interest, as are formation of semantic memories and whether this depends upon the episodic memory store. The psychological contribution to memory disorders is likely to garner increasing attention, not just in psychogenic fugue and focal retrograde amnesia, but also in interaction with clearly neurological factors, as will the deficits that give rise to pathological false memory. Progress will be made through neuropsychological studies of patients, together with neuroscientific techniques – preferably employed in concert – resulting in better understanding of the causes of memory disorders.

See also: Amnesia, Declarative and Nondeclarative Memory; Amnesia, Functional; Memory, Semantic; Memory, Short Term and Working.

Further Reading

Aggleton, JP and Brown, MW (2006). Interleaving brain systems for episodic and recognition memory. *Trends in Cognitive Sciences* 10: 455–463.

Baddeley, A, Kopelman, MD, and Wilson, B (eds.) (2002). *Handbook for Memory Disorders.* 2nd edn. Chichester: Wiley.

Cohen, NJ, Poldrack, RA, and Eichenbaum, H (1998). Memory for items and memory for relations in the procedural/declarative memory framework. *Memory* 6: 6689–6699.

Fotopoulou, A, Solms, M, and Turnbull, O (2004). Wishful reality distortions in confabulation: A case report. *Neuropsychologia* 42: 727–744.

Hodges, J (2006). Alzheimer's centennial legacy: Origins, landmarks and the current status of knowledge concerning cognitive aspects. *Brain* 129: 2811–2822.

Kopelman, MD (2000). Focal retrograde amnesia and the attribution of causality: An exceptionally critical review. *Cognitive Neuropsychology* 17: 585–621.

Kopelman, MD (2002). Disorders of memory. *Brain* 125: 2151–2190.

Mayes, A, Montaldi, M, and Migo, E (2007). Associative memory and the medial temporal lobes. *Trends in Cognitive Sciences* 11(3): 126–135.

Mishkin, M, Vargha-Khadem, F, and Gadian, DG (1998). Amnesia and the organization of the hippocampal system. *Hippocampus* 8: 212–216.

Moscovitch, M, Nadel, L, Winocur, G, et al. (2006). The cognitive neuroscience of remote episodic, semantic and spatial memory. *Current Opinion in Neurobiology* 16: 179–190.

Neary, D, Snowden, J, and Mann, D (2005). Frontotemporal dementia. *Lancet Neurology* 4: 771–780.

Schacter, DL and Slotnick, SD (2004). The cognitive neuroscience of memory distortion. *Neuron* 44: 149–160.

Schnider, A (2003). Spontaneous confabulation and the adaptation of thought to ongoing reality. *Nature Reviews Neuroscience* 4: 662–671.

Squire, LR (2006). Lost forever or temporarily misplaced? The long debate about the nature of memory impairment. *Learning and Memory* 13: 522–529.

Squire, LR and Schacter, DL (2002). *Neuropsychology of Memory*, 3rd edn. New York: Guilford Press.
Warrington, EK (1975). The selective impairment of semantic memory. *Quarterly Journal of Experimental Psychology* 27: 635–657.
Yonelinas, AP (2002). The nature of recollection and familiarity: A review of 30 years of research. *Journal of Memory and Language* 46: 441–517.

Relevant Websites

http://www.neuroskills.com – Centre for NeuroSkills, Traumatic Brain Injury Resource Guide.
http://www.gluck.edu – Memory Disorders Project, Rutgers University (Newark, NJ, USA).

Memory, Autobiographical

E. Svoboda and B. Levine

Facets of memory have been subjected to scientific scrutiny for well over a century, but a surprisingly small proportion of this research has directly examined the most human of all memory processes—memory for information and experiences pertaining to one's own life, or autobiographical memory. Although the encoding, retention, and retrieval processes discovered in laboratory studies are relevant to our everyday autobiographical memory experiences, autobiographical memory has an added layer of complexity. Unlike the word lists or pictures studied in the laboratory, it is implicated in one's protracted self-awareness across time and self-identity. Indeed, it is this close connection to the self that makes autobiographical memory an unpopular topic among experimentalists, who prefer a greater degree of control over the encoding process than can be achieved in an autobiographical memory study.

Like other memory domains, autobiographical memory is not unitary. Contrasting autobiographical systems and processes can be identified in healthy people and can be affected differentially by brain disease. Storage and retrieval of autobiographical information depends on complex and widely distributed mechanisms. Generation of autobiographical information is a reconstructive, strategic, and often fallible cognitive operation that is affected by both the characteristics of the subject and the nature of the information being retrieved.

The Cognitive Neuroscience of Autobiographical Memory

Recollection of perceptual, cognitive, and emotional details allows one to reexperience a prior event that is specific in time and place. Knowledge of facts and themes from one's autobiography, on the other hand, relates to self-identity but is not time locked to any single prior episode. These reexperiencing and self-knowledge components overlap with the domains of episodic and semantic memory that have influenced experimental memory research.

The Episodic/Semantic Distinction within Autobiographical Memory

Episodic memory was defined by Tulving as the retrieval of an event specific in time and place and has been traditionally assessed through tests of word lists, text, or pictures. Semantic memory was defined as the retrieval of undated, generic knowledge about the world and oneself, for which standard assessment includes tests of vocabulary, object naming, and recognition of famous faces and news events. Within the framework of autobiographical memory, episodic autobiographical memory refers to the reexperiencing of specific past episodes and their details, and semantic autobiographical memory refers to factual information about oneself (e.g., schools attended, previous jobs, skills, and personality traits). In comparison to semantic autobiographical memory, episodic autobiographical reexperiencing probably evolved relatively late, is unique to humans, and stabilizes late in development (at approximately age 4). Episodic and semantic memory can be dissociated in patients with brain disease and in healthy adults with functional neuroimaging.

Conway and colleagues have also proposed a model of autobiographical memory that overlaps with the episodic/semantic distinction. In the Self Memory Model, autobiographical memory is organized into levels of knowledge specificity: life time periods, general events, and event-specific knowledge. Life time periods (knowledge about primary school, university, and working for company X) and general events (themes of repeated events, single extended events, or a clustering of activities thematically related by a goal) broadly overlap with semantic autobiographical memory, whereas event-specific knowledge (episodic fragments such as sensory and perceptual details) is analogous to episodic autobiographical memory.

Strategic Retrieval Processes in Autobiographical Remembering

Recollection of autobiographical episodes is a complex multistage cyclic retrieval process that does not necessarily result in a high-fidelity representation of the original experience. The frontal lobes serve a controlling and monitoring function in this process. In the first step, a memory template is developed in response to internal or external cues and demands. Following search initiation, sensory and phenomenal properties are brought to consciousness through patterns of transregional neocortical activation. The medial temporal lobes (including the hippocampus) probably contain the indices or "combinatory codes" to these regions. The resulting pattern is verified against the original template until a satisfactory outcome occurs, which may require numerous cycles of template elaboration and verification of activation patterns. Reexperiencing may also occur more spontaneously through associative or direct activations in response to highly specific or elaborate cues (e.g., odor). Autobiographical memories are thus not stored as distinct units but are rather diffusely represented and reactivated through hippocampal–neocortical interaction. Access to semantic knowledge, either personal or public, which is by definition free of temporal and contextual components, is thought to be less dependent on hippocampal–neocortical interactions.

Since autobiographical memory is reconstructive in nature, faulty retrieval attempts may occur, specific details may be lost or inconsistently retrieved, and the description may change with changes in personal goals and self-schemas. In cases of frontal brain damage, this distortion can reach pathological levels in the form of confabulation. More subtle forms of memory distortion can be observed in healthy people. Researchers have manipulated false memory by exploiting the tendency of individuals to create a coherent and internally consistent representation of experience.

Autobiographical Retrieval across the Life Span

The pattern of autobiographical memory retrieval varies across the life span. What is referred to as the life span retrieval curve is most evident when subjects are asked to recall freely and date memories that come to mind in response to a list of cue words. The number of memories recalled across the life span is represented by a retrieval curve with three components. First, there is an overall decrease in memories recalled over time, with superior autobiographical recall for memories occurring in recent years. Second, there is a reduction of memories during early childhood years referred to as childhood amnesia. The third component, observed in middle-aged and older adults, is an increase in recall of memories from adolescence and young adult years, known as the reminiscence bump. The latter component may be related to memory enhancement of events that are both novel and important in the formulation and stabilization of one's self-identity and personal goals.

Autobiographical Memory in Patients with Neuropsychological Disorders

Contributions of the Medial Temporal, Diencephalic, and Basal Forebrain Regions

Selective impairment of specific memory systems or processes in patients with amnesia provides useful information about the organization of memory in the brain. One clear finding from such studies is that episodic memory is more sensitive to brain damage than is semantic memory. This finding is consistent with the previously described conceptualization of autobiographical episodic and semantic retrieval processes. That is, retrieval of personal semantic information derives from stable memory traces that are more redundantly represented than those traces mediating episodic reexperiencing.

Patients with classic forms of anterograde amnesia due to medial temporal, diencephalic, or basal forebrain damage are severely impaired in the acquisition, retention, and retrieval of novel experiences. These structures act as bottleneck regions during the encoding and retrieval of episodes. The hippocampus and related medial temporal lobe structures play an important role in the binding of spatial and other contextual event details that are represented throughout the neocortex. Damage to the medial temporal region results in the loss of contextual specificity that contributes to the recollection of unique episodes. Retrieval of general or semantic information that is independent of contextual specificity is less prone to disruption. Medial temporal lobe damage is associated with a temporal gradient of retrograde amnesia (originally described by Ribot) by which information acquired relatively recently is more vulnerable to damage than remotely acquired information. The precise nature and determinants of this gradient are currently under debate. The temporal extent of retrograde amnesia is related to the amount of medial temporal damage. Recent evidence suggests that the gradient most aptly describes the pattern of remote semantic memory loss and that remote episodic memory follows a more temporally extensive gradient.

Damage to the diencephalic structures, either by focal lesions or more commonly by Wernicke–Korsakoff syndrome due to chronic alcoholism, causes a temporally extensive retrograde amnesia. The basal forebrain, the final bottleneck structure, has projections to other systems important to memory, namely the hippocampal and amygdalar systems. Numerous pathways that have been linked to memory pass through or nearby this region. Due to its anatomical complexity, its contributions to memory are not well understood.

Although a semantic deficit can be demonstrated in amnesic patients, it is almost invariably less severe than the episodic deficit. New knowledge and skills (e.g., motor tasks and computer knowledge) can be acquired with repeated trials under conditions of minimal interference, even in severe amnesics who cannot form new episodic memories. Such patients can therefore show remarkable demonstrations of learning in the absence of recollection of any learning episode.

Retrograde amnesia is nearly always accompanied by anterograde amnesia that is greater in degree, although an increasing number of cases of disproportionate (also called isolated or focal) retrograde amnesia are being reported. An exception to this pattern can be found in patients with bilateral inferolateral temporal cortical damage (e.g., semantic dementia), in which semantic memory is more impaired.

Prefrontal Contributions to Autobiographical Amnesia

The prefrontal cortex is involved in the organization, storage, search, retrieval, and reconstruction of autobiographical memories. Patients with prefrontal damage often show autobiographical memory deficits due to impairments in one or more of these processes. These patients, however, derive more benefit from retrieval support than do patients with medial temporal lobe damage.

Frontal lesions also appear to be requisite to amnesic syndromes in which self-awareness is clearly disrupted, most notably in confabulation. Confabulation is the unintentional recollection of erroneous information that can be either plausible or completely bizarre. In either case, the patient is unaware or unconcerned about his or her memory deficits and will hold his or her views with absolute conviction. Confabulation is most frequently reported for autobiographical information, although it has also been reported for semantic information. In amnesics, confabulation is typically associated with damage to the ventromedial frontal region, prefrontal cortex, and basal forebrain, although damage to these regions does not necessarily imply the presence of confabulation. Confabulation occurs with greater frequency in conjunction with Wernicke–Korsakoff syndrome and hemorrhage after a ruptured communicating artery aneurysm, but it may also accompany trauma to the frontal lobes, herpes simplex encephalitis, frontal lobe dementia, and cerebral infarction. Confabulations differ from delusions in that they occur in the context of amnesia or a transient confusional state rather than in the context of psychosis.

The predominant explanation of confabulation is that it is a symptom of impaired search and monitoring processes during memory retrieval. These processes are also of particular importance in successful autobiographical remembering. Without the proper functioning of these mechanisms, memories and their fragments may be retrieved out of context, out of order, or be overly influenced by the immediate social or physical environment. The ability to differentiate real events from thought content or imagined events may also be impaired.

Psychogenic Retrograde Amnesia in Autobiographical Memory

Psychogenic or functional amnesia is the sudden loss of autobiographical memory and personal identity, and it is commonly precipitated by a traumatic event, severe stress, or depression. Individuals are often unaware of their previous lives and unconcerned about their amnesic condition. In the fugue state, a person may wander for days in pursuit of a particular destination or goal, usually related to precipitating circumstances, unaware and oblivious to his or her lack of identity or personal history. Although episodic autobiographical memory is predominantly affected in psychogenic amnesia, recollection of semantic or general information (e.g., famous faces and news events) may or may not be impaired. The extent of autobiographical memory loss may encompass an entire lifetime or a specific stressful event or time period. Autobiographical memory loss in these cases is usually temporary. Memory for ongoing events during the amnesic state is temporarily intact, but this information may be lost upon recovery. Psychogenic symptoms vary from case to case because they are idiosyncratic in nature. Many cases of psychogenic amnesia have a history of brain disease, giving rise to speculation that retrograde amnesia is neither purely organic nor psychogenic but a mixture of the two.

Functional Imaging of Autobiographical Remembering

With the recent development of functional imaging techniques, a handful of studies have investigated the neuroanatomical correlates of autobiographical remembering in healthy adults. Brain activity studied *in vivo* during autobiographical remembering has begun to extend the knowledge from neuropsychological research to normal autobiographical memory. Consistent with the roles of prefrontal and hippocampal structures in patients with brain disease, imaging studies have demonstrated the activation of these areas in healthy adults during autobiographical recollection. Further investigation is required to clarify the differential contributions of the right and left hemispheres as well as possibly distinct dorsal/ventral and medial/lateral contributions from the frontal lobes.

Assessment of Autobiographical Memory

Although autobiographical memory impairment can have significant implications for patients' quality of life, it is typically not assessed or is informally assessed using one or two questions. Detailed neuropsychological test batteries often leave autobiographical memory unexamined. Although it is obviously difficult to assess such inherently subjective information, impoverished autobiographical recollection can be reliably detected. In cases of suspected confabulation, verification against significant others' reports is required.

Two widely used tools for the assessment of autobiographical memory are the Crovitz technique and the Autobiographical Memory Interview (AMI). The Crovitz technique is used extensively in the experimental study of autobiographical memory. The basic testing procedure comprises giving subjects a list of words and asking them to recall an event related to each word. The administration and scoring of this instrument, however, vary from laboratory to laboratory. The AMI is the only commercially available clinical measure. It is a semistructured interview that separately assesses episodic and personal semantic autobiographical memory across three broad lifetime periods. Each episode or component is given a qualitative 0–3 rating reflecting the degree of reexperiencing conveyed by the patient's recollection.

See also: Memory, Episodic; Memory, Explicit/Implicit; Memory, Semantic; Memory, Spatial; Transient Global Amnesia.

Further Reading

Conway, MA and Pleydell-Pearce, CW (2000). The construction of autobiographical memories in the self-memory system. *Psychol. Rev.* 107: 261–288.

Kapur, N (1999). Syndromes of retrograde amnesia: A conceptual and empirical synthesis. *Psychol. Bull.* 125: 800–825.

Kopelman, MD, Wilson, BA, and Baddeley, AD (1989). The Autobiographical Memory Interview: A new assessment of autobiographical and personal semantic memory in amnesic patients. *J. Clin. Exp. Neuropsychol.* 11: 724–744.

Rubin, DC, Rahhal, TA, and Poon, LW (1998). Things learned in early adulthood are remembered best. *Mem. Cognit.* 26: 3–19.

Tulving, E (1989). Remembering and knowing the past. *Am. Sci.* 77: 361–367.

Memory, Episodic

J. H. Kramer

Although human memory systems encompass several different types of learning phenomena, episodic memory is what most people are referring to when they discuss memory. Episodic memory is our ability to learn, store, and later retrieve new information, and it is often referred to as recent memory or anterograde memory. Recent models of memory place episodic memory within the declarative memory system, which refers to memories that are directly accessible to conscious recollection. Retrieval of information from declarative memory is usually intentional and done with the awareness of the individual. Episodic memory specifically refers to memory for events or episodes in one's life that are associated with a particular time and place. Episodic memory can be contrasted with semantic memory, which is another component of the declarative memory system and refers to a person's fund of general information. Unlike episodic memory, semantic memory holds information that does not depend on a particular time or place. Thus, knowing that Cleopatra was a queen of Egypt is part of semantic memory; remembering a time when one saw Shakespeare's *Anthony and Cleopatra* is part of episodic memory. Similarly, learning a list of words is a function of episodic memory; knowing what the words mean depends on semantic memory.

Episodic memory is a complex set of cognitive operations and is mediated by multiple neurological pathways and systems. To illustrate some of these components, consider a friend's account of a recent trip to Europe. She describes how the trip began in Paris and then continued to Nice, Monaco, Venice, Vienna, and finally Frankfurt. She also recounts a boat trip on the Seine during which a tour guide informed her that the Eiffel Tower was completed in 1889 and is 300 m high. She exclaims that Venice was one of the trip's highlights and describes in detail the view of St. Mark's Basilica from her hotel window.

Extensive research with primate and neurological patients has demonstrated that your friend's ability to store information about events that occurred several months previously depends on the integrity of structures in the medial temporal lobes. One of the first structures linked to new learning was the hippocampus, a small structure shaped like a seahorse tucked deep in the medial portion of each temporal lobe. Patients with bilateral lesions in the hippocampus typically present with dense amnesia or an inability to learn new information. Old information and basic perceptual and intellectual functioning can be entirely unaffected. Controlled lesion studies with primates also revealed that even incomplete damage to the hippocampus can produce significant memory impairment. More extensive experiments have shown that the hippocampus is just one part of an extensive information processing network that contributes to memory performance. Information being processed in all parts of the neocortex projects to parahippocampal gyrus, perirhinal cortex, and entorhinal cortex prior to being sent to the hippocampus. The hippocampus has been subdivided into key components: Information projects first to the dentate gyrus and then to the C3 and C1 regions. Information leaving the hippocampus enters the subiculum and entorhinal cortex prior to being projected back to the cortex. Projections to the cortex are widely distributed, with multiple cortical regions contributing to a memory trace. Because memories are stored in multiple cortical regions, memories can be triggered by initial access to only a limited portion of the memory; this explains why memories for specific events are preserved following focal cortical lesions. Although the hippocampus appears critical for normal memory function, damage to other parts of the medial temporal system can also impair memory. Similarly, damage to the hippocampus alone does not seem to impair memory as much as when there is concurrent damage to entorhinal and perirhinal cortex.

Your friend recalled several facts that were verbal in nature and some images of St. Mark's Basilica that were visual in nature. Hemispheric specialization of memory largely parallels that of cognitive operations in general, with verbal memory predominately mediated by the left hippocampus and visual memory predominately mediated by the right hippocampus. Memories are typically multimodal, however, and both hemispheres generally contribute to the formation of new memory traces.

One of the mechanisms by which learning occurs in this information-processing system may be long-term potentiation, which is a long-term increase in synaptic sensitivity and postsynaptic output that occurs when a neural loop has been activated. This change in synaptic activity can last for hours or days after the original stimulus has disappeared, thereby leading many neuroscientists to suggest that long-term potentiation may be the basis for more permanent synaptic changes and the formation of a durable memory trace. Ironically, the role of the medial temporal system in long-term storage of information may be time limited. Several studies have shown that damage to the hippocampus may not affect retrieval of information that was learned months or years prior to the lesion. Patients with focal amnesia typically present with intact memory for old semantic and autobiographical facts. This implies that the medial temporal system may serve to link together previously unconnected cortical sites; once these neural loops are established, however, the hippocampus is no longer necessary for activation of that memory.

Your friend's account of her European trip also illustrates other features of episodic memory. She not only recalled several facts about the Eiffel Tower but also could specify where and when she learned them. This is an example of source memory. Source memory is memory for the source of a fact or message (e.g., who said something rather than what was said). The frontal lobes appear to be the critical structure for this kind of learning. In one study, patients with frontal lobe lesions recalled as many facts as their age-matched controls and younger subjects, but they frequently attributed facts to incorrect sources. A study of Huntington's disease patients, who have subcortical and frontal dysfunction, also demonstrated impaired memory for the source of learned information, even though fact recall did not differ significantly between early stage Huntington's patients and an age- and education-equated group of healthy control subjects. In contrast, although Alzheimer's disease patients recall fewer facts than healthy controls, when they remember information, they attribute their learning to the correct source.

The frontal lobes are also important for other aspects of episodic memory. In recounting her travels, your friend was able to report on where her trip began, where she went next, and so on. This depends on the ability to store and retrieve not only the events but also when they occurred in relationship to other events. Patients with frontal lobe lesions are impaired at placing items in the correct temporal order, even when memory for the items is intact, and may have difficulty giving biographical details or stating recent U.S. presidents in the correct chronological order. Temporal ordering and source memory are examples of contextual memory—that is, encoding not just the events but also the context within which they occur—and it appears that frontal structures provide the foundation for this cognitive skill. The frontal lobes also play a key role in how information to be learned is organized during encoding and retrieval. For example, in one study using positron emission tomography in normals, activation in left prefrontal cortex was linked to semantic clustering, which is a measure of active regrouping of words into semantic categories during free recall.

Episodic memory is a complex cognitive ability subserved by multiple brain systems, and it can therefore be disrupted by several different types of neurological disorders. The hippocampus and surrounding structures play a central role in new learning, so disorders causing hippocampal pathology are almost always associated with significant deficits in new learning. Perhaps the most common disorder producing extensive hippocampal damage is Alzheimer's disease. The neuropathological changes of Alzheimer's disease—neuritic plaques, neurofibrillary tangles, and neuronal cell loss—typically begin in the medial temporal lobe (entorhinal cortex and hippocampus), which explains why episodic memory is so impaired in Alzheimer's disease patients. Herpes encephalitis also differentially affects the temporal lobes and can produce severe amnesia. The hippocampus is also very sensitive to oxygen and glucose deprivation. Consequently, events that produce acute anoxia, such as cardiac arrest, drowning, and asphyxiation, commonly result in damage to the hippocampus and deficits in episodic memory. Another type of memory disorder thought to be linked to the medial temporal lobe system is transient global amnesia, which is a syndrome in which a previously well person suddenly becomes confused and amnesic for a period of usually less than 24 hr. Language, attention, visuospatial skills, and semantic memory are well preserved. Blood flow studies have shown changes in the medial temporal lobes, presumably due to ischemia in the vertebrobasilar system.

Structural damage in other areas of the brain can also produce episodic memory impairment. Studies of patients with Korsakoff's disease and patients with focal injury have shown that lesions in the dorsal–medial nucleus of the thalamus can produce an amnesia as severe as that following hippocampal damage. Neurological disorders such as multiple sclerosis, Huntington's disease, Parkinson's disease, progressive supranuclear palsy, and subcortical ischemic vascular disease can also compromise normal memory functions. In these disorders, the neurological damage is in subcortical structures such as the basal ganglia, midbrain, and white matter, and the rich interconnections between subcortical structures and the frontal lobes are disrupted. The nature of the episodic memory impairment in these subcortical syndromes tends to be different than the amnesia following medial temporal injury. Medial temporal injury interferes with the consolidation of new information; consequently, new information is rapidly forgotten after relatively short delay periods. In subcortical syndromes, patients may have difficulty learning new material because of slowed information processing and inefficient encoding. They are better able to retain what they have learned, however, and their recognition memory is often better than their spontaneous recall.

Individual differences in episodic memory abilities have also been a subject of considerable research. Age is a very strong predictor of how well information is stored and retrieved. Significant improvement in recall levels, recognition, and application of learning strategies (e.g., organization and rehearsal) occurs during childhood and into early adolescence. Large cross-sectional and longitudinal studies have further suggested that age-related declines in memory performance begin in the fourth and fifth decades of life and continue throughout the life span. Although atrophic changes in the hippocampus may explain some of the age-related changes in episodic memory, cognitive psychologists have also found that older normals are less likely to spontaneously organize information to be learned than are younger normals. For example, younger subjects cluster together list items that share semantic properties to a much greater degree than do older subjects. Several researchers have also found that source and temporal order memory are more affected by normal aging than is fact memory, further suggesting that changes in the frontal lobes may also contribute to age-related episodic memory decline.

Gender differences in episodic memory have also been studied. Females tend to outperform males on a host of verbal memory tasks, whereas studies examining visuospatial memory have yielded less consistent results. These frequently reported sex differences in verbal episodic memory have generated considerable debate regarding their underlying mechanisms. Estrogen has been considered as one possible contributing factor. Experimental studies in postmenopausal women have generally found a protective effect of estrogen on verbal memory, and longitudinal studies found that women who were estrogen users performed better on verbal memory tasks than nonusers of similar age.

Advances in our understanding of the cognitive and neuroanatomical bases of episodic memory have made important contributions to clinical practice and the differentiation of learning and memory disorders, and they offer a framework for future research aimed at improving episodic memory functions.

See also: Memory, Autobiographical; Memory, Explicit/Implicit; Memory, Semantic; Memory, Spatial.

Further Reading

Brandt, J, Bylsma, FW, Aylward, EH, et al. (1995). Impaired source memory in Huntington's disease and its relation to basal ganglia atrophy. *J. Clin. Exp. Neuropsychol.* 17: 868–877.

Caine, D and Watson, JD (2000). Neuropsychological and neuropathological sequelae of cerebral anoxia: A critical review. *J. Int. Neuropsychol. Soc.* 6: 86–99.

Goldman, WP, Winograd, E, Goldstein, FC, et al. (1994). Source memory in mild to moderate Alzheimer's disease. *J. Clin. Exp. Neuropsychol.* 16: 105–116.

Janowsky, JS, Shimamura, AP, and Squire, LR (1989). Source memory impairment in patients with frontal lobe lesions. *Neuropsychologia* 27: 1043–1056.

Savage, CR, Deckersbach, T, Heckers, S, et al. (2001). Prefrontal regions supporting spontaneous and directed application of verbal learning strategies: Evidence from PET. *Brain* 124: 219–231.

Sherwin, BB (2000). Oestrogen and cognitive function throughout the female lifespan. *Novartis Found. Symp.* 230: 188–196.

Shimamura, AP, Janowsky, JS, and Squire, LR (1990). Memory for the temporal order of events in patients with frontal lobe lesions and amnesic patients. *Neuropsychologia* 28: 803–813.

Squire, LR and Kandel, E (2000). *Memory: From Mind to Molecules.* New York: Scientific American Library.

Strupp, M, Bruning, R, Wu, RH, et al. (1998). Diffusion-weighted MRI in transient global amnesia: Elevated signal intensity in the left mesial temporal lobe in 7 of 10 patients. *Ann Neurol.* 43: 164–170.

Memory, Explicit/Implicit

B. J. Cherry

Memory is the capacity to utilize facts, events, and skills previously experienced or learned. This mental process can be performed either consciously or unconsciously in humans. Explicit memory is remembering that is conscious and effortful, such as in trying to recall someone's name. Implicit memory, on the other hand, refers to remembering that is outside of an individual's awareness and is considered automatic. Knowing how to deal a deck of cards or ride a bike exemplifies this type of memory. Individuals with certain neurological conditions have demonstrated dissociations between the two types of memory, suggesting multiple mechanisms and/or locations for these memory processes.

Explicit Memory

Tasks

Memory for words, paragraphs, digits, and/or objects has been used to study episodic memory or memory for facts and events within a temporal context (**Table 1**). For example, individuals are asked to recall, recognize, and/or draw stimuli previously seen or heard. Individuals may be asked to read a series of words then report them back. Recall may be immediate or after some delay (minutes or days). Subjects may also be asked to identify among a series of words, digits, or objects those that they have seen before—a process called recognition memory. Recognition is less effortful than recall, as reflected in better memory performance for recognition than recall tasks. Individuals may also view or copy line drawings and then be asked to reconstruct them from memory.

Table 1 Examples of Explicit and Implicit Memory

Explicit memory: conscious, effortful
Episodic: knowledge, facts, events within a temporal context
Semantic: knowledge, facts
Working: manipulation of information held in temporary storage
Source: knowledge of when, where, or from whom information is acquired
Metamemory: awareness of one's memory capabilities and strategies; monitoring, control
Implicit memory: unconscious, automatic
Procedural: skill learning, habits, with and without a motor component
Associative (classic conditioning, learned conditioned response probabilistic associations, artificial grammar, category learning): knowledge of associations or categories over multiple trials without explicit awareness of rules or learning
Priming: change in reaction time or accuracy in response to prior exposure to a stimulus

To assess semantic memory or memory for knowledge and facts, individuals may be asked to name common objects. Alternatively, they may be asked to perform a fluency task; that is, to name as quickly as possible either items from a particular category or any objects that begin with a particular letter. The number of items generated in a short period of time (usually 1 or 2 min) is a measure of this type of memory function.

Working memory refers to the manipulation of information held in temporary store, such as adding 317 and 286 without the aid of paper and pencil. Tasks typically used to assess this type of memory are two-component or dual tasks, such as reading a series of sentences and then attempting to recall the last word from each sentence. Source memory (knowing the context in which information was acquired) and metamemory (the awareness of one's memory capabilities and strategies) are assessed with direct questions to individuals regarding where and when they learned a particular fact or by having them rate their confidence in regard to knowing certain information or not.

Biological Bases of Explicit Memory

Neuroanatomical loci for explicit episodic and semantic memory are the medial temporal area and diencephalic midline structures. This includes the hippocampal formation, entorhinal cortex, parahippocampal cortex, and perirhinal cortex. In addition, "word-finding" difficulties on fluency tasks used to assess semantic memory are often found in patients with left hemisphere frontal lesions.

Working memory is associated with prefrontal cortex. There is also frontal cortex involvement for recall of source and temporal order information (e.g., when information is on the "tip of the tongue").

Implicit Memory

Procedural and associative learning and memory are acquired over multiple trials (with the possible exception of taste aversion), whereas priming can occur after a single trial. Different implicit memory tasks may also be dissociable within certain populations or within subgroups of populations (e.g., Alzheimer's or Parkinson's disease), suggesting that independent processes and/or different anatomical substrates are required to perform these processes.

Implicit Memory Tasks

Procedural learning tasks reflect motor skills learning and include such tasks as pursuit rotor and mirror drawing. Associative learning refers to classic conditioning in which individuals learn an association between an unconditioned and conditioned stimulus to produce a conditioned response. Pavlov's dogs are a classic example. In humans (as well as in rabbits), individuals can learn to blink to a tone alone after a series of trials in which a tone is paired with an air puff to the eye. Associative learning can also include cognitive associations such as probabilistic associations, artificial grammar learning, and category level learning. Subjects learn a set of associations over a series of trials—for example, forecasting the weather based on cues, learning an artificial grammar system by being shown a series of letter strings adhering to a novel grammar system, or classifying novel stimuli after exposure to a series of training stimuli. Patients with amnesia and other individuals with explicit memory impairment can perform these tasks without specific knowledge of training sessions or recognition of stimuli used in individual trials.

Priming is an unconscious change in performance due to prior exposure to a stimulus. This change most typically facilitates memory but can also be inhibitory. Tasks commonly used to assess priming include fragment-stem completion and repetition priming. Fragment-stem completion involves exposure to a list of words and then completion of a list of fragment stems (e.g., someone may respond "street" to the stimulus "str____"). Individuals are more likely to complete stems with words from a prior list rather than generate new words. Stimuli used in repetition priming can be either words or pictures, with prior exposure typically eliciting either faster or more accurate responses over a series of trials.

Biological Bases of Implicit Memory

Motor skills learning and memory, including procedural memory and sequence learning, occur primarily in motor cortex, basal ganglia, and the supplementary motor area. Classic condition associative learning and memory, perhaps the best studied pathways in mammals, involve regions of the cerebellum. In addition, the hippocampus has a modulating effect on some conditioned responses. For example, ablation of the hippocampus does not affect the learned response, whereas electrical or chemical modification of the hippocampus does. Probabilistic classification is most likely related to functioning of the caudate nucleus. For example, both Huntington's and Parkinson's disease patients are impaired on this task and have known caudate nucleus pathology. Artificial grammar and category learning may depend on neocortical functioning. Loci for category learning may also include the striatum.

There may be two types of priming: perceptual and conceptual priming. Perceptual priming refers to the presemantic form and structure of the stimulus and is considered modality specific. It is associated with right extrastriate occipital cortex for visual presentation and the sensory cortex relevant for the task plus the striatum for stimuli presented in other modalities. Conceptual priming refers to activation of the semantic store or stimulus meaning, with locations most likely involving left temporal cortex and/or polymodal association cortices.

Memory Impairment in Clinical Populations

A loss of memory is the inability to remember past events, facts, or knowledge. Clinical conditions for which memory losses are common are organic amnesia, traumatic brain injury, Alzheimer's disease, stroke, mental retardation, Down's syndrome, Korsakoff's syndrome (memory loss due to alcoholism), Huntington's disease, and Parkinson's disease. Various clinical conditions demonstrate dissociations between explicit and implicit memory systems. Moreover, dissociations have been demonstrated within these classification systems as well. For example, loss of explicit memory and relative sparing of implicit memory are well documented in patients with amnesia, traumatic brain injury, and Korsakoff's and Down's syndrome. A loss of implicit memory has been evidenced in patients with Huntington's and Parkinson's disease. A hallmark clinical feature of Alzheimer's disease is explicit memory loss. This may be episodic or semantic or both. Certain implicit memory processes may be impaired as well, such as classic conditioning, whereas other implicit memory tasks may remain intact.

Noted brain injury cases also demonstrate dissociations between different aspects of memory. For example, patient HM underwent surgery in 1953 for intractable epilepsy. Surgeons removed parts of his temporal lobes, including the hippocampus. The seizures stopped, but HM no longer had the ability to transfer information from short- to long-term memory. Thus, he could meet and carry on a conversation with someone, but if the person left and returned a few minutes later, he had no memory of meeting that person. He could, however, perform certain implicit memory tasks, such as mirror tracing.

Life Span and Risk of Memory Impairment

Memory problems are different during different stages of the life span. There is evidence that both children and older adults demonstrate age-related increases and decreases in explicit memory, respectively, whereas implicit memory is relatively intact in both age groups. Even children with mental retardation and those with Down's syndrome show impaired explicit but spared implicit memory.

Age-related declines in explicit memory begin to occur in approximately the fourth decade. Classic conditioning (associative learning) also shows decline beginning at approximately this time. In addition, the risk of diseases associated with memory loss increases with age. For example, there is increased risk of stroke-related dementia and memory impairment as well as dementia due to Parkinson's disease. Also, Alzheimer's disease increases exponentially with age. The prevalence of Alzheimer's disease is approximately 6–8% at age 65, whereas estimates of prevalence range from 20 to 50% after age 85. Finally, Down's syndrome patients who survive to the age of 35 begin to exhibit both the behavioral and neuropathological features typical of Alzheimer's disease.

See also: Alzheimer's Disease; Memory, Autobiographical; Memory, Episodic; Memory, Semantic; Memory, Spatial.

Further Reading

Anooshian, LJ (1998). Implicit and explicit memory in childhood: A review of relevant theory and research. *Child Study J.* 28: 17–52.
Cabeza, R, Kapur, S, Craik, FIM, et al. (1997). Function neuroanatomy of recall and recognition: A PET study of episodic memory. *J. Cogn. Neurosci.* 9: 254–265.
Fleischman, DA and Gabrieli, JDE (1998). Repetition priming in normal aging and Alzheimer's disease: A review of findings and theories. *Psychol. Aging* 13: 88–119.
Reder, LM (ed.) (1996). *Implicit Memory and Metacognition.* Mahwah, NJ: Erlbaum.
Schacter, DL, Chie, C-YP, and Ochsner, KN (1993). Implicit memory: A selective review. *Annu. Rev. Neurosci.* 16: 159–182.
Shimamura, AP (1995). Memory and frontal lobe function. In: Gazzaniga, MS (ed.) *The Cognitive Neurosciences.* Cambridge, MA: MIT Press.
Squire, LR and Zola, SM (1996). Structure and function of declarative and nondeclarative memory systems. *Proc. Natl. Acad. Sci. USA* 93: 13515–13522.
Vicari, S, Bellucci, S, and Carlesimo, GA (2000). Implicit and explicit memory: A function dissociation in persons with Down syndrome. *Neuropsychologia* 38: 240–251.

Memory, Semantic

A. Martin, National Institute of Mental Health, Bethesda, MD, USA

Published by Elsevier Ltd.

Introduction

'Semantic memory' refers to a major division of long-term memory that includes knowledge of facts, events, ideas, and concepts. As such, it covers a vast terrain, ranging from information about historical and scientific facts, details of public events, and mathematical equations to the information that allows us to identify objects and understand the meaning of words. Semantic memory can be distinguished from episodic/autobiographical memory by an absence of temporal and spatial details about the context of learning. In relation to episodic memory, semantic memory is considered to be both a phylogenically and an ontologically older system. Although many animals, especially mammals and birds, acquire information about the world, they are assumed to lack the neural machinery to consciously recollect detailed episodes of their past. Finally, although retrieval of semantic memory often requires explicit, conscious mediation, the organization of semantic memory can also be revealed via implicit tasks such as semantic priming.

Semantic Memory and the Medial Temporal Lobe Memory System

Studies of patients with amnesia due to damage to the medial temporal lobes have established three broadly agreed on facts about the functional neuroanatomy of semantic memory. First, like episodic memory, acquisition of semantic memories is dependent on medial temporal lobe structures, including the hippocampal region (CA fields, dentate gyrus, and subiculum) and surrounding neocortex (parahippocampal, entorhinal, and perirhinal cortices). Damage to these structures results in deficient acquisition of new facts and public events and the extent of this deficit is roughly equivalent to the deficit for acquiring personal information about day-to-day occurrences. However, despite broad agreement that acquiring semantic memories requires medial temporal lobe structures, there is disagreement concerning the role of the hippocampal region. One position, championed by Larry Squire and colleagues, holds that the hippocampus is necessary for acquiring semantic information. In contrast, others have argued that acquisition of semantic memories can be accomplished by the surrounding neocortical structures alone; participation of the hippocampus is not necessary. Recent studies have favored the hippocampal position by showing that carefully selected patients with damage limited to the hippocampus are impaired in learning semantic information, and that the impairment is equivalent to their episodic memory deficit. One potentially important caveat to this claim comes from studies of individuals who have sustained damage to the hippocampus at birth or during early childhood. These cases of developmental amnesia have disproportionately better semantic than episodic memories, suggesting that the hippocampal region may not be necessary for acquiring semantic information. Reconciliation of this issue will depend on direct comparison of adult onset and developmental amnesias with regard to extent of medial temporal lobe damage and its behavioral consequences.

The second major finding established by studies of amnesic patients is that the medial temporal lobe structures have a time-limited role in the retrieval of semantic memories. Retrieval of information about public events shows a temporally graded pattern with increasing accuracy for events further in time from the onset of the amnesia. Conceptual information about the meaning of objects and words acquired many years prior to the amnesia onset remains intact as assessed by both explicit and implicit tasks. Third, semantic memories of all types are stored in the cerebral cortex. In amnesic patients, impairments in semantic memory for information acquired prior to amnesia onset are directly related to the extent of damage to cortex outside the medial temporal lobes.

Cortical Lesions and the Breakdown of Semantic Memory

Studies of semantic memory in amnesia have concentrated largely on measures of public event knowledge. The reason for this is that these tasks allow memory performance to be assessed for events known to have occurred either prior to, or after, amnesia onset. These measures also allow performance to be evaluated for events that occurred at different times prior to amnesia onset to determine if the memory impairment shows a temporal gradient – a critical issue for evaluating theories of memory consolidation. Because these patients have either no or, more commonly, limited damage to regions outside the medial temporal lobes, they are not informative about how semantic information is organized in the cerebral cortex. To address this issue, investigators have turned to patients with relatively focal lesions compromising different cortical areas. In contrast to the studies of amnesic patients, these studies have focused predominantly on measures designed to probe knowledge of object concepts.

Object Concepts

An object concept refers to the representation (i.e., information stored in memory) of an object category (a class of objects in the external world). Concepts are central to all aspects of cognition; they are the glue that holds cognition together. The primary function of a concept is to allow us to quickly draw inferences about an object's properties. That is, identifying an object as, for example, a 'hammer' means that we know that this is an object used to pound nails, so that we do not have to rediscover this property each time the object is encountered. Object concepts are hierarchically organized, with the broadest knowledge represented at the superordinate level, more specific knowledge at an intermediary level referred to as the 'basic level,' and the most specific information at the subordinate level. For example, 'dog' is a basic-level category that belongs to the superordinate categories 'animals' and 'living things,' and has subordinate categories such as 'poodle' and 'collie.' As established by Eleanor Rosch and others in the 1970s and 1980s, the basic level has a privileged status. It is the level used nearly exclusively to name objects (e.g., 'dog' rather than 'poodle'). It is also the level at which we are fastest to verify category membership (i.e., we are faster to verify that a picture is a 'dog' rather than an 'animal' or a 'poodle'). It is also the level at which subordinate category members share the most properties (e.g., collies and poodles have similar shapes and patterns of movement). Finally, the basic level is the easiest level at which to form a mental image (you can easily imagine an elephant but not an 'animal'). Studies of patients with cortical damage have documented the neurobiological reality of this hierarchical scheme and the central role of the basic level for representing objects in the human brain.

Semantic Dementia and the General Disorders of Semantic Memory

Several neurological conditions can result in a relatively global or general disorder of conceptual knowledge. These disorders are considered general in the sense that they cut across multiple category boundaries; they are not category specific. Many of these patients suffer from a progressive neurological disorder of unknown etiology referred to as semantic dementia (SD). General disorders of semantic memory are also prominent in patients with Alzheimer's disease (who, compared to SD patients, typically have a greater episodic memory impairment), and can also occur following left hemisphere stroke, prominently involving the left temporal lobe. The defining characteristics of this disorder, initially described by Elizabeth Warrington and colleagues in the mid-1970s, are deficits on measures designed to probe knowledge of objects and their associated properties. These deficits include impaired object naming (with errors typically consisting of semantic errors – retrieving the name of another basic-level object from the same category, or retrieval of a superordinate category name), impaired generation of the names of objects within a superordinate category, and an inability to retrieve information about object properties – including sensory-based information (shape, color) and functional information (motor-based properties related to the object's customary use, but this may include other kinds of information not directly related to sensory or motor properties). The impairment is not limited to stimuli presented in a single modality, like vision, but rather extends to all tasks probing object knowledge regardless of stimulus presentation modality (visual, auditory, tactile) or format (words, pictures). The semantic deficit is hierarchical in the sense that broad levels of knowledge are often preserved, while specific information is impaired. Thus, these patients can sort objects into superordinate categories, having, for example, no difficulty indicating which are animals, which are tools, which are foods, and the like. The difficulty is manifest as a problem distinguishing among the basic-level objects as revealed by impaired performance on measures of naming and object property knowledge.

Recent studies have expanded our understanding of SD in two important ways: one is related to location of neuropathology, the other to functional characteristics of the disorder. The initial neuropathological and imaging studies of SD indicated prominent atrophy of the temporal lobes, especially to the anterolateral sector of the left temporal lobe, including the temporal polar cortex inferior and middle temporal gyri, and the most anterior extent of the fusiform gyrus. However, recent advances in neuroimaging that allow for direct and detailed comparison of brain morphology in SD patients relative to healthy controls have shown that the atrophy extends more posteriorally along the temporal lobe than previously appreciated. In fact, the amount of atrophy in ventral occipitotemporal cortex, including the posterior portion of the fusiform gyrus, has been reported to be as strongly related to the semantic impairment in SD as is atrophy in the most anterior regions of the temporal lobes.

The other major advance in our understanding of SD is that it is not as global a conceptual disorder as initially thought. Rather, certain domains of knowledge may be preserved, and the pattern of impaired and preserved knowledge appears to be related to the locus of pathology. Specifically, left-sided atrophy seems to impair information about all object categories except person-specific knowledge (i.e., information about famous people), which, in turn, is associated with involvement of the right anterior temporal lobes. Also relatively spared is knowledge of number and mathematical concepts, and information about motor actions needed to use familiar tools. Both of these knowledge domains are associated with left posterior parietal cortex.

Category-Specific Disorders of Semantic Memory

Although reports of cases of relatively circumscribed knowledge disorders date back over 100 years, the modern era of the study of category-specific disorders began in the early 1980s with the seminal reports of Warrington and colleagues. Category-specific disorders have the same functional characteristics as does SD, except that the impairment is largely limited to members of a single superordinate object category. For example, a patient with a category-specific disorder for 'animals' will have greater difficulty naming and retrieving information about members of this superordinate category relative to members of other superordinate categories (e.g., tools, furniture, flowers). Similar to patients with SD, patients with category-specific disorders have difficulty distinguishing among basic-level objects (e.g., between dog, cat, horse), thereby suggesting a loss or degradation of information that uniquely distinguishes among members of the superordinate category (e.g., four-legged animals).

Although a variety of different types of category-specific disorders have been reported (e.g., for fruits and vegetables), most common have been reports of patients with relatively greater knowledge deficits for animate entities (especially animals) than for a variety of inanimate object categories. While less common, other patients show the opposite dissociation of a greater impairment for inanimate manmade objects (including common tools) than for animals and other living things.

Models of category-specific disorders

Two major theoretical positions have been advanced to explain these disorders. Following the explanation posited by Warrington for her initial cases, most current investigators assume that category-specific deficits are a direct consequence of an object property-based organization of conceptual knowledge, an idea that was prominent in the writings of Karl Wernicke, Sigmund Freud, and other behavioral neurologists during the late nineteenth and early twentieth centuries. The central idea is that object knowledge is organized in the brain by sensory (e.g., form, motion, color, smell, taste) and motor properties associated with the object's use, and in some models, by other functional/verbally mediated properties, such as where an object is typically found. In this view, category-specific semantic disorders occur when a lesion disrupts information about a particular property or set of properties critical for defining, and for distinguishing among, category members. Thus damage to regions that store information about object form, and form-related properties like color and texture, will produce a disorder for animals. This is because visual appearance is assumed to be a critical property for defining animals, and because the distinction between different animals is assumed to be heavily dependent on knowing about subtle differences in their visual forms. A critical prediction of sensory/motor-based models is that the lesion should affect knowledge of all object categories with this characteristic, not only animals. In a similar fashion, damage to regions that store information about how an object is used should produce a category-specific disorder for tools, and all other categories of objects defined by how they are manipulated.

The alternative to these property-based theories is the domain-specific view championed most recently by Alfonso Caramazza and colleagues. On this account, our evolutionary history provides the major constraint on the organization of conceptual knowledge in the brain. Specifically, the theory proposes that selection pressures have resulted in dedicated neural machinery for solving, quickly and efficiently, computationally complex survival problems. Likely candidate domains offered are animals, conspecifics, plant life, and possibly tools. Property-based and category-based accounts are not mutually exclusive. For example, it is certainly possible that concepts are organized by domains of knowledge, implemented in the brain by large-scale property-based systems. Much of the functional neuroimaging evidence (to be discussed later) is consistent with this view.

Functional neuroanatomy of category-specific disorders

There is considerable variability in the location of lesions associated with category-specific disorders for animate and inanimate entities. Nevertheless, some general tendencies can be observed. In particular, category-specific knowledge disorders for animals are disproportionately associated with damage to the temporal lobes. The most common etiology is herpes simplex encephalitis, a viral condition with a predilection for attacking anteromedial and inferior (ventral) temporal cortices. Category-specific knowledge disorders for animals also have been reported following focal, ischemic lesions to the more posterior regions of ventral temporal cortex, including the fusiform gyrus. In contrast, category-specific knowledge disorders for tools and other manmade objects have been most commonly associated with focal damage to lateral frontal and parietal cortices of the left hemisphere. However, it is important to stress that the lesions in patients presenting with category-specific knowledge disorders are often large and show considerable variability in their location from one patient to another. As a result, these cases have been relatively uninformative for questions concerning the organization of object memories in cerebral cortex. In contrast, recent functional neuroimaging studies of the intact human brain have begun to shed some light on this thorny issue.

Organization of Conceptual Knowledge: Neuroimaging Evidence

The functional neuroanatomy of semantic memory has been explored using a wide variety of experimental approaches and paradigms. The overarching goal of these studies has been to identify brain regions that show a heightened response during a conceptual or semantic processing task (e.g., is the object a living thing?) versus performing a nonsemantic, but equally difficult, task (e.g., does the object's name contain the letter 'p'?) with the same set of stimuli. Assigning a particular brain region a role in semantic processing is further strengthened when the activity is associated with semantic task performance, regardless of physical differences in the stimuli used to denote the objects (i.e., visual or auditory, pictures or words). As a result, activity in these brain regions can be linked to conceptual processes and not features of stimulus input modality or format.

Studies based on this type of approach have consistently isolated two regions, the left ventrolateral prefrontal cortex (VLPFC) and the ventral and lateral regions of the temporal lobes (typically stronger in the left than in the right hemisphere). Detailed evaluations of left VLPFC have shown that this region is critically involved in the top-down control of semantic memory. Specifically, left VLPFC is responsible for guiding retrieval and post-retrieval selection of conceptual information stored in posterior temporal and perhaps other cortical regions. This neuroimaging finding is consistent with studies of patients with left inferior frontal lesions that have word-retrieval difficulties, but retain concept knowledge of the words they have difficulty retrieving. In contrast, a large body of evidence has linked activity in posterior regions of the temporal lobes to memory representations, especially concerning conceptual representations of specific properties associated with concrete objects.

Object Knowledge Is Organized by Sensory and Motor-Based Properties

One source of evidence concerning the organization of object property information comes from property production tasks. In these tasks, individuals are presented with an object, denoted either by a picture or the object's name, and are required to generate a word denoting a specific property associated with that object. Several studies have shown that generating an action associate (e.g., saying 'pull' in response to a child's wagon) elicits heightened activity in premotor cortex as well as in a posterior region of the left lateral temporal cortex, centered on the middle temporal gyrus (pMTG) just anterior to primary visual motion-sensitive cortex. In contrast, relative to action word generation, color word generation (e.g., saying 'red' for the child's wagon) activates the fusiform gyrus, anterior to regions associated with passive perception of color. Subsequent studies have shown that tasks requiring finer perceptual discrimination of colors, or perceiving more complex patterns of object motion, elicit activity in the same temporal lobe regions active when color or action knowledge is retrieved. The findings from these and similar studies suggest two important points. First, that information about different types of object-associated properties (e.g., color, action) is represented in different anatomical regions. Second, these regions directly overlap with sites that mediate perception of these object properties. A number of studies have replicated these two basic points using property verification tasks requiring subjects to answer yes/no questions about the relation between a particular object and property. These studies have linked retrieval of information about visual, auditory, and tactile properties to regions associated with processing within each of these sensory modalities. Similarly, retrieval of object use-associated information has been linked to motor regions active when objects are actually manipulated. These studies suggest that the same neural systems are involved, at least in part, in perceiving, acting on, and knowing about specific object properties.

Neural Networks for Animate Entities and Tools

A large number of studies have addressed questions concerning how information about different object categories is represented in the brain. Many of these studies were motivated by the neuropsychological evidence for category-specific disorders discussed in the preceding sections. As a result, these studies have concentrated on the neural systems for perceiving and knowing about two broad domains: animate agents (living things that move on their own), and tools (manmade objects with a close association between their function and motor movements associated with their use). These studies have provided evidence for four major points about the organization of conceptual knowledge. First, information about a specific object category is not represented in a single cortical region, but rather is represented by a network of discrete regions that may be widely distributed throughout the brain. Second, the informational contents of these regions are related to specific properties associated with the object. Third, some of these property-based regions are automatically active when objects are identified, thus suggesting that object perception is associated with the automatic retrieval of a limited set of associated properties that may be necessary and sufficient to identify that object. These properties prominently include information about what the object looks like, how it moves, and, for a tool, its use. Fourth, this object property-based information is stored in sensory and motor systems active when that information was acquired.

Conceptual representations of animate entities have been most strongly linked to two regions of temporal lobe cortex, the lateral region of the fusiform gyrus, located on the ventral surface of the temporal lobe (including the fusiform face area; FFA), and the posterior region of the superior temporal sulcus (pSTS), located on the lateral surface of the temporal lobe (**Figure 1**). Activation of these regions is typically stronger in the right, rather than in the left, hemisphere. In contrast, conceptual representations of tools have been linked to four regions. Included in this network are the medial portion of the fusiform gyrus, pMTG (as discussed previously in relation to generating action words), and posterior parietal and ventral premotor

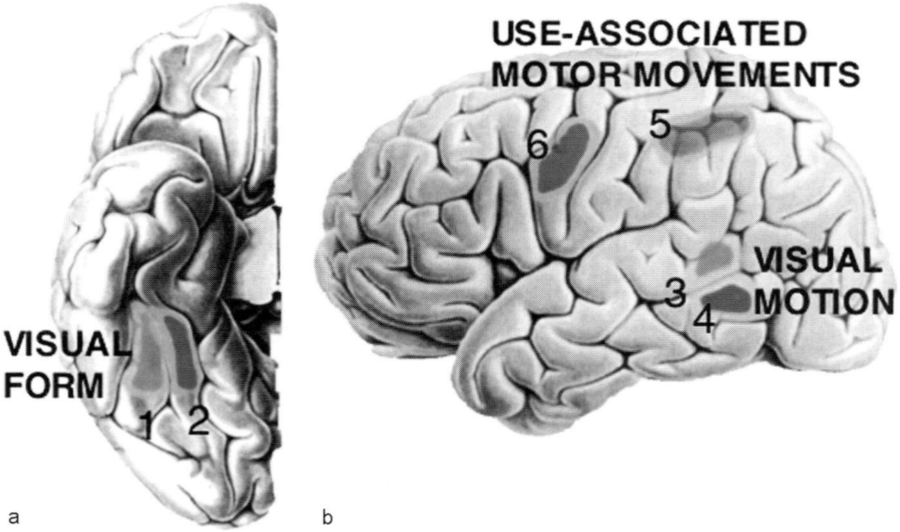

Figure 1 Schematic illustration of location of regions showing category-related activity for animate entities (red) and tools (blue). (a) Ventral view of the right hemisphere, showing relative location of regions assumed to represent visual form and form-related properties such as color and texture of animate entities (1, lateral region of the fusiform gyrus, including, but not limited to the fusiform face area) and tools (2, medial region of the fusiform gyrus). (b) Lateral view of the left hemisphere, showing relative location of regions assumed to represent biological motion (3, posterior region of the superior temporal sulcus) and rigid motion vectors typical of tools (4, posterior region of the middle temporal gyrus). Also shown are the relative locations of the posterior parietal (5, typically centered on the intraparietal sulcus) and ventral premotor (6) regions of the left hemisphere assumed to represent information about the motor movements associated with using tools. (See color plate 32.)

cortices. Activity in these regions is typically stronger in the left, rather than in the right, hemisphere (**Figure 1**).

Activity in these networks transcends stimulus features, thus strengthening the claim that these regions are involved in conceptual processing. For example, category-related activity in the lateral region of the fusiform gyrus has been shown not only in response to pictures of people and animals, but also to the written and heard names of animals, human voices, animal-associated sounds (like the moo of a cow), and when simply imagining faces. In addition, category-related activity in the lateral fusiform gyrus has been found in response to degraded and abstract visual stimuli such as humanlike stick figures, point light displays interpreted as human figures in motion, degraded pictures of objects when misinterpreted as faces, and when simple geometric shapes in motion are interpreted as depicting social interactions. Similarly, category-related activity in the more medial region of the fusiform gyrus has been shown not only in response to pictures of tools, but also to the written and heard names of tools and to tool-associated sounds (like the banging of a hammer). In addition, category-related activity in the medial fusiform gyrus has been observed in response to degraded and abstract visual stimuli such as point light displays interpreted as depicting tools in motion, and when simple geometric shapes in motion are interpreted as depicting mechanical interactions. Taken together, these findings indicate that the critical determinant of differential activity in these regions is the conceptual interpretation assigned to a stimulus (e.g., as a person, animal, or tool), not the physical characteristics of the stimulus, *per se*.

Linking Category-Related Representations to Sensory and Motor Properties

Neuroimaging studies also have provided evidence about the functional role of regions showing category-related activity. The two regions in the posterior region of the temporal lobe that show a stronger response to animate rather than inanimate objects – the lateral region of the fusiform gyrus and pSTS – have been linked to representing the visual form and the flexible, fully articulated, patterns of motion associated with animate objects, respectively. These findings are consistent with a large body of neurophysiological data from studies of monkeys showing that neurons in inferior temporal cortex and STS are differentially tuned to visual form and biological motion, respectively. In contrast, the two regions in the posterior region of the human temporal lobe that show a stronger response to tools than to animate objects – the medial region of the fusiform gyrus and pMTG – have been linked to representing the visual form and rigid, unarticulated patterns of motion typically associated with manipulable manmade objects.

Other studies have provided evidence linking the representation of tools to two regions of the dorsal action-processing stream – the left posterior parietal cortex and left ventral premotor cortex. These findings are consistent with data from monkey neurophysiology showing that neurons in ventral premotor and parietal cortices respond both when monkeys grasp objects and when they see objects that they have had experience manipulating. Along with pMTG, functional brain imaging studies in humans have shown that these dorsal regions are active when individuals retrieve information about the functional properties of objects, suggesting that information about how objects are used is stored in these regions. Support for this claim comes from recent neuropsychological investigations linking impaired knowledge of tools and their associated actions to damage to either left pMTG, posterior parietal, or premotor cortices.

Finally, recent studies have shown that the category-related, property-based neural systems discussed here are not only active when objects are encoded into memory, but also that this activity is reinstated prior to recalling that information at a later time. These findings underscore the central role that these systems play in memory encoding, storage, and retrieval.

See also: Cognition, An Overview of Neuroimaging Techniques; Memory Disorders.

Further Reading

Caramazza, A and Shelton, JR (1998). Domain-specific knowledge systems in the brain: The animate–inanimate distinction. *Journal of Cognitive Neuroscience* 10: 1–34.

Damasio, H, Tranel, D, Grabowski, T, et al. (2004). Neural systems behind word and concept retrieval. *Cognition* 92: 179–229.

Forde, EME and Humphreys, GW (2002). *Category Specificity in the Brain and Mind.* Hove and New York: Psychology Press.

Garrard, P and Hodges, JR (1999). Semantic dementia: Implications for the neural basis of language and meaning. *Aphasiology* 13: 609–623.

Manns, JR, Hopkins, RO, and Squire, LR (2003). Semantic memory and the human hippocampus. *Neuron* 38: 127–133.

Martin, A (2007). The representation of object concepts in the brain. *Annual Review of Psychology* 58: 25–45.

Martin, A and Caramazza, A (eds.) (2003). *The Organization of Conceptual Knowledge in the Brain: Neuropsychological and Neuroimaging Perspectives.* Hove and New York: Psychology Press.

Murphy, GL (2002). *The Big Book of Concepts.* Cambridge, MA: The MIT Press.

Polyn, SM, Natu, VS, Cohen, JD, et al. (2005). Category-specific cortical activity precedes retrieval during memory search. *Science* 310: 1963–1966.

Vargha-Khadem, F, Gadian, DG, Watkins, KE, et al. (1997). Differential effects of early hippocampal pathology on episodic and semantic memory. *Science* 277: 376–380.

Warrington, EK (1975). The selective impairment of semantic memory. *Quarterly Journal of Experimental Psychology* 27: 635–657.

Warrington, EK and Shallice, T (1984). Category specific semantic impairments. *Brain* 107: 829–854.

Memory, Short Term and Working

B. R. Postle, University of Wisconsin – Madison, Madison, WI, USA
T. Pasternak, University of Rochester, Rochester, NY, USA

Introduction

Definition

Short-term memory (STM) refers to the active retention (for humans, the 'keeping in mind') of information when it is not accessible from the environment. Working memory can be thought of as 'STM+,' the '+' referring to the ability to manipulate or otherwise transform this information, to protect it in the face of interference, and to use it in the service of such high-level behaviors as planning, reasoning, and problem solving. STM and working memory are of central importance to the study of high-level cognition because they are believed to be critical contributors to such essential cognitive functions and properties as language comprehension, learning, planning, reasoning, and general fluid intelligence.

Historical Backdrop

The modern study of working memory began with the work of Jacobsen, who, in the 1930s, demonstrated that large bilateral lesions of the prefrontal cortex (PFC) in the monkey produced profound deficits in spatial working memory, and thus Jacobsen ascribed to the PFC a function he termed "immediate memory." A subsequent study, however, revealed that this deficit could be erased by darkening the testing cage and thus reducing interference during the memory delay. These results highlighted a critical question, still the subject of an active debate, which is whether PFC plays a critical role in storage in addition to its role in behavioral control.

The early 1970s witnessed two developments that were seminal in shaping contemporary conceptions of working memory. The first was the observation made by Joaquin Fuster that individual neurons in PFC of monkeys, trained to compare visual stimuli separated by a memory delay, exhibit sustained activity throughout that delay. This observation suggested a neural correlate of two potent ideas from physiological psychology – that of a PFC-dependent immediate memory and that of a reverberatory mechanism for "a transient 'memory'" proposed by psychologist Donald Hebb. The second development, which occurred in the field of human cognitive psychology, was the multiple component model of working memory proposed by Alan Baddeley and Graham Hitch. In its initial instantiation this model comprised two independent buffers for the storage of verbal and of visuospatial information, and a central executive to control attention and to manage information in the buffers. Prompted by these two developments, the neuroscientific and the psychological study of working memory each proceeded along parallel, but largely independent, paths until the late 1980s, when a third important advance occurred.

The third advance was the conceptual integration of the neuroscientific and psychological traditions of working memory research, proposed by Patricia Goldman-Rakic, that the sustained delay-period neural activity in PFC and the storage buffers of the multiple-component model of Baddeley and Hitch were cross-species manifestations of the same fundamental mental phenomenon. This association between prefrontal cortex and working memory has been very influential in systems and cognitive neuroscience.

Current State of Working Memory Research

A growing body of evidence provided by behavioral, physiological, and neuroimaging studies indicates that information about sensory stimuli may be stored in a segregated, feature-selective manner, and that the relevant cortical regions include relatively early stages of sensory cortical processing. The principle emerging from this work is that the same brain regions that are responsible for the precise sensory encoding of information also contribute to its short-term retention. In the remaining portions of this article we briefly describe these recent advances, with the emphasis on working memory for fundamental dimensions of sensory stimuli.

Visual Working Memory

In the laboratory, the ability to briefly retain visual information can be measured with delayed discrimination tasks. In the simplest version of such tasks, individuals discriminate between two stimuli, the sample and the test, separated by a temporal delay of various durations, and report whether and how the test differs from the previously seen sample. The results of such experiments have revealed that fundamental stimulus features, such as orientation, contrast, size, or speed, can be faithfully preserved for many seconds, although the duration of this preservation often differs for different features. For example, stimulus size or orientation can be retained accurately longer than can luminance contrast. This difference suggests that different stimulus attributes may be retained by separate, feature-selective mechanisms. More direct support for feature-selective storage mechanisms comes from studies that have used interference consisting of an irrelevant stimulus (a 'memory mask') introduced during the delay separating S1 and S2. With this procedure, determination of the parameters that maximize the interfering effects of the mask can provide insights into the nature of the remembered stimulus and thus into the mechanisms involved in its short-term retention. For example, the memory for spatial frequency of gratings (size) can be disrupted only if the masking stimulus is of a different spatial frequency, irrespective of its orientation. This selective interference suggests that information about spatial frequencies may be preserved by mechanisms that are narrowly tuned for that stimulus attribute, and closely associated with its processing, but distinct from mechanisms concerned with stimulus orientation. Similar specialization is seen within the domain of visual motion, in that stimulus speed can be preserved by the mechanisms that are relatively narrowly tuned for speed, independently of stimulus direction.

Representation of visual motion in memory appears to be localized in space in a manner consistent with properties of neurons in cortical area MT, a region specialized in processing of visual motion, thereby supporting the idea that neurons processing visual motion may also be involved in its short-term storage. Overall, behavioral studies of mechanisms that preserve basic attributes of visual stimuli can be characterized as narrowly tuned, spatially localized filters, supporting a model of working memory that involves the contribution of sensory cortical areas.

A close link between visual processing and storage is also suggested by the consequences of cortical damage. For example, damage to motion processing area MT in monkeys results in deficits in remembering motion direction, but only when the remembered stimuli require area MT for their encoding (**Figure 1**). Similarly, damage to inferotemporal cortex, associated with processing of complex shapes, results in deficits in remembering such shapes. Humans with focal lesions in the occipitotemporal cortical area, implicated in processing of specific visual features, also have difficulties remembering these features.

The activity of visual cortical neurons during working memory tasks also attests to their role in sensory maintenance. Such tasks similar to the delayed discrimination tasks described earlier, require the comparison of two stimuli separated by a memory delay. When such stimuli consist of moving random-dot stimuli and the monkeys are required to identify and remember the dot direction, the activity of MT neurons during the memory delay shows selectivity reflecting the remembered direction. This activity is pronounced early in memory delay but weakens toward its end and does not correlate with the animals' decision, suggesting that additional neural mechanisms are needed to account for the maintenance of motion signals. However, at the time of the comparison and decision, these neurons are strongly affected by the remembered direction, suggesting that throughout the task they have access to the remembered direction, and thus are likely to participate in the circuitry subserving storage. Similar behavior has been observed in inferotemporal (IT) cortex, associated with the processing of complex shapes, in that stimulus-selective activity occurs not only in response to specific shapes but also during the memory delay. During the comparison phase of the task, these neurons, like neurons in area MT, reflect the remembered shape. This type of activity is consistent with the possibility that visual cortical neurons actively participate the circuitry subserving storage of signals they process, although the nature of this participation awaits further study.

Functional imaging studies of visual working memory indicate that regions of the visual system are differentially recruited by working memory tasks, depending on the stimulus dimension that must be remembered. For example, working memory for the location versus the identity of visual stimuli, such as color patches and geometric shapes, recruits domain-specific memory-related activity in posterior cortical regions associated with the 'where' and 'what' visual streams, respectively. For location memory this includes dorsal occipital cortex, the intraparietal sulcus, and superior parietal lobule, whereas for object identity it includes ventral temporal and occipital cortex. Location memory tasks also typically recruit frontal regions associated with oculumotor control – the frontal eye fields and the supplementary eye fields.

Within the ventral streams, delay-period activity is segregated in a category-specific manner. For example, multiple images of faces and of naturalistic scenes can be presented as samples, with a postsample cue indicating which is the to-be-remembered category. When individuals are cued to remember the faces, delay-period activity is selectively elevated in the fusiform face area (FFA). When they are cued to remember scenes, delay-period activity is selectively elevated in the parahippocampal place area (PPA). Another study of working memory for faces featured three delay periods interposed between the presentation of the first and second, second and third, and third and fourth stimuli. The logic was that the multiple distracting events in this task might serve to 'weed out' from the first delay period activity that was not involved directly in storage, because only regions with activity necessary for retaining the information to the end of the trial would maintain their activity across distracting stimuli. The results revealed that the posterior fusiform gyrus was the only region that retained the relevant signal during the last delay, immediately preceding the decision. Still other studies of working memory for faces have varied memory load (i.e., the number of items to be remembered), on the

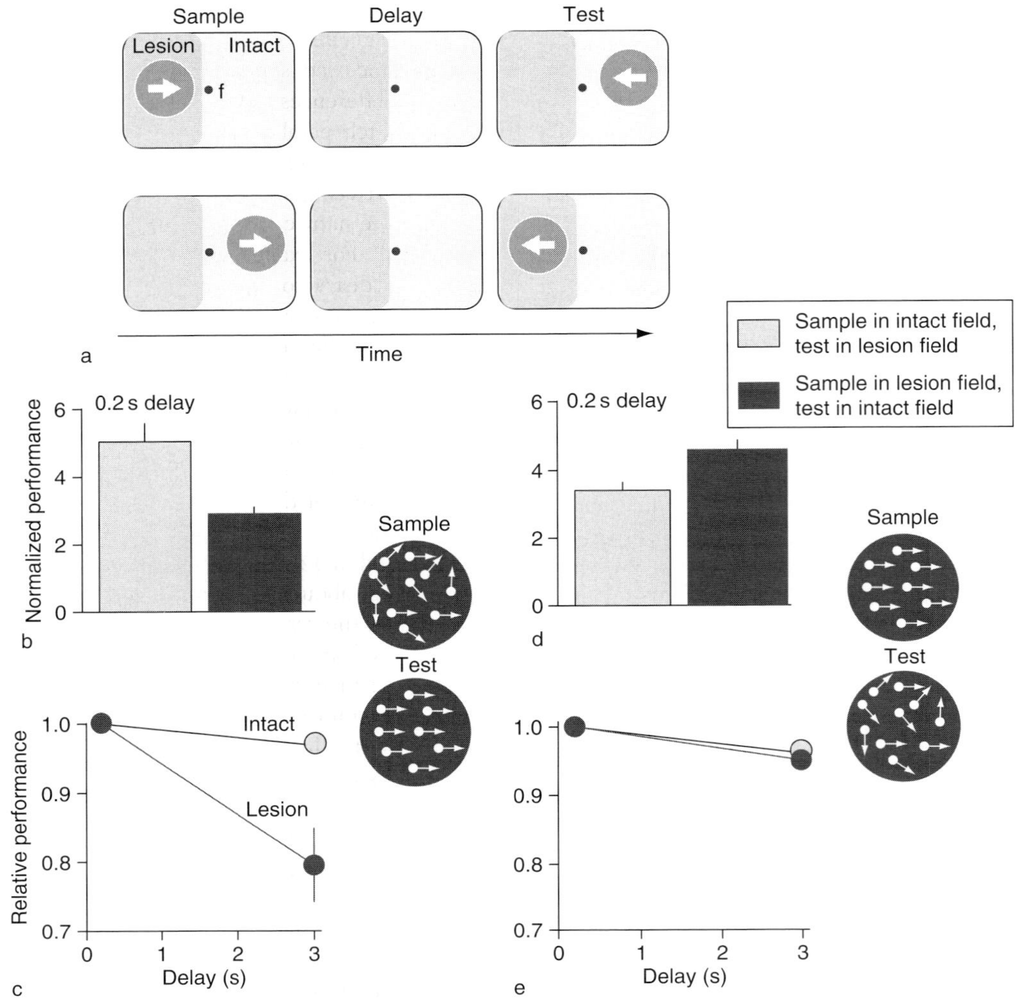

Figure 1 The role of cortical areas processing visual motion in remembering motion direction. (a) Monkeys with unilateral lesions of motion processing areas MT/MST performed a task requiring integration of complex motion and remembering its direction. In this task, sample and test stimuli were separated by a delay and positioned in opposite hemifields, so that one was placed in the lesioned and the other in the corresponding location in the intact hemifield. The monkeys reported whether sample and test moved in the same or in different directions by pressing one of two response buttons. During each trial the monkeys fixated a small target at the center of the display (dark gray dot) while attending to moving random dots (indicated by arrows) presented in the periphery. (b, d) Normalized direction range thresholds (1/(360-range threshold)/360) measured when the delay between sample and test was minimal (0.2 s). The sample or the test stimulus was composed of dots moving in a range of directions, while the other stimulus contained only coherent motion (stimulus configurations shown to the right of each set of plots). Performance was decreased whenever the stimulus containing noncoherent motion, and thus requiring integration, was placed in the lesioned field, demonstrating the importance of areas MT/MST for motion integration. (c, e) Effect of memory delay on performance for two direction range tasks. Performance was measured with both stimuli placed in the intact (light gray circles) or in the lesioned hemifields (dark gray circles), either by varying the range of directions in the sample, while the test moved coherently (left plots), or by varying the range of directions in the test, while the sample moved coherently (right plots). Thresholds were normalized to the data measured at a 0.2 s delay. Error bars are SEM. A delay-specific deficit was present only when the remembered stimulus (sample) contained a broad range of directions and required integration. This result demonstrates that stimulus conditions requiring motion integration depend on intact areas MT/MST. However, coherently moving random dots can be discriminated and remembered at a normal level even in the absence of areas MT/MST. This shows that a cortical area involved in processing of sensory signals is also involved in their storage. Adapted from Bisley JW and Pasternak T (2000) The multiple roles of visual cortical areas MT/MST in remembering the direction of visual motion. *Cerebral Cortex* 10: 1053–1065.

logic that storage-related activity is sensitive to variations in load. These studies confirmed the importance of posterior fusiform gyrus in short-term storage.

Studies of working memory for spatial location have also addressed the mechanisms that support storage. One of these is attention-based rehearsal, a mechanism hypothesized to contribute to the short-term retention of locations via covert shifts of attention to the to-be-remembered location. These studies presented sample stimuli in one or the other visual hemifield while individuals fixated a central spot. Delay-period activity was greater in the hemisphere contralateral to the target location, an effect comparable to what one sees in studies of attention. This lateralized delay-period bias was strongest in extrastriate regions, decreased in magnitude across the parietal cortex, and was no longer reliable in frontal cortex. A second mechanism for the short-term retention of location information is prospective motor coding – the formulation, and then retention, of a motor plan for the acquisition of a target with, say, a saccade or a grasp. Electrophysiology studies in monkeys and neuroimaging studies in humans that encourage a prospective strategy localize this activity to frontal oculomotor regions, to prefrontal cortex, and to the caudate nucleus.

Tactile Working Memory

As with visual stimuli, tactile stimuli can be faithfully represented in working memory. Delayed discrimination of vibration stimuli can be performed with delays of many seconds, although the accuracy of this discrimination is maximal at short delays and decreases rapidly during the first 5 s of the delay. At longer delays, however, performance does not continue to deteriorate, suggesting that a two-stage memory process might be involved. Delayed discrimination of vibration stimuli can be disrupted by the application of transcranial magnetic stimulation (TMS) to human primary somatosensory cortex (area S1) during the initial portion of the delay period. This effect not only implicates area S1 in storage of vibration information, but also demonstrates the vulnerability of the storage mechanism early in the delay, an effect also observed in studies of working memory for visual motion.

In the awake behaving monkey, electrophysiological evidence for delay-period activity in S1 is mixed, with some laboratories reporting evidence in favor of it and others failing to find it. In area S2, however, there is no such equivocality, with strong evidence for stimulus frequency-specific activity persisting far into the delay period. Furthermore, responses of S2 neurons to the test stimulus contain information about the remembered stimulus, thereby reflecting the relationship between the two stimuli.

The ability to recognize and remember objects based on tactile input has also been studied with human neuroimaging. For example, positron emission tomography (PET) studies have revealed activation in the parietal operculum (area S2), an associative somatosensory area, during working memory tasks involving vibratory stimuli or palpated wire forms.

Auditory Working Memory

Although humans discriminate both pitch and loudness of sounds with high accuracy and remember these dimensions for many seconds, memory for pitch and loudness decline at different rates, suggesting that the two dimensions may be processed separately in auditory memory. The observed differences in the precision of memory for intensity and pitch parallel the findings in vision for contrast and spatial frequency (see earlier). As with vision, the use of interfering stimuli during the memory delay has revealed the nature of representation of auditory stimuli in memory. For example, memory for pitch can be disturbed by distractor tones, but only if these tones are within a narrow range of frequencies, relative to the frequency of the remembered stimulus, supporting the existence of separate pitch memory modules. Furthermore, sound frequency is likely to be stored separately from its location, suggesting that auditory memory obeys the same patterns as does auditory perception for physical parameters of the remembered stimuli.

In the auditory cortex, neuronal activity during the delay period of a delayed two-tone discrimination carries information about the frequency of the sample tone. In addition, the response to the second tone depends on whether its frequency matches that of the first, implicating neurons in auditory cortex in the circuitry subserving working memory for tone frequency. Participation of auditory cortex in auditory working memory is also supported by studies of the human using magnetoencephalography (MEG).

Memory-related activity has also been seen in associative auditory cortex of humans during tasks requiring memory for differences in pitch and tonal sequences; the right superior temporal lobe was associated with tonal sequences, and pitch judgments were associated with increased right frontal lobe activation. Interestingly, the auditory cortex appears to be maximally active early in the delay, whereas regions in the supramarginal gyrus and parts of the cerebellum are activated later, suggesting that for audition, too, working memory may be accomplished in multiple stages.

The involvement of regions processing auditory information in working memory is also supported by selective deficits in patients with damage to auditory associative cortex in the right temporal lobe. These patients are impaired primarily on tone discrimination with long, distracted delays.

Multiple Encoding in Working Memory

It seems unlikely that the representational bases of working memory are limited to the domain in which stimuli are perceived. In addition to the multiple serially ordered stages in working memory for visual, tactile, and auditory domains, sensory information can also be represented in parallel in multiple formats. Thus, as reviewed earlier, working memory for location can be accomplished via

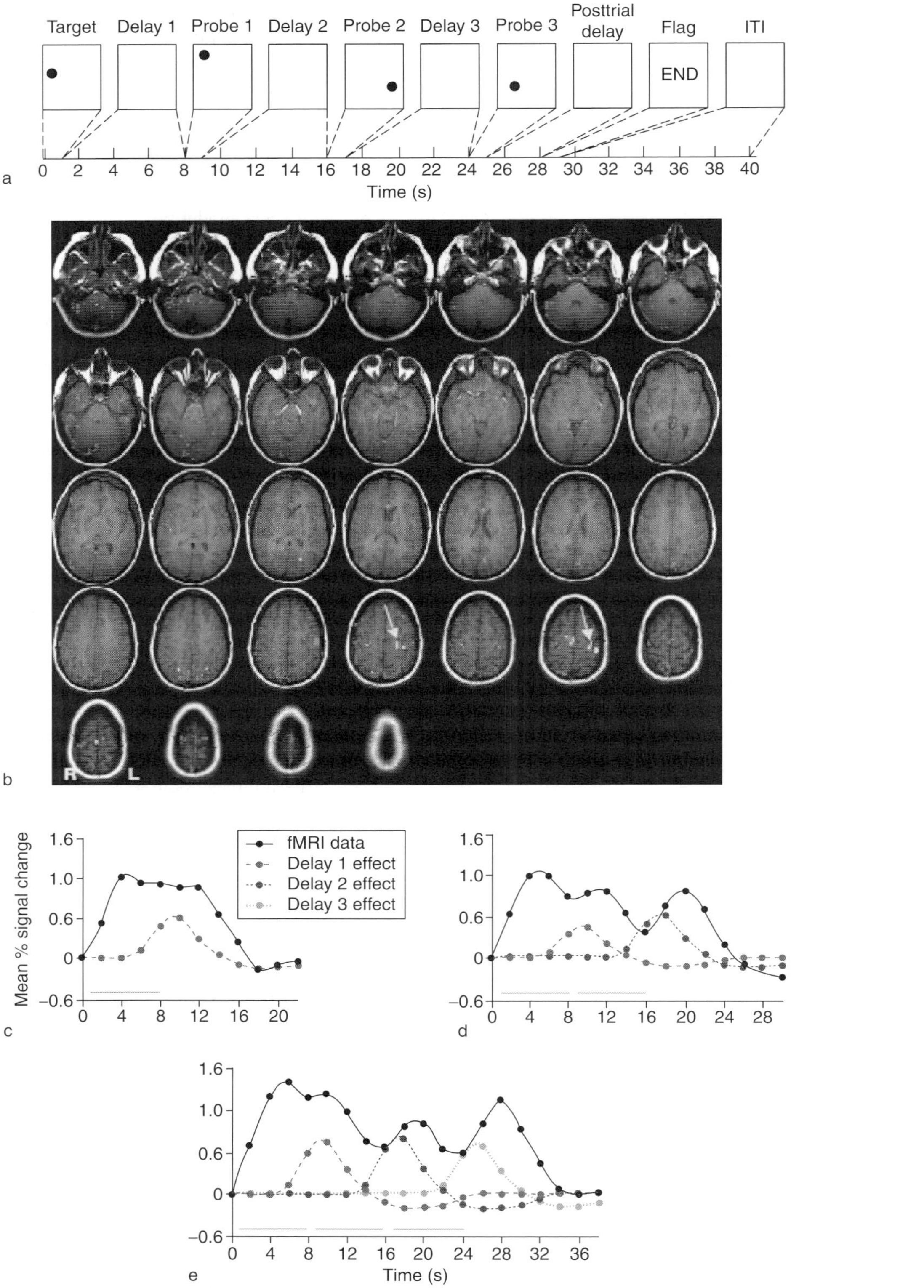

Figure 2 A functional magnetic resonance imaging experiment demonstrating sustained memory-related activity for location across multiple delay periods. (a) Behavioral task. Individuals view and encode the target location, then, after a 7 s delay, indicate with a button press whether the probe does or does not appear in the same location. One-third of the trials end after probe 1. On two- and three-delay trials, the offset of probe 1 is followed by another delay period, after which individuals evaluate the location of probe 2 with respect to the target. On one- and two-delay trials, the 'END' message appears at times 12 and 20 s, respectively. (b) Results from a single representative individual. Voxels in red showed sustained delay-period activity for delay 1 only. Voxels in blue are the subset

retrospective sensory memory-based mechanism, as well as a prospective motor planning mechanism. Analogously, there is growing evidence that working memory for visual identity recruits verbal (and, perhaps, semantic) representations in addition to the ventral stream visual mechanisms already discussed.

Working Memory and Prefrontal Cortex

For many years PFC has been strongly associated with the storage of sensory information in working memory. Consistent with this idea are the facts that PFC is directly interconnected with cortical areas processing fundamental sensory dimensions, and that PFC neurons often display stimulus-related activity during the memory delay. However, a growing body of evidence suggests that PFC is more likely to play a key role in directing attention to behaviorally relevant sensory signals and in making decisions concerning these signals, than in directly supporting their retention in short-term and working memory. Consistent with this view is the fact that extensive damage to prefrontal cortex does not eliminate the ability to perform simple short-term memory tasks, such as the digit span and spatial span variants of immediate serial recall. The limited effect of such lesions is apparent on delay tasks if during the memory period there is no interference and no requirement to keep track of multiple items. Also consistent with this view is the finding that although the delay activity of PFC neurons recorded in monkeys performing a delayed direction discrimination task (see earlier) was direction-specific, it did not predict decisions about stimulus direction that they made at the end of the trial. The contribution of these neurons to the task became apparent only after the end of the memory delay, when the monkeys compared test direction with that of the remembered sample. Furthermore, direction selectivity in PFC neurons, prevalent during the task, was greatly reduced when the monkeys were not required to use the information about stimulus direction. This work showed that PFC neurons are capable of gating sensory signals according to their behavioral relevance, it but does not support the key role for PFC neurons in the maintenance of these signals. Other studies, designed to isolate the contributions of attention and response selection from those of sensory storage, indicate a stronger role for the former in PFC.

In the human neuroimaging literature there is some debate about stimulus domain- or category-specific segregation of delay-period activity in PFC – for example, comparable patterns of delay-period activity during tasks involving memory for location versus memory for objects or memory for faces versus memory for scenes. The same is true for tasks that involve haptic object encoding versus those that involve visual object encoding. Similarly, in tasks requiring cross-modal integration, individual PFC neurons can be active during the memory delay following the presentation of different stimulus modalities. These examples suggest that PFC assists early-level sensory processing regions to form supramodal mental representations of objects and/or of task contingencies when the relevant stimuli belong to more than one sensory domain.

Another strategy for evaluating the neural basis of sensory storage is to require the retention of information across multiple delay periods interrupted with intervening distracting stimuli. This approach has revealed that neurons in the monkey PFC, but not IT cortex, could sustain a representation of the sample stimulus across multiple delays. Robust sample-specific activity across multiple delay periods is not limited to PFC, however, and has also been observed in other regions, including the temporal pole and the entorhinal cortex of the medial temporal lobe. Functional magnetic resonance imaging (fMRI) studies in humans remembering faces showed that only posterior fusiform gyrus retains sustained activity across all three delay periods, although many regions displayed activity during the first delay period. An analogous result was seen in the individuals remembering spatial locations, with distraction-spanning delay-period activity distributed across multiple areas, including intraparietal sulcus, superior parietal lobule, frontal eye fields, and supplementary eye fields in frontal cortex (**Figure 2**). Finally, repetitive TMS (rTMS) applied to PFC has failed to disrupt working memory performance, but has altered performance when applied to parietal cortex.

Although the weight of evidence is inconsistent with a storage role for PFC, virtually every electrophysiological and neuroimaging study of primate working memory finds delay-period activity in this region of the brain. Thus, it is important to address the role of this activity. If this activity does not represent the storage of information, what are alternative explanations of its function? One possibility is that PFC plays an important role in

of voxels with delay-period activity sustained across delay 1 and delay 2. Voxels in yellow are the still smaller subset with delay-period activity sustained across all three delays. Note that although many regions, including the prefrontal cortex, show delay-period activity during delay 1, only dorsal-stream parietal and frontal oculomotor regions sustain this delay-period activity across all three delays. Arrows highlight the voxels from left frontal eye field (the activity of which is shown in panels c, d, and e). (c) Activity from three-delay voxels in the left frontal eye field, averaged across one-delay trials. 'Delay 1 effect' reflects the estimated magnitude of delay 1 activity. Gray bar along the horizontal axis indicates the duration of the delay period. (d) Activity from these same frontal eye field voxels averaged across two-delay trials. Graphical conventions are the same as in panel b. (e) Activity from these same frontal eye field voxels averaged across three-delay trials. Graphical conventions are the same as in panel c. Adapted from Postle BR (2006) Distraction-spanning sustained activity during delayed recognition of locations. *NeuroImage* 30: 950–962. (See color plate 34.)

the control of potentially disrupting effects of distraction and interference during working memory tasks. Lesion, electrophysiology, and fMRI studies have all provided evidence that dorsolateral PFC can accomplish this by controlling the gain of activity in sensory processing regions, such that the delay-period processing of potentially distracting stimuli is suppressed. Analogously, a region of ventrolateral PFC has been implicated in the control of proactive interference, the deleterious effect of previous mental activity on current task performance. In addition, an important function of delay activity in PFC may be the attentional selection of task-relevant information, as well as in planning for the response. This is consistent with the well-characterized role for PFC in the biasing of stimulus–response circuits so that novel or less salient behaviors can be favored over well-learned associations and behavioral routines. Finally, the potential role of PFC in the integration of cognitive and motivational factors is supported by the modulation of delay-period activity of its neurons during spatial memory tasks by the type of the anticipated reward.

Conclusion

The emerging picture of the neural basis of working memory is of a class of behaviors that does not depend on one or more functionally specialized regions. Rather, working memory is supported by the coordinated activity of circuits responsible for the sensory processing of the critical information, and, to varying degrees, those that control the flexible allocation of attention and the selection of task-relevant behavior.

See also: Cognition, An Overview of Neuroimaging Techniques.

Further Reading

Baddeley, A (1992). Working memory. *Science* 255: 556–559.

Bisley, JW and Pasternak, T (2000). The multiple roles of visual cortical areas MT/MST in remembering the direction of visual motion. *Cerebral Cortex* 10: 1053–1065.

Cowan, N (2005). *Working Memory Capacity.* Hove, UK: Psychology Press.

Fuster, J (1995). *Memory in the Cerebral Cortex.* Cambridge, MA: MIT Press.

Goldman-Rakic, PS (1995). Cellular basis of working memory. *Neuron* 14: 477–485.

Hebb, D (1949). *Organization of Behavior.* New York: Wiley.

Miller, EK and Cohen, JD (2001). An integrative theory of prefrontal cortex function. *Annual Review of Neuroscience* 24: 167–202.

Pasternak, T and Greenlee, M (2005). Working memory in primate sensory systems. *Nature Reviews Neuroscience* 6: 97–107.

Petrides, M (2000). Dissociable roles of mid-dorsolateral prefrontal and anterior inferotemporal cortex in visual working memory. *Journal of Neuroscience* 20: 7496–7503.

Postle, BR (2006). Distraction-spanning sustained activity during delayed recognition of locations. *NeuroImage* 30: 950–962.

Postle, BR (2006). Working memory as an emergent property of the mind and brain. *Neuroscience* 139: 23–38.

Postle, BR and Hamidi, M (in press) Nonvisual codes and nonvisual brain areas support visual working memory. *Cerebral Cortex Advance Access.* published online on December 5, 2006.

Romo, R and Salinas, E (2003). Flutter discrimination: Neural codes, perception, memory and decision making. *Nature Reviews Neuroscience* 4: 203–218.

Todd, J and Marois, R (2005). Posterior parietal cortex activity predicts individual differences in visual short-term memory capacity. *Cognitive, Affective & Behavioral Neuroscience* 5(2): 144–155.

Zaksas, D and Pasternak, T (2006). Directional signals in the prefrontal cortex and area MT during a working memory for visual motion task. *Journal of Neuroscience* 26: 11726–11742.

Memory, Spatial

L. F. Jacobs

Spatial memory, the memory for the spatial location and organization of objects in our environment, plays a critical role in daily life. Even the momentary loss of memory for the location one's keys, glasses, or daily parking place can be unsettling. The dramatic degeneration of spatial memory in neurological disorders such as Alzheimer's disease greatly disrupts a person's ability to function and control his or her life.

Spatial Memory and Spatial Cognition

Spatial memory is one component of spatial cognition (**Fig. 1**). Spatial cognition embraces a range of mental representations of spatial relations in the external world. It includes the manipulation and orientation of single objects (e.g., mental rotation and knowing the location of an object relative to a reference point such as the body)

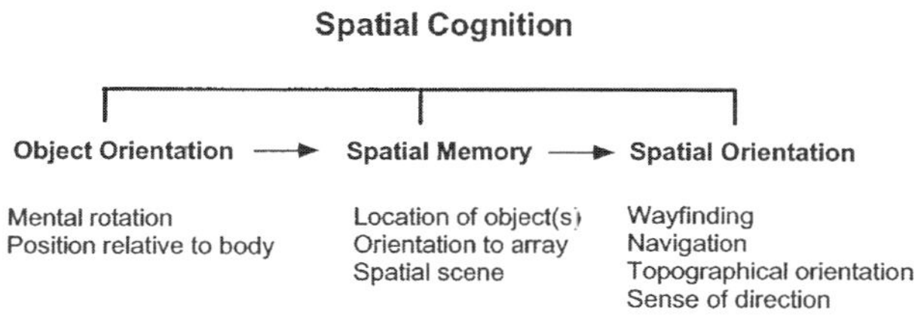

Figure 1 The relationship of spatial memory to other forms of spatial cognition.

and spatial orientation, which is orienting in large-scale space (e.g., spatial navigation and way finding). Together, these cognitive abilities are used to manipulate, recall, and navigate through space, whether in the real world or in mental imagery. The different abilities are also dependent on each other. Remembering the location of an object may require that one remember its orientation in space, and being able to remember the location of objects is necessary for large-scale spatial navigation. Thus, these three subcategories of spatial cognition are related in a hierarchical fashion. They are also mediated by different neural structures, as discussed later. Hence, spatial cognition is not a unitary trait that can be assessed with a single test; it is a complex of cognitive abilities that can function in concert or independently. Therefore, different neurological insults can produce a wide variety of changes in spatial cognition. To determine which subsystem has been affected, one must identify the kind of spatial cognition that has been damaged.

The location of an object can be remembered in reference to different kinds of spatial information (**Fig. 2**). First, the object can be coincident with a conspicuous landmark or beacon. Second, the object's location can be remembered as a triangulation from an array of objects. Here, the subject has to remember not only what objects are where but also how they are oriented (e.g., vertical or horizontal). If they are being viewed from a novel vantage point, the subject may have to mentally rotate them to determine the triangulation. Finally, the object's location may be encoded as in the direction of a distant landmark or compass mark; this is a landmark that is so far away that the navigator cannot use it to determine distance accurately—only direction.

Space can also be encoded using different reference frames according to the situation. For example, one can encode a location relative to one's own body, such as to one's left or right. This egocentric encoding, mediated largely by the parietal cortex, is different from that of structures, such as hippocampus, that mediate orientation in a global sense, independent from one's body. An example of such allocentric encoding is a mental image of the layout of a city. A spatial memory encoding of an object's position can be either egocentric or allocentric, depending on the frame of reference.

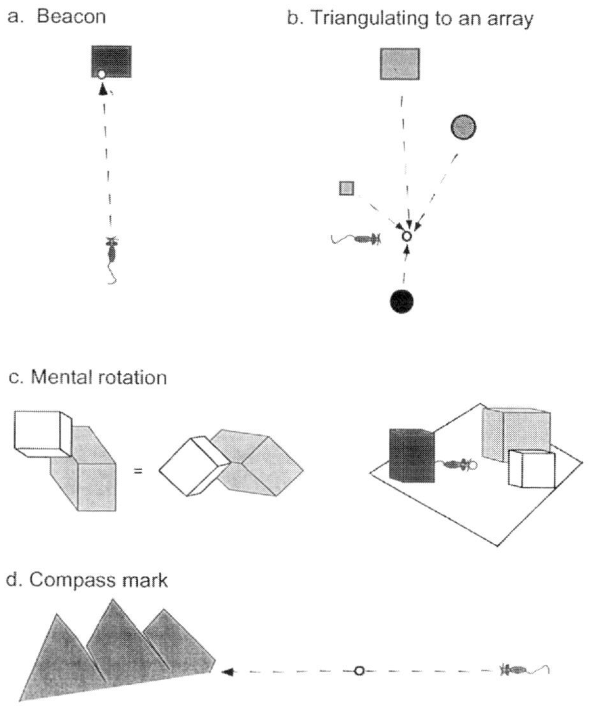

Figure 2 Mechanisms underlying spatial memory. (a) Orienting toward a beacon, an object whose location is coincident with that of the goal's. (b) Triangulating toward an array, where the location of a goal is defined relative to nearby landmarks. (c) Mental rotation of landmarks in an array. (d) Orienting toward a compass mark, a landmark that supplies directional information, like a compass.

Localization and Function of Spatial Memory

Just as spatial cognition is not a single phenomenon but a complex of cognitive abilities, so too is memory composed of several systems organized in hierarchical levels, all mediated by different brain structures. As with other types of memory, spatial memory can be classified as short (i.e., minutes or hours) or long term (i.e., weeks to months). An important component of working or short-term memory, as proposed by Baddeley, is a visuospatial scratch pad. This "structure" encodes the memory of object locations, a memory that may last only a few seconds before it is forgotten or rehearsed and consolidated into long-term memory. Like short-term verbal memory, short-term memory for object locations is subject to interference, giving credence to the notion of a short-term spatial memory system. In humans, there is additional lateralization of spatial memory, given the specialization of the right cerebral hemisphere for spatial processing.

Neural Encoding of Spatial Memory

Neuroimaging studies in humans suggest that both the right posterior parietal cortex and the right lateral prefrontal cortex are important in the processing of spatial working memory. However, the right medial temporal lobe, including the hippocampus, has been implicated in long-term spatial memory.

Behavioral studies of memory for object locations typically require subjects to study groups of stimulus items located on an array and then to recall and replace those objects after a delay interval (**Fig. 3**). This technique was developed by Brenda Milner in the 1980s while studying patients who underwent unilateral temporal lobectomies for the treatment of epilepsy. Patients were asked to view 16 toy objects laid out on an array and to estimate a price for each object. After a delay, the subjects were then asked to recall each object from memory and then to place each object in its original location. After a long delay, both the right and the left lobectomy patients were impaired on the object recall task, with the left patients performing worse than the right patients. In the object location task, however, the right lobectomy patients were severely impaired, whereas the left lobectomy patients performed at normal levels.

Although spatial memory impairment only occurs with right medial temporal lobe damage, deficits in visual memory and object recall have also been demonstrated, making it difficult to completely dissociate spatial memory from other types of memory. Long-term spatial memory appears to be dissociable among cerebral hemispheres, even within the same temporal lobe. Nunn and colleagues replicated the Milner study but included a temporal titration procedure. Here, the delay between viewing the array and recall was varied for the right and left lobectomy groups. In this way, they could match performance on the object location (spatial) memory function with the object recall (nonspatial) memory function. Only the right temporal lobectomy patients were impaired on the spatial version of the task.

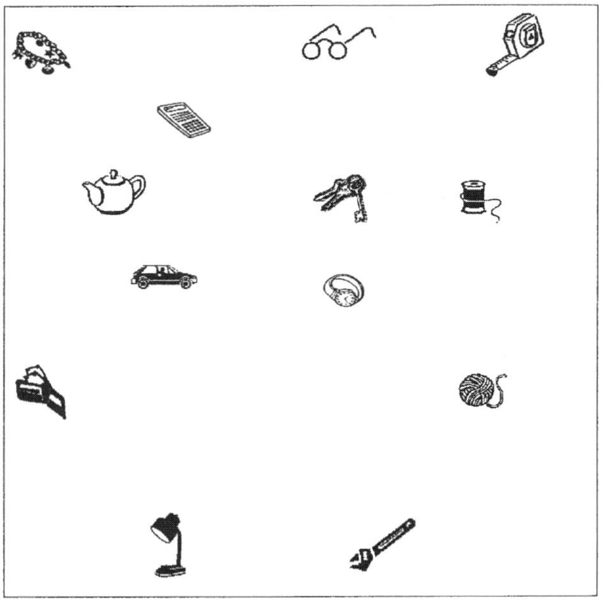

Figure 3 Spatial memory recall task developed by Brenda Milner. In this task, subjects are asked to recall the location of household objects that they have seen previously arrayed on an open surface.

Also at issue are the exact medial temporal structures involved in spatial memory and their relative roles. Although focal lesion studies have laid the groundwork for models of hippocampal involvement in human spatial memory, they are flawed because control of lesion size is almost impossible, leading to variability within studies of the structures involved. This is alleviated somewhat by lesion analysis, a procedure measuring the size of the lesions, and only subjects with specific lesion measurements are included in the study. Nunn et al. included only those patients with specific hippocampal lesions that did not encroach upon surrounding structures to demonstrate the importance of right hippocampus in spatial memory. Functional neuroimaging studies have also been utilized to study spatial memory, but different results have been obtained from different laboratories and/or different techniques (positron emission tomography and functional magnetic resonance imaging). The cognitive/behavioral research is generally consistent, however, with the view that the right hippocampus is specialized in some way for spatial memory, although it does not have an exclusive role in this capacity.

This raises the issue of the independence of spatial memory from other types of memory. Even if spatial memory can be dissociated in this way, this does not mean that spatial memory is a separate memory system. Its status, however, is currently a matter of debate. For example, some argue that spatial memory may serve as the foundation for broad concepts such as episodic memory, whereas others argue that it is simply a subcomponent of the broader declarative memory system. These questions are at the forefront of an active area of research and are being pursued employing many techniques, including electrophysiological recordings in laboratory rodents and humans, genetic and pharmacological lesions in rodents, and neuroimaging studies in humans.

Evidence from Animal Models of Spatial Memory

Data from nonhuman animals offer an important perspective on the nature of spatial memory. There are two complementary lines of evidence, one from patterns of space use in wild animals and the other from neurophysiological recordings from laboratory rodents orienting in space.

Studies of the natural patterns of space use in wild rodents and wild birds have found a remarkable pattern:

The larger the territory or the greater the need for spatial memory, the larger the hippocampus is relative to the whole brain in that species. Thus, small rodents and birds that store food like squirrels (e.g., kangaroo rats and chickadees), putting a single seed in a cache and returning weeks later to retrieve it, have relatively larger hippocampi than closely related species that do not store food in this way. Within species, individuals of the sex that must search widely for mates or nest sites during the breeding season (e.g., voles and cowbirds) also have a relatively larger hippocampus. Thus, data from the naturally occurring patterns of hippocampal size in both birds and mammals indicate the role of the hippocampus in spatial cognition.

More direct evidence comes from neurophysiological studies of spatial memory in the laboratory rodent. Recordings from single hippocampal neurons during exploration of a novel place have led to a sophisticated understanding of the role of the hippocampus in this process. Much of this work began with the theory of the hippocampus as a cognitive map, first proposed by John O'Keefe and Lynn Nadel in 1978. This theory developed from O'Keefe's finding that pyramidal neurons in the rat hippocampus are active only in a particular point in space, such as only at the end of one arm of a radial arm maze (**Fig. 4a**). These "place cells" have receptive fields that can be altered by changing the environment. As shown in **Fig. 4b**, if the landmarks around the outside of the radial arm maze are rotated, the place fields also rotate, firing only when the rat is in the same spatial position relative to those landmarks. Thus, neural activity in hippocampal place cells closely parallels the spatial behavior of the rodent.

Experimental lesions of the hippocampus also confirm its role in spatial memory. After a lesion, the rodent will make repeated revisits in the radial arm maze. In the water maze, although the rodent can learn a path to the platform after many trials, it cannot quickly adapt its behavior if released from a novel start point, but must painstakingly memorize a new route.

Hormonal Influences

Male and female humans and laboratory rats show a remarkable difference in the visual cues that they use to orient. In rats, Williams has shown that male performance on the radial arm maze is severely disrupted if the maze is curtained, even if positional landmarks are still visible. Female performance is only slightly impaired under this condition. In contrast, if the positional landmarks are removed or randomized female performance is severely impaired, whereas this manipulation has less effect on male performance. For example, if male and female rats were trained on a radial arm maze (**Fig. 4b**), female performance would be completely disrupted if the landmarks were randomized. In contrast, males would continue to orient to other cues, such as the geometrical shape of the room.

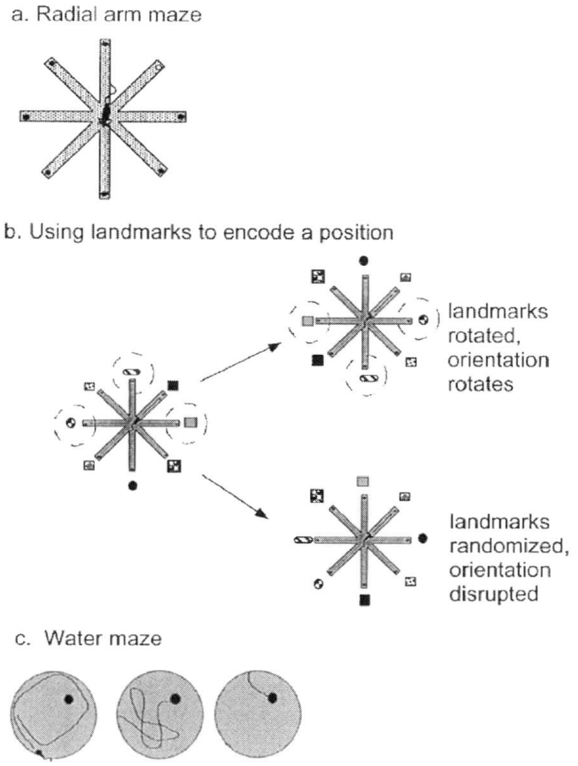

Figure 4 Methods used to study spatial memory in laboratory animals. (a) Radial arm maze developed by David S. Olton. The goal of this task is to retrieve eight rewards, each placed on the end of a maze arm (•). Over several days, the rodent naturally learns to avoid revisiting an arm that has recently been explored (○). Performance is quantified as the number of revisits per trial. The same maze can also be used to study long-term memory by training the rodent that only a certain subset of arms are ever rewarded. Performance on this task is quantified as the number of incorrect visits, either to never-baited arms or arms already visited in that trial. (b) The use of landmarks by laboratory rodents to encode a position in space on the radial arm maze. The unique shapes represent unique local landmarks. The dashed line encircles three of the landmarks available during training to facilitate the visualization of the manipulations. After rats learn the landmarks, they are either rotated or randomized. After rotation (top), the rats simply rotate their orientation and continue to orient accurately. After randomization (bottom), the rats must completely relearn the maze. Note that the circles with dashed lines could also represent the shape and location of three place fields encoded by three hippocampal neurons; place fields would rotate with the landmarks. (c) Water maze developed by Richard G. M. Morris. The goal of this task is to find a hidden platform whose surface is several centimeters beneath the water's surface. Until the platform is found, the rodent must keep swimming. Over the course of several trials in a few days, the rodent learns to take increasingly shorter paths to the platform, even when it is released from a different location on each trial. Representative swim paths from three points during the learning of the task are shown, arranged chronologically from left to right. •, hidden platform location.

Similar patterns are seen in humans: There are female or male advantages on different spatial tasks. The largest sex difference, and one that has been documented in different cultures and age groups, is mental rotation. However, in the recall of the relative position of objects, women are more accurate than men. This is seen for the recall of a large number of objects ($>$20), whether drawn on a sheet of paper or actual objects in a small room such as an office. In contrast, Postma demonstrated a male advantage when the absolute location of fewer objects ($<$10) must be recalled.

The explanation for this difference may lie in the preference of males to encode in terms of direction and distance and females to encode in terms of relative position. The same effect is seen in map recall studies. When given fictitious maps to remember, women remember more distinctive landmarks, whereas men are more accurate at reproducing accurate Euclidean directions and distances. Men and women also differ in their response to virtual mazes, with men navigating more accurately by direction of movement, whereas women are more accurate regarding the identity and location of landmarks. Recent neuroimaging studies of this phenomenon suggest that both men and women employ right hippocampal activation during virtual maze navigation. However, there are subtle sex differences in the parallel involvement of the prefrontal and parietal cortices during navigation. Unfortunately, results from imaging are contradictory, and further research is needed before any strong conclusions can be drawn regarding the neural basis of such sex differences in spatial navigation.

Effects of Aging

As with other types of memory, the accuracy of spatial memory recall declines with age. The parameters surrounding the objects to be remembered, however, have a major effect on this age difference in recall.

A common technique to study changes with aging is the recall of distinctive objects or patterns on a small matrix (e.g., 5×5) on a display board or computer screen. Performance is measured as the number of objects recalled after a delay. Older subjects show reduced accuracy on this task compared to young adults, particularly when the task is set up as incidental learning. In this case, subjects are not instructed to remember but simply do so incidentally while paying attention to another instruction (e.g., estimate the cost of the object). However, even when instructed to remember (intentional learning), a deficit is seen in older subjects. Older subjects do particularly poorly when the objects to be remembered are similar to each other (e.g., all poker chips compared to different household objects). A similar age difference in spatial memory recall is seen on more naturalistic tasks, such as placing objects on maps. Again, there is an added effect if the learning is incidental, not intentional, and an effect of type of object: Real objects are recalled more readily than paper-and-pencil versions of the same task. Evidence suggests that objects are also confused if they are too similar to each other in type (e.g., tool vs furniture), suggesting that the semantic encoding of an object contributes to age-related declines in recall.

See also: Alzheimer's Disease; Memory, Autobiographical; Memory, Episodic; Memory, Explicit/Implicit.

Further Reading

Baddeley, A (1993). *Your Memory: A User's Guide,* 2nd ed. London: Penguin.

de Haan, EHF, Kappelle, LJ, and Postma, A (2001). Varieties of human spatial memory: A meta-analysis on the effects of hippocampal lesions. *Brain Res. Rev* 35: 295–303.

Jacobs, LF (1996). Sexual differentiation and cognitive function. In: Blakemore, C and Iversen, S (eds.) *Gender and Society.* Oxford: Oxford Univ. Press.

Kausler, DH (1994). *Learning and Memory in Normal Aging.* San Diego: Academic Press.

Kimura, D (1999). *Sex and Cognition.* Cambridge, MA: MIT Press.

Kolb, B and Whishaw, IQ (1996). Spatial behavior. In *Human Neuropsychology*. 4th ed. New York: Freeman.

Isgor, C and Sengelaub, DR (1998). Prenatal gonadal steroids affect adult spatial behavior, CA1 and CA3 pyramidal cell morphology in rats. *Horm. Behav* 34: 183–198.

Nunn, JA, Graydon, FJX, Polkey, CE, et al. (1999). Differential spatial memory impairment after right temporal lobectomy demonstrated using temporal titration. *Brain* 122: 47–59.

O'Keefe, J and Nadel, L (1978). *The Hippocampus as a Cognitive Map.* Oxford: Oxford Univ. Press.

O'Keefe, J, Burgess, N, Donnett, JG, et al. (1998). Place cells, navigational accuracy, and the human hippocampus. *Philos. Trans. R. Soc. London B* 353: 1333–1340.

Sherry, DF and Hampson, E (1997). Evolution and the hormonal control of sexually dimorphic spatial abilities in humans. *Trends Cogn. Sci.* 1: 50–56.

Sherry, DF, Jacobs, LF, and Gaulin, SJC (1992). Adaptive specialization of the hippocampus. *Trends Neurosci.* 15: 298–303.

Squire, LR (1987). *Memory and Brain.* Oxford: Oxford Univ. Press.

Williams, CL and Meck, WH (1993). Organizational effects of gonadal hormones induce qualitative differences in visuospatial navigation. In: Haug, M, Whalen, RE, Aron, C, and Oslen, KL (eds.) *The Development of Sex Differences and Similarities in Behavior.* Dordrecht: Kluwer.

Mental Retardation

E. H. Sherr and D. M. Ferriero

Almost no disease category arouses more controversy within the medical field than mental retardation because it raises issues such as eugenics and the balance between nature (genetics) and nurture in influencing a behavioral phenotype. Even the term is subject to critique. Major issues that impact these affected individuals are highlighted along with recent advances in the genetics and pathophysiology of mental retardation.

In 1992, the American Association on Mental Retardation stated that "mental retardation . . . is characterized by significantly subaverage intellectual functioning, existing concurrently with related limitations in . . . adaptive skill areas." This definition recognizes that it is possible and meaningful to measure an individual's cognitive abilities and that mental retardation is a composite of a deficiency in these abilities and in the practical application of adaptive skills that are essential for participating in society. Any definition of a deficiency in cognitive skills must be normative. Thus, an IQ of 70 merely reflects the percentile within the total population who scored at that level. For most standardized tests this corresponds to two standard deviations below the mean. This has served as a practical cutoff for mental retardation, with mild mental retardation equal to an IQ between 50 and 70, moderate to severe <50, and borderline mental retardation between 71 and 80. Therefore, these terms reflect society's threshold for a minimal level of intelligence and daily functioning. If this threshold is utilized as a "litmus test" to instigate a search for causes and to initiate a network of educational and support services, then we have begun to address the needs of these vulnerable members of our society. However, the treatment of the mentally retarded throughout history, even in the past century in the United States, has frequently reflected less well-intentioned motivations.

History

The plight of individuals with mental retardation has been dependent on the customs and beliefs of the era and the locale. In ancient Greece and Rome, infanticide was common and children with disabilities were sold for entertainment or amusement (the circus of P. T. Barnum offered similar fates for the physically unusual). The Middle Ages provided only minimal relief for the mentally retarded because they were frequently sold into slavery or abandoned. However, with the Age of Enlightenment there was a shift in the attitude and treatment of the mentally retarded. In 1690, John Locke published *Essay Concerning Human Understanding*, in which he put forth his theory that the mind was a *tabla rasa*; this theory would have a significant impact on the care and training of individuals with mental retardation. He was also the first to draw a distinction between mental retardation and mental illness: "Herein seems to lie the difference between idiots and madmen, that madmen put wrong ideas together and reason from them, but idiots make very few or no propositions and reason scarce at all."

The modern era in the education and care of individuals with mental retardation began with the work of French physician Jean Marc Itard (1774–1838). He was famous for his attempts to educate a child found in the mountains outside Aveyron whom he named Victor. The systematic training program that he developed for Victor, although it achieved minimal success, inspired the work of Edouard Seguin. Seguin also undertook the training of a cognitively impaired child and in 1837 established a program for "educating" these children at the Salpetriere in Paris. Seguin immigrated to the United States in 1848 and founded an organization that became the American Association on Mental Retardation.

In 1905, Alfred Binet and Theodore Simon created the first intelligence test. This was used as a screen for students in French schools. In 1911, Henry Goddard translated the test into English, and in 1916 Lewis Terman of Stanford University refined the test into what became known as the Stanford–Binet. Intimately connected with these advances, however, was the rise of the eugenics movement in the United States. Goddard published *The Kallikak Family: A Study in the Heredity of Feeble-Mindedness* (1913), which promulgated views about the coheritability of criminality and mental retardation. The eugenics movement reached its zenith in the United States at this time. As many as 27 states had involuntary sterilization laws, and immigration was markedly curtailed by the Immigration Restriction Act of 1924 primarily to prevent the entry of potential "dysgenics" from southern and eastern Europe. It is in this light that we must interpret the current advances in genetic technology. As we are reminded by George Santayana, "those who forget the past are condemned to repeat it."

Positive change occurred for individuals with mental retardation after World War II. The National Association for Retarded Children was founded in 1950 and has been a strong advocate for support services, research, and enhanced rights for retarded individuals. Between 1950 and 1975, enrollment of mentally retarded children in special education programs in the United States increased from less than 50,000 to more than 1.3 million. This movement culminated in the passing of the Education for All Handicapped Children Act, now titled the Individuals with Disabilities Education Act. This act guarantees appropriate education and intervention for all children with disabilities from birth to age 21. Recent U.S. Census Bureau data show that 5,339,400 children are receiving services through this act. Despite these impressive recent gains, there remains much to be done. For instance, testing for certain metabolic disorders is inconsistent from state to state, thus resulting in missed opportunities to prevent new cases of mental retardation. These missed opportunities are even more prevalent in countries less prosperous than the United States.

Epidemiology

As stated previously, mental retardation is functionally defined as the combination of intelligence two standard deviations below the mean and poor adaptive skills. The Wechsler Intelligence Scale for Children III and most other standardized intelligence tests utilize similar scales, thus allowing for quantitative classification of mild, moderate to severe, and borderline mental retardation. Numerous population-based studies have estimated the prevalence of mental retardation. The majority of these studies have found that mild mental retardation affects 15 per 1000 individuals and that moderate to severe mental retardation affects approximately one-third of these individuals or 5 per 1000. There is variability between populations that reflects neonatal and prenatal genetic and metabolic screening programs. Some variability exists as a result of higher consanguinity and levels of nutrition and poverty, and other differences reflect cultural biases toward testing and labeling intellectually challenged children. Most of these individuals come to medical attention because of delays in developmental milestones, particularly speech; however, some continue to be detected as late as 10 years of age.

Many mildly retarded or borderline individuals are able to function independently and are active members of the workforce. However, some require full-time assistance and the care of multidisciplinary medical teams (the cardiac, neurological, and endocrine issues of Down's patients provide a compelling example). The care of the mentally retarded represents a significant percentage of overall health care expenditures. A recent Dutch study determined that the economic costs to society for mental retardation were nearly equal to those for heart disease, stroke, and cancer combined, thus highlighting the need for prevention, early detection, and treatment.

Etiology

The known causes of mental retardation are too numerous to be delineated here; **Table 1** is a list of the more common etiologies. Generally, etiologies are classified into the following categories: prenatal, perinatal, and postnatal. The prenatal group includes known genetic syndromes, central nervous system malformations (which overlap with many other causes), and toxic (e.g., fetal alcohol syndrome) and infectious causes. Perinatal conditions include birth asphyxia, stroke, and meningitis. Using this classification, a recent study of mental retardation in school-age children in metropolitan Atlanta found that 87% of children with mild mental retardation and 57% of moderate to severely affected children did not have identified causes. A similar skew was reported in a landmark Swedish study of all children born in Göteborg between 1966 and 1970, although the percentages of known diagnoses were higher. In many studies, a significant percentage of children with no identifiable diagnosis have a strong family history. Recent discoveries highlight the continued importance that careful genetic analysis will have on the diagnosis and treatment of the mentally retarded.

Table 1 Categories and causes of Mental Retardation

Category	*Causes*
Prenatal	Genetic
	Chromosomal (e.g., trisomy 21, mosaics, translocations)
	Mutant gene (e.g., fragile X, Rubinstein–Taybi, Coffin–Lowry)
	Metabolic (e.g., phenylketonuria, galactosemia, Smith–Lemli–Opitz)
	Acquired
	Fetal alcohol syndrome
	Other maternal subtance abuse
	Nutritional (e.g., rubella, toxoplasmosis, CMV)
	Unknown
	Syndrome (e.g., Schinzel–Giedeon, FG and KBG syndromes)[a]
	Multiple congenital anomaly and mental retardation
Perinatal	Birth asphyxia
	Infection (HSV encephalitics or group B Strep meningitis)
	Stroke (embolic or hemorrhagic)
	Very low birth weight, extreme prematurity
	Metabolic (e.g., hypoglycemia, hyperbilirubinemia)
Postnatal environmental	Toxins (e.g., lead)
	Infection (*H. influenza* b meningitis, arbovirus encephalitis)
	Trauma (consider nonaccidental)
Undetermined	Familial
	Nonfamilial

[a]These are labeled as unknown; they are mostly likely genetic but can be acquired.

Genetics

Since the description of "mongolism" by J. Langdon Down in 1866 and the discovery of trisomy 21 by Lejeune in 1960, considerable progress has been made in uncovering genetic causes of mental retardation. Currently, there are 948 separate entries for mental retardation in the *Online Mendelian Inheritance of Man*. Many of these are rare single gene disorders resulting in mental retardation through a metabolic defect or through aberrations early in embryology. Examples of these disorders include tyrosinemia and holoprosencephaly, respectively. The majority of syndromes do not have an identified causative gene. Most individuals with mental retardation cannot be given a syndromic diagnosis, despite a family history. Recent work, however, has identified a previously unrecognized chromosomal mutation that may be second only to Down's syndrome as a common genetic cause of mental retardation.

In 1995, Jonathan Flint and colleagues reported the development of a system by Southern blot analysis (and now refined to a fluorescence *in situ* hybridization approach) that could detect submicroscopic deletions or rearrangements at the ends of chromosomes. It had been known for some time that these telomeric regions are more susceptible to translocations and deletions. These investigators showed that these "subtelomeric" rearrangements could be detected sensitively by their methods and that a not insignificant percentage of patients with mental retardation were found to have these chromosomal changes. A recent study by this group systematically addressed this association and reported that 7% of patients with mental retardation and some dysmorphic features and 0.5% of patients with isolated mental retardation have these deletions or translocations, which were not detected by traditional 600-band karyotyping. Moreover, they discovered that in approximately 50% of these cases, one parent had a previously undetected balanced translocation. This generation transfer has important genetic counseling implications. This approach should provide an important clinical tool for diagnosing mental retardation and also will provide more general information on gene alleles that can cause mental retardation. Indeed, a recent paper by Higgins et al. that reported a family with nonsyndromic mental retardation localized to the telomeric region of chromosome 3q is a confirmation of this potential.

Another area in which there has been considerable progress in the identification of disease-causing mutations is X-linked mental retardation (**Fig. 1**). This reflects years of work that began with the recognition that familial mental retardation is more common in males, with an average reported ratio of 1.2:1. Fragile X is the most common X-linked disorder of mental retardation. Identified by the susceptibility of metaphase chromosomes to breakage in the presence of folate, this disorder (and its *in vitro* "fragility") is caused by methylation of an expanded CCG repeat and subsequent inactivation of the *fmr1* gene. This encodes a protein (fmrp) thought to be involved in mRNA transport and regulation of protein translation. Interestingly, the triplet repeat region can be demethylated *in vitro* with 5-azadeoxycytidine, leading to normal transcription of the gene. This might pave the way for the development of pharmacological therapy for these patients. Another "fragile" site, FRAXE, has also been linked to mental retardation; the gene *fmr2* encodes a putative transcription factor. Although mental retardation is rarely associated with methylation-based inactivation of

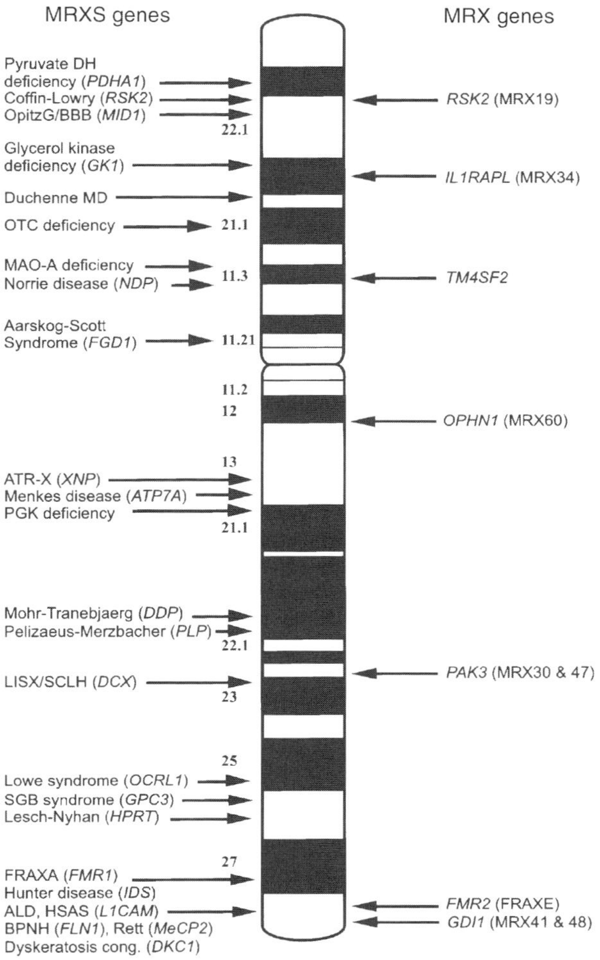

Figure 1 Map of the X chromosome (G banding) with localization of cloned genes responsible for syndromic (MRXS) and nonsyndromic (MRX) mental retardation transmitted in an X-linked fashion. The syndrome name is followed by the name of the gene in brackets for MRXS, whereas for MRX genes the name is followed by the number of the MRX family in brackets in which mutations of that gene were found. OTC, ornithine transcarbamylase; MAO-A, monoamino oxidase A; PGK, phosphoglycerol kinase; LISX/SCLH, lissencephaly X/subcortical laminar heterotopia; SGB, Simpson–Golabi–Behmel; ALD, adrenoleukodystrophy; HSAS, hydrocephalus with stenosis of the aqueduct of Silvius; BPNH, bilateral periventricular nodular heterotopia (reprinted with permission of Dr. Ben Oostra).

this gene, there are reports linking microdeletions of *fmr2* with mental retardation and premature ovarian failure.

Many families have been reported in which individuals affected by mental retardation span multiple generations. Multiplex families that have an autosomal mode of inheritance are usually not large enough to permit localization of the causative mutation by classic genetic analysis. This analysis is simplified when the inheritance pattern implicates the X chromosome, and numerous families have been documented with an X-linked form of mental retardation. Many of these families do not have detectable physical or medical features to accompany the cognitive impairment. Therefore, the terms nonsyndromic or isolated mental retardation apply. As a first approximation, the genes causing mental retardation may be directly involved in synaptic plasticity. To date, six genes (including *fmr2*) have been implicated in the pathogenesis of mental retardation: *OPHN1*, *GDI1*, *PAK3*, *IL1RAPL*, and *TM4SF2*. The first three have been indirectly implicated in neurite outgrowth and synaptic vesicle recycling. The last two are cell surface molecules; *TM4SF2* is part of a class of proteins called tetraspanins, which have been shown to play a role in cell–cell signaling. It will be interesting to determine if any of these mutations shed light on general mechanisms of synaptic plasticity and if the pathways identified by this research will inform studies on the more common polygenic forms of mental retardation.

Conclusion

During the past 50 years, there has been considerable progress in the services and rights accorded to individuals with mental retardation. Also, much information has been learned regarding the genetic causes of mental retardation. We hope that the rapid advances in biotechnology will lead to meaningful treatments for these individuals.

See also: Cognitive Impairment; Intelligence; Mental Status Testing.

Further Reading

Cabezas, DA, Arena, JF, Stevenson, RE, et al. (1999). XLMR database. *Am. J. Med. Genet.* 85: 202–205.
Higgins, JJ, Rosen, DR, Loveless, JM, et al. (2000). A gene for nonsyndromic mental retardation maps to chromosome 3p25–pter. *Neurology* 55: 335–340.
Knight, SJ, Regan, R, Nicod, A, et al. (1999). Subtle chromosomal rearrangements in children with unexplained mental retardation. *Lancet* 354: 1676–1681.
McKusick, VA (2000). *Online Mendelian Inheritance in Man, OMIM.* Baltimore, MD/Bethesda, MD: McKusick–Nathans Institute for Genetic Medicine, Johns Hopkins University/National Center for Biotechnology Information, National Library of Medicine. http://www.ncbi.nlm.nih.gov/omim.
Micklos, D and Witkowski, J (2000). *Image Archive on the American Eugenics Movement.* Cold Spring Harbor, NY: Cold Spring Harbor Laboratory. http://vector.cshl.org/eugenics.

Mental Status Testing

K. P. Rankin

The mental status examination (MSE) is a standard component of health care practice for general medical practitioners, neurologists, and mental health professionals. It should be used to evaluate the cognitive and psychiatric status of any patient who is known or suspected to have neurological or psychiatric symptoms. Because it functions largely as a screening tool, the MSE not only can help identify aspects of the patient's mental health that are in need of more detailed investigation but also can elicit information that alerts practitioners to the need for referral to a specialist. Although a variety of structured MSE instruments exist and can be quite useful for aspects of the assessment, unstructured or semistructured forms of the MSE are best able to provide a comprehensive picture of an individual patient's functioning. Clinicians can expand or contract the unstructured MSE to provide information that is more applicable to their specialty, and they may tailor it to focus in on particular areas of suspicion for a single patient. The three main components of the MSE—history, psychiatric status, and cognitive status—are described here.

History

Whenever possible, a comprehensive MSE should involve taking a history before the formal mental status testing begins. The primary goal of this history should be to obtain current and past information pertaining to the patient's behavioral, neurological, and psychiatric status. An attempt should always be made to elicit a clear timeline from the patient for any problem because diagnostic accuracy in mental disorders often relies on factors such as age of onset, rate of progression, episodicity, duration, and frequency.

The history should begin with a complete description of the patient's current complaints and symptoms, and the interviewer should be sure to fully investigate changes or problems in the areas of behavior, cognition, and psychological status, including current stressors. Next, a medical history should be taken, again with a particular focus on medical issues that pertain to cognitive and psychiatric functioning. Questions should be asked regarding general medical disease or injury, neurological disease or injury, medications, seizures, head injury, toxic exposure, and substance use (including alcohol, tobacco, caffeine, and drug use). Third, the interviewer should obtain a psychiatric history from the patient, including any past or present diagnoses, assessment, and treatment. Fourth, any relevant social history should be noted. This should include educational attainment, vocational history (including military service), and a criminal history to provide information about any significant behavioral problems. Lastly, the patient's family history should be obtained. This will focus on any significant history of neurological or psychiatric problems in family members, but it should also obtain information about general medical conditions that could impact neurological status (e.g., hypertension and stroke). It may also be helpful to ask the patient about family members with behavioral oddities because the proverbial "funny uncle" may have had an undiagnosed neurological or psychiatric disease.

Psychiatric Status

Making an assessment of the patient's psychiatric status is the first phase of the formal mental status examination. It relies heavily on behavioral observation on the part of the interviewer, and much of the information will have already been gathered as an implicit part of the history-taking process. Psychiatric status is the foundation for the rest of the MSE because a patient who is seriously disordered in this domain may not be able to perform well on the cognitive portion of the examination. Interpretation of patients' higher level functioning must be guided by an awareness of the psychiatric factors that may be limiting them.

Appearance

Although this has been a standard component of mental status examination in the past, it has recently become a controversial category due to accusations of clinician insensitivity and bias. Thus, evaluation in this area should be done cautiously, avoiding statements that could be interpreted as solely the opinion of the examiner (e.g., "attractive") and focusing on aspects of appearance that have direct relevance to the issue of the patient's mental status. Common inclusions in this category are statements about the patient's apparent level of consciousness (alert, drowsy, stuporous, etc.), apparent age (differentiated from actual age), eye contact, clothing, hygiene and grooming, position (sitting or lying down), as well as indication of any physical abnormalities, disabilities, or relevant features not included elsewhere.

Attitude

This is an assessment of the patient's degree of cooperation with the assessment process as well as their attitude toward the clinician. Any positive or negative deviation from the norm should be noted, including hostility, guardedness, apathy, eagerness, or jocularity; otherwise, the patient is usually described as cooperative. A statement is often made in this section noting whether or not the clinician was able to establish rapport with the patient, with an indication if the patient was particularly engaging or inappropriate (e.g., seductive, disinhibited, or abusive).

Motor Activity/Behavior

Most items in this category correspond with observations of gross neurological function. Statements should be made about the patient's general level of activity (from restless hyperactivity to bradykinesia, or abnormally slow movement), coordination, gait, and posture (e.g., spasticity or rigidity). Any unusual motor behavior should also be included, such as tremor, rhythmic movements, tics, or abnormal facial expression. This may also include odd mannerisms or behaviors such as frequent grimacing or a tendency to place objects from throughout the room in their mouth (hyperorality).

Mood

There are many different definitions of mood; however, one analogy used in the psychotherapy-oriented disciplines is that mood is distinguished from affect as climate is distinguished from weather. It is less variable and superficial than affect and represents the deeper, more typical emotional tone experienced by the patient over a longer period of time (days to weeks). Thus, mood is best derived primarily from history and patient self-report, unless the clinician has opportunity to observe the patient over the course of multiple visits.

Affect

This is the visible, expressed emotional state of the patient during the evaluation. Facial expression, tone of voice, content of speech, physical tension, and posture may all be used to form a statement about the patient's affect.

Extreme fluctuations in affect (labile affect), as well as the absence of normal variation (flattened affect), are important and should be noted. It is standard practice to include a statement comparing affect to mood, and any disjunction among modalities should be noted (e.g., smiling broadly while discussing an emotionally upsetting event, or tearfulness in the context of reportedly positive mood).

Thought Process

This is an assessment of the quality of the patient's thought, particularly with regard to its degree of connection and organization. Common observations include whether the patient's thought process is linear and understandable or whether the patient evidences significant tangentiality (getting off topic), flight of ideas, perseveration (repeatedly returning to the same topic or word), loose associations, or circumstantiality (excessive attention to detail, usually at the expense of the main topic of conversation). Echolalia, neologisms, and clang associations (connecting words because of their sound rather than their meaning; e.g., "cuff tough rebuff") are examples of disordered thought processes occurring at the level of words or short phrases.

Thought Content

This category includes observations about the nature of the patient's thoughts as well as perceptions. Delusions, hallucinations, homicidal or suicidal ideation, obsessions, and compulsive thoughts are commonly described in this section. Any significant preoccupation, paranoia, or phobia should be noted here, along with any dissociative phenomena, such as derealization or depersonalization.

Cognitive Status

As with the psychiatric portion of the MSE, each component of the cognitive status evaluation builds upon what has preceded it. Impairment in language, for instance, must be considered in the evaluation of abstract reasoning because the patient may be able to clearly conceptualize their response but cannot communicate it. The cognitive component of the MSE is more scripted than the history or psychiatric status examination, and it relies heavily on the patient's performance of various tasks. A number of structured cognitive examinations have been created to provide comprehensive screening; however, flexibility in response to an individual patient's pattern of cognition will always provide a more complete, accurate assessment. Some of the most widely used structured MSEs include versions of the Folstein Mini-Mental State Exam (**Table 1**), although it has an updated version, the 3MS. The American Neuropsychiatric Association also recommends the use of the Neurobehavioral Cognitive Status Examination, updated under the name COGNISTAT. For dementia screening in older patients, the Mattis Dementia Rating Scale is quite thorough.

Table 1 Mini-Mental State[a]

Maximum points	*Question*
5	What is the: Year? Season? Date? Day? Month?
5	Where are we: State (Country)? County (Province)? City? Hospital (Place)? Floor (Street)?
3	Name three objects (Apple, Penny, Table) using 1 second to say each. Then ask the patient to repeat all three after you have said them. 1 point for each correct. Then repeat them until the patient learns them. Count the number of trials and record ——.
5	Serial 7's: Subtract 7 from 100 and stop at 5 answers. 1 point for each correct. OR, Spell "WORLD" backwards. Number correct is the number of letters in correct order (e.g., "dlorw" = 3 points).
3	Ask for the names of the three objects (Apple, Penny, Table). 1 point for each correct.
2	Point to a pencil and a watch. Ask the patient to name them as you point.
1	Have the patient repeat the phrase, "No ifs, and, or buts."
3	Have the patient follow a three-stage command, only after all three steps have been given: "Take the paper in your right hand, fold it in half, and put it on the floor."
1	Write "CLOSE YOUR EYES" in large letters. Show this to the patient and ask them to do what it says.
1	Have the patient write a sentence spontaneously.
1	Have the patient copy the intersecting pentagons below.

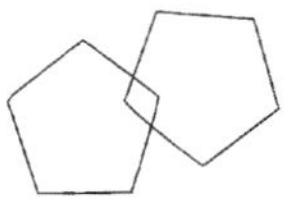

Total: 30

[a]From Folstein et al. (1975).

Attention

If the patient is having difficulty maintaining attention and concentration, this will be observable by the clinician. The patient may miss questions or instructions, or they may become easily distracted. Simple attention can best be quantified using a digit repetition task, in which the patient is asked to repeat back increasingly longer sequences of digits. Adult patients should be able to repeat back five to seven digits; if they are unable to repeat a span of five digits after two trials, their attention is probably impaired.

Orientation

The three major domains to which the patient should be oriented are person (who they are), place (location and how they got there), and time (date and time of day). Orientation is actually a measure of recent memory functioning because it is dependent on attending to and learning the continually changing facts about one's environment. It may be assessed by asking the patient questions about the city, state, name of the hospital, and floor of the building on which the interview is taking place as well as the full date, day of the week, season, and time of day.

Language

A number of aspects of both expressive and receptive language can be assessed fairly easily during the course of the MSE. First, the patient's spontaneous speech should be rated for fluency (i.e., are their words unusually slow or halting), prosody (rising and falling voice inflection), appropriate grammatical structure, articulation, and gross comprehension. Then, more structured assessments are usually done. Repetition is assessed by having the patient repeat simple and then more complex words and phrases after the examiner (e.g., "No ifs, ands, or buts"). Verbal fluency can be assessed by having the patient name as many animals as they can in 1 min. Normal adults should name approximately 18–22 animals, decreasing slightly in the elderly. An assessment of confrontation naming can be done by simply pointing at various objects around the office and asking the patient to name them. However, structured stimulus booklets (such as Kaplan's *Boston Naming Test*) are available that contain pictures of objects that are increasingly difficult to name. Utilizing such structured assessments is preferable due to their sensitivity as well as the availability of extensive normative data. The patient's comprehension can be assessed by asking them to follow grammatically complex commands (e.g., "Before touching your chin, point to your eye") and answer complex statements (e.g., "If a lion was killed by a tiger, which animal is dead?"). Finally, an assessment for alexia and agraphia can be done by asking the patient to read and write various words or sentences. Spontaneous writing as well as writing to dictation should be assessed.

Construction

Assessment of visuospatial skills in the MSE is usually limited to construction tasks, in which the patient is asked to either copy drawings or draw objects from memory. Mental status examinations often include only one complex two-dimensional drawing, a pair of interlocking pentagons. This is usually scored on a pass–fail basis, allowing the patient to "pass" if both of the pentagons have five angles of any shape and they intersect. Ideally, however, the patient should be asked to copy multiple stimuli that begin simply (e.g., a diamond or a circle) and become more complex (e.g., a cube), moving from two to three dimensions. Common errors include rotation, perseveration (drawing the same component repeatedly), and stimulus-bound behavior, in which the patient attempts to draw their copy immediately next to or even on top of the stimulus picture. For drawing on command, patients are often asked to draw the face of a clock that indicates the time 11:10. This measure is particularly sensitive to visuospatial neglect, micrographia, and spatial disorganization. Errors in correctly reproducing the time may suggest attentional problems, memory deficits, or executive dysfunction.

Memory

Both verbal and nonverbal memory should be assessed in a thorough MSE. Remote verbal memory for autobiographical information can be obtained by asking the patient for information about their childhood. Both recent and remote semantic memory can be assessed by asking the patient questions about important world events or famous people from successive decades of their life, including the current year. When a patient has recent memory loss, it is helpful diagnostically to ascertain the time period in the patient's life in which their memories become fragmented (e.g., the patient can tell detailed stories about the Vietnam war but cannot identify any U.S. presidents after Ford).

There are a number of ways to assess patients' ability to learn new information during the course of an MSE, all of which include a learning trial followed by memory assessment after a delay. Clinicians often name three or four words, ask the patient to repeat the words back, then ask the patient to remember them for later. After performing a different task for 30 sec to 10 min, the examiner asks the patient to recall the objects. Another way to assess new learning that is particularly useful when the patient has a language deficit is to show the patient five small objects (such as a coin, pen, or comb) and then hide the objects around the office, showing the patient each hiding place. Then, after a delay of 5 min, the clinician asks the patient where the objects are located. Patients younger than age 60 should be able to find four or all five of the objects. This test can also be done with stimuli that are more salient to the patient, such as money. Visuospatial memory can be assessed by asking the patient to draw one or more of the visuoconstruction stimuli from memory 5–10 min after they copied them. Assessment with more complex stimuli provides greater sensitivity to mild memory impairment.

Higher Cognitive Functioning

There are a variety of tasks that can be done during a MSE that elicit information regarding the patient's higher level functions. For instance, abstract reasoning can be assessed by asking the patient to explain similarities (e.g., "How are an eye and an ear alike?") or by asking the patient to interpret proverbs. These are scored according to both the degree of concreteness and the accuracy of the patient's answers. Another aspect of higher function, calculation, can easily be assessed by asking the patient to perform a series of math problems either on paper or mentally (although the latter relies on complex attention and working memory in addition to calculation skills). The patient's judgment can also be assessed by both listening carefully during the history and asking the patient questions about how they would behave in situations requiring good judgment and reasoning (e.g., "If you were stranded in the Denver airport with only one dollar, what would you do?"). The patient's level of insight can also be described in this section, although it is most often assessed during the history by asking questions about the nature of the patient's symptoms in order to determine the patient's level of awareness of their problems.

Conclusion

There are as many ways to conduct an MSE as there are individual patients, but an assessment containing the previously discussed components will be both thorough and edifying. A good MSE can render a valuable snapshot of the patient that guides the clinician toward providing the best assessment, diagnosis, and treatment.

See also: Cognitive Impairment.

Further Reading

Folstein, MF, Folstein, SE, and McHugh, PR (1975). ''Mini-Mental State'': A practical method for grading the cognitive state of patients for the clinician. *J. Psychiatr. Res.* 12: 189–198.
Kaplan, EF, Goodglass, H, and Weintraub, A (1983). *The Boston Naming Test,* 2nd ed. Philadelphia: Lea & Febiger.
Kiernan, RJ, Mueller, J, and Langston, JW (1987). The Neurobehavioral Cognitive Status Examination: A brief but quantitative approach to cognitive assessment. *Ann. Intern. Med* 107: 481–485.
Malloy, PF, Cummings, JL, Coffey, CE, et al. (1997). Cognitive screening instruments in neuropsychiatry: A report of the committee on research of the American Neuropsychiatric Association. *J. Neuropsychiatr. Clin. Neurosci* 9: 189–197.
Mattis, S (1988). *Dementia Rating Scale: Professional Manual.* Odessa, FL: Psychological Assessment Resources.
Strub, RL and Black, FW (2000). *The Mental Status Examination in Neurology.* Philadelphia: Davis.
Teng, EL and Chui, HC (1987). The Modified Mini-Mental State (3MS) Examination. *J. Clin. Psychiatry* 48: 314–318.

Morphology, Disorders of

G. Jarema and G. Libben, University of Montreal, Montreal, Quebec, Canada

Introduction

Aphasia can have a profound impact on an individual's ability to recognize the meanings of words and to retrieve the word forms that correspond to particular meanings that he or she wishes to express. It can also affect how words are built up and taken apart in language production and comprehension. The reason for this is that, in English and other languages, most words are not atomic units, but rather are complex structures made up of simpler meaningful forms called morphemes. Consider the word *form* itself. Although in the English language it can be used as a simple monomorphemic word, it also appears in the prefixed multimorphemic forms *inform*, *reform*, and *deform*. It can be suffixed in the words *forming*, *formation*, and *formless*. It can also occur as part of a compound word *freeform*, and in very complex structures such as *well-formedness*. For unimpaired language users, the comprehension and production of such multimorphemic words pose little difficulty. Rather, the morphological ability that is an integral part of language competency provides distinct advantages. It allows us to create and understand a very large number of words from a relatively small number of morphemes. It allows us to co-index words in our vocabulary on the basis of the morphemes that they share, so that words such as *blueberry*, *strawberry*, and *raspberry* are automatically represented as types of *berry*. It also provides us with a substantial head start in the understanding of new words. If one knows that *aphasia* is the loss of language ability as a result of damage to the brain, then it is morphological ability that most likely enables us to infer that the term *aphasics* refers to individuals with this language loss.

In some ways, however, morphological ability can be considered to be a double-edged sword for lexical comprehension and production. The fact that the words *blueberry, strawberry,* and *raspberry* may be represented in the mind in terms of the morphemes that they share also carries with it the danger that one may be selected or activated instead of the other. The fact that the morphological complexity can have both advantages and disadvantages for language processing has led to considerable interest among both psycholinguists and neurolinguists, which has contributed a great deal to our overall understanding of the fundamental nature of lexical processing as well as the underlying components of language disturbance in aphasia. In the sections below, we review the current state of knowledge on the types of morphological difficulties that aphasic patients encounter and the manner in which those difficulties differ depending on the area of damage to the brain and the resulting aphasic syndrome. We also consider the ways in which morphological deficits vary depending on the language involved. Languages such as English, Chinese, Finnish, and Hebrew differ markedly in their morphological complexity as well as in the manner in which they form multimorphemic words from simpler units of meaning. We will also see that not all areas of morphology are equally affected. Inflectional morphology, the type of morphology that typically encodes the tense of a verb (e.g., *jump* → *jumped*) or the number of a noun (e.g., *tree* → *trees*), is usually more impaired in aphasia than derivational morphology, which creates words with new meanings and new grammatical categories (e.g., *teach* → *teacher*).

The diversity of morphological difficulties encountered by aphasic patients reveals to us the extraordinary complexity of this aspect of the language system. In the latter part of this article, we explore the ways in which knowledge acquired from the study of aphasic performance can help us to understand the consequences of this complexity for unimpaired lexical processing and how morphological ability may be instantiated in the human brain.

Types of Morphological Errors in Aphasia

Morphological errors, or morphological paraphasias, observed in the performances of individuals with aphasia are classically characterized in terms of omissions and substitutions of bound grammatical morphemes. Thus, inflectional suffixes such as the English tense marker-*ed* are reported as being omitted (e.g., *closed* → *close*) or substituted (e.g. *closed* → *closing*) in aphasic productions. Similarly, derivational affixes such as the prefix *un*-may give rise to omissions (e.g., *undo* → *do*) or substitutions (e.g., *undo* → *redo*).

Importantly, morphological paraphasias rarely violate the well-formedness principles of a language. Thus, erroneous productions are phonotactically legal, i.e., they result in phonological sequences that exist in the language. They also do not deviate from grammatical well-formedness. For example, an inflectional suffix will be replaced by another inflectional suffix (e.g., *he danced* → *he dances*), but not by a derivational suffix (*dancer*). Furthermore, as this example illustrates, a verbal inflection will be exchanged with another verbal inflection. Substitutions are thus generally within category (here inflections) and within paradigm (here verbal suffixes). This clearly indicates that aphasic patients have not lost their linguistic knowledge. Rather, they are unable to select the required morpheme during language production.

With respect to inflectional morphology, it has been shown that nouns and verbs may be spared or impaired differentially. One patient may have greater difficulty with inflected forms of verbs than of nouns (e.g., Caramazza and Hillis, 1991; Tsapkini et al., 2002; Shapiro and Caramazza, 2003a), while another may exhibit the opposite pattern (Shapiro et al., 2000). However, selective difficulties with verb vs. noun processing may also derive from impaired semantic knowledge about actions (e.g., Pulvermüller, 1999; Tranel et al., 2001).

While aphasic patients tend to omit or substitute lexical constituents in compound words (e.g., *horseshoe* → *horse* or *horse-iron*), as observed for English (Libben, 1993, 1998; Badecker, 2001), Italian (Delazer and Semenza, 1998), and Chinese (Packard, 1990), they can exhibit a dissociation in their ability to process closed-class morphology in compounds vs. noun phrases. Thus a study of Italian-speaking agrammatic aphasics has shown that whereas patients were impaired in their production of noun–adjective agreement in noun phrases (e.g., *febbre strana* 'strange fever'), their performance improved significantly on analogous compounded constructions (e.g., *febbre gialla* 'yellow fever') (Mondini et al., 2002). This result indicates that inflectional morphology is more stable within lexicalized complex structures such as compounds than within a corresponding syntactic phrase and bears on the theoretical import of the dissociation observed between intact morphological performance on words produced in isolation vs. impaired morphological performance on words produced within a sentential context (Nespoulous et al., 1988; Caramazza and Hillis, 1989; De Bleser et al., 1996). Indeed, selectively impaired morphology in the production of sentences, but not in isolated words, points to an underlying deficit at the syntactic level of processing. However, the reported existence of impaired performance on words produced in isolation (e.g., Miceli and Caramazza, 1988) is not amenable to such an interpretation and casts doubt on a strictly syntactic account of impaired functional categories. Such an account is nevertheless attractive because it offers an explanation of why not all types of inflectional affixes are equally affected in aphasia. For example, in a series of recent studies investigating the performance of Hebrew- and Arabic-speaking agrammatic aphasic patients, tense was found to be impaired whereas (subject–verb) agreement was found to be spared (Freedman and Grodzinsky, 1997, 2000; Friedman, 2000, 2001). While tense has been shown to be more vulnerable than agreement across several languages (e.g., Goodglass, 1993 for English; Höhle, 1995 for German; Benedet et al., 1998 for Spanish; Kolk, 2000 for Dutch), other studies did not replicate this finding (e.g., Stavrakaki and Kouvava, 2003 for Greek). These inconclusive results underscore the role of crosslinguistic variation in the study of morphological breakdown in aphasia.

Do Patterns of Morphological Impairment Differ across Languages?

Until the 1980s, our understanding of morphological impairments in aphasia, indeed of aphasic deficits in general, was largely based on investigations of English-speaking patients. Yet the English language features a relatively poor inflectional morphology and relies heavily on word order to assign argument structure (e.g., to assign the role of agent to a noun), in contrast to, for example, Turkish, a highly agglutinative language that relies mainly on case marking to assign sentence roles. The Cross-Language Aphasia Study by Menn and Obler (1990a) was the first systematic study that brought together narrative data across typologically differing languages, including Finnish, Hebrew, and Japanese. Parallel analyses of the 14 corpora of spontaneous speech presented in that study demonstrated the role of language variation in the manifestations of morphological impairments in agrammatism, a type of disorder commonly associated with Broca's aphasia.

Crosslinguistic differences have also been central to the account of aphasic deficits proposed by Bates and collaborators (for a review, see Bates et al., 1991). Evidence from both research groups indicates that the degree and nature of morphological deficits vary considerably from one language to another. According to Bates et al., error probability is directly related to the strength of a particular form in a language. Thus, in Hungarian and Turkish (MacWhinney et al., 1991), case marking was found to be well preserved (a finding also reported by Niemi et al., 1990 for Finnish). Furthermore, on the receptive side, grammatical redundancy (the presence of several different cues to sentence comprehension, including inflectional markers) was shown to augment comprehension performance to near-normal levels, leading the authors to conclude that the accessibility of morphological cues is reduced in aphasia. In sum, on that account morphology will be spared or impaired relative to the importance of a given marker in the language and depending on the processing resources still available to the patient. These resources may be reduced due to perceptual, attentional, and/or mnemonic limitations. The interpretation put forth by Menn and Obler (1990b) was that agrammatic aphasic patients suffer from an impoverished capacity to integrate information required by complex syntactic computations, resulting in "degraded or blurred specifications of bound grammatical morphemes." Blurred specifications result in misselection errors and heavily degraded specifications result in the use of default forms.

Much debate has surrounded the issue of how omissions and substitutions pattern across languages in aphasia. It has been observed that in languages such as English, omissions of affixes tend to be more frequent than substitutions, while in languages such as Greek (Kehayia et al., 1990), one only finds substitutions. This has led to the claim that problematic affixes are omitted only if the resulting form is a word in the language (e.g. *book* is still a word when omitting the plural marker-*s* in *books*), otherwise the affix is substituted. In Greek, for example, the form *anthrop*-resulting from the omission of the suffix-*os* in *anthropos* 'man' is not a word, as is the case with all unaffixed nominal stems, and would therefore never be produced by aphasic patients. Legally bare, or zero-inflected, forms have been claimed to represent the default form in aphasia (Grodzinsky, 1984); however, patients with a morphological deficit do not systematically revert to omissions when the resulting form is a word in the language. For example, a Polish-speaking aphasic patient having difficulties with the past tense form of verbs did not produce the bare form of the imperative, but rather misselected another inflected form of the verb (Jarema and Kadzielawa, 1990). This speaks against an account according to which patients systematically omit bound morphemes when the language allows bare forms and points toward an interaction with other factors, such as form frequency, but not affix frequency (Faroqi-Shah and Thompson, 2004; but for the opposite pattern, see Centeno et al., 1996 for Spanish and Penke, 2003 for German) or distance from the target item, as measured by the number of features that separate the erroneous item from the target (Menn and Obler, 1990b).

What Do Morphological Deficits in Aphasia Tell Us about Normal Morphological Processing?

Without a doubt, most research on morphological processing in healthy adults has centered on the question of whether multimorphemic words are processed in terms of their constituent morphemes. Positions regarding this question have ranged from the view that all multimorphemic words are routinely and automatically decomposed into their constituents in word recognition (Taft, 2004) to the view that morphological decomposition is simply a backup procedure to be used when whole-word recognition fails (Butterworth, 1983). Over the past years, a number of intermediate positions have emerged. One position is that whole-word processing and morphological processing are carried out simultaneously (Schreuder and Baayen, 1995) as separate routes. For high frequency words, the whole-word route typically 'wins the race' whereas for less frequent words, particularly those with high frequency morphological constituents, the decomposition route has an advantage. This basic notion – that some types of word are decomposed but others are not – has been extended to a wide variety of morphological distinctions, including derivation vs. inflection, regularity vs. irregularity, and semantic transparency vs. semantic opacity.

Evidence from aphasia has a special role to play in our understanding of whether such distinctions do indeed play a role in determining whether words are processed as wholes or in terms of their constituent morphemes. The reason for this is that, in contrast to the apparently effortless and errorless manner in which multimorphemic words are processed by normal healthy adults, persons with aphasia often show selective difficulty on particular types of morphological constructions as well as error patterns that reveal underlying processes of morphological decomposition.

The performance dissociations seen in aphasia between derived words and inflected words serve as an excellent first example, although the exact characteristics that distinguish between inflectional morphology and derivational morphology are still a matter of debate (see Bybee, 1985). It seems that inflected words would be much more likely to be composed and decomposed on line than derived words. Inflectional morphology has been described (Anderson, 1982) as that aspect of morphology that is relevant to syntax and, as such, involves obligatory adjustments to a morphological stem so that it 'fits' into a sentence. Derivational morphology, on the other hand, is essentially a type of word formation process, resulting in either the creation of a word with a new meaning or of a new word having a different lexical category. These new words would seem much more likely to be represented in a manner that is distinct from their inflectional counterparts. The available data from aphasia seems to support such a view. There is evidence that derivational and inflectional morphology can, for example, be selectively impaired. Miceli and Caramazza (1988) reported the case of F.S., an Italian-speaking patient who showed inflectional errors both in spontaneous speech and in repetition. F.S.'s performance on derived words, on the other hand, was unimpaired. Moreover, F.S. did not only show difficulty with inflected words. He also produced words that involved inappropriate combinations of morphological stems and affixes. The authors reasoned that such errors could only be possible if the multimorphemic inflected forms were composed on line.

In general, aphasic patients have much more difficulty with inflected words than with derived words, suggesting that the former are much more likely to be composed and decomposed on line. However, derived words can also be selectively impaired in aphasia. De Bleser and Bayer (1986) reported the case of a patient who showed difficulties with derived words but not inflected ones. Luzzatti and de Bleser (1996) reported a patient, M.G., who showed unimpaired lexical processing for inflected and derived words but very poor performance on compounds. Another patient in the same study, D.R., also showed difficulties with compounds, but in this case with impaired performance on inflected but not derived words. Two unusual cases of a selective deficit in derivational morphology were reported by Marangolo et al. (2003). The two patients presented in that study had similar right hemisphere lesions and showed intact linguistic abilities at all levels, including inflectional and derivational morphology, with the exception of a deficit in deriving nouns from verbs (but not nouns from adjectives, or verbs from nouns). Both patients substituted target deverbal nouns with participles. For example, for the verb *liberare* 'to free', they produced the participle *liberato* 'set free', instead of the noun *liberazione* 'liberation', but had no difficulty in producing the infinitive *liberare* when presented with *liberazione*. These results are interesting in several respects. First, they confirm previously reported dissociations between inflectional and derivational impairment; second, they bring to light the existence of highly selective deficits in the domain of morphology; and third, they reveal that a lesion in the right hemisphere **can** induce a morphological impairment and that the right hemisphere **does** contribute to morphological processing. Evidence from these studies thus suggests that the nature of morphological deficits in aphasia can be quite specific and correlate with the linguistic distinctions among the categories of inflection, derivation, and compounding.

Inflected words are the best candidates for obligatory morphological decomposition, particularly when they involve regular suffixation (Clahsen, 1999; Pinker, 1999). Studies have largely focused on past tense formation in regular verbs (e.g., *greet-greeted*) vs. irregular verbs (e.g., *teach-taught*). Patients are reported to have difficulties with regular verbs more than irregular ones, and vice versa (Ullman et al., 1997; Marslen-Wilson and Tyler, 1997, 1998). The regular–irregular dissociation has also been reported to co-occur for both verbs and nouns (Miozzo, 2003). In that study, the patient produced regular forms such as *walked* and *gloves* accurately, but had difficulties with irregular forms such as *found* and *children*. These dissociations demonstrate that patients can be selectively impaired for either regular or irregular inflection.

The data from aphasia also offers evidence that derived words may be processed online in terms of their morphological constituents. Libben (1990) described an agrammatic patient, J.Z., who produced repetition errors with derived words such as *irregularity*, but had no difficulty with ones such as *unhappiness*. The crucial difference between these subtypes of derivation is that in the case of *irregularity* the addition of affixes to the root involves segmental and stress changes. In the case of words such as *unhappiness*, the derivational prefixes and suffixes are simply added to the root. The author concluded that J.Z.'s decreased performance on the former type of derived words resulted from the increased computational demand created by the nonneutral affixes in on-line composition. This conclusion was supported by the fact that J.Z. repeated words such as *irregularity* as 'un-regular-ity,' with unchanged stress and an unchanged prefix.

Studies of aphasic performance with compound words, as well, show evidence of automatic and obligatory morphological decomposition. Semenza et al. (1997) found that, in naming compound words, aphasic errors typically involve the erroneous production of another compound, rather than an inflected or derived word. This suggests that even though performance is impaired, aphasics have access to the morphological structure of compound targets. Badecker (2001) reported the case of an aphasic patient whose compound naming was characterized by the presence of reversal errors (e.g., *firewood* → *woodfire*). For such errors to occur, it was reasoned that the compound words would have to be represented and processed in terms of their constituent morphemes.

One category of compound word that might be particularly revealing of underlying processes involved in morphological computation is the category of semantically opaque compounds. Such compounds, e.g., *Sunday*, are those for which the whole word meaning is not obviously related to the meanings of both morphological constituents. Thus, an opaque compound such as *Sunday* may be contrasted to a more semantically transparent compound such as *sunburn*. It has been claimed that only transparent compounds are automatically decomposed into their constituents. Some evidence from aphasia, however, suggests that, although there may be a fundamental difference between semantically transparent and opaque compounds, that difference may result from the fact that both are automatically and obligatorily decomposed in lexical processing. Indeed, Blanken (2000) found evidence of morphological composition for both types of compounds in German. A study by Libben (1998) reported a patient, R.S., who had particular difficulty processing opaque compounds. The paraphrase task revealed that her comprehension of opaque compounds such as *butterfly* involved the activation of both whole word and constituent meanings, so that she described it as "a pretty fly, it's yellow." The *yellow* descriptor was analyzed as being related to the constituent *butter*, whereas the descriptor *pretty* referred to the whole word meaning. A similar effect was reported by McEwen et al. (2001). They examined the deep dyslexic patient J.O., who also showed evidence of whole word and constituent blending in a reading task. Thus, in reading *pancake*, she produced 'cake, breakfast, syrup.' Both of these studies suggest that difficulties encountered in the processing of semantically opaque compounds may result from problems in 'turning morphemes off' rather than 'turning them on' (see Semenza and Mondini, forthcoming for a complete review of compound processing in aphasia).

Taken together, the studies we have reviewed point to the view that multimorphemic words are not processed as atomic units, but rather, their constituent subunits are routinely and automatically activated during word production and comprehension. This brings us to the question of why aphasic patients may have selective difficulties with inflected, derived, and compound words. We suggest the following possibility: in the case of inflected words, which are most often transparent in form and in meaning, the morphological deficit is likely to involve difficulties of morpheme access and combination. This can also be the case in derivation, particularly for low frequency words and those that involve phonological changes at the morpheme boundary. As we have suggested above, however, the evidence from semantic transparency effects in compounds suggests that a lexical processing impairment can result not only from difficulties in activating morphemes, but also from difficulties in deactivating them (Libben et al., 2004). Thus, as we have noted above, automatic morphological processing ability can be considered to be a 'double-edged sword' for the language processing system, and a considerable challenge for persons with aphasia.

Do Patterns of Morphological Impairment Differ across Aphasic Syndromes?

Morphological deficits are found in two major aphasic syndromes: Broca's, or nonfluent, aphasia and Wernicke's, or fluent, aphasia. Morphological paraphasias are characteristic of sentence production and comprehension, as well as of single-word naming, reading, writing, and repetition. However, whereas morphological impairments are considered to be one of the defining feature of agrammatism in Broca's aphasia, this is not the case with paragrammatism in Wernicke's aphasia, a clinical disorder characterized by the massive production of paraphasias of all types (semantic, phonological, and morphological). This asymmetry is even more apparent in the case of jargonaphasia, a severe form of Wernicke's aphasia, in which patients produce affixed neologisms in which stems of words are abstruse but feature preserved (i.e., recoverable and contextually appropriate) inflections (e.g., Butterworth and Howard, 1987; Caplan et al., 1972), as well as derivations (e.g., Semenza et al., 1990). Affixes also appear to be preserved in the misspellings of patients suffering from an acquired dysgraphia. It was thus observed that word stems, but not affixes, are spelled erroneously (for a discussion, see Badecker and Caramazza, 1998). Probing Dutch- and English-speaking Broca's and Wernicke's aphasic patients, Bastiaanse and Edwards (2004) found that both groups of patients produce finite (inflected) verbs less accurately than infinitives. However, Broca's aphasics made more inflectional errors, while Wernicke's aphasics made more semantic errors.

In sum, morphological deficits do vary across clinically defined aphasic disorders, which leads to the question whether brain areas typically damaged in a given syndrome subserve morphological processing.

Is There a Morphology Center in the Brain?

Dissociations in the processing of multimorphemic words, brought to light by numerous behavioral studies over the past two decades, have spurred the question of whether different morphological operations involve different anatomical substrates. The classical lesion-based approach to the study of the relationship between language and the brain has proven problematic on several accounts. First, the same language disorder can be induced by varying lesion sites, and second, a specific lesion can induce different aphasic profiles. Thus the type of deficit does not unequivocally predict the locus of the lesion, and vice versa.

The development of imaging techniques, such as fMRI (functional magnetic resonance imaging), has raised hopes about uncovering the neural correlates of language functions. Imaging studies probe the loci of cerebral activation *in vivo* while manipulating linguistic dimensions that yield differential performances and are associated with distinct neuropathologies. Two such dimensions have received much attention in both neurologically healthy and brain-damaged populations: grammatical category, more specifically the verb–noun contrast, and morphological regularity, more specifically the regular vs. irregular past tense contrast. However, due in part to the as yet unresolved shortcomings of imaging techniques (e.g., poor temporal resolution, limitations of the subtractive method in the case of fMRI; for a discussion see Démonet et al., 1996), results from these studies remain inconclusive. Moreover, whether aphasic patients recruit the same neural substrate as non-brain-damaged individuals when processing multimorphemic words remains an open question. Overlap, albeit partial, between selective cortical activation in neurologically healthy individuals processing inflected verbs and lesions in patients with impaired verb morphology has been viewed as supporting the hypothesis that the same neural system is involved (Tyler et al., 2004).

Several recent studies have attempted to address the issue of cerebral activation in aphasic performance. Laine et al. (1999), for example, demonstrated in a PET (positron emission tomography) study that decoding complex (regular case-inflected) words relative to simple words in Finnish increases activation in Broca's area, suggesting that the left anterior dominance reported for the production of regular morphology (Ullman et al., 1997) also holds for comprehension, even though production and comprehension deficits can dissociate (Miceli, 1999). Ullman et al. (1997) reported a patient with an anterior aphasia showing more difficulties with the **regular** past tense, while patients with a posterior aphasia showed the opposite pattern, i.e., more impaired irregular forms. By contrast, Shapiro and Caramazza (2003b) described an agrammatic patient with a lesion primarily in the left frontal lobe who exhibited more difficulty in producing **irregular** forms of verbs, thus contradicting the hypothesis that anterior damage results in greater difficulty with regular forms.

In light of these and other conflicting results, it thus appears that linking fine-grained distinctions of morphological processing to specific brain regions may be premature. However, as we have seen throughout this discussion, disorders of morphology in aphasia show that aphasic syndromes map quite specifically onto distinctions in morphological structure. Our expectation is that, as brain-imaging techniques develop, we will find that the relation between morphology and the brain results primarily from the interaction of computational demands made by different aspects of morphological structure and the availability of those specific computational resources subsequent to brain damage.

Bibliography

Anderson, SR (1982). 'Where's morphology?' *Linguistic Inquiry* 13: 571–613.

Badecker, W (2001). 'Lexical composition and production of compounds: evidence from errors in naming.' *Language and Cognitive Processes* 16: 337–366.

Badecker, W and Caramazza, A (1998). 'Morphology and aphasia.' In: Spencer, A and Zwicky, AM (eds.) *The handbook of morphology*, pp. 390–405. Oxford: Blackwell.

Bastiaanse, R, Hugen, J, Kos, M, and van Zonneveld, R (2002). 'Lexical, morphological, and syntactic aspects of verb production in agrammatic aphasics.' *Brain and Language* 80: 142–159.

Bastiaanse, R and Thompson, CK (2003). 'Verb and auxiliary movement in agrammatic Broca's aphasia.' *Brain and Language* 84: 286–305.

Bastiaanse, R and Edwards, S (2004). 'Word order and finiteness in Dutch and English Broca's and Wernicke's aphasia.' *Brain and Language* 89: 91–107.

Bates, E, Wulfeck, B, and MacWhinney, B (1991). 'Cross-linguistic research in aphasia: an overview.' *Brain and Language* 41: 123–148.

Benedet, MJ, Christiansen, JA, and Goodglass, H (1998). 'A cross-linguistic study of grammatical morphology in Spanish- and English-speaking agrammatic aphasics.' *Cortex* 34: 309–336.

Blanken, G (2000). 'The production of nominal compounds in aphasia.' *Brain and Language* 74: 84–102.

Butterworth, B (1983). 'Lexical representation.' In: Butterworth, B (ed.) *Language production*, pp. 257–294. New York: Academic Press.

Butterworth, B and Howard, D (1987). 'Paragrammatism.' *Cognition* 26: 1–37.

Bybee, JL (1985). *Morphology: a study of the relation between meaning and form.* Philadelphia: John Benjamins.

Caplan, D, Kellar, L, and Locke, S (1972). 'Inflection of neologism in aphasia.' *Brain* 95: 169–172.

Caramazza, A and Hillis, AE (1989). 'The disruption of sentence production: some dissociations.' *Brain and Language* 36: 625–650.

Caramazza, A and Hillis, AE (1991). 'Lexical organization of nouns and verbs in the brain.' *Nature* 349: 788–790.

Centeno, J, Obler, LK, Cairns, H, Garro, L, and Merrifield, P (1996). 'Frequency effects on verb inflection use by agrammatic Spanish-speaking subjects.' *Brain and Language* 5: 47–50.

Clahsen, H (1999). 'Lexical entries and rules of language: a multidisciplinary study of German inflections.' *Behavioral and Brain Science* 22: 991–1060.

De Bleser, R and Bayer, J (1986). 'German word formation and aphasia.' *Linguistic Review* 5: 1–40.

De Bleser, R, Bayer, J, and Luzzatti, C (1996). 'Linguistic theory and morphosyntactic impairment in German and Italian aphasics.' *Journal of Neurolinguistics* 9: 175–185.

Delazer, M and Semenza, C (1998). 'The processing of compound words: a study in aphasia.' *Brain and Language* 61: 54–62.

Démonet, JF, Fiez, JA, Paulesu, E, Petersen, SE, and Zatorre, RJ (1996). 'PET studies of phonological processing: a critical reply to Poeppel.' *Brain and Language* 55: 352–379.

Faroqi-Shah, Y and Thompson, CK (2004). 'Semantic, lexical, and phonological influences on the production of verb inflections in agrammatic aphasia.' *Brain and Language* 89: 484–498.

Friedmann, N (2000). 'Moving verbs in agrammatic production.' In: Bastiaanse, R and Grodzinsky, Y (eds.) *Grammatical disorders in aphasia: a neurolinguistic perspective*, pp. 152–170. London: Whurr.

Friedmann, N (2001). 'Agrammatism and the psychological reality of the syntactic tree.' *Journal of Psycholinguistic Research* 30: 71–90.

Friedmann, N and Grodzinsky, Y (1997). 'Tense and agreement in agrammatic production: pruning the syntactic tree.' *Brain and Language* 56: 397–425.

Friedmann, N and Grodzinsky, Y (2000). 'Split inflection in neurolinguistics.' In: Friedemann, M-A and Rizzi, L (eds.) *The acquisition of syntax: studies in comparative developmental linguistics*, pp. 84–104. Harlow, England: Longman.

Goodglass, H (1993). *Understanding aphasia.* London: Academic Press.

Grodzinsky, Y (1984). 'The syntactic characterization of agrammatism.' *Cognition* 16: 99–120.

Höhle, B (1995). *Aphasie und Sprachproduktion: Sprachstörungen bei Broca-und Wernicke-Aphasikern.* Opladen, Germany: Westdeutscher Verlag.

Jarema, G and Kadzielawa, D (1990). 'Agrammatism in Polish: a case study.' In: Menn and Obler (eds.) 817–893.

Kehayia, E, Jarema, G, and Kadzielawa, D (1990). 'Cross-linguistic study of morphological errors in aphasia: evidence from English, Greek, and Polish.' In: Nespoulous, J-L and Villard, P (eds.) 140–155.

Kolk, H (2000). 'Canonicity and inflection in agrammatic sentence production.' *Brain and Language* 74: 558–560.

Laine, M, Rinne, JO, Krause, BJ, Teräs, M, and Sipila, H (1999). 'Brain activation during encoding of inflected words.' *Brain and Language* 69: 305–318.

Libben, G (1990). 'Morphological representation and morphological deficits in aphasia.' In: Nespoulous, J-L and Villard, P (eds.) 20–31.

Libben, G (1993). 'A case of obligatory access to morphological constituents.' *The Nordic Journal of Linguistics* 16: 111–121.

Libben, G (1994). 'How is morphological decomposition achieved?' *Language and Cognitive Processes* 9: 369–391.

Libben, G (1998). 'Semantic transparency in the processing of compounds: consequences for representation, processing, and impairment.' *Brain and Language* 61: 30–44.

Libben, G and Buchanan, L (forthcoming). 'Morphology, semantics, and the mental lexicon: the failure of deactivation hypothesis.' *Logos and Language.*

Luzzatti, C and De Bleser, R (1996). 'Morphological processing in Italian agrammatic patients: eight experiments in lexical morphology.' *Brain and Language* 54: 26–74.

MacWhinney, B and Osman-Sagi, J (1991). 'Inflectional marking in Hungarian aphasics.' *Brain and Language* 41: 165–183.

MacWhinney, B, Osman-Sagi, J, and Slobin, DI (1991). 'Sentence comprehension in aphasia in two clear case-marking languages.' *Brain and Language* 41: 234–249.

Marangolo, P, Incoccia, C, Pizzamiglio, L, Sabatini, U, Castriota-Scanderbeg, A, and Burani, C (2003). 'The right hemisphere involvement in the processing of morphologically derived words.' *Journal of Cognitive Neuroscience* 15: 364–371.

Marslen-Wilson, WD and Tyler, LK (1997). 'Dissociating types of mental computation.' *Nature* 387: 592–594.

Marslen-Wilson, WD and Tyler, LK (1998). 'Rules, representation, and the English past tense.' *Trends in Cognitive Sciences* 2: 428–435.

McEwen, S, Westbury, C, Buchanan, L, and Libben, G (2001). 'Semantic information is used by a deep dyslexic to parse compounds.' *Brain and Cognition* 46: 201–205.

Menn, L and Obler, LK (eds.) (1990a). *Agrammatic aphasia: a cross-language narrative sourcebook* 3 vols). Amsterdam: John Benjamins.

Menn, L and Obler, LK (1990b). 'Cross-language data and theories of agrammatism.' In: Menn and Obler (eds.) 1369–1389.

Miceli, G (1999). 'Grammatical deficits in aphasia.' In: Denes, G and Pizzamiglio, L (eds.) *Handbook of clinical and experimental neuropsychology*, pp. 245–272. Hove, England: Psychology Press.

Miceli, G and Caramazza, A (1998). 'Dissociation of inflectional and derivational morphology.' *Brain and Language* 35: 24–65.

Miozzo, M (2003). 'On the processing of regular and irregular forms of verbs and nouns: evidence from neuropsychology.' *Cognition* 87: 101–127.

Mondini, S, Jarema, G, Luzzatti, C, Burani, C, and Semenza, C (2002). 'Why is "Red Cross" different from "Yellow Cross"? A neuropsychological study of noun–adjective agreement within Italian compounds.' *Brain and Language* 81: 621–634.

Nespoulous, J-L and Villard, P (eds.) (1990). *Morphology, phonology and aphasia.* New York: Springer.

Nespoulous, J-L, Dordain, M, Perron, C, Ska, B, Bub, D, Caplan, D, Mehler, J, and Lecours, AR (1998). 'Agrammatism in sentence production without comprehension deficits: reduced availability of syntactic structures and/or of grammatical morphemes? A case study.' *Brain and Language* 33: 273–295.

Niemi, J, Laine, M, Hänninen, R, and Koivuselkä-Sallinen, P (1990). 'Agrammatism in Finnish: two case studies.' In: Menn and Obler (eds.) 1013–1085.

Packard, JL (1990). 'Agrammatism in Chinese: a case study.' In: Menn, L and Obler, LK (eds.) 1191–1223.

Penke, M (2003). *On the morphological basis of syntactic deficits*. Paper presented at the Academy of Aphasia, Vienna.

Pinker, S (1999). *Words and rules: the ingredients of language.* London: Weidenfeld & Nicolson.

Pulvermüller, F (1999). 'Words in the brain's language.' *Behavioral and Brain Sciences* 22: 253–336.

Schreuder, R and Baayen, RH (1995). 'Modeling morphological processing.' In: Feldman, LB (ed.) *Morphological aspects of language processing*, pp. 345–364. Hillsdale, NJ: Erlbaum.

Semenza C & Mondini S (forthcoming). 'The neuropsychology of compound words.' In: Libben G & Jarema G (eds.) *The representation and processing of compound words.* Oxford: Oxford University Press.

Semenza, C, Butterworth, B, Panzeri, M, and Ferreri, T (1990). 'Word formation: new evidence from aphasia.' *Neuropsychologia* 28: 499–502.

Semenza, C, Luzzatti, C, and Carabelli, S (1997). 'Morphological representation of compound nouns: a study on Italian aphasic patients.' *Journal of Neurolinguistics* 10: 33–43.

Shapiro, K and Caramazza, A (2003a). 'Grammatical processing of nouns and verbs in left frontal cortex?' *Neuropsychologia* 41: 1189–1198.

Shapiro, K and Caramazza, A (2003b). 'Looming a loom: evidence for independent access to grammatical and phonological properties in verb retrieval.' *Journal of Neurolinguistics* 16: 85–111.

Shapiro, K, Shelton, J, and Caramazza, A (2000). 'Grammatical class in lexical production and morphological processing: evidence from a case of fluent aphasia.' *Cognitive Neuropsychology* 17: 665–682.

Stavrakaki, S and Kouvava, S (2003). 'Functional categories in agrammatism: evidence from Greek.' *Brain and Language* 86: 129–141.

Taft, M (2004). 'Morphological decomposition and the reverse base frequency effect.' *Quarterly Journal of Experimental Psychology A* 57: 745–765.

Tranel, D, Adolphs, R, Damasio, H, and Damasio, AR (2001). 'A neural basis for the retrieval of action words.' *Cognitive Neuropsychology* 18: 655–672.

Tsapkini, K, Jarema, G, and Kehayia, E (2002). 'A morphological processing deficit in verbs but not in nouns: a case study in a highly inflected language.' *Journal of Neurolinguistics* 15: 265–288.

Tyler L K, Bright P, Fletcher P & Stamatakis E A (2004). 'Neural processing of nouns and verbs: the role of inflectional morphology.' *Neuropsychologia* 42: 512–523.

Ullman, MT, Corkin, S, Coppola, M, Hickok, G, Growdon, J H, Koroshetz, WJ, and Pinker, SJ (1997). 'A neural dissociation within language: evidence that the mental dictionary is part of declarative memory, and that grammatical rules are processed by the procedural system.' *Journal of Cognitive Neuroscience* 9: 266–276.

N

Neuropragmatics, Disorders and Neural Systems

B. Stemmer, Université de Montréal, Montreal, Canada

Introduction

When we hear or utter something like "That was very smart of you" we may interpret this to mean *Well done, you are a clever person* on one occasion, or, *You are an idiot* on another. The way we interpret or phrase these utterances goes beyond the traditional players in linguistics, that is, phonetics, morphology, syntax and semantics, and also involves the *unsaid.* The way language is used and interpreted while taking into consideration the characteristics of the speaker and hearer and the effects of contextual and situational variables has been subsumed under the notion linguistic pragmatics. It also includes aspects of discourse, inasmuch as the production and interpretation of discourse also relies on pragmatics. The study of how the brain comprehends and produces linguistic pragmatic behavior has become known as neuropragmatics.

Frequently discussed issues in the study of neuropragmatics relate to which aspects of pragmatics are preserved or impaired in individuals with brain pathology. Findings from such research are generally used in several ways such as specifying the functional (pragmatic) abilities of the patients (e.g., for diagnostic or therapeutic purposes), testing psycholinguistic models of processing or gaining insights into the neural substrates underlying the pragmatic impairment. Advances in neuroimaging technologies have made it possible to study the latter two aspects also in healthy populations.

This chapter will introduce the reader to research in neuropragmatics with a focus on pragmatic disorders in *acquired* brain pathologies and the neural systems involved (see also Chapter 28 for a focus on traumatic brain injury (TBI) patients; see Chapter 37 for a focus on autism and Asperger syndrome).

Pragmatic Disorders in Adult Clinical Populations

Affective prosody, aspects of discourse (e.g., conversational and narrative style, cohesion and coherence), non-literal language (such as "indirect" speech acts or humor) or figurative language (e.g., metaphor, idioms, irony and so forth) are the most frequently investigated pragmatic aspects of linguistic communication in patients with acquired brain pathologies. A broad range of patients have been investigated that shows problems with these different aspects of pragmatics.

Discourse

Before sophisticated brain imaging methods were yet available, individuals with lesions in the right hemisphere (usually due to a stroke) were the most investigated patient population. What made this patient group so interesting to researchers was an observed dissociation between their impaired communicative abilities and well-preserved linguistic abilities. For example, difficulties with topic maintenance, identification and extraction of relevant themes, structure organization and discourse cohesion and coherence as well as the use of prosody to interpret the emotional content of discourse have been characterized as reflecting the conversational and narrative discourse of some right hemisphere damaged (RHD) patients (for summaries see Brownell & Martino, 1998; Myers, 2005). Not all studies report these impairments, however (e.g., Brady et al., 2005). And similar discourse problems have also been described in other patient populations although the underlying cause was explained differently. The discourse problems of RHD patients have mainly been attributed to difficulties with integrating information or drawing appropriate inferences. At times, the question was also raised whether attention or affective impairments observed in some RHD patients were the underlying cause, without, however, clear answers. In some patients with Alzheimer's disease impaired attention and memory functions were more clearly associated with problems in drawing inferences between textual content and real world knowledge (Chapman et al., 1998). Executive functions and social behavior, that is, abilities closely mediated by the frontal lobe, have been suggested to underlie the inability of patients with frontotemporal dementia to establish global coherence (Ash et al., 2006). The discourse problems of patients with a lesion in the left hemisphere have been mainly ascribed to their linguistic impairment (for a summary see Wright & Newhoff, 2005).

Another disorder that produces impairments similar to RHD patients is schizophrenia. Schizophrenia patients have been shown to display difficulties with topic maintenance, distinction of relevant from non-relevant content in narrative discourse and with turn taking and decoding implied meaning in conversation (for a summary see Meilijson et al., 2004; Mitchell & Crow, 2005). Early work proposed that the discourse difficulties of schizophrenic patients rest in their inability to share reality with their interlocutor, to use conventional social norms to guide their speech or to mindread. Some authors suggest that the underlying cause for these difficulties is based on their abnormal lateralization of language – with what are normally left hemisphere language functions being lateralized to the right hemisphere or being more equally distributed between the hemispheres (Mitchell & Crow, 2005; see Chapter 29, this volume).

To sum up, despite different disease etiologies and differences in the underlying pathophysiologies several patient groups display similar problems in discourse production and comprehension. This would seem to indicate that the discourse "symptoms" are not specific to a certain disease but rather that different causes can underlie similar pragmatic impairments. The explanations for the observed discourse impairments vary widely depending on the pathological population (for a more detailed discussion see Section 3). Although it is not always clear which neural systems are impaired in these different patient populations, what they seem to have in common (in very general terms) is an implication of the frontal lobes (see also Chapter 28).

Non-literal Language and Figurative Language

Aside from discourse phenomena, another aspect of pragmatics that has received particular attention concerns the interpretation of "the unsaid", as reflected in non-literal language such as "indirect" speech acts (requests) or humor, or in figurative language such as metaphor, sarcasm and irony, or in idioms. Classical models have assumed that the comprehension of literal utterances required just one processing step while non-literal or figurative language involved at least two (or more) processing steps, that is computing the literal meaning first, rejecting it as contextually inappropriate and finally re-interpreting the utterance and arrive at the intended meaning.

Indirect Requests

The concept of indirectness has been a key feature of investigations in several neuropsychological studies with RHD patients. The underlying assumption in early studies has been that "indirect" requests (e.g., uttering *I am cold* as a request to close the window) is more abstract and requires more complex or different inferencing processes and thus more processing steps than "literal" or "direct" language (*Close the window, please*). While early studies claimed that RHD patients had problems understanding "indirect" requests, this claim had to be modified as subsequent studies using different designs and theoretical frameworks only partially supported the earlier findings (for a review see Stemmer, 2008). RHD patients were able to produce or comprehend indirect requests but showed difficulties to establish a relationship between request types (non-conventional indirect requests) and the supporting material. These studies also pointed out the importance of distinguishing subtypes of the target phenomena (e.g., direct requests, conventional indirect requests, non-conventional indirect requests) as these may be processed differently and thus may also implicate different neural systems.

Other patient groups that have been shown to be impaired in their abilities to appropriately interpret non-conventional indirect requests (*Awfully dry air in here* meaning *I am thirsty*) are patients with schizophrenia (Corcoran, 2003) and patients with TBI, especially such patients with frontal lobes damage and executive dysfunctions (see Chapter 28).

Other Non-literal and Figurative Language

The comprehension of figurative language or other nonliteral language is similar to understanding non-conventional indirect requests inasmuch as such figurative or non-literal language also implies comprehending "the unsaid". Complex meta-representational abilities are required that involve making inferences at various levels of complexity and integrating a wide range of information sources. It is thus not surprising that impairments have been described in several patient populations. These include difficulties in the interpretation of metaphors in patients with RHD and in schizophrenia patients (for summaries see Champagne Lavau et al., 2006; Mitchell & Crow, 2005) but not patients with Alzheimer's disease in the early stages (Papagno, 2001). Problems recognizing and appropriately interpreting sarcasm and irony have also been shown in TBI patients with frontal lobe damage and with executive impairment despite at least partially intact mindreading abilities (e.g., McDonald, 1999). Although RHD patients have been able to correctly identify sarcastic remarks in the context of a multiple choice task, they have shown difficulties with tasks involving lies and ironic joke stories, that is, tasks that require second-order meta-representational judgments (Winner et al., 1998).

Similar to figurative language, joke comprehension also involves the generation of inferences drawing on contextual, knowledge and experiential factors. In addition to these more cognitive elements, apprehension, unexpectedness, surprise and appreciation are other elements in joke comprehension. Early behavioral studies reported problems with joke interpretations in RHD and left hemisphere damage (LHD) patients (for a summary see Stemmer, 2008). A later study that investigated patients with right, left or bilateral frontal lesions reported impairments in specific aspects of the humor task with such impairment being evident only in a subgroup of patients with frontal lobe lesions (Shammi & Stuss, 1999). Patients with schizophrenia have also displayed difficulties with joke comprehension. Schizophrenia patients in remission, however, performed much better than those with the active disease suggesting that medication may have interfered with joke comprehension in these patients (Corcoran et al., 1997; Drury et al., 1998).

Mentalizing or Mindreading

The ability to infer other peoples' mental states, thoughts and feelings has been referred to as mentalizing or mindreading, that is, the person is said to have a theory of mind (ToM) (for details see Chapters 28 and 37, this volume). ToM is typically evaluated using first-order and second-order belief tasks that involve reasoning about mental states such as assessing a person's ability to infer that someone can have a mistaken belief that is different from one's own true belief (e.g., see Chapters 28 and 37). In this context, it is important to mention that ToM has been used both as a *descriptive* tool, and, at the same time, served as an *explanatory* model. We will first focus on the descriptive level before taking up the topic again in Section 3.

A variety of tasks have been used to test patients with dementia, RHD, schizophrenia and other pathologies. The similarity of findings is striking, in the sense that those patient groups that have been shown to be impaired in nonliteral and figurative language production and comprehension also display problems with high-order ToM tasks.

ToM and Dementia

Patients with the frontal variant of frontotemporal dementia (Pick's disease) show changes in personality and behavior such as lack of empathy, socially inappropriate behavior, lack of personal awareness and insight while their memory capacities are relatively spared in the early stages. This is in contrast to patients with Alzheimer's disease who typically present with impairment of episodic memory and of semantic and attentional processing while, in the early stages, personality and social behavior is intact. Comparing these two patients groups on mindreading tasks can thus provide insights into the dependency of mindreading on these skills. Frontotemporal dementia patients show poor performance on a broad spectrum of mentalizing and classical ToM tasks despite good general comprehension and memory abilities (Gregory et al., 2002; Lough et al., 2006). Such patients are also impaired in moral reasoning, emotion processing and empathy (Lough et al., 2006). Patients with Alzheimer's disease also perform poorly on mentalizing and ToM tasks, although in a more selective manner. For example, they showed difficulties only with the second-order false belief task and faux pas task (Gregory et al., 2002). Furthermore, while non-verbal psychological reasoning was impaired, physical reasoning was intact (Verdon et al., 2007). It thus seems that both frontal lobe and memory skills affect mindreading tasks, *albeit* to different extents. Frontal lobe impairment has a more detrimental and a variable effect, possibly due to the broad range of skills mediated by the frontal lobes whereas memory impairments particularly affect those mindreading tasks that generate a high processing load.

Another question concerns the relationship of executive functions and mindreading. There is some indication that executive functions contributed to the poor performance of patients with the frontal variant of frontotemporal dementia although they did not seem sufficient to explain all the problems observed (Snowden et al., 2003; Lough et al., 2006). The nature and extent of differently involved neural systems seems to be equally important.

ToM and Schizophrenia

An impairment in social functioning is one of the most disabling clinical features in schizophrenia and the more severe and acute the symptoms the more severe the mentalizing impairment (e.g., Corcoran et al., 1997; for a review see Lee et al., 2004). There is currently an inconsistency as to whether specific items of schizophrenia symptomatology (or different types of schizophrenia) relate to impaired mentalizing abilities. Impairment in mentalizing and empathy in schizophrenia seems to be independent of generalized cognitive deficits although no final evaluation of this relationship can yet be given.

ToM and RHD

Some studies have investigated ToM behavior in RHD patients with, however, ambiguous findings or interpretations (for a summary see Siegal & Varley, 2002). For example, in one study some RHD patients demonstrated problems in attributing second-order beliefs; this performance varied, however, in the sense that the RHD patients sometimes responded correctly to the second-order belief questions and failed at other times (Winner et al., 1998). In addition, some of the non-brain-damaged control participants also performed poorly on the second-order belief tasks. Another study investigated the hypothesis that people with RHD show a deficit in ToM in the context of otherwise intact reasoning skills (Happé et al., 1999). Compared to the LHD patients with Broca type aphasia and a healthy control group, the RHD group performed less well on stories and cartoons that required mentalizing abilities but similarly well on stories and cartoons that did not require mentalizing abilities.

Although the authors suggested a dedicated cognitive system for ToM and a role for the right hemisphere in *adult* ToM, like most other studies, the results are difficult to interpret due to the high heterogeneity of the patient groups. One of the few studies that compared patient groups according to lesion localization was that by Stuss and colleagues (Stuss et al., 2001). These authors investigated stroke patients with lesions in right, left and bilateral focal frontal and non-frontal regions using visual perspective-taking and a deception task, both implicating first-order attributions. In the visual perspective-taking task, first level direct inferences did not pose problems for any patient group. However, inferences in a transfer condition showed significant differences for the right frontal group compared to all other groups. For the deception task, the right frontal group did not show any problems, although combined right and left frontal patients displayed significant difficulties with the task. In addition, the right medial (inferior and superior) frontal areas and the right anterior cingulate correlated with the number of errors. The authors concluded that the frontal lobes are implicated in some aspects of ToM and that different neural systems may be implicated in different ToM tasks.

Summary

Difficulties with the production and/or interpretation of discourse, non-literal and figurative language and mentalizing have been described in several pathological populations. When interpreting these empirical findings, it is important to realize not only the benefits of patient studies but also their limitations. The number of subjects investigated is usually relatively small but the most important problem is the great heterogeneity of the patients in terms of age, education, time post-onset and disease severity. Equally problematic is the poor information on the neuropsychological tasks, inadequate information on the lesion site and functional severity exhibited by the patients. All these negative factors are then combined with analysis of the patients as group (see also Stuss et al., 2001). As a consequence, general conclusions need to be made with caution and studies need to be replicated. With these cautionary words in mind, what seems to emerge from the patient studies is that the frontal lobes do play an important role in pragmatic processing. Although many studies with RHD patients do not carefully distinguish between frontal and non-frontal lesions, the majority of included RHD included in these studies have frontal lesions and the studies that directly address this issue show the role/involvement of the frontal lobes. Findings from TBI patients with lesioned frontal lobes support the notion that the frontal lobes are critical for the production and interpretation of higher language functions (see Chapter 28) as do research results from patients with frontotemporal dementia and schizophrenia (for a discussion of hemispheric asymmetry and impaired neural substrates in schizophrenia see also Chapter 29, this volume; Mitchell & Crow, 2005).

Although research based on lesion studies has shown the relevance of the frontal lobes in linguistic pragmatics, the functional subdivision of the frontal lobes has rarely been considered. The different pathologies that produce overlapping pragmatic disorders suggest that pragmatic disorders are not disease specific. It seems more likely that the extent and nature of lesions to the neural systems and the resulting (faulty or modified) processing will affect functional systems that contribute in a variety of ways to aspects of pragmatic behavior. Various pathologies will then produce at times similar and at other times different impairments.

Explaining Linguistic Pragmatic Impairments in Clinical Populations

Numerous hypotheses and theories have been advanced to explain linguistic pragmatic difficulties; there has, however, been limited interest in establishing an appropriate theoretical framework. The earliest explanations suggested that RHD patients had problems integrating pieces of information into a coherent whole or difficulties in generating inferences. More recent explanations have suggested that a faulty ToM underlies their problems. In previous work, we have argued that inference generation *per se* is not a theory and that *the mental model hypothesis* as advanced by Johnson-Laird (for a summary see Stemmer & Cohen, 2002) encompasses other suggested hypotheses or theories. The failure of RHD patients to ignore the implausibility of absurd logical syllogisms has, however, been interpreted as contradiction of the mental model hypothesis (McDonald, 2000). This seems a rather limited view of the mental model hypothesis and it does not seem justified to refute the hypothesis on these grounds alone.

The empirical validity of three theories that attempt to explain pragmatic language impairment in autism, RHD patients and TBI patients was discussed by Martin and McDonald (2003), that is *ToM* as a component of *social inference theory*, the *weak central coherence hypothesis* (WCCH) and the *executive dysfunction account*. These authors show that none of the three positions sufficiently accounts for the pragmatic impairments observed across different patient populations. For ToM it is pointed out that there is a close relationship between the concept of ToM and pragmatic understanding – and this makes it difficult to define the causal relationship between the two. Others have criticized that the ToM framework inappropriately intellectualizes everyday social activities, as experiments are conducted to test the ability to represent the intentions of others instead of observing and analyzing the intentionality in spontaneous social interactions

(Leudar et al., 2004). For example, discrepancies have been found between patients' poor performance on ToM tasks in the laboratory and good performance in managing intentionality in interactions outside of the laboratory (McCabe, 2004). Finally, ToM is but one domain of social cognition and its application to patients has mostly been limited to processes used to perceive other people. Other components of social cognition that also need consideration are the perception of self and social knowledge that enables people to manage everyday life. (For a summary see Beer & Ochsner, 2006.)

The WCCH refers to the inability to use context to derive meaning; this inability reflects the failure of a central system to integrate small pieces of information with a globally coherent pattern of information. A problem already mentioned for ToM also pertains to the WCCH: it is used to describe and, at the same time, explain pragmatic deficits. Another shortcoming of the WCCH is that it cannot be applied to explain pragmatic behavior across populations (Martin & Crow, 2003).

The executive dysfunction account is based on the observation that disturbances in executive functions often reflect impairments of the frontal lobe. Executive functions have been conceptualized as the central executive of the information-processing system and as such include the control of attention, goal setting (initiating, planning, problem solving, strategic behavior) as well as that of cognitive flexibility (attention shifting, working memory, self-monitoring, self-regulation) (Stuss & Alexander, 2000). The question is thus whether these specific cognitive abilities underlie pragmatic impairments, or – as some have suggested – especially ToM abilities. While some studies report a relationship between executive dysfunctions and pragmatic impairment, or ToM in particular, others do not – and yet again others have not investigated this issue (for a summary see Martin & Crow, 2003; see also Mitchell & Crow, 2005; Champagne Lavau et al., 2006).

In sum, despite numerous studies of pragmatic disorders, there is currently no agreement on how to best explain the impairments. Several factors contribute to this situation: an important and inherent problem in the majority of studies across patient populations is the grouping of patients – despite great heterogeneity. Another problem relates to the ambiguity of the stimuli used and yet other problems refer to the lack of adequate consideration of testing different theoretical positions and failing to cross-reference findings in other clinical populations. In addition, various researchers use different methods of assessment which thus target different aspects of pragmatics. The same holds for neuropsychological assessment. Finally, as already mentioned, target concepts (e.g., inferencing, ToM, executive functions) are frequently used to describe as well as explain the phenomenon and this leads to circularity of the arguments advanced.

Neural Systems Underlying Pragmatic Abilities

With the technological advancement in neuroimaging, it is now possible to correlate pragmatic task performance with brain activation in healthy as well as in pathological populations and specify in more detail the neural systems involved. The majority of studies have used the functional magnetic resonance imaging (fMRI) technique, as it is particularly suitable to investigate the neural systems implicated (see **Box 1** for the relevance of electroen-cephalogram/event-related potential (EEG/ERP) studies).

Neural Systems in Discourse Processing

Based on lesion studies, text and discourse processing, and especially inferencing and integration processes, are often associated with the right hemisphere, although the findings are not always clear cut (see Section 2). So far, neuroimaging studies with healthy populations have not provided much evidence for this assumption. Text processing has been associated with left hemisphere dominance or the involvement of both hemispheres, and studies on coherence and inferencing have also produced controversial results (for a detailed review and discussion the reader is referred to Chapter 16; see **Box 2** for a summary). Similar to sentence processing, activation of inferior frontal and temporal regions have been described in most studies indicating (the intuitively plausible observation) that similar neural systems that underlie sentence processes are also recruited during text and discourse processes. Other neural systems have also been activated; some of them may reflect the recruitment of cognitive processes (such as attention, memory or control processes) involved in the task. So far it has been difficult to determine the neural systems that are specific to text or discourse, or, even more basic, whether such specific systems exist.

Neural Systems in Non-literal and Figurative Language

Different processing mechanisms have been suggested for different subtypes of non-literal and figurative items (e.g., conventional versus novel metaphors) and it is thus possible that these may also implicate different neural systems. A behavioral study using the divided visual field technique showed the involvement of the right hemisphere in the comprehension of novel but not of conventional metaphors (Faust & Mashal, 2007). Further support comes from a neuroimaging study with fMRI that contrasted conventional and novel metaphors (Mashal et al., 2005). The right homolog of Wernicke's area was viewed as playing a special role in the processing of novel metaphors conjointly with the activation of other regions, suggesting a basic network for the processes of reading and

Box 1 One or two steps to interpret language?

When someone tells us that ''Dutch trains are white'' we can either take the sentence at face value, or, if we are Dutch or an observant traveler, world knowledge tells us that this is not true as Dutch trains are yellow. How do we get to the insight that the sentence is not true and the speaker possibly joking or a liar? By first computing a local context-independent meaning of the sentence from its phonology, syntax and semantics, and then, in a next step, integrating this meaning with our world knowledge? Or do we do this – as some researchers claim – in one step? Peter Hagoort and his colleagues have performed a series of experiments tackling the question whether we use two steps to arrive at the meaning of a sentence or whether we combine in one step the linguistic information with the information from prior discourse, the speaker, the situational and our world knowledge. For example, in one study they presented violated sentences where the violation could be recognized on linguistic bases alone or only when world knowledge was applied (see the following figure). Using the event-related potential and fMRI technique they showed that the N400 effects obtained for both conditions were identical in onset and peak latency suggesting that lexical–semantic knowledge and general world knowledge were both integrated in the same time-frame during sentence interpretation [panel (a) in the figure]. In addition, the fMRI data identified a common activation are in the left inferior frontal gyrus for both conditions [panel (b) in the figure].

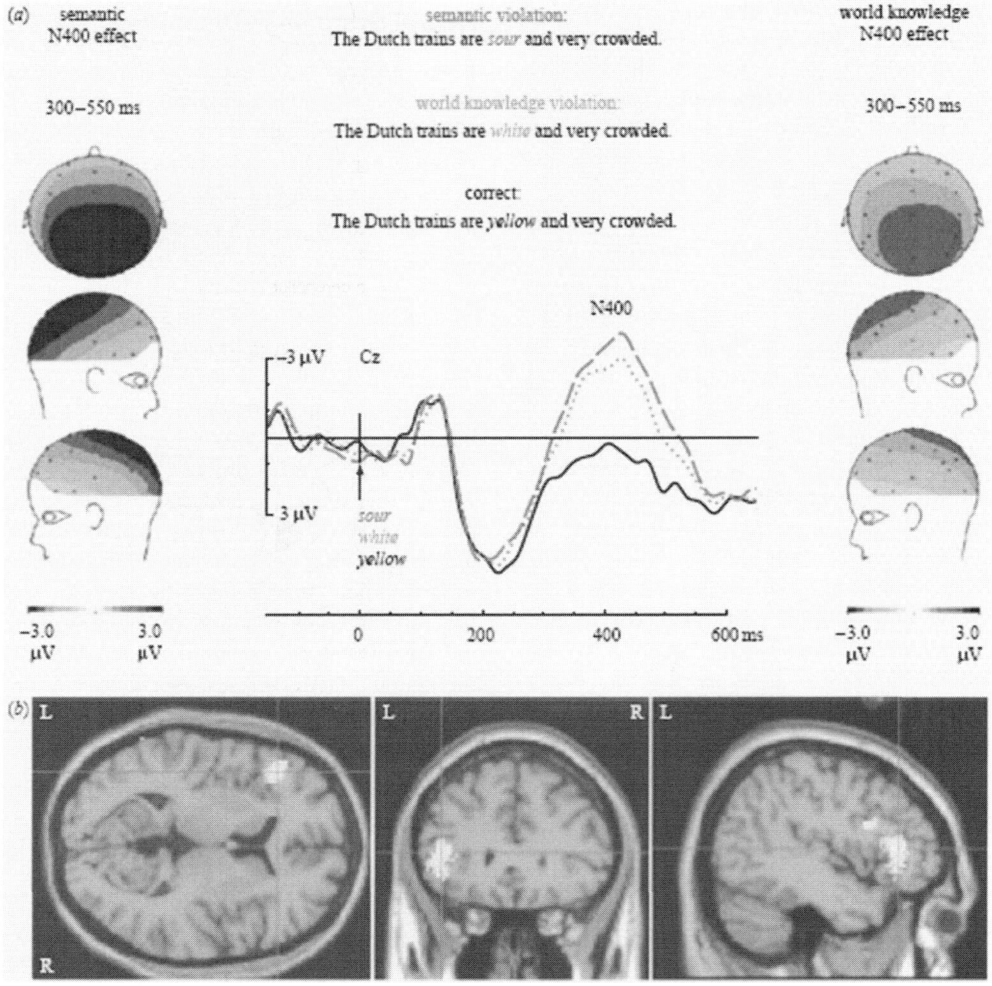

Source: Figure taken from Hagoort & van Berkum (2007) (Fig. 4, p. 805). Printed by permission of The Royal Society. (See color plate 31.)

Hagoort, P., & van Berkum, J. (2007). Beyond the sentence given. *Philosophical Transactions of the Royal Society B, 362*, 801–811.

Hagoort, P., Hald, L., Bastiaansen, M., & Petersson, K.M. (2004). Integration of word meaning and world knowledge in language comprehension. *Science, 304*, 438–441.

Box 2 Neuroimaging of discourse

Generally, left or bilateral activation has been observed much more frequently than specific right hemisphere activation. In addition to the activation of classical language areas in the left hemisphere (inferior frontal gyrus, superior, middle, inferior temporal gyri and angular gyrus) in most studies, other areas are also activated. Whether these are specific to discourse is currently not clear. The figure summarizes the areas of brain activation that have been identified in different neuroimaging studies on aspects of discourse. The localization is approximate and symbols close to each other may, in fact, overlap. For exact localization the reader is referred to the original studies. Note that the studies are not directly comparable due to different methodological details.

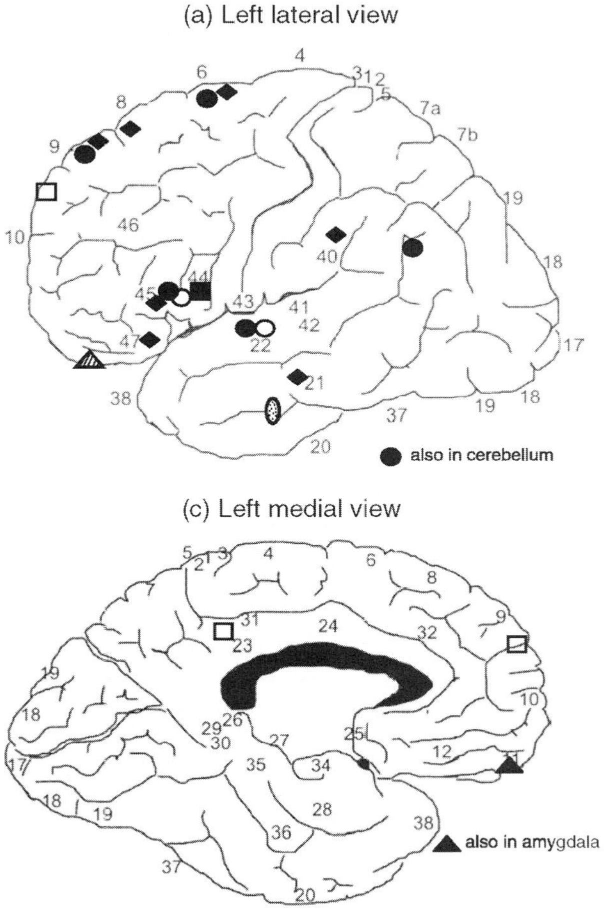

Symbols:

Caplan, R., & Dapretto, M. (2001). Making sense during conversation: an fMRI study. *Neuroreport, 12*, 3625–3632: ○ reasoning (L-IFG BA44,45; L-STG BA22) ● topic maintenance (bilateral with RH bias: BA44/45, BA22; R-DLPFC BA46,9; L-PL BA39; L-SMA BA6)

Ferstl, E.C., & von Cramon, Y. (2001). The role of coherence and cohesion in text comprehension: an event-related fMRI study. *Cognitive Brain Research, 11*, 325–340: □ coherence building L-PCC/IPC BA23/31; L-frontomedian wall/SFG BA9,10), ■ task difficulty: L-IFS/IPCS BA44

Ferstl, E.C., Rinck, M., & von Cramon, D.Y. (2005). Emotional and temporal aspects of situation model processing during text comprehension: An event-related fMRI study. *Journal of Cognitive Neuroscience, 17*(5), 724–739: Δ local detection of inconsistencies (R-ATL), ▲ (hatched) integration of inconsistencies (bilateral vlPFC BA47/1; ▲ emotional involvement (bilateral vmPFC/supraorbital sulcus + amygdaloid complex)

Kuperberg, G.R., Lakshmanan, B.M., Caplan, D.N., & Holcomb, P.J. (2006). Making sense of discourse: An fMRI study of causal inferencing across sentences. *Neuroimage, 33*(1), 343–361: ◆ generation and integration of causal inferences: L-IFG BA45,47, L-MFG BA6/9, L-IPL BA40; L-MTG BA21; L-SFG BA9; R-SFG BA6/8/9 St. George, Kutas, Martinez, & Sereno, 1999: (dotted oval) untitled condition (bilateral ITS; R-MTS)

L, R: left, right; BA: Brodman area; ATL: anterior temporal lobe; DLPF: dorsolateral prefrontal cortex; IFS: inferior frontal sulcus; IFG: inferior frontal gyrus; IPC: inferior precuneus; IPCS: inferior precental sulcus; IPL: inferior parietal lobule; ITS: inferior temporal sulcus; MFG: middle frontal gyrus; MTG: middle temporal gyrus; MTS: middle temporal sulcus; PCC: posterior cingulate cortex; SFG: superior frontal gyrus; SMA: supplementary motor area; STG: superior temporal gyrus; vlPFC: ventrolateral prefrontal cortex; vmPFC: ventromedial prefrontal cortex.

Box 3 Neuroimaging of non-literal and figurative language

Similar to the discourse tasks (see **Box 2**), non-literal and figurative language tasks activate the classical language areas. There is currently no agreement to which extent the other activated brain areas are specific to metaphor processing and how they interact with other cortical or subcortical systems. The latter aspect also applies to discourse processing although some proposals have recently been made. Humorous stimuli but not metaphoric stimuli also activated brain regions associated with affective processing. The reader should be aware that the studies are not directly comparable due to different methodological details. Note that localization is approximate and symbols close to each other may, in fact, overlap. For exact localization see original studies.

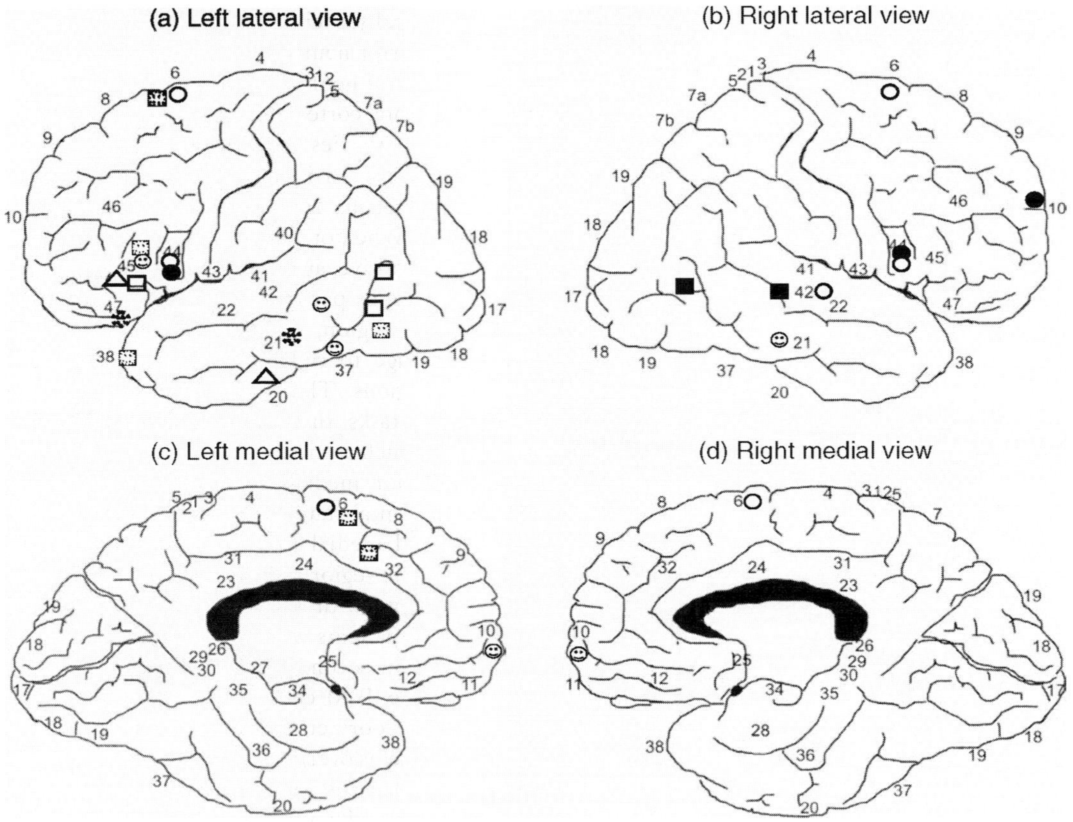

Symbols for figurative language studies:

Eviatar, Z., & Just, M.A. (2006). Brain correlates of discourse processing: An fMRI investigation of irony and conventional metaphor comprehension. Neuropsychologia, 44, 2348–2359: □ conventional metaphors (L-IFG, L-ITG, R-ITG, L-IESC) ■ ironic statements (R-STG, R-MTG)

Mashal, N., Faust, M., & Hendler, T. (2005). The role of the right hemisphere in processing nonsalient metaphorical meanings: Application of principal components analysis to fMRI data. Neuropsychologia, 43, 2084–2100: ○ novel metaphors (bilateral Broca BA44; R-Wernicke (BA22/44), bilateral insula BA13; bilateral SMA BA6) ● conventional metaphors (bilateral Broca BA44; R-SFG BA10)

Rapp, A.M., Leube, D.T., Erb, M., Grodd, W., & Kircher, T.T. J. (2004). Neural correlates of metaphor processing. Cognitive Brain Research, 20, 395–402: △ metaphors (L-IFG BA47/45)

Symbols for joke/humor studies:

Goel, V., & Dolan, R.J. (2001). The functional anatomy of humor: segregating cognitive and affective components. Nature Neuroscience, 4(3), 237–238: ☺ joke (mvPFC BA10/11, bilateral cerebellum); cognition: (L-posterior MTG BA21/37, L-posterior ITG BA37, R-posterior MTG BA21, L-IFG BA44/45)

Mobbs, D., Greicius, M.D., Abdel-Azim, E., Menon, V., & Reiss, A.L. (2003). Humor modulates the mesolimbic reward centers. Neuron, 40, 1041–1048: ⊡ bilateral ventral tegmental area, Ncl. accumbens, amygdala; L-IFG BA44/45, L-TOJ BA37, L-temporal pole BA38)

Moran, J.M., Gagan, S.W., Adamas, R.B.Jr., Janata, P., & Kelley, W. (2004). Neural correlates of humor detection and appreciation. Neuroimage, 21, 1055–1060: ⚇ humor appreciation: bilateral insular cortex, bilateral amygdala); humor detection: L-posterior MTG BA21, L-IFG BA47)

Watson, K.K., Matthews, B.J., & Allman, J.M. (2007). Brain activation during sight gags and language-dependent humor. Cerebral Cortex, 17, 314–324: ☺ L-midbrain, bilateral amygdala (common network for both types of humor)

(The numbers indicate the approximate site of Brodman areas).

L, R: left, right; BA: Brodman area; IESC: inferior extrastriate cortex; IFG: inferior frontal gyrus; ITG: inferior temporal gyrus; MTG: middle temporal gyrus; mvPFC: medial ventral prefrontal cortex; SFG: superior frontal gyrus; SMA: supplementary motor area; STG: superior temporal gyrus; TOJ: temporo-occipital junction comprehension (see **Box 3**). Another study reported an overlapping network in the classical left language areas and specific (mostly left) frontal and temporal networks for conventional metaphoric and specifically activated right temporal areas for ironic statements (Eviatar & Just, 2006; see also **Box 3**). In disagreement with the Mashal et al. (2005) study, only left inferior frontal activation for simple novel metaphors was reported by Rapp et al., 2004. Yet another study using the ERP and divided visual field techniques found that both hemispheres were associated with metaphor processing (Coulson & van Petten, 2007).

Using the repetitive transmagnetic stimulation (rTMS) technique only left temporal and left frontal regions have been associated with opaque idiom comprehension, (Oliveri et al., 2004). No disruption, however, was observed with right frontal stimulation. While this study speaks to the importance of these regions in opaque idiom comprehension, it cannot exclude the possibility that other left or right hemisphere regions contribute to the comprehension process inasmuch as no other areas were stimulated.

Taken together, these studies suggest an activation of classical language areas conjointly with specific regions in the prefrontal and temporal cortices that are differently activated for various types of figurative language. Whether these regions or neural systems are specific for figurative language remains currently unanswered. It seems likely that, depending on task and stimuli demand, and on individual characteristics, attention, memory and control networks are initiated to various degrees.

Behavioral lesion studies have frequently been interpreted to point to an involvement of the right hemisphere in non-literal and figurative language, although findings have not always been straightforward. Based on current neuroimaging studies it is difficult to provide an evaluation – at least at this point they do not seem to support a special role for the right hemisphere.

Another aspect that deserves attention is the affective component involved in pragmatic processing. At least one characteristic that distinguishes humor and joke comprehension from figurative language is its affective component. It is thus not surprising that a cognitive and an affective system were identified in an fMRI study on joke processing. The cognitive system was implicated in "getting the joke" and the affective system in joke appreciation (Goel & Dolan, 2001; see also **Box 3**). It is thus plausible to assume that when affect is involved (and not necessarily only in the form of a joke) in pragmatic processing, the neural systems associated with affect will be recruited. Subsequent humor and joke studies confirmed and further specified these distinctive systems and identified yet another network suggestive of the implication of the reward system (ventral tegmental area, medial ventral prefrontal cortex (PFC), Ncl. accumbens) in joke and humor comprehension (for a summary see **Box 3**).

Neural Systems in Mindreading (ToM)

In Section 2, it was suggested that patients with difficulties in mindreading show some involvement of the frontal lobes. Difficulties with mindreading may result from an abnormal interaction between the frontal lobe and their functionally connected cortical and subcortical areas. Here we will now focus on studies directly addressing the issue of neural systems underlying mindreading and, more generally, social cognition (see **Box 4** for mindreading and mirror neurons).

A series of neuroimaging studies have implicated the medial frontal cortex in mindreading although – similar to behavioral studies – evidence relating to laterality remains controversial (for summaries see Siegal & Varley, 2002; Lee et al., 2004; Amodio & Frith, 2006; see also **Figure 1**. When other aspects of social cognition such as visual, cognitive and affective domains are considered, neural systems partially overlap – but also differ within the frontal region, as has been shown in stroke patients with damage to right, left or bilateral frontal or non-frontal regions. The findings suggest that those social cognition tasks that preferentially implicate cognitive processes such as visual perspective-taking, recruit lateral and superior medial frontal regions, while the ability to infer mental states implicates affective connections of the ventral medial frontal cortex to the amygdala and other limbic regions (Stuss et al., 2001). The observation that patients with schizophrenia (with negative symptoms) and patients with ventromedial PFC damage were impaired on second-order affective ToM tasks but not in cognitive ToM conditions would support such a view (Shamay-Tsoory et al., 2007). The extent to which these neural systems overlap is currently not clear. There is also evidence that the neural substrates of mindreading and empathy (i.e., the attribution of emotion) share the same frontal–temporal network – *albeit* with different weighting of subcomponents. While the empathy network relies more on temporal/amygdala and orbitofrontal areas, the mindreading network depends on medial frontal cortex (Lee et al., 2004). Based on a review of neuropsychological and neuroimaging studies on aspects of social cognition, it has been suggested that the anterior regions of the medial frontal cortex are associated with metacognitive representations that enable us to "think about thinking", such as reflecting on what others think of us or on the values that people attach to actions and outcomes (for a review see Amodio & Frith, 2006; see **Figure 1**). In more caudal regions of the medial frontal cortex value is associated with actions while in the more orbital region value is associated with outcomes.

Summary

The nature and extent of the neural systems implicated in pragmatic processing largely depend on which aspects

Box 4 Mirror neurons and mindreading

A mirror neuron is a neuron that fires both when an individual performs an action and when the individual observes the same action performed by another individual. In other words, the neuron "mirrors" or imitates the action of another person, as though the observer were performing the action herself. Thus, mirror neurons have been associated with imitative behavior and action. As can be seen in the following figure, a core circuit for imitation has been identified: the posterior superior temporal sulcus is associated with a high-order visual description of the action to be imitated, the parietal component with the motor aspects of the imitated action and the frontal component with the goal of the imitated action (for a review see Iacoboni & Dapretto, 2006). Researchers have observed that the mirror neuron system not only codes for action but also for the intention associated with it, and a link was thus established between the mirror neuron system and social cognition (but see Jacob & Jeannerod., 2005 for a critique). It has even been proposed that mirror neurons are key elements in the understanding of the intentions of others associated with everyday actions. Some disorders, like autism, have been explained with a disruption of the activity of the mirror neuron system. Whether the mirror neuron hypothesis can explain other pathologies that implicate disorders of social cognition remains to be seen.

Does the mirror neuron system give us some indication on the question whether language related aspects of social cognition are lateralized? As a special high-order motor system the mirror neuron system tends to be bilaterally represented. However, empirical research suggests that the left hemisphere – with its specialization for specific language components – has a multimodal (visual, auditory) mirror neuron system, whereas the right hemisphere has only a visual mirror neuron system.

IPL: inferior parietal lobe; PF: prefrontal; PFG: prefrontal gyrus; PMC: posterior medial cortex; IFG: inferior frontal gyrus; STS: superior temporal sulcus; MNS: mirror neuron system.

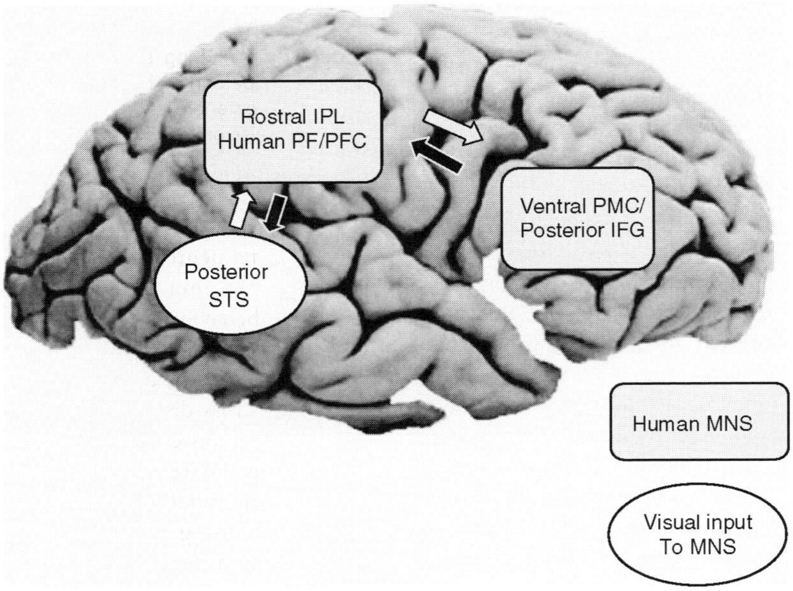

Source: Figure adapted by permission from Iacoboni, & Dapretto. (2006). *Nature Reviews Neuroscience*. Macmillan Publishers Ltd., © 2007.

Iacoboni, M., & Dapretto, M. (2006). The mirror neuron system and the consequences of its dysfunction. *Nature Reviews Neuroscience, 7*, 942–951.

Jacob, P., & Jeannerod, M. (2005). The motor theory of social cognition: A critique. *Trends in Cognitive Sciences, 9*, 21–25.

of pragmatics are in focus, the demands the experimental tasks make on the brain system, and, last but not least, the individual characteristics of the individual. It seems unlikely that there is a *single* neural system responsible for linguistic pragmatic behavior. Instead, pragmatic behavior evolves from an interaction of neural systems necessary for the task at hand – in both a bottom–up and top–down fashion. The classical language areas are involved and so are attention and memory (fronto-temporal-parietal systems), monitoring (cingulate cortex) and emotion networks (fronto-limbic-systems). The medial PFC is particularly involved if aspects of social cognition are implicated in pragmatic behavior. The special role of the PFC is generally undisputed. However, the contributing role of its subsystems is still unclear and present research findings are limited and difficult to reconcile. Some tasks that were hypothesized (based on behavioral studies) to involve the right hemisphere have been shown in neuroimaging studies to rely on left or bilateral hemisphere systems. What seems to evolve is that if the brain detects inconsistencies and/or task demands increase, then the right hemisphere is recruited. Generally, however, based

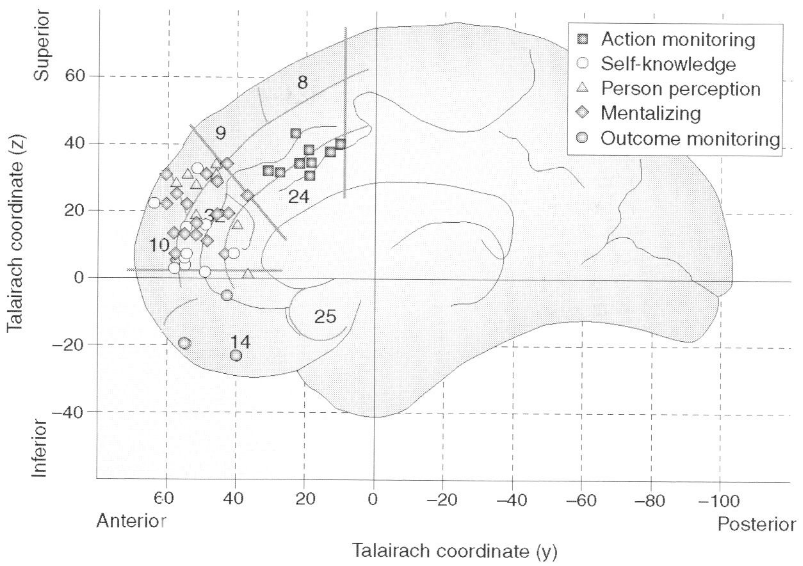

Figure 1 The figure shows activations in the medial frontal cortex during action monitoring, social cognition and outcome monitoring. The meta-analysis suggests that social cognition tasks (including self-knowledge, person perception, mentalising) activate areas in the anterior rostral medial frontal cortex (arMFC). Monitoring of actions activate the posterior rostral region of the MFC (prMFC) while monitoring of outcomes involves the orbital MFC (oMFC). Figure reprinted by permission from Macmillan Publishers Ltd: *Nature Review Neuroscience*, D.M. Amodio & C.D. Frith (2006). © 2007.

on current neuroimaging studies, the specific contribution of the right hemisphere to pragmatic behavior still remains elusive.

We have seen the importance of including psycholinguistic theories to ensure finer graded stimulus construction (e.g., not all metaphors are alike and thus need not necessarily implicate the same processing mechanisms) and its impact on (different) neural systems. Individual differences and variability (e.g., in arousal, affective and cognitive systems) have only rarely been considered although it can be assumed that they also play an important role. Experimental designs that are based on carefully constructed stimuli and carefully analyzed tasks (instead of undifferentiated assumptions on stimulus and task similarity) might be one way to achieve better predictions and test hypotheses on the sufficiency and necessity of the recruited neural systems. And finally, one question that remains unanswered is the very basic one of whether what we test in experimental conditions also applies outside the laboratory.

Challenges and Future Directions

Linguistic pragmatic behavior is a complex phenomenon with many different aspects. Understanding its processing mechanisms and underlying neural systems requires a cross-disciplinary endeavor – an approach often espoused but in practice still less than optimal. Although research questions from (psycho-)linguistics, philosophical, social cognition and neuroscience research increasingly converge in an effort to unravel how the brain deals with linguistic pragmatic behavior, theory and models discussed in each of these disciplines are less easily reconciled. Hence, one challenge lies in the effort to develop theories and models that satisfy cross-disciplinary standards, which would then serve to test more specific predictions and hypotheses. Besides the theoretical framework, we also need to be guided by methodological, technical and paradigm standards when using neuroimaging techniques. Currently, these are as different and numerous as the number of neuroimaging laboratories that exist. Without some minimal consensus, comparison of studies will remain vague or impossible. Related to this is the requirement to replicate studies – a common and necessary practice in research – an activity which, however, rarely occurs in pragmatic research using hemodynamic techniques. Finally, we need to consider individual variability and differences which have been mostly neglected.

Another dimension that needs development is a more optimal combination of imaging studies to make best use of the strength and limitations of each method. While such a combination of methods has become more and more common in other research areas, it is still rare in pragmatic research. Complementary information could also be gained by investigating pragmatic behavior in patient populations using neuroimaging techniques.

Many neuroimaging studies report areas of activation without much consideration of possible interactions with other brain regions. The relationship between identified cortical and subcortical regions and their organization in interrelated neural systems might be equally important. Advances in diffusion and fiber tracking imaging might help to elucidate these issues.

A final issue concerns the ecological validity of our findings. We need to verify whether what we test in the laboratory also applies to "real life". This implies, on the one hand, the development of laboratory tasks that better simulate real world behavior (e.g., by using virtual reality techniques), while, on the other hand, applying real world findings to laboratory tests.

Acknowledgments

This work was supported by the Canada Research Chair Program. Thanks go to F.A. Rodden and H.A. Whitaker for helpful suggestions to earlier drafts.

References

Amodio, DM and Frith, CD (2006). Meeting of minds: The medial frontal cortex and social cognition. *Nature Reviews Neuroscience* 7: 268–277.

Ash, S, Moore, P, Antani, BS, McCawley, G, Work, M, and Grossman, M (2006). Trying to tell a tale. Discourse impairments in progressive aphasia and frontotemporal dementia. *Neurology* 66: 1405–1413.

Beer, JS and Ochsner, KN (2006). Social cognition: A multi level analysis. *Brain Research* 1079: 98–105.

Brady, M, Armstrong, L, and Mackenzie, C (2005). Further evidence on topic use following right hemisphere brain damage: Procedural and descriptive discourse. *Aphasiology* 19(8): 731–747.

Brownell, HH and Martino, G (1998). Deficits in inference and social cognition. The effects of right hemisphere brain damage on discourse. In: Beeman, M and Chiarello, C (eds.) *Right hemisphere language comprehension: Perspectives from cognitive neuroscience*, pp. 309–328. Mahwah, NJ: Lawrence Erlbaum.

Champagne Lavau, M, Stip, E, and Joanette, Y (2006). Social cognition deficit in schizophrenia: Accounting for pragmatic deficits in communication abilities? *Current Psychiatry Reviews* 2: 309–315.

Chapman, SB, Highley, AP, and Thompson, JL (1998). Discourse in fluent aphasia and Alzheimer's disease. *Journal of Neurolinguistics* 11: 55–78.

Corcoran, R (2003). Inductive reasoning and the understanding of intention in schizophrenia. *Cognitive Neuropsychiatry* 8(3): 223–235.

Corcoran, R, Cahill, C, and Frith, CD (1997). The appreciation of visual jokes in people with schizophrenia: A study of "mentalizing" ability. *Schizophrenia Research* 24: 319–327.

Coulson, S and van Petten, C (2007). A special role for the right hemisphere in metaphor comprehension? ERP evidence from hemifield presentation. *Brain Research* 1146: 128–145.

Drury, VM, Robinson, EJ, and Birchwood, M (1998). "Theory of mind" skills during an acute episode of psychosis and following recovery. *Psychological Medicine* 28: 1101–1112.

Eviatar, Z and Just, MA (2006). Brain correlates of discourse processing: An fMRI investigation of irony and conventional metaphor comprehension. *Neuropsychologia* 44: 2348–2359.

Faust, M and Mashal, N (2007). The role of the right cerebral hemisphere in processing novel metaphoric expressions taken from poetry: A divided visual field study. *Neuropsychologia* 45: 860–870.

Goel, V and Dolan, RJ (2001). The functional anatomy of humor: Segregating cognitive and affective components. *Nature Neuroscience* 4(3): 237–238.

Gregory, C, Lough, S, Stone, V, Erzinclioglu, S, Martin, L, Baron-Cohen, S, and Hodges, JR (2002). Theory of mind in patients with frontal variant frontotemporal dementia and Alzheimer's disease: Theoretical and practical implications. *Brain* 125(4): 752–764.

Happé, F, Brownell, H, and Winner, E (1999). Acquired "theory of mind" impairments following stroke. *Cognition* 70: 211–240.

Lee, KH, Farrow, TFD, Spence, SA, and Woodruff, PWR (2004). Social cognition, brain networks and schizophrenia. *Psychological Medicine* 34: 391–400.

Leudar, I, Costall, A, and Francis, D (2004). Theory of mind: A critical assessment. *Theory and Psychology* 14(5): 571–578.

Lough, S, Kipps, CM, Treise, C, Watson, P, Blair, JR, and Hodges, JR (2006). Social reasoning, emotion and empathy in frontotemporal dementia. *Neuropsychologia* 44: 950–958.

Martin, I and McDonald, S (2003). Weak coherence, no theory of mind, or executive dysfunction? Solving the puzzle of pragmatic language disorders. *Brain and Language* 85(3): 451–466.

Mashal, N, Faust, M, and Hendler, T (2005). The role of the right hemisphere in processing nonsalient metaphorical meanings: Application of principal components analysis to fMRI data. *Neuropsychologia* 43: 2084–2100.

McCabe, R (2004). On the inadequacies of theory of mind explanations of schizophrenia. Alternative accounts of alternative problems. *Theory and Psychology* 14(5): 738–752.

McDonald, S (1999). Exploring the process of inference generation in sarcasm: A review of normal and clinical studies. *Brain and Language* 68: 486–506.

McDonald, S (2000). Exploring the cognitive basis of right-hemisphere pragmatic language disorders. *Brain and Language* 75: 82–107.

Meilijson, SR, Kasher, A, and Elizur, A (2004). Language performance in chronic schizophrenia: A pragmatic approach. *Journal of Speech, Language and Hearing Research* 47: 695–713.

Mitchell, RLC and Crow, TJ (2005). Right hemisphere language functions and schizophrenia: The forgotten hemisphere? *Brain* 128: 963–978.

Myers, P (2005). Profiles of communication deficits in patients with right cerebral hemisphere damage: Implications for diagnosis and treatment. *Aphasiology* 19: 1147–1160.

Oliveri, M, Romero, L, and Papagno, C (2004). Left but not right temporal involvement in opaque idiom comprehension: A repetitive transcranial magnetic stimulation study. *Journal of Cognitive Neuroscience* 16(5): 848–855.

Papagno, C (2001). Comprehension of metaphors and idioms in patients with Alzheimer's disease. A longitudinal study. *Brain* 124: 1450–1460.

Rapp, AM, Leube, DT, Erb, M, Grodd, W, and Kircher, TTJ (2004). Neural correlates of metaphor processing. *Cognitive Brain Research* 20: 395–402.

Shamay-Tsoory, SG, Aharon-Peretz, J, and Levkovitz, Y (2007). The neuroanatomical basis of affective mentalizing in schizophrenia: Comparison of patients with schizophrenia and patients with localized prefrontal lesions. *Schizophrenia Research* 90: 274–283.

Shammi, P and Stuss, D (1999). Humour appreciation: A role of the right frontal lobe. *Brain* 122: 657–666.

Siegal, M and Varley, R (2002). Neural systems involved in "theory of mind" *Nature Reviews Neuroscience* 3: 463–471.

Snowden, JS, Gibbons, ZC, Blackshaw, A, Doubleday, E, Thompson, J, Craufurd, D, Foster, J, Happé, F, and Nearly, D (2003). Social cognition in frontotemporal dementia and Huntington's disease. *Neuropsychologia* 41: 688–701.

Stemmer, B (2008). Neuropragmatics. In: Ball, MJ, Perkins, M, Mueller, N, and Howard, S (eds.) *Handbook of clinical linguistics*, pp. 61–78. Oxford: Blackwell.

Stemmer, B and Cohen, H (2002). Neuropragmatique et lésions de l'hémisphère droit. *Psychologie de l'Interaction* 13(14): 15–46.

Stuss, DT and Alexander, MP (2000). Executive functions and the frontal lobes: A conceptual view. *Psychological Research* 63: 289–298.

Stuss, DT, Gallup, GG, and Alexander, MP (2001). The frontal lobes are necessary for "theory of mind" *Brain* 124: 279–286.

Verdon, C-M, Fossati, P, Verny, M, Dieudonné, Teillet, L, and Nadel, J (2007). Social cognition: An early impairment in dementia of the Alzheimer type. *Alzheimer Disease and Associated Disorders* 21(1): 25–30.

Winner, E, Brownell, H, Happé, F, Blum, A, and Pincus, D (1998). Distinguishing lies from jokes: Theory of mind deficits and discourse

interpretation in right hemisphere brain-damaged patients. *Brain and Language* 62: 89–106.
Wright, HH and Newhoff, M (2005). Pragmatics. In: LaPointe, LL (ed.) *Aphasia and related neurogenic language disorders*, pp. 237–248. New York: Thieme.

Further Reading

Mason, RA and Just, MA (2006). Neuroimag ng contributions to the understancing of discourse processes. In: Traxler, M and Gernsbacher, MA (eds.) *Handbook of Psycholinguistics*, pp. 765–799. Amsterdam: Elsevier.
Ferstl, EC (2007). The functional neuroanatomy of text comprehension: What's the story so far? In: Schmalhofer, F and Perfetti, CA (eds.) *Higher level language processes in the brain: Inference and comprehension processes*, pp. 53–102. Mahwah, NJ: Erlbaum.
Both chapters discuss the neural systems implicated in discourse processing. Although the interpretation of the correlation between behavioral and neuroimaging do not always coincide and are, at times, disputable, the chapters provides a basis for further evaluation, verification and discussion.
Stuss, D and Knight, R (2002). *Principles of frontal lobe function.* Oxford: Oxford University Press.
The collection of articles provides an excellent summary on the different aspects of frontal lobe functions – from a theoretical as well as clinical perspective.

Neuropsychological Testing

D. C. Delis, University of California at San Diego, La Jolla, CA, USA; and San Diego veterans Affairs Healthcare System, San Diego, CA, USA

Introduction

The psychometric assessment of cognitive and motor functions has proved to have considerable utility in the diagnosis of neurological and psychiatric disorders. Many insidious disorders that evade early identification using the most advanced medical technologies (e.g., neuroimaging; electroencephalography, EEG) can often be effectively diagnosed using neuropsychological testing. Following are examples of neurological conditions that depend heavily on neuropsychological assessment for accurate diagnosis:

- Individuals with early Alzheimer's disease often have normal neurological examinations, magnetic resonance imaging (MRI) and computed tomography (CT) brain scans, and EEG findings. However, studies have found that neuropsychological testing has proved to be one of the most effective procedures for the earliest diagnosis of this pervasive disorder.
- Some elderly patients with severe depression present with memory complaints and low scores on mental status exams that are comparable to those of patients with early Alzheimer's disease, thereby making it difficult to distinguish between these two conditions. However, neuropsychological tests can differentiate between the qualitatively different memory profiles of depressed individuals versus those of early Alzheimer's patients with approximately 95% accuracy.
- Children with fetal alcohol syndrome (FAS), who often have significant deficits in cognitive development, are typically first identified by their facial dysmorphic features. However, many children who are exposed to alcohol *in utero* have normal facial features but go on to develop levels of cognitive impairment that are comparable to those of children with FAS. Neuropsychological testing is important for identifying children who were prenatally exposed to alcohol but who do not have the facial dysmorphic features in order to determine if they should receive early educational interventions for cognitive impairments.
- Some individuals who have had serious head traumas suffer brain damage and cognitive impairments and yet have normal findings on neuroimaging. Other individuals can have head trauma without brain damage, but exaggerate cognitive deficits for external incentive. Neuropsychologists have developed empirically based methods for distinguishing between head-injured individuals with bona fide cognitive deficits secondary to brain damage versus head-injured individuals without permanent brain damage who attempt to feign cognitive impairment on cognitive testing.

Historical Perspective

The field of clinical neuropsychology evolved in the 1940s through the 1960s primarily as a tool to aid in addressing the very broad question of whether a patient had organicity or brain damage. The need to address this general question was important at that time, because CT and MRI brain scans had not yet been developed. In addition, the primary focus of the neurological examination has always involved testing of reflexes and senses, both of which are mediated by the sensorimotor cortex and connecting pathways. This focus leaves vast regions of the brain that can be damaged but without altering sensorimotor functions. Instead, neuropathology in these other regions often affects cognitive skills. When brain damage is subtle to moderate, the decline in cognitive functions can also be mild to moderate. Neurologists and other physicians often conduct a 'mental status exam,' which is a cursory assessment of cognitive skills, such as asking the patient to remember three words. Such brief, nonstandardized exams usually are capable of identifying patients with severe brain damage, but they frequently fail to identify patients with mild to moderate neurocognitive dysfunction.

The need to identify individuals with mild to moderate brain damage outside the sensorimotor circuitry was one of the primary reasons why psychologists began studying neurological patients. Since the early 1900s, psychologists have been armed with powerful methodologies for rigorously measuring subtle differences in mental abilities. The fields of psychometrics and IQ testing, two of the most important contributions in the history of psychology, have long provided clinicians with the means for reliably measuring the development of intellectual and cognitive functions in children and adolescents. In the hands of the neuropsychologist, these methodologies offer the ideal procedures for gauging even subtle declines in intellectual and cognitive functions in individuals with brain dysfunction.

The pioneers in this area were a handful of psychologists during the 1940s through the 1960s; working at a time before there was a field of clinical neuropsychology, these psychologists had the vision to see the tremendous utility of adapting psychometric tests to the assessment of cognitive decline in brain-damaged patients. These early leaders included, among others, Arthur Benton, Kurt Goldstein, Harold Goodglass, Ward Halstead, Donald Hebb, Edith Kaplan, Alexander Luria, Brenda Milner, Ralph Reitan, Andre Rey, Hans-Lukas Teuber, Elizabeth Warrington, and David Wechsler. In administering a wide variety of cognitive tests to patients with focal brain damage, psychologists soon discovered another vital contribution of their methodologies: more accurate characterizations of neuropsychological syndromes with different profiles of cognitive strengths and weaknesses. This work resurrected the importance of the early writings (late 1800s and early 1900s) of neurologists on the aphasias, agnosias, apraxias, and other syndromes, and brought a psychometric rigor to the descriptions of these syndromes. In addition, the emergence of cognitive science in the 1960s also brought more sophisticated experimental procedures for isolating and studying the integrity of specific cognitive processes in patients with focal brain lesions.

In modern times, the need for neuropsychologists to identify organicity or brain damage *per se* has decreased with the development of more sensitive structural and functional neuroimaging techniques. Although there continues to be some neurological disorders (e.g., Alzheimer's disease) that begin with such microscopic lesions that neuropsychological testing is still required for early detection, neuroimaging will likely soon be capable of detecting these insidious disorders as well. However, with advances in the detection of more subtle neurological conditions, and with such diverse individual differences in how similar levels of brain damage can affect cognitive functions, there continues to be growing need for clinical neuropsychologists to document each patient's profile of cognitive and motor strengths and weaknesses. In this context, clinical neuropsychology has become a flourishing field of practice.

The Basic Premise of Neuropsychological Testing

As a general rule, cognitive and motor functions tend to fall within the normal range of the bell curve in an individual with a healthy brain, with some relative strengths and weaknesses. However, when one or more regions of the brain have been damaged by injury or disease, the cognitive and motor functions that are mediated at least in part by those regions often will become significantly impaired. Accordingly, the clinical neuropsychologist will typically administer to a patient with known or suspected brain damage 20–30 different tests assessing attention, language skills, math abilities, visual–spatial functions, new learning and memory, problem solving, abstract thinking, and other cognitive and motor skills. In past research, these tests were administered to large numbers of neurologically intact individuals (the normative group) and to patients with different types of brain damage; the neuropsychologist uses these normative and clinical data to draw conclusions about whether a patient's raw scores on the tests fall within the expected or impaired ranges. This determination is not an exact science, since many neurologically normal individuals will have some test scores that fall in the impaired range, and some brain-damaged patients, especially if they have relatively high premorbid cognitive skills, may have few scores in the impaired range. Nevertheless, by examining the patient's profile of cognitive and motor strengths and weaknesses, the neuropsychologist can make inferences about the integrity of different brain regions and can begin to formulate hypotheses about the presence or absence of different neurological disorders.

What Comprises a Neuropsychological Evaluation?

The typical neuropsychological evaluation takes 6–8 h. For most teenagers and adults, the examination can be completed in a day, with ample breaks. For younger children, older adults, or patients whose endurance has been significantly compromised by a neurological, medical, or psychiatric condition, the examination can be conducted across two or three sessions.

In the morning and early afternoon hours of a 1-day exam, patients are typically administered the cognitive and motor tests when they are usually more alert. Some neuropsychologists administer the tests themselves, whereas others employ a trained psychological technician to administer the tests; both approaches are acceptable in the field, since the tests have standardized administration procedures. In the afternoon, patients who have adequate cognitive skills are often administered a psychological inventory designed to assess their self-reported emotional functioning. In addition, a comprehensive clinical interview is also typically conducted. In this era of managed care, many patients are first given neuropsychological screening exams, which usually vary from 30 min to 3 h in duration. If a patient exhibits some evidence of cognitive impairment on the screening exam, then more extensive neuropsychological testing may be conducted.

Selection of Tests

Neuropsychologists typically select tests that have empirically documented reliability and validity; adequate, updated normative data; and empirically demonstrated utility in identifying neurocognitive deficits in brain-damaged patients. Modern neuropsychological tests often contain improvements over their predecessors by the incorporation of constructs from cognitive science, thereby making the tests more sensitive to the assessment of specific cognitive processes. Some neuropsychologists use a 'battery approach,' meaning that they will administer all tests or subtests that comprise a particular battery or scale (e.g., all subtests of the Wechsler Memory Scale-III). Other neuropsychologists use an 'eclectic approach,' meaning that they will pick and choose only certain tests or subtests from different batteries or scales (e.g., many psychologists administer only two subtests of the Wechsler Memory Scale-III: the Logical Memory subtest and the Visual Reproduction subtest). In addition, some neuropsychologists adopt a 'fixed approach,' meaning that they try to give the same tests to all patients, whereas other neuropsychologists use a 'flexible approach,' meaning that they will tailor the selection of tests administered to each patient based on the patient's presenting problems and referral question. These different approaches are all acceptable in the field, provided that the major domains of cognitive, motor, and behavioral functions are adequately covered by the tests selected. **Table 1** lists a number of tests that are commonly used by neuropsychologists to assess cognitive and motor functions in children and adults.

The Clinical Interview

A critical part of the neuropsychological evaluation is the clinical interview. A comprehensive survey of possible risk factors for brain damage should be explored in the interview. In addition, many factors beyond brain damage *per se* can affect performance on rigorous psychometric tests of cognitive and motor skills, and these factors should also be covered in the interview. Important areas to explore in the interview include early developmental problems (e.g., pregnancy and delivery complications; prenatal exposure to alcohol, drugs, or other teratogenic agents; delays in achieving developmental milestones as an infant or toddler); cultural factors (e.g., English as a second language, being raised in another country); educational history (e.g., level and type of education obtained, history of learning disability or attention problems); occupational history (e.g., the degree to which an individual's work requires higher level thinking skills); history of medical illnesses that are risk factors for brain dysfunction (e.g., hypertension, diabetes); history of head injury or loss of consciousness; past and current psychiatric disorders; past and current alcohol and drug use; current medications (e.g., narcotic analgesics); current emotional state; current physical state (e.g., headaches and other pain symptoms, which can affect performance on psychometric tests); and family history of medical and psychiatric disorders (e.g., a family history of Alzheimer's disease is a risk factor for this disorder). Based on information gathered in the clinical interview, the neuropsychologist attempts to identify which risk factors may be present in an individual and how they may affect the person's performances on the cognitive and motor tests.

Another step in the clinical interview is to ask the patient, and family members if they are available, about their perceptions of the patient's cognitive complaints, the onset of the problems, and whether the problems have changed over time. Sometimes this information can be helpful in evaluating, for instance, whether a patient's cognitive difficulties started abruptly, as with a stroke, or gradually, as in Alzheimer's disease. However, the self-reported cognitive difficulties of patients and their family members often fail to correlate with objective test results. For example, depressed patients sometimes report severe memory difficulties when their actual scores on objective tests of memory may be normal or near normal.

Finally, the clinical interview allows the neuropsychologist to observe directly patients' emotional demeanor and behavioral functioning at a time when they are discussing their problems and symptoms. These observations can be valuable for identifying whether a psychiatric component is contributing to a patient's presentation.

Test-Taking Effort

Scores on difficult cognitive and motor tests are valid only if the examinee exerts adequate effort in taking them. An important part of the neuropsychological evaluation is the assessment of the individual's motivation to perform well

Table 1 Examples of commonly used neuropsychological tests for adults and children

Domain	*Representative test*
Adults	
Intellectual functions	Wechsler Adult Intelligence Scale-III
Learning and memory	California Verbal Learning Test-II
	Rey Auditory Verbal Learning Test
	Rey Osterrieth Complex Figure Test
	Warrington Recognition Memory Test
	Wechsler Memory Scale-III
Visuospatial abilities	Block Design Subtest (WAIS-III)
	Hooper Visual Organizational Test
	Judgment of Line Orientation
	Rey Osterrieth Complex Figure Test
Language	Boston Diagnostic Aphasia Exam
	Boston Naming Test
	Controlled Oral Word Association Test
	Token Test
	Vocabulary Subtest (WAIS-III)
Executive functions	Category Test
Abstraction ability	Delis–Kaplan Executive Function System
	Similarities Subtest (WAIS-III)
	Trail Making Test
	Verbal Fluency Tests
	Wisconsin Card Sorting Test
Attention	Digit Span Subtest (WAIS-III)
	Digit Vigilance Test
	Spatial Span (WMS-III)
Motor Functions	Finger Tapping Test
	Grooved Pegboard Test
	Grip Strength (Hand Dynamometer)
Emotional/behavioral functions	Beck Depression Inventory
	Hamilton Depression Scale
	Millon Clinical Personality Inventory
	Minnesota Multiphasic Personality Inventory-II
Screening instruments	Kaplan Baycrest Neurocognitive Assessment
	Mattis Dementia Rating Scale
	MicroCog
	Repeatable Battery for the Assessment of Neuropsychological Status
Academic achievement	Wechsler Individual Achievement Test
	Wide Range Achievement Test-III
Children	
Intellectual functions	Cognitive Assessment System
	Wechsler Intelligence Scale for Children-IV
	Woodcock–Johnson Tests of Cognitive Ability
Specific neuropsychological domains	California Verbal Learning Test–Children's Version
	Children's Memory Scale
	Delis-Kaplan Executive Function System
	NEPSY Neuropsychological Battery
	Peabody Picture Vocabulary Test-III
	Wide Range Assessment of Memory and Learning
	WISC-III as a Neuropsychological Instrument
Emotional/behavioral functions	Child Behavior Checklist
	Personality Inventory for Children

on the tests. Some individuals exert minimal effort on neuropsychologist tests for secondary gain. For example, an inmate may intentionally perform poorly on memory tests to support his or her claim of amnesia for the accused crime. As another example, an individual involved in litigation related to a car accident may claim that he or she suffered a brain injury in the accident. When this individual undergoes a neuropsychological evaluation, he or she may fail to exert adequate effort on the tests, with the hope of looking 'brain damaged' and obtaining a large settlement. The frequency with which individuals have been found to exaggerate cognitive problems on neuropsychological tests has been reported to be as high as 30% of cases referred in the context of forensic evaluations.

Neuropsychologists have developed a number of tools for evaluating an individual's test-taking effort, including specific cognitive 'malingering' tests, analysis of typical and atypical profiles of neurocognitive dysfunction, consistency of test findings and profiles across repeat evaluations, and examination of whether a patient's low scores on neuropsychological tests are consistent with how he or she is functioning in everyday life. Even with these procedures, however, it is sometimes difficult to identify a clever patient who is feigning cognitive difficulties, especially if he or she does so to a mild degree (more blatant forms of exaggeration are easier to detect). As reported in the literature, some individuals have admitted to having been 'coached' by their attorneys as to which tests are designed to detect malingering, prior to their neuropsychological evaluations. In addition, individuals can learn about malingering tests on the Internet. For these reasons, neuropsychologists strive to use different methods for the detection of inadequate effort and to stay one step ahead of public knowledge by developing new effort-testing techniques.

Premorbid Level of Cognitive Functioning

The most common reason that patients are referred for a neuropsychological evaluation is to determine whether they have acquired brain damage from some neurological insult, and, if so, whether they have experienced a decline in their level of cognitive functioning from a premorbid (preexisting) state. However, inferences about declines in cognitive functioning must include estimates of the individual's level of cognitive functioning before the onset of the insult. Neuropsychologists employ several techniques for estimating or correcting for premorbid level of cognitive functioning, including the following approaches:

- Testing overlearned cognitive skills that tend to be resilient to the effects of more diffuse brain damage and that correlate significantly with preexisting IQ (e.g., tests of individual word reading or vocabulary level are good predictors of premorbid verbal IQ).
- Developing normative test data that are corrected not only for age but also for education level, a strong predictor of premorbid IQ.
- Obtaining prior scholastic test scores from the individual's school records, since these scores correlate robustly with an individual's verbal IQ as an adult.
- Using regression analyses based on key demographic variables, such as education and occupation levels, to derive formulas for estimating premorbid IQ.

The estimation of premorbid level of cognitive functioning is a difficult task. Each method should be considered as a tool that may or may not be useful or even appropriate for a particular patient. For instance, the use of education-corrected norms can be invaluable for one patient and misleading for another. Following are three case examples that illustrate this point:

- A physician with 20 years of education and a premorbid IQ of 130 suffers a left hemisphere stroke. While her postinjury scores on language tests are within the average (normal) range for her normative age group, these scores fall in the impaired range for her education group (i.e., compared to age-matched individuals with approximately 20 years of education). In this case, the education-corrected norms are warranted because they provide an empirically based method for documenting evidence of acquired cognitive decline in this individual.
- A self-made businessman has a premorbid IQ of 130 but left high school after his sophomore year because his father was killed in a car accident and he had to begin working to help support his family. As an adult, this individual suffers a left hemisphere stroke and obtains scores on language tests that fall in the average (normal) range using both age- and education-corrected norms (i.e., compared to age-matched individuals with approximately 10 years of education). However, these standardized scores are likely misleading, because they are obtained from a normative reference group that likely has a lower mean premorbid verbal IQ than that of the patient. For this individual, it would have been more appropriate to use one or more of the other methods to estimate the patient's premorbid level of cognitive functioning (e.g., obtain school records to see if scholastic test scores are available for this individual; administer a single-word reading test).
- At birth, an individual suffers a brain insult secondary to delivery complications. In school, he is found to have an IQ that falls in the borderline mentally retarded range. He completes only 8 years of education. As an adult, he is evaluated by a neuropsychologist who scores the test findings using education-corrected norms (i.e., his raw scores are compared to age-matched individuals with approximately 8 years of education). The patient's standardized scores using these norms fall in the low-average range and the neuropsychologist claims that the patient does not have brain damage. However, the use of education-corrected norms is inappropriate for this case. The patient's relatively low education level was likely one of the 'effects' of his early brain insult (not the cause), and to correct his scores for a low level of education essentially negates one of the main effects of his brain damage. For this individual, age-corrected norms would be more appropriate to document that the patient shows evidence of cognitive impairment (i.e., borderline mental retardation) relative to his age-matched peers.

As a general rule, prior scholastic or IQ test scores that are obtained from a patient's school records when he or she was around 10 years of age or older are often the best method for estimating premorbid level of intellectual functioning, because achievement and IQ scores tend to be relatively stable across the life span. In addition, each person's premorbid functioning should be estimated individually, given that there are significant individual differences in IQ level among people with similar levels of education. Other factors that contribute to discrepancies in IQ among people with similar levels of education include motivation to achieve in school (e.g., a person with average IQ and high motivation may achieve a high level of education, whereas a person with superior IQ and low motivation may drop out of school early); differences in the quality of the education (e.g., university-based graduate school versus private professional graduate school); and English as a second language (e.g., a highly educated person may have learned English as a second language and, as a result, obtain only average scores on English-based verbal tests, despite achieving a relatively high level of education). Unfortunately, for the majority of patients evaluated, school test results are not accessible, necessitating the use of one of the other methods for estimating premorbid functioning. Finally, it is important to note that the different methods for estimating premorbid mental abilities may apply to certain domains of cognitive functioning but not to others. For example, the ability to read individual words of varying difficulty has been found to be a significant predictor of verbal IQ. However, verbal IQ tends to have relatively low correlations with executive functions and memory skills (accounting for 0–16% of the variance). Thus, while current reading ability can be a useful predictor of premorbid verbal IQ, it tends to be less effective in predicting premorbid level of executive functions and memory skills.

Analysis of Test Performance

After the neuropsychological tests have been administered, raw scores are summed for each test and converted to standardized scores. In addition to these quantitative scores, many neuropsychologists also examine test performance for qualitative features that may be pathognomonic of brain dysfunction. For instance, a patient may speak primarily in content words and omit the little grammatical words of language (e.g., the patient says, "Hospital . . . Monday" when trying to say that he came into the hospital on Monday). This qualitative feature of the patient's language, when seen consistently, is pathognomonic of a type of language disorder called Broca's aphasia, and likely reflects a brain injury in the posterior region of the left frontal lobe. As another example, a patient may omit most details and features from the left side of his drawings (see **Figure 1**); this neurobehavioral syndrome, known as left hemi-inattention, typically occurs following brain damage to posterior regions of the right hemisphere.

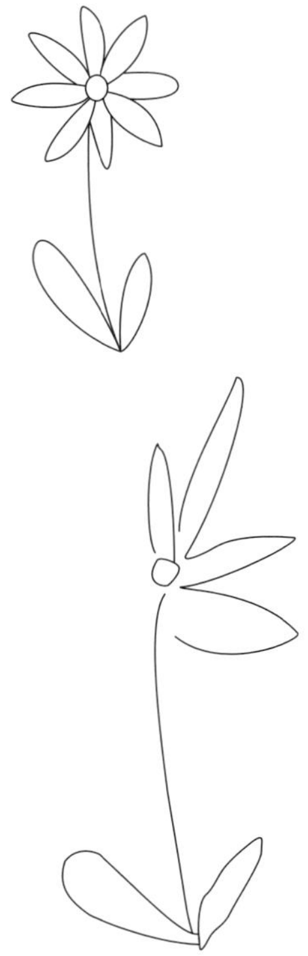

Figure 1 An individual who suffered a cerebral vascular accident in the right parietal lobe was asked to copy a model drawing of a daisy (top). The patient's drawing (bottom) illustrates left hemi-inattention.

Emotional, Behavioral, and Personality Testing

The neuropsychological evaluation typically goes beyond the assessment of cognitive and motor skills, and also includes psychometric testing of emotional, behavioral, and personality functioning. Many neuropsychologists administer tests such as the Minnesota Mutiphasic Personality Inventory-2 (MMPI-2) or the Beck Depression Inventory as part of their standard evaluation, given that the patient has the cognitive capacity to take them. These tests assist the neuropsychologist in determining whether a patient has a psychiatric disturbance, which, in turn, may be affecting his or her performance on the neuropsychological tests. Most practicing neuropsychologists obtain their doctoral degrees in clinical psychology before receiving specialized training in neuropsychology, and this training enables them to conduct general psychodiagnostic assessments as part of their neuropsychological evaluations.

Final Interpretations and Recommendations

The heart of the neuropsychological evaluation, and the most difficult part, is drawing final conclusions about the presence, nature, extent, and causes of a patient's cognitive, motor, and behavioral difficulties and, if necessary, formulating recommendations for helping the patient. Just because a patient obtains test scores that fall in the impaired range does not mean that he or she has brain damage.

The first step in the interpretation process is to determine whether a patient's test scores are valid (using techniques discussed earlier) and internally consistent (e.g., if a patient has a word-finding deficit, then he or she should exhibit difficulty on any task that places extensive demands on precise naming ability). If the test scores appear valid and consistent, the neuropsychologist then attempts to characterize the patient's profile of cognitive–motor strengths and weaknesses. Based on an estimate of the patient's premorbid level of cognitive functioning, the neuropsychologist opines whether the patient's weaknesses represent acquired deficits. Next, the neuropsychologist, drawing upon his or her knowledge of brain–behavior relationships, tries to decide whether the patient's profile of cognitive–motor strengths and weaknesses is typical of particular types and locations of brain dysfunction. The neuropsychologist then must weigh all of the patient's risk factors for acquired brain damage, such as a recent head trauma or stroke, history of medical illnesses that may compromise brain functioning, history of serious psychiatric disorder, past alcohol or drug abuse, or a family history of a genetically based neurological disorder (e.g., Alzheimer's disease). In considering these different risk factors, the neuropsychologist tries to determine whether the patient's cognitive–motor profile is more likely to be associated with one risk factor than another, or with multiple risk factors.

Before a final conclusion can be reached about the presence of neurocognitive dysfunction, the neuropsychologist must rule out all possible explanations for the patient's low test scores, going beyond brain damage *per se*, such as educational and cultural factors, current medications, current emotional and physical state, and level of motivation to perform well on the tests. In addition, the neuropsychologist must conduct a psychodiagnostic evaluation to determine whether the patient has a psychiatric disorder and, if so, whether this disorder is contributing to the patient's cognitive difficulties. After integrating, analyzing, and synthesizing this extensive and varied body of information, the neuropsychologist is then in a position to proffer his final impressions about the presence or absence of brain dysfunction and its sequelae. If the neuropsychological data strongly implicate a neurological disorder, such as Alzheimer's disease, then it falls within the neuropsychologist's purview to make those diagnoses.

At the end of the report, the neuropsychologist will typically offer recommendations for the patient. Common areas of recommendations include the following approaches:

- Additional neurological, medical, or psychiatric examinations, consultations, or procedures (e.g., MRI brain scan; psychotropic medication consultation).
- Speech therapy or cognitive rehabilitation.
- Individual or family psychotherapy or other behavioral interventions.
- Educational interventions and programs (especially for children and young adults).
- Vocational testing and counseling.
- Social work consultation to address the patient's living situation and the need for various levels of assistance and supervision with activities of daily living.
- Repeat neuropsychological evaluation in the future to determine the status of the patient's cognitive functioning over time.

When feasible, the neuropsychologist often will meet with the patient and his or her family to discuss the findings of the evaluation and the need for the various recommended interventions.

Repeat Neuropsychological Testing

The readministration of the same or similar neuropsychological tests to a patient at a later time can serve several clinically useful purposes. As an example, for patients suspected of having a progressive dementia such as Alzheimer's disease, the first neuropsychological testing provides baseline data. The repeat testing, which usually is done 9–12 months later, affords an objective measure of whether the patient exhibits a decline in cognitive functions typical of a progressive disease. Some neuropsychological tests may show practice effects on repeat testing, which is an improvement in performance from having taken the same or similar tasks at an earlier time. However, the inexorable progression of a disorder such as Alzheimer's disease typically overrides any improvement in scores related to practice effects.

Repeat testing also is helpful for charting the recovery of neurocognitive functions over time following a brain insult, such as a stroke or brain injury. Recovery of brain functions tends to occur relatively slowly, with a 1-year time period often used as the benchmark for the vast majority of the recovery to have occurred. By comparing a patient's test scores obtained a few months after an injury with those obtained a year or more postinjury, the neuropsychologist, after factoring in practice effects, can provide objective data about the patient's recovery process. Other important reasons for conducting repeat testing include monitoring improvement in cognitive functions following various interventions, such as cognitive rehabilitation and pharmacological treatment, and determining the validity of an individual's test scores by examining the consistency of his or her profile of cognitive and motor strengths and weaknesses over time.

Common Referral Questions for Adults

Adult patients typically are referred for a neuropsychological evaluation by neurologists, neurosurgeons, clinical psychologists, psychiatrists, primary care physicians, speech pathologists, other health professionals, and attorneys. The following examples of consult questions illustrate some of the reasons why adult patients undergo neuropsychological testing:

- To assist in evaluating whether a patient with increasing cognitive difficulties, as reported by the patient, family members, or health professionals, has an insidious neurological disorder. Examples of these disorders include multiple sclerosis, brain tumor, idiopathic hydrocephalus, white-matter ischemic changes, and Alzheimer's disease.
- To evaluate whether a patient who has had a risk factor for brain damage does, in fact, exhibit cognitive–motor deficits or emotional–behavioral changes consistent with brain dysfunction. Examples of these risk factors include head trauma, chronic alcohol or drug abuse, certain medical illnesses (e.g., hypertension, diabetes, kidney failure, HIV infection), certain psychiatric disorders (e.g., schizophrenia), and exposure to neurotoxic agents.
- To assess the presence, nature, and extent of cognitive–motor deficits and emotional–behavioral changes in patients with known brain pathology. These patients are referred after it has been determined, usually from the neurological examination and neuroimaging, that they have had, for instance, a cerebral vascular accident or have a brain tumor, Parkinson's disease, probable Alzheimer's disease, or MRI- or CT scan-confirmed brain damage following a head trauma. The question for these patients is not whether they have brain damage, but rather the presence, nature, and extent of cognitive, motor, and behavioral sequelae of their brain dysfunction.
- To assist neurosurgeons in several ways, such as in evaluating whether a patient with intractable seizures and in need of resection of the epileptogenic focus has language skills localized in this general brain region (this testing usually involves a Wada procedure, where one cerebral hemisphere at a time is anesthetized during cognitive screening); in conducting pre- and postsurgery evaluations to determine whether a neurosurgical procedure (e.g., insertion of a shunt tube to relieve hydrocephalus; resection of a brain tumor) alters cognitive–motor functions for better or worse; and in reevaluating cognitive functions over a period of several years in a hydrocephalus patient who has received a shunt in order determine if the shunt has continued to function normally.
- To evaluate the cognitive functions of individuals with more serious psychiatric disorders that often have a neurological component (e.g., schizophrenia).
- To provide recommendations regarding the patient's capacity to return to work or to receive vocational retraining in a new occupation that would be best suited for the patient, given his or her profile of cognitive strengths and weaknesses.
- To offer recommendations for cognitive rehabilitation (e.g., teaching the patient memory compensatory strategies).
- To assist in determining whether a patient with brain dysfunction has the cognitive, motor, and behavioral capacity to perform important activities of daily living (e.g., ability to drive a car, handle finances, prepare meals, live independently, comply with medication regimens, care for self).
- To make recommendations regarding the best living situation for the patient in light of his or her cognitive, motor, and behavioral deficits (e.g., independent, assisted-living, or nursing-home placement).

Common Referral Questions for Children

Neuropsychological evaluations are generally more difficult to conduct for children than for adults. Just as children differ in their physical growth rates, they also differ in the development of their cognitive and motor functions. It is sometimes difficult to determine whether a 'cognitive deficit' in a child represents a permanent impairment or simply a lag or delay in the development of that ability. In addition, the classic brain–behavior relationships that have been documented in adults do not always apply to children, making it difficult to localize cognitive deficits to particular brain regions. For example, a lesion in the left superior temporal gyrus can result in a Wernicke's (fluent) aphasia in an adult and in a nonfluent aphasia in a child. Finally, some children present with pronounced attention problems, hyperactivity, or other behavioral disturbances that make it difficult for the child to focus on the psychometric tests and provide valid test responses.

Despite the challenges inherent in child neuropsychology, this area of practice has become one of the fastest growing disciplines within the field. Referrals for child neuropsychological evaluations usually are made by pediatricians, pediatric neurologists, clinical psychologists, school psychologists, speech therapists, educators, and sometimes parents. Many of the referral questions for children are similar to those for adults, such as assessing whether the apparent onset of new cognitive difficulties reflects an insidious neurological disorder (e.g., brain tumor); evaluating whether a known risk factor for brain damage (e.g., birth complications, head trauma, lead exposure) has, in fact, resulted in cognitive, motor, or behavioral dysfunction; and assessing the presence, nature, and extent of cognitive, motor, and behavioral changes in patients with known brain pathology (e.g., childhood seizure disorder). Following are examples of other specific reasons why children are referred for neuropsychological testing:

- To determine whether a child who is struggling academically in school has a learning disability. Neuropsychological research has documented different types of learning disabilities (e.g., verbal vs. nonverbal) that may reflect neurodevelopmental abnormalities in distinct brain regions.
- To assess whether a child whose mother abused alcohol or drugs or consumed other teratogenic agents during her pregnancy (e.g., certain medications) exhibits cognitive, motor, or behavioral deficits suggestive of prenatal brain damage (e.g., FAS).
- To assist educators in developing the best educational program for a child based on the child's profile of cognitive and behavioral strengths and weaknesses.
- To assess recovery of function in a child who has suffered a documented traumatic brain injury and to provide recommendations for cognitive remediation and educational assistance.

Conclusions

Clinical neuropsychology has become one of the fastest growing disciplines in psychology. Neuropsychological testing not only provides an empirically rigorous method for assisting in the diagnosis of neurological, medical, and psychiatric patients, it also enhances our scientific understanding of one of the great mysteries of life, namely, the generation of mental processes from brain structures.

See also: Cognition, An Overview of Neuroimaging Techniques.

Further Reading

Benton, AL (1980). Psychological testing for brain damage. In: Kaplan, HI, Freedman, AM, and Badock, BJ (eds.) *Comprehensive Textbook of Psychiatry,* vol. 1. ch. 12. Baltimore, MD: Williams & Wilkins.

Delis, DC, Kaplan, E, and Kramer, JH (2001). *The Delis-Kaplan Executive Function System.* San Antonio, TX: The Psychological Corporation.

Delis, DC, Kramer, JH, Kaplan, E, et al. (2000). *The California Verbal Learning Test,* 2nd edn. San Antonio, TX: The Psychological Corporation.

Goodglass, H and Kaplan, E (1983). *The Assessment of Aphasia and Related Disorders.* Philadelphia, PA: Lea & Febiger.

Grant, I and Adams, K (eds.) (1996). *Neuropsychological Assessment of Neuropsychiatric Disorders,* 2nd edn. New York: Oxford University Press.

Heaton, RK, Grant, I, and Matthew, CG (1991). *Comprehensive Norms for an Expanded Halstead–Reitan Battery.* Odessa, FL: Psychological Assessment Resources.

Heilman, K and Valenstein, E (eds.) (1993). *Clinical Neuropsychology,* 3rd edn. New York: Oxford University Press.

Kaplan, E, Fein, D, Morris, R, et al. (1991). *WAIS-R as a Neuropsychological Instrument.* New York: Psychological Corporation.

Larrabee, GL (ed.) (2005). *Forensic Neuropsychology.* New York: Oxford University Press.

Lezak, MD, Howieson, DB, Loring, DW, et al. (2005). *Neuropsychological Assessment,* 4th edn. New York: Oxford University Press.

Luria, AR (1980). *Higher Cortical Functions in Man,* 2nd edn, New York: Basic Books.

Massman, PJ, Delis, DC, Butters, N, et al. (1992). The subcortical dysfunction hypothesis of memory deficits in depression: Neuropsychological validation in a subgroup of patients. *Journal of Clinical and Experimental Neuropsychology* 14: 687–706.

Mattson, SN, Riley, EP, Gramling, L, et al. (1997). Heavy prenatal alcohol exposure leads to IQ deficits with or without all of the features of fetal alcohol syndrome. *Journal of Pediatrics* 131: 718–721.

Spreen, O and Strauss, E (1998). *A Compendium of Neuropsychological Tests: Administration, Norms, and Commentary,* 2nd edn. New York: Oxford University Press.

Squire, L and Butters, N (eds.) (1992). *Neuropsychology of Memory,* 2nd edn. New York: Guilford Press.

P

Parkinson's Disease and Language

A. I. Tröster, University of North Carolina School of Medicine, Chapel Hill, NC, USA

Introduction to Parkinson's Disease

Parkinson's disease (PD) is a neurodegenerative disorder that afflicts primarily persons older than 50 years of age. Among Western populations, it affects about 2% of those 65 years of age and older. It is important to note that PD is not the same as parkinsonism. Parkinsonism refers to a constellation of four signs (gait instability, rigidity or stiffness, tremor, and bradykinesia, or a slowing of movement) that are observable in numerous conditions. In contrast, PD is a specific disease and is the most common of the parkinsonian syndromes, accounting for about 75% of cases. In PD there is a progressive and marked loss of cells in the substantia nigra that project to deep brain structures called the caudate nucleus and the putamen (which is disproportionately affected early in the disease), collectively referred to as the striatum. Because these cells are the principal source of the neurotransmitter dopamine, treatment early on is by drugs that either mimic the action of dopamine (dopamine agonists) or provide the chemical building block that is converted into dopamine in the brain by enzymes (levodopa).

The proportion of persons having alterations in mental/cognitive functions early in the disease remains debated, but a recent epidemiological study found that almost 40% of persons with PD already have cognitive alterations detectable on formal neuropsychological evaluation at the time of disease diagnosis. Of course, these cognitive changes are most often subtle and detectable only on careful testing; clinically meaningful cognitive alterations probably occur in a small minority of patients this early in the disease course. Early on in PD, the cognitive alterations typically involve executive functions and working memory and are most readily observed on tasks that require the person to spontaneously develop and deploy efficient information processing, encoding, and retrieval strategies. It is thought that the nigrostriatal, and possibly mesocortical, dopaminergic reductions underlie these early cognitive alterations. With disease progression, multiple neurotransmitter systems become compromised, and it is likely that this multiplicity of changes, along with both cortical and subcortical pathology, underlies the more severe cognitive changes, or dementia, estimated to occur in 20–40% of patients. The dementia of PD has been referred to as a 'subcortical dementia,' given its core features of slowed thinking (bradyphrenia), impaired recall, executive dysfunction, apathy, and depression. Although the concept of 'subcortical dementia' is subject to criticism because neurodegenerative dementias eventually fail to respect anatomical boundaries, and because dementia in PD may be manifestations of different neuropathological entities, the term remains a clinically useful shorthand. For the aphasiologist and linguist, this distinction is of particular relevance because subcortical dementias, in contrast to cortical dementias such as Alzheimer disease, are not associated with frank aphasia.

Language in Parkinson's Disease

Motor speech abnormalities are often evident in mid- to late PD. The disease can affect each of the speech production systems, including respiration, phonation, articulation, resonance, and prosody. Features of the parkinsonian hypokinetic dysarthria are variable but include one or more of imprecise articulation of consonants, variable (including too fast and too slow) rate of speech, short bursts of speech, breathy or harsh voice, and reduced or monotonous loudness and pitch. Speech intelligibility can also be diminished by excessive salivation and swallowing difficulties.

In contrast to motor speech abnormalities, frank aphasia is very rare in PD. Though certain aspects of language are compromised in PD patients with dementia, the subtle alterations in performance on language and communication tasks observed in patients without dementia are often attributed to diminished attention and working memory, or inefficient information processing strategy development and deployment. The language task on which PD patients' performance has been studied most frequently is verbal fluency. Far fewer studies have addressed naming to confrontation, repetition, and the production and comprehension of complex syntax.

Verbal fluency tasks require persons to orally generate (or sometimes write) as many words as possible within a time limit. The task is constrained in one of several ways; for example, requiring that words begin with a specific letter of the alphabet, or belong to a semantic category, such as animals. Patients with PD and dementia, not surprisingly, perform more poorly on these tasks than do patients without dementia. Indeed, PD patients without dementia may demonstrate intact performance. When patients without dementia do perform below expected levels, there is a tendency for them to perform more poorly on letter category fluency tasks than on semantic category fluency tasks. The reason for this is debated but may reflect the specific letters and categories (some inherently more difficult than others) chosen for the task. Alternatively, poorer performance on letter than on semantic category tasks may be a manifestation of the retrieval deficits of PD because letter fluency tasks place greater demands on systematic word search and retrieval strategies than do semantic category fluency tasks. Several studies have attempted to identify the cognitive mechanisms underlying fluency deficits in PD. Presumably an efficient strategy on verbal fluency tasks involves the retrieval of highly related words from a subcategory (e.g., domestic animals) and then switching to a new subcategory (e.g., wild animals), rather than attempting to retrieve low-frequency and more tenuously related exemplars from the same subcategory. Researchers have quantified these two related processes of clustering (retrieving consecutive words that are semantically or phonemically related) and switching (shifting between subcategories). Given the role of the frontal lobes and basal ganglia in cognitive efficiency, and the pathology of frontal-subcortical circuits in PD, it is not astonishing that clustering (related primarily to integrity of semantic networks and the temporal lobes) tends to be relatively preserved, whereas switching (related to cognitive flexibility) is relatively diminished in PD. What remains less clear is whether diminished switching is a consequence or cause of reduced verbal fluency output.

Two other types of verbal fluency tasks may be especially sensitive to PD: alternating word fluency (requiring retrieval of consecutive words from alternate semantic or letter categories) and verb fluency tasks requiring naming of actions. Alternating fluency may be especially sensitive to PD because the task places a premium on working memory, a memory system that has limited capacity, is of limited duration, requires executive functions, and is compromised early in PD. Verb fluency may lend its sensitivity to the observation that retrieval of verbs is probably relatively more reliant on the frontal lobes, whereas noun retrieval depends especially on the temporal lobes.

Performance on visual confrontation naming tasks, requiring naming of pictured or actual objects, is preserved in PD without dementia, but a few studies report subtle naming impairments in early PD. Patients with obvious cognitive impairment, in contrast, do show naming impairments. However, in comparison to Alzheimer disease, a prototypical cortical dementia, the naming impairment is less severe and emerges later in PD. A few studies have characterized the types of naming errors made by patients with PD. One study comparing groups of patients with Alzheimer disease and PD with dementia equated for overall severity of cognitive impairment found that the Alzheimer disease patients made more phonemic errors (mispronunciations or distortions sharing at least one syllable with the target word) and 'don't know' responses. Both patient groups made more semantic errors than the control group, but unlike the Alzheimer and normal control groups, the PD with dementia group's semantic errors were largely associative (meaning the provided word described an action, function, or physical attribute of the target, a contextual associate, or a subordinate or proper noun example of the target).

These findings indicate that in patients with PD and dementia, category knowledge is available but insufficient to generate item names. That such subtle category knowledge deficits might be evident already in PD without dementia was indicated by the finding that the proportion of associative semantic errors in PD is intermediate to that of normal elderly and PD patients with dementia. The proclivity of PD patients to make associative errors differentiates them from normal elderly, whose limited errors tend to be within category errors, meaning the response is from the same semantic category as the target but visually dissimilar (e.g., misnaming 'asparagus' as 'cauliflower').

Other subtle linguistic impairments observed in PD include those in syntactic comprehension and production. The mechanisms underlying the subtle sentence comprehension deficits in PD remain controversial, but proposed ones include grammatical processing deficits, slowed information processing, and diminished attention or working memory. Some have observed the spontaneous speech output of mild PD patients to be syntactically simplified and characterized by a smaller proportion of grammatical sentences. When provided with cards with words and asked to construct a meaningful sentence, patients with PD tend to make 'capture' errors, linking two highly related words, although such a construction precludes a meaningful sentence (e.g., 'the hair brush long clogged' instead of 'long hair clogged the brush').

A few studies have examined PD patients' comprehension of complex sentences by varying the nature and location of a clause embedded in the sentences. Sentences containing a subject-relative, center-embedded clause ('the man who called the sheriff is responsible') are easier to understand than those containing object-relative, center-embedded clauses ('the man who the sheriff called is responsible'). About 45–65% of PD patients without dementia demonstrate difficulty comprehending the noncanonical, object-centered, clause-containing sentences, but the cognitive mechanisms underlying these comprehension difficulties are a matter of speculation. Preliminary functional neuroimaging data implicate attentional and information processing resource limitations in PD sentence comprehension deficits. Activations of the left anteromedial prefrontal cortex, striatum, and right posterior–lateral temporal cortex were reduced during sentence processing in patients with PD, and striatal and anteromedial activations have respectively been associated with information processing speed and attention.

There may also be mild phonetic impairment in early PD. For example, patients may have trouble detecting phonetic errors in words, regardless of the clausal structure of sentences. In addition, errors in the temporal organization and coordination of American Sign Language used by persons with PD have also been interpreted as reflecting a phonetic deficit.

Pragmatics (the study of discourse within social context) has rarely been studied in PD. However, persons with PD relative to healthy elderly individuals may show poorer conversational appropriateness, turn taking, prosody, and proxemics (the perception and use of personal space). Though the pragmatics rating score of PD patients has been related to performance on tests of 'frontal lobe function' such as the Stroop and Tower of London tasks, it is unknown to what extent motor, speech, motivational, and emotional factors (such as apathy and depression) might underlie diminished pragmatic communication skills. Whether patients with PD generally develop pragmatic compensatory strategies, as has been observed among three deaf and mute patients with PD using sign language, is still to be determined.

Effect of Neurosurgical Treatments on Language

Surgical treatments of PD, similar to drug treatments, are symptomatic rather than curative. Early ablative interventions were associated with considerable cognitive morbidity, but more recent unilateral ablative interventions, regardless of whether they are targeting the thalamus, subthalamic nucleus (STN), or globus pallidus (GPi), appear considerably safer. The most common compromise after modern unilateral pallidotomy occurs in verbal fluency.

Deep brain stimulation (DBS) involves unilateral or bilateral implantation of electrodes and the application of high-frequency electrical stimulation from an implanted pulse generator to thalamus, GPi, or STN. Unilateral and bilateral thalamic and GPi DBS are cognitively safe, although declines in verbal fluency are possible. As in pallidotomy and GPi DBS, verbal fluency decrements appear to be the most commonly reported changes after STN DBS. Although motor speech changes may contribute to altered fluency, it appears that switching among categories rather than clustering is altered, indicating a possible executive cognitive basis for the deficit.

Bibliography

Crosson, B (1992). *Subcortical functions in language and memory.* New York: Guilford.

Crosson, B, Zawacki, T, Brinson, G, Lu, L, and Sadek, JR (1997). 'Models of subcortical functions in language: current status.' *Journal of Neurolinguistics* 10: 277–300.

Grossman, M, Carvell, S, Stern, MB, Gollomp, S, and Hurtig, HI (1992). 'Sentence comprehension in Parkinson's disease: the role of attention and memory.' *Brain and Language* 42: 347–384.

Grossman, M, Cooke, A, DeVita, C, Lee, C, Alsop, D, Detre, J, Gee, J, Chen, W, Stern, MB, and Hurtig, HI (2003). 'Grammatical and resource components of sentence processing in Parkinson's disease: an fMRI study.' *Neurology* 60: 775–781.

Jankovic, JJ and Tolosa, E (eds.) (2002). *Parkinson's disease & movement disorders,* 4th edn. Philadelphia: Lippincott Williams and Wilkins.

McNamara, P and Durso, R (2003). 'Pragmatic communication skills in patients with Parkinson's disease.' *Brain and Language* 84: 414–423.

Murdoch, BE (2001). 'Subcortical brain mechanisms in speech and language.' *Folia Phoniatrica et Logopaedica* 53: 233–251.

Pillon, B, Boller, F, Levy, R, and Dubois, B (2001). 'Cognitive deficits and dementia in Parkinson's disease.' In: Boller, F and Cappa, SF (eds.) *Handbook of neuropsychology,* 2nd edn., pp. 311–371. Amsterdam: Elsevier.

Schulz, GM and Grant, MK (2000). 'Effects of speech therapy and pharmacologic and surgical treatments on voice and speech in Parkinson's disease: a review of the literature.' *Journal of Communication Disorders* 33: 59–88.

Tröster, AI and Fields, JA (2003). 'The role of neuropsychological evaluation in the neurosurgical treatment of movement disorders.' In: Tarsy, D, Vitek, JL, and Lozano, AM (eds.) *Surgical treatment of Parkinson's disease and other movement disorders*, pp. 213–240. Totowa, NJ: Humana.

Troyer, AK, Moscovitch, M, Winocur, G, Leach, L, and Freedman, M (1998). 'Clustering and switching on verbal fluency tests in Alzheimer's and Parkinson's disease.' *Journal of the International Neuropsychological Society* 4: 137–143.

Woods, SP, Field, JA, and Tröster, AI (2002). 'Neuropsychological sequelae of subthalamic nucleus deep brain stimulation in Parkinson's disease: a critical review.' *Neuropsychology Review* 12: 111–126.

PET Research of Language

B. Horwitz, National Institutes of Health, Bethesda, MD, USA
R. J. S. Wise, Imperial College London, Hammersmith Hospital, London, UK

Introduction

In 1988 Petersen and colleagues published an article in *Nature* on single word processing. This important article demonstrated how a relatively new brain imaging technique, positron emission tomography (PET), could enable one to make inferences about some aspects of the neural basis for a number of singularly human cognitive functions. Unlike earlier PET studies that examined sensory processing and whose findings could be related to non-human neurophysiological and neuroanatomical data, the paper by Petersen and colleagues provided a window into the functioning of the brain of healthy human subjects during a high-level cognitive task with a spatio-temporal resolution and area of coverage that other brain imaging methods (e.g., the non-tomographic xenon-133 inhalation method) could not match. This type of data, therefore, offered the promise that the neural underpinnings for uniquely human cognitive functions, especially those related to language processing, could now be explored in living, healthy subjects. Furthermore, this method seemed capable of enabling researchers to explore the functional abnormalities in patients with various kinds of language disorders. Since then, there has been an explosion of research investigations of language using PET, and – since the mid-1990s – an analogous technique called functional magnetic resonance imaging (fMRI) (see Cabeza & Kingstone, 2001, for a comprehensive review).

As the other chapters in this book make clear, a variety of methods are used to understand the neural basis of language processing. Until the advent of functional brain imaging, most knowledge concerning the neurobiological correlates of language processing was derived from neuropsychological investigation of brain damaged patients or by electrical stimulation and recording from individuals undergoing neurosurgery. More recently, techniques like transcranial magnetic stimulation, which can produce "virtual" lesions, have become valuable tools for studying the brain basis of linguistic cognition. However, PET and fMRI (and also electro(magneto)encephalography (EEG/MEG)) have produced an extraordinary wealth of new data that have added considerable information about the functional neuroanatomy of specific cognitive functions (and dysfunctions).

Why are functional brain imaging data so important for understanding neurolinguistics? First, they, of course, permit one to directly have a measure of brain functional activity that can be related to brain structure and to behavior. Second, they can be acquired non-invasively (or in the case of PET, relatively non-invasively, since radioactive isotopes must be injected into the blood stream; see Rodden and Stemmer, 2008, for details) from healthy normal subjects, as well as from patients with brain disorders. Third, because these data are obtained simultaneously from much of the brain, they are quite unique for investigating not just what a single brain area does, but also how brain regions work together during the performance of individual tasks. This latter point is important because the traditional methods used to understand the neural basis of language investigate one "object" at a time (e.g., the ideal brain damaged patient has a single localized brain lesion). The potential to assess how brain regions interact to implement specific neurolinguistic and other cognitive functions has necessitated the development of network analysis methods, and has given rise to a new paradigm in which cognitive functions are conceived as being mediated by distributed interacting neural elements (Mesulam, 1998; Horwitz et al., 1999).

The various functional brain imaging methods are reviewed in Rodden and Stemmer, 2008 (see **Box 1** for a brief overview of PET analysis methods). In subsequent sections of this chapter, we will focus on the use of PET to study the neural processes involved in language functioning. We will begin with some remarks contrasting the advantages and disadvantages of PET versus fMRI. We will then discuss a few of the important PET studies of the past decade that will illustrate the kinds of issues for which PET is the most appropriate hemodynamic functional imaging modality. Our last section will address where we see the field going.

PET Versus fMRI – Some Methodological Issues

fMRI has a number of advantages over PET, and these advantages have led to fMRI becoming the predominant modality for functional neuroimaging studies of language (see **Functional Magnetic Resonance Imaging (fMRI)**

Box 1 PET analysis methods

There are two primary approaches toward analyzing PET (and fMRI) data. The first, called the subtraction paradigm (Horwitz, 1994), proposes that different brain regions are engaged in different functions, and is implemented by comparing the functional signals between two scans (in its most simple formulation), each representing a different experimental condition. The brain locations of the large signal differences between the two scans are assumed to correspond to the brain regions differentially involved in the two conditions. The second method, the covariance paradigm, rests on the notion that a task is mediated by a network of interacting brain regions and that different tasks utilize different functional networks (Horwitz, 1994). By examining the covariance in brain activity between different pairs of brain areas (i.e., the functional connectivity), information is obtained about which areas are important nodes in the network under study and how these nodes are functionally connected (see **Box 2** for an example of functional connectivity analysis of PET data applied to single word reading in normal and dyslexic subjects).

Besides functional connectivity, functional neuroimaging studies can also involve the related concept of effective connectivity. Because two brain regions may show a strong functional connectivity whether or not they are anatomically linked (e.g., the two may receive direct inputs from a third region), methods have been employed to evaluate the effective connectivity, which is the direct effect that activity in one region has on a second (i.e., the functional strength of the anatomical link between the two regions in a given task). The effective connections between a set of brain regions can be obtained by combining the regions' functional connections with a model of the anatomical links between them using techniques such as structural equation modeling (McIntosh et al., 1994) or dynamic causal modeling (Friston et al., 2003).

Friston, KJ, Harrison, L, and Penny, W (2003). Dynamic causal modelling. *Neuroimage* 19: 1273–1302.

Horwitz, B (1994). Data analysis paradigms for metabolic-flow data: Combining neural modeling and functional neuroimaging. *Human Brain Mapping* 2: 112–122.

McIntosh, AR, Grady, CL, Ungerleider, LG, Haxby, JV, Rapoport, SI, and Horwitz, B (1994). Network analysis of cortical visual pathways mapped with PET. *Journal of Neuroscience* 14: 655–666.

Research on Language). The three most important advantages are better spatial resolution, better temporal resolution, and not requiring the injection of radioactive substances into the subjects being scanned. This last one allows more scans to be performed in a single subject, and it also means that fMRI can be performed in a non-medical environment, since intravenous lines are not necessary.

However, the use of PET to image regional cerebral blood flow (rCBF) has a number of significant advantages over fMRI, and these advantages are particularly important for addressing key issues in language functioning. First, unlike PET, the gradient coils that are employed in conventional fMRI scanning are quite loud, and can interfere with a subject hearing auditory inputs and with the ability of investigators to record a subject's vocal output. Moreover, the noise produced by the scanner also can reduce the sensitivity of auditory neural responses to auditory inputs even if the subject can hear them. Although fMRI scanning protocols such as sparse sampling (also called clustered acquisition) can overcome some of these problems, they impose limits on the kinds of experimental designs one can employ.

Another significant problem with using fMRI to study language function is that image artifacts occur if the subjects speak. First, speaking results in a susceptibility artifact that is particularly strong in anterior and ventral brain areas. Second, the movement itself can lead to image artifacts, although image preprocessing algorithms can usually deal with these effectively. Although speaking-induced susceptibility artifacts can be distinguished from neurally induced activity (fMRI signal changes due to neural activity are not instantaneous because of the hemodynamic delay, whereas the artifactual signal change arising from speaking is), nevertheless, this problem means that continuous language production cannot be imaged. PET does not have this problem.

Finally, a number of investigators have shown that the left anterior temporal cortex plays a significant role in language processing (Spitsyna et al., 2006; see below for more information), and this area, especially the region around the temporal pole, is particularly sensitive to the fMRI susceptibility artifact. Consequently, in many fMRI studies, data from this area may not be usable. It has been shown that the susceptibility artifact can be reduced by using higher spatial resolution (Devlin et al., 2000), but that in turn often results in limited coverage of other brain areas.

The net effect of these limitations in using fMRI is that imaging studies of speech comprehension and language production, especially beyond the word level, are more readily done employing PET than fMRI, and as will be shown below, important findings continue to be reported.

Crucial PET Findings

In this section we will discuss PET studies that have addressed questions concerning hemispheric differences and anterior–posterior differences in language comprehension and the brain areas involved in speech and sign language.

Language Comprehension

We will highlight in this subsection recent PET studies that have addressed two fundamental questions concerning the brain organization associated with language comprehension: (1) hemispheric differences and (2) anterior–posterior differences.

Hemispheric Differences

It was apparent from the earliest PET studies of speech perception that when subjects heard speech relative to a baseline of silence, activity was almost equally distributed between the left and right superior temporal gyri (e.g., see Petersen et al., 1988; Wise et al., 1991). This absence of asymmetry indicated that a crude subtractive methodology was not going to replicate the asymmetry evident from clinical observations, namely that impaired comprehension after aphasic stroke was a consequence of left hemisphere lesions, particularly those centered around the lateral (Sylvian) sulcus (Caplan, 1987). Yet if the early PET studies did not demonstrate anything "special" about the response of the left superior temporal gyrus (STG) (which is the location of unimodal primary and association auditory cortex) to heard words, this was hardly surprising. Spoken language is the most complex sound that we routinely encounter, and over the range of spectral and temporal detail conveyed by speech we can detect phonemes, syllables, stress, and variations in amplitude and pitch. These convey verbal information, in the form of phonetic cues and features, obviously, but also non-linguistic information that both supports comprehension of the verbal message and allows the listener to deduce the affect, sex, age, and individual identity of the speaker. Further, the categorical perception of a sequence of sounds as a word, irrespective of whether the "perceptual unit" is at the level of phonemes or syllables, is remarkably robust, and we can tolerate considerable distortions to speech before it becomes totally incomprehensible. This redundancy in the speech signal suggests that many separate cues and features are processed in parallel, and perception and comprehension is further assisted by top-down processing; we hear next what we expect to hear, given the sense of what has gone before. Moreover, the evidence from neurological cases suggests that although pure word deafness is often only observed after bilateral superior temporal lesions, left-sided lesions alone can result in impaired speech perception, and this impairment does not occur after purely right-sided lesions (Griffiths et al., 1999).

Therefore, the hypothesis was that a refined study design would show with functional imaging that left hemisphere activity predominated over right during speech perception and comprehension. As Scott and Johnsrude (2003) emphasized, the selection of the baseline condition is critical. There have been a series of PET studies which used a variety of non-linguistic acoustic stimuli as the baseline condition; for example, pure tones (Demonet et al., 1992), signal correlated noise – the time-amplitude envelopes of speech filled with white noise, resulting in some temporal but no spectral information – (e.g., Zatorre et al., 1992; Mummery et al., 1999), reversed speech signal (speech played backwards) (Crinion et al., 2003), and spectrally rotated speech (Scott et al., 2000). The advantages and disadvantages of these baseline stimuli have been reviewed in Scott and Wise (2004). One problem with non-linguistic baseline stimuli is that even when they match speech closely in terms of acoustic complexity, they invariably distort or abolish affective prosody and information about the speaker. Therefore, a contrast of speech against one of these baseline stimuli will include responses to both verbal and non-verbal information carried by the speech signal. The review also discusses the use of unfamiliar foreign languages, which, while they might appear to be the best unintelligible baseline to contrast with intelligible native speech, as they will include prosodic and speaker information, nevertheless they also include the confound of unfamiliar phonemes and different rules for combining phonemes; for example, the Japanese word structure is strictly CVCV, whereas English allows a CCCVCCC structure. What influence these confounds will have on observed activity in a functional imaging study is largely unknown. Given such considerations, one can see, why fMRI might compound such subtle problems with its added noise.

Nevertheless, left lateralization of signal in response to speech perception and comprehension has been increasingly observed. One of the first PET studies that demonstrated clear lateralization used a combination of intelligible and unintelligible sentences in a 2×2 factorial design (Scott et al., 2000). Sentences presented as clear speech were acoustically matched with the same sentences after spectral rotation (inversion) to render them unintelligible. A further set of sentences was distorted by a technique known as noise-vocoding (Shannon et al., 1995), whereby temporal information is largely preserved but the spectral information is reduced to a few broad frequency bands (six in this study). Perceptually, this distorted speech, which simulates the acoustic information reaching the auditory nerve after a cochlear implant, sounds like a harsh whisper, and it is intelligible after a brief period of familiarization. The "matched" baseline stimulus for the noise-vocoded sentences were made by spectral inversion. The data demonstrated that the left STG responded equally to speech, rotated speech and noise-vocoded speech relative to rotated noise-vocoded speech. This was interpreted as a response to phonetic cues and features, present in both versions of intelligible sentences and also present in the unintelligible rotated speech, but not in the rotated noise-vocoded sentences. Intelligibility, confined to the clear and noise-vocoded speech, activated a left anterior region, centered on the superior temporal sulcus. The main response of the right temporal lobe across contrasts was to clear speech and its spectrally rotated version, stimuli that contained a strong sense of pitch and intonation. Therefore, this study demonstrated a left–right asymmetry in the responses to speech and stimuli that were derived from speech. It also demonstrated a rostral–caudal asymmetry, with intelligibility activating the anterolateral left temporal cortex.

Anterior–Posterior Differences

According to the clinical literature on aphasic stroke, one might have predicted that intelligibility would activate Wernicke's area or adjacent cortex in the posterior temporal lobe and inferior parietal lobe – lesions in this region are associated with poor comprehension after aphasic stroke. It remains the view of many that the functional imaging data supports the observations on stroke aphasia, and that lexical semantics is dependent on left temporo-parietal cortex (e.g., Hickok & Poeppel, 2004). However, a growing interest in the functional organization of non-human primate auditory cortex has indicated the existence of an anterior auditory pathway, a "what" pathway (Rauschecker & Tian, 2000; Husain et al., 2004), and thus, by extension, maybe an auditory verbal "what" pathway in the human (Scott & Johnsrude, 2003). The use of magnetic resonance imaging techniques to display human white matter tracts *in vivo* has led to a reappraisal of the effects of lobar stroke on brain function, when damage to both a cortical area and projection pathways, long and short, contribute to the observed behavioral impairment (Catani & ffytche, 2005). PET has been used to demonstrate that an infarct in Wernicke's area has an impact on the function in the ipsilateral hemisphere, in the intact anterior temporal cortex (Crinion et al., 2006).

The proposal that anterior temporal lobe cortex is involved in word comprehension finds strong support from the clinical observations on patients with the neurodegenerative condition known as semantic dementia where predominantly anterior temporal lobe atrophy is associated with a progressive, and ultimately profound, loss of semantic knowledge (see Grossman, 2008, for more on semantic dementia). The deficit is not confined only to language comprehension, but it does affect comprehension at the single content word level. This last point is important, because there is a functional imaging literature, mainly from fMRI, that equates anterior temporal lobe activity with comprehension at the sentence and narrative level. For example, Humphries et al. (2006) equates the posterior and anterior temporal lobes with lexical semantics and syntax, respectively, although the authors do indicate that the functional distinction is relative and not absolute. Nevertheless, there is an issue about the context in which the stimuli are presented. To illustrate, the study by Spitsyna et al. (2006) investigated automatic (implicit) comprehension of sentences and/or narratives, without an associated task demand. Under these circumstances, it would appear that there is a relative increase in the strength of the response of the anterior temporal to verbal meaning conveyed within the context of sentences and narratives (see Xu et al., 2005). Left anterior temporal lobe activation can also be seen in response to single words when there is an explicit task demand based on selecting and retrieving word meaning (Sharp et al., 2004).

Figure 1 gives an example of the results that can be extracted from a PET study of implicit language comprehension that uses different modalities of stimulus presentation and a range of different baseline conditions – for more details, see Spitsyna et al. (2006). Narratives were presented either as speech or as written text. The modality-specific baseline conditions were rotated speech and text-like arrays of false fonts. A further baseline task, an odd/ even decision on serially presented numbers 1–10, was included to unmask language processing activity that is associated with "passive" baseline tasks. The use of an "active" baseline condition reduces the medial and lateral activity associated with what has been termed the default mode of brain function, which includes medial prefrontal activity associated with "self-referential thoughts," the kind of stimulus-independent thoughts that may occupy the awake brain unengaged by attention to external stimuli (Gusnard et al., 2001). As stimulus-independent thoughts will include retrieval of both episodic and semantic memories, their intrusion during a baseline task will mask activity associated with declarative memory processes under investigation with the activation task. The effect of using an active baseline task, devoid of meaning (other than simple number semantics) is to considerably increase the extent of activity observed with speech and reading comprehension (**Figure 1**). Such a contrast reveals both anterior and posterior temporal lobe regions, reconciling the separate location of areas associated with access to meaning from the literature on aphasic stroke and semantic dementia. Although the function of these two regions is almost certainly not identical, it would appear probable that their functions are complementary – and the hypothesis is that future connectivity studies will demonstrate integration of their activity during language comprehension.

A third area activated in common was the anterior fusiform gyrus. As this region responded to both heard and written language, its response was polymodal, and its activity may represent that of polymodal perirhinal (paralimbic) cortex. This region is located at the end of a ventral, and strongly left-lateralized, "stream" of activity associated with reading (Spitsyna et al., 2006). Early in this "stream" is the area that has become known as the visual word form area (McCandliss et al., 2003), although the specificity of this region for the processing of written words alone has been challenged (Price & Devlin, 2003). Nevertheless, a lesion of this area, or its connection to left and right primary visual cortex, reliably results in the condition known as pure alexia – poor single word reading, accompanied by laborious covert or overt letter-by-letter reading and a reversed spelling strategy to allow any written comprehension at all.

In summary, the results of these PET comprehension studies lead to the conclusion that verbal comprehension uses unimodal processing streams that converge in

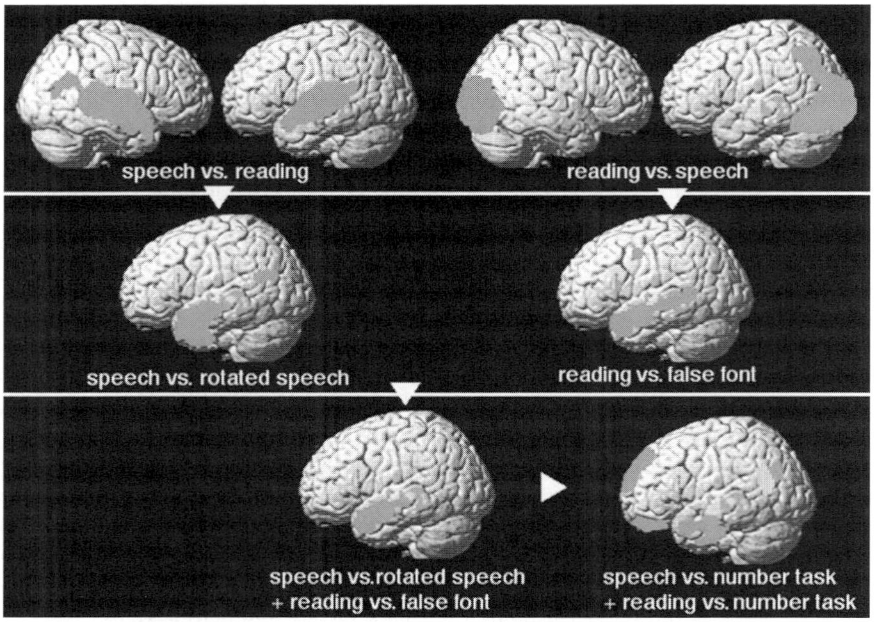

Figure 1 Activity evoked by narratives, both spoken and written, rendered onto the left and right cerebral hemispheres (group averaged data, n = 11 normal subjects). Solid red regions are located over the lateral and inferior surfaces of the hemispheres, hatched red regions are located over the medial surfaces. The contrasts of speech with reading and reading with speech demonstrated bilateral, symmetrical activity in the superior temporal gyri and the occipital lobes, respectively. The asymmetry in posterior parietal cortex (left > right) during reading is the consequence of visual attention and reading saccades being directed to the right in left-to-right readers. Contrasting speech with its modality-specific baseline condition of spectrally inverted (rotated) speech, and reading with its modality-specific baseline condition of text-like arrays of false font, demonstrated activity centered around the superior temporal sulcus, predominantly lateralized to the left. The conjunction of activity for these two contrasts was centered over left anterolateral temporal cortex – a region that responded to intelligible language independent of modality. By using an alternative baseline condition (number task), an explicit task on simple number semantics (an odd/even decision on randomly presented numbers, 1–10), activity was also demonstrated in the anterior fusiform gyrus (the ''basal'' language area) and just ventral to the angular gyrus. There was also prominent activity in the left superior frontal gyrus, orbito-frontal cortex and in retrosplenial cortex (hatched region). The rationale for using the number task as an alternative baseline condition is described in the text. Data from Spitsyna et al. (2006). (See color plate 33.)

both anterior and posterior cortical regions in the left temporal lobe.

Language Production

As mentioned earlier, imaging studies in which the participants are required to produce overt language, especially output beyond a single word, are particularly difficult to do with fMRI, and therefore PET has continued to be used for these investigations. We will discuss some of these studies in this subsection. The focus will be on PET studies requiring continuous language production.

Propositional Language Production

Speech of any kind, whether single word repetition, counting (one form of non-propositional speech) or normal narrative speech production (propositional speech), activates the supplementary motor area (SMA), bilateral primary sensorimotor cortex, the left anterior insula/frontal operculum, basal ganglia and thalamus, and bilateral paravermal cerebellum (Wise et al., 1999; Braun et al., 2001; Blank et al., 2002).

Focusing on propositional speech, Braun et al. (1997, 2001) used PET measurements of rCBF to evaluate functional brain activity during spontaneous narrative speech and several other tasks involving speech-like features. Each subject performed several tasks, including narrative speech, which consisted of recounting a series of events from memory (e.g., talking about a vacation), and a control task that consisted of producing laryngeal and oral articulatory movements and associated sounds devoid of linguistic content. Compared to a resting state, the orolaryngeal motor control task activated bilaterally dorsal posterior frontal operculum (pars opercularis), pre- and postcentral gyrus and primary and anterior auditory cortex. Compared to the orolaryngeal motor control task, the speech condition activated a large number of regions in the left hemisphere, including regions in the anterior and ventral frontal operculum (pars opercularis, triangularis, orbitalis), pre-SMA, lateral premotor cortex, dorsolateral prefrontal cortex, anterior cingulate and insula. Bilateral activations were observed in posterior superior and middle temporal cortex. Another recent PET study of propositional speech production in normal subjects found a similar set of activated regions (Blank et al., 2002).

Horwitz and Braun (2004) used these data to examine the functional interactions of some of these areas during language production (see **Box 2** for details about how functional connectivity is evaluated for PET data). The question addressed was the specificity of brain areas traditionally associated with language, since many such regions are located near motor and auditory areas and are often activated in non-language tasks (e.g., for the data discussed in the previous paragraph, the pars opercularis was activated by both the speech condition and the orolaryngeal task). Functional connectivity within each condition was calculated using reference voxels corresponding to language areas significantly activated for narrative speech compared to the orolaryngeal motor control task. We chose left hemisphere perisylvian regions in the posterior STG (likely corresponding to what classically has been called Wernicke's area) and in the inferior frontal cortex (near or in what classically has been denoted as Broca's area). The posterior STG area had strong functional links during speech with left inferior parietal and frontal perisylvian regions, with left middle and inferior temporal gyri, and with the anterior cingulate/supplementary motor area. Most of these strong functional connections were absent in the motor control task, especially the link to frontal perisylvian regions. The left frontal opercular region had significantly large functional connections during speech with other language-associated areas in the left hemisphere, including regions in posterior temporal and inferior parietal cortex. Generally, these strong functional connections were absent during the motor control task even though the frontal opercular area was activated in the motor control task when compared to the rest condition. Furthermore, the strong functional interactions between the frontal opercular region in the left hemisphere were to both left and right hemisphere posterior superior temporal gyri regions. This result is consistent with the model proposed by Braun et al. (2001) that hypothesizes that language production proceeds from early bilateral posterior cortical stages of lexical access to later left-lateralized anterior stages of articulatory-motor encoding.

Box 2 PET data functional connectivity analysis

The central idea behind functional connectivity analysis is that activities that covary together indicate that the neurons generating the activities may be interacting. As indicated in Box 1, two neural entities are said to be functionally connected if their activities are correlated. Functional connectivity does not necessarily imply a causal link, whereas effective connectivity does.

For rCBF PET activation data, some investigators calculate interregional functional connectivity by correlating rCBF data within a task condition and across subjects. The reasoning behind this method starts with the fact that subjects perform tasks with different abilities, as shown by differences in accuracy, reaction time and other measures of performance. This subject-to-subject variability suggests that the activity of the brain network mediating a task also varies from subject to subject.

An example of this approach is Horwitz et al. (1998), where PET functional connectivity analysis was applied to normal and dyslexic subjects. The task consisted of pronouncing pseudowords. In agreement with the classic neurologic model for reading, which is based on studies of alexic patients, rCBF in the left angular gyrus showed strong functional connectivity with rCBF in visual association areas in occipital and temporal cortex, and with rCBF in language areas in superior temporal and inferior frontal cortex. In contrast, these strong functional connections were absent in subjects with developmental dyslexia, indicating that dyslexia is characterized by a functional disconnection of the angular gyrus that mirrors the anatomical disconnection seen in alexia, a finding supported by other investigators using fMRI (Pugh et al., 2000) and diffusion tensor imaging of white matter (Klingberg et al., 2000).

Horwitz, B, Rumsey, JM, and Donohue, BC (1998). Functional connectivity of the angular gyrus in normal reading and dyslexia. *Proceedings of the National Academy of Science* 95: 8939–8944.

Klingberg, T, Hedehus, M, Temple, E, Salz, T, Gabrieli, JD, Moseley, ME, and Poldrack, RA (2000). Microstructure of temporo-parietal white matter as a basis for reading ability: Evidence from diffusion tensor magnetic resonance imaging. *Neuron* 25(2): 493–500.

Pugh, KR, Mencl, WE, Shaywitz, BA, Shaywitz, SE, Fulbright, RK, Constable, RT, Skudlarski, P, Marchione, KE, Jenner, AR, Fletcher, JM, Liberman, AM, Shankweiler, DP, Katz, L, Lacadie, C, and Gore, JC (2000). The angular gyrus in developmental dyslexia: Task-specific differences in functional connectivity within posterior cortex. *Psychological Science* 11(1): 51–56.

Broca's Area for Speech and Sign Language

Are the locations in the brain of language regions related to the fact that most human languages employ speech? That is, Wernicke's area is near auditory cortex, and Broca's area is just anterior to the mouth area of motor cortex. Not all linguistic functions, however, use audition as input and mouth movement as output; sign languages, in particular, employ vision and limb movement. To investigate aspects of this issue, a human PET study in hearing adults whose parents were deaf and who were fluently bilingual for speech and America Sign Language (ASL) was performed and showed that narrative production by both languages activated a common set of language areas (Braun et al., 2001). The tasks used were the same type as discussed above: for speech – narrative speech and an orolaryngeal motor control task; for ASL – extemporaneously recounting a story using ASL was the narrative language task along with a limb–facial motor control task devoid of linguistic content. The areas activated by both narrative tasks, which access the modality-independent aspects of language use, included left frontal operculum and bilateral perisylvian cortex in the STG, but common sites of activation also extended to a number of extrasylvian areas presumably involved in paralinguistic functions (declarative memory, attention, visual imagery) that are engaged at the level of discourse.

One of the classical language regions is Broca's area in the inferior frontal gyrus, which consists of two cytoarchitectonically defined regions – Brodmann's areas (BA) 44 and 45. Recently, it has become possible to investigate these subdivisions using probabilistic brain maps (see Amunts, 2008, for details). These maps were derived by histological analysis that determined the locations and spatial extents of BA44 and BA45 in the left and right hemispheres of 10 individual brains, after which the cytoarchitectonic data were transposed to a common space so as to form a probabilistic atlas, where voxel value indicates the percentage of brains having that location as BA44 or BA45. The above PET data were used to investigate the role that these two cytoarchitectonic subdivisions of Broca's region play in language production in the bilingual (English-ASL) subjects discussed above (Horwitz et al., 2003). The probabilistic atlas data were applied to the PET data for the two narrative tasks and the two motor control tasks (see **Figure 2**). This allowed us to determine the probability that BA44 or BA45 was activated during each language production task relative to its motor control task. It was found that BA45, not BA44, is activated by both speech and signing. It was BA44, not BA45, that was activated by the two motor control tasks (relative to a resting condition). The same patterns of activation were found for oral language production in a group of English speaking monolingual subjects. These findings thus implicate BA45 as the part of Broca's area that represents the conceptual-language interface that is fundamental to the modality-independent aspects of language generation.

In summary, these studies demonstrate that language production, whether in the form of speech or ASL, share a widespread group of modality-independent brain regions, which include not only classical perisylvian language regions in the left hemisphere, but also areas that extend beyond the traditional regions. Furthermore, speech and ASL production seem to engage the same cytoarchitectonically defined parts of Broca's area. Finally, during speech production, there is a strong functional connectivity between Broca's and Wernicke's areas in the left hemisphere.

Challenges and Future Directions

In spite of the extensive use of fMRI during the past decade, the above discussion makes it clear that the use of PET to measure rCBF has continued to provide valuable and essentially unique information about the brain organization in humans of language-related processes. However, although we envision that PET will continue to be used in the future, we suspect that more and more there will be a shift away from this technology toward an even more extensive use of fMRI, in spite of the difficulties we discussed in the early sections of this chapter. New hardware and software developments are likely to mitigate some of fMRI's disadvantages in so far as language and auditory studies are concerned.

However, the *real future* of using neuroimaging to assess language functioning lies, we believe, in a totally different direction. It does not lie in just performing more tasks that try to fractionate the linguistic processes into even finer and more subtle detail, although there surely will be a number of studies that do this. It does not lie in just improving the spatial and temporal resolution of neuroimaging technology, although that will surely be accomplished. Rather, we believe that the future of neuroimaging lies in combining multi-modality data acquisition with computational neural modeling.

In neuroscience, as in other areas of biology, there now exists the ability to acquire large quantities of data at multiple spatial and temporal scales of investigation (molecules to the brain as a whole; milliseconds to a lifetime). Because no one method transcends all the different levels, investigators often have trouble interpreting and understanding their particular subset of data in terms of all the other relevant data that others acquired. This makes it difficult to frame a single, unified account relating specific behaviors to their underlying neural mechanisms. We saw a simple example of this problem in the language comprehension section: the bilateral results of the first PET studies seemed at variance with the results of human lesion studies that seemed to demonstrate a strong left hemisphere lateralization of language comprehension. Although more careful experimental design seems to have resolved this issue, it is not clear that experiment alone will always work. What is needed is a formal way to systematically relate multiple data sets (i.e., fMRI, PET, MEG, lesion, behavior, neuroanatomical, perhaps even neuron electrophysiological data), thus bridging the various spatiotemporal levels of neuroscientific investigation. It has been argued that computational neural modeling provides the way to do this (Horwitz, 2004, 2005; Horwitz & Braun, 2004). Already there have been a number of studies in which various types of computational modeling have been combined with human imaging data, including studies of auditory object processing (Husain et al., 2004), mirror neurons (Arbib et al., 2000), and sentence processing (Just et al., 1999). The first two of these used biologically realistic neural modeling to related neural activity to fMRI/PET data, and the last used a cognitive model of sentence comprehension to explain how fMRI activation levels varied as a function of sentence complexity in three brain areas (Broca, Wernicke and dorsolateral prefrontal cortex). These modeling efforts, if successful, result in either a way to understand the neural mechanisms that underlie specific linguistic functions (in the case of using neurobiological models) or to understand the brain locations for specific cognitive components of a linguistic function. Ultimately, the goal will be to provide a

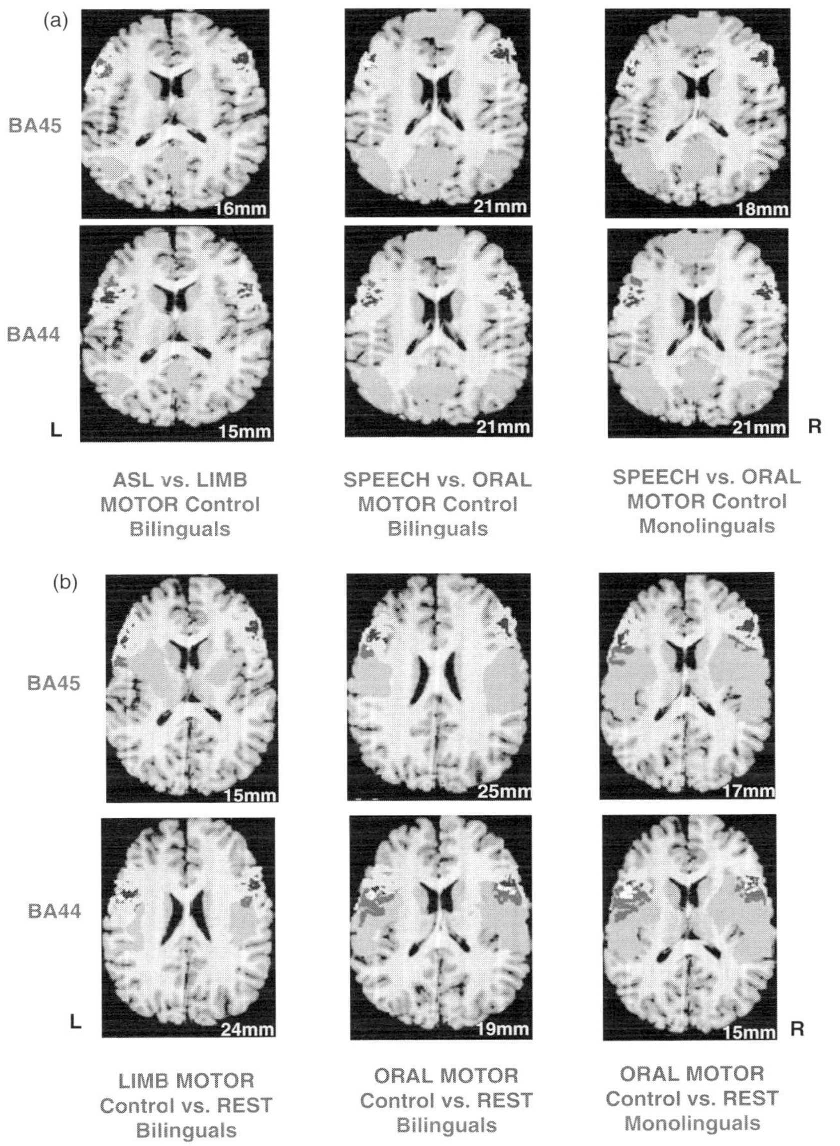

Figure 2 (a) Activations of BA45 (top row) and BA44 (bottom row) during production of language narratives compared to a motor control task; and (b) activation of BA45 (top) and BA44 (bottom) comparing each motor control task to a resting condition. Shown are representative horizontal slices (left side of each image corresponds to the left side of the brain; the level in mm superior to the AC-PC plane (z-coordinate of Talairach & Tournoux atlas, 1988) is indicated on each slice). Images displayed in the two columns on the left are from the bilingual (English and ASL) subjects, and those in the column on the right are from the monolingual English speakers. Voxels in dark blue correspond to core parts of the specific Brodmann area, those in light blue to peripheral voxels. Voxels significantly more active in one condition compared to a second ($Z > 2.33$) are shown in green. Voxels in the peripheral part of a Brodmann area that had a significant PET activation are displayed in red, and core voxels that were significantly activated are shown in yellow. From Horwitz et al. (2003) [Talairach, J., & Tournoux, P. (1988). *Co-planar stereotaxic atlas of the human brain* (M. Rayport, Trans.). New York: Thieme.] (See color plate 35.)

unified account of the neural mechanisms supporting language processing.

Acknowledgments

We wish to thank Dr. Allen Braun for useful discussions. This work was supported, in part, by the NIDCD Intramural Research Program.

References

Arbib, MA, Billard, A, Iacoboni, M, and Oztop, E (2000). Synthetic brain imaging: Grasping, mirror neurons and imitation. *Neural Networks* 13(8–9): 975–997.

Amunts, K (2008). Architectonic Language Research. *Handbook of the Neuroscience of Language*, pp 33–43. Oxford: Elsevier.

Blank, SC, Scott, SK, Murphy, K, Warburton, E, and Wise, RJ (2002). Speech production: Wernicke, Broca and beyond. *Brain* 125: 1829–1838.

Braun, AR, Guillemin, A, Hosey, L, and Varga, M (2001). The neural organization of discourse: An H215O-PET study of narrative production in English and American sign language. *Brain* 124: 2028–2044.

Braun, AR, Varga, M, Stager, S, Schulz, G, Selbie, S, Maisog, JM, Carson, RE, and Ludlow, CL (1997). Altered patterns of cerebral activity during speech and language production in developmental stuttering. An H215O positron emission tomography study. *Brain* 120: 761–784.

Cabeza, R and Kingstone, A (eds.) (2001). *Handbook of functional neuroimaging of cognition.* Cambridge, MA: MIT Press.

Caplan, D (1987). *Neurolinguistics and Linguistic Aphasiology: An Introduction.* Cambridge: Cambridge Univ. Press.

Catani, M and ffytche, DH (2005). The rises and falls of disconnection syndromes. *Brain* 128: 2224–2239.

Crinion, JT, Lambon-Ralph, MA, Warburton, EA, Howard, D, and Wise, RJ (2003). Temporal lobe regions engaged during normal speech comprehension. *Brain* 126: 1193–1201.

Crinion, JT, Warburton, EA, Lambon-Ralph, MA, Howard, D, and Wise, RJ (2006). Listening to narrative speech after aphasic stroke: The role of the left anterior temporal lobe. *Cerebral Cortex* 16: 1116–1125.

Demonet, J-F, Chollet, F, Ramsay, S, Cardebat, D, Nespoulous, J-L, Wise, R, Rascol, A, and Frackowiak, R (1992). The anatomy of phonological and semantic processing in normal subjects. *Brain* 115: 1753–1768.

Devlin, JT, Russell, RP, Davis, MH, Price, CJ, Wilson, J, Moss, HE, Matthews, PM, and Tyler, LK (2000). Susceptibility-induced loss of signal: Comparing PET and fMRI on a semantic task. *Neuroimage* 11: 589–600.

Griffiths, TD, Rees, A, and Green, GGR (1999). Disorders of human complex sound processing. *Neurocase* 5: 365–378.

Grossman, M (2008). Langugage in Dementia. *Handbook of the Neuroscience of Langauge*, pp 279–287. Oxford: Elsevier.

Gusnard, DA, Akbudak, E, Shulman, GL, and Raichle, ME (2001). Medial prefrontal cortex and self-referential mental activity: Relation to a default mode of brain function. *Proceedings of the National Academy of Science* 98(7): 4259–4264.

Hickok, G and Poeppel, D (2004). Dorsal and ventral streams: A framework for understanding aspects of the functional anatomy of language. *Cognition* 92: 67–99.

Horwitz, B (2004). Relating fMRI and PET signals to neural activity by means of large-scale neural models. *Neuroinformatics* 2: 251–266.

Horwitz, B (2005). Integrating neuroscientific data across spatiotemporal scales. *Comptes rendus Biologies* 328: 109–118.

Horwitz, B and Braun, AR (2004). Brain network interactions in auditory, visual and linguistic processing. *Brain and Language* 89: 377–384.

Horwitz, B, Tagamets, M-A, and McIntosh, AR (1999). Neural modeling, functional brain imaging, and cognition. *Trends in Cognitive Science* 3: 91–98.

Horwitz, B, Amunts, K, Bhattacharyya, R, Patkin, D, Jeffries, K, Zilles, K, and Braun, AR (2003). Activation of Broca's area during the production of spoken and signed language: A combined cytoarchitectonic mapping and PET analysis. *Neuropsychologia* 41(14): 1868–1876.

Humphries, C, Binder, JR, Medler, DA, and Liebenthal, E (2006). Syntactic and semantic modulation of neural activity during auditory sentence comprehension. *Journal of Cognitive Neuroscience* 18: 665–679.

Husain, FT, Tagamets, M-A, Fromm, SJ, Braun, AR, and Horwitz, B (2004). Relating neuronal dynamics for auditory object processing to neuroimaging activity. *Neuroimage* 21: 1701–1720.

Just, MA, Carpenter, PA, and Varma, S (1999). Computational modeling of high-level cognition and brain function. *Human Brain Mapping* 8: 128–136.

McCandliss, BD, Cohen, L, and Dehaene, S (2003). The visual word form area: Expertise for reading in the fusiform gyrus. *Trends in Cognitive Science* 7(7): 293–299.

Mesulam, M-M (1998). From sensation to cognition. *Brain* 121: 1013–1052.

Mummery, CJ, Ashburner, J, Scott, SK, and Wise, RJ (1999). Functional neuroimaging of speech perception in six normal and two aphasic subjects. *Journal of the Acoustical Society of America* 106: 449–457.

Petersen, SE, Fox, PT, Posner, MI, Mintun, M, and Raichle, ME (1988). Positron emission tomographic studies of the cortical anatomy of single-word processing. *Nature* 331: 585–589.

Price, CJ and Devlin, JT (2003). The myth of the visual word form area. *Neuroimage* 19(3): 473–481.

Rauschecker, JP and Tian, B (2000). Mechanisms and streams for processing of ''what'' and ''where'' in auditory cortex. *Proceedings of the National Academy of Science* 97(22): 11800–11806.

Rodden, FA and Stemmer, B (2008). A brief introduction to common neuroimaging techniques. *Handbook of the Neuroscience of Language*, pp 57–67. Oxford: Elsevier.

Scott, SK, Blank, CC, Rosen, S, and Wise, RJ (2000). Identification of a pathway for intelligible speech in the left temporal lobe. *Brain* 123: 2400–2406.

Scott, SK and Johnsrude, IS (2003). The neuroanatomical and functional organization of speech perception. *Trends in Neuroscience* 26(2): 100–107.

Scott, SK and Wise, RJ (2004). The functional neuroanatomy of prelexical processing in speech perception. *Cognition* 92: 13–45.

Shannon, RV, Zeng, FG, Kamath, V, Wygonski, J, and Ekelid, M (1995). Speech recognition with primarily temporal cues. *Science* 270: 303–304.

Sharp, DJ, Scott, SK, and Wise, RJ (2004). Monitoring and the controlled processing of meaning: Distinct prefrontal systems. *Cerebral Cortex* 14: 1–10.

Spitsyna, G, Warren, JE, Scott, SK, Turkheimer, FE, and Wise, RJ (2006). Converging language streams in the human temporal lobe. *Journal of Neuroscience* 26: 7328–7336.

Wise, R, Chollet, F, Hadar, U, Friston, K, Hoffner, E, and Frackowiak, R (1991). Distribution of cortical neural networks involved in word comprehension and word retrieval. *Brain* 114: 1803–1817.

Wise, RJ, Greene, J, Büchel, C, and Scott, SK (1999). Brain regions involved in articulation. *Lancet* 353(9158): 1057–1061.

Xu, J, Kemeny, S, Park, G, Frattali, C, and Braun, A (2005). Language in context: Emergent features of word, sentence, and narrative comprehension. *Neuroimage* 25: 1002–1015.

Zatorre, RJ, Evans, AC, Meyer, E, and Gjedde, A (1992). Lateralization of phonetic and pitch discrimination in speech. *Science* 256: 846–849.

Further Reading

Brown, CM and Hagoort, P (1999). *The neurocognition of language.* Oxford: Oxford University Press.
This book presents a series of articles on the cognitive neuroscience of language by experts in the field, including several articles that use functional neuroimaging methods. There are also several articles that discuss functional brain imaging methodology. Thus, this book places neuroimaging results in the context of other studies of language function.

Cabeza, R and Nyberg, L (1997). Imaging cognition: An empirical review of PET studies with normal subjects. *Journal of Cognitive Neuroscience* 9: 1–26.
This review article provides a very nice overview of PET results obtained from studies of higher-order cognitive processes, including attention, perception, language, and memory. The review shows the set of brain regions that are consistently activated by each cognitive function. Thus, this article places PET studies of language in the context of PET studies of other cognitive functions.

Demonet, JF, Thierry, G, and Cardebat, D (2005). Renewal of the neurophysiology of language: Functional neuroimaging. *Physiological Review* 85(1): 49–95.
This is a review of functional brain imaging studies of language. Besides having a good section on brain imaging methodology, this review also includes a discussion of language and brain plasticity, thus incorporating information about developmental disorders, post-lesion recovery of function, and language reorganization in neurodegenerative diseases.

Vigneau, M, Beaucousin, V, Herve, PY, Duffau, H, Crivello, F, Houde, O, Mazoyer, B, and Tzourio-Mazoyer, N (2006). Meta-analyzing left hemisphere language areas: Phonology, semantics, and sentence processing. *Neuroimage* 30(4): 1414–1432.
The title of this review explains exactly what the article is about. The meta-analysis covers PET and fMRI studies from 1992 to 2004. The authors conclude that their results argue for the notion of large-scale language networks, rather than a modular organization of language in the left cerebral hemisphere.

Phonological Impairments, Sublexical

H. W. Buckingham, Louisiana State University, Baton Rouge, LA, USA
S. S. Christman, University of Oklahoma, Oklahoma City, OK, USA

Introduction

In the present contribution to this volume, we will briefly discuss some recent work in neurolinguistic modeling that once again considers the human language cerebral system as a functional mosaic, more diffuse in its overall functional operation and slightly more parallel in its chronometry. Here, we will pay specific attention to phoneme structure and prosody – namely the units commonly referred to as tonemes. This allows us explore prosody in a very digital/analytical way, where fundamental frequency control looks to be a property of the left hemisphere. Prosody is a multifunctional dynamic, not fully right-nor left-hemisphere-specific. We will then present some analysis of recent sublexical studies of paraphasia and point to some inconsistencies and weaknesses of each, concentrating on syllable structure complexity and how that complexity and its linguistic control is extremely important in drawing finer distinctions among aphasic deficits – among error types as well as among aphasic types. As we will argue, it is most often the case that differently categorized aphasics (especially those who are clearly in the posterior/sensory fluent groups of Wernicke's as well as conductions and subgroupings of these) will likely produce from time to time, and certainly in differing numbers, most sublexical error types. The challenge, therefore, is to find instances of **significantly** differing quantitative groupings among the error types for different subject groupings. There is ample evidence that most studies demonstrate precisely this kind of dissociation. To this, we will simply reiterate the obvious: these statistically differing groupings within error types are qualitative in the sense of statistics, but quantitative, still, in the sense of the error types themselves. We will subsequently point out that this, in turn, is why Freud's 'continuity thesis' keeps rearing its ugly head in the study of paraphasia in brain damage and why investigators continue to allude to the slips-of-the-tongue in nonpathologically involved speakers. Lastly, we will consider some recent work in the aphasic production of neologisms, how and where they may be generated, by whom, under what circumstances, whether they involve anomia or not, and how they resolve to more recognizable language. We will pay close attention to whether or not the appearance of the neologism adumbrates a lexical block, or whether it adumbrates something that is actually quite different: the strictly phonological transformation or deformation of a form that by definition must have been retrieved at some higher level of production. Lastly, we will follow the logical predictions of neology recovery from these two accounts.

Functional Metabolic Mosaics

To begin with, we would emphasize that many of the recent findings from positron emission tomography as well as from functional magnetic resonance imaging and magnetoencephalography have provided support for theories developed long before these advances in the technology of cerebral observation: theories such as motor–sensory reverberatory circuitry and function in ongoing speech production with interconnective physiology and a left hemisphere specificity. The origins of these theories date as far back as the monograph of Karl Wernicke (1874). There is much evidence from imaging work that John Hughlings-Jackson (1866) was quite correct in his assumption that the nondominant hemisphere was actively involved in many aspects of language comprehension and that its role was increasingly observed in the resolution of aphasia. Furthermore, there now exists incontrovertible evidence from imaging for earlier motor theories of speech perception as well as for other theories that postulate the leading role that acoustic memory of one sort or another has in speech production. One can go even further into history (Hartley, 1749) for the establishment of strong motor–sensory associations in terms of 'muscle sense.' Such strong associative connections and the theories they stemmed from would certainly accord with parallel cerebral metabolic mosaics so often revealed during the production of phonological segments and during the perception of the same.

Two modern neurolinguistic investigators, David Poeppel and Greg Hickok (e.g., Hickok, 2000), have designed a model based on their own imaging work and that of others that is bilateral for comprehension, thereby bringing the nondominant hemisphere into the total picture for language perception, including more than simply prosody and pragmatics – both of which also play important roles in the overall picture of online language processing, which for them begins with the introduction of an auditory signal that very importantly spreads to both hemispheres initially and only then gets parceled out in terms of what processing of that auditory signal can remain in the right and what processing is forced to dominant hemisphere analysis, and why. In fact, it may very well be that what is being seen in the metabolism of the right hemisphere during comprehension are precisely those computations of intonation and schematic knowledge access from memory stores so crucial in our understanding of spoken language. Poeppel and Hickok are careful to chart all relevant studies that demonstrate a clear role for the nondominant hemisphere for comprehension: the Wada test, split brain studies, and single cell recordings.

Before going on, we want to emphasize that in these imaging studies what we actually see is metabolism, and only metabolism. In order to infer what may have been the work task, intricate statistical subtractions must be performed on the signal to ferret out the clutter, so to speak. The timing of events must be closely controlled as well so that we can be sure that the biochemically marked nutrients are introduced and arrive at the cerebral zones so their magnetic fields can be scanned radiographically, etc. (see Uttal, 2001 for a sober evaluation of recent scanning technology and about some of the limitations of the paradigm).

Hickok (2000) focuses upon the functional neuroanatomy of conduction aphasia and uses the right hemisphere for comprehension and the left temporal zones for the strictly phonological (with emphasis on sublexical processing) auditory element, which in turn fits into the acoustic–motor reverberatory system. Holding to previous models scaffolded on techniques other than imaging, he suggests two types of physiological interconnectionistic routes – in short, the insula or the arcuate fasciculus, which as we have known for over 100 years courses through the opercular regions of the temporal, parietal, and frontal lobes. This, in turn, allows the Poeppel/Hickok model to again reach into preimaging models and to suggest that there are two kinds of conduction aphasias, one perhaps involving lesions in and around the supramarginal gyrus (SMG) in such a way that the lesion would extend to the operculum, thereby interfering in one way or another with smooth acoustic–motor cooperation between Wernicke's area and Broca's area. An old notion, to be sure. Lesions to the left posterior supratemporal plane (location of sound-based representations), including Heschl's gyrus (BA 41) and the planum temporale (PT), slightly inferior to the SMG, may produce a more anterior type of conduction aphasia. In any event, Hickok and Poeppel do point out that activation levels of the auditory signal, although bilateral, tend to be somewhat stronger in the left.

Other recent significant studies of the perception of phonemic elements, called tonemes, have been carried out by Jack Gandour and his colleagues. In one (Gandour et al., 2000), the investigators looked at the perception of tone in speakers of three languages: Thai, Chinese, and English.

Tonemes are very short stretches of fast fluctuating fundamental frequencies over the range of a vowel production. As a simple example, the segmental stretch of a CV, such as /ma/, may have a number of differing tone patterns over the /a/, such that a 'high-falling' fundamental frequency (Fo) pattern shift will give you one word, while the /a/ with a tone pattern of 'low-rising' will give you quite another. These represent minimal phonemic pair distinctions and like minimal pair distinctions call for close, digital, and highly analytical processing skills upon the acoustic spectrum. In these kinds of studies, success on the part of the subjects depends upon the ability to **link** those analytical analyses of the perceptual system **with words** in their language. Each 'tone language' has its own set of parameters that fit to the lexicon. Linguists frequently define pitch as Fo, and therefore what is involved physically is a set of fast-changing pitches. Pitch, however, tends to avoid mention of something so communicative that it would serve as the sole element to distinguish one word from another in some languages. The term 'toneme' is therefore applied to a rapid pitch change that calls up in the minds of the listener different words. Thai and Chinese are tone languages, English is not.

The method of study was PET, and there were three to four subjects for each language. The subjects were asked to simply listen to the prosodic, fast fluctuations of Fo and to press a 'same' or 'different' button if they thought they heard the same pitch pattern or not. For tonemes, only Thai patterns were chosen for this study.

Several earlier imaging studies have shown activation in the left opercular regions of the frontal lobe, very near Broca's area, during phonemic perception. Recall that most consider both areas 44 and 45 *en toto* to be Broca's area (see Foundas et al., 1998, for an extremely close and detailed neuroanatomical study of pars triangularis [45] and pars opercularis [44], using volumetric MRI). The Gandour et al. (2000) study now shows this for the perception of the toneme, if you will, a phoneme of prosody. All subjects showed similar metabolic mosaics for the perception of rapidly changing pitch patterns that were **non**linguistic. However, only the Thai speakers revealed a significantly added component to the mosaic of metabolism when the pitch changes matched the tonemes of Thai. They were not only perceiving the rapid pitch changes, and therefore able to press same or different buttons, they were 'hearing' words. That is to say, the perception was linguistic. And, crucially, that added metabolic zone was in the left frontal operculum. Both the Chinese speakers and the English speakers revealed similar patterns of metabolism, but no added left Broca's area metabolism.

Another equally sophisticated and significant study along somewhat similar lines is found in Hseih et al. (2001). Here, however, there were 10 Chinese speakers and 10 English speakers, and all were analyzed as they perceived consonants and vowels, as well as pitches (nonspeech but physically similar to tones) and tones. The general metabolic mosaic patterns were different with each group of speakers, thus providing evidence that the cerebral metabolic patterns were largely reflective of the fact that Chinese and English involve different linguistic experiences. Subjects either listened passively or were instructed to do 'same–different' responding by clicking left or right, same vs. different. Subjects still had to click in the passive condition, but they simply had to alternate from one to the other for each presentation – a mindless task involving similar digit movements.

The findings here show a task-dependent mosaic of metabolic functioning that reflects how acoustic, segmental, and suprasegmental signals may or may not directly tap into linguistic significance, with nondominant hemisphere mechanisms activated for cues that eventually work themselves into dominant hemisphere activation. Broca's area on the left was activated for the Chinese-speaking group for consonants, vowels, tones, and pitches, while the right Broca's area was activated for English speakers on the pitch task. Since pitch is nonlinguistic on all views for English, this finding makes sense and again shows the role of the nondominant hemisphere in processing auditory stimuli at the beginning. Those pitches are extremely rapid as well, but can be processed by the right as long as they do not tap into anything linguistically meaningful. Chinese speakers, on the other hand, appear to process temporal and spectral signals in the left, not the right. Lateral effects are not predictable for very complex processing of rapid temporal and spectral change. Pitch patterns, then, along with temporal/spectral signals for consonants and vowels, are as likely to be in right or left hemisphere for this or that language. Hsieh et al. (2001: 240) write, "Pitch processing is lateralized to the left hemisphere only when the pitch patterns are phonologically significant to the listener; otherwise to the right hemisphere when the pitch patterns are linguistically irrelevant." Recall that in the previous study, only the Thai speaking group showed left activation (also in and around Broca's area) for the pitches that fit to the Thai tonemic system. Chinese speakers in that study showed absolutely no left Broca's area effect. Again, Chinese **is** a tone language, but the substrate of pitches is not the same as in Thai. One further finding (among the many others that we cannot go into here) was that the Chinese group showed increased metabolism in the left premotor cortex as well as the gyral zones of Broca's area (44 and 45) on the four tasks, while only the vowel condition activated left Broca's area significantly for English speakers. The pitch condition for English speakers in this study gave rise to increased metabolism in the **right** Broca's homologue. Again, we see a picture of right and left processing for auditory input, but where that auditory processing directly connects with linguistic significance for some language, that processing will drift leftwards or otherwise be attracted to the dominant hemisphere by the strength and dominance of the language processor. Now, therefore, we have growing evidence that the left Broca's area is involved in linguistic perception. In addition to this, there is increasing evidence as well that left posterior regions are involved in linguistic production.

We witness several lines of evidence in modern neurolinguistics that strengthen the classical aphasia notion that the posterior sensory auditory cortex is in many ways directly involved in speaking. Buckingham and Yule (1987) have related the architectonic findings of Galaburda of giant Betz cells under the planum temporale in level III. Not only does this system connect with the arcuate fibers in the operculum, but these regions as well show large concentrations of acetylcholine in the left temporal lobe. Since that neurotransmitter is found as well in large concentrations in left basal ganglia in right-handed people, it is assumed that it plays a motor role as well for articulation, and thus would be well situated for such a function in the left planum. In addition, Square et al. (1997) speak increasingly of a 'posterior' apraxia of speech (AOS), which would agree with older theories of Liepmann (1905) and with more recent models such as the one presented by Doreen Kimura (1982). There has always been a certain amount of tension in theories of AOS as to just how much of its nature is phonetic and how much is phonological. This question would only make sense, of course, if there were a certain metric that would keep the two apart, with clearly demarcated domains that would allow for an 'interface' of the two. We have already seen a complex array of interactions between the sensory and the motor for production and perception, both functionally and neuroanatomically. The brain may very well turn out to be unable to enforce a strict compartmentalization between the two, and this would in turn lend support to the claims of certain phonologists such as John Ohala (1990) that in fact there is no such thing as a phonetics–phonology 'interface,' since the two are fully intertwined. The whole issue may turn out to be moot more than originally thought. Finally, stemming from the recent evidence for old functional notions of the arcuate fasciculus, that tract's motor–sensory mediation capacity has led to its establishment as part and parcel of a subvocal rehearsal mechanism that is crucially involved in short-term operational verbal memory.

Recent Linguistic Aphasiological Studies of Sublexical Units

Most studies of segmental paraphasias in modern terms include reference to syllable structure as well as syllable complexity. Phonotactic patterns are closely scrutinized, but the interaction between phonotactics and the sonority scale are often only loosely defined and only marginally used as a comparative analytic metric. For example, many investigators (e.g., Nickels and Howard, 2004) measure syllable complexity largely by canonical form and nothing else. An aphasic who reduced complexity of syllable structure would simply change a CCVCC to perhaps a CVC, a CV, or a VC. A simple assumption would be that a CV is less complex than a CCV. The sonority hierarchy, however, provides the aphasiologist with a more powerful way to measure syllable complexity that goes beyond phonotactics. Universal (not absolute) sonority ranking, going from least to most sonorous, is: **O**bstruent **N**asal **L**iquid **G**lide **V**owel. The distance from O to V is 4, from O to N is 1, from N to G is 2, and so forth. Onset structures have a crescendo architecture, while coda structures have a decrescendo architecture, the vowel being the nucleus of the syllable with maximum sonority. The most powerful complexity metric is the 'dispersion' principle embedded in this theory. The calculation of dispersion is done by summing the inverses of the squared values of all the distances of all elements in the initial demisyllable (the Cs and the V). The dispersion value for an initial demisyllable, such as the /pli/ of the word /pliz/, would be the following. From O to L has a distance value of 2; from O to V has a distance of 4, while the distance from L to V is 2. The dispersion value here would be: .56. Now, note for instance, that if you measure the dispersion of the CV /yu/, you get 1/1 = 1.00, a higher value than calculated for the CCV /pli/. There is a smoother and more steady crescendo going from O, then to L, then to V. This is not the case for the /yu/. The principle prefers sequences of two segments that differ as much as possible on sonority ranking. Lower dispersion values are less marked in initial demisyllables. Sonority relates to amplitude, resonance, vocalicness, and vocal tract opening. Sharp discontinuities in these features is what is preferred: maximum contrast (see Ohala, 1992, where he stresses maximum discontinuity, which to him renders the sonority principle totally redundant, or, at best, derivative). There is very little contrast between a glide and a vowel; they are contiguous. Even more nonpreferred would be a sequence of two segments of the same sonority value, a 'flat' sequence, flat meaning that there is no crescendo nor descrescendo. Other than /s/ plus another obstruent in English, which are numerous (/s/ is often considered 'extrasyllabic' by some phonologists, and thus that problem would vanish), often processes intervene to shift the syllable structure to a more preferred situation. Often, for instance, when two vowels end up together, a glottal stop intervenes to break up that undesirable sequence.

In a recent study, Nickels and Howard (2004) used a powerful statistic to discover the crucial factor correlating with word production errors (phonemic paraphasia). They could dissociate the effects of number of segments in a word, number of syllables in a word, and the syllable complexity of the word. Admittedly, the three are often conflated in studies of paraphasia that simply put the onus on 'word length' for degree of paraphasia. Number of segments and number of syllables often intercorrelated, for instance. A greater number of syllables would allow for the possibility of more complex syllables. The authors' statistic was such that it leveled out syllable complexity, showing ultimately that only number of syllables correlated with degree of accuracy in lexical realization. The problem, of course, is that without considering sonority and its dispersion measurement, the simple use of canonical forms to measure syllable complexity is weak at best, and as we saw above, actually wrong in many of its predictions of complexity, a CV in some cases being more complex that a CCV.

Furthermore, note that not all CVs are if equal complexity. A /pa/ (OV) = .06; a /na/ (NV) = .11; a /ra/ (LV) = .25, and a /ya/ (GV) = 1.

In two recent studies by Romani and Calabrese (1998) and Romani et al. (2002), the principle of sonority and dispersion were closely charted in the analysis of a nonfluent patient (Romani and Calabrese, 1998), and then in the 2002 study that patient contrasted with a typical fluent paraphasic speaker, with a CT scan demonstrating a two-year-old CVA in the left temporoparietal area. The previous 1998 study had clearly shown that the nonfluent errors simplified structures clearly along the lines of predictions from sonority: more segmental transformations creating less complexity in terms of sonority and syllable simplifications that followed sonority predictions as well. In that study, Romani and Calabrese importantly emphasize that since this patient was nonfluent with great articulatory difficulty, there is reason to believe that sonority patterns are grounded in motor speech execution. Christman (1992, 1994), on the other hand, showed that neologisms in a fluent aphasic also tend to follow the patterns of sonority. Neologistic structures abide quite rigidly to the architecture of sonority, and consequently they demonstrate that the principle filters up into the phonology, or otherwise becomes phonologized. In this way, sonority in the big picture can be at work in both fluent and nonfluent aphasic production. Romani et al.'s (2002) fluent subject did not show such simplification tendencies and to that effect did not reveal as much influence from sonority. In general, the 2002 comparison study reported the following main differences between the nonfluent DB and the fluent MM:

1. The majority of DB's errors, but not MM's errors, gave rise to simpler syllables.
2. Most of DB's errors involved consonants; MM's did not.
3. DB's substitutions were closer to the target and were influenced by frequency.

4. DB's errors were largely paradigmatic substitutions, while MM's were more involved with linear sequencing of segments.
5. MM showed no specific tendencies toward differential errors among vowels. DB, however, made the fewest errors on /a/; /a/ is the most sonorous of the vowels, since it has the most aperture.

In addition to sonority patterns, there are metrical patterns as well, and they, too, have distinct complexity levels. The trochee pattern of Strong-Weak is the most frequent meter for two syllable words in English and is likely a very frequent rhythmic template in all human languages. Iambs are somewhat more complex, since the initial syllables are unstressed, initiation thereby being more difficult. Note that many children's deletions as well as aphasics' are focused on unstressed – and most often reduced – syllables. Goodglass (1978) was one of the first aphasia researchers to point out that utterance-initial weak stresses are abnormally difficult for many types of patients, especially the nonfluent Broca's aphasics. He extended this observation to sentence-initial unstressed function words, such as *the* in a phrase *the book is on the table.* Here he noted the extreme difficulties many Broca's aphasics had with producing the initial *the,* and thus initiating the sentence. He pointed out, however, that the patient could much more easily produce noninitial, unstressed *the,* internal to the sentence. It turns out that there is a metrical account for the differential deletability of the two *the* function words, and that the same account works as well for explaining why children who delete unstressed schwas most often delete the initial ones in words such as *banana.* Metrical feet are assigned in algorithmic fashion to a stretch of syllables or words from right to left. Details aside, *nana* gets a trochaic foot (SW), but the first syllable is not assigned a foot, and is therefore referred to as an 'unfooted' schwa. The theory now says that the second schwa is 'protected' by being within a foot unit. Of the two unstressed schwas, therefore, the unfooted one is more vulnerable to apocope. At the sentential level, a similar situation arises. Going from right to left, *table* is a trochee; *on the* is a trochee; *book is* is a trochee as well. There is no foot that can be assigned to the initial *the,* so that it is 'unfooted.' An unfooted function word such as the first article *the* in the sentence, is therefore more vulnerable than the internal *the,* which is protected by the trochaic foot domain *on the.* In the final tally, these new findings from the phonology of the syllable, of metrics, and of the suprasegmental constraints on rhythm and cadence have allowed us to better appreciate that AOS has as much to do with loss of rhythm and cadence of speech, and that they in turn cause many of the articulatory derailments seen in that syndrome. It also allows us to appreciate even further that the phonemic paraphasias of Wernicke's and conduction aphasics take place at levels much higher in the linguistic production system. Metrical and syllabic phonology have led to the postulation of frames or templates into which contents may be inserted: phonemes or words. The picture is one of empty slots within these templatic frames and the access of the contents to fill those slots. Finally, each element, structure or unit may be dissociated from any other. The syllable itself is typically considered as an encasement with slots labeled as onset, rime, nucleus, and coda and groups of segments placed there as segments in production. It is stressed that syllables themselves are not subject to productive sequencing, but rather their contents are. Levelt et al. (1999) constructs both phonological/syllabic frames and metrical frames. There has been a long-standing article of faith held by many psycholinguists, which claims that when phonemes move in linear ordering errors they move from and to the same syllabic constituent slots: onsets move to onset positions, nuclei move to nuclei positions and codas move to coda positions. This has been variously called 'the syllable constraint condition.' For Levelt, this constraint is overly lopsided in that according to his numbers 80% of English language slips-of-the-tongue involve syllable onsets, but these are crucially word onsets as well. According to Levelt's numbers, slips not involving word onsets, "... are too rare to be analyzed for adherence to a positional constraint" (Levelt, 1999: 21). He rules out on other principles the nucleus to nucleus observation, claiming that phonotactic constraints are operating here, since a vowel → consonant will not likely result in a pronounceable string. In addition, Levelt feels that vowels and coda consonants operate under more tightly controlled conditions whereby "... segments interact with similar segments." Phonologists have observed that there are often fewer coda consonants than onset consonants, which is especially true for a language like Spanish. The number of vowels in a language is always smaller than the total number of consonants. In any event, there is ample evidence (also see Shattuck-Hufnagel, 1987) that onsets are much less 'tied' to the syllable than are codas, which being sister nodes of the nucleus, both dominated by the rime, are much more 'glued' to the vowel of the syllable. In terms of a qualitatively different status for word onsets, there is evidence that the word onset position is significantly more involved in the phonemic carryover errors in recurrent perseveration (e.g., Buckingham and Christman, 2004).

Two new notions of the nature of segmental targets have been introduced recently. One is seen in Square (1997) with her 'movement formulae.' These are stored in posterior left temporoparietal cortex and seem very much like the centuries-old memories of articulatory procedures of Jean-Baptiste Bouillaud (1825). Targets are now understood by some as idealized gestures for sound production and that voluntary speech would involve the access of these stored gestural engrams for articulation. Both of these conjure up theories of embodiment and both are forms of representative memory (see Glenberg, 1997 for a cogent treatment of memory and embodiment).

Goldman et al. (2001) have analyzed the effect of the phonetic surround in the production of phonemic paraphasias in the spontaneous speech of a Wernicke's aphasic. Through the use of a powerful statistic, the authors were able to control for chance occurrence of a 'copy' of the error phoneme either in the past context or in the future context. The idea was that there could be a context effect that caused the phonemic paraphasia to occur. Chance baselines were established, and it was found that relative to this baseline, the 'error-source' distances were shorter than expected for anticipatory transpositions but not for perseverative transpositions. That could be taken to mean that anticipatory errors are more indicative of an aphasia than perseveratory errors in that this patient seemed more unable to inhibit a copy of an element in line to be produced a few milliseconds ahead. Thus, this could be taken to support the claim that anticipatory bias in phonemic paraphasia correlates with severity. The authors also observed that many but not all anticipatory errors involved word onsets, mentioned earlier in this review as vulnerable to movement or substitution. The much larger distances between error and source for perseverations could have been due to slower decay rates of activated units whereby they return to their resting states. The patient's anterior/perseveration ratios measured intermediate between a nonaphasic error corpus and that of a more severe aphasic speaker. One troubling aspect of this study was that a source was counted in the context whether or not it shared the same word or syllable position as the error. This may represent a slight stumbling block in interpreting the findings, since, Levelt notwithstanding, it would imply that syllable position had no necessary effect. The authors, however, presented their findings with caution, especially so because some recent work (Martin and Dell, 2004) has demonstrated a strong correlation between anticipatory errors and normality vs. perseveratory errors and abnormality. It is a long-noted fact that slips-of-the-tongue in normal subjects are more anticipatory than perseverative. Perseveration is furthermore felt by many to be indicative of brain damage. Martin and Dell (2004) set up an anticipation ratio, which is obviously higher in normality through slips. They also find that more severe aphasics produce more perseverative paraphasias than anticipations, but that the ratio increases throughout recovery such that in the later stages of recovery patients produce fewer and fewer perseverations as opposed to anticipations: the anticipatory effect grows as the patients approach normality. On the logic that the improving aphasic should move in the direction of the normal subject, the anticipatory ratio should increase. It may very well turn out that the anticipatory error will ultimately serve as a metric to measure recovery over time in aphasia.

Recovery from the Production of Neologisms

The question may be, and has been, asked: neologisms: from whence? From the beginning, it was simply thought that they stemmed from a complex array of literal or phonemic paraphasias. That is, it had originally been taken as an article of faith that neologisms originated from words that had been phonemically transformed to the extent that any transparency between error and target word was obliterated. There has never been any question that this account is not a logical one, especially given the prevalence of phonemic paraphasia in fluent aphasia. Since the days of Wernicke (1874), M. Allen Starr (1889), the late 19th-century linguists, through Arnold Pick (1931/1973) and up to the present (see Buckingham, 1989), error typologies have included anticipatory errors, perseverative errors, exchanges, and substitutions of phonemes in both normal subjects (slips-of-the-tongue) and aphasics. The phonemic paraphasia theory of neology was dubbed by Buckingham (1977) as 'the conduction theory,' since conduction aphasics are marked by their phonemic paraphasias. This was the theory implied in the Boston Aphasia Exam and specifically invoked in Kertesz and Benson (1970) for the neologism. Note very importantly that this account for the production of neologisms implies, if it does not say so outright, that the problem is not with the retrieval of the word but rather with the phonological realization of that word. For this theory to hold true, the target word would presumably have to have been retrieved from the lexicon, because it must serve as the input to the component that transforms it.

Another possible account of neologisms would be to claim that straight away the patient had a word block whereby no target word would be forthcoming, and that nonetheless, the patient continued talking or stopped responding. The question then becomes, how in this circumstance could the patient produce what would then be a surrogate for or a 'masker' of the unaccessed word. By what aspects of phonetic production could the speaker produce the surrogate. The issue was introduced in modern neurolinguistic studies in Alajouinine (1956), Kertesz and Benson (1970), Buckingham and Kertesz (1976), and Butterworth (1979). Butterworth called this second account of neology 'the anomia theory,' and suggested the metaphor of a 'random generator' as a principle device that could produce a phonetic form in light of retrieval failure.

Butterworth had studied with Freida Goldmann-Eisler (1968), who had analyzed large stretches of spontaneous speech and had looked closely at the on-going lexical selection processes online. She had noted time delays before the production of nouns of high information (i.e., low redundancy) in the speech of normal subjects. Time delays for her indicated the action of word search, and that search would obviously be a bit more automatic and fast, to the extent that the word sought was highly redundant, therefore carrying less information. Butterworth very cleverly extended his mentor's methods to the analysis of neologistic jargon stretches of spontaneous speech in Wernicke's aphasia. What he found was extremely interesting. Before neologisms that were totally opaque as to any possible target (subsequently termed 'abstruse' neologisms by A. R. Lecours (1982)), Butterworth noted clear delays of up to 400 ms before their production. Crucially, he did not notice this delay before phonemic paraphasias, where targets could nevertheless be clearly discerned, nor before semantic substitutions, related to the target. This indicated failed retrieval for Butterworth and he went on to suggest that perseverative processes and nonce word production capabilities could play a role in this 'random generator.' It was 'random' for Butterworth, since his analysis of the actual phonemic makeup of neologisms did not follow the typical patterns of phoneme frequency in English. He never implied that 'random' meant helter skelter; he knew enough about phonotactic constraints in aphasic speech. Neither did he imply that the patient actually, with premeditated intentionality, produced the surrogate. The whole issue was subsequently treated in Buckingham (1981, 1985, 1990).

Each of these accounts of neology makes different predictions concerning recovery. The conduction theory predicts that as the patient recovers, target words will slowly but surely begin to reappear. Paraphasic infiltration will lessen throughout the months and ultimately the word forms will be less and less opaque. In the endstage of recovery, there should be no anomia. The theory also predicts that the error distributions in the acute stage will produce some errors with mild phonemic transformation, others with more, others with a bit more, etc., up to the completely opaque ones, i.e., a nonbimodal distribution. The anomia theory, on the other hand, predicts a bimodal distribution with neologisms on one end and more or less simple phonemic paraphasia on the other, and few in the middle that were more severe but not enough to render word recognizability opaque. The anomia theory predicts that during recovery patients with that underlying problem will generally show fewer and fewer neologisms, gaining better monitoring capacity to note the neologisms, perhaps ultimately holding back the surrogate productions as a mark of improvement in the aphasia. It is also highly likely that as the patient improves, the perseverations will lessen (e.g., Martin and Dell, 2004). What is clearly predicted at the endstage, however, is that the anomia may very well remain, but now with more stammering, pausing, and halting. This, then, would be more in the line of what a normal speaker might do when faced with word-finding difficulties. Unhampered with additional sequelae, this is more or less what the 'pure' anomic will do.

These predictions remained untested in the clinic until Kohn and Smith (1994) and Kohn et al. (1996). Essentially, and more specifically in 1996, Kohn and colleagues observed and described patients who, in the acute stages of their aphasia, produced neologisms. One group recovered to mild phonemic paraphasia with no noted anomia, while the other group no longer produced neologisms in the later recovery stages. This second group of patients, when producing the neology initially, appeared to Kohn and colleagues (1996: 132) to be invoking some kind of "... backup mechanism for 'reconstructing' a phonological representation when either partial or no stored phonological information about a word is made available to the production system."

Most connectionists have an easier time with the conduction theory of neologisms and in general only provide this one account of their generation. They generally weaken in varying degrees the connection strengths between the lexical and the phonemic levels in their models, while keeping decay rates at normal levels. They can thus quite easily simulate a gamut of phonemic errors (and also they can simulate segmental slips-of-the-tongue), the more severe bordering on the opaque. Their paradox, however, would be that the simple paraphasias would not render target words opaque, and thus interlevel transparency would be maintained between word and phoneme. On the other hand, with a bit more connection weight reduction, opaque forms may begin to be produced, and to the extent they are opaque, interlevel transparency will disappear. Connectionists often make the claim that interlevel transparency reveals qualitatively different kinds of errors – or even different kinds of patients. Some have called errors that do not show between-level communication 'stupid,' while those that nevertheless reveal interlevel connectivity have been called 'smart.' Note that both kinds of patients in Kohn and colleagues' study would start out with 'stupid' errors. Neologisms have no transparency concerning some target. But, by the anomia account, the errors would remain 'stupid' even into recovery, as long as the anomia was there, unless some semantically related errors began to appear; some probably did. On the other hand, by the conduction account, the errors would start off 'stupid' but end up 'smart.' Connectionists will have to tell us whether this scenario is a puzzle for them or not. Again, most connectionist modelers opt for the conduction theory of neologisms (e.g., Gagnon and Schwartz, 1996; Hillis et al., 1999). As an example of the conduction theory for neologisms in connectionist modeling, Hillis et al. (1999: 1820) wrote, "This proposal would account for her phonemic paraphasias (when few nontarget subword units are activated) and neologisms (when many nontarget subword units are activated)." That is to say, few phonemic errors result in simple paraphasia, where the target is not rendered opaque, while many phonemic errors result in a neologism, where the target is, indeed, rendered opaque. The problem of the neologism, however, is still with us, and especially so if we do not admit at least two error routes – perhaps even a third, but time does not permit further consideration.

Conclusions

We have considered a vast array of findings on sublexical linguistic elements, their brain locations and tight sensory–motor links. We have claimed that many new imaging studies have conjured up and vindicated several earlier theories laid down long before the modern technology before us in the neurosciences. We have seen the motor–sensory interface in the functional linguistic descriptions of phoneme level production and perception, and we have even seen that much new work with modern technology has served to sharpen our understanding at somewhat closer levels, but nonetheless has vindicated much previous thinking – back to the Haskins Labs and even further back to the classic aphasia models of the late 1800s. The focus upon the perisylvian region in the left hemisphere has not changed, and in fact there is even more growing interest in charting the anatomy and function of the arcuate fasciculus, the opercular regions, and the insula. At a slight remove from the physical system, we have discussed and compared various new findings and principles in the phonetics and phonology of segments, syllables, and meter and how they impact on sublexical processing in aphasia. Finally, we considered the enigma of the neologism and provided evidence that there are at least two quite reasonable accounts of how they may be produced and under what conditions they may appear. This leads to a consideration of how recovery from neology may take different paths as the patient improves language control. Many questions remain.

Bibliography

Alajouanine, T (1956). 'Verbal realization in aphasia.' *Brain* 79: 1–28.

Bouillaud, JB (1825). 'Recherches cliniques propres à démontrer que la perte de la parole correspond à la lésion des lobes antérieures du cerveau, et à confirmer l'opinion de M. Gall, sur le siège de l'organe du langage articulé.' *Archives Générales Medicales* 8: 25–45.

Buckingham, HW (1977). 'The conduction theory and neologistic jargon.' *Language and Speech* 20: 174–184.

Buckingham, HW (1981). 'Where do neologisms come from?' In: Brown, JW (ed.) *Jargonaphasia*, pp. 39–62. New York: Academic Press.

Buckingham, HW (1985). 'Perseveration in aphasia.' In: Newman, S and Epstein, R (eds.) *Current perspectives in dysphasia*, pp. 113–154. Edinburgh: Churchill Livingstone.

Buckingham, HW (1989). 'Phonological paraphasia.' In: Code, C (ed.) *The characteristics of aphasia*, pp. 89–110. London: Taylor & Francis.

Buckingham, HW (1990). 'Abstruse neologisms, retrieval deficits and the random generator.' *Journal of Neurolinguistics* 5: 215–235.

Buckingham, HW and Kertesz, A (1976). *Neologistic jargonaphasia.* Amsterdam: Swets & Zeitlinger.

Buckingham, HW and Yule, G (1987). 'Phonemic false evaluation: theoretical and clinical aspects.' *Clinical Linguistics and Phonetics* 1: 113–125.

Buckingham, HW and Christman, SS (2004). 'Phonemic carryover perseveration: word blends.' *Seminars in Speech and Language* 25: 363–373.

Butterworth, B (1979). 'Hesitation and the production of verbal paraphasias and neologisms in jargon aphasia.' *Brain and Language* 18: 133–161.

Christman, SS (1992). 'Abstruse neologism formation: parallel processing revisited.' *Clinical Linguistics and Phonetics* 6: 65–76.

Christman, SS (1994). 'Target-related neologism formation in jargon aphasia.' *Brain and Language* 46: 109–128.

Foundas, AL, Eure, KF, Luevano, LF, and Weinberger, DR (1998). 'MRI asymmetries of Broca's area: the pars triangularis and pars opercularis.' *Brain and Language* 64: 282–296.

Gagnon, D and Schwartz, MF (1996). 'The origins of neologisms in picture naming by fluent aphasics.' *Brain and Cognition* 32: 118–120.

Gandour, J, Wong, D, Hsieh, L, Weinzapfel, B, VanLancker, D, and Hutchins, GD (2000). 'A cross-linguistic PET study of tone perception.' *Journal of Cognitive Neuroscience* 12: 207–222.

Glenberg, AM (1997). 'What memory is for.' *Behavioral and Brain Sciences* 20: 1–55.

Goldmann, RE, Schwartz, MF, and Wilshire, CE (2001). 'The influence of phonological context in the sound errors of a speaker with Wernicke's aphasia.' *Brain and Language* 78: 279–307.

Goldman-Eisler, F (1968). *Psycholinguistics: experiments in spontaneous speech.* London: Academic Press.

Goodglass, H (1978). *Selected papers in neurolinguistics.* Munchen: Wilhelm Fink Verlag.

Hartley, D (1749/1976). *Observations on man: his frame, his duty and his expectations.* Delmar, NY: Scholars' Facsimiles & Reprints.

Hickok, G (2000). 'Speech perception, conduction aphasia, and the functional neuroanatomy of language.' In: Grodzinsky, Y, Shapiro, LP, and Swinney, D (eds.) *Language and the brain: representation and processing. Multidisciplinary studies presented to Edgar Zurif on his 60th birthday*, pp. 87–104. San Diego: Academic Press.

Hillis, A, Boatman, D, Hart, J, and Gordon, B (1999). 'Making sense out of jargon: a neurolinguistic and computational account of jargon aphasia.' *Neurology* 53: 1813–1824.

Hsieh, L, Gandour, J, Wong, D, and Hutchins, G (2001). 'Functional heterogeneity of inferior frontal gyrus is shaped by linguistic experience.' *Brain and Language* 76: 227–252.

Hughlings-Jackson, J (1866). 'Notes on the physiology and pathology of language: remarks on those cases of disease of the nervous system, in which defect of expression is the most striking symptom.' *Medical Times and Gazette* 1 Reprinted in *Brain* 38. Also in Taylor, J (ed.) (1958). *Selected writings of John Hughlings-Jackson*, Vol. II. London: Hodder & Stoughton.

Kertesz, A and Benson, DF (1970). 'Neologistic jargon: a clinicopathological study.' *Cortex* 6: 362–386.

Kimura, D (1982). 'Left-hemisphere control of oral and brachial movements and their relation to communication.' *Philosophical Transactions of the Royal Society of London B* 298: 135–149.

Kohn, S and Smith, K (1994). 'Distinctions between two phonological output disorders.' *Applied Psycholinguistics* 15: 75–95.

Kohn, S, Smith, K, and Alexander, M (1996). 'Differential recovery from impairment to the phonological lexicon.' *Brain and Language* 52: 129–149.

Lecours, AR (1982). 'On neologisms.' In: Mehler, J, Walker, E, and Garrett, M (eds.) *Perspectives on mental representation: experimental and theoretical studies of cognitive processes and capacities*, pp. 217–247. Hillsdale, NJ: Erlbaum.

Levelt, WJM, Roelofs, A, and Meyer, AS (1999). 'A theory of lexical access in speech production.' *Behavioral and Brain Sciences* 22: 1–75.

Liepmann, H (1905). 'Die linke Hemisphare und das Handeln.' *Munchener Medizinische Wochenschrift* 49: 2322–2326,

2375–2378. Translated into English by Kimura, D (1980). In *Translations from Liepmann's essays on apraxia.* Research Bulletin #506. London, Ontario: Dept. of Psychology, University of Western Ontario.
Martin, N and Dell, G (2004). 'Perseverations and anticipations in aphasia: primed intrusions from the past and future.' *Seminars in Speech and Language* 25: 349–362.
Nickels, L and Howard, D (2004). 'Dissociating effects of number of phonemes, number of syllables, and syllabic complexity on word production in aphasia: it's the number of phonemes that counts.' *Cognitive Neuropsychology* 21: 57–78.
Ohala, J (1990). 'There is no interface between phonology and phonetics: a personal view.' *Journal of Phonetics* 18: 153–171.
Ohala, J (1992). 'Alternatives to the sonority hierarchy for explaining segmental sequential constraints.' In: Ziolkowski, M, Noske, M, and Deaton, K (eds.) *Papers from the 26th Regional Meeting of the Chicago Linguistic Society, vol. 2. The parasession on the syllable in phonetics and phonology*, pp. 319–338. Chicago: Chicago Linguistic Society.
Pick, A (1931). 'Aphasia.' In: *Handbuch der normalen und pathologischen* 15. Heidelberg: Springer-Verlag. Translated into English and edited by Brown, JW (1973). Aphasia. Springfield, Ill: Charles C. Thomas.
Romani, C and Calabrese, A (1998). 'Syllable constraints on the phonological errors of an aphasic patient.' *Brain and Language* 64: 83–121.
Romani, C, Olson, A, Semenza, C, and Grana, A (2002). 'Patterns of phonological errors as a function of a phonological versus an articulatory locus of impairment.' *Cortex* 38: 541–567.
Shattuck-Hufnagel, S (1987). 'The role of word-onset consonants in speech production planning: new evidence from speech error patterns.' In: Keller, E and Gopnik, M (eds.) *Motor and sensory processes of language*, pp. 17–51. Hillsdale, NJ: Erlbaum.
Square, PA, Roy, EA, and Martin, RE (1997). 'Apraxia of speech: another form of praxis disruption.' In: Rothi, LJG and Heilman, KM (eds.) *Apraxia: the neuropsychology of action*, pp. 173–206. Hove: East Sussex, UK: Psychology Press.
Starr, M A (1889) . 'The pathology of sensory aphasia, with an analysis of fifty cases in which Broca's center was not diseased.' *Brain* 12: 82–102.
Uttal, WR (2001). *The new phrenology: the limits of localizing cognitive processes in the brain.* Cambridge: The MIT Press.
Wernicke, K (1874). *The aphasia symptom complex: a psychological study on an anatomic basis.* Breslau: Cohn & Weigert. Translated into English by Egger, GH (1977). *Wernicke's works on aphasia: A sourcebook and review.* The Hague: Mouton. 91–145.

Phonological, Lexical, Syntactic, and Semantic Disorders in Children

D. L. Molfese, M. J. Maguire, V. J. Molfese, N. Pratt, E. D. Ratajczak, L. E. Fentress, and P. J. Molfese,
University of Louisville, Louisville, KY, USA

Brain Measures Common to the Study of Language Disabilities

A variety of procedures is currently used to investigate brain processes underlying language disabilities. These include functional magnetic resonance imaging (fMRI), MRI, positron emission tomography (PET), magnetoelectroencephalography (MEG), and event-related potentials (ERPs). Each procedure, of course, has its strengths and weaknesses. MRI provides information concerning the morphology of brain structures, whereas fMRI monitors hemodynamic processes, such as changes in brain functions reflected during extended periods of language processing. PET operates in a somewhat similar fashion but tracks the flow of radioactive elements injected into the blood to identify areas actively engaged in a language task. MEG can detect small fluctuations in the brain's magnetic field in response to task demands, and ERPs, a portion of the ongoing EEG that is time locked to the onset of a stimulus event, can reflect rapid changes in the brain's encoding and processing of a speech sound, word, or even sentence. All procedures enable investigators to map linguistic and cognitive functions onto brain structures (Fonaryova Key et al., in press).

Although studies of brain processing usually use one of these procedures, it is clear that much is to be gained from using a combination of procedures. For example, the high temporal sensitivity of ERP techniques can provide a means for determining the sequential relationships that exist between the specific areas of brain activation identified through fMRI (Georgiewa et al., 2002). Moreover, convergence in source localization across fMRI, MEG and ERP procedures ensures that solutions are not biased by particular approaches but may reflect different aspects of what occur in the brain in response to stimulus input or task demands (see Hugdahl et al., 1998).

In general, differences are noted in brain responses and structures for different disabilities (Harter et al., 1988a, 1988b), but there are similarities across disabilities as well. Brain differences could relate to general cognitive processing differences (e.g., attention) that may be impaired in some types of disabilities (Holcomb et al., 1986), or brain differences could reflect the involvement of different structures in response to task demands. Generally, brain structure and functional differences have been thought to be related to poor language function in general (Molfese and Segalowitz, 1988) and to dyslexia in particular (Eckert et al., 2001; Frank and Pavlakis, 2001). Orton (1937) as well as Travis (1931) held the belief that early signs of lateralization serve to identify children at risk for developmental language disorders. More recent investigations continue to indicate that differences in cerebral asymmetry associated with atypical organization of the left hemisphere are a marker for dyslexic children (Heim and Keil, 2004). However, although reports often link hemisphere differences and language disorders, current thinking indicates that the pathology as well as the neurophysiology of developmental language disabilities are a great deal more complex than originally thought and extend well beyond the classically defined language areas of the brain (Eden et al., 1996). For example, some point to the neural circuitry to account for brain organizational differences between impaired and nonimpaired children, as well as between children with different types of language disabilities (Eden et al., 1996; Leonard et al., 2002; Sarkari et al., 2002). For example, dyslexic readers fail to exhibit the usual network of anterior and posterior brain areas over left hemisphere regions, whereas children with attention deficit hyperactivity disorder appear to have an abnormality in the prefrontal and striatal regions.

For the purposes of this present chapter, the review of brain structures and functions involved in language disabilities is limited to autism, developmental dyslexia, Down syndrome, specific language impairment (SLI), and Williams syndrome. Links between brain and behavior in these developmental disabilities are highlighted.

Autism

Autism is a neurodevelopmental disorder characterized by impairments in language, communication, imagination, and social relations (American Psychiatric Association, 1994). Estimates of occurrence in the general population range from approximately 1 in 200 to 1 in 1000 (Fombonne, 1999). Although nearly 25% of children with autism have essentially normal vocabulary and grammatical abilities (Kjelgaard and Tager-Flusberg, 2001), another 25% may remain mute for their entire lives (Lord and Paul, 1997). Many underlying language problems found in autistic children are believed to be linked to social and emotional deficits. Although the leading causes of autism remain unknown, the interplay of multiple genes with multiple environmental factors is considered a factor (Akshoomoff et al., 2002).

General Brain Imaging Results for Autism

Most imaging studies of children with autism are carried out with sedated children and thus focus on brain structures rather than functional differences (Rapin and Dunn, 2003). Even so, structural differences noted in autistic populations are often contradictory. The most consistent findings include increased cerebellar hemisphere, parietotemporal lobe, and total brain volume. Current research findings also show that the size of the amygdala, hippocampus, and corpus callosum may differ from that of normals (see Brambilla et al., 2003, for a review).

Social – Brain Difference and Autism

Neurologically, many of the social aspects of language acquisition (e.g., social orienting, joint attention and responding to emotional states of others) are tied to differences in the medial temporal lobe (amygdala and hippocampal), which is larger in autistic children than in age-matched controls (Brambilla et al., 2003; Sparks et al., 2002). This brain region is thought to be related to performance on deferred imitation tasks – a skill that may be important in language acquisition (Dawson et al., 1998). Further, the increase in amygdala size may have consequences for important skills such as discriminating facial expressions (Adophs et al., 1995; Whalen et al., 1998) and joint attention (Sparks et al., 2002). Both skills appear to be important for language acquisition and are often impaired or absent in autism.

Phonology and Autism

A shift in the latency of the first positive peak in the ERP (P1) and the following first large negative peak (N1) to speech sounds in typically developing children is believed to result from maturational changes related to synaptogenesis, myelinogenesis, and dendritic pruning, possibly reflecting cortical auditory system maturation (Bruneau et al., 1997; Eggermont, 1988; Houston and McClelland, 1985). Findings with autistic children for these two ERP peaks are mixed: some studies report longer N1 latencies in children with autism (Dunn et al., 1999; Seri et al., 1999), whereas others report shorter N1 latencies with autistic children (Oades et al., 1988) or no differences between autistic and control children (Kemner et al., 1995; Lincoln et al., 1995).

Using MEG, the N1 correlate is the M100 or N1m. Gage et al. (2003) found that the M100 shifted in latencies in the left and right hemispheres with age for typically developing children listening to tones but occurred only in the left hemisphere for autistic children. This neural activation was localized to the supratemporal sites, reflecting activity of the auditory cortex. Overall, children with autism also exhibited delayed M100 latencies compared to controls, indicating a fundamental difference in the auditory processing of autistic children.

Semantics and Autism

When given a semantic (meaning) categorization task, autistic children exhibit no differences in the N400 between deviant and target words, unlike age-matched controls

(Dunn et al., 1999). Surprisingly, autistic children's categorizing errors were not higher than controls, indicating that although the autistic children could categorize based on semantics, they could not attend to the global context and could not discern that one ending was more common than another. As a result, their brains appeared not to process out-of-category words as 'deviant.'

Many autistic children have limited word knowledge and limited comprehension of meaning in connected speech (Dunn et al., 1999). Mental words, such as 'think', 'believe,' and 'know,' are rarely part of the autistic child's vocabulary (Happe, 1995), which is speculated to be caused by differences in the limbic system and as reflecting consistent with the problems of these children in processing emotional information (Dawson et al., 1998).

Dyslexia

Developmental dyslexia refers to the abnormal acquisition of reading skills during the normal course of development despite adequate learning and instructional opportunities and normal intelligence. Estimates are that 5–10% of school-age children fail to learn to read normally (Habib, 2000). Dyslexia can exist in isolation, but more commonly it occurs with other disabilities, such as dyscalculia (mathematic skill impairment) and attention deficit disorder, both with and without hyperactivity. Studies of dyslexia usually indicate the involvement of left-hemisphere perisylvian areas during the reading process. The specific areas identified vary somewhat depending on the component of reading being engaged in but overall the extrastriate visual cortex, inferior parietal regions, superior temporal gyrus, and inferior frontal cortex appear to be activated.

When one examines specific skills, visual word form processing is associated with occipital and occipitotemporal sites, whereas reading-relevant phonological processing has been associated with superior temporal, occipitotemporal, and inferior frontal sites of the left hemisphere. However, there is some variation in the scientific reports. For example, although some studies report a hemisphere asymmetry in the area of the planum temporale related to dyslexia (Frank and Pavlakis, 2001), others report no such effect (Heiervang et al., 2000).

A number of studies have identified brain anatomical differences that distinguish dyslexic from normal brains (see Hynd and Semrud-Clikeman [1989] for an earlier review). For example, Eckert et al. (2003), using MRI scans, reported that dyslexics exhibited significantly smaller right anterior lobes of the cerebellum, pars triangularis bilaterally, and brain volume than controls. Correlation analyses showed that these neuroanatomical measurements relate to reading, spelling and language measures of dyslexia (see also Grunling et al., 2004). Although earlier studies report hemisphere differences in the region of the planum temporale between dyslexics and controls, more recent studies investigating the morphology of the perisylvian cortical area in a clinical sample of children failed to find morphological differences at this locale that were associated with the diagnosis of dyslexia (Hiemenz and Hynd, 2000). Scientists have also reported differences between dyslexics and controls in the corpus callosum – the band of fibers connecting the two hemispheres (von Plessen et al., 2002). These researchers reported differences in the posterior midbody/isthmus region that contains interhemispheric fibers from primary and secondary auditory cortices – a finding that converges with other reports of developmental differences during the late childhood years, coinciding with reading skill development.

General Brain Imaging Results for Dyslexia

There are general consistencies across phonological, semantic, and syntactic processing in that enhanced activation of the left extrastriate cortex is found when visuospatial, orthographic, phonologic, and semantic processing demands are placed on the dyslexic group (Backes et al., 2002).

Researchers argue that variations in brain processing relate to language and cultural factors – a finding that parallels behavioral investigations of language differences. For example, using fMRI, Siok et al. (2004) reported that functional disruption of the left middle frontal gyrus is associated with impaired reading of the Chinese language (a logographic rather than alphabetic writing system). No disruption was found for the left temporoparietal brain regions. Siok et al. argue that such differences reflect two deficits during reading: the conversion of the orthography (characters) to syllables, and the mapping of the orthography onto the semantics. Both processes, the authors argue, are mediated by the left middle frontal gyrus that coordinates and integrates various information about written Chinese characters in verbal and spatial working memory (see also Eckert et al., 2001; Grigorenko, 2001).

Phonology and Dyslexia

Dyslexic readers show less activation of both the temporal and the prefrontal cortex during phonologic processing (Backes et al., 2002). Intriguingly, similar areas of lowered activation are seen in other populations with reading problems, reinforcing the notion that inferior frontal and superior temporal brain areas support reading skills (e.g., neurofibromatosis; see Backes et al., 2002).

When magnetic source imaging (MSI) was employed during phonological tasks, Papanicolaou et al. (2003) reported consistent brain maps across children that differentiate between dyslexic and nondyslexic children in the left and right posterior temporal regions. Moreover, following reading interventions with the dyslexic children, brain sources shifted from the right to the left hemisphere, indicating that intervention 'normalizes' as the child's brain moves from an ineffective to a more efficient use of brain structures and pathways (Simos et al., 2002; for replication, see Temple et al., 2003).

MEG investigations into the perception of speech cues such as voice onset time (VOT) indicate that children with dyslexia experienced a sharp peak of relative activation in right temporoparietal areas between 300 and 700 milliseconds poststimulus onset, a point markedly later in time (~500 milliseonds) relative to normal readers. This increased late activation in right temporoparietal areas was correlated with reduced performance on phonological processing measures (Breier et al., 2003). Further, there are data indicating an early relation between the perception of speech cues in early infancy and the emergence of reading disorders as late as 8 years of age (Molfese & Molfese, 1985; Molfese, 2000; Molfese et al., 2005; Lyytinen et al., 2003). These studies indicate that infants who go on to develop normal language skills generate ERPs over left frontal and temporal brain regions that discriminate between speech sounds, whereas ERPs collected from infants at risk for developing a reading disorder fail to discriminate between these same sounds.

In phonological related tasks such as rhyming, fMRI differences are found between dyslexic and control children (Corina et al., 2001). During phonological judgment, dyslexics generated more activity than controls in right than left inferior temporal gyrus and in left precentral gyrus (see Georgiewa et al. [1999] for replication). During lexical judgment, dyslexics showed less activation than controls in the bilateral middle frontal gyrus and more activation than controls in the left orbital frontal cortex. In an ERP study paralleling this study, Lovrich et al. (1996) reported that rhyme processing produced more pronounced group differences than semantic processing at about 480 milliseconds, with a relatively more negative distribution for the impaired readers at centroparietal sites. By 800 milliseconds, the impaired readers displayed a late positivity that was delayed in latency and that was of larger amplitude at frontal sites than that for the average readers.

When brain activation patterns were studied in dyslexic and nonimpaired children during pseudoword and real-word reading tasks that required phonologic analysis, differences were noted in posterior brain regions, including parietotemporal sites and sites in the occipitotemporal area. Reading skill overall was positively correlated with the magnitude of activation in the left occipitotemporal region – an area similarly found to discriminate between adult groups of readers and nonreaders (Shaywitz et al., 2002). A similar effect was demonstrated using MEG (Simos et al., 2000).

Semantics and Dyslexia

During lexical judgment, less activation in bilateral middle frontal gyrus and more activation in left orbital frontal cortex occurred for dyslexic compared to nondyslexic children (Corina et al., 2001). In a related task, in which children read words and pronounceable nonwords, fMRI results detected a hyperactivation of the left inferior frontal gyrus in dyslexic children. ERPs collected from the same children converged with the fMRI findings and showed topographic difference between groups at the left frontal electrodes in a time window of 250–600 milliseconds after stimulus onset. A related study by Molfese et al. (in press) reported similar findings, as well as a slower rate of word processing over left hemisphere electrode sites in dyslexic children compared to normal and advanced readers.

Reading and Dyslexia

Relatively few studies have investigated brain activation when the child is reading continuous text (Backes et al., 2002). One exception is a report by Johnstone et al. (1984), who monitored silent and oral reading, noting that reading difficulty affected the central and parietal ERPs of dyslexics but not the controls. In addition, different patterns of asymmetry were found for the two groups in silent compared to oral reading at midtemporal placements.

Down Syndrome

Down syndrome (DS) is characterized by a number of physical characteristics and learning impairments, as well as IQ scores that may range from 50 to 60. Individuals with DS typically are microcephalic and have cognitive and speech impairments, as well as neuromotor dysfunction. In addition, problems generally occur in language, short-term memory, and task shifting. Typical language problems involve delays in articulation, phonology, vocal imitation, mean length utterance (MLU), verbal comprehension, and expressive syntax. Spontaneous language is often telegraphic, with a drastic reduction in the use of function words: articles, prepositions, and pronouns (Chapman et al., 2002). Language deficits may arise from abnormalities noted within the temporal lobe (Welsh, 2003). Individuals afflicted with DS commonly suffer from a mild to moderate hearing loss (78% of DS children have a hearing loss; Stoel-Gammon, 1997), which may partially account for the delay in phonological processing and poor articulation.

DS occurs in approximately 1 in 800–1,000 live births. Ninety to 95% of cases are caused by a full trisomy of chromosome 21, and 5% result from translocation or mosaicism. Considerable individual variability exists in cognitive development among those afflicted, with the greatest deficits in development observed with full trisomy–21, where specific genes have been associated with brain development, specifically the cerebellum development, and produce Alzheimer-type neuropathology, neuronal cell loss, accelerated aging, and so on (Capone, 2001). Individuals with DS commonly exhibit neuropathology resembling that seen in Alzheimer disease, with some patients showing symptoms beginning as early as age 35 years.

General Brain Imaging Results for DS

Brains of DS individuals appear to have a characteristic morphologic appearance that includes decreased size and weight, a foreshortening of the anterior–posterior diameter, reduced frontal lobe volume, and flattening of the occiput. The primary cortical gyri may appear wide, whereas secondary gyri are often poorly developed or absent, with shallow sulci and reduced cerebellar and brain stem size (Capone, 2004). MRI studies indicate a volume reduction for the whole brain, with the cerebral cortex, white matter, and cerebellum totaling 18% (Pinter et al., 2001a). Hippocampal dysfunction occurs in DS (Pennington et al., 2003), perhaps because of the reduced size of the hippocampus, as determined by MRI (Pinter et al., 2001b), and the cerebral cortex has fewer neurons at all cortical layers. In addition, dendritic spines appear longer and thinner than in matched controls (Capone, 2004; Seidl et al., 1997). Studies using MEG indicate atypical cerebral specialization, showing a greater activation of the right hemisphere in DS when compared to normal controls (Welsh, 2002). This greater activation is confirmed by PET studies (Nadel, 2003), indicating that the brain of the DS individual is working harder to process information, although less effectively.

Brain morphology in DS does not differ dramatically from normals throughout the first 6 months of life. Delayed myelination occurring within the cerebral hemispheres, basal ganglia, cerebellum, brain stem, and nerve tracts (fibers linking frontal and temporal lobes) occurs after 6 months (Nadel, 2003; Capone, 2004). Other critical periods of brain development affected by DS include neuronal differentiation, proliferation, and organization. A reduction in neuronal number and density was noted for most brain areas examined, specifically within interneurons and pyramidal neurons. However, this differs on a case-to-case basis and has been hypothesized as a potential explanation for the spectrum of neurodevelopment impairment observed (Capone, 2004).

Phonology and DS

Research of neural function indicates that in DS there may be a delay in the development of the auditory system (Nadel, 2003). Phonological delays exhibited in DS cases are often linked to differences in anatomy and central nervous system development in DS. In addition, limits on auditory working memory and hearing may account for deficits observed in phonological processing (Tager-Flusberg, 1999).

Semantics and DS

Dichotic listening tasks involving DS children generally result in a left-ear advantage, indicating that these individuals use their right hemisphere to process for speech (Welsh, 2002). On the basis of such findings, Capone (2004) argued that difficulties in semantic processing in DS occur from a reduction in cerebral and cerebellar volume. In addition, the corpus callosum is thinner in the DS brain in the rostral fifth, the area associated with semantic communication. Welsh (2002) speculated that the thinner corpus callosum isolates the two hemispheres from each other, making it more difficult to integrate verbal information.

Vocabulary growth in DS children is delayed increasingly with age (Chapman, 2002). Studies using dichotic listening tasks report a left-ear advantage for DS, indicating that lexical operations are carried out primarily in the right hemisphere, a finding opposite to that found with normal developing children. In fact, individuals with DS who exhibit the most severe language deficits demonstrate the most atypical ear advantage (Welsh, 2002).

Syntax and DS

Children with DS exhibit a delay in syntax production that generally becomes evident with the emergence of two-word utterances, and syntax is often more severely impaired than lexical development (Chapman, 1997). Verbal short-term memory may be affected, limiting the ability to understand syntactic relations. Research on short-term memory points to hippocampal dysfunction in DS children (Pinter et al., 2001a). MRI studies of adults with DS highlight the possibility that reductions in volume size observed in DS may contribute to the development of language and memory deficits. It has been hypothesized that the cause of language deficits observed in children with DS are primarily related to memory and learning and are most associated with deficits observed in the hippocampal region (Nadel, 2003).

Specific Language Impairment

It is estimated that approximately 7% of the 5-year-old population is characterized with specific language impairment (SLI), and that SLI is three times more likely in males than females. The basic criteria underlying this disorder include normal intelligence (IQ of 85 or higher), language impairment (language test score of −1.25 sd (standard deviation) or lower), no neurological dysfunctions or structural anomalies, successful completion of a hearing screening, and no impairment in social interactions. Speculations as to causes focus on the biological and environmental issues, but with no resolution. Because of the heterogeneity of the phenotype, it is difficult to study this population as a single unit (Leonard, 1998). As a consequence, results and conclusions resulting from any particular study are limited to the specific subset of SLI under study.

Phonology and SLI

A phonological processing delay exists in children with SLI, where the children have a problem distinguishing similar spoken sounds (i.e., /b/ vs. /p/) from one another, as well as show lower accuracy in processing speech sounds at rapid ISI (interstimulus intervals). Improvement occurs with age in SLI children; however, the plateau reached is still below normal levels. ERP patterns of older SLI children in comparison with same-age and younger control children show a correlation in brain wave patterns to that of the younger population in response to auditory tone presentation. An auditory immaturity hypothesis is indicated as a basis for the delay in phonological processing in SLI. This hypothesis points to the auditory system as the basis for developmental delays found in SLI children (Bishop et al., 2004). In fact, an fMRI study showed that individuals with SLI had less activation in brain regions specific to language processing as well as phonological awareness (Hugdahl et al., 2004). Furthermore, MMN (mismatch negativity), a region of the ERP that is an indicator of stimulus discrimination, indicates a deficit in discrimination of CV (consonant–vowel) syllables that differ in the place of articulation in SLI children (Uwer et al., 2002). Infants as early as 8 weeks of age who are at risk for SLI are already showing MMN delays in their latency response when presented with auditory speech sounds (Friedrich, 2004). These findings indicate that delays in discrimination skills are present from an early stage of development.

Semantics and SLI

Semantic abilities are problematic in SLI. Investigations into the neural substrate of these issues have made some headway in recent years. In particular, the N400 (Kutas and Hillyard, 1980), a large negative component of the ERP that correlates with semantic ability and occurs approximately 400 milliseconds after a stimulus begins, is altered in populations of SLI children, as well as in their parents. This brain component is enhanced in fathers of SLI children compared to controls in response to the unexpected ending of a sentence (Ors et al., 2001). For example, the N400 response is normally larger in response to the last word in the sentence, 'The train runs on the banana' than if the final word is 'track.' Atypical N400 amplitudes also are found in children with other language deficits (Neville et al., 1993). MEG studies have pinpointed the lateral temporal region as the origin of the N400 response (Simos et al., 1997). Intracortical depth recordings in response to written words point to the medial temporal structures near the hippocampus and amygdala (Smith et al., 1986).

William's Syndrome

William's-Beuren syndrome (WS) results from a rare genetic deficit (about 1 in 20 000 births) caused by a microdeletion on chromosome 7 (Levitin et al., 2003). This genetic etiology present in WS allows researchers to identify developmental abnormalities associated with WS from birth. Characteristics of WS include dysmorphic facial features, mental retardation, and a unique behavioral phenotype (Bellugi et al., 1999, 2000; Levitin et al., 2003). Recently, Mervis and colleagues (Mervis, in press; Mervis et al., 2003) have formulated a cognitive profile for WS by analyzing the relative weaknesses and strengths often associated with the genetic syndrome. Markers for this profile include a very low IQ and weakness in visuospatial construction, as well as strengths in recognition of faces, verbal memory, and language abilities. These findings have been replicated by other researchers (Galaburda et al., 2003).

Anatomical Aspects of WS

MRI studies note anatomical differences in brain morphology in WS that include a bilateral decrease in the dorsal posterior regions in both hemispheres with an increase in the superior temporal gyrus, frontal lobe, and amygdala (Galaburda et al., 2003). Schmitt et al. (2001a) recorded MRI images in 20 individuals with WS (age: 19–44 years) compared to 20 age- and gender-matched participants. In WS adults, the midsagittal corpus callosum was reduced in total area, and within the corpus callosum, the isthmus and splenium were disproportionately smaller. However, the frontal lobe and cerebellum were similar in size to those of controls (Schmitt et al., 2001b). The decrease in volume within the corpus callosum and the parietal lobe has led many researchers to speculate that these findings could explain visuospatial weaknesses in this population (Schmitt et al., 2001a; Eckert et al., 2005). Other studies indicate abnormal clustering of neurons in the visual cortex (Lenhoff et al., 1997). In contrast, the language strength predominately found in WS children may be caused, based on the MRI data, by the relatively unimpaired frontal lobe and cerebellum and the enlarged planum temporale (auditory region), particularly in the left hemisphere (Lenhoff et al., 1997; Bellugi et al., 1999, 2000).

Semantics and WS

Studies indicate that WS children are capable of semantic organization, although the onset is often delayed (Mervis and Bertrand, 1997; Mervis, in press). WS children tend to list low-frequency words when asked to complete the task (Mervis, in press). In studies of lexical and semantic processing, unique ERP patterns are recorded from WS children to auditory stimuli during a sentence completion task that includes anomaly words at the end of the sentence (Bellugi et al., 2000). In general, the expected component at N400 associated with anomaly words in WS was more evenly distributed across the scalp, with no hemispheric interaction (Bellugi et al., 2000). This finding is unusual, given the left-hemisphere activation common in typically developing children (Bellugi et al., 2000). In addition, during the positive peak at 50 milliseconds, WS individuals produced an abnormally large spike. A 'smaller than normal' negative peak at 100 milliseconds and a large positive peak at 200 milliseconds can be seen in the WS population, but not within normal controls (Bellugi et al., 1999).

Phonology and WS

Little research has examined the neural bases for phonological processing in children with WS. A current study by Fornaryova Key et al. (in progress) examined the brain's response to speech syllables (/ba/ and /ga/) in eight children with WS (age: 4.03–4.64 years). The results indicate that the left hemispheric of WS children is engaged in discriminating between different speech sounds, rather than showing the lack of hemisphere differences that Bellugi et al. (2000) would predict. In addition, variations in the second large positive ERP component (P2) to speech sounds correlated highly with a range of language and verbal abilities, such as those needed for performance on the Matrices subtest of the K-BIT.

Syntax and WS

In normal, age-matched controls, ERP responses to nouns, adjectives, and verbs (or open-class words) tend to invoke a N400 peak in the right posterior lobe. Words like articles, conjunctions, and prepositions (or close-class words) elicit an early negativity peak in the anterior portion of the left hemisphere (Bellugi et al., 1999). Using ERPs to open and closed-class word stimuli, WS subjects do not display the typical evoked pattern at the N400 peak for open-class words in the right hemisphere, but instead, a negativity in the left hemisphere was found (see Bellugi et al., 1999). For closed-class words, the typical left-hemisphere pattern found in normal subjects is not found in individuals with WS (Bellugi et al., 1999). These findings indicate that the neural functional organization for syntactic processing is different for individuals with WS, even though results from MRI studies report similar frontal lobe and cerebellum sizes to matched age and sex controls (Bellugi et al., 1999, 2000).

Summary and Conclusion

Across the five developmental disability areas reviewed here, much is already known about the underlying neural bases for some impaired phonological processes, but exceptionally little is known concerning the neural underpinnings of other deficits involving syntactical processing. At the same time, in areas where some research is available, it is evident that language deficits are not unique to a single syndrome and do not result from the dysfunction in a single, discrete brain structure. Rather, language disorders are multidimensional and involve neural processes that arise out of complex interactions between multiple cortical brain regions, and neural pathways, as well as from genetic factors whose phenotypic expression is mitigated through dynamic environmental factors. There are, no doubt, other as-yet-unknown factors. Clearly, we are still in the earliest stages of our quest to understand the complex relationships that exist between developmental language disabilities and the brain. Lest we get discouraged, it is important to keep in mind is that we at least have begun that quest.

Acknowledgments

This work was supported in part by grants to D. L. M. (NIH/NHLB HL01006, NIH/NIDCD DC005994, NIH/NIDA DA017863) and V. J. M. (DOE R215R000023, HHS 90XA0011).

Bibliography

Adolphs, R, Tranel, D, Damasio, H, and Damasio, AR (1995). 'Fear and the human amygdala.' *Journal of Neuroscience,* 15: 5879–5891.
Akshoomoff, N, Pierce, K, and Courchesne, E (2002). 'The neurobiological basis of autism from a developmental perspective.' *Development and Psychopathology* 14: 613–634.
Alt, M, Plante, E, and Creusere, M (2004). 'Semantic features in fast mapping: performance of preschoolers with specific language impairment versus preschoolers with normal language.' *Journal of Speech, Language and Hearing Research* 47: 407–420.
American Psychiatric Association (1994). *Diagnostic and statistical manual of mental disorders,* 4th edn. Washington, DC: American Psychiatric Association.
Backes, W, Vuurman, E, Wennekes, R, Spronk, P, Wuisman, M, van Engelshoven, J, and Jolles, J (2002). 'Atypical brain activation of reading processes in children with developmental dyslexia.' *Journal of Child Neurology* 17: 867–871.
Bellugi, U, Lichtenberger, L, Mills, D, Galaburda, A, and Korenber, JR (1999). 'Bridging cognition, the brain and molecular genetics: evidence from Williams syndrome.' *Trends in Neuroscience* 22(5): 197–207.
Bellugi, U, Lichtenberger, L, Jones, W, and Lai, Z (2000). 'I. The neurocognitive profile of Williams syndrome: a complex pattern of strengths and weaknesses.' *Journal of Cognitive Neuroscience* 12(1): 7–29.
Billingsley, RL, Jackson, EF, Slopis, JM, Swank, PR, Mahankali, S, and Moore, BD 3rd(2003). 'Functional magnetic resonance imaging of phonologic processing in neurofibromatosis 1.' *Journal of Child Neurology,* 18: 731–740.
Bishop, DVM and McArthur, GM (2004). 'Immature cortical responses to auditory stimuli in specific language impairment: evidence from ERPs to rapid tone sequences.' *Developmental Science* 7: 11–18.
Brambilla, P, Hardan, A, Ucelli di Nemi, S, Perez, J, Soares, JC, and Barale, F (2003). 'Brain anatomy and development in autism: review of structural MRI studies.' *Brain Research Bulletin* 61: 557–569.
Breier, JI, Simos, PG, Fletcher, JM, Castillo, EM, Zhang, W, and Papanicolaou, AC (2003). 'Abnormal activation of temporoparietal language areas during phonetic analysis in children with dyslexia.' *Neuropsychology* 17: 610–621.
Bruneau, N, Roux, S, Guerin, P, and Barthelemy, C (1997). 'Temporal prominence of auditory evoked potentials (N1 wave) in 4–8-year-old children.' *Psychophysiology* 34: 32–38.
Buckley, S (2000). 'Teaching reading to develop speech and language.' Presented at the 3rd International Conference on Language and Cognition in Down Syndrome, Portsmouth, UK.

Camarata, S and Yoder, P (2002). 'Language transactions during development and intervention: theoretical implications for developmental neuroscience.' *International Journal of Neuroscience* 20: 459–465.

Capone, GT (2001). 'Down syndrome: advances in molecular biology and the neurosciences.' *Developmental and Behavioral Pediatrics* 22: 40–59.

Capone, GT (2004). 'Down syndrome: genetic insights and thoughts of early intervention.' *Infants and Young Children* 17: 45–58.

Chapman, RS (1997). 'Language development in children and adolescents with Down syndrome.' *Mental Retardation and Developmental Disabilities Research Reviews* 3: 307–312.

Chapman, RS, Hesketh, LJ, and Kistler, DJ (2002). 'Predicting longitudinal change in language production and comprehension in individuals with Down syndrome: hierarchical linear modeling.' *Journal of Speech, Language, and Hearing Research* 45: 902–915.

Corina, DP, Richards, TL, Serafini, S, Richards, AL, Steury, K, Abbott, RD, Echelard, DR, Maravilla, KR, and Berninger, VW (2001). 'fMRI auditory language differences between dyslexic and able reading children.' *Neuroreport* 12: 1195–1201.

Dawson, G, Meltzoff, AN, and Osterling, J (1998). 'Children with autism fail to orient to naturally occuring social stimuli.' *Journal of Autism and Developmental Disorders* 28(6): 479–485.

Dawson, G, Webb, S, Schellenberg, GD, Dager, S, Friedman, S, Aylward, E, and Richards, T (2002). 'Defining the broader phenotype of autism: genetic, brain, and behavioral perspectives.' *Development and Psychopathology* 14: 581–611.

Dunn, M, Vaughan, H, Jr., Kreuzer, J, and Kurtzberg, D (1999). 'Electrophysiologic correlates of semantic classification in autistic and normal children.' *Developmental Neuropsychology* 16: 79–99.

Eckert, MA, Hu, D, Eliez, S, Bellugi, U, Galaburda, A, Korenberg, J, Mills, D, and Reiss, AL (2005). 'Evidence for superior parietal impairment in Williams syndrome.' *Neurology* 64(1): 152–153.

Eckert, MA, Leonard, CM, Richards, TL, Aylward, EH, Thomson, J, and Berninger, VW (2003). 'Anatomical correlates of dyslexia: frontal and cerebellar findings.' *Brain* 126: 482–494.

Eckert, MA, Lombardino, LJ, and Leonard, CM (2001). 'Planar asymmetry tips the phonological playground and environment raises the bar.' *Child Development* 72: 988–1002.

Eden, GF, VanMeter, JW, Rumsey, JM, and Zeffiro, TA (1996). 'The visual deficit theory of developmental dyslexia.' *Neuroimage* 4: S108–S117.

Eggermont, JJ (1988). 'On the rate of maturation of sensory evoked potentials.' *Electroencephalography and Clinical Neurophysiology* 70: 293–305.

Fombonne, E (1999). 'The epidemiology of autism: a review.' *Psychological Medicine* 29: 768–786.

Fonaryova Key, AP, Dove, GO and Maguire, MJ (In press). 'Linking brainwaves to the brain: an ERP primer.' *Developmental Neuropsychology.*

Fonaryova Key, AP, Mervis, C and Molfese, DL (in progress). 'ERPs to speech sounds over the left hemisphere are linked to language and cognitive abilities in 4-year-old children with Williams syndrome.

Frank, Y and Pavlakis, SG (2001). 'Brain imaging in neurobehavioral disorders.' *Pediatric Neurology* 25: 278–287.

Freidrich, M, Weber, C, and Freiderici, DD (2004). 'Electrophysiological evidence for delayed mismatch response in infants at risk for specific language impairment.' *Psychophysiology* 41: 772–782.

Gage, NM, Siegel, B, and Roberts, TPL (2003). 'Cortical auditory system maturational abnormalities in children with autism disorder: an MEG investigation.' *Developmental Brain Research* 144: 201–209.

Galaburda, AM, Hollinger, D, Mills, D, Reiss, A, Korenberg, J R, and Bellugi, U (2003). 'Williams syndrome: A summary of cognitive, electrophysiological, anatomofunctional, microanatomical and genetic findings.' *Revista de Neurologia* 36(1): 132–137.

Georgiewa, P, Rzanny, R, Gaser, C, Gerhard, UJ, Vieweg, U, Freesmeyer, D, Mentzel, HJ, Kaiser, WA, and Blanz, B (2002). 'Phonological processing in dyslexic children: a study combining functional imaging and event related potentials.' *Neuroscience Letters* 318: 5–8.

Georgiewa, P, Rzanny, R, Hopf, JM, Knab, R, Glauche, V, Kaiser, WA, and Blanz, B (1999). 'fMRI during word processing in dyslexic and normal reading children.' *Neuroreport* 10: 3459–3465.

Grigorenko, EL (2001). 'Developmental dyslexia: an update on genes, brains, and environments.' *Journal of Child Psychology and Psychiatry* 42: 91–125.

Grunling, C, Ligges, M, Huonker, R, Klingert, M, Mentzel, HJ, Rzanny, R, Kaiser, WA, Witte, H, and Blanz, B (2004). 'Dyslexia: the possible benefit of multimodal integration of fMRI- and EEG-data.' *Journal of Neural Transmission* 111: 951–969.

Habib, M (2000). 'The neurological basis of developmental dyslexia: an overview and working hypothesis.' *Brain* 123: 2373–2399.

Happe, FGE (1995). 'The role of age and verbal ability in the theory of mind task performance of subjects with autism.' *Child Development* 66: 843–855.

Harter, MR, Anllo-Vento, L, Wood, FB, and Schroeder, MM (1988a). 'Separate brain potential characteristics in children with reading disability and attention deficit disorder: color and letter relevance effects.' *Brain and Cognition* 7: 115–140.

Harter, MR, Diering, S, and Wood, FB (1988b). 'Separate brain potential characteristics in children with reading disability and attention deficit disorder: relevance-independent effects.' *Brain and Cognition* 7: 54–86.

Heiervang, E, Hugdahl, K, Steinmetz, H, Inge Smievoll, A, Stevenson, J, Lund, A, Ersland, L, and Lundervold, A (2000). 'Planum temporale, planum parietale and dichotic listening in dyslexia.' *Neuropsychologia* 38: 1704–1713.

Heim, S and Keil, A (2004). 'Large-scale neural correlates of developmental dyslexia.' *European Child and Adolescent Psychiatry* 13: 125–140.

Hiemenz, JR and Hynd, GW (2000). 'Sulcal/gyral pattern morphology of the perisylvian language region in developmental dyslexia.' *Brain and Language* 74: 113–133.

Holcomb, PJ, Ackerman, PT, and Dykman, RA (1986). 'Auditory event-related potentials in attention and reading disabled boys.' *International Journal of Psychophysiology* 3: 263–273.

Houston, HG and McClelland, RJ (1985). 'Age and gender contributions to intersubject variability of the auditory brainstem potentials.' *Biological Psychiatry* 20: 419–430.

Hugdahl, K, Gunderson, H, Brekke, C, Thomsen, T, and Morten-Rimol, L (2004). 'fMRI brain activation in a Finnish family with specific language impairment compared with a normal control group.' *Journal of Speech, Language, and Hearing Research* 47: 162–172.

Hugdahl, K, Heiervang, E, Nordby, H, Smievoll, AI, Steinmetz, H, Stevenson, J, and Lund, A (1998). 'Central auditory processing, MRI morphometry and brain laterality: applications to dyslexia.' *Scandanavian Audiology Supplement* 49: 26–34.

Hynd, GW and Semrud-Clikeman, M (1989). 'Dyslexia and brain morphology.' *Psychological Bulletin* 106: 447–482.

Johnstone, J, Galin, D, Fein, G, Yingling, C, Herron, J, and Marcus, M (1984). 'Regional brain activity in dyslexic and control children during reading tasks: visual probe event-related potentials.' *Brain and Language* 21: 233–254.

Joseph, J, Noble, K, and Eden, G (2001). 'The neurobiological basis of reading.' *Journal of Learning Disabilities* 34: 566–579.

Kemner, C, Verbaten, MN, Cuperus, JM, and Camfferman, G (1995). 'Auditory event-related brain potentials in autistic children and three different control groups.' *Biological Psychiatry* 38: 150–165.

Kjelgaard, MM and Tager-Flusberg, H (2001). 'An investigation of language impairment in autism: implications for genetic subgroups.' *Language and Cognitive Processes* 16: 287–308.

Kutas, M and Hillyard, SA (1980). 'Reading senseless sentences: brain potentials reflect semantic incongruity.' *Science* 207: 203–205.

Lenhoff, HM, Wang, PP, Greenberg, F, and Bellugi, U (1997). 'Williams syndrome and the brain.' *Scientific American* 277(6): 68–73.

Leonard, CM, Lombardino, LJ, Walsh, K, Eckert, MA, Mockler, JL, Rowe, LA, Williams, S, and DeBose, CB (2002). 'Anatomical risk factors that distinguish dyslexia from SLI predict reading skill in normal children.' *Journal of Communicative Disorders* 35: 501–531.

Leonard, L (1998). *Children with specific language impairment.* Cambridge, MA: MIT Press.

Levitin, DJ, Menon, V, Schmitt, JF, Eliez, S, White, CD, Glover, GH, Kadis, J, Korenberg, JR, Bellugi, U, and Reiss, AL (2003). Neural correlates of auditory perception in Williams syndrome: an fMRI study. *Neuroimage* 18(1): 74–82.

Lincoln, AJ, Courchesne, E, Harms, L, and Allen, M (1995). 'Sensory modulation of auditory stimuli in children with autism and receptive developmental language disorder: event related brain potential evidence.' *Journal of Autism and Developmental Disorders* 25: 521–539.

Lincoln, AJ, Courchesne, E, Harms, L, and Allen, M (1995). 'Sensory modulation of auditory stimuli in children with autism and receptive developmental language disorder: event related brain potential evidence.' *Journal of Autism and Developmental Disorders* 25: 521–539.

Lord, C and Paul, R (1997). 'Language and communication in autism.' In: Cohen, DJ and Volkmar, FR (eds.) *Handbook of autism and pervasive development disorders,* 2nd edn. New York: Wiley.

Lovrich, D, Cheng, JC, and Velting, DM (1996). 'Late cognitive brain potentials, phonological and semantic classification of spoken words, and reading ability in children.' *Journal of Clinical and Experimental Neuropsychology* 18: 161–177.

Lyytinen, H, Leppänen, PHT, Richardson, U, and Guttorm, TK (2003). 'Brain functions and speech perception in infants at risk for dyslexia.' In: Csépe, V (ed.) *Dyslexia: different brain, different behaviour*, pp. 113–152. Dordrecht: Kluwer.

Marchman, VA, Wulfeck, B, and Weismer, SE (1999). 'Morphological productivity in children with normal language and SLI: a study of the English past tense.' *Journal of Speech, Language and Hearing Research* 42: 206–219.

Mervis, C (in press). 'Recent research on language abilities in Williams–Beuren syndrome: a review.' In: Morris, CA, Wang, PP, and Lenhoff, H (eds.) *Williams–Beuren Syndrome: Research and Clinical Perspectives*. Baltimore, MD: Johns Hopkins University Press.

Mervis, CB, and Bertrand, J (1997). 'Developmental relations between cognition and language: evidence from Williams syndrome.' In: Adamson, LB, and Romski, MA (eds.) *Communication and language acquisition: discoveries from atypical development.* New York: Brookes. 75–106.

Mervis, CB, Robinson, BF, Rowe, ML, Becerra, AM, and Klein-Tasman, BP (2003). 'Language abilities of individuals who have Williams syndrome.' In: Abbeduto, L (ed.) *International Review of Research in Mental Retardation,* vol. 27. Orlando, Fl: Academic Press. 35–81.

Molfese, DL (2000). 'Predicting dyslexia at 8 years using neonatal brain responses.' *Brain and Language* 72: 238–245.

Molfese, DL, and Betz, JC (1988). 'Electrophysiological indices of the early development of lateralization for language and cognition and their implications for predicting later development.' In: Molfese, DL, and Segalowitz, SJ (eds.) *The developmental implications of brain lateralization for language and cognitive development.* New York: Guilford Press. 171–190.

Molfese, DL and Molfese, VJ (1985). 'Electrophysiological indices of auditory discrimination in newborn infants: the bases for predicting later language development.' *Infant Behavior and Development* 8: 197–211.

Molfese, DL, Fonaryova Key, A, Kelly, S, Cunningham, N, Terrell, S, Fergusson, M, Molfese, V, and Bonebright, T (In press). 'Dyslexic, average, and above average readers engage different and similar brain regions while reading.' *Journal of Learning Disabilities.*

Molfese, DL, Fonaryova Key, AP, Maguire, MJ, Dove, GO, and Molfese, VJ (2005). 'Event-related evoked potentials (ERPs) in speech perception.' In: Pisoni, D and Remez, R (eds.) *Handbook of speech perception.* London: Blackwell.

Nadel, L (2003). 'Down's syndrome: a genetic disorder in biobehavioral perspective.' *Genes, Brain and Behavior* 2: 156–166.

Neville, HJ, Coffey, SA, Holcomb, PJ, and Tallal, P (1993). 'The neurobiology of sensory and language processing in language-impaired children.' *Journal of Cognitive Neurosciences* 5: 235–253.

Oades, RD, Walker, MK, and Geffen, LB (1988). 'Event-related potentials in autistic and healthy children on an auditory choice relation time task.' *International Journal of Psychophysiology* 6(1): 25–37.

Ors, M, Lindgren, M, Berglund, C, Hagglund, K, Rosen, I, and Blennow, G (2001). 'The N400 component in parents of children with specific language impairment.' *Brain and Language* 77: 60–71.

Orton, S (1937). *Reading, writing and speech problems in children.* New York: Horton.

Papanicolaou, AC, Simos, PG, Breier, JI, Fletcher, JM, Foorman, BR, Francis, D, Castillo, EM, and Davis, RN (2003). 'Brain mechanisms for reading in children with and without dyslexia: a review of studies of normal development and plasticity.' *Developmental Neuropsychology* 24: 593–612.

Pennington, BF, Moon, J, Edgin, J, Stedron, J, and Nadel, L (2003). 'The neuropsychology of Down syndrome: evidence for hippocampal dysfunction.' *Child Development* 74: 75–93.

Pinter, JD, Brown, WE, Eliez, S, Schmitt, J, Capone, GT, and Reiss, AL (2001a). 'Amygdala and hippocampal volumes in children with Down syndrome: a high-resolution MRI study.' *Neurology* 56: 972–974.

Pinter, JD, Stephan, E, Schmitt, J, Capone, GT, and Reiss, AL (2001b). 'Neuroanatomy of Down's syndrome: a high-resolution MRI study.' *The American Journal of Psychiatry* 158: 1659–1671.

Rapin, I and Dunn, M (2003). 'Update on the language disorders of individuals on the autistic spectrum.' *Brain and Development* 25: 166–172.

Sarkari, S, Simos, PG, Fletcher, JM, Castillo, EM, Breier, JI, and Papanicolaou, AC (2002). 'Contributions of magnetic source imaging to the understanding of dyslexia.' *Seminars in Pediatric Neurology* 9: 229–238.

Schmitt, JF, Eliez, S, Warsofsky, LS, Bellugi, U, and Reiss, AL (2001a). 'Corpus callosum morphology of Williams syndrome: relation to genetics and behaviour.' *Developmental Medicine and Child Neurology* 43(3): 155–159.

Schmitt, JF, Eliez, S, Warsofsky, LS, Bellugi, U, and Reiss, AL (2001b). 'Enlarged cerebellar vermis in Williams syndrome.' *Journal of Psychiatric Research* 35(4): 225–229.

Seidl, R, Hauser, E, Bernert, G, Marx, Freilinger, M, and Lubec, G (1997). 'Auditory evoked potentials in young patients with Down syndrome. Event-related potentials (P3) and histaminergic system.' *Cognitive Brain Research* 5: 301–309.

Seri, S, Cerquiglini, A, Pisani, F, and Curatolo, P (1999). 'Autism in tuberous sclerosis: Evoked potential evidence for a deficit in auditory sensory processing.' *Clinical Neurophysiology* 110: 1825–1830.

Shaywitz, BA, Shaywitz, SE, Pugh, KR, Mencl, WE, Fulbright, RK, Skudlarski, P, Constable, RT, Marchione, KE, Fletcher, JM, Lyon, GR, and Gore, JC (2002). 'Disruption of posterior brain systems for reading in children with developmental dyslexia.' *Biological Psychiatry* 52: 101–110.

Simos, PG, Breier, JI, Fletcher, JM, Foorman, BR, Bergman, E, Fishbeck, K, and Papanicolaou, AC (2000). 'Brain activation profiles in dyslexic children during non-word reading: a magnetic source imaging study.' *Neuroscience Letters* 290: 61–65.

Simos, PG, Fletcher, JM, Bergman, E, Breier, JI, Foorman, BR, Castillo, EM, Davis, RN, Fitzgerald, M, and Papanicolaou, A C (2002). 'Dyslexia-specific brain activation profile becomes normal following successful remedial training.' *Neurology* 58: 1203–1213.

Simos, PG, Basile, LFH, and Papanicolaou, AC (1997). 'Source localization of the N400 response in a sentence-reading paradigm using evoked magnetic fields and magnetic resonance imaging.' *Brain Research* 762: 29–39.

Siok, WT, Perfetti, CA, Jin, Z, and Tan, LH (2004). 'Biological abnormality of impaired reading is constrained by culture.' *Nature* 431: 71–76.

Smith, ME, Stapleton, JM, and Halgren, E (1986). 'Human medial temporal lobe potentials evoked in memory and language tasks.' *Electroencephalography & Clinical Neurophysiology* 63: 145–159.

Sparks, GF, Friedman, SD, Shaw, DW, Aylward, EH, Echelard, D, Artru, AA, Maravilla, KR, Giedd, HN, Munson, J, Dawson, G, and Dager, SR (2002). 'Brain structural abnormalities in young children with autism spectrum disorder.' *Neurology* 59: 184–192.

Stoel-Gammon, C (1997). 'Phonological development in Down syndrome.' *Mental Retardation and Developmental Disabilities Research Reviews* 3: 300–306.

Stoel-Gammon, C (2001). 'Down syndrome: developmental patterns and intervention strategies.' *Down Syndrome Research and Practice* 7: 93–100.

Tager-Flusberg, H (1999). 'Language development in atypical children.' In: Barrett, M (ed.) *The development of language*, pp. 311–348. London: UCL Press.
Temple, E, Deutsch, GK, Poldrack, RA, Miller, SL, Tallal, P, Merzenich, MM, and Gabrieli, JD (2003). 'Neural deficits in children with dyslexia ameliorated by behavioral remediation: evidence from functional MRI.' *Proceedings of the National Academy of Science USA* 100: 2860–2865.
Travis, L (1931). *Speech pathology.* New York: Appleton-Century.
Uwer, R, Albert, R, and von Suchodoletz, W (2002). 'Automatic processing of tones and speech stimuli in children with specific language impairment.' *Developmental Medicine and Child Neurology* 44: 527–532.
von Plessen, K, Lundervold, A, Duta, N, Heiervang, E, Klauschen, F, Smievoll, AI, Ersland, L, and Hugdahl, K (2002). 'Less developed corpus callosum in dyslexic subjects – a structural MRI study.' *Neuropsychologia* 40: 1035–1044.
Welsh, TN, Digby, E, and Simon, D (2002). 'Cerebral specialization and verbal-motor integration in adults with and without Down syndrome.' *Brain and Language* 84: 153–169.
Whalen, PJ, Rauch, SL, Etcoff, NL, McInerney, SC, Lee, MB, and Jenike, MA (1998). 'Masked presentation of emotional face expression modulates amygdala activity without explicit knowledge.' *Journal of Neuroscience* 18: 411–418.

Phonology

L. Phengrasamy and B. Miller

Language is a complex and intricate system within the brain and relies on other systems to complete the process of communication, such as the motor speech system. Speech production is an important part of language and communication processes. A study of the spoken language system is called phonology. The sounds placed together or the systematic organization of selected speech sounds to form vocalized words in individual languages is part of phonology.

Three distinct phonological processes have an affect on sound production. One is the set of sounds used in a language. An example is the tonal production of words in Chinese. The tone of similar-sounding words gives each word its different meaning. Another process is the arrangement of sounds to produce distinct and understandable words. The third process that affects sound production is that of sound addition and deletion.

Within the phonological processes there are physical elements. The "articulatory" organs, which are attributed to sound production, comprise the tongue, lips, palate, and teeth. These articulatory organs are controlled by the pyramidal tract, the nervous system pathway that controls voluntary muscle movements. The physical elements are further broken down into two categories for which these processes are responsible. The resonance and articulation of sounds involve the hard palate and teeth. For example, a missing tooth can cause a person to have trouble with pronunciation because they lack the sharpness in sound production with the /s/ and /z/. The soft palate, lips, and tongue are responsible for phonetic components such as the pronouncing of vowels, consonant, and the consonant–vowel syllables. Each vowel is produced based on the positioning of the tongue and the shape of the lips. Consonants are produced with the help of the levator veli palatani muscle, which controls the soft palate, and the narrowing of the vocal tract. These organs are important to the phonological process of speech. Also, the size of the articulatory organs plays a role in one's ability to make precise speech articulation.

Disorders

A type of disorder that interferes with phonological processes is called dysarthria. It is a motor problem but more specifically a neurological disorder of speech (articulation) caused by damage to the motor cortex (located in the frontal lobe) or the cranial nerves. Not only can dysarthria be caused by lesions to the upper motor neurons but also any weakness or malfunctioning to any structures related to speech production can be caused by a series of lesions that occur at different levels in the nervous system: to the upper motor neurons bilaterally at any level, from the cortex to the nuclei of the cranial nerves; to the extrapyramidal system; to the cerebellum; and to the lower motor neurons. Dysarthria is defined as any disturbance of articulation or speech, but a more refined definition is needed to distinguish it from other speech disorder such as speech apraxia. In a more narrow definition, dysarthria is a motor speech disturbance of phonation, articulation, and resonance due to the abnormal neuromusculature actions that change the speed, strength, range, timing, or accuracy of the speech output. The symptoms of dysarthria are slurred speech or paralysis of the speech musculature.

There are many types of dysarthria, depending on the affected structure. One subtype of dysarthria is paralytic dysarthria, categorized by paralysis of the lower motor neurons of the cranial nerves. An example is paralysis of the hypoglossal nerve that controls the articulatory movements resulting in the impairment of movements of the tongue. The inability to move the tongue results in loss of controlled speech. There are other types of disorders of the tongue that prevent precise phonological output, such as Beckwith–Wiedeman syndrome, which also causes difficulty in producing precise articulation or speech. A feature associated with Beckwith–Wiedeman syndrome is macroglossia (enlargement of the tongue). This enlargement prevents the patient from placing their tongue within the oral space either when resting or when speaking, thus preventing the tongue from functioning properly during speech. Macroglossia can be resolved through surgical reduction and with the help of a speech pathologist.

A lesion of the upper motor neuron in the motor cortex or in the fiber tracts that originate from the motor cortex causes another type of dysarthria called spastic dysarthria. This type of dysarthria is characterized by inaccurate speech production of consonants, monopitch, and reduced stress speech. A weak voice in spastic dysarthric is due to excessive muscle tone.

A cerebellar lesion produces a type of dysarthria called ataxic dysarthria. The symptoms of ataxic dysarthria are the incoordination of speech due to reduced muscle tone, thus causing slowness, and inaccuracy in timing, range, force, and direction of speech actions. Therefore, it is unlike spastic dysarthria, in which there is weak speech production, but there is more uncoordinated speech in ataxic dysarthria.

A lesion in the basal ganglia causes hypokinetic dysarthria. This subtype of dysarthria is caused by rigidity and/or reduced range of movements. One of the prominent symptoms of hypokinetic dysarthria is the "inappropriate silences" caused by trouble initiating movements. In addition to the symptoms mentioned previously, dysphonia (involuntary contractions of the laryngeal muscles) can also be associated with dysarthria. An early sign of hypokinetic dysarthria is breathiness and reduction in loudness. In particular, there are three forms of dysphonia—adductor, abductor, and mixed—that have either a neurogenic (a neurological lesion) or psychogenic (psychological stress) cause. The adductor type is a more common spasmodic dysphonia and is differentiated by a strained, tight, and strangled voice. The abductor type generates a breathy voice, which can be found in some hypokinetic dysarthria. The mixed type of dysphonia produces intermittent strained and breathy qualities.

Conclusion

The study of phonology provides a better understanding of the correlation between the motor cortex, cranial nerves, and the articulatory organs. The motor cortex is the control center for speech production, and if there is an insult to this area then controlled speech production will be difficult to retain. This also holds for the cranial nerves, which provide the connection from the motor cortex to the articulatory organs. If speech disorder is the result of a damaged articulatory system, then controlled speech production may be restored to a certain degree.

Tests have been developed to help diagnose probable speech disorder and locate problematic areas of speech production. Neurologists use these tests to diagnose speech disorders such as dysarthria in patients with dementia. Phonology is one of the more concrete areas of language and language problems.

See also: Language and Discourse; Memory, Semantic; Reading and Acquired Dyslexia; Speech Disorders, Overview.

Further Reading

Bentin, S (1989). Electrophysiological studies of visual word perception, lexical organization, and semantic processing: A tutorial review. *Lang. Speech* 32: 205–220.

Bernthal, JE and Bankson, NW (1988). *Articulation and Phonological Disorders.* Englewood Cliffs, NJ: Prentice-Hall.

Bosman, AM, van Leerdam, M, and de Gelder, B (2000). The/O/in OVER is different from the/O/in OTTER: Phonological effects in children with and without dyslexia. *Dev. Psychol.* 36: 817–825.

Duffy, JR (1995). *Motor Speech Disorders: Substrates, Differential Diagnosis, and Management.* Mosby: St. Louis.

Fiez, JA (1997). Phonology, semantics, and the role of the left inferior prefrontal cortex. *Hum. Brain Mapping* 5: 79–83.

Fiez, JA and Raichle, ME (1997). Linguistic processing. *Int. Rev. Neurobiol* 41: 233–254.

Grunwell, P (1987). *Clinical Phonology.* Baltimore: Williams & Wilkins.

Honjo, I (1999). *Language Viewed from the Brain.* New York: Karger.

Jenkins, L (2000). *Biolinguistics.* New York: Cambridge Univ. Press.

Moller, KT (1994). Dental-occlusal and other conditions and speech. In: Bernthal, JE and Bankson, NW (eds.) *Child Phonology: Characteristics, Assessment, and Intervention with Special Populations*, pp. 3–28. New York: Thieme.

Muma, JR (1978). *Language Handbook.* Englewood Cliffs, NJ: Prentice-Hall.

Primary Progressive Aphasia in Nondementing Adults

O. Selnes, Johns Hopkins University School of Medicine, Baltimore, MD, USA
M. Harciarek, University of Gdansk, Gdansk, Poland

Primary progressive aphasia (PPA) is a focal degenerative condition with decline in one or more language functions and asymmetric atrophy involving the perisylvian regions of the left hemisphere. The clinical syndrome is characterized by a slow, insidious decline in specific aspects of language functioning, with onset typically in the fifth or sixth decade of life. The earliest symptoms are often so subtle that only the patient or family members can detect them. Unlike aphasia due to stroke, the onset is not accompanied by an acute neurological event. Despite gradual worsening of language functions, nonlinguistic aspects of cognition may remain relatively intact for several years. Both a nonfluent variety leading to mutism and a fluent subtype with predominantly semantic impairment are now recognized. Although early cases of focal deterioration of language functions were described by pioneers of aphasia research such as Arnold Pick (Luzzatti and Poeck, 1991), it was Mesulam who proposed to differentiate this syndrome from Alzheimer's disease and thus revived interest in a clinical phenomenon that had been largely forgotten (Mesulam, 1982). The majority of cases reported in the literature have involved English speakers, although there have been reports of a few French-, Standard German-, Japanese-, Italian-, and Dutch-speaking patients as well.

Terminology

Mesulam initially suggested the term "slowly progressive aphasia" to characterize this form of progressive language deterioration. Subsequently, other terminologies have been proposed, including progressive aphasia without dementia, progressive nonfluent aphasia, and progressive language impairment without dementia. Currently, the most widely accepted term appears to be primary progressive aphasia (Mesulam, 2001; Kertesz et al., 1994).

Clinical Features

The earliest cognitive symptoms in patients who are eventually diagnosed with PPA are most commonly related to word-finding difficulties. With progression, loss of fluency often takes place, whereas comprehension remains relatively intact. Although the majority of patients with progressive aphasia evolve into a nonfluent aphasia, a subset may also have fluent aphasia. Patients with PPA typically do not complain of memory changes during the early stages of their illness, although some patients mistakenly think of their inability to retrieve words as loss of memory. The progressive decline in speech fluency is accompanied by a similar deterioration of written language functions, and thus difficulties with spelling are frequently an early feature. Patients with PPA differ from patients with early Alzheimer's disease in that not only do they have insight into the progressive decline in their language functions, but they are also profoundly concerned and disturbed by these changes. In rare cases, the earliest symptoms may be limited to articulatory changes, which over time progress to a marked dysarthria, aphasia, and nonfluency (Selnes et al., 1996; Broussolle et al., 1996; Cohen et al., 1993). In some patients, symptoms may remain limited to language functions for more than 10 years, whereas others progress to a more generalized intellectual decline after 2 to 3 years. Patients with PPA do not have any of the marked personality changes, or difficulties with activities of daily living or self-care, that are commonly seen in other degenerative disorders.

Linguistic and Neuropsychological Features

There may be considerable heterogeneity in the language symptoms of patients with PPA, but a slowly progressive dysnomia is by far the most common presenting symptom (Westbury and Bub, 1997; Jodzio, 1999). Some patients have significant difficulties with word retrieval in their spontaneous speech, but may perform nearly normally on standardized measures of confrontation naming, such as the Boston Naming test (Kaplan et al., 1983). Naming performance is strongly determined by word frequency, and certain classes of words, such as names of flowers, animals, and vegetables, are often most vulnerable during the early stages of the illness. Patients with nonfluent PPA have been shown to have disproportionate difficulties with naming verbs, whereas those with fluent aphasia have more difficulties with nouns (Hillis et al., 2004).

Comprehension of everyday conversational speech is typically well preserved during the first few years after symptom onset, although formal testing will demonstrate mild abnormalities in a significant subset of the patients. Repetition is generally spared for several years, with some studies reporting mild deficits after 8 or 9 years of progression. This suggests that the underlying disease process does not typically involve white matter tracts during the early stages of the illness. The evolution of reading deficits shows a temporal trend similar to that of the repetition impairment, consistent with the observation that the underlying disease process tends to spare the most posterior cortical regions during the early stages of the illness (Karbe et al., 1993).

The nonlinguistic features of PPA by definition emerge several years after the first language symptoms. Because performance on standardized neuropsychological measures often depends on verbal abilities, it can sometimes be difficult to separate specific neuropsychological deficits from the underlying progressive aphasia. Therefore, nonverbal measures of memory, such as the Warrington Recognition memory test, are preferable to standard verbal list-learning tests of memory. With disease progression, patterns of cognitive abnormalities consistent with executive functioning (attention/working memory; abstraction/cognitive flexibility) are often noted (Zakzanis, 1999).

Differential Diagnosis

Because the earliest symptoms of PPA are so subtle that they are noticeable only to the patient, some patients may be mistakenly thought to have a functional illness when they first approach their physicians. With progression, the language changes can be documented by careful neuropsychological testing. Performance on standard mental status screening tests such as the Mini Mental State Exam, usually remains normal, however. Additionally, normal performance on tests of memory, calculations, visuoconstruction, and executive functions will help differentiate PPA from early Alzheimer's disease. Although most patients with frontotemporal dementia do not have aphasia, subgroups with prominent early speech and language changes are now recognized. Semantic dementia is a form of frontotemporal dementia that presents with progressive loss of semantic knowledge and dysnomia (Snowden et al., 1992). Motor neuron disease may also present with a nonfluent, progressive aphasia, although with a more rapid progression (Catani et al., 2003). The absence of significant personality and behavioral changes may help distinguish patients with PPA from other patients with frontotemporal dementia syndrome. Patients with corticobasal degeneration may occasionally present with an initial aphasia, but subsequent development of unilateral motor symptoms or apraxia will differentiate these patients from those with PPA. Other conditions that may present with an initial isolated, progressive aphasia include Creutzfeldt-Jakob disease (Mandell et al., 1989; Kirk and Ang, 1994). Other focal degenerative disorders with selective involvement of higher cortical functions include slowly progressive pure dysgraphia (Luzzi and Piccirilli, 2003), slowly progressive pure word deafness (Otsuki et al., 1998), progressive prosopagnosia, and slowly progressive apraxia (Otsuki et al., 1997). Although the great majority of reported cases of PPA have been sporadic, a few cases of familial progressive aphasia have been reported. Neuropathological findings in cases of progressive aphasia have been varied and do not typically correspond to any of the classic neuropathological disorders. Most of the reported cases have had diffuse or focal neuronal loss, cortical gliosis, or focal spongiform changes.

Laboratory Testing

Brain imaging with MRI is typically the first step in the evaluation of patients with PPA. This will help exclude neoplasms or other structural causes of cognitive impairment. Routine blood studies to rule out thyroid and parathyroid disease should be performed. Although rare, progressive dysarthria and dysphagia may be associated with hypoparathyroid disease (Cheek et al., 1990). Serum vitamin B12, folate, and methylmalonic acid should also be included in the initial work-up. Detailed language and cognitive testing may help confirm the diagnosis, even relatively early in the disease progression (Gorno-Tempini et al., 2004; Croisile et al., 2003; Kertesz et al., 2003).

Radiological Features

The principal radiologic feature of PPA is an asymmetric focal atrophy in the perisylvian language areas of the dominant hemisphere (Sinnatamby et al., 1996). This pattern of atrophy may not become apparent, however, until the disease has progressed for some time (**Figure 1**). Positron-emission tomography (PET) studies of PPA have documented a heterogeneous pattern of hypometabolism involving principally the frontal, temporal, and parietal regions of the dominant hemisphere. In approximately one-third of the PET studies reported to date, bilateral abnormalities were found.

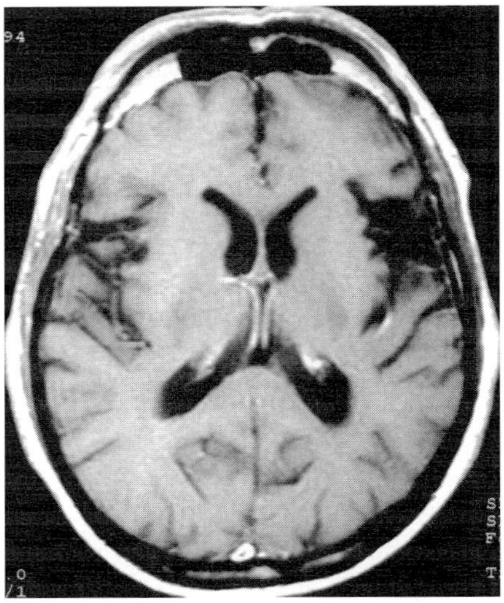

Figure 1 Magnetic resonance imaging scan of a patient with a four-year history of primary progressive aphasia. The scan demonstrates an asymmetrical distribution of atrophy involving the perisylvian areas, with greater atrophy in the left hemisphere (left side of the photograph is the right side of the brain).

Treatment

There are no specific medical treatments currently available that will reverse or slow the progression of the language symptoms, nor are there systematic studies of the efficacy of cholinergic medications in patients with PPA. Medical treatments typically focus on the management of associated symptoms, including depression, anxiety, or agitation. These symptoms may surface during the later stages of the illness. Speech therapy is typically offered during the earlier stages, and treatment focuses on the specific language functions that are impaired. An alternative to speech therapy is the use of augmentative communication devices. These are generally useful as long as the patient's general cognitive skills are reasonably intact. No systematic trials of speech therapy have been reported for patients with PPA.

Prognosis and Complications

At present, there is no known disease-modifying treatment for the degenerative diseases that may be associated with the clinical syndrome of PPA. The long-term prognosis of primary progressive aphasia is variable. Some patients have survived for as long as 14 years, but the average length of survival after diagnosis is considerably shorter.

See also: Dementia and Language; Speech Impairments in Neurodegenerative Diseases/Psychiatric Illnesses; Speech Processes in Dysarthria.

Bibliography

Broussolle, E, Bakchine, S, Tommasi, M, Laurent, B, Bazin, B, Cinotti, L, et al. (1996). 'Slowly progressive anarthria with late anterior opercular syndrome: A variant form of frontal cortical atrophy syndromes.' *Journal of Neurological Science* 144: 44–58.

Catani, M, Piccirilli, M, Geloso, MC, Cherubini, A, Finali, G, Pelliccioli, G, et al. (2003). 'Rapidly progressive aphasic dementia with motor neuron disease: A distinctive clinical entity.' *Dementia and Geriatric Cognitive Disorders* 17: 21–28.

Cheek, JC, Riggs, JE, and Lilly, RL (1990). 'Extensive brain calcification and progressive dysarthria and dysphagia associated with chronic hypoparathyroidism.' *Archives of Neurology* 47: 1038–1039.

Cohen, L, Benoit, N, VanEeckhout, P, Ducarne, B, and Brunet, P (1993). 'Pure progressive aphemia.' *Journal of Neurology, Neurosurgery and Psychiatry* 56: 923–924.

Croisile, B, Astier, JL, and Beaumont, C (2003). 'Routine clinical diagnosis of primary progressive non-fluent aphasia.' *Revue Neurologique* 159: 1009–1015.

Gorno-Tempini, ML, Dronkers, NF, Rankin, KP, Ogar, JM, Phengrasamy, L, Rosen, HJ, et al. (2004). 'Cognition and anatomy in three variants of primary progressive aphasia.' *Annals of Neurology* 55: 335–346.

Hillis, AE, Oh, S, and Ken, L (2004). 'Deterioration of naming nouns versus verbs in primary progressive aphasia.' *Annals of Neurology* 55: 268–275.

Jodzio, K (1999). *Primary progressive aphasia.* Gdansk: Gdansk University Press.

Kaplan, E, Goodglass, H, and Weintraub, S (1983). *The Boston naming test.* (2nd edn.). Lea & Febiger: Philadelphia.

Karbe, H, Kertesz, A, and Polk, M (1993). 'Profiles of language impairment in primary progressive aphasia.' *Archives of Neurology* 50: 193–201.

Kertesz, A, Davidson, W, McCabe, P, Takagi, K, and Munoz, D (2003). 'Primary progressive aphasia: Diagnosis, varieties, evolution.' *Journal of the International Neuropsychological Society* 9: 710–719.

Kertesz, A, Hudson, L, Mackenzie, IR, and Munoz, DG (1994). 'The pathology and nosology of primary progressive aphasia.' *Neurology* 44: 2065–2072.

Kirk, A and Ang, LC (1994). 'Unilateral Creutzfeldt-Jakob disease presenting as rapidly progressive aphasia.' *Canadian Journal of Neurological Sciences* 21: 350–352.

Luzzatti, C and Poeck, K (1991). 'An early description of slowly progressive aphasia.' *Archives of Neurology* 48: 228–229.

Luzzi, S and Piccirilli, M (2003). 'Slowly progressive pure dysgraphia with late apraxia of speech: A further variant of the focal cerebral degeneration.' *Brain and Language* 87: 355–360.

Mandell, AM, Alexander, MP, and Carpenter, S (1989). 'Creutzfeldt-Jakob disease presenting as isolated aphasia.' *Neurology* 39: 55–58.

Mesulam, M-M (1982). 'Slowly progressive aphasia without generalised dementia.' *Annals of Neurology* 11: 592–598.

Mesulam, MM (2001). 'Primary progressive aphasia.' *Annals of Neurology* 49: 425–432.

Otsuki, M, Soma, Y, Sato, M, Homma, A, and Tsuji, S (1998). 'Slowly progressive pure word deafness.' *European Neurology* 39: 135–140.

Otsuki, M, Soma, Y, Yoshimura, N, and Tsuji, S (1997). 'Slowly progressive limb-kinetic apraxia.' *European Neurology* 37: 100–103.

Selnes, OA, Holcomb, HH, and Gordon, B (1996). 'Progressive dysarthria: Structural and functional brain correlations.' *American Journal of Psychiatry* 153: 309–310.

Sinnatamby, R, Antoun, NA, Freer, CE, Miles, KA, and Hodges, JR (1996). 'Neuroradiological findings in primary progressive aphasia: CT MRI and cerebral perfusion SPECT.' *Neuroradiology* 38: 232–238.

Snowden, JS, Neary, D, Mann, DM, Goulding, PJ, and Testa, HJ (1992). 'Progressive language disorder due to lobar atrophy.' *Annals of Neurology* 31: 174–183.

Westbury, C and Bub, D (1997). 'Primary progressive aphasia: A review of 112 cases.' *Brain and Language* 60: 381–406.

Zakzanis, KK (1999). 'The neuropsychological signature of primary progressive aphasia.' *Brain and Language* 70: 70–85.

Procedural Learning in Humans

K. Foerde and R. A. Poldrack, University of California at Los Angeles, Los Angeles, CA, USA

Multiple Memory Systems

Human long-term memory consists of multiple distinct types, which appear to rely on separable mechanisms that can be localized to distinct regions of the brain. Early evidence for multiple forms of long-term memory came from studies of patients with neurological damage to the medial temporal lobe (MTL) or related diencephalic structures. Such individuals suffer from a global amnesia characterized by the inability to remember new events or learn new facts (anterograde amnesia), as well as a loss of memory for events prior to the neurological insult (retrograde amnesia), without any deficits in attention, perception, language, or reasoning. This form of memory has been termed 'declarative' or 'explicit' in recognition of the fact that its contents are generally available to conscious awareness and require attention for learning. However, beginning in the late 1960s it became clear that many forms of learning were normal even in the face of dense amnesia. The term 'procedural' was applied to these spared forms of memory because they appeared to reflect changes in how a task was performed ('knowing how') without the necessity of conscious memory for how this learning occurred ('knowing that'). More recently, the term 'nondeclarative memory' has been proposed to cover a broader set of memory phenomena that are spared in amnesia.

Nondeclarative memory encompasses a number of heterogeneous mnemonic functions, one of which is procedural learning, a term that we will use to refer specifically to the acquisition of new skills or abilities which are general to a task domain. As opposed to declarative memory, the knowledge acquired through procedural learning is not necessarily available to conscious awareness, but is instead tied to the routines or procedures involved in task performance. Whereas declarative memory is generally tested through direct assessment about details of a specific episode, procedural learning is observed indirectly as facilitation of performance after training.

Types of Procedural Learning

In the following discussion, we divide procedural learning into the domains of motor, perceptual, and cognitive skills for the sake of organization. These distinctions mainly arise as a result of the tasks used to assess procedural learning. However, it should be recognized that these categories are primarily heuristic and may not necessarily reflect fundamental neurobiological distinctions.

Motor Skill Learning

Motor skill learning involves improvement in the speed and/or accuracy of motor movements with practice. Across the wide range of tasks that have been examined, motor skill learning has commonly been dissociated from declarative memory by showing that amnesic patients can learn the skills normally.

Sequence learning

Motor sequence learning is perhaps the most studied motor skill task. In this paradigm, study participants respond manually to the spatial location of a visual stimulus. In implicit sequence-learning paradigms, the stimuli appear in a regular sequence during training, but the participant is not alerted to this regularity. With practice, participants respond more quickly to these sequences compared to randomly ordered stimuli. A substantial proportion of neurologically intact persons routinely report being unaware of the underlying sequence; although the role of awareness remains controversial, awareness of the sequence does not appear to be necessary for learning the skill. Amnesic patients can also show normal learning in this paradigm. In contrast, patients with basal ganglia damage exhibit specific deficits in motor sequence learning. Most neuroimaging studies of implicit motor sequence learning have observed striatal activity, consistent with a role for the striatum in sequence learning. In addition, imaging studies have reported activity in the supplementary motor area (SMA), which is likely involved in motor planning, and the parietal lobe, which appears to be involved in spatial aspects of the task (**Figure 1**).

Explicit learning of sequences has been examined using a procedure in which participants learn a sequence through trial and error. This type of learning engages regions similar to implicit learning as well as additional prefrontal regions. However, with extended practice, sequence performance becomes more automatic and relies less on prefrontal mechanisms.

With increasing practice, a shift in activity from anterior to posterior cortical and subcortical regions has been observed in several functional magnetic resonance imaging (fMRI) studies. Neurophysiological studies in monkeys have also observed such anterior–posterior shifts in the striatum. Anterior striatal regions are critical for processing feedback, whereas posterior regions appear to

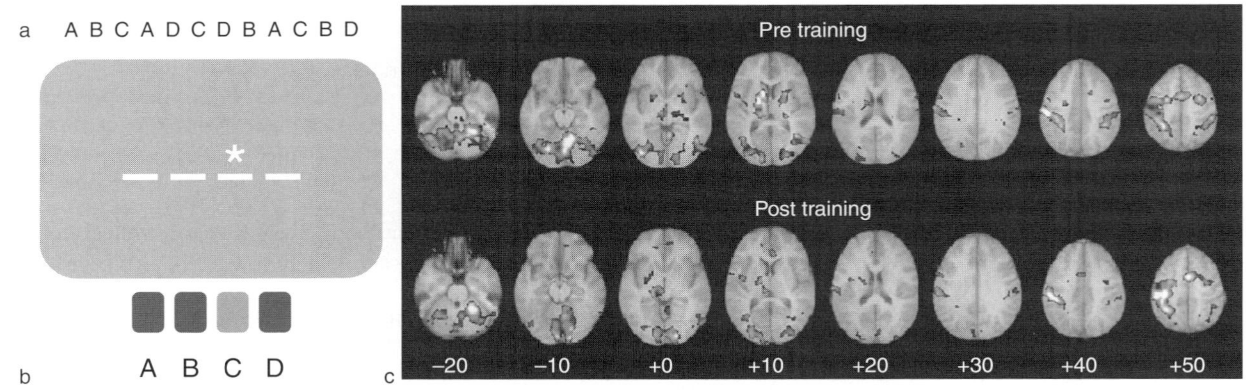

Figure 1 (a) Example of repeating sequence used in a serial reaction time (SRT) task. (b) Participants press a button corresponding to the spatial location of the onscreen asterisk. (c) Results from a fMRI study of SRT performance. Participants in this study were trained on an SRT task for three 1 h sessions (top row, brain images prior to the training session; bottom row, brain images after training). Reproduced from Poldrack RA, Sabb F, Foerde K, et al. (2005). The neural correlates of automaticity during motor skill learning. *Journal of Neuroscience* 25: 5356–5364, with permission. Copyright 2005 by the Society for Neuroscience. (See color plate 36.)

be related to performance of the learned skill *per se*. Findings regarding contributions of the cerebellum are currently mixed. Based on work with patients, neuroimaging studies, and neurophysiological studies, it has been suggested that the cerebellum may be important for the execution of well-learned motor sequence skills rather than the acquisition.

Rotary pursuit

In rotary pursuit tasks the participant tracks a small target on a rotating platter with a stylus. The profile of impairment in patients is mixed, with intact performance in amnesics, impairment in Huntington's disease, and some evidence of deficits in Parkinson's disease (PD). According to neuroimaging studies the SMA and posterior parietal cortex are involved in learning; these regions are similar to those engaged in sequence-learning tasks. Striatum and cerebellum activity has been observed in relation to motor execution on a rotary pursuit task, but thus far increases or decreases related to learning have not been observed in these regions.

Mirror tracing

Mirror tracing requires subjects to trace the outline of geometric figures while viewing the figures reflected in a mirror. Tracing becomes faster and less error prone with practice. Amnesic patients and PD patients exhibit normal learning on the task, whereas patients with cerebellar damage do not.

Motor adaptation

Motor adaptation tasks generally involve adjusting motor behavior in response to an artificial perturbation. In prism adaptation tasks, participants, fitted with prism spectacles that displace the visual field, must learn to reach for objects. In another paradigm, they are required to move a cursor to a target while interacting with a manipulandum that applies a predictable force. They learn to adjust their movements to compensate for the displacement. The parietal cortex appears to be involved in learning in these paradigms, consistent with the importance of spatial translation for accurate behavior. Furthermore, the cerebellum may be important for the acquisition of these types of motor skills. Through the cerebellum's involvement in error correction for movements, specifically the ability to use execution error information to adapt internal models, it allows improvement on subsequent trials. The striatum also appears to play a role in processing errors online, but is perhaps more involved in adapting current behavior and movement goals without affecting adaptation of internal models (**Figure 2**).

Perceptual Skill Learning

Perceptual skills involve the development of new abilities to recognize or distinguish perceptual stimuli. We do not discuss perceptual learning for low-level perceptual features or expertise in object and face recognition, but limit our discussion to forms of perceptual skill that have been directly dissociated from declarative memory.

Mirror reading

Mirror reading has been used extensively to test the acquisition of perceptual skills. Participants are exposed to spatially transformed (e.g., mirror-reversed) text. Amnesic patients show normal acquisition of mirror-reading skill without the ability to remember specific words. There is some evidence that the basal ganglia are important for learning the mirror-reading task, but the results are inconsistent. Neuroimaging studies have implicated both parietal regions and the striatum in mirror-reading skill learning.

Perceptual categorization

In perceptual categorization tasks, participants must learn to categorize multidimensional visual stimuli (e.g., Gabor patches varying in spatial frequency and orientation; see **Figure 3(a)**). In so-called information integration

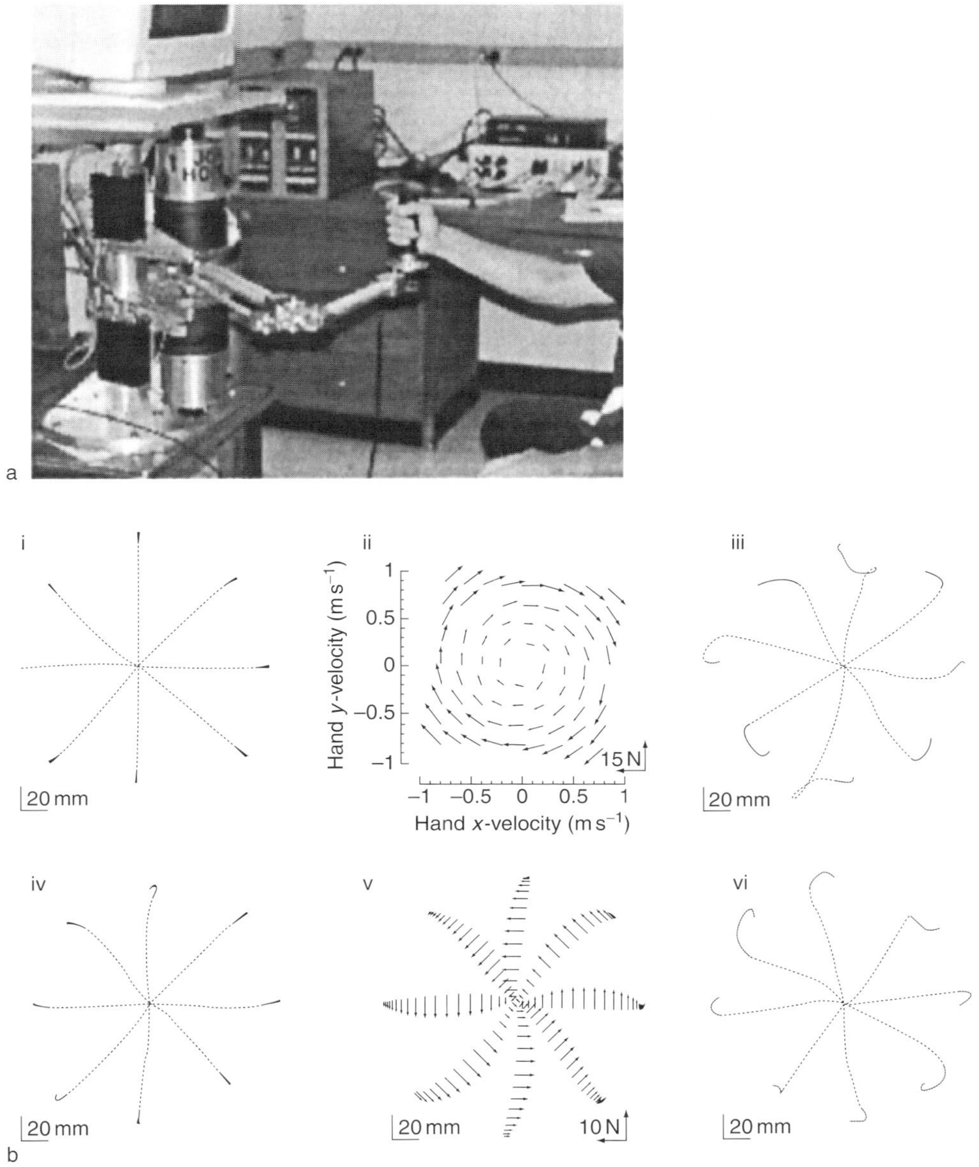

Figure 2 (a) Experimental setup for a motor adaptation task. The manipulandum is a very low-friction, planar mechanism powered by two high-performance torque motors. The study participant grips the handle of the robot. The handle houses a force transducer. The video monitor facing the participant displays a cursor corresponding to the position of the handle. A target position is displayed, and the participant makes a reaching movement. With practice, the participant learns to compensate for the forces produced by the robot. (b) (i) Hand path of a typical participant in the null field (the points in all hand paths are 10 ms apart). (ii) An example of a force field produced by the robot. (iii) Hand path of an untrained participant in the field. (iv) Hand path after 300 movements in the field. The trajectory in the field converges to the trajectory observed in the null field. (v) Forces produced by a typical trained participant to counter the effect of the force field as a function of hand position for each movement. These forces are the projection of the forces measured at the interaction point between the participant and robot onto a direction perpendicular to the direction of target. (vi) While training in the field, random targets are presented with null field conditions. The results are aftereffects. (a) Adapted from Shadmehr R and Brashers-Krug T (1997) Functional stages in the formation of human long-term motor memory. *Journal of Neuroscience* 17: 409–419, with permission. Copyright 1997 by the Society for Neuroscience.

categorization tasks, categories are delineated by a linear or nonlinear decision boundary involving multiple perceptual dimensions, and no simple verbal rule describes the category. Amnesics can learn perceptual categories even with difficult nonlinear decision bounds. Basal ganglia disorders consistently impair learning of categories with nonlinear bounds, with inconsistent deficits in learning of linear-bound categories.

Visual prototype learning

In prototype learning, participants study a set of dot patterns (see **Figure 3(b)**), which are distortions of a prototype,

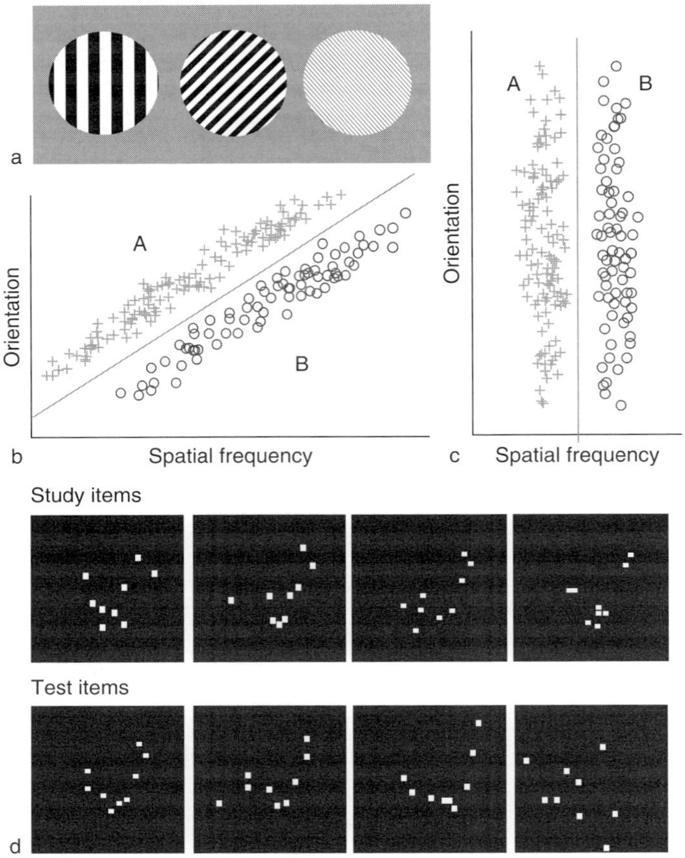

Figure 3 (a) Gabor patches used in perceptual categorization experiments. Spatial frequency and orientation vary from trial to trial. (b) Plot of stimuli that might be used in an information-integration category-learning task. Each plus symbol denotes the spatial frequency and orientation of an exemplar from category A and each circle denotes a category B exemplar. The diagonal line indicates the optimal decision bound, which requires integrating information about orientation and spatial frequency prior to making a decision. (c) Plot of stimuli that might be used in a rule-based category-learning task. The vertical line is the optimal category boundary, a rule that can easily be verbalized. (d) Examples of study items and test items used to assess classification learning of dot patterns. Study items were high distortions of a prototype dot pattern. The test items, illustrated left to right, were presentations of the training prototype, low and high distortions of the training prototype, and random dot patterns. (a–c) Adapted from Ashby FG and Maddox WT (2005) Human category learning. *Annual Review of Psychology* 56: 149–178, with permission. (d) Reproduced from Reber PJ, Stark CEL, and Squire LR (1998) Cortical areas supporting category learning identified using functional MRI. *Proceedings of the National Academy of Sciences of the United States of America* 95: 747–750, with permission. Copyright 1998 by the National Academy of Sciences, USA.

without being told about the presence of a category. Participants are then required to decide for subsequent test items whether the items are from the same category as the study items. Amnesic patients are able to normally classify new distortions of the prototype among distortions of different prototypes, but are significantly worse than neurologically intact controls at recognizing studied patterns. Patients with basal ganglia damage are not impaired at dot pattern classification. Imaging studies have suggested that this type of learning may rely upon early perceptual systems, as classifying new distortions of the learned prototype is associated with decreased activity in occipital cortex (BA 17/18) compared to distortions of unstudied prototypes. This seems specific to incidental learning, as classification of new category members after intentional learning is associated with increased activity in the MTL and prefrontal regions.

Cognitive Skill Learning

Cognitive skill learning involves the development of new task procedures or classification abilities, which are not closely tied to new perceptual or motor abilities.

Category learning

Cognitive skills are often acquired through performance of tasks requiring classification of novel stimuli; whereas the examples discussed earlier involved development of new perceptual categories, the tasks discussed here are more abstract. In some tasks, participants simply learn by observing a number of category exemplars, whereas other tasks involve learning from feedback on a trial-by-trial basis.

Probabilistic classification learning

In this commonly used paradigm, cues are probabilistically associated with categories. The most common cover story (the 'weather prediction task') is that participants must predict the weather based on a set of cards. Participants are shown individual cues or combinations of the cues and must predict the outcome (rain or sunshine) on each trial, based on feedback provided after each response; however, this feedback is probabilistic. The complexity of the task (as well as the probabilistic feedback) makes it difficult to simply memorize the cue-outcome association on each trial, and participants routinely report feeling unable to learn the task. However, they customarily attain around 70–80% optimal responses within less than 100 training trials. Amnesics are sometimes able to perform this task as well as normal controls do, but they have poorer memory for the details of the testing episode. In contrast, patients with basal ganglia damage are consistently impaired at probabilistic classification, but have intact memory for the testing episode. This deficit appears to be related to the need to process feedback, which relies upon dopaminergic prediction error signals. Neuroimaging data have confirmed the involvement of the basal ganglia in classification learning, while also suggesting that, sometimes, normal persons might rely upon the MTL to perform the task. Learning under dual-task conditions can reduce the reliance upon the MTL and drive study participants to rely on the basal ganglia to perform the task instead (**Figure 4**).

Artificial grammar learning

In the artificial grammar paradigm, participants incidentally process letter strings produced using an underlying set of rules (usually a finite-state grammar). After a short delay participants are told that the items were produced according to a set of rules and they must classify a new set of items according to whether or not they follow the same rules.

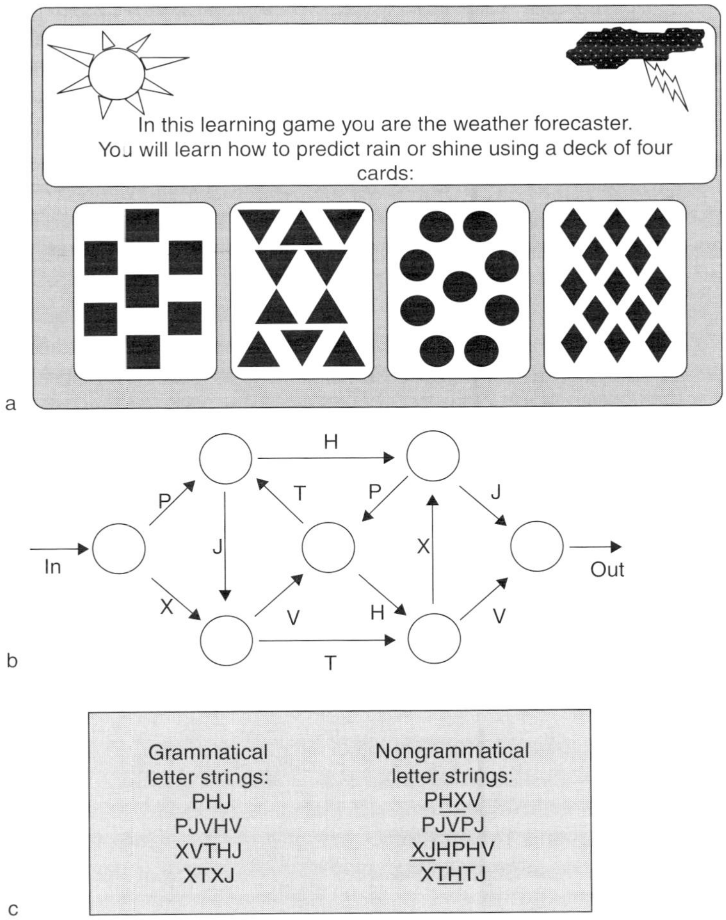

Figure 4 (a) Example of stimuli used in probabilistic classification tasks. One or more of the cards are presented on each trial and a prediction of sunny or rainy outcome is made. (b) Finite-state grammar used to generate letter strings. (c) Examples of grammatical and nongrammatical letter strings that participants would attempt to classify. (a) Reproduced from Knowlton BJ, Mangels JA, and Squire LR (1996) A neostriatal habit learning system in humans. *Science* 273: 1399–1402, with permission. Copyright 1996 by AAAS.
(b, c) Reproduced from Skosnik PD, Mirza F, Gitelman DR, et al. (2002) Neural correlates of artificial grammar learning. *NeuroImage* 17: 1306–1314, with permission. Copyright 2002 by Elsevier.

Amnesics show normal grammar learning on this task, yet have poor recognition for individual letter strings, whereas basal ganglia pathology does not appear to lead to impaired artificial grammar learning (AGL) performance. There are multiple forms of knowledge that can underlie learning in this task, including knowledge about specific features (such as chunks of letter strings) as well as more abstract rules for generating the strings. One fMRI study found activity in the caudate associated with rule knowledge and in the hippocampus in association with chunk knowledge. However, amnesics can acquire both of these forms of knowledge normally, suggesting that neither requires the MTL, even though it is active in imaging studies. Neuroimaging studies have found activation in prefrontal and occipital regions during classification of grammatical versus ungrammatical items, suggesting that those regions may be involved in expressing grammar knowledge in the task.

Tower puzzle tasks

Procedural learning of a planning skill has been assessed in neurologically impaired populations by using several variations of a problem-solving task (e.g., Towers of Hanoi, London, and Toronto). The Tower puzzles involve three pegs and disks of varying size (or color). The goal is to move all of the disks from the right peg to the left peg, such that the disks end up in the same configuration as on the starting peg. Disks must be moved one at a time and a larger (or darker) disk may not be placed upon a smaller (or lighter) disk. This class of tasks has been used extensively to test cognitive procedural learning, and initial reports indicated that amnesics could solve this problem, whereas patients with basal ganglia damage were impaired. Follow-up studies in amnesics have not consistently confirmed intact learning on these tasks, whereas the deficits in patients with basal ganglia pathology have been largely confirmed. Imaging has shown increased activity in both basal ganglia and prefrontal regions as task complexity increases, suggesting that the involvement of those regions may be closely related to the planning demands of the task rather than learning *per se*.

Characteristics of Procedural Learning

The heterogeneity of behaviors that are supported by procedural learning mechanisms makes it difficult to formulate general principles regarding procedural learning. We focus herein on a number of general features of procedural learning, though there seem to be exceptions to each potential principle.

Automaticity

One general characteristic of procedural learning may be that skills can become automatic with extensive practice, where automaticity refers to the ability to perform a task without the need for executive control. Automaticity is often defined in terms of dual-task performance: if performance of a skill is insensitive to interference from a secondary task, then it is considered automatic. It has long been suggested that the need for executive processes differs between early and late stages of learning. Many studies find that executive control is necessary for learning a skill, although in some domains it appears that executive control is not necessary at any point in learning. Other studies find that interference with executive control processes may affect only the performance, but not the acquisition of a skill. Whatever the role of executive control in early learning, it is clear that procedural learning leads to automaticity in a way that is qualitatively different from declarative memory.

Awareness

The role of awareness in procedural learning is perhaps the most controversial issue surrounding the concept of multiple memory systems. The first difficulty is that the term can refer either to the online awareness of what is being learned (e.g., the grammatical rules in the artificial grammar paradigm, or the particular sequence in the motor sequence-learning task) or to later declarative memory for what was learned. The ability of amnesics to learn skills in the absence of declarative memory for the learning event or insight into their newly acquired abilities provides strong evidence that at least some forms of skill are independent of later declarative memory. Disentangling the role of online awareness from procedural learning is more difficult, since any test for awareness during learning will potentially contaminate the person's strategy for performing the task. Imaging has proved useful in this domain, by showing that the neural basis of performance differs for skills that are learned with awareness versus those learned without awareness. Thus it appears that there are differences in the degree to which procedural learning requires online awareness of task contingencies, but this issue will remain controversial until there is an adequate account of the functional role of awareness in learning.

Long-Term Retention

Although rates of retention in procedural learning have not been extensively investigated, in some cases procedural learning has been characterized by remarkably long-term retention. Studies of mirror tracing, mirror reading, and AGL have all reported skill retention in excess of 1 year, in amnesics as well as normal controls. Studies of motor sequence learning have reported retention after 1–2 weeks, though one study reported a failure to retain sequence knowledge at 1 year. Whereas forgetting of declarative memories is thought to occur primarily due to interference, this factor may be less relevant for procedural learning. Study participants are unlikely to have much experience outside of the laboratory with the kinds of tasks involved in procedural learning studies (e.g., categorizing dot patterns) and thus there may be less possibility for interference than for declarative memories. Some studies also suggest that procedural memories may become resistant to interference over time due to a consolidation process that requires some number of hours following learning. Interference has mainly been studied in the context of motor adaptation. Other skills (e.g., sequence learning) rely on different neural substrates and the representations may change differently over time.

Neural Bases of Procedural Learning

Much knowledge regarding the neural basis of procedural learning initially came from neuropsychological studies. Early studies of amnesic patients revealed that procedural learning does not require intact MTL structures. Studies in Parkinson's and Huntington's disease patients with damage to the basal ganglia, and other patients with damage to the cerebellum, have shown that both of these brain structures may be important substrates of procedural learning. Neuroimaging has provided additional evidence regarding the neural basis of procedural learning and has highlighted the fact that learning involves dynamic changes in brain activity with practice. There has sometimes been a lack of convergence between neuropsychological data and imaging data, which may reflect the fact that activation in neuroimaging does not indicate that a region is necessary for task performance. On the other hand, imaging studies in healthy populations have revealed that healthy individuals may approach tasks differently than damaged populations do because they have multiple representations or types of knowledge available. Here we outline the major brain structures known to be involved in procedural learning.

Striatum

The striatum appears to be the most widely involved brain structure in procedural learning, based on both lesion evidence and functional imaging results. One potential role for the striatum is in the acquisition of stimulus–response (S–R) associations, likely dependent upon dopamine-modulated synaptic plasticity at corticostriatal synapses. Tasks such as classification learning, which involve learning of responses to specific stimuli based on feedback, are impaired in patients with Huntington's disease (damaging striatal neurons) and PD (disrupting the dopaminergic system). Further, the impairment in PD on classification tasks appears to be specific to learning from feedback. Thus, the reinforcement learning mechanisms supported by the striatum may play an important role in procedural learning.

Feedback does not play a critical role in sequencing tasks, but the basal ganglia also appear to be important for developing unitized action sequences. Through repeated performance of a motor sequence, individual responses become chained into a single chunk or an action sequence. In this way common actions can be executed quicker and more reliably. For example, a forgotten telephone number or password might be successfully completed if one knows the first elements. A chunking mechanism might account for improved performance of motor sequences and perhaps also on Tower puzzles, where optimal performance requires multiple moves in a particular sequence. The best evidence for basal ganglia involvement in such a chunking mechanism comes from recordings from neurons in rodent striatum. During repeated performance of a task, the pattern of neural activity changed from activity occurring throughout the task procedure to activity occurring only at the onset and the offset of the task procedure. A more efficient representation of repeated behaviors could allow more automatic or habit-like performance.

The role of the striatum in procedural learning is increasingly being parsed into more specific functions and related to subregions within the striatum. For example, processing feedback in response to actions is consistently tied to the head of the caudate nucleus, whereas motor learning appears to rely upon the putamen. Separate parallel corticostriatal loops are tied to performance of tasks in various domains, but these loops also communicate throughout the striatum. Different tasks probably rely on the various functions of the basal ganglia to a different degree. Generally, it has been suggested that the basal ganglia may be critical in open-loop skill learning, where behavior is initiated by internally generated plans and subsequently received feedback guides future behavior.

Several neuroimaging studies have found that striatal activity during procedural learning is associated with decreased MTL activity. The meaning of this MTL decrease is not fully understood, but it has been suggested that regions involved in learning declarative knowledge and those involved in procedural learning may be in competition to control behavior. Interestingly, some studies of classification learning and sequence learning using neuroimaging in patients with striatal pathology have observed MTL activity during learning rather than the striatal activity found in normal controls. Thus, for some of these tasks it appears that other strategies may be available when procedural learning is compromised.

Cerebellum

In contrast to the striatum, the cerebellum has been proposed as critical in closed-loop skill learning, where continuous external feedback guides behavior (e.g., mirror tracing), or when novel mappings between motor behavior and visual cues are required (e.g., motor adaptation tasks). As such, a function of the cerebellum may also be thought of as processing feedback, but specifically monitoring and optimizing movements in response to online sensory feedback.

Cerebral Cortex

Several other regions are consistently associated with procedural learning. Whereas the necessity of cerebellum and basal ganglia structures has been studied in various patient populations, the involvement of other regions is generally observed using neuroimaging. Although imaging does not allow inference about necessity, imaging results have generally suggested that procedural learning involves changes in the same areas that are necessary for task performance. For example, the SMA, premotor areas, and primary motor cortex are involved in learning motor skills. Occipital lobe and temporal lobe visual regions are involved in visual perceptual tasks, such as prototype learning. Parietal regions are engaged when tasks require processing of spatial information. These results are consistent with the notion that procedural learning involves online changes in the neural networks involved in task performance. Additionally, prefrontal regions are generally involved during the early stages of learning, likely providing executive control over novice performance.

Conclusion

Although much is still to be learned about how procedural learning is acquired and develops with training, it is clear that humans have a remarkable capacity for acquiring a wide range of skills. These skills can sometimes be retained for years without continued practice and often generalize beyond the studied materials. Conscious memory for the learning event is not necessary, as numerous demonstrations of intact procedural learning by amnesics have shown. The striatum and cerebellum appear to play general roles in procedural learning and, depending on the task, various sensory–motor cortical regions might also be important. Future studies will be needed to further explore how activity changes with practice and better understand what these changes mean.

Further Reading

Ashby, FG, and Maddox, WT (2005). Human category learning. *Annual Review of Psychology* 56: 149–178.

Cohen, NJ and Squire, LR (1980). Preserved learning and retention of pattern-analyzing skill in amnesia: Dissociation of knowing how and knowing that. *Science* 210(4466): 207–210.

Corkin, S (1968). Acquisition of motor skill after bilateral medial temporal-lobe excision. *Neuropsychologia* 6: 255–265.

Eichenbaum, HE and Cohen, NJ (2001). *From Conditioning to Conscious Recollection: Memory Systems of the Brain.* New York: Oxford University Press.

Foerde, L, Knowlton, BJ, and Poldrack, RA (2006). Distraction modulates the engagement of competing memory systems. *Proceedings of the National Academy of Sciences of the United States of America* 103: 11778–11783.

Karni, A, Meyer, G, Jezzard, P, et al. (1995). Functional MRI evidence for adult motor cortex plasticity during motor skill learning. *Nature* 377: 155–158.

Knowlton, BJ, Mangels, JA, and Squire, LR (1996). A neostriatal habit learning system in humans. *Science* 273: 1399–1402.

Poldrack, RA, Sabb, F, Foerde, K, et al. (2005). The neural correlates of automaticity during motor skill learning. *Journal of Neuroscience* 25: 5356–5364.

Poldrack, RA and Willingham, DB (2006). Functional neuroimaging of skill learning. In: Cabeza, R and Kingstone, A (eds.) *Handbook of Neuroimaging of Cognition,* 2nd edn., pp. 113–148. Cambridge, MA: MIT Press.

Reber, PJ, Stark, CEL, and Squire, LR (1998). Cortical areas supporting category learning identified using functional MRI. *Proceedings of the National Academy of Sciences of the United States of America* 95: 747–750.

Saint-Cyr, JA, Taylor, AE, and Lang, AE (1988). Procedural learning and neostriatal dysfunction in man. *Brain* 111: 941–959.

Salmon, D and Butters, N (1995). Neurobiology of skill and habit learning. *Current Opinion in Neurobiology* 5: 184–190.

Shadmehr, R and Brashers-Krug, T (1997). Functional stages in the formation of human long-term motor memory. *Journal of Neuroscience* 17: 409–419.

Shadmehr, R and Holcomb, HH (1997). Neural correlates of motor memory consolidation. *Science* 277(5327): 821–825.

Skosnik, PD, Mirza, F, Gitelman, DR, et al. (2002). Neural correlates of artificial grammar learning. *NeuroImage* 17: 1306–1314.

Squire, LR (1992). Memory and the hippocampus: A synthesis from findings with rats, monkeys, and humans. *Psychological Review* 99(2): 195–231.

Proper and Common Names, Impairments

C. Semenza, University of Trieste, Trieste, Italy

The distinction between common and proper names is a fundamental one in lexical semantics. The two categories, in fact, are distinguishable from one another since they have a different type of reference. This fact has been shown to impinge on the kind of processing each category undergoes. Neuropsychological research in the past 20 years has indeed uncovered a series of phenomena that critically contribute to the understanding of how proper names are processed in the brain with respect to common names. These findings could be interpreted in light of past and current philosophical and linguistic theories on the nature of proper and common names, that, in turn, received empirical support. Thus, the role of a very important dimension, that of the amount of 'sense' in Frege's (1892) terms, was highlighted, and it became possible to distinguish semantics referring to individuals from general semantics.

Relevant philosophical and linguistic theories can be summarized as follows. Proper names are thought to relate to their reference in a 'token' (individual) as opposed to 'type' (categorical) fashion, which is the case for common nouns. In other words, while proper names refer to individual entities, common nouns refer to categories of items. According to philosophers like Frege (1892) or, more recently, Kripke (1980), proper names are pure referring expressions, in that they carry little if any sense or connotation beyond that of the reference. In other words, proper names do not entail any description of the entity they designate. Changing basic features and properties over time does not change the proper name of a given single entity. Another way of expressing this fact is to tell that proper names have an arbitrary relation with their reference. As Semenza et al. (1998) have observed, a name designating a category applies to a set of attributes that overlap or interact with each other via high-probability connections. In the set of attributes labeled by a proper name, instead, attributes combine together incidentally, being related to each other only by virtue of belonging to entities that are unique. This distinction resembles closely that universally made between semantic and episodic memory mechanisms, but with an important difference: the mechanisms in question are more peripheral and operate at the lexical level.

In neuropsychology, cases were discovered whereby, as a result of a brain lesion, patients were affected by selective anomia for proper names, with normal retrieval of common names. Cases of the reverse pattern – proper name selective sparing – have also been reported.

Anomia for proper names, in general, affects retrieval in all testing conditions and comes in different varieties, the most common (so-called 'pure proper name anomias') being those originating with a deficit at a postsemantic level (i.e., failure to access the name's phonological form from an intact semantic system, e.g., Semenza and Zettin, 1988, 1989; Lucchelli and De Renzi, 1992; Hittmair-Delazer et al., 1994). The phonological level itself seems to be spared in these patients, since they maintain the ability to read aloud irregularly spelled proper names. This type of anomia comes in two different subtypes: one concerns all proper names, while the other is limited to people's names only. It is still unclear whether proper names other than people's ones are easier than the latter or rather have particular properties that may help in circumventing the deficit. Most of these patients seem little if not at all sensitive to phonemic as well as semantic cueing, but a combination of both types of cue has been shown to yield some improvement. Cases, however, have been reported of patients showing a significant improvement when aided with a phonological cue (e.g., Lucchelli and De Renzi, 1992; Otsuka et al., 2005). Other cases have been shown, instead, to derive from a problem within the semantic system (e.g., Miceli et al., 2000), where information about individual people seems to be selectively lost with respect to information about other entities, or from the isolation of information on individual entities from both the general semantic system and the output lexicon (Van der Linden et al., 1995; Semenza et al., 1998). Thus, while some patients cannot retrieve the name but have no problem showing they know everything else about the individual, other less frequently observed patients seem to be selectively impaired in the semantic store containing all the information about that individual, including the corresponding name. In 'isolation' cases the information was available but could only be triggered by providing the proper name itself. A last variety, only very recently described, is that of 'prosopanomia' (Semenza et al., 2003), a face-specific optic aphasia, where patients cannot retrieve the names of people by just looking at their faces but they can do so on definition. They have no trouble recognizing the face, but like optic aphasics, they seem instead unable to retrieve enough semantic information from the visual stimulus (in this case, specifically, only from faces) to activate the name.

Anomias for proper names arising at the retrieval level are also important for their concomitant symptoms. While, at least in the purest cases, they seem to come as the only reported symptom, careful neuropsychological assessment systematically uncovers a revealing constellation of associated deficits. Semenza and Zettin (1989) first showed that their proper name anomic could not retrieve a member of an arbitrarily related word pair given the other. The same patient and similar ones could not retrieve 'token' information arbitrarily connected with other information, such as known phone numbers of people, titles of wordless pieces of music, dates of known events, etc. This finding provides support for theories of proper names as pure referring expressions, whose link with the entity they represent is arbitrary, nondescriptive (i.e., unlike with common nouns, not implying attributes), and thus devoid of sense.

Cases of selective sparing of proper names are more complicated than proper name anomias and do not seem to tell a straightforward story. Two main factors contribute to this state of uncertainty and, consequently, to the difficulty in identifying the nature of the functional deficit. First, in general, sparing of proper names has been found in otherwise very severely affected patients. This fact has seriously hampered the possibility of testing the patients in the desirable level of detail. Second, the conditions in which proper names are selectively spared appears to differ widely from case to case; in fact, unlike in cases of the most common (postsemantic) proper name anomia, which all look rather similar, no single reported case of proper name sparing closely resembles any of the others. For instance, the first such case ever observed (McKenna and Warrington, 1978) concerned only the names of nations. In another case, reported by Cipolotti et al. (1993), the patient could be tested only in writing, where he could retrieve only names of countries and famous people. In the case reported by Semenza and Sgaramella (1993), the patient could not retrieve any name, and selective preservation of proper names emerged only in the middle of a gibberish jargon, and, more clearly, after phonemic cueing in picture naming. In contrast, Cipolotti's (2000) patient showed proper name superiority just for countries and only in oral naming and reading aloud. In another case (Schmidt et al., 2004), preserved sparing was shown only in the written condition in a patient whose articulation was totally impaired. This patient showed semantic knowledge about items whose (common) name he could not retrieve and never committed paragraphias; these facts led the authors to suggest that the functional deficit could be located in accessing, from an intact semantic level, an intact orthographic lexicon. Unfortunately, the patient's extremely severe articulation problems prevented assessing the status of his phonological lexicon. In the case described by Lyons et al. (2002), the patients not only missed common nouns but also the correspondent semantic information: in contrast, the patient showed a normal ability to retrieve people's names and the corresponding biographical information.

With one exception, none of the patients with proper name sparing described in the literature truly mirrors reported cases of anomia for proper names. Because of the severity of the cases, only limited testing results are available for any one patient, so it has been very difficult to locate the deficit at a particular processing stage.

This review thus shows that a convincing double dissociation in the processing of proper and common names, the clearest evidence for separate systems, has not been described at all processing stages. The only exception is indeed constituted by two cases, the proper name anomia studied by Miceli et al. (2000) and the proper name selective sparing reported by Lyons et al. (2002). These cases really mirror each other, insofar the former, as reported above, missed the knowledge of the semantics of individual entities while preserving knowledge of categorical entities, while the latter, instead, showed exactly the reverse pattern.

Strangely, the most frequent pattern of proper name anomia (i.e., where the defect has been located at the postsemantic lexical activation level) is not clearly mirrored by any case of proper name sparing. Before Miceli et al. (2000) and Lyons et al. (2002) had described their patients, the lack of a double dissociation could be taken as meaning that the processing of the two categories follows the same path. Semenza (1997), however, warned against this last interpretation by pointing out that the patients reported in Semenza and Zettin (1988, 1989) could retrieve virtually all items in their presumed premorbid vocabulary, and were well within, if not superior to, normal level in the retrieval of common names. They could indeed retrieve very difficult abstract names and correctly name in a minute a high number of items from odd common name categories. In contrast, they were profoundly impaired with proper names to the point that they could retrieve only their own name and that of a few family members. The fact that they were unable to retrieve the names of people they had known all their lives and met almost every day indicates that this dissociation cannot be determined by low frequency or familiarity of such items; rather, it suggests that proper names have a separate processing pathway.

The problem remains of why, with about two dozen cases of anomia for proper names described in literature, their selective sparing is still so hard to find. One possible explanation is that the retrieval of proper names is simply more difficult than the retrieval of common nouns. This position is widely held and anecdotally supported, but experimental confirmation has been difficult to obtain (Cohen and Burke, 1993). In fact, the main methods used in the past to demonstrate proper names' relative difficulty with respect to common names proved to be largely inadequate. It is indeed very hard if not impossible to match for perceptual difficulty visual stimuli consisting of pictures of faces (for proper names) and pictures of objects (for common names). Diary studies, instead, collecting participants' naming failures in a given period of time, were hampered by the obvious fact that one often hardly notices missing a common name, while missing a proper name may cause serious embarrassment.

Thus, the best available evidence for proper names being indeed more difficult to process rests mainly on two types of relatively recent observations. One concerns the so called 'baker–Baker' paradox: it is easier to learn that a face belongs to a baker than it is to learn that the same face belongs to a Mr Baker (McWeeny et al., 1987; Cohen, 1990). This effect cannot be attributed to differences in the phonological form or frequency of occurrence of occupations versus proper names. Another methodology – repetition of supraspan lists of words – shows a significantly weaker priority effect when the list is composed of proper names than when it is composed of common nouns matched to proper names for frequency, length and phonological complexity (Hittmair-Delazer et al., 1994; Semenza et al., 1996; Pelamatti et al., 2003). This effect widens with age and exposure to high altitude and comes to an extreme with Alzheimer's disease.

Proper name recognition has also been studied in neuropsychology. A selective deficit in proper name recognition *vis-à-vis* sparing of the comprehension of common names was first reported by Verstichel et al. (1996) in a patient who showed the same dissociation in output. Sparing in recognition of proper names relative to common ones has also been reported (Saffran et al., 1980; Van Lanker and Klein, 1990), generally after major damage to the left hemisphere.

Once established that proper and common names follow different functional pathways, an important and debated issue concerns localization of proper name processing in the brain. Reported investigations so far employed lateralization techniques, ERPs (Evoked Response Potentials), neuroimaging, and classic clinical–anatomical correlation.

Ohnesorge and Van Lanker (2001), reviewing findings via lateralization techniques on proper name recognition, came to the following conclusions: greater accuracy is found in the right visual field for both common proper names; famous proper names are overall more accurately recognized; no field difference exists for famous proper names in categorization tasks and for more familiar items. The authors suggested that both hemispheres can process famous proper names and that the right hemisphere contributes to personal name recognition because it may be specialized for items of 'personal relevance.'

An ERP study carried out by Proverbio et al. (2001) revealed that tacit retrieval of a proper name phonological form is reflected in a strong activation of left anterior temporal and left centrofrontal areas, while the same task shows greater involvement of occipitotemporal areas with common names.

Neuroimaging studies (Damasio et al., 1996; Gorno Tempini et al., 1998; Rotschtein et al., 2005) seem to indicate a critical role of the left temporal pole in naming of faces and that proper name categorization depends on the left–anterior middle–temporal region.

Finally, the anatomoclinical correlation method (Semenza et al., 1995; Yasuda et al., 2000) allowed researchers to reach the following conclusions: a) in proper name anomias, the left temporal lobe is often damaged; b) several cases are determined by left-sided lesions clearly outside the temporal lobe, including the basal ganglia, the thalamus, and the occipital lobe; c) the left temporal lobe is most often damaged also in selective sparing of proper names; and d) at least one case of selective sparing of proper names followed a lesion in the left temporal pole. The most recent review (Yasuda et al., 2000) thus concluded that various aspects of proper name retrieval may be sustained by different structures differently participating in a complex network: existing speculations about the specific role of each of these structures remains at present unwarranted.

In summary, localization studies lead to the suggestion that a dedicated module dealing with proper name retrieval probably exists, but it is either subject to great interindividual variation or it is distributed throughout a large portion of the left hemisphere.

Bibliography

Cipolotti, L (2000). 'Sparing of country and nationality names in a case of modality-specific oral output impairment: implications for theories of speech production.' *Cognitive Neuropsychology* 17: 709–729.

Cipolotti, L, McNeill, JE, and Warrington, EK (1993). 'Spared written naming of proper nouns: a case report.' *Memory* 1(4): 289–311.

Cohen, G (1990). 'Why it is difficult to put names to faces?' *British Journal of Psychology* 81: 287–297.

Cohen, G and Burke, DM (1993). 'Memory for proper names: a review.' *Memory* 1(4): 249–264.

Damasio, H, Grabowski, TJ, Tranel, D, Hichwa, RD, and Damasio, A (1996). 'A neural basis for lexical retrieval.' *Nature* 380: 499–505.

Frege, G (1892). 'Über Sinn und Bedeutung.' In: Patzig, G (ed.) *Funktion, Begriff, Bedeutung*, pp. 40–65. Gottingen: Vandenhoek und Ruprecht.

Gorno Tempini, ML, Price, CJ, Josephs, O, Vandenberghe, R, Cappa, SF, Kapur, N, and Frackowiak, RSJ (1998). 'The neural system sustaining face and proper name processing.' *Brain* 121: 2103–2118.

Hittmair-Delazer, M, Denes, G, Semenza, C, and Mantovan, M C (1994). 'Anomia for people's names.' *Neuropsychologia* 86: 345–358.

Kripke, S (1980). *Naming and necessity.* Oxford: Basil Blackwell.

Lucchelli, F and De Renzi, E (1992). 'Proper name anomia.' *Cortex* 28: 221–230.

Lyons, F, Hanley, JR, and Kay, J (2002). 'Anomia for common names and geographical names with preserved retrieval of names of people: a semantic memory disorder.' *Cortex* 38: 23–35.

McKenna, P and Warrington, EK (1978). 'Category-specific naming preservation: a single case study.' *Journal of Neurology, Neurosurgery and Psychiatry* 41: 571–574.

McWeeny, KH, Young, A, Hay, DC, and Ellis, AW (1987). 'Putting names to faces.' *British Journal of Psychology* 78: 143–144.

Miceli, G, Capasso, R, Daniele, A, Esposito, T, Magarelli, M, and Tomaiuolo, F (2000). 'Selective deficit for people names following left temporal damage: an impairmant of domain-specific conceptual knowledge.' *Cognitive Neuropsychology* 17(6): 489–516.

Ohnesorge, C and Van Lanker, D (2001). 'Cerebral laterality for famous proper nouns: visual recognition by normal subjects.' *Brain and Language* 77: 135–165.

Otsuka, Y, Suzuki, K, Fujii, T, Miura, R, Endo, K, Kondo, H, and Yamadori, A (2005). 'Proper name anomia after left temporal subcortical hemorrage.' *Cortex* 41: 39–47.

Pelamatti, G, Pascotto, M, and Semenza, C (2003). 'Verbal free recall in high altitude: proper names vs. common names.' *Cortex* 39: 97–103.

Proverbio, AM, Lilli, S, Semenza, C, and Zani, A (2001). 'ERP indexes of functional differences in brain activation during proper and common names retrieval.' *Neuropsychologia* 39: 815–827.

Rotschtein, P, Henson, RNA, Treves, A, Driver, J, and Dolan, RJ (2005). 'Morphing Marilyn into Maggie dissociates physical and identity face representations in the brain.' *Nature Neuroscience* 8(1): 107–113.

Saffran, EM, Bogyo, LC, Schwartz, MF, and Marin, OSM (1980). 'Does deep dyslexia reflect right hemisphere reading?' In: Colthearth, M, Patterson, K, and Marshall, JC (eds.) *Deep dyslexia.* London: Routledge and Kegan.

Schmidt, D, Buchanan, L, and Semenza, C (2004). 'Sparing of proper names and dates in aphasia.' *Brain and Language* 91: 9–10.

Semenza, C (1997). 'Proper-name-specific aphasias.' In: Goodglass, H and Wingfield, A (eds.) *Anomia.* San Diego: Academic Press.

Semenza, C and Sgaramella, TM (1993). 'Production of proper names: a clinical case study of the effects of phonemic cueing.' *Memory* 1(4): 265–280.

Semenza, C and Zettin, M (1988). 'Generating proper names: a case of selective inability.' *Cognitive Neuropsychology* 5(6): 711–721.

Semenza, C and Zettin, M (1989). 'Evidence from aphasia for proper names as pure referring expressions.' *Nature* 342(6250): 678–679.

Semenza, C, Nichelli, F, and Gamboz, N (1996). 'The primacy effect in free recall of lists of common and proper names: a study on young, elderly and Alzheimer disease subjects.' *Brain and Language* 55: 45–47.

Semenza, C, Sartori, G, and D'Andrea, J (2003). 'He can tell which master craftsman blew a Venetian vase, but he cannot name the

Pope: a patient with a selective difficulty in naming faces.' *Neuroscience Letters* 352: 73–75.
Semenza, C, Zettin, M, and Borgo, F (1998). 'Names and identification: an access problem.' *Neurocase* 4: 45–53.
Valentine, T, Brennen, T, and Bredart, S (1996). *The cognitive psychology of proper names: on the importance of being earnest.* London: Routledge.
Van der Linden, M, Bredart, S, and Schweich, M (1995). 'Developmental disturbance of access to biographical information and people's names: a single case study.' *Journal of the International Neuropsychological Society* 1: 589–595.
Van Lanker, D and Klein, K (1990). 'Preserved recognition of familiar personal names in global aphasia.' *Brain and Language* 39: 511–529.
Verstichel, P, Cohen, L, and Crochet, G (1996). 'Associated production and comprehension deficits for people's names following left temporal lesion.' *Neurocase* 2: 221–234.
Yasuda, K, Nakamura, T, and Beckam, B (2000). 'Brain processing of proper names.' *Aphasiology* 14(11): 1067–1089.

Prosopagnosia

M. J. Farah and T. E. Feinberg

Visual agnosia, the acquired disorder of visual object recognition, does not always affect the recognition of all types of stimuli equally. Patients with prosopagnosia have particular difficulty recognizing faces. To the extent that they can recognize familiar people, they rely on nonfacial cues such as voice, distinctive clothing, or hairstyle. The disorder can be so severe that even close friends and family members will not be recognized. Indeed, the failure of recognition extends even to the patient's own face. One extremely high-functioning prosopagnosic man related the following story: While at a conference attended by many of his colleagues, he rounded a corner in the hotel and found himself walking toward someone. Assuming it was a colleague, he greeted the man but got nothing in response but a stare. Finally, he understood the man's apparently bizarre behavior: He was facing himself in a floor-to-ceiling mirror.

Historical Background

According to De Renzi, the Italian ophthalmologist Antonio Quaglino in 1867 provided the first formal description of a prosopagnosic patient. Quaglino described a 54-year-old man with a right hemisphere stroke who displayed an inability to recognize the faces of persons previously known to him. Although this patient displayed a left hemianopia and achromatopsia, he retained good central vision and was able to read small print. On this basis, Quaglino argued that his patient suffered from a specific disorder of face recognition that could not be ascribed to a more basic perceptual disorder. In a 1947 report, Bodamer reaffirmed the existence of prosopagnosia as a distinct clinical entity, and he suggested it be called prosopagnosia, from the Greek word *prosopon*, which means face.

How Selective is Prosopagnosia?

In general, prosopagnosics have some degree of difficulty recognizing objects other than faces, but their difficulty with faces is the most significant aspect of their agnosia. Much of the recent research on prosopagnosia has addressed whether the face recognition impairment in prosopagnosia is most salient simply because faces are the most difficult types of objects to recognize or because it is truly disproportionate to patients' object recognition difficulties even when difficulty is taken into account. The answer to this question about prosopagnosia has important implications for our understanding of the normal human visual system. If all types of visual stimuli are recognized using a single general-purpose system, then it should not be possible for brain damage to impair face recognition disproportionately. On the other hand, if face recognition is disproportionately impaired, this suggests that the human brain has a specialized face recognition system, which when damaged leads to prosopagnosia.

In order to determine whether prosopagnosia is truly selective for faces, and hence whether the human brain has specialized mechanisms for recognizing faces, the prosopagnosic's performance on faces and nonface objects must be assessed relative to the difficulty of these stimuli for normal subjects. The first researchers to address this issue directly were McNeil and Warrington. They studied case WJ, a middle-aged professional man who became prosopagnosic following a series of strokes. After becoming prosopagnosic, WJ made a career change and became a sheep farmer. He eventually came to recognize many of his sheep, although he remained unable to recognize most humans. The authors noted the potential implications of this dissociation for the question of whether human face recognition is "special," and they designed an ingenious experiment to exploit WJ's newfound career. They assembled three groups of photographs of human faces and sheep faces of a different breed, and they attempted to teach subject names for each face. Normal subjects performed at intermediate levels in all conditions. Normal subjects, even those who, like WJ, worked with sheep, performed better with the human faces than with sheep faces. In contrast, WJ performed poorly with the human faces and performed normally with sheep faces. These data suggest that WJ's recognition impairment does not affect the recognition of all groups of visually similar patterns but is selective for human faces.

Similar results were obtained by Farah et al. using common objects rather than faces of another species to compare with human face recognition. The subject was LH, a well-educated professional man who has been prosopagnosic since an automobile accident in college. LH related the story presented at the beginning of this entry of mistaking his own reflection for another person. This investigation employed a recognition memory paradigm in which LH and control subjects first studied a set of photographs of faces and nonface objects, such as forks, chairs, and eyeglasses. Subjects were then given a larger set of photographs and asked to make "old"/"new" judgments about them. This larger set was designed so that for each face and nonface object in the old set there was a highly similar item in the new set. For example, one of the study items was an upholstered swiveling desk chair with arms. Among the larger set of test photos, there were two upholstered swiveling desk chairs with arms, one of the old chair and one of a new chair. Whereas normal subjects performed equally well with the faces and nonface objects, LH showed a significant performance disparity, performing worse with faces than with objects. A disproportionate impairment with faces was also found in a second experiment, in which the nonface stimuli were drawn from a single large and visually homogeneous category, namely eyeglass frames.

The general conclusion of the studies of WJ and LH is that prosopagnosia represents the selective loss of visual mechanisms necessary for face recognition and not necessary (or less necessary) for other types of object recognition.

Neuroanatomy

What are the anatomical substrates of face recognition in the human brain? Studies of prosopagnosic patients provide important evidence. The studies on the patients described previously, WJ and LH, are not very informative regarding localization because the patients' damage was widespread (multiple strokes and closed head injury, respectively). Surveys of the lesions in larger groups of prosopagnosics are more helpful in regard to localization because the regions of overlap among different patients can be identified.

De Renzi et al. reviewed published cases of prosopagnosia with autopsy data, along with recent cases and data from living patients whose brain damage was mapped using both structural magnetic resonance imaging (MRI) and positron emission tomography (PET). Their findings supported a ventral temporo-occipital localization of face recognition. Although most prosopagnosics had bilateral lesions, some patients became prosopagnosic after unilateral right hemisphere damage. The possibility of hidden left hemisphere dysfunction in these cases was reduced by the PET scan finding of normal metabolic activity in the left hemisphere. DeRenzi et al. concluded that there is a spectrum of hemispheric specialization for face recognition in normal right-handed adults. Although the right hemisphere may be relatively better at face recognition than the left, most people have a degree of face recognition ability in both hemispheres. Nevertheless, in a minority of cases, face recognition is so focally represented in the right hemisphere that a unilateral lesion will lead to prosopagnosia.

The lesion sites associated with prosopagnosia are, as a group, clearly different from the lesions that cause associative object agnosia in the absence of prosopagnosia. The latter syndrome is almost invariably associated with a unilateral left hemisphere lesion, although it is confined to approximately the same intrahemispheric region. These findings accord well with the growing literature on functional neuroimaging of normal subjects. For example, Kanwisher et al. used MRI to compare regional brain activity while subjects viewed photographs of faces and objects. An objects-minus-faces subtraction revealed areas more responsive to objects than faces, and the reverse revealed an area more responsive to faces than objects. Both types of stimuli activated inferior temporo-occipital regions, with face-specific activation confined to part of the right fusiform gyrus. A follow-up study by Kanwisher and coworkers identified the same fusiform face area and systematically verified its specificity for faces by comparing responses to faces and to scrambled faces, houses, and hands.

Conclusion

Prosopagnosia is a subtype of visual agnosic disturbance that can be dissociated neuropsychologically from other visual recognition disturbances, such as visual object agnosia and alexia. On the basis of lesion studies in prosopagnosic patients and supporting evidence from functional imaging investigations in normal subjects, medial occipito-temporal regions, especially of the right hemisphere, are implicated in the pathophysiology of prosopagnosia and in face recognition abilities in general.

See also: Agnosia.

Further Reading

De Renzi, E (1997). Prosopagnosia. In: Feinberg, TE and Farah, M (eds.) *Behavioral Neurology and Neuropsychology*, pp. 245–255. New York: McGraw-Hill.

De Renzi, E, Perani, D, Carlesimo, GA, et al. (1994). Prosopagnosia can be associated with damage confined to the right hemisphere—An MRI and PET study and a review of the literature. *Neuropsychologia* 32: 893–902.

Farah, M (1991). Patterns of co-occurrence among the associative agnosias: Implications for visual object representation. *Cogn. Neuropsychol.* 8: 1–19.

Farah, MJ, Klein, KL, and Levinson, KL (1995). Face perception and within-category discrimination in prosopagnosia. *Neuropsychologia* 33: 661–674.

Feinberg, TE, Rothi, LJ, and Heilman, KM (1986). Multimodal agnosia after unilateral left hemisphere lesion. *Neurology* 36: 864–867.

Feinberg, TE, Schindler, FJ, Ochoa, E, et al. (1994). Associative visual agnosia and alexia without prosopagnosia. *Cortex* 30: 395–412.

Kanwisher, N, Chun, MM, McDermott, J, et al. (1996). Functional imaging of human visual recognition. *Brain Res. Cogn. Brain Res.* 5: 55–67.

Kanwisher, N, McDermott, J, and Chun, MM (1997). The fusiform face area: A module in human extrastriae cortex specialized for face perception. *J. Neurosci.* 17: 4302–4311.

McNeil, JE and Warrington, EK (1993). Prosopagnosia: A face-specific disorder. *Q. J. Exp. Psychol.* 46A: 1–10.

Quaglino, A (1867). Empeligia sinistra con amaurosi-Guarigione-Perdita totale della percezione dei colori e della memoria della configurazione degli oggetti. Annotazione alla medesima di GB Borelli. *G. Ital. Oftalmol.* 10: 106–117.

R

Reading and Acquired Dyslexia

H. B. Coslett

The archaeological record suggests that the uniquely human capacity to read developed during the past 4000 years. Because this period is generally considered to be too brief for evolutionary processes to have played a significant role, it appears that reading is not supported by a dedicated processing mechanism but is dependent on preexisting capacities to process complex visual stimuli and language. In this entry, the visual and linguistic processes by which written words are thought to be identified are reviewed and specific syndromes of acquired dyslexia resulting from disruption of these processes are discussed.

Processes Involved in Reading

Reading requires that the visual system efficiently process a complicated stimulus that, at least for alphabetic languages, is composed of smaller meaningful units—letters. In part because the number of letters is small in relation to the number of words, there is often a considerable visual similarity between words (e.g., "structure" vs "stricture"). Additionally, the position of letters within the letter string is also critical to word identification (e.g., "mast" vs "mats"). Therefore, it is perhaps not surprising that reading places a substantial burden on the visual system and that disorders of visual processing or visual attention may substantially disrupt reading.

Normal readers recognize written words so rapidly and effortlessly that one might suspect that a word is identified as a unit, much as we identify an object. The evidence, however, suggests otherwise. Normal reading appears to require that letters be identified as alphabetic symbols. Support for this claim comes from demonstrations that presenting words in an unfamiliar form—for example, by alternating the case of the letters (e.g., "wOrD") or introducing spaces between words (e.g., "w o r d")—does not substantially influence reading speed or accuracy. Data from these and other studies indicate a stage of word identification in which the graphic form (whether printed or written) is transformed into a string of alphabetic characters ("W-O-R-D"), sometimes referred to as abstract letter identities. Finally, it should be noted that in normal circumstances letters are not processed in a strictly serial fashion but letter strings are processed in parallel (provided they are not too long).

Controversy persists regarding the mechanisms by which a visual word form contacts its meaning and sound (or pronunciation). Dual-route models of reading postulate three procedures by which a written word may be pronounced. The first is a semantic procedure by which the letter string contacts an entry in a stored catalog of familiar words, or visual word form system. Meaning is subsequently accessed directly from the visual word form system. With this procedure, which in some respects is similar to looking up a word in a dictionary, access to the sound of the word is achieved only after the meaning of the word has been established. Dual-route accounts also incorporate a second "lexical" mechanism by means of which stored word forms contact phonology directly without accessing meaning. Finally, dual-route models of reading also assume that the letter string can be converted directly to a phonological form by means of the application of a set of learned correspondences between orthography and phonology. On this account, meaning may then be accessed from the phonological form of the word. Although originally formulated as a "box and arrow" model, Coltheart and colleagues developed a fully specified, computer-instantiated dual-route model of reading.

In recent years, a fundamentally different conceptual approach to reading has been developed by Seidenberg and McClelland and subsequently elaborated by Plaut et al. This account belongs to the general class of parallel distributed processing or connectionist models. Sometimes referred to as the triangle model, this approach incorporates a semantically based reading procedure but differs from dual-route accounts in that it eschews word-specific stored information (e.g., visual word forms and output phonological representations). Rather, subjects are assumed to learn how written words map onto spoken words through repeated exposure to letter strings. Learning of word pronunciations is achieved by means of the development of a mapping between letters and sounds generated on the basis of experience with many different letter strings. The probabilistic mapping between letters and sounds is assumed to provide the means by which both familiar and unfamiliar words are pronounced.

Acquired Dyslexias

Acquired dyslexias are disorders of reading observed in previously literate individuals as a consequence of brain dysfunction. A useful starting point in the discussion of these disorders is the distinction between peripheral and central dyslexias. The former are conditions characterized by a deficit in the processing of visual aspects of the stimulus that prevent the patient from reliably matching a familiar word to the visual word form. In contrast, central dyslexias reflect impairment to the "deeper" or "higher" reading functions by which visual word forms mediate access to meaning or speech production mechanisms.

Peripheral Dyslexias

Alexia without agraphia (pure alexia; letter-by-letter reading) is among the most common of the peripheral reading disturbances. It is associated with a left hemisphere lesion that blocks direct visual input to the reading mechanisms in the left hemisphere. Some patients seem to be unable to read at all, whereas others do so slowly and laboriously by means of a process that involves serial letter identification (often termed letter-by-letter reading). This form of alexia is pure in the sense that patients with the disorder often speak and write normally. Recent work suggests that many patients with this disorder exhibit implicit reading in that they access information about written words of which they are unaware.

Neglect dyslexia is a disorder characterized by a failure to process part of the letter string. Patients with neglect dyslexia may read "cowboy" as "boy" or "house" as "use." In most instances, the disorder is associated with impaired identification of the left side of the letter string. However, recent work suggests that many patients with left hemisphere lesions exhibit less dramatic but clinically significant neglect of word ends.

Attentional dyslexia is a disorder characterized by at least relatively preserved reading of single words but impaired reading of words in the context of other words or letters. By one account, attentional dyslexia is attributed to poor control of a filtering mechanism that normally serves to suppress input from unattended words or letters in the display. Loss of precision regarding letter location may also contribute to the disorder.

Central Dyslexias

Deep dyslexia is the most extensively investigated of the central dyslexias and, in many respects, the most compelling. Perhaps the most dramatic manifestation of deep dyslexia is the production of semantic errors. For example, when shown the word "desk," a deep dyslexic may respond "table." Deep dyslexics also typically produce visual errors (e.g., "skate" read as "scale") and morphological errors in which a prefix or suffix is added, deleted, or substituted (e.g., "scolded" read as "scolds" or "governor" read as "government").

Additional features of the syndrome include a greater success in reading words of high (e.g., "table") compared to low (e.g., "destiny") imageability. Patients with this disorder exhibit a part of speech effect such that nouns are read better than modifiers, which in turn are read more accurately than verbs. Functors or short words (e.g., "that," "which," and "because") are particularly difficult for deep dyslexics. One deep dyslexic, for example, was able to read the word "chrysanthemum" but not "the." Finally, all deep dyslexics exhibit a substantial impairment in the pronunciation of nonword letter strings (e.g., "flig").

Deep dyslexia is generally attributed to an impairment in the ability to read by phonoligic mediation (e.g., sounding out) with a reliance on the semantically based reading procedure. Whether this process is dependent on abnormal left hemisphere reading procedure or reflects processing by the right hemisphere remains controversial.

Phonological dyslexia is a disorder in which reading of real words may be nearly intact or only mildly impaired. For example, patients with this disorder correctly read 85–95% of real words. Most errors in response to real words bear a visual similarity to the target word (e.g., "topple" read as "table").

The striking aspect of the performance of phonological dyslexics is a substantial impairment in the oral reading of nonword letter strings (e.g., "chust"). Most errors to nonwords involve the substitution of a visually similar real word (e.g., "phope" read as "phone") or the incorrect application of print-to-sound correspondences [e.g., "stime" read as "stim" (to rhyme with "him")].

In the dual-route model of reading, the account for this disorder is relatively straightforward. Good performance with real words suggests that the processes involved in normal lexical reading (i.e., visual analysis, the visual word form system, semantics, and the phonological output lexicon) are at least relatively preserved. The impairment in nonword reading suggests that the print-to-sound translation procedure is disrupted.

Surface dyslexia is characterized by the relatively preserved ability to read words with regular or predictable grapheme-to-phoneme correspondences but substantially impaired reading of words with irregular or exceptional print-to-sound correspondences. Surface dyslexics typically read words such as "state," "hand," "mosquito," and "abdominal" quite well, but they exhibit substantial problems reading words such as "colonel," "yacht," "island," and "borough," the pronunciation of which cannot be derived by sounding-out strategies. Errors to irregular words usually consist of "regularizations"; for example, surface dyslexics may read "colonel" as "kollonel."

The fact that the regularity of print-to-sound correspondences significantly influences performance in surface dyslexia suggests that patients with this disorder rely on phonics or print-to-sound correspondences.

Acknowledgments

This work was supported by the National Institute of Deafness and Other Communication Disorders Grant RO1 DC2754.

See also: Agrammatism; Agraphia; Language and Discourse; Phonology.

Further Reading

Coltheart, M (1996). Phonological dyslexia: Past and future issues. *Cogn. Neuropsychol.* 13.
Coltheart, M (1998). Pure alexia: Letter-by-letter reading. *Cogn. Neuropsychol.* 15.
Coltheart, M, Patterson, K, and Marshall, JC (eds.) (1980). *Deep Dyslexia.* London: Routledge Kegan Paul.
Funnell, E (ed.) (2000). *Case Studies in the Neuropsychology of Reading.* Hove, UK: Psychology Press.
Patterson, KE, Marshall, JC, and Coltheart, M (eds.) (1985). *Surface Dyslexia.* London: Routledge Kegan Paul.
Plaut, DC, McClelland, JL, Seidenberg, MS, et al. (1996). Understanding normal and impaired word reading: Computational principles in quasi-regular domains. *Psychol. Rev.* 103: 56–115.
Rastle, K and Coltheart, M (1999). Serial and strategic effects in reading aloud. *J. Exp. Psychol. Hum. Percep. Performance* 25: 482–503.

Recovery of Language after Stroke or Trauma in Adults

S. S. Christman and F. R. Boutsen, The University of Oklahoma Health Sciences Center, Oklahoma City, OK, USA

Introduction

Research efforts in the realm of recovery from aphasia have generally been directed toward (a) identification of salient neurologic and anagraphic factors predictive of recovery, (b) investigation of recovery mechanisms associated with different lesion sites, etiologies, and aphasia symptom clusters using modern imaging techniques, (c) determination of the relative roles of the two cerebral hemispheres in recovery, and (d) explication of the role of behavioral and pharmacological treatments in facilitating recovery from acute, subacute, and chronic aphasia. Current thought on these topics will be discussed herein. Space limitations prohibit discussions of attention, memory, and motor speech recovery, even though deficits in attention and memory may underlie some symptoms of aphasia and even though improvements in all of these domains may parallel and, to some extent, perhaps explain, individual differences in recovery from aphasia (Crosson, 2000a, 2000b; Haarman and Kolk, 1991; Kolk, 1995; Kolk and Weijts, 1996; Tseng et al., 1993). Discussion will focus on recovery from classic acquired aphasia (e.g., that which is associated with CVA or focal trauma) in monolingual speakers rather than recovery from the 'non-acquired' (progressive) aphasias arising from degenerative disease (Kertesz et al., 1994; Mesulam, 1982; Weintraub et al., 1990) or neoplastic proliferation. Recovery phenomena in bilingual speakers with aphasia or in those with crossed aphasia will also not be addressed, though readers are encouraged to investigate these phenomena (cf. Paradis, 2000; Paradis and Goldblum, 1989).

It should be noted that while many acquired aphasic syndromes have been identified and studied in modern research, aphasia is nevertheless a somewhat individualized disorder of impaired information processing, specific to that subsystem of cognition serving language (Davis, 2000; Porch, 1994, 2001). Recovery from acquired aphasia has been thought to depend on a variety of neurological factors, including type of aphasia, severity of initial aphasia, site of neurological lesion, extent of neurological lesion, time postonset, etiology, and presence of concomitant disorders (Basso, 1992). A variety of anagraphic or personal factors such as the age, gender, handedness, and psychosocial characteristics of affected individuals also influences the speed and extent of recovery (Basso, 1992; Hemsley and Code, 1996; LaPointe, 1999). An important additional factor influencing aphasia resolution is the type, frequency, and intensity of speech–language treatment received (Basso, 1992; Carlomango et al., 2001; Weiller et al., 1995). Research in recovery supports the notion of language as a well-distributed function with some localizable aspects, illustrates the limitations of aphasia typologies in capturing recovery phenomena, and establishes the superiority of neurological (vs. anagraphic) factors as those most predictive of recovery. It also pushes the recovery envelope beyond conventional limits by providing evidence for neural reorganization and functional improvement in chronic aphasia when intensive treatment paradigms are applied (Hillis and Heidler, 2002; Pulvermuller et al., 2001).

Aphasia: Localized and Distributed

Aphasia has been defined as "a selective impairment of the cognitive system specialized for comprehending and formulating language, leaving other cognitive capacities relatively intact." (Davis, 2000: 16–17). It is an acquired disorder of language processing arising most often in adults as a consequence of cerebro-vascular accident (CVA) or 'stroke' in the language-dominant hemisphere of the brain's cerebral cortex or subcortex (Benson and Ardila, 1996; Brown, 1980; Davis, 2000). There are many types of aphasias, and their symptoms are somewhat predictable from basic principles of brain–language organization. These principles establish that there are strong relationships between normal mental functions (such as language, attention, and memory) and either localized regions of the brain or collections of reciprocal, highly parallel neural networks that are widely distributed across brain regions (Chollet and Weiller, 2000; Howard et al., 1992; Kertesz, 1991; Mesulam, 1990).

Distributed neural networks are comprised of interconnected neurosynaptic circuits, some elements of which may be distant, but all of which converge on local nodal processing zones that are crucial for network operations (Mesulam, 1990). Wernicke's area (minimally Brodmann Area 22 but see Bogen and Bogen, 1976), a region of the cerebral cortex in the superior temporal gyrus of the dominant language hemisphere (the left cerebrum in most individuals) is one such nodal region for the distributed circuitry dedicated to the auditory comprehension of language (Mesulam, 1990). This area also plays an important role in semantic and phonological processing (Kertesz, 1991). Broca's area (typically Brodmann Areas 44–45), a region of the cerebral cortex in the posterior, inferior area of the third frontal convolution of the dominant language hemisphere, is another nodal region whose function is essential for motor speech planning/programming (Mesulam, 1990; Van der Merwe, 1997), for some forms of semantic processing, and for some aspects of syntax construction and interpretation (Kertesz, 1991). Wernicke's and Broca's regions are frequently coactive during language processing (Van der Merwe, 1997) and, when damaged, frequently lead to distinctly different but persistent symptoms of aphasia. Damage to the more widely distributed elements of the auditory comprehension or syntactic processing circuitries may also impair the adequacy of those functions but usually not to the extent that is found when damage to the nodal (Wernicke's or Broca's) zones occurs (Mesulam, 1990).

Other important speech and language processing circuits support those associated with Wernicke's and Broca's areas and yield aphasic outputs when damaged. Individual differences notwithstanding, strokes involving large portions of the frontal language cortex (especially Broca's area, or zones anterior–superior to or deep to Broca's area), and/or portions of the basal ganglia typically cause the so-called 'nonfluent' types of aphasia such as Broca's aphasia, transcortical motor aphasia, mixed transcortical aphasia, global aphasia, and striato-capsular aphasia (Benson and Ardila, 1996; Goodglass and Kaplan, 1983; LaPointe, 1997). These disorders may vary somewhat in severity and symptomatology, but as a group they are characterized by nonfluent speech, relatively few phonemic paraphasias (sound substitutions, omissions, additions, or misorderings), difficulty accessing content words (particularly verbs), and disturbed comprehension and production of complex syntactic forms. Sentence production is usually described as telegraphic or agrammatic, lacking intact syntactic constituent structures and characterized by the omission of free and bound grammatical morphemes (Berndt, 1998; Caplan, 1987, 1992; Kean, 1985; Kearns, 1997).

Strokes involving posterior cortical language zones (especially Brodmann Areas 22, 37, 39, 40) and/or the thalamus, on the other hand, frequently cause the more 'fluent' aphasias such as Wernicke's aphasia, transcortical sensory aphasia, conduction aphasia, anomic aphasia, and thalamic aphasia (Benson and Ardila, 1996; Goodglass and Kaplan, 1983; LaPointe, 1997). These disorders frequently are identified by impaired auditory comprehension, severe word-finding deficits (particularly for nouns), copious production of phonemic paraphasias and neologisms, and syntax production deficits characterized by substitutions (more often than omissions) of free and bound grammatical morphemes (Benson and Ardila, 1996; Buckingham, 1989; Caplan, 1987, 1992; Christman and Buckingham, 1989; Gonzales-Rothi, 1997; Simmons-Mackie, 1997). Recovery from aphasia is an incremental process characterized by a reduction of symptoms and an improvement in language comprehension, production, or integration.

Discussions of recovery from aphasia frequently link physiological and behavioral concepts, inadvertently suggesting that localizing and/or measuring changes in the activity of normal and lesioned brain areas is akin to localizing and/or assessing improvements in normal and disordered mental functions. John Hughlings Jackson (1874), however, cautions otherwise (Kertesz, 1991) as do Chollet and Weiller (2000: 587) who note that, "... recovery corresponds to improvement of clinical function in patients and not necessarily to any changes in cerebral activation patterns as they can be observed with modern neuroimaging techniques." It is therefore important to be careful in the attribution of causality to any of the neurological changes accompanying functional improvements in aphasia. It is a *sine qua non* in the philosophy of science that 'correlation' does not and cannot mean 'causation.' Despite this caveat, a thriving line of research suggests that neural reorganization and reduction in aphasia symptoms may correlate even in patients with chronic aphasia (Pulvermuller et al., 2001).

While there are correlations between specific brain areas and associated linguistic functions, there is sufficient functional overlap or redundancy in distributed language processing networks to permit several different neural structures to perform a particular operation on different occasions (Kertesz, 1991). One such occasion may be when brain damage provides an opportunity for nonnodal, or even latent, circuits to assume (albeit less efficiently) the function of a damaged network (Chollet and Weiller, 2000) during recovery. Localizing function is perhaps least controversial for nodal brain areas but even then, functional localization is not fixed because the brain retains some plasticity or capacity for reorganization across the lifespan (Brown, 1980, 1982; Chollet and Weiller, 2000). The extent to which portions of nodal zones can recover function, the extent to which distributed (nonnodal) network circuitry can continue a function, and the extent to which nondedicated or formerly nonparticipatory circuits can assume new functions comprise some of the issues investigated in the research on the neural mechanisms underlying recovery from aphasia.

Recovery: A Continuous Phenomenon

A Framework for Understanding Recovery

Recovery from acquired aphasia is evident when language processing skills improve to levels beyond those extant immediately after the onset of stroke. Recovery is therefore defined operationally in behavioral terms and cannot be directly attributed to specific changes in poststroke neurophysiology (Chollet and Weiller, 2000; Porch, 1994, 2001). Porch (1994: 175) described aphasia from this kind of cybernetic perspective, arguing that neurological insults reduce the brain's ability to,

> "store, switch, and monitor, and to do the many other steps necessary for the brain to receive, assimilate, and send information. Since these processes cannot be observed directly, they must be assessed by exposing the patient to standard tasks . . . and then the clinician, by carefully noting the response characteristics of the patient, can make inferences about the relative efficiency of various 'brain circuits.' "

This approach views aphasia less as a loss of morphosyntactic, semantic, and phonological knowledge per se and more as a disorder of an individual's ability to accurately, responsively, completely, promptly, and efficiently utilize the computational processes underlying language processing (Porch, 1994, 2001). Computational failures of these kinds lead to the types of linguistic errors (e.g., semantic or phonemic paraphasias, agrammatic or paragrammatic syntax), comprehension deficits, response delays (e.g., long or short, filled or silent latencies), and unintelligible utterances (e.g., neologisms) that characterize the aphasias. In this paradigm, recovery is observed when language tasks are processed more accurately, responsively, completely, promptly, and efficiently than they were previously. Therapeutic improvement is accomplished by repeatedly stimulating damaged language systems with performance tasks that are challenging but achievable (Porch, 1994, 2001; Schuell, 1974). The assumption underlying this approach is that when damaged neural networks are properly stimulated, repeated activation of those networks ultimately increases their internal activation strength, in consequence yielding faster and more accurate language processing over time. Many current models of parallel language processing in artificial intelligence systems support this conclusion (cf. Martin and Dell, 2004), but the precise nature of the brain–language interface remains elusive. To the extent that the cybernetic metaphor can be extended to actual neurological activity, however, this remains the fundamental principle underlying recovery from aphasia.

As Kertesz (1988) affirms, aphasia is a dynamic disorder, a disorder in evolution. When aphasia is viewed as a constellation of symptoms, with each symptom moving along an independent recovery continuum over time, it is not surprising that chronic symptom profiles may differ significantly from acute symptom profiles. Aphasia taxonomies are problematic for representing the nature of change underlying aphasia recovery, because their use suggests that aphasic speakers somehow metamorphose from one type of aphasia to another (from Global to Broca's type, for example). A more logical conceptualization is that initial poststroke phenomena such as edema and diaschisis compromise the function of multiple local and distant circuits within the language processing network, and across related networks, yielding numerous initial symptoms that may not persist over time. Diaschisis, the state of 'shock' into which hypoperfused neurons enter after a brain injury, spreads along neuroanatomical pathways away from an initial site of lesion, reducing function in the many brain areas that may be served by those pathways (Chollet and Weiller, 2000). Cerebrocerebellar connections, for example, allow damage to the cerebrum to suppress metabolic function in remote cerebellar locations. Although the relationship between diaschisis and aphasic symptoms is not fully understood, it is suspected that as edema and diaschisis resolve during the process of spontaneous recovery, some initial symptoms of aphasia will disappear (Cappa, 2000). As language processing networks are stimulated through use, a number of neural mechanisms may contribute to improved processing over time. As Rosenbek et al. (1989) note, however, a core of aphasia symptoms will persist in most individuals.

The principle that local neural networks participate in larger-scale networks is consistent with the observation that diverse lesion sites (affecting diverse neural networks) can yield similar symptoms (e.g., naming is mediated redundantly across right and left peri-Sylvian cortex, as well as across some subcortical structures, so anomic behavior arises unsurprisingly from lesions to multiple cortical and subcortical sites). Individual differences in language network configurations may be genetically coded, may reflect neural reorganization following cortical injury, may depend on the age at which a language was learned, and may depend on an individual's gender, handedness, or intrinsic learning style. Individual differences suggest the likelihood that identically located lesions across individuals may not yield identical symptom complexes, and suggest the converse as well – that different lesion sites across individuals may occasionally yield similar symptom complexes (Kertesz, 1991). These factors confound the study of recovery in aphasia, making it difficult to match subjects in group studies, but also making it difficult to generalize findings from single subject studies where an individual subject has been his own control. These methodological difficulties, combined with the ambiguities inherent in typology change over time, make it difficult to compare studies of recovery. Nevertheless, a review of the recovery literature suggests that there are some factors that can reliably predict recovery from aphasia.

The Aphasia Recovery Curve

The classic recovery curve in aphasia can be described as one of gradual inclination and progressive deceleration within the first year postonset (Porch, 1994, 2001). Although there is little agreement as to the exact time course for recovery, the greatest improvement in language function is generally seen within the first three months postonset (Kertesz, 1988). Although some have suggested that little change in language function will occur past that time (Basso, 1992), recent studies suggest otherwise (Pulvermuller et al., 2001). Recovery plateaus are generally apparent within six months to one year postonset. The parallel of the aphasia recovery curve with that of spontaneous (biological) recovery has prompted numerous aphasia treatment studies (Basso, 1992), many of which suggest that language recovers best in response to purposeful, intensive stimulation, whether delivered by educated professionals or caregiving significant others. Other studies, however, have shown that many patients with aphasia recover functional language even without directed intervention (Basso, 1992).

Different recovery mechanisms may be at work at different overlapping 'stages' of the recovery continuum. While neural reorganization can occur soon after stroke, especially with peripheral or small cortical lesions (Chollet and Weiller, 2000; Merzenich et al., 1983; Coq and Xerri, 1999; Jenkins and Merzenich, 1987; Jenkins et al., 1990; Weiller et al., 1992). Hillis and Heidler (2002) suggest that this, together with the learning of compensatory strategies, is more likely a mechanism associated with later stages of recovery from aphasia. They further suggest that it is the reperfusion of surviving (but nonfunctional) ischemic tissue surrounding an area of infarct (i.e., reperfusion of the 'ischemic penumbra') that probably accounts for early resolution of aphasic symptoms, even in severe cases, during the first few (1–3) days following stroke. To test this premise, Hillis and Heidler (2002) investigated early recovery of lexical-semantics (reflected via spoken word comprehension) in 18 patients with aphasia secondary to posterior left hemisphere stroke. They hypothesized that if initial hypoperfusion of Wernicke's area causes poor word comprehension, speedy reperfusion of that area should accompany improved comprehension soon after stroke.

Patients meeting the criteria for lexical-semantic deficit (10 men, 8 women, all right-handed, mean age 61 years) were assessed once with magnetic resonance imaging techniques of perfusion-weighted imaging (PWI) and diffusion-weighted imaging (DWI) at Day 1 of stroke onset and again at Days 2–5 (mean Day 3) postonset. Perfusion levels of ten anterior and posterior left hemisphere cortical zones (Brodmann Areas 10/11, 18/19, 20, 22, 37, 38, 39, 44, 45) were evaluated on each assessment. Lexical-semantic tasks (word comprehension and production) were given on Day 1 and at follow up. Thirteen of the eighteen subjects demonstrated early recovery of lexical-semantics. All 13 of these subjects showed a corresponding statistically significant reperfusion of Area 22 (Wernicke's area) to the exclusion of the other Brodmann areas studied. None of the five subjects with poor lexical-semantic recovery demonstrated reperfusion of Wernicke's area. This double dissociation, and in the coincident absence of evidence for neural reorganization in subjects studied, suggests a crucial role for reperfusion of an ischemic penumbra (in this case, Wernicke's area), in early recovery of lexical-semantics in aphasia.

Hillis and Heidler (2002) argued that whereas rapid neural reorganization has been documented in the sensory cortex following peripheral limb amputation and in the sensory-motor cortex following small focal lesions, less rapidity is observed when cortical lesions are large and/or when damaged functions (such as lexical-semantic processing) are complex and widely distributed. They suggested that in most cases of aphasia, recovery can be characterized as a three-stage process mediated by different neurological mechanisms and benefiting from different approaches to intervention. The first, acute, phase of recovery occurs during the first few days after stroke and is characterized primarily by reperfusion of the ischemic penumbra and/or reduction of diaschisis (Cappa, 2000). Intervention at this stage of recovery is best managed medically with input provided to patients and families from speech-language pathologists who can share information and counseling with regard to the nature of recovery from aphasia. The second or subacute stage of recovery may begin several days after onset and continue for months or even years. Neural reorganization is thought to account for most aspects of recovery at this stage and rehabilitation efforts are directed toward the provision of intensive therapies for language stimulation.

The third or chronic stage of recovery follows the completion of neural reorganization and probably involves the establishment of new pathways to link language processing zones that have become functionally disconnected as a consequence of stroke. In the chronic phase of recovery, speech-language intervention may yield improved behavioral outcomes in motivated patients who receive intensive daily treatment and/or who are receptive to learning compensatory strategies for managing compromised language skills (Hillis and Heidler, 2002; Pulvermuller et al., 2001). As Hillis and Heidler, (2002: 893) noted, "These stages are likely overlapping, in that one language function might be recovering in one stage, while another language function is recovering in another stage, in the same individual." This phenomenon explains why some patients initially diagnosed with one type of aphasia, such as Wernicke's or conduction aphasia, may eventually recover to another type such as anomic aphasia, the residual symptom profile apparent when, for example, initial auditory comprehension problems, phonemic jargon, and verbal repetition deficits improve but aphasic word finding difficulties persist (Simmons and Buckingham, 1992).

Neurologic Factors in Aphasia Recovery

Mechanisms of Recovery

The mechanisms of neurological change during recovery from stroke are thought to contribute to recovery from aphasia, although the degree of causality remains unclear (Cappa, 2000; Cappa et al., 1997). Chollet and Weiller (2000) described four mechanisms of cerebral reorganization made apparent from a decade of poststroke neuroimaging studies: spontaneous neural reorganization, recruitment of remote brain areas (including the cerebral hemisphere contralateral to the site of stroke), extension of specialized areas into neighboring cortex, and increased neurological activity in lesioned areas. Spontaneous neural reorganization in stroke patients can be observed with Positron Emission Tomography (PET) as changes in patterns of cerebral metabolism (increased and/or decreased) relative to patterns exhibited by normal controls (Weiller et al., 1992). Metabolic changes unrelated to diaschisis can be observed soon after stroke onset and may account for the rapid improvement seen in the postacute phase of recovery from aphasia (Chollet and Weiller, 2000). PET studies have provided some evidence that the right hemisphere (remote to lesioned left temporal cortex) is activated during language processing in patients with good (vs. poor) recovery from Wernicke's aphasia (Weiller et al., 1995), although studies have also shown that some normal, nonaphasic individuals show right hemisphere activation during similar language tasks (Frackowiak, 1997). With regard to cortical extension, it has been well-documented that lesions to motor pathways and the motor cortex can influence the activity of undamaged motor zones. Cortical areas that have become underactivated because of limb paralysis, for example, may become re-dedicated to the function of remaining intact limbs or other moveable structures that are represented nearby on a cortical motor map (Cohen et al., 1991; Nudo et al., 1996; Weiller et al., 1992; Weiller et al., 1993; Pons et al., 1991). Finally, with regard to increased activity of nonspared cortical areas, evidence suggests that, at least with regard to the hierarchically organized motor system, damage to lower-order structures leads to increased compensatory activity of associated higher-order structures in the system. It is interesting to speculate that a highly integrated but nevertheless hierarchically conceived language system (cf. Brown, 1982) might show much the same pattern of neural reorganization after stroke.

This observation is consistent with Melulam's assertion that distributed activation networks can demonstrate spontaneous learning and is certainly consistent with the work of Mazzoni and colleagues (1992), who were able to quantify spontaneous recovery from aphasia in 45 first-time stroke patients. Assessments of oral and written expression, as well as auditory–verbal and reading comprehension were conducted at 15 days postonset, one month post-onset, three to four months postonset, and six to seven months postonset.

Mazzoni et al.'s (1992) findings across subjects, in summary, were the following:

1. Oral comprehension recovery began early at two weeks postonset, continued throughout the first year after stroke, and was independent of initial aphasia type, severity, or size of lesion. Reading comprehension was maximal within the first month postonset.
2. Recovery rates for expression were slower than for comprehension and differed according to aphasia type. Fluent aphasias showed uniform improvement from two weeks postonset onward; nonfluent aphasias began to improve only at the three to four month poststroke

period. Apraxia of speech may have confounded results in the latter group.
3. Fluent patients and all patients with moderately severe aphasias improved significantly in all four language modalities (verbal expression, listening comprehension, reading, writing). Nonfluent patients and those with initially severe aphasias showed limited improvement in verbal expression and no recovery of written language.
4. Patients with small lesions of moderate size showed significant recovery across modalities. Patients with moderately sized lesions improved in all modalities except written expression. Patients with large lesions only showed improvement in auditory comprehension.

Their main conclusions were that (1) the dominant language hemisphere has good potential for assisting with auditory comprehension but not verbal expression, and that (2) the posterior site of lesion correlates with increased aphasia severity, which in turn predicts poor recovery. Because auditory comprehension deficits frequently characterize the posterior aphasias, the findings of Mazzoni and colleagues present aphasiologists with a conundrum for future study.

The Role of the Contralateral Cortex in Recovery

There are many approaches to measuring the role of the cerebral hemispheres in the recovery from aphasia. According to Cappa and Vallar (1992), the most widely used physiological approach to lateralization studies is examination of auditory evoked potentials to linguistic stimuli. Thomas et al. (1997) suggested that electroencephalography (EEG) provides a reliable and robust method for assessing changes in lateralization of language functions during recovery, and Cappa (2000) noted the important role that Positron Emission Tomography (PET) and functional Magnetic Resonance Imaging (fMRI) technologies have played in recent aphasia studies. Recovery research varies across a number of important factors, including subject characteristics (e.g., subject age, language, etiology), numbers of subjects per study, type of aphasia examined, nature of symptoms tested, stage of recovery studied, and method of brain assessment used, among others. This variety creates difficulties in the comparison of findings across studies, but there are nevertheless some general (occasionally conflicting) conclusions that can be drawn about the role of the two cerebral hemispheres in recovery from aphasia. They may be summarized as follows: right-hemisphere activity in areas homologous to damaged left-hemisphere zones is frequently observed early in recovery for both anterior and posterior language zones. In later stages of successful recovery, increased activity in damaged left-hemisphere zones, with concommitant diminution of right-hemisphere activation, is often apparent, especially in frontal language areas (Thomas et al., 1997). With temporal-parietal damage, however, a pattern of persistent right-hemisphere activation, even amidst increased left-hemisphere activity, is frequently present in aphasic patients regaining auditory comprehension and semantic processing skills (Thomas et al., 1997; Weiller et al., 1995). At the very least, these principles suggest the desirability of ipsilateral recovery after left-hemisphere damage, but they do not clarify the role of contralateral hemisphere activity during recovery from left-hemisphere damage (Cappa, 2000).

It has been suggested that novel right-hemisphere activity subsequent to left-hemisphere aphasia reflects a variety of possible favorable and nonfavorable behavioral and/or neurological phenomena including, (a) compensatory language processing activity via activation of latent language-capable circuits, (b) disinhibition of the contralateral cortex resulting in 'maladaptive' functional reorganization, and (c) recruitment of additional cognitive resources (attention, memory) to those normally needed for language processing (Belin et al., 1996; Cappa, 2000; Thomas et al., 1997; Weiller et al., 1995).

The work of Papanicolaou and colleagues (1984, 1987, 1988) has shown that chronic aphasics (with LH language dominance) show a larger right-hemisphere response to language stimuli than do either normals or right-hemisphere impaired subjects. Computerized Axial Tomography (CAT) and regional blood flow studies conducted by Knopman (1984) have shown increased and extensive activation of the right-hemisphere cortex during listening tasks at six months (compared to three months) postonset for aphasic speakers who had sustained damage to the left temporoparietal cortex and who still presented with partial deficits in auditory comprehension. Conversely, their subjects whose left-dominant auditory association cortex was spared and who had recovered completely from initial auditory comprehension deficits, showed the predicted left posterior pattern of activation for listening tasks. These findings indicated that for the latter subject group, early comprehension impairments and their resolution were most likely due to disruption and then recovery of ipsilateral neural networks distant to the focal site of lesion. For the former subject group, however, structural damage to left hemisphere local networks dedicated to auditory comprehension precluded recovery of function by that region. Partial functional recovery in their case depended upon assumption of function by capable and diffuse, but less efficient, neural networks in the contralateral hemisphere.

When these studies are compared with those evaluating recovery of frontal function, and in particular, recovery of speech fluency (Vallar et al., 1988), it would seem that the undamaged left-rather than the right-hemisphere cortex is primarily responsible for recovery from nonfluent aphasia (and perhaps associated speech apraxia). This conclusion is supported by the work of

Thomas et al. (1997) whose EEG studies of eleven patients with Broca's and Wernicke's aphasias showed an initially right-hemisphere activation pattern in Broca's aphasia shifting with increased recovery to a left-hemisphere frontal pattern. Their patients with Wernicke's aphasia, on the other hand, showed a permanent right-hemisphere shift for tasks in which all patients (fluent and nonfluent) had to search for synonyms to orally presented nouns. Other case studies, however, such as those conducted by Thulborn and colleagues (1999), cited MRI findings to suggest that nonfluent Broca's and fluent Wernicke's aphasias both recover auditory comprehension skills via increased and persistent activation from right-hemisphere homologous zones. Again, differences in subject and methodological variables may account for differences in findings across recovery studies.

The time course for assumption of function by the nondominant cortex for lexical-semantic tasks is not known, although the work of Demeurisse and Capon (1991) has suggested that significant right-hemisphere activity can be observed at three months postonset and Thulborn et al. (1999) have suggested that it can be detected at three days poststroke. Bushnell et al. (1989) have determined by Single Photon Emission Computerized Tomography (SPECT) analysis that extensive left-hemisphere hypoperfusion at one month postonset correlates inversely with degree of recovery at three months postonset. Interestingly, a SPECT study of subcortical aphasia by Vallar et al. (1988) has shown that reduced left-cortical hypoperfusion correlates with poor language recovery, suggesting that hemispheric mechanisms mediate recovery from subcortical, as well as cortical, aphasias. Cappa and Vallar (1992) suggest the superiority of Positron Emission Tomography (PET) scanning as the method of choice for investigating neurological correlates of recovery, but cite PETs limited availability as problematic.

One study that challenges the aforementioned conclusions about cortical neurophysiology and recovery, however, has employed PET technology to evaluate whether improvements in auditory comprehension can be linked to improvements in right or left temporoparietal regional glucose metabolism after stroke. Metter et al. (1992) evaluated eight right-handed male subjects who sustained single vascular lesions (sites not given), who had no previous histories of stroke, and who originally presented a variety of mild to severe aphasias. Each patient was scanned twice, first at one month postonset, and again at no sooner than six months postonset. Results showed that six of the eight patients showed improved left-hemisphere temporoparietal glucose metabolism, although the amount of improvement varied across subjects. The highest metabolism rates were found for Wernicke's regions rather than for parietal zones in the six improved subjects. Increased glucose metabolism was also observed in these subjects across the right-hemisphere cortex, with increased metabolism of the right-temporoparietal cortex correlating significantly with left homologous zones. Metabolic findings correlated closely with improved scores on the *Western Aphasia Battery* (WAB) (Kertesz, 1982). Assuming (cautiously) that metabolic change over time may reflect change in brain function, Metter et al.'s (1992) findings support the general hypothesis that recovery of comprehension is dependent on recovery of, and/or assumption of function in, the left and right posterior cortex. The contributions of left- and right-hemisphere recovery may not be independent, but may, "interact in such a way as to facilitate the recovery of comprehension" (Metter et al., 1992: 357).

Ansaldo et al. (2002) concur that both cerebral hemispheres contribute to recovery from aphasia, though not necessarily at the same time nor to the same degree. In a case study of a young woman with Broca's aphasia secondary to a left fronto–parietal hematoma, Ansaldo and colleagues examined the role of the right and left hemispheres in the processing of nouns and verbs of high and low imageability. A computer-driven lexical decision lateralization task allowed the experimenters to determine that by four months after the onset of Broca's aphasia, the right hemisphere participated more than the left in the comprehension of highly imageable nouns and verbs. By eight months postonset, the right hemisphere was additionally active in the recognition of low imageability words. By a year postonset, however, no distinct lateralization pattern was apparent; the left and right hemispheres participated equally in lexical decision tasks, and oral expression began to show considerable improvement as well. The authors suggest that, in accordance with findings by Karbe et al. (1998), right-hemisphere compensatory activity is needed less over time as impaired left hemisphere processing slowly improves (see Cao et al., 1999). Results also point to the recovery of the left-hemisphere Broca's area in the improvement of verbal expression.

If verbal expression depends on sufficient amounts of left-hemisphere frontal cortex for recovery, then large lesions will yield initially severe nonfluent aphasias that will not ameliorate; if large lesions destroy significant amounts of left temporoparietal cortex, the potential for recovery of auditory comprehension is good with right hemisphere assumption of function. However, among even the most severe of nonfluent aphasias, global aphasia, different recovery profiles can be seen (Ferro, 1992). In a CAT study of 54 Portugese, right-handed, firsttime stroke patients, Ferro (1992) showed that five different lesion locations yielded acute global aphasia: (1) large fronto–temporo–parietal lesions, with or without subcortical extension, (2) anterior, suprasylvian, frontal lesions with or without subcortical damage, (3) large subcortical infarcts, (4) posterior, suprasylvian, parietal infarcts, with or without subcortical extension, and (5) a double lesion composed of a frontal and a temporal infarct. Although patients with lesions from the first location tended to have initially more severe aphasias than patients with the other four lesion loci, language and neuropsychological profiles conducted at one month postonset revealed similar functional profiles across all five groups. By six months postonset, recovery profiles revealed that (1) patients with the first type of lesion had the poorest prognosis, retaining global aphasia and showing limited improvement, (2) patients with lesion locations 2, 3, and 4 showed variable degrees of recovery, improving to Broca's or transcortical aphasia or showing only anomic or speech apraxia deficits, (3) patients with exclusively deep lesions had the best prognosis and some with subcortical and anterior infarcts recovered completely, and (4) patients with lesion location number 5 showed only modest improvement (Ferro, 1992: 427). Ferro noted that while other anatomical sites may also yield global aphasia, his groupings were notable for the similarity of symptoms across groups and the differential recovery patterns identifiable by group, despite the diversity of lesion sites. Ferro (1992) specifically addressed the compatibility of his findings with those of Mesulam (1990), whereby anatomically diverse lesions to a large-scale distributed network, such as that subserving language, are quite capable of yielding transient and relatively similar-looking dysfunctions of the whole network. Further, unless the system sustains massive damage, or damage to a completely dedicated (or modular) local component, recovery should be expected if sufficient stimulation is provided to the damaged processing system.

Anagraphic Factors in Aphasia Recovery

With regard to anagraphic, or personal history, factors, Basso (1992, 2003) suggests that handedness, gender, and even age are not significant prognostic factors. In her recent text *Aphasia and Its Therapy*, Basso (2003: 192) examines the factors influencing recovery and states that, "To my knowledge, no study has tackled the problem of the possible influence of personal factors (age, sex, handedness, and educational level) on the effect of rehabilitation. However, they have been studied in relation to spontaneous recovery and ... we can safely conclude that the most recent investigations have not demonstrated that they have an important role in recovery (for a review, see Cappa, 1998)." Part of the difficulty in establishing the positive contribution of personal factors to recovery is that it is difficult to isolate them as causative influences in recovery studies. There may be an interaction, for example, between age, aphasia type, and severity of aphasia. An interesting demographic reviewed by Coppens (1991) reveals that Wernicke's aphasia (a frequently severe aphasia associated with poorer recovery than Broca's aphasia (Kertesz, 1988)) is linked more often to older individuals, whereas Broca's aphasia occurs more frequently in younger patients. Although the reason for this remains unclear, common sense would suggest a generally poorer prognosis for older patients due to the increased likelihood of concomitant disease in that population.

The Role of Rehabilitation in Recovery

There appears to be some direct evidence that neural reorganization and functional recovery from aphasia are linked, particularly when reorganization is induced by language rehabilitation training. Further, it appears that neural changes can occur and be detected within minutes of training. Musso and colleagues (1999) studied four stroke patients with auditory comprehension deficits and left hemisphere Wernicke's aphasia in order to address these issues. Assessments of auditory comprehension skills (using a short form of the *Token Test*) were obtained during each of 12 consecutive PET scans, after each of which patients underwent intensive eight-minute language comprehension training sessions. Training-induced improvements on *Token Test* performance were noted across scanning sessions and were correlated with increased activity of the posterior portion of the right superior temporal gyrus and the posterior portion of the left precuneus in subjects studied, suggesting a role for the right hemisphere in recovery from left hemisphere Wernicke's aphasia.

It should be noted that the language training activities used by Musso et al. (1999) included five different comprehension tasks presented in varying order and at increased levels of complexity on successive training trials. Tasks required patients to perform actions with objects, to match pictures with objects, to evaluate the semantic correctness of sentences, to evaluate the phonological correctness of sentences, and to match pictures with descriptive sentences. The training tasks tapped into a number of the component linguistic processes and input/output modalities (e.g., auditory, visual, tactile) involved in language comprehension, processes whose supportive circuitries are normally distributed across many regions of the left and right cerebral hemispheres (especially with regard to semantics). The increasing complexity of the assessment and training tasks across time also placed considerable demands on patients' attention and memory systems, some aspects of which are thought to be mediated by the right hemisphere. Musso and colleagues raise an important point as they interpret their findings: the right-hemisphere activity they recorded might reflect that hemisphere's contribution to language comprehension *per se*, or it might reflect its role in short-term verbal memory (Paulesu et al., 1993), a deficit in which may contribute to aphasic language comprehension impairments (Wilson et al., 1989; Wilson et al., 1995; Hermann, 1992). It is also difficult to know whether the increase in posterior right-hemisphere activity during repeated testing really reflects right-hemisphere activation or left-hemisphere inhibition of right-hemisphere activity, a point that emphasizes the complex nature of language processing across disparate brain areas (Thomas et al., 1997).

Important advances in the treatment in chronic aphasia suggest renewed hope for individuals in whom fluent or nonfluent aphasia has persisted beyond six months postonset. A novel treatment approach dubbed Constraint-Induced Movement Therapy ('CI therapy') has been shown to be effective in improvement of poststroke limb motor skills (Duncan, 1997; Leipert et al., 2000) and may have beneficial application in aphasia rehabilitation. Constraint-induced therapy appears to foster neural reorganization in impaired limbs. Soon after stroke, there is frequently a decrease in the cortical representation of limbs having paralyzed or disused muscles; restraining intact limbs while forcing impaired limbs to perform premorbid functions seems to yield an improved representation of damaged limbs and facilitate neuroplastic changes associated with improved use of those structures (see Liepert et al., 2000 for review).

Part of the beneficial effect of CI therapy for improvement of motor skills may be attributed to the brief but intensive structure of the therapy design (e.g., restraint of a nonaffected limb for 90% of waking hours across 12 days of treatment, 8 days of which also included six hours of behavioral training in the use of the nonrestrained affected limb) (Leipert et al., 2000). While the application of this model to aphasia rehabilitation is somewhat awkward, it has proven useful in the few studies conducted to date. One of the most compelling of those studies was conducted by Pulvermuller et al. (2001) with 17 right-handed (three premorbidly ambidextrous) aphasic stroke patients who were monolingual speakers of German. Patients had sustained focal lesions in the territory of the middle cerebral artery; most were diagnosed with Broca's aphasia but four patients exhibited Wernicke's aphasia and three patients exhibited other types of aphasia (transcortical, conduction, and anomic types). The 17 predominantly male subjects with aphasia were randomly assigned to either a constraint-induced treatment group (N = 10; five with moderate aphasia, three with severe aphasia, two with mild aphasia; six with Broca's aphasia, two with Wernicke's aphasia, one with transcortical aphasia, one with anomic aphasia; mean age = 55.4 yrs; mean time postonset = 98.2 months) or a conventional treatment group (N = 7; four with moderate aphasia, one with severe aphasia, two with mild aphasia; four with Broca's aphasia, two with Wernicke's aphasia, one with conduction aphasia; mean age = 53.9 yrs; mean time postonset = 24.0 months). Both treatment groups received the same total amount of therapy time, although the delivery structure was organized differently per group: the CI therapy group received 3–4 hours of speech–language therapy per day for 10 days (mean hours of treatment = 31.5), whereas the conventional treatment group received an equivalent number of treatment hours (mean = 33.9) distributed across 3–5 weeks.

The treatment approach used with the CI group was similar to that of the PACE (Promoting Aphasics' Communicative Effectiveness) method (for a description, see Davis and Wilcox, 1985), where speakers must communicate effectively across a barrier about a hidden referent (picture or object). Importantly, and unlike the conventions of PACE therapy, patients with aphasia in the CI group were required to use only verbal communication, the modality that was most difficult for them after the onset of aphasia. They were required to perform systematic massed practice of speech acts that were extremely difficult for them, and they were not allowed to use compensatory techniques or other communicative modalities that would more easily allow them to exchange information. Patients assigned to the conventional treatment group received intervention described by Pulvermuller et al. (2001) as a syndrome-specific standard approach to aphasia rehabilitation based on classic principles established by Hildred Schuell (1974) and targeting skills in naming, verbal repetition, sentence completion, following instructions, and conversation.

The results of the Pulvermuller et al. (2001) study revealed that subjects in the CI treatment group performed significantly better on a posttreatment administration of the *Aachen Aphasia Test* (Huber et al., 1983) than did the subjects in the conventional treatment group. The CI subjects also appeared to have a greater improvement in everyday communication skills than did subjects in the conventional treatment group. This finding was particularly intriguing given that the subjects in the CI treatment group had, on average, exhibited chronic aphasia for almost four times the average duration of that of the conventional treatment group. It is not often the case that patients with moderate-severe aphasia improve so rapidly during the course of treatment. More typical is the Pulvermuller et al. (2001) finding for the subjects in the conventional treatment group, where no significant gains in language performance were apparent during therapy posttesting.

Pulvermuller and colleagues (2001) were careful to note that the design of their study did not allow them to determine whether the most beneficial treatment factor for patients in the CI group was the massed practice component, the constraints on responding to treatment stimuli, or the apparent communicative relevance of the therapeutic tasks. They did suggest, however, that the combination of all three may stimulate neural mechanisms underlying brain plasticity, heretofore suppressed by learned nonuse of verbal language, to aid recovery even in people whose aphasia had lasted, on average, eight or more years. Whether these results can be generalized to other patient populations (such as those who are older) is not known.

New behavioral treatment paradigms such as constraint-induced therapy or computer-assisted interventions (Aftonomos et al., 1997) give hope to individuals with chronic aphasia – those who have traditionally been advised that recovery stops after six months to a year postonset. Another exciting trend with the potential to improve recovery is the pharmacological management of acute, subacute, and chronic aphasia, especially when such potentially useful medications as piracetam, bromocriptine, and dextroamphetamine, among others, are combined with speech–language therapy. The following recent sources provide more information on this topic: Bragoni et al. (2000), Deberdt, (1994), Greener et al. (2001), Huber (1999), Muller and von Crammon (1994), Troisi et al. (2002), Walker-Batson et al. (2001).

Conclusion

Research investigating the mechanisms of recovery in aphasia proceeds from several different and occasionally overlapping lines of evidence: neuroimaging studies, lateralization studies, and treatment studies. Each approach provides a unique perspective on the reemergence of language function after stroke, but some conclusions can be drawn from findings across various types of studies. Basso (1992) acknowledged the interdependence of lesion site and size with aphasia type and initial severity, and suggested the superiority of initial severity for predicting aphasia prognosis. She noted that traumatic aphasia generally has a better prognosis than vascular aphasia, and that among vascular etiologies, hemorrhage generally predicts the poorest recovery.

Whereas improvement can generally be predicted for aphasic speakers as a group, it is relatively difficult to predict recovery for individual patients, especially during the acute (two weeks postonset) period of illness; findings are mixed as to whether outcome severity can be predicted well during the acute phase of aphasia (Wallesch et al., 1992). Initial communication ratings for spontaneous speech may be more reliable than semantic, syntactic, or phonological factors in outcome prediction: poor initial communication abilities may predict poor recovery, because impaired communication suggests the presence of other limbic, reticular, and/or cognitive deficits that, if present, would exacerbate an aphasia.

Initial severity of aphasia (past the two-week post-stroke milestone) nevertheless remains the single most reliable predictor of aphasia recovery. With respect to lesion site, although it is tied to aphasia type, it generally has more influence on initial severity than on the degree of ultimate recovery (Basso, 1992). Mohr et al. (1978) and Brunner et al. (1982) have suggested that lesions relegated solely to Broca's area most often create transient and moderate aphasia, whereas lesions to Wernicke's cortex are associated with severe and persistent aphasia. Posterior extent of lesion appears to influence initial severity, and thus long-term outcome, regardless of whether lesion sites are focused in the frontal or temporal–parietal cortex (Basso, 1992). Findings from Ludlow et al. (1986) concur, illustrating that of 39 patients with traumatic Broca's aphasia, those whose initial lesions extended farther posteriorly remained aphasic 15 years post-onset while those whose lesions extended more anteriorly had fully recovered. It is tempting to conclude that because posterior extension usually impacts auditory comprehension, recovery of comprehension must lag behind expression. However, the opposite appears to be the case. According to Basso (1992: 345) "... a higher percentage of patients improve in comprehension than production and ... in oral than in written language."

Mesulam (1990) reminds us that Broca's and Wernicke's type aphasias each have associated receptive and expressive deficits. So regardless of aphasia type, we should expect expressive deficits to outlast deficits in comprehension simply because the active formulation and expression of language is a more complex cognitive exercise than that which is needed for comprehension (Mazzoni et al., 1992). Why, then, should lesions that extend farther into the posterior auditory associative cortex yield initially more severe and ultimately more persistent aphasias than those that extend into the motor cortex?

The answers to this and other questions related to aphasia recovery are not known, but they may ultimately be found in studies of poststroke brain neurophysiology that examines the differential contributions of the dominant and nondominant language cortex (and subcortex) to language recovery. Studies investigating the nature of neural reorganization after stroke and research defining the specific role that speech–language rehabilitation plays in recovery from subacute and chronic aphasia will provide important advances in our understanding of recovery from aphasia.

Bibliography

Aftonomos, LB, Steele, RD, and Wertz, RT (1997). 'Promoting recovery in chronic aphasia with an interactive technology.' *Archives of Physical Medicine and Rehabilitation* 78(8): 841–846.

Ansaldo, AI, Arguin, M, and Lecours, AR (2002). 'Initial right hemisphere take-over and subsequent bilateral participation during recovery from aphasia.' *Aphasiology* 16(3): 287–304.

Basso, A (1992). 'Prognostic factors in aphasia.' *Aphasiology* 6(4): 337–348.

Basso, A (2003). *Aphasia and its therapy.* Oxford: Oxford University Press.

Belin, P, Van Eeckhout, P, Zilbovicius, M, Remy, P, Francois, C, Guillaume, S, Chain, F, Rancurel, G, and Samson, Y (1996). 'Recovery from nonfluent aphasia after melodic intonation therapy: a PET study.' *Neurology* 47: 1504–1511.

Benson, DF and Ardila, A (1996). *Aphasia: a clinical perspective.* New York: Oxford University Press.

Berndt, RS (1998). 'Sentence processing in aphasia.' In: Sarno, MT (ed.) *Acquired aphasia,* 2nd edn., pp. 229–268. New York, NY: Academic Press.

Bogen, JE and Bogen, GM (1976). 'Wernicke's region – where is it?' *Annals of the New York Academy of Sciences* 280: 834–843.

Bragoni, M, Altieri, M, DiPiero, V, Padovani, A, Mostardini, C, and Lenzi, GL (2000). 'Bromocriptine and speech therapy in non-fluent chronic aphasia after stroke.' *Neurological Sciences* 21(1): 19–22.

Brown, J (1980). 'Brain structure and language production: a dynamic view.' In: Caplan, D (ed.) *Biological studies of mental processes.* Cambridge, MA: MIT Press. 287–300.

Brown, J (1982). 'Hierarchy and evolution in neurolinguistics.' In: Arbib, MA, Caplan, D, and Marshall, JC (eds.) *Neural models of language processes.* New York: Academic Press. 447–467.

Brunner, RJ, Kornhuber, HH, Seemuller, S, Surger, B, and Wallesch, CW (1982). 'Basal ganglia participation in language pathology.' *Brain and Language* 16: 281–299.

Buckingham, HW (1989). 'Phonological paraphasia.' In: Code, C (ed.) *The characteristics of aphasia*, pp. 89–110. London: Taylor and Francis.

Bushnell, DL, Gupta, S, Mlcoch, AG, and Barnes, WE (1989). 'Prediction of language and neurological recovery after cerebral infarction with SPECT imaging using N-isopropyl-p (I–123) Iodoamphetamine.' *Archives of Neurology* 46: 665–669.

Cao, Y, Vikingstad, EM, George, KP, Johnson, AF, and Welch, K (1999). 'Cortical language activation in stroke patients recovering from aphasia with functional MRI.' *Stroke* 30(11): 2331–2340.

Caplan, D (1987). *Neurolinguistics and linguistic aphasiology.* New York: Cambridge University Press.

Caplan, D (1992). *Language: structure processing and disorders.* Cambridge, MA: MIT Press.

Cappa, SF (1998). 'Spontaneous recovery from aphasia.' In: Stemmer, B and Whitaker, HA (eds.) *Handbook of neurolinguistics*, pp. 535–545. San Diego: Academic Press.

Cappa, SF (2000). 'Recovery from aphasia: why and how.' *Brain and Language* 71: 39–41.

Cappa, SF and Vallar, G (1992). 'The role of the left and right hemispheres in recovery from aphasia.' *Aphasiology* 6(4): 359–372.

Cappa, SF, Perani, D, Grassi, F, Bressi, S, Alberoni, M, Franceschi, M, Bettinardi, V, Todde, S, and Fazio, F (1997). 'A PET follow-up study of recovery after stroke in acute aphasics.' *Brain and Language* 56(1): 55–67.

Carlomango, S, Pandolfi, M, Labruna, L, Colombo, A, and Razzano, C (2001). 'Recovery from moderate aphasia in the first year poststroke: effect of type of therapy.' *Archives of Physical Medicine and Rehabilitation* 82(8): 1073–1080.

Chollet, F and Weiller, C (2000). 'Recovery of neurological function.' In: Mazziotta, JC, Toga, AW, and Frackowiak, RSJ (eds.) *Brain mapping: the disorders*, pp. 587–597. San Diego: Academic Press.

Christman, SS and Buckingham, HW (1989). 'Jargonaphasia.' In: Code, C (ed.) *The characteristics of aphasia*, pp. 111–130. London: Taylor and Francis.

Cohen, L, Bandinelli, SM, Findley, TW, and Hallet, M (1991). 'Motor reorganization after limb amputation in man.' *Brain* 114: 615–627.

Coppens, P (1991). 'Why are Wernicke's aphasia patients older than Broca's? A critical review of the hypotheses.' *Aphasiology* 5: 279–290.

Coq, JO and Xerri, C (1999). 'Acute reorganization of forepaw representation in the rat SI cortex after focal injury: neuroprotective effects of piracetam treatment.' *European Journal of Neuroscience* 11: 2597–2608.

Crosson, B (2000a). 'Systems that support language processes: attention.' In: Nadeau, SE, Gonzalez-Rothi, LJ, and Crosson, B (eds.) *Aphasia and language: theory to practice*, pp. 372–398. New York: The Guilford Press.

Crosson, B (2000b). 'Systems that support language processes: verbal working memory.' In: Nadeau, SE, Gonzalez-Rothi, LJ, and Crosson, B (eds.) *Aphasia and language: theory to practice*, pp. 399–420. New York: The Guilford Press.

Davis, GA (2000). *Aphasiology: disorders and clinical practice.* Boston: Allyn and Bacon.

Davis, G and Wilcox, J (1985). *Adult aphasia rehabilitation.* San Diego: College-Hill Press.

Deberdt, W (1994). 'Interaction between psychological and pharmacological treatment in cognitive impairment.' *Life Sciences* 55: 25–26, 2057–2066.

Demeurisse, G and Capon, A (1991). 'Brain activation during a linguistic task in conduction aphasia.' *Cortex* 27: 285–294.

Duncan, PW (1997). 'Synthesis of intervention trials to improve motor recovery following stroke.' *Topics in Stroke Rehabilitation* 3: 1–20.

Ferro, JM (1992). 'The influence of infarct location on recovery from global aphasia.' *Aphasiology* 6(4): 415–430.

Frackowiak, R (1997). 'The cerebral basis of functional recovery.' In: Frackowiak, R, Friston, KJ, Frith, CD, Dolan, RJ, and Mazziotta, JC (eds.) *Human brain function*, pp. 275–300. London: Academic Press.

Gonzales-Rothi, LJ (1997). 'Transcortical motor, sensory, and mixed aphasias.' In: LaPointe, LL (ed.) *Aphasia and related neurogenic language disorders,* 2nd edn., pp. 91–111. New York: Thieme.

Goodglass, H and Kaplan, E (1983). *The assessment of aphasia and related disorders,* 2nd edn. Philadelphia: Lea & Febiger.

Greener, J, Enderby, P, and Whurr, R (2001). 'Pharmacological treatment for aphasia following stroke.' Review. *Cochrane Database of Systematic Reviews* 4. CD000424.

Haarman, HJ and Kolk, HHJ (1991). 'Syntactic priming in Broca's aphasia: evidence for slow activation.' *Aphasiology* 5: 247–263.

Hemsley, G and Code, C (1996). 'Interactions between recovery in aphasia, emotional and psychosocial factors in subjects with aphasia, their significant others and speech pathologists.' *Disability and Rehabilitation* 18(11): 567–584.

Hermann, BP, Seidenberg, M, Haltiner, A, and Wyler, AR (1992). 'Adequacy of language function and verbal memory performance in unilateral temportal lobe epilepsy.' *Cortex* 28: 423–433.

Hillis, AE and Heidler, J (2002). 'Mechanisms of early aphasia recovery.' *Aphasiology* 16(9): 885–895.

Howard, D, Patterson, K, Wise, RJ, Brown, WD, Friston, KJ, and Weiller, C (1992). 'The cortical localization of the lexicons: PET evidence.' *Brain* 115: 1779–1782.

Huber, W (1999). 'The role of piracetam in the treatment of acute and chronic aphasia (Review).' *Pharmacopsychiatry* 32(1): 38–43.

Huber, W, Poeck, K, Weniger, D, and Willmes, K (1983). *Aachener aphasie test (AAT).* Handanweisung Gottingen, Germany: Beltz Verlag.

Jackson, JH (1874). 'On the nature of the duality of the brain.' Reprinted in Taylor, J (ed.) *Selected writings of John Hughlings Jackson,* vol. 2, 1958. London: Hodder & Stoughton. 129–145.

Jenkins, WM and Merzenich, MM (1987). 'Reorganization of neocortical representations after brain injury: a neurophysiological model of the bases of recovery from stroke.' *Progress in Brain Research* 71: 249–268.

Jenkins, WM, Merzenich, MM, and Recanzone, G (1990). 'Neocortical representation dynamics in adult primates: implications for neuropsychology.' *Neuropsychologia* 28: 573–584.

Karbe, H, Thiel, A, Weber-Luxemburger, G, Herholz, K, Kessler, J, and Heiss, WD (1998). 'Brain plasticity in poststroke aphasia: what is the contribution of the right hemisphere?' *Brain and Language* 64: 215–230.

Kean, M-L (1985). *Agrammatism.* Orlando, FL: Academic Press.

Kearns, KP (1997). 'Broca's aphasia.' In: LaPointe, LL (ed.) *Aphasia and related neurogenic language disorders,* 2nd edn., pp. 1–41. New York: Thieme.

Kertesz, A (1982). *The Western aphasia battery.* New York, NY: Grune and Stratton.

Kertesz, A (1988). 'What do we learn from recovery from aphasia?' *Advances in Neurology* 47: 277–292.

Kertesz, A (1991). 'Language cortex.' *Aphasiology* 5(3): 207–234.

Kertesz, A, Hudson, L, MacKenzie, IRA, and Munoz, DG (1994). 'The pathology and nosology of primary progressive aphasia.' *Neurology* 44: 2065–2072.

Knopman, DS, Selnes, OA, Niccum, N, and Rubens, AB (1984). 'Recovery of naming in aphasia: relationship to fluency, comprehension and CT findings.' *Neurology* 3411: 1461–1470.

Kolk, H (1995). 'A time-based approach to agrammatic production.' *Brain and Language* 50: 282–303.

Kolk, H and Weijts, M (1996). 'Judgements of semantic anomaly in agrammatic patients: Argument movement, syntactic complexity, and the use of heuristics.' *Brain and Language* 54: 86–135.

LaPointe, LL (ed.) (1997). *Aphasia and related neurogenic language disorders,* 2nd edn. New York: Thieme.

LaPointe, LL (1999). 'Quality of life with aphasia.' *Seminars in Speech and Language* 20(1): 5–16, quiz 16–17.

Leipert, J, Bauder, H, Miltner, WHR, Taub, E, and Weiller, C (2000). 'Treatment-induced cortical reorganization after stroke in humans.' *Stroke* 36(1): 1210–1216.

Ludlow, CL, Rosenberg, J, Fair, C, Buck, D, Schesselman, S, and Salazar, A (1986). 'Brain lesions associated with nonfluent aphasia fifteen years following penetrating head injury.' *Brain* 109: 55–80.

Martin, N and Dell, GS (2004). 'Perseverations and anticipations in aphasia: primed intrusions from the past and future.' *Seminars in Speech and Language* 25(4): 349–362.

Mazzoni, M, Vista, M, Pardossi, L, Avila, L, Bianchi, F, and Moretti, P (1992). 'Spontaneous evolution of aphasia after ischaemic stroke.' *Aphasiology* 6(4): 387–396.

Merzenich, MM, Kaas, JH, Wall, JT, Nelson, RJ, Sur, M, and Felleman, D (1983). 'Topographic reorganization of somatosensory cortical areas 3b and 1 in adult monkeys following restricted deafferentation.' *Neuroscience* 8: 33–55.

Mesulam, M-M (1982). 'Slowly progressive aphasia without dementia.' *Annals of Neurology* 11: 592–598.

Mesulam, M-M (1990). 'Large-scale neurocognitive networks and distribution processing for attention, language, and memory.' *Annals of Neurology* 28: 597–603.

Metter, EJ, Jackson, CA, Kempler, D, and Hanson, WR (1992). 'Temporoparietal cortex and the recovery of language comprehension in aphasia.' *Aphasiology* 6: 349–358.

Mohr, JP, Pessin, MS, Finkelstein, S, Funkestein, HH, Duncan, GW, and Davies, KR (1978). 'Broca aphasia: pathology and clinical.' *Neurology* 28: 311–324.

Muller, U and von Crammon, DY (1994). 'The therapeutic potential of bromocriptine in neuropsychological rehabilitation of patients with acquired brain damage.' Review. *Progress in Neuro-Psychopharmacology and Biological Psychiatry* 18(7): 1103–1120.

Musso, M, Weiller, C, Kiebel, S, Muller, SP, Bulau, P, and Rijntjes, M (1999). 'Training-induced brain plasticity in aphasia.' *Brain* 122(9): 1781–1790.

Nudo, R, Wise, BM, SiFuentes, F, and Miliken, GW (1996). 'Neural substrates for the effects of rehabilitative training on motor recovery after ischemic infarct.' *Science* 272: 1791–1794.

Papanicolaou, AC, Levin, HS, and Eisenberg, HM (1984). 'Evoked potential correlates of recovery from aphasia after focal left hemisphere injury in adults.' *Neurosurgery* 14(4): 412–415.

Papanicolaou, AC, Moore, BD, Deutsch, G, Levin, HS, and Eisenberg, HM (1988). 'Evidence for right-hemisphere involvement in recovery from aphasia.' *Archives of Neurology* 45: 1025–1029.

Papanicolaou, AC, Moore, BD, Levin, HS, and Eisenberg, HM (1987). 'Evoked potential correlates of right hemisphere involvement in language recovery following stroke.' *Archives of Neurology* 4(5): 521–524.

Paradis, M (2000). 'Generalizable outcomes of bilingual aphasia research.' Review. *Folia Phoniatrica et Logopedica* 52: 1–354–64.

Paradis, M and Goldblum, MC (1989). 'Selective crossed aphasia in a trilingual aphasic patient followed by reciprocal antagonism.' *Brain and Language* 36(1): 62–75.

Paulesu, E, Frith, CD, and Frackowiak, RS (1993). 'The neural correlates of the verbal component of working memory.' *Nature* 362: 342–345.

Pons, T, Garraghty, PE, Ommaya, AK, Kaas, JH, Taub, E, and Miskin, M (1991). 'Massive cortical reorganization after sensory deafferentation in adult macaques.' *Science* 252: 1857–1860.

Porch, BE (1994). 'Treatment of aphasia subsequent to the Porch Index of Communicative Ability (PICA).' In: Chapey, R (ed.) *Language intervention strategies in adult aphasia,* 3rd edn., pp. 178–183. Baltimore: Williams & Wilkins.

Porch, BE (2001). 'Treatment of aphasia subsequent to the Porch Index of Communicative Ability (PICA).' In: Chapey, R (ed.) *Language intervention strategies in adult aphasia,* 4th edn., pp. 663–674. Philadelphia: Lippincott, Williams & Wilkins.

Pulvermuller, F, Neininger, B, Elbert, T, Mohr, B, Rockstroh, B, Koebbel, P, and Taub, E (2001). 'Constraint-induced therapy of chronic aphasia after stroke.' *Stroke* 32(7): 1621–1626.

Rosenbek, JC, LaPointe, LL, and Wertz, RT (1989). *Aphasia: a clinical approach.* Boston, MA: College-Hill Press, Inc.

Schuell, H (1974). *Aphasia theory and therapy: selected lectures and papers of Hildred Schuell.* Baltimore: University Park Press.

Simmons, N and Buckingham, HW (1992). 'Recovery in jargonaphasia.' *Aphasiology* 6(4): 403–414.

Simmons-Mackie, N (1997). 'Conduction aphasia.' In: LaPointe, LL (ed.) *Aphasia and related neurogenic language disorders,* 2nd edn., pp. 63–90. New York: Thieme.

Thomas, C, Altenmuller, E, Marckmann, G, Kahrs, J, and Dichgans, J (1997). 'Language processing in aphasia: changes in lateralization patterns during recovery reflect cerebral plasticity in adults.' *Electroencephalography and Clinical Neurophysiology* 102(2): 86–97.

Thulborn, KR, Carpenter, PA, and Just, MA (1999). 'Plasticity of language-related brain function during recovery from stroke.' *Stroke* 30(4): 749–754.

Troisi, E, Paolucci, S, Silvestrini, M, Matteis, M, Vernieri, F, Grasso, MG, and Caltagirone, C (2002). 'Prognostic factors in stroke rehabilitation: the possible role of pharmacological treatment.' *Acta Neurologica Scandinavica* 105(2): 100–106.

Tseng, C-H, McNeil, MR, and Milenkovic, P (1993). 'An investigation of attention allocation deficits in aphasia.' *Brain and Language* 45(2): 276–296.

Vallar, G, Sterzi, R, and Basso, A (1988). 'Left hemisphere contribution to motor programming of aphasic speech: a reaction time experiment in aphasic patients.' *Neuropsychologia* 26: 511–519.

Vallar, G, Perani, D, Cappa, SF, Messa, C, Lenzi, GL, and Fazio, F (1988). 'Recovery from aphasia and neglect after subcortical stroke: neuropsychological and cerebral perfusion study.' *Journal of Neurology Neurosurgery and Psychiatry* 51: 1269–1276.

Van der Merwe, A (1997). 'A theoretical framework for the characterization of pathological speech sensorimotor control.' In: McNeil, MR (ed.) *Clinical management of sensorimotor speech disorders*, pp. 1–25. New York: Thieme.

Walker-Batson, D, Curtis, S, Natarajan, R, Ford, J, Dronkers, N, Salmeron, E, Lai, J, and Unwin, DH (2001). 'A double-blind, placebo-controlled study of the use of amphetamine in the treatment of aphasia.' *Stroke* 32(9): 2093–2098.

Wallesch, C-W, Bak, T, and Schulte-Monting, J (1992). 'Acute aphasia: patterns and prognosis.' *Aphasiology* 6(4): 373–386.

Weiller, C, Chollet, F, Friston, KJ, Wise, RJ, and Frackowiak, RS (1992). 'Functional reorganization of the brain in recovery from striatocapsular infarction in man.' *Annals of Neurology* 31(5): 463–472.

Weiller, C, Ramsay, S, Wise, RJS, Friston, KJ, and Frackowiak, RSJ (1993). 'Individual patterns of functional reorganization in the human cerebral cortex after capsular infarction.' *Annals of Neurology* 33: 181–189.

Weiller, C, Isensee, C, Rijintjes, M, Huber, W, Mueller, S, Bier, D, Butschka, K, Woods, RP, Noth, J, and Diener, HC (1995). 'Recovery from Wernicke's aphasia – a PET study.' *Annals of Neurology* 37: 723–732.

Weintraub, S, Rubin, NP, and Mesulam, M-M (1990). 'Primary progressive aphasia: longitudinal course, neurological profile, and language features.' *Archives of Neurology* 47: 1329–1335.

Wilson, BA, Baddeley, AD, and Cockburn, JM (1989). 'How do old dogs learn new tricks: teaching a technological skill to brain injured people.' *Cortex* 25: 115–119.

Wilson, BA, Baddeley, AD, and Kapur, N (1995). 'Dense amnesia in a professional musician following herpes simplex virus encephalitis.' *Journal of Clinical Experimental Neuropsychology* 17: 668–681.

Remediation of Language Disorders in Adults

L. R. Cherney, Northwestern University, Chicago, IL, USA

Since the reports of Paul Broca in 1861 and 1865 and Carl Wernicke in 1874, there has been a long-standing interest in the nature of aphasia and the relationship between language and the brain. Yet, interest in language remediation in adults grew slowly, and it was only after World War II that most treatment strategies and techniques were developed (Basso, 2003). Today, there are many approaches to language rehabilitation for adults with acquired aphasia, and it is this heterogeneity that poses a challenge for practicing clinicians who must select the appropriate treatments for their patients.

There have been several attempts to categorize the numerous approaches to language remediation in adults. Based on a literature review of articles that were published in five major journals and that spanned approximately 20 years (1971–1991), Horner and colleagues (1994) identified six models of aphasia treatment, each of which are discussed below. Similarly, Basso (2003) presented a taxonomy of approaches to aphasia rehabilitation and their theoretical underpinnings. Basso's classification, which was based on historical trends in the latter half of the 20th century, closely agrees with the categories identified by Horner et al. (1994). Yet any taxonomy is a simplification – it is not always clear where one approach ends and another begins, so some therapies may be consistent with more than one approach. For example, Horner and colleagues note that of the articles they reviewed, the majority (21.7%) used a hybrid approach or multitheoretic approach. Other language therapies may not fit into any of the approaches, particularly when therapies from different countries worldwide are considered (Holland and Forbes, 1993). Nevertheless, the following six categories serve as a guide to the rich and varied treatments for aphasia. Selection of treatments occurs with consideration of patient-specific factors such as type, severity, and chronicity of the aphasia, the presence of associated impairments, and the patient's communication environments.

Taxonomy of Language Remediation Approaches

1. The Stimulation-Facilitation Approach is a term that is often used synonymously with Hildred Schuell, who proposed and supported this approach (Schuell et al., 1964; Duffy and Coelho, 2001). It is based on the philosophy that, in aphasia, language is not lost, but rather cannot be accessed. Aphasia is considered to be unidimensional in nature so individuals with aphasia differ only in terms of severity, not in type of aphasia. Therefore, language rehabilitation can be essentially the same for all patients. Since the auditory modality is of prime importance in language processing and is also a key area of deficit in aphasia, treatment involves repetitive, intensive auditory stimulation. The auditory stimulation, which is designed to elicit a maximum number of responses, is sometimes paired with stimulation in other modalities. Error responses are not corrected but are followed by additional stimulation, which, if adequate, is likely to elicit a correct response.

2. In contrast to the premise that aphasia is unidimensional, proponents of the Modality Model view language as modality-bound, with aphasia being characterized as a modality-specific performance deficit that may involve one or more modalities. The goal of treatment is to remediate the specific input or output modalities, singly or in combination. One way that this can be accomplished is by systematically pairing weak and strong modalities to 'deblock' impaired performance. This principle can be applied regardless of the specific modality that is being treated. For example, when confrontation naming is difficult, repetition may be used to help the patient produce the correct response; then immediately after deblocking has occurred through the use of repetition, the target response may be accessed in the previously inaccessible modality (i.e., confrontation naming) (Weigl, 1961, cited in Basso, 2003).

Luria's functional reorganization approach, which has widely influenced aphasia research and therapy, is consistent with the modality model (Horner et al., 1994). According to Luria (1963, 1970), when brain tissue is destroyed, its original function cannot be restored to its previous form but can be performed by means of a partially new neural organization. Therapy is therefore directed towards reorganization and transfer of the function to other brain structures or functional systems. With intersystemic organization, new functional systems are created through the use of other undamaged links, and the impaired function is carried out at a different level of the same functional system, either at a lower and more automatic level or at a higher and more voluntary level. Precise identification of which modalities are damaged and which are preserved makes it possible to develop and implement different training procedures.

3. The Processing Approach is based on the cognitive neuropsychological models of normal language processes that have been developed for specific language tasks such as reading, spelling, naming, or sentence production

(Hillis, 2001). These information processing models assume that a complex cognitive function consists of a system of distributed and interconnected modules or mental representations that allow for processing of different types of information in cascade fashion. The representations and processes do not necessarily correspond to locations in the brain, but reflect functional components of a cognitive operation. Rehabilitation begins for each individual patient with identifying which cognitive processes and representations underlying the language task are impaired and which processes and representations are intact. For example, the task of reading words aloud involves the graphemic input lexicon, while repetition of words involves the phonological input lexicon. However, both tasks involve the semantic system and the phonological output lexicon. By comparing performance across tasks, inferences about the integrity of these cognitive processes can be made. Treatment then focuses on either the remediation of the impaired cognitive processes, compensation via the intact cognitive processes, or both. The primary contribution of the Processing Approach is that it guides the choice of interventions; however, it does not provide direct motivation for specific treatment strategies (Hillis, 2001). There are many studies, mostly single case descriptions, in which cognitive analyses have been used to focus treatment; examples can be found in Hillis (2002).

4. Several treatment approaches are based on the premise that the minor hemisphere (i.e., the hemisphere that is nondominant for language) has specific abilities, such as visual-spatial, affective-prosodic, and paralinguistic abilities, that can be used to facilitate communication. Melodic Intonation Therapy (MIT) is perhaps the best known of these treatment approaches (Sparks, 2001). It is a hierarchically structured program that uses intonation and rhythm to increase the patient's ability to independently produce high-probability phrases and sentences. The steps of MIT range from intoning a melodic line and hand tapping to answering questions using drilled phrases and sentences. Other remediation approaches that are consistent with the Minor Hemisphere Mediation Model utilize drawing as a communicative function (Lyon, 1995) and encourage humor within the therapy session (Simmons-Mackie, 2004).

5. The Linguistic (Neurolinguistic) approach is based on the principle that language has an internal organization that can be described by a specialized system of rules. In aphasia, there is disruption of lexical-semantic, syntactic, and/or phonologic performance. Treatment therefore focuses on restoring language performance, using neurolinguistic principles that are specific for each linguistic impairment. For example, the Sentence Production Program for Aphasia (Helm-Estabrooks and Nicholas, 2000) systematically trains syntax using a story completion format. Selection of syntactic structures was based on a study of agrammatism that identified a hierarchy of difficulty across 14 grammatical constructions, with imperative intransitive statements being the easiest and future tense statements the most difficult. Another sentence-production training program, Cuing Verb Treatments, is based on the notion that the verb is the central constituent in sentence structure (Loverso et al., 1986, cited in Thompson, 2001). In this approach, verbs are presented as the central core of the simple active sentence; patients are trained to produce the verb and, in response to a wh-question cuing strategy, also specific sentence constituents (usually noun phrases) that are assigned to various thematic roles by the verb (e.g., agent, theme).

Based on aspects of formal linguistic theory and neurolingusitic research and consistent with Chomsky's conceptual framework, Thompson and colleagues have developed a series of treatment strategies that use the underlying canonical form of complex sentences to improve sentence production (Thompson, 2001). Procedures target the underlying linguistic representations of sentences rather than treating the surface representation that is manifested in word order. Subjects are taught to recognize the verb, its arguments, and the arguments' thematic roles in active declarative forms of noncanonical sentences. Instruction concerning the movement of various sentence constituents are provided, and subjects are taken through the proper movement to derive the surface form of target sentences such as wh-questions. Additional morphemes required in the surface form of various sentences are provided and inserted into sentence frames. Once the noncanonical form is derived, subjects are required to orally produce them.

6. In the Functional Communication or Pragmatic approach, therapists are not interested in the accuracy of the linguistic message but focus on the patient's ability to communicate the intent of the message. Communication involves more than just speaking and understanding – it reflects the application of pragmatic rules and the ability to use language in a context. Therefore, treatment includes compensatory strategies for circumventing communication breakdown as well as strategies for communication breakdown repair. One of the best-known pragmatic approaches is PACE (Promoting Aphasic's Communicative Effectiveness) (Davis and Wilcox, 1985). In the PACE technique, four major treatment principles have been delineated in an attempt to incorporate rules of natural communication into semi-structured treatment: the clinician and patient participate equally as senders and receivers of messages; the interaction incorporates the exchange of new information between clinician and patient; patients freely choose the channels through which they will communicate, such as words, gestures, drawing, or any other communication device; and the clinician's feedback is based on the patient's success in communicating the message. Extending treatment into natural communication settings and ensuring a positive communication environment through partner training, removal of environmental barriers to participation, and conversational supports are also consistent with a functional approach (Kagan, 1998; Lubinski, 2001).

Biological Approach to Language Remediation

As we acquire new knowledge about aphasia and brain-behavior relations, additional approaches to treatment that are not easily categorized with the present taxonomy are emerging. For example, Small (2004) has advocated for a biological model of aphasia rehabilitation, in which the goal of remediation is to alter brain anatomy and physiology so that language function can be restored. In order to effect the necessary neural changes, both novel biological treatments and speech-language treatment are necessary. While the biological treatment stimulates or repairs the injured brain area, language treatments are provided to retrain the new circuitry and integrate it with the preserved, existing tissue.

Intervening in the biology of the brain will have direct effects on language recovery. Pharmacotherapy is the most frequently used biological therapy for aphasia. To date, the effects of three groups of neurotransmitters on language deficits in aphasia have been investigated: dopamine agonists such as bromocriptine (Gupta and Mlcoch, 1992; Gupta et al., 1995); dextro-amphetamine and other agents that affect catecholamine systems (Walker-Batson et al., 2001); and the nootropic agent, piracetam (Huber et al., 1997). While its mechanism is not fully understood, it has been suggested that piracetam exerts its effect by improving cognition through cholinergic and excitatory amine neurotransmission (Huber et al., 1997). While pharmacotherapy is not yet proven, Small (2004) suggests that it has promise, but only when accompanied by concommitant language therapy.

Another example of a biological therapy for language remediation in adults is repetitive transcranial magnetic stimulation (rTMS) (Martin et al., 2004). Based on the premise that overactivity of the right hemisphere language homologues may be maladaptive and interfere with, rather than promote, aphasia recovery, rTMS was applied to the right hemisphere to reduce its cortical excitability. Preliminary results obtained in four individuals with chronic nonfluent aphasia indicated improved picture naming following 10 sessions of rTMS. Other types of cortical stimulation techniques and even neural transplantation may, in the future, provide promise – especially when linked with intensive language treatment (Small, 2004).

Treatment Efficacy and Effectiveness

Any discussion about language remediation in adults must also address the basic question of whether aphasia treatment works. To date, the historical record of clinical outcomes for treatments of aphasia is extensive (Cherney and Robey, 2001). Over time, experimental methodologies in the field of aphasia have improved (e.g., measuring the change in communication behavior from pre-test to post-test; controlling for time post onset; setting clear exclusion and inclusion criteria to establish homogeneous groups; introducing no-treatment control groups using deferred treatment groups; random assignment; and controls on the type(s), amount, and duration of treatment), so that findings have become less ambiguous and support the conclusion that treatment for aphasia is both efficacious and effective. While there are relatively few randomized clinical trials of aphasia treatment (Greener et al., 2000), over 100 single-subject aphasia treatment studies have appeared in the literature. In addition, meta-analyses applied to the aphasia treatment literature have concluded that aphasia treatment is effective (Greenhouse et al., 1990; Whurr et al., 1992; Robey, 1994, 1998). The latter meta-analyses (Robey, 1994, 1998), based on 21 studies and 55 studies respectively, have suggested several other conclusions, such as:

- recovery of treated individuals was, on average, nearly twice as extensive as the recovery of untreated individuals when treatment was begun before 3 months post onset
- treatment brought about appreciable gains, even when begun after 3 months post onset
- treatment brought about large effects even in individuals with severe aphasia
- treatment exceeding 2 hours of treatment per week brought about greater treatment effects.

Future research in the area of language remediation for adults is likely to focus on the development of new and innovative treatments that are theoretically based and demonstration of their efficacy and effectiveness, using rigorous scientific methodologies.

Bibliography

Basso, A (2003). *Aphasia and its therapy.* Oxford: Oxford University Press.

Chapey, R (ed.) (2001). *Language intervention strategies in aphasia and related neurogenic communication disorders,* 4th edn. Philadelphia: Lippincott Williams & Wilkins.

Cherney, LR and Robey, RR (2001). 'Aphasia treatment: recovery, prognosis and clinical effectiveness.' In: Chapey, R (ed.) 148–172.

Davis, G and Wilcox, M (1985). *Adult aphasia rehabilitation: applied pragmatics.* Windsor: NFER-Nelson.

Duffy, JR and Coelho, CA (2001). 'Schuell's stimulation approach to rehabilitation.' In: Chapey, R (ed.) 341–382.

Greener, J, Enderby, P, and Whurr, R (2000). 'Speech and language therapy for aphasia following stroke.' *The Cochrane Database of Systematic Reviews* 2, CD000424.

Greenhouse, JB, Fromm, D, Iyengar, S, et al. (1990). 'The making of a meta-analysis: a quantitative review of the aphasia treatment literature.' In: Wachter, KW and Straf, ML (eds.) *The future of meta-analysis.* New York: Russell Sage Foundation.

Gupta, SR and Mlcoch, AG (1992). 'Bromocriptine treatment of nonfluent aphasia.' *Archives of Physical Medicine and Rehabilitation* 73: 373–376.

Gupta, SR, Mlcoch, AG, Scolaro, MS, et al. (1995). 'Bromocriptine treatment of nonfluent aphasia.' *Neurology* 45: 2170–2173.

Helm-Estabrooks, N and Nicholas, M (2000). *Sentence production program for aphasia.* Austin, TX: Pro-Ed.

Hillis, AE (2001). 'Cognitive neuropsychological approaches to rehabilitation of language disorders.' In: Chapey, R (ed.) 513–523.

Hillis, AE (2002). *The handbook of adult language disorders: integrating cognitive neuropsychology, neurology, and rehabilitation.* New York: Psychology Press.

Holland, AL and Forbes, M (1993). *Aphasia treatment: world perspectives.* San Diego, CA: Singular Publishing Group.

Horner, J, Loverso, FL, and Rothi, LG (1994). 'Models of aphasia treatment.' In: Chapey, R (ed.) *Language intervention strategies in adult aphasia,* (3rd edn.), pp. 135–145. Baltimore: Williams & Wilkins.

Huber, W, Willmes, K, Poeck, K, et al. (1997). 'Piracetam as an adjuvant to language therapy for aphasia: a randomized double-blind placebo controlled pilot study.' *Archives of Physical Medicine and Rehabilitation* 78: 245–250.

Kagan, A (1998). 'Supported conversation for adults with aphasia: methods and resources for training conversation partners.' *Aphasiology* 12: 816–830.

Lubinski, R (2001). 'Environmental systems approach in adult aphasia.' In: Chapey, R (ed.) 269–296.

Luria, AR (1963). *Restoration of function after brain injury.* Oxford: Pergamon Press.

Luria, AR (1970). *Traumatic aphasia.* The Hague: Mouton.

Lyon, JG (1995). 'Drawing: its value as a communication aid for adults with aphasia.' *Aphasiology* 9: 33–50.

Martin, PI, Naeser, MA, Theoret, H, et al. (2004). 'Transcranial magnetic stimulation as a complementary treatment for aphasia.' *Seminars in Speech and Language* 25(2): 181–191.

Nadeau, SE, Rothi, LJG, and Crosson, B (eds.) (2000). *Aphasia and language: theory to practice.* New York: The Guilford Press.

Robey, RR (1994). 'The efficacy of treatment for aphasic persons: a meta-analysis.' *Brain and Language* 47: 582–608.

Robey, RR (1998). 'A meta-analysis of clinical outcomes in the treatment of aphasia.' *Journal of Speech Language Hearing Research* 41: 172–187.

Schuell, H, Jenkins, JJ, and Jimenez-Pabon, E (1964). *Aphasia in adults.* New York: Harper & Row.

Simmons-Mackie, N (2004). 'Just kidding! Humour and therapy for aphasia.' In: Duchan, JF and Byng, S (eds.) *Challenging aphasia therapies*, pp. 101–117. New York: Psychology Press.

Small, SL (2004). 'A biological model of aphasia rehabilitation: pharmacologic perspectives.' *Aphasiology* 18: 473–492.

Sparks, RW (2001). 'Melodic intonation therapy.' In: Chapey, R (ed.) 703–717.

Thompson, CK (2001). 'Treatment of underlying forms: a linguistic specific approach for sentence production deficits in agrammatic aphasia.' In: Chapey, R (ed.) 605–628.

Walker-Batson, D, Curtis, S, Natarajan, R, et al. (2001). 'A double-blind, placebo-controlled study of the use of amphetamine in the treatment of aphasia.' *Stroke* 32: 2093–2098.

Whurr, R, Lorch, MP, and Nye, C (1992). 'A meta-analysis of studies carried out between 1946 and 1988 concerned with the efficacy of speech and language treatment for aphasic patients.' *European Journal of Disorders of Communication* 27: 1–17.

S

Sensory Aging, Hearing

M. K. Pichora-Fuller, University of Toronto, Mississauga, ON, Canada
E. MacDonald, University of Toronto, Toronto, ON, Canada

Presbycusis

Causes

The term presbycusis, or presbyacusis, refers to age-related hearing loss. There are many causes of hearing loss in older people, including environmental factors such as exposure to noise and ototoxic drugs, genetic factors, and generalized effects of aging such as cell damage and neural degeneration. Many age-related hearing impairments are types of sensorineural hearing loss involving damage to the cochlea, or inner ear. The hallmark of this damage is the elevation of the thresholds of audibility for high-frequency pure tones.

Our knowledge of cochlear pathology, its effects on perception, and many issues pertaining to treatment and rehabilitation can be generalized across the adult age range. In addition to types of cochlear damage that are common to adults across the age range, the peripheral and central auditory systems of older adults may also be damaged in ways that are not typical in younger adults. Furthermore, older adults often exhibit perceptual deficits that are disproportionate to the problems observed in younger adults with similar hearing thresholds. Importantly, studies of several species of mammals have demonstrated that hearing declines as a function of chronological age, even when all genetic and potentially damaging environmental effects have been carefully controlled.

The classification of subtypes of presbycusis, defined according to the particular structures of the auditory system that are affected by age, has continued to be refined for over four decades. Unfortunately, there is not a straightforward correspondence between damage to particular structures and perceptual deficits. Damage at multiple sites likely contributes to the differences in auditory processing that are observed between younger and older adults with similar hearing thresholds. Although high-frequency pure-tone threshold elevation is very common in older adults, the more age-specific structural and perceptual aspects of presbycusis have been the focus of most research conducted in the past decade.

Prevalence

The prevalence of hearing loss increases with age and is greater in males than in females. The prevalence of presbycusis, based on audiometric pure-tone threshold data, ranges from almost 50% to over 80%, depending on the sample, age, and the definition of hearing loss. Some reports indicate that hearing loss is the third most common chronic disability in senior citizens. About three-quarters of those who have impaired hearing are over the age of 75 years.

Age-related hearing loss characterized by high-frequency threshold elevations can begin in the fourth decade of life. The degree of hearing loss and the range of frequencies affected continue to increase with age. The specific prevalence estimates based on pure-tone thresholds depend on the degree of loss and on which frequencies are used to determine the inclusion criteria. One explanation for the greater prevalence of hearing loss in males is that their cumulative exposure to noise, including industrial and military noise, is typically greater than that of females. Age cohorts may also differ in history of noise exposure associated with wars and changing industrial practices, as well as changes in longevity.

In industrialized countries, a century ago, fewer than 1 in 20 persons lived to age 65 years, but by 1980, there were 1 in 10, and by 2030, 1 in 5 persons will be over age 65 years. As the baby-boom generation enters retirement age and longevity increases, with the fastest growing age group now being those over the age of 85 years, because hearing loss increases with age, estimates of the prevalence of hearing loss increase for the coming decades.

In general, self-reported hearing loss yields prevalence estimates that are lower than those based on pure-tone thresholds measured objectively in the clinic. A typical finding is that by 65 years of age, over one-third of adults report hearing problems, and the prevalence of hearing loss has been reported to be as high as 80% for the frail elderly living in residential care facilities. The most obvious explanation for this apparent discrepancy in the estimates based on subjective and objective measures is that the effect of hearing loss on functioning in everyday life depends greatly on the individual's auditory ecology and not only on the degree of hearing impairment.

Research Issues

Most early research on presbycusis was confounded by the high degree of correlation between high-frequency hearing loss and age. More recent studies of the effects of age on auditory perception have attempted to minimize this confound by matching younger and older adults as closely as possible for audiometric thresholds, by simulating the effects of hearing loss in younger listeners with normal hearing, or by amplifying sound so that it is equally audible to younger and older listeners. By controlling better for the effects of audibility it has been possible to isolate changes in auditory perception that are specific to aging.

Studies of nonhuman mammal species have enabled researchers to differentiate between the effects on the peripheral auditory system of genetic factors, environmental factors, and aging *per se*. A high degree of variability in hearing thresholds in quiet-reared gerbils and patterns of hearing loss in different strains of mice suggest that there is a strong genetic component in age-related hearing loss. A consistent finding is that heritability coefficients for age-related hearing loss in humans are strong (0.22–0.55), especially for mother/daughter and sister/sister relationships, with magnitudes similar to those reported for hypertension and hyperlipidemia. Whereas in studies of humans it is virtually impossible to eliminate the role of environmental factors that are known to cause hearing loss, it has been possible to rear animals in quiet and to control their diet and acoustical environment so that the effects of aging can be isolated.

Animal models have greatly advanced our understanding of age-related changes in peripheral auditory anatomy and physiology and how these changes relate to changes in pure-tone thresholds. Nevertheless, the auditory central nervous system, from the brain stem to the cortex, also undergoes significant age-related changes. It is more difficult to compare the nature and consequences of these changes across species, especially with regard to the perception of complex signals such as speech or music. Studies of the human central auditory system using electrophysiological techniques, such as evoked potentials and brain imaging, are beginning to address questions concerning age-related changes in the more cortical aspects of auditory perception.

Anatomy and Physiology

The main structures of the peripheral auditory system are the outer, middle, and inner ear. The effects of aging on auditory perception result mainly from changes in the inner ear and the auditory nervous system.

Outer Ear and Middle Ear

The outer ear, including the pinna, concha, and the ear canal to the ear drum, does not undergo any age-related change that significantly affects auditory perception in everyday life. Two outer ear conditions that may affect hearing testing are cerumen buildup and collapsing ear canals. Buildup of cerumen, or ear wax, may impede the perception of sound and possibly cause tinnitus, or ringing in the ears; however, cerumen can be safely removed by a qualified health professional. The cartilage of the outer ear loses rigidity, with the consequence that the ear canal may collapse if pressure is applied to the pinna. Collapsing canals occur in about a third of older adults. The occlusion produced when the ear canal collapses impedes the transmission of high-frequency sounds such that thresholds measured using circumaural earphones may over-estimate the degree of hearing loss. This testing artifact can be avoided by using insert earphones. A tester can easily identify a collapsing ear canal by pressing on the pinna with a finger and observing a change in the shape of the opening of the ear canal.

The middle ear cavity, from the ear drum to the inner ear, is normally air filled and contains a chain of three ossicles. The middle ear structures transduce the airborne acoustical sound vibrations arriving at the ear drum into mechanical vibrations that are relayed to the fluid-filled inner ear. Some older adults have hearing loss resulting from middle ear damage that developed earlier in their lifetime; however, the middle ear does not undergo any changes specifically related to age that significantly affect auditory perception in everyday life or during hearing testing.

Inner Ear

The high-frequency threshold elevations commonly observed in older adults may be partially the result of environmental factors such as exposure to noise or ototoxic drugs, rather than age *per se*. Losses due to such environmental factors are characterized by damage to and loss of the outer hair cells of the cochlea, or inner ear. In the normal cochlea, the outer hair cells have a gain-control function that enables low-intensity sounds to be heard. The outer hair cells are motile and under efferent control. Their status is evaluated clinically by testing otoacoustic emissions. Importantly, there is less change in otoacoustic emissions with age than would be expected if outer hair cell damage were the only pathology contributing to the high-frequency hearing loss typical of presbycusis.

In addition to outer hair cell damage resulting from environmental factors rather than to age *per se*, there are two subtypes of presbycusis in which cochlear pathology is attributable specifically to aging. One subtype of presbycusis, sensory loss, characterized by atrophy or degeneration of the sensory receptor cells, the inner hair cells, and supporting cells, is now considered to be of only minor importance in the aged ear. A second subtype of presbycusis, metabolic loss, characterized by atrophy and degeneration of the lateral wall of the cochlea, especially the stria vascularis and spiral ligament, is now considered to be the predominant and most distinctive lesion of the aging ear.

The stria vascularis has a dense capillary network and an exceptionally high metabolic rate. There are significant losses of strial capillaries in aging animals. Age-related changes in the stria vascularis affect the basic mechanoelectric transduction process of the cochlea, the generation of electrochemical gradients, and the regulation of cochlear ionic homeostasis. Specifically, there is an age-related decrease in the endocochlear potential and in the gain of the cochlear amplifier. Importantly, metabolic presbycusis accounts for high-frequency threshold elevations, but is not observed in cases of noise-induced or ototoxic hearing loss. Furthermore, animal studies show that there can be at least temporary reversals of age-related threshold elevations on the order of 20–40 dB when the endocochlear potential is increased by the introduction of a direct current voltage into the scala media of the cochlea.

Auditory Nerve

A third subtype of presbycusis, neural loss, is characterized by loss of spiral ganglion neurons and pronounced degeneration of the auditory nerve. In quiet-reared gerbils and other species, spiral ganglion cell density decreases and the average volume of the surviving cells also decreases in older compared to younger ears. In aging gerbils, reduced slopes of the input–output functions are observed for the compound action potential of the auditory nerve and for the auditory brain stem response. Such reduced amplitudes of physiological responses in aging ears to moderate to high-level signals, in cases in which there are only small changes in auditory thresholds, are consistent with reduced synchronization of neural firing. Importantly, these changes have been observed in the presence of intact inner hair cells, consistent with age-related primary degeneration of the auditory nerve, as opposed to degeneration secondary to loss of sensory receptor cells, as is observed in cases of noise-induced or ototoxic hearing loss.

Perception

Auditory aging alters the perception of sound. The most commonly reported problem of older adults is difficulty understanding speech in noise. For the most part, the perceptual consequences of high-frequency hearing loss due to environmental factors are well known and will be the same for older adults as for younger adults. The perceptual consequences of the three subtypes of presbycusis are less well known, but seem to be distinctive. Importantly, older adults often find it more challenging than do their younger counterparts with similar audiograms when listening in complex acoustical environments, even though they have little or no problem listening in quiet situations. Furthermore, these problems can occur even if the audiometric thresholds of the older adults are within the normal range for speech or if sound is adequately amplified by hearing aids.

Psychoacoustic studies have documented changes in how older adults perceive the basic dimensions of sound. Studies have also documented age-related declines in speech perception and spoken language comprehension in more realistic, complex listening conditions. In humans, it has been difficult to distinguish the perceptual consequences of outer hair cell damage due to environmental factors from the perceptual consequences of the three subtypes of presbycusis, because most older adults have a combination of these pathologies. Insight into how the perceptual abilities of older adults resemble, or differ from, those of younger adults have been provided by studies in which the pure-tone thresholds of younger and older adults are matched as closely as possible, especially in the low-frequency range from 250 to 3000 Hz that is most important for speech perception.

Psychoacoustics

Absolute auditory thresholds

Compared to a population of human adults with normal hearing, the perceptual decline that defines the degree of hearing loss is the increase in absolute thresholds. The absolute threshold of audibility is the lowest intensity at which a sound is detectable. Clinically, these thresholds are measured for pure-tone frequencies at octave intervals between 125 and 8000 Hz and they are plotted on an audiogram in decibels referenced to standards based on population hearing level (HL) norms, or dB HL. The typical hearing loss associated with presbycusis is characterized by normal thresholds, less than or equal to 25 dB HL, in the low-frequency range, and a sloping high-frequency hearing loss with thresholds increasing progressively with frequency. **Figure 1** depicts the common progression of audiometric pure-tone threshold hearing loss with age for males and females.

An increase in high-frequency absolute thresholds, and thus a decline in sensitivity, can affect perception and function in everyday life; for example, some speech sounds, especially consonants, become inaudible. In addition, such hearing loss is usually associated with alterations in the perception of the physical dimensions of

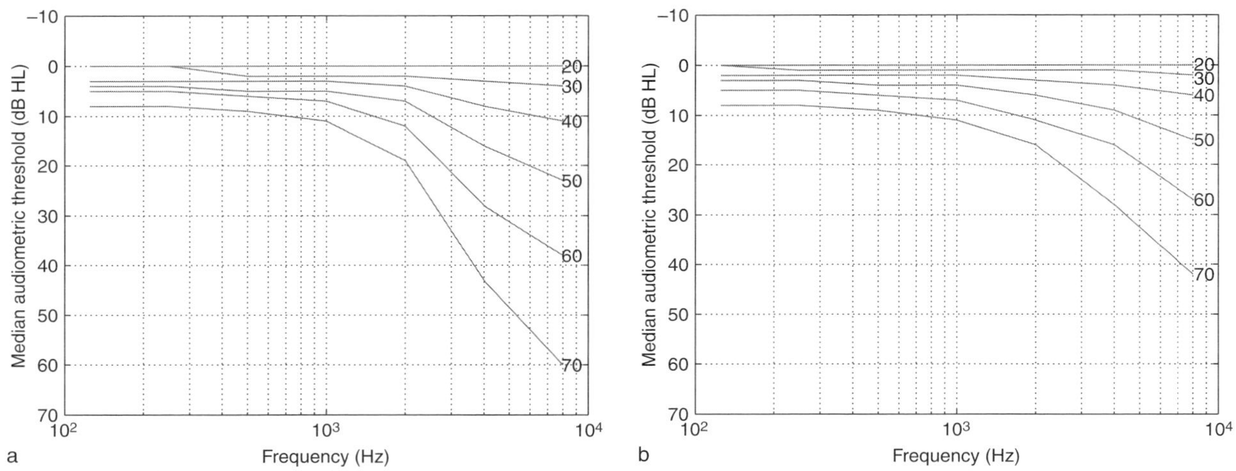

Figure 1 Median thresholds in decibel 'hearing level' (dB HL; i.e., relative to normal hearing in 18-year-olds) as a function of age for males (a) and females (b), based on population data from the International Standards Organization (ISO 7029).

suprathreshold sounds. The main physical dimensions of suprathreshold sound are frequency, intensity, and duration. In general, variations in the frequency of sound are perceived as variations in pitch, while variations in the intensity of sound are perceived as loudness. Older adults often exhibit changes in suprathreshold perception that are not predictable from their audiometric thresholds.

Frequency selectivity and discrimination

The cochlea is tonotopically arranged such that different regions respond maximally to different frequencies (i.e., there is place coding of frequency). The characteristic frequency, or the frequency that elicits the maximum response, is highest in the basal region of the cochlea (nearest to the middle ear) and it decreases more or less logarithmically with distance along the cochlea, with the most apical region having the lowest characteristic frequency. The tuning of the cochlear response to different frequencies has been examined using psychoacoustic experiments in humans and physiological measurements in mammals. The frequency tuning of the cochlea is often characterized in terms of auditory filter properties. The auditory filters of listeners with outer hair cell loss are broader than are those of listeners with normal hearing. The degree to which the auditory filters are broadened is correlated with degree of audiometric hearing loss.

A perceptual consequence of broadened auditory filters, or decreased frequency selectivity, is an increased susceptibility to masking of one signal by a simultaneous competing signal, especially masking signals lower in frequency than the target signal. Listeners with outer hair cell loss often have difficulty understanding speech in noise because of their increased susceptibility to masking. The deleterious effects of the upward spread of masking continue to undermine speech perception in noise, especially when the noise is the speech of other talkers, even when hearing aids amplify sound sufficiently to restore the audibility, because both the target and any competing signals are amplified.

The effect of outer hair cell loss on ability to discriminate sequentially presented tones differing in frequency is less clear. While frequency discrimination is usually adversely affected, there is significant variability among individuals, and the size of the just-noticeable frequency difference is generally not well correlated with the degree of threshold hearing loss.

In general, older adults with normal audiograms for low-frequencies do not discriminate sequentially presented tones of different frequencies as well as younger adults do. Importantly, these age-related differences in frequency discrimination do not appear to vary with presentation level and they are larger for low-frequency pure tones than for high-frequency tones. The place coding of frequency is dominant for high frequencies while temporal coding is dominant at low frequencies. Temporal coding of low frequencies is possible because the timing of the firing of primary auditory neurons is phase-locked to the signal which causes the movement of the cochlear structures. Thus, the synchronized timing of the firing of auditory neurons provides a cue that can be used to code low frequencies. At higher frequencies, the speed of firing needed for this type of coding exceeds the limits of the neural response. The pattern of age-related declines in frequency discrimination is consistent with disruptions in temporal coding, rather than with the disruptions in place coding associated with outer hair cell damage that results in high-frequency threshold elevations.

Loudness and intensity discrimination

Loudness recruitment is a phenomenon that is observed with almost all cases of outer hair cell loss. This phenomenon refers to an increased rate of growth in perceived loudness as the intensity level of a signal is increased. Consider an individual with a unilateral hearing loss – that is, one ear with normal thresholds and abnormally elevated thresholds in the other ear. While the range of audible sound levels will be different for both ears, the full range of perceived loudness will be the same (i.e., from barely audible to painfully loud). In the case of complete recruitment, once a tone becomes audible in the ear with elevated thresholds, the perceived loudness of that tone will grow faster there than in the normal ear as the level of the tone is increased, until the sound level is sufficiently high to produce the same perceived loudness in both ears. Overrecruitment or underrecruitment can also occur in some cases of cochlear hearing loss; respectively, these refer to the perceived loudness of a sound presented at a high level as being either greater or less in the impaired ear compared to the normal ear.

Typically, when tested at low intensity levels relative to their absolute thresholds, listeners with cochlear hearing loss who have recruitment discriminate smaller intensity differences compared to listeners with normal absolute thresholds. This is the basis of the behavioral tests sometimes used in the clinical evaluation of cochlear hearing loss characterized by recruitment. However, when tested at high intensity levels relative to their absolute thresholds, listeners with recruitment discriminate intensity differences that are similar, or sometimes larger, compared to young adults with normal audiograms.

Older adults with normal audiograms in the low-frequency range often exhibit larger intensity discrimination thresholds than do younger adults, with the largest age-related differences in intensity discrimination occurring for low-frequency tones. For high-frequency tones, loudness is mostly coded by the spread of activation along the length of the cochlea; that is, the overall rate of neural firing increases because activation occurs at more places in the cochlea. However, coding of loudness for low-frequency tones is influenced by temporal cues based on the number of neurons firing synchronously. The pattern of larger age-related threshold differences for low-frequency tones than for high-frequency tones is not consistent with the disruptions in place coding associated with outer hair cell damage resulting in high-frequency threshold elevations, but it is consistent with an age-related decline in neural synchrony.

Temporal processing

The pattern of age-related differences in frequency and intensity discrimination for low frequencies is consistent with declines in auditory temporal processing. Age-related declines in temporal processing undermine the coding of the durational and transitional time-varying properties of the input signal and the extraction of signals from noise.

The gap detection threshold, the smallest gap between two sound markers that a listener can detect, is the most common measure of temporal resolution. Many older adults do not detect gaps until the gaps are significantly longer than those that can be detected by younger adults. Notably, age-related differences in gap detection thresholds are not associated with absolute threshold elevations. The effect of age on gap detection threshold is more pronounced when the markers surrounding the gap are shorter than 10 ms, when the gap is nearer to the onset or offset of the signal, and when the markers differ in frequency composition.

Older adults are also significantly worse than younger adults in discriminating the duration of two tones. The effect of age on duration discrimination is more pronounced when the target tone is embedded in a sequence of tones. There are also significant age-related declines in the discrimination and recall of the temporal order of short sequences of sounds, especially when the sounds are presented at fast rates.

Synchrony or periodicity coding is another aspect of auditory temporal processing that declines with age. Loss of neural synchrony is implicated by the pattern of age-related differences in frequency and intensity discrimination, as well as by the pattern of age-related differences in masking-level differences. Other evidence pointing to loss of periodicity coding in older adults is that they have more difficulty than do younger adults in detecting mistuned harmonics in complex sounds and in segregating concurrently presented sounds.

Speech Processing

Like listeners of any age who have outer hair cell loss, audiometric thresholds explain nearly all of the problems encountered by older adults when they listen to speech in relatively quiet environments. However, specifically age-related deficits seem to be most apparent in difficult or complex auditory perception tasks, such as when speech is presented rapidly or in noisy or reverberant conditions, particularly in a background of interrupted or modulated noise, or when there is competing speech, even from a single talker.

Importantly, age-related deficits are much larger for temporally complex conditions compared to spectrally complex conditions. There is growing evidence that age-related declines in auditory temporal processing account for the disproportionate difficulties in understanding speech in noise that are experienced by older adults, including those for whom the audibility of speech is not a problem because they have normal audiometric thresholds throughout the speech frequency range up to 3000 Hz.

Declines in auditory temporal processing affect the ability of older adults to use different types of speech cues. At the sentence level, prosodic cues, such as syllable stress and rhythmic patterning, impart syntactic and affective information. At the word level, gaps and durations serve phonemic contrasts that enable word recognition (e.g., the stop consonant gap of [p] distinguishes the words split and slit). At the subphonemic level, periodicity cues derived from the voice fundamental frequency and harmonic structure contribute to voice quality and talker identification. Older adults exhibit deficits at all levels of speech processing that can be related to declines in auditory temporal processing.

Interactions between Auditory and Cognitive Processing

There is a strong correlation between sensory and cognitive aging. The difficulties of older adults in understanding spoken language in complex listening conditions may be exacerbated by the effect of age on cognitive processing, including declines in working memory and attention. As the listening condition becomes more adverse, it becomes more cognitively demanding for listeners of any age to process heard information. However, older adults demonstrate preserved knowledge and better ability, compared younger adults, to use contextual cues to compensate for difficulty hearing in challenging listening conditions.

Rehabilitation

In quiet, older adults with outer hair cell loss exhibit perceptual deficits resembling those of younger adults with comparable loss. Beyond the difficulties in speech perception explained by loss of audibility, many older adults also have problems attributable to subtypes of presbycusis involving declines in temporal processing. Currently, hearing aids are unable to correct for these declines; however, other assistive listening technology which enables the segregation of sound sources can reduce the challenge of listening in complex acoustical environments. Other forms of rehabilitation focus on training the older person and their communication partners to use strategies to avoid and cope with everyday listening challenges.

See also: Deafness.

Further Reading

Cilento, B, Norton, S, and Gates, G (2003). The effects of aging and hearing loss on distortion-product otoacoustic emissions. *Otolaryngology, Head and Neck Surgery* 129: 382–389.
Davis, AC (1995). *Hearing Impairment in Adults.* London: Whurr Publishers Ltd.
Frisina, DR, Frisina, RD, Snell, KB, et al. (2001). Auditory temporal processing during aging. In: Hof, PR and Mobbs, CV (eds.) *Functional Neurobiology of Aging*, pp. 565–579. New York: Academic Press.
Gallacher, J (2005). Hearing, cognitive impairment and aging: A critical review. *Reviews in Clinical Gerontology* 14: 199–209.
International Organization for Standardization (2000). *ISO 7029–2000: Acoustics – Statistical Distribution of Hearing Thresholds as a Function of Age,* 2nd edn. Geneva: International Organization for Standardization.
Kiessling, J, Pichora-Fuller, MK, Gatehouse, S, et al. (2003). Candidature for and delivery of audiological services: Special needs of older people. *International Journal of Audiology* 42(supplement 2): 2S92–2S101.
Moore, BCJ (1998). *Cochlear Hearing Loss.* London: Whurr Publishers Ltd.
Pichora-Fuller, MK and Carson, AJ (2000). Hearing health and the listening experiences of older communicators. In: Hummert, ML and Nussbaum, J (eds.) *Communication, Aging, and Health: Linking Research and Practice for Successful Aging*, pp. 43–74. Mahwah, NJ: Lawrence Erlbaum Associates.
Pichora-Fuller, MK and Singh, G (2006). Effects of age on auditory and cognitive processing: Implications for hearing aid fitting and audiological rehabilitation. *Trends in Amplification* 10: 29–59.
Schneider, BA and Pichora-Fuller, MK (2000). Implications of perceptual deterioration for cognitive aging research. In: Craik, FIM and Salthouse, TA (eds.) *The Handbook of Aging and Cognition,* 2nd edn., pp. 155–219. Mahwah, NJ: Lawrence Erlbaum Associates.
Vaughan, N and Fausti, S (eds.) (2006). The aging auditory system: Considerations for rehabilitation. Proceedings from the National Center for Rehabilitative Auditory Research (NCRAR), 2005. *Seminars in Hearing* 27(4): 213–352.
Willott, JF (1991). *Aging and the Auditory System: Anatomy, Physiology, and Psychophysics.* San Diego: Singular.

Sentence Comprehension

M. C. MacDonald and R. S. Sussman, University of Wisconsin–Madison, Madison, WI, USA

Introduction

When people talk to each other, they translate their ideas into a series of sounds (or in the case of signed languages, gestures), and the recipient of the message must take this string of essentially arbitrary sounds or movements and interpret it as a discrete, abstract message. As such, processes of language comprehension run the gamut, from the earliest stages of perception of a speech sound or gesture to high-level inferences concerning the implications of the messages that have been comprehended. Sentence comprehension forms a middle ground in this sequence and concerns the processes by which a language perceiver transforms a linear string of words into an understanding of the essential sentence meaning.

The meaning of a sentence can be thought of as a hierarchically organized structure connecting and relating the meanings of individual elements to create propositional meaning. For example, in the sentences in example 1, a comprehender must understand that Silvia is the one doing the giving (that is, that Silvia has the thematic role of Agent in the sentence), that Mom is receiving something (Mom has the Recipient role), and the flowers are the thing being given (the Theme role). Although the three sentences in 1 have quite different word orders, these basic role assignments remain the same.

1a. Silvia gave some flowers to Mom.
1b. Silvia gave Mom some flowers.
1c. Mom was given some flowers by Silvia.

As this example illustrates, the role that any individual element will play in the event that is being described is determined by the sort of sentence structure it occurs in, as well as the position it occupies within that structure. Moreover, words and phrases toward the ends of utterances may have an effect on how the beginning of a sentence must be interpreted. Consider example 2:

2. I saw her fly . . .
   a. the fighter jet.
   b. was open.

Before listeners have heard the end of the utterance, they cannot be sure whether the phrase 'her fly' is the beginning of an embedded clause describing the actions of a pilot or a noun phrase denoting the front closure of a woman's pants. Sentence comprehension has the property of immediacy of interpretation: people begin interpreting language as soon as they hear it; listeners do not wait to find out how an utterance will end before they assign at least a tentative interpretation to its beginning. Immediacy of interpretation is an essential feature of the comprehension process because the acoustic speech signal is fleeting, and memory for unanalyzed acoustic information is strictly limited. Thus the memory of the input signal will be lost if it is not rapidly converted to a meaningful representation. The same is essentially true in reading, despite the fact that words on a page, unlike a speech signal, are available for reprocessing. If comprehenders did not advance beyond a visual or phonological (sound-based) representation of the written input for the early part of a sentence, then processing later parts of a sentence would simply create interference in the representation of the initial sequence. Thus, sentence comprehension proceeds through the rapid development of an initial interpretation of a sentence, with enrichment and adjustment of this interpretation as the sentence unfolds. The key research questions have concerned the nature of that preliminary interpretation and the mechanisms for its enrichment and revision. These issues have typically been addressed in investigations of sentence comprehension processes by adult native speakers of a language, but the work has clear overlap with studies of child language acquisition, comprehension processes in second language acquisition, and the nature of impairments in these processes following brain injury.

The first attempt to develop a theory of the processes executed during sentence comprehension emerged in the 1960s through a collaboration between linguist Noam Chomsky and psychologist George Miller, who tried to integrate the rapidly developing field of generative linguistics with studies of cognitive processes. The derivational theory of complexity (DTC) was built on Chomsky's transformational grammar, which posited that the structure of a sentence (the surface structure) was related to a meaning-based representation (a deep structure) through a series of transformations. The DTC posited that during the process of sentence comprehension, people mentally worked through the various sentence transformations to convert a perceived sentence to its deep structure, from which sentence meaning could then be extracted. The more transformations that had to be undone to arrive at the deep structure, the longer the sentence comprehension process should take. For example, the passive sentence above 1c was hypothesized to need at least one more transformation than the active sentence 1a, yielding the prediction that passive sentences should take longer to comprehend than their active counterparts. Whereas early studies found good support for these predictions, later work suggested that the number of posited transformations had essentially no value in predicting comprehension difficulty. As a result, not only did the DTC fall out of favor as an account of sentence comprehension processes, but many psychologists became disillusioned with the idea that formal linguistic theories of the structure of language could offer insight into accounts of language comprehension.

More currently, research in sentence comprehension has addressed the cognitive processes, assumptions, and information that underlie the mechanisms and strategies of understanding everyday language in real time. This focus on the precise timing of comprehension processes emerges from a general interest in modularity claims within language research. Applied to sentence comprehension, the key modularity question concerns whether the many levels of language representation (sound, word, sentence, discourse, etc.) interact to derive sentence meaning or whether processes operate autonomously on different levels, saving any cross-level integration for the final stage of processing. Sentence comprehension research, situated between research on lexical (word) processing and the interpretation of entire conversations or texts, can be viewed as spanning three subfields – syntactic ambiguity resolution, syntactically complex utterances, and the relating of sentences to the broader discourse or text, including the interpretation of referentially dependent expressions such as pronouns.

Ambiguity Resolution

Language is rife with ambiguities at all levels of representation, and sentence comprehension research addresses the challenges presented by lexical ambiguity and syntactic ambiguity. Lexical ambiguities arise when a word has more than one meaning, as in example 3. Because the word 'glasses' can denote either eyewear or kitchenware, the intended meaning of the sentence is not obvious. Syntactic ambiguities, on the other hand, arise when a sequence of words is at least temporarily compatible with more than one sentence structure and more than one set of thematic roles and relations among the participants of the action. In example 4 below, the prepositional phrase 'with a lollipop' could be interpreted as modifying either the main verb of the sentence, as in 4a, such that the lollipop is the instrument used to tease the boy, or as modifying the object of the sentence, as in 4b. Lexical ambiguity and syntactic ambiguity frequently interact, as in example 2, in which the lexical ambiguity of the words 'her' and 'fly' created a syntactic ambiguity.

3. Phil wiped off the glasses.
4. The surly teenager teased the boy with the lollipop.
   a. The surly teenager teased the boy by using a lollipop (as bait).
   b. The surly teenager teased the boy who was holding the lollipop.

The modularity debate in syntactic ambiguity resolution has concerned the time course over which information is brought to bear on an ambiguity. Listeners must attach at least a partial interpretation to each word of an utterance as soon as it is encountered. The question then is, given that they have not yet heard the end of the utterance, on what information are they basing their interpretations? When do they integrate the information into their understanding of the unfolding utterance? Are certain types of information more useful (or used) than others?

One approach to these questions is exemplified by Lyn Frazier and colleagues' Garden Path model. 'Garden path' refers to an initial misinterpretation of a sentence, followed by a moment of surprise when later information in the sentence reveals that the initial interpretation was incorrect. The Garden Path model is a modular, two-stage approach in which the first-stage parser (the syntactic interpretation component of the comprehension system) develops an initial syntactic structure for the input, guided by only the lexical categories of the input words (noun, verb, etc.), the syntactic rules of the language, and structure-based heuristics that direct structure building when the given lexical categories can combine in more than one way within the syntax of the language. The structure-building heuristics typically favor syntactically simpler interpretations over more-complex ones. At some later point, a second stage integrates semantic and contextual information into the representation, and if this information conflicts with the initial interpretation built by the parser, the conflict may trigger a revision and reanalysis of the input. The guiding assumption of this and other 'syntax-first' models was that the demands of immediacy of interpretation could not be satisfied if all information were used in developing the initial interpretation, because probabilistic information, such as the implications of the prior context or the likelihood of the speaker's conveying a particular meaning, was too complex and would take too long to compute to be applied rapidly. The first-stage parser, with access to minimal and rapidly available information, was therefore seen as serving the function of getting a syntactic interpretation started, leaving additional time for the second-stage system to finish computations.

The preeminent role accorded to the syntactic parser in the Garden Path model and other syntax-first models is accompanied by a prediction for sentence comprehension behavior during the interpretation of ambiguous sentences: namely that all nonsyntactic factors such as the context in which a sentence is produced, the actual words used, the relative frequency of its constructions with respect to the words involved, the prosodic features of the utterance, and so on, will affect the course of sentence comprehension only secondarily, in the second stage of processing. The alternative, constraint-based approach argues that the preference for one interpretation over another during comprehension of an ambiguous sentence emerges from the rapid combination of many probabilistic constraints, with no privileged role for syntactic information. Proponents of this approach explicitly reject the notion that nonsyntactic information is somehow harder to compute. A key observation of this approach is that different types of information tend to be correlated. For example, a verb's meaning is strongly related to the kinds of nouns and prepositional phrases (such as 'with a lollipop') it tends to appear with in sentences. As a result, even weak cues can combine with other correlated cues and have a strong effect on interpretation preferences.

Both the constraint-based and modular accounts have primarily been assessed with online measures, that is, precise, time-locked measures of comprehension processes as the sentence progresses, in order to look for behavioral evidence consistent with either early interaction or two modular subprocesses. A significant body of work in the 1980s and 1990s used measures of reading time during comprehension of written ambiguous sentences. Some early work using eye movement monitoring (eye tracking) during reading claimed to find evidence of a modular, two-stage interpretation system, with the earliest eye fixations on a region of text guided by operations of the first-stage parser, and later fixations on the text and rereading were driven by second-stage semantic integration processes. This view was motivated in part by studies in which manipulations of semantic information in syntactically ambiguous sentences were found to affect late eye fixations but not early ones. Subsequent studies suggested that at least some delayed effects of nonsyntactic information in eye fixation patterns were attributable to weak or infelicitous contexts or other biases in the ambiguous stimuli. More-robust manipulations of context have shown clear evidence of use of nonsyntactic information very early. These results challenged the modular claims for isolated subprocesses during sentence comprehension. Additional evidence for the constraint-based approach comes from studies of comprehenders' eye fixations on visual scenes while listening to spoken language related to the scene. Patterns of eye fixations suggest that information in the visual scene affects the early stages of interpreting ambiguous sentences. These results offer a powerful challenge to claims for modularity in sentence comprehension: not only does nonsyntactic information in the linguistic signal appear to constrain early syntactic ambiguity resolution, but even nonlinguistic information (such as from the visual scene) has a powerful early effect.

Complex Sentence Interpretation

A second area of investigation in sentence comprehension is syntactically complex sentences. The sentences in example 5 show two different types of relative clause. The example in 5a is known as a subject relative because the head of the relative clause (the element modified by the relative clause, here 'the reporter') is the subject of the attacking action in the relative clause. The object relative clause (also known as a center embedded clause) in 5b has a similar word order, but here the head of the relative clause ('the reporter') is the direct object of 'attacked' rather than the one doing the attacking.

5a. Subject relative: The reporter that attacked the senator admitted the error.
5b. Object relative: The reporter that the senator attacked admitted the error.

Despite the clauses' identical words and highly similar word order, sentences containing object relatives are typically much more difficult to comprehend than those with subject relatives. The added comprehension difficulty is not thought to reflect ambiguity resolution processes. The explanation of processing difficulty for object relatives varies, but the dominant view is that comprehenders encounter two unintegrated nouns (e.g., 'The reporter that the senator') before a verb, thus creating a working memory load in which two nouns must be held in memory while waiting for verb information that relates them. By contrast, in subject relatives such as 5a, the alternating pattern of nouns and verbs permits rapid integration of these sentence elements, reducing the memory burden. A minority view holds that object relative clauses are more difficult than the subject relatives because the object relative structure is unlike other sentence structures in the language, effectively leading to ambiguity in how to interpret them. If so, then relative clause interpretation may be a form of ambiguity resolution, similar to that in the more widely recognized syntactic ambiguities discussed above.

Because of their syntactic complexity and their presumed dependence on working memory processes, relative clause structures have been a popular choice in investigations of sentence comprehension in atypical populations, including patients with aphasia, Alzheimer's disease, or other forms of dementia. The relationship between memory processes and relative clause comprehension has also been investigated in children, for whom both the ability to interpret relative clauses and the ability to perform well on working memory tasks develops fairly late.

Referentially Dependent Expressions and Links to Discourse Representations

Referentially dependent expressions are those which do not directly refer to something in the world but typically refer instead to some previously mentioned entity. For example, in 6a, we know that 'John' refers to a person, and we can interpret 'John' in this way even if we don't know him personally. By contrast, the pronoun 'he' does not refer directly to someone in this way but instead acquires its meaning indirectly, by being linked to the expression 'John.' This linking process is a form of ambiguity resolution, as the referent of a pronoun is not always clear. For example in 6b, 'he' might refer to either 'John' or 'Javier.' Research on pronoun comprehension spans both the ambiguity resolution processes that identify the correct referent of a pronoun and the consequences of pronominal reference – that is, how the comprehender's representation of the sentence changes as a result of having identified the referent of a pronoun.

6a. John went to the store after he got off work.
6b. John called Javier after he got off work.

The processes of pronoun reference resolution have a character similar to that of the processes of syntactic ambiguity resolution in that comprehenders appear to integrate a variety of probabilistic constraints to converge on the correct referent of a pronoun, including order of mention (earlier mentioned referents are more likely to be pronoun referents than later ones, at least within a sentence), grammatical role of referents (subjects of sentences are more likely to be referents than are other roles), and parallelism in grammatical role (nouns with the same grammatical role as the pronoun – e.g., both are subjects or both are objects – are more likely to be referents). These three constraints all serve to promote 'John' rather than 'Javier' as the referent of 'he' in example 6b.

In addition, the syntactic structure surrounding a referentially dependent expression may constrain the choice of referent. In 7a, the reflexive 'himself' must refer to John, while in 7b, the pronoun 'him' must not.

7a. John likes himself.
7b. John likes him.

These patterns of permissible co-reference have led to the hypothesis that syntactic structures define possible domains of reference, that is, the regions in which a referentially dependent expression may find a referent or may be blocked from finding a referent. Specifically, reflexives must find a referent within their own syntactically defined domain; pronouns must find a referent outside that domain. In examples 7a and 7b, this domain is the complete sentence. Thus, in 7a, 'himself' refers to the only possible referent within the relevant syntactic domain: 'John.' In 7b, 'him' can refer to any male entity except John. Extensive work within the field of linguistics has been devoted to defining these syntactic domains of reference, and modular accounts of pronoun resolution have suggested that these syntactic constraints have a privileged, early effect on pronominal reference resolution. However, recent work within both linguistics and sentence comprehension suggests that the syntactic domains are not so clear as originally thought, nor do they have a privileged status in referent resolution during comprehension. Online behavioral measures of referential interpretation (e.g., using eye tracking to monitor looks to displays of possible referents) confirm this intuition. These results suggest that while syntactic structure is certainly a factor in defining the preferred referents of pronouns and reflexives, other factors – such as point-of-view information or the specific lexical biases of other words in the construction – may also influence early stages of interpretation.

When someone identifies the referent of a pronoun, the mental representation of the sentence appears to be updated to reflect the re-mention (via pronoun) of a previously mentioned entity in the discourse. For example, when a comprehender has determined that 'he' must refer to 'John' in the examples above, the representation of 'John' appears to become more prominent in the discourse representation, as evidenced by shorter reaction times to the word 'John' compared with control conditions just after the pronoun has been comprehended. Moreover, other previously mentioned entities in the discourse (such as 'Javier' in 6b) appear to be inhibited and yield slower reaction times, as the pronoun indicates a shift toward focus on the referent in the ongoing linguistic input. The work provides time-locked data concerning the processes of memory updating during the comprehension process.

Sentence Comprehension Methodologies

Research in sentence comprehension employs both online behavioral and brain imaging methodologies. Behavioral measures in sentence comprehension typically assess processing difficulty, as indexed by assessments of response time, errors, or both. The most common behavioral method has been reading times of particular words or regions within a sentence as a measure of processing difficulty. The focus on reading rather than comprehension of spoken sentences emerged out of the necessity to have a continuous measure of comprehension processes as the linguistic signal unfolds over time. Because reading proceeds at the comprehender's own pace, continuous measures of processing difficulty can be obtained from assessments of reading time, whereas there is no listening-time equivalent for spoken sentence comprehension.

In reading comprehension studies, the immediacy assumption holds that the reader is building an interpretation of the sentence as each new word or phrase is read. When the reader encounters a word or words that do not fit with this interpretation, this new material should take longer to read than in cases in which the material easily fits into the ongoing sentence interpretation. Comparing reading times of critical regions across different constructions yields a measure of the relative difficulty of integration of new material into the comprehender's interpretation of the sentence so far, which in turn sheds light on the interpretations that must have been developed by the reader in order for this difficulty to arise. The two primary reading measures are self-paced reading, in which the comprehender reads text on a computer screen and is allowed to see only a small portion of a sentence at a time, pressing a key to see each new word or region, and eye tracking, in which the entire sentence can be viewed while a device records the location and duration of eye fixations. Both measures yield data concerning the overall length of time spent reading a region, but eye tracking also yields data concerning the patterns of eye movements through a sentence, including patterns of rereading previously read text. Some researchers have interpreted different sorts of fixations within this sequence (e.g., the first fixation to a region vs. the second fixation or looks back to a region after reading later regions) as corresponding to the integration of different sources of information (syntactic, semantic, pragmatic, etc.) into the reader's interpretation of the sentence.

Eye movements have also been used to provide a time-locked measure of spoken sentence comprehension in the visual world paradigm, in which comprehenders view an array of objects or a scene on a computer and listen to speech referring to the scene, such as instructions to act on certain objects in view. Eye fixations on elements of the scene reflect their current state of understanding of the spoken material and its relationship to the visual environment. For instance, listeners who hear a sentence containing the verb 'eat' are more likely to look at edible items in a visual display than are listeners who heard a sentence that featured the verb 'take.' By manipulating both the visual display and the language accompanying it, researchers can investigate how context and language interact during spoken sentence comprehension.

Measures of brain activity as rendered by positron-emission tomography, functional magnetic resonance imaging (fMRI), magnetoencephalography, and event-related potentials (ERPs) have also been used to assess online sentence comprehension, often accompanied by an explicit task to encourage attention to the stimuli, such as to judge the sensibility of sentences. As with studies using behavioral measures, researchers typically compare materials that are similar save for one critical manipulation, such as contrasts between sensible sentences and scrambled words or between subject and object relative clauses.

Various fMRI studies of sentence comprehension have revealed a large number of areas that appear to be crucial to the comprehension process, beyond those that are important in interpretation of isolated words. These sentence-specific areas are believed to be important for interpreting the syntax of the sentence, identifying the thematic roles, and linking the sentence representation to prior knowledge. Whereas studies of patients with brain injury have named the left hemisphere as the site of virtually all language processes in most individuals, imaging studies have tended to find bilateral activation of a number of frontal and temporal brain regions during sentence comprehension, often with somewhat greater levels of activation in the left hemisphere than in the homologous area on the right. The fMRI studies of sentence comprehension have not factored heavily into the research issues addressing the time course of processing described above, which have been the focus of many behavioral studies in sentence comprehension. The temporal resolution of the blood oxygen level-dependent (BOLD) signal in fMRI, with about a 5 s latency, is not an appropriate instrument to address the precise time course of processes which behavioral data suggest operate on the order of a few dozen milliseconds.

The shorter latency of ERPs makes them more applicable to issues concerning the time course of comprehension, and some measures are thought to map onto specific comprehension processes. For instance, an early left anterior negativity is thought to be associated with syntactic difficulty, while negativity approximately 400 ms after stimulus onset is hypothesized to be an indicator of semantic discord. A more generalized process of information integration has been tentatively linked to a positivity 600 ms after stimulus onset. It should be emphasized, however, that these connections between activation patterns and specific comprehension processes are by no means uncontroversial and are at best only loosely understood.

See also: Language Development; Sentence Production; Word Learning; Word Recognition.

Suggested Reading

Altmann, G (1998). Ambiguity in sentence processing. *Trends in Cognitive Sciences* 2(4): 146–152.

Ferreira, F, Bailey, K, and Ferraro, V (2002). Good-enough representations in language comprehension. *Current Directions in Psychological Science* 11: 11–15.

Frazier, L (1987). Sentence processing: A tutorial review. In: Coltheart, M (ed.) *Attention and Performance XII: The Psychology of Reading*, pp. 559–586. Hove, UK: Lawrence Erlbaum.

Garnham, A (2001). *Mental Models and the Interpretation of Anaphora.* Philadelphia: Psychology Press.

Gibson, E (1998). Linguistic complexity: Locality of syntactic dependencies. *Cognition* 68: 1–76.

Henderson, J and Ferreira, F (2004). *The Interface of Language, Vision, and Action: Eye Movements and the Visual World.* New York: Psychology Press.

Kaan, E and Swaab, T (2002). The brain circuitry of syntactic comprehension. *Trends in Cognitive Sciences* 6(8): 350–356.

Lewis, RL, Vasishth, S, and VanDyke, JA (2006). Computational principles of working memory in sentence comprehension. *Trends in Cognitive Sciences* 10: 447–454.

MacDonald, MC, Pearlmutter, NJ, and Seidenberg, MS (1994). The lexical nature of syntactic ambiguity resolution. *Psychological Review* 101: 483–506.

MacDonald, MC and Seidenberg, MS (2006). Constraint satisfaction approaches to lexical and sentence comprehension. In: Traxler, M and Gernsbacher, MA (eds.) *Handbook of Psycholinguistics*, pp. 581–612. New York: Academic Press.

Pickering, M and van Gompel, R (2006). Syntactic parsing. In: Traxler, M and Gernsbacher, MA (eds.) *Handbook of Psycholinguistics*, pp. 455–504. New York: Academic Press.

Runner, JT, Sussman, RS, and Tanenhaus, MK (2006). Assigning referents to reflexives and pronouns in picture noun phrases: Experimental tests of binding theory. *Cognitive Science* 30: 1–49.

Tanenhaus, M, Spivey-Knowlton, M, and Hanna, J (2000). Modeling thematic and discourse context effects with a multiple constraints approach: Implications for the architecture of the language comprehension system. In: Crocker, M, Pickering, M, and Clifton, C, Jr. (eds.) *Architectures and Mechanisms for Language Processing*, pp. 90–118. Cambridge, UK: Cambridge University Press.

Townsend, D and Bever, T (2001). *Sentence Comprehension: The Integration of Habits and Rules.* Cambridge, MA: MIT Press.

Trueswell, JC and Tanenhaus, MK (2004). *Approaches to Studying World-Situated Language Use: Bridging the Language-as-Product and Language-as-Action Traditions.* Cambridge, MA: MIT Press.

Sentence Production

V. S. Ferreira, University of California at San Diego, La Jolla, CA, USA

Introduction

Sentence production refers to the ability of speakers of natural language to assemble known words into larger structured phrases or sentences. These phrases and sentences have two critical and related properties: They are grammatically well formed, as speakers generally do not produce 'the cat were happy' or 'cat happy the were,' and they convey the relational meaning of a sentence, or 'who did what to whom,' that the words by themselves cannot. For example, there is no single word (or, more precisely, morpheme – the smallest meaningful unit of language) that conveys 'the cat was happy'; one must assemble a sentence to relate one lexically denoted meaning, happiness, to another, the cat.

This article reviews different issues in sentence production research, roughly following a historical sequence. It begins with the first insights into sentence production from speech error evidence, followed by empirical and theoretical issues that have emerged from laboratory study, and moves on to more recent investigations of naturalistic issues. The article closes with a brief discussion of the neuroscience of sentence production.

Initial Insights: Evidence from Speech Errors

Compared with its sibling fields of language acquisition and language comprehension, research on language production in its current form began later and more slowly. This is likely due primarily to methodological challenges. In language comprehension at least, it is obvious how to precisely control the input to the system. For language production, however, it was not obvious how to get speakers to produce the sentences that were necessary for theory development and testing.

This methodological roadblock was overcome in the 1970s, through the pioneering work of Vicki Fromkin and Merrill Garrett. They sidestepped this input problem by amassing and exploring relatively large corpora of naturally occurring speech errors or slips of the tongue. These researchers made two critical discoveries that allowed speech error evidence to reveal the workings of sentence production mechanisms. First, they recognized that speech errors were often the (bungled) products of cognitive mechanisms involved in core language processing. At least for a relatively large class of errors, an utterance like 'that log could use another fire' is not a 'slip of the mind,' because speakers know when they make such errors, so they are not the result of bad conceptual knowledge. It is also (ironically) not a 'slip of the tongue,' because speech errors are unaffected by very peripheral articulatory or acoustic properties of speech. Instead, such errors are 'slips of the sentence production mechanism,' revealing the basic processing and representations speakers use to put sentences together. Second, Fromkin and Garrett discovered that when analyzed *en masse*, speakers slipped into consistent patterns, and these hinted at how sentence production mechanisms encoded nonlinguistic thought into phrases and sentences.

In a series of analyses published from the mid-1970s onward, Merrill Garrett used speech error evidence to lay a foundation for a theory of sentence production, the general outline of which can be recognized in most theories to this day. Garrett's initial investigations looked primarily at movement errors – slips in which one or more elements that a speaker intends are positioned in the wrong place. 'That log could use another fire' is a movement error because though the speaker intended to use 'log' and 'fire,' each word was produced in the place of the other and so were 'moved' with respect to the speaker's original intention. The same is true of 'I met someone who had a spet pider,' but with respect to the positioning of the sound 's.' Garrett first noticed that such movement errors clustered into two types. One typically involved words, like the log/fire error above, though larger units like phrases can be involved. In these errors, the words moved about as far as speakers could plan and nearly always came from the same part of speech (so that nouns traded places with nouns, verbs with verbs, and so forth). Such errors were also largely insensitive to the properties of the sounds of words. The other type of movement error typically involved individual speech sounds, like 'spet pider,' though again larger units like morphemes can be involved. In these, sounds rarely moved more than two or three words and exchanged between words of any part of speech. Also, the movement patterns in these errors were highly sensitive to the properties of the sounds of words, such as stress level or whether they were consonants or vowels.

These and related patterns of errors led Garrett to posit that sentence production proceeds through two distinct stages, sketched in **Figure 1**. The first type of error reflects the organization of the first stage of sentence production, called functional processing, in which

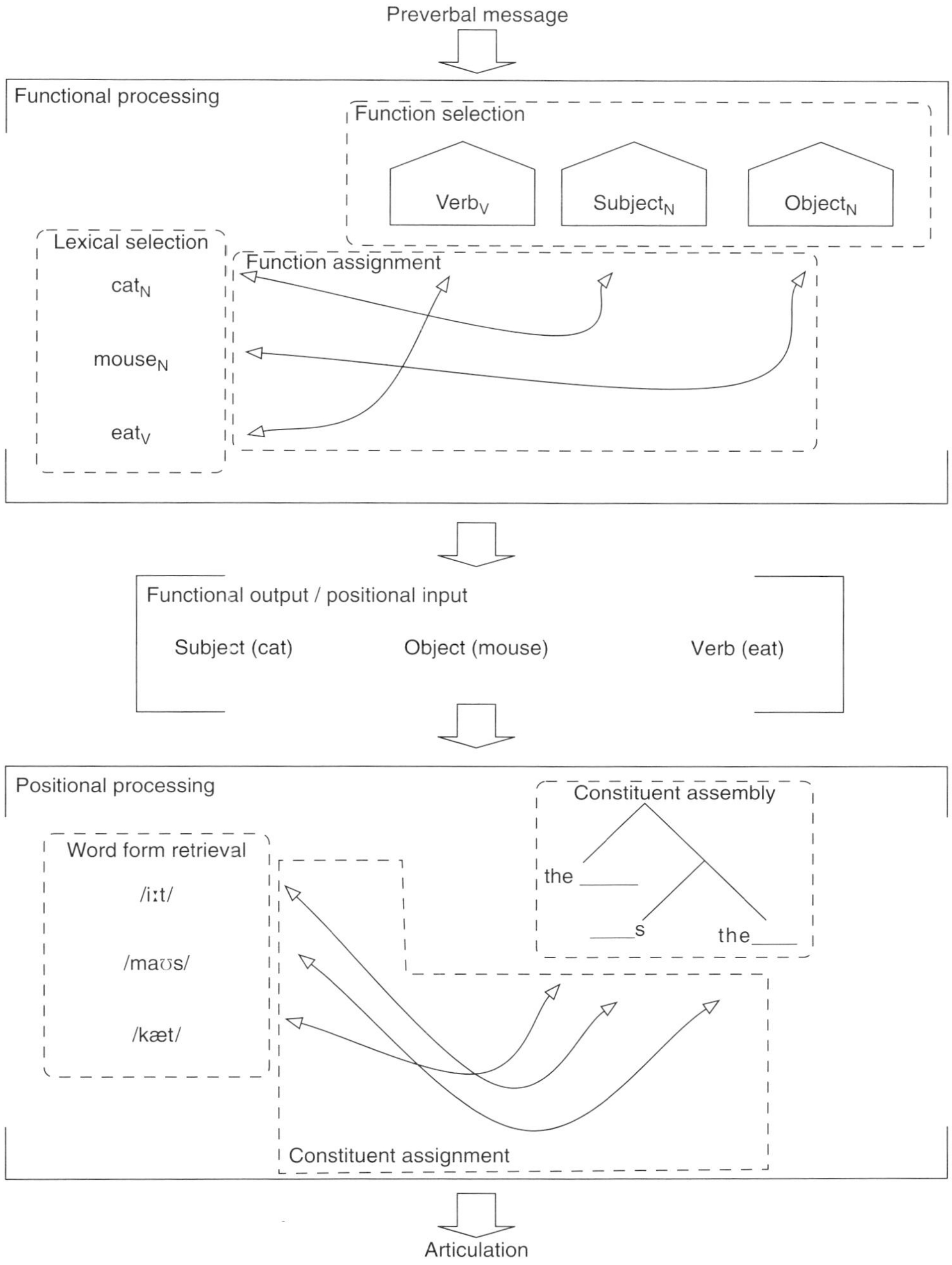

Figure 1 Sketch of the architecture of sentence production, as proposed by Garrett. Processing flow begins with the preverbal message (top), proceeds through functional processing and then positional processing, and concludes with articulation (bottom). V, verb; N, noun.

speakers assign words on the basis of their part of speech (noun, verb) to grammatical functions such as 'subject of the sentence.' These words are not phonologically defined, which is the reason why errors involving words are not sensitive to how they sound. According to Garrett, the processing dynamics at the functional level are independent of the spoken order of words. This explains why misplaced words can move large distances: what determines whether two units are processed at about the same time, and so might exchange, is unrelated to whether those units are adjacent in the eventual utterance. The second type of error reflects the organization of the next stage of sentence production, termed positional processing, at which speakers configure words into hierarchical constituent structures that determine their order in the spoken utterance. At positional processing, segmental content (individual speech sounds) is specified, whereas functional information is not represented.

Though basic outlines of Garrett's proposal are still current, certain details of Garrett's proposals have been scrutinized. One prominent effort was a series of empirical and theoretical speech error studies carried out by Gary Dell. Dell first identified patterns of speech errors that revealed mutual influence or interactions among representations at different stages of processing. In particular, Dell showed that when one word replaces another that is similar in meaning, the words are more likely than chance to be similar also in sound. He also showed that when speakers erred in producing the individual sounds of words, the outcomes were more likely to constitute a known word than chance would predict. These patterns can be accommodated by assuming that processing at one level of sentence production is influenced by processing at other levels. So the phonological similarity of semantically related substituting words can be explained if representations at the analog of Garrett's positional level – phonologically defined words – are able to influence selection at the analog of Garrett's functional level – semantically selected and syntactically defined words. The tendency for sound errors to result in real words can be explained if the representations of words other than the one a speaker intends to say can influence the ongoing selection of individual sounds that a speaker does intend to say. Later, Dell developed a comprehensive connectionist model of the sentence production process that explained these observations and more. In connectionist models, knowledge structures are represented as units that become activated as a function of degree of evidence supporting those knowledge structures and are interconnected to represent the relationships among the knowledge structures. Dell's model could explain not only the speech error patterns already described but other, even less intuitive effects, such as the fact that sound errors are more likely to result in known words more as speech rate slows (because representations at different levels have more time to influence one another).

The Move to the Laboratory

The theory developed by Garrett proved seminal. Garrett's theory was important not only for investigations of speech errors; it succeeded in bootstrapping a laboratory sentence production enterprise as well. Recall that the primary impediment to developing a science of sentence production was the search for a valid way to elicit controlled, theoretically informative sentences. With Garrett's model, based as it was on face-valid evidence from speech errors, laboratory techniques further removed from natural production could confirm their own validity. This allowed laboratory investigations of sentence production to flourish until today, when diverse laboratory techniques are used to explore diverse theoretical issues. These issues are discussed next.

Scope of Planning

One of the first laboratory investigations of sentence production explored a simple question that has proven to have a rather complex answer: When speakers produce sentences, how far do they plan in advance, and what are the linguistic units they plan with? If freely speaking participants are asked to press buttons on hearing randomly presented tones, their responses are slowest at the ends of linguistic units called basic clauses, provided that they are about to produce more sentence material. A basic clause is a part of a sentence that includes a verb and all its directly associated arguments; thus, speakers evidently plan speech one basic clause at a time (fitting well with Garrett's claims regarding functional processing). Analyses of patterns of pausing in natural speech later verified this conclusion.

Subsequent work has revealed, however, that these original conclusions were likely too simple. Two factors complicate the story. First, the scope of planning seems different for different levels of sentence production. Early, during semantic and functional processing, the scope of planning is likely broader than later, during phonological and positional processing. Second, the scope of planning appears to be highly sensitive to task circumstances and speaker strategies. It is interesting that as production becomes more constrained and formulaic, speakers seem to plan ahead less. The idea is that speakers plan as little as they can get away with; when production is highly constrained and formulaic, speakers can be confident that they can come up with linguistic material to produce 'on the fly' and so can plan ahead less. With free-form production, speakers are less confident that they will be able to formulate on the fly, and so they plan ahead more. Relatedly, speakers are able to plan the same basic utterance about twice as fast (presumably because they plan ahead less) when given tight deadlines to begin speaking as they are if allowed to begin speaking whenever they like.

Accessibility Effects

Recall that Garrett assumed that functional processing is not affected by the order of words in the eventual utterance. A heavily investigated set of effects that revisits this assumption is termed accessibility effects. When speakers produce sentences, they tend to mention easily retrieved or highly accessible material sooner, leaving harder-to-retrieve or less accessible material to be mentioned later. For example, Kay Bock discovered that speakers choose different syntactic structures to allow semantically primed words to be mentioned as the subjects of their sentences. Thus, speakers tend to say, 'The lightning struck the church' if semantically primed by 'thunder,' but 'The church was struck by lightning' when semantically primed by 'worship' – first retrieved, first spoken. This seems inconsistent with Garrett's assumption that functional processing is insensitive to the eventual orders of words in sentences.

Yet with reasonable assumptions, the core of Garrett's claim can be preserved. Specifically, one can claim that words that are accessible (e.g., because they are semantically primed) are selected sooner during functional processing (see the left box in **Figure 1**) and so are assigned to 'higher' grammatical functions (where 'subject' is higher than 'object,' for example). Across languages, higher grammatical functions tend to be mentioned earlier in sentences, and so these assumptions can accommodate accessibility effects without requiring that functional processing directly reference the eventual positions of words in sentences. Further support for this assumption comes from demonstrations that accessibility manipulations that are more meaning-based (e.g., differences in semantic priming or the imageability of words) more readily influence function assignment (e.g., whether something is produced as a subject or object); in contrast, manipulations that are more form-based (e.g., the lengths of words) influence word order independent of function assignment (e.g., the order of words in a conjunction like 'salt and pepper'). This fits with Garrett's original division of production into a meaning-based functional system and a form-based positional system.

Within models of sentence production, accessibility effects are generally motivated by incrementality – that sentences are produced piecemeal from beginning to end. Incrementality implies that if one part of a sentence becomes accessible before another, production is most efficient if the part that is accessible sooner is mentioned sooner and the part that is accessible later is mentioned later.

Grammatical Agreement

Another topic that can be couched within Garrett's framework is agreement, referring to when the form of one element in a sentence depends on some property of another element. In English, this arises with subject–verb agreement: One says, 'the cat was happy' and 'the cats were happy,' such that the form of the verb ('was' or 'were') depends on the plurality of the subject ('cat' or 'cats').

The core agreement-related object of study is attraction, in which some irrelevant part of a sentence influences agreement. For example, when given a subject noun phrase like 'The key to the cabinets' and asked to complete it, subjects are likely to say 'The key to the cabinets were lost,' with the verb ('were') agreeing with the local noun 'cabinets' rather than the subject noun 'key.' The empirical enterprise has primarily been to assess the properties of local nouns that do and do not cause such attraction. One factor that powerfully causes attraction is grammatical plurality: Local nouns that are grammatically plural (like 'cabinets') cause plural-agreeing verbs to be produced rather than singular-agreeing verbs. Curiously, this effect is asymmetrical, such that grammatically singular local nouns do not cause attraction (in utterances like 'The keys to the cabinet was/were . . .'). This has led to the proposal that in English, plurality is marked – it is an explicit feature that is associated with a noun argument; the singular, in contrast, is unmarked, such that nouns default to being singular when not otherwise specified.

Given the robust effect of plurality on attraction, the question arises whether properties that are correlated with plurality, such as plurals' meaning (they are usually more numerous than the singular, like 'keys' vs. 'key') or sound (the '-s' at the ends of words), cause attraction errors. Generally, such properties are much less potent (if influential at all) compared with true grammatical plurality. For example, local nouns that denote collectives but are not grammatically plural ('The general of the army . . .') do not cause attraction, nor do local nouns that sound like plurals but are not ('The petal on the rose . . .'). In contrast, local nouns that denote single entities but are grammatically plural ('The ad for the scissors . . .') cause attraction, as do nouns that are plural but do not sound that way ('The trap for the mice . . .').

Comprehensive theories of agreement are currently the subject of active debate, the details of which are beyond the scope of this article. The weight of evidence suggests that within Garrett's model, agreement processing should arise within positional processing. Some properties of attraction fit in with this, including the above-noted insensitivity to semantic correlates of plurality and the sensitivity to the hierarchical structure of sentences. However, given that positional processing has a phonological character, additional assumptions may be needed to explain why attraction is insensitive to phonological factors.

Syntactic Priming

A heavily investigated phenomenon in sentence production that does not fit as neatly into Garrett's framework is termed syntactic priming (sometimes called structural or syntactic persistence). When a speaker produces or comprehends a sentence with a particular syntactic structure, the speaker is then more likely to use that structure rather than a reasonable alternative. For example, after hearing a prepositional dative structure ('The doctor gave the hat to the sailor'), speakers are likely to use another prepositional dative ('The ballerina showed the cake to the boxer') rather than a double-object structure ('The ballerina showed the boxer the cake').

Evidence has shown that at core, syntactic priming reflects the repetition of the syntactic structures of sentences. Properties correlated with syntactic structure either do not affect priming or affect priming independent of syntactic repetition. Such inconsequential properties include aspects of meaning (e.g., the order of agents and themes and recipients), sounds (e.g., rhythm or auditory structure), or words (especially syntactically relevant words like 'to') of sentences. Syntactic priming is enhanced by repeating meaningful words (especially verbs) in sentences but is reliable even without such repetition.

Three different theories of syntactic priming dominate current scientific discourse. One views priming as implicit learning, such that comprehending or producing particular structures (quasi-) permanently strengthens the knowledge of those structures, thereby resulting in repetition. Supporting this view are the observations that priming can be notably long-lived (surviving the comprehension and production of at least ten intervening neutral trials), is independent of explicit memory, and is evident in patients with anterograde amnesia. Another views priming as reflecting recent shorter-term activation of knowledge structures representing syntax. Supporting this is the observation that priming can be short-lived, especially when meaningful words are repeated from prime to target sentences. A third view is that priming is a force to coordinate knowledge structures among interlocutors in order to promote communicative success. Supporting this is the finding that priming is sensitive to conversational variables (such as the linguistic capabilities of the participants or whether participants are speakers, hearers, or side participants).

Earlier, syntactic priming was described as ill-fitting with respect to Garrett's framework. The reason is that priming operates similarly at both functional and positional processing. For example, the selection of an active rather than a passive sentence form – a sentence choice involving different assignments of grammatical functions – is influenced by priming in the same way as the selection of 'on the table is a book' versus 'the book is on the table' – a function-independent structure choice. Furthermore, to date, no aspect of priming has been revealed to dissociate along functional–positional lines (unlike accessibility effects, as noted earlier). Thus, though priming might affect the two separate processing stages identically, a more parsimonious proposal might be that the two stages should be collapsed into one.

The Separation of Words and Syntax

An area of active controversy in sentence production concerns the relationship between lexical and syntactic knowledge. At one extreme of a theoretical continuum, lexical knowledge could ground syntactic knowledge, such that the structure of a sentence is organized around the structures permitted by a particular verb, for example. These are termed lexically based theories. At the other extreme, lexical knowledge could be separate from syntactic knowledge, such that syntactic structures are constructed independently to obey communicative and grammatical constraints, and then words are slotted into those structures. These are termed frame-based theories. Between these are closed-class immanence accounts, whereby some words – closed-class or function words in particular, like 'the' and 'to' and 'by' – ground syntactic knowledge, with other words 'slotted in' as in the independent syntactic account.

Evidence from syntactic priming can be taken to support either extreme. Frame-based theories are supported by the fact that syntactic priming is observed even when no words are repeated between prime and target. Lexically based theories are supported by the fact that repeated words boost priming. Closed-class immanence accounts are supported especially by neuropsychological evidence showing that with breakdown of syntactic knowledge, speakers' use of function words is especially compromised.

From the Lab to the Wild

A current trend in sentence production work since the migration to the lab is toward evaluating issues of relevance to naturally produced sentences.

Corpora

The analysis of collections of natural speech, or language corpora, has a long tradition in sentence production research, with its current incarnation beginning with the publication of the famous Brown corpus in 1967. Ready access to greater computational power has allowed more-recent corpus work to take a considerable leap. Also, powerful statistical techniques such as mixed-effects modeling have allowed corpus researchers to isolate the influence of specific theoretically interesting factors while taking into account confounded uninteresting factors. The Linguistic Data Consortium at the University of Pennsylvania is a useful source of corpus data.

Nonverbal Devices

Because of its laboratory tradition (and perhaps because of the emphasis on reading in sentence comprehension research), most investigations of sentence production have focused on issues relevant to 'idealized' utterances – sentences with an uninterrupted delivery characteristic of a prepared speech or words on a page. However, natural language is rife with disfluencies – violations of idealized delivery – including fillers like 'uh' and 'um,' backtracking, self-interruptions, and so forth. The lore was that such violations are nuisance factors, to be avoided or ignored. Recent work has challenged this assumption, instead identifying the performance factors that underlie disfluency. These performance factors seem to be metalinguistic, largely reflecting the state of mind of the speaker (e.g., an 'uh' and 'um' indicate that the speaker is having difficulty thinking of the material).

Gesture also sometimes conveys metalinguistic information. Some gesture simply accompanies the rhythm of a spoken sentence (what are sometimes called beat gestures). Other gesture conveys physical properties of the matter under discussion (e.g., 'The fish I caught was THAT big!'). Yet other gesture conveys information redundant with that in the speech signal, for example, the path along which an object is traveling. With the trend toward more naturalistic research, investigations of gesture are becoming more prominent.

Spoken sentence production has one other critical nonverbal property: because it is presented in a perceptually graded medium (sound), some of the acoustic properties of a sentence can vary independent of the lexical and syntactic properties (a situation that holds for signed languages as well). The higher-order structure of such acoustic properties is termed the prosody (e.g., rhythm and stress) of a sentence. Research suggests that these two levels of higher-order structure, syntactic and prosodic, are related but independent. Prosodic structure gets some of its characteristics from syntactic structure, but it is sensitive to its own pressures (including the facts that it must respect other acoustic properties of sentences that syntactic structure does not and that it represents a lower dimensionality of structure, without recursive properties).

Communicating Discourse Properties

Though sentences are the basic units of certain aspects of communication, they rarely occur in isolation. Rather, sentences are typically parts of discourses such as a story or conversation. Critically, devices within sentences help them cohere into discourses. This is sometimes termed the information structure of a sentence, referring to the linguistic devices that help convey the foreground and background status of referents in sentences. A systematic and universal example of a discourse device in sentence production is given–new ordering, whereby speakers tend to produce already described (given) information before newly introduced (new) information; accordingly, addressees can take early mention to indicate that they should already know a referent and later mention to indicate that they should add a referent to their discourse models. Note that such information–structure effects bear a tight relationship to the above-described accessibility effects. Indeed, it is reasonable to suppose that at least given–new ordering could emerge directly from accessibility if given items are more accessible than new.

The Neuroscience of Sentence Production

Thus far, this article has included little on the neuroscience of sentence production. Regarding traditional neuropsychology, this is because the range of work that has been done is extensive and detailed and involves its own set of phenomena and debates. A useful recent review is included in the recommended readings. An especially commendable characteristic of the primary literature on the neuropsychology of sentence production is that it has made very close contact with the core theories of normal sentence production outlined here.

Only a handful of studies have used techniques for assessing online neurological functioning (such as fMRI, PET, or EEG) to better understand mechanisms of sentence production. One major reason for this gap is (again) methodological: most techniques for assessing ongoing neural functioning are disrupted by head motion. It is difficult to investigate sentence production unless speakers actually produce sentences, and for spoken production, this requires the movement of the head and jaw. These challenges have begun to be overcome, however, and the cognitive neuroscience of sentence production promises to be an exciting avenue of research in the future.

Currently, debates in the cognitive neuroscience of sentence production have largely concerned the precise localization of general sentence production abilities. At this point, it is clear that brain regions within Brodmann areas 44 and 45 and adjacent regions are implicated in processes that combine words into grammatical sentences, as opposed to processes that just list words or simpler structures. Going forward, cognitive neuroscience investigations would (like the traditional neuropsychological literature) gain by making greater contact with the rich and well-established range of theories on normal sentence production.

See also: Aphasia, Sudden and Progressive; Language Development; Language, Cortical Processes; Sentence Comprehension; Speech Production, Adult; Word Production.

Further Reading

Bock, JK (1982). Toward a cognitive psychology of syntax: Information processing contributions to sentence formulation. *Psychological Review* 89: 1–47.
Bock, JK (1986). Meaning, sound, and syntax: Lexical priming in sentence production. *Journal of Experimental Psychology: Learning, Memory, and Cognition* 12: 575–586.
Bock, JK (1986). Syntactic persistence in language production. *Cognitive Psychology* 18: 355–387.
Bock, JK (1995). Producing agreement. *Current Directions in Psychological Science* 8: 56–61.
Clark, HH (1996). *Using Language*. Cambridge, UK: Cambridge University Press.
Dell, GS (1986). A spreading-activation theory of retrieval in sentence production. *Psychological Review* 93: 283–321.
Ferreira, F (1993). The creation of prosody during sentence production. *Psychological Review* 100: 233–253.
Ferreira, VS and Slevc, LR (2007). Grammatical encoding. In: Gaskell, MG (ed.) *The Oxford Handbook of Psycholinguistics*, pp. 453–469. Oxford, UK: Oxford University Press.
Fromkin, VA (ed.) (1973). *Speech Errors as Linguistic Evidence*. The Hague: Mouton.

Garrett, MF (1975). The analysis of sentence production. In: Bower, GH (ed.) *The Psychology of Learning and Motivation,* vol. 9, pp. 133–177. New York: Academic Press.
Griffin, ZM and Ferreira, VS (2006). Properties of spoken language production. In: Traxler, MJ and Gernsbacher, MA (eds.) *Handbook of Psycholinguistics,* 2nd edn. Amsterdam: Academic Press.
Indefrey, P, Brown, CM, Hellwig, F, et al. (2001). A neural correlate of syntactic encoding during speech production. *Proceedings of the National Academy of Sciences of the United States of America* 98(10): 5933–5936.
Levelt, WJM (1989). *Speaking: From Intention to Articulation*. Cambridge, MA: MIT Press.
Pickering, MJ and Garrod, S (2004). Toward a mechanistic psychology of dialogue. *Behavioral and Brain Sciences* 27(2): 169–226.
Schütze, CT and Ferreira VS (eds.) (2007). *MIT Working Papers in Linguistics 53: The State of the Art in Speech Error Research: Proceedings of the LSA Institute Workshop.* Cambridge, MA: MITWPL.

Relevant Website

http://www.ldc.upenn.edu – The Linguistic Data Consortium.

Sign Language, Disorders of

A. Okrent, The University of Chicago, Chicago, IL, USA

Sign Language Breaks Down by Linguistic Levels

Sign languages, like spoken languages, are not just collections of symbols but complex systems of communication in which smaller units of structure are organized on multiple levels. The units, and the principles of their combination, differ according to the level at which they operate: phonetics, phonology, morphology, syntax, semantics, or discourse. Sign language can be disrupted at one or more of these levels due to brain injury or disease.

Most data on disorders of sign language come from signers of American Sign Language. A number of signers with Parkinson's disease, left hemisphere brain damage, and right hemisphere brain damage have been studied. Rigorous clinical tests of their language skills as well as analysis of their spontaneous language use have revealed that even though sign language is quite unlike spoken language in its physical properties, it breaks down according to the same linguistic properties that spoken language does. Although signs are dependent on arm and hand movements, Parkinson's disease, a movement disorder, disrupts these movements only at the phonetic level. Although signing makes extensive use of visuospatial processing, a domain generally handled by the right hemisphere, it is left hemisphere damage that causes the most severe disruption to signing. Right hemisphere damage leaves grammar intact but disrupts language at the discourse level. For the most part, disorders of sign language and disorders of spoken language that arise from similar causes are manifested in similar ways. A description of the nature of language breakdown at each level follows.

Parkinson's Disease: Disruption of Phonetics

Parkinson's disease involves the degeneration of dopamine-producing cells in the brain, leading to problems with the control of movement. The dysfunction of motor processes supporting spoken language in people with Parkinson's results in errors at the level of articulation. This is also true for sign language. Timing, rhythm, volume, and melody in the execution of language may be disrupted, but deeper levels of linguistic structure are spared.

Signs are formed from sublexical contrastive specifications for handshape, movement, orientation, and location. Case studies of signers with Parkinson's have shown that these signers preserve the required phonemic contrasts in the sublexical parameters but alter other features of production. The overall effect of this alteration is that the signing space becomes smaller and movements are less pronounced. For example, the handshape of a sign may be produced in a lax manner, with fingers less tightly closed than they should be (see **Figure 1**), but it will not be replaced by another, phonologically distinct handshape. Another characteristic of Parkinsonian signing is the distalization of joint movement. In this case, a sign that normally moves outward with a motion of the elbow will be produced instead with an outward motion of the wrist. The proper, contrastive direction of movement is preserved, but in a way that demands less energy and coordination.

Disruptions to temporal aspects of signing are also observed in signers with Parkinson's disease, imparting a monotone quality. In normal signing, handshape changes that occur within signs (i.e., the change from an open to

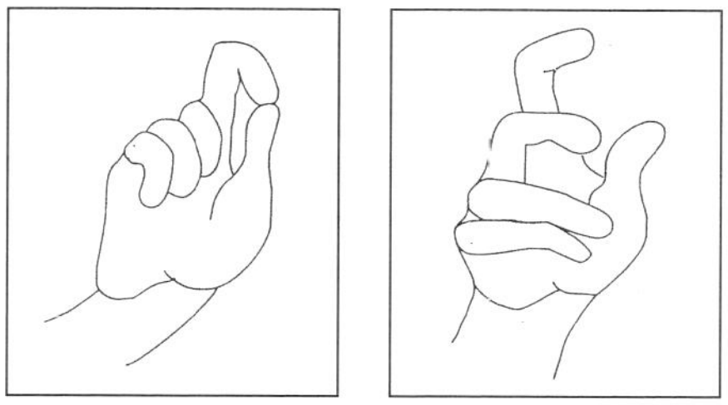

Figure 1 Well-articulated handshape and correct but poorly articulated handshape produced by signer with Parkinson's disease. On the left is a good 'b0' handshape, and on the right, a lax 'b0' handshape. Adapted from an article by Brentari D & Poizner H (1994). Published in *Language and Cognitive Processes 9*, by Psychology Press Ltd. (http://www.psypress.co.uk/journals.asp).

a closed hand in the sign MISS) are spread over the entire duration of the sign, while handshape changes that occur between signs (i.e., the change from an open hand in WILL to a closed hand in WORK) take a smaller proportion of the transition time. Signers with Parkinson's spread intersign handshape changes over the entire transition between signs, making them temporally indistinguishable from within-sign changes. Pauses between signs are also slowed, making them look more like phrase and utterance-final pauses. In signers without Parkinson's disease, the durations of these three types of pauses are much more distinct.

Aphasia: Disruption of Phonology, Morphology, Syntax, and Semantics

Damage to certain areas in the left hemisphere of the brain results in aphasia – a significant impairment in producing or understanding language. While aphasia can be accompanied by problems with perception, motor skills, or ability to use symbols, it can also occur independently of these problems. Aphasic behaviors display evidence of a language malfunction at the level of grammar.

Although aphasic syndromes do not conform to a one-to-one correspondence between location of brain injury and type of language deficit, they have been classified into two general categories: expressive and receptive. Expressive aphasia, also known as Broca's aphasia, is characterized by slow, effortful production and lack of closed-class words and grammatical markers, while comprehension is left relatively intact. Expressive aphasia occurs with damage to the inferior frontal lobe. In receptive aphasia, also known as Wernicke's aphasia, speech is fluent but peppered with odd word choices and grammatical mistakes. Comprehension of speech is also impaired. It is associated with damage to the posterior temporal lobe near the sylvian fissure.

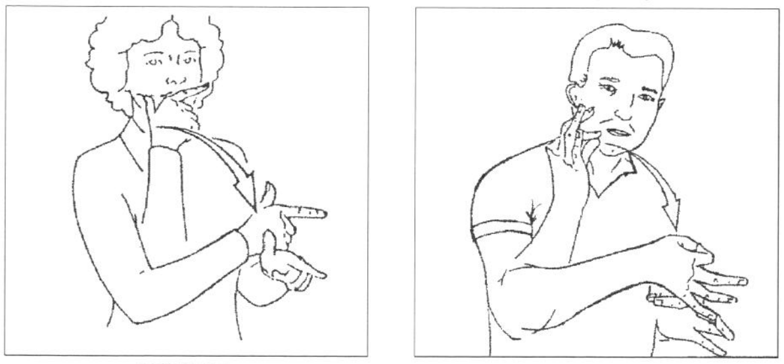

Figure 2 Phonemic paraphasia. The aphasic signer had replaced the correct 'L' handshape with an 'F' handshape. The picture on the left shows someone signing SISTER correctly; the picture on the right shows *SISTER signed by someone with phonemic paraphasia, who uses the 'F' handshape instead of 'L.' Reprinted with permission from Elsevier from Corina D P, Poizner H, Feinberg T et al. (1992). 'Dissociation between linguistic and non-linguistic gestural systems: a case for compositionality.' *Brain and Language 43*, 414–447.

Poizner et al. (1987) closely analyzed the language abilities of three signers with left hemisphere damage and three with right hemisphere damage. One of the left-brain-damaged signers, who had a large left frontal lesion, exhibited a classic case of expressive aphasia with severe dysfluency and complete lack of grammatical inflections in her signing. The others, whose lesions were more posterior, fit the profile of receptive aphasia. Since the Poizner et al. (1987) study, the number of brain-damaged signers studied linguistically has more than doubled.

Phonology

Phonological disorders affect the constrastive structure of signs rather than features of their execution. Unlike signers with Parkinson's disease, who modify sublexical components of signs without altering their distinctive features, aphasic signers make complete substitutions in handshape, location, and movement. Such substitutions are referred to as phonemic paraphasias. The most common phonemic paraphasia involves a substitution in the handshape specification for a sign. **Figure 2** shows one such error, in which the correct 'L' handshape in the sign SISTER was replaced by an 'F' handshape. In this error one distinctive feature has been replaced with another. By contrast, in the example from Parkinson's disease (see **Figure 1**), distinctive features are all preserved, although their articulation is distorted.

Morphology

In American Sign Language, multiple morphemes are pronounced simultaneously. For example, a plain lexical verb is inflected for object agreement by moving toward a location in space associated with the object. The grammatical function of aspect is indicated by combining a lexical verb with a specific movement pattern. Aphasic signers may fail to use agreement or aspect morphology at all, as in the case of the expressive aphasic, or they may use the morphological system incorrectly. One signer with posterior damage had signing that was full of morphological errors such as the inappropriate use of the morpheme for habitual aspect, resulting in the ungrammatical sign *BRILLIANT[habitual aspect], meaning something like 'always brillianting.'

Syntax

Sign language syntax involves two types of behavior that is known to be served by the right hemisphere: facial expressions and spatial cognition. In signers, damage to the left hemisphere does not affect these behaviors in general, but it does disrupt them when they are used for linguistic purposes. A limited set of facial expressions is used to indicate syntactic functions and relations between clauses. For example, a conditional clause is marked by an eyebrow raise that lasts the duration of the clause. Aphasic signers can fail to produce this type of facial expression but have no problem making facial expressions to show emotions and attitudes. Signers with right hemisphere damage, in contrast, lack affective facial expressions but use grammatical ones correctly.

Syntactic roles are set up at locations in the space in front of the signer. Signs for pronouns and verbs refer to these roles by pointing to those locations. While right hemisphere damage can cause severe problems with nonlinguistic visuospatial processing in signers, it is the left hemisphere damage of aphasia that disrupts the use of space in syntax. Aphasic signers may fail to point to the relevant locations at all, or they may point to the wrong locations (see **Figure 3**).

Semantics

Left-hemisphere-damaged signers can also have deficits at the level of semantics. These deficits can take the form of semantic paraphasia, in which an intended sign is replaced by another sign related to it in meaning. For example, BED may be signed for CHAIR, or YEAR may be signed instead of HOUR. In these cases, the signs are correctly formed but miss the target meaning. In a different type of semantic error, one signer produced a semantic blend. He made the sign for TREE, but with the

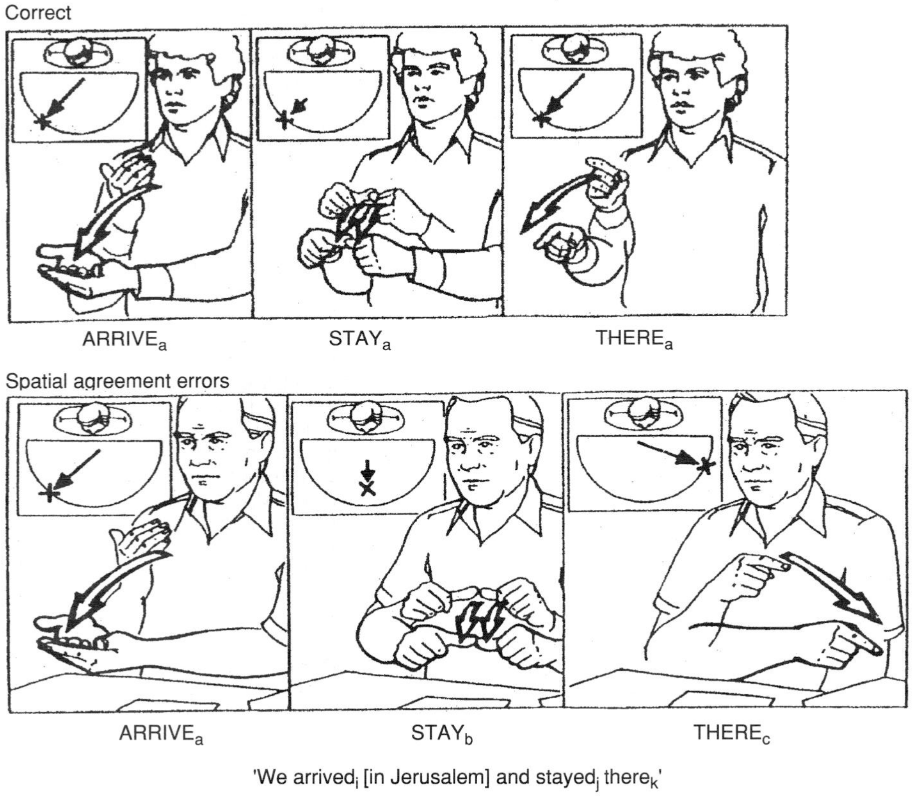

Figure 3 Incorrect use of spatial agreement as performed by aphasic signer. The correct use is shown in the upper strip: left pane: ARRIVE$_a$; center pane: STAY$_a$; right pane: THERE$_a$. Spatial agreement errors are shown in the lower strip: left pane: ARRIVE$_a$; center pane: STAY$_b$; right pane: THERE$_c$. The sentence being signed is 'We arrived$_i$ [in Jerusalem] and stayed$_j$ there$_k$.' Adapted from Poizner H, Klima E S & Bellugio U (1987). *What the hands reveal about the brain*. Published by the MIT Press.

'G' handshape from the sign GREEN instead of the proper, open handshape. In this case the form produced is not an actual sign but a blend of two signs with related meanings.

In general, aphasia in sign language is evidence of a dissociation of the linguistic facts of sign language from the physical facts. Left-hemisphere-damaged signers can often perform elaborate meaningful pantomime without any difficulty, but their signing comes out labored and full of errors. Aphasia affects the ability to communicate through signs only if those signs are part of a linguistic system. Further, it affects the system in specific ways, interpretable with respect to levels of structure.

Right Hemisphere Damage: Disruption of Discourse

For spoken language, right hemisphere damage is not associated with disruption of speech or grammar, but it can cause problems for linguistic communication at the level of discourse. People with this type of damage may be difficult to understand because they speak in a flat, affectless manner without appropriate prosody or facial expressions. They also often fail to make connections between topics, or they go into too much detail in their descriptions. Their visuospatial abilities are also often impaired, something that doesn't necessarily have an effect on spoken language but that has the potential to cause unique problems for a spatially dependent sign language.

As is the case for spoken language, the quality of sign language discourse is impaired with right hemisphere damage. Signers with right hemisphere damage perform normally on tests of phonological structure, and their spontaneous production is grammatical, but their narratives sometimes have a confusing, unnatural quality. They may include frequent off-topic comments and display unusual attention to detail. These narratives also seem flat, lacking in emotion and personal involvement, because, as mentioned above, affective facial expressions are absent.

Right hemisphere damage may also lead to a lack of cohesion in discourse because spatial reference is not maintained. The agreement of verbs with the spatial locations of their subjects and objects is a syntactic function operating at the level of the sentence. The consistency of those positions across sentences is a function of discourse. One signer with right hemisphere damage was reported to inflect verbs for agreement correctly within sentences, but she was unable to maintain locations for referents over the course of a narrative.

Sign Language and Spoken Language

The overall pattern of language disorder in sign language closely matches that of spoken language. The match is not perfect, however. The location of lesions resulting in receptive aphasia for sign language appears to be more posterior than for spoken language, and right hemisphere damage does sometimes result in comprehension deficits for spatialized syntax. There is evidence from studies of normal signers that some degree of neural reorganization of language takes place in people who acquire sign language early in life, so it is to be expected that brain damage will affect sign language differently in some cases. However, similar types of brain damage overwhelmingly lead to similar outcomes. Parkinson's disease disrupts signing at the phonetic level, left hemisphere damage disrupts it at grammatical levels, and right hemisphere damage disrupts it at the discourse level.

Bibliography

Brentari, D and Poizner, H (1994). 'A phonological analysis of a deaf Parkinsonian signer.' *Language and Cognitive Processes* 9: 69–100.

Brentari, D, Poizner, H, and Kegl, J (1995). 'Aphasic and Parkinsonian signing: differences in phonological disruption.' *Brain and Language* 48: 69–105.

Corina, DP (1998). 'Aphasia in users of signed language.' In: Coppens, P, Lebrun, Y, and Basso, A (eds.) *Aphasia in atypical populations*, pp. 261–310. Hillsdale, NJ: Lawrence Erlbaum.

Corina, DP (1999). 'Neural disorders of language and movement: evidence from American Sign Language.' In: Messing, LS and Campbell, R (eds.) *Gesture, speech, and sign*, pp. 27–43. Oxford: Oxford University Press.

Corina, DP, Bellugi, U, and Reilly, J (1999). 'Neuropsychological studies of linguistic and affective facial expressions in deaf signers.' *Language and Speech* 42: 307–331.

Corina, DP, Kritchevsky, M, and Bellugi, U (1996). 'Visual language processing and unilateral neglect: evidence from American Sign Language.' *Cognitive Neuropsychology* 13: 321–351.

Corina, DP, Poizner, H, Feinberg, T, et al. (1992). 'Dissociation between linguistic and non-linguistic gestural systems: a case for compositionality.' *Brain and Language* 43: 414–447.

Emmorey, K (1996). 'The confluence of space and language in signed languages.' In: Bloom, P, Peterson, M, Nadel, L, et al. (eds.) *Language and space*, pp. 171–209. Cambridge, MA: MIT Press.

Hickok, G, Bellugi, U, and Klima, ES (1998a). 'The neural organization of language: evidence from sign language aphasia.' *Trends in Cognitive Sciences* 2: 129–136.

Hickok, G, Bellugi, U, and Klima, ES (1998b). 'What's right about the neural organization of sign language? A perspective on recent neuroimaging results.' *Trends in Cognitive Sciences* 2: 465–468.

Hickok, G, Wilson, M, Clark, K, et al. (1999). 'Discourse deficits following right hemisphere damage in deaf signers.' *Brain and Language* 66: 233–248.

Kegl, J and Poizner, H (1997). 'Crosslinguistic/crossmodal syntactic consequences of left hemisphere damage: evidence from an aphasic signer and his identical twin.' *Aphasiology* 11: 1–37.

Neville, HJ, Bavelier, D, Corina, DP, et al. (1998). 'Cerebral organization for language in deaf and hearing subjects: biological constraints and effects of experience.' *Proceedings of the National Academy of Sciences USA* 95: 922–929.

Newman AJ, Bavelier D, Corina DP, et al. (2002). 'A critical period for right hemisphere recruitment in American Sign Language processing.' *Nature Neuroscience 5*, 76–80.

Poizner, H and Kegl, J (1992). 'Neural basis of language and motor behavior: perspectives from American Sign Language.' *Aphasiology* 6: 219–256.

Poizner, H, Klima, ES, and Bellugi, U (1987). *What the hands reveal about the brain.* Cambridge, MA: MIT Press.

Speech Disorders, Overview

S. Hari and B. L. Miller

Speech is a form of communication that is unique to humans. Production of speech involves a process wherein a concept is formed and then expressed. This is externalized as speech that requires concurrent motor functions of respiration, phonation, articulation, and prosody. Speech disorders can result from a disruption in language, although pure speech disorders occur when language is normal. When speech is disrupted in association with abnormalities in language, the disorder is referred to as an aphasia.

Dysarthria refers to an impairment in the motor aspect of speech where language is spared. An intact articulatory system is required for adequate speech production, and injury anywhere along the articulatory route can lead to dysarthria. The anatomy necessary for articulation consists of the lungs, which are required to maintain a controlled airflow, the larynx and soft palate, which are used for voice production, and the lips, tongue, teeth, and jaws. The motor cerebral cortex generates impulses that are transmitted to cranial nerves VII and IX–XII that innervate the articulatory muscles. This action is integrated in the basal ganglia and cerebellum en route. Articulation, represented in the posterior frontal region bilaterally, is directly connected to Broca's area (frontal lobe, dominant hemisphere). The corpus callosum connects Broca's area to the nondominant motor cortex. Hence, the articulatory patterns required to produce normal speech are bilaterally controlled.

Dysarthria results from a number of neurological conditions at various levels in the pathway. Muscular causes, such as myasthenia gravis, polymyositis, and muscular dystrophies, produce slurred speech. This is due to dysfunction of muscles of respiration and articulation.

Lower motor neurons consist of motor nuclei of cranial nerves with the nerve fibers to the neuromuscular junction. Also included are nerves from the anterior horn cells of the spinal cord. Disorders affecting the lower cranial nerves, such as Bell's palsy and neoplasms, or the motor nuclei, such as poliomyelitis, motor neuron disease, and neoplasms such as gliomas, produce flaccid dysarthria. Bulbar palsy refers to involvement of the motor nuclei of lower cranial nerves located in the medulla (bulb). This produces dysarthria, dysphonia, and dysphagia. The soft palate is weak, producing a hypernasal sound. Lesions caused by cerebrovascular accidents, motor neuron disease, and degenerative conditions affecting the corticobulbar fibers (i.e., from the cortex to the bulb) produce pseudobulbar palsy. This is associated with spasticity and emotional lability in addition to dysarthria.

The basal ganglia control movement, tone, and posture. Involvement of these structures as in Parkinson's disease results in speech that is low in volume, monotonous, and hypernasal. Excessive salivation contributes to slurred speech. Involuntary movements, such as chorea and athetosis seen in Huntington's disease and Wilson's disease, cause dysarthria that is associated with jerky movements of articulatory and respiratory muscles.

The cerebellum plays an important role in coordination of movements and also influences muscle tone. Stroke, multiple sclerosis, and cerebellar degenerations result in dysarthria. This is characterized by slurring, jerking, and difficulty pronouncing consonants. Staccato speech results from poor control of rhythm. Improper emphasis on syllables results in scanning speech.

Dysarthria can result from lesions of the motor areas of the cerebral cortex that control muscles of the face and those used for speech. This may coexist with expressive aphasia. Apraxia or an inability to use orofacial muscles for speech in the absence of weakness can be seen in cortical lesions.

Drowsiness and confusion seen in metabolic or toxic encephalopathies also cause dysarthria. Transient dysarthria can be a manifestation of migraines or transient ischemic attacks. Some types of dementia present with poverty of speech and decreased speed. Speech arrest can be a manifestation of seizures.

Passage of air through the larynx produces sound or phonation. The strength, tone, pitch, and resonance are dependent on the laryngeal structure and neuromuscular control of laryngeal and respiratory systems. Dysphonia refers to weakness or hoarseness of voice. A number of nonneurological causes, such as laryngitis and hysteria, result in dysphonia. Neuromuscular causes of dysphonia include myasthenia gravis, in which the quality of voice worsens with use. Damage to the recurrent laryngeal nerve due to neck surgery or carcinomatous infiltration produces dysphonia. Dysphonia is seen in Parkinson's disease and bulbar and pseudobulbar palsy.

Management of speech disorders consists of identifying the etiology followed by prompt institution of speech therapy. This is preferably done early in the course because dysarthria can cause a tremendous psychological burden.

See also: Agrammatism; Anomia; Language and Discourse; Phonology.

Further Reading

Adler, CH and Ahlaskog, HA (2000). *Parkinson's Disease and Movement Disorders. Diagnosis and Treatment Guidelines for the Practicing Physician.* Clifton, NJ: Humanae Press.

Freed, DB (2000). *Motor Speech Disorders, Diagnosis and Treatment.* London, UK: Singular Thomson Learning.

Kent, RD (2000). Research on speech motor control and its disorders: A review and prospective. *J. Commun. Disord* 33: 391–427.

Urban, PP, Wicht, S, Vukurevic, G, et al. (2001). Dysarthria in acute ischemic stroke: Lesion topography, clinicoradiologic correlation and etiology. *Neurology* 56: 1021–1027.

Speech Impairments in Neurodegenerative Diseases/Psychiatric Illnesses

A. Wisniecki, University of Connecticut, Storrs, and Pfizer Global Research and Development, Groton, CT, USA
M. Cannizzaro, Pfizer Global Research and Development, Groton, CT, USA and NeuroSolutions, Inc., Montreal, QC, Canada
H. Cohen, NeuroSolutions, Inc., and Université de Québec à Montréal, Montréal, QC, Canada
P. J. Snyder, University of Connecticut, Storrs, CT, USA; Pfizer Global Research and Development, Groton, CT, USA; Université de Québec à Montréal, Montréal, QC, Canada

The ability to speak using the structured rule-governed system of language is a uniquely human characteristic. With an ease and simplicity that is regularly taken for granted, spoken communication imparts information regarding a speaker's message by orchestrating the language domains of semantics, syntax, morphology, phonology, and pragmatics. Typically one thinks of the spoken message as being contained solely within this linguistic code. However, there is also a great deal of information conveyed through associated paralinguistic content as well as through the motor processes of the speech act itself. The speech signal is essentially a highly interlinked and well-organized conglomeration of acoustic energy that can be represented by time, frequency, and intensity information. These domains allow for quantitative physical measurement of the signal as well as qualitative perceptual judgments by listeners. Such qualitative and quantitative assessments of speech each provide a wealth of information about an individual, ranging from his or her sex, age, and cultural and socioeconomic background, to physical health and emotional state.

The process of speech production itself, that is, the generation of the appropriate sounds necessary to convey a speaker's message, is inordinately complex. Simply put, this intricate process involves the coordination of over 100 individual muscles, numerous cranial and spinal nerves, cortical and subcortical neural areas, and the cognitive processes necessary to generate meaningful sound combinations from the raw physiological materials. That is, when respiration, phonation, articulation, resonance, and prosody are combined in a well-executed manner, the end product is a clear and meaningful speech code that contains a message. However, a breakdown anywhere in these interdependent physiological systems, spanning from the diaphragm to the cortex and to the outermost border of the lips, can lead to measurable changes in the speech acoustic output. The neurological and physiological substrates necessary for speech production may be altered by a wide variety of neurological or psychiatric disease processes, often altering the final acoustical properties of speech in a somewhat predictable manner. Hence, measurable information in the acoustic output of individual patients may provide valuable clues for diagnosing certain diseases, following the course of disease progression, assessing response to medical treatment, or a combination of these.

Certain voice features may change in healthy people as a result of their emotional state (e.g., anger), fatigue, or pharmacological intervention (e.g., in response to the sedative effects of alcohol). In addition, changes in speech and voice patterns may reflect certain pathological changes resulting from disease processes. For example, in 1817, James Parkinson described individuals suffering from the disease that today bears his name as showing changes in their speech that made them "become scarcely intelligible" (Parkinson, 1817).

Although the voice and speech production changes associated with various diseases are readily detected on a perceptual level, studying them in an objective and quantitative manner can be a logistically difficult task. Systematic attempts to classify and measure voice characteristics date back to the 1960s. Not surprisingly, these analyses were often compromised by the limitations of the technology of the time. With the advent of modern computing platforms and applications, and with affordable access to high-fidelity digital recording techniques, the analysis of voice acoustical properties has become more accurate, reliable, practical, and relatively inexpensive.

Recording and Data Processing Equipment

It is now possible to record research-quality acoustic information directly to a computer hard drive using a high-quality microphone, an external analog-to-digital converter (e.g., a sound card), and a simple digital connection. The acoustic signal is captured by the microphone (preferably a condenser microphone with response characteristics in the 20–20,000-Hz frequency range), converted to digital code by the sound card (i.e., preferably an external device that does not rely on the computer for power, processing, or clock information), and transmitted to the computer via simple digital connection (e.g., Firewire/USB). In this way the data can be stored in digital format and analyzed for their acoustic content without a loss of information. Recording quality is affected by the equipment and should be sufficiently high to capture and accurately represent the acoustic properties of the human voice. A sampling rate of at least 22 kHz with 16-bit intensity quantization is both appropriate and widely available.

Because a great number of different measurements can be made from a short sample of speech, the software package used for analysis is dependent on the needs of the researcher and his or her particular area of interest. There are many commercially available (e.g., Kay Elemetrics Computerized Speech Laboratory, Kay Elemetrics Corp., 2004) as well as free 'shareware' programs available (*PRAAT*; Boersma and Weenik, 2004) for computerized speech analyses. These programs generally provide a package of recording, manipulation, and analysis tools with easy-to-use graphic user interfaces, designed to extract frequency, intensity, and time measures from acoustic samples.

Neurobiology of Speech Production in Common Neurodegenerative Disorders

The production of speech is a voluntary process that relies heavily on motor areas in the prefrontal cortex, the primary motor cortex, premotor cortex, associative motor areas, and Broca's area. Important connections that lead to the transfer of cortical motor commands to the lower motor neurons include the corticobulbar and corticospinal tracts, collectively known as the internal capsule. Typically, localized damage to these upper motor neurons results in spastic dysarthria, whereas damage to the lower motor neurons results in a flaccid dysarthria (Duffy, 1995).

Of the many subcortical structures, the one crucially involved in any voluntary motor activity, including speech production, is the basal ganglia and its functional circuitry. The basal ganglia include several nuclei: the caudate, putamen, two parts of globus pallidus (internal and external) and two compartments of substantia nigra (pars reticulata and pars compacta), subthalamic nucleus, ventral tegmental area, and nucleus accumbens. Of these, the caudate and putamen are, together, referred to as the striatum. The striatum receives its major afferents from cortex (excitatory glutamatergic projections) and substantia nigra pars compacta (dopaminergic projections). The major output structure of the basal ganglia is the thalamus (especially the ventrolateral portion), which in turn provides feedback and modulates cortical activity. The basal ganglia exert influence on the thalamus via two pathways; a direct pathway, which sends inhibitory signals, and an indirect pathway, to which it sends excitatory signals (Murdoch, 2001). Although the exact role of separate components of the basal ganglia on speech is poorly understood, the system is known to be responsible for maintaining postural stability and static muscle contraction – providing a framework for voluntary skilled movements and the regulation of amplitude, velocity, and the initiation of movements, as well as sequencing of movements (Duffy, 1995). Damage to the basal ganglia can often result in either hypokinetic or hyperkinetic dysarthria.

Another structure that also plays a role in speech production, especially the fluency of speech production, is the cerebellum. The cerebellum has connections with both primary and premotor cortex via the ventral thalamic nuclei, and it also gains access to the corticobulbar and corticospinal tracts (Duffy, 1995). It is able to coordinate and modify both planned and ongoing speech movements. Damage to cerebellum produces an ataxic dysarthria.

Voice and speech production reflect complex motor activity, thinking processes, and emotional processes. Therefore, certain neurological disorders related to those processes tend to affect speech as well. As a consequence, language, speech, and voice analysis may provide a noninvasive and inexpensive window into underlying neurological pathologies.

Speech and Voice Acoustic Characteristics in Neurodegenerative Diseases

Parkinson Disease

Parkinson disease (PD) is a progressive neurodegenerative disorder that affects the motor system and cognitive functioning. The selective destruction of the nigrostriatal dopaminergic neurons leads to a disruption of the basal ganglia circuitry, thus leading to the outward symptomatic presentation associated with the disease. The underlying pathology is manifest in several classic motor symptoms: bradykinesia (motor slowness), akinesia (difficulties in movement initiation), rigidity (stiffness in muscles), and resting tremor, which occurs in the absence of voluntary motor behavior (Barbeau, 1986). The underlying neurodegeneration is also associated with affected speech musculature compromising muscles responsible for respiration, laryngeal control, and articulation. The associated speech and voice impairment in PD is collectively termed hypokinetic dysarthria. Perceptually, hypokinetic dysarthria is characterized by monopitch, monoloudness, reduced stress, imprecise consonants, and inappropriate silences. In addition, hypokinetic dysarthria is characterized by hoarse, breathy quality of voice and short rushes of speech (Darley et al., 1972). The acoustic findings of Parkinsonian speech, reflecting monopitch and monoloudness, include a decrease in fundamental frequency (F_0) variability and range, with increased F_0 variability found on vowel prolongation tasks, and a decrease in maximum intensity range and laryngeal respiratory coordination deficits (e.g., voice onset time). In addition, there is a smaller distinction between different vowel productions as measured from decreased acoustic differentiation and resonant energy transitions in vowel–consonant production than in control subjects, reflecting the imprecise consonant production (Goberman and Coelho, 2002).

Interestingly, hypokinetic dysarthria is the only type of dysarthria characterized by increased speed of reading, most likely related to the phenomenon of festination. The increased reading rate is achieved by compromising articulation accuracy. However, with the progression of the disease, this compensation is not sufficient to maintain typical speech rate. As the disease process becomes more severe, articulation is less precise, and reading rates become slower. The inability to initiate movement of articulators is reflected in the increased number and duration of pauses. Prosody measures are characterized by decreased intensity variability and fundamental frequency variability, adding to the perceptual monotonous and reduced loudness of Parkinsonian speech.

Huntington Disease

Huntington disease (Huntington chorea) is a genetic neurodegenerative disease that affects the basal ganglia and parts of the cortex. The selective destruction of GABAergic neurons within the caudate nucleus, and later the substantia nigra, leads to the disruption of the basal ganglia system, and ultimately disinhibition of the thalamus (Murdoch, 2001). The cardinal symptom of the disease is chorea, a variety of uncontrollable involuntary movements, accompanied by bradykinesia of voluntary movements and dementia later in the course of the disease (Strange, 1996).

These involuntary movements interfere with speech production. Speech deficits frequently associated with Huntington disease are known collectively as hyperkinetic dysarthria. Perceptual analysis of choreic speech is predominantly characterized by intermittently harsh voice with a strain-strangled voice quality. In addition, imprecise consonants, prolonged intervals, irregular pitch fluctuations, variable speaking rate, inappropriate silences, distorted vowels, and uncontrolled variations in loudness have also been reported (Darley et al., 1972).

Acoustically, vowel prolongation tasks have revealed the presence of lower-frequency segments, vocal arrests, and reduced maximum vowel duration, as well as an increased standard deviation of fundamental frequency in patients with Huntington disease (Ramig, 1986; Zwirner et al., 1991). Some studies revealed normal values for shimmer and jitter accompanied by low values of harmonic-to-noise ratio (Ramig, 1988), whereas others found jitter to be significantly higher in a Huntington diseased voice, with the other perturbation measures unchanged (Zwirner et al., 1991).

A number of acoustic studies have focused on the speech motor timing deficits in this disease. The most prominent features observed in a consonant vowel production within the context of a sentence included increased variability of sentence utterance duration and voice onset time (Hertrich and Ackermann, 1994). The measurements of alternating motion rates also revealed increased syllabic durational variability as well as increased syllable duration (Ackerman et al., 1995).

Progressive Supranuclear Palsy (Steele-Richardson-Olszewski Syndrome)

Progressive supranuclear palsy is a neurodegenerative disorder characterized by the presence of neurofibrillary tangles and cerebral atrophy, and with the exception of the frontal lobes, the cortex is generally unaffected. However, degeneration is observed in a number of subcortical nuclei, including parts of basal ganglia (subthalamic nucleus, substantia nigra, and globus pallidus), red nucleus, and superior colliculli, as well as in a number of brain stem nuclei (Duffy, 1995).

The symptomatic picture of the early stages of the disease is very similar to PD. Patients experience rigidity, bradykinesia, and postural instability. The distinguishing feature, usually developing later in the course of the disease, is a gaze palsy that manifests as a paralysis of vertical downward gaze. Speech disturbances are not typically the predominating complaint in most patients at the time of the diagnosis, and they may take a form of generalized dysarthria with the presence of dysphagia. However, there is no single type of dysarthria characteristic for the disease. Usually patients present with a mixed dysarthria with varying degrees of hypokinetic, spastic, and to a lesser extent, ataxic elements (Duffy, 1995). Interestingly, the presence of dysarthria becomes a useful way to distinguish between PSP and PD. Perceptually, the prominent speech characteristics related to the PSP occur more often than in PD and include monopitch hoarseness, nasal emission, excess and equal stress, hypernasality, imprecise articulation, and slow rate (Duffy, 1995). To date, there is a marked lack of systematic, quantitative studies of voice changes in patients with Progressive Supranuclear Palsy.

Multiple Sclerosis

Multiple sclerosis (MS) is a progressive inflammatory neurodegenerative disease. The main pathology involves destruction of myelin and myelin-producing oligodendrocytes, which result in an accumulation of sclerotic plaques and impaired neural transmission. The destruction leads to multiple white-matter lesions throughout the brain stem, cerebrum, and cerebellum. As a consequence, a variety of symptoms can be observed ranging from motor and sensory disturbances to visual symptoms and cognitive impairments (Smith and McDonald, 1999).

Depending on the location of the lesions, patients with MS often present with a variety speech impairments. In general, the mixed form of dysarthria, including spastic and ataxic components, has been most often reported in MS. On a perceptual level, the most frequently observed characteristics of voice and speech were changes in loudness control, voice quality, articulation, emphasis, and pitch control (Darley et al., 1972).

In an acoustic analysis of a sustained vowel phonation, voice samples of patients with MS were characterized by increased long-term phonatory instability, as measured by fluctuations of fundamental frequency and amplitude (Hartelius et al., 1997). Temporal characteristic as measured by alternating motion rate (AMR) and sequential motion rate (SMR) tasks were shown to be a distinct features in MS patients. In general, voice samples of people diagnosed with MS were distinguished by longer gap duration and slower diadokinetic rate for both AMRs and SMRs, as well as longer syllable duration, observed in AMRs. In addition, analysis of energy characteristics revealed reduced vocal intensity in MS group (Tjaden and Watling, 2003). However, only a few attempts have been made to quantify the observed speech changes using systematic measurements such as acoustic analysis.

Acoustic Speech Characteristics in Psychiatric Diseases

Methods of acoustic quantification have also been applied to the speaking behaviors of persons with psychiatric disorders, most notably depression and schizophrenia. This avenue of research makes inherent sense, as much depressive and schizophrenic symptomatology is assessed clinically using subjective rating scales designed to elicit verbal responses. Under these circumstances a number of rating items from which the clinical impressions are made are influenced by linguistic and paralinguistic aspects of the interview process. For example, in depression, the Hamilton Rating Scale for Depression (HSRD; Hamilton, 1980) guides the clinicians' judgment in rating depressed mood, psychomotor retardation, and anxiety based on subjective assessments of speech, voice, and communication. Similarly, the Positive and Negative Symptom Scale (PANSS; Kay, 1987) for schizophrenia contains a number of rating items related to speech and verbal behavior. Specific items related to clinical evaluation of the client's speech are found in the assessment areas of excitement, blunted affect, emotional withdrawal, poor rapport, lack of spontaneity and conversational flow, stereotyped thinking, motor retardation, disturbance of volition, poor attention, and preoccupation. Both the PANSS and the HRSD are considered gold standards for clinical assessment of their respective disorders, and the inclusion of such a large number of items related to spoken communication behavior indicates the pervasiveness of these traits in schizophrenia and depression.

Schizophrenia

Predominantly negative-symptom schizophrenia (NSZ) can be characterized by a number of atypical reductions in observed behavior, including communication behavior. Classically observed outward manifestations in spoken (e.g., linguistic production) and pragmatic/paralinguistic (e.g., body language, intonation, and prosody) aspects of communication are related to affective flattening, anhedonia, alogia, and avolition (the *Diagnostic and Statistical Manual of Mental Disorders* summarized characterization of NSZ), implying an effect on both affect and cognition. Atypical communication can have an effect on clinical assessment, as it may influence rater scoring on a number of items from subjective behavioral rating scales (e.g., PANSS) including items such as blunted affect, emotional withdrawal, poor rapport, social withdrawal, reduced flow of conversation, and motor retardation, to name a few (Alpert, 1996). Although these rating scales are invaluable in their ability to help clinicians assess symptomatology, the addition of objective and quantifiable measures of disease severity and therapeutic treatment response are desirable and possible through speech and voice acoustic measurement.

In the most basic terms, physical quantitative measurements of communication behavior, using aspects of frequency, intensity, and time, support and extend the clinical impressions of atypical communication used clinically (Alpert, 1996). This adds clinical value by providing repeatable quantification of observed symptomatology.

The literature surrounding acoustic investigations in persons with schizophrenia has revealed a number of consistent themes. Flat affect, alogia, and asociality (as measured by the PANSS scale) are strongly related to restricted speech output, monotonous speech, pause in speech, energy variation, utterance duration, and inflection (both in dB and Hz) (Dworkin, 1996; Alpert et al., 1997, 2000; Puschel et al., 1998). In addition, acoustic measures have shown great promise in identifying treatment response by demonstrating a larger treatment effect than those seen with traditional rating scales (Alpert, 1996). It has also been demonstrated that specific measures of acoustic inflection are sensitive enough to differentiate between antipsychotic compounds (Olanzapine vs. Haloperidol; Remoxipride vs. Haloperidol), whereas rating scales were not able to detect this difference (Alpert M, Smith R C, Pouget E R, Allan E, and Sisson C, unpublished data). Bidirectional changes in the speech acoustic characteristics between drug conditions have also led researchers to the conclusion that different mechanisms of drug action that may be at work, though rating scales were not able to make this distinction (Alpert et al., unpublished data; Alpert et al., 2002). Acoustic measures were able to separate the different drug groups at outcome while the rating scales failed to show a difference.

In a recent acoustic investigation in our laboratory, we have successfully demonstrated measurable differences in cognitive behavior and motor slowing by comparing persons with NSZ to a control group. Speech pause behavior in a simple counting and picture description task have indicated that average pause length was indicating of motor retardation, whereas global measures of pause were indicative of the increased cognitive linguistic demands of the picture description task. The analyses of longitudinal within-subject change data from this study are still ongoing.

Major Depression

The relationship between subjective estimates of the severity of major depression and observed qualitative or quantitative changes in speech production has been documented in a number of investigations. For example, Stassen et al. (1998) found a strong correlation between change in clinical ratings of symptom severity and several key voice acoustic measures. This finding was consistent in more than 74% of the researchers' patients undergoing inpatient pharmacologic treatment for severe Major Depressive Disorder (MDD). Stassen et al. (1998) reported that fundamental frequency amplitude and mean pause duration were among the voice acoustic variables that most closely tracked with improvement in symptom severity, as measured by the 17-item HDRS (Hamilton, 1980) over the first few weeks of treatment. The former acoustic measure relates to the muscular and respiratory effort exerted to control phonatory intensity and rate, whereas the latter measure relates to motor timing and the execution of speech movements. These findings corroborate earlier reports that increased speech pause time and total speech time are associated with higher scores on the HDRS and other scales of psychomotor speed and subject self-rating of mood (Teasdale et al., 1980; Hardy et al., 1984). Longitudinal design studies by Ellgring and Scherer (1996) and Stassen (1998) have demonstrated similar results, using measures of speech rate, pause duration, and minimum fundamental frequency.

Regardless of the specific pharmacologic mechanisms of action of the antidepressant medications used in these studies, several speech acoustical measures consistently track with subtle changes in symptom severity. Moreover, these measures seem to be sensitive to early symptomatic improvement, as well as to the degree of response to drug intervention (Stassen et al., 1998). The observed changes seen in these voice acoustical measures quite likely reflect changes in the modulation of both serotonergic and dopaminergic neurotransmitter systems in response to treatment of MDD. Previous literature supports the conclusion that two general aspects of speech and voice, specifically, motor timing and fundamental frequency, are closely related to mood states as measured by both subject self-report and clinician-administered rating scales (Stassen et al., 1998).

The Clinical Utility and Application of Speech and Voice Acoustical Analyses

Acoustic correlates of neurological and psychiatric disorders have a realistic potential to provide complementary, sensitive methods for the early detection of the onset, progression, and severity of several disease states, as well as providing a means to objectively track symptomatic changes induced by therapeutic intervention (e.g., behavioral or pharmacological therapy, or both). There are no known risks related to the use of voice signal capture and analysis. On the contrary, a speech behavioral assessment may provide a rapid, nonintrusive, inexpensive, and relatively effort-free way to obtain objective data regarding disease progression and treatment response. It is noninvasive by nature, and in carefully controlled circumstances, it can provide a large amount of meaningful data. In addition, because altered communication ability is both bothersome and frustrating for so many patients who suffer from the diseases described above, the measurement of an improvement in speech quality is both desirable and encouraging for patients and families alike.

Despite the promising potential applications of this technology, the available literature on this subject remains equivocal and fraught with contradictory results. This variability in published results may actually reflect the high sensitivity of the measurements, the complexity of the speech production system, and the intersubject as well as intrasubject variability inherent in this type of research. Thus, there is a need for more normative data related to acoustical changes associated with neurodegenerative diseases, and improved consistency in methodology across laboratories, so that future results are more readily comparable.

Certain normative profiles have been recently provided in an article by Kent and colleagues (2003) and may help with enhancing the clinical utility of the acoustic analyses of voice disorders. Once the normative rules are applied in experiments across different laboratories, what today is perceived as conflicting results may in the future yield information about different aspects of the same disease. In summary, the acoustic analysis of voice is a research technique with great potential as a diagnostic tool for a variety of neurological and psychiatric disorders.

See also: Classical Tests for Speech and Language Disorders; Speech Processes in Dysarthria.

Bibliography

Ackermann, H, Hertrich, I, and Hehr, T (1995). 'Oral diadochokinesis in neurological dysarthrias.' *Folia Phoniatr Logop* 47: 15–23.
Alpert, M, Kotsaftis, A, and Pouget, ER (1997). 'At issue: speech fluency and schizophrenic negative signs.' *Schizophrenia Bulletin* 23(2): 171–177.
Alpert, M, Rosenberg, SD, Pouget, ER, and Shaw, RJ (2000). 'Prosody and lexical accuracy in flat affect schizophrenia.' *Psychiatry Research* 97(2–3): 107–118.
Alpert, M, Pouget, ER, Sison, C, Yahia, M, and Allan, E (1995). 'Clinical and acoustic measures of the negative syndrome.' *Psychopharmacology Bulletin* 31(2): 321–326.
Alpert, M, Smith, RC, Pouget, ER, Allan, E, and Sison, C (2002). (Unpublished data).
Barbeau, A (1986). 'Parkinson's Disease: clinical features and etiopathology.' In: Vinkel, PJ, Bruyn, GW, and Klawns, HL (eds.) *Handbook of Clinical Neurology, vol 5 (49): Extrapyramidal Disorders.* Elsevier Science Publishers.
Boersma, P and Weenik, D (2003). *Praat (Version 4.1.9).* [computer software]. Amsterdam: Institute of Phonetic Sciences.
Darley, FL, Brown, JR, and Goldstein, PNP (1972). 'Dysarthria in multiple sclerosis.' *Journal of Speech and Hearing Research* 15: 229–245.
Duffy, JR (1995). *Motor speech disorders.* St Louis, MO: Mosby-Year Book.
Dworkin, RH, Clark, SC, Amador, XF, and Gorman, JM (1996). 'Does affective blunting in schizophrenia reflect affective deficit or neuromotor dysfunction?' *Schizophrenia Research* 20(3): 301–306.
Ellgring, H and Scherer, KR (1996). 'Vocal indicators of mood change in depression.' *Journal of Nonverbal Behaviors* 20: 83–110.
Goberman, A and Coelho, CA (2002). 'Acoustic analysis of Parkinsonian speech I: speech characteristics and L-Dopa therapy.' *NeuroRehabilitation* 17(3): 237–246.
Hamilton, M (1980). 'Rating depressive patients.' *Journal of Clinical Psychiatry* 41(12 Pt 2): 21–24.
Hardy, P, et al. (1984). 'Speech pause time and the retardation rating scale for depression (ERD). Towards a reciprocal validation.' *Journal of Affective Disorders* 6(1): 123–127.
Hartelius, L, Buder, EH, and Strand, EA (1997). 'Long-term phonatory instability in individuals with multiple sclerosis.' *Journal of Speech and Hearing Research* 40: 1056–1072.
Hertrich, I and Ackermann, H (1994). 'Acoustic analysis of speech timing in Huntington's disease.' *Brain and Language* 47: 182–196.
Kent, RD, Vorperian, HK, Kent, JF, and Duffy, JR (2003). 'Voice dysfunction in dysarthria: application of the Multi-Dimensional Voice Program.' *Journal of Communication Disorders* 36: 281–306.
Kay, SR, Fiszbein, A, and Olper, LA (1987). 'The positive and negative symptom scale (PANSS) for schizophrenia.' *Schizophrenia Bulletin* 13: 261–276.
Murdoch, BE (2001). 'Subcortical brain mechanisms in speech and language.' *Folia Phoniatrica et Logopaedica* 53: 233–351.
Parkinson, J (1817). *An essay on the shaking palsy.* London, Sherwood, Neely and Jones.
Puschel, J, Stassen, HH, Bomben, G, Scharfetter, C, and Hell, D (1998). 'Speaking behavior and speech sound characteristics in acute schizophrenia.' *Journal of Psychiatric Research* 32(2): 89–97.
Ramig, LA (1986). 'Acoustic analyses of phonation in patients with Huntington's disease. Preliminary report.' *The Annals of Otology, Rhinology, and Laryngology* 95: 288–293.
Ramig, LA, Titze, IR, Scherer, RC, and Ringel, SP (1988). 'Acoustic analysis of voices of patients with neurologic disease: rational and preliminary data.' *The Annals of Otology, Rhinology, and Laryngology* 97: 164–172.
Smith, KJ and McDonald, WI (1999). 'The pathophysiology of multiple sclerosis: The mechanisms underlying the production of symptoms and the natural history of the disease.' *The Royal Society of London* 345: 1649–1673.
Stassen, HH, et al. (1998). 'The speech analysis approach to determining onset of improvement under antidepressants.' *European Neuropsychopharmacology* 8(4): 303–310.
Strange, PG (1996). *Brain biochemistry and brain disorders.* New York: Oxford University Press.
Teasdale, JD, et al. (1980). 'Speech rate as a measure of short-term variation in depression.' *British Journal of Social and Clinical Psychology* 19(3): 271–278.
Tjaden, K and Watling, E (2003). 'Characteristics of diadochokinesis in multiple sclerosis and Parkinson's disease.' *Folia Phoniatrica et Logopaedica* 55: 241–256.
Zwirner, P, Murry, T, and Woodson, GE (1991). 'Phonatory function of neurologically impaired patients.' *Journal of Communication Disorders* 24: 287–300.

Speech Processes in Dysarthria

F. R. Boutsen, University of Oklahoma, Oklahoma City, OK, USA

In an era when the terms 'speech' and 'language' were used interchangeably, and Broca and Wernicke's constructs of 'aphemia' and 'aphasia symptom complex' found harmonious reconciliation in localizationist theories of language, Kussmaul (1881) broke tradition by asserting that the seat of speech is most likely not confined to a cerebral convolution. Furthermore, unlike his contemporaries, he drew a clear distinction between the neurological disorders of speech and language. In what is conceivably the first classification of neurogenic communication disorders, he defined as separate from aphasia a group of articulation disorders that were due to organic or psychic disturbances of the central nervous system (CNS). These articulation disorders he labeled dysarthria, which were to be distinguished from the dyslalias that resulted from peripheral lesions and/or malformations of the articulators or the cranial nerves (Grewel, 1957).

Overall, Kussmaul's broad neurological roadmap, albeit provocative for its time, did not much more than delimit the concept of dysarthria, confining it to the CNS apart from language and functional/organic speech disorders. It was not until later that more refined neurological classification schemes began to also assert a coupling between the still fairly amorphous dysarthria symptom complex and etiologies that were bound within levels or components of the central nervous system. For example, Zentay (1937), Froeshels (1943), and Luschsinger and Arnold (1949) classified the etiologies associated with dysarthria at four levels within the central nervous system (the corticobulbar, cortico-strio-pallido-rubro-bulbar, frontopontine, and cerebellar levels). Growing consideration of speech processes, other than 'articulation,' as well as a broadening array of 'dysarthric' symptoms needing theoretical cover, soon stretched and refined the four-level classification schemes to include the peripheral nervous system (PNS) and subdivisions within the neuroanatomic levels. The classifications of Peacher (1950) and Grewel (1957), perhaps, best embodied this trend. In seminal papers, these authors formulated what even by today's standards can be regarded as a modern neurological perspective on dysarthria.

Peacher and Grewel defined dysarthrias, with the exclusion of developmental, somatic, or psychogenic speech disorders, as disturbances of the speaking system resulting from neurological disorders that involve the cortical, subcortical, brainstem, and spinal levels. Physiologically, the aforementioned disorders were proposed to yield distinct motor deficits that in turn patterned different dysarthria types. Those enumerated in Grewel's theory included dysarthrias associated with flaccid or spastic paralysis, rigidity, discoordination, lack of sensation, difficulty with praxis, and disinhibition (as seen in echolalia).

Though conspicuous in some places of their theory, the objective to link the varied phenomenology of dysarthria to neuroanatomical levels was not the sole organizing principle in either of the aforementioned frameworks. This is because the proposed divisional lesions of the nervous system that they argued were capable of framing a dysarthria type were also undergirded by views concerning the neuroanatomical levels of the 'normal' speech mechanism if not the various processes that partake in it. The theoretical requirement that a neuroanatomical map of dysarthria would be consistent with that underlying normal speech processes was perhaps most strongly articulated by Peacher (1950). He argued that while clinically, it might be anticipated that dysarthria presents varying degrees of dysfunction in articulation, phonation, resonation and respiration, speech rhythm needs inclusion as well. He felt its incorporation was justified in view of normal speech data reported by Stetson (1932) who had shown that speech rhythm was 'peripherally' dependent on the respiratory cycle. He further cited clinical evidence including Monrad Krohn's (1947) observation of 'dysprosody' in extrapyramidal disorders as well as the well-known failure of rhythm to develop in the congenitally deaf.

While Peacher assigned a critical role to the 'peripheral' processes of audition and respiration in speech rhythm, he also hypothesized this function to be dependent on integrative functions, which, like those for speech, if disturbed produce deficits that are to be distinguished from dysarthria. Here Peacher's general account of the speech process as well as his classification differs from that of Grewel. Borrowing from Froment (1924), Grewel conceived speech to unfold in two successive stages: that of praxis and that of execution. This latter process, defined as the release of a series of reflexes, was dependent on intact sensibility and required coordination of the successive stages of the speaking procedure (respiration, phonation, articulation). Along these lines, Grewel, unlike Peacher, defined, as was shown above, apraxia of speech as a subtype, albeit at the margins, of dysarthria. In addition, in further contrast with Peacher, Grewel accorded the (integrative) processes of attention and memory a more penetrating role in speech. In his view, disturbance in these processes could complicate the dysarthric symptoms.

Finally, apart from these theoretical differences, Peacher and Grewel both claimed that a neurological perspective on dysarthria lacked diagnostic power and therapeutic relevance if it was not also complemented by detailed speech analysis. In this regard, they proposed some procedural guidelines for the diagnosis of dysarthria and provided an initial broad description of the speech symptoms in the various dysarthria types. Even so, realizing that descriptions of dysarthric speech were subjective and at best impressionistic, Peacher (1950) called for a resurveying of the entire field using principles of experimental phonetics and speech pathology.

Though not yet employing an experimental method, Darley et al. (1969a, 1969b) attempted to do just that in the first systematic and comprehensive study of the audible characteristics of the dysarthrias. The raw data in this investigation comprised reading samples of 212 patients with dysarthria whose neurological diagnosis fell in one of seven categories: pseudobulbar palsy, bulbar palsy, amyotrophic lateral sclerosis, cerebellar lesions, parkinsonism, dystonia, and choreoathetosis. These neurological disorders were a likely choice, as they had been the subject of earlier dysarthria investigations in some form or another. Listening to the tapes, Darley and his colleagues tried to capture the distinct phenomenology of the dysarthrias, not within neuroanatomic levels as had been done before, but within the audible domain. Toward this goal, they conceptualized a series of speech and voice dimensions along which to rate the speech samples. These dimensions were not inspired by a phonetic or prosodic theory, but rather by the requirement that they could be more or less directly perceived, reflect a minimum of interpretation and data reduction, or in other words had high face validity. A direct consequence of this phenomenological approach was that prosodic processes such as coarticulation, resyllabification, syllable lengthening/shortening, and pitch declination remained largely outside the scope of the analysis. Also, similar to what occurred in the neurological perspective on dysarthria before, the initial set of dimensions quickly had to be expanded to more fully capture the diverse universe of the audible symptoms in dysarthria.

Ultimately, Darley et al. settled for 38 dimensions along seven major categories. They included pitch (level, breaks, tremor, or mono), loudness (level, decay, alternating, excessively varied, or mono), vocal quality (harsh/wet hoarseness, continuous/transient breathiness, strained voice, hypo/hypernasality, and nasal emission) audible aspects of respiration (forced inhalation or exhalation, audible inspiration, grunt at end of expiration), prosody (rate, short phrases, increased overall/segmental rate, variable rate, reduced/excessive stress, silences, short rushes of speech), and articulation (imprecise consonants, vowel distortion, prolonged/repeated phonemes, irregular articulatory breakdown). In addition, speech samples were rated along two overall dimensions: intelligibility and bizarreness. Overall, it can be seen that apart from the general impression dimensions, the perceptual categories rated by Darley et al. tapped dysfunction(s) along more or less the same major components/processes of speech, as were outlined within the neurological perspective on dysarthria.

The results of Darley et al.'s (1969a) investigation revealed imprecise consonants, pitch level, mono-pitch, mono-loudness, rate, and hypernasality to be prominent across the groups. Interestingly, consonants appeared more vulnerable than vowels. The results further showed that for a given neurological disease, not only did a single dimension turn out to be unique, also the cooccurrence of several dimensions was distinct. The five basic 'perceptual' patterns that thus were found were given physiological labels and termed flaccid, spastic, ataxic, hypokinetic, and hyperkinetic dysarthria. This labeling, reminiscent of that fashioned by the neurological perspective on dysarthria, found further elaboration and justification in Darley et al. (1969b, 1975). In Darley et al. (1969b), they mapped the cooccurrent dimensions (clusters) on neuromuscular deficits. They are summarized in **Table 1**.

Table 1 Clusters of dysarthric speech dimensions and proposed associated neuromuscular deficits (Darley et al., 1969b)

Cluster	*Deficit*
Articulatory inacccuracy	Inaccurate direction of movement
Prosodic excess	No direct physiological implication
Prosodic insufficiency	Restricted range of movement
Articulatory/resonatory incompetence	Impaired force of muscle contraction and reduced range of movement
Phonatory stenosis	Biased hypertonus
Phonatory/reonatory incompetence	Reduction in contraction force
Phonatory–prosodic insufficiency	Hypotonia

As can be seen there, Darley et al. (1969b, 1975) asserted a movement deficit as the basis for each cluster except for prosodic excess. Later, in their now classic monograph, Darley et al. (1975) went on to define the dysarthrias along with apraxia of speech within the concept of motor speech disorders. Unlike Peacher and Grewel, before, they drew a clear separation between apraxia of speech and dysarthria. Apraxia of speech in their view involved a deficit in one of three hierarchically organized conceptual motor stages (processes), including purpose formulation, movement planning, and programming that were separate, physiologically and anatomically, from the processes that involve movement execution (and control) and considered within the response province of dysarthria. The former processes were, except for the global cortical process of purpose formulation, considered left lateralized and had no direct neuromuscular implication or a prosodic consequence. Dysarthric processes, on the other hand, involved motor execution at the exclusion of sensory processes and were relegated to upper motor neurons (bilaterally), as well as extrapyramidal, cerebellar, and lower motor neurons.

The Mayo Classification has remained the gold standard in motor speech disorders for almost 40 years. Duffy's (1995) recent update of the theory added unilateral upper motor neuron dysarthria to the classification, but was otherwise faithful to Darley et al.'s founding principles. Like Darley et al., he underscored the need for a strict adherence to a 'perceptual' roadmap guiding the classification of dysarthria and a pure motor interpretation of its neurophysiological underpinnings in accordance with a three-stage model of speech production, involving cognitive-linguistic, programming, and execution phases.

Within the last decade, Van der Merwe (1997) and Boutsen (Boutsen, 2003; Boutsen and Christman, 2002) have challenged some basic tenets of the Mayo classification. In line with research showing that the cerebellum and basal ganglia (BG) are involved with cognitive, linguistic, and motor aspects of speech, they argue that a sharp distinction between apraxia of speech and dysarthria is not tenable even in neurophysiological terms. In addition, underscoring the sensorimotor nature of speech, they assigned a pivotal role to audition and proprioception in speech disorders and argued that context specificity plays a role in motor speech disorders. Boutsen maintained in this regard that speech contexts variably tap into prosodic goals that are intrinsic or extrinsic to the language. His theory further argues that those strategies (processes) that serve goals across linguistic domains in a language-specific manner are predominantly elaborated by left hemisphere–right cerebellar circuitry, while those that serve to communicate pragmatic effect are lateralized in right hemisphere–left cerebellar circuitry. Accordingly, dysarthrias, if lateralized, may show differential impairment of these processes. In addition, in line with evidence that the role of the BG and the cerebellum changes fundamentally from childhood to adolescence, this theory predicts that the processes in adult dysarthria may not have much bearing on those observed in developmental dysarthria.

See also: Classical Tests for Speech and Language Disorders; Speech Impairments in Neurodegenerative Diseases/Psychiatric Illnesses.

Bibliography

Boutsen, F (2003). 'Prosody: the music of language and speech.' *ASHA Leader* 5: 7–9.

Boutsen, F and Christman, S (2002). 'Prosody in apraxia of speech.' *Seminars in Speech and Language* 23: 245–256.

Darley, F, Aronson, AE, and Brown, JR (1969a). 'Differential diagnostic patterns of dysarthria.' *Journal of Speech and Hearing Research* 12: 249–269.

Darley, F, Aronson, AE, and Brown, JR (1969b). 'Clusters of deviant dimensions in the dysarthrias.' *Journal of Speech and Hearing Research* 12: 462–496.

Darley, F, Aronson, AE, and Brown, JR (1975). *Motor speech disorders.* Philadelphia: W. B. Saunders.

Duffy, JR (1995). *Motor speech disorders: substrates, differential diagnosis, and management.* St. Louis, MO: Mosby-Year Book.

Froeshels, E (1943). 'A contribution of the pathology and therapy due to certain cerebral lesions.' *Journal of Speech Disorders, 1943* 8: 301–321.

Froment, J (1924). 'Comment étudier les troubles du langage.' *Congrès des médecins alienistiques et neurologiques de France.* Brussels.

Grewel, F (1957). 'Classification of dysarthrias.' *Acta Psychiatrica Scandinavica* 32: 325–337.

Kussmaul, A (1881). *Die storungen der sprache.* Leipzig: F. W. C. Vogel.

Luchsinger, R and Arnold, GE (1949). *Lehrbuch der Stimm-und Sprachheilkunde.* Vienna: Springer-Verlag.

Monrad Krohn, GH (1947). 'The prosodic quality of speech and its disorders.' *Acta Psychiatrica et Neurologica* 22: 255–269.

Peacher, WG (1950). 'The etiology and differential diagnosis of dysarthria.' *Journal of Speech and Hearing Disorders* 15: 252–265.

Stetson, RH (1932). 'Speech movements in action.' *Transactions of the American Laryngological Association* 55: 29–41.

Van der Merwe, A (1997). 'A theoretical framework for the characterization of pathological speech sensori motor control.' In: McNeil, M (ed.) *Clinical management of sensorimotor speech disorders*, pp. 1–25. Thieme: Stuttgart.

Zentay, PJ (1937). 'Motor disorders of the central nervous system and their significance for speech.' *Journal of Speech Disorders* 2: 131–138.

Speech Production, Adult

S. M. Barlow and S. Stumm, University of Kansas, Lawrence, KS, USA

Introduction

The adult speech motor control system (including the chest wall (abdomen and rib cage), larynx, velopharynx, tongue, jaw, and lips) represents an anatomically diverse collection of connective tissue–muscle subsystems regulated by a phylogenetically elaborated and distributed neural system. More than 100 muscles are involved in the precise and rapid timing of these muscle subsystems to produce temporally complex speech sounds which are characterized by transitions as short as 10 ms, articulatory velocities approaching 20 cm s^{-1}, and an average speaking rate of approximately 8–12 sounds per second. As a sensorimotor skill, speech is performed with speed and accuracy, improved with practice, highly adaptive in achieving spatiotemporal goals, and relegated to automaticity in the adult speaker. Speech also exhibits the Hebbian principle of motor equivalence, which is defined as the capacity of the motor control system to achieve the same goal or end product with considerable variation among individual components that contribute to that output. In achieving a particular vocal tract goal, the specific contributions of individual speech articulators may vary from one production of a particular element to another, as long as the desired end product is achieved.

Compensatory vowel articulation – presumably involving the operation of motor equivalence between the lips, tongue, and jaw – is defined as the ability of speakers to generate acceptable vowel qualities despite a fixed position of the mandible or other structures. Producing vowels which require a relatively closed jaw position, such as /i/ or /u/, with a spacer held between the teeth fixing the jaw into a very open position confronts a speaker with a new, or at least unfamiliar, task compared with producing the same vowel under normal, nonconstrained conditions. Remarkably, speakers are able to produce vowels which are acoustically correct with regard to formant frequency locations at the first glottal pulse. These studies clearly demonstrate that the tongue is capable of reorganizing motor output to achieve the acoustic product. At least for adult speakers, goal-oriented motor reorganization appears to require no learning since speakers are able to produce the correct vowels under bite-block conditions on the very first attempt, only a few seconds after inserting the bite-block and being cued for what vowel to produce.

Damage to select areas of the nervous system involved in the selection, sequencing, and activation of articulatory muscles will degrade speech production and may reduce intelligibility. Measurement of articulatory muscle performance variables, including kinematics, is central to advancing our understanding of the development of speech movements over the life span and the response to neurological disease and traumatic injury.

Vocal Tract Dynamics

Generating the source excitation and shaping the anterior portion of the vocal tract to achieve a sequence of acoustic targets involves coordinated muscle actions and movements of the chest wall, larynx, velopharynx, tongue, jaw, and lips. The integrity of the underlying performance anatomy (including contractile elements, connective tissue, bone, and the neural substrate) is central to a discussion of motor proficiency during speech. In some instances, the accurate positioning of one structure (i.e., the lower lip) may be dependent on another structure (i.e., the mandible). Motor goal acquisition often involves reorganization of motor patterns for individual structures during the course of speech production. Kinematic studies of speech typically involve recording from multiple structures in an attempt to understand the trading relations between structures, patterns of organization, and reorganization during development or following brain injury or neurological disease. Feedback and predictive or 'forward looking' neural mechanisms are hypothesized to play an important role in the acquisition and maintenance of speech movements.

Measures of Muscle Output

Activation of the articulatory muscles yields a number of measurable outputs, including force, displacement, heat, vibration, and electrical activity. Speech kinematic variables typically studied include the amplitude of displacement, velocity, acceleration, phase and relative timing among multiple articulators, spatiotemporal variability, phase relations to electromyography muscle patterns, and spectral properties of movement (frequency domain).

Methods and Studies of Speech Kinematics

X-Ray Tracking of Orofacial Movements

The X-ray microbeam is a computer-controlled system available in the United States and Japan that uses a narrow beam of X-rays to localize and track the two-dimensional movements of small gold pellets attached to select speech structures, including the lips, jaw, tongue, soft palate, and eustachian tube. Two additional pellets are attached to the bridge of the nose and a maxillary incisor to serve as reference points that are immobile relative to the skull. The focal X-ray beam (0.4 mm diameter) is scanned at a high rate across a pellet producing a recognizable 'shadow' that is registered on a sodium iodide crystal detector. The path of the X-ray beam toward a pellet is determined by predictions of the position of the pellet generated by current and previous locations.

The X-ray microbeam system has been used successfully to study the relation between speech rate and velocity profiles of movements of the lower lip and tongue tip during the production of stop consonants in young normal adults. Fast speaking rates yielded symmetrical, single-peaked velocity functions, whereas slow speech produced asymmetrical, multipeaked velocity profiles. Speech produced at fast rates appears to involve unitary movements that may be preprogrammed and executed with little or no dependence on sensorimotor integration, whereas articulatory gestures produced at slow speaking rates may be influenced by feedback mechanisms.

X-ray microbeam data have also been combined with cinefluorography to examine the displacement of the tongue body during opening articulatory gestures in deaf and hearing subjects. Speech samples consisted of consonant–vowel–consonant syllables embedded within a carrier phrase. Displacement patterns in deaf and hearing subjects were examined for variation in vocalic contexts between subjects. Deaf speakers had less flexible tongue bodies as a result of compensatory and incorrectly learned principles for constraining tongue movement during speech.

The question of functional regionality within the tongue during speech and swallowing was studied by quantifying the strength of coupling among four different tongue locations. Tongue-surface movement patterns characterized by calculating the covariance between the vertical displacement time histories of all possible pellet pairs show that speech and swallowing kinematics are clustered into distinct groups based on their coupling profiles.

Orofacial Magnetometry

Alternating magnetic field devices known as magnetometers have been used to capture elements of speech production where movements of the face, jaw, tongue, soft palate, and chest wall are tracked in real time. Part of the magnetometer's appeal in speech physiology research and clinical application is due to the fact that the kinematics of intraoral structures (tongue and velopharynx) can be observed and recorded in real time without the biohazards associated with radiological imaging methods (i.e., cineradiography). Historically, the study of speech kinematics has been problematic because movements within the mouth are difficult to measure and visualize.

Orofacial magnetometry is also a valuable therapeutic tool. For example, individuals with hearing loss can observe a visual feedback analog of their tongue movements on a computer in real time. This approach can be applied to the rehabilitation of certain forms of dysarthria, craniofacial disorders, or second language acquisition.

Optical Three-Dimensional Tracking of the Face

Developmental studies of lip and jaw coordination during speech production have benefited directly from the emergence of sophisticated multichannel video-based movement tracking systems. High-speed video cameras are used to register marker location using either reflective markers or infrared source tracking. An algorithm has been developed by researchers at Purdue University to index the spatial and temporal variability in the kinematic trajectory patterns for facial articulators during repeated productions of select speech utterances. When applied to the development of functional synergies among labial–mandibular systems, they found that the time course of development for speech motor coordination is protracted and does not reach 'adult-like' performance until after age 14 years for both males and females, with males lagging on the spatiotemporal variability index.

Tracking Tongue Movements

From the late 1940s through the mid-1970s, our understanding of tongue movements in adult speakers relied heavily on studies using radiography and tongue contact devices such as the dynamic palatometer. Since then, technological advances have been made in optics, magnetometry, ultrasound, X-ray microbeam, and functional magnetic resonance imaging (fMRI) for tracking the tongue during speech and swallowing.

Palatometry has been used to show that each vowel in English is associated with a unique stationary linguapalatal contact map. For example, during the stable contact portion of [i], the tongue is in contact with sensors extending from the cuspid–bicuspid region of the palate to the posterior border of the alveolar ridge. During the [ae], the contact is against the most posteriolateral sensors. Diphthongs are characterized by movements between two stable monophthong positions. Optical and contact pattern (tongue–palate) tracking devices have been used in training or retraining vowel space and consonant production in hearing-impaired adults.

Ultrasonic Imaging of the Tongue

Ultrasound provides real-time images of the tongue surface in a digital video format during speech and swallowing. Images are combined with estimates of the hard palate boundary using ultrasound during the production of command swallows to establish a reference within headspace for coregistration among subjects and calculation of select phonetic measures.

Ultrasound results indicate that cross-sectional tongue shape is directly related to the position of the tongue and the lateral and sagittal shape of the tongue. In general, midsagittal grooving is evident for all vowel types, with posterior grooves being deeper than anterior grooves. Posterior grooving is greater in the /p/ context than in the /s/ context. Grooving for vowels in the /p/ context demonstrated a continuum, whereas in the anterior /s/ context two groups of vowels were identified (high group/shallower grooves and back group with deeper grooves). In the anterior /s/ context, tongue shape for /i/ and /u/ was convex.

Considerable progress has been made with high-speed three-dimensional (3-D) reconstruction of tongue ultrasonic images. In adult speakers, this work has focused on defining predictable mathematical relations between midsagittal tongue contour shapes and up to five cross-sectional (coronal) contours. A concatenation of these coronal slices permits the reconstruction of a 3-D tongue surface. When compared among four tongue shape phonemic categories (i.e., front raising /i/, back raising /ŋ/, continuous grooving /ae/, and two point displacement /l/), it was found that transitional values exist that predict tongue arching versus midsagittal tongue grooving. Even better predictions are possible using three anterior coronal slices in which strong correlations exist between midline displacement and groove depth to arch height. Knowledge of both category and midsagittal displacement provides good prediction of coronal tongue shape.

Tracking Velar and Laryngeal Movements

Kinematic studies of the 'invisible valves' of speech, including the velopharynx and larynx, is technically challenging due to small size and inaccessibility. Acceptable sampling methods in humans usually reflect a concession between the invasiveness of the instrument and the quality of the acquired signals. Whereas it is acceptable to attach small sensors to the lips and jaw in the form of radio-opaque pellets, reflective balls or tape, infrared diodes, cantilevers, or magnetic coils to the rib cage or abdomen, no such electromechanical device or sensor is acceptable to the delicate tissue boundary of the human vocal fold because this would disrupt the behavior and health of the organism. Instead, techniques have evolved that rely on imaging, acoustics, and/or fluid mechanics. These procedures are described in the following sections.

Velopharynx

The velopharynx (VP) is a complex muscular valve that is strategically situated to divert acoustic and aerodynamic energy through the oral and nasal cavities. The size of the velar port determines the oral or nasal nature of speech sounds. Movements of the velum, lateral pharyngeal walls, and the posterior pharyngeal wall collectively determine the size of the velar port.

Methods aimed at measuring the size and/or movements of the velum and lateral and posterior pharyngeal walls roughly fall into one of two categories: direct and indirect. Direct methods include imaging techniques such as cineradiography, video nasendoscopy, and electromechanical, optomechanical transduction of velar displacement. These transducers for measuring velar activity and radiographic imaging techniques share a common limitation in only resolving movement in a single plane. In most radiographic studies, discrete points are tracked on a frame-by-frame basis, which is useful in resolving velocity and displacement profiles. However, because the radiographic methods are limited to one plane or slice through the velopharynx, one is never certain if closure has occurred. Velar apertures may exist at locations opposite the lateral pharyngeal walls on one or both sides. The patterns of VP closure are highly variable both within and across adult speakers.

Complete VP closure is not always obtained during vowel production. Pioneering work aimed at characterizing normal patterns of VP closure using cineflourographic techniques revealed that high vowels exhibit greater VP closure than low vowels, regardless of consonant context. Complete closure of the VP is not always present during production of the low vowels nor attained on vowels adjacent to a nasal consonant (assimilation). Speech rate is another factor which can significantly influence the degree of VP closure.

Flexible fiberoptic nasoendoscopy is a powerful imaging tool which helps to resolve some of the uncertainty regarding the dynamics of the velopharyngeal port. Advanced camera, fiberoptics, and digital recording technology provides high-resolution color images of the velopharynx in real time during speech production. Image recognition software routines assist the investigator in accurate identification of tissue boundaries and kinematic properties of the velopharynx, including computation of portal area and boundary velocity, displacement, and calibration schemes for scaling distance. This information will be invaluable for studies of velopharyngeal motor control in patients with sensorimotor speech disorders.

Aerodynamic measures of velopharyngeal port function offer some unique perspectives on the fluid dynamics of this valve during speech in adults and children. Current aerodynamic protocols and instrumentation provide reasonably accurate estimates of the subglottal driving air pressures (P_s) and airflows acting on the velopharynx during speech in fluid mechanics terms without the biohazards associated with radiation or the invasiveness of a fiberoptic bundle inserted into the nasal cavity. Area functions, resistance (impedance) estimates, and temporal pattern studies have been used effectively to characterize the activity of the velopharynx during speech.

Numerous reports have described some of the temporal relations between pressure–flow variables during nasal-plosive blends to stress the velopharyngeal mechanism and reveal the coarticulatory dynamics between velopharynx and other upper airway structures in normal and cleft palate speakers. For example, studies of VP aerodynamics in repaired cleft palate adults and normal controls revealed that the magnitude of mean intraoral air pressures tends to be slightly less than that of control speakers. Articulatory timing errors were evident as the nasal airflow pulse overlapped into the rising phase and peak of the pressure pulse associated with /p/ in the word 'hamper.' A decrease in respiratory effort may represent a compensatory strategy used by patients with repaired cleft palates to achieve adequate velopharyngeal closure and minimize shunting (air leak) through the velopharyngeal port. This conclusion was based on careful study of the temporal relations between the airflow and pressure curves associated with production of the nasal-plosive blend.

Laryngeal Kinematics

The larynx represents a microcosm of the entire speech mechanism in that it provides a sound source in coordination with the respiratory system, acts as a dynamic 'articulator' capable of rapid adductor and abductor adjustments, modulates pitch (male f_0 ~125 Hz, female f_0 ~225 Hz), and conveys emotion and personal identity. Endoscopy is an important tool in the assessment of laryngeal movement disorders affecting speech/voice. Laryngeal aerodynamics is a useful adjunct which provides quantitative data on the articulatory dynamics of laryngeal engagement for consonant–vowel transitions, vocal efficiency, and chest wall function for P_s regulation. Use of fiberoptic nasopharyngoscopy, laryngoscopy, and stroboscopy in conjunction with low-light cinematography allows observation of the dynamic processes of speech production. This technique allows the investigator to visualize the overall articulatory dynamics of the larynx during speech and other behaviors such as swallowing, coughing, and respiration. Information obtained during the nasendoscopic examination has proved to be useful for biofeedback in the remediation of select laryngeal and velopharyngeal impairments affecting speech.

Videokymography

A relatively new technique that takes advantage of digital video recording and processing in strip kymography (the recording of wavelike motions or undulations) of the glottis is videokymography (VKG). This method permits visualization of the individual cycles of phonation by analyzing only a small segment of the vibrating vocal folds. Developed in The Netherlands by Drs. Harm Schutte and Jan Švec of the University of Groningen, VKG uses a modified charge-coupled device camera to record images of selected cross-sections of the vocal folds during motion. The position of the horizontal measuring line is maintained throughout the analysis. VKG systems use standard videolaryngoscopic setups with a continuous light source and record images to a digital storage device. In place of recording the entire image of the vocal fold, however, VKG systems allow for the collection of a single line of the image (orthogonal to the longitudinal axis of the fold) at rates of 8 kHz, thus allowing for sampling rates great enough to cover the entire frequency range of fold oscillation. Successive lines are temporally aligned and cascaded in real time on a conventional monitor, thus showing the vibratory pattern of the selected region of interest on the vocal fold for a preselected time period. The resulting 'kymogram' displays a spatiotemporal image of the vocal folds at the scanned line over time. Videokymography and digital kymography allow for true cycle-by-cycle analysis of vocal fold vibratory patterns. Analysis of the resulting kymograms can provide information on right–left vocal fold asymmetries, open and closed quotients, ventricular fold and/or mucous interference, mucosal wavefront propagation, frequency, amplitude, speed quotient, and within-cycle perturbations.

Electroglottography (EGG) has been used with success to assess laryngeal activity. This instrument consists of a flexible neck collar supporting an array of electrodes and a signal conditioning unit. In EGG, a small DC bias current is fed through the tissues of the neck and the conditioning unit senses changes in the electrical resistance in the region of the larynx. Essentially, the EGG signal is correlated with vocal fold contact area and is regarded as a useful assessment technique in drawing inferences about patterns of vocal fold vibration during speech.

Electroglottographic measures have been used to measure timing between voiced segments and for analysis of the cycle-by-cycle dynamics of voicing, and they are usually obtained in combination with inverse filtered flow signals (AC flow) for the purpose of detailing the organization and timing of the open and closed phases of the glottis during voice production. Because information derived from EGGs is based on the vocal segment and changes in vocal fold contact area, it offers limited information concerning the aeromechanical events underlying vocal fold engagement. Furthermore, the reliability and validity of the EGG signal associated with the early phases of laryngeal engagement are questionable. The beginning phases of arytenoid rotation are associated with displacement of the vocal folds in glottal space. During this interval, one would not expect appreciable increases in vocal fold contact area until arytenoid advancement results in actual tissue approximation. Therefore, the EGG output during this phase of engagement may yield little or no output signal even though significant displacements of the vocal folds have occurred.

Laryngeal Aerodynamics

The utility and noninvasive nature of aerodynamics is underscored in adults with neurogenic speech disorders. Voice disorders range from hyperfunctional (excessive medial compression, hard glottal attack, and groping voice quality) to hypofunctional (soft glottal attack, breathy, and soft or weak voice) and disturbances in the timing and coordination of arytenoid–VF medialization (basal ganglia (BG), cerebellar disease, upper motor neuron syndrome, and others). For example, speakers with Parkinson's disease often exhibit air loss when attempting to engage (adduct) the vocal folds for voice production. In contrast, patients with adductor spasmodic dysphonia manifest exaggerated medial compression of the vocal processes of the arytenoids. This pattern of hyperadduction may include the ventricular or false folds and results in a sudden interruption of the breath stream during voicing. Disruption of this important articulatory adjustment due to neural and/or biomechanical factors can dramatically influence the manner in which the vital capacity is used for speech. In cases of slow or mechanically limited engagement, significant portions of the lung vital capacity may be wasted by a defective laryngeal articulatory apparatus independently from the pressure–flow dynamics associated with voice production.

Real-time digital speech aerodynamic recording and analysis tools are available to measure articulatory proficiency during laryngeal engagement and phonation. This technique, based on the simultaneous sampling of intraoral air pressure, translaryngeal airflow, and voice acoustic signals, has been used effectively to reveal the reorganization of laryngeal function in patients with amyotrophic lateral sclerosis, idiopathic Parkinson's disease following posteroventral pallidotomy, and bilateral subthalamic nucleus deep brain stimulation. The magnitude and time course of translaryngeal flow, described mathematically as air volume and flow rate declination functions, are presumed to reflect the underlying kinematics of vocal fold adduction toward the phonatory phase. Measures of pressure–flow dynamics and laryngeal airway resistance can also be determined for the phonatory phase of syllable production to provide for a comprehensive evaluation of the articulatory dynamics of laryngeal behavior. The net result of a hypokinetic adductory mechanism is that lung volume is wasted during translation of the arytenoids to achieve vocal fold approximation. The lung volume available for speech is depleted and overall utterance length is decreased. Therefore, the evaluation of laryngeal function in patients with sensorimotor speech disorders benefits from an analysis of the kinematic properties of transitory (engagement–disengagement) and phonatory (voice efficiency) phases.

Chest Wall Kinematics

The chest wall includes, except for the lungs and airways, all parts of the respiratory apparatus – the rib cage, diaphragm, and the abdomen and its contents – and is regarded as one of the principal articulatory systems that provide a pressure–flow source to support speech and voice production. The rib cage and diaphragm constitute the thoracic cavity. The abdominal cavity is defined by the diaphragm and abdominal wall bounding an incompressible mass of liquid. According to Hixon's model, the chest wall is reduced to a two-structure model consisting of the rib cage and 'diaphragm-abdomen.' Isovolume maneuvers are used to calibrate the chest wall size against lung volumes and involve equal and opposite volume displacement by the surfaces of the abdomen and rib cage under a closed system. Movement outputs from the rib cage and abdomen can be adjusted to account for the difference in volume displacements from these two parts. Once the chest wall has been calibrated, lung volume calibrations can be achieved by measuring integrated flow at the airway opening during simultaneous chest wall kinematic measurements to establish the relationship between chest wall movement and various static inspiratory or expiratory lung volumes.

Magnetometry

Changes in the anterior–posterior diameters of the rib cage and abdomen are transduced with two-channel electromagnetic devices consisting of small coils (2×0.5 cm) set up in pairs, one for signal generation and the other for sensing changes in inductance due to displacement. The generator coils are attached midline on the anterior surface of the chest wall at the level of the nipples and to the abdomen immediately above the umbilicus. An alternative transducer system that has been used to measure chest wall kinematics is the strain gage belt pneumograph. Setup is simple and involves a clip gage attached to a circumferential belt with an elastic strap.

Speech breathing kinematics using magnetometers has been studied in individuals with profound hearing impairments, voice disorders, motor neuron disease, flaccid paralysis, parkinsonian dysarthria, cerebellar ataxic dysarthria, traumatic brain and spinal cord injury, and in a variety of normal subgroups in which factors such as age, body type, and sex are the dependent variables.

Functional Neural Systems for Speech Motor Control

The encoding of force and movement by the brain is central to models of movement and highly relevant to our understanding of speech motor control. The relation between force control and neural firing patterns in primate motor cortex is strongly correlated with the rate and direction of force change and preferred torque directions. Primary motor cortex has also been shown to encode functional muscle synergies. The cortical mechanisms involved in the regulation of muscle dynamics during the early phases of force recruitment have been shown for orofacial muscles. The complex articulatory force dynamics evident among facial muscles during speech is similar in many ways to the precise movements and forces generated by hand and fingers during manipulation. During speech production, the muscles of the perioral system exhibit a streaming repertoire of phasic adjustments in force from resting tonic activation to approximately 10% of the maximum voluntary contraction level.

Mounting evidence also suggests that the sensorimotor cortex may participate in the modulation of the reflexive compensatory motor responses in lip muscles during speech. The orofacial apparatus appears to utilize mechanosensory information differentially for the early versus later phases of lip force output. During speech articulation, longer latency reflex actions presumably involving primary motor cortex correct for the effects of external movement disturbances. Mechanical inputs delivered to a dynamically contracting lip muscle produce a compound evoked perioral response characterized by phases of excitation and suppression that are absent during static force conditions. Under these conditions, compensatory lip movements demonstrate a well-calibrated readjustment.

Velocity is one kinematic variable which has been explored in some detail and appears to have a definable neural network. Positron emission tomography mapping of regional cerebral blood flow has demonstrated a velocity subcircuit within the motor control system, including the bilateral sensorimotor cortex, BG (putamen and globus pallidus (GP)), and the ipsilateral cerebellum. Increases in velocity are associated with parallel increases in BG activation. The BG motor circuit may be preferentially involved in controlling or monitoring the scale and/or dynamics of arm movements and may also control articulatory movements at lower frequencies. A dysfunctional BG circuit (i.e., Parkinson's disease (PD)) may result in hypophonia (lowered speech volume) and bradykinesia. Functional brain imaging of patients with PD during velocity control tasks reveals a significant disruption to the BG circuitry which may partially account for the pathophysiology of bradykinesia. Unilateral lesions of the GP internal and GP external result in slowness of movement and abnormal co-contraction of agonist and antagonist muscles and often impair movements of the orofacial, laryngeal, and chest wall systems for speech production.

A positive relation also exists between increases in speech rate and cerebellar activation, suggesting this brain structure plays a significant role in the velocity of articulatory movements within the frame of time-critical adjustments. Motor speech symptoms resulting from cerebellar pathology may reflect a distorted process of articulatory planning and coordination. Cerebellar posterior lobe syndrome is often associated with speech that is perceived as having an 'intoxicated-like' quality.

The brain imaging and neurocomputational literature is proliferating rapidly with studies of speech production and sensorimotor control of the upper airway. The production of simple vowels and simple oral movements results in similar activation patterns among cortical and subcortical motor systems. More complex, polysyllabic utterances are associated with additional activation of the bilateral cerebellum, presumably reflecting increased demands on speech motor control, and additional activation of the bilateral temporal cortices thought to subserve phonological processing.

The hemodynamic effects associated with paced syllable production during fMRI have been compared with passive listening of pacing signals. Cerebral structures associated with speech motor control included the supplementary motor area (SMA), primary sensorimotor regions, dorsolateral prefrontal cortex (including Broca's area), anterior insula, thalamus, putamen/pallidum, and cerebellar hemispheres. Dorsolateral prefrontal and intrasylvian cortex displayed lateralization toward the left side, whereas the other components showed a bilateral activation pattern. The cerebral correlates of speech motor control based on connectivity analyses appear to be organized into two separate networks – motor preparation (SMA, dorsolateral frontal cortex (Broca's area), anterior insula, and superior cerebellum) and a motor execution processor (sensorimotor cortex, BG, thalamus, and inferior cerebellum). Broca's area is thought to contribute to orthographic-to-phonological transformation, whereas motor cortex, SMA, and the cerebellum play critical roles in phonetic encoding and articulation of speech. Functional imaging studies show that pre-SMA and SMA are engaged in the control of externally triggered movements. Moreover, SMA shows a frequency effect and may indicate that this region is involved in the generation of the motor program for an entire spoken word, with the level of activation in SMA influenced by how often this motor program is implemented. Motor cortex appears to represent articulatory gestures at the syllable or phoneme sequence level. Clinical data support this dichotomy of motor preparation/motor execution.

Speech production is dependent on auditory, somatosensory, and visual feedback for its development and maintenance. These mechanisms are also crucial to invoke mechanisms of plasticity following a sudden insult to the brain (ischemia reperfusion or hemorrhage) or during the course of a progressive neuromotor disease (i.e., PD). A simulation has been developed to test many of these conditions as given by the Directions into Velocities of Articulators (DIVA) model of speech motor control, shown schematically in **Figure 1**. The DIVA model includes a feed-forward network, composed of the premotor and primary motor cortices and cerebellum, and feedback control systems which encode auditory and somatosensory inputs with comparator functions to assist in the specification of speech articulatory velocity and position. A central feature of the DIVA model that differentiates it from other computational models of speech production is that all components of the model have been associated with specific neuroanatomical loci. The DIVA model generates simulated fMRI activations associated with small populations of synchronously firing neurons from the model's cell activities during computer simulation. It features adaptive control mechanisms to effect the learning of auditory and somatosensory consequences during babbling or syllable productions which are eventually incorporated into feed-forward mechanisms. According to the DIVA model, outputs from premotor cortex (left frontal operculum) and cerebellum to motor cortex constitute feed-forward motor commands for syllable production. In infants, feed-forward commands for a syllable are tuned on each production attempt. Initial attempts rely heavily on auditory feedback. With changes in body plan (i.e., growth of the speech articulators), the auditory feedback control system continues to provide corrective tuning of the feedback controller over the life span. Consistent with research in other laboratories, it is clear that somatosensory information is central to achieving the precision requirements of speech movements, including consonant and vowel position targets. The neural control of stiffness appears to be a key factor to consider for the somatosensory precision involved in speech production.

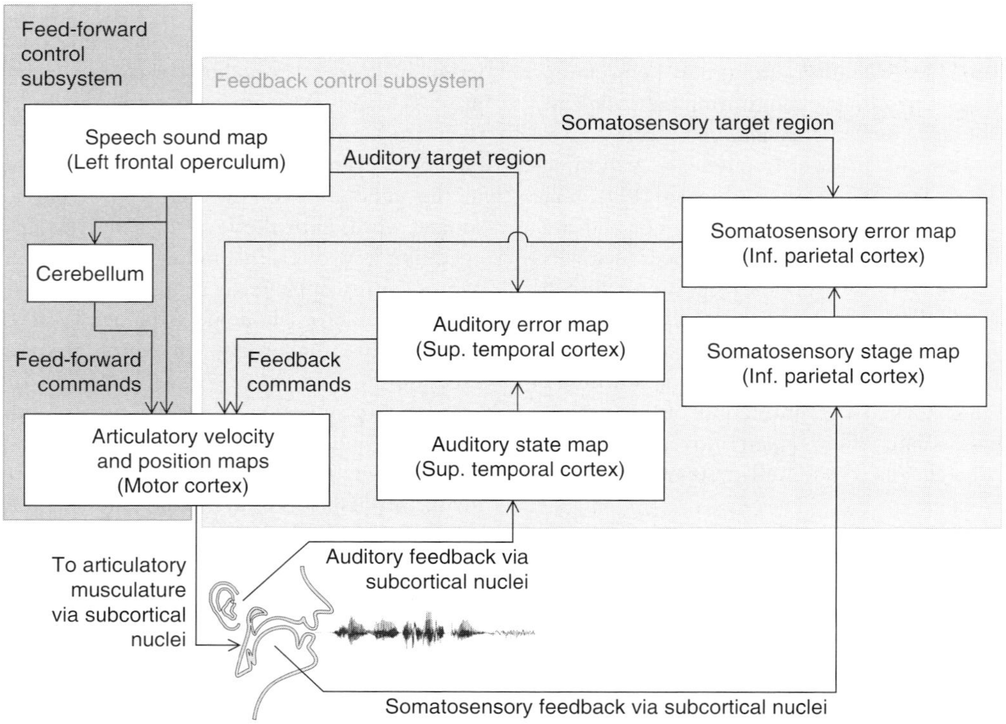

Figure 1 Schematic of the DIVA model of speech acquisition and production. Projections to and from the cerebellum are simplified for clarity. Reproduced from Guenther FH (2006) Cortical interactions underlying the production of speech sounds. *Journal of Communication Disorders* 39: 350–365, with permission.

Future work by the developers of the DIVA model will incorporate the anterior cingulate cortex, SMA, BG, and anterior insula into the scheme of feedback and feed-forward control of speech movements.

See also: Sentence Production; Word Production.

Further Reading

Adams, SG, Weismer, G, and Kent, RD (1993). Speaking rate and speech movement velocity profiles. *Journal of Speech and Hearing Research* 36: 41–54.
Baken, RJ (1992). Electroglottography. *Journal of Voice* 6: 98–110.
Barlow, SM, Farley, GR, and Andreatta, RD (1999). Neural systems in speech physiology. *Handbook of Clinical Speech Physiology*, pp. 101–165. San Diego: Singular Publishing.
Cunnington, R, Windischberger, C, Deecke, L, and Moser, E (2002). The preparation and execution of self-initiated and externally-triggered movement: A study of event-related fMRI. *NeuroImage* 15: 373–385.
Estep, M and Barlow, SM (2007). Modulation of the trigeminofacial pathway during syllabic speech. *Brain Research* 1171: 67–74.
Gracco, VL, Tremblay, P, and Pike, B (2005). Imaging speech production using MRI. *NeuroImage* 26: 294–301.
Guenther, FH, Ghosh, SS, and Tourville, JA (2006). Neural modeling and imaging of the cortical interactions underlying syllable production. *Brain and Language* 96: 280–301.
Hixon, TJ (1987). Respiratory function in speech. In: Hixon, TJ (ed.) *Respiratory Function in Speech and Song*, pp. 1–54. Boston: Little, Brown.
Levelt, WJM (1989). Speaking: *From Intention to Articulation*. Cambridge, MA: MIT Press.
Ludlow CL and Bassich CJ (1984) Relationships between perceptual ratings and acoustic measures of hypokinetic speech. In: McNeil MR, Rosenbet JC, and Aronson AE (eds.) *The Dysarthrias*, pp. 163–195. San Diego: College-Hill Press.
Munhall, K (2006). Speech production: The force of your words. *Current Biology* 16(21): 922–923.
Nasir, SM and Ostry, DJ (2006). Somatosensory precision in speech production. *Current Biology* 16: 1918–1923.
Perkell, JS, Cohen, MH, Svirsky, MA, Matthies, ML, Garabieta, I, and Jackson, MTT (1992). Electromagnetic midsagittal articulometer systems for transducing speech articulatory movements. *Journal of the Acoustical Society of America* 92: 3078–3096.
Riecker, A, Mathiak, K, Wildgruber, D, et al. (2005). fMRI reveals two distinct cerebral networks subserving speech motor control. *Neurology* 64: 700–706.
Schutte, HK, Svec, JG, and Sram, F (1998). First results of clinical application of videokymography. *Laryngoscope* 108(8): 1206–1210.
Smith, A, Johnson, M, McGillem, C, and Goffman, L (2000). On the assessment of stability and patterning of speech movements. *Journal of Speech, Language, and Hearing Research* 43: 277–286.
Soros, P, Sokoloff, LG, Bose, A, McIntosh, AR, Graham, SJ, and Stuss, DT (2007). Clustered functional MRI of overt speech production. *NeuroImage* 32: 376–387.
Stone, M, Epstein, MA, and Iskarous, K (2004). Functional segments in tongue movement. *Clinical Linguistics & Phonetics* 18: 507–522.
Turner, RS, Desmurget, M, Grethe, J, Crutcher, MD, and Grafton, ST (2003). Motor subcircuits mediating the control of movement extent and speed. *Journal of Neurophysiology* 90(6): 3958–3966.
Turner, RS, Grafton, ST, McIntosh, AR, DeLong, MR, and Hoffman, JM (2003). The functional anatomy of parkinsonian bradykinesia. *NeuroImage* 19: 163–179.

Sturge–Weber–Dimitri Syndrome and Language

S. Rémillard and H. Cohen, Université du Québec à Montréal, Montréal, Canada

The association of cerebral leptomeningeal angioma and facial nevus flammeus in the territory of the first branch of the trigeminal nerve ipsilateral to the angioma is known as Sturge–Weber syndrome (SWS). The cases with absence of a facial angioma are usually considered to be variants of the syndrome. This is a rare congenital neurocutaneous syndrome of unknown origin that occurs in both sexes with a frequency of approximately 1 per 50 000 (e.g., Comi, 2003). Sturge first described this disorder in 1879. In 1922, Weber described a similar clinical case and advocated the use of the term 'encephalotrigeminal angiomatosis' to describe it. It is characterized by leptomeningeal angiomatosis, glaucoma, and ipsilateral facial capillary hemangioma (port-wine stain) in the ophthalmic division of the trigeminal nerve (Aicardi, 1992). The facial nevus flammeus is present in 98% of children with SWS and it is visible at birth (Sujansky and Conradi, 1995b). It usually affects the upper eyelid and the forehead. The stain is caused by an overabundance of capillaries just beneath the surface of the affected skin. The angioma is typically located on the parietal and occipital lobes. It has been suggested that the angioma results from the failure of the primitive cephalic venous plexus to regress and properly mature in the first trimester of development (Comi, 2003). Normally, this vascular plexus forms in the sixth week and regresses at approximately the ninth week of gestation.

SWS is also characterized by neurological manifestations, which include focal or diffuse seizures (Kramer et al., 2000), abnormal cerebral glucose metabolism (Lee et al., 2001; Maria et al., 1998; Pfund et al., 2003; Pinton et al., 1997), enlargement of the choroid plexus (Guermazi et al., 2000), progressive atrophy and calcification of the brain (Comi, 2003; Jay, 2000; Shamoto and Chugani, 1997), and recurrent stroke-like episodes (see Thomas-Sohl et al., 2003, for a review of clinical symptoms and management). Hemianopia, progressive hemiparesis, motor deficits, developmental delay, and mental retardation are other dysfunctions associated with this neurological disorder. Mental retardation is present in approximately 50% of children with SWS (Sujansky and Conradi, 1995a) and clinical severity of signs and symptoms varies widely from one patient to another (Maria et al., 1998).

It has been hypothesized that two main complications of SWS may explain the progressive neurological deficits associated with the disorder: the occurrence of seizures and cerebral ischemia. Thus, repeated seizure activity is associated with developmental delay, permanent hemiparesis, and mental retardation. In addition, venous stasis and recurrent episodes of venular thrombosis may be responsible for neurological deteriorations (cerebral calcification, gliosis of the cortex and white matter) and postnatal hemispheric atrophy (Comi, 2003; Kramer et al., 2000; Portilla et al., 2002).

Epilepsy affects over 80% of the children with SWS (Sujansky and Conradi, 1995a; Ville et al., 2002). In a majority of children, onset occurs during the first year of life. Of the children who did not develop seizures during their first 2 years of life, only 14% developed seizures subsequently. It has been suggested that onset of seizures during the first 2 years of life and the presence of uncontrollable seizures are responsible for the developmental deterioration of previously normally functioning children with SWS (Roach, 1992). Thus, according to Sujansky and Conradi (1995a), later age of seizure onset is a favorable prognostic indicator. Contrary to these observations, Kramer et al. (2000) showed that cognitive delay is significantly correlated with seizure intensity, rather than the age of onset.

When seizures are unihemispheric and intractable to medication, hemispherectomy is strongly recommended. This type of surgery is used in an attempt to control seizures and to prevent neurological deterioration (Kossoff et al., 2002). Generally, bilateral angiomatosis is a contraindication to epilepsy surgery because a more diffuse region of epileptogenesis, which is not resectable, is more probable and the seizure prognosis may thus be unfavorable (Arzimanoglou et al., 2000; Roach et al., 1994). Nevertheless, according to some authors, epilepsy surgery in SWS should not be used too restrictively (Tuxhorn and Pannek, 2002). Tuxhorn and Pannek presented two bilateral cases of SWS that showed good seizure control and remission of epileptic encephalopathy after functional hemispherectomy.

Language development in SWS has not been well studied. Nevertheless, a few case studies have shown that language impairments associated with this syndrome result principally from epilepsy and following hemispherectomy. Vargha-Khadem et al. (1997) described the case of a 9 year old boy diagnosed with SWS affecting the left hemisphere, in which seizure activity is the cause for arrested speech development. This boy, named Alex, experienced his first epileptic episode 6 days after birth. Despite having normal hearing, Alex did not develop speech, and his utterances, at 33 months of age, were still limited to babbling. Furthermore, his intellectual development was globally delayed. Between the ages of 4 and 8 years, Alex attempted to communicate with gestures.

At age of 8 years 6 months, Alex underwent a successful left hemispherectomy. Interestingly, 10 months after surgery, Alex suddenly began to develop speech and, by age 10, could converse with copious and appropriate speech. This child achieved remarkable linguistic competence with an isolated right hemisphere and he speaks clearly and fluently with grammatically correct sentences. However, in the domain of receptive language, Alex showed poor comprehension of more complex grammatical sentences, as assessed by the Token Test (De Renzi and Vignolo, 1962) and the Clinical Evaluation of Language Functions-Revised (CELF-R; Semel et al., 1987). Other cognitive dysfunctions have been noted in Alex's case, such as reading, writing, and arithmetic. At age 13, his performance in these cognitive areas was still at the basal level (i.e., $<$6 years).

Mariotti et al. (1998) described the linguistic abilities of a woman with SWS who underwent early removal of her left hemisphere, at age 3. Extensive assessment of her linguistic abilities was conducted when she was 20. In contrast to Alex's case, her performance, when compared to mentally retarded controls matched for age, education, and IQ, showed fluent spontaneous speech with intact pragmatic abilities, normal articulation, prosody, and phrase length, and grammatically correct sentences. Reading and writing on copy were also normal, although writing on dictation was slightly impaired. As in Alex's case, however, she showed a marked impairment in more complex syntactic comprehension of sentences, low IQ, and poor memory span.

These observations in the case of SWS and hemispherectomy indirectly suggest a necessary integrity of the left cerebral hemisphere to adequately process morphosyntactic aspects of language. However, not all authors agree with this interpretation on the issue of cerebral hemispheric specialization of function (e.g., Bishop, 1988; Mariotti et al., 1998; Vargha-Khadem et al., 1997). Rather, they attribute the observed deficits to a low IQ and limited verbal memory span in children with SWS. Mariotti et al. (1998) suggested that failure of syntactic tasks could be merely the expression of a generic cognitive impairment (such as poor lexical knowledge) and not of specific linguistic damage. Thus, it is unclear whether the language dysfunction seen in SWS can be ascribed to a low IQ and poor working memory.

See also: Anatomical Asymmetries Versus Variability of Language Areas of the Brain.

Bibliography

Aicardi, J (1992). *Diseases of the nervous system in childhood.* Cambridge: Cambridge University Press.

Arzimanoglou, AA, Andermann, F, Aicardi, J, Sainte-Rose, C, Beaulieu, M-A, Villemure, J-G, Olivier, A, and Rasmussen, Th (2000). 'Sturge–Weber syndrome: Indications and results of surgery in 20 patients.' *Neurology* 55: 1472–1479.

Bishop, DVM (1988). 'Can the right hemisphere mediate language as well as the left? A critical review on recent research.' *Cognitive Neuropsychology* 5: 353–367.

Comi, AM (2003). 'Pathophysiology of Sturge–Weber syndrome.' *Journal of Child Neurology* 18: 509–516.

De Renzi, E and Vignolo, LA (1962). 'The token test: A sensitive test to detect receptive disturbances in aphasics.' *Brain* 85: 665–678.

Guermazi, A, De Kerviler, E, Zagdanski, AM, and Frija, J (2000). 'Diagnostic imaging of choroid plexus disease: Pictorial review.' *Clinical Radiology* 55: 503–516.

Jay, V (2000). 'Sturge–Weber syndrome.' *Pediatric and Developmental Pathology* 3: 301–305.

Kossoff, EH, Buck, CE, and Freeman, JM (2002). 'Outcomes of 32 hemispherectomies for Sturge–Weber syndrome worldwide.' *Neurology* 59: 1735–1738.

Kramer, U, Kahana, E, Shorer, Z, and Ben-Zeev, B (2000). 'Outcome of infants with unilateral Sturge–Weber syndrome and early onset seizures.' *Developmental Medicine and Child Neurology* 42: 756–759.

Lee, JS, Asano, E, Muzik, O, Chugani, DC, Juhasz, C, Pfund, Z, Philip, S, Behen, M, and Chugani, HT (2001). 'Correlation between clinical course and FDG PET findings.' *Neurology* 57: 189–195.

Maria, BL, Neufeld, JA, Rosain, LC, Ben-David, K, Drane, WE, Quisling, RG, and Hamed, LM (1998). 'High prevalence of bihemispheric structural and functional defects in Sturge–Weber syndrome.' *Journal of Child Neurology* 13: 595–605.

Mariotti, P, Iuvone, L, Torrioli, MG, and Silveri, MC (1998). 'Linguistic and non-linguistic abilities in a patient with early left hemispherectomy.' *Neuropsychologia* 36: 1303–1313.

Pfund, Z, Kagawa, K, Juhasz, C, Shen, C, Lee, JS, Chugani, DC, Muzik, O, and Chugani, HT (2003). 'Quantitative analysis of gray- and white-matter volumes and glucose metabolism in Sturge–Weber syndrome.' *Journal of Child Neurology* 18: 119–126.

Pinton, F, Chiron, C, Enjolras, O, Motte, J, Syrota, A, and Dulac, O (1997). 'Early single photon emission computed tomography in Sturge–Weber syndrome.' *Journal of Neurology, Neurosurgery, and Psychiatry* 63: 616–621.

Portilla, P, Husson, B, Lasjaunias, P, and Landrieu, P (2002). 'Sturge–Weber disease with repercussion on the prenatal development of the cerebral hemisphere.' *American Journal of Neuroradiology* 23: 490–492.

Roach, ES (1992). 'Neurocutaneous syndromes.' *Pediatric Clinical North America* 39: 591–620.

Roach, ES, Riela, AR, Chugani, HAT, Shinnar, S, Bodensteiner, JB, and Freeman, J (1994). 'Sturge–Weber syndrome: Recommendations for surgery.' *Journal of Child Neurology* 9: 190–193.

Semel, E, Wiig, EH, and Secord, W (1987). *CELF-R: Clinical evaluation of language functions – Revised.* London: Psychological Corporation.

Shamoto, H and Chugani, H (1997). 'Glucose metabolism in the human cerebellum: An analysis of crossed cerebellar diaschisis in children with unilateral cerebral injury.' *Journal of Child Neurology* 12: 407–414.

Sujansky, E and Conradi, S (1995a). 'Sturge–Weber syndrome: Age of onset of seizures and glaucoma and the prognosis for affected children.' *Journal of Child Neurology* 10: 49–58.

Sujansky, E and Conradi, S (1995b). 'Outcome of Sturge–Weber syndrome in 52 adults.' *American Journal of Medical Genetics* 57: 35–45.

Thomas-Sohl, KA, Vaslow, DF, and Maria, BL (2003). 'Sturge–Weber syndrome: A review.' *Pediatric Neurology* 30: 303–310.

Tuxhorn, IEB and Pannek, HW (2002). 'Epilepsy surgery in bilateral Sturge–Weber syndrome.' *Pediatric Neurology* 26: 394–397.

Vargha-Khadem, F, Carr, LJ, Isaacs, E, Brett, E, Adams, C, and Mishkin, M (1997). 'Onset of speech after left hemispherectomy in a nine-year-old boy.' *Brain* 120: 159–182.

Ville, D, Enjolras, O, Chiron, C, and Dulac, O (2002). 'Prophylactic antiepileptic treatment in Sturge–Weber disease.' *Seizures* 11: 145–150.

Synesthesia and Language

J. Ward, University of London, London, UK
R. Cytowic, Washington, DC, USA

Sharing a Greek root with anesthesia, meaning 'no perception,' synesthesia (*syn* 'together' + *aisthēsis* 'perception') means 'joined perception,' wherein two or more senses are coupled such that a voice, for example, is not only heard but also felt, seen, tasted, or even sensed in multiple modalities. Individuals who undergo such automatic crossmodal perceptions are called 'synesthetes.' For a long time, synesthesia endured reflexive hostility from critics, who insisted it could not possibly be real, at best conceding the subjective experience as nothing more than a learned association or metaphoric speech. Doubts regarding its genuineness as a neurological phenomenon have been thoroughly answered.

Cytowic (1997, 2002a) elucidated general properties: synesthetic experience is involuntarily elicited, consistent, memorable, affect laden, perceptually simple, and spatial. Stroop interference confirms that synesthetic associations are automatic (Smilek and Dixon, 2002) whereas lawful segregations such as perceptual grouping, popout, and stereoptic fusion confirm their early perceptual nature (Ramachandran and Hubbard, 2001a; Palmeri et al., 2002), and xenon, PET, and MRI methods have diversely shed light on the functional landscape of synesthetic experience. The phenomenon is more common than once believed, occurring in at least one in 2000 individuals by population prevalence estimate (Baron-Cohen et al., 1996) and ten times as many by less sound surveys. Forty percent have more than one type of synesthesia (polymodal), and females predominate by more than three to one.

Despite an overall impression that synesthetic experiences are perceptual, some two-thirds of instances are actually triggered by hearing, reading, or thinking of letters, integers, or words (**Table 1**).

We first review evidence that graphemes and phonemes – the building blocks of language – can trigger synesthetic experiences of color and taste. Secondly, we consider the interplay between synesthesia and concept formation. We conclude that synesthesia is not a mere curiosity in a few brains, but widespread with broad implications and possible use as an experimental probe for understanding metaphor and language evolution.

Colored Graphemes

The naming convention of putting synesthetic sense before its stimulus yields the terms 'color-lexical,' 'color-graphemic,' and 'color-phonemic' synesthesia. Graphemic is the most common type, wherein letters, numerals and, less often, punctuation, Braille, and musical symbols automatically evoke color sensations; phonemes trigger just 10% of cases. Individuals characteristically describe colors in precise detail (e.g., 'dirty, dull yellow' or 'deepest violet with sparkles'). Colors remain consistent over years, whereas nonsynesthetes asked to generate letter–color associations are only about 30% consistent after an interval of a week. Consistency over time is the most commonly used measure of authenticity. An example of colored graphemes is shown in **Figure 1**.

Word colors are variously derived from constituent graphemes. In some, the first letter dominates, thus *psychology*, *photograph*, and *poetry* all share the same color as the letter P. Other synesthetes base word colors on consonant or vowel composition. A double dissociation exists between consonant and vowel influences on word color (Ward et al., 2005), demonstrating how synesthesia can inform theories of language by suggesting, in this instance, that consonant–vowel coding may be an intrinsic property of graphemic representation (see also Ward and Romani, 2000).

Upper- and lower-case letters usually, but not always, evoke identical colors, whereas Arabic numerals are seen differently from Roman ones. Navon figures reveal attentional influences: for example, a black numeral 5 target

Table 1 Typological distribution

Graphemes → Color	68.8%
Time Units → Color	23.3%
Music Sounds → Color	19.2%
General Sounds → Color	14.0%
Musical Notes → Color	10.6%
Phonemes → Color	10.6%
Tastes → Color	7.1%
Smell → Color	6.9%
Pain → Color	6.3%
Sound → Taste	5.6%
Personalities → Color	4.8%
Touch → Color	3.9%
Temperatures → Color	2.7%
Vision → Taste	2.3%
Sound → Smell	1.6%
Vision → Sound	1.6%
Orgasms → Color	1.1%
Vision → Smell	1.1%
Vision → Touch	1.1%

A distribution of the types of synaesthesia based on 588 cases. Approximately 40% of individuals have multiple types of synaesthesia. For simplification, the table does not include types of synaesthesia affecting less than 1% of the sample.

Figure 1 An example of a synesthete's colored graphemes. (See color plate 37.)

composed of smaller 2s is seen as green, say, when the subject attends to the global configuration, but as orange when attending to its constituent 2s. As each synesthete has idiosyncratic associations, experiments must be tailored to the individual; nonetheless, regularities do exist. Synesthesia is also observed for scripts that do not use the Roman alphabet (see e.g., Mills et al., 2002).

Sir Francis Galton first noted synesthesia's strong heritability in 1883 (Baron-Cohen et al., 1996) and contemporary evidence suggests that mammalian neonates, including humans, are born with synesthesialike responses (Maurer, 1997). Yet graphemes and words are cultural symbols acquired later in life. Because synesthesia takes on an extraordinary variety of forms, any general theory must account for it in terms of both neural development and acquired experience (e.g., of one's own particular language).

Gustatory Phonemes

One can only speculate about the relative rarity of synesthesia induced by phonemic patterns (**Table 1**). Grapheme recognition exists from about age 3 to 4 years (Frith, 1985). Possibly, color-graphemic synesthesia begins as color-phonemic and then undergoes conceptual reorganization according to accepted phoneme-to-grapheme conversion rules and literacy acquisition. There is no *a priori* reason why infant synesthetic brains should not undergo the same reorganization pressures as others. Prospectively testing this conjecture would be difficult but not impossible.

Subject JIW tastes flavors in his mouth whenever he hears, reads, speaks, or thinks about words (Ward and Simner, 2003). *Safety* tastes of "toast lightly buttered," *Phillip* tastes of "oranges not quite ripe." As with other types of synesthesia, his sensations are stable over time and he is significantly more consistent than controls asked to generate or memorize word–food associations. Detailed analysis of his word–taste associations shows that words containing common patterns of phonemes (rather than graphemes) tend to produce the same taste. For example, *marriage*, *village*, and *college* all contain a common phonemic rhyme and all elicit a taste of sausage sandwiches. In contrast to color-graphemic synesthetes, there is no relationship between the taste assigned to graphemes and that assigned to words, and words sharing the first letter tend not to produce the same taste.

Notably, not only do words with similar phonemes evoke similar tastes but also the phonemes tend to be present in the form of the word corresponding to that taste. Thus, *Sydney* tastes of kidney, *auction* tastes of Yorkshire Pudding, *super* tastes of tomato soup, and so on. It is as if the phonological forms of food-related vocabulary have served as a template for deriving synesthetic associations for other words. This again points to the need for better understanding of the interplay between innate and environmental factors. This trend is found for all other known cases, comprising three cases from the historical literature and seven published contemporary cases (see Ward et al., 2005).

What biological reason could explain why graphemic properties preferentially elicit color whereas phonological ones elicit tastes? Ramachandran and Hubbard (2001a) proposed an 'adjacency theory.' In color-graphemic synesthesia, they emphasized that the grapheme recognition region on the left fusiform gyrus lies adjacent to area V4, which concerns color perception. Only left V4 activates in individuals who see color in response to spoken words (Nunn et al., 2002). Synesthetes might plausibly cross-activate these regions because of either unusual projections or lack of inhibition between them. Others have similarly referred to the assumed cross-activation of grapheme and color regions in synesthetes as a breakdown of modularity (Baron-Cohen et al., 1993) or as anomalous binding of modules (Cytowic, 2002b, 2003).

The gustatory cortex is bilaterally located in the frontal and parietal opercula and the insula. This is certainly not adjacent to the grapheme recognition region on the left fusiform gyrus, perhaps explaining why graphemic properties of words have little influence on synesthetic tastes. Nor are the Wernicke phonemic regions any closer. Even though all sensory modalities and the visceral milieu are represented in the insula, which also responds to both speech perception and production (Wise et al., 1999), adjacency alone appears inadequate as a general synesthetic mechanism. As the phonological associations derive from a single semantic category, 'food,' we may speculate on the necessary recruitment of additional brain areas (for example, anterior temporal regions supporting semantic memory). One inference follows that synesthesia does not localize to a discrete locus in the sense of classical neurology but rather is supported by a network of structures (Cytowic, 2002a, 2003).

Structure versus Meaning

We have so far concentrated on the internal structure of words – both graphemic and phonological. But what about meaning? Marks (1978) showed that systematic correspondences exist among dimensions of a given sense for synesthetes and nonsynesthetes alike. For example, both say that louder tones are brighter than soft tones, higher ones are smaller than lower ones, and that low tones are both larger and darker than high ones. The perceptual similarities that yield such orderly relationships among pitch, loudness, brightness, and size (**Figure 2**) can be described in psychophysical terms such as temporal coding or opponent processing, and may be rooted in fundamental similarities of phenomenal experience. For example, von Békésy (1959) first noted physiological similarities between hearing and touch. **Figure 3** is an illustrative painting of two bars of music from a synesthete, in which different shades, shapes and positions may correspond to different notes.

The demonstration of regular congruences between many (though not all) qualitative aspects of experience in different modalities has led to the idea of a continuum from perception → synesthesia → metaphor → abstract language, as perceptual similarities, synesthetic equivalences, and metaphoric identities in turn become available to the more abstract knowledge that is embodied in language (Cytowic, 2002b; Marks et al., 1987; Ramachandran and Hubbard, 2001b). For example, a tone of 2000 Hz may be labeled 'high' pitched and one of 100 Hz labeled 'low' pitched. Why do we use a spatial metaphor for pitch? The pitch–space association is not strictly linguistic, because Stroop-like interference exists between pitch and space in perceptual judgment tasks (Bernstein and Edelstein, 1971) and infants are sensitive to this correspondence (Wagner et al., 1981). In this instance, a basic crossmodal correspondence has entered into metaphorical language and has perhaps even influenced the development of Western musical notation (increasing pitch associated with higher position on the stave).

An even stronger claim is that these correspondences could have provided an early protolanguage during human evolution (Cytowic, 2002b; Ramachandran and Hubbard, 2001b). Humans seem able to agree crossculturally upon the assignment of certain symbols to represent objects (see, e.g., Davis, 1961) or upon how one domain can be expressed in terms of another (e.g., colors and emotions; D'Andrade and Egan, 1974). Kohler (1947) presented participants with two shapes and asked them to decide which one was called 'takete' and which one was called 'maluma.' Participants tended to associate rounder visual forms with

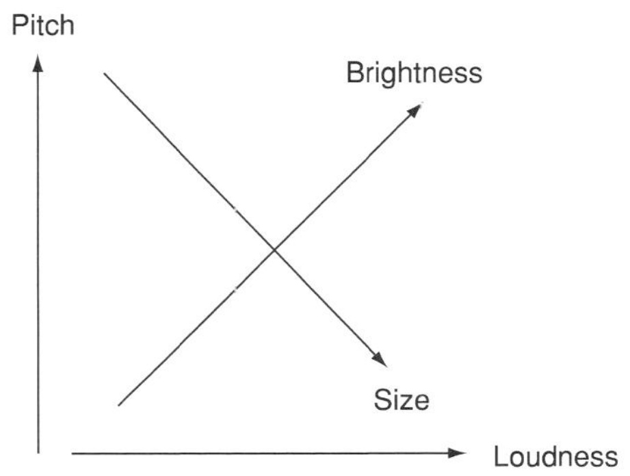

Figure 2 The higher the pitch and/or louder the sound the 'brighter' it is judged to be, and the lower the pitch and louder the sound the 'larger' it is judged to be.

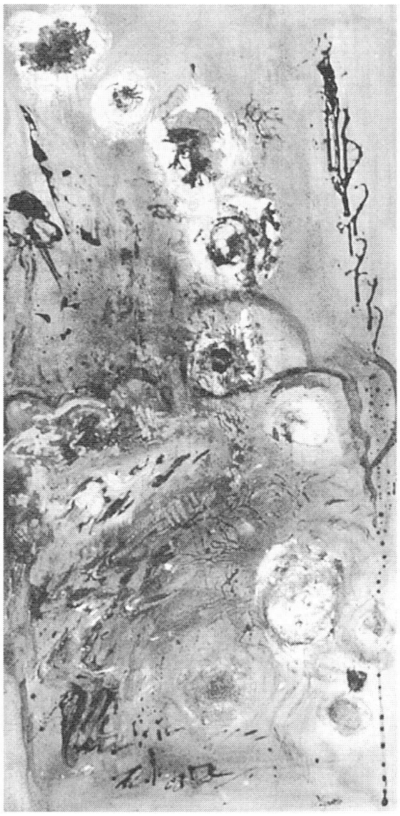

Figure 3 A painting of two bars of music from a music-to-color synesthete. (See color plate 38.)

'maluma,' and more angular forms with 'takete.' This trend appears to be crosscultural insofar as a group of people in Tanzania showed a similar associative bias.

Even though each synesthete's responses are idiosyncratic, their associations are not arbitrary. Although our understanding of this is incomplete, many researchers concur that the orderly topographic mapping characteristic of many cortical areas likely underlies this nonarbitrariness. Synesthetic associations may lay bare other properties of cognitive representation that may not be immediately apparent to the nonsynesthete. This is considered in the final section below.

Semantic Categories as Synesthetic Inducers

Certain semantic categories may have a privileged status in synesthetic induction. Such categories include numbers and other ordinal representations (days, months, etc.), vocabulary used to denote perceptual categories (e.g., color words, food names), and names of familiar people, which may be imbued with color via their affective status to the perceiver.

The term 'number form' is somewhat of a misnomer given that the configurations concern not only integers, but any concept involving serial order. Thus, the perceptual qualities of spatial location, shape, and, often, color become synesthetically joined to semantically ordered sets such as integers, months, days, the alphabet, shoe sizes, temperature, and so forth (see **Figures 4** and **5** for examples). Ordinality and configuration both suggest participation of the angular gyrus in this type of synesthesia. There is evidence that we all implicitly represent numbers in a visuospatial format: nonsynesthetes are faster at making judgments about small numbers (e.g., 1, 2) with their left and faster at making judgments about larger numbers (e.g., 8, 9) with their right hand (see, e.g., Dehaene et al., 1993).

A special category for synesthetes experiencing color is color names – red, yellow, green, etc. Gray et al. (2002) report that some synesthetes cannot inhibit a word's conceptual color. Thus, *red* may evoke a red synesthesia despite all other R words being green. In other cases, *red* may elicit a green synesthesia – a phenomenon the authors call the 'alien color effect.' It possibly arises from competition between different levels of representation (graphemic versus lexical-semantic) in the process of mapping synesthetic color.

Gustatory synesthetes presented with food names (e.g., *beef*, *cheese*) typically experience the appropriate sensation (e.g., the word *cheese* elicits a cheesy taste). There is little evidence for an 'alien taste effect' in which the word *cheese* would produce a taste of beef. Meaning appears more

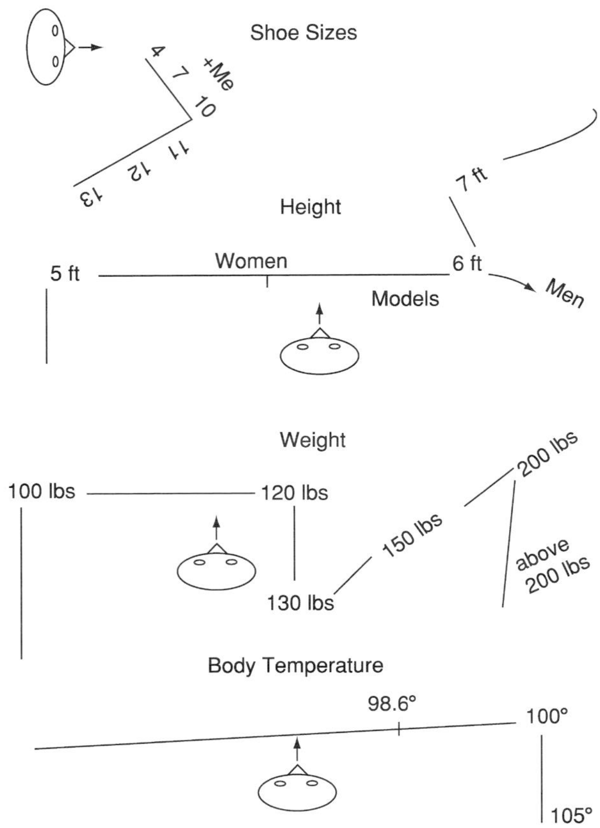

Figure 4 An example of spatial 'forms' for shoe sizes, height, weight, and body temperature, reprinted from Cytowic (2002a), MIT Press.

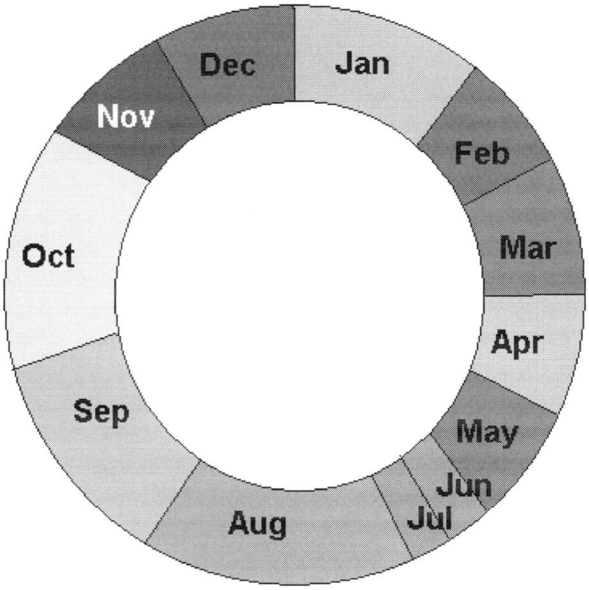

Figure 5 A colored spatial form for months of the year. (See color plate 39.)

operative in gustatory than in color synesthesia, and although phonological factors influence synesthetic taste, the phonemic patterns themselves derive from the words used to represent the semantic category of food, as pointed out above.

Another special semantic category is people's names (Ward, 2004; Weiss et al., 2001). GW experiences people's names as colored depending on whether she is personally familiar with anyone so christened. Using colors to describe people is a common feature of many natural languages (Asch, 1955). However, GW does so significantly more consistently than controls and shows Stroop-like interference when the names are printed in incongruous ink colors. Perhaps the emotional context determines both the presence of color and the particular color evoked by acquaintances. Indeed, GW reports synesthetic colors with other emotional words (e.g., hatred, marriage). This case again illustrates the interaction between language and more basic crossmodal correspondences between color and emotion.

In conclusion, there is likely to be a reciprocal relationship between synesthesia and language. At one level, the representational units of language (graphemes, phonemes, and words) may acquire a perceptual dimension in the minds and brains of synesthetes. At another level, the existence of seemingly universal crossmodal correspondences may guide both the formation of certain types of synesthetic correspondence (e.g., between number and space, pitch and lightness) and also the way that we speak about and conceptualize the world around us.

Bibliography

Asch, SE (1955). 'On the use of metaphor in the description of persons.' In: Werner, H (ed.) *On expressive language.* Worcester, MA: Clark University Press.

Baron-Cohen, S and Harrison, JE (eds.) (1997). *Synaesthesia: classic and contemporary readings.* Oxford: Blackwell.

Baron-Cohen, S, Harrison, J, Goldstein, LH, and Wyke, M (1993). 'Coloured speech perception: is synaesthesia what happens when modularity breaks down?' *Perception* 22: 419–426.

Baron-Cohen, S, Burt, L, Smith-Laittan, F, Harrison, J, and Bolton, P (1996). 'Synaesthesia: prevalence and familiality.' *Perception* 25: 1073–1079.

Bernstein, IH and Edelstein, BA (1971). 'Effects of some variations in auditory input upon visual choice reaction time.' *Journal of Experimental Psychology* 87: 241–246.

Cytowic, RE (1997). 'Synaesthesia: Phenomenology and neuropsychology: a review of current knowledge.' In: Baron-Cohen and Harrison (eds.).

Cytowic, RE (2002a). *Synesthesia: a union of the senses,* 2nd edn. Cambridge, MA: MIT Press.

Cytowic, RE (2002b). 'Touching tastes, seeing smells – and shaking up brain science.' *Cerebrum* 4: 7–26.

Cytowic, RE (2003). 'Synesthesia: anomalous binding of qualia and categories.' In: Adelman, G and Smith, BH (eds.) *Encyclopedia of neuroscience,* 3rd edn. New York: Elsevier.

D'Andrade, R and Egan, M (1974). 'The colors of emotions.' *American Ethnologist* 1: 49–63.

Davis, R (1961). 'The fitness of names to drawings: a cross-cultural study in Tanganyika.' *British Journal of Psychology* 52: 259–268.

Dehaene, S, Bossini, S, and Giraux, P (1993). 'The mental representation of parity and numerical magnitude.' *Journal of Experimental Psychology: General* 122: 371–396.

Frith, U (1985). 'Beneath the surface of developmental dyslexia.' In: Patterson, K and Marshall, J (eds.) *Surface dyslexia: neuropsychological and cognitive studies of phonological reading.* Hillsdale, NJ: Lawrence Erlbaum Associates.

Gray, JA, Chopping, S, Nunn, J, Parslow, D, Gregory, L, Williams, S, Brammer, MJ, and Baron-Cohen, S (2002). 'Implications of synaesthesia for functionalism.' *Journal of Consciousness Studies* 9: 5–31.

Kohler, W (1947). *Gestalt psychology,* 2nd edn. New York: LiveRight.

Marks, LE (1978). *The unity of the senses.* London: Academic Press.

Marks, LE, Hammeal, RJ, and Bornstein, MH (1987). 'Perceiving similarity and comprehending metaphor.' *Monographs of the Society for Research in Child Development* 52: 1–93.

Maurer, D (1997). 'Neonatal synaesthesia: implications for the processing of speech and faces.' In: Baron-Cohen, S and Harrison, JE (eds.).

Mills, CB, Viguers, ML, Edelson, SK, Thomas, AT, Simon-Dack, SL, and Innis, JA (2002). 'The color of two alphabets for a multilingual synesthete.' *Perception* 31: 1371–1394.

Nunn, JA, Gregory, LJ, Brammer, M, Williams, SCR, Parslow, DM, Morgan, MJ, Morris, RG, Bullmore, ET, Baron-Cohen, S, and Gray, JA (2002). 'Functional magnetic resonance imaging of synaesthesia: activation of V4/V8 by spoken words.' *Nature Neuroscience* 5(4): 371–375.

Palmeri, TJ, Blake, R, Marois, R, Flanery, MA, and Whetsell, W (2002). 'The perceptual reality of synesthetic colors.' *Proceedings of the National Academy of Science of the United States of America* 99: 4127–4131.

Ramachandran, VS and Hubbard, EM (2001a). 'Psychophysical investigations into the neural basis of synaesthesia.' *Proceedings of the Royal Society of London B* 268: 979–983.

Ramachandran, VS and Hubbard, EM (2001b). 'Synaesthesia: a window into perception, thought and language.' *Journal of Consciousness Studies* 8: 3–34.

Smilek, D and Dixon, MJ (2002). 'Towards a synergistic understanding of synaesthesia: combining current experimental findings with synaesthetes' subjective descriptions'. *Psyche 8*.

von Békésy, G (1959). 'Similarities between hearing and skin sensations.' *Psychological Review* 66: 1–22.

Wagner, S, Winner, E, Cicchetti, D, and Gardner, H (1981). '"Metaphorical" mapping in human infants.' *Child Development* 52: 728–731.

Ward, J (2004). 'Emotionally mediated synaesthesia.' *Cognitive Neuropsychology* 21: 761–772.

Ward, J and Romani, C (2000). 'Ortho-syllables and consonant–vowel encoding in acquired dysgraphia.' *Cognitive Neuropsychology* 17: 641–663.

Ward, J and Simner, J (2003). 'Lexical-gustatory synaesthesia: linguistic and conceptual factors.' *Cognition* 89: 237–261.

Ward, J, Simner, J, and Auyeung, V (2005). 'A comparison of lexical-gustatory and grapheme–colour synaesthesia.' *Cognitive Neuropsychology* 22: 28–41.

Weiss, PH, Shah, NJ, Toni, I, Zilles, K, and Fink, GR (2001). 'Associating colours with people: a case of chromatic-lexical synaesthesia.' *Cortex* 37: 750–753.

Wise, RJS, Greene, J, Buchel, C, and Scott, SK (1999). 'Brain regions involved in articulation.' *Lancet* 353: 1057–1061.

Relevant Websites

http://home.comcast.net/~sean.day/html/types.htm – Source of data for **Table 1**.

www.syn.ucl.ac.uk – research group site.

T

The Intracarotid Amobarbital Test (Wada Test) and Complementary Procedures to Evaluate Language Before Epilepsy Surgery

A. I. Tröster and K. R. Mohn, University of North Carolina, Chapel Hill, NC, USA

Introduction

The exact frequency of treatment-resistant or medically intractable epilepsy is unknown, but approximately 20–40% of individuals with epilepsy do not respond adequately to treatment with anticonvulsant medications (Aicardi & Shorvon, 1997). As one might imagine, uncontrolled seizures are both psychologically and socially disruptive. Patients often avoid situations in which having a seizure would prove embarrassing or dangerous and many such patients are either underemployed or unemployed. Surgical intervention affords patients with pharmacologically intractable epilepsy – most often temporal lobe epilepsy (TLE) – the opportunity to eliminate (or reduce) seizure activity. Although the potential benefits of surgery are appealing (e.g., increased quality of life and reduced cost of treatment), the removal of the tissue involved in seizures within the temporal cortex is not without risk as structures critical to language and memory are embedded within the temporal lobe. Therefore, to avoid postoperative language disruption or aphasia, the treatment team must ascertain whether the unoperated portions of the brain can support language. The most widely used method or "gold standard" for determining which side of the brain is relatively more important for language (language dominance) is the intracarotid amobarbital test (IAT), a method employing selective anesthetization of brain areas. This chapter details the basic elements of the IAT, its methodological pitfalls, and the advent of "less invasive" alternatives to determine hemispheric language dominance.

Historical Background

IAT was first described by Juhn Wada (1949), and thus, is often referred to as the "Wada test." Wada originally developed this technique to study the spread of epileptiform discharges (abnormal electrical activity) between the left and right halves of the brain in patients undergoing unilateral electroconvulsive therapy (a somewhat controversial treatment for mood disorders wherein a seizure is induced by electrodes placed on the patient's head). Wada observed that when the presumed language-dominant hemisphere was injected with amobarbital, and anesthetized, the result was a disruption of spoken language or expressive aphasia. Clinically, this pharmacological method of determining the language-dominant hemisphere allowed physicians to apply electroconvulsive therapy selectively to the contralateral (opposite, subdominant) hemisphere, thereby reducing the risk of cognitive dysfunction. Based on his observations of psychiatric patients, Wada reasoned that this technique might also be useful in determining hemispheric language dominance (and minimizing cognitive morbidity) in neurosurgical candidates. Working as a fellow with Rasmussen at the Montreal Neurological Institute, the procedure was first introduced there into the preoperative evaluation of persons with medically refractory epilepsy.

Current Clinical use of the IAT

At present, the IAT is generally used for three purposes in epilepsy surgery centers. The relative importance of these purposes (and the weight given to IAT test results in determinations with respect to whether or not to operate) differs, however, from center to center. These purposes are: First, determination of which brain hemisphere is dominant for language in order to reduce postoperative language impairment. Second, determination of the adequacy of memory performance in the unoperated hemisphere in order to predict which persons are at risk for amnesia (memory loss) after temporal lobe resection. Third, corroboration of the presumed side of seizure onset as determined by other diagnostic methods (e.g., electroencephalography (EEG), video EEG telemetry and ictal semiology, structural and functional radiography). This chapter focuses on the assessment of language lateralization. With respect to IAT in the evaluation of memory, there are several recent reviews that are suggested in the further readings section.

As is outlined in the next section, the IAT is an invasive procedure and neurological complications during the procedure are possible such as stroke, embolism, and transient global amnesia. This understandably results in controversy about its use. Despite the risks involved, the IAT remains an integral component of the comprehensive presurgical evaluation of patients with intractable epilepsy. A worldwide survey of 39 epilepsy centers between the years 1995 and 1997 indicated that over 2000 IAT procedures were performed with pre-surgical candidates (Lüders, 2001). Moreover, capacity to perform the IAT is one criterion required of epilepsy centers under the current National Association of Epilepsy Centers (NAEC, 2001) guidelines.

Rationale Underlying the IAT Procedure

In the simplest terms, the underlying rationale for employing the IAT procedure is to determine how well one hemisphere of the brain can support cognitive functions, such as language, when the other hemisphere is "put to sleep" or anesthetized. The most widely used anesthetic agent is sodium amobarbital, which crosses the blood–brain barrier (a functional obstruction in the brain's circulatory system which usually keeps harmful substances out of brain tissue) easily, allowing for a rapid anesthetic effect. The amobarbital is, however, not injected directly into the patient's head or neck, but rather, in most Wada test procedures, the drug is injected into the internal carotid artery (ICA) via a thin tube (catheter) inserted in the femoral artery (see **Figure 1** for an illustration of this procedure). Pharmacological inactivation of brain areas occurs in the regions of vascular supply of the ipsilateral (same-sided) anterior and middle cerebral arteries, and the anterior choroidal artery, thereby affecting areas of the frontal and temporal lobes pertinent to speech and language functions; the anterior one-third of the hippocampus is also affected. Thus, if the amobarbital is injected into the left ICA, the left anterior portions of the brain will be anesthetized. When supplementary information is desired about memory function, one can separately anesthetize the occipitoparietal and posterior mesiotemporal regions by similar injection into the posterior cerebral artery (PCA). Potential advantages of selective anesthesia of the PCA supplied areas include the possibility of assessing memory in the absence of significant sedation or aphasia, and the possibility of observing language-related impairments (such

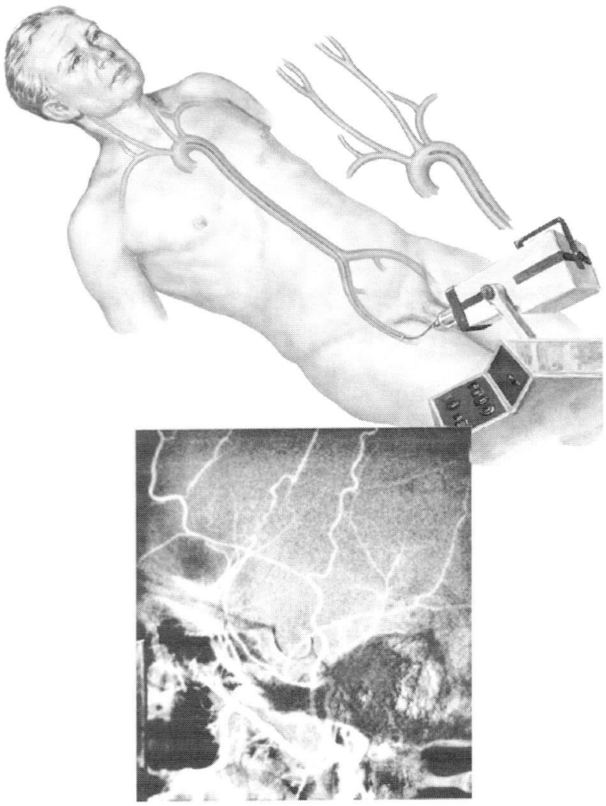

Figure 1 Femorocerebral angiography is the means by which amobarbital is delivered to the patient's ICA, allowing anesthetization of one cerebral hemisphere. *Source*: Reprinted from Frank H. Netter. The Netter Collection of Medical Illustrations – Nervous, © 1984, Elsevier Inc. All Rights Reserved.

as dyslexia) which may not be revealed by ICA injection. Many centers, however, feel that there is possibly a greater risk of stroke or vasospasm with PCA than with ICA injection, and that the additional risk of injury with multiple injections, outweighs the benefits of PCA and other "superselective" injections.

Because injection of amobarbital into an ICA temporarily inactivates only part of one cerebral hemisphere, the IAT allows one to assess independently the cognitive functions served by each hemisphere; that is, it is assumed that disruptions of language and memory during the IAT are a consequence of the temporary "lesioning" of the injected hemisphere, and that IAT mimics the effects that surgery on the injected hemisphere might have. As discussed above, this is particularly important in the surgical treatment of TLE, in which the tissue excised may be adjacent to or embedded within cortical tissue which supports language and memory functions. Moreover, because there is a greater incidence of atypical speech development (i.e., right hemisphere or bilateral representation) in those with known neurologic dysfunction, such as epilepsy, it is important to evaluate, rather

Box 1 Why do we need the Wada test: How typical is atypical language lateralization?

Language is lateralized in the left cerebral hemisphere for most humans. There are, however, a small percentage of individuals with "atypical" lateralization, meaning that language is represented either bilaterally or in the right hemisphere. There is disagreement among scholars about what atypical lateralization indicates. Some believe that it a rare variant of "normal," that is, without any prior neurologically relevant incidents (Knecht et al., 2000); others, however, contend that atypical lateralization generally stems from early brain insult or developmental aberration (Miller et al., 2003). Unfortunately, there are too few studies that have examined language lateralization in individuals with normal developmental and neurologic histories to adequately test either hypothesis. That being said, it is also well recognized that individuals with a history of early insult to the left hemisphere are more likely to develop atypical cerebral distribution of language (such as those with left TLE). This is attributed to the human brain's tendency to reorganize in order to accommodate language (albeit sometimes at the expense of other functions such as spatial abilities). For example, in examining the Wada results from 170 patients with known neurological insults before that age of 15, Miller et al. found that approximately 14% of these patients had atypical speech lateralization (Miller et al., 2005). Interestingly, they found that atypical language lateralization was more frequent in females (19 women versus 5 men). The authors suggest that this could indicate overall greater plasticity in the female brain.

Knecht, S, Deppe, M, Dräger, B, Bobe, L, Lohmann, H, Ringelstein, E-B, et al. (2000). Language lateralization in healthy right handers. *Brain* 123: 74–81.

Miller, JW, Dodrill, CB, Born, DE, and Ojemann, GA (2003). Atypical speech is rare in individuals with normal developmental histories. *Neurology* 60: 1042–1044.

Miller, JW, Jaydev, S, Dodrill, CB, and Ojemann, GA (2005). Gender differences in handedness and speech lateralization related to early neurologic insults. *Neurology* 65: 1974–1975.

than presume language lateralization in individual patients (**Box 1**).

Components of the IAT Procedure

IAT procedures vary from center to center, but often share several general features. Before the IAT, a baseline cognitive evaluation may be performed on the day of the IAT or in the preceding days. Such a baseline evaluation provides a basis for comparing cognitive test performances during the IAT relative to "normal" and familiarizes the patient with the test procedures. Before the IAT commences, angiography (radiographic visualization of cerebral blood vessels) is performed to identify any abnormalities or developmental variations in the blood vessels, and to determine whether there is a potential for cross-flow of amobarbital into the other hemisphere (as one might imagine, the presence of anesthetic in both hemispheres would complicate interpretation of test findings). A pre-IAT arteriogram is pictured in **Figure 2**.

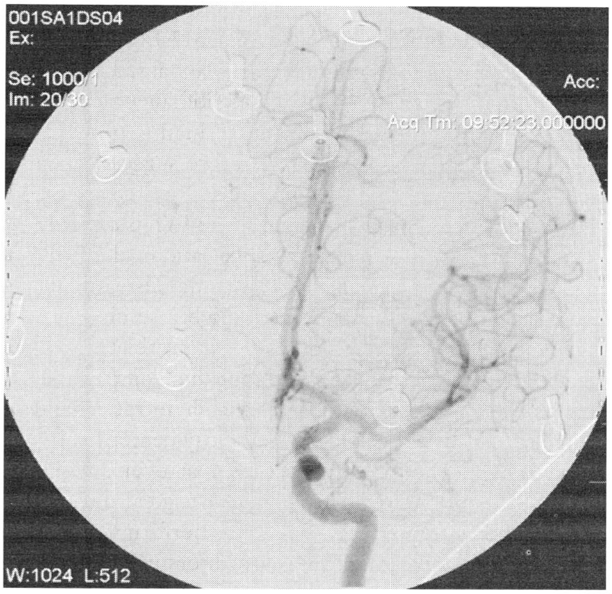

Figure 2 Arteriogram of ICA completed before Wada testing to visualize the patient's vasculature. This procedure helps the team determine whether there are any abnormalities in the vessels which would increase the risk of amobarbital flowing into unintended areas of the brain.

At centers evaluating memory and language lateralization, stimuli (e.g., words and objects) are often presented before the amobarbital injection so that recall of the items can be tested during the partial anesthesia. Most centers among those carrying out IATs on both cerebral hemispheres first examine the hemisphere for which surgery is planned, while others may inject the left ICA first (given the likelihood that language functions will be lateralized in the left hemisphere).

At the time of injection the supine patient is instructed to hold his or her arms straight up, and to begin counting. Upon injection, the patient's arm opposite the side of the injection becomes limp (if it does not, an inadequate dose of drug was injected, or the tip of the catheter may have slipped down resulting in drug delivery to the external carotid). When the language-dominant hemisphere is affected, a global aphasia typically results and speech is arrested or dysarthric (the patient will stop counting or slur). Because only one hemisphere is affected, the patient does not become unconscious (as in general anesthesia), but the extent of alteration in consciousness or somnolence, varies among patients.

There is significant variability among centers in the extent to which (and how) speech and language functions are tested (Benbadis, 2001). These functions are generally evaluated by tasks measuring expressive and receptive (comprehension) abilities including: automatic speech (e.g., months of the year), visual confrontation naming (e.g., objects, pictures, or colors), following verbal commands, repetition of words and phrases, and reading. The most widely used measure of language is naming to visual presentation (Rausch et al., 1993), because dysnomia (difficulty naming pictured or actual objects) is a feature of most aphasic syndromes.

The second ICA is injected 30 min to 24 h after the first injection to ensure that the amobarbital has cleared from the first-injected hemisphere. The test procedure is repeated, typically using test materials that are different (to avoid a practice effect), but comparable in difficulty to those used during the first injection.

Some IAT protocols involve the use of functional imaging (e.g., EEG or single photon emission computed tomography (SPECT)) to ascertain drug effect and to visualize the distribution of the amobarbital within the injected hemisphere. Protocols typically involve monitoring the extent of hemiparesis to determine the duration of the anesthesia (the effects of the anesthesia generally last between 90 and 300 s) and to ensure that assessment was conducted during adequate anesthesia (Benbadis, 2001) so that results are valid.

Problems and Considerations in IAT Protocol Administration and Interpretation

Although the rationale underlying the IAT seems straightforward, the performance and interpretation of the tests are not. Both the determination of speech dominance and that of memory representation are subjective. Protocols for the IAT vary from center to center, making meaningful data comparisons difficult. Additionally, given the invasiveness of the procedure, there is a lack of IAT data derived from subjects without neurological abnormalities that might alter lateralization and localization of functions (normals). Consequently, there are no data with which to compare the results of patients being considered for surgery. While there has been a recent push toward increasing the uniformity of the comprehensive pre-surgical evaluation (Haut et al., 2002), some important between-center differences still exist. The protocol differences which most affect interpretation of IAT language test results are discussed below. For a comprehensive review of intersite similarities and differences with regards to the IAT procedure, we direct the reader to a published survey of surgical centers at the *1992 Palm Desert International Epilepsy Conference* (Rausch et al., 1993).

Unilateral versus Bilateral IAT

The majority of centers conduct some form of the IAT before surgically removing the seizure focus, although some centers perform only unilateral IAT to either confirm left-hemisphere language presence or to establish the extent of dysfunction when the hemisphere slated for surgery is anesthetized (Rausch et al., 1993). Many would contend that candidates who undergo surgery based on results obtained from a single injection may be at greater risk for postoperative language deficits. Wellmer et al. (2005) argue, however, that bilateral IAT is often redundant. In their retrospective review of 107 cases having undergone bilateral IAT, results from the unilateral IATs performed on the side of intended surgery would have accurately lateralized language in over 80% of cases. The 20% of patients for whom unilateral IAT is insufficient to document language lateralization (in this case roughly 21 individuals) might argue, however, that avoiding potential loss of language is well worth the possible redundancy of bilateral IAT!

Drugs and Administration Methods

Most frequently, sodium amobarbital is the anesthetic agent of choice. Intermittent shortages in amobarbital, mostly due to manufacturing problems (Buchtel et al., 2002; Grote & Meador, 2005; Jones-Gotman et al., 2005) have lead to delays in scheduling epilepsy surgery. Consequently, and because in some countries amobarbital is not available, several other anesthetic agents have been explored. Methohexital (Brevital) has a similar anesthetic effect, but is shorter-lived and requires reinjection (Buchtel et al., 2002). Patients reportedly demonstrate less sedation with methohexital and less time is required between administrations to each hemisphere (both hemispheres can be evaluated within 2h). This drug is usually injected along with an anticonvulsant, however, because of its epileptogenic potential. Etomidate has also been successfully used in place of amobarbital. Jones-Gotman et al. (2005) described using a constant infusion of this similarly short-lived drug until critical language and memory tests have been completed. Infusion offers two advantages: avoiding changing levels of anesthesia between re-administrations and allowing examiners to determine the length of anesthesia. Unfortunately, renal insufficiency has been a reported side effect of etomidate, causing concerns about its use with critically ill patients (Grote & Meador, 2005). Another short-acting anesthetic used in the course of Wada testing is propofol (also used by some as an anesthetic during epilepsy surgery), although the incidence of complications may be unacceptably high, having occurred in 19 of 58 patients in one series (Mikuni et al., 2005).

Drug parameters – for example, amobarbital dosages and concentration, volume of amobarbital and saline mixture, rate of delivery (steady or incremental), and method of delivery (hand or automated injection) – also vary widely (Rausch et al., 1993) and can lead to discrepant findings. Drug parameters affect the extent and duration of anesthesia. For instance, a faster rate or larger volume of injection will typically perfuse a more extensive vasculature, thus compromising more domains of function whereas smaller volumes or slower rates of injection will lead to a greater concentration of drug in a smaller area, possibly leading to more intense or prolonged drug effects. Further, the desired level of anesthetization is the result of a fine balance; it should not be so sedating or persistent that the patient cannot respond, yet should be sufficient to create a condition modeling as closely as possible the effects of surgery. Finally, drug effect should be long enough to permit presentation of an adequate number of test items, allowing the evaluation team to make valid inferences from test results.

Interpretation of the IAT is predicated on the assumption that brain regions supplied by the anterior and middle cerebral arteries are inactivated during anesthesia. A neuro-imaging study by Hart et al. (1993) suggests that this assumption is not always warranted. Using SPECT, they found that there is great interindividual variability in the regions actually perfused by amobarbital after ICA injection. Further, there will occasionally be cross-filling of the contralateral hemisphere or the posterior circulation, leaving uncertainty about the neural bases of elicited responses and deficits (Hart et al., 1993). Although some centers estimate likelihood of cross-flow of amobarbital into the contralateral hemisphere or perfusion of other territories by amobarbital during angiography (which traces the perfusion of contrast media) before the IAT procedure, the correlation between contrast medium and amobarbital distribution is limited by differences in methods of injection (e.g., Rausch et al., 1993).

Determination of Adequacy of Anesthesia and Timing of Stimulus Presentation

Among many features of IAT protocols that differ across centers are the determinations of when an adequate drug effect to begin testing is evident, timing of stimulus presentation, types of stimuli and response formats, and criteria used to infer adequacy of language and memory. It is agreed across centers that presentation of stimuli is contingent on sufficient hemispheric anesthesia. In order to achieve a model of how the brain will function if tissue were removed, testing should occur during adequate drug effect. Unfortunately, the means of determining onset and duration of adequate anesthesia differ across centers. One or more of the following might be used to infer acceptable level of anesthesia: contralateral hemiparesis, grip strength, loss of antigravity tone, and marked EEG slowing. Yet, other centers simply present stimuli during a predetermined, standard interval (e.g., within the first 300 s) (Rausch et al., 1993). Even if sufficiency of anesthetic effect were similarly defined across centers, disagreement might remain about the timing of stimulus presentation. When the speech-dominant hemisphere is injected, and speech arrest ensues, some clinicians wait for speech to return before proceeding with testing (*note*: speech arrest may reflect motor speech disruption rather than language deficit and may also interfere with the ability to respond during memory testing), whereas others continue stimulus presentation regardless of speech difficulty.

Criteria to Establish Hemispheric Language Dominance

What exactly constitutes evidence for language representation in a cerebral hemisphere? Benbadis et al. (1998) described two popular ways of determining hemispheric dominance (often referred to as the "laterality index") during IAT. One method is based on speech arrest alone and another is based on language task performance. In the calculation relying on speech arrest, duration of muteness after injection of each hemisphere is calculated and then compared across the two hemispheres by an equation: $(L-R)/(L+R)$. Using this method, the laterality index varies from -1 (strong right hemisphere dominance) to $+1$ (strong left hemisphere dominance). Alternatively, laterality indices based on language performance first calculate a percentage correct score on a battery of language tests obtained during anesthetization of each hemisphere (using tests evaluating, e.g., comprehension of commands, naming, phrase repetition, and sentence reading). The following equation is then employed ($P_L - P_R$), where P represents the percentage correct score after left and right hemisphere injections (testing the right and left hemisphere functions, respectively). Using this approach, scores vary from -100 (strong right hemisphere dominance) to $+100$ (strong left hemisphere dominance).

Although these two methods appear generally comparable, Benbadis et al. (1998) warn that this is not the case. In a study of 21 patients, there was no significant correlation between the laterality index as calculated by speech arrest and the laterality index as calculated by performances on measures of language ability. Benbadis et al. did, however, find a strong relationship between lateral dominance as determined by language performance (the latter equation) and dominance as visualized by functional magnetic resonance imaging (fMRI). This suggests that speech arrest might not be a sufficient criterion for determining language dominance.

IAT in Pediatric Populations

Research exploring the IAT in pediatric populations is extremely limited and little has been published on this topic (most attention has been focused on less invasive techniques such as fMRI). Discussion of IAT in children and adolescents is frequently couched in terms of adult research findings. The few published empirical studies suggest that the IAT protocol might need to be modified

Box 2 What can the IAT tell us about language representation in bilingual individuals?

Several studies have shown that the interhemispheric organization of both languages in bilingual individuals is complementary, that is, hemispheric dominance for the two languages is similar (Berthier et al., 1990; Gomez-Tortosa et al., 1995). Intrahemispheric organization of the native and second languages, however, is likely different. Berthier (1990) described a case study in which a bilingual patient demonstrated the ability to speak his second language (English) 1 min before he was able to speak his native tongue (Spanish) after injection of amobarbital into the left middle cerebral artery. Based on this observation, the author speculated that the second language might be organized within the central sylvian core, whereas the first language might be represented in more distal perisylvian regions. Electrical stimulation studies (for review, see Ojemann, 1983) offer an opposing view, however, demonstrating that object naming in the second language tends to be more peripheral from the sylvian fissure and represented in a larger area. Thus, one might conclude, assuming that amobarbital effects dissipate earlier in more distant areas, that Berthier et al.'s (1990) findings actually indicate the first language to be more centrally located.

Berthier, ML, Starkstein, SE, Lylyk, P, and Leiguarda, R (1990). Differential recovery of languages in a bilingual patient: A case study using selective amytal test. *Brain and Language* 38: 449–453.

Gomez-Tortosa, E, Martin, EM, Gaviria, M, Charbel, F, and Ausman, JI (1995). Selective deficit of one language in a bilingual patient following surgery in the left perisylvian area. *Brain and Language* 48: 320–325.

Ojemann, GA (1983). Brain organisation for language from the perspective of electrical stimulation mapping. *Behavioral and Brain Sciences* 6: 189–230.

for children and adolescents. Szabo and Wyllie (1993) noted that language dominance was established in all children who had bilateral injections and at least borderline intelligence, but in only about half of the children with mental retardation. Westerveld et al. (1994) reported more encouraging data. Using amobarbital doses of 100 or 130 mg, they considered IAT to yield unambiguous data concerning language dominance in children as young as 7 years.

Validation and Reliability Studies

Despite differences in protocols, a multicenter study of seven epilepsy centers found a high degree of interrater reliability for language lateralization with IAT (Haut et al., 2002) and the validity of the IAT to establish hemispheric language dominance is well accepted (Dodrill, 1993). The interesting question raised is whether it is sufficient to carry out the IAT to avoid postoperative language deficits? Specifically one might ask whether cases undergoing IAT also require intra-operative cortical mapping using electrical stimulation, and whether this leads to better outcomes (fewer postoperative language or cognitive declines) than in cases not undergoing language mapping. Among left-hemisphere language-dominant patients who underwent IAT and then conservative left temporal lobe resection without language mapping, no significant postoperative language decrements were observed by Davies et al. (1995). In a follow-up study of 162 patients who underwent temporal lobectomy without mapping, Hermann et al. (1994) observed a postoperative dysnomia in 7% of left lobectomy patients. Moreover, an association between later age at onset of epilepsy and postoperative dysnomia was observed in the left lobectomy group undergoing language mapping. These findings suggest that mapping after IAT may still be a prudent course of action (even though most patients fare well) given that a subgroup of individuals do experience postoperative dysnomia. Furthermore, intraoperative mapping may be especially important in persons with bilateral language representation, because such patients are more likely than left-hemisphere language-dominant patients to have multiple, non-contiguous language areas in the left hemisphere (Jabbour et al., 2005). Intraoperative right hemisphere language mapping may also be helpful in identifying what are assumed to be accessory language areas in those persons with IAT-demonstrated bilateral language representation (Jabbour et al., 2005).

Supplementary and Alternative Techniques for Establishing Language Lateralization

Some centers consider surface EEG during IAT helpful in locating and monitoring the slowing of brain activity after amobarbital injection. Some centers also perform the IAT after intracranial electrode implantation so as to permit EEG recording directly from subdural grid and/or strip electrodes, as well as deep electrodes implanted in the mesial temporal lobes. Electrocortical stimulation mapping of language cortex is also frequently employed before resection, especially when IAT results are ambiguous (Jabbour et al., 2005; Kho et al., 2005).

Because of the IAT's invasive nature and limitations, many clinicians and researchers have explored the use of alternative technologies, such as functional neuroimaging, to provide information about language lateralization in surgical candidates. For example, studies have been published examining the usefulness and accuracy of lateralization determination with near-infrared spectroscopy (NIS), magnetoencephalography (MEG), and positron emission tomography (PET). All of these techniques rely on computing metabolic or blood flow changes correlated with performance of language tasks. Among the studies that compared functional imaging with results of IAT,

Box 3 The Wada test and American Sign Language

As in investigations involving bilingual persons, sign language studies in non-deaf individuals also indicate interhemispheric organization of signed and spoken language to be similar, at least in that the same hemisphere is dominant for both forms of communication. The existence of subtle interhemispheric differences in the organization of signed and spoken language, however, has not been settled by amobarbital studies (instead we would direct the reader to numerous studies published using techniques such as cortical stimulation mapping, fMRI, and PET). On the one hand, some studies have found that sign language is characterized by greater bilateral representation than spoken language (e.g., Homanet al., 1982). In contrast, several other studies have found that the interhemispheric organization of signed and spoken language to be complementary and highly similar (e.g., Mateer et al., 1984).

Because a substantial portion of deaf individuals apparently have experienced some cortical reorganization (Wolff et al., 1994), reports of IAT results in deaf individuals are of particular significance. That is, such studies provide tentative data that speak to the issue of whether findings from normal-hearing individuals concerning the organization of sign language apply to deaf individuals. Complete left-hemisphere dominance has been found in a right-handed individual for American Sign Language, signed English, and finger spelling (Wolff et al., 1994). Thus, evidence of bilateral representation for sign language was not found.

Homan RW, Criswell, E, Wada, JA and Ross, ED (1982). Hemispheric contributions to manual communication (signing and finger-spelling). *Neurology* 32: 1020–1023.

Mateer, CA, Rapport, RL, and Kettrick, C (1984). Cerebral organization of oral and signed language responses: Case study evidence from amytal and cortical stimulation studies. *Brain and Language* 21: 123–135.

Wolff, AB, Sass, KJ, and Keiden, J (1994). Case report of an intracarotid amobarbital procedure performed for a deaf patient. *Journal of Clinical and Experimental Neuropsychology* 16: 15–20.

agreement ranged from 88% to 91% (Hunter et al., 1999; Bowyer et al., 2005).

The most widely explored potential alternative to the IAT is fMRI. fMRI allows visualization of changes in the flow of oxygenated blood within neural tissue. In the brain, changes in blood oxygen level have been shown to be related to neural activity. Consequently, fMRI is often used to infer localization of brain activity by comparing the location and extent of blood oxygenation while persons are engaged in particular language tasks versus activity observed during rest or a comparison task. In general, fMRI indicates hemispheric dominance through the use of laterality indices that compare the ratio of pixels (small areas within an image) activated during language tasks in one hemisphere to those in the other hemisphere. Hemispheric dominance for a function can be also inferred from comparisons of the activation of specific, homologous regions in each hemisphere (often referred to as "regions of interest" or "ROIs"). It remains unclear which method of inferring language dominance from fMRI yields results more consistent with those of the IAT and electrical stimulation.

Table 1 The Wada Test versus fMRI

	Wada	*fMRI*
Advantages	Mimics temporary lesion Well-established as valid measure of hemispheric language dominance	Non-invasive procedure May establish intrahemispheric language organization Less time restraint, allowing for more extensive batteries
Disadvantages	Invasive procedure Short length of anesthesia precludes extensive batteries Lack of standardization among protocols No normative database with healthy controls	Lack of standardization among protocols Difficulty statistically determining essential versus non-essential language areas Less effective for determining lateralization in individuals with mixed or right dominance

fMRI has several advantages over IAT (see **Table 1**). Most importantly, fMRI is non-invasive and therefore does not pose physical risks to patients. This is a particularly attractive feature when dealing with medically compromised patients and pediatric populations. fMRI also allows for repeated test sessions, if necessary, and there are fewer drawbacks to creating a normative database with healthy controls, given less procedural risks. Additionally, most major medical centers have fMRI capability, making it a more appealing alternative than other functional technologies such as PET. Deblaere et al. (2004) reported the ability to determine language lateralization with relatively low field strength (1 Tesla magnetic force), a field strength available in many clinical settings. Finally, fMRI potentially imposes less time constraints (e.g., one is not restricted to 300 s or less of anesthetization), allowing use of a more extensive battery of tests that evaluate more language functions.

In addition to the procedural advantages, fMRI can provide a visual estimate of the cortical areas involved in language for any given individual. Thus, fMRI allows for an intrahemispheric language map that can help determine the functionality of specific areas targeted for surgical resection. This is particularly useful given that usually limited amounts of tissue are removed, rather than the entire temporal lobe or hemisphere. fMRI can also provide information about the spectrum or continuum of lateralization which is not as well characterized by IAT.

Initial studies comparing IAT and fMRI have been promising, with language lateralization concordance rates exceeding 90% (Binder et al., 1996; Lehéricy et al., 2000; Woermann et al., 2003). Benke et al. (2006) found fMRI to accurately identify language dominance in persons with right TLE; however, concordance rates were poor for individuals with left TLE and left or mixed hemispheric language dominance.

The use of fMRI for determining language lateralization is not without criticism. Most importantly, fMRI cannot mimic a lesion like IAT. Thus, it is difficult if not impossible to ascertain whether unoperated tissue can truly support language. Moreover, functional imaging is based on the assumption that "active areas" are responsible for or involved in concurrent behaviors (such as producing or comprehending language). While many of the associations observed between activities in specific brain regions and particular behaviors in functional imaging are consistent with our knowledge of brain–behavior relationships (often gleaned from lesion studies), functional imaging inferences are based on a correlation from which causation cannot be inferred. In short, when a portion of the brain "lights up" during a specific task on fMRI, we cannot be entirely sure that the association is meaningful. Loring et al. (2002) further explain the challenge of distinguishing between essential and nonessential areas using fMRI in analyzing the location and parameters of "eloquent cortex" in eight adults. The authors noted that they were less likely to find random activations during language tasks if more conservative statistical methods were employed (i.e., raising the threshold for statistical significance). However, using these conservative methods they were also less likely to find activations among areas known to be associated with language functions. Another issue is how to interpret *decreased* activation during language tasks compared to control tasks.

Lack of standardized test batteries to assess language dominance is also a criticism of fMRI studies. Among published studies, the tasks employed are varied and range from semantic decision tasks (i.e., distinguishing between words and non-words) (Binder et al., 1996) to covert word generation (i.e., thinking of as many words from a certain category as possible within 1 min) (Woermann et al., 2003), making comparisons between protocols difficult. Further, lack of standardized test batteries presents a challenge similar to IAT procedures: which task or tasks best demonstrate language dominance? Rutten et al. (2002) have suggested using a combined analysis of several language tasks to improve detection of hemispheric dominance. The authors reported more reliable and robust concordance with IAT findings using combined task analysis compared with analysis of any individual language task (Rutten et al., 2002).

Challenges and Future Directions

So one might ask: what is the future of the Wada test? Will it be replaced by functional imaging for determination of language lateralization? Certainly, fMRI is a safer technology than IAT, but does it afford less risk of language loss postoperatively? Data suggest a high concordance rate between fMRI and IAT, but mostly in cases of left hemisphere language dominance. Unfortunately, if concordance rates are examined separately for persons with right, left, and mixed hemispheric language representations, fMRI struggles to accurately define language representation in persons with right and mixed dominance. It is possible that functional imaging will surpass the accuracy of IAT in determining language lateralization (it already provides important information about intrahemispheric language mapping); however, it will require the establishment of a standardized protocol. While researchers may achieve this goal, they will be hard pressed to replace the one most impressive feature of the IAT: glimpsing into the patient's future by inflicting a temporary lesion.

References

Aicardi, J and Shorvon, SD (1997). Intractable epilepsy. In: Engels, J and Pedley, TA (eds.) *Epilepsy: A comprehensive textbook*, pp. 1325–1331. Philadelphia, PA: Lippincott-Raven.

Benbadis, SR (2001). Intracarotid amobarbital test to define language lateralization. In: Lüders, HO and Comair, YG (eds.) *Epilepsy surgery*, 2nd edn., pp. 525–529. Philadelphia, PA: Lippincott Williams & Wilkins.

Benbadis, SR, Binder, JR, Swanson, SJ, Fischer, M, Hammeke, TA, Morris, GL, et al. (1998). Is speech arrest during Wada testing a valid method for determining hemispheric representation of language? *Brain and Language,* 65, pp 441–446.

Benke, T, Koylu, B, Visani, P, Kamer, E, Brenneis, C, Bartha, L, et al. (2006). Language lateralization in temporal lobe epilepsy: A comparison between fMRI and the Wada test. *Epilepsia* 47: 1308–1319.

Binder, JR, Swanson, SJ, Hammeke, TA, Morris, GL, Mueller, WM, Fischer, M, et al. (1996). Determination of language dominance using functional MRI: A comparison with the Wada test. *Neurology* 46: 978–984.

Bowyer, SM, Moran, JE, Weiland, BJ, Mason, KM, Greenwald, ML, Smith, BJ, et al. (2005). Language laterality determined by MEG mapping with MR-FOCUSS. *Epilepsy and Behavior* 6: 235–241.

Buchtel, HA, Passaro, EA, Selwa, LM, Deveikis, J, and Gomez-Hassan, D (2002). Sodium methohexital (Brevital) as an anesthetic in the Wada test. *Epilepsia* 43: 1056–1061.

Davies, KG, Maxwell, RE, Beniak, TE, Destafney, E, and Fiol, ME (1995). Language function after temporal lobectomy without stimulation mapping of cortical function. *Epilepsia* 36: 130–136.

Deblaere, K, Boon, PA, Vandenmaele, P, Tieleman, A, Vonck, K, Vingerhoets, G, et al. (2004). MRI language dominance assessment in epilepsy patients at 1.0 T: Region of interest analysis and comparison with intracarotid amytal testing. *Neuroradiology* 46: 413–420.

Dodrill, CB (1993). Preoperative criteria for identifying eloquent brain: Intracarotid amytal for language and memory testing. *Neurosurgery Clinics of North America* 4: 211–216.

Grote, CL and Meador, K (2005). Has amobarbital expired? Considering the future of the Wada. *Neurology* 65: 1692–1693.

Hart, J, Lewis, PJ, Lesser, RP, Fisher, RS, Monsein, LH, Schwerdt, P, et al. (1993). Anatomic correlates of memory from intracarotid amobarbital injections with technetium Tc 99 mm

hexamethylpropyleneamine oxime SPECT. *Archives of Neurology* 50: 745–750.
Haut, SR, Berg, AT, Shinnar, S, Cohen, HW, Bazil, CW, Sperling, MR, et al. (2002). Interrater reliability among epilepsy centers: Multicenter study of epilepsy surgery. *Epilepsia* 43: 1396–1401.
Hermann, BP, Wyler, AR, Somes, G, and Clement, L (1994). Dysnomia after left anterior temporal lobectomy without functional mapping: Frequency and correlates. *Neurosurgery* 35: 52–56.
Hunter, KE, Blaxton, TA, Bookheimer, SY, Figlozzi, C, Gaillard, WD, Grandin, C, et al. (1999). ^{15}O water positron emission tomography in language localization: A study comparing positron emission tomography visual and computerized region of interest analysis with the Wada test. *Annals of Neurology* 45: 662–665.
Jabbour, RA, Hempel, A, Gates, JR, Zhang, W, and Risse, G (2005). Right hemisphere mapping in patients with bilateral language. *Epilepsy and Behavior* 6: 587–592.
Jones-Gotman, M, Sziklas, V, Djordjevic, J, Dubeau, F, Gotman, J, Angle, M, et al. (2005). Etomidate speech and memory test (eSAM): A new drug and improved intracarotid procedure. *Neurology* 65: 1723–1729.
Kho, KH, Leijten, FSS, Rutten, G, Vermeulen J, van Rijen, P, and Ramsey, NF (2005). Discrepant findings for Wada test and functional magnetic resonance imaging with regard to language function: Use of electrocortical stimulation mapping to confirm results. *Journal of Neurosurgery* 102: 169–173.
Lehéricy, S, Cohen, L, Bazin, B, Samson, S, Giacomini, E, Rougetet, L, et al. (2000). Functional MR evaluation of temporal and frontal language dominance compared with the Wada test. *Neurology* 54: 1625–1633.
Loring, DW, Meador, KJ, Allison, JD, Pillai, JJ, Lavin, T, Lee, GP, et al. (2002). Now you see it, now you don't: Statistical and methodological considerations in fMRI. *Epilepsy and Behavior* 3: 539–547.
Lüders, HO (2001). Protocols and outcome statistics from epilepsy surgery centers. In: Lüders, HO and Comair, YG (eds.) *Epilepsy surgery,* 2nd edn., pp. 973–977. Philadelphia, PA: Lippincott Williams & Wilkins.
Mikuni, N, Takayama, M, Satow, T, Yamada, S, Hayashi, N, Nishida, N, et al. (2005). Evaluation of adverse effects in intracarotid propofol injection for Wada test. *Neurology* 65: 1813–1816.
Rausch, R, Silfevenius, H, Wieser, H, Dodrill, C, Meador, K, and Jones-Gotman, M (1993). Intraarterial amobarbital procedures. In: Engel, J (ed.) *Surgical treatment of the epilepsies,* 2nd edn., pp. 341–357. New York: Raven Press.
Rutten, GJM, Ramsey, NF, van Rijen, PC, Alpherts, WC, and van Veelen, CWM (2002). fMRI-determined language lateralization in patients with unilateral or mixed language dominance according to the Wada test. *Neuroimage* 17: 447–460.
Szabo, CA and Wyllie, E (1993). Intracarotid amobarbital testing for language and memory dominance in children. *Epilepsy Research* 15: 239–246.
The National Association of Epilepsy Centers (NAEC) (2001). Guidelines for essential services, personnel, and facilities in specialized epilepsy centers in the United States. *Epilepsia* 42: 804–814.
Wada, J (1949). A new method for the deterioration of the side of the cerebral speech dominance: A preliminary report on the intracarotid injection of sodium amytal in man. *Igaku Seibutsugaku* 14: 221–222.
Wellmer, J, Fernandez, G, Linke, DB, Urbach, H, Elger, CE, and Kurthen, M (2005). Unilateral intracarotid amobarbital procedure for language lateralization. *Epilepsia* 46: 1764–1772.
Westerveld, M, Zawacki, T, Sass, KJ, Spencer, S, Novelly, RA, and Spencer, DD (1994). Intracarotid amytal procedure evaluation of hemispheric speech and memory function in children and adolescents. *Journal of Epilepsy* 7: 295–302.
Woermann, FG, Jokeit, H, Luerding, R, Freitag, H, Schulz, R, Guertler, M, et al. (2003). Language lateralization by Wada test and fMRI in 100 patients with epilepsy. *Neurology* 61: 699–701.

Further Reading

The following two references are suggested for the reader who has an interest in learning more about the use of the Wada test for memory lateralization.
Akanuma, N, Koutroumanidis, M, Adachi, N, Alarcon, G, and Binnie, CD (2003). Presurgical assessment of memory-related brain structures: The Wada test and functional neuroimaging. *Seizure* 12: 346–358. Akanuma et al. focus on the role of the Wada test in pre-surgical evaluation of memory in epilepsy candidates. They also explore the use of other functional imaging techniques in identifying extratemporal regions important in memory functioning.
Simkins-Bullock, J (2000). Beyond speech lateralization: A review of the variability, reliability, and validity of the intracarotid amobarbital procedure and its nonlanguage uses in epilepsy surgery candidates. *Neuropsychology Review* 10: 41–74. Simkins-Bullock provides a comprehensive review of the Wada for nonlanguage purposes (such as memory evaluation), addressing the future of the IAT along with her predictions for future research.

Transcranial Magnetic Stimulation (TMS) as a Tool for Studying Language

K. E. Watkins, University of Oxford, Oxford, UK
J. T. Devlin, University College London, London, UK

Introduction

Until the advent of transcranial magnetic stimulation (TMS), interfering with brain function was limited to studies of patients. The pioneering work of Wilder Penfield and others in the areas of electrocorticography and Wada testing were critical in extending our understanding of the neural basis of language. Limited conclusions could be drawn from these studies, however, as they were based on patients with neurological conditions usually of long standing, which may have altered the brain organization due to recovery or compensatory processes. TMS offers an extension and advancement of these early methods by allowing us to examine language organization in normal healthy individuals. This non-invasive technique tests the *necessity* of an area for a cognitive task

Box 1 What is transcranial magnetic stimulation?

A transcranial magnetic stimulation (TMS) coil is comprised of windings of metal wire encased in plastic and connected to a capacitor. A brief electric current is discharged through the wires, producing a rapidly changing magnetic field orthogonal to the plane of the coil. When placed over the scalp, the field is unimpeded by the skull, fluid and meninges surrounding the brain and, by simple electromagnetic induction, causes a current to flow in neurons lying parallel to the plane of the coil. In the cortex, this is most likely to cause spiking or depolarization in axons whose orientation is tangential to the cortical surface, that is those lying parallel to the surface, or running perpendicular to the cortical thickness on the crown of a gyrus or bank of a sulcus (Rothwell, 1997).

A single pulse of TMS over the primary motor or visual cortex can be used to elicit positive phenomena such as motor-evoked potentials (MEPs) or phosphenes, respectively (Barker et al., 1985). When delivered to other cortical regions, TMS can disrupt neural activity by introducing noise into the local circuitry and interfering with behavior. These negative effects are typically measured by changes in error rates or response latencies (Walsh & Rushworth, 1999).

With high-frequency repetitive TMS (rTMS), trains of pulses are delivered at fixed inter-pulse intervals of between 20 and 200 ms (50–5 Hz frequency) disrupting function for the duration of the stimulation, on the order of seconds or less. This is useful if we are unsure when precisely to stimulate. Once an area has been shown to be involved in a particular cognitive function or behavior, more precise relationships with time can be determined using single pulses. Low-frequency rTMS (1 Hz or less) delivered for several minutes (typically 10–15), disrupts the function of a brain area and these effects outlast the stimulation itself usually for durations similar to the stimulation time.

Barker, AT, Jalinous, R, and Freeston, IL (1985). Non-invasive magnetic stimulation of human motor cortex. *Lancet* 1(8437): 1106–1107.

Rothwell, JC (1997). Techniques and mechanisms of action of transcranial stimulation of the human motor cortex. *Journal of Neuroscience Methods* 74(2): 113–122.

Walsh, V, and Rushworth, MFS (1999). The use of transcranial magnetic stimulation in neuropsychological testing. *Neuropsychologia* 37: 125–135.

unlike others that measure the *correlation* between brain function and a cognitive task either in space, for example, functional magnetic resonance imaging (FMRI) and positron emission tomography (PET), or in time, for example, electroencephalograms (EEG) and magnetoencephalography (MEG). TMS is often referred to as providing a "virtual" lesion, the effects of which are brief and reversible. In addition to interfering with brain function, it can provide new correlates of brain function such as measures of cortical excitability; these measures may be more sensitive to brain function than measures of blood flow and correlated electrical activity.

Here, we summarize the use of TMS in studies of the cognitive and neural basis of language processing. We begin with TMS studies of hemispheric dominance for language and use these to describe the various ways in which TMS is applied (see **Box 1**). This introductory section on language dominance is followed by TMS studies of the classic language circuit, which have examined the role of Wernicke's area in lexical processing, and Broca's area in phonology and semantics. We then describe studies that have explored areas outside this classic circuit examining the role of the motor system in speech perception and differences in processing of nouns and verbs following motor and prefrontal cortex stimulation. Finally, in conjunction with other imaging techniques, we describe how TMS is being used to assess reorganization of function in the brains of patients with aphasia.

Assessing Hemispheric Specialization for Language with TMS

Some of the earliest uses of TMS in the study of language assessed hemispheric specialization, lateralization or "dominance." This is unsurprising given the need for a non-invasive replacement for the sodium amobarbital (or Wada) technique used in patients who are about to undergo neurosurgery (see Chapter 3, this volume). These studies provide a useful introduction to the different ways in which TMS can be used both to interfere with brain function and to provide a correlate of the involvement of a brain area in a function (see **Box 1**).

High-Frequency rTMS

In the first TMS studies of language dominance, high-frequency rTMS was applied in 10-s trains of different frequencies over left and right hemisphere language regions (Pascual-Leone et al., 1991). Left inferior frontal gyrus (LIFG) stimulation caused speech interruption in all patients; none had speech problems during right hemisphere stimulation. One patient described the effect of TMS as follows: "I could move my mouth and I knew what I wanted to say, but I could not get the numbers to my mouth" (Pascual-Leone et al., 1991, p. 699). The concordance between the results of TMS and Wada testing in these first six patients gave great confidence to the use of TMS for non-invasive studies of language lateralization. Unfortunately, this early success has not been consistently replicated calling into question the reliability of TMS as an alternative to Wada testing.

For example, recent studies of speech lateralization in healthy participants (Stewart et al., 2001; Aziz-Zadeh et al., 2005) demonstrate that both hemispheres may contribute to the execution of speech with additional areas in the left hemisphere involved in other language production processes. Stimulation over posterior inferior frontal sites in the left or right hemisphere results in speech arrest in association with an electromyographic (EMG) response (i.e., a muscle twitch) in the face muscles. This suggests that the motor representations of the articulators are stimulated.

In contrast, stimulation over a more anterior location in the left, but not right, inferior frontal cortex also produces speech arrest but no EMG response. This suggests that stimulation of Broca's area itself results in impaired processes required for language production.

Low-Frequency rTMS

Language lateralization varies across individuals and is particularly important consideration for studies of patients with aphasia. Low-frequency rTMS was used to assess the effects of this variation in a group of normal healthy participants (Knecht et al., 2002). Hemispheric lateralization during word generation was initially established using a blood flow method called transcranial Doppler ultrasonography. One-Hz rTMS stimulation (for 10 min at 110% of the motor threshold (MT); see **Box 2**) over Wernicke's area increased response times on a word-picture matching tasks in individuals with left, but not right, language dominance as established by transcranial Doppler ultrasonography. Conversely, stimulation over the right hemisphere homolog of Wernicke's area increased response times for those with right, but not left hemisphere dominance. Importantly, the disruptive effect of the TMS interference was related to the degree of language lateralization. TMS had less of an effect in participants with bilateral language organization and a greater effect in those who were strongly lateralized.

Box 2 Intensity of stimulation: thresholds

The intensity of stimulation is an important consideration in transcranial magnetic stimulation (TMS) studies, although the choices can be somewhat arbitrary. In the motor and the visual cortex, the effects of stimulus intensity can be directly measured and thresholds established. These represent the percentage of maximum stimulator output required to elicit an motor-evoked potential (MEP) or a phosphene, respectively. The most commonly used threshold is the motor threshold (MT), typically established as the percentage of stimulator output required to elicit an MEP of size > 50 μV in more than 5 out of 10 consecutive pulses. Motor and visual thresholds are most likely related to skull thickness and therefore serve to normalize the stimulation across individuals. To some extent, however, an individual's resting "excitability" will be related to their threshold. When recruiting participants for TMS studies, it is important to consider factors that might raise their cortical excitability and lower threshold, such as a personal or family history of epilepsy, caffeine, alcohol or drug intake, sleep deprivation, hunger or anxiety. Screening for these factors can reduce the likelihood of an adverse event such as a seizure (see Wassermann, 1998 for details). Interestingly, however, motor and visual thresholds appear uncorrelated (Stewart et al., 200⁻). This may be due to differences in skull thickness overlying these regions, or it may reflect differences in the anatomy of the brain region targeted. For instance, the functional area may lie deeper within the sulcus in one region and on the crown of the gyrus in the other. Also, more often than not we wish to stimulate areas outside the visual and motor systems where it is not possible or practical to determine a threshold. In such cases, arbitrary choices are often made with respect to stimulus intensity, which is worth considering when reviewing the results of TMS studies.

Stewart, L, Walsh, V, and Rothwell, JC (2001). Motor and phosphene thresholds: A transcranial magnetic stimulation correlation study. *Neuropsychologia* 39(4): 415–419.

Wassermann, EM (1998). Risk and safety of repetitive transcranial magnetic stimulation: Report and suggested guidelines from the International Workshop on the Safety of Repetitive Transcranial Magnetic Stimulation, June 5–7, 1996. *Electroencephalography and Clinical Neurophysiology* 108: 1–16.

Single-Pulse TMS and EMG

Finally, single-pulse TMS and EMG can be used to measure motor excitability during language tasks. Such a measure may be more sensitive than those obtained with other techniques, which usually assess a proxy of neural activity such as blood flow. In one study, the motor excitability of the hand area of motor cortex was measured under the following conditions: reading aloud, reading silently, spontaneous speech or production of non-speech vocal sounds (Tokimura et al., 1996). The size of the motor-evoked potential (MEP) elicited in the hand muscle by TMS was facilitated (reflecting increased motor excitability) during speech production but was only clearly lateralized for the reading condition. In contrast, the silent reading condition and the non-speech sound production did not result in changes in excitability. This suggests increased motor excitability in primary motor areas during speech production, a perhaps unsurprising result. We used similar methods to examine motor excitability in the representation of speech articulators during speech perception rather than production (Watkins et al., 2003). We found that during listening to speech or viewing speech-related lip movements, the size of the MEP in the lip muscles elicited by single pulses of TMS (120% MT) was facilitated, but only for stimulation over the left hemisphere and not the right (see **Figure 1(a)** and **(b)**). Also, MEPs measured in the hand muscle in response to single-pulse TMS over the hand representation in the left motor cortex showed no change during any of the speech perception or control conditions (see **Figure 1(c)**). The results of these studies offer an intriguing possibility for non-invasive study of language lateralization using TMS.

Summary

We have described a series of studies that illustrate the variety of ways in which TMS is used to examine hemispheric dominance for speech and language processing. However, it is important to point out the limitations of TMS for such assessments. Unlike sodium amobarbital, which affects the entire middle cerebral artery territory in one hemisphere for several minutes, TMS only affects a small brain area for a very brief time. In addition, not all speech sites are equally accessible to stimulation as they may be located at different depths from the scalp or

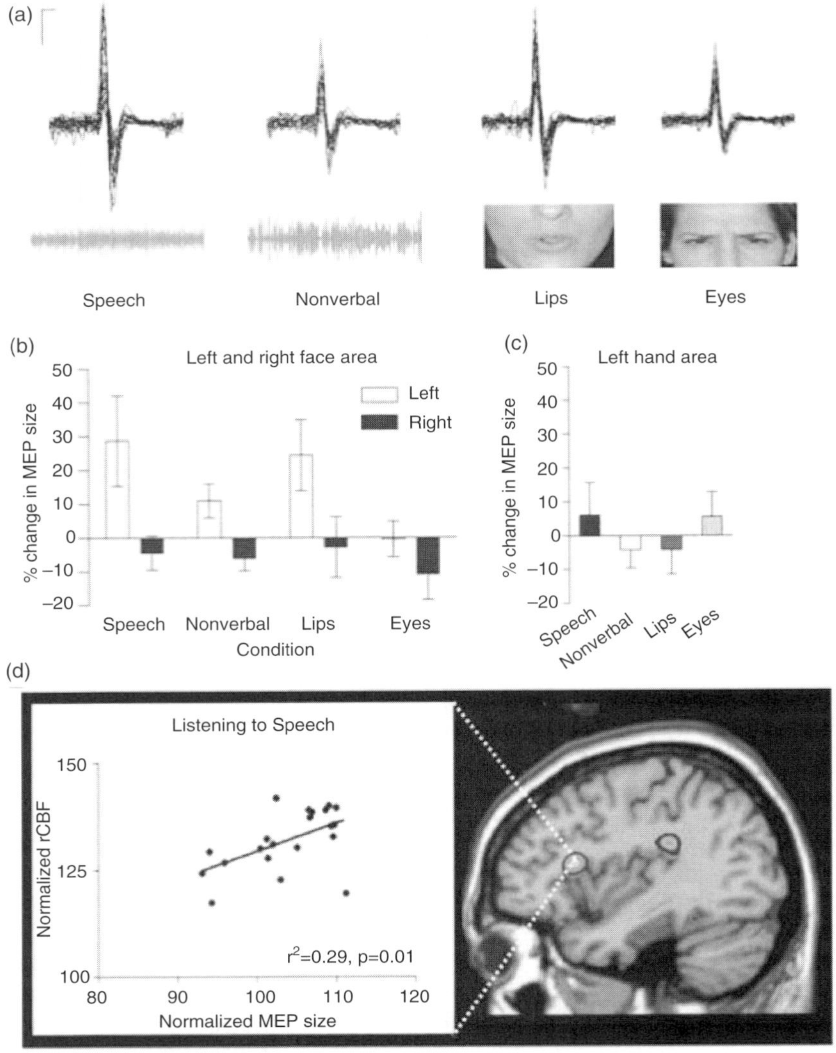

Figure 1 Motor excitability during speech perception. (a) Data from stimulation of the left primary motor face area in a single subject when listening to speech, listening to non-verbal sounds, viewing speech and viewing eye movements. During the listening conditions, subjects viewed a screen of noise and during viewing conditions, subjects heard auditory white noise. EMG recordings from individual trials are superimposed and the dotted line indicates the time of stimulation. The horizontal bar represents 10 ms and the vertical bar 0.5 mV. (b) Average MEP sizes for the same four stimulus conditions with stimulation to the left and right face area. (c) Average MEP sizes for the four stimulus conditions with stimulation to the hand area of motor cortex. The *x*-axis through the 0% level represents the mean MEP size in the control condition and error bars represent standard error of the mean. Panels (a)–(c) are modified from Watkins et al. (2003), with permission. (d) The relation between regional cerebral blood flow in Broca's area and the size of the MEP evoked by single-pulse TMS over the mouth region of primary motor cortex (left panel). On the right, an activation map showing the anatomical location of the significant positive relationship illustrated in the graph. *Source*: From Watkins & Paus (2004), with permission.

oriented differently in the two hemispheres. It is difficult, therefore, to make a fair comparison between hemispheres with regard to their involvement or relative involvement in speech production. Also, stimulating the scalp over peri-Sylvian language areas can be painful for the participant when it produces muscle twitches on the head or stimulates cranial nerves such as the trigeminal bundle. All these effects limit the efficacy of TMS for studies of language dominance (see **Box 3**).

Different Effects of TMS on Task Performance: Posterior Temporal Cortex and Picture Naming

The effects of TMS are usually observed in increased reaction times or decreased accuracy of responses, often in comparison with either unstimulated trials or stimulation over control sites. Decreases in reaction times due to stimulation are frequently reported, which emphasizes

Box 3 Advantages and disadvantages of transcranial magnetic stimulation

- Advantages
  - Participants act as their own controls, allowing comparisons to be made before, during or after stimulation. This avoids the potential confounds associated with neuropsychological studies of patients with lesions, such as compensatory plasticity, the large and varied extents of naturally occurring lesions, and damage to subjacent fibers-of-passage.
  - TMS can be used to examine the timing of information processing within a brain area with a temporal resolution of tens of milliseconds (Amassian, 1989; Schluter et al., 1998).
  - In conjunction with positron emission tomography (PET), functional magnetic resonance imaging (fMRI) or electroencephalograms (EEG), or by using more than one coil, one can examine functional connectivity between brain regions and within cognitive systems.
  - In patients, one can assess whether brain activity revealed by functional imaging is compensatory or maladaptive.
  - TMS offers the possibility of treatment in patients with speech and language disorders.
- Disadvantages
  - TMS is limited to brain areas at or near the cortical surface because the effect of the stimulation reduces with distance from the coil.
  - The brief passage of current through the coil produces a loud click and a sensation on the scalp, both of which can affect the experimental results and need to be controlled for (Walsh & Rushworth, 1999).
  - When stimulation affects peripheral nerves or muscles, it can cause discomfort or sometimes pain.
  - Areas outside of primary motor or visual cortices can be difficult to locate accurately because there is no obvious physiological response to measure such as MEP or phosphene induction.

Amassian, VE (1989). Suppression of visual perception by magnetic coil stimulation of human occipital cortex. *Electroencephalography and Clinical Neurophysiology* 74: 458–462.

Schluter, ND, Rushworth, MF, Passingham, RE, and Mills, KR (1998). Temporary interference in human lateral premotor cortex suggests dominance for the selection of movements. A study using transcranial magnetic stimulation. *Brain* 121: (Pt 5), 785–799.

Walsh, V, and Rushworth, MFS (1999). The use of transcranial magnetic stimulation in neuropsychological testing. *Neuropsychologia* 37: 125–135.

the importance of baselines and comparison conditions to separate regionally specific facilitation effects from more global ones. These facilitatory effects are difficult to interpret, however, and it may be controversial to conclude from such results that an area is *necessary* for a task. It is striking that many reports of facilitatory effects are associated with Wernicke's area stimulation, suggesting that this may be a special case (Topper et al., 1998; Mottaghy et al., 1999; Andoh et al., 2006). All of these studies suggest involvement of an area in a task but it may be controversial to conclude in all cases that a necessary role has been demonstrated. Below we review a set of studies that have examined lexical retrieval using word-picture matching or picture naming, yielding a set of apparently contradictory results. We use these studies firstly to illustrate the differential effects of TMS on behavior and secondly to demonstrate how different control conditions and control stimulation sites can aid interpretation of some of these behavioral results.

Increased picture-naming latencies were observed during stimulation over the left posterior infero-temporal cortex (BA37) using short (600 ms) trains of rTMS (10 Hz at 75% maximum stimulator output) (Stewart et al., 2001). These increases were found relative to stimulation over the right homologous region and the vertex during performance of the same task. Also, the effect of TMS was selective to this task as it did not affect word and non-word reading or color naming. These results are straightforward and consistent with previous functional imaging findings confirming that the posterior inferior-temporal cortex region is necessary for picture naming.

In another picture-naming study, however, very different behavioral effects of TMS were observed. Stimulation (20-Hz rTMS for 2 s at 55% maximum output) over Wernicke's area in this case decreased naming latencies (Mottaghy et al., 1999). Stimulation over Broca's area and the visual cortex had no affect leading the authors to conclude that stimulation at a low intensity "preactivated" or primed Wernicke's area. The explanation of priming, either of representations in Wernicke's area or of those more remotely located, seems a parsimonious one, but as yet there is no physiological explanation for TMS-induced behavioral facilitation.

In some studies the interpretation of results is even more complicated. For instance, one study (Drager et al., 2004) tested participants on a word-picture verification task before and after a 10-min session of 1-Hz rTMS delivered over one of five locations (Broca's and Wernicke's areas, their right hemisphere homologs, and midline occipital cortex). They also included a sham-TMS control condition, which produces TMS pulses with the coil turned 90° away from the scalp. Reaction times after the 10 min of 1-Hz TMS were consistently faster than those before stimulation regardless of the site, which suggests a non-specific arousal effect of TMS. The authors re-calculated site-specific reaction times relative to the mean across all five sites following stimulation (rather than relative to reaction times before stimulation), to reveal an inhibitory effect of stimulation in Wernicke's area and a facilitatory effect in Broca's area. It is interesting to note that had there been only a single control condition (for example mid-line occipital or sham stimulation), it would have been difficult to separate these regional effects from the overall facilitation effect.

TMS Studies of Semantic and Phonological Processing in LIFG

Several recent studies have used TMS to address the role of different portions of the LIFG in semantic and phonological processing (Devlin et al., 2003; Nixon et al., 2004; Gough et al., 2005). Functional imaging studies commonly report activity in anterior portions of the LIFG during semantic processing tasks but the presence of semantic deficits in patients with lesions in this area is not clearly established.

In a simple semantic task such as deciding whether a visually presented word referred to a man-made (e.g., "kennel") or natural object (e.g., "dog"), TMS (10 Hz for 300 ms at 110% MT) over anterior LIFG increased reaction times relative to trials with no TMS; there was no effect of TMS on reaction times for simple judgements concerning the visual properties of the presented words (Devlin et al., 2003). In a similar study, using fMRI-guided rTMS (7 Hz for 600 ms at 100% MT) over anterior LIFG, response times for decisions based on word meanings were significantly slowed relative to trials with no TMS; there were no effects over two other control sites (Kohler et al., 2004). Taken together, these studies support the claim that anterior LIFG is necessary for semantic processing.

A number of studies have also confirmed a necessary role for LIFG in phonological processing. In one study of phonological working memory participants saw a word on a computer screen (e.g., "knees") and then held it in memory during a 1–2 s delay before deciding whether it sounded the same as a subsequently presented non-word (e.g., "neaze") (Nixon et al., 2004). Stimulation (10 Hz for 500 ms at 120% MT) was applied over posterior LIFG during the delay period and selectively increased the error rate during the phonological task, but not during a comparable visual working memory task. Similarly rTMS (5 Hz for 2.4 s at 115% MT) over posterior LIFG increased response times for a phonological working memory task requiring silent reading and syllable counting of a visually presented word (Aziz-Zadeh et al., 2005).

Taken together the results of these TMS studies of LIFG significantly extend the previous neuroimaging results by demonstrating that anterior LIFG is *necessary* for semantic processing while the posterior LIFG is *necessary* for phonological processing. It is possible, however, that the LIFG acts as a single functional region required for both semantic and phonological processing. Alternately, there may be sub-regions within LIFG specialized for semantic and phonological processing but co-activated due to incidental processing. The TMS results described above do not distinguish between these possibilities. Therefore, to test for a double dissociation between semantic and phonological processing within LIFG, Gough et al. (2005) designed the following TMS experiment. Two letter strings were presented simultaneously on a computer screen and participants made a semantic (e.g., same meaning? "idea-notion"), phonological (e.g., sound the same? "nose-knows") or visual decision (e.g., look the same? "fwtsp-fwtsp") decision. Compared to no stimulation, TMS of anterior LIFG selectively increased response times when participants made semantic but not phonological decisions. Conversely, stimulation of posterior LIFG selectively interfered with phonological but not semantic decisions (**Figure 2**). Neither site of stimulation affected the response times in the visual control task. In other words, the authors demonstrated a functional double dissociation for semantic and phonological processing within LIFG in sites separated by less than 3 cm. Although this double dissociation was first suggested by functional imaging, it required the spatial precision of TMS to independently disrupt the regions and clarify their distinct contributions to word processing.

Speech Perception and the Motor System

A recent series of studies used TMS to measure the excitability of the motor system during speech perception. These studies largely arose out of renewed interested in motor theories of perception related to the neurophysiological findings of mirror neurons in the monkey brain (Fadiga et al., 2005; see Chapter 23, this volume). These neurons fire not only when the monkey performs an action but also when the monkey sees or hears an action being performed, thereby providing a functional link between perception and action. Using single pulses of TMS over the cortical motor representation of a muscle of interest (the tongue or the lips), the size of the MEP elicited by TMS at a fixed intensity provides an index of the excitability of the motor system, which is compared across conditions. During passive listening to stimuli with or without consonant sounds that required tongue movements in their production, MEPs were measured from the tongue (Fadiga et al., 2002). MEP size increased when subjects listened to words and non-words containing the labiodental "rr" phoneme as in the Italian word "terra" but not those with the "ff" phoneme as in the Italian word "zaffo." In a similar experiment measuring MEP sizes in the lip muscle (orbicularis oris), MEP size increased when subjects listened to continuous prose passages or viewed lip movements during continuous speech (Watkins et al., 2003), but was unchanged during listening to non-verbal stimuli or watching eye and brow movements.

The two TMS studies described above suggest a functional connection between speech perception and the motor system underlying speech production, but they do not provide any anatomical information to suggest how this link is mediated. By combining TMS with PET, we investigated the brain regions that mediate the change in motor excitability during speech perception (Watkins & Paus, 2004). Motor excitability was measured by eliciting

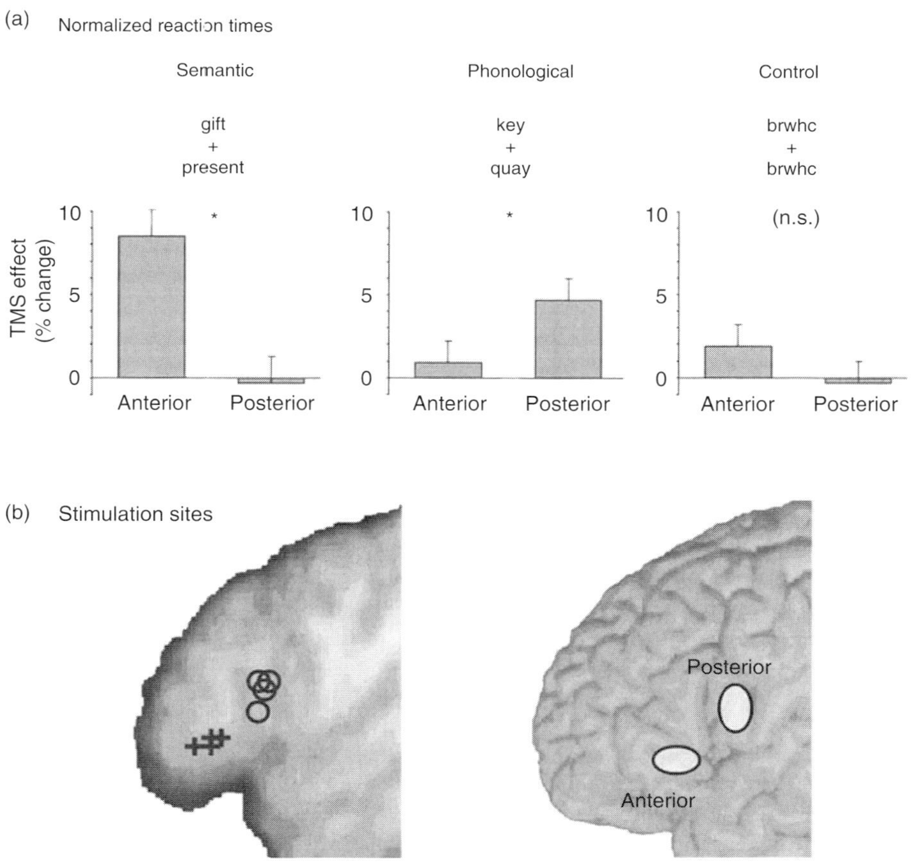

Figure 2 Effects of stimulation on anterior and posterior LIFG. (a) The bar plots show the mean normalized TMS effects as percent change in reaction times from the non-TMS baseline during synonym judgments (left), homophone judgments (middle) and visual matching (right). Error bars indicate the standard error of the mean and significant differences are indicated with an *($p<0.05$). (b) The bottom panel shows the location of stimulation sites for four participants on their mean structural image with anterior locations marked with crosses and posterior locations marked with circles. Next to it is a 3D rendering with the stimulation sites shown as ovals representing the spatial 85% confidence interval. Stimulation sites were on average 2.5 cm apart on the cortical surface. *Source*: From Gough et al. (2005) with permission.

MEPs in the orbicularis oris muscle due to TMS over the face area of left motor cortex. As before, MEP size increased during auditory speech perception. The MEP sizes were then regressed against regional cerebral blood flow measures across the whole brain obtained during the TMS. This analysis revealed that increased motor excitability during speech perception correlated with blood flow increases in the posterior part of the LIFG (Broca's area; see **Figure 1(d)**). In other words, Broca's area plays a central role in linking speech perception with speech production, consistent with theories that emphasize the integration of sensory and motor representations in understanding speech (Liberman & Mattingly, 1985).

The results from these studies show that increased motor excitability of the speech production system is specific to the muscle used in production, that this effect is lateralized to the left hemisphere and that the changes are mediated by neurons in Broca's area. These increases may reflect covert imitative mechanisms, rapid internal speech or a correlate of the perception process. Whether this in some way aids speech perception or comprehension remains to be tested.

Representation of Actions and Verbs in the Motor System and Frontal Cortex

A series of studies have examined the role of motor areas in the neural representation of actions and verbs. Two such studies have used TMS over the primary motor representations of different effectors to elicit MEPS while subjects processed actions. In the first study, subjects listened to sentences related to hand-actions (e.g., "he sewed the skirt"), foot-actions (e.g., "he jumped the rope") or more abstract actions (e.g., "he forgot the date"), while MEPs were measured from the hand and foot muscles (Buccino et al., 2005). The size of the MEPs in specific muscles used to produce the actions were specifically modulated when listening to sentences referring to actions involving those muscles rather than actions involving other muscles or abstract actions. In another study, subjects received single pulses of TMS over the left motor cortex representation of the arm or leg while they made lexical decisions (Pulvermüller et al., 2005). Reaction times were decreased to lexical decisions for actions related to arms (e.g., "folding") and legs (e.g. "stepping"), respectively. As noted above, however, the interpretation of facilitatory effects of TMS is not straightforward. The authors suggest that the decrease in response times may be due to partial activation of the representation of actions related to the specific areas being stimulated.

Neuropsychological studies in patients with brain lesions show selective impairments for nouns and verbs suggesting that their neural representations may be spatially distinct. TMS studies offer an opportunity to test this hypothesis in the normal healthy brain. In one study, the authors postulated that verb-specificity may be due to the close relationship between verbs and actions and used TMS to investigate the role of left dorso–lateral prefrontal cortex (DLPFC) in action naming (Cappa et al., 2002). A set of Italian speaking participants were shown pictures of common objects and asked to either name the object (e.g., "telefono" [a telephone]) or the associated action ("telefonare" [a telephone]). rTMS (20 Hz for 500 ms at 90% MT) of left DLPFC decreased naming latencies for verbs relative to right DLPFC and sham stimulation (coil is placed perpendicular rather than tangential to the skull, thereby providing similar sensory effects of TMS but no stimulation). In contrast, the latencies for object naming were unaffected. Based on this condition-specific facilitation effect, the authors suggested that verbs may be preferentially impaired by left frontal lesions because damage to DLPFC affects action observation and representation which are more tightly linked with verbs than nouns.

Other studies, however, call this interpretation into question (Shapiro et al., 2001). In one study, participants were asked to inflect nouns and verbs (e.g., "song"→"songs" or "sing"→"sings") either before or after 10 min of 1-Hz stimulation over left DLPFC. Reaction times were significantly slowed for verbs, but not nouns. In order to determine whether this effect was due to the action-related meaning of the verbs, a second experiment used pseudowords (e.g., "flonk") treated as either nouns or verbs. Because pseudowords do not have any associated meaning, the authors reasoned that TMS would only affect reaction times if the region was important for processing the grammatical class of verbs rather that words with action-related meanings. DLPFC stimulation selectively slowed reaction times only in the verb condition – a finding interpreted as evidence for a neuroanatomical basis for grammatical categories *per se* rather than a by-product of the differences in meaning between nouns and verbs.

It is not entirely clear how to reconcile these findings. In both cases, DLPFC stimulation preferentially affected verbs relative to nouns, although in one case this manifested as facilitation (Cappa et al., 2002) and in the other, inhibition (Shapiro et al., 2001). Further work will be necessary to determine the range of verbs and tasks that engage DLPFC. For instance, are the effects modulated by the amount of "action" inherent in the verb? In other words, do "running" and "throwing" require greater DLPFC involvement than "thinking" or "sleeping"? If so, the functional link between hand or leg motor regions and specific action words may be mediated via DLPFC in much the same way the ventrolateral prefrontal cortex mediates the link between perceiving speech and the mouth region of motor cortex (Watkins and Paus, 2004).

TMS Studies in Patients with Aphasia

Several researchers have investigated the role of the right inferior frontal gyrus (IFG) in recovery from non-fluent aphasia due to left hemisphere stroke (Martin et al., 2004; Naeser et al., 2005a; Naeser et al., 2005b; Winhuisen et al., 2005). Functional imaging studies have frequently shown increased right hemisphere activity in patients with aphasia. The question of interest here is whether the abnormal level of right hemisphere activity reflects a successful compensatory mechanism aiding recovery of function or a maladaptive one, which impedes recovery. An initial study in four chronic non-fluent patients used 1-Hz rTMS (90% MT for 10 mins) to test four different sites in the right hemisphere (Martin et al., 2004). The targeted sites were anterior IFG, posterior IFG, mouth area of primary motor cortex and posterior superior temporal gyrus. Only stimulation over anterior IFG led to an improvement in naming accuracy and reaction times. In a follow-up study, the patients were given 20 min of 1-Hz rTMS at 90% MT daily for 2 weeks (Naeser et al., 2005b). Significant improvements on naming accuracy and reaction times were seen immediately after the 10th treatment session and these effects persisted for at least 2 months in all patients and for 8 months in one of the patients (Naeser et al., 2005a).

In a similar experiment, a group of 14 patients with brain tumors were examined using PET functional imaging and high-frequency rTMS (4 Hz at MT) during verb generation (Thiel et al., 2005). Brain activity revealed by PET was compared in the left and right IFG. The location of maximum activity on the PET scan in these areas was then targeted with TMS while patients attempted to generate verbs. LIFG stimulation resulted in increased latencies for all controls and 10 out of 14 patients; a further three patients did not respond to the presented noun; and one patient produced a verb unrelated to the presented noun. In contrast, right IFG stimulation resulted in increased latencies in only 5 of the 14 patients and none of the controls. Laterality indices calculated for the brain activity in IFG were significantly lower in the patients who showed TMS interference for right IFG stimulation.

That is, those with right hemisphere dominance in the PET study were impaired at verb generation when the right IFG was stimulated. The authors concluded that in these five patients, right hemisphere activity was necessary for language function – a conclusion which cannot be drawn from the imaging data alone.

Although TMS provides some support for the idea that homologous regions assume lost language functions following left hemisphere lesions (Thiel et al., 2005; Winhuisen et al., 2005), it also demonstrates that, at the very least, the story is considerably more complicated. For one thing, TMS confirms the importance of residual left hemisphere function, as suggested by previous functional imaging studies. In fact, left hemisphere stimulation interfered with performance more consistently than right hemisphere stimulation, which only affected the subset of patients with the strongest rightward asymmetries. The reason for these asymmetries remains unclear, but one factor likely to play a role is premorbid language organization (Knecht et al., 2002). Another complicating finding is that in some cases, right hemisphere stimulation interfered with performance (Thiel et al., 2005; Winhuisen et al., 2005) while in others, it improved performance (Martin et al., 2004; Naeser et al., 2005a; Naeser et al., 2005b). There are, of course, significant differences between the studies including the types of patients (i.e., chronic non-fluent versus fluent aphasics) and the type of TMS (i.e., long trains of low-frequency versus short bursts of high-frequency TMS). Nonetheless, the findings support the idea that one cannot draw a simple conclusion regarding right hemisphere involvement in recovery. Understanding these differences poses a major challenge for cognitive neuroscience and may require adopting more sophisticated models of recovery that move beyond the simple notions of "homologous transfer of function" and "necessary and sufficient" brain regions.

Challenges and Future Directions

As illustrated here, TMS has already begun to offer novel and important insights into the cognitive and neural basis of language processing. When used to produce "virtual" lesions, TMS can assess whether an area is necessary for a task by demonstrating inhibitory effects on behavior. In contrast, behavioral facilitation (Cappa et al., 2002; Sakai et al., 2002; Pulvermüller et al., 2005) is not readily explained in terms of externally induced neuronal firing and consequently, a significant challenge will be to elucidate the physiological mechanisms underlying these effects. Without this explanation, interpretation of such results will remain speculative and controversial. TMS can also provide a useful measure of cortical excitability for identifying functional links between language and the motor system, which, for instance, demonstrate a close link between speech perception and the motor cortex areas responsible for producing speech (Fadiga et al., 2002; Watkins et al., 2003; Watkins and Paus, 2004). A critical test of this relationship will be to determine whether this functional link in some way aids speech perception or comprehension. Finally, recent developments in TMS methodology offer novel opportunities for investigating cortical connectivity (Paus et al., 1997), and suggest that the application of these tools could help to trace the neural circuitry underlying human language processing. In short, the field seems poised to expand enormously in virtually all areas of language research, building on the early successes and developing novel methods capable of answering an even wider range of questions.

References

Andoh, J, Artiges, E, Pallier, C, Riviere, D, Mangin, JF, Cachia, A, Plaze, M, Paillere-Martinot, ML, and Martinot, JL (2006). Modulation of language areas with functional MR image-guided magnetic stimulation. *Neuroimage* 29(2): 619–627.

Aziz-Zadeh, L, Cattaneo, L, Rochat, M, and Rizzolatti, G (2005). Covert speech arrest induced by rTMS over both motor and nonmotor left hemisphere frontal sites. *Journal of Cognitive Neuroscience* 17(6): 928–938.

Buccino, G, Riggio, L, Melli, G, Binkofski, F, Gallese, V, and Rizzolatti, G (2005). Listening to action-related sentences modulates the activity of the motor system: A combined TMS and behavioral study. *Brain Research. Cognitive Brain Research* 24(3): 355–363.

Cappa, SF, Sandrini, M, Rossini, PM, Sosta, K, and Miniussi, C (2002). The role of the left frontal lobe in action naming: rTMS evidence. *Neurology* 59(5): 720–723.

Devlin, JT, Matthews, PM, and Rushworth, MF (2003). Semantic processing in the left inferior prefrontal cortex: A combined functional magnetic resonance imaging and transcranial magnetic stimulation study. *Journal of Cognitive Neuroscience* 15(1): 71–84.

Drager, B, Breitenstein, C, Helmke, U, Kamping, S, and Knecht, S (2004). Specific and nonspecific effects of transcranial magnetic stimulation on picture-word verification. *European Journal of Neuroscience* 20(6): 1681–1687.

Fadiga, L, Craighero, L, Buccino, G, and Rizzolatti, G (2002). Speech listening specifically modulates the excitability of tongue muscles: A TMS study. *European Journal of Neuroscience* 15(2): 399–402.

Fadiga, L, Craighero, L, and Olivier, E (2005). Human motor cortex excitability during the perception of others' action. *Current Opinions in Neurobiology* 15(2): 213–218.

Gough, PM, Nobre, AC, and Devlin, JT (2005). Dissociating linguistic processes in the left inferior frontal cortex with transcranial magnetic stimulation. *Journal of Neuroscience* 25(35): 8010–8016.

Knecht, S, Floel, A, Drager, B, Breitenstein, C, Sommer, J, Henningsen, H, Ringelstein, EB, and Pascual-Leone, A (2002). Degree of language lateralization determines susceptibility to unilateral brain lesions. *Nature Neuroscience* 5(7): 695–699.

Kohler, S, Paus, T, Buckner, RL, and Milner, B (2004). Effects of left inferior prefrontal stimulation on episodic memory formation: A two-stage fMRI–rTMS study. *Journal of Cognitive Neuroscience* 16(2): 178–188.

Liberman, AM and Mattingly, IG (1985). The motor theory of speech perception – revised. *Cognition* 21: 1–36.

Martin, PI, Naeser, MA, Theoret, H, Tormos, JM, Nicholas, M, Kurland, J, Frengi, F, Seekins, H, Doron, K, and Pascual-Leone, A (2004). Transcranial magnetic stimulation as a complementary treatment for aphasia. *Seminars in Speech and Language* 25(2): 181–191.

Mottaghy, FM, Hungs, M, Brugmann, M, Sparing, R, Boroojerdi, B, Foltys, H, Huber, W, and Topper, R (1999). Facilitation of picture naming after repetitive transcranial magnetic stimulation. *Neurology* 53(8): 1806–1812.

Naeser, MA, Martin, PI, Nicholas, M, Baker, EH, Seekins, H, Helm-Estabrooks, N, Cayer-Meade, C, Kobayashi, M, Theoret, H, Fregni, F, Tormos, JM, Kurland, J, Doron, KW, and Pascual-Leone, A (2005a). Improved naming after TMS treatments in a chronic, global aphasia patient – case report. *Neurocase* 11(3): 182–193.

Naeser, MA, Martin, PI, Nicholas, M, Baker, EH, Seekins, H, Kobayashi, M, Theoret, H, Fregni, F, Maria-Tormos, J, Kurland, J, Doron, KW, and Pascual-Leone, A (2005b). Improved picture naming in chronic aphasia after TMS to part of right Broca's area: An open-protocol study. *Brain and Language* 93(1): 95–105.

Nixon, P, Lazarova, J, Hodinott-Hill, I, Gough, P, and Passingham, R (2004). The inferior frontal gyrus and phonological processing: An investigation using rTMS. *Journal of Cognitive Neuroscience* 16(2): 289–300.

Pascual-Leone, A, Gates, JR, and Dhuna, A (1991). Induction of speech arrest and counting errors with rapid-rate transcranial magnetic stimulation. *Neurology* 41: 697–702.

Paus, T, Jech, R, Thompson, CJ, Comeau, R, Peters, T, and Evans, AC (1997). Transcranial magnetic stimulation during positron emission tomography: A new method for studying connectivity of the human cerebral cortex. *Journal of Neuroscience* 17(9): 3178–3184.

Pulvermüller, F, Hauk, O, Nikulin, VV, and Ilmoniemi, RJ (2005). Functional links between motor and language systems. *European Journal of Neuroscience* 21(3): 793–797.

Sakai, KL, Noguchi, Y, Takeuchi, T, and Watanabe, E (2002). Selective priming of syntactic processing by event-related transcranial magnetic stimulation of Broca's area. *Neuron* 35(6): 1177–1182.

Shapiro, KA, Pascual-Leone, A, Mottaghy, FM, Gangitano, M, and Caramazza, A (2001). Grammatical distinctions in the left frontal cortex. *Journal of Cognitive Neuroscience* 13(6): 713–720.

Stewart, L, Meyer, BU, Frith, U, and Rothwell, J (2001). Left posterior BA37 is involved in object recognition: A TMS study. *Neuropsychologia* 39: 1–6.

Stewart, L, Walsh, V, Frith, U, and Rothwell, JC (2001). TMS produces two dissociable types of speech disruption. *Neuroimage* 13: 472–478.

Thiel, A, Habedank, B, Winhuisen, L, Herholz, K, Kessler, J, Haupt, WF, and Heiss, WD (2005). Essential language function of the right hemisphere in brain tumor patients. *Annals of Neurology* 57(1): 128–131.

Tokimura, H, Tokimura, Y, Oliviero, A, Asakura, T, and Rothwell, JC (1996). Speech-induced changes in corticospinal excitability. *Annals of Neurology* 40(4): 628–634.

Topper, R, Mottaghy, FM, Brugmann, M, Noth, J, and Huber, W (1998). Facilitation of picture naming by focal transcranial magnetic stimulation of Wernicke's area. *Experimental Brain Research* 121: 371–378.

Watkins, K and Paus, T (2004). Modulation of motor excitability during speech perception: The role of Broca's area. *Journal of Cognitive Neuroscience* 16(6): 978–987.

Watkins, KE, Strafella, AP, and Paus, T (2003). Seeing and hearing speech excites the motor system involved in speech production. *Neuropsychologia* 41(8): 989–994.

Winhuisen, L, Thiel, A, Schumacher, B, Kessler, J, Rudolf, J, Haupt, WF, and Heiss, WD (2005). Role of the contralateral inferior frontal gyrus in recovery of language function in poststroke aphasia: A combined repetitive transcranial magnetic stimulation and positron emission tomography study. *Stroke* 36(8): 1759–1763.

Further Reading

Devlin, JT and Watkins, KE (2007). Stimulating language: Insights from TMS. *Brain* 130(3): 610–622.

The paper provides a comprehensive review of TMS studies of language. It covers the literature published since 1991 when TMS was first introduced as a tool to study language. Further details of many of the studies reviewed here are provided with a specific focus on studies that have extended our understanding of either the cognitive or the neural basis of language.

Robertson, EM, Theoret, H, and Pascual-Leone, A (2003). Studies in cognition: The problems solved and created by transcranial magnetic stimulation. *Journal of Cognitive Neuroscience* 15(7): 948–960.

This paper reviews the potential problems associated with the use of TMS in cognitive studies and provides a critical discussion of the limitations of the method.

Sack, AT (2006). Transcranial magnetic stimulation, causal structure-function mapping and networks of functional relevance. *Current Opinion in Neurobiology* 16(5): 593–599.

This paper provides further detail on recent advances in the combination of TMS with other imaging modalities.

Transient Global Amnesia

B. L. Miller, K. Lee, and H. A. Miller

Transient global amnesia (TGA) is a syndrome characterized by the sudden loss of the ability to remember. Unlike other amnestic syndromes, TGA is temporary and does not last long. Patients with TGA tend to be middle-aged, usually 50 or older, and both sexes are affected. Some spells are precipitated by intense exercise, but in many instances TGA occurs without precipitants. Typical spells last minutes to hours, although episodes that last for many hours have been described. Transient spells of amnesia can occur with epilepsy, arterial or venous ischemia, migraine, high altitude, hypoglycemia, and head trauma, but most cases of TGA have no known etiology. When a patient first presents, ruling out some or all of the treatable causes for amnesia may be necessary, after which a diagnosis of TGA can be made.

Individuals who are affected by TGA no longer remember the ongoing events of their lives, and the ability to lay down episodic memories (memories with a temporal and spatial component) is transiently interrupted. Within seconds, patients with TGA forget what is told to them. They ask repetitive questions, reflecting their inability to remember what has been told to them and what they have seen and experienced. Some patients appear unsettled and worried, suggesting that they have at least limited awareness that there is something wrong. However, they rarely possess a complete awareness of the fact that they are unable to remember. Typically, the TGA victim repeatedly asks friends and family members the same questions, such as "Where am I?" or "Why are we here?" Along with this loss of new learning, patients often have problems with older memories. This retrograde amnesia can date back months to years, and this can further exacerbate the confusion that accompanies many cases of TGA.

Formal neuropsychological studies of TGA demonstrate normal attention, working memory, language, drawing, visual perception, and frontal executive abilities. The diagnosis of TGA must be questioned if significant problems exist in any of these cognitive spheres. Patients with confusional states are easily distinguished from those with TGA because they exhibit alterations in alertness, awareness, and attention—spheres that are normal in TGA. Comprehensive studies of memory during TGA show abnormal encoding or storage. Studies on retrograde memory with TGA are lacking, but some patients show loss of memories that date back many years.

TGA has proven difficult to study because of the short duration of the episodes. Using functional imaging techniques such as single photon emission computerized tomography, positron emission computerized tomography, and functional magnetic resonance imaging, dysfunction in medial temporal lobe structures has been documented in some cases of TGA, whereas in others the medial thalamic region is the site of abnormality. Temporal lobe epilepsy can cause transient dysfunction of the medial temporal lobes and needs to be considered in any patient who has suffered from TGA. Symptoms and signs that make epilepsy more likely include automatisms, auras, repeated episodes, and abnormalities in the medial temporal lobes detected by electroencephalography or neuroimaging. Similarly, subtle brain trauma will precipitate transient episodes of amnesia, and this potential cause needs to be explored in the history. However, in most cases of TGA epilepsy and head trauma are not serious considerations. The three leading hypotheses regarding TGA are that it is caused by posterior cerebral artery ischemia leading to medial temporal dysfunction, increased venous pressure leading to medial thalamic hypoperfusion, and spreading hypometabolism of Leao secondary to migraine.

The posterior cerebral arteries both send a small branch to the medial temporal lobe and permanent amnestic syndromes can occur with infarction of the territory of these vessels. Some cases of TGA represent transient ischemic attacks that involve posterior cerebral territory. However, the vast majority of patients in whom an evaluation for cerebrovascular risk factors is sought show no abnormalities in the posterior circulation, suggesting that transient ischemic attacks due to atherosclerosis or cardiac emboli are not causal. For this reason, some have suggested that spasm of medial temporal lobe vasculature is the mechanism for TGA. This would explain why the blood vessels appear normal after an attack.

Because some cases of TGA occur with intense exercise during which the Valsalva maneuver occurs, it has been suggested that increased venous pressure is transmitted to the memory areas in the brain, which in turn leads to transient dysfunction in these regions. This mechanism is difficult to prove and would not explain many of the cases in which exercise is not a precursor to TGA.

Finally, with migraine aura there is a spreading wave of cortical hypometabolism that begins in the occipital cortex and spreads rostally. This stereotyped metabolic change is called the wave of Leao and is present with classic migraines. This hypometabolism accounts for the visual auras that typify migraine and classically precede the migraine headache. TGA is a rare finding with migraines, but it has been reported.

TGA is almost always a benign syndrome and rarely leads to serious medical complications. Recurrence is unusual, but repeated episodes of TGA have been reported in some individuals. The medical evaluation for a single episode of TGA needs to be tailored to the individual patient, and some will require a comprehensive assessment for cerebrovascular risk factors of head trauma and epilepsy. During the next decade, discoveries should emerge regarding the etiology, pathogenesis, treatment, and prevention of TGA. Importantly, research on this condition should facilitate a better understanding of the anatomical structures involved with memory.

See also: Memory, Autobiographical; Memory, Episodic.

Further Reading

Eustache, F, Desgranges, B, Aupee, AM, et al. (2000). Functional neuroanatomy of amnesia: Positron emission tomography studies. *Microsc. Res. Tech.* 51: 94–100.

Lewis, SL (1998). Aetiology of transient global amnesia. *Lancet* 352: 397–399.

Litch, JA and Bishop, RA (2000). High-altitude global amnesia. *Wilderness Environ. Med.* 11: 25–28.

Zeman, AZ and Hodges, JR (1997). Transient global amnesia. *Br. J. Hosp. Med.* 58: 257–260.

Turner's Syndrome

J. Ross

Turner's syndrome (TS), described by Dr. Henry Turner in 1938, is a human genetic disorder associated with monosomy X, the absence of the second X chromosome in females. Common chromosomal abnormalities associated with TS include complete monosomy X and a variety of more complicated abnormalities involving the X chromosome with mosaicism for a second cell line seen in 28–67% of subjects in several large series. The incidence of all TS-associated karyotypes is estimated to be approximately 1 in 3000–5000 live-born girls, but monosomy X may be present in as many as 2% of all conceptions, with fewer than 1% of all 45,X embryos surviving to term. Estimates for TS prevalence in the United States range from 28,000 to 75,000.

The X chromosome abnormality can arise through several different mechanisms. It may be the consequence of nondysjunction, chromosome breakage, and loss during oogenesis or spermatogenesis. Alternatively, this chromosomal anomaly can develop early in conception as a result of an error in mitosis, such as anaphase lag or mitotic nondysjunction. The mitotic error is not associated with advanced maternal age. Studies of parental origin of the retained X in 45,X TS reveal that the paternally derived X chromosome is lost twice as often as the maternally derived X chromosome because 45,Y, unlike 45,X, is uniformly lethal to the fetus.

TS features are associated not only with complete monosomy X but also with partial deletions of either the short (Xp) or long (Xq) arm. One of the most common features is gonadal dysgenesis or ovarian failure, which results in decreased circulating estrogen, incomplete pubertal development, and infertility. Other characteristic physical features of TS include short stature and any of a variety of specific somatic abnormalities, such as webbed neck, high arched palate, increased carrying angle of the elbows (cubitus valgus), short fourth or fifth metacarpals, aortic coarctation, renal malformations, multiple pigmented nevi, lymphedema, impaired glucose tolerance, autoimmune thyroid disease, and hypertension. Short stature is generally apparent, starting in early childhood. Adult height measurements of TS women who did not receive growth hormone treatment ranges from 146 to 148.5 cm. Growth is improved with growth hormone therapy.

Certain physical features (cubitus valgus, short metacarpals, and edema) are noted in childhood and persist into adulthood, whereas other physical features (nevi) are noted during adolescence and adulthood. Complex multifactorial features, such as impaired glucose tolerance and hypertension, also tend to start as early as adolescence or are diagnosed in adulthood.

Neuroanatomical and Neurophysiological Aspects

Neurophysiological and neuroanatomical differences between Turner females and normal female controls are consistent with multifocal brain abnormalities, without pathognomonic findings of TS. Data from electrophysiological, neuroanatomical, and positron emission tomography studies support an early, sustained abnormality of cerebral substrate, either as a primary factor or secondary to the endocrine and/or genetic influences. In electrophysiological studies, TS girls and adults have evoked potentials that differ from those of normal controls. Anatomical studies (magnetic resonance imaging and autopsy) have shown differences between TS adults and normal controls, particularly in the right posterior (temporal, parietal, and occipital lobes) regions. Detailed neuroanatomical magnetic resonance imaging studies of 30 girls with TS and female controls showed differences in the right posterior regions (parietal and temporal) and the left parietal–perisylvian region in the Turner subjects.

These findings in patients with TS suggest to some investigators an anomalous hemispheric maturation because the right hemisphere is underdeveloped relative to the usual symmetry seen in normal age-matched girls. Others support an alternative hypothesis for the etiology of the cognitive profile of TS patients that is consistent with a more diffuse brain abnormality. Current knowledge suggests that females with TS have diffuse right cerebral hemispheric dysfunction.

Neurocognitive Profile

TS is not typically associated with general mental retardation, unlike other common chromosome disorders such as Down's syndrome (trisomy 21). Verbal abilities in TS are generally normal; however, specific deficits in visual–spatial/perceptual abilities, nonverbal memory function, motor function, executive function, and attentional abilities occur in TS children and adults of varying races and socioeconomic status. TS children with mosaicism tend to be less severely affected than TS girls with the 45,X karyotype. TS-associated psychosocial difficulties occur in the areas of maturity and social skills. The constellation of neurocognitive deficits observed in TS is most likely multifactorial and related to a complex interaction between genetic abnormalities, hormonal deficiencies, and other unspecified determinants of cognitive ability.

TS-associated spatial difficulties that emerge in childhood may be secondary to poor visual memory and motor incoordination. TS young adults perform worse than their controls in immediate and delayed recall on the Rey–Osterrieth Complex Figure Test, consistent with impaired visual memory. This could involve visual working memory as opposed to long-term memory storage. Alternatively, some problems may be secondary to processing and perceptual organization of complex visual material.

Psychomotor coordination continues to be depressed throughout adolescence. The time required for performance of cognitive tasks with limited motor requirements does not appear to change over a wide age range. In contrast, the time required for performance of tasks that require motor planning decreases as girls with TS become adults. These changes may reflect positive estrogen effects associated with estrogen replacement therapy in adolescence.

TS-associated deficits in the ability to make discriminations based on visual perception, to perceptually integrate spatial configurations, and to manipulate mental representations of objects in space are apparent across wide age ranges. Given that these measures require minimal motor involvement, the impaired performance observed indicates that spatial difficulties persist independently of a motor component. Measures sensitive to distractibility and attention (WISC-R or WAIS-R Arithmetic subtest and Digit Span) are also relatively impaired in TS children, adolescents, and adults. TS females tend to have more difficulty on Digits Backward, which contains a visuospatial component, compared with Digits Forward, consistent with their relatively greater difficulties with spatial than verbal tasks.

Approximately 75% of individuals with TS experience arithmetic difficulties, including problems with both fact retrieval and procedural knowledge components of arithmetic. The procedural knowledge problems appear to persist into adulthood, whereas fact retrieval skills improve with age and tend to be normal by adolescence. Problems with short-term or working memory have been considered the core deficit for many of the cognitive problems experienced by TS girls; however, recent studies also indicate that some TS girls achieve more poorly in school than expected based on their intellectual and neurocognitive profiles.

Converging neurophysiological and neuroanatomical results support the presence of TS-specific "hallmark" visual–spatial/perceptual dysfunction. A subset of the neurocognitive deficits (visual–spatial/perceptual abilities) are genetically determined and result from abnormal expression of one or more X chromosome genes. In addition, a different subset of these neurocognitive deficits (memory, reaction time, and speeded motor function) result from estrogen deficiency and are at least somewhat reversible with estrogen treatment. In contrast, the visual–spatial/perceptual deficits are relatively consistent across wide age ranges and are not reversible with estrogen treatment. The TS-associated psychosocial problems are most likely linked to these core neurocognitive deficits and do not reflect a separate and independent component of the syndrome.

TS Psychosocial Profile

Immaturity and attention deficits have been observed in younger TS girls, who also had fewer friends, spent less time with friends, and did not get along as well with peers compared to control girls. The TS girls also engaged in fewer social activities and had less involvement in athletic pursuits. The younger girls do not appear to have an increase in psychopathology. For adolescent TS girls, immaturity and anxiety appear to be the central issues. They have more problems in school and with peer relationships than age-matched girls with idiopathic short stature. Moreover, samples of both TS girls and women endorse a less positive sense of self-concept than that of girls with idiopathic short stature or normative samples of women. Recent studies revealed a decline in self-concept for TS girls as they moved from childhood into early adolescence, with an improvement in self-esteem during the adolescent years. One factor thought to influence self-esteem was estrogen treatment. Adolescent TS girls treated with estrogen showed an improvement from baseline self-esteem scores not seen in an untreated comparison group. Adolescence has been thought to be a particularly high-risk period for girls with TS, given their delay in pubertal development and short stature. TS adolescents consistently differed from controls in the area of social functioning. Social difficulties were reported by the adolescents on a self-perception scale as well as by mothers' report of social competence and social problems. Mothers of TS girls endorsed symptoms suggestive of past attention deficit hyperactivity disorder and current depressive disorders more frequently than did parents of control girls.

Studies of the social functioning of adult women with TS indicate that these women tend to be well educated and productively employed. However, the adult women tend to live with their parents longer than siblings or age-matched peers, are less likely to be married, and marry later in life. Self-esteem problems appear to persist into adulthood. Adult women report lowered self-esteem in some but not all domains, and in one sample self-esteem was significantly associated with the women's ratings of their overall health status. When the data across studies of adult TS women are combined, the prevalence rates for psychiatric diagnoses (2–6%) are similar to those reported in epidemiological studies of U.S. adults (3.7–7.6%).

Research on social development has documented adjustment problems in the areas of social maturity, social relationships, and self-esteem. Difficulties in these three areas seem to be the primary psychosocial risks for TS females.

Conclusions, Limitations, and Future Directions

Females with TS are faced with unique challenges that may influence their ability to excel in school and social settings. Growth delay, the need to initiate pubertal changes via estrogen replacement therapy, the knowledge of impaired fertility, and, in some cases, the presence of other physical problems all contribute to increased risk of self-consciousness and difficulties with social adaptation. TS children and adults have to handle differential treatment within their environment, especially if they are short. Environmental factors may play an important role in increasing risk for social immaturity, just as hearing impairments may contribute to subsequent learning problems. Estrogen appears to play a role in both neurocognitive and behavioral realms, although the mechanisms involved may be different.

TS research has progressed significantly during the past decade. The field has moved from descriptive reports based on single individuals or small clinical samples to the use of experimental designs with larger, more diverse, and representative samples. Some longitudinal studies are also under way. The longitudinal elucidation of individual developmental profiles seems critical given the considerable individual variability observed. This degree of variability among individuals with TS in all domains (karyotype or genetic constitution, physical attributes, and neurocognitive and social functioning) suggests the need to identify risk and protective factors contributing to the heterogeneity in the phenotype.

Finally, sufficient progress has been made in our understanding of TS women to inform and justify the use of early preventive interventions to minimize potential problems. Last, and perhaps most important, is participation in patient advocacy groups such as the Turner Syndrome Society of the United States (http://www.turner-syndrome-us.org). This can provide important new information for TS adults and families as well as a supportive peer group.

See also: Mental Status Testing.

Further Reading

McCauley, E, Ross, JL, Kushner, H, et al. (1995). Self-esteem and behavior in girls with Turner syndrome. *J. Dev. Behav. Pediatry* 16: 82–88.

Pavlidis, K, McCauley, E, and Sybert, V (1995). Psychosocial and sexual functioning of adult women with Turner syndrome. *Clin. Genet.* 47: 85–89.

Romans, SM, Stefanatos, G, Roeltgen, DP, et al. (1998). The transition to young-adulthood in Ullrich-Turner syndrome: Neurodevelopmental changes. *Am. J. Med. Genet.* 79: 140–147.

Ross, JL, Stefanatos, G, and Roeltgen, D (1995). Ullrich-Turner syndrome: Neurodevelopmental changes from childhood through adolescence. *Am. J. Med. Genet.* 57: 1–9.

Ross, JL, McCauley, E, and Roeltgen, D (1996). Self-concept and behavior in adolescent girls with Turner syndrome: Potential estrogen effects. *J. Clin. Endocrinol. Metab.* 8: 926–931.

Ross, JL, Roeltgen, D, Feuillan, P, et al. (1998). Estrogen effects on nonverbal processing speed and motor function in girls with Turner syndrome. *J. Clin. Endocrinol. Metab.* 83: 3198–3204.

V

Visual Associative Memory

H. M. Kimura, K. Nakahara, and Y. Miyashita, University of Tokyo School of Medicine, Tokyo, Japan

Associative Memory in Vision: An Elementary Model for Declarative Memory Networks

A significant aspect of high-level cognitive function in humans is our ability to categorize and memorize declarative knowledge and experiences in associative networks that can be reactivated on demand by both internal and external cues. In seeking to better understand the neuronal mechanisms underlying these processes, visual associative memory offers an attractive model that is readily accessible to empirical neurophysiological approaches.

The primate visual system is divided into two functionally and anatomically distinct streams: the dorsal stream and the ventral stream. The dorsal stream, which conveys information from early visual areas to the posterior parietal cortex, is involved in processing the location and motion of visual objects (i.e., where); interruption of this stream disrupts the perception of the spatial relations among objects. On the other hand, the ventral stream conveys information from early visual areas to the inferior temporal (IT) cortex and is involved in processing color and shape (i.e., what); interruption of this stream affects the ability to recognize objects and discriminate among them. In monkeys, bilateral excision of the anterior IT cortex causes severe deficits in visual object recognition and impairs visual pattern discrimination, whereas more posterior, temporal-occipital lesions produce more severe perceptual deficits. Similarly, patients who have undergone right anterior temporal lobectomy show mild impairment in perceptual tasks such as the Mooney Closure Faces Test (in which subjects are asked to visually organize a percept of a face from degraded images), but show markedly impaired recognition memory of complex visual patterns which cannot be verbalized. These deficits are unrelated to the extent of hippocampal removal during the temporal lobectomy. Moreover, electrical stimulation of the temporal lobes of conscious epileptic patients during brain surgery induces vivid, almost hallucinatory memories (i.e., faces of friends and sounds of music), suggesting that electrical input to the putative memory storehouse reactivates the memory records.

These findings suggest that the IT cortex contributes to the representation and storage of visual memories. If this is so, then how are visual associative links represented within the IT cortex? This article focuses on the neuronal substrates and mechanisms underlying visual associative long-term memory (LTM), mainly revealed by single-unit recordings from the brains of monkeys performing memory tasks. We first introduce neurophysiological evidence for neuronal representations of visual associative memories in the monkey IT cortex. We then present single-unit recordings indicating that neural activity within the monkey IT cortex also contains the retrieval signal of visual associative memories. Finally, we discuss how the visual association is recalled from memory by reactivation of the neuronal representation, focusing on two different processes mediating memory retrieval: automatic memory retrieval signaling, which is conveyed backwardly from the limbic cortex to the temporal neocortex, and active retrieval signaling, which is conveyed as top-down signaling from the prefrontal cortex (PFC) to the IT cortex.

Neuronal Correlates of Associative Memory in the Monkey Inferior Temporal Cortex

Inferior Temporal Neurons Establishing Visual Associative Links

The neuronal correlates of visual associative LTM were first identified by Miyashita and Sakai in the monkey IT cortex. They recorded from single neurons while the subjects performed a pair-association (PA) task, which is a well-known neuropsychological test widely used in humans to assess dysfunction of the medial temporal

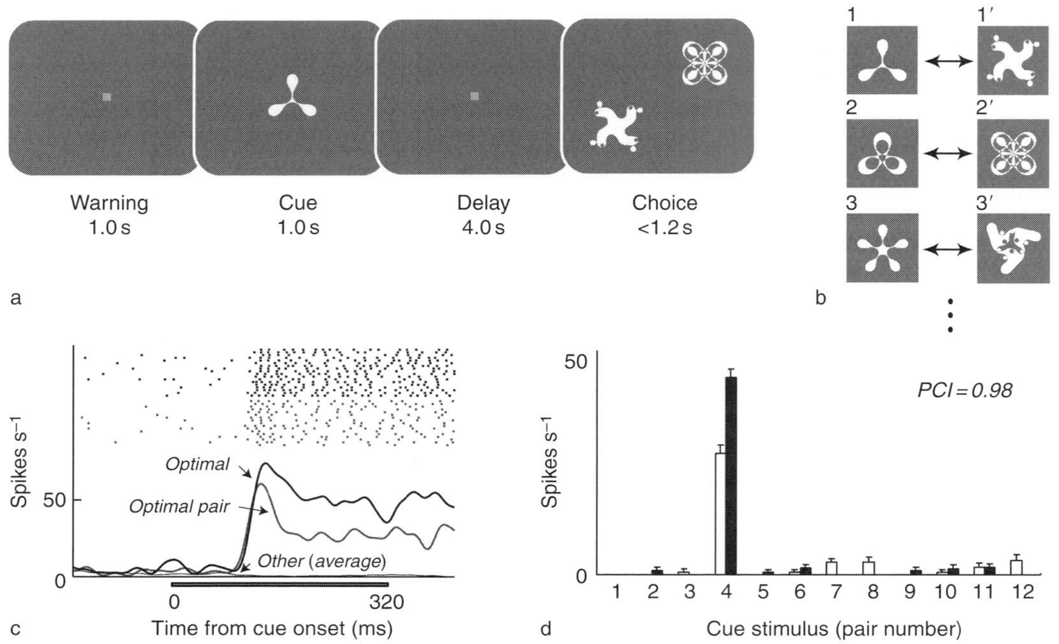

Figure 1 Pair-association (PA) task for monkeys used by Sakai and Miyashita: (a) sequence of events within a trial; (b) examples of paired associates used in the task (the monkeys learned to retrieve the other member of the associated pair for each cue picture); (c) rastergrams of neural discharges in each trial (upper) and spike density functions (SDF, lower) obtained from a single neuron; (d) mean discharge rates during the cue period (60–320 ms from the cue onset). As shown in (a), after a lever press by the monkey initiating a new trial, there is a warning, a green square (1 s); then a cue, one of the Fourier descriptors that serves as the cue stimulus (1 s); then a delay, a green square (4 s); and then a choice of two stimuli, the paired associate of the cue and one from a different pair. Fruit juice was given as a reward for correctly touching the paired associate. In (c), the optimal trial (the strongest response) is shown as the thick black line and optimal-pair trial (the second strongest response) is shown as the thick gray line. The trials are aligned at the cue onset. The thin black line denotes the averaged responses in the other trials. The duration of the cue period was 320 ms. In (d), 12 pairs of stimuli are labeled on the abscissa. The open and filled bars in pair 1, for example, refer to the responses to stimulus 1 and 1′, respectively. Error bars denote SEM. PCI, pair-coding index. (c, d) Reproduced from Naya Y, Yoshida M, and Miyashita Y (2003) Forward processing of long-term associative memory in monkey inferotemporal cortex. *Journal of Neuroscience* 23: 2861–2871. Copyright 2003, with permission from the Society for Neuroscience. (See color plate 40.)

lobe system. In the PA task, the monkeys were trained to memorize associations between computer-generated paired pictures that had no apparent geometric similarity (**Figures 1(a)** and **1(b)**). At the start of each trial, one of the pictures was presented as a cue (i.e., 1 in **Figure 1(b)**). After a delay interval, during which no stimulus was presented, the subject was presented with a choice between the paired associate of the cue (i.e., 1′) and a stimulus from another pair. Using this approach, two classes of task-related neuronal activities were identified in the IT cortex. In one class of neurons, the strongest and second strongest responses during the cue period were ascribed to particular paired pictures (pair-coding neurons; **Figures 1(c)** and **1(d)**). The other type of neurons not only responded to an optimal stimulus during the cue period, but also was active during the blank delay period after the paired associate of the optimal picture was presented as a cue. This delay activity gradually increased until the choice stimuli appeared (target-recall activity; see the section titled 'Two types of sustained activities in the delay period'). This pattern of activity includes the ability of IT neurons to acquire selectivity for visual patterns through associative learning and to establish links between neuronal representations of different stimuli that have a semantic association but no geometrical relationship. Neurophysiological studies of monkeys by other groups lend additional support to this notion of the properties of the IT cortex. For instance, the Logothetis and Tanaka research groups reported that the visual stimulus selectivity of neurons in TE showed a training effect – the proportion of neurons responsive to trained stimuli was significantly greater in trained monkeys than in control untrained monkeys. In addition, Erickson and Desimone recorded single neurons in the perirhinal area of the IT cortex while monkeys performed a visual cue-choice association task and found that the correlation relating responses to a familiar cue and a choice stimulus is highly significant.

Forward Processing of Long-Term Associative Memory

The IT cortex comprises two cytoarchitectonically distinct but mutually interconnected areas: TE and A36 (**Figure 2**). TE is a unimodal neocortical area located at the final stage of the ventral visual stream devoted to object vision. By contrast, A36 is a limbic polymodal association area and a component of the medial temporal-lobe memory system, which is involved in the formation of declarative memory. The respective roles played by these two areas in the neuronal representation of associative memory were analyzed in terms of the pair-coding responses of neurons. A correlation coefficient was calculated for each neuron between the mean firing rate during the cue period to one stimulus and the mean firing rate during the cue period to the paired associate of that stimulus (pair-coding index (PCI)). If a single neuron in a population showed a pattern of stimulus selectivity that was independent of the stimulus pairs, the mean value of the PCIs would be expected to approach 0 as the number of neurons in the population increased. This analysis showed that the PCI values for A36 neurons were significantly higher ($P < 0.001$) than those for TE neurons (**Figure 3(a)**) and that the percentage of neurons which showed significantly positive PCIs at the single-neuron level (pair-coding neurons) was also much higher in A36 (33%) than TE (4.9%). However, the general stimulus selectivities of the cue-selective neurons (as measured by R^2 and kurtosis in **Figures 3(b)** and **3(c)**) did not differ between the two areas, indicating that the associative memory is represented in a highly specific change of neuronal stimulus selectivity (as measured by the PCI).

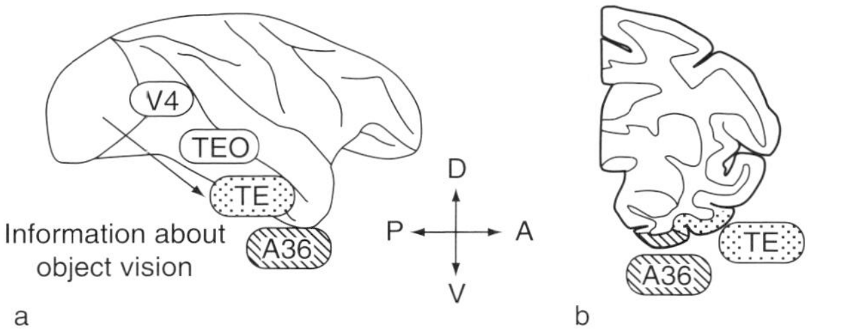

Figure 2 Macaque brain: (a) lateral view; (b) coronal cross section. A36, area 36 (hatched); TE, area TE (dotted); TEO, area TEO; V4, visual area 4; D, dorsal; V, ventral; A, anterior; P, Posterior. Reprinted from Naya Y, Yoshida M, and Miyashita (2001) Backward spreading of memory-retrieval signal in the primate temporal cortex. *Science* 291: 616–664, with permission from American Association for the Advancement of Science.

Next, the time courses of the responses of TE and A36 pair-coding neurons were compared, and it was observed that most of the pair-coding neurons in A36 began to encode the association between paired stimuli as soon as they exhibited stimulus selectivity (called type 1 neurons); the remaining pair-coding neurons in A36 began to encode the association 20–30 ms after they began to show stimulus selectivity (type 2 neurons). This suggests that type 1 neurons encode the associative memory by directly

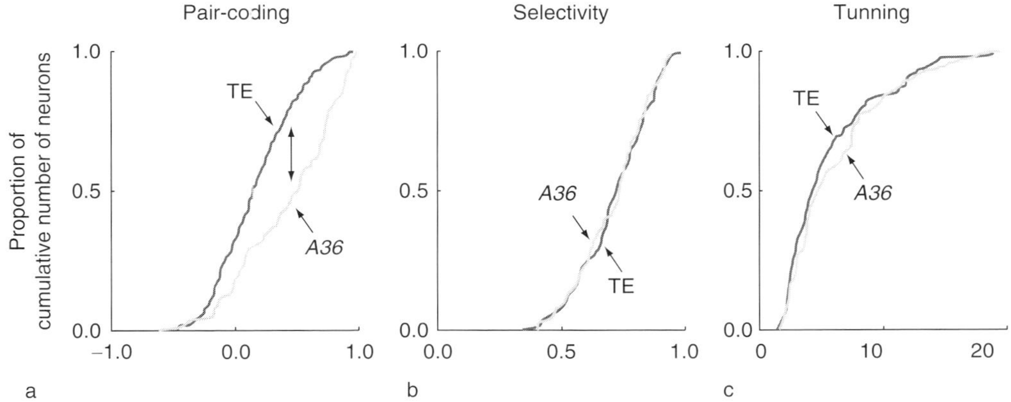

Figure 3 Response correlation to paired associates and general response properties of cue-selective neurons in A36 (light gray) and TE (dark gray): (a) cumulative frequency histogram of PCIs for A36 ($n = 76$) and TE ($n = 347$) neurons; (b) cumulative frequency histogram of R^2; (c) cumulative frequency histogram of kurtosis. In (a), the PCIs for A36 neurons were significantly higher than those for TE neurons ($P < 0.001$; Kolmogorov-Smirnov test). In (b), R^2 provides an estimate of how much of the variance in firing rate can be accounted for by the factor of stimulus. In (c), kurtosis provides a measure of the sharpness of the stimulus selectivity. Neither the R^2 ($P < 0.99$) nor kurtosis ($P = 0.41$) significantly differs between A36 and TE neurons. The equations used are:

- In (a), $\mathrm{PCI} = \sum[(x_i - \mu)(x_{i'} - \mu')]/\{\sum[(x_i - \mu)^2]\sum[(x_i - \mu)^2]\}^{1/2}$, ($i = 1, \ldots, 12$); where x_i is the mean cue response for the ith stimulus (the ith and i'th pictures belong to a pair), and μ and μ' are the average of x_i and $x_{i'}$., respectively.
- In (b), $R^2 = \sum m_j(x_j - \mu_{tot})^2/\sum(x_{j,k} - \mu_{tot})^2 (j = 1, \ldots, 12, 1', \ldots, 12';\ k = 1 - m_j)$;
- In (c), kurtosis $= \sum(x_j - \mu_{tot})^4/\{\sum(x_j - \mu_{tot})^2\}^2 (j = 1, \ldots, 12, 1', \ldots, 12';\ k = 1 - m_j)$, where in the last two equations, $x_{j,k}$ is the cue response in the kth trial for the jth stimulus; x_j is the mean cue response for the jth stimulus; m_j is the total number of the trials for the jth stimulus; and μ_{tot} is the average of the cue responses across the total trials.

A36, area 36; TE, area TE; PCI, pair-coding index. Reproduced from Naya Y, Yoshida M, and Miyashita Y (2003) Forward processing of long-term associative memory in monkey inferotemporal cortex. *Journal of Neuroscience* 23: 2861–2871. Copyright 2003, with permission from the Society for Neuroscience.

combining the feed-forward input from TE, whereas type 2 neurons more likely encode the association memory using feedback input from other higher areas (see the section titled 'Active retrieval: Top-down signal from the prefrontal cortex in executive control of memory retrieval') or intrinsic input from other A36 neurons.

Collectively then, the findings presented so far indicate that the association between the representations of paired-associates proceeds forward through the anatomical hierarchy of the IT cortex and suggest selective convergence onto a single A36 neuron from two groups of TE neurons that separately encode each paired picture.

Retrieval Signaling in Visual Association Memory

Two Types of Sustained Activities in the Delay Period

In the IT cortex, two types of sustained activities were found in the delay period when the subject retrieved and maintained the target stimulus from LTM. One population of IT neurons exhibits a stimulus selectivity pattern during the delay period that was similar to that during the cue period. That is to say, this sustained activity in optimal trials (i.e., the trials in which the optimal stimulus was presented as a cue stimulus) related to the cue stimulus itself – cue-holding activity (**Figures 4(a)** and **4(b)**). On the other hand, another population of neurons exhibits target-recall activities, which was elicited by the paired associate of the cue stimulus rather than by the cue stimulus itself as previously discussed (**Figures 4(c)** and **4(d)**). This sustained activity in optimal-pair trials (i.e., the trials in which the paired associate of the optimal stimulus was presented as a cue stimulus) is induced only when the subject retrieves and maintains the optimal stimulus in mind and thus reflects the memory of the optimal stimulus. To further characterize the cue-holding and target-recall activities, the responses to all of the cue stimuli were considered. The partial correlation coefficients relating delay activity to the responses to a particular cue stimulus (cue-holding index (CHI)) and to its paired associate (pair-recall index (PRI)) were calculated for each neuron. CHI and PRI values are bounded by −1 and 1; a large CHI implies cue-holding activity as shown in **Figures 4(a)** and **4(b)** (CHI = 0.95, PRI = −0.47), whereas a large PRI implies target-recall activity as shown in **Figures 4(c)** and **4(d)** (CHI = −0.01, PRI = 0.64).

Then, how are these two types of delay activities, cue-holding and target-recall, represented in TE and A36? The comparison of the delay activities between individual TE

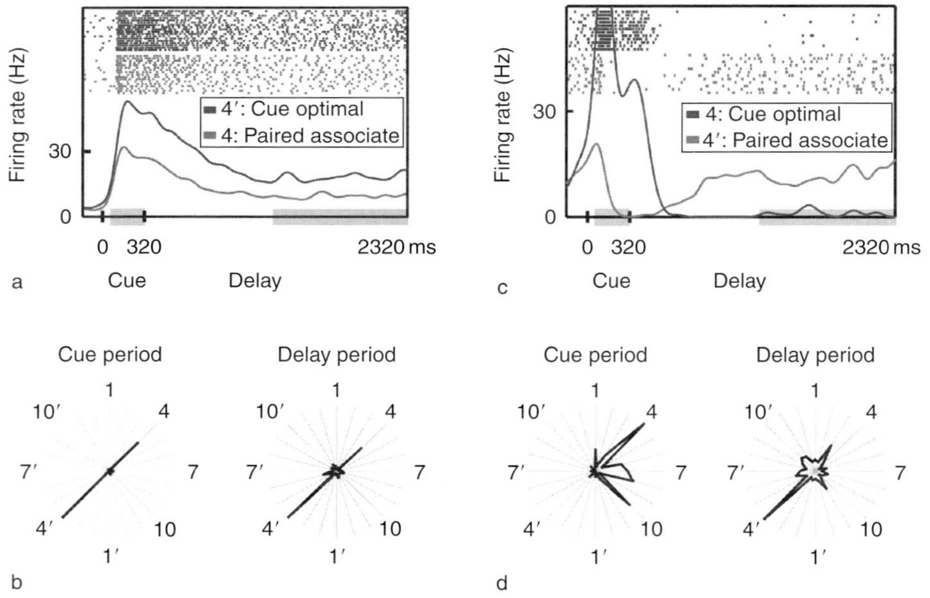

Figure 4 Examples of delay-selective neurons: (a) A36 raster displays and spike density functions; (b) A36 polar plots of mean discharge rates; (c) TE raster displays and spike density functions; (d) TE polar plots of mean discharge rates. In (a,c) , trials using the cue-optimal stimulus as the cue (optimal trials, green) and those using the paired associate as the cue (optimal-pair trials, red) were aligned at the cue onset. In (b) and (d), mean discharge rates during the cue and delay periods (60–320 ms and 1320–2320 ms; gray boxes in (a) and (c), respectively) are shown in polar plots for each cue presentation. The responses to stimuli and to their paired associates are indicated by radial lines. The discharge rates were normalized based on the maximum values for each period ((b) cue period, 44.0 Hz at stimulus 4′; delay period, 18.6 Hz at stimulus 4′; (d) cue period, 48.7 Hz at stimulus 4; delay period, 18.7 Hz at stimulus 4′). A36, area 36; TE, area TE. Reproduced from Naya Y, Yoshida M, Takeda M, Fujimichi R, and Miyashita Y (2003) Delay-period activities in two subdivisions of monkey inferotemporal cortex during pair association memory task. *European Journal of Neuroscience* 18: 2915–2918. Copyright 2003, with permission from Blackwell Publishing Ltd. (See color plate 41.)

and A36 neurons during a PA task in terms of their signal content provided the answer to this question. A comparison of the CHI and PRI values for TE and A36 neurons revealed that in TE the PRIs for the delay-selective neurons were significantly higher than the CHIs. In A36, by contrast, the PRIs for the delay-selective neurons were not different from the CHIs. Moreover, the CHIs were significantly lower in TE than in A36, whereas the PRIs did not significantly differ in the two areas. This suggests that the delay activity of TE neurons preferentially represents the paired associate that is retrieved from LTM, not the cue stimulus itself, whereas the delay activity of A36 neurons retained not only the paired associate but also the cue stimulus.

Active Maintenance of Associative Mnemonic Signaling in the Monkey Inferior Temporal Cortex

In another study focusing on delay activity with the aim of determining the contribution made by IT neurons to the persistence of internal representations, single units were recorded from neurons in the IT cortex while monkeys performed a sequential type of PA task in which distractor stimuli interrupted the delay period between a cue stimulus and the target stimulus (the paired associate of the cue stimulus) (**Figure 5(a)**). Some delay-selective neurons exhibited, in optimal trials, cue-holding activity during the first delay period. This sustained discharge was attenuated when the distractor stimulus was presented (compare the two light-gray shaded areas in **Figure 5(b)**). During optimal-pair trials, the neuronal discharge of the same cell was weak throughout the trial (**Figure 5(c)**). However, during optimal-pair trials another type of neuron exhibited target-recall activity during the first delay period, and the significant activity was still sustained during the second delay period (compare the two light-gray shaded areas in **Figure 5(e)**). During optimal trials, by contrast, the neuronal discharge of the same cell was weak both during the first and the second delay periods (**Figure 5(d)**). These results mean that the cue-holding activity tends to be attenuated by the subsequent distractor stimulus (in fact, this activity is replaced by that elicited by the distractor stimulus) during the second delay period (i.e., after the presentation of the distractor stimulus); on the other hand, the target-recall activity continues to signal the target stimulus information, even after an intervening distractor.

A population analysis of all the delay-selective neurons recorded is shown in **Figures 5(f)** and **5(g)**. Partial regression coefficients (β) were used to relate the neuronal discharge during the first delay period and second delay periods to the discharge elicited by the cue and target. A larger value of β means that the delay activities convey more information about the cue or target.

The scatterplots relates the β values for the cue (**Figure 5(f)**) and target (**Figure 5(g)**) stimuli during the first and second delay periods. Note that the values for the cue stimulus lie below the orthogonal line, whereas those for the target stimulus lie around it. This indicates that the target stimulus information signaled by delay activity is more resistant to the distractor stimulus than the cue stimulus information and suggests that, whereas LTM-derived information required for upcoming behavior (i.e., target stimulus) is actively maintained in IT neurons, visually derived information tends to be updated irrespective of behavioral relevance (i.e., cue stimulus and distractor stimulus).

Global Network of Memory Retrieval

Thus far, we have provided evidence as to how visual associative memory is stored and represented in the IT cortex. We next discuss how these mnemonic representations are reactivated during memory retrieval. The evidence summarized shows that memory retrieval can be processed either within the IT cortex or via an interaction between the PFC and the IT cortex.

Everyone knows from experience that sometimes recollection is effortless but that at other times one must make an effort to recall successfully. Here, we refer to the former as automatic retrieval and to the latter as active retrieval. Visual associative memories can be retrieved from the IT cortex by either of these two processes.

Automatic Retrieval: Backward Spreading of the Memory-Retrieval Signal in the Temporal Cortex

During a PA task, groups of neurons in both TE and A36 show target-recall activity. The responses of representative A36 neuron and TE neuron are shown in **Figures 6(a)** and **6(c)**. One stimulus elicited the strongest response during the cue period (perceptual signal), and the latencies of the response in TE neurons were significantly shorter than those in A36 neurons (TE, median 77 ms; A36, median 89 ms; Kolmogorov–Smirnov test, $P < 0.05$). Moreover, the paired-associate stimulus of a cue stimulus elicits the highest delay activity in A36 and TE neurons, although the onset of the target-recall tonic activity was later in TE than in A36 (**Figures 6(a)** and **6(c)**).

To compare the properties of the target-recall activities between TE and A36 neurons, the time courses were analyzed. In this analysis, an instantaneous PRI at time plot t (PRI(t)) was defined as partial correlation coefficients relating instantaneous firing rates at time t in the response to each cue stimulus to the responses to its paired associate. Then the time courses of the average PRI(t) across the population of stimulus-selective neurons in A36 and TE were determined. The average PRI(t) for the A36 neurons began to increase within the cue period and developed over

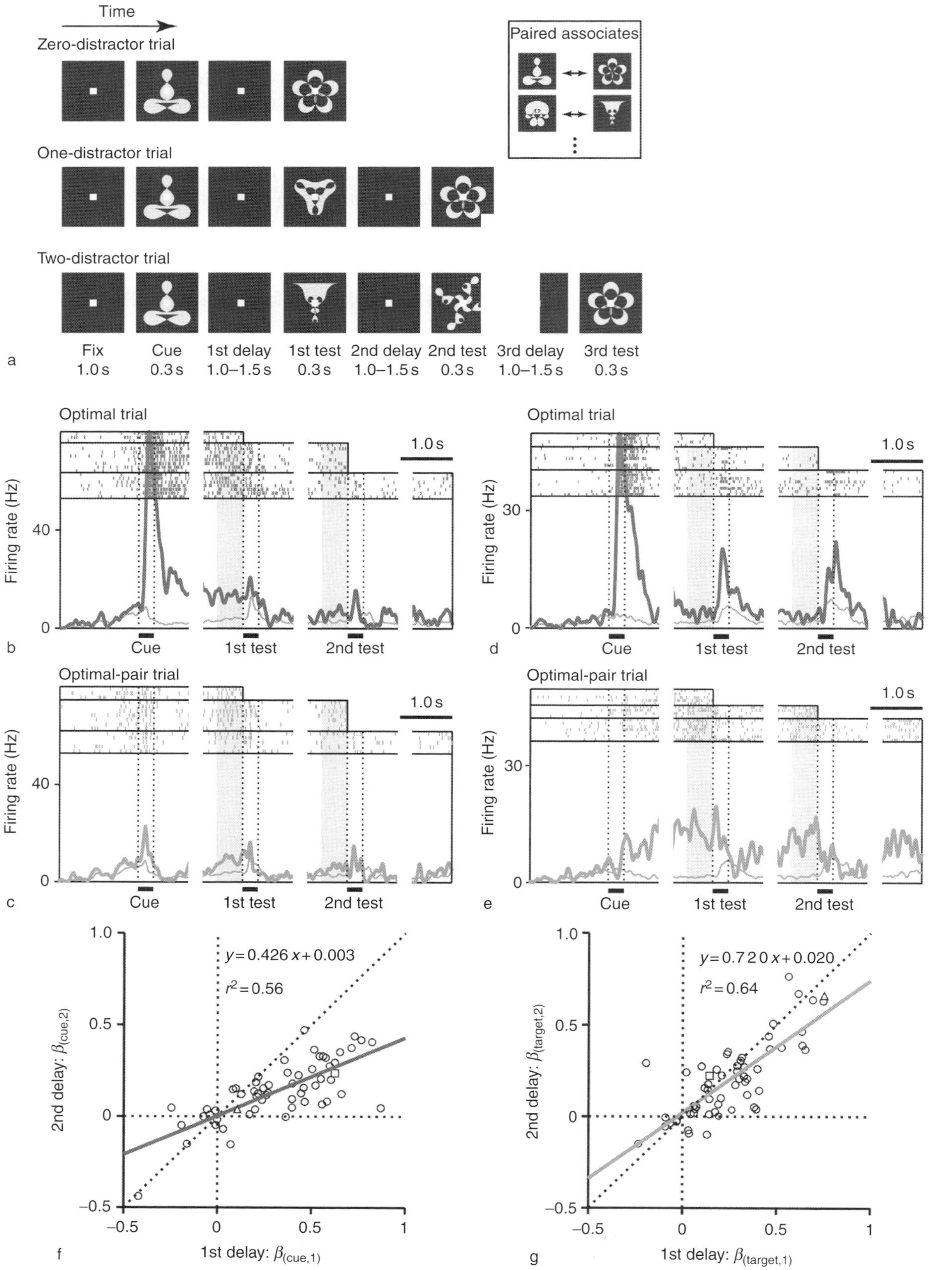

Figure 5 (Continued)

a comparatively rapid time course (**Figure 6(b)**). On the other hand, the PRI(t) for the TE neurons increased slowly, reaching a plateau in the middle of the delay period (**Figure 6(d)**). Apparently, even though the visual signal reaches TE before it reaches A36, the memory retrieval signal emerges first in A36 and then TE neurons are gradually recruited to represent the sought target. The implication of this finding is that backward projections from A36 to TE may underlie the activation of TE neurons that represent mnemonic information retrieved from LTM.

Active Retrieval: Top-Down Signal from the Prefrontal Cortex in Executive Control of Memory Retrieval

Memory retrieval can be regulated by top-down processes that have been implicated in executive functions, such as planning. For instance, examination of an epileptic patient with a selective posterior callosotomy revealed that although sensory stimuli confined to the nondominant right hemisphere could not be transferred to the left hemisphere for naming, semantic features of those stimuli could be described using the expressive language system of the left hemisphere. This observation suggests that top-down processes originating in the PFC can regulate the retrieval of LTM from the modality-specific posterior association cortex, even in the absence of direct sensory input.

To test that idea, the posterior corpus callosum (CC) and the anterior commissure were transected in monkey subjects (the posterior split-brain paradigm), after which the monkeys' performances on a PA task were evaluated. The critical question was whether the PFC of these monkeys could instruct the contralateral hemisphere, via the intact anterior CC, to retrieve LTM when sensory interaction between posterior cortical areas was prevented. In the posterior-split-brain monkey, each hemisphere receives bottom-up visual information only from the contralateral visual hemifield, and LTM acquired through learning pair association does not transfer interhemispherically via the anterior CC. Nonetheless, information about the cue stimulus presented to one hemisphere was transmitted through the anterior CC, enabling the target stimulus specified by the cue to be retrieved from the other hemisphere. Thus, we can conclude that, although visual LTM is stored in the temporal cortex, memory retrieval is under the executive control of the PFC.

The existence of top-down signaling from the PFC to the temporal cortex and its contribution to the active retrieval process have been demonstrated using single-unit recordings from the IT cortex of posterior-split-brain monkeys. In these animals, IT neurons in one hemisphere were activated by bottom-up visual inputs when an object was presented in the visual hemifield contralateral to the recording site (**Figure 7(a)**). When the object was presented in the ipsilateral hemifield, however, these neurons did not receive the bottom-up visual inputs (**Figure 7(b)**), so any neural activation should reflect top-down inputs from the PFC. And, in fact, a considerable number of IT neurons received top-down signals from the PFC (**Figure 7(c)**). The neurons were activated not only by contralateral presentation of stimuli but also by ipsilateral presentation of stimuli. The stimulus selectivity of the bottom-up response was similar to that of the top-down response. The onset latency of neuronal responses was significantly longer under the top-down than the bottom-up condition, and top-down responses were abolished after transection of the remaining anterior CC (full-split).

The memory retrieval is a complicated process; it is not just the process of cueing and interrogation of the memory store (a narrow sense of memory retrieval), but it is also bound up with the updating of memory information in working memory and evaluation or monitoring of this information. Recent positron emissions tomography (PET) and functional magnetic resonance imaging (fMRI) studies carried out in humans while they performed a memory retrieval task confirmed that the PFC is involved in these

Figure 5 Sequential-type paired-association task. (a) The procedure; (b,c) rastergrams and SDFs of the optimal trials and optimal-pair trials showing representative neurons exhibiting cue-holding activity; (d,e) rastergrams and SDFs of the optimal trials and optimal-pair trials showing representative neurons exhibiting target-recall activity; (f) scatterplot of the effect of the cue stimulus on neuronal activity during the delay epoch; (g) scatterplot of the effects of the target stimulus on neuronal activity during the delay epoch. As shown in (a), after the fixation spot, one of the pictures was presented as the cue stimulus. During the delay epoch that followed the cue stimulus, one, two, or three test stimuli were presented. After each delay period, the paired associate of the cue stimulus (target stimulus) or a distractor stimulus was presented as the test stimulus. In (b–e), gray lines indicate average SDFs in trials in which the other pictures were presented as cue stimuli. Data from correct trials are aligned on the onset of the cue, first-test, and second-test stimuli. Light-gray shading indicates the first and second delay periods for analysis. In the optimal trials, neuronal discharge (cue-holding activity) declined from the first to the second delay period (b). In the optimal-pair trials, strong neuronal discharge (target-recall activity) was observed during both the first and second delay periods (e). In (f), the scatterplot relates the changes in the β values for the cue stimulus from the first delay (x axis) to the second delay (y axis) period across the population of delay-selective neurons ($n = 59$). The regression slope is significantly positive ($t = 8.58$, $p < 0.01$). In (g), the regression slope for the β values for the target stimulus is significantly positive ($t = 9.95$, $p < 0.01$) and steeper than that for β values for the cue stimulus ($F = 11.57$, $p < 0.01$). The open triangles in (f, g) represent the data from the neurons in (b,c) and the open squares represent the data from the neurons in (d,e). SDF, spike density function. Reproduced from Takeda M, Naya Y, Fujimichi R, Takeuchi D, and Miyashita Y (2005) Active maintenance of associative mnemonic signal in monkey inferior temporal cortex. *Neuron* 48: 839–848. Copyright 2005, with permission from Elsevier. (See color plate 42.)

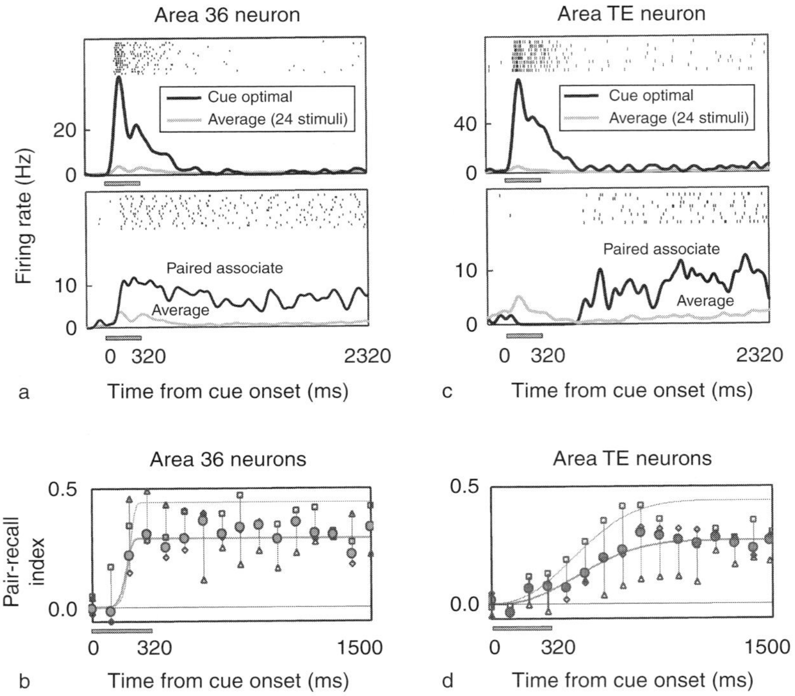

Figure 6 Neuronal activity related to memory retrieval during the paired-association task: (a) activity of a representative A36 neuron; (b) temporal dynamics of average PRI(*t*) for the population of stimulus-selective A36 neurons ($n = 45$); (c) activity of a representative TE neuron; (d) temporal dynamics of average PRI(*t*) for the population of stimulus-selective TE neurons ($n = 69$). In (a) and (c), SDFs are aligned at the cue onset in trials where the cue-optimal stimulus served as the cue (top) and in trials where its paired associate served as the cue (bottom). Black lines indicate responses to the cue-optimal stimulus (top) or its paired associate (bottom); gray lines indicate mean responses to all stimuli. In (b) and (d), mean values of PRI(*t*) are plotted every 100 ms (solid circle, total; diamond, monkey 1; open square, monkey 2; open triangle, monkey 3). Thick lines (green and red, respectively) indicate the best-fit Weibull functions for the population-averaged PRI(*t*) in the two areas. Thin lines indicate this for the neurons whose PRI(*t*) increased above the 5% significance level. PRI, paired-recall index; SDF, spike density function. Reprinted from Naya Y, Yoshida M, and Miyashita Y (2001) Backward spreading of memory-retrieval signal in the primate temporal cortex. *Science* 291: 661–664, with permission from American Association for the Advancement of Science. (See color plate 43.)

component processes. In that context, Fletcher and Henson investigated the roles of three regions of the lateral frontal cortex: the ventrolateral frontal cortex (VLFC; Brodmann's area (BA) 44, 45, 47), the dorsolateral frontal cortex (DLFC; BA 9, 46), and the anterior frontal cortex (AFC; BA 8, 10). In paired associate-cued retrieval tasks, activation of the VLFC contributed to updating and maintaining working memory (WM), within which the cue must be maintained along with possible responses retrieved from LTM. The DLFC, on the other hand, was involved in selecting, manipulating, and monitoring information already active in WM. Because efficient interaction between the VLFC and DLFC is necessary to meet the demands of the task, a meta-level of control is needed to coordinate them. Such control was attributed to the AFC, which optimally selects between the processes or goals of the VLFC and DLFC in order to maximize task performance. Earlier anatomical studies showed that BA 47/12 (an area within the VLFC) is strongly connected with the IT cortical region, which suggests that the top-down retrieval signaling from the PFC to the IT cortex seen in the single-unit study previously summarized may have originated from the homolog of BA 47/12 in the monkey PFC.

The actual retrieval processes are even more complicated than we mentioned in the preceding paragraph; they may entail encoding processes (i.e., when we remember something, we inevitably encode it again at the same time, and vice versa). Consequently, it is important to reevaluate the previous neuroimaging studies from the viewpoints that the memory retrieval process can be seen at different levels of the definition. Questions that remain include, are there the prefrontal regions which are specifically involved in retrieval processes in the narrowest definition? If yes, what signals are exchanged between these areas and the areas related to monitoring or selection or encoding? And which prefrontal area controls these complicated processes of across-areal communication? Future research should provide answers to these and other questions, enabling a fuller understanding and appreciation of the neuronal mechanisms responsible for the management of semantic memories in primate brains.

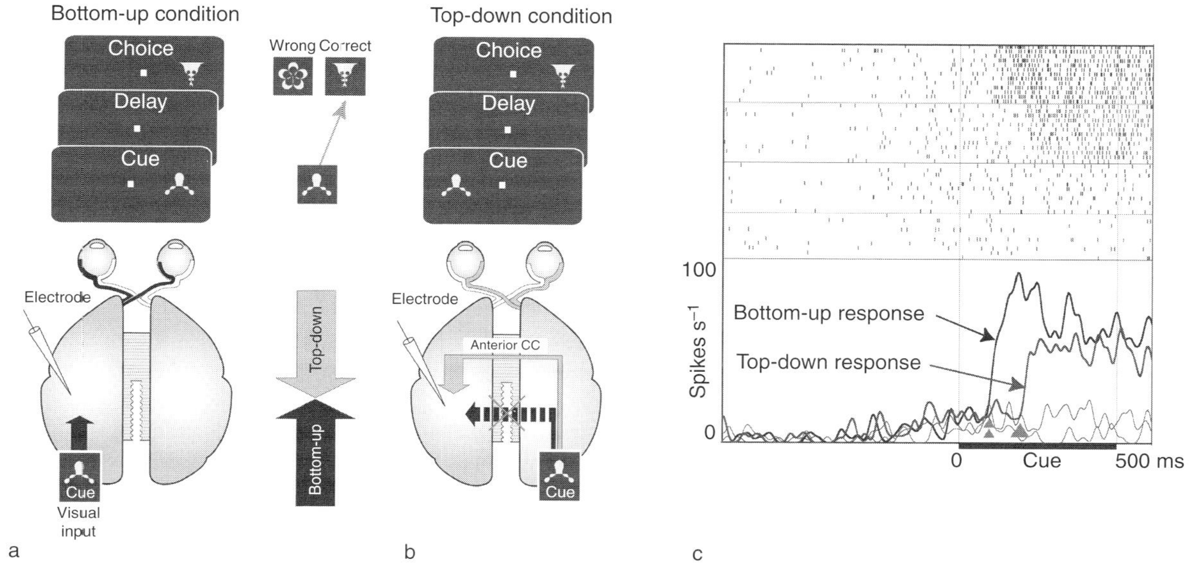

Figure 7 Experimental design measuring neuronal activity in monkeys: (a) bottom-up condition; (b) top-down condition; (c) activity of a single IT neuron under the top-down condition (top-down, blue; bottom-up, black). As shown in (a), in the bottom-up condition visual stimuli (cue and choice pictures) were presented in the hemifield contralateral to the recording site (electrode) in the IT cortex. The monkey was required to make the correct choice specified by the cue. Fixation was required throughout each trial ($< 0.6°$). Bottom-up sensory signals (black arrow) were detected in this condition. As shown in (b), in the top-down condition, the cue was presented in the hemifield ipsilateral to the recording site, but the choice was presented contralaterally. In posterior-split-brain monkeys, sensory signals do not reach the visual areas in the opposite hemisphere. In this condition, only top-down signals (blue arrow) can activate IT neurons through top-down connections from the prefrontal cortex. In (c), the raster displays and SDFs are aligned at the cue onset. In the SDFs, the thick lines show responses to the optimal cue; the thin lines show responses to a null cue. The onset of the top-down response (arrowhead) was later than the onset of the bottom-up response (doubled arrowhead). CC, corpus callosum; IT, inferior temporal; SDF, spike density function. Modified from Tomita H, Ohbayashi M, Nakahara K, Hasegawa I, and Miyashita Y (1999) Top-down signal from prefrontal cortex in executive control of memory retrieval. *Nature* 401: 699–703, Copyright 1999 with permission from Macmillan Publishers Ltd. (See color plate 44.)

See also: Amnesia, Declarative and Nondeclarative Memory; Memory, Semantic.

Further Reading

Brown, MW and Aggleton, JP (2001). Recognition memory: What are the roles of the perirhinal cortex and hippocampus? *Nature Reviews Neuroscience* 2: 51–61.

Buckner, RL and Wheeler, ME (2001). The cognitive neuroscience of remembering. *Nature Reviews Neuroscience* 2: 624–634.

Fletcher, PC and Henson, RN (2001). Frontal lobes and human memory: Insights from functional neuroimaging. *Brain* 124: 849–881.

Milner, B (1990). Right temporal-lobe contribution to visual perception and visual memory. In: Iwai, R and Mishkin, M (eds.) *Vision, Memory and the Temporal Lobe*, pp. 43–53. New York: Elsevier.

Miyashita, Y (2004). Cognitive memory: Cellular and network machineries and their top-down control. *Science* 306: 435–440.

Murray, EA and Bussey, TJ (1999). Perceptual-mnemonic functions of the perirhinal cortex. *Trends in Cognitive Science* 3: 142–151.

Naya Y, Yoshida M, and Miyashita Y (2001) Backward spreading of memory-retrieval signal in the primate temporal cortex. *Science* 291: 661–664.

Naya, Y, Yoshida, M, and Miyashita, Y (2003). Forward processing of long-term associative memory in monkey inferotemporal cortex. *Journal of Neuroscience* 23: 2861–2871.

Naya Y, Yoshida M, Takeda M, Fujimichi R, and Miyashita Y (2003). Delay-period activities in two subdivisions of monkey inferotemporal cortex during pair association memory task. *European Journal of Neuroscience* 18: 2915–2918.

Petrides, M (2000). Frontal lobes and memory. In: Boller, F and Grafman, J (eds.) *Handbook of Neuropsychology*, pp. 67–84. Amsterdam: Elsevier.

Ranganath, C and D'Esposito, M (2005). Directing the mind's eye: Prefrontal, inferior and medial temporal mechanisms for visual working memory. *Current Opinion in Neurobiology* 15: 175–182.

Simons, JS and Spiers, HJ (2003). Prefrontal and medial temporal lobe interactions in long-term memory. *Nature Reviews Neuroscience* 4: 637–648.

Squire, LR, Stark, CEL, and Clark, RE (2004). The medial temporal lobe. *Annual Review of Neuroscience* 27: 279–306.

Takeda, M, Naya, Y, Fujimichi, R, Takeuchi, D, and Miyashita, Y (2005). Active maintenance of associative mnemonic signal in monkey inferior temporal cortex. *Neuron* 48: 839–848.

Tanaka, K (1997). Mechanisms of visual object recognition: Monkey and human studies. *Current Opinion in Neurobiology* 7: 523–529.

Tomita, H, Ohbayashi, M, Nakahara, K, Hasegawa, I, and Miyashita, Y (1999). Top-down signal from prefrontal cortex in executive control of memory retrieval. *Nature* 401: 699–703.

Wagner, AD, Desmond, JE, Glover, GH, and Gabrieli, JD (1998). Prefrontal cortex and recognition memory: Functional-MRI evidence for context-dependent retrieval process. *Brain* 121: 1985–2002.

W

Word Learning

J. Snedeker, Harvard University, Cambridge, MA, USA

Word learning is often considered the simplest and least controversial aspect of language development. Although theorists fiercely debate the ontogenetic and phylogenetic origins of grammar, everyone agrees that words must be learned by observing the contexts in which they are used. No other theory can explain how English-speaking children come to use 'shoe' to label footwear, whereas young French speakers use the same sequence of sounds to label cabbage. However, this self-evident truth masks a host of questions about how learning occurs and the knowledge that children bring to the problem.

Defining the Problem

To understand word learning, we need to know both what a word is and which aspects of words are learned. Surprisingly, neither question has a clear answer. There are two difficulties in defining what a word is.

The first is determining what information is included as part of a word. By all definitions, each word (or lexical entry) consists of a symbol that is paired with a concept. In the case of spoken languages, these symbols consist of phonological representations. For example, my lexical entry for 'cat' includes the phoneme sequence /kæt/ which is linked to some conceptual representation of catness. Literate individuals also store the written form of words they are familiar with. In addition, language users have other knowledge of words that could be a part of the lexical entry. Much of this knowledge is related to the grammatical environments in which a word appears. For example, our knowledge of English allows us to recognize that "I have a cat" is a grammatical sentence, whereas "I like to cat" is not. In dictionaries, we capture these facts by assigning words to grammatical categories which are listed with each definition (e.g., 'cat' is a noun and not a verb). Many have argued that grammatical categories are also stored in the mental lexicon. However, our knowledge of the relation between lexical items and grammatical structure extends beyond syntactic categories. For example, we know that a verb such as 'roll' can appear in a transitive sentence ("I rolled the ball"), whereas a verb such as 'fall' cannot ("I fell the ball"). This has led many to propose that individual lexical entries contain detailed grammatical information about the contexts of word use. Others have argued that the concepts with which words are associated allow us to derive these structural facts, eliminating the need for their storage.

The second definitional difficulty is determining how to individuate words: Which chunks of linguistic material are entered in our mental lexicons? How large are these chunks, and where does one entry end and the next begin? Clearly, words such as 'cat' that consist of a single morpheme (meaningful unit) will have to be stored because they cannot be derived in any way. However, we also store morphemes that are not whole words (-ness or-ed), some words that are made of multiple morphemes (e.g., 'walked' or 'happiness'), and idioms that consist of multiple words ('kick the bucket'). The fact that many phonological forms have several meanings creates further uncertainty about what constitutes a lexical entry. In the case of homonyms, these meanings are not related and clearly must be stored separately (e.g., river bank vs. savings bank). However, in the case of polysemes, the different meanings are related (e.g., line up vs. telephone line), and it is unclear whether the alternatives are two separate words, two ways of thinking about a single lexical entry, or two subentries of a single lexical item. Problems of this kind have led some theorists to reject the metaphor of the lexicon as the list of entries and to argue instead that the lexicon is a generative system for linking forms to meanings.

Once we have defined a word, we can ask what it means to learn one. Which aspects of a lexical entry are learned and which can be derived? Which parts of the entry precede word learning and which are the result of it? All theorists agree that children must learn the mapping between the phonological form and the concept. Although there are some minor islands of systematicity (e.g., in English words beginning with *sn-* are related to the nose), these mappings are largely arbitrary and vary across languages; thus, they must be learned. There is more controversy about the role of learning in our ability to represent the phonological form of the word or to represent the concept with which it is associated.

Adults and older children clearly represent speech in terms of stable phonological categories and thus simply have to learn the sequence of phonemes that is linked to a particular concept. The nature of infants' phonological representations has been more controversial. Because infants sometimes fail to distinguish between two novel words that are similar but phonologically distinct (e.g., 'bim' and 'dim'), it has been suggested that infants have less precise, gestalt representations of words and only develop phonological representations as their lexicons grow. However, infants can succeed in learning phonologically similar words in more supportive contexts and have more difficulty comprehending a known word when a single phoneme has been altered. One possible interpretation is that infants represent word forms in the same way as older children but have difficulty attending to and encoding these forms when the task is challenging.

Many developmental psychologists have argued that word learning involves concept acquisition. Children do not merely map words to existing concepts; instead, they use the recurring word form as a cue to form a new category. This theory is compatible with the Whorfian hypothesis because the concepts that the learner acquires depend on the concepts that are lexicalized in the learner's language. This theory could potentially explain why children learn concrete words early and more abstract words later, or why labels for objects generally appear before predicates. However, theories of this kind face two challenges. First, it is unclear how a child could learn what a word means if he or she did not already have access to the concept that the word encodes. To recognize that a word reliably co-occurs with a particularly category of entities, one must be able to represent those entities as a class. In other words, you cannot not learn that /kæt/ means cat unless you already have a representational arsenal that allows you to distinguish cats from noncats. Second, the course of lexical development in cognitively advanced learners suggests that conceptual limitations play little role in early word learning. Children who are internationally adopted as preschoolers must learn a new language in context similar to that of infant language learners. If the course of infant word learning is shaped by the conceptual limitations of babies, then we would expect that older children, free from such limitations, would be able to learn more verbs and abstract words during the initial phases of lexical development. However, internationally adopted preschoolers acquire words in approximately the same order as infant learners, suggesting that early vocabulary development is largely independent of cognitive development.

Word Learning across Development

Children learning both signed and spoken languages generally produce their first word at approximately 12 months of age. By adulthood, the typical person knows approximately 60 000 words. Although this averages out to approximately 9 words a day, the actual pace of word learning varies across development. As **Figure 1** illustrates, the initial pace of word learning is quite slow, with the average child learning approximately 2 words a week between 12 and 16 months of age. Until recently, many observers believed that there was a sudden acceleration in word learning at approximately 18 months of age (often called the vocabulary spurt). However, closer examination has revealed that the pace of word learning increases gradually throughout the toddler and preschool years. In literate societies, this steady acceleration continues into the school years as children encounter new words while reading. The pace of word learning begins to decelerate

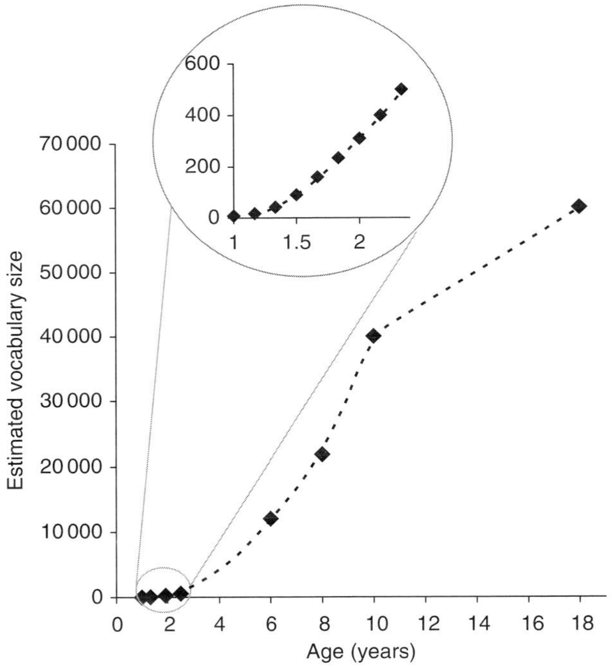

Figure 1 Vocabulary growth throughout development. The vocabulary estimates for 12- to 30-month-olds are from Fenson L, Dale PS, Reznick JS, Bates E, Thal DJ, and Pethick SJ (1994) Variability in early communicative development. *Monographs of the Society for Research in Child Development* 59: 1–173. The estimates for 6- to 10-year-olds are from Anglin J (1993) Vocabulary development: A morphological analysis. *Monographs of the Society for Research in Child Development* 238: 1–166. The estimate for adults is based on the figure cited by Aitchinson J (1994) *Words in the Mind: An Introduction to the Mental Lexicon*, 2nd edn. Oxford, UK: Blackwell.

sometime between 8 and 18 years, presumably because older children encounter fewer unknown words. There is no evidence for a critical period in word learning: Adults do as well or better than children in most experimental word learning tasks and we can readily learn new words throughout our lives.

As children's vocabularies grow, they also change. The first words that children learn are typically labels for people ('mommy' or 'daddy'), animal names ('kitty'), social words ('hi' or 'uh-oh'), or utterances used in common routines ('peek-a-boo'). Although verbs, prepositions, and other relational words appear in early vocabularies, they may have more limited meanings for infants than they do for adults and older children. For example, many 1-year-olds say 'more' to request the recurrence of an event or object, but there is no evidence that children of this age understand that 'more' is a term that quantifies the amount in one set relative to another.

The early vocabularies of children learning English are dominated by nouns, most of which label people, animals, or objects. Even though adults speak to young children in full sentences, complete with verbs and grammatical words, these elements are massively underrepresented in children's early vocabularies. The proportion of nouns in the child's lexicon varies from language to language depending on whether subjects and objects are mandatory and whether the verb appears in a perceptually salient position (e.g., at the beginning or end of the utterance). Nevertheless, in every language that has been systematically studied, nouns are overrepresented in children's vocabularies relative to their rate of occurrence in the input, whereas verbs are underrepresented. This suggests that nouns, particularly those that label objects or people, are easier for children to learn than verbs or other relational words. Some theorists have attributed this to the greater conceptual complexity of verbs, whereas others attribute it to the nature of the information needed to identify the meanings of nouns and verbs.

There is considerable variability in how rapidly children learn words. At 16 months of age, the median vocabulary size for middle-class children in the US, is approximately 40 words. However, 10% of children produce no words, whereas another 10% produce more than 150 words. Early in development, vocabulary size is a better predictor of vocabulary composition than age. As the child's vocabulary grows from 50 to 200 words, the proportion of these words that are nouns increases. Verbs and adjectives begin to appear in greater numbers between 100 and 400 words. Grammatical words (such as articles, pronouns, prepositions, and auxiliaries) increase in frequency at approximately 400 words. Between 16 and 30 months, the size of a child's productive vocabulary is tightly correlated with the grammatical complexity of the child's speech. Initially, children primarily produce one-word utterances. When their productive vocabulary reaches 50–200 words, they begin combining words into short phrases. From 300 to 500 words, grammatical morphemes appear and the child's utterances increase in length and complexity. These relations are preserved in internationally adopted preschoolers, suggesting that the correlation is not a side effect of global maturational or cognitive changes. In bilingual children, these relations hold within a language but not between languages, suggesting that lexical development facilitates grammatical development or vice versa. During the school years, lexical development and reading are closely linked. A child's vocabulary when he or she enters school is a strong predictor of later reading achievement, and subsequent vocabulary development is correlated with the amount that the child reads.

Word Learning as Induction

How do children learn the meanings of words? Most people who have thought about the problem long enough have come up with essentially the same solution: Word learning is a form of induction. Learners generate hypotheses based on the situation in which the new word occurs. As the learner observes new instances of the word, hypotheses are eliminated or strengthened, allowing him or her to close in on the correct meaning.

Although this mechanism clearly plays a role in word learning, it cannot be the entire story. First, even very young children can learn some words after hearing them used in just one context. Second, many words, particularly verbs and other relational terms, are often used in the absence of the event being labeled (e.g., when parents tell children to "go to sleep," both parties are typically awake).

Finally, the account of word learning given previously is subject to the mid-century critiques of empiricism voiced by philosophers such as W. V. O. Quine and Nelson Goodman. Learning simply cannot be unconstrained induction because any finite set of observations is consistent with an infinite set of hypotheses. To take Quine's example, the set of observations that would allow one to learn that a word ('gavagai') means rabbit is also compatible with the hypothesis that it means undetached rabbit parts (or temporal rabbit slices). Thus, a full account of lexical development requires more than merely stating that word learning is induction. In the past 25 years, developmental psycholinguists have begun to flesh out this story by identifying three ways in which children and adults can tame the induction problem and learn the meanings of words.

Constraints and Biases on Hypothesized Meanings

The first way to tame induction is by limiting the range of meanings that are considered as possible hypotheses.

Many theoretically possible meanings may be ruled out simply because children cannot or do not think of them – for word learning or any other purpose. Quine's example of undetached rabbit parts is presumably ruled out by cognitive constraints of this kind. However, such constraints cannot explain how the learner rules out more plausible alternatives such as white, fluffy, hopping, tail, animal, or Flopsie. All these hypotheses are plausible ones, meanings which the learner could eventually link to some other phonological form. Children, however, are biased learners who privilege some of these hypotheses over others.

The nature of these biases has been explored with an experimental paradigm called the word extension task. In this task, children are shown a novel object (e.g., a blue kidney-shaped piece of plaster) which is labeled with a novel word ("This is my dax"). Then they are given a small set of test objects (e.g., a blue circular piece of plaster and a red kidney-shaped piece of wood) and asked to find another example of the target word ("Can you give me the dax?"). The child's response allows the experimenter to infer how the child is interpreting the novel word.

Through tasks such as this one, researchers have discovered that children (and adults) have a strong bias to assume that a new word refers to a whole object rather than one of its parts, its properties, or the relations that it is involved in. When children have mapped a word to an object, they will extend it to other objects of the same kind rather than to other objects that are involved in the same event (e.g., extending from a birthday cake to other cakes rather than to birthday presents and birthday candles). In the case of novel artifacts, they typically extend the word to objects of the same shape rather than to objects of the same material or same color. However, when a word is applied to a novel animal, children are more conservative, preferring referents that have the same color or texture and the same shape.

These biases should aid the child in learning count nouns (such as 'cat,' 'book,' or 'car'), but they might hinder the acquisition of adjectives, verbs, relational nouns, and labels for substances and parts of objects. For example, if little Johnny were to hear the word 'silver' applied to Mommy's car, his bias to map words to whole objects could lead him to incorrectly conclude that 'silver' means car. One additional constraint, often called mutual exclusivity, may help learners overcome this bias. Young children are reluctant to map a second label to an object for which they already have a label. Thus, if little Johnny has already learned that cars are called 'car,' he is likely to reject the hypothesis that 'silver' means car and consider other possibilities.

The existence of these biases is uncontroversial, but their origins are not. Current research in this area focuses on two issues. The first is domain specificity. Are these biases unique to word learning or do they reflect more general properties of cognition? Perhaps the bias to link words to whole objects reflects the centrality of objects in early cognition rather than any preconceptions about the nature of words. Similarly, mutual exclusivity in word learning could result from a more general principle of communication which leads learners to assume that speakers will use known forms of reference whenever possible. The second issue is whether these biases are available at the onset of word learning. Some theorists suggest that these biases are learned as the child acquires words and notices the properties that are typically used in word extension. For example, children may learn their first artifact labels by trial and error. After learning many of these words, a child may notice that these labels are generally extended by shape and develop a bias to extend new words in this way. Several pieces of evidence support this account. The shape bias for novel artifacts increases as vocabulary size grows, and toddlers who are taught categories that are extended on the basis of shape develop this bias more quickly and are more successful at learning count nouns.

Social Cues to Reference

Children can also tame the induction problem by using their implicit understanding of social interactions to make inferences about the communicative intentions of the speaker. These inferences can help the child identify the object or event to which the speaker is referring, thus simplifying the problem of word learning. The best studied social cue to word meaning is the speaker's direction of gaze. When speakers are talking about objects that are visible, they often look at that object at roughly the same time as they are mentioning it. By approximately 18 months of age, children will map a word to the object that the speaker was looking at, even when they themselves were examining a different object when the word was spoken. Infants can also identify the referent of a word when the speaker points at the object or moves it as it is labeled.

Other abilities appear to require a more complex representation of the interaction. When a speaker labels an action before performing it, young children prefer to link the label to an intentional action rather than an accidental one. When a speaker uses a novel label, children assume that she is referring to an object that was introduced while she was gone rather than an object that she saw before.

Research on the use of social cues has explored two questions. First, what role do these cues play in word learning? Are they necessary or merely facilitory? Several lines of evidence demonstrate that children can learn words in the absence of any single social cue. For example, infants can learn the mapping between an object and a word from a videotape in which the person who is producing the word is never visible. The ability of blind children to acquire words at approximately the same age as sighted children provides further evidence that visual access to social cues (such as pointing or gaze direction) is not necessary for successful word learning. Of course, it is possible that these learning contexts contain other cues that allow the child to infer the referential intentions of the speaker. A second and related question is whether infants' use of social cues reflects an understanding of the mental states of the speaker rather than simple associations or low-level attentional processes. Do infants make use of eye gaze because they know that it reflects the speaker's knowledge and communicative intentions, or have they merely learned that gaze is a reliable predictor of which object a word will be associated with?

Sentential Contexts as Cues to Word Meanings

The final way in which children tame the problem of word learning is by using the sentential context in which a word occurs to narrow down the set of possible hypotheses. Sentential contexts provide three kinds of information. First, they identify the syntactic category of a novel word. Because syntactic categories are systematically (but imperfectly) linked to semantic categories, they provide information about the kind of meaning that the word is likely to have. For example, 1-year-olds who are shown a doll and told that 'this is a zav' interpret the novel word as a common noun and extend it to other similar dolls. In contrast, those who hear 'this is Zav' interpret it as a proper noun and refuse to extend it. Similarly, by approximately 2½ years of age, young children have learned to extend mass nouns ('this is some dax') to entities that are made of the same substance and to extend adjectives ('this is a daxy one') to objects that share a common property.

Second, sentential contexts provide information about the number and kinds of arguments that a predicate can take which constrain the kind of meaning that the predicate has. For example, verbs of self-generated motion (e.g., 'dance') often appear with just one argument (the subject); verbs of contact (e.g., 'hit') or caused motion (e.g. 'push') usually appear with a subject and a direct object; and verbs of transfer (e.g., 'send') appear with three arguments (subject, direct object, and indirect object). Young children use these connections between syntax and semantics to learn the meanings of unknown words. For example, 2-year-olds who hear a transitive utterance such as "She is blicking her around" expect the verb to have a meaning such as 'push,' whereas those who hear an intransitive utterance such as "They are blicking around" expect the verb to have a meaning such as 'dance.'

Finally, sentential contexts contain known words which provide information about the other entities or relations that are involved in the event under discussion. For example, if children hear an utterance such as 'John is eating a dax,' they can infer that a dax is probably a kind of food, and they can direct their attention to John to ascertain precisely what kind of food it might be. Although cues of this kind tightly constrain word learning, their availability depends on the child having already learned some of the other content words in the utterance.

Current research on the role of sentential contexts centers on two issues. First, when do children begin to use each of these cues? Some cues have an influence on infants as young as 13 months of age (e.g., use of word in count noun syntax), but other cues appear to have little effect even in preschoolers. For example, in several studies 2- and 3-year-olds have failed to use verbal morphology ("Look gorping!") to map the word to the action (e.g., waving) that is being performed. The second active area of research explores how these cues are acquired. One possibility is that by learning words from particular categories, children discover a direct association between specific grammatical contexts and particular aspects of word meaning. The second possibility is that children's word learning is guided by universal linkages between syntax and semantics. Children must learn the grammatical morphemes that mark each syntactic category (e.g., that 'a dax' is a count noun in English and 'une dax' is a count noun in French) but the connection between particular syntactic categories and patterns of word extension comes for free. These theories make different predictions about when these cues should be learned and whether the semantic relations in question are likely to be linked to observable properties (e.g., count nouns pick out shape-based categories) or more abstract properties that are tightly linked to the syntax (e.g., count nouns pick out individuated entities).

Final Words

During the past 25 years, researchers have demonstrated that young children make use of all three of the previously discussed strategies to learn words. The challenge in the future will be to understand how these strategies work together throughout development. It may be useful to think of constraints, social cues, and structural contexts as complementary mechanisms rather than competing hypotheses. The three strategies account for different aspects of word learning. For example, social cues allow children to identify the referent of the phrase, whereas constraints on hypotheses and structural cues provide guidance about how this referent is being construed.

The order in which these abilities emerge during development may explain why early vocabularies are dominated by nouns but contain few verbs, and why children's mastery of verbs coincides with the emergence of grammar. Many social cues and constraints may be available at the onset of word learning. These abilities do not necessarily depend on prior linguistic knowledge, and their use extends well beyond the linguistic domain (e.g., knowledge of object kinds constrains reasoning as well as word learning, and eye gaze provides information about a person's knowledge outside of the linguistic domain). These abilities would primarily facilitate the acquisition of nouns: Most word learning constraints and biases apply to object categories and most social cues function to pick out objects in space. In contrast, the use of structural contexts necessarily requires some grammatical knowledge and thus can only be used after language acquisition is underway. This information source is particularly useful for learning verbs and other predicates (which occur in richer structural contexts). Thus, efficient verb learning may emerge only when children have acquired enough grammatical and lexical knowledge to make use of sentential contexts during word learning.

See also: Language Development; Language, Cortical Processes; Lexical Impairments Following Brain Injury; Word Production; Word Recognition.

Further Reading

Baldwin, DA (1991). Infants' contribution to the achievement of joint reference. *Child Development* 62: 875–890.
Bates, E, Dale, PS, and Thal, D (1995). Individual differences and their implications for theories of language development. In: Fletcher, P and MacWhinney B (eds.) *The Handbook of Child Language*, pp. 96–151. Oxford, UK: Blackwell.
Bates, E and Goodman, JC (1997). On the inseparability of grammar and the lexicon: Evidence from acquisition, aphasia and real-time processing. *Language and Cognitive Processes* 12(5/6): 507–586.
Bloom, P (2000). *How Children Learn the Meanings of Words.* Cambridge, MA: MIT Press.
Caselli, MC, Casadio, P, and Bates, E (1999). A comparison of the transition from first words to grammar in English and Italian. *Journal of Child Language* 26: 69–111.
Gentner, D and Boroditsky, L (2001). Individuation, relativity and early word learning. In: Bowerman, M and Levinson S (eds.) *Language Acquisition and Conceptual Development.* Cambridge, UK: Cambridge University Press.
Gillette, J, Gleitman, H, Gleitman, L, and Lederer, A (1999). Human simulation of vocabulary learning. *Cognition* 73: 135–151.
Gleitman, LR (1990). The structural sources of word meaning. *Language Acquisition* 1: 3–55.
Hall, DG and Waxman, SR (2004). *Weaving a Lexicon.* Cambridge, MA: MIT Press.
Markman, EM (1989). *Categorization and Naming in Children.* Cambridge, MA: MIT Press.
Naigles, L (1990). Children use syntax to learn verb meanings. *Journal of Child Language* 17: 357–374.
Smith, LB, Jones, SS, Landau, B, Gershkoff-Stowe, L, and Samuelson, L (2002). Object name learning provides on-the-job training for attention. *Psychological Science* 13: 13–19.
Snedeker, J, Geren, J, and Shafto, C (2007). Starting over: International adoption as a natural experiment in language development. *Psychological Science* 18: 79–87.
Waxman, SR (1999). Specifying the scope of 13-month-olds' expectations for novel words. *Cognition* 70: B35–B50.

Word Production

R. J. Hartsuiker, Ghent University, Ghent, Belgium
G. Vigliocco, University College London, London, UK

Introduction

Please say the name of the item pictured in **Figure 1**.

Research on word production is concerned with the mental processes and representations that are involved during the 1000–1200 ms that it probably took from seeing the picture to uttering the word 'banana.' In picture naming, this involves the initial process of visual processing, followed by core processes of identifying the concept, retrieving the appropriate word from memory, determining the word's phonological structure (e.g., the word has three syllables) and content (e.g., the first speech sound is a /b/), and planning a speech motor program, which controls articulation.

Historically, language production has been the subject of less research than language comprehension, and this holds for both research studying the word level and the sentence level. However, in recent years there has been an increase in interest in production. This increased interest is accompanied by important methodological innovation. Until fairly recently, the main source of data informing the field of word production research was corpora of spontaneously occurring speech errors. Although this work has allowed the development of influential production theories,

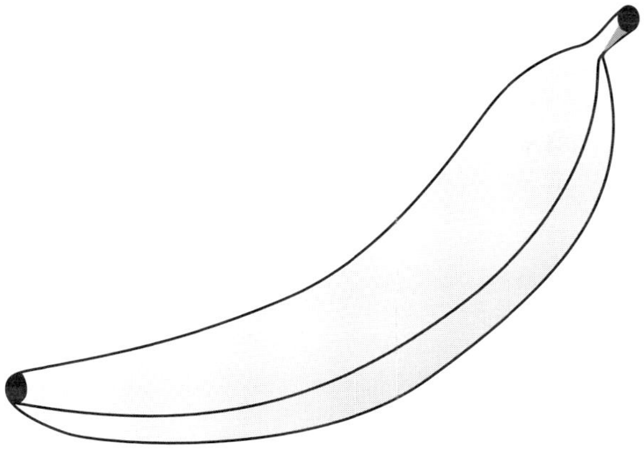

Figure 1 Picture of an everyday object. From the picture set presented in Rossion B and Pourtois G (2004) Revisiting Snodgrass and Vanderwart's object set: The role of surface detail in basic-level object recognition. *Perception 33: 217–236.*

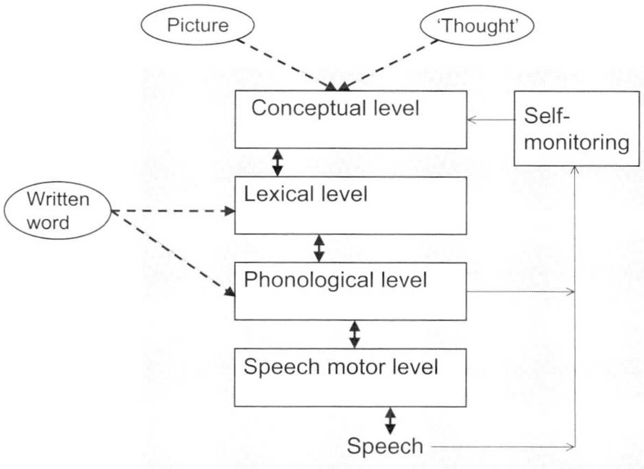

Figure 2 Overview of core word production processes (against the gray background) and lead-in stimuli, such as pictures, words, and thoughts.

in particular Merrill Garrett's theory of language production, observational methods suffer from important problems, such as collector biases, the infrequency of errors, and the issue of whether the corpus is representative of the language as a whole. Methodological improvements have made it possible to study word production under laboratory conditions, considering normal, fluent production as well as the production of errors and allowing researchers to focus on the time course of the production process. Moreover, despite methodological obstacles (e.g., the need to control for movement artifacts), word production can now be studied while registering the speakers' eye-movements, event-related potentials, or Bold signals.

The Functional Architecture of Word Production

Word production is a multistage process. That is, given the intention to say something, representations need to be selected or constructed in a sequence of processing levels. Each of these processing levels is specialized and represents a particular type of knowledge, such as meaning or form. Although there is consensus in the field about this hierarchical organization, there is considerable debate about whether the processing stages are strictly sequential or whether they interact to some degree (see below). This multistage nature of word production is sometimes overlooked. For example, some studies of word recognition use the task of word naming, neglecting the fact that this task also recruits production.

A blueprint of word production is provided in **Figure 2**. The figure shows the core processing levels (against the blue background) and several sources of input to this system. Imagine that a speaker will produce the word 'banana,' perhaps so as to name a picture or, in a more naturalistic situation, because the person is thinking about a banana and wants to say something about it. The following sections describe the route that processing takes from seeing to saying, excepting details of articulation.

Conceptual Preparation

The first core processing level is the conceptual level. Here, a representation referring to a banana becomes activated, and representations of related concepts (e.g., 'apple,' 'pear,' 'fruit,' 'peel' (part of a banana), 'canoe' (looks like a banana)) are also somewhat activated. There is no consensus on the precise nature of the conceptual representations used for production. Some researchers argue for distributed conceptual representations, so that a given concept can be characterized by a constellation of features (either 'macrofeatures' that carry meaning themselves, such as 'yellow,' 'sweet,' 'long,' or in certain connectionist models, 'microfeatures' without any intrinsic meaning). In these views, similarity among concepts is determined on the bases of features that are shared across concepts and features that are instead specific for a given concept. Other researchers, however, argue for localist concepts, so that there would be a single, indivisable representation for each concept. On such 'semantic network' accounts, concepts are connected via meaningful links that indicate category membership (e.g., a banana is a fruit) and properties (e.g., a banana has a yellow color). Similar concepts have links to the same categories and properties.

Do speakers of different languages activate identical concepts when they are preparing to say a word? Probably not. Languages differ in what they require their speakers to think about. For example, English often captures the manner of motion in a verb, whereas Spanish needs to add such information in an additional phrase. Research has shown that such differences influence the type of information speakers recall from a description (e.g., of a cartoon) they recently provided, suggesting that when verbalizing events, conceptual information is activated in a language-specific way.

Lexical Processing

The activated concept will send activation to the lexical level, and if all goes well, the lexical representation for banana will become the most active representation at this level. If there was always a one-to-one relation between concepts and words, it would not be necessary to postulate different processing levels for them. However, there are many situations in which there is no one-to-one relation between concepts and words. For example, there are concepts such as 'the actions of two people maneuvering for one armrest in a movie theater or airplane seat' for which we do not have a word. Moreover, as discussed above, which concepts are verbalized can differ across languages.

At the lexical level, the word activated by the concept (the 'target word') enters into a competition with other activated words, usually words with a similar meaning. The word with the most activation will be selected, and the time to select the correct word and the chance of making a lexical selection error depend on the activation level of competitor words. This mechanism of selection by competition is nicely illustrated by results from the picture–word interference paradigm, one of the most frequently employed paradigms in word production research. In these experiments, participants are instructed to name pictures with single words while ignoring a 'distracter word' that is presented either simultaneously with the picture or shortly (e.g., 150 ms) before or after the picture. A consistent finding is that semantically related distracters (e.g., 'apple' for the picture of a banana) delay picture-naming onsets compared with unrelated distracters (e.g., 'chair' for the picture of the banana). This delay can be explained as follows: Both the written words 'apple' and 'chair' directly activate their corresponding representations at the lexical level (**Figure 2**). However, the picture's concept (for banana) activates the related concept (for apple) but not the unrelated concept (for chair). Therefore, the lexical representation of 'apple' receives additional input from and is a stronger competitor for 'banana' than is 'chair.' Computer models of word production that incorporate this mechanism can mimic the temporal costs caused by semantic relatedness.

How many lexical levels are there? Some researchers argue that the lexical level should be subdivided into two levels, namely, a lemma level and a word form level, whereas others postulate only a single lexical level. In the two-level view, lemmas are lexical representations containing or pointing to lexical-syntactic information (e.g., gender) and semantic information, but not phonological information. Furthermore, there are different versions of two-level theories. Thus, in his seminal book *Speaking*, Willem Levelt suggested that the lemma representation of a word contained semantic and syntactic information and pointed to the word form representation that contained morphological and phonological information. But in a more recent version of Levelt's theory, the lemma is considered void of content; it connects the conceptual level to the level of word forms and is connected to (rather than contains) syntactic information.

There is much evidence that appears to support a division into a lemma level and a word form level. One source of observational evidence concerns the occurrence of word substitution errors. These are related to the intended word either in its meaning or in its form, suggesting that there are two types of retrieval processes that can derail: (1) lemma selection, which is driven by semantic information and can lead to semantic errors, and (2) word form selection, which can lead to phonologically conditioned errors. For example:

1. I want whipped cream on my mushrooms. (intended: strawberries)
2. I've got some whipped cream on my mushroom. (intended: mustache)

In addition, picture–word interference studies show distinct effects of semantically related distracters, which slow down picture naming (see above), and phonologically related distracters, which speed up picture naming. The difference in polarity of these effects is consistent with the notion of different processing levels.

Further evidence comes from the so-called tip-of-the-tongue (TOT) phenomenon. This phenomenon, strikingly described by William James in 1890, entails the inability to produce a word one is certain to know. Studies that have elicited this phenomenon in the laboratory demonstrated that speakers in a TOT state reliably know syntactic information about a word (e.g., whether an Italian noun's grammatical gender is masculine or feminine) while being unable to retrieve phonological information about the word. This suggests that speakers have succeeded in retrieving the lemma (and can therefore activate the syntactic information associated with it) but have failed to retrieve the word form. It is interesting that brain-damaged patients who suffer from an inability to name objects or events likewise demonstrate syntactic knowledge of the words they cannot name.

A final source of support for the distinction between lemmas and word forms comes from studies of morphological processing. A model with two such levels rather naturally lends itself to the representation of morphologically complex words. For example, a Dutch complex verb like *opgeven* (to give up) would have a separate lemma from a simplex verb like *geven* (to give). This is syntactically motivated as these verbs are syntactically different. At the word form level, however, overlapping inflectional forms of *geven* and *opgeven* would be shared, for example, *geeft* in the third-person, present-tense forms *geeft op* and *geeft*. In line with this hypothesis, Dutch speakers have a naming latency advantage when saying *geeft op* compared with *veegt op* (sweeps up), although these verb–particle combinations occur equally frequently. The advantage is that *geeft op* shares a word form with a very frequent verb, whereas *veegt op* shares a word form with an infrequent verb.

This subdivision into lemmas and word forms has been challenged by Alfonso Caramazza and colleagues, who proposed that the conceptual level is directly connected to the level of word forms and that both these levels are independently connected to syntactic information (**Figure 3**). In addition to a network of phonological word forms (employed in speaking), there would be orthographic word forms (used in writing). Much evidence that supports the distinction between lemmas and word forms is also consistent with Caramazza's framework.

Phonological Processing

Most theories assume a level of word forms, at which words are represented in terms of their speech sounds. It is conceivable that an error at this level leads to a malapropism, a phonologically governed word substitution error, like the Dutch error *ondergoed* (underwear) instead of *onderzoek* (research). Perhaps surprisingly, the next processing step involves breaking up the word form into its constituents, such as its phonological segments and metrical structure. Why doesn't the processor simply use the just-retrieved complete word form to guide articulation? An important reason is that speakers normally do not produce words in their citation forms. Rather, in connected speech, words are merged, and syllables can cross word boundaries. For example, in natural speech, one does not say "and Oliver" but "n doliver."

An influential model of the processes involved in phonologically encoding words was proposed by Gary Dell (**Figure 4**). This model, analogous to McClelland and Rumelhart's seminal Interactive Activation Model of word recognition, postulates localist representations for different phonological units (such as words, syllables, and phonological clusters); processing proceeds by spreading activation from a target unit. Selection takes place at the phoneme level, so that after a given number of time steps of activation spreading (determined by speech rate), the most highly active phoneme unit is selected in separate pools of units. These pools correspond to the onset (initial consonants), nucleus (vowel), and coda (final consonants) of the syllable.

If all goes well, phoneme units corresponding to the intended word are selected, but whenever a competing phoneme has a higher activation level than the intended one, a speech error occurs. There are several reasons an unintended phoneme can win the competition. It may have residual activation because it has been recently selected and the activation has not decayed yet. It is also possible that the unit needs to be selected in an upcoming syllable but is activated too early. Finally, a phoneme may be randomly active because the system is intrinsically noisy.

Dell's model successfully accounts for naturalistic speech error data. For example, the model simulates effects of speech rate on the number of errors; the so-called lexical bias effect (by which errors tend to form existing words more often than chance would predict); and the distribution of speech errors, so that anticipations (in which a phoneme is said too early; e.g., 'bake my bike' (intended: take my bike)) outnumber perseverations (in which a phoneme is repeated in a subsequent word; e.g., 'she pulled a pantrum' (intended: she pulled a tantrum)), which in turn outnumber exchanges (in which phonemes from different words are swapped; e.g., 'waple malnut' (intended: maple walnut)).

However, Dell's model has two limitations. First, the model is restricted to accounting for the outcome of phonological encoding (correct or error) but not for the

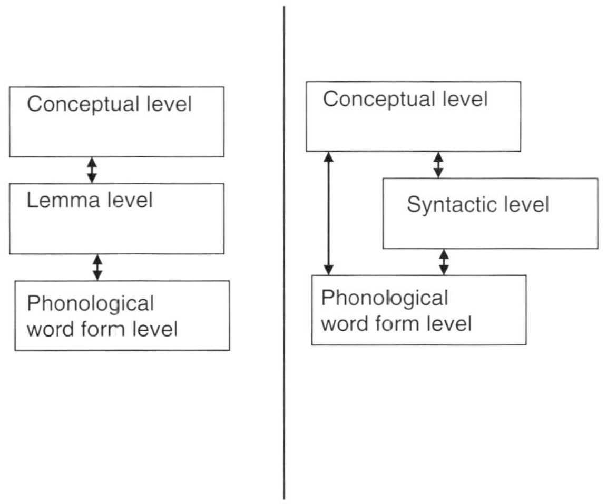

Figure 3 Lexical representations according to Levelt and colleagues (left panel) and Caramazza and colleagues (right panel).

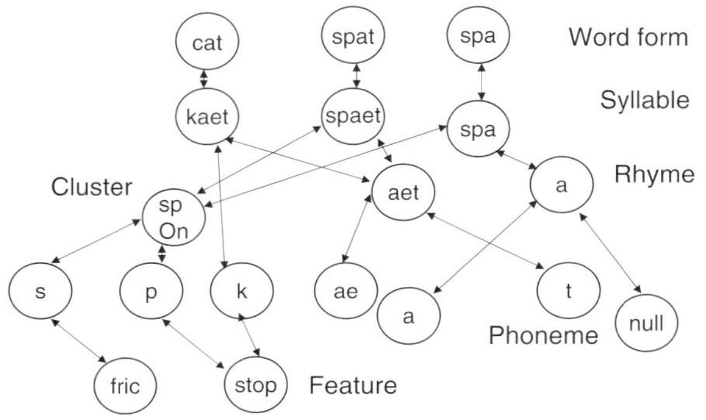

Figure 4 Gary Dell's 1986 model of word production.

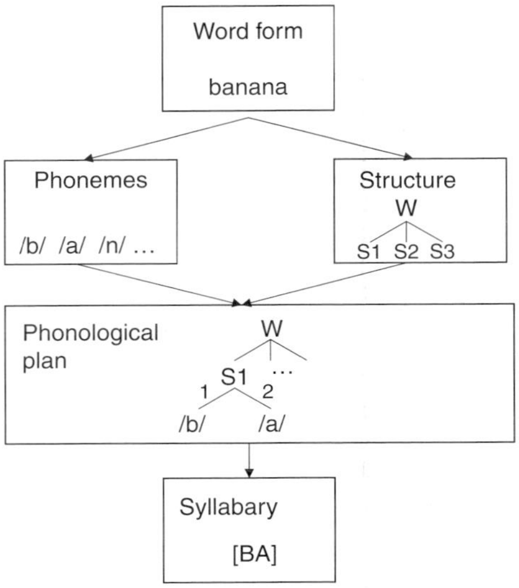

Figure 5 The WEAVER++ model's architecture of phonological encoding.

time course of processing. Another limitation is that the model does not have a mechanism for the resyllabification processes that take place in connected speech: it produces words in citation form only. Ardi Roelofs, Willem Levelt, and colleagues therefore extended their theory of lexical access to phonological encoding. This new model, WEAVER++ (**Figure 5**), complements Dell's: it provides an account of reaction time data (e.g., results from picture–word interference experiments) but does not account for speech errors.

WEAVER++ assumes that the word form is broken down into its parts in two parallel processing streams, one that retrieves individual phonemes and one that retrieves the metrical frame. The latter frame specifies the number of syllables of the word and the location of stress. These processes take place in parallel for all constituent syllables of the phonological word, which is usually defined as a content word (like 'banana') and any function words (e.g., 'a,' 'the,' 'it') that are phonologically 'glued' to it. Based on these representations and on the language's resyllabification rules (not shown in the figure), a syllabified, phonological plan for the phonological word is constructed. Finally, information now associated with syllable representations (e.g., that the onset of the first syllable is /b/ and its rhyme is /a/) serves as input to the 'syllabary,' a repository of motor programs that guide the articulation of individual syllables.

This model has successfully simulated reaction time data, mostly from experiments that used the picture–word interference paradigm or the implicit priming paradigm (a task in which speakers produce blocks of words with (experimental condition) or without (control condition) phonological overlap). Note, however, that some assumptions of the WEAVER++ model are controversial. In particular, there is no compelling evidence in support of the mental syllabary.

Self-Monitoring

Speakers monitor whether the words they produce conform to what they wanted to say. This verbal self-monitoring system inspects not only a speaker's overt speech but also speech before articulation (internal speech). That internal speech is monitored is evident from data on self-interruptions. Speakers can interrupt their errors so quickly that they could not have detected the error in their overt speech. Despite recent attempts to formulate precise computational models of the monitoring process, it is still unclear how monitoring establishes that something is an error. This issue has important theoretical repercussions, in particular with respect to the question of whether the processing levels in production have the characteristic of modular stages or whether there is cross-talk between different levels (see the next section).

Information Flow in the Functional Architecture: Modularity versus Interactivity

A debate that has divided the word production literature for decades concerns whether processing levels are modular (i.e., encapsulated from other levels) or not. There are two aspects to this issue. First, models differ in whether they assume that only the selected representation at level $n-1$ activates representations at the next level, n (the modular stance), or whether processing at these levels overlaps somewhat in time so that all representations activated at level $n-1$ send some activation to level n. The latter mechanism is usually referred to as 'cascading of activation.' Second, models differ in whether they assume that activation flow is unidirectional (from level $n-1$ to level n), or whether there is also a return flow of activation (from level n to level $n-1$). The latter mechanism is usually referred to as 'feedback of activation.' Note that even theorists who propose full interactivity (cascading and feedback) limit it to local interactivity. There appears to be no direct (cross-) talk between level $n-2$ and level n.

In contrast to conclusions of several studies in the early 1990s, there is now overwhelming evidence for cascading of activation. For example, picture–word interference studies using homophone targets (e.g., a picture of a (toy) ball) showed facilitation when the distracter was related to the other meaning of the target name (e.g., 'dance'). This demonstrates that the distracter activated the lemma for the 'dance' meaning of 'ball' and that this lemma cascaded activation to the word form 'ball,' thereby speeding up selection of this word form.

The existence of feedback remains disputed. Data from speech errors appear to support feedback. For example, the lexical bias effect on phonological speech errors suggests that feedback from the phonological level activates representations of existing words, increasing the probability that they are selected. It is important that Dell's model, which incorporates feedback links, simulates the lexical bias effect, as well as effects of speech rate on the magnitude of this bias. However, a competing account of the lexical bias assumes unidirectional activation flow and explains the effect as the result of covert error repair. On that story, the monitoring system uses criteria such as, is this a word? and is therefore more likely to detect and intercept nonsense errors than errors that form existing words. It is difficult to reject such accounts, because the mechanisms of error detection remain underspecified. Note that recent evidence suggests a third possibility, one by which monitoring biases interact with an underlying pattern of errors, which is shaped by feedback.

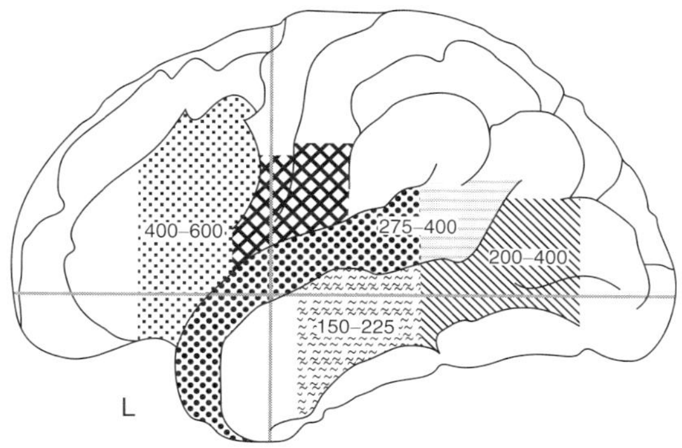

Figure 6 Proposed localization of brain regions involved in word production processes. The numbers refer to Indefrey's and Levelt's estimates of the moments of time during which these areas would be active, given the task of picture naming. Adapted from *Cognition*, 92, Indefrey P and Levelt WJM, The spatial and temporal signatures of word production components, pp. 101–144 (2004), with permission from Elsevier.

Neural Correlates of the Functional Architecture

What are the neural systems engaged in word production? It has long been known from patient studies that language processing takes place in a brain network that is largely left-lateralized and surrounds the perisylvian fissure. Modern brain imaging techniques allow for a more fine-grained localization of brain areas involved in production, although only very recently have studies begun to address overt production, thanks to the advent of data acquisition and analysis techniques that reduce susceptibility to movement artifacts.

A recent meta-analysis considered 85 imaging studies (mostly positron-emission tomography and functional magnetic resonance imaging) in which participants were engaged in tasks like picture naming, verb generation (e.g., "Generate as many verbs as you can applying to a particular noun"), word naming, pseudoword naming, and so on. These tasks differ in the extent to which they involve different processing components (**Figure 2**). The logic of the meta-analysis was that if a certain brain region genuinely subserves a certain process, then this region should be active in all tasks that involve this process. That study suggested several localizations of production processes (**Figure 6**).

Conceptual processing and lemma selection are subserved by an area in the middle of middle temporal gyrus. Word form retrieval is localized in the posterior part of the middle and superior temporal gyri (Wernicke's area). Phonological encoding is localized in the left posterior inferior gyrus (Broca's area). Articulation is subserved by several regions, including bilateral sensory and motor areas. Finally, self-monitoring is localized in the superior temporal gyri of both hemispheres.

A more detailed neuroanatomical hypothesis concerning the brain network(s) subserving word production has been proposed by Hanna Damasio and colleagues on the basis of imaging and lesion data. In this view, word naming is achieved in the following manner: Conceptual retrieval corresponds to engagement of intermediary regions in higher-order association cortices. The brain network subserving conceptual activation can differ (at least partially) depending on the semantic category of the stimulus (e.g., animals vs. famous people) and recruits regions outside the 'language' network, for example, in left inferior temporal areas. Once conceptual activation is achieved, naming a stimulus from a particular conceptual category is dependent on intermediary structures for 'words.' These intermediary structures correspond to the neural substrate of semantic representations. Finally, structures which support the implementation of word forms (the classical language areas located in the left perisylvian region, including Broca's and Wernicke's areas) are engaged. These structures correspond to the neural substrate of phonological word forms and the processes engaged in their retrieval.

Consider **Figure 7**. When an individual is shown a picture of a cup or a picture of a familiar person (e.g., John F. Kennedy) and is asked to name the item, there will be activation of the appropriate 'concept' intermediary regions, which will promote concept retrieval. Activation in the concept intermediary regions leads to activation in the corresponding 'word' intermediary region, which in turn promotes the retrieval of lexical knowledge required for word production. This is likely to require auditory structures (areas 41/42; 22), which overlap in part with Wernicke's area. This step can be considered to closely correspond to the retrieval of word forms. Finally, somatomotor (3/1/2; 40; 44/45) structures are engaged for the phonetic sequencing and production of the actual spoken name; these structures overlap in part with Broca's area.

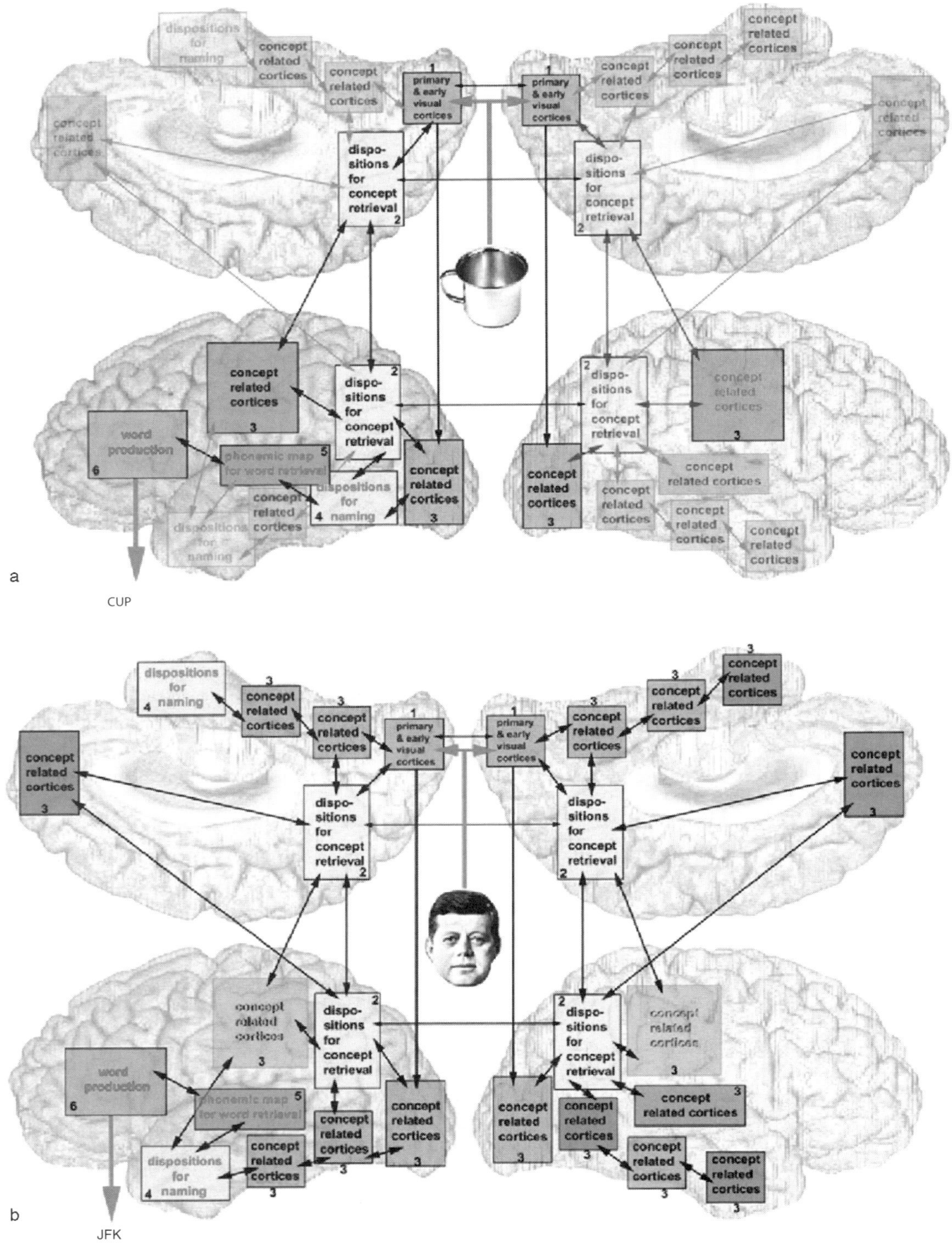

Figure 7 Reprinted from *Cognition*, 92, Damasio H, Tranel D, Grabowsky TJ, Adolphs R, and Damasio HR, Neural systems behind word and concept retrieval, pp. 179–229 (2004), with permission from Elsevier. (See color plate 45.)

Summary and Future Directions

There is broad consensus in the literature on the functional architecture of word production, and recent imaging and patient studies have led to suggestions about the localization of global processing components in the brain. However, important lacunae in our knowledge remain. These include the nature of conceptual representations, the number of levels of lexical representation, the existence of a mental syllabary, the workings of the self-monitor, and the existence of direct feedback between processing levels.

It is important to note that word production research studies the production of isolated words, neglecting that words are usually parts of sentences and that sentences are parts of conversations. A consideration of these higher levels raises important further questions. For example, one debate in the literature concerns the scope of planning in language production: Do we produce one word at a time, or can the production system plan multiple words in parallel? Another debate concerns the interface between words and sentence level syntax: Do words constrain the syntactic structure of the rest of the sentence, or do syntactic planning mechanisms recruit words that fit the syntactic requirements?

It is also important to note that word production has concentrated mainly on production of spoken words. However, people have several modalities at hand for word production, including typing, handwriting, and signing. Issues regarding the number of levels that are shared or separate between modalities remain largely unexplored. Finally, with bilingualism being the rule rather than the exception in Earth's population, many speakers have two or more lexicons to choose from, which raises important new questions about the functional organization and processing mechanisms in bilingual people.

See also: Language in Aged Persons; Language, Auditory Processes; Lexical Impairments Following Brain Injury; Sentence Production; Speech Production, Adult; Word Learning.

Further Reading

Caramazza, A (1997). How many levels of processing are there in lexical access? *Cognitive Neuropsychology* 14: 177–208.
Damasio, H, Tranel, D, Grabowsky, TJ, Adolphs, R, and Damasio, HR (2004). Neural systems behind word and concept retrieval. *Cognition* 92: 179–229.
Dell, GS (1986). A spreading-activation theory of retrieval in sentence production. *Psychological Review* 93: 283–321.
Fromkin, VA (ed.) (1980). *Errors in Linguistic Performance: Slips of the Tongue, Ear, Pen, and Hand.* New York: Academic Press.
Garrett, MF (1975). The analysis of sentence production. In: Bower, GH (ed.) *The Psychology of Learning and Motivation*, pp. 133–177. New York: Academic Press.
Harley, T (2001). *The Psychology of Language: From Data to Theory.* Hove, England: Psychology Press.
Indefrey, P and Levelt, WJM (2004). The spatial and temporal signatures of word production components. *Cognition* 92: 101–144.
Levelt, WJM (1989). *Speaking: From Intention to Articulation.* Cambridge, MA: MIT Press.
Levelt, WJM, Roelofs, A, and Meyer, AS (1999). A theory of lexical access in speech production. *Behavioral and Brain Sciences* 22: 1–75.
Roelofs, A, Meyer, AS, and Levelt, WJM (1998). A case for the lemma/lexeme distinction in models of speaking: Comment on Caramazza and Miozzo (1997). *Cognition* 69: 219–230.
Vigliocco, G and Hartsuiker, RJ (2002). The interplay of meaning, sound, and syntax in sentence production. *Psychological Bulletin* 128: 442–472.

Word Recognition

J. Zevin, Weill Medical College of Cornell University, New York, NY, USA

It is intuitive to think of the word as a basic unit of language. Dictionaries, for example, list the definitions of individual words. But in fact, they list multiple definitions for most, because what a word means is determined in large part by its context. Consider, for example, that the phrases 'a chocolate bar,' 'a sports bar,' or 'to bar entry' each use the word 'bar' to refer to very different things. Furthermore, words are not even the smallest unit at which regularities between sound and meaning are encoded: new words can be created generatively by a process of 'derivational morphology.' For example, once we know what a 'blog' is, we have little difficulty guessing what a 'blogger' does or what the 'blogosphere' might be, even on first hearing. Thus, although it is natural to think of words as representing a stable correspondence between a linguistic form (spoken or written) and a meaning or concept, in fact, both the status of words as units of linguistic form and their relationship to particular meanings are something of an oversimplification. Fortunately, despite these definitional issues about what a word is, and what one is actually doing when one 'recognizes a word,' much is known about how words are recognized in both spoken and written language.

Factors That Influence Word Recognition

The recognition of individual words presented in isolation is arguably not very representative of typical language use. Nonetheless, it has formed the basis for a vast empirical literature, in part because various properties of words are readily quantified, manipulated, and controlled. Large databases of text called corpora can be used to determine how frequently words occur in the language and to quantify their similarity to other words. These properties can then be used to develop experimental materials used in studies that test how rapidly and accurately words can be recognized and whether there is an effect of a particular measurable factor.

Frequency

The more frequently a word occurs in the language, the more rapidly it is recognized. This is true of both written and spoken words, across a wide range of psycholinguistic tasks. The relationship between frequency and response efficiency is consistent with the power law of practice such that, for example, a word that is seen only 10 times per million is processed much less efficiently than a word that is seen 50 times per million, whereas the difference between a word that is seen 110 times and a word seen 150 times is much smaller. This power law holds for a wide range of psychological phenomena, and its role here suggests an important role for domain-general learning mechanisms in vocabulary acquisition.

A factor related to frequency is age of acquisition. Unlike other aspects of language, word-learning ability is not thought to decline during development. There is evidence, however, that the age at which words are learned has an influence on word recognition: Words learned earlier in life are processed more efficiently than words learned later in life. One difficulty in establishing this effect, however, is that words learned earlier in life tend to be easier for a host of reasons that also influence adult processing. Nonetheless, a number of carefully controlled studies have shown independent effects of age of acquisition in some aspects of word recognition.

It has been suggested that the number of times a word occurs is less important than its 'contextual diversity' – the number of different discourse contexts in which it occurs. Whether as a result of frequency or contextual diversity, it is clear that factors regarding the number and context of experiences with a word predict performance in a manner consistent with general models of learning and memory.

Neighborhood Effects

The 'neighborhood' of a word is the set of words that can be made by changing one or more speech sounds (for spoken words) or one letter (for written words). 'Neighborhood size' is thus an index of similarity to other words. Interestingly, this factor influences auditory and visual word recognition differently. In auditory word recognition, similarity to other words slows down response latency, but larger neighborhood size results in faster responses to written words. This difference is likely due to the task constraints of reading and listening. Because spoken words unfold over time, spoken word recognition under time pressure seems to involve activating multiple candidate words that are consistent with the auditory input at a given time. Therefore, if the goal is to identify a specific word, similarity to many other words will result in greater confusion.

In visual word recognition, in contrast, the facilitatory effect of having many neighbors is related to the fact that written words are processed in parallel – that is, all of the letters of the word are seen at once. Words with common combinations of letters are, all else being equal, more visually familiar than words with unusual combinations of letters and therefore easier to recognize. Neighborhood effects for pseudowords, such as GLORP, that can be read aloud but do not correspond to real written words are highly task dependent. When subjects are asked to read pseudowords aloud, neighborhood size has a facilitatory effect, just as it does with words. However, in a lexical decision task, large neighborhood size slows down responses to pseudo-words. That is, people find it more difficult to determine that an item such as BREN, which has at least 15 neighbors, is not a word than an item such as FNER, which has none.

Mapping from Spelling to Sound in Visual Word Recognition

Visual word recognition depends in large part on being able to determine the pronunciation of a word from its written form. One factor that influences how easily this can be done is the regularity of the mapping from spelling to sound. Consider a word such as DOLL. Arriving at the correct pronunciation benefits from experience with words such as DOT and GOLF, in which the O is pronounced in the same way. On the other hand, DOLL is very similar to words such as ROLL, TOLL, and KNOLL, in which the letter O is assigned a different pronunciation. The fact that similar written forms map onto disparate phonological forms makes mapping difficult, and in fact words that contain such inconsistent mappings between spelling and sound are more difficult to read than words that contain entirely consistent mappings.

Interestingly, regularity in spelling-to-sound mappings varies greatly among languages. Some, such as Korean and Serbo-Croatian, employ perfectly regular mappings from spelling to sound, such that each sound in the language is represented by a single character. Chinese characters, at the opposite extreme, contain only highly probabilistic information about pronunciation. English – the language in which by far the most research has been conducted – represents something of an intermediate case. This has consequences for how visual word recognition is accomplished in these languages and even for how reading disorders manifest. In English, it is common for dyslexic children to have trouble with 'decoding' (i.e., being able to read novel pseudo-words), whereas in Italian (a highly regular writing system) the main deficit in dyslexia is slow reading speed.

Word Recognition Influences Lower Levels of Processing

In both spoken and written language, words can be described as composed of parts. For example, the word KNEW is written with four letters and pronounced with two or three phonemes (a 'phoneme' is the linguistic term for a single speech sound, and KNEW can be pronounced /nu/ or /nju/ depending on one's dialect). The ease with which these parts can be identified, particularly in print, makes it tempting to assume that word recognition proceeds in a strictly serial fashion, starting with the identification of individual parts and proceeding to the identification of the whole word. In fact, there is abundant evidence that knowledge of whole words has a strong influence on recognition of smaller units.

Fluent comprehension of language frequently depends on making decisions based on incomplete information. For example, most telephones carry a signal that discards much of the information carried in speech, and yet we are rarely aware of the ambiguities this introduces, for example, between the first sounds in the words 'think' and 'fink.' In fact, a great deal of early research on speech perception was done at Bell Labs to address this kind of issue. One reason we are so good at word recognition is that we are able to engage what are called 'top-down' processes – for example, guessing what the next word will be or using our knowledge that some patterns are more consistent with a specific context or even general properties of our language. The influence of our knowledge of words on perception of smaller 'grain sizes,' or units of information, is part of a general pattern: Sentence and even discourse-level context can influence how we recognize individual words, and knowledge of the speech sounds of our language influences how we perceive particular sounds. As discussed later, however, there is some controversy regarding whether top-down influences affect perception directly or are implicated only when we make decisions about what we have heard.

Phoneme Restoration and the Ganong Effect

Lexical effects on phoneme perception can, in appropriate circumstances, result in rather compelling auditory illusions. For example, when presented with a sentence in which a consonant has been replaced with white noise, people readily identify all words in the sentence and furthermore are frequently unable to determine which sound was manipulated. This is termed the 'phoneme restoration effect' because it is as if the manipulated speech sound were restored by the listener. A similar effect is named after its discoverer, William F. Ganong III: When ambiguous speech sounds are presented as stimuli in categorical perception experiments (e.g., an utterance halfway between 'pink' and 'bink'), people are more likely to identify the stimulus as a word. This is interesting because unlike the tasks typically used to study the phoneme restoration effect, in this case the experiment explicitly requires participants to pay attention to individual speech sounds, and yet there is a strong influence of lexical knowledge.

Although these effects clearly demonstrate that lexical knowledge influences how speech sounds are perceived, there is also abundant evidence that fine phonetic detail has an influence on how rapidly words are recognized. To some extent we hear what we are somehow 'prepared' to hear, but there is also an effect of what is actually impinging on our ears. Manipulations much subtler than replacing an entire phoneme with white noise – for example, splicing in the same sound from a different word – result in slower performance in a wide range of word recognition tasks. Furthermore, the strength of both the Ganong and phoneme restoration effects can be influenced by various stimulus parameters. Finally, there is some question as to whether or not identification of these 'smaller units' is a necessary precursor to identifying spoken words. In fact, a number of distinct theories share the assumption that identification of individual speech sounds is epiphenomenal to the goal of distinguishing words from one another.

The Reicher–Wheeler Effect and 'Interactive Activation'

In the late 1960s, GM Reicher and Daniel D Wheeler each independently discovered the 'word superiority effect.' In a series of experiments, they consistently found that people were much better at identifying letters that appeared in words than when they appeared in random letter strings or when they appeared by themselves. The interactive activation model was developed in 1981 by David Rumelhart and James McClelland in part to explain these phenomena, and it remains influential in current research. It was one of the first models of a psychological process that was implemented on a computer and made quantitative predictions based on an architecture loosely inspired by facts about information processing in the brain.

The interactive activation model simulates human word recognition with a set of interconnected nodes that represent increasingly large 'grain sizes' or units from visual features that make up letters, to letters themselves, to whole words. Processing in the model is simulated as passing activation – an analogy to electrochemical impulses transmitted across synapses in real neural systems – forward from levels representing smaller units and, critically, backward from larger levels to smaller. The feedback connections were critical to capturing the word superiority effect: When the visual features for a known word were activated, this would partially activate the corresponding letters, which in turn would partially activate all of the words in which they were contained. When the active letters were consistent with a known word, the feedback from the word level would be stronger and more coherent than when they were not, resulting in a word superiority effect. This remains the dominant explanation of the word superiority effect in reading, although the role of feedback in perception of spoken words is more controversial.

Word Recognition Models and Controversies in Cognitive Psychology and Neuroscience

Word recognition is often a paradigmatic case for cognitive psychology and cognitive neuroscience because it provides a setting in which phenomena of clear relevance to larger theoretical issues can be readily observed. Many issues of theoretical debate are relatively abstract, and so pursuing computational models of increasing sophistication and addressing specific phenomena in word recognition has been one important way these debates have moved forward. Thus, although they remain largely unresolved, no discussion of word recognition would be complete without touching on these issues.

Interactive Processing with Feedback or Autonomous, Feed-Forward Processing?

The necessity of feedback touches on a long-standing issue of contention in cognitive psychology: Is the architecture of cognition correctly described as a set of modular, domain-specific processing units dedicated to particular tasks? Or is it more of an interactive system in which processing units at multiple levels influence one another bidirectionally? Spoken word recognition is an area of research in which this question is being actively pursued.

The influence of lexical knowledge on perception of smaller units of speech is well characterized. One model that addresses these phenomena, the TRACE model, is based on the interactive activation model. In fact, TRACE uses the same principles as the interactive activation model, but instead of visual features and letters, this model identifies words based on auditory features and phonemes. In this model, the influence of lexical knowledge on speech perception is the result of feedback from the word level to lower levels of representation.

An alternative model, the MERGE model, argues that such feedback is never necessary for word recognition and could, in fact, prevent the hearer from being able to detect mispronunciations. As noted previously, lexical effects can result in compelling auditory illusions under some conditions, but it is more usual for so-called 'bottom-up' processes to drive perception. The MERGE model addresses lexical influences on phonological perception by attributing these effects to a phonetic decision stage that is task specific. That is, when asked to make a decision about which speech sound was presented, people pool information from both phoneme-level and word-level representations in a third, decision stage that is not used in typical spoken word recognition.

Both models can explain much of the relevant data, and in fact it remains controversial which is more accurate or complete. The distinction between these two models reflects a division between interactionist and modular theories of cognition that is found throughout the cognitive psychology. Interactionist theories stress the role of feedback because it is consistent with a particular view of brain function – specifically that information processing involves pooling multiple, interacting sources of information, and that 'partial products' of processing at one level can influence processing at other levels. In contrast, modular theories emphasize the autonomy of processing subsystems because this is thought to be critical for rapid, automatic processing.

'Words and Rules' or 'Constraint Satisfaction'?

One point of consensus among theorists who study visual word recognition is that there are at least two pathways involved in word reading: One that links written words directly with their pronunciations and another that links them with their meanings. The two dominant theoretical frameworks in the field differ sharply, however, in the mechanisms they propose to underlie these pathways. The contrasts are very revealing with respect to the differences between two rival schools of cognitive psychology (especially psycholinguistics) and their differing approaches to interpreting data and elaborating theories of language processing.

In the 'words and rules' view (this moniker is taken from a popular book by Steven Pinker that describes a similar debate – with many of the same participants – regarding morphological processing; the most important example of this approach to reading is Max Coltheart's 'dual route' model), reading is accomplished by two separate mechanisms with entirely different computational properties. The 'lexical route' is an associative network of words similar to the interactive activation model. The 'sublexical route' comprises a set of rules for translating letters into sounds. Whereas the lexical route is activated in parallel, and is sensitive to fine-grained statistics of the lexicon such as the frequency of individual words, the sublexical route operates in serial and applies spelling-to-sound rules that, though based on statistics of the lexicon, are discrete and categorical in their application (so that no matter how many times it has seen the word MIND, it will always arrive at a pronunciation that rhymes with PINNED by applying the rules for M, I, N, and D in serial).

An important feature of this view is that the different pathways are conceived as entirely distinct processing mechanisms. This reflects a theoretical commitment to the notion of modularity, with an emphasis on the assertion that cognitive functions are subserved by highly specialized processing units. Note, however, that this model differs from MERGE in that it permits both feedback and cascading activation, albeit only in the lexical route. This model also reflects the influence of cognitive neuropsychology in its early development. The distinction between lexical and sublexical routes was initially motivated by a series of neuropsychological observations of double dissociations. Some stroke patients present with specific difficulty reading exception words that do not follow typical spelling-to-sound correspondence patterns, such as PINT, but are relatively unimpaired at reading novel pseudowords, such as GLORP. Other patients present with a complementary pattern of deficit: relatively spared performance on exception words and gross impairment on pseudowords.

The constraint satisfaction approach views the division of labor in visual word recognition differently. (This approach is often referred to as the parallel distributed processing approach, after the style of computational model that is used to implement the theory; the most recent version of this model by Harm and Seidenberg directly addresses the notion of division of labor.) In this view, mappings from spelling to sound and spelling to meaning are acquired and processed by the same basic mechanism, operating over different types of information. Mappings from spelling to sound are not conceived as a set of categorical rules abstracted from the statistics of the input but, rather, as a set of probabilistic constraints that reflect these statistics. In this way, consistency effects resulting from multiple grain sizes – letters, combinations of letters such as PH that map onto single sounds, and still larger possible units – can be accounted for (e.g., the influence of ROLL and POLL on DOLL discussed previously). Mappings from spelling to meaning are acquired with the same learning mechanism. However, because associations between spelling and meaning (in English, at least) are more arbitrary than associations between spelling and sound, the result of this learning process tends to be more word specific. That is, different factors influence the mapping from spelling to sound and the mapping from spelling to meaning as a result of the same learning mechanism applied to different types of problem, not as a result of different processing mechanisms in the two pathways.

In this view, observed dissociations between nonword and exception word reading are the result of damage to regions involved in mapping from spelling to sound and spelling to meaning, respectively. This further predicts that patients who lose the ability to read 'exception' words may also have difficulties with word meanings more generally, and that patients who have difficulty with decoding are likely to have difficulties with more general aspects of speech sounds. These associations are found throughout the neuropsychological literature, and in fact, the cases of dissociation are, despite their importance in theory building, relatively rare. Furthermore, because constraint satisfaction models are implemented as systems that learn, they have been able to provide an explanation of the link between phonological deficits and reading difficulties observed in developmental dyslexia.

Neuroanatomy of Word Recognition

Aside from modality-specific sensory regions engaged by particular stimulus types – visual regions involved in perceiving text and auditory regions involved in perceiving speech – a number of brain regions have been consistently shown to be involved in word recognition. Data from both neuropsychological studies of patients with brain lesions and studies using neuroimaging techniques such as positron emission tomography, functional magnetic resonance imaging, and electroencephalography provide insights into the network of brain regions involved in perceiving and understanding words.

Superior Temporal Gyrus and Superior Temporal Sulcus

Superior temporal gyrus (STG) is the site of auditory association cortex (and a site of multisensory integration) and thus necessarily plays some role in spoken word recognition. Evidence that its role extends beyond that of higher-level perceptual processing was found as early as 1871 by Karl Wernicke. He discovered that lesions in the posterior portion of the left STG were associated with the loss of the ability to comprehend and produce spoken words. More recently, it has been found that this phenomenon of 'Wernicke's aphasia' is observed to result from brain damage to a broad variety of sites; furthermore, damage to traditional Wernicke's area does not always result in aphasic symptoms.

Neuroimaging studies of healthy subjects have found evidence for a role in processing of word meanings for both anterior and posterior STG as well as superior temporal sulcus (STS; the sulcus that divides the STG from the middle temporal gyrus). The STS, in particular, responds more strongly to interpretable speech than to a range of stimuli matched on lower level acoustic dimensions. The STS is also a likely site of integration between print and sound in visual word recognition.

Inferior Frontal Gyrus

Although the involvement of inferior frontal gyrus in language processing was initially described by Paul

Broca in 1861, its precise function is the subject of continuing research even today. This region is known to be involved in multiple aspects of word recognition, including both semantic and phonological processing. Critically, it is not thought to be involved in purely perceptual or bottom-up processes involved in word recognition. Instead, activity in this region is thought to reflect effortful processing, as in tasks that require comparing the meanings or pronunciations of multiple words. One active area of investigation concerns whether subdivisions of the inferior frontal gyrus are functionally distinct with respect to their role in word processing; because this region also plays a role in many forms of working memory, its activity is also related to general task difficulty.

The 'Visual Word Form Area'

A region of left ventral temporal cortex, on the fusiform gyrus, is involved in processing the printed forms of words. Evidence that this region plays a role in early visual processing of written words comes from studies using a wide range of techniques. Within less than 200 ms after a stimulus is presented, electrophysiological responses in this region differentiate words from nonlinguistic visual stimuli. Patients with brain damage in this region present with alexia – an inability to read, often with a spared ability to write. Furthermore, metabolic neuroimaging techniques consistently show a role for this region in reading. Whether activity in this region is specific to words is under debate, as is its specific function, although anatomical and functional evidence suggests that it intermediates among lower level visual information and the phonological and semantic processes involved in recognizing visual words. Bilateral ventral temporal cortex has been implicated in many tasks involving perceptual expertise for visual stimuli. Specialization for text in this region may thus be understood as an example of perceptual expertise.

Summary

Behavioral research has established a number of key phenomena in word recognition: Many factors that influence the efficiency of computing meaning from sound – and both meaning and sound from text – have been discovered. Sophisticated computational models have provided mechanistic explanations for these findings while, largely in parallel, research in cognitive neuroscience and neuropsychology has revealed gross aspects of the neuroanatomy of word recognition and has begun to explore finer-grained detail of how these processes are accomplished in the brain. Although serious controversies remain, these multiple different avenues of research together have provided important insights about the word recognition and about many broader issues in the study of cognition.

See also: Dyslexia, Neurodevelopmental Basis; Language Development; Language, Auditory Processes; Language, Cortical Processes; Sentence Comprehension; Word Learning; Word Production.

Further Reading

Coltheart, M, Rastle, K, Perry, C, Langdon, R, and Ziegler, J (2001). DRC: A dual route cascaded model of visual word recognition and reading aloud. *Psychological Review* 108: 204–256.

Ganong, WF (1980). Phonetic categorization in auditory word perception. *Journal of Experimental Psychology: Human Perception and Performance* 6: 110–125.

Harm, MW and Seidenberg, MS (2004). Computing the meanings of words in reading: Cooperative division of labor between visual and phonological processes. *Psychological Review* 111: 662–720.

McClelland, J and Elman, J (1986). The TRACE model of speech-perception. *Cognitive Psychology* 18: 1–86.

McClelland, JL and Rumelhart, DE (1981). An interactive activation model of context effects in letter perception: Part 1. An account of basic findings. *Psychological Review* 88: 375–407.

Norris, D, McQueen, J, and Cutler, A (2000). Merging information in speech recognition: Feedback is never necessary. *Behavioral and Brain Sciences* 23: 299–325.

Written Language, Acquired Impairments of

C. Luzzatti, Universita' degli Studi di Milano-Bicocca, Milan, Italy
H. A. Whitaker, Northern Michigan University, Marquette, MI, USA

Introduction

An adult individual who acquired normal reading and spelling skills may lose these abilities after cerebral damage. Reading and spelling may be impaired either in isolation after a lesion to the brain areas that are specifically involved in storing or processing orthographic representations, or in accompaniment with aphasia, i.e., in association with more general language disorders.

Phylogenetic Observations

Language is a function that has developed during the natural evolution from the primate to the human species. The phylogenetic and ontogenetic development underlying language acquisition is based on neuroanatomical and functional units that are genetically determined. This assumption is clearly demonstrated for the acquisition of oral language, but the generalization to the functional units specifically devoted to the processing of written language is more difficult to maintain. In fact, the use of written language has emerged much more recently, i.e., not much earlier than 6000 years ago, and – even more crucially – part of the human population is still illiterate or has become literate only during the last few generations. Despite that, every child has the identical capacity of acquiring the ability to read and write, irrespective of the degree of literacy achieved by his/her social and ethnic group.

Writing Systems

Populations from different parts of the world developed different systems for transcribing oral language representations in a sequence of written symbols. Even if such a distinction is clearly too simplistic, the writing systems adopted all around the world may be distinguished along the major dichotomy of ideographic and alphabetic writing systems. In ideographic writing systems, symbols correspond to the meaning of words. In alphabetic writing systems, each symbol (or set of symbols) corresponds to a sound (or set of sounds).

The major advantage of alphabetic systems derives from their regularity and from the possibility of combining few (usually 20–50) symbols in strings of letters. However, it must be kept in mind that, in particular for languages whose orthography has been codified several centuries ago (such as French or English), the correspondence between symbols and sounds (graphemes and phonemes) may not be regular anymore.

The major advantage of ideographic systems (e.g., the Chinese one) derives from the possibility that a unique written code may be shared (i.e., may be understood) by many populations speaking fully different dialects or languages. However, most ideographic writing systems are in fact intermediate systems, where ideograms are mixed with characters or parts of characters bearing morphological and/or phonological information.

Reading and Spelling Impairments in Classical Aphasiology

The first model of reading and spelling and of the cerebral implementation of written language was developed by Carl Wernicke (1874) based on the reading and spelling deficits observed in aphasic patients.

A few years later (1883), Charcot developed his famous anatomofunctional model in which he represented oral and written input and output modalities as symmetric and independent processing units (**Figure 1**).

A symmetric independent organization of written language with respect to oral language was rejected by Lichtheim (1885), who proposed a dependent asymmetric model (see **Figure 2**) in which a reading (O) and a spelling center (E) both depend upon a center of auditory images of words (A). In a later study, Wernicke (1885–1886) partly accepted Lichtheim's diagram, but suggested a reanalysis of the operations underlying the processing of written language: he first excluded a symmetrical organization with respect to oral language, but he also refuted the notion of a complete subordination of written to oral language. In his final model, he opposed a diagram of written language in which letters are the atomic processing units to a model of oral language in which words are the atomic units (*wir sprechen nicht buchstabierend*, 'we do

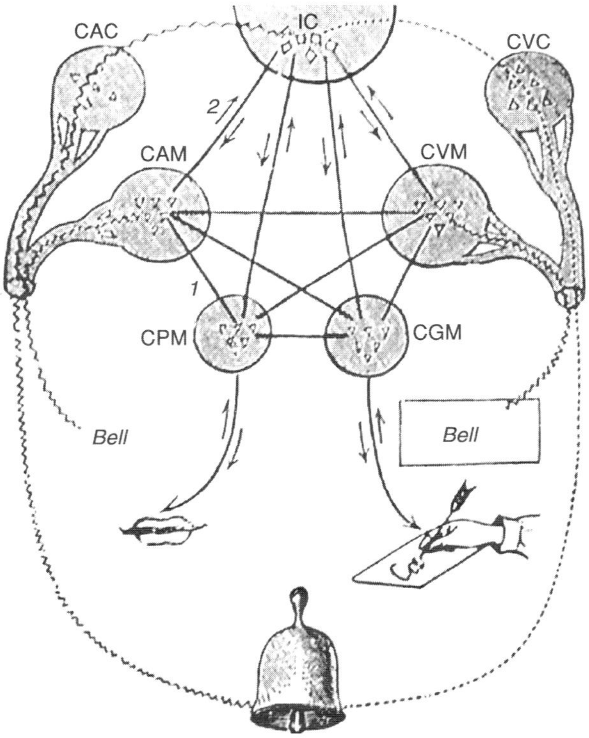

Figure 1 Charcot's diagram (1883). The sound of a bell is identified through the common auditory center (CAC); the spoken word *bell* is identified through the center of auditory memory of words (CAM); the image of a bell is identified through the common visual center (CVC); the written word *bell* is identified through the center of visual memory of words (CVM); the word *bell* is pronounced through the center of articulatory movements (CPM); the word *bell* is written through the center of graphic movements (CGM); the concept of a bell is stored in the ideatory center (IC).

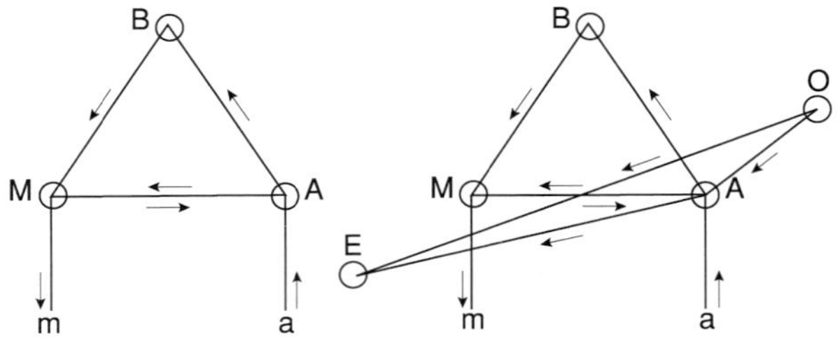

Figure 2 Lichtheim's (1885) model of oral and written language. Left, oral language. Right, oral + written language: dependent asymmetric model in which a reading (O) and a spelling center (E) depend both on the center of auditory images of words (A).

not speak letter-by-letter [in fact sound-by-sound]'). To support his hypothesis, he introduced an abstract unit (gamma), which is neither sensory nor motor, but allows the mapping of oral lexical units to the corresponding letter strings and the mapping of letter strings to the corresponding (oral) words (for an extensive discussion of Wernicke's [1885–1886] thought, see De Bleser and Luzzatti, 1989). (It must be underlined that at that time, the linguistic theory did not conceive yet of a segmentation of words into further abstract units of representation, i.e., the phonemes.)

Pure Forms of Reading and Writing Disorders

On the basis of clinical descriptions and later autopsy of two patients suffering from isolated impairment of written language, Déjerine (1891, 1892) developed an anatomo-functional model of reading and spelling that remained unchallenged until the second half of the 20th century. In the first patient, suffering from a reading and spelling disorder in absence of any deficit of oral language (alexia with agraphia), the lesion causing the impairment was confined to the left angular gyrus. The second patient suffered from right hemianopia and complete alexia with the exception of single digits (pure alexia, i.e., alexia without agraphia); the lesion in this case involved the left occipital lobe, extending to the splenium of the corpus callosum.

On the basis of his clinical observations, Déjerine developed an anatomical model of written language. In his diagram (see **Figure 3**) the angular gyrus is considered to be the store of all acquired orthographic representations (using his terminology, the center of visual memories, CVM). The visual images of letters and words are perceived either in the left or the right occipital visual center (OVC) and projected to CVM for identification and further on to the center of auditory memories (CAM, i.e., Wernicke's area) for lexical (and semantic) access. Letter and word naming would require the further connection to the motor center of word articulation (MCA, i.e., Broca's area). On the contrary, written spelling would flow from CAM to CVM and further on to the hand motor center (HMC) where the graphic motor patterns of letters are stored.

Following Déjerine functional-anatomical model, alexia with agraphia would be caused by a damage to the CVM, while pure alexia by damage to the left OVC and isolation of CVM from the contralateral right OVC, due to the splenial lesion of the corpus callosum.

Cognitive Models of Reading

Déjerine's anatomical and functional model remained for many decades the standard reference for the analysis and explanation of reading and writing impairments. However, the qualitative analysis of the reading performance of some aphasic patients (Marshall and Newcombe, 1966, 1973) pointed out that none of the classical models could account for several of the phenomena, such as the emergence of semantic substitutions, grammatical class effects (better performance on nouns than on function words), imageability effects (better performance on concrete words), and word frequency effects (better performance on higher frequency words). Furthermore, the classical models did not consider some aspects of reading performance such as selective damage of irregular words or the inability of some patients to read regular nonwords (possible but nonlexical orthographic strings). These observations were consistent with the model of reading (the logogen model) developed in this period by Morton (1969, 1980).

Dual Route Models of Reading

The ability a normal subject has to read regular nonlexical strings as well as words with irregular or unpredictable orthography (e.g., *yacht*, *pint*, or the ambiguous pronunciation of the letter string EA in *dear*, *bear*, *heart*, or *steak*) suggest two complementary reading procedures, a subword level and a lexical level (**Figure 4**).

The subword-level procedure allows the conversion of a string of graphemes into their corresponding phonemic string. The route is based on basic sublexical orthographic-to-phonological conversion rules, and accounts for reading regular words (i.e., words with fully predictable pronunciation such as *dog* or *cake*) and nonlexical but possible orthographic strings (nonwords), such as *balt* or *mable*.

The lexical procedure assumes the existence of two lexical stores listing the orthographic and phonological representations of words whose orthography and/or phonology have already been learned by an individual. Naming a written word requires the activation of its orthographic form in an orthographic input lexicon.

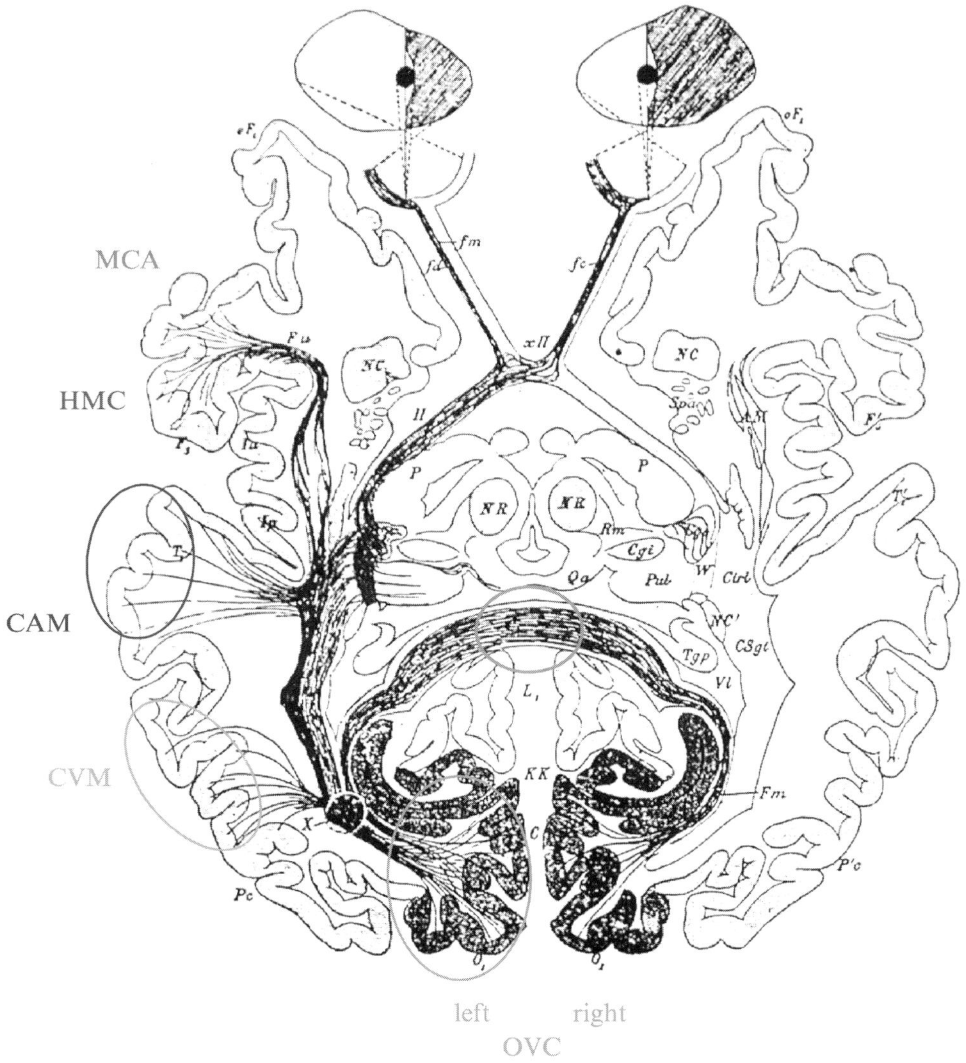

Figure 3 Déjerine's anatomical model of written language. CVM: center of visual memories; OVC: occipital visual center; CAM: center of auditory memories (i.e., the Wernicke's area); MCA: motor center of word articulation (i.e., Broca's area); HMC: hand motor center. Alexia with agraphia would be caused by a damage to CVM, while pure alexia by damage to the left OVC and isolation of CVM from the controlateral right OVC.

This lexical unit activates the underlying conceptual knowledge and later on the corresponding phonological representation from a lexical mental store (the phonological output lexicon).

The lexical route is quicker than the subword-level procedure and automatically activates word meaning, but can be used only for words whose orthography is already known by a subject, and not for nonlexical orthographic strings, and is finally the only possible route to read words with irregular or unpredictable orthography.

The phonemic string generated along either reading route is further conveyed to the phonemic buffer, a short-term store interfacing the phononogical representations with those devoted to the articulatory planning.

Lexical Analogy Models

In English, words containing letter strings with ambiguous pronunciation (*veal, deaf, steak*) are named more slowly than words with no ambiguity (Glusko, 1979). This difference has been explained as an interaction of subword-level procedures even when reading highly frequent words, and indicates that both word and nonwords are read accessing the phonological lexical representations of known words. Words stored in the orthographic lexicon would be linked for orthographic similarity. A written string (word or nonword) would activate all linked lexical strings. This would allow, by analogy, pronunciation of nonwords.

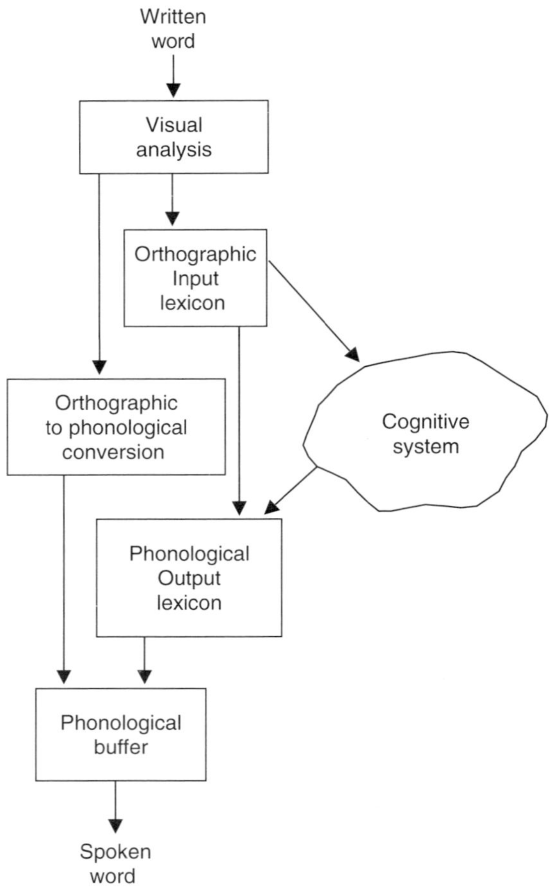

Figure 4 Dual-route model of reading. Lexical and subword-level routes of reading.

Reading Impairments in a Cognitive Neuropsychological Frame

The dual route information processing model described so far predicts the possible impairment of either reading route, namely selective damage to either the subword level, or the lexical reading procedure. In fact, some patients suffering from acquired language impairments show exactly the predicted pattern of damage.

Phonological or Surface Dyslexia

Damage to the grapheme-to-phoneme conversion rules is usually called phonological dyslexia, while damage to the lexical route goes under the label of surface dyslexia (**Figure 5**). **Table 1** summarizes the principal aspects of these two major types of reading impairment.

Direct Dyslexia

The observation of patients who could read irregular words but not understand them (e.g., the case W. L. P. of Schwartz et al., 1980) suggested a direct connection of the orthographic input lexicon to the phonological output lexicon, by-passing the underlying conceptual knowledge.

Deep Dyslexia

As already mentioned, some patients make semantic reading errors (e.g., they read *dog* instead of *hound* or *tree* instead of *wood*). Semantic paralexia is a phenomenon observed in some cases presenting with the pattern of errors similar to that described for phonological dyslexia (selective damage to the subword-level reading route); this reading impairment may be associated with grammatical class effects (nouns are read better than verbs or function words) and imageability effects (concrete words are read better than abstract words). Together, this peculiar type of reading disorder is called deep dyslexia. It often characterizes the reading performance of severe agrammatic patients. One explanation for this is the emergence of right hemisphere linguistic abilities after extensive damage to the left hemisphere language areas (Coltheart, 1980, 2000).

Letter-by-Letter Reading

This type of reading impairment usually appears in isolation from other language disorders and corresponds to the classical concept of pure alexia (Déjerine, 1892). Patients are unable to name a target word either through the lexical or the subword-level route. However, they may still be able to name the letters of words, but the procedure is typically slow and often ineffective. There is a strong word length effect, but no word frequency or word class effect (Patterson and Kay, 1982; Kinsbourne and Warrington, 1962; Coslett and Saffran, 1989).

Neglect Dyslexia

Another type of reading impairment arises in association with visuospatial neglect, due to a hemi-inattention and/or a left side representational impairment of the visual field, body, and extrapersonal space. In a word-naming task, patients neglect the left side of words. Reading errors may be either omissions (e.g., *race* for ***terrace***) or substitutions (e.g., *window* for ***meadow***). When reading a string of words, patients usually start from the middle of the string, leaving out the left side of it; they are often unaware of their impairment (anosognosia).

Diagnosis of Reading Impairments

To analyze the nature of an acquired reading impairment, three major tasks should be used: lexical decision, semantic judgment, and reading aloud. In a lexical decision task patients are asked to decide whether strings of letters are

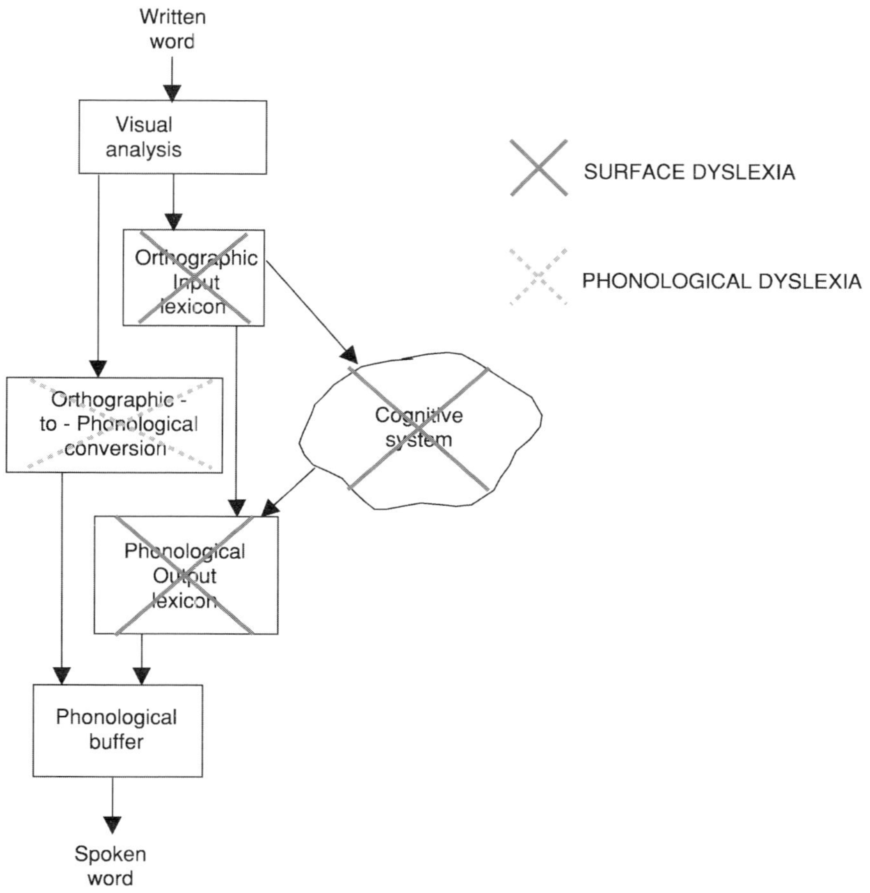

Figure 5 Dual-route model of reading. Functional lesions causing phonological and surface dyslexia.

Table 1 Principal patterns of damage characterizing phonological and surface dyslexia[a]

	Phonological dyslexia	*Surface dyslexia*
Regular words	+	+
Irregular words	+	−(→regular)
Nonwords	−	+
Lexical effects (WF, Gram. class, Concr.)	yes	no
Length effect	no	yes

[a]The symbol + indicates no or mild disorder, the symbol − indicates more severe disorder. WF = word frequency; Gram. class = grammatical class; Concr. = concreteness; → regular = regularization of irregular words.

real words or nonwords. In a semantic judgment task, patients are asked to make decisions about the meaning of words they may not be able to read (e.g., whether a certain word refers to an edible or nonedible item). According to contemporary reading models, a reading task should include words with both regular and irregular letter-to-sound correspondence and nonwords. The second set of stimuli should only be read along the lexical route, the third along the grapheme-to-phoneme conversion route, while the first set may be read along both routes. Lists of words should also vary by grammatical class, word length, word frequency, and morphological complexity (cf. the PALPA test by Kay et al., 1992). The National Adult Reading Test (NART; see Nelson, 1982) assesses the ability to read words with irregular letter-to-sound correspondence. It has been standardized on a large sample of English-speaking normal adults. As expected, the NART score correlates highly with the education level.

Clinical Neuropsychological Classification of the Spelling Impairments

During the first half of the 20th century, clinical neuropsychologists distinguished six types of spelling disorders: aphasic agraphia, alexia with agraphia (see Déjerine's model of written language), pure agraphia, apraxic agraphia, callosal agraphia, and visuospatial agraphia.

Aphasic Agraphia

The spelling impairment mirrors the clinical aspects of the oral language impairment. In addition to the deficit that arises from the right hand motor impairment that often co-occur with language dysfunction, most aphasic patients suffer from a widespread writing disorder with letter omissions, substitutions, perseverations, and spontaneous repairs. Severe fluent language impairments often assume the characteristics of a jargon agraphic output (neologisms), while nonfluent language impairments are often in association with a deficit in realizing the orthographic strokes of letters.

Alexia with Agraphia

See 'Pure forms of reading and writing disorders.'

Pure Agraphia

This is the type of spelling impairment predicted and described by Charcot (1883) in his early model under the label of motor aphasia of the hand. It is a damage to orthographic representations and therefore involves handwriting as well as oral spelling or writing on a keyboard. It has been described for left parietal and in some rare cases for left frontal lesions.

Apraxic Agraphia

In this type of writing impairment oral spelling and typing on a keyboard are spared. The inability to realize letter symbols may follow either a failure to retrieve letter forms from memory or to a difficulty in realizing these forms graphically and combining individual letter strokes appropriately. The disorder cannot be traced back to an ideomotor or constructional apraxic deficit, since both types of apraxia may not involve writing abilities and, vice versa, apraxic agraphia may emerge without any major apraxic deficit.

Callosal Agraphia

This type of impairment is usually caused by anteromedial damage to the corpus callosum. Agraphia appears in this case for the left hand only (due to a disconnection from left-hemisphere writing centers). It is often associated with left-hand apraxia and left-hand tactile anomia.

Visuospatial (Neglect) Agraphia

By analogy to neglect dyslexia (see above), there is also a spelling disorder that may arise in association with left spatial neglect. Patients may produce writing and spelling errors that only involve the left side of words. This phenomenon was interpreted as a left-side neglect of mental orthographic representations (Baxter and Warrington, 1983).

Cognitive Models of Spelling

In analogy to the dual route models of reading, cognitive psychologists have also developed dual route models to describe the spelling performance of normal adult subjects. These models assume two independent procedures, a lexical route along which words are processed as a whole, and a subword-level routine based on phoneme-to-grapheme conversion rules (see **Figures 6** and **7**). A dual-route model offers the best account so far for the ability of a literate subject to spell both irregular words and legal nonwords. Once again, the major evidence for a dual-route model of spelling derives from the observation of aphasic patients suffering from acquired spelling disorders (Beauvois and Dérouesné, 1981; Shallice, 1981; Baxter and Warrington, 1985; Harris and Coltheart, 1986; Patterson, 1986).

As with the lexical route of word naming, the lexical route of writing (to dictation) implies two stores listing the phonological and orthographic lexical knowledge of a subject and another lexical semantic store. After auditory analysis, input words activate phonological lexical knowledge stored in the phonological input lexicon. Stored lexical knowledge spreads activation to the underlying conceptual knowledge, which in turns activates the orthographic output knowledge stored in the orthographic output lexicon.

This procedure allows one to spell regular and irregular words whose orthography had already been learned, but cannot be used when spelling new words or nonwords;

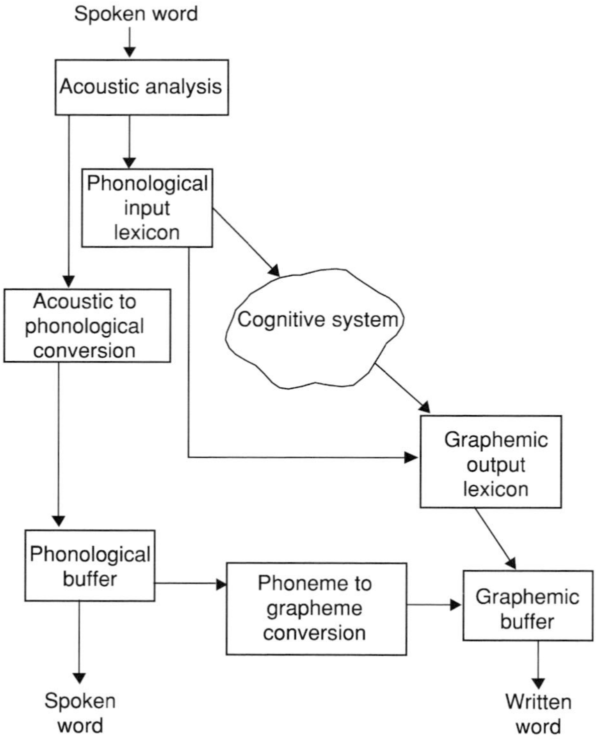

Figure 6 Dual-route model of spelling. Lexical and subword-level routes of spelling.

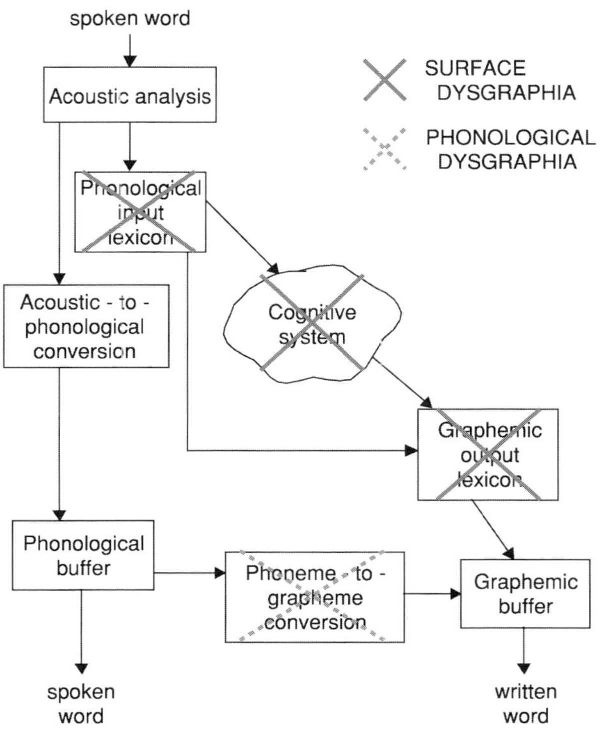

Figure 7 Dual-route model of spelling. Functional lesions causing phonological and surface dysgraphia.

it is the only procedure available for spelling irregular words.

Sub-word-level procedures permit one to convert a string of sounds into its corresponding orthographic string, following phoneme-to-grapheme conversion rules. This procedure allows one to spell regular words and nonlexical phonemic strings (nonwords).

The routine can be divided in several sequential components: after auditory analysis, the continuous flow of sounds has to be segmented and further translated into the underlying phonemic string (auditory-to-phonological conversion); the string is then reassembled in the phonemic buffer, and then conveyed to sequential translation by the phoneme-to-grapheme conversion rules into its appropriate graphemic string.

Both spelling procedures feed the graphemic buffer, a short-term memory store controlling the temporal sequencing of the selected graphemic string, and interfacing the abstract orthographic units with more peripheral processing units underlying different output modalities (handwriting, writing on a keyboard, and oral spelling).

Spelling Impairments in a Cognitive Neuropsychological Frame

The spelling disorder an adult subject may acquire after focal brain damage is caused by an impairment of the lexical and/or the subword-level spelling route.

Table 2 Principal patterns of damage characterizing phonological and surface dysgraphia[a]

	Phonological dysgraphia	*Surface dysgraphia*
Regular words	+	+
Irregular words	+	−(→regular)
Nonwords		+
Lexical effects (WF, Gram. class., Concret.)	yes	no
Length effects	no	yes

[a]The symbol + indicates no or mild damage, the symbol − more severe impairment. WF = word frequency; Gram. class = grammatical class; Concr. = concreteness; → regular = regularization of irregular words.

Damage to phoneme-to-grapheme conversion procedures causes a spelling impairment that is usually called phonological dysgraphia. The alternate pattern of impairment is called surface dysgraphia and follows damage to the lexical route of spelling. **Table 2** summarizes the contrasting phenomena characterizing these two types of dysgraphia.

Deep Dysgraphia

By analogy to reading impairments, there is a subtype of phonological dysgraphia called deep dysgraphia, which is characterized by the emergence of semantic errors. The spelling impairment in deep dysgraphia is usually associated with grammatical class (nouns are spelled better than verbs or function words) and imageability effects (concrete words are spelled better than abstract words).

Graphemic Buffer Disorders

This is a spelling disorder in which graphemic substitutions predominate. However, with respect to the previous types of dysgraphia, in graphemic buffer dysgraphia the orthosyllabic structure of the stimulus is preserved (vowels are substituted to other vowels, consonants are substituted by consonants, and the structure of clusters and doubled consonants is preserved). A comparable impairment emerges both for words and nonwords. This set of phenomena suggests that substitutions arise at an advanced stage of the spelling processes, i.e., in a phase where the orthosyllabic structure of the stimulus to be spelled has already been formed.

Peripheral Dysgraphia (Allographic Dysgraphia)

This is a set of writing impairments originating at a peripheral stage with respect to the graphemic output buffer. It usually involves handwriting, leaving oral spelling and the ability to write on a keyboard unimpaired. Some patients are unable to distinguish lower- and upper-case letters, mixing these two sets of characters during handwriting.

This impairment must be distinguished from apraxic dysgraphia (see above), because the output observed in allographic dysgraphia may be fluent and letter shapes are typically well formed.

Diagnosis of Spelling Impairments

In analogy to reading tasks, writing tasks should contain several sets of items, i.e., words with regular spelling, words with irregular spelling, and nonwords. Words should vary for grammatical class, word length, word frequency and morphological complexity. Finally, patients should be tested for oral and written spelling, copying, delayed copying, and repetition. Cognitive neuropsychologists studying patients for their writing disabilities usually devise their own lists of items designed specifically to test certain aspects of the patient under study.

Spelling abilities may be assessed in English-speaking subjects using the PALPA test (Kay et al., 1992). The test includes writing and spelling of regular and irregular words (from different grammatical classes and of variable length and frequency), writing and spelling of nonwords, and written naming of object pictures.

Bibliography

Baxter, DM and Warrington, KE (1983). 'Neglect dysgraphia.' *Journal of Neurology, Neurosrgery and Psychiatry* 46: 1073–1078.

Baxter, DM and Warrington, KE (1985). 'Category specific phonological dysgraphia.' *Neuropsychologia* 23: 653–666.

Beauvois, MF and Derouesné, J (1981). 'Lexical ortographic agraphia.' *Brain* 104: 21–49.

Charcot, JM (1883). *Le differenti forme di afasia.* Milan: Vallardi.

Coltheart, M (1980). 'Deep dyslexia: a right hemisphere hypothesis.' In: Coltheart, M, Patterson, KE, and Marshall, JC (eds.) *Deep dyslexia*, pp. 326–380. London: Routledge and Kegan Paul.

Coltheart, M (2000). 'Deep dyslexia is right-hemisphere reading.' *Brain & Language* 71: 299–309.

Coltheart, M, Patterson, K, and Marshall, JC (eds.) (1980). *Deep dyslexia.* London: Routledge and Kegan Paul.

Coslett, HB and Saffran, EM (1989). 'Evidence for preserved reading in "pure alexia".' *Brain* 112: 327–359.

De Bleser, R and Luzzatti, C (1989). 'Models of reading and writing and their disorders in classical German aphasiology.' *Cognitive Neuropsychology* 6: 501–513.

Déjerine, JJ (1891). 'Sur un cas de cécité verbale avec agraphie suivi d'autopsie.' *Mémoires de la Société de Biologie* 3: 197–201.

Déjerine, JJ (1892). 'Contribution à l'étude anatomo-pathologique et clinique des différentes variétés de cécité verbale.' *Comptes Rendus Hebdomadaires des Séances et Mémoires de la Société de Biologie (Paris)* 4: 61–90.

Glushko, RJ (1979). 'The organization and activation of orthographic knowledge in reading aloud.' *Journal of Experimental Psychology: Human Perception and Performance* 5: 674–691.

Harris, M and Coltheart, M (1986). *Language processing in children and adults.* London: Routledge and Kegan Paul.

Kay, J, Lesser, R, and Coltheart, M (1992). *PALPA: Psycholinguistic assessment of language processing in aphasia.* Hove, UK: Lawrence Erlbaum.

Kinsbourne, M and Warrington, EK (1962). 'A disorder of simultaneous form perception.' *Brain* 85: 461–485.

Lichtheim, L (1885). 'Über Aphasie.' *Deutsches Archiv für klinische Medizin* 36: 204–268. (On Aphasia. *Brain 7*, 433–484, 1885.)

Marshall, JC and Newcombe, F (1966). 'Syntactic and semantic errors in paralexia.' *Neuropsychologia* 4: 169–176.

Marshall, JC and Newcombe, F (1973). 'Patterns of paralexia a psycholinguistic approach.' *Journal of Psycholinguistic Research* 2: 175–199.

Morton, J (1969). 'The interaction of information in word recognition.' *Psychological Review* 76: 165–178.

Morton, J (1980). 'The logogen model and ortographic structure.' In: Frith, U (ed.) *Cognitive processes in spelling.* London: Academic Press.

Nelson, HE (1982). *The National Adult Reading Test (NART): Test manual.* Windsor, UK: NFER-Nelso.

Patterson, KE (1986). 'Lexical but nonsemantic spelling.' *Cognitive Neuropsychology* 3: 341–367.

Patterson, KE and Kay, J (1982). 'Letter by letter reading: psychological description of a neurological syndrome.' *Quarterly Journal of Experimental Psychology* 34a: 411–441.

Schwartz, MF, Saffran, EM, and Marin, OSM (1980). 'Fractionating the reading process in dementia: evidence from word-specific print-to-sound associations.' In: Coltheart, M, Patterson, K, and Marshall, JC (eds.) *Deep dyslexia.* London: Routledge & Kegan Paul.

Shallice, T (1981). 'Phonological agraphia and the lexical route in writing.' *Brain* 104: 413–429.

Wernicke, C (1874). *Der aphasische Symptomencomplex. Eine Psychologische Studie auf anatomischer Basis.* Breslau: Cohn & Weigert.

Wernicke, C (1885, 1886). 'Die Neueren Arbeiten über Aphasie.' *Fortschritte der Medizin* 3: 824–830; *4*, 371–377; *4*, 463–482 ('Recent contributions on aphasia.' *Cognitive Neuropsychology 6*, 547–569, 1989).

Subject Index

A

B

C

D

E

F

G

H

I

M

N

O

P

Q

R

S

T

U

V

W

X

Y

Z

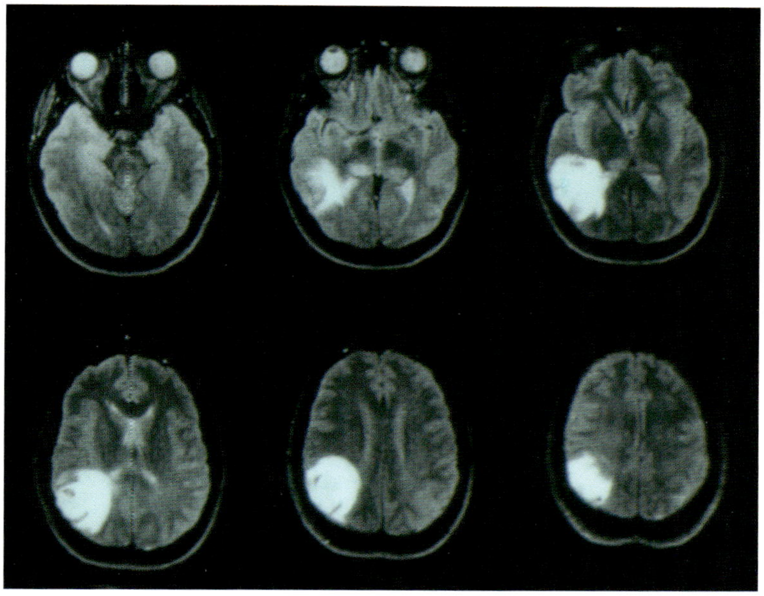

Plate 1 (*see page 18*)

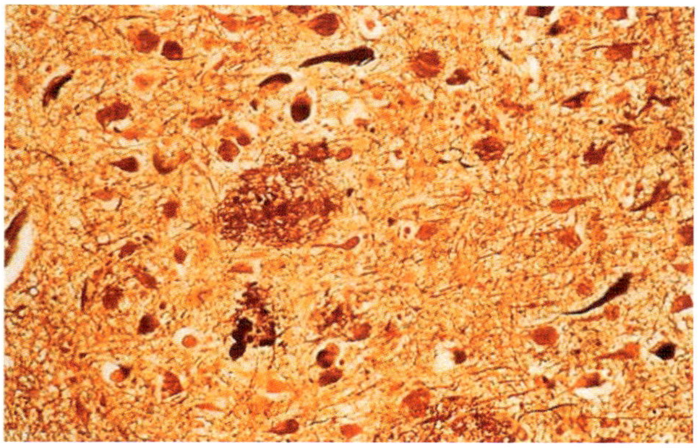

Plate 2 Bielschowsky silver staining reveals a typical Alzheimer's plaque (left of center). Several neurofibrillary tangles are also present (*see page 20*).

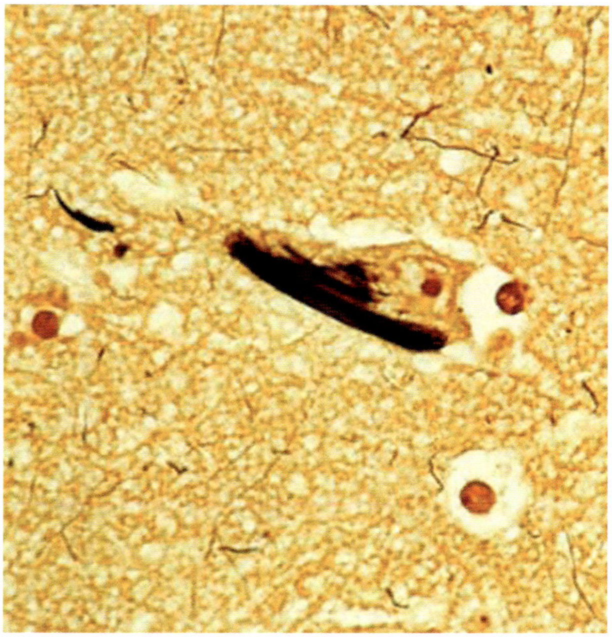

Plate 3 Magnified view of a neurofibrillary tangle (Bielschowsky stain) (*see page 21*).

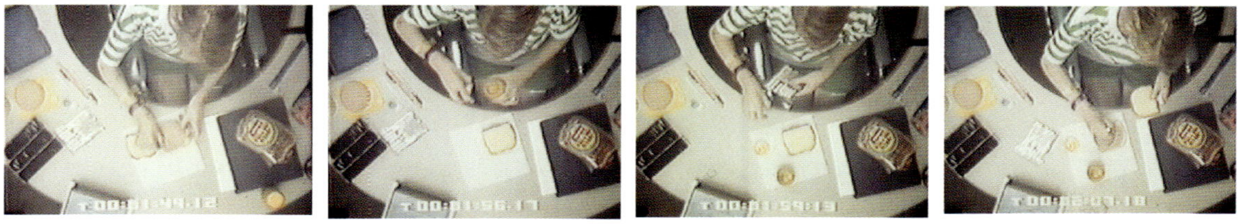

Plate 4 Photographs of a patient with conceptual apraxia making a sandwich with meat and mustard. She correctly places meat on a slice of bread, closes the sandwich, and cpens a mustard jar. She replaces the mustard jar, reaches into a package of marking pens, retrieves a yellow marker, and proceeds to color the meat yellow (*see page 57*).

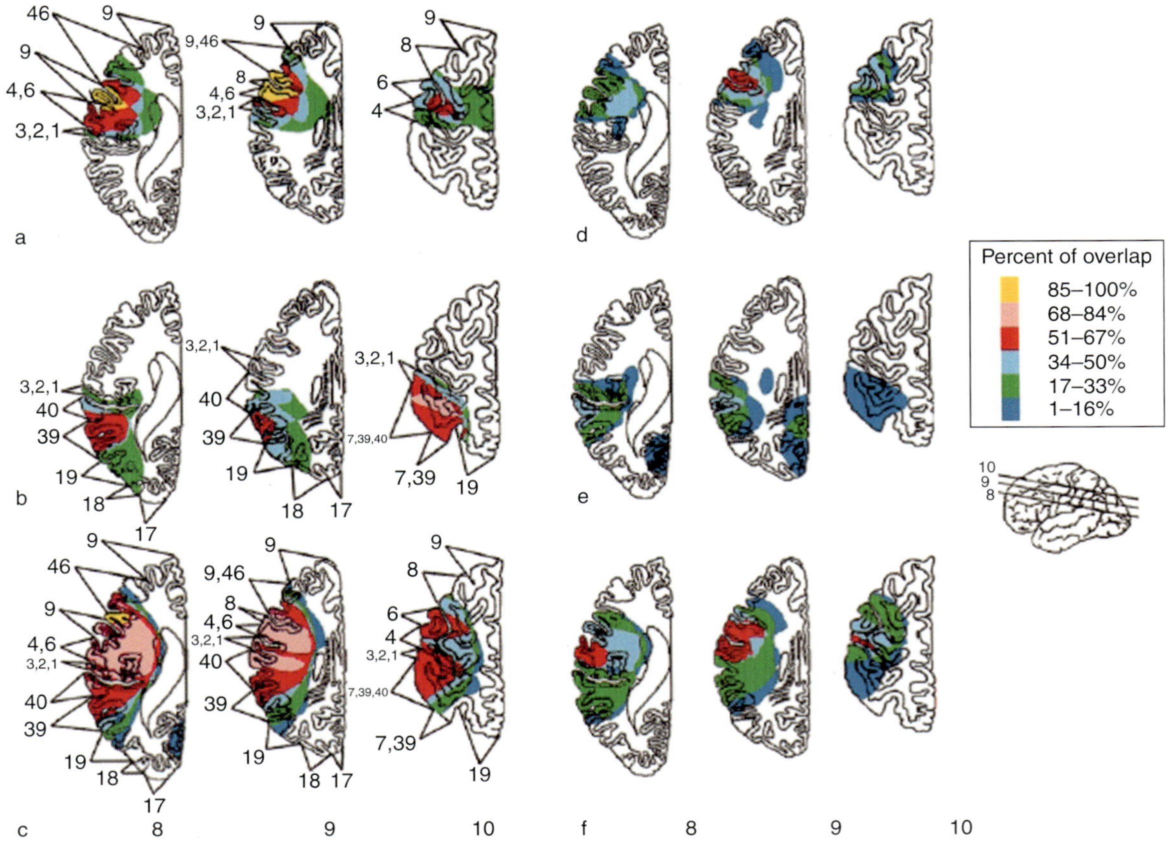

Plate 5 Maximal lesion overlap from 17 apraxic patients is shown in dorsolateral and inferior parietal regions. From Haaland KY, Harrington DL, and Knight RT (2000) Neural representations of skilled movement. *Brain* 123: 2306–2313. (*see page 58*).

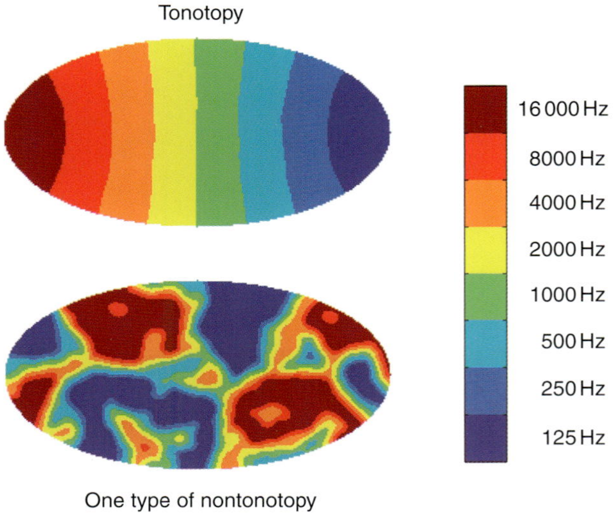

Plate 6 Model tonotopic and nontonotopic representations of sound frequency in a cortical area (*see page 68*).

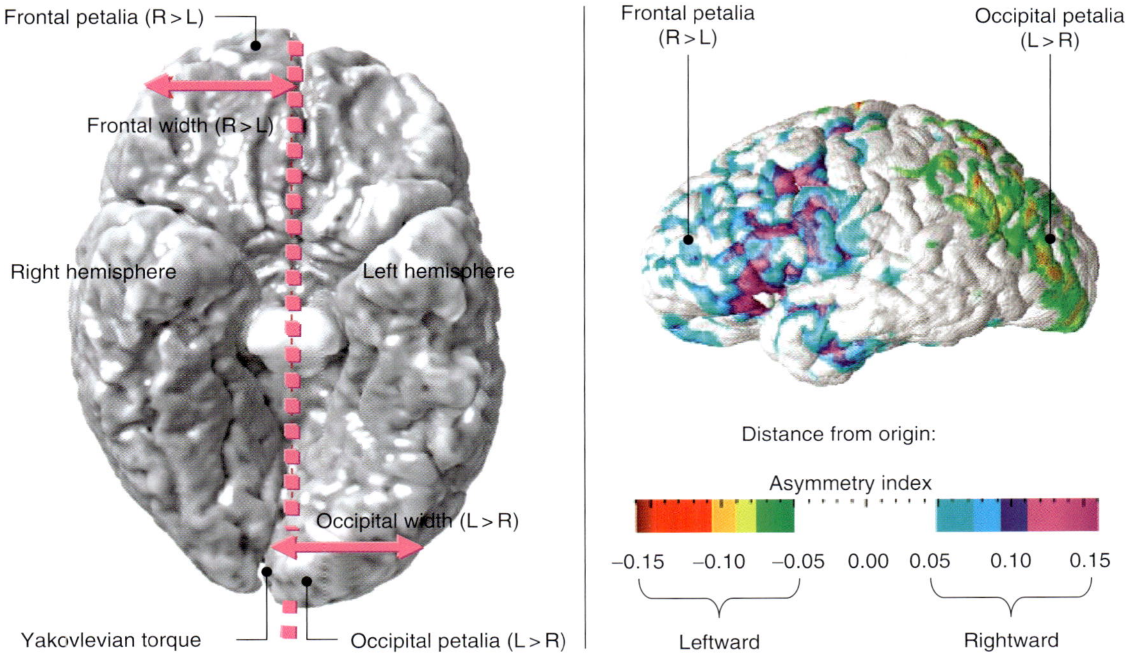

Plate 7 Petalia asymmetry. (Left) A three-dimensional rendering of the inferior surface of the human brain exaggerated to illustrate prominent asymmetries found in the gross anatomy of the two brain hemispheres. Noticeable protrusions of the hemispheres, anteriorly (R > L) and posteriorly (L > R), are observed, as well as differences in the widths of the frontal (R > L) and occipital lobes (L > R). A twisting effect is also observed, known as Yakovlevian torquxe, in which the left occipital lobe is splayed across midline and skews the interhemispheric fissure in a rightward direction. (Right) The magnitude and direction of hemispheric shape differences, which are estimated by measuring distances from a central point (origin) in the brain to thousands of spatially equivalent cortical surface locations in each hemisphere and by comparing these distances using an asymmetry index. The color scale illustrates anterior protrusions of hemispheric shape in the right hemisphere and posterior protrusions of hemispheric shape in the left hemisphere in one individual (*see page 93*).

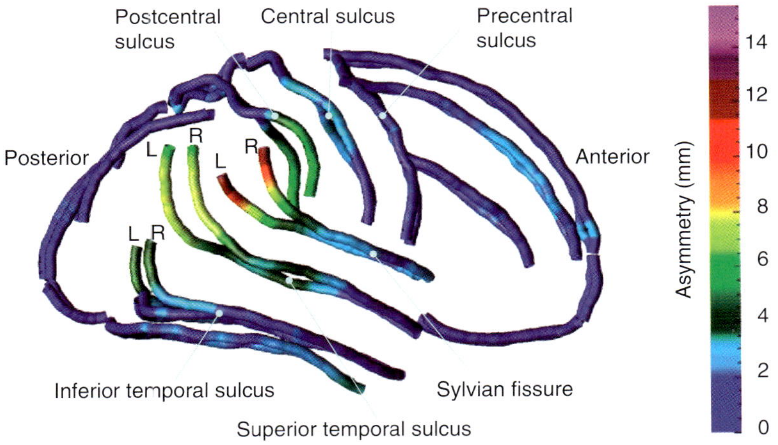

Plate 8 MRI of a 55-year-old patient. Note the marked atrophy in the parieto-occipital region (*see page 94*).

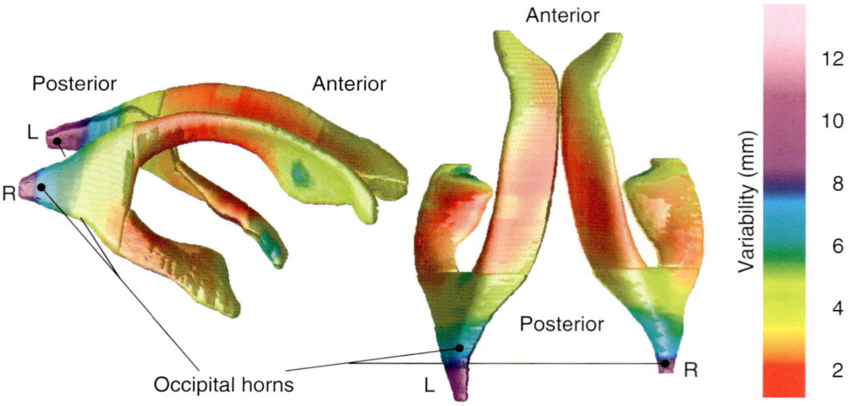

Plate 9 Ventricular asymmetry. The anatomy of the lateral ventricles is shown across subjects ($N = 40$) in three-dimensional view. These maps of average ventricular anatomy show that the left ventricle is larger than the right ventricle. The anatomic asymmetry is clearly localized to the occipital horn, which extends (on average) 5.1 mm more posteriorly on the left than the right. This is consistent with the petalia and torque effects described previously. This asymmetry may go unnoticed in individual subjects due to the high intersubject variability of anatomy (*see page 95*).

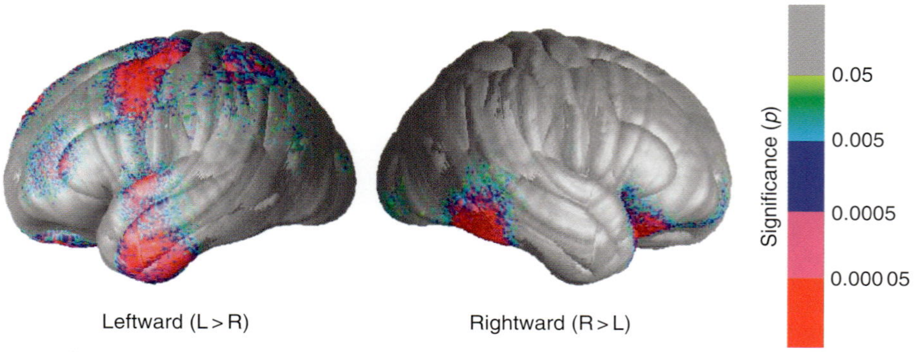

Plate 10 Cortical thickness asymmetry. Statistical maps demonstrating significant hemispheric differences of cortical thickness in a large sample of subjects ($N = 60$). The left brain demonstrates leftward (L > R) asymmetries in the anterior temporal lobe, including the inferior, middle, and superior temporal gyri and the precentral gyrus extending anteriorly to adjacent regions. Two additional larger clusters favoring the left are apparent in the middle frontal gyrus and superior parietal lobe (extending more diffusely inferiorly, covering the inferior parietal lobe and supramarginal gyrus). Smaller clusters of leftward asymmetry are evident in superior frontal regions very close to the midline extending along the longitudinal fissure and in the orbital gyrus. The right brain demonstrates significant rightward asymmetries (R > L) in the posterior inferior temporal lobe and inferior frontal gyrus (comprising the pars orbitalis, triangularis, and opercularis and extending into the extreme anterior tip of the temporal lobe) and near the frontal pole. In general, leftward asymmetries are spread over larger regions than rightward asymmetries (*see page 95*).

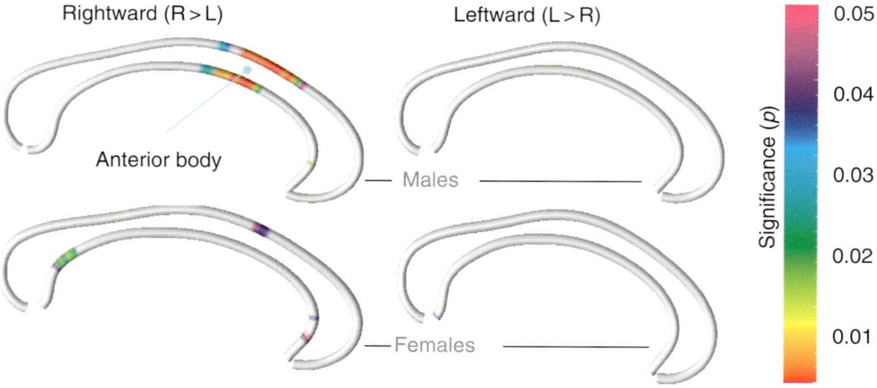

Plate 11 Callosal asymmetry. Statistical maps demonstrating significant gender-specific asymmetries in a large sample of subjects (30 men and 30 women). Differences between callosal thicknesses were measured in the left and right hemispheres several millimeters apart from the midsagittal plane. Rightward asymmetries are largely increased in men, supporting the assumption of a sexually dimorphic organization of male and female brains that involves hemispheric relations and is reflected in the organization and distribution of callosal fibers (*see page 97*).

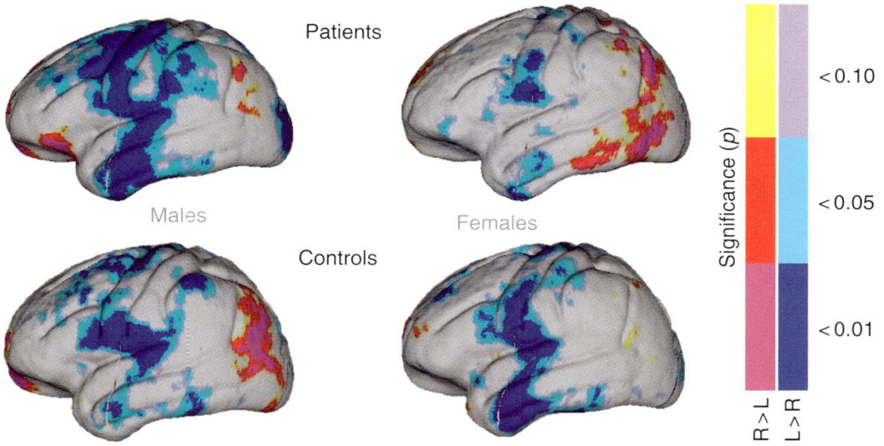

Plate 12 Cortical thickness asymmetry in schizophrenia. Statistical maps show significant hemispheric differences in cortical thickness within groups defined by sex and a diagnosis of schizophrenia ($N = 150$). The patterns of cortical thickness asymmetries appear similar in all groups (leftward asymmetries of thickness in sensorimotor and perisylvian cortices and rightward cortical thickness asymmetries in posterior temporoparietal cortices). Notably, these patterns were not shown to differ statistically in patients with schizophrenia compared to demographically similar healthy comparison subjects (*see page 98*).

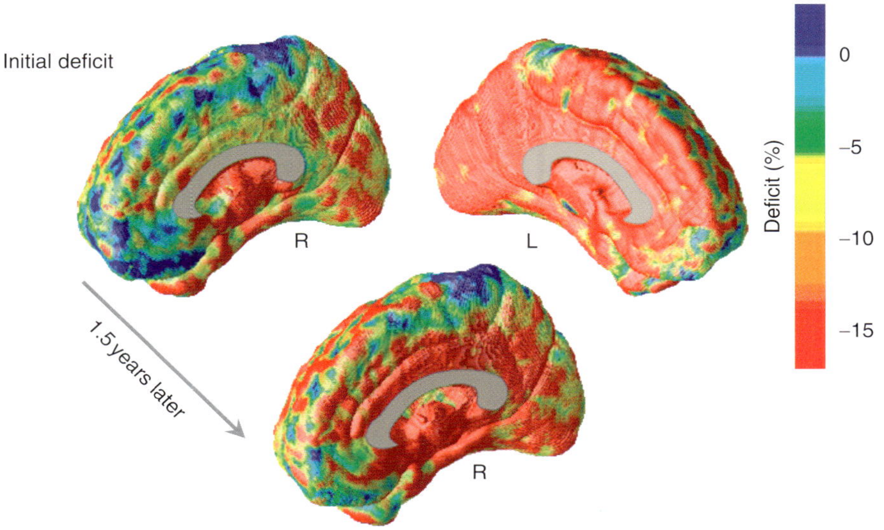

Plate 13 Asymmetrical progression of Alzheimer's disease. These maps show the average profile of GM loss in a group of patients with mild to moderate Alzheimer's disease ($N = 17$) compared to a group of healthy age- and gender-matched controls ($N = 14$). Initially, the right hemisphere (R) is much less severely affected than the left (L), but after 1.5 years the deficit progresses to encompass more of the right hemisphere (*see page 98*).

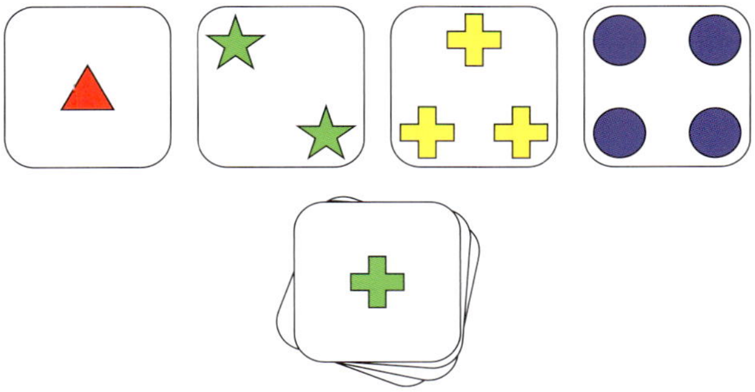

Plate 14 WCST: the participant is presented with four prototype cards and given a stack of cards to match to one of the prototypes by placing it beneath the prototype in a separate pile. The participant is not told the sorting rule (color, shape, or number) but has to figure it out on the basis of feedback from the examiner (i.e., a statement indicating that the match was correct or incorrect). If participants make a mistake, they must try again with the next card. Following ten correct sorts, unbeknownst to the participant, the rule changes, and the participant must again figure out the operative sorting rule based on feedback (*see page 134*).

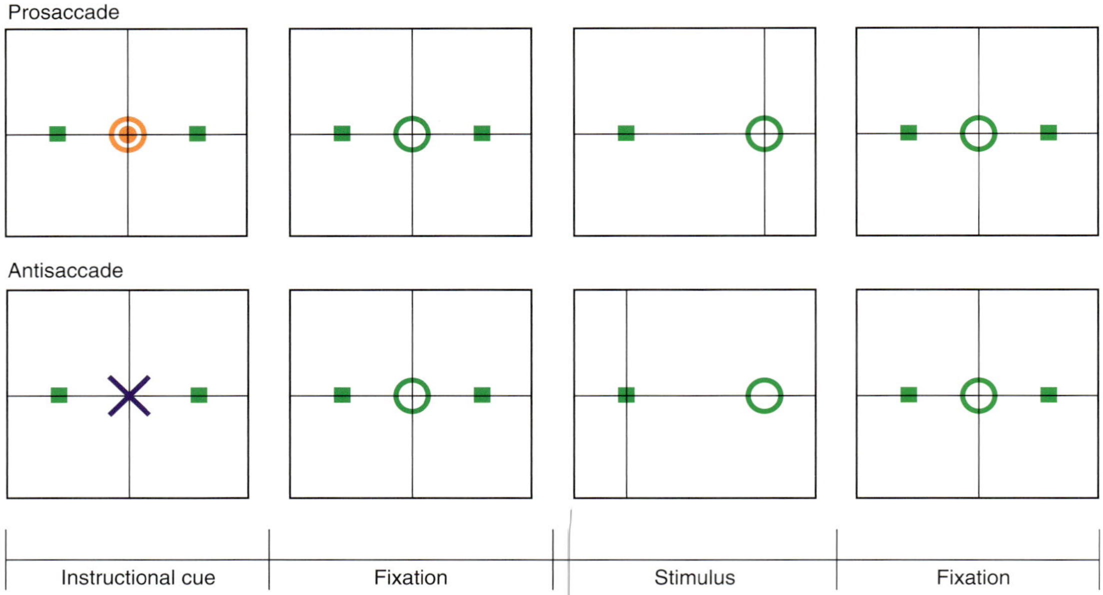

Plate 15 An example antisaccade paradigm. The cross hair represents the point of regard. A trial begins with a visual cue instructing either a prosaccade or an antisaccade (in this case an orange circle for prosaccades and a blue X for antisaccades). Following the disappearence of the cue, participants maintain fixation on the center until a stimulus appears over one of the two peripheral dots, the side randomly determined. Participants are instructed to look toward the suddenly appearing stimulus on prosaccade trials. For antisaccade trials, they are instructed to look in the opposite direction. After stimulus offset, fixation returns to the center as participants await the beginning of the next trial. While prosaccades are a relatively automatic response, antisaccades require executive control. To perform an antisaccade correctly one must suppress the prepotent response of looking toward a suddenly appearing stimulus (i.e., prosaccade) and generate the novel behavior of looking in the opposite direction. Out come measurements include directional accuracy of the saccadic eye movement and latency to initiate the saccade. Individuals with schizophrenia generally perform normally on prosaccade trials but show increased errors (failures of inhibition) and, depending on task parameters, may also show increased latency for correct responses on antisaccade trials (*see page 135*).

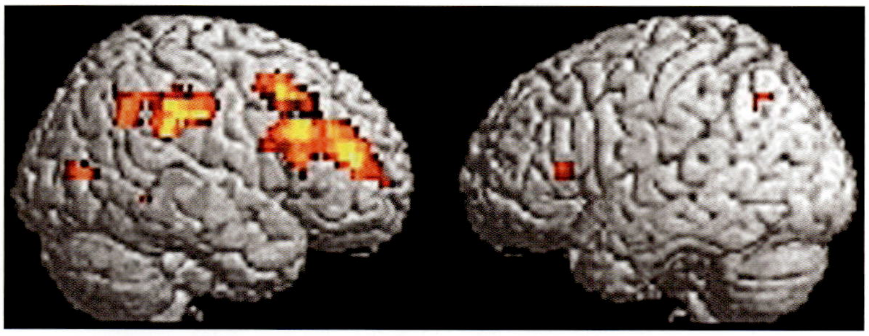

Plate 16 Regions of increased, inefficient fMRI activation in the unaffected siblings of schizophrenia patients relative to demographically matched control participants during performance of a working memory paradigm. Behavioral performance did not discriminate between the groups, but fMRI activation did, suggesting that imaging indices may be more sensitive to genetic risk for schizophrenia. Regions of increased activation include right dorsolateral and ventrolateral prefrontal cortices. Statistical group difference maps are rendered onto canonical single-participant lateral brain surfaces. Adapted from figure 2 in Callicott JH, Egan MF, Mattay VS, et al. (2003) Abnormal fMRI response of the dorsolateral prefrontal cortex in cognitively intact siblings of patients with schizophrenia. *American Journal of Psychiatry* 160: 709–719 (*see page 139*).

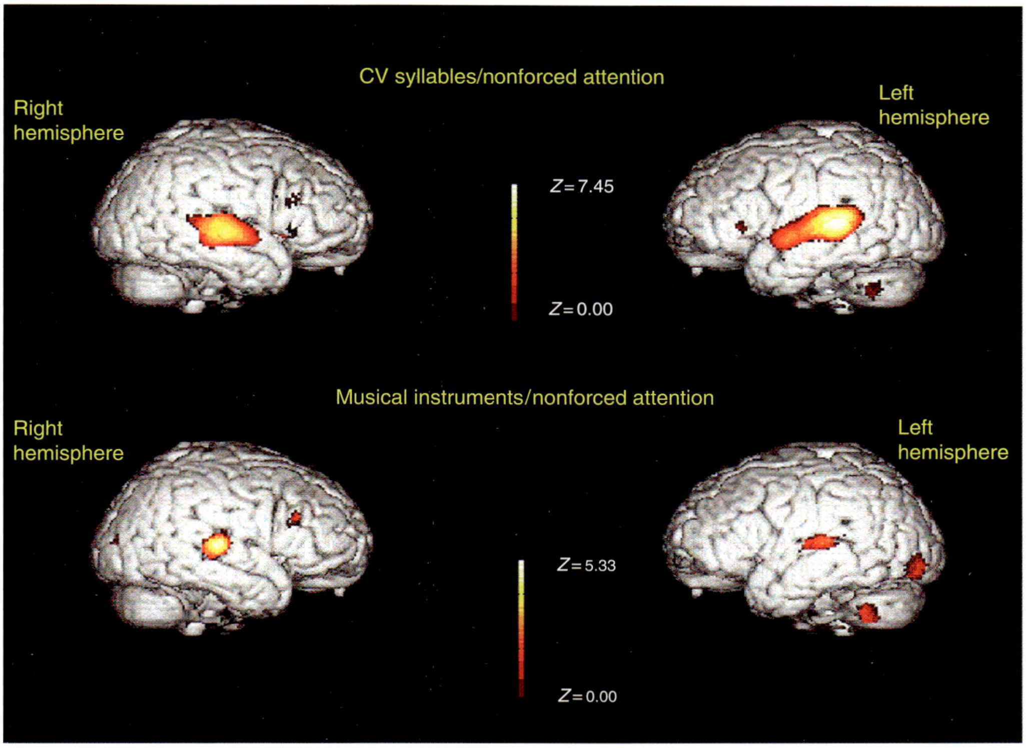

Plate 17 ^{15}O-PET brain activation data in response to CV syllables and musical stimuli. Note the leftward asymmetry for the CV syllable stimuli, and rightward asymmetry for the musical stimuli. Reproduced from Hugdahl K, Brønnick K, Law I, et al. (1999) Brain activation during dichotic presentations of consonant–vowel and musical instruments stimuli: A ^{15}O-PET study. *Neuropsychologia* 37: 431–440, with permission from Elsevier (*see page 165*).

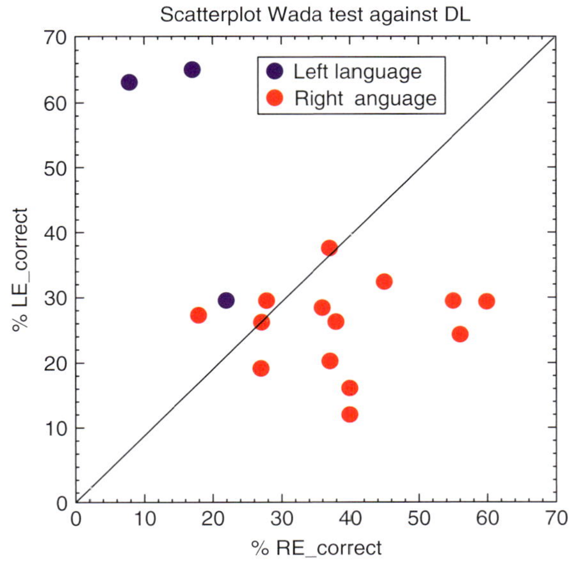

Plate 18 Wada test validation of DL scores from 17 adolescent epileptic patients. Overall, 94% of the group was correctly classified. Data courtesy of Göran Carlsson and Paul Uvebrant, Kiel, Germany, and Göteborg, Sweden (*see page 166*).

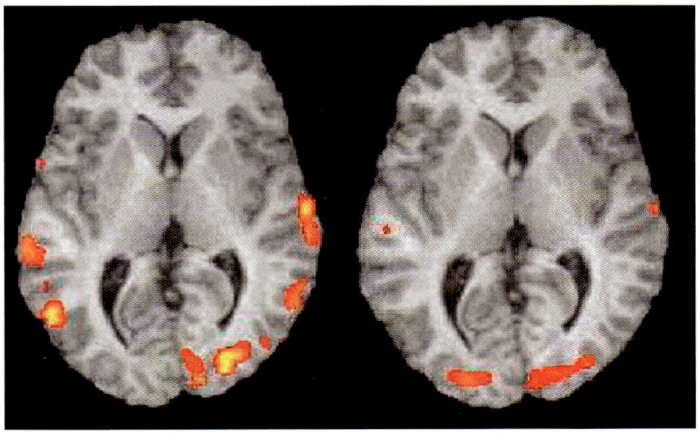

Plate 19 Horizontal sections of the brain reveal that typical adult readers (left) display activity in visual cortex, including area MT/V5, during the perception of visual motion. Adults with dyslexia (right) lack this activity. From Eden GF, VanMeter JW, Rumsey JW, Maisog J, and Zeffiro TA (1996) Abnormal processing of visual motion in dyslexia revealed by functional brain imaging. *Nature* 348: 66–69 (*see page 186*).

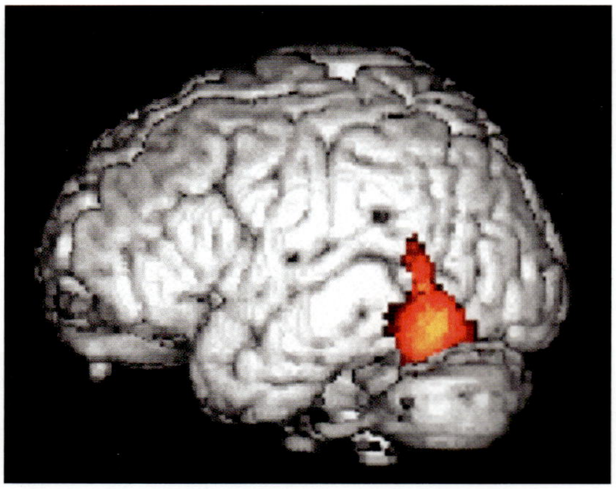

Plate 20 An example of a brain examined at postmortem. The individual was diagnosed as having had dyslexia. Developmental anomalies consist of neuronal ectopias and architectonic dysplasias. Adapted from Galaburda AM, Sherman GF, Rosen GD, Aboitiz F, and Geschwind N (1985) Developmental dyslexia: Four consecutive patients with cortical anomalies. *Annals of Neurology* 18: 222–233 (*see page 187*).

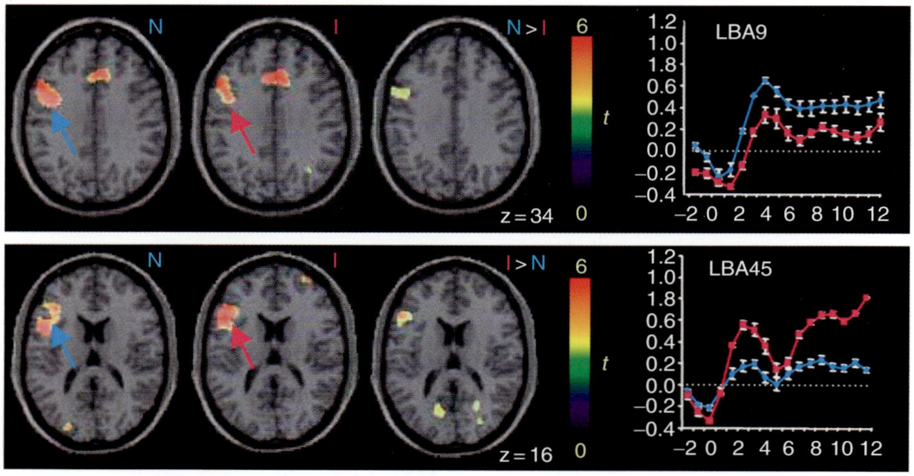

Plate 21 During a homophone judgment task, Chinese normal (blue) and impaired readers (red) differ in brain activity in left-middle frontal gyrus (top panel) and inferior frontal gyrus. From Siok WT, Perfetti CA, Jin Z, and Tan LH (2004) Biological abnormality of impaired reading is constrained by culture. *Nature* 431(7004): 71–76 (*see page 188*).

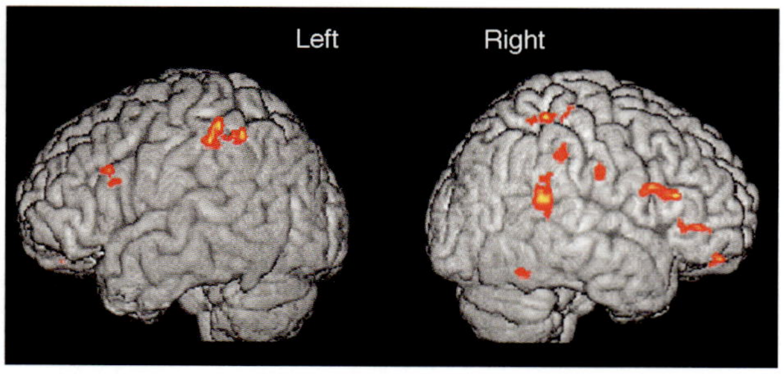

Plate 22 Functional anatomy of phonological manipulation following reading remediation (Group X Session interaction) revealed increases during phonological manipulation in left parietal cortex and fusiform gyrus. Right hemisphere increases included posterior superior temporal sulcus/gyrus and parietal cortex. Reprinted from Eden GF, Jones KM, Cappell K, et al. (2004) Neural changes following remediation in adult developmental dyslexia. *Neuron* 44(3): 411–422 (*see page 190*).

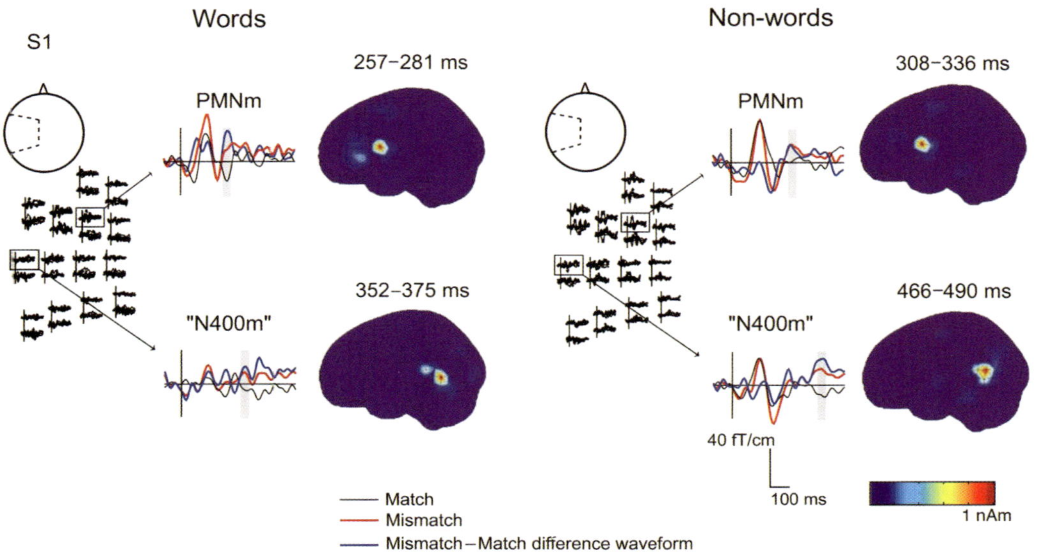

Plate 23 Phonological mapping negativity (PMN) and semantic N400. MEG responses to words (left) and non-words (right) for one participant for those left-hemisphere channels showing maximum amplitude for the magnetic PMN (PMNm) and the N400-like response. The corresponding estimates of the PMN- and N400m-like response sources (over a 25 ms time window centered at the peak of the response) are depicted in the brain images. The gray vertical bars indicate the 50 ms time periods within which significant PMNm- and N400m-like responses occurred. *Source*: Modified after Kujala et al., 2004 (*see page 193*).

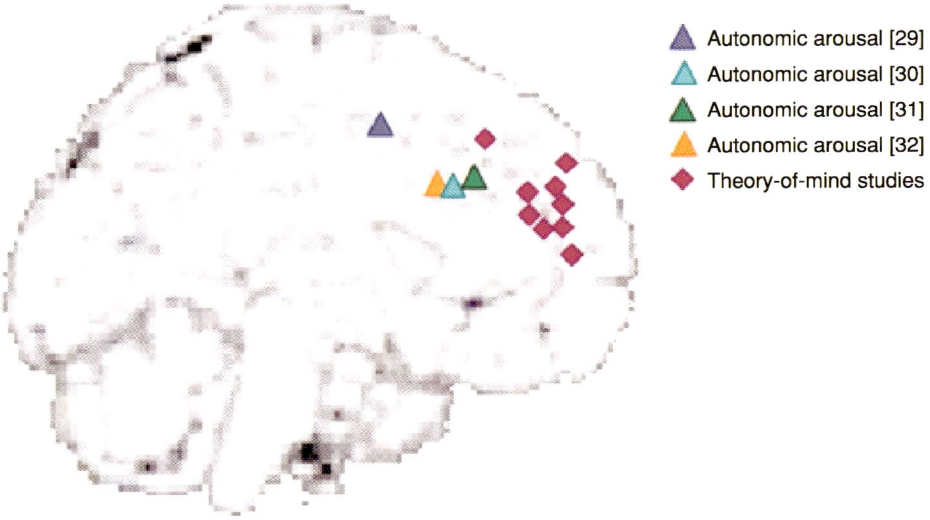

Plate 24 A summary and display of areas of activation found in the medial prefrontal cortex (anterior paracingulate) during theory-of-mind tasks. Also displayed are areas of activation in other areas of the medial prefrontal cortex (the anterior cingulate cortex) found to be associated with autonomic arousal, cognitive demand, and response conflict. [29] Critchley H D et al. (2000). 'Cerebral correlates of autonomic cardiovascular arousal: a functional neuroimaging investigation in humans.' *Journal of Physiology London 523*, 259–270. [30] Critchley H D et al. (2001). 'Neural activity in the human brain relating to uncertainty and arousal during anticipation.' *Neuron 29*, 537–545. [31] Duncan J and Owen A M (2000). 'Common regions of the human frontal lobe recruited by diverse cognitive demands.' *Trends in Neuroscience 23*, 475–483. [32] Barch D M et al. (2001). 'Anterior cingulate cortex and response conflict: effects of response modality and processing domain.' *Cerebellum Cortex 11*, 837–848. Taken from Gallagher HL & Frith C D (2003). 'Functional imaging of 'theory of mind'.' *Trends in Cognitive Science 7(2),* 77–83. © Elsevier, with permission (*see page 233*).

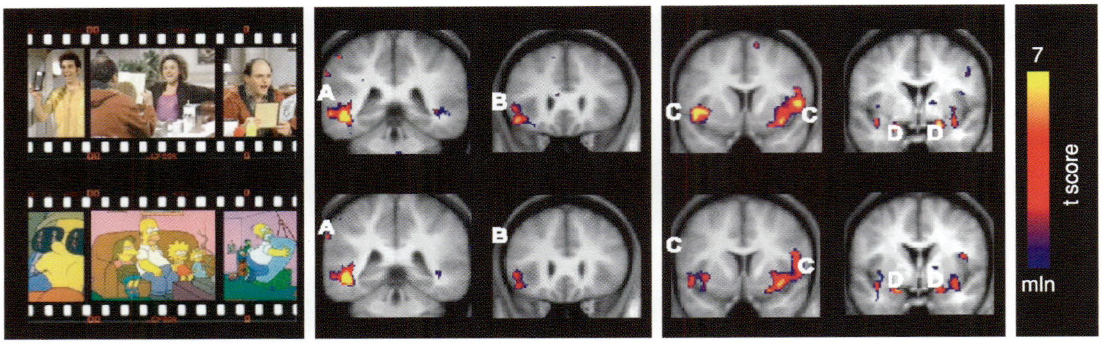

Plate 25 Displayed are averaged activation maps based on subjects viewing *Seinfeld* (upper panel) and *The Simpsons* (lower panel) sitcoms. A functional dissociation between humor detection and humor appreciation was described. In the coronal brain images, the left side of the image corresponds to the left hemisphere. In both studies, humor detection led to greater activation in the left posterior middle temporal gyrus and the left inferior frontal gyrus. By contrast, humor appreciation yielded greater activation bilaterally in the insular cortex and the amygdala. Taken from Moran et al. (2004). 'Neural correlates of human detection and appreciation.' *Neuroimage 21*, 1055–1060. © Elsevier, with permission (*see page 234*).

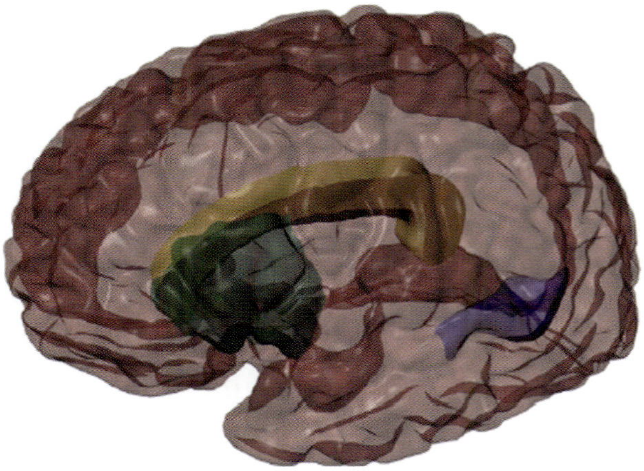

Plate 26 Anatomical sites of the classical language areas identified in a transparent surface model of the human cerebral cortex. Broca's speech area (green) and Wernicke's language-comprehension area (blue) are identified on a transparent surface model of the human cerebral cortex. All cortical regions are interconnected through the corpus callosum (yellow) with corresponding systems in the opposite brain hemisphere. From Toga A W and Thompson P M (2003). Mapping brain asymmetry. Reproduced with permission from Nature Reviews Neuroscience. Copyright (2003) Macmillan Magazines Ltd., www.nature. com/reviews (*see page 236*).

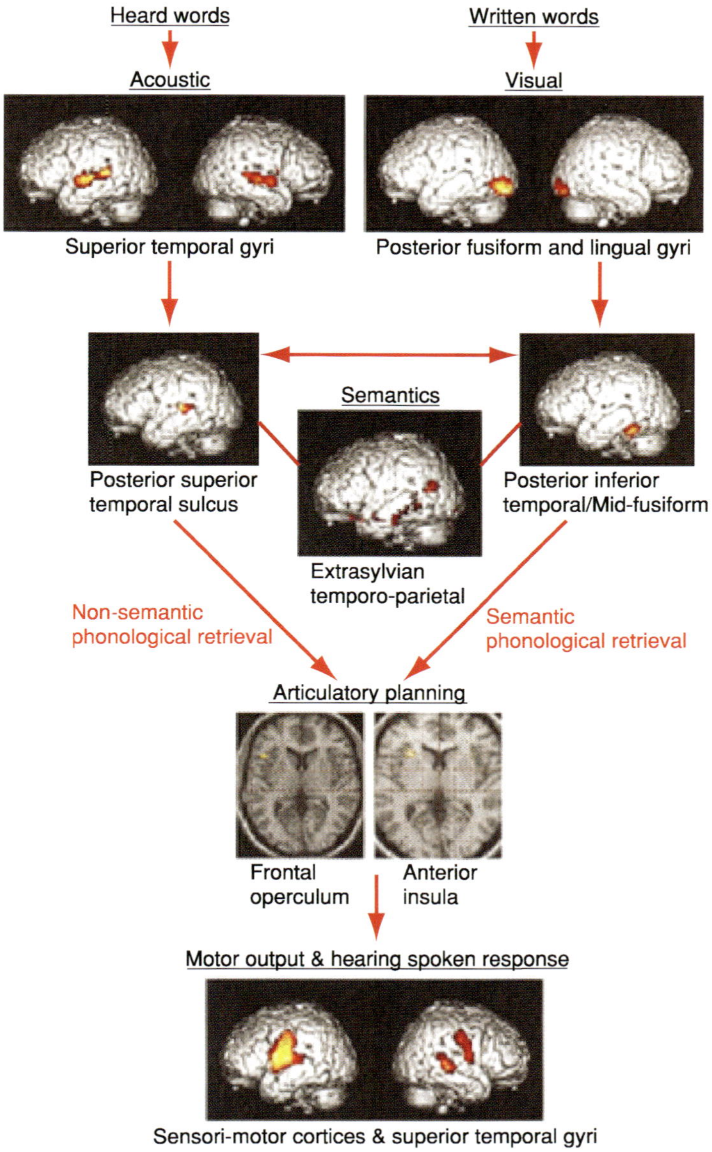

Plate 27 Summary of the results of functional imaging studies on word repetition, word retrieval, and word reading. The top row shows brain areas activated during the acoustic processing of heard words and visual processing of written words. Activation is predominantly bilateral. The second row, left side, shows brain activation related to the phonological processing of speech sounds relative to environmental sounds. In the center, semantic decisions relative to phonological decisions on the same words are shown, and the right side shows activation associated with retrieving the name (via lexical semantics) relative to seeing visual controls and saying 'Okay' or 'Yes.' Note that the activation is predominantly left lateralized. The third row presents transverse slices and shows activation in the left anterior insula and left frontal operculum during phonological output. Bilateral activation is shown in the fourth row and exhibits motor areas for articulation and auditory processing of spoken response for reading aloud relative to reading silently. The red arrows connect these areas to indicate the proposed model of auditory and visual word processing. From Price C J (2000). 'The anatomy of language: contributions from functional neuroimaging.' *Journal of Anatomy 197(5)*, 335–359. Reproduced with permission from Blackwell Publishing (*see page 237*).

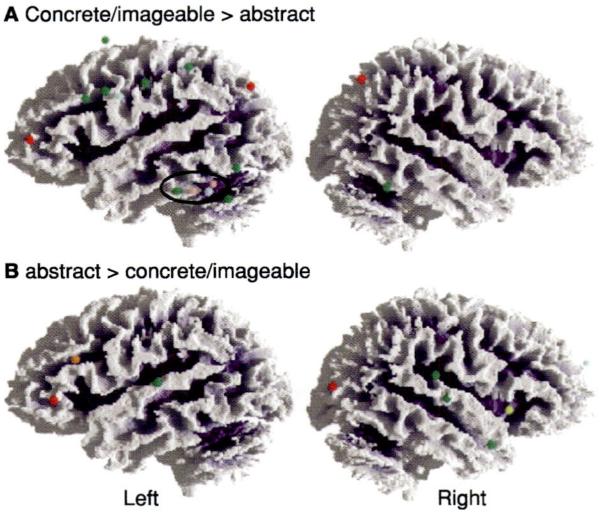

Plate 28 Fiebach and Friederici (2003) visualized brain areas exhibiting greater activity for concrete words than for abstract words (A) or greater activity for abstract than for concrete words (B). Each colored dot represents the results of a particular study reviewed by Fiebach and Friederici. Note that medial and subcortical activations are not displayed. Reproduced with permission from Fiebach C J and Friederici A D (2003). 'Processing concrete works: fMRI evidence against a specific right-hemisphere involvement.' *Neuropsychologia 42*, 62–70. © Elsevier (*see page 238*).

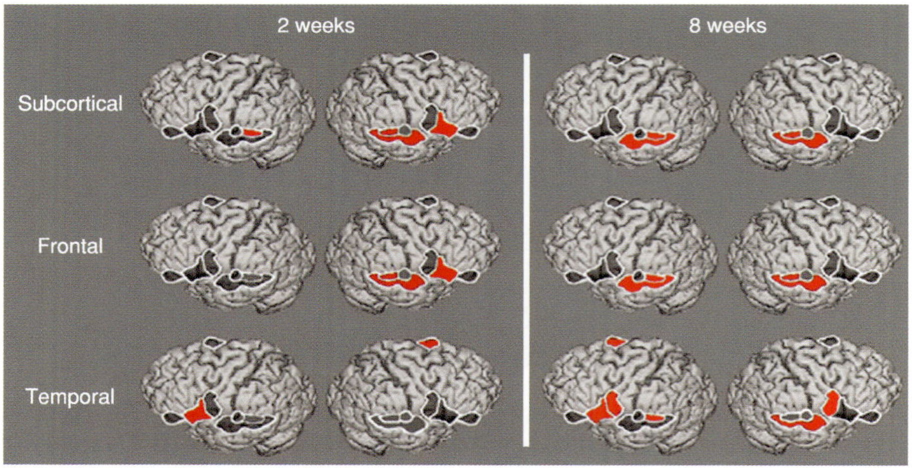

Plate 29 Results of a PET study in left hemisphere stroke patients with various aphasic syndromes. The patient group with subcortical and frontal lesions improved substantially and activated the right hemisphere (inferior frontal and right superior temporal gyri) at baseline. Left superior temporal gyrus activation occurred at follow-up. Patients with temporal lesions improved only in word comprehension and activated the left Broca area and supplementary motor areas at baseline. Precentral gyrus bilaterally and right superior temporal gyrus were activated at follow-up but not the left superior temporal gyrus. Reproduced with permission from Heiss et al. (2003). 'Disturbance and recovery of language function: correlates in PET activation.' *Neuroimage 20(1)*, 542–549. © Elsevier (*see page 241*).

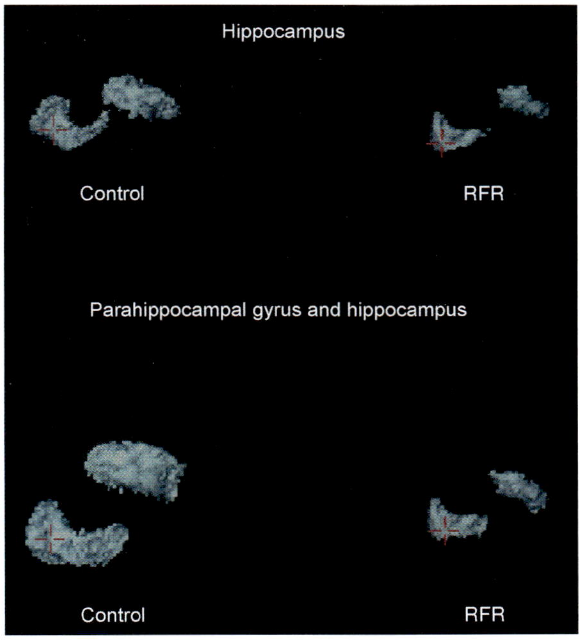

Plate 30 Three-dimensional surface renderings of the hippocampi (top) and the combined parahippocampal and hippocampal structures (bottom) in a healthy control volunteer (left) and in a herpes encephalitis patient (right). These images are taken from planimetric segmentations of the structures from three-dimensional magnetic resonance images. Reproduced from Kopelman MD, Lasserson D, Kingsley DR, et al. (2003) Retrograde amnesia and the volume of critical brain structures. *Hippocampus* 13: 879–891, with permission (*see page 318*).

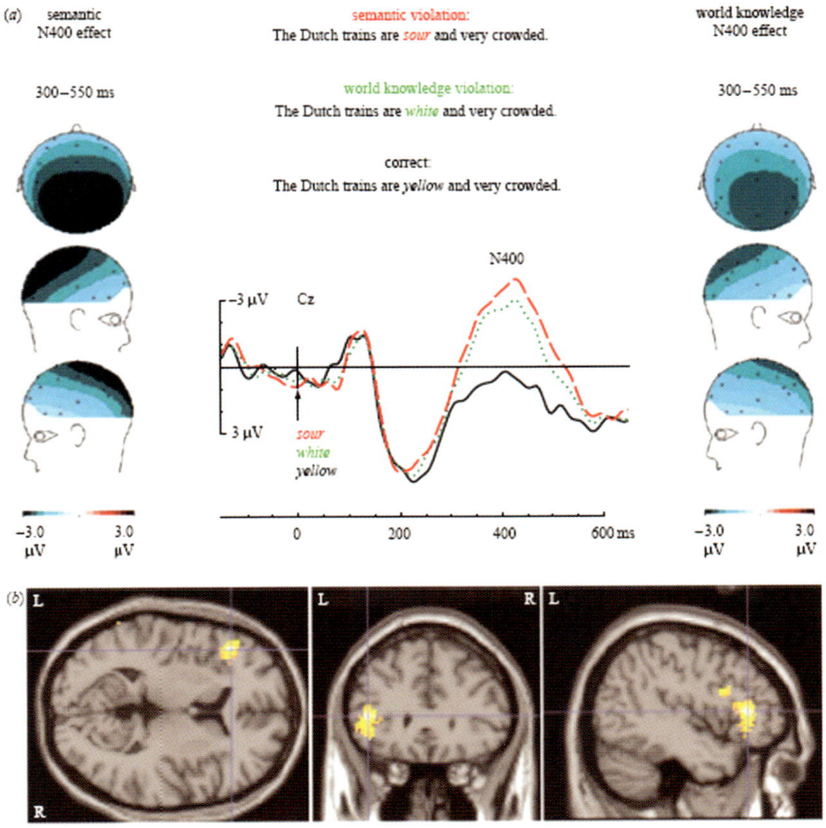

Plate 31 *Source*: Figure taken from Hagoort & van Berkum (2007) (Fig. 4, p. 805). Printed by permission of The Royal Society (*see page 372*).

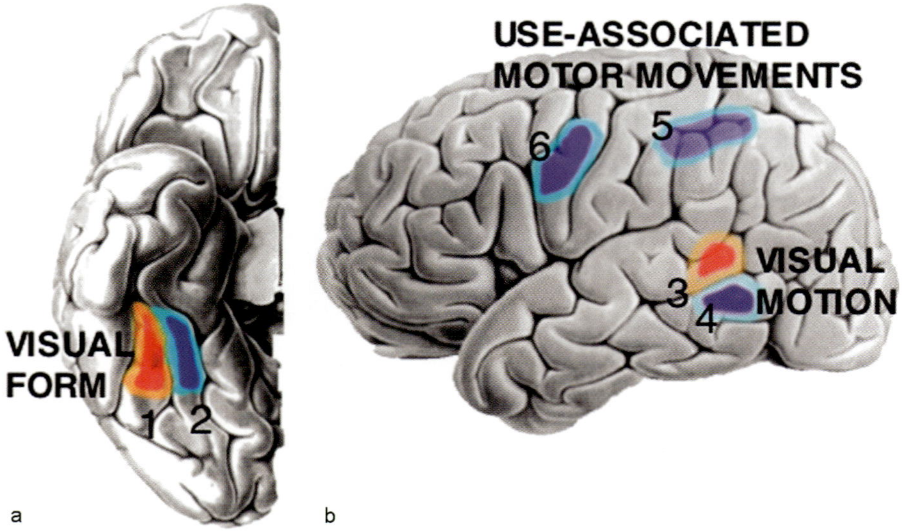

Plate 32 Schematic illustration of location of regions showing category-related activity for animate entities (red) and tools (blue). (a) Ventral view of the right hemisphere, showing relative location of regions assumed to represent visual form and form-related properties such as color and texture of animate entities (1, lateral region of the fusiform gyrus, including, but not limited to the fusiform face area) and tools (2, medial region of the fusiform gyrus). (b) Lateral view of the left hemisphere, showing relative location of regions assumed to represent biological motion (3, posterior region of the superior temporal sulcus) and rigid motion vectors typical of tools (4, posterior region of the middle temporal gyrus). Also shown are the relative locations of the posterior parietal (5, typically centered on the intraparietal sulcus) and ventral premotor (6) regions of the left hemisphere assumed to represent information about the motor movements associated with using tools (*see page 338*).

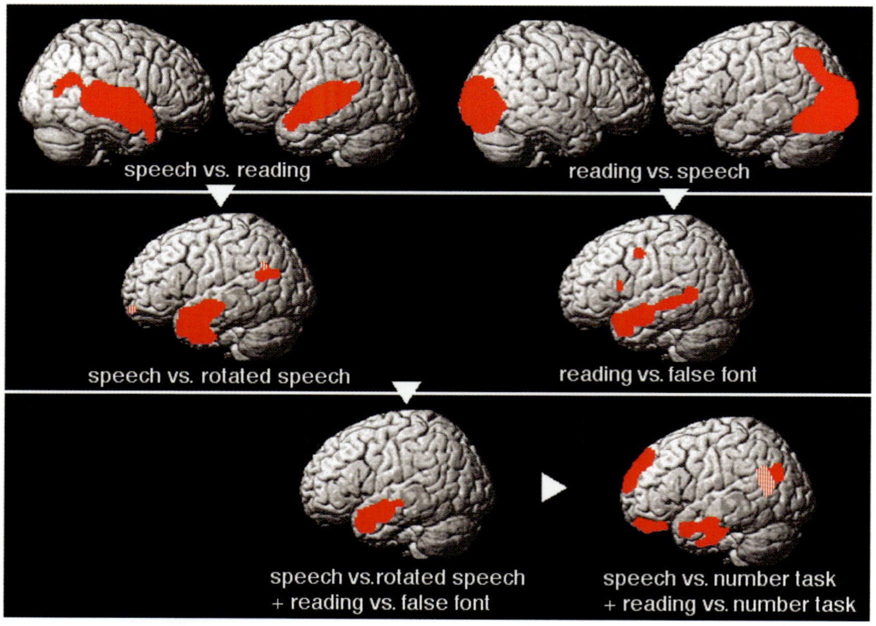

Plate 33 Activity evoked by narratives, both spoken and written, rendered onto the left and right cerebral hemispheres (group averaged data, n = 11 normal subjects). Solid red regions are located over the lateral and inferior surfaces of the hemispheres, hatched red regions are located over the medial surfaces. The contrasts of speech with reading and reading with speech demonstrated bilateral, symmetrical activity in the superior temporal gyri and the occipital lobes, respectively. The asymmetry in posterior parietal cortex (left > right) during reading is the consequence of visual attention and reading saccades being directed to the right in left-to-right readers. Contrasting speech with its modality-specific baseline condition of spectrally inverted (rotated) speech, and reading with its modality-specific baseline condition of text-like arrays of false font, demonstrated activity centered around the superior temporal sulcus, predominantly lateralized to the left. The conjunction of activity for these two contrasts was centered over left anterolateral temporal cortex – a region that responded to intelligible language independent of modality. By using an alternative baseline condition (number task), an explicit task on simple number semantics (an odd/even decision on randomly presented numbers, 1–10), activity was also demonstrated in the anterior fusiform gyrus (the "basal" language area) and just ventral to the angular gyrus. There was also prominent activity in the left superior frontal gyrus, orbito-frontal cortex and in retrosplenial cortex (hatched region). The rationale for using the number task as an alternative baseline condition is described in the text. Data from Spitsyna et al. (2006) (*see page 396*).

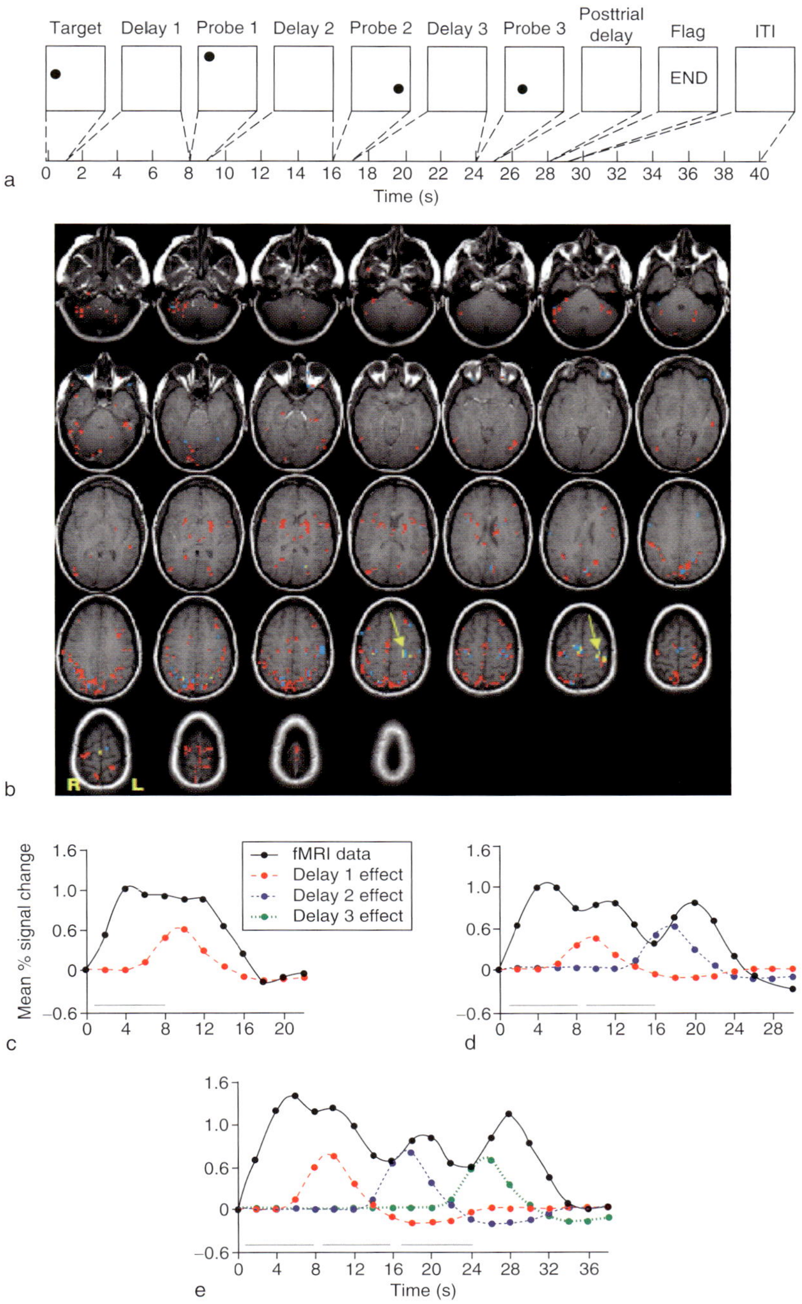

Plate 34 A functional magnetic resonance imaging experiment demonstrating sustained memory-related activity for location across multiple delay periods. (a) Behavioral task. Individuals view and encode the target location, then, after a 7 s delay, indicate with a button press whether the probe does or does not appear in the same location. One-third of the trials end after probe 1. On two- and three-delay trials, the offset of probe 1 is followed by another delay period, after which individuals evaluate the location of probe 2 with respect to the target. On one- and two-delay trials, the 'END' message appears at times 12 and 20 s, respectively. (b) Results from a single representative individual. Voxels in red showed sustained delay-period activity for delay 1 only. Voxels in blue are the subset of voxels with delay-period activity sustained across delay 1 and delay 2. Voxels in yellow are the still smaller subset with delay-period activity sustained across all three delays. Note that although many regions, including the prefrontal cortex, show delay-period activity during delay 1, only dorsal-stream parietal and frontal oculomotor regions sustain this delay-period activity across all three delays. Arrows highlight the voxels from left frontal eye field (the activity of which is shown in panels c, d, and e). (c) Activity from three-delay voxels in the left frontal eye field, averaged across one-delay trials. 'Delay 1 effect' reflects the estimated magnitude of delay 1 activity. Gray bar along the horizontal axis indicates the duration of the delay period. (d) Activity from these same frontal eye field voxels averaged across two-delay trials. Graphical conventions are the same as in panel b. (e) Activity from these same frontal eye field voxels averaged across three-delay trials. Graphical conventions are the same as in panel c. Adapted from Postle BR (2006) Distraction-spanning sustained activity during delayed recognition of locations. *NeuroImage* 30: 950–962. (*see page 344*).

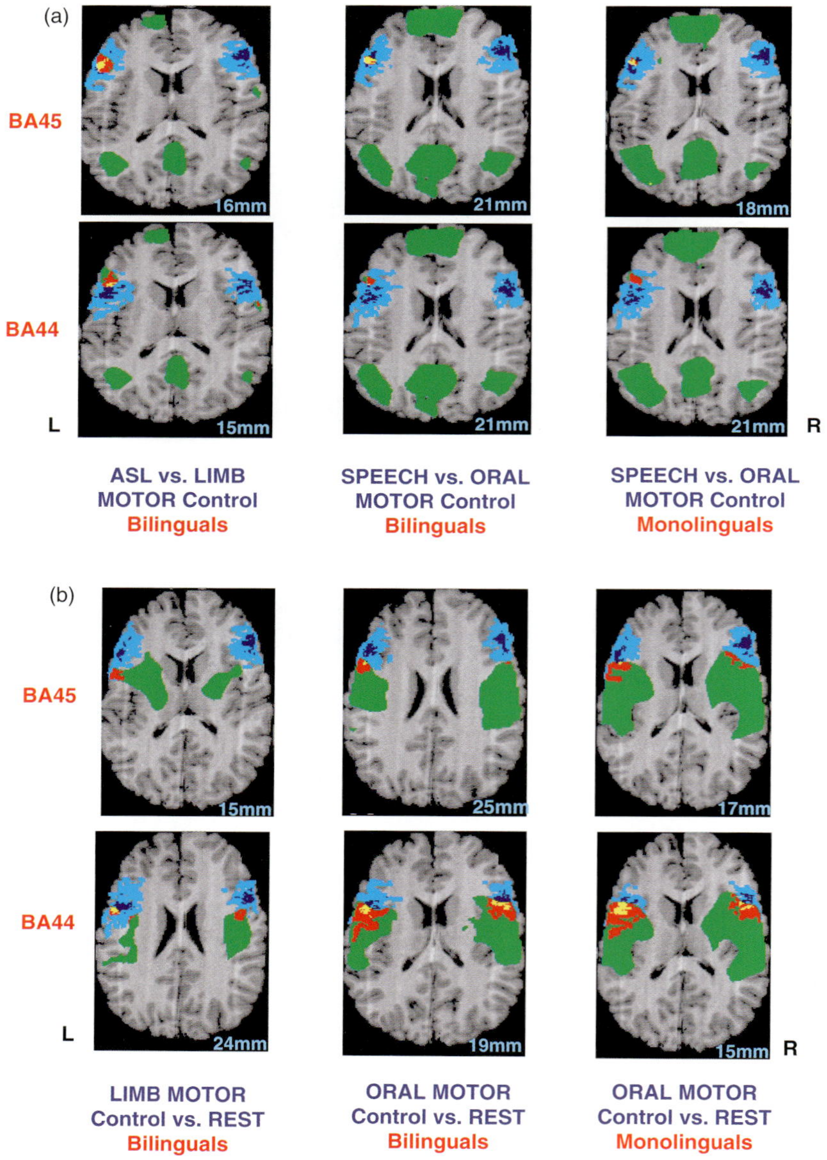

Plate 35 (a) Activations of BA45 (top row) and BA44 (bottom row) during production of language narratives compared to a motor control task; and (b) activation of BA45 (top) and BA44 (bottom) comparing each motor control task to a resting condition. Shown are representative horizontal slices (left side of each image corresponds to the left side of the brain; the level in mm superior to the AC-PC plane (*z*-coordinate of Talairach & Tournoux atlas, 1988) is indicated on each slice). Images displayed in the two columns on the left are from the bilingual (English and ASL) subjects, and those in the column on the right are from the monolingual English speakers. Voxels in dark blue correspond to core parts of the specific Brodmann area, those in light blue to peripheral voxels. Voxels significantly more active in one condition compared to a second ($Z > 2.33$) are shown in green. Voxels in the peripheral part of a Brodmann area that had a significant PET activation are displayed in red, and core voxels that were significantly activated are shown in yellow. From Horwitz et al. (2003) [Talairach, J., & Tournoux, P. (1988). *Co-planar stereotaxic atlas of the human brain* (M. Rayport, Trans.). New York: Thieme.] (*see page 399*).

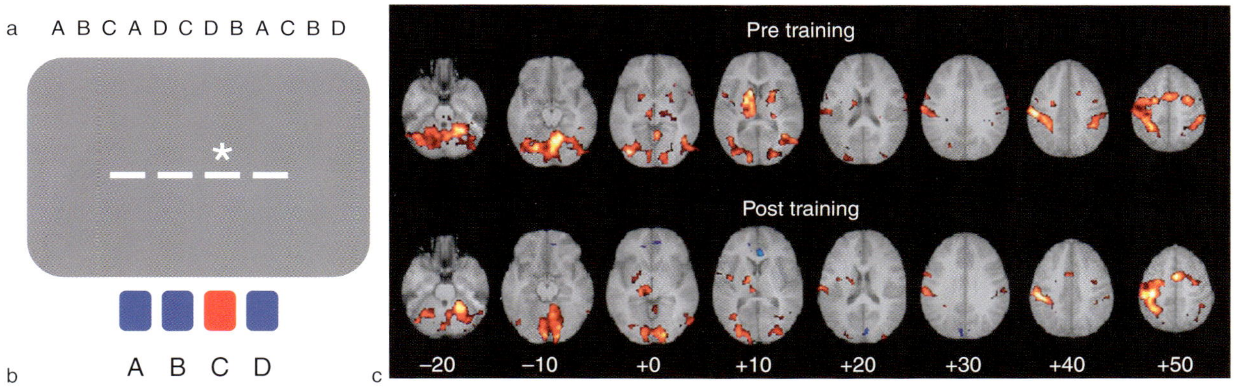

Plate 36 (a) Example of repeating sequence used in a serial reaction time (SRT) task. (b) Participants press a button corresponding to the spatial location of the onscreen asterisk. (c) Results from a fMRI study of SRT performance. Participants in this study were trained on an SRT task for three 1 h sessions (top row, brain images prior to the training session; bottom row, brain images after training). Reproduced from Poldrack RA, Sabb F, Foerde K, et al. (2005). The neural correlates of automaticity during motor skill learning. *Journal of Neuroscience* 25: 5356–5364, with permission. Copyright 2005 by the Society for Neuroscience (*see page 424*).

Plate 37 An example of a synesthete's colored graphemes (*see page 496*).

Plate 38 A painting of two bars of music from a music-to-color synesthete (*see page 497*).

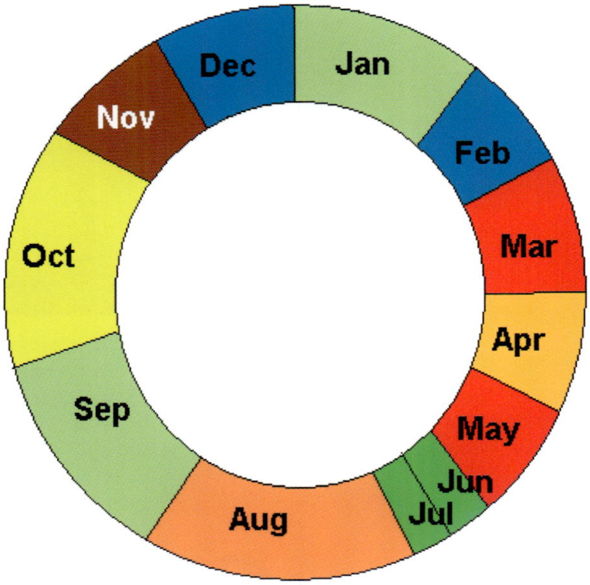

Plate 39 A colored spatial form for months of the year (*see page 498*).

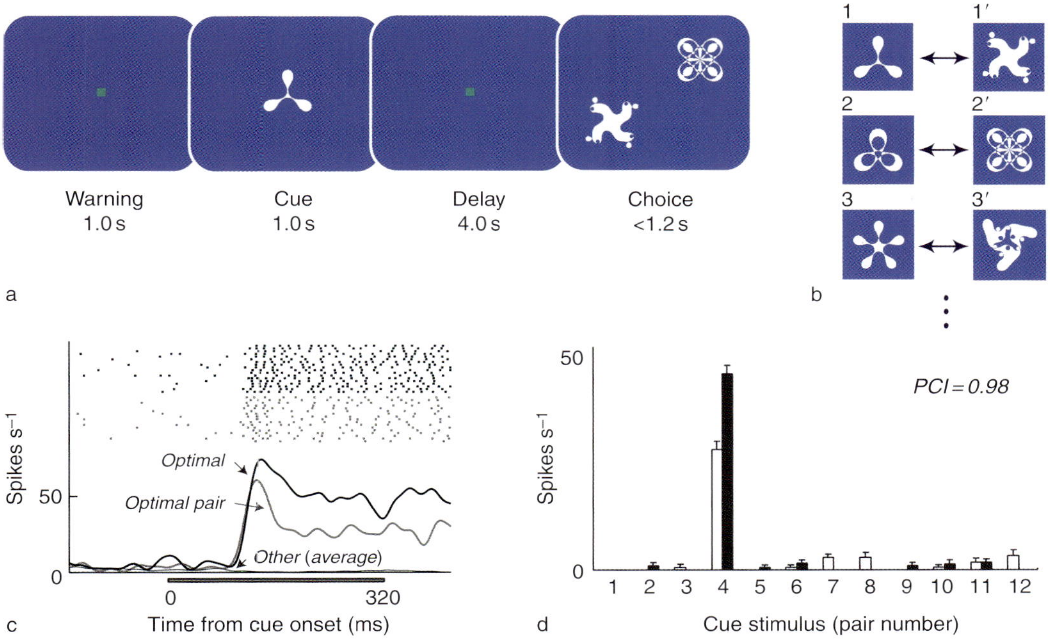

Plate 40 Pair-association (PA) task for monkeys used by Sakai and Miyashita: (a) sequence of events within a trial; (b) examples of paired associates used in the task (the monkeys learned to retrieve the other member of the associated pair for each cue picture); (c) rastergrams of neural discharges in each trial (upper) and spike density functions (SDF, lower) obtained from a single neuron; (d) mean discharge rates during the cue period (60–320 ms from the cue onset). As shown in (a), after a lever press by the monkey initiating a new trial, there is a warning, a green square (1 s); then a cue, one of the Fourier descriptors that serves as the cue stimulus (1 s); then a delay, a green square (4 s); and then a choice of two stimuli, the paired associate of the cue and one from a different pair. Fruit juice was given as a reward for correctly touching the paired associate. In (c), the optimal trial (the strongest response) is shown as the thick black line and optimal-pair trial (the second strongest response) is shown as the thick gray line. The trials are aligned at the cue onset. The thin black line denotes the averaged responses in the other trials. The duration of the cue period was 320 ms. In (d), 12 pairs of stimuli are labeled on the abscissa. The open and filled bars in pair 1, for example, refer to the responses to stimulus 1 and 1′, respectively. Error bars denote SEM. PCI, pair-coding index. (c, d) Reproduced from Naya Y, Yoshida M, and Miyashita Y (2003) Forward processing of long-term associative memory in monkey inferotemporal cortex. *Journal of Neuroscience* 23: 2861–2871. Copyright 2003, with permission from the Society for Neuroscience (*see page 524*).

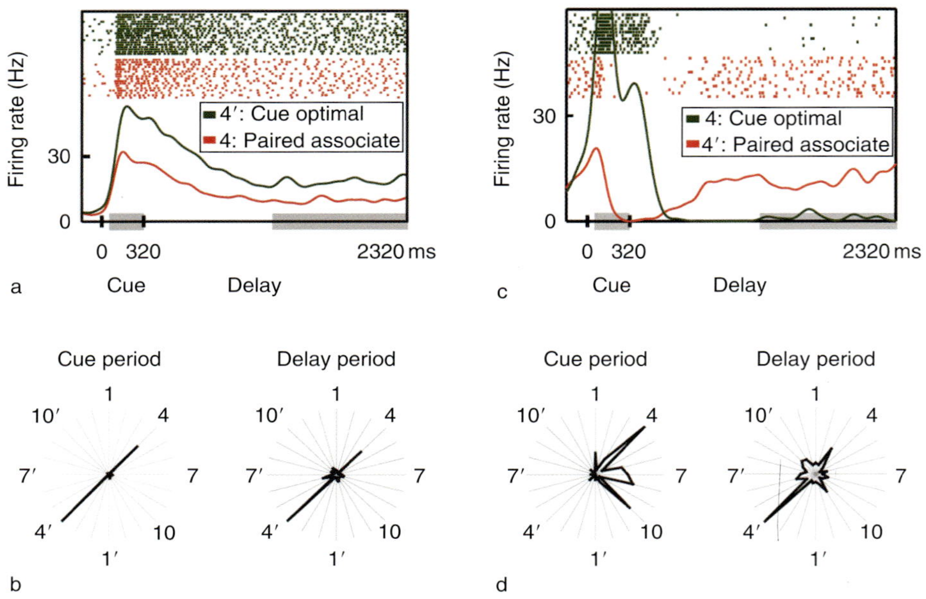

Plate 41 Examples of delay-selective neurons: (a) A36 raster displays and spike density functions; (b) A36 polar plots of mean discharge rates; (c) TE raster displays and spike density functions; (d) TE polar plots of mean discharge rates. In (a,c) , trials using the cue-optimal stimulus as the cue (optimal trials, green) and those using the paired associate as the cue (optimal-pair trials, red) were aligned at the cue onset. In (b) and (d), mean discharge rates during the cue and delay periods (60–320 ms and 1320–2320 ms; gray boxes in (a) and (c), respectively) are shown in polar plots for each cue presentation. The responses to stimuli and to their paired associates are indicated by radial lines. The discharge rates were normalized based on the maximum values for each period ((b) cue period, 44.0 Hz at stimulus 4′; delay period, 18.6 Hz at stimulus 4′; (d) cue period, 48.7 Hz at stimulus 4; delay period, 18.7 Hz at stimulus 4′). A36, area 36; TE, area TE. Reproduced from Naya Y, Yoshida M, Takeda M, Fujimichi R, and Miyashita Y (2003) Delay-period activities in two subdivisions of monkey inferotemporal cortex during pair association memory task. *European Journal of Neuroscience* 18: 2915–2918. Copyright 2003, with permission from Blackwell Publishing Ltd (*see page 526*).

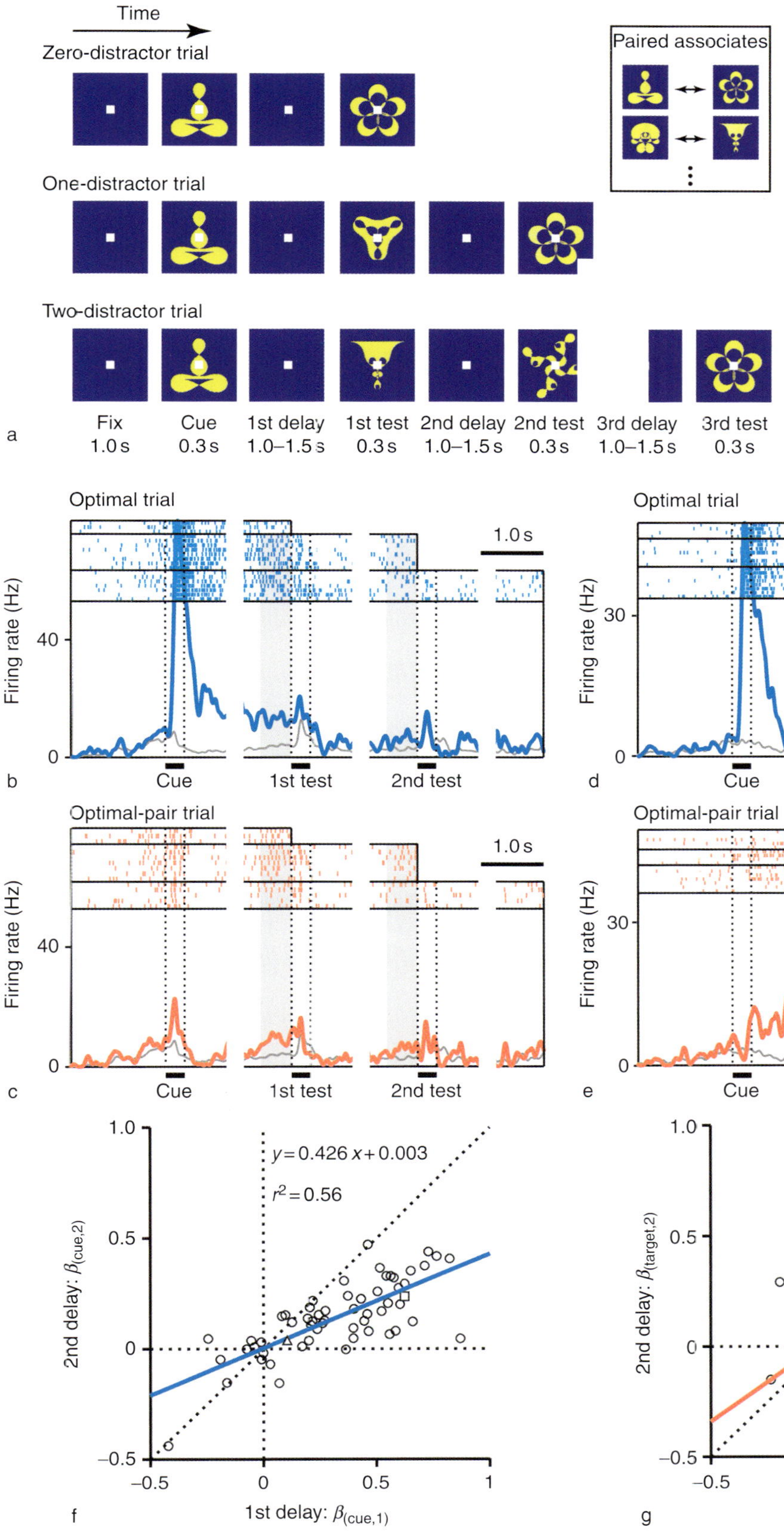

Plate 42 (see over for legend)

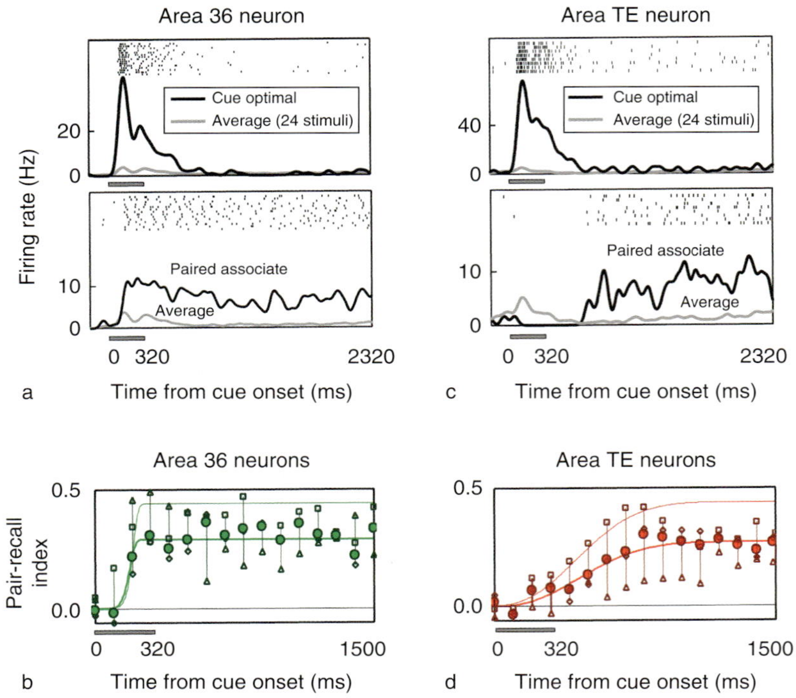

Plate 43 Neuronal activity related to memory retrieval during the paired-association task: (a) activity of a representative A36 neuron; (b) temporal dynamics of average PRI(*t*) for the population of stimulus-selective A36 neurons ($n = 45$); (c) activity of a representative TE neuron; (d) temporal dynamics of average PRI(*t*) for the population of stimulus-selective TE neurons ($n = 69$). In (a) and (c), SDFs are aligned at the cue onset in trials where the cue-optimal stimulus served as the cue (top) and in trials where its paired associate served as the cue (bottom). Black lines indicate responses to the cue-optimal stimulus (top) or its paired associate (bottom); gray lines indicate mean responses to all stimuli. In (b) and (d), mean values of PRI(*t*) are plotted every 100 ms (solid circle, total; diamond, monkey 1; open square, monkey 2; open triangle, monkey 3). Thick lines (green and red, respectively) indicate the best-fit Weibull functions for the population-averaged PRI(*t*) in the two areas. Thin lines indicate this for the neurons whose PRI(*t*) increased above the 5% significance level. PRI, paired-recall index; SDF, spike density function. Reprinted from Naya Y, Yoshida M, and Miyashita Y (2001) Backward spreading of memory-retrieval signal in the primate temporal cortex. *Science* 291: 661–664, with permission from American Association for the Advancement of Science (*see page 530*).

Plate 42 Sequential-type paired-association task. (a) The procedure; (b,c) rastergrams and SDFs of the optimal trials and optimal-pair trials showing representative neurons exhibiting cue-holding activity; (d,e) rastergrams and SDFs of the optimal trials and optimal-pair trials showing representative neurons exhibiting target-recall activity; (f) scatterplot of the effect of the cue stimulus on neuronal activity during the delay epoch; (g) scatterplot of the effects of the target stimulus on neuronal activity during the delay epoch. As shown in (a), after the fixation spot, one of the pictures was presented as the cue stimulus. During the delay epoch that followed the cue stimulus, one, two, or three test stimuli were presented. After each delay period, the paired associate of the cue stimulus (target stimulus) or a distractor stimulus was presented as the test stimulus. In (b–e), gray lines indicate average SDFs in trials in which the other pictures were presented as cue stimuli. Data from correct trials are aligned on the onset of the cue, first-test, and second-test stimuli. Light-gray shading indicates the first and second delay periods for analysis. In the optimal trials, neuronal discharge (cue-holding activity) declined from the first to the second delay period (b). In the optimal-pair trials, strong neuronal discharge (target-recall activity) was observed during both the first and second delay periods (e). In (f), the scatterplot relates the changes in the β values for the cue stimulus from the first delay (*x* axis) to the second delay (*y* axis) period across the population of delay-selective neurons ($n = 59$). The regression slope is significantly positive ($t = 8.58$, $p < 0.01$). In (g), the regression slope for the β values for the target stimulus is significantly positive ($t = 9.95$, $p < 0.01$) and steeper than that for β values for the cue stimulus ($F = 11.57$, $p < 0.01$). The open triangles in (f, g) represent the data from the neurons in (b,c) and the open squares represent the data from the neurons in (d,e). SDF, spike density function. Reproduced from Takeda M, Naya Y, Fujimichi R, Takeuchi D, and Miyashita Y (2005) Active maintenance of associative mnemonic signal in monkey inferior temporal cortex. *Neuron* 48: 839–848. Copyright 2005, with permission from Elsevier (*see page 528*).

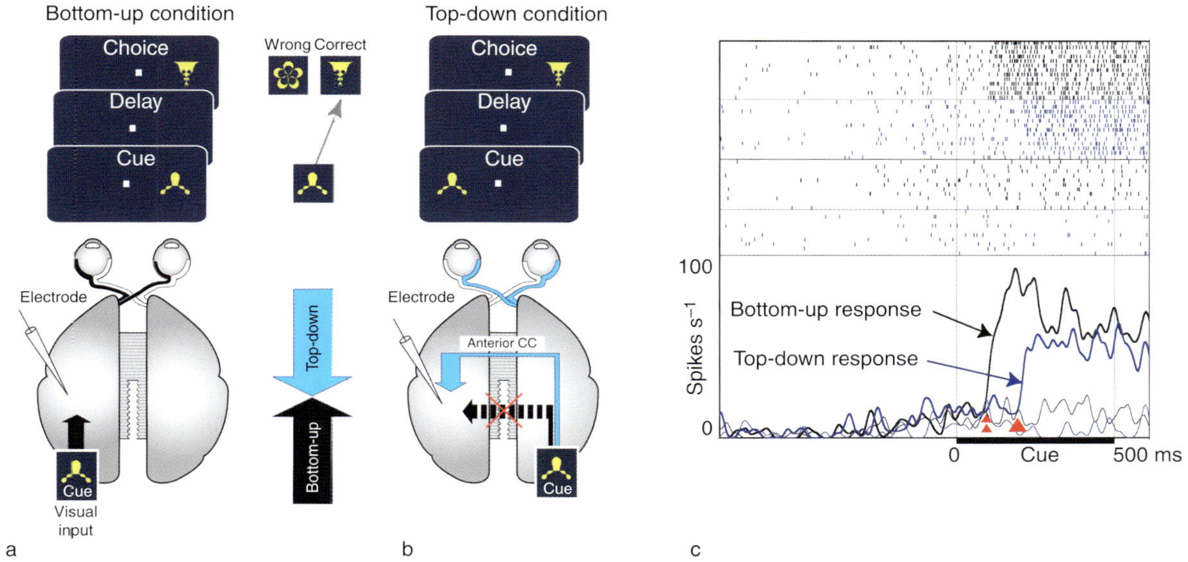

Plate 44 Experimental design measuring neuronal activity in monkeys: (a) bottom-up condition; (b) top-down condition; (c) activity of a single IT neuron under the top-down condition (top-down, blue; bottom-up, black). As shown in (a), in the bottom-up condition visual stimuli (cue and choice pictures) were presented in the hemifield contralateral to the recording site (electrode) in the IT cortex. The monkey was required to make the correct choice specified by the cue. Fixation was required throughout each trial ($< 0.6°$). Bottom-up sensory signals (black arrow) were detected in this condition. As shown in (b), in the top-down condition, the cue was presented in the hemifield ipsilateral to the recording site, but the choice was presented contralaterally. In posterior-split-brain monkeys, sensory signals do not reach the visual areas in the opposite hemisphere. In this condition, only top-down signals (blue arrow) can activate IT neurons through top-down connections from the prefrontal cortex. In (c), the raster displays and SDFs are aligned at the cue onset. In the SDFs, the thick lines show responses to the optimal cue; the thin lines show responses to a null cue. The onset of the top-down response (arrowhead) was later than the onset of the bottom-up response (doubled arrowhead). CC, corpus callosum; IT, inferior temporal; SDF, spike density function. Modified from Tomita H, Ohbayashi M, Nakahara K, Hasegawa I, and Miyashita Y (1999) Top-down signal from prefrontal cortex in executive control of memory retrieval. *Nature* 401: 699–703, Copyright 1999 with permission from Macmillan Publishers Ltd (*see page 531*).

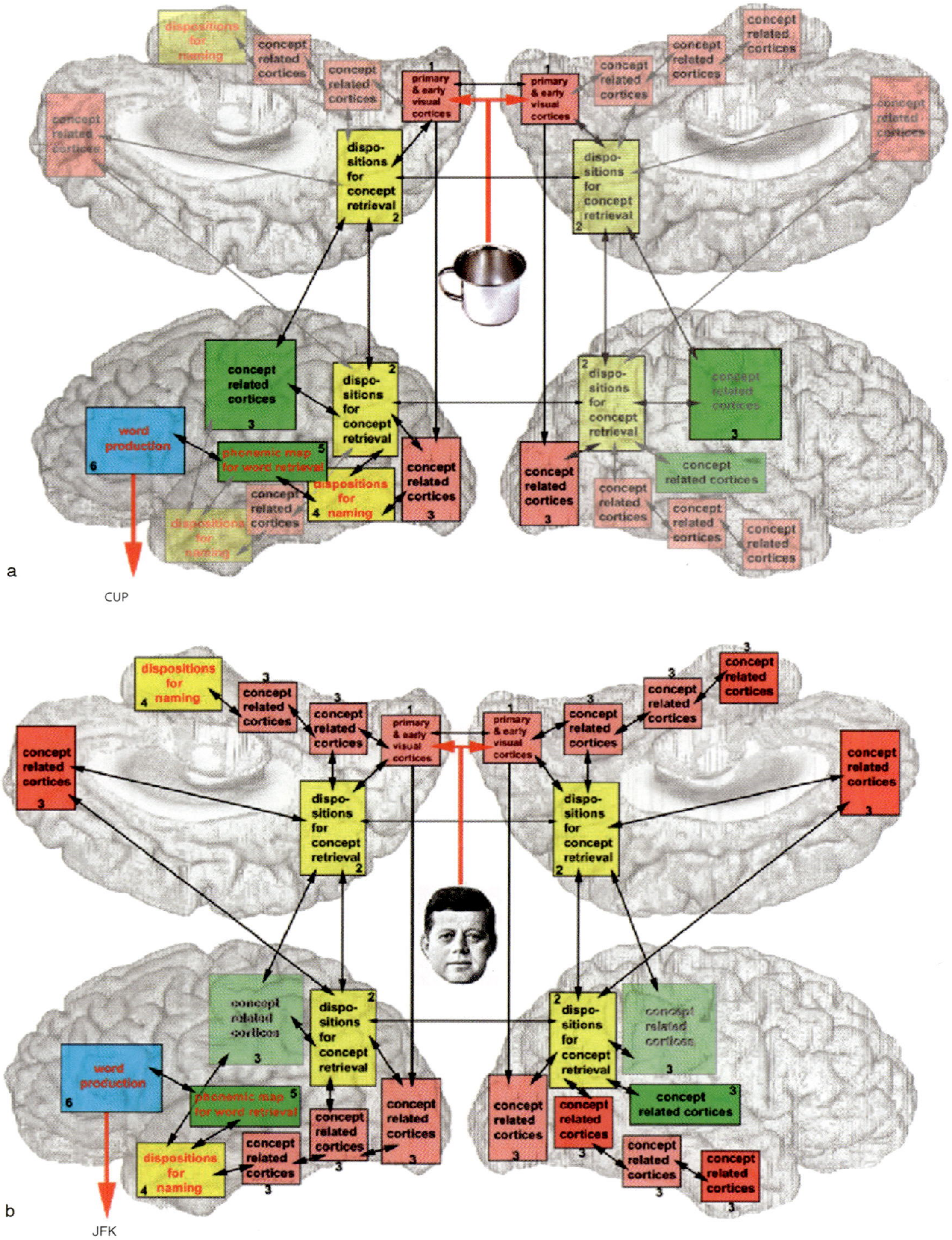

Plate 45 Reprinted from *Cognition*, 92, Damasio H, Tranel D, Grabowsky TJ, Adolphs R, and Damasio HR, Neural systems behind word and concept retrieval, pp. 179–229 (2004), with permission from Elsevier (*see page 544*).